Ethical Issues

Western Philosophical and Religious Perspectives

Terrence Reynolds
Georgetown University

THOMSON

™

WADSWORTH

Australia • Canada • Mexico • Singapore • Spain • United Kingdom • United States

THOMSON
WADSWORTH

Publisher: *Holly J. Allen*
Philosophy Editor: *Steve Wainwright*
Assistant Editors: *Lee McCracken, Barbara Hillaker*
Technology Project Manager: *Julie Aguilar*
Marketing Manager: *Worth Hawes*
Marketing Assistant: *Andrew Keay*
Advertising Project Manager: *Laurel Anderson*
Executive Art Director: *Maria Epes*
Print/Media Buyer: *Lisa Claudeanos*

Composition Buyer: *Ben Schroeter*
Permissions Editor: *Stephanie Lee*
Production Service: *Matrix Productions*
Copy Editor: *Victoria Nelson*
Cover Designer: *Yvo Riezebos*
Cover Image: *Getty Images*
Compositor: *Cadmus*
Text and Cover Printer: *Transcontinental/Louiseville*

Printed in Canada
1   2   3   4   5   6   7   09   08   07   06   05

For more information about our products,
contact us at:
Thomson Learning Academic Resource Center
1-800-423-0563

For permission to use material from this text
or product, submit a request online at
http://www.thomsonrights.com.
Any additional questions about permissions
can be submitted by email to
thomsonrights@thomson.com.

Library of Congress Control Number: 2004116737

ISBN: 0-534-51847-8

Thomson Higher Education
10 Davis Drive
Belmont, CA 94002-3098
USA

Asia (including India)
Thomson Learning
5 Shenton Way
#01-01 UIC Building
Singapore 068808

Australia/New Zealand
Thomson Learning Australia
102 Dodds Street
Southbank, Victoria 3006
Australia

Canada
Thomson Nelson
1120 Birchmount Road
Toronto, Ontario M1K 5G4
Canada

UK/Europe/Middle East/Africa
Thomson Learning
High Holborn House
50–51 Bedford Road
London WC1R 4LR
United Kingdom

Latin America
Thomson Learning
Seneca, 53
Colonia Polanco
11560 Mexico
D.F. Mexico

Spain (including Portugal)
Thomson Paraninfo
Calle Magallanes, 25
28015 Madrid, Spain

Contents

Preface

The idea for this collection originated some years ago when I had the privilege of teaching *Religious Ethics and Moral Issues* under the tutelage of John P. Reeder, Jr., at Brown University. The course was structured with an introductory series of essays on ethical theory that acquainted the diverse student population with the terminology of ethical discourse and provided them with the conceptual tools necessary to appreciate the subtlety of moral decision making. At the conclusion of the first portion of the course, students were well versed in the theories of Immanuel Kant, John Stuart Mill, and Aristotle and were also aware of the fundamental objections that had been leveled at each of these thinkers. Moreover, students also began to wrestle with the principles, norms, and convictions that gave shape to their own moral judgments. Following the introduction to ethical theory, the course moved on to examine moral problems in the areas of sexual ethics, abortion, issues related to war, and euthanasia/suicide, though other dilemmas could be substituted at the teacher's discretion. In my experience, the course was so profoundly rewarding to students that I vowed, if given the opportunity, to teach a comparable class. This volume is an attempt to bring together a sufficient breadth and depth of readings to serve as a primary, or only, text for such a course.

Thanks are owed to several persons who helped make this collection possible. First, I wish to thank John P. Reeder, Jr., whose passion for teaching and whose understanding of how courses ought to be structured to create and sustain student engagement taught me lessons I have never forgotten. He was a wonderful mentor and remains a very good friend. I wish also to thank Steve Wainwright, the religion editor at Wadsworth Press, for his unusual patience and his never-ending good will throughout this process. I'm also indebted to the reviewers who assessed the initial proposal for this volume; their constructive suggestions were invaluable in the shaping of a richer, and more complete, collection of essays. Thanks are also in order for Walter Conser, an old and dear friend from the University of North Carolina at Wilmington. Having roomed together at the annual meetings of the AAR/SBL for over twenty years, Walter and I have been through much together, and his unfailing support and encouragement have meant more to me than I have ever said, or he has ever realized. Truly, he has been a friend like no other, and I thank him deeply for it. Britt Borgstrom, my assistant in the project, also offered support, editorial assistance, and a welcome hand with the preparation of the final manuscript. For all of that, and for her cheerfulness, I thank her as well. In the end, this collection has only come into being because of the students I have enjoyed teaching so much at Brown, Connecticut College, the U.S. Coast Guard Academy, and Georgetown University. I owe them a debt of gratitude for their passion for the moral life and for their patience with me. I could not have asked for better companions in the quest for understanding.

Introduction

There is no paucity of anthologies on moral dilemmas in the current market, but I think that the collection of essays I have assembled is distinctive, nonetheless. Over the years I have come both to admire many of the available collections and also to find them structurally unsuited for my pedagogical needs. These anthologies are praiseworthy for their breadth of coverage, but their very strength, in my view, constitutes their weakness. In attempting to offer essays on issues as diverse as sexual ethics; affirmative action; poverty; animal rights; abortion; environmental concerns; capital punishment; euthanasia; suicide; world hunger; just war; corporate responsibility; pornography; discrimination in the workplace; issues of gender, race, and ethnicity; cloning; and others, along with some treatment of ethical theory, such collections succeed in covering a commendable breadth of topics but at the cost of sufficient depth of treatment. The result is that most anthologies offer only a few essays on any given topic, and instructors are forced to ask students to purchase several texts, often at prohibitive cost.

In this volume I have tried to provide an introduction to ethical theory and limit the number of issues addressed to only seven, with much deeper and more diverse coverage of each. Instructors using my anthology for an introductory course in ethics could begin with a thorough exploration of ethical theory and move on to examine, in genuine detail, any four or five issues of their choosing. The essays are arranged in each section according to the arguments of the authors; those in support of a given perspective are listed in sequence, as are those who are generally opposed. I have found that teaching a course in this manner is pedagogically sound and invites students into a serious conversation with a broad range of thinkers on issues of interest to them. Reading six to eight essays on abortion is far more fruitful than a cursory examination of two or three and enables students to formulate and constructively reshape their own positions with far greater nuance and complexity. In the end, students develop their ability to propose and defend their arguments on moral issues with a high level of skill and sophistication.

In addition to breaking with the more standard arrangement of essays, I've also chosen not to limit selections to philosophers or religious thinkers. Philosophers and religious thinkers, it seems to me, speak out of distinctive webs of belief and ought to be in conversation with one another. The public arena should be occupied with consistent, coherent perspectives in dialogue, whatever their theological or nontheological presuppositions. This anthology, therefore, brings together Western thinkers from both secular and religious perspectives to debate controverted issues in the moral life. I have found that exposing students to such a wide-ranging conversation engages and challenges them in ways that a more monolithic collection cannot. Further, my students come from a wide variety of backgrounds and beliefs and expect a broader conversation than some anthologies have been able to provide. Because students will face a world in which philosophers do not merely engage other philosophers and religious thinkers do not converse only with the like minded, a critical exposure of these thinkers' positions to a wider range of perspectives can only be an enriching intellectual experience.

Any anthology is open to criticism for any number of omissions, and this volume is no exception. For example, critics could object that insufficient attention is paid to the voices of historicism, feminism, and virtue ethics. From this perspective, the collection might appear predominantly linear, logical, and based on the sort of reasoning associated with notions of objectivity and justice in ethics. These objections are serious, and I have tried to address them by including thinkers whose views reflect these concerns, both in the theoretical and applied portions of the text. At the same time, however, I have tried to focus on essays that accurately reflect the cultural debates currently taking place. In short, my purpose has been to familiarize students with these significant theoretical concerns in order to sensitize them to the ambiguities inherent in contemporary moral conversations. Without dramatically altering the nature of the text, I could do no more.

Others could object that the collection largely overlooks classical thinkers, that it is limited to Western thought, or that minority voices are inadequately represented in the debates. These objections also strike me as fair and indisputably accurate. I plead guilty with an explanation, since these shortcomings reflect the editorial choices I have consciously made in preparing this collection. In choosing to collect essays into a coherent volume, one must make choices and recognize that one's selections may not suit the pedagogical interests of all. It was my decision to concentrate on Western thought and the contemporary debates to which my students will be contributing, and I made the selections with that end in view. As for the critique that the volume does not give sufficient voice to minority positions, I have attempted to include such perspectives in the collection as much as possible without diminishing the focus of the volume on the more widely defended positions in the current conversations. No anthology can be exhaustive, but I stand by my choices and know from experience that the selections deeply engage students from a wide diversity of backgrounds and perspectives.

As I've said, the collection begins with a section on ethical theory. Without some attention to the terminology at work in the discourse of ethics and to the normative theories that inform our moral thinking, subsequent discussions of moral issues degenerate swiftly into a superficial, and largely uncritical, sharing of opinions. Included in this section are seminal selections from Immanuel Kant (ethical formalism), John Stuart Mill (utilitarianism), and Aristotle (virtue ethics), because an acquaintance with these classical normative ethical theories is indispensable for understanding ethics. To provide reflections on the role of religious belief in the nature and practice of the moral life, I've included essays by Louis Dupré and Ronald Green. In addition, I've chosen essays by Carol Gilligan, Stanley Hauerwas and David Burrell, and myself, each of which argues in its own way against the possibility of objectivity in ethics. As all three of these essays suggest, none of us is free from sociohistorically formed perspectives, worldviews, webs of belief, or linguistic conceptions that shape our moral vision. Armed with an introductory appreciation of ethical theory and the complexity of ethical discourse, students are better equipped to apply their theoretical preferences to a variety of moral issues.

In the sections that follow, students are exposed to a broad range of perspectives on issues related to sexual ethics, abortion, the conduct of war, euthanasia and suicide, environmental ethics, capital punishment, and human cloning. In every section students are forced to wrestle with some of the finest thinkers in the field and to reflect on the ethical principles on which they ground their moral judgments. The essays are intended to engage students in a stimulating debate between opposing views and to help them appreciate how their own perspectives fare in the discussion. At the end of each section of the course, they are also required to write papers of five to seven pages in which they propose and defend their own moral judgments in the face of serious scrutiny. These papers encourage students to formulate their thoughts carefully and in dialogue with others, an exercise that enables them to achieve an advanced level of understanding and expression. Whether students change their thinking dramatically, adapt their thinking to make their positions more defensible, or come to appreciate more fully the strength of their initial judgments, they consistently report that the exercise is challenging and intellectually satisfying.

I fully realize that it is impossible to cover all the issues included in this volume with sufficient attention, but the breadth of readings in each section is sufficient to give four or five topics careful scrutiny in a given semester and to acquaint students with the subtlety of the debate they have inspired. In undertaking such a project, one always hopes that others will benefit from the fruits of one's labor, and it is my wish that the selection of essays I've included will be viewed as balanced, demanding, and provocative, and that these essays will be as engaging in other classrooms as they have been in mine.

Part 1
Ethical Theory

1. Utilitarianism: General Remarks

JOHN STUART MILL

In his essay *Utilitarianism* (1879), John Stuart Mill (1806–1873) traces the development of moral principles to the desire of humankind to create and sustain its own happiness. Persuaded early in life by the writings of Jeremy Bentham, Mill believed that, although persons may interpret the meaning of happiness somewhat differently and may desire different goods, happiness itself remains an end in itself, the one intrinsic value sought by all. Happiness is not a means to another end; it is pursued for its own sake. Moral laws or rules, though they may appear to be absolute and inviolable, have, in fact, been established in the service of happiness. Justice, for example, produces such extraordinary levels of security and peace of mind, both indispensable to happiness, that it is sometimes mistakenly thought to be an absolute requirement of morality. But justice is only so highly valued, Mill argues, because of its utility in serving the pursuit of happiness. On rare occasions, Mill could envision justice giving way to injustice if long-term utility, or overall happiness, required it. Thus, for Mill, acts are not right or wrong in themselves but are only right or wrong insofar as, compared to other available options, they can be said to maximize aggregate utility or minimize aggregate disutility.

There are few circumstances among those which make up the present condition of human knowledge more unlike what might have been expected, or more significant of the backward state in which speculation on

From John Stuart Mill, *Utilitarianism*, 7th ed. (London: Longmans, Green, 1879), pp. 1–7.

the most important subjects still lingers, than the little progress which has been made in the decision of the controversy respecting the criterion of right and wrong. From the dawn of philosophy, the question concerning the *summum bonum*, or, what is the same thing, concerning the foundation of morality, has been accounted the main problem in speculative thought, has occupied the most gifted intellects and divided them into sects and schools carrying on a vigorous warfare against one another. And after more than two thousand years the same discussions continue, philosophers are still ranged under the same contending banners, and neither thinkers nor mankind at large seem nearer to being unanimous on the subject that when the youth Socrates listened to the old Protagoras and asserted (if Plato's dialogue be grounded on a real conversation) the theory of utilitarianism against the popular morality of the so-called sophist.

It is true that similar confusion and uncertainty and, in some cases, similar discordance exist respecting the first principles of all the sciences, not excepting that which is deemed the most certain of them—mathematics, without much impairing, generally indeed without impairing at all, the trustworthiness of the conclusions of those sciences. An apparent anomaly, the explanation of which is that the detailed doctrines of a science are not usually deduced from, nor depend for their evidence upon, what are called its first principles. Were it not so, there would be no science more precarious, or whose conclusions were more insufficiently made out, than algebra, which derives none of its certainty from what are commonly taught to learners as its elements, since these, as laid down by some of its most eminent teachers, are as full of fictions as English law, and of mysteries as theology. The truths which are ultimately accepted as the first principles of a science are really the last results of metaphysical analysis practiced on the elementary notions with which the science is conversant; and their relation to the science is not that of foundations to an edifice, but of roots to a tree, which may perform their office equally well though they be never dug down to and exposed to light. But though in science the particular truths precede the general theory, the contrary might be expected to be the case with a practical art, such as morals or legislation. All action is for the sake of some end, and rules of action, it seems natural to suppose, must take their whole character and color from the end to which they are subservient. When we engage in a pursuit, a clear and precise conception of what we are pursuing would seem to be the first thing we need, instead of the last we are to look forward to. A test of right and wrong must be the means, one would think, of ascertaining what is right or wrong, and not a consequence of having already ascertained it.

The difficulty is not avoided by having recourse to the popular theory of a natural faculty, a sense or instinct, informing us of right and wrong. For—besides that the existence of such a moral instinct is itself one of the matters in dispute—those believers in it who have any pretensions to philosophy have been obliged to abandon the idea that it discerns what is right or wrong in the particular case in hand, as our other senses discern the sight or sound actually present. Our moral faculty, according to all those of its interpreters who are entitled to the name of thinkers, supplies us only with the general principles of moral judgments; it is a branch of our reason, not of our sensitive faculty, and must be looked to for the abstract doctrines of morality, not for perception of it in the concrete. The intuitive, no less than what may be termed the inductive, school of ethics insists on the necessity of general laws. They both agree that the morality of an individual action is not a question of direct perception, but of the application of a law to an individual case. They recognize also, to a great extent, the same moral laws, but differ as to their evidence and the source from which they derive their authority. According to the one option, the principles of morals are evident a priori, requiring nothing to command assent except that the meaning of the terms be understood. According to the other doctrine, right and wrong, as well as truth and falsehood, are questions of observation and experience. But both hold equally that morality must be deduced from principles; and the intuitive school affirm as strongly as the inductive that there is a science of morals. Yet they seldom attempt to make out a list of the a priori principles which are to serve as the premises of the science; still more rarely do they make any effort to reduce those various principles to one first principle or common ground of obligation. They either assume the ordinary precepts of morals as of a priori authority, or they lay down as the common groundwork of those maxims some generality much less obviously authoritative than the maxims themselves, and which has never succeeded in gaining popular acceptance. Yet to support their pretensions there ought either to be some one fundamental principle or law at the root of all morality, or, if there be several, there should be a determinate order of precedence among them; and the one principle, or the rule for deciding between the various principles when they conflict, ought to be self-evident.

To inquire how far the bad effects of this deficiency have been mitigated in practice, or to what extent the moral beliefs of mankind have been vitiated or made uncertain by the absence of any distinct recognition of an ultimate standard, would imply a complete survey and criticism of past and present ethical doctrine. It would, however, be easy to show that whatever steadiness or consistency these moral beliefs have attained has been mainly due to the tacit influence of a standard not recognized. Although the nonexistence of an acknowledged first principle has made ethics not so much a guide as a consecration of men's actual sentiments, still, as men's sentiments, both of favor and of aversion, are greatly influenced by what they suppose to be the effects of things upon their happiness, the principle of utility, or, as Bentham latterly called it, the greatest happiness principle, has had a large share in forming the moral doctrines even of those who most scornfully reject its authority. Nor is there any school of thought which refuses to admit that the influence of actions on happiness is a most material and even predominant consideration in many of the details of morals, however unwilling to acknowledge it as the fundamental principle of morality and the source of moral obligation. I might go much further and say that to all those a priori moralists who deem it necessary to argue at all, utilitarian arguments are indispensable. It is not my present purpose to criticize these thinkers; but I cannot help referring, for illustration, to a systematic treatise by one of the most illustrious of them, the *Metaphysics of Ethics* by Kant. This remarkable man, whose system of thought will long remain one of the landmarks in the history of philosophical speculation, does, in the treatise in question, lay down a universal first principle as the origin and ground of moral obligation; it is this: "So act that the rule on which thou actest would admit of being adopted as a law by all rational beings." But when he begins to deduce from this precept any of the actual duties of morality, he fails, almost grotesquely, to show that there would be any contradiction, any logical (not to say physical) impossibility, in the adoption by all rational beings of the most outrageously immoral rules of conduct. All he shows is that the *consequences* of their universal adoption would be such as no one would choose to incur.

On the present occasion, I shall, without further discussion of the other theories, attempt to contribute something toward the understanding and appreciation of the Utilitarian or Happiness theory, and toward such proof as it is susceptible of. It is evident that this cannot be proof in the ordinary and popular meaning of the term. Questions of ultimate ends are not amenable to direct proof. Whatever can be proved to be good must be so by being shown to be a means to something admitted to be good without proof. The medical art is proved to be good by its conducing to health; but how is it possible to prove that health is good? The art of music is good, for the reason, among others, that it produces pleasure; but what proof is it possible to give that pleasure is good? If, then, it is asserted that there is a comprehensive formula, including all things which are in themselves good, and that whatever else is good is not so as an end but as a means, the formula may be accepted or rejected, but is not a subject of what is commonly understood by proof. We are not, however, to infer that its acceptance or rejection must depend on blind impulse or arbitrary choice. There is a larger meaning of the word "proof", in which this question is as amenable to it as any other of the disputed questions of philosophy. The subject is within the cognizance of the rational faculty; and neither does that faculty deal with it solely in the way of intuition. Considerations may be presented capable of determining the intellect either to give or withhold its assent to the doctrine; and this is equivalent to proof.

We shall examine presently of what nature are these considerations; in what manner they apply to the case, and what rational grounds, therefore, can be given for accepting or rejecting the utilitarian formula. But it is a preliminary condition of rational acceptance or rejection that the formula should be correctly understood. I believe that the very imperfect notion ordinarily formed of its meaning is the chief obstacle which impedes its reception, and that, could it be cleared even from only the grosser misconceptions, the question would be greatly simplified and a large proportion of its difficulties removed. Before, therefore, I attempt to enter into the philosophical grounds which can be given for assenting to the utilitarian standard, I shall offer some illustrations of the doctrine itself, with the view of showing more clearly what it is, distinguishing it from what it is not, and disposing of such of the practical objections to it as either originate in, or are closely connected with, mistaken interpretations of its meaning. Having thus prepared the ground, I shall afterwards endeavor to throw such light as I can call upon the question considered as one of philosophical theory. . . .

2. *What Utilitarianism Is*

JOHN STUART MILL

A passing remark is all that need be given to the ignorant blunder of supposing that those who stand up for utility as the test of right and wrong use the term in that restricted and merely colloquial sense in which utility is opposed to pleasure. An apology is due to the philosophical opponents of utilitarianism for even the momentary appearance of confounding them with anyone capable of so absurd a misconception; which is the more extraordinary, inasmuch as the contrary accusation, of referring everything to pleasure, and that, too, in its grossest form, is another of the common charges against utilitarianism; and, as has been pointedly remarked by an able writer, the same sort of persons, and often the very same persons, denounce the theory "as impracticably dry when the word 'utility' precedes the word 'pleasure,' and as too practicably voluptuous when the word 'pleasure' precedes the word 'utility.'" Those who know anything about the matter are aware that every writer, from Epicurus to Bentham, who maintained the theory of utility meant by it, not something to be contradistinguished from pleasure, but pleasure itself, together with exemption from pain; and instead of opposing the useful to the agreeable or the ornamental, have always declared that the useful means these, among other things. Yet the common herd, including the herd of writers, not only in newspapers and periodicals, but in books of weight and pretension, are perpetually falling into this shallow mistake. Having caught up the word "utilitarian," while knowing nothing whatever about it but its sound, they habitually express by it the rejection or the neglect of pleasure in some of its forms: of beauty, of ornament, or of amusement. Nor is the term thus ignorantly misapplied solely in disparagement, but occasionally in compliment, as though it implied superiority to frivolity and the mere pleasures of the moment. And this perverted use is the only one in which the word is popularly known, and the one from which the new generation are acquiring their sole notion of its meaning. Those who introduced the word,

but who had for many years discontinued it as a distinctive appellation, may well feel themselves called upon to resume it if by doing so they can hope to contribute anything toward rescuing it from this utter degradation.

The creed which accepts as the foundation of morals, Utility, or the Greatest Happiness Principle, holds that actions are right in proportion as they tend to promote happiness, wrong as they tend to produce the reverse of happiness. By happiness is intended pleasure and the absence of pain; by unhappiness, pain and the privation of pleasure. To give a clear view of the moral standard set up by the theory, much more requires to be said; in particular, what things it includes in the ideas of pain and pleasure, and to what extent this is left an open question. But these supplementary explanations do not affect the theory of life on which this theory of morality is grounded—namely, that pleasure and freedom from pain are the only things desirable as ends; and that all desirable things (which are as numerous in the utilitarian as in any other scheme) are desirable either for pleasure inherent in themselves or as means to the promotion of pleasure and the prevention of pain.

Now such a theory of life excites in many minds, and among them in some of the most estimable in feeling and purpose, inveterate dislike. To suppose that life has (as they express it) no higher end than pleasure—no better and nobler object of desire and pursuit—they designate as utterly mean and groveling, as a doctrine worthy only of swine, to whom the followers of Epicurus were, at a very early period, contemptuously likened; and modern holders of the doctrine are occasionally made the subject of equally polite comparisons by its German, French, and English assailants.

When thus attacked, the Epicureans have always answered that it is not they, but their accusers, who represent human nature in a degrading light, since the accusation supposes human beings to be capable of no pleasures except those of which swine are capable. If this supposition were true, the charge could not be gainsaid, but would then be no longer an imputation;

John Stuart Mill, *Utilitarianism,* 7th ed. (London: Longmans, Green, 1879), pp. 8–38.

for if the sources of pleasure were precisely the same to human beings and to swine, the rule of life which is good enough for the one would be good enough for the other. The comparison of the Epicurean life to that of beasts is felt as degrading, precisely because a beast's pleasures do not satisfy a human being's conceptions of happiness. Human beings have faculties more elevated than the animal appetites and, when once made conscious of them, do not regard anything as happiness which does not include their gratification. I do not indeed consider the Epicureans to have been by any means faultless in drawing out their scheme of consequences from the utilitarian principle. To do this in any sufficient manner, many Stoic, as well as Christian, elements require to be included. But there is no known Epicurean theory of life which does not assign to the pleasures of the intellect, of the feelings and imagination, and of the moral sentiments a much higher value as pleasures than to those of mere sensation. It must be admitted, however, that utilitarian writers in general have placed the superiority of mental over bodily pleasures chiefly in the greater permanency, safety, uncostliness, etc., of the former—that is, in their circumstantial advantages rather than in their intrinsic nature. And on all these points utilitarians have fully proved their case; but they might have taken the other and, as it may be called, higher ground with entire consistency. It is quite compatible with the principle of utility to recognize the fact that some kinds of pleasure are more desirable and more valuable than others. It would be absurd that, while in estimating all other things quality is considered as well as quantity, the estimation of pleasure should be supposed to depend on quantity alone.

If I am asked what I mean by difference of quality in pleasures, or what makes one pleasure more valuable than another, merely as a pleasure, except it being greater in amount, there is but one possible answer. Of two pleasures, if there be one to which all or almost all who have experience of both give a decided preference, irrespective of any feeling of moral obligation to prefer it, that is the more desirable pleasure. If one of the two is, by those who are competently acquainted with both, placed so far above the other that they prefer it, even though knowing it to be attended with a greater amount of discontent, and would not resign it for any quantity of the other pleasure which their nature is capable of, we are justified in ascribing to the preferred enjoyment a superiority in quality so far outweighing quantity as to render it, in comparison, of small account.

Now it is an unquestionable fact that those who are equally acquainted with and equally capable of appreciating and enjoying both do give a most marked preference to the manner of existence which employs their higher faculties. Few human creatures would consent to be changed into any of the lower animals for a promise of the fullest allowance of a beast's pleasures; no intelligent human being would consent to be a fool, no instructed person would be an ignoramus, no person of feeling and conscience would be selfish and base, even though they should be persuaded that the fool, the dunce, or the rascal is better satisfied with his lot than they are with theirs. They would not resign what they possess more than he for the most complete satisfaction of all the desires which they have in common with him. If they ever fancy they would, it is only in cases of unhappiness so extreme that to escape from it they would exchange their lot for almost any other, however undesirable in their own eyes. A being of higher faculties requires more to make him happy, is capable probably of more acute suffering, and certainly accessible to it at more points, than one of an inferior type; but in spite of these liabilities, he can never really wish to sink into what he feels to be a lower grade of existence. We may give what explanation we please of this unwillingness; we may attribute it to pride, a name which is given indiscriminately to some of the most and to some of the least estimable feelings of which mankind are capable; we may refer it to the love of liberty and personal independence, an appeal to which was with the Stoics one of the most effective means for the inculcation of it; to the love of power or to the love of excitement, both of which do really enter into and contribute to it; but its most appropriate appellation is a sense of dignity, which all human beings possess in one form or other, and in some, though by no means in exact, proportion to their higher faculties, and which is so essential a part of the happiness of those in whom it is strong that nothing which conflicts with it could be otherwise than momentarily an object of desire to them. Whoever supposes that this preference takes place at a sacrifice of happiness—that the superior being, in anything like equal circumstances, is not happier than the inferior—confounds the two very different ideas of happiness and content. It is indisputable that the being whose capacities of enjoyment are low has the greatest chance of having them fully satisfied; and a highly endowed being will always feel that any happiness which he can look for, as the world is constituted, is imperfect. But he can learn to bear its imperfections, if they are at all bearable; and they will not make him envy the being who is indeed unconscious of the imperfections, but only because he feels not at all the good which those imperfections qualify. It is better to be a human being dissatisfied than a pig satisfied; better to be Socrates dissatisfied than a fool satisfied. And if the fool, or the pig, are of a different opinion, it is because they only know their own side of the question. The other party to the comparison knows both sides.

It may be objected that many who are capable of the higher pleasures occasionally, under the influence of temptation, postpone them to the lower. But this is quite compatible with a full appreciation of the intrinsic superiority of the higher. Men often, from infirmity of character, make their election for the nearer good, though they know it to be the less valuable; and this no less when the choice is between two bodily pleasures than when it is between bodily and mental. They pursue sensual indulgences to the injury of health, though perfectly aware that health is the greater good. It may be further objected that many who begin with youthful enthusiasm for everything noble, as they advance in years, sink into indolence and selfishness. But I do not believe that those who undergo this very common change voluntarily choose the lower description of pleasures in preference to the higher. I believe that, before they devote themselves exclusively to the one, they have already become incapable of the other. Capacity for the nobler feelings is in most natures a very tender plant, easily killed, not only by hostile influences, but by mere want of sustenance; and in the majority of young persons it speedily dies away if the occupations to which their position in life has devoted them, and the society into which it has thrown them, are not favorable to keeping that higher capacity in exercise. Men lose their high aspirations as they lose their intellectual tastes, because they have not time or opportunity for indulging them; and they addict themselves to inferior pleasures, not because they deliberately prefer them, but because they are either the only ones to which they have access or the only ones which they are any longer capable of enjoying. It may be questioned whether anyone who has remained equally susceptible to both classes of pleasures ever knowingly and calmly preferred the lower, though many, in all ages, have broken down in an ineffectual attempt to combine both.

From this verdict of the only competent judges, I apprehend there can be no appeal. On a question which is the best worth having of two pleasures, or which of two modes of existence is the most grateful to the feelings, apart from its moral attributes and from its consequences, the judgment of those who are qualified by knowledge of both, or, if they differ, that of the majority among them, must be admitted as final. And there needs be the less hesitation to accept this judgment respecting the quality of pleasures, since there is no other tribunal to be referred to even on the question of quantity. What means are there of determining which is the acutest of two pains, or the intensest of two pleasurable sensations, except the general suffrage of those who are familiar with both? Neither pains nor pleasures are homogeneous, and pain is always heterogeneous with pleasure. What is there to decide whether a particular pleasure is worth purchasing at the cost of a particular pain, except the feelings and judgment of the experienced? When, therefore, those feelings and judgment declare the pleasures derived from the higher faculties to be preferable *in kind*, apart from the question of intensity, to those of which the animal nature, disjoined from the higher faculties, is susceptible, they are entitled on this subject to the same regard.

I have dwelt on this point as being part of a perfectly just conception of Utility or Happiness considered as the directive rule of human conduct. But it is by no means an indispensable condition to the acceptance of the utilitarian standard; for that standard is not the agent's own greatest happiness; but the greatest amount of happiness altogether; and if it may possibly be doubted whether a noble character is always the happier for its nobleness, there can be no doubt that it makes other people happier, and that the world in general is immensely a gainer by it. Utilitarianism, therefore, could only attain its end by the general cultivation of nobleness of character, even if each individual were only benefited by the nobleness of others, and his own, so far as happiness is concerned, were a sheer deduction from the benefit. But the bare enunciation of such an absurdity as this last renders refutation superfluous.

According to the Greatest Happiness Principle, as above explained, the ultimate end, with reference to and for the sake of which all other things are desirable (whether we are considering our own good or that of other people), is an existence exempt as far as possible from pain, and as rich as possible in enjoyments, both in point of quantity and quality; the test of quality and the rule for measuring it against quantity being the preference felt by those who, in their opportunities of experience, to which must be added their habits of self-consciousness and self-observation, are best furnished with the means of comparison. This, being, according to the utilitarian opinion, the end of human action, is necessarily also the standard of morality; which may accordingly be defined, the rules and precepts for human conduct, by the observance of which an existence such as has been described might be, to the greatest extent possible, secured to all mankind; and not to them only, but, so far as the nature of things admits, to the whole sentient creation.

Against this doctrine, however, arises another class of objectors who say that happiness, in any form, cannot be the rational purpose of human life and action; because, in the first place, it is unattainable; and they contemptuously ask, What right hast thou to be happy?—a question which Mr. Carlyle clinches by the addition, What right, a short time ago, hadst thou even *to be*? Next they say that men can do *without* happiness; that all noble human beings have felt this, and could not have become noble but by learning the lesson of *Entsagen,* or renunciation; which lesson, thoroughly learned and submitted to, they affirm to be the beginning and necessary condition of all virtue.

The first of these objections would go to the root of the matter were it well founded; for if no happiness is to be had at all by human beings, the attainment of it cannot be the end of morality or of any rational conduct. Though, even in that case, something might still be said for the utilitarian theory, since utility includes not solely the pursuit of happiness, but the prevention or mitigation of unhappiness; and if the former aim be chimerical, there will be all the greater scope and more imperative need for the latter, so long at least as mankind think fit to live and do not take refuge in the simultaneous act of suicide recommended under certain conditions by Novalis. When, however, it is thus positively asserted to be impossible that human life should be happy, the assertion, if not something like a verbal quibble, is at least an exaggeration. If by happiness be meant a continuity of highly pleasurable excitement, it is evident enough that this is impossible. A state of exalted pleasure lasts only moments or in some cases, and with some intermissions, hours or days, and is the occasional brilliant flash of enjoyment, not its permanent and steady flame. Of this the philosophers who have taught that happiness is the end of life were as fully aware as those who taunt them. The happiness which they meant was not a life of rapture, but moments of such, in an existence made up of few and transitory pains, many and various pleasures, with a decided predominance of the active over the passive, and having as the foundation of the whole not to expect more

from life than it is capable of bestowing. A life thus composed, to those who have been fortunate enough to obtain it, has always appeared worthy of the name of happiness. And such an existence is even now the lot of many during some considerable portion of their lives. The present wretched education and wretched social arrangements are the only real hindrance to its being attainable by almost all.

The objectors perhaps may doubt whether human beings, if taught to consider happiness as the end of life, would be satisfied with such a moderate share of it. But great numbers of mankind have been satisfied with much less. The main constituents of a satisfied life appear to be two, either of which by itself is often found sufficient for the purpose: tranquillity and excitement. With much tranquillity, many find that they can be content with very little pleasure; with much excitement, many can reconcile themselves to a considerable quantity of pain. There is assuredly no inherent impossibility of enabling even the mass of mankind to unite both, since the two are so far from being incompatible that they are in natural alliance, the prolongation of either being a preparation for, and exciting a wish for, the other. It is only those in whom indolence amounts to a vice that do not desire excitement after an interval of repose; it is only those in whom the need of excitement is a disease that feel the tranquillity which follows excitement dull and insipid, instead of pleasurable in direct proportion to the excitement which preceded it. When people who are tolerably fortunate in their outward lot do not find in life sufficient enjoyment to make it valuable to them, the cause generally is caring for nobody but themselves. To those who have neither public nor private affections, the excitements of life are much curtailed, and in any case dwindle in value as the time approaches when all selfish interests must be terminated by death; while those who leave after them objects of personal affection, and especially those who have also cultivated a fellow-feeling with the collective interests of mankind, retain as lively an interest in life on the eve of death as in the vigor of youth and health. Next to selfishness, the principal cause which makes life unsatisfactory is want of mental cultivation. A cultivated mind—I do not mean that of a philosopher, but any mind to which the fountains of knowledge have been opened, and which has been taught, in any tolerable degree, to exercise its faculties—finds sources of inexhaustible interest in all that surrounds it: in the objects of nature, the achievements of art, the imaginations of poetry, the incidents of history, the ways of mankind, past and present, and their prospects in the future. It is possible, indeed, to become indifferent to all this, and that too without having exhausted a thousandth part of it, but only when one has had from the beginning no moral or human interest in these things and has sought in them only the gratification of curiosity.

Now there is absolutely no reason in the nature of things why an amount of mental culture sufficient to give an intelligent interest in these objects of contemplation should not be the inheritance of everyone born in a civilized country. As little is there an inherent necessity that any human being should be a selfish egotist, devoid of every feeling or care but those which center in his own miserable individuality. Something far superior to this is sufficiently common even now, to give ample earnest of what the human species may be made. Genuine private affections and a sincere interest in the public good are possible, though in unequal degrees, to every rightly brought up human being. In a world in which there is so much to interest, so much to enjoy, and so much also to correct and improve, everyone who has this moderate amount of moral and intellectual requisites is capable of an existence which may be called enviable; and unless such a person, through bad laws or subjection to the will of others, is denied the liberty to use the sources of happiness within his reach, he will not fail to find this enviable existence, if he escapes the positive evils of life, the great sources of physical and mental suffering—such as indigence, disease, and the unkindness, worthlessness, or premature loss of objects of affection. The main stress of the problem lies, therefore, in the contest with these calamities from which it is a rare good fortune entirely to escape; which, as things now are, cannot be obviated, and often cannot be in any material degree mitigated. Yet no one whose opinion deserves a moment's consideration can doubt that most of the great positive evils of the world are in themselves removable, and will, if human affairs continue to improve, be in the end reduced within narrow limits. Poverty, in any sense implying suffering, may be completely extinguished by the wisdom of society combined with the good sense and providence of individuals. Even that most intractable of enemies, disease, may be indefinitely reduced in dimensions by good physical and moral education and proper control of noxious influences, while the progress of science holds out a promise for the future of still more direct conquests over this detestable foe. And every advance in that direction relieves us from some, not only of the chances which cut short our own lives, but, what

concerns us still more, which deprive us of those in whom our happiness is wrapt up. As for vicissitudes of fortune and other disappointments connected with worldly circumstances, these are principally the effect either of gross imprudence, of ill-regulated desires, or of bad or imperfect social institutions. All the grand sources, in short, of human suffering are in a great degree, many of them almost entirely, conquerable by human care and effort; and though their removal is grievously slow—though a long succession of generations will perish in the breach before the conquest is completed, and this world becomes all that, if will and knowledge were not wanting, it might easily be made—yet every mind sufficiently intelligent and generous to bear a part, however small and inconspicuous, in the endeavor will draw a noble enjoyment from the contest itself, which he would not for any bribe in the form of selfish indulgence consent to be without.

And this leads to the true estimation of what is said by the objectors concerning the possibility and the obligation of learning to do without happiness. Unquestionably it is possible to do without happiness; it is done involuntarily by nineteen-twentieths of mankind, even in those parts of our present world which are least deep in barbarism; and it often has to be done voluntarily by the hero or the martyr, for the sake of something which he prizes more than his individual happiness. But this something, what is it, unless the happiness of others or some of the requisites of happiness? It is noble to be capable of resigning entirely one's own portion of happiness, or chances of it; but, after all, this self-sacrifice must be for some end; it is not its own end; and if we are told that its end is not happiness but virtue, which is better than happiness, I ask, would the sacrifice be made if the hero or martyr did not believe that it would earn for others immunity from similar sacrifices? Would it be made if he thought that his renunciation of happiness for himself would produce no fruit for any of his fellow creatures, but to make their lot like his and place them also in the condition of persons who have renounced happiness? All honor to those who can abnegate for themselves the personal enjoyment of life when by such renunciation they contribute worthily to increase the amount of happiness in the world; but he who does it or professes to do it for any other purpose is no more deserving of admiration than the ascetic mounted on his pillar. He may be an inspiriting proof of what men *can* do, but assuredly not an example of what they *should*.

Though it is only in a very imperfect state of the world's arrangements that anyone can best serve the happiness of others by the absolute sacrifice of his own, yet, so long as the world is in that imperfect state, I fully acknowledge that the readiness to make such a sacrifice is the highest virtue which can be found in man. I will add that in this condition of the world, paradoxical as the assertion may be, the conscious ability to do without happiness gives the best prospect of realizing such happiness as is attainable. For nothing except that consciousness can raise a person above the chances of life by making him feel that, let fate and fortune do their worst, they have not power to subdue him; which, once felt, frees him from excess of anxiety concerning the evils of life and enables him, like many a Stoic in the worst times of the Roman Empire, to cultivate in tranquillity the sources of satisfaction accessible to him, without concerning himself about the uncertainty of their duration any more than about their inevitable end.

Meanwhile, let utilitarians never cease to claim the morality of self-devotion as a possession which belongs by as good a right to them as either to the Stoic or to the Transcendentalist. The utilitarian morality does recognize in human beings the power of sacrificing their own greatest good for the good of others. It only refuses to admit that the sacrifice is itself a good. A sacrifice which does not increase or tend to increase the sum total of happiness, it considers as wasted. The only self-renunciation which it applauds is devotion to the happiness, or to some of the means of happiness, of others, either of mankind collectively or of individuals within the limits imposed by the collective interests of mankind.

I must again repeat what the assailants of utilitarianism seldom have the justice to acknowledge, that the happiness which forms the utilitarian standard of what is right in conduct is not the agent's own happiness but that of all concerned. As between his own happiness and that of others, utilitarianism requires him to be as strictly impartial as a disinterested and benevolent spectator. In the golden rule of Jesus of Nazareth, we read the complete spirit of the ethics of utility. "To do as you would be done by," and "to love your neighbor as yourself," constitute the ideal perfection of utilitarian morality. As the means of making the nearest approach to this ideal, utility would enjoin, first, that laws and social arrangements should place the happiness or (as, speaking practically, it may be called) the interest of every individual as nearly as possible in harmony with the interest of the whole; and, secondly, that education and opinion, which have so vast a power over human character, should so use that power as to establish in the mind of every individual an indissoluble association between his own happiness and the good of the whole, especially between his own happiness and the practice of such modes of conduct, negative and positive, as regard for the universal happiness prescribes; so that not only he may be unable to conceive the possibility of happiness to himself, consistently with conduct opposed to the general good, but also that a direct impulse to promote the general good may be in every individual one of the habitual motives of action, and the sentiments connected therewith may fill a large and prominent place in every human being's sentient existence. If the impugners of the utilitarian morality represented it to their own minds in this its true character, I know not what recommendation possessed by any other morality they could possibly affirm to be wanting to it; what more beautiful or more exalted developments of human nature any other ethical system can be supposed to foster, or what springs of action, not accessible to the utilitarian, such systems rely on for giving effect to their mandates.

The objectors to utilitarianism cannot always be charged with representing it in a discreditable light. On the contrary, those among them who entertain anything like a just idea of its disinterested character sometimes find fault with its standard as being too high for humanity. They say it is exacting too much to require that people shall always act from the inducement of promoting the general interest of society. But this is to mistake the very meaning of a standard of morals and confound the rule of action with the motive of it. It is the business of ethics to tell us what are our duties, or by what test we may know them; but no system of ethics requires that the sole motive of all we do shall be a feeling of duty; on the contrary, ninety-nine hundredths of all our actions are done from other motives, and rightly so done if the rule of duty does not condemn them. It is the more unjust to utilitarianism that this particular misapprehension should be made a ground of objection to it, inasmuch as utilitarian moralists have gone beyond almost all others in affirming that the motive has nothing to do with the morality of the action, though much with the worth of the agent. He who saves a fellow creature from drowning does what is morally right, whether his motive be duty or the hope of being paid for his trouble; he who betrays the friend that trusts him is guilty of a crime, even if his object be to serve another friend to whom he is under greater obligations.[1] But to speak only of actions done from the motive of duty, and in direct obedience to principle: it is a misapprehension of the utilitarian mode of thought to conceive it as implying that people should fix their minds upon so wide a generality as the world, or society at large. The great majority of good actions are intended not for the benefit of the world, but for that of individuals, of which the good of the world is made up; and the thoughts of the most virtuous man need not on these occasions travel beyond the particular persons concerned, except so far as is necessary to assure himself that in benefiting them he is not violating the rights, that is, the legitimate and authorized expectations, of anyone else. The multiplication of happiness is, according to the utilitarian ethics, the object of virtue: the occasions on which any person (except one in a thousand) has it in his power to do this on an extended scale—in other words, to be a public benefactor—are but exceptional; and on these occasions alone is he called on to consider public utility; in every other case, private utility, the interest or happiness of some few persons, is all he has to attend to. Those alone the influence of whose actions extends to society in general need concern themselves habitually about so large an object. In the case of abstinences indeed—of things which people forbear to do from moral considerations, though the consequences in the particular case might be beneficial—it would be unworthy of an intelligent agent not to be consciously aware that the action is of a class which, if practiced generally, would be generally injurious, and that this is the ground of the obligation to abstain from it. The amount of regard for the public interest implied in this recognition is no greater than is demanded by every system of morals, for they all enjoin to abstain from whatever is manifestly pernicious to society.

The same considerations dispose of another reproach against the doctrine of utility, founded on a still grosser misconception of the purpose of a standard of morality and of the very meaning of the words "right" or "wrong." It is often affirmed that utilitarianism renders men cold and unsympathizing; that it chills their moral feelings toward individuals; that it makes them regard only the dry and hard considerations of the consequences of actions, not taking into their moral estimate the qualities from which those actions emanate. If the assertion means that they do not allow their judgment respecting the rightness or wrongness of an action to be influenced by their opinion of the qualities of the person who does it, this is a complaint not against utilitarianism, but against any standard or morality at all; for certainly no known ethical standard decides an action to be good or bad because it is done by a good or bad man, still less because done by an amiable, a brave, or a benevolent man, or the contrary. These considerations are relevant, not to the estimation of actions, but of persons; and there is nothing in the utilitarian theory inconsistent with the fact that there are other things which interest us in persons besides the rightness and wrongness of their actions. The Stoics, indeed, with the paradoxical misuse of language which was part of their system, and by which they strove to raise themselves above all concern about anything but virtue, were

---

[1]An opponent, whose intellectual and moral fairness it is a pleasure to acknowledge (the Rev. J. Llewellyn Davies), has objected to this passage, saying, "Surely the rightness or wrongness of saving a man from drowning does depend very much upon the motive with which it is done. Suppose that a tyrant, when his enemy jumped into the sea to escape from him, saved him from drowning simply in order that he might inflict upon him more exquisite tortures, would it tend to clearness to speak of that rescue as 'a morally right action'? Or suppose again, according to one of the stock illustrations of ethical inquiries, that a man betrayed a trust received from a friend, because the discharge of it would fatally injure that friend himself or someone belonging to him, "would utilitarianism compel one to call the betrayal 'a crime' as much as if it had been done from the meanest motive?"

I submit that he who saves another from drowning in order to kill him by torture afterward does not differ only in motive from him who does the same thing from duty or benevolence; the act itself is different. The rescue of the man is, in the case supposed, only the necessary first step of an act far more atrocious than leaving him to drown would have been. Had Mr. Davies said, "The rightness or wrongness of saving a man from drowning does depend very much"—not upon the motive, but—"upon the *intention*," no utilitarian would have differed from him. Mr. Davies, by an oversight too common not to be quite venial, has in this case confounded the very different ideas of Motive and Intention. There is no point which utilitarian thinkers (and Bentham preeminently) have taken more pains to illustrate than this. The morality of the action depends entirely upon the intention—that is, upon what the agent *wills to do*. But the motive, that is, the feeling which makes him will so to do, if it makes no difference in the act, makes none in the morality; though it makes a great difference in our moral estimation of the agent, especially it if indicates a good or bad habitual *disposition*—a bent of character from which useful, or from which hurtful actions are likely to arise.

fond of saying that he who has that has everything; that he, and only he, is rich, is beautiful, is a king. But no claim of this description is made for the virtuous man by the utilitarian doctrine. Utilitarians are quite aware that there are other desirable possessions and qualities besides virtue, and are perfectly willing to allow to all of them their full worth. They are also aware that a right action does not necessarily indicate a virtuous character, and that actions which are blamable often proceed from qualities entitled to praise. When this is apparent in any particular case, it modifies their estimation, not certainly of the act, but of the agent. I grant that they are, notwithstanding, of opinion that in the long run the best proof of a good character is good actions; and resolutely refuse to consider any mental disposition as good of which the predominant tendency is to produce bad conduct. This makes them unpopular with many people, but it is an unpopularity which they must share with everyone who regards the distinction between right and wrong in a serious light; and the reproach is not one which a conscientious utilitarian need be anxious to repel.

If no more be meant by the objection than that many utilitarians look on the morality of actions, as measured by the utilitarian standards, with too exclusive a regard, and do not lay sufficient stress upon the other beauties of character which go toward making a human being lovable or admirable, this may be admitted. Utilitarians who have cultivated their moral feelings, but not their sympathies, nor their artistic perceptions, do fall into this mistake; and so do all other moralists under the same conditions. What can be said in excuse for other moralists is equally available for them, namely, that, if there is to be any error, it is better that it should be on that side. As a matter of fact, we may affirm that among utilitarians, as among adherents of other systems, there is every imaginable degree of rigidity and of laxity in the application of their standard; some are even puritanically rigorous, while others are as indulgent as can possibly be desired by sinner or by sentimentalist. But on the whole, a doctrine which brings prominently forward the interest that mankind have in the repression and prevention of conduct which violates the moral law is likely to be inferior to no other in turning the sanctions of opinion against such violations. It is true, the question "What does violate the moral law?" is one on which those who recognize different standards of morality are likely now and then to differ. But difference of opinion on moral questions was not first introduced into the world by utilitarianism, while that doctrine does supply, if not always an easy, at

all events a tangible and intelligible, mode of deciding such differences.

It may not be superfluous to notice a few more of the common misapprehensions of utilitarian ethics, even those which are so obvious and gross that it might appear impossible for any person of candor and intelligence to fall into them; since persons, even of considerable mental endowment, often give themselves so little trouble to understand the bearings of any opinion against which they entertain a prejudice, and men are in general so little conscious of this voluntary ignorance as a defect that the vulgarest misunderstandings of ethics doctrines are continually met with in the deliberate writings of persons of the greatest pretensions both to high principle and to philosophy. We not uncommonly hear the doctrine of utility inveighed against a *godless* doctrine. If it be necessary to say anything at all against so mere an assumption, we may say that the question depends upon what idea we have formed of the moral character of the Deity. If it be a true belief that God desires, above all things, the happiness of his creatures, and that this was his purpose in their creation, utility is not only not a godless doctrine, but more profoundly religious than any other. If it be meant that utilitarianism does not recognize the revealed will of God as the supreme law of morals, I answer that a utilitarian who believes in the perfect goodness and wisdom of *God* necessarily believes that whatever God has thought fit to reveal on the subject of morals must fulfill the requirements of utility in a supreme degree. But others besides utilitarians have been of opinion that the Christian revelation was intended, and is fitted, to inform the hearts and minds of mankind with a spirit which should enable them to find for themselves what is right, and incline them to do it when found, rather than to tell them, except in a very general way, what it is; and that we need a doctrine of ethics, carefully followed out, to *interpret* to us the will of God. Whether this opinion is correct or not, it is superfluous here to discuss; since whatever aid religion, either natural or revealed, can afford to ethical investigation is as open to the utilitarian moralist as to any other. He can use it as the testimony of God to the usefulness or hurtfulness of any given course of action by as good a right as others can use it for the indication of a transcendental law having no connection with usefulness or with happiness.

Again, utility is often summarily stigmatized as an immoral doctrine by giving it the name of Expediency, and taking advantage of the popular use of that term to contrast it with Principle. But the expedient, in the sense in which it is opposed to the Right, generally means that which is expedient for the particular interest of the agent himself; as when a minister sacrifices the interests of his country to keep himself in place. When it means anything better than this, it means that which is expedient for some immediate object, some temporary purpose, but which violates a rule whose observance is expedient in a much higher degree. The Expedient, in this sense, instead of being the same thing with the useful, is a branch of the hurtful. Thus it would often be expedient, for the purpose of getting over some momentary embarrassment, or attaining some object immediately useful to ourselves or others, to tell a lie. But inasmuch as the cultivation in ourselves of a sensitive feeling on the subject of veracity is one of the most useful, and the enfeeblement of that feeling one of the most hurtful, things to which our conduct can be instrumental; and inasmuch as any, even unintentional, deviation from truth does that much toward weakening the trustworthiness of human assertion, which is not only the principal support of all present social well-being, but the insufficiency of which does more than any one thing that can be named to keep back civilization, virtue, everything on which human happiness on the largest scale depends—we feel that the violation, for a present advantage, of a rule of such transcendent expediency is not expedient, and that he who, for the sake of convenience to himself or to some other individual, does what depends on him to deprive mankind of the good, and inflict upon them the evil, involved in the greater or less reliance which they can place in each other's words, acts the part of one of their worst enemies. Yet that even this rule, sacred as it is, admits of possible exceptions is acknowledged by all moralists; the chief of which is when the withholding of some fact (as of information from a malefactor, or of bad news from a person dangerously ill) would save an individual (especially an individual other than oneself) from great and unmerited evil, and when the withholding can only be effected by denial. But in order that the exception may not extend itself beyond the need, and may have the least possible effect in weakening reliance on veracity, it ought to be recognized and, if possible, its limits defined; and, if the principle of utility is good for anything, it must be good for weighing these conflicting utilities against one another and marking out the region within which one or the other preponderates.

Again, defenders of utility often find themselves called upon to reply to such objections as this—that there is not time, previous to action, for calculating and weighing the effects of any line of conduct on the general happiness. This is exactly as if anyone were to say that it is impossible to guide our conduct by Christianity because there is not time, on every occasion on which anything has to be done, to read through the Old and New Testaments. The answer to the objection is that there has been ample time, namely, the whole past duration of the human species. During all that time mankind have been learning by experience the tendencies of actions; on which experience all the prudence as well as all the morality of life are dependent. People talk as if the commencement of this course of experience had hitherto been put off, and as if, at the moment when some man feels tempted to meddle with the property or life of another, he had to begin considering for the first time whether murder and theft are injurious to human happiness. Even then I do not think that he would find the question very puzzling; but, at all events, the matter is now done to his hand. It is truly a whimsical supposition that, if mankind were agreed in considering utility to be the test of morality, they would remain without any agreement as to what is useful, and would take no measures for having their notions on the subject taught to the young and enforced by law and opinion. There is no difficulty in proving any ethical standard whatever to work ill if we suppose universal idiocy to be conjoined with it; but on any hypothesis short of that, mankind must by this time have acquired positive beliefs as to the effects of some actions on their happiness; and the beliefs which have thus come down are the rules of morality for the multitude, and for the philosopher until he has succeeded in finding better. That philosophers might easily do this, even now, on many subjects; that the received code of ethics is by no means of divine right; and that mankind have still much to learn as to the effects of actions on the general happiness, I admit or rather earnestly maintain. The corollaries from the principle of utility, like the precepts of every practical art, admit of indefinite improvement, and, in a progressive state of the human mind, their improvement is perpetually going on. But to consider the rules of morality as improvable is one thing; to pass over the intermediate generalization entirely and endeavor to test each individual action directly by the first principle is another. It is a strange notion that the acknowledgment of a first principle is inconsistent with the admission of secondary ones. To inform a traveler respecting the place of his ultimate destination is not to forbid the use of landmarks and direction-posts on the way. The proposition that happiness is the end and aim of morality does not mean that no road ought to be laid down to that goal, or that persons going thither should not be advised to take one direction rather than another. Men really ought to leave off talking a kind of nonsense on this subject, which they would neither talk nor listen to on other matters of practical concernment. Nobody argues that the art of navigation is not founded on astronomy because sailors cannot wait to calculate the Nautical Almanac. Being rational creatures, they go to sea with it ready calculated; and all rational creatures go out upon the sea of life with their minds made up on the common questions of right and wrong, as well as on many of the far more difficult questions of wise and foolish. And this, as long as foresight is a human quality, it is to be presumed they will continue to do. Whatever we adopt as the fundamental principle of morality, we require subordinate principles to apply it by; the impossibility of doing without them, being common to all systems, can afford no argument against any one in particular; but gravely to argue as if no such secondary principles could be had, and as if mankind had remained till now, and always must remain, without drawing any general conclusions from the experience of human life is as high a pitch, I think, as absurdity has ever reached in philosophical controversy.

The remainder of the stock arguments against utilitarianism mostly consist in laying to its charge the common infirmities of human nature, and the general difficulties which embarrass conscientious persons in shaping their course through life. We are told that a utilitarian will be apt to make his own particular case an exception to moral rules, and, when under temptation, will see a utility in the breach of a rule, greater than he will see in its observance. But is utility the only creed which is able to furnish us with excuses for evildoing and means of cheating our own conscience? They are afforded in abundance by all doctrines which recognize as a fact in morals the existence of conflicting considerations, which all doctrines do that have been believed by sane persons. It is not the fault of any

creed, but of the complicated nature of human affairs, that rules of conduct cannot be so framed as to require no exceptions, and that hardly any kind of action can safely be laid down as either always obligatory or always condemnable. There is no ethical creed which does not temper the rigidity of its laws by giving a certain latitude, under the moral responsibility of the agent, for accommodation to peculiarities of circumstances; and under every creed, at the opening thus made, self-deception and dishonest casuistry get in. There exists no moral system under which there do not arise unequivocal cases of conflicting obligation. These are the real difficulties, the knotty points both in the theory of ethics and in the conscientious guidance of personal conduct. They are overcome practically, with greater or with less success, according to the intellect and virtue of the individual; but it can hardly be pretended that anyone will be the less qualified for dealing with them, from possessing an ultimate standard to which conflicting rights and duties can be referred. If utility is the ultimate source of moral obligations, utility may be invoked to decide between them when their demands are incompatible. Though the application of the standard may be difficult, it is better than none at all; while in other systems, the moral laws all claiming independent authority, there is no common umpire entitled to interfere between them; their claims to precedence one over another rest on little better than sophistry, and, unless determined, as they generally are, by the unacknowledged influence of consideration of utility, afford a free scope for the action of personal desires and partialities. We must remember that only in these cases of conflict between secondary principles is it requisite that first principles should be appealed to. There is no case of moral obligation in which some secondary principle is not involved; and if only one, there can seldom be any real doubt which one it is, in the mind of any person by whom the principle itself is recognized.

3. On the Connexion between Justice and Utility

JOHN STUART MILL

In all ages of speculation, one of the strongest obstacles to the reception of the doctrine that Utility or Happiness is the criterion of right and wrong, has been drawn from the idea of Justice. The powerful sentiment, and apparently clear perception, which that word recalls with a rapidity and certainty resembling an instinct, have seemed to the majority of thinkers to point to an inherent quality in things; to show that the Just must have an existence in Nature as something absolute—generically distinct from every variety of the Expedient, and, in idea, opposed to it, though (as is commonly acknowledged) never, in the long run, disjoined from it in fact.

In the case of this, as of our other moral sentiments, there is no necessary connexion between the question of its origin, and that of its binding force. That a feeling is bestowed on us by Nature, does not necessarily legitimate all its promptings. The feeling of justice might be a peculiar instinct, and might yet require, like our other instincts, to be controlled and enlightened by a higher reason. If we have intellectual instincts, leading us to judge in a particular way, as well as animal instincts that prompt us to act in a particular way, there is no necessity that the former should be more infallible in their sphere than the latter in theirs: it may as well happen that wrong judgments are occasionally suggested by those, as wrong actions by these. But though it is one thing to believe that we have natural feelings of justice, and another to acknowledge them as an ultimate criterion of conduct, these two opinions are very closely connected in point of fact. Mankind are always predisposed to believe that any subjective feeling, not otherwise accounted for, is a revelation of some objective reality. Our present object is to determine whether the reality, to which the feeling of justice corresponds, is one which needs any such special revelation; whether the justice or injustice of an action is a thing intrinsically peculiar, and distinct from all its other qualities, or only a combination of certain of those qualities, presented under a peculiar aspect. For

the purpose of this inquiry, it is practically important to consider whether the feeling itself, of justice and injustice, is *sui generis* like our sensations of colour and taste, or a derivative feeling, formed by a combination of others. And this it is the more essential to examine, as people are in general willing enough to allow, that objectively the dictates of justice coincide with a part of the field of General Expediency; but inasmuch as the subjective mental feeling of Justice is different from that which commonly attaches to simple expediency, and, except in extreme cases of the latter, is far more imperative in its demands, people find it difficult to see, in Justice, only a particular kind or branch of general utility, and think that its superior binding force requires a totally different origin.

To throw light upon this question, it is necessary to attempt to ascertain what is the distinguishing character of justice, or of injustice: what is the quality, or whether there is any quality, attributed in common to modes of conduct designated as unjust (for justice, like many other moral attributes, is best defined by its opposite), and distinguishing them from such modes of conduct as are disapproved, but without having that particular epithet of disapprobation applied to them. If, in everything which men are accustomed to characterize as just or unjust, some one common attribute or collection of attributes is always present, we may judge whether this particular attribute or combination of attributes would be capable of gathering round it a sentiment of that peculiar character and intensity by virtue of the general laws of our emotional constitution, or whether the sentiment is inexplicable, and requires to be regarded as a special provision of Nature. If we find the former to be the case, we shall, in resolving this question, have resolved also the main problem: if the latter, we shall have to seek for some other mode of investigating it.

To find the common attributes of a variety of objects, it is necessary to begin by surveying the objects themselves in the concrete. Let us therefore advert successively to the various modes of action, and arrangements of human affairs, which are classed, by universal or widely spread opinion, as Just or as

John Stuart Mill, *Utilitarianism*, 7th ed. (London: Longmans, Green, 1879), pp. 39–51.

Unjust. The things well known to excite the sentiments associated with those names are of a very multifarious character. I shall pass them rapidly in review, without studying any particular arrangement.

In the first place, it is mostly considered unjust to deprive anyone of his personal liberty, his property, or any other thing which belongs to him by law. Here, therefore, is one instance of the application of the terms just and unjust in a perfectly definite sense, namely, that it is just to respect, unjust to violate, the *legal rights* of anyone. But this judgment admits of several exceptions, arising from the other forms in which the notions of justice and injustice present themselves. For example, the person who suffers the deprivation may (as the phrase is) have *forfeited* the rights which he is so deprived of: a case to which we shall return presently. But also,

Secondly, the legal rights of which he is deprived may be rights which *ought* not to have belonged to him; in other words, the law which confers on him these rights, may be a bad law. When it is so, or when (which is the same thing for our purpose) it is supposed to be so, opinions will differ as to the justice or injustice of infringing it. Some maintain that no law, however bad, ought to be disobeyed by an individual citizen; that his opposition to it, if shown at all, should only be shown in endeavouring to get it altered by competent authority. This opinion (which condemns many of the most illustrious benefactors of mankind, and would often protect pernicious institutions against the only weapons which, in the state of things existing at the time, have any chance of succeeding against them) is defended, by those who hold it, on grounds of expediency; principally, on that of the importance, to the common interest of mankind, of maintaining inviolate the sentiment of submission to law. Other persons, again, hold the directly contrary opinion, that any law, judged to be bad, may blamelessly be disobeyed, even though it be not judged to be unjust, but only inexpedient; while others would confine the licence of disobedience to the case of unjust laws: but again, some say, that all laws which are inexpedient are unjust; since every law imposes some restriction on the natural liberty of mankind, which restriction is an injustice, unless legitimated by tending to their good. Among these diversities of opinion, it seems to be universally admitted that there may be unjust laws, and that law, consequently, is not the ultimate criterion of justice, but may give to one person a benefit, or impose on another an evil, which justice condemns. When, however, a law is thought to be unjust, it seems always to be regarded as being so in the same way in which a breach of law is unjust, namely, by infringing somebody's right; which, as it cannot in this case be a legal right, receives a different appellation, and is called a moral right. We may say, therefore, that a second case of injustice consists in taking or withholding from any person that to which he has a *moral right.*

Thirdly, it is universally considered just that each person should obtain that (whether good or evil) which he *deserves*; and unjust that he should obtain a good, or be made to undergo an evil, which he does not deserve. This is, perhaps, the clearest and most emphatic form in which the idea of justice is conceived by the general mind. As it involves the notion of desert, the question arises what constitutes desert? Speaking in a general way, a person is understood to deserve good if he does right, evil if he does wrong; and in a more particular sense, to deserve good from those to whom he does or has done good, and evil from those to whom he does or has done evil. The precept of returning good for evil has never been regarded as a case of the fulfilment of justice, but as one in which the claims of justice are waived, in obedience to other considerations.

Fourthly, it is confessedly unjust to *break faith* with any one: to violate an engagement, either express or implied, or disappoint expectations raised by our own conduct, at least if we have raised those expectations knowingly and voluntarily. Like the other obligations of justice already spoken of, this one is not regarded as absolute, but as capable of being overruled by a stronger obligation of justice on the other side; or by such conduct on the part of the person concerned as is deemed to absolve us from our obligation to him, and to constitute a *forfeiture* of the benefit which he has been led to expect.

Fifthly, it is, by universal admission, inconsistent with justice to be *partial*; to show favour and preference to one person over another, in matters to which favour and preference do not properly apply. Impartiality, however, does not seem to be regarded as a duty in itself, but rather as instrumental to some other duty; for it is admitted that favour and preference are not always censurable, and indeed the cases in which they are condemned are rather the exception than the rule. A person would be more likely to be blamed than applauded for giving his family or friends no superiority in good offices over strangers, when he could do so without violating any other duty; and no one thinks it unjust to seek one person in preference to another as a friend, connexion, or companion. Impartiality where rights are concerned is of course obligatory, but this is involved in the more general obligation of giving to every one his right. A tribunal, for example, must be impartial, because it is bound to award, without regard to any other consideration, a disputed object to the one of two parties who has the right to it. There are other cases in which impartiality means, being solely influenced by desert; as with those who, in the capacity of judges, preceptors, or parents, administer reward and punishment as such. There are cases, again, in which it means, being solely influenced by consideration for the public interest; as in making a selection among candidates for a government employment. Impartiality, in short, as an obligation of justice, may be said to mean, being exclusively influenced by the considerations which it is supposed ought to influence the particular case in hand; and resisting the solicitation of any motives which prompt to conduct different from what those considerations would dictate.

Nearly allied to the idea of impartiality is that of *equality,* which often enters as a component part both into the conception of justice and into the practice of it, and, in the eyes of many persons, constitutes its essence. But in this, still more than in any other case, the notion of justice varies in different persons, and always conforms in its variations to their notion of utility. Each person maintains that equality is the dictate of justice, except where he thinks that expediency requires inequality. The justice of giving equal protection to the rights of all, is maintained by those who support the most outrageous inequality in the rights themselves. Even in slave countries it is theoretically admitted that the rights of the slave, such as they are, ought to be as sacred as those of the master; and that a tribunal which fails to enforce them with equal strictness is wanting in justice; while, at the same time, institutions which leave to the slave scarcely any rights to enforce, are not deemed unjust, because they are not deemed inexpedient. Those who think that utility requires distinctions of rank, do not consider it unjust that riches and social privileges should be unequally dispensed; but those who think this inequality inexpedient, think it unjust also. Whoever thinks that government is necessary, sees no injustice in as much inequality as is constituted by giving to the magistrate powers not granted to other people. Even among those who hold levelling doctrines, there are as many questions of justice as there are differences of opinion about expediency. Some Communists consider it unjust that the produce of the labour of the community should be shared on any other principle than that of exact equality; others think it just that those should receive most whose needs are greatest; while others hold that those who work harder, or who produce more, or whose services are more valuable to the community, may justly claim a larger quota in the division of the produce. And the sense of natural justice may be plausibly appealed to in behalf of every one of these opinions.

Among so many diverse applications of the term Justice, which yet is not regarded as ambiguous, it is a matter of some difficulty to seize the mental link which holds them together, and on which the moral sentiment adhering to the term essentially depends.

. . . We do not call anything wrong, unless we mean to imply that a person ought to be punished in some way or other for doing it; if not by law, by the opinion of his fellow creatures; if not by opinion, by the reproaches of his own conscience. This seems the real turning point of the distinction between morality and simple expediency. It is a part of the notion of Duty in every one of its forms, that a person may rightfully be compelled to fulfil it. Duty is a thing which may be *exacted* from a person, as one exacts a debt. Unless we think that it might be exacted from him, we do not call it his duty. Reasons of prudence, or the interest of other people, may militate against actually exacting it; but the person himself, it is clearly understood, would not be entitled to complain. There are other things, on the contrary, which we wish that people should do, which we like or admire them for doing, perhaps dislike or despise them for not doing, but yet admit that they are not bound to do; it is not a case of moral obligation; we do not blame them, that is, we do not think that they are proper objects of punishment. How we come by these ideas of deserving and not deserving punishment, will appear, perhaps, in the sequel; but I think there is no doubt that this distinction lies at the bottom of the notions of right and wrong; that we call any conduct wrong, or employ instead, some other term of dislike or disparagement, according as we think that the person ought, or ought not, to be punished for it; and we say that it would be right to do so and so, or merely that it would be desirable or laudable, according as we would wish to see the person whom it concerns, compelled or only persuaded and exhorted, to act in that manner.

This, therefore, being the characteristic difference which marks off, not justice, but morality in general, from the remaining provinces of Expediency and Worthiness; the character is still to be sought which distinguishes justice from other branches of morality. Now it is known that ethical writers divide moral duties into two classes, denoted by the ill-chosen expressions, duties of perfect and of imperfect obligation; the latter being those in which, though the act is obligatory, the particular occasions of performing it are left to our choice; as in the case of charity or beneficence, which we are indeed bound to practise, but not towards any definite person, nor at any prescribed time. In the more precise language of philosophic jurists, duties of perfect obligation are those duties in virtue of which a correlative *right* resides in some person or persons; duties of imperfect obligation are those moral obligations which do not give birth to any right. I think it will be found that this distinction exactly coincides with that which exists between justice and the other obligations of morality. In our survey of the various popular acceptations of justice, the term appeared generally to involve the idea of a personal right—a claim on the part of one or more individuals, like that which the law gives when it confers a proprietary or other legal right. Whether the injustice consists in depriving a person of a possession, or in breaking faith with him, or in treating him worse than he deserves, or worse than other people who have no greater claims, in each case the supposition implies two things—a wrong done, and some assignable person who is wronged. Injustice may also be done by treating a person better than others; but the wrong in this case is to his competitors, who are also assignable persons. It seems to me that this feature in the case— a right in some person, correlative to the moral obligation—constitutes the specific difference between justice, and generosity or beneficence. Justice implies something which it is not only right to do, and wrong not to do, but which some individual person can claim from us as his moral right. No one has a moral right to our generosity or beneficence, because we are not morally bound to practise those virtues towards any given individual. And it will be found with respect to this as with respect to every correct definition, that the instances which seem to conflict with it are those which most confirm it. For if a moralist attempts, as some have done, to make out that mankind generally, though not any given individual, have a right to all the good we can do them, he at once, by that thesis, includes generosity and beneficence within the category of justice. He is obliged to say, that our utmost exertions are *due* to our fellow creatures, thus assimilating them to a debt; or that nothing less can be a sufficient *return* for what society does for us, thus classing

the case as one of gratitude; both of which are acknowledged cases of justice. Wherever there is a right, the case is one of justice, and not of the virtue of beneficence: and whoever does not place the distinction between justice and morality in general where we have now placed it, will be found to make no distinction between them at all, but to merge all morality in justice.

The sentiment of justice, in that one of its elements which consist of the desire to punish, is thus, I conceive, the natural feeling of retaliation or vengeance, rendered by intellect and sympathy applicable to those injuries, that is, to those hurts, which wound us through, or in common with, society at large. This sentiment, in itself, has nothing moral in it; what is moral is, the exclusive subordination of it to the social sympathies, so as to wait on and obey their call. For the natural feeling tends to make us resent indiscriminately whatever any one does that is disagreeable to us; but when moralized by the social feeling, it only acts in the directions conformable to the general good: just persons resenting a hurt to society, though not otherwise a hurt to themselves, and not resenting a hurt to themselves, however painful, unless it be of the kind which society has a common interest with them in the repression of.

It is no objection against this doctrine to say, that when we feel our sentiment of justice outraged, we are not thinking of society at large, or of any collective interest, but only of the individual case. It is common enough certainly, though the reverse of commendable, to feel resentment merely because we have suffered pain; but a person whose resentment is really a moral feeling, that is, who considers whether an act is blameable before he allows himself to resent it—such a person, though he may not say expressly to himself that he is standing up for the interest of society, certainly does feel that he is asserting a rule which is for the benefit of others as well as for his own. If he is not feeling this—if he is regarding the act solely as it affects him individually—he is not consciously just; he is not concerning himself about the justice of his actions. This is admitted even by anti-utilitarian moralists. When Kant (as before remarked) propounds as the fundamental principle of morals, 'So act, that thy rule of conduct might be adopted as a law by all rational beings,' he virtually acknowledges that the interest of mankind collectively, or at least of mankind indiscriminately, must be in the mind of the agent when conscientiously deciding on the morality of the act. Otherwise he uses words without a meaning: for, that a rule even of utter selfishness could not *possibly* be adopted by all rational beings—that there is any insuperable obstacle in the nature of things to its adoption—cannot be even plausibly maintained. To give any meaning to Kant's principle, the sense put upon it must be, that we ought to shape our conduct by a rule which all rational beings might adopt *with benefit to their collective interest.*

To recapitulate: the idea of justice supposes two things; a rule of conduct, and a sentiment which sanctions the rule. The first must be supposed common to all mankind, and intended for their good. The other (the sentiment) is a desire that punishment may be suffered by those who infringe the rule. There is involved, in addition, the conception of some definite person who suffers by the infringement; whose rights (to use the expression appropriated to the case) are violated by it. And the sentiment of justice appears to me to be, the animal desire to repel or retaliate a hurt or damage to oneself, or to those with whom one sympathizes, widened so as to include all persons, by the human capacity of enlarged sympathy, and the human conception of intelligent self-interest. From the latter elements, the feeling derives its morality; from the former, its peculiar impressiveness, and energy of self-assertion.

I have, throughout, treated the idea of a *right* residing in the injured person, and violated by the injury, not as a separate element in the composition of the idea and sentiment, but as one of the forms in which the other two elements clothe themselves. These elements are, a hurt to some assignable person or persons on the one hand, and a demand for punishment on the other. An examination of our own minds, I think, will show, that these two things include all that we mean when we speak of violation of a right. When we call anything a person's right, we mean that he has a valid claim on society to protect him in the possession of it, either by the force of law, or by that of education and opinion. If he has what we consider a sufficient claim, on whatever account, to have something guaranteed to him by society, we say that he has a right to it. If we desire to prove that anything does not belong to him by right, we think this done as soon as it is admitted that society ought not to take measures for securing it to him, but should leave it to chance, or to his own exertions. Thus, a person is said to have a right to what he can earn in fair professional competition; because society ought not to allow any other person to hinder him from endeavouring to earn in that manner as much as he can. But he has not a right to three hundred a year, though he may happen to be earning it; because society

is not called on to provide that he shall earn that sum. On the contrary, if he owns ten thousand pounds three percent stock he *has* a right to three hundred a year; because society has come under an obligation to provide him with an income of that amount.

To have a right, then, is, I conceive, to have something which society ought to defend me in the possession of. If the objector goes on to ask why it ought, I can give him no other reason than general utility. If that expression does not seem to convey a sufficient feeling of the strength of the obligation, nor to account for the peculiar energy of the feeling, it is because there goes to the composition of the sentiment, not a rational only but also an animal element, the thirst for retaliation; and this thirst derives its intensity, as well as its moral justification, from the extraordinarily important and impressive kind of utility which is concerned. The interest involved is that of security, to every one's feelings the most vital of all interests. Nearly all other earthly benefits are needed by one person, not needed by another; and many of them can, if necessary, be cheerfully foregone, or replaced by something else; but security no human being can possibly do without; on it we depend for all our immunity from evil, and for the whole value of all and every good, beyond the passing moment; since nothing but the gratification of the instant could be of any worth to us, if we could be deprived of everything the next instant by whoever was momentarily stronger than ourselves. Now this most indispensable of all necessaries, after physical nutriment, cannot be had, unless the machinery for providing it is kept unintermittedly in active play. Our notion, therefore, of the claim we have on our fellow creatures to join in making safe for us the very groundwork of our existence, gathers feelings round it so much more intense than those concerned in any of the more common cases of utility, that the difference in degree (as is often the case in psychology) becomes a real difference in kind. The claim assumes that character of absoluteness, that apparent infinity, and incommensurability with all other considerations, which constitute the distinction between the feeling of right and wrong and that of ordinary expediency and inexpediency. The feelings concerned are so powerful, and we count so positively on finding a responsive feeling in others (all being alike interested), that *ought* and *should* grow into *must,* and recognised indispensability becomes a moral necessity, analogous to physical, and often not inferior to it in binding force.

. . . Justice is a name for certain classes of moral rules, which concern the essentials of human well-being more nearly, and are therefore of more absolute obligation, than any other rules for the guidance of life; and the notion which we have found to be of the essence of the idea of justice, that of a right residing in an individual, implies and testifies to this more binding obligation.

The moral rules which forbid mankind to hurt one another (in which we must never forget to include wrongful interference with each other's freedom) are more vital to human well-being than any maxims, however important, which only point out the best mode of managing some department of human affairs. They have also the peculiarity, that they are the main element in determining the whole of the social feelings of mankind. It is their observance which alone preserves peace among human beings: if obedience to them were not the rule, and disobedience the exception, every one would see in every one else a probable enemy, against whom he must be perpetually guarding himself. What is hardly less important, these are the precepts which mankind have the strongest and the most direct inducements for impressing upon one another. By merely giving to each other prudential instruction or exhortation, they may gain, or think they gain, nothing: in inculcating on each other the duty of positive beneficence they have an unmistakable interest, but far less in degree: a person may possibly not need the benefits of others; but he always needs that they should not do him hurt. Thus the moralities which protect every individual from being harmed by others, either directly or by being hindered in his freedom of pursuing his own good, are at once those which he himself has most at heart, and those which he has the strongest interest in publishing and enforcing by word and deed. It is by a person's observance of these, that his fitness to exist as one of the fellowship of human beings, is tested and decided; for on that depends his being a nuisance or not to those with whom he is in contact. Now it is these moralities primarily, which compose the obligations of justice. The most marked cases of injustice, and those which give the tone to the feeling of repugnance which characterizes the sentiment, are acts of wrongful aggression, or wrongful exercise of power over some one; the next are those which consist in wrongfully withholding from him something which is his due; in both cases, inflicting on him a positive hurt, either in the form of direct suffering, or of the privation of some good which he had reasonable ground either of a physical or of a social kind, for counting upon.

The same powerful motives which command the observance of these primary moralities, enjoin the punishment of those who violate them; and as the impulses of self-defence, of defence of others, and of vengeance, are all called forth against such persons, retribution, or evil for evil, becomes closely connected with the sentiment of justice, and is universally included in the idea. Good for good is also one of the dictates of justice; and this, though its social utility is evident, and though it carries with it a natural human feeling, has not at first sight that obvious connexion with hurt or injury, which, existing in the most elementary cases of just and unjust, is the source of the characteristic intensity of the sentiment. But the connexion, though less obvious, is not less real. He who accepts benefits, and denies a return of them when needed, inflicts a real hurt, by disappointing one of the most natural and reasonable of expectations, and one which he must at least tacitly have encouraged, otherwise the benefits would seldom have been conferred. The important rank, among human evils and wrongs, of the disappointment of expectation, is shown in the fact that it constitutes the principal criminality of two such highly immoral acts as a breach of friendship and a breach of promise. Few hurts which human beings can sustain are greater, and none wound more, than when that on which they habitually and with full assurance relied, fails them in the hour of need; and few wrongs are greater than this mere withholding of good; none excite more resentment, either in the person suffering, or in a sympathizing spectator. The principle, therefore, of giving to each what they deserve, that is, good for good as well as evil for evil, is not only included within the idea of Justice as we have defined it, but is a proper object of that intensity of sentiment, which places the Just, in human estimation, above the simply Expedient.

Most of the maxims of justice current in the world, and commonly appealed to in its transactions, are simply instrumental to carrying into effect the principles of justice which we have now spoken of. That a person is only responsible for what he has done voluntarily, or could voluntarily have avoided; that it is unjust to condemn any person unheard; that the punishment ought to be proportioned to the offence, and the like, are maxims intended to prevent the just principle of evil for evil from being perverted to the infliction of evil without justification. The greater part of these common maxims have come into use from the practice of courts of justice, which have been naturally led to a more complete recognition and elaboration than was likely to suggest itself to others, of the rules necessary to enable them to fulfil their double function, of inflicting punishment when due, and of awarding to each person his right.

That first of judicial virtues, impartiality, is an obligation of justice, partly for the reason last mentioned; as being a necessary condition of the fulfilment of the other obligations of justice. But this is not the only source of the exalted rank, among human obligations, of those maxims of equality and impartiality, which, both in popular estimation and in that of the most enlightened, are included among the precepts of justice. In one point of view, they may be considered as corollaries from the principles already laid down. If it is a duty to do to each according to his deserts, returning good for good as well as repressing evil by evil, it necessarily follows that we should treat all equally well (when no higher duty forbids) who have deserved equally well of us, and that society should treat all equally well who have deserved equally well of it, that is, who have deserved equally well absolutely. This is the highest abstract standard of social and distributive justice; towards which all institutions, and the efforts of all virtuous citizens, should be made in the utmost possible degree to converge. But this great moral duty rests upon a still deeper foundation, being a direct emanation from the first principle of morals, and not a mere logical corollary from secondary or derivative doctrines. It is involved in the very meaning of Utility, or the Greatest-Happiness Principle. That principle is a mere form of words without rational signification, unless one person's happiness, supposed equal in degree (with the proper allowance made for kind), is counted for exactly as much as another's. Those conditions being supplied, Bentham's dictum, 'everybody to count for one, nobody for more than one,' might be written under the principle of utility as an explanatory commentary. The equal claim of everybody to happiness in the estimation of the moralist and the legislator, involves an equal claim to all the means of happiness, except in so far as the inevitable conditions of human life, and the general interest, in which that of every individual is included, set limits to the maxim; and those limits ought to be strictly construed. As every other maxim of justice, so this, is by no means applied or held applicable universally; on the contrary, as I have already remarked, it bends to every person's ideas of social expediency. But in whatever case it is deemed applicable at all, it is held to be the dictate of justice. All persons are deemed to have a *right* to equality of treatment, except when some recognised social expediency requires the reverse. And hence all social inequalities which have ceased to be considered expedient, assume the character not of simple inexpediency, but of injustice, and appear so tyrannical, that people are apt to wonder how they ever could have been tolerated; forgetful that they themselves perhaps tolerate other inequalities under an equally mistaken notion of expediency, the correction of which would make that which they approve seem quite as monstrous as what they have at last learnt to condemn. The entire history of social improvement has been a series of transitions, by which one custom or institution after another, from being a supposed primary necessity of social existence, has passed into the rank of an universally stigmatized injustice and tyranny. So it has been with the distinctions of slaves and freemen, nobles and serfs, patricians and plebians; and so it will be, and in part already is, with the aristocracies of colour, race, and sex. . . .

4. *Fundamental Principles of the Metaphysics of Morals*

IMMANUEL KANT

In this selection from *The Foundation of the Metaphysic of Morals* (1785), Immanuel Kant (1724–1804) discusses the indispensable value of a good will, or the disposition of one's character to pursue the requirements of duty. A good will, he argues, is a precondition for genuine happiness. For Kant, morality is to be found in the moral law and the categorical imperatives it establishes. Arguing that our rational autonomy is the source of our moral understanding, Kant insists that reason can direct us to the moral law and develops three formulations of the Law to assist reason in discerning one's moral duty: (1) the maxim by which one chooses to act must be such that it could become a universal law; (2) in all actions, one must always treat humanity, including oneself, as an end in itself, and never as a means to an end; (3) all rational agents should be understood as possessing a universally legislating will, such that all should acknowledge their actions as in accord with the moral law. According to Kant, actions are right or wrong in themselves without references to consequences, and a rational agent is obliged to seek out the moral law and act as duty requires.

Preface

As my concern here is with moral philosophy, I limit the question suggested to this: Whether it is not of the utmost necessity to construct a pure moral philosophy, perfectly cleared of everything which is only empirical, and which belongs to anthropology? for that such a philosophy must be possible is evident from the common idea of duty and of the moral laws. Everyone must admit that if a law is to have moral force, *i.e.* to be the basis of an obligation, it must carry with it absolute necessity; that, for example, the precept, "Thou shalt not lie," is not valid for men alone, as if other rational beings had no need to observe it; and so with all the other moral laws properly so called; that, therefore, the basis of obligation must not be sought in the nature of man, or in the circumstances in the world in which he is placed, but *à priori* simply in the conceptions of pure reason; and although any other precept which is founded on principles of mere experience may be in certain respects universal, yet in as far as it rests even in the least degree on an empirical basis, perhaps only as to a motive, such a precept,

while it may be a practical rule, can never be called a moral law.

Thus not only are moral laws with their principles essentially distinguished from every other kind of practical knowledge in which there is anything empirical, but all moral philosophy rests wholly on its pure part. When applied to man, it does not borrow the least thing from the knowledge of man himself (anthropology), but gives laws *à priori* to him as a rational being. No doubt these laws require a judgment sharpened by experience, in order on the one hand to distinguish in what cases they are applicable, and on the other to procure for them access to the will of the man, and effectual influence on conduct; since man is acted on by so many inclinations that, though capable of the idea of a practical pure reason, he is not so easily able to make it effective *in concreto* in his life.

A metaphysic of morals is therefore indispensably necessary; not merely for speculative reasons, in order to investigate the sources of the practical principles which are to be found *à priori* in our reason, but also because morals themselves are liable to all sorts of corruption, as long as we are without that clue and supreme canon by which to estimate them correctly. For in order that an action should be morally good, it is not enough that it *conform* to the moral law, but it must also be done *for the sake of the law,* otherwise that conformity

From *The Foundations of the Metaphysic of Morals,* translated by T. K. Abbott (this translation first published in 1873).

21

is only very contingent and uncertain; since a principle which is not moral, although it may now and then produce actions conformable to the law, will also often produce actions which contradict it. Now it is only in a pure philosophy that we can look for the moral law in its purity and genuineness (and, in a practical matter, this is of the utmost consequence): we must, therefore, begin with pure philosophy (metaphysic), and without it there cannot be any moral philosophy at all. That which mingles these pure principles with the empirical does not deserve the name of philosophy (for what distinguishes philosophy from common rational knowledge is, that it treats in separate sciences what the latter only comprehends confusedly); much less does it deserve that of moral philosophy, since by this confusion it even spoils the purity of morals themselves, and counteracts its own end.

First Section: *Transition from the Common Rational Knowledge of Morality to the Philosophical*

The Good Will

Nothing can possibly be conceived in the world, or even our of it, which can be called good, without qualification, except a Good Will. Intelligence, wit, judgment, and the other *talents* of the mind, however they may be named, or courage, resolution, perseverance, as qualities of temperament, are undoubtedly good and desirable in many respects; but these gifts of nature may also become extremely bad and mischievous if the will which is to make use of them, and which, therefore, constitutes what is called *character*, is not good. It is the same with the *gifts of fortune*. Power, riches, honour, even health, and the general well-being and contentment with one's condition which is called *happiness*, inspire pride, and often presumption, if there is not a good will to correct the influence of these on the mind, and with this also to rectify the whole principle of acting, and adapt it to its end. The sight of a being who is not adorned with a single feature of a pure and good will, enjoying unbroken prosperity, can never give pleasure to an imperial rational spectator. Thus a good will appears to constitute the indispensable condition even of being worthy of happiness.

There are even some qualities which are of service to this good will itself, and may facilitate its action, yet which have no intrinsic unconditional value, but always presuppose a good will, and this qualifies the esteem that we justly have for them, and does not permit us to regard them as absolutely good. Moderation in the affections and passions, self-control, and calm deliberation are not only good in many respects, but even seem to constitute part of the intrinsic worth of the person; but they are far from deserving to be called good without qualification, although they have been so unconditionally praised by the ancients. For without the principles of a good will, they may become extremely bad; and the coolness of a villain not only makes him far more dangerous, but also directly makes him more abominable in our eyes than he would have been without it.

A good will is good not because of what it performs or effects, not by its aptness for the attainment of some proposed end, but simply by virtue of the volition, that is, it is good in itself, and considered by itself is to be esteemed much higher than all that can be brought about by it in favour of any inclination, nay, even of the sum-total of all inclinations. Even if it should happen that, owing to special disfavour of fortune, or the niggardly provision of a step-motherly nature, this will should wholly lack power to accomplish its purpose, if with its greatest efforts it should yet achieve nothing, and there should remain only the good will (not, to be sure, a mere wish, but the summoning of all means in our power), then, like a jewel, it would still shine by its own light, as a thing which has its whole value in itself. Its usefulness or fruitlessness can neither add to nor take away anything from this value. It would be, as it were, only the setting to enable us to handle it the more conveniently in common commerce, or to attract to it the attention of those who are not yet connoisseurs, but not to recommend it to true connoisseurs, or to determine its value.

Why Reason Was Made to Guide the Will

There is, however, something so strange in this idea of the absolute value of the mere will, in which no account is taken of its utility, that notwithstanding the thorough assent of even common reason to the idea, yet a suspicion must arise that it may perhaps really be the product of mere high-blown fancy, and that we may have misunderstood the purpose of nature in assigning reason as the governor of our will. Therefore we will examine this idea from this point of view.

In the physical constitution of an organized being, that is, a being adapted suitably to the purposes of life, we assume it as a fundamental principle that no organ for any purpose will be found but what is also the fittest and best adapted for that purpose. Now in a being which has reason and a will, if the proper object of nature were its *conservatism*, its *welfare*, in a word, its *happiness*, then nature would have hit upon a very bad arrangement in selecting the reason of the creature to carry out this purpose. For all the actions which the creature has to perform with a view to this purpose, and the whole rule of its conduct, would be far more surely prescribed to it by instinct, and that end would have been attained thereby much more certainly than it ever can be by reason. Should reason have been communicated to this favoured creature over and above, it must only have served it to contemplate the happy constitution of its nature, to admire it, to congratulate itself thereon, and to feel thankful for it to the beneficent cause, but not that it should subject its desires to that weak and delusive guidance, and meddle bunglingly with the purpose of nature. In a word, nature would have taken care that reason should not break forth into *practical exercise*, nor have the presumption, with its weak insight, to think out for itself the plan of happiness, and of the means of attaining it. Nature would not only have taken on herself the choice of the ends, but also of the means, and with wise foresight would have entrusted both to instinct.

And, in fact, we find that the more a cultivated reason applies itself with deliberate purpose to the enjoyment of life and happiness, so much the more does the man fail of true satisfaction. And from this circumstance there arises in many, if they are candid enough to confess it, a certain degree of *misology*, that is, hatred of reason, especially in the case of those who are most experienced in the use of it, because after calculating all the advantages they derive, I do not say from the invention of all the arts of common luxury, but even from the sciences (which seem to them to be after all only a luxury of the understanding), they find that they have, in fact, only brought more trouble on their shoulders, rather than gained in happiness; and they end by envying, rather than despising, the more common stamp of men who keep closer to the guidance of mere instinct, and do not allow their reason much influence on their conduct. And this we must admit, that the judgment of those who would very much lower the lofty eulogies of the advantages which reason gives us in regard to the happiness and satisfaction of life, or who would even reduce them below zero, is by no means morose or ungrateful to the goodness with which the world is governed, but that there lies at the root of these judgments the idea that

our existence has a different and far nobler end, for which, and not for happiness, reason is properly intended, and which must, therefore, be regarded as the supreme condition to which the private ends of man must, for the most part, be postponed.

For as reason is not competent to guide the will with certainty in regard to its objects and the satisfaction of all our wants (which it to some extent even multiplies), this being an end to which an implanted instinct would have led with much greater certainty; and since, nevertheless, reason is imparted to us as a practical faculty, *i.e.* as one which is to have influence on the *will*, therefore, admitting that nature generally in the distribution of her capacities has adapted the means to the end, its true destination must be to produce a *will*, not merely good as a *means* to something else, but *good in itself*, for which reason was absolutely necessary. This will then, though not indeed the sole and complete good, must be the supreme good and the condition of every other, even of the desire of happiness. Under these circumstances, there is nothing inconsistent with the wisdom of nature in the fact that the cultivation of the reason, which is requisite for the first and unconditional purpose, does in many ways interfere, at least in this life, with the attainment of the second, which is always conditional, namely, happiness. Nay, it may even reduce it to nothing, without nature thereby failing in her purpose. For reason recognizes the establishment of a good will as its highest practical destination, and in attaining this purpose is capable only of a satisfaction of its own proper kind, namely, that from the attainment of an end, which end again is determined by reason only, notwithstanding that this may involve many a disappointment to the ends of inclination.

The First Proposition of Morality

We have then to develop the notion of a will which deserves to be highly esteemed for itself, and is good without a view to anything further, a notion which exists already in the sound natural understanding, requiring rather to be cleared up than to be taught, and which in estimating the value of our actions always takes the first place, and constitutes the condition of all the rest. In order to do this, we will take the notion of duty, which includes that of a good will, although implying certain subjective restrictions and hindrances. These, however, far from concealing it, or rendering it unrecognizable, rather bring it out by contrast, and make it shine forth so much the brighter.

I omit here all actions which are already recognized as inconsistent with duty although they may be useful for this or that purpose, for with these the question whether they are done *from duty* cannot arise at all, since they even conflict with it. I also set aside those actions which really conform to duty, but to which men have *no* direct *inclination;* performing them because they are impelled thereto by some other inclination. For in this case we can readily distinguish whether the action which agrees with duty is done *from duty,* or from a selfish view. It is much harder to make this distinction when the action accords with duty, and the subject has besides a *direct* inclination to it. For example, it is always a matter of duty that a dealer should not overcharge an inexperienced purchaser; and wherever there is much commerce the prudent tradesman does not overcharge, but keeps a fixed price for everyone, so that a child buys of him as well as any other. Men are thus *honestly* served; but this is not enough to make us believe that the tradesman has so acted from duty and from principles of honesty: his own advantage required it; it is out of the question in this case to suppose that he might besides have a direct inclination in favour of the buyers, so that, as it were, from love he should give no advantage to one over another. Accordingly the action was done neither from duty nor from direct inclination, but merely with a selfish view.

On the other hand, it is a duty to maintain one's life; and, in addition, everyone has also a direct inclination to do so. But on this account the often anxious care which most men take for it has no intrinsic worth, and their maxim has no moral import. They preserve their life *as duty requires,* no doubt, but not *because duty requires.* On the other hand, if adversity and hopeless sorrow have completely taken away the relish for life; if the unfortunate one, strong in mind, indignant at his fate rather than desponding or dejected, wishes for death, and yet preserves his life without loving it—not from inclination or fear, but from duty—then his maxim has a moral worth.

To be beneficent when we can is a duty; and besides this, there are many minds so sympathetically constituted that, without any other motive of vanity or self-interest, they find a pleasure in spreading joy around them, and can take delight in the satisfaction of others so far as it is their own work. But I maintain that in such a case an action of this kind, however proper, however amiable it may be, has nevertheless no true moral worth, but is on a level with other inclinations, *e.g.* the inclination to honour, which, if it is happily directed to that which is in fact of public utility and accordant with duty, and consequently honourable, deserves praise and encouragement, but not esteem. For the maxim lacks the moral import, namely, that such actions be done *from duty,* not from inclination. Put the case that the mind of that philanthropist was clouded by sorrow of his own, extinguishing all sympathy with the lot of others, and that while he still has the power to benefit others in distress, he is not touched by their trouble because he is absorbed with his own; and now suppose that he tears himself out of this dead insensibility, and performs the action without any inclination to it, but simply from duty, then first has his action its genuine moral worth. Further still; if nature has put little sympathy in the heart of this or that man; if he, supposed to be an upright man, is by temperament cold and indifferent to the sufferings of others, perhaps because in respect of his own he is provided with the special gift of patience and fortitude, and supposes, or even requires, that others should have the same—and such a man would certainly not be the meanest product of nature—but if nature had not specially framed him for a philanthropist, would he not still find in himself a source from whence to give himself a far higher worth than that of a good-natured temperament could be? Unquestionably. It is just in this that the moral worth of the character is brought out which is incomparably the highest of all, namely, that he is beneficent, not from inclination, but from duty.

To secure one's own happiness is a duty, at least indirectly; for discontent with one's condition, under a pressure of many anxieties and amidst unsatisfied wants, might easily become a great *temptation to transgression of duty.* But here again, without looking to duty, all men have already the strongest and most intimate inclination to happiness, because it is just in this idea that all inclinations are combined in one total. But the precept of happiness is often of such a sort that it greatly interferes with some inclinations, and yet a man cannot form any definite and certain conception of the sum of satisfaction of all of them which is called happiness. It is not then to be wondered at that a single inclination, definite both as to what it promises and as to the time within which it can be gratified, is often able to overcome such a fluctuating idea, and that a gouty patient, for instance, can choose to enjoy what he likes, and to suffer what he may, since, according to his calculation, on this occasion at least, he has [only] not sacrificed the enjoyment of the present moment to a possibly mistaken expectation of a happiness which is supposed to be found in health. But even in this case, if the general desire for happiness did not influence his will, and supposing that in his particular case health was not a necessary element in this calculation, there yet remains in this, as in all other cases, this law, namely, that he should promote his happiness not from inclination but from duty, and by this would his conduct first acquire true moral worth.

It is in this manner, undoubtedly, that we are to understand those passages of Scripture also in which we are commanded to love our neighbour, even our enemy. For love, as an affection, cannot be commanded, but beneficence for duty's sake may; even though we are not impelled to it by any inclination—nay, are even repelled by a natural and unconquerable aversion. This is *practical* love, and not *pathological*—a love which is seated in the will, and not in the propensions of sense—in principles of action and not of tender sympathy; and it is this love alone which can be commanded.

The Second Proposition of Morality

The second proposition is: That an action done from duty derives its moral worth, *not from the purpose* which is to be attained by it, but from the maxim by which is it determined, and therefore does not depend on the realization of the object of the action, but merely on the *principle of volition* by which the action has taken place, without regard to any object of desire. It is clear from what precedes that the purposes which we may have in view in our actions, or their effects regarded as ends and springs of the will, cannot give to actions any unconditional or moral worth. In what, then, can their worth lie, if it is not to consist in the will and in reference to its expected effect? It cannot lie anywhere but in the *principle of the will* without regard to the ends which can be attained by the action. For the will stands between its *à priori principle,* which is formal, and its *à posteriori* spring, which is material, as between two roads, and as it must be determined by something, it follows that it must be determined by the formal principle of volition when an action is done from duty, in which case every material principle has been withdrawn from it.

The Third Proposition of Morality

The third proposition, which is a consequence of the two preceding, I would express thus: *Duty is the necessity of acting from respect for the law.* I may have *inclination* for an object as the effect of my proposed action, but I cannot have *respect* for it, just for this reason, that it is an effect and not an energy of will. Similarly, I cannot have respect for inclination, whether my own or another's; I can at most, if my own, approve it; if another's, sometimes even love it; *i.e.* look on it as favourable to my own interest. It is only what is connected with my will as a principle, by no means as an effect—what does not subserve my inclination, but overpowers it, or at least in case of choice excludes it from its calculation—in other words, simply the law of itself, which can be an object of respect, and hence a command. Now an action done from duty must wholly exclude the influence of inclination, and with it every object of the will, so that nothing remains which can determine the will except objectively the *law,* and subjectively *pure respect* for this practical law, and consequently the maxim[1] that I should follow this law even to the thwarting of all my inclinations.

Thus the moral worth of an action does not lie in the effect expected from it, nor in any principle of action which requires to borrow its motive from this expected effect. For all these effects—agreeableness of one's condition, and even the promotion of the happiness of others—could have been also brought about by other causes, so that for this there would have been no need of the will of a rational being; whereas it is in this alone that the supreme and unconditional good can be found. The pre-eminent good which we call moral can therefore consist in nothing else than *the conception of law* in itself, *which certainly is only possible in a rational being,* in so far as this conception, and not the expected effect, determines the will. This is a good which is already present in the person who acts accordingly, and we have not to wait for it to appear first in the result.

The Supreme Principle of Morality: The Categorical Imperative

But what sort of law can that be, the conception of which must determine the will, even without paying any regard to the effect expected from it, in order that this will may be called good absolutely and without qualification? As I have deprived the will of every impulse which could arise to it from obedience to any law, there remains nothing but the universal conformity of its actions to law in general, which alone is to serve the will as a principle, *i.e.* I am never to act otherwise than so *that I could also will that my maxim should become a universal law.* Here, now, it is the simple conformity to law in general, without assuming any particular law applicable to certain actions, that serves the will as its principle, and must so serve it, if duty is not to be a vain delusion and a chimerical notion. The common reason of men in its practical judgments perfectly coincides with this, and always has in view the principle here suggested. Let the question be, for example: May I when in distress make a promise with the intention not to keep it? I readily distinguish here between the two significations which the question may have: Whether it is prudent, or whether it is right, to make a false promise? The former may undoubtedly often be the case. I see clearly indeed that it is not enough to extricate myself from a present difficulty by means of this subterfuge, but it must be well considered whether there may not hereafter spring from this lie much greater inconvenience than that from which I now free myself, and as, with all my supposed *cunning*, the consequences cannot be so easily foreseen but that credit once lost may be much more injurious to me than any mischief which I seek to avoid at present, it should be considered whether it would not be more *prudent* to act herein according to a universal maxim, and to make it a habit to promise nothing except with the intention of keeping it. But it is soon clear to me that such a maxim will still only be based on the fear of consequences. Now it is a wholly different thing to be truthful from duty, and to be so from apprehension of injurious consequences. In the first case, the very notion of the action already implies a law for me; in the second case, I must first look about elsewhere to see what results may be combined with it which would affect myself. For to deviate from the principle of duty is beyond all doubt wicked; but to be unfaithful to my maxim of prudence may often be very advantageous to me, although to abide by it is certainly safer. The shortest way, however, and an unerring one, to discover the answer to this question whether a lying promise is consistent with duty, is to ask myself, Should I be content that my maxim (to extricate myself from difficulty by a false promise) should hold good as a universal law, for myself as well as for others? and should I be able to say to myself, "Every one may make a deceitful promise when he finds himself in a difficulty from which he cannot otherwise extricate himself"? Then I presently become aware that while I can will the lie, I can by no means will that lying should be a universal law. For with such a law there would be no promises at all, since it would be in vain to allege my intention in regard to my future actions to those who would not believe this allegation, or if they over-hastily did so, would pay me back in my own coin. Hence my maxim, as soon as it should be made a universal law, would necessarily destroy itself.

I do not, therefore, need any far-reaching penetration to discern what I have to do in order that my will may be morally good. Inexperienced in the course of the world, incapable of being prepared for all its contingencies, I only ask myself: Canst thou also will that thy maxim should be a universal law? If not, then it must be rejected, and that not because of a disadvantage accruing from myself or even to others, but because it cannot enter as a principle into a possible universal legislation, and reason extorts from me immediate respect for such legislation. I do not indeed as yet *discern* on what this respect is based (this the philosopher may inquire), but at least I understand this, that it is an estimation of the worth which far outweighs all worth of what is recommended by inclination, and that the necessity of acting from *pure* respect for the practical law is what constitutes duty, to which every other motive must give place, because it is the condition of a will being good *in itself*, and the worth of such a will is above everything.

Thus, then, without quitting the moral knowledge of common human reason, we have arrived at its principle. And although, no doubt, common men do not conceive it in such an abstract and universal form, yet they always have it really before their eyes, and use it as the standard of their decision.

Second Section: Transition from Popular Moral Philosophy to the Metaphysic of Morals

The Impossibility of an Empirical Moral Philosophy

If we have hitherto drawn our notion of duty from the common use of our practical reason, it is by no means to be inferred that we have treated it as an empirical notion. On the contrary, if we attend to the experience of men's conduct, we meet frequent and, as we ourselves allow, just complaints that one cannot find a single certain example of the disposition to act from pure duty. Although many things are done in *conformity* with what *duty* prescribes, it is nevertheless always doubtful whether they are done strictly *from duty*, so as to have a moral worth. Hence there have at all times been philosophers who have altogether denied that this disposition actually exists at all in human actions, and have ascribed everything to a more or less refined self-love. Not that they have on that account questioned the soundness of the conception of morality; on the contrary, they spoke with sincere regret of the frailty and corruption of human nature, which though noble enough to take as its rule an idea so worthy of respect, is yet too weak to follow it, and employs reason, which ought to give it the law, only for the purpose of providing for the interest of the inclinations, whether singly or at the best in the greatest possible harmony with one another.

In fact, it is absolutely impossible to make out by experience with complete certainty a single case in which the maxim of an action, however right in itself, rested simply on moral grounds and on the conception of duty. Sometimes it happens that with the sharpest self-examination we can find nothing beside the moral principle of duty which could have been powerful enough to move us to this or that action and to so great a sacrifice; yet we cannot from this infer with certainty that it was not really some secret impulse of self-love, under the false appearance of duty, that was the actual determining cause of the will. We like then to flatter ourselves by falsely taking credit for a more noble motive; whereas in fact we can never, even by the strictest examination, get completely behind the secret springs of action; since, when the question is of moral worth, it is not with the actions which we see that we are concerned, but with those inward principles of them which we do not see.

Moreover, we cannot better serve the wishes of those who ridicule all morality as a mere chimera of human imagination overstepping itself from vanity, than by conceding to them that notions of duty must be drawn only from experience (as from indolence, people are ready to think is also the case with all other notions); for this is to prepare for them a certain triumph. I am willing to admit out of love of humanity that even most of our actions are correct, but if we look closer at them we everywhere come upon the dear self which is always prominent, and it is this they have in view, and not the strict command of duty which would often require self-denial. Without being an enemy of virtue, a cool observer, one that does not mistake the wish for good, however lively, for its reality, may sometimes doubt whether true virtue is actually found anywhere in the world, and this especially as years increase and the judgment is partly made wiser by experience, and partly also more acute in observation. This being so, nothing can secure us from falling away altogether from our ideas of duty, or maintain in the soul a well-grounded respect for its law, but the clear conviction that although there should never have been actions which really sprang from such pure sources,

yet whether this or that takes place is not at all the question; but that reason of itself, independent on all experience, ordains what ought to take place, that accordingly actions of which perhaps the world has hitherto never given an example, the feasibility even of which might be very much doubted by one who founds everything on experience, are nevertheless inflexibly commanded by reason; that, [for example], even though there might never yet have been a sincere friend, yet not a whit the less is pure sincerity in friendship required of every man, because, prior to all experience, this duty is involved as duty in the idea of a reason determining the will by *à priori* principles.

When we add further that, unless we deny that the notion of morality has any truth or reference to any possible object, we must admit that its law must be valid, not merely for men, but for all *rational creatures generally,* not merely under certain contingent conditions or with exceptions, but *with absolute necessity,* then it is clear that no experience could enable us to infer even the possibility of such apodictic laws. For with what right could we bring into unbounded respect as a universal precept for every rational nature that which perhaps holds only under the contingent conditions of humanity? Or how could laws of the determination of *our* will be regarded as laws of the determination of the will of rational beings generally, and for us only as such, if they were merely empirical, and did not take their origin wholly *à priori* from pure but practical reason?

Nor could anything be more fatal to morality than that we should wish to derive it from examples. For every example of it that is set before me must be first itself tested by principles of morality, whether it is worthy to serve as an original example, *i.e.* as a pattern, but by no means can it authoritatively furnish the conception of morality. Even the Holy One of the Gospels must first be compared with our ideal of moral perfection before we can recognize Him as such; and so He says of Himself, "Why call ye Me [whom you see] good; none is good [the model of good] but God only [whom ye do not see]." But whence have we the conception of God as the supreme good? Simply from the *idea* of moral perfection, which reason frames *à priori,* and connects inseparably with the notion of a free will. Imitation finds no place at all in morality, and examples serve only for encouragement, *i.e.* they put beyond doubt the feasibility of what the law commands, they make visible that which the practical rule expresses more generally, but they can never authorize us to set aside the true original which lies in reason, and to guide ourselves by examples.

From what has been said, it is clear that all moral conceptions have their seat and origin completely *à priori* in the reason, and that, moreover, in the commonest reason just as truly as in that which is in the highest degree speculative; that they cannot be obtained by abstraction from any empirical, and therefore merely contingent knowledge; that it is just this purity of their origin that makes them worthy to serve as our supreme practical principle, and that just in proportion as we add anything empirical, we detract from their genuine influence, and from the absolute value of actions; that it is not only of the greatest necessity, in a purely speculative point of view, but is also of the greatest practical importance, to derive these notions and laws from pure reason, to present them pure and unmixed, and even to determine the compass of this practical or pure rational knowledge, *i.e.* to determine the whole faculty of pure practical reason; and, in doing so, we must not make its principles dependent on the particular nature of human reason, though in speculative philosophy this may be permitted, or may even at times be necessary; but since moral laws ought to hold good for every rational creature, we must derive them from the general concept of a rational being. In this way, although for its *application* to man morality has need of anthropology, yet, in the first instance, we must treat it independently as pure philosophy, *i.e.* as metaphysic, complete in itself (a thing which in such distinct branches of science is easily done); knowing well that unless we are in possession of this, it would not only be vain to determine the moral element of duty in right actions for purposes of speculative criticism, but it would be impossible to base morals on their genuine principles, even for common practical purposes, especially of moral instruction, so as to produce pure moral dispositions, and to engraft them on men's minds to the promotion of the greatest possible good in the world.

But in order that in this study we may not merely advance by the natural steps from the common moral judgment (in this case very worthy of respect) to the philosophical, as has been already done, but also from a popular philosophy, which goes no further than it can reach by groping with the help of examples, to metaphysic (which does not allow itself to be checked by anything empirical, and as it must measure the whole extent of this kind of rational knowledge, goes as far as ideal conceptions, where even examples fail us), we must follow and clearly describe the practical faculty of reason, from the general rules of its determination to the point where the notion of duty springs from it.

Imperatives: Hypothetical and Categorical

Everything in nature works according to laws. Rational beings alone have the faculty of acting according *to the conception* of laws, that is according to principles, *i.e.* have a *will*. Since the deduction of actions from principles requires *reason*, the will is nothing but practical reason. If reason infallibly determines the will, then the actions of such a being which are recognized as objectively necessary are subjectively necessary also; *i.e.* the will is a faculty to choose *that only* which reason independent on inclination recognizes as practically necessary, *i.e.* as good. But if reason of itself does not sufficiently determine the will, if the latter is subject also to subjective conditions (particular impulses) which do not always coincide with the objective conditions; in a word, if the will does not *in itself* completely accord with reason (which is actually the case with men), then the actions which objectively are recognized as necessary are subjectively contingent, and the determination of such a will according to objective laws is *obligation*, that is to say, the relation of the objective laws to a will that is not thoroughly good is conceived as the determination of the will of a rational being by principles of reason, but which the will from its nature does not of necessity follow.

The conception of an objective principle, in so far as it is obligatory for a will, is called a command (of reason), and the formula of the command is called an Imperative.

All imperatives are expressed by the word *ought* [or *shall*], and thereby indicate the relation of an objective law of reason to a will, which from its subjective constitution is not necessarily determined by it (an obligation). They say that something would be good to do or to forbear, but they say it to a will which does not always do a thing because it is conceived to be good to do it. That is practically *good*, however, which determines the will by means of the conceptions of reason, and consequently not from subjective causes, but objectively, that is on principles which are valid for every rational being as such. It is distinguished from the *pleasant*, as that which influences the will only by means of sensation from merely subjective causes, valid only for the sense of this or that one, and not as a principle of reason, which holds for every one.

A perfectly good will would therefore be equally subject to objective laws (viz. laws of good), but could not be conceived as *obliged* thereby to act lawfully, because of itself from its subjective constitution it can only be determined by the conception of good. Therefore no imperatives hold for the Divine will, or in general for a *holy* will; *ought* is here out of place, because the volition is already of itself necessarily in unison with the law. Therefore imperatives are only formulae to express the relation of objective laws of all volition to the subjective imperfection of the will of this or that rational being, *e.g.* the human will.

Now all *imperatives* command either *hypothetically* or *categorically.* The former represent the practical necessity of a possible action as means to something else that is willed (or at least which one might possibly will). The categorical imperative would be that which represented an action as necessary of itself without reference to another end, *i.e.,* as objectively necessary.

Since every practical law represents a possible action as good, and on this account, for a subject who is practically determinable by reason, necessary, all imperatives are formulae determining an action which is necessary according to the principle of a will good in some respects. If now the action is good only as a means *to something else,* then the imperative is *hypothetical;* if it is conceived as good *in itself* and consequently as being necessarily the principle of a will which of itself conforms to reason, then it is *categorical.*

Thus the imperative declares what action possible by me would be good, and presents the practical rule in relation to a will which does not forthwith perform an action simply because it is good, whether because the subject does not always know that it is good, or because, even if it know this, yet its maxims might be opposed to the objective principles of practical reason.

Accordingly the hypothetical imperative only says that the action is good for some purpose, *possible* or *actual.* In the first case it is a Problematical, in the second an Assertorial practical principle. The categorical imperative which declares an action to be objectively necessary in itself without reference to any purpose, *i.e.* without any other end, is valid as an Apodictic (practical) principle.

Whatever is possible only by the power of some rational being may also be conceived as a possible purpose of some will; and therefore the principles of action as regards the means necessary to attain some possible purpose are in fact infinitely numerous. All sciences have a practical part, consisting of problems expressing that some end is possible for us, and of imperatives directing how it may be attained. These may, therefore, be called in general imperatives of Skill. Here there is no question whether the end is rational and good, but only what one must do in order to attain it. The

precepts for the physician to make his patient thoroughly healthy, and for a poisoner to ensure certain death, are of equal value in this respect, that each serves to effect its purpose perfectly. Since in early youth it cannot be known what ends are likely to occur to us in the course of life, parents seek to have their children taught a *great many things,* and provide for their *skill* in the use of means for all sorts of arbitrary ends, of none of which can they determine whether it may not perhaps hereafter be an object to their pupil, but which it is at all events *possible* that he might aim at; and this anxiety is so great that they commonly neglect to form and correct their judgment on the value of the things which may be chosen as ends.

There is *one* end, however, which may be assumed to be actually such to all rational beings (so far as imperatives apply to them, viz. as dependent beings), and, therefore, one purpose which they not merely *may* have, but which we may with certainty assume that they all actually *have* by a natural necessity, and this is *happiness.* The hypothetical imperative which expresses the practical necessity of an action as means to the advancement of happiness is Assertorial. We are not to present it as necessary for an uncertain and merely possible purpose, but for a purpose which we may presuppose with certainty and *à priori* in every man, because it belongs to his being. Now skill in the choice of means to his own greatest well-being may be called *prudence,* in the narrowest sense. And thus the imperative which refers to the choice of means to one's own happiness, *i.e.* the precept of prudence, is still always *hypothetical;* the action is not commanded absolutely, but only as means to another purpose.

Finally, there is an imperative which commands a certain conduct immediately, without having as its condition any other purpose to be attained by it. This imperative is Categorical. It concerns not the matter of the action, or its intended result, but its form and the principle of which it is itself a result; and what is essentially good in it consists in the mental disposition, let the consequence be what it may. This imperative may be called that of Morality.

There is a marked distinction also between the volitions on these three sorts of principles in the *dissimilarity* of the obligation of the will. In order to mark this difference more clearly, I think they would be most suitably named in their order if we said they are either *rules* of skill, or *counsels* of prudence, or *commands* (*laws*) of morality. For it is *law* only that involves the conception of an *unconditional* and objective necessity, which is consequently universally valid; and commands are laws which must be obeyed, that is, must be followed, even in opposition to inclination. *Counsels*, indeed, involve necessity, but one which can only hold under a contingent subjective condition, *viz.* they depend on whether this or that man reckons this or that as part of his happiness; the categorical imperative, on the contrary, is not limited by any condition, and as being absolutely, although practically, necessary, may be quite properly called a command. We might also call the first kind of imperative *technical* (belonging to art), the second *pragmatic* (to welfare), the third *moral* (belonging to free conduct generally, that is, to morals).

The Rational Ground of Hypothetical Imperatives

Now arises the question, how are all these imperatives possible? This question does not seek to know how we can conceive the accomplishment of the action which the imperative ordains, but merely how we can conceive the obligation of the will which the imperative expresses. No special explanation is needed to show how an imperative of skill is possible. Whoever wills the end, wills also (so far as reason decides his conduct) the means in his power which are indispensably necessary thereto. This proposition is, as regards the volition, analytical; for, in willing an object as my effect, there is already thought the causality of myself as an acting cause, that is to say, the use of the means; and the imperative educes from the conception of volition of an end the conception of actions necessary to this end. Synthetical propositions must no doubt be employed in defining the means to a proposed end; but they do not concern the principle, the act of the will, but the object and its realization. [For example], that in order to bisect a line on an unerring principle I must draw from its extremities two intersecting arcs; this no doubt is taught by mathematics only in synthetical propositions; but if I know that it is only by this process that the intended operation can be performed, then to say that if I fully will the operation, I also will the action required for it, is an analytical proposition; for it is one and the same thing to conceive something as an effect which I can produce in a certain way, and to conceive myself as acting in this way.

If it were only equally easy to give a definite conception of happiness, the imperatives of prudence would correspond exactly with those of skill, and would likewise be analytical. For in this case as in that, it could be said, whoever wills the end, wills also (according to the dictate of reason necessarily) the

indispensable means thereto which are in his power. But, unfortunately, the notion of happiness is so indefinite that although every man wishes to attain it, yet he never can say definitely and consistently what it is that he really wishes and wills. The reason of this is that all the elements which belong to the notion of happiness are altogether empirical, *i.e.* they must be borrowed from experience, and nevertheless the idea of happiness requires an absolute whole, a maximum of welfare in my present and all future circumstances. Now it is impossible that the most clear-sighted and at the same time most powerful being (supposed finite) should frame to himself a definite conception of what he really wills in this. Does he will riches, how much anxiety, envy, and snares might he not thereby draw upon his shoulders? Does he will knowledge and discernment, perhaps it might prove to be only an eye so much the sharper to show him so much the more fearfully the evils that are now concealed from him, and that cannot be avoided, or to impose more wants or his desires, which already give him concern enough. Would he have long life? who guarantees to him that it would not be a long misery? would he at least have health? how often has uneasiness of the body restrained from excesses into which perfect health would have allowed one to fall? and so on. In short, he is unable, on any principle, to determine with certainty what would make him truly happy; because to do so he would need to be omniscient. We cannot therefore act on any definite principles to secure happiness, but only on empirical counsels, [for example] of regimen, frugality, courtesy, reserve, &c., which experience teaches do, on the average, most promote well-being. Hence it follows that the imperatives of prudence do not, strictly speaking, command at all, that is, they cannot present actions objectively as practically *necessary;* that they are rather to be regarded as counsels (*consilia*) than precepts (*praecepta*) of reason, that the problem to determine certainly and universally what action would promote the happiness of a rational being is completely insoluble, and consequently no imperative respecting it is possible which should, in the strict sense, command to do what makes [for happiness]; because happiness is not an ideal of reason but of imagination, resting solely on empirical grounds, and it is vain to expect that these should define an action by which one could attain the totality of a series of consequences which is really endless. This imperative of prudence would, however, be an analytical proposition if we assume that the means to happiness could be certainly assigned; for it is distinguished from the imperative of skill only by this, that in the latter the end is merely possible, in the former it is given; as, however, both only ordain the means to that which we suppose to be willed as an end, it follows that the imperative which ordains the willing of the means to him who wills the end is in both cases analytical. Thus there is no difficulty in regard to the possibility of an imperative of this kind either.

The Rational Ground of the Categorical Imperative

On the other hand, the question, how the imperative of *morality* is possible, is undoubtedly one, the only one, demanding a solution, as this is not at all hypothetical, and the objective necessity which it presents cannot rest on any hypothesis, as is the case with the hypothetical imperatives. Only here we must never leave out of consideration that we *cannot* make out *by any example*, in other words empirically, whether there is such an imperative at all; but it is rather to be feared that all those which seem to be categorical may yet be at bottom hypothetical. For instance, when the precept is: Thou shalt not promise deceitfully; and it is assumed that the necessity of this is not a mere counsel to avoid some other evil, so that it should mean: Thou shalt not make a lying promise, lest if it become known thou shouldst destroy thy credit, but that an action of this kind must be regarded as evil in itself, so that the imperative of the prohibition is categorical; then we cannot show with certainty in any example that the will was determined merely by the law, without any other spring of action, although it may appear to be so. For it is always possible that fear of disgrace, perhaps also obscure dread of other dangers, may have a secret influence on the will. Who can prove by experience the non-existence of a cause when all that experience tells us is that we do not perceive it? But in such a case the so-called moral imperative, which as such appears to be categorical and unconditional, would in reality be only a pragmatic precept, drawing our attention to our own interests, and merely teaching us to take these into consideration.

We shall therefore have to investigate *à priori* the possibility of a categorical imperative, as we have not in this case the advantage of its reality being given in experience, so that [the elucidation of] its possibility should be requisite only for its explanation, not for its establishment. In the meantime it may be discerned beforehand that the categorical imperative alone has the purport of a practical law: all the rest may indeed be called *principles* of the will but not laws, since whatever is only necessary for the attainment of some arbitrary purpose may be considered as in itself contingent, and we can at any time be free from the precept if we give up the purpose: on the contrary, the unconditional command leaves the will no liberty to choose the opposite; consequently it alone carries with it that necessity which we require in a law.

Secondly, in the case of this categorical imperative or law of morality, the difficulty (of discerning its possibility) is a very profound one. It is an *à priori* synthetical practical proposition;[2] and as there is so much difficulty in discerning the possibility of speculative propositions of this kind, it may readily be supposed that the difficulty will be no less with the practical.

First Formulation of the Categorical Imperative: Universal Law

In this problem we will first inquire whether the mere conception of a categorical imperative may not perhaps supply us also with the formula of it, containing the proposition which alone can be a categorical imperative; for even if we know the tenor of such an absolute command, yet how it is possible will require further special and laborious study, which we postpone to the last section.

When I conceive a hypothetical imperative, in general I do not know beforehand what it will contain until I'am given the condition. But when I conceive a categorical imperative, I know at once what it contains. For as the imperative contains besides the law only the necessity that the maxims[3] shall conform to this law, while the law contain no conditions restricting it, there remains nothing but the general statement that the maxim of the action should conform to a universal law, and it is this conformity alone that the imperative properly represents as necessary.

There is therefore but one categorical imperative, namely, this: *Act only on that maxim whereby thou canst at the same time will that it should become a universal law.*

Now if all imperatives of duty can be deduced from this one imperative as from their principle, then, although it should remain undecided whether what is called duty is not merely a vain notion, yet at least we shall be able to show what we understand by it and what this notion means.

Since the universality of the law according to which effects are produced constitutes what is properly called *nature* in the most general sense (as to form), that is the existence of things so far as it is determined by general laws, the imperative of duty may be expressed thus: *Act as if the maxim of thy action were to become by thy will a universal law of nature.*

Four Illustrations

We will now enumerate a few duties, adopting the usual division of them into duties to ourselves and to others, and into perfect and imperfect duties.

1. A man reduced to despair by a series of misfortunes feels wearied of life, but is still so far in possession of his reason that he can ask himself whether it would not be contrary to his duty to himself to take his own life. Now he inquires whether the maxim of his action could become a universal law of nature. His maxim is: From self-love I adopt it as a principle to shorten my life when its longer duration is likely to bring more evil than satisfaction. It is asked then simply whether this principle founded on self-love can become a universal law of nature. Now we see at once that a system of nature of which it should be a law to destroy life by means of the very feeling whose special nature it is to impel to the improvement of life would contradict itself, and therefore could not exist as a system of nature; hence that maxim cannot possibly exist as a universal law of nature, and consequently would be wholly inconsistent with the supreme principle of all duty.

2. Another finds himself forced by necessity to borrow money. He knows that he will not be able to repay it, but sees also that nothing will be lent to him, unless he promises stoutly to repay it in a definite time. He desires to make this promise, but he has still so much conscience as to ask himself: Is it not unlawful and inconsistent with duty to get out of a difficulty in this way? Suppose, however, that he resolves to do so, then the maxim of his action would be expressed thus: When I think myself in want of money, I will borrow money and promise to repay it, although I know that I never can do so. Now this principle of self-love or of one's own advantage may perhaps be consistent with my whole future welfare; but the question now is, Is it right? I change then the suggestion of self-love into a universal law, and state the question thus: How would it be if my maxim were a universal law? Then I see at once that it could never hold as a universal law of nature, but would necessarily contradict itself. For supposing it to be a universal law that everyone when

he thinks himself in a difficulty should be able to promise whatever he pleases, with the purpose of not keeping his promise, the promise itself would become impossible, as well as the end that one might have in view in it, since no one would consider that anything was promised to him, but would ridicule all such statements as vain pretences.

3. A third finds in himself a talent which with the help of some culture might make him a useful man in many respects. But he finds himself in comfortable circumstances, and prefers to indulge in pleasure rather than to take pains in enlarging and improving his happy natural capacities. He asks, however, whether his maxim of neglect of his natural gifts, besides agreeing with his inclination to indulgence, agrees also with what is called duty. He sees then that a system of nature could indeed subsist with such a universal law although men (like the South Sea islanders) should let their talents rest, and resolve to devote their lives merely to idleness, amusement, and propagation of their species—in a word, to enjoyment; but he cannot possibly *will* that this should be a universal law of nature, or be implanted in us as such by a natural instinct. For, as a rational being, he necessarily wills that his faculties be developed, since they serve him, and have been given him, for all sorts of possible purposes.

4. A fourth, who is in prosperity, while he sees that others have to contend with great wretchedness and that he could help them, thinks: What concern is it of mine? Let everyone be as happy as Heaven pleases, or as he can make himself; I will take nothing from him nor even envy him, only I do not wish to contribute anything to his welfare or to his assistance in distress! Now no doubt if such a mode of thinking were a universal law, the human race might very well subsist, and doubtless even better than in a state in which everyone talks of sympathy and good-will, or even takes care occasionally to put it into practice, but, on the other side, also cheats when he can, betrays the rights of men, or otherwise violates them. But although it is possible that a universal law of nature might exist in accordance with that maxim, it is impossible to *will* that such a principle should have the universal validity of a law of nature. For a will which resolved this would contradict itself, inasmuch as many cases might occur in which one would have need of the love and sympathy of others, and in which, by such a law of nature, sprung from his own will, he would deprive himself of all hope of the aid he desires.

These are a few of the many actual duties, or at least what we regard as such, which obviously fall into two classes on the one principle that we have laid down. We must be *able to will* that a maxim of our action should be a universal law. This is the canon of the moral appreciation of the action generally. Some actions are of such a character that their maxim cannot without contradiction be even *conceived* as a universal law of nature, far from it being possible that we should *will* that it *should* be so. In others this intrinsic impossibility is not found, but still it is impossible to *will* that their maxim should be raised to the universality of a law of nature, since such a will would contradict itself. It is easily seen that the former violate strict or rigorous (inflexible) duty; the latter only laxer (meritorious) duty. Thus it has been completely shown by these examples how all duties depend as regards the nature of the obligation (not the object of the action) on the same principle.

Transgressions of the Moral Law

If now we attend to ourselves on occasion of any transgression of duty, we shall find that we in fact do not will that our maxim should be a universal law, for that is impossible for us; on the contrary, we will that the opposite should remain a universal law, only we assume the liberty of making an *exception* in our own favour or (just for this time only) in favour of our inclination. Consequently if we considered all cases from one and the same point of view, namely, that of reason, we should find a contradiction in our own will, namely, that a certain principle should be objectively necessary as a universal law, and yet subjectively should not be universal, but admit of exceptions. As, however, we at one moment regard our action from the point of view of a will wholly conformed to reason, and then again look at the same action from the point of view of a will affected by inclination, there is not really any contradiction, but an antagonism of inclination to the precept of reason, whereby the universality of the principle is changed into a mere generality, so that the practical principle of reason shall meet the maxim half way. Now, although this cannot be justified in our own impartial judgment, yet it proves that we do really recognize the validity of the categorical imperative and (with all respect for it) only allow ourselves a few exceptions, which we think unimportant and forced from us.

The Need for an A Priori *Proof* of the Categorical Imperative

We have thus established at least this much, that if duty is a conception which is to have any import and real legislative authority for our actions, it can only be expressed in categorical, and not at all in hypothetical imperatives. We have also, which is of great importance, exhibited clearly and definitely for every practical application the content of the categorical imperative, which must contain the principle of all duty if there is such a thing at all. We have not yet, however, advanced so far as to prove *à priori* that there actually is such an imperative, that there is a practical law which commands absolutely of itself, and without any other impulse, and that the following of this law is duty.

With the view of attaining to this it is of extreme importance to remember that we must not allow ourselves to think of deducing the reality of this principle from the *particular attributes of human nature.* For duty is to be a practical, unconditional necessity of action; it must therefore hold for all rational beings (to whom an imperative can apply at all), and *for this reason only* be also a law for all human wills. On the contrary, whatever is deduced from the particular natural characteristics of humanity, from certain feelings and propensions, nay, even, if possible, from any particular tendency proper to human reason, and which need not necessarily hold for the will of every rational being; this may indeed supply us with a maxim, but not with a law; with a subjective principle on which we may have a propension and inclination to act, but not with an objective principle on which we should be *enjoined* to act, even though all our propensions, inclinations, and natural dispositions were opposed to it. In fact, the sublimity and intrinsic dignity of the command in duty are so much the more evident, the less subjective impulses favour it and the more they oppose it, without being able in the slightest degree to weaken the obligation of the law or to diminish its validity.

Here then we see philosophy brought to a critical position, since it has to be firmly fixed, notwithstanding that it has nothing to support it in heaven or earth. Here it must show its purity as absolute director of its own laws, not the herald of those which are whispered to it by an implanted sense or who knows what tutelary nature. Although these may be better than nothing, yet they can never afford principles dictated by reason, which must have their source wholly *à priori* and thence their commanding authority, expecting everything from the supremacy of the law the due respect for it, nothing from inclination, or else condemning the man to self-contempt and inward abhorrence.

Thus every empirical element is not only quite incapable of being an aid to the principle of morality, but is even highly prejudicial to the purity of morals; for the proper and inestimable worth of an absolutely good will consists just in this, that the principle of action is free from all influence of contingent grounds, which alone experience can furnish. We cannot too much or too often repeat our warning against this lax and even mean habit of thought which seeks for its principle amongst empirical motives and laws; for human reason in its weariness is glad to rest on this pillow, and in a dream of sweet illusions (in which, instead of Juno, it embraces a cloud) it substitutes for morality a bastard patched up from limbs of various derivation, which looks like anything one chooses to see in it; only not like virtue to one who has once beheld her in her true form.[4]

The question then is this: Is it a necessary law *for all rational beings* that they should always judge of their actions by maxims of which they can themselves will that they should serve as universal laws? If it is so, then it must be connected (altogether *à priori*) with the very conception of the will of a rational being generally. But in order to discover this connexion we must, however reluctantly, take a step into metaphysic, although into a domain of it which is distinct from speculative philosophy, namely, the metaphysic of morals. In a practical philosophy, where it is not the reasons of what *happens* that we have to ascertain, but the laws of what *ought to happen*, even although it never does, *i.e.* objective practical laws, there it is not necessary to inquire into the reason why anything pleases or displeases, how the pleasure of mere sensation differs from taste, and whether the latter is distinct from a general satisfaction of reason; on what the feeling of pleasure or pain rests, and how from its desires and inclinations arise, and from these again maxims by the co-operation of reason: for all this belongs to an empirical psychology, which would constitute the second part of physics, if we regard physics as the *philosophy* of nature, so far as it is based on *empirical laws*. But here we are concerned with objective practical laws, and consequently with the relation of the will to itself so far as it is determined by reason alone, in which case whatever has reference to anything empirical is necessarily excluded; since if *reason of itself alone* determines the conduct (and it is the possibility of this that we are now investigating), it must necessarily do so *à priori*.

Second Formulation of the Categorical Imperative: Humanity as an End in Itself

The will is conceived as a faculty of determining one-self to action *in accordance with the conception of certain laws*. And such a faculty can be found only in rational beings. Now that which serves the will as the objective ground of its self-determination is the *end*, and if this is assigned by reason alone, it must hold for all rational beings. On the other hand, that which merely contains the ground of possibility of the action of which the effect is the end, this is called the *means*. The subjective ground of the desire is the *spring*, the objective ground of the volition is the *motive*; hence the distinction between subjective ends which rest on springs, and objective ends which depend on motives valid for every rational being. Practical principles are *formal* when they abstract from all subjective ends; they are *material* when they assume these, and therefore particular springs of action. The ends which a rational being proposes to himself at pleasure as *effects* of his actions (material ends) are all only relative, for it is only their relation to the particular desires of the subject that gives them their worth, which therefore cannot furnish principles universal and necessary for all rational beings and for every volition, that is to say practical laws. Hence all these relative ends can give rise only to hypothetical imperatives.

Supposing, however, that there were something *whose existence* has *in itself* an absolute worth, something which, being *an end in itself,* could be a source of definite laws, then in this and this alone would lie the source of a possible categorical imperative, *i.e.* a practical law.

Now I say: man and generally any rational being *exists* as an end in himself, *not merely as a means* to be arbitrarily used by this or that will, but in all his actions, whether they concern himself or other rational beings, must be always regarded at the same time as an end. All objects of the inclinations have only a conditional worth; for if the inclinations and the wants founded on them did not exist, then their object would be without value. But the inclinations themselves being sources of want are so far from having an absolute worth for which they should be desired, that, on the contrary, it must be the universal wish of every rational being to be wholly free from them. Thus the worth of any object which is *to be acquired* by our action is always conditional. Beings whose existence depends not on our will but on nature's, have nevertheless, if they are nonrational beings, only a relative value as means, and are therefore called *things;* rational beings, on the contrary, are called *persons,* because their very nature points them out as ends in themselves, that is as something which must not be used merely as means, and so far therefore restricts freedom of action (and is an object of respect). These, therefore, are not merely subjective ends whose existence has a worth *for us* as an effect of our action, but *objective ends,* that is things whose existence is an end in itself: an end moreover for which no other can be substituted, which they should subserve *merely* as means, for otherwise nothing whatever would possess *absolute worth;* but if all worth were conditioned and therefore contingent, then there would be no supreme practical principle of reason whatever.

If then there is a supreme practical principle or, in respect of the human will, a categorical imperative, it must be one which, being drawn from the conception of that which is necessarily an end for everyone because it is *an end in itself,* constitutes an *objective* principle of will, and can therefore serve as a universal practical law. The foundation of this principle is: *rational nature exists as an end in itself.* Man necessarily conceives his own existence as being so: so far then this is a *subjective* principle of human actions. But every other rational being regards its existence similarly, just on the same rational principle that holds for me[5]: so that it is at the same time an objective principle, from which as a supreme practical law all laws of the will must be capable of being deduced. Accordingly the practical imperative will be as follows: *So act as to treat humanity, whether in thine own person or in that of any other, in every case as an end withal, never as means only.* We will now inquire whether this can be practically carried out.

Four Illustrations

To abide by the previous examples:

Firstly, under the head of necessary duty to oneself: He who contemplates suicide should ask himself whether his actions can be consistent with the idea of humanity *as an end in itself.* If he destroys himself in order to escape from painful circumstances, he uses a person merely as *a means* to maintain a tolerable condition up to the end of life. But a man is not a thing, that is to say, something which can be used merely as means, but must in all his actions be always considered as an end in himself. I cannot, therefore, dispose in any way of a man in my own person so as to mutilate him, to damage or kill him. (It belongs to ethics proper to define this principle more precisely, so as to

avoid all misunderstanding, *e.g.* as to the amputation of the limbs in order to preserve myself; as to exposing my life to danger with a view to preserve it, &c. This question is therefore omitted here.)

Secondly, as regards necessary duties, or those of strict obligation, towards others; he who is thinking of making a lying promise to others will see at once that he would be using another man *merely as a mean,* without the latter containing at the same time the end in himself. For he whom I propose by such a promise to use for my own purposes cannot possibly assent to my mode of acting towards him, and therefore cannot himself contain the end of this action. This violation of the principle of humanity in other men is more obvious if we take in examples of attacks on the freedom and property of others. For then it is clear that he who transgresses the rights of men intends to use the person of others merely as means, without considering that as rational beings they ought always to be esteemed also as ends, that is, as beings who must be capable of containing in themselves the end of the very same action.[6]

Thirdly, as regards contingent (meritorious) duties to oneself; it is not enough that the action does not violate humanity in our own person as an end in itself, it must also *harmonize with* it. Now there are in humanity capacities of greater perfection which belong to the end that nature has in view in regard to humanity in ourselves as the subject: to neglect these might perhaps be consistent with the *maintenance* of humanity as an end in itself, but not with the *advancement* of this end.

Fourthly, as regards meritorious duties towards others: the natural end which all men have is their own happiness. Now humanity might indeed subsist, although no one should contribute anything to the happiness of others, provided he did not intentionally withdraw anything from it; but after all, this would only harmonize negatively, not positively, with *humanity as an end in itself,* if everyone does not also endeavour, as far as in him lies, to forward the ends of others. For the ends of any subject which is an end in himself, ought as far as possible to be *my* ends also, if that conception is to have its *full* effect with me.

Third Formulation of the Categorical Imperative: The Autonomy of the Will as Universal Legislator

This principle, that humanity and generally every rational nature is *an end in itself* (which is the supreme limiting condition of every man's freedom of action), is not borrowed from experience, *firstly,* because it is universal, applying as it does to all rational beings whatever, and experience is not capable of determining anything about them; *secondly,* because it does not present humanity as an end to men (subjectively), that is as an object which men do of themselves actually adopt as an end; but as an objective end, which must as a law constitute the supreme limiting condition of all our subjective ends, let them be what we will; it must therefore spring from pure reason. In fact the objective principle of all practical legislation lies (according to the first principle) in *the rule* and its form of universality which makes it capable of being a law (say, *e.g.,* a law of nature); but the *subjective* principle is in the *end;* now by the second principle the subject of all ends is each rational being inasmuch as it is an end in itself. Hence follows the third practical principle of the will, which is the ultimate condition of its harmony with the universal practical reason, viz.: the idea 'of' *the will of every rational being as a universally legislative will.*

On this principle all maxims are rejected which are inconsistent with the will being itself universal legislator. Thus the will is not subject simply to the law, but so subject that it must be regarded *as itself giving the law,* and on this ground only, subject to the law (of which it can regard itself as the author).

In the previous imperatives, namely, that based on the conception of the conformity of actions to general laws, as in a *physical system of nature,* and that based on the universal *prerogative* of rational beings as *ends* in themselves—these imperatives just because they were conceived as categorical, excluded from any share in their authority all admixture of any interest as a spring of action; they were, however, only *assumed* to be categorical, because such an assumption was necessary to explain the conception of duty. But we could not prove independently that there are practical propositions which command categorically, nor can it be proved in this section; one thing, however, could be done, namely, to indicate in the imperative itself by some determinate expression, that in the case of volition from duty all interest is renounced, which is the specific criterion of categorical as distinguished from hypothetical imperatives. This is done in the present (third) formula of the principle, namely, in the idea of the will of every rational being as a *universally legislating will.*

For although a will *which is subject to laws* may be attached to this law by means of an interest, yet a will which is itself a supreme lawgiver so far as it is such cannot possibly depend on any interest, since a will so dependent would itself still need another law restricting the interest of its self-love by the condition that it should be valid as universal law.

Thus the *principle* that every human will is *a will which in all its maxims gives universal laws,*[7] provided it be otherwise justified, would be very *well adapted* to be the categorical imperative, in this respect, namely, that just because of the idea of universal legislation it is *not based on any interest,* and therefore it alone among all possible imperatives can be *unconditional.* Or still better, converting the proposition, if there is a categorical imperative (*i.e.,* a law for the will of every rational being), it can only command that everything be done from maxims of one's will regarded as a will which could at the same time will that it should itself give universal laws, for in that case only the practical principle and the imperative which it obeys are unconditional, since they cannot be based on any interest.

Looking back now on all previous attempts to discover the principle of morality, we need not wonder why they all failed. It was seen that man was bound to laws by duty, but it was not observed that the laws to which he is subject are *only those of his own giving,* though at the same time they are *universal,* and that he is only bound to act in conformity with his own will; a will, however, which is designed by nature to give universal laws. For when one has conceived man only as subject to a law (no matter what), then this law required some interest, either by way of attraction or constraint, since it did not originate as a law from *his own* will, but this will was according to a law obliged by *something else* to act in a certain manner. Now by this necessary consequence all the labour spent in finding a supreme principle of *duty* was irrevocably lost. For men never elicited duty, but only a necessity of acting from a certain interest. Whether this interest was private or otherwise, in any case the imperative must be conditional, and could not by any means be capable of being a moral command. I will therefore call this the principle of *Autonomy* of the will, in contrast with every other which I accordingly reckon as *Heteronomy.*

The Kingdom of Ends

The conception of every rational being as one which must consider itself as giving in all the maxims of its will universal laws, so as to judge itself and its actions from this point of view—this conception leads to another which depends on it and is very fruitful, namely, that of a *kingdom of ends.*

By a *kingdom* I understand the union of different rational beings in a system by common laws. Now since it is by laws that ends are determined as regards their universal validity, hence, if we abstract from the personal differences of rational beings, and likewise from all the content of their private ends, we shall be able to conceive all ends combined in a systematic whole (including both rational beings as ends in themselves, and also the special ends which each may propose to himself), that is to say, we can conceive a kingdom of ends, which on the preceding principles is possible.

For all rational beings come under the *law* that each of them must treat itself and all others *never merely as means,* but in every case *at the same time as ends in themselves.* Hence results a systematic union of rational beings by common objective laws, i.e., a kingdom which may be called a kingdom of ends, since what these laws have in view is just the relation of these beings to one another as ends and means. It is certainly only an ideal.

A rational being belongs as a *member* to the kingdom of ends when, although giving universal laws in it, he is also himself subject to these laws. He belongs to it *as sovereign* when, while giving laws, he is not subject to the will of any other.

A rational being must always regard himself as giving laws either as member or as sovereign in a kingdom of ends which is rendered possible by the freedom of will. He cannot, however, maintain the latter position merely by the maxims of his will, but only in case he is a completely independent being without wants and with unrestricted power adequate to his will.

Morality consists then in the reference of all action to the legislation which alone can render a kingdom of ends possible. This legislation must be capable of existing in every rational being, and of emanating from his will, so that the principle of this will is, never to act on any maxim which could not without contradiction be also a universal law, and accordingly always so to act *that the will could at the same time regard itself as giving in its maxims universal laws.* If now the maxims of rational beings are not by their own nature coincident with this objective principle, then the necessity of acting on it is called practical necessitation, i.e. *duty.* Duty does not apply to the sovereign in the kingdom of ends, but it does to every member of it and to all in the same degree.

The practical necessity of acting on this principle, *i.e.* duty, does not rest at all on feelings, impulses, or inclinations, but solely on the relation of rational beings to one another, a relation in which the will of a rational being must always be regarded as *legislative,* since otherwise it could not be conceived as *an end in itself.* Reason then refers every maxim of the will, regarding it as legislating universally, to every other will and also to every action towards oneself; and this not on account of any other practical motive or any future advantage, but from the idea of the *dignity* of a rational being, obeying no law but that which he himself also gives.

In the kingdom of ends everything has either Value or Dignity. Whatever has a value can be replaced by something else which is *equivalent;* whatever, on the other hand, is above all value, and therefore admits of no equivalent, has a dignity.

Whatever has reference to the general inclinations and wants of mankind has a *market value;* whatever, without presupposing a want, corresponds to a certain taste, that is to a satisfaction in the mere purposeless play of our faculties, has a *fancy value;* but that which constitutes the condition under which alone anything can be an end in itself, this has not merely a relative worth, *i.e.* value, but an intrinsic worth, that is *dignity.*

Now morality is the condition under which alone a rational being can be an end in himself, since by this alone it is possible that he should be a legislating member in the kingdom of ends. Thus morality, and humanity as capable of it, is that which alone has dignity. Skill and diligence in labour have a market value; wit, lively imagination, and humour, have fancy value; on the other hand, fidelity to promises, benevolence from principle (not from instinct), have an intrinsic worth. Neither nature nor art contains anything which in default of these it could put in their place, for their worth consists not in the effects which spring from them, not in the use and advantage which they secure, but in the disposition of mind, that is, the maxims of the will which are ready to manifest themselves in such actions, even though they should not have the desired effect. These actions also need no recommendation from any subjective taste or sentiment, that they may be looked on with immediate favour and satisfaction: they need no immediate propension or feeling for them; they exhibit the will that performs them as an object of an immediate respect, and nothing but reason is required to *impose* them on the will; not to *flatter* it into them, which, in the case of duties, would be a contradiction. This estimation therefore shows that the worth of such a disposition is dignity, and places it infinitely above all value, with which it cannot for a moment be brought into comparison or competition without as it were violating its sanctity.

What then is it which justifies virtue or the morally good disposition, in making such lofty claims? It is nothing less than the privilege it secures to the rational being of participating in the giving of universal laws, by which it qualifies him to be a member of a possible kingdom of ends, a privilege to which he was already destined by his own nature as being an end in himself, and on that account legislating in the kingdom of ends; free as regards all laws of physical nature, and obeying those only which he himself gives, and by which his maxims can belong to a system of universal law, to which at the same time he submits himself. For nothing has any worth except what the law assigns it. Now the legislation itself which assigns the worth of everything must for that very reason possess dignity, that is an unconditional incomparable worth; and the word *respect* alone supplies a becoming expression for the esteem which a rational being must have for it. *Autonomy* then is the basis of the dignity of human and of every rational nature.

The Autonomy of the Will as the Supreme Principle of Morality Autonomy of the will is that property of it by which it is a law to itself (independently on any property of the objects of volition). The principle of autonomy then is: Always so to choose that the same volition shall comprehend the maxims of our choice as a universal law. We cannot prove that this practical rule is an imperative, *i.e.,* that the will of every rational being is necessarily bound to it as a condition, by a mere analysis of the conceptions which occur in it, since it is a synthetical proposition; we must advance beyond the cognition of the objects to a critical examination of the subject, that is of the pure practical reason, for this synthetic proposition which commands apodictically must be capable of being cognized wholly *à priori*. This matter, however, does not belong to the present section. But that the principle of autonomy in question is the sole principle of morals can be readily shown by mere analysis of the conceptions of morality. For by this analysis we find that its principle must be a categorical imperative, and that what this commands is neither more nor less than this very autonomy.

Heteronomy of the Will as the Source of All Spurious Principles of Morality If the will seeks the law which is to determine it *anywhere else* than in the fitness of its maxims to be universal laws of its own dictation, consequently if it goes out of itself and seeks this law in the character of any of its objects, there always results *heteronomy*. The will in that case does not give itself the

law, but it is given by the object through its relation to the will. This relation, whether it rests on inclination or on conceptions of reason, only admits of hypothetical imperatives: I ought to do something *because I wish for something else*. On the contrary, the moral, and therefore categorical, imperative says: I ought to do so and so, even though I should not wish for anything else. [For example], the former says: I ought not to lie if I would retain my reputation; the latter says: I ought not to lie although it should not bring me the least discredit. The latter therefore must so far abstract from all objects that they shall have no *influence* on the will, in order that practical reason (will) may not be restricted to administering an interest not belonging to it, but may simply show its own commanding authority as the supreme legislation. Thus, [for example], I ought to endeavour to promote the happiness of others, not as if its realization involved any concern of mine (whether by immediate inclination or by any satisfaction indirectly gained through reason), but simply because a maxim which excludes it cannot be comprehended as a universal law in one and the same volition.

Third Section: Transition from the Metaphysic of Morals to the Critique of Pure Practical Reason

The Concept of Freedom Is the Key That Explains the Autonomy of the Will The will is a kind of causality belonging to living beings in so far as they are rational, and *freedom* would be this property of such causality that it can be efficient, independently on foreign causes *determining* it; just as *physical necessity* is the property that the causality of all irrational beings has of being determined to activity by the influence of foreign causes.

The preceding definition of freedom is *negative*, and therefore unfruitful for the discovery of its essence; but it leads to a *positive* conception which is so much the more full and fruitful. Since the conception of causality involves that of laws, according to which, by something that we call cause, something else, namely, the effect, must be produced [laid down]; hence, although freedom is not a property of the will depending on physical laws, yet it is not for that reason lawless; on the contrary, it must be a causality acting according to immutable laws, but a peculiar kind; otherwise a free will would be an absurdity. Physical necessity is a heteronomy of the efficient causes, for every effect is possible only according to this law, that something else determines the efficient cause to exert its causality. What else then can freedom of the will be but autonomy, that is, the property of the will to be a law to itself? But the proposition: The will is in every action a law to itself, only expresses the principle, to act on no other maxim than that which can also have as an object itself as a universal law. Now this is precisely the formula of the categorical imperative and is the principle of morality, so that a free will and a will subject to moral laws are one and the same.

On the hypothesis, then, of freedom of the will, morality together with its principle follows from it by mere analysis of the conception. However, the latter is a synthetic proposition; viz., an absolutely good will is that whose maxim can always include itself regarded as a universal law; for this property of its maxim can never be discovered by analysing the conception of an absolutely good will. Now such synthetic propositions are only possible in this way: that the two cognitions are connected together by their union with a third in which they are both to be found. The *positive* concept of freedom furnishes this third cognition, which cannot, as with physical causes, be the nature of the sensible world (in the concept of which we find conjoined the concept of something in relation as cause to *something else* as effect). We cannot now at once show what this third is to which freedom points us, and of which we have an idea *à priori*, nor can we make intelligible how the concept of freedom is shown to be legitimate from principles of pure practical reason, and with it the possibility of a categorical imperative; but some further preparation is required.

Freedom Must be Presupposed as a Property of the Will of All Rational Beings It is not enough to predicate freedom of our own will, from whatever reason, if we have not sufficient grounds for predicating the same of all rational beings. For as morality serves as a law for us only because we are *rational beings*, it must also hold for all rational beings; and as it must be deduced simply from the property of freedom, it must be shown that freedom also is a property of all rational beings. It is not enough, then, to prove it from certain supposed experiences of human nature (which indeed is quite impossible, and it can only be shown *à priori*), but we must show that it belongs to the activity of all rational beings endowed with a will. Now I say every being that cannot act except *under the idea of freedom* is just for that reason in a practical point of view really free, that is to say, all laws which are inseparably connected with freedom have the same force for him as if his will had been shown to be

free in itself by a proof theoretically conclusive.[8] Now I affirm that we must attribute to every rational being which has a will that it has also the idea of freedom and acts entirely under this idea. For in such a being we conceive a reason that is practical, that is, has causality in reference to its objects. Now we cannot possibly conceive a reason consciously receiving a bias from any other quarter with respect to its judgments, for then the subject would ascribe the determination of its judgment not to its own reason, but to an impulse. It must regard itself as the author of its principles independent on foreign influences. Consequently as practical reason or as the will of a rational being it must regard itself as free, that is to say, the will of such a being cannot be a will of its own except under the idea of freedom. This idea must therefore in a practical point of view be ascribed to every rational being.

Of the Interest Attaching to the Ideas of Morality We have finally reduced the definite conception of morality to the idea of freedom. This latter, however, we could not prove to be actually a property of ourselves or of human nature; only we saw that it must be presupposed if we would conceive a being as rational and conscious of its causality in respect of its actions, *i.e.*, as endowed with a will; and so we find that on just the same grounds we must ascribe to every being endowed with reason and will this artribute of determining itself to action under the idea of its freedom.

Now it resulted also from the presupposition of this idea that we became aware of a law that the subjective principles of action, *i.e.* maxims, must also be so assumed that they can also hold as objective, that is, universal principles, and so serve as universal laws of our own dictation. But why, then, should I subject myself to this principle and that simply as a rational being, thus also subjecting to it all other beings endowed with reason? I will allow that no interest *urges* me to this, for that would not give a categorical imperative, but I must *take* an interest in it and discern how this comes to pass; for this "I ought" is properly an "I would," valid for every rational being, provided only that reason determined his actions without any hindrance. But for beings that are in addition affected as we are by springs of a different kind, namely sensibility, and in whose case that is not always done which reason alone would do, for these that necessity is expressed only as an "ought," and the subjective necessity is different from the objective.

It seems, then, as if the moral law, that is, the principle of autonomy of the will, were properly speaking only presupposed in the idea of freedom, and as if we could not prove its reality and objective necessity independently. In that case we should still have gained something considerable by at least determining the true principle more exactly than had previously been done; but as regards its validity and the practical necessity of subjecting oneself to it, we should not have advanced a step. For if we were asked why the universal validity of our maxim as a law must be the condition restricting our actions, and on what we ground the worth which we assign to this matter of acting—a worth so great that there cannot be any higher interest; and if we were asked further how it happens that it is by this alone a man believes he feels his own personal worth, in comparison with which that of an agreeable or disagreeable condition is to be regarded as nothing, to these questions we could give no satisfactory answer.

We find indeed sometimes that we can take an interest in a personal quality which does not involve any interest of external condition, provided this quality makes us capable of participating in the condition in case reason were to effect the allotment; that is to say, the mere being worthy of happiness can interest of itself even without the motive of participating in this happiness. This judgment, however, is in fact only the effect of the importance of the moral law which we before presupposed (when by the idea of freedom we detach ourselves from every empirical interest); but that we ought to detach ourselves from these interests, *i.e.,* to consider ourselves as free in action and yet as subject to certain laws, so as to find a worth simply in our own person which can compensate us for the loss of everything that gives worth to our condition; this we are not yet able to discern in this way, nor do we see how it is possible so to act—in other words, *whence the moral law derives its obligation.*

It must be freely admitted that there is a sort of circle here from which it seems impossible to escape. In the order of efficient causes we assume ourselves free, in order that in the order of ends we may conceive ourselves as subject to moral laws: and we afterwards conceive ourselves as subject to these laws, because we have attributed to ourselves freedom of will: for freedom and self-legislation of will are both autonomy, and therefore are reciprocal conceptions, and for this very reason one must not be used to explain the other or give the reason of it, but at most only for logical purposes to reduce apparently different notions of the same object to one single concept (as we reduce different fractions of the same value to the lowest terms).

The Two Points of View

One resource remains to us, namely, to inquire whether we do not occupy different points of view when by means of freedom we think ourselves as causes efficient *à priori,* and when we form our conception of ourselves from our actions as effects which we see before our eyes.

It is a remark which needs no subtle reflection to make, but which we may assume that even the commonest understanding can make, although it be after its fashion by an obscure discernment of judgment which it calls feeling, that all the "ideas" that come to us involuntarily (as those of the senses) do not enable us to know objects otherwise than as they affect us; so that what they may be in themselves remains unknown to us, and consequently that as regards "ideas" of this kind even with the closest attention and clearness that the understanding can apply to them, we can by them only attain to the knowledge of *appearances,* never to that of *things in themselves.* As soon as this distinction has once been made (perhaps merely in consequence of the difference observed between the ideas given us from without, and in which we are passive, and those that we produce simply from ourselves, and in which we show our own activity), then it follows of itself that we must admit and assume behind the appearance something else that is not an appearance, namely, the things in themselves; although we must admit that as they can never be known to us except as they affect us, we can come no nearer to them, nor can we ever know what they are in themselves. This must furnish a distinction, however crude, between a *world of sense* and the *world of understanding,* of which the former may be different according to the difference of the sensuous impressions in various observers, while the second which is its basis always remains the same. Even as to himself, a man cannot pretend to know what he is in himself from the knowledge he has by internal sensation. For as he does not as it were create himself, and does not come by the conception of himself *à priori* but empirically, it naturally follows that he can obtain his knowledge even of himself only by the inner sense, and consequently only through the appearances of his nature and the way in which his consciousness is affected. At the same time beyond these characteristics of his own subject, made up of mere appearances, he must necessarily suppose something else as their basis, namely, his *ego,* whatever its characteristics in itself may be. Thus in respect to mere perception and receptivity of sensations he must reckon himself as belonging to the *world of sense;* but in respect of whatever there may be of pure activity in him (that which reaches consciousness immediately and not through affecting the senses) he must reckon himself as belonging to the *intellectual world,* of which, however, he has no further knowledge. To such a conclusion the reflecting man must come with respect to all the things which can be presented to him: it is probably to be met with even in persons of the commonest understanding, who, as is well known, are very much inclined to suppose behind the objects of the sense something else invisible and acting of itself. They spoil it, however, by presently sensualizing this invisible again; that is to say, wanting to make it an object of intuition, so that they do not become a whit the wiser.

Now man really finds in himself a faculty by which he distinguishes himself from everything else, even from himself as affected by objects, and that is *Reason.* This being pure spontaneity is even elevated above the *understanding.* For although the latter is a spontaneity and does not, like sense, merely contain intuitions that arise when we are affected by things (and are therefore passive), yet it cannot produce from its activity any other conceptions than those which merely serve *to bring the intuitions of sense under rules,* and thereby to unite them in one consciousness, and without this use of the sensibility it could not think at all; whereas, on the contrary. Reason shows so pure a spontaneity in the case of what I call Ideas [Ideal Conceptions] that it thereby far transcends everything that the sensibility can give it, and exhibits its most important function in distinguishing the world of sense from that of understanding, and thereby prescribing the limits of the understanding itself.

For this reason a rational being must regard himself *qua* intelligence (not from the side of his lower faculties) as belonging not to the world of sense, but to that of understanding; hence he has two points of view from which he can regard himself, and recognize laws of the exercise of his faculties, and consequently of all his actions: *first,* so far as he belongs to the world of sense, he finds himself subject to laws of nature (heteronomy); *secondly,* as belonging to the intelligible world, under laws which, being independent on nature, have their foundation not in experience but in reason alone.

As a reasonable being, and consequently belonging to the intelligible world, man can never conceive the causality of his own will otherwise than on condition of the idea of freedom, for independence on the determining causes of the sensible world (an independence which Reason must always ascribe to itself) is freedom. Now the idea of freedom is inseparably connected with the conception of *autonomy,* and this again with the universal principle of morality which is ideally the foundation of all actions of *rational* beings, just as the law of nature is of all phenomena.

Now the suspicion is removed which we raised above, that there was a latent circle involved in our reasoning from freedom to autonomy, and from this to the moral law, [namely]: that we laid down the idea of freedom because of the moral law only that we might afterwards in turn infer the latter from freedom, and that consequently we could assign no reason at all for this law, but could only [present] it as a *petitio principii* which well-disposed minds would gladly concede to us, but which we could never put forward as a provable proposition. For now we see that when we conceive ourselves as free we transfer ourselves into the world of understanding as members of it, and recognize the autonomy of the will with its consequence, morality; whereas, if we conceive ourselves as under obligation, we consider ourselves as belonging to the world of sense, and at the same time to the world of understanding.

How Is a Categorical Imperative Possible? Every rational being reckons himself *qua* intelligence as belonging to the world of understanding, and it is simply as an efficient cause belonging to that world that he calls his causality a *will.* On the other side he is also conscious of himself as a part of the world of sense in which his actions, which are mere appearances [phenomena] of that causality, are displayed; we cannot, however, discern how they are possible from this causality which we do not know; but instead of that, these actions as belonging to the sensible world must be viewed as determined by other phenomena, namely, desires and inclinations. If therefore I were only a member of the world of understanding, then all my actions would perfectly conform to the principle of autonomy of the pure will; if I were only a part of the world of sense, they would necessarily be assumed to conform wholly to the natural laws of desires and inclinations, in other words, to the heteronomy of nature. (The former would rest on morality as the supreme principle, the latter on happiness.) Since, however, *the world of understanding contains the foundation of the world of sense, and consequently of its laws also,* and accordingly gives the law to my will (which belongs wholly to the world of understanding) directly, and must be conceived as doing so, it follows that, although on the one side I must regard myself as a being belonging to the world of sense, yet on the other side I must recognize myself as subject as an intelligence to the law of the world of understanding, *i.e.* to reason, which contains this law in the idea of freedom, and therefore as subject to the autonomy of the will: consequently I must regard the laws of the world of understanding as imperatives for me, and the actions which conform to them as duties.

And thus what makes categorical imperatives possible is this, that the idea of freedom makes me a member of an intelligible world, in consequence of which, if I were nothing else, all my actions *would* always conform to the autonomy of the will; but as I at the same time intuite myself as a member of the world of sense, they *ought* so to conform, and this *categorical* "ought" implies a synthetic *à priori* proposition, inasmuch as besides my will as affected by sensible desires there is added further the idea of the same will, but as belonging to the world of the understanding, pure and practical of itself, which contains the supreme condition according to Reason of the former will; precisely as to the intuitions of sense there are added concepts of the understanding which of themselves signify nothing but regular form in general, and in this way synthetic *à priori* propositions become possible, on which all knowledge of physical nature rests.

The practical use of common human reason confirms this reasoning. There is no one, not even the most consummate villain, provided only that he is otherwise accustomed to the use of reason, who, when we set before him examples of honesty of purpose, of steadfastness in following good maxims, of sympathy and general benevolence (even combined with great sacrifices of advantages and comfort), does not wish that he might also possess these qualities. Only on account of his inclinations and impulses he cannot attain this in himself, but at the same time he wishes to be free from such inclinations which are burdensome to himself. He proves by this that he transfers himself in thought with a will free from the impulses of the sensibility into an order of things wholly different from that of his desires in the field of the sensibility; since he cannot expect to obtain by that wish any gratification of his desires nor any position which would satisfy any of his actual or supposable inclinations (for this would destroy the pre-eminence of the very idea which wrests that wish from him): he can only expect a greater intrinsic worth of his own person. This better person, however, he imagines himself to be when he transfers himself to the point of view of a member of the world of the understanding, to which he is involuntarily forced by the idea of free-

dom, *i.e.,* of independence on *determining* causes of the world of sense; and from this point of view he is conscious of a good will, which by his own confession constitutes the law for the bad will that he possesses as a member of the world of sense—a law whose authority he recognizes while transgressing it. What he morally "ought" is then what he necessarily "would" as a member of the world of the understanding, and is conceived by him as an "ought" only inasmuch as he likewise considers himself as a member of the world of sense.

The question then: How a categorical imperative is possible can be answered to this extent that we can assign the only hypothesis on which it is possible, namely, the idea of freedom; and we can also discern the necessity of this hypothesis, and this is sufficient for the *practical exercise* of reason, that is, for the conviction of the *validity of this imperative,* and hence of the moral law; but how this hypothesis itself is possible can never be discerned by any human reason. On the hypothesis, however, that the will of an intelligence is free, its *autonomy,* as the essential formal condition of its determination, is a necessary consequence.

Endnotes

1. A *maxim* is the subjective principle of volition. The objective principle (*i.e.* that which would also serve subjectively as a practical principle to all rational beings if reason had full power over the faculty of desire) is the practical *law.*

2. I connect the act with the will without presupposing any condition resulting from any inclination, but *à priori,* and therefore necessarily (though only objectively, *i.e.* assuming the idea of a reason possessing full power over all subjective motives). This is accordingly a practical proposition which does not deduce the willing of an action by mere analysis from another already presupposed (for we have not such a perfect will), but connects it immediately with the conception of the will of a rational being, as something not contained in it.

3. A maxim is a subjective principle of action, and must be distinguished from the *objective principle,* namely, practical law. The former contains the practical rule set by reason according to the conditions of the subject (often its ignorance or its inclinations), so that it is the principle on which the subject *acts;* but the law is the objective principle valid for every rational being, and is the principle on which it *ought to act* that is an imperative.

4. To behold virtue in her proper form is nothing else but to contemplate morality stripped of all admixture of sensible things and of every spurious ornament of reward or self-love. How much she then eclipses everything else that

appears charming to the affections, every one may readily perceive with the least exertion of his reason, if it be not wholly spoiled for abstraction.

5. This proposition is here stated as a postulate. The ground of it will be found in the concluding section.

6. Let it not be thought that the common: *quod tibi non vis fieri, &c.,* [that which you do not wish to be done to you, do not do to others] could serve here as the rule or principle. For it is only a deduction from the former, though with several limitations; it cannot be a universal law, for it does not contain the principle of duties to oneself, nor of the duties of benevolence to others (for many a one would gladly consent that others should not benefit him, provided only that he might be excused from showing benevolence to them), nor finally that of duties of strict obligation to one another, for

on this principle the criminal might argue against the judge who punishes him, and so on.

7. I may be excused from adducing examples to elucidate this principle, as those which have already been used to elucidate the categorical imperative and its formula would all serve for the like purpose here.

8. I adopt this method of assuming freedom merely *as an idea* which rational beings suppose in their actions, in order to avoid the necessity of proving it in its theoretical aspect also. The former is sufficient for my purpose; for even though the speculative proof should not be made out, yet a being that cannot act except with the idea of freedom is bound by the same laws that would oblige a being who was actually free. Thus we can escape here from the onus which presses on the theory.

5. *Nicomachean Ethics*

ARISTOTLE

Aristotle (384–322 B.C.), was a Greek physician and philosopher whose seminal work on the virtues continues to exert a profound influence on ethical thinkers. In his *Nicomachean Ethics,* he discusses the relationship between ethics and human flourishing. According to Aristotle, persons attain human excellence through their participation in well-ordered communities in which they are given the opportunity to develop virtuous lives. Communities shape persons of virtue and are shaped and improved by them in turn. Unlike intellectual virtues, which can simply be learned, moral virtues such as courage, patience, justice, and prudence must be practiced regularly until they become engrained in one's character. As Aristotle explains, virtue is to be found in living in moderation between the vice of deficiency on one hand and the vice of excess on the other. Bringing a virtuous character to the moral life enables one to foster excellence in oneself and in others, and to move toward happiness or human well-being.

Book I

Chapter 1 Every art and every scientific inquiry, and similarly every action and purpose, may be said to aim at some good. Hence the good has been well defined as that at which all things aim. But it is clear that there is a difference in ends; for the ends are sometimes

activities, and sometimes results beyond the mere activities. Where there are ends beyond the action, the results are naturally superior to the action.

As there are various actions, arts, and sciences, it follows that the ends are also various. Thus health is the end of the medical art, a ship of shipbuilding, victory of strategy, and wealth of economics. It often happens that a number of such arts or sciences combine for a single enterprise, as the art of making bridles and all such other arts as furnish the implements of horsemanship

From *Aristotle's Nicomachean Ethics,* translated by James E. C. Weldon (Macmillan, 1897).

combine for horsemanship, and horsemanship and every military action for strategy; and in the same way, other arts or sciences combine for others. In all these cases, the ends of the master arts or sciences, whatever they may be, are more desirable than those of the subordinate arts or sciences, as it is for the sake of the former that the latter are pursued. It makes no difference to the argument whether the activities themselves are the ends of the action, or something beyond the activities, as in the above-mentioned sciences.

If it is true that in the sphere of action there is some end which we wish for its own sake, and for the sake of which we wish everything else, and if we do not desire everything for the sake of something else (for, if that is so, the process will go on *ad infinitum,* and our desire will be idle and futile), clearly this end will be good and the supreme good. Does it not follow then that the knowledge of this good is of great importance for the conduct of life? Like archers who have a mark at which to aim, shall we not have a better chance of attaining what we want? If this is so, we must endeavor to comprehend, at least in outline, what this good is, and what science or faculty makes it its object.

It would seem that this is the most authoritative science. Such a kind is evidently the political, for it is that which determines what sciences are necessary in states, and what kinds should be studied, and how far they should be studied by each class of inhabitant. We see too that even the faculties held in highest esteem, such as strategy, economics, and rhetoric, are subordinate to it. Then since politics makes use of the other sciences and also rules what people may do and what they may not do, it follows that its end will comprehend the ends of the other sciences, and will therefore be the good of mankind. For even if the good of an individual is identical with the good of a state, yet the good of the state is evidently greater and more perfect to attain or to preserve. For though the good of an individual by himself is something worth working for, to ensure the good of a nation or a state is nobler and more divine.

These then are the objects at which the present inquiry aims, and it is in a sense a political inquiry. . . .

Chapter 2 As every science and undertaking aims at some good, what is in our view the good at which political science aims, and what is the highest of all practical goods? As to its name there is, I may say, a general agreement. The masses and the cultured classes agree in calling it happiness, and conceive that "to live well" or "to do well" is the same thing as "to be happy." But as to what happiness is they do not

agree, nor do the masses give the same account of it as the philosophers. The former take it to be something visible and palpable, such as pleasure, wealth, or honor; different people, however, give different definitions of it, and often even the same man gives different definitions at different times. When he is ill, it is health, when he is poor, it is wealth; if he is conscious of his own ignorance, he envies people who use grand language above his own comprehension. Some philosophers, on the other hand, have held that, besides these various goods, there is an absolute good which is the cause of goodness in them all. It would perhaps be a waste of time to examine all these opinions; it will be enough to examine such as are most popular or as seem to be more or less reasonable.

Chapter 3 Men's conception of the good or of happiness may be read in the lives they lead. Ordinary or vulgar people conceive it to be a pleasure, and accordingly choose a life of enjoyment. For there are, we may say, three conspicuous types of life, the sensual, the political, and, thirdly, the life of thought. Now the mass of men present an absolutely slavish appearance, choosing the life of brute beasts, but they have ground for so doing because so many persons in authority share the tastes of Sardanapalus. Cultivated and energetic people, on the other hand, identify happiness with honor, as honor is the general end of political life. But this seems too superficial an idea for our present purpose; for honor depends more upon the people who pay it than upon the person to whom it is paid, and the good we feel is something which is proper to a man himself and cannot be easily taken away from him. Men too appear to seek honor in order to be assured of their own goodness. Accordingly, they seek it at the hands of the sage and of those who know them well, and they seek it on the ground of their virtue; clearly then, in their judgment at any rate, virtue is better than honor. Perhaps then we might look on virtue rather than honor as the end of political life. Yet even this idea appears not quite complete; for a man may possess virtue and yet be asleep or inactive throughout life, and not only so, but he may experience the greatest calamities and misfortunes. Yet no one would call such a life a life of happiness, unless he were maintaining a paradox. But we need not dwell further on this subject, since it is sufficiently discussed in popular philosophical treatises. The third life is the life of thought, which we will discuss later.

The life of money making is a life of constraint; and wealth is obviously not the good of which we are in quest; for it is useful merely as a means to something else. It would be more reasonable to take the things mentioned before—sensual pleasure, honor, and virtue—as ends than wealth, since they are things desired on their own account. Yet these too are evidently not ends, although much argument has been employed to show that they are. . . .

Chapter 5 But leaving this subject for the present, let us revert to the good of which we are in quest and consider what it may be. For it seems different in different activities or arts; it is one thing in medicine, another in strategy, and so on. What is the good in each of these instances? It is presumably that for the sake of which all else is done. In medicine this is health, in strategy victory, in architecture a house, and so on. In every activity and undertaking it is the end, since it is for the sake of the end that all people do whatever else they do. If then there is an end for all our activity, this will be the good to be accomplished; and if there are several such ends, it will be these.

Our argument has arrived by a different path at the same point as before; but we must endeavor to make it still plainer. Since there are more ends than one, and some of these ends—for example, wealth, flutes, and instruments generally—we desire as means to something else, it is evident that not all are final ends. But the highest good is clearly something final. Hence if there is only one final end, this will be the object of which we are in search; and if there are more than one, it will be the most final. We call that which is sought after for its own sake more final than that which is sought after as a means to something else; we call that which is never desired as a means to something else more final than things that are desired both for themselves and as means to something else. Therefore, we call absolutely final that which is always desired for itself and never as a means to something else. Now happiness more than anything else answers to this description. For happiness we always desire for its own sake and never as a means to something else, whereas honor, pleasure, intelligence, and every virtue we desire partly for their own sakes (for we should desire them independently of what might result from them), but partly also as means to happiness, because we suppose they will prove instruments of happiness. Happiness, on the other hand, nobody desires for the sake of these things, nor indeed as a means to anything else at all.

If we start from the point of view of self-sufficiency, we reach the same conclusion; for we assume that the final good is self-sufficient. By self-sufficiency we do not mean that a person leads a solitary life all by himself, but that he has parents, children, wife and friends and fellow citizens in general, as man is naturally a social being. Yet here it is necessary to set some limit; for if the circle must be extended to include ancestors, descendants, and friends' friends, it will go on indefinitely. Leaving this point, however, for future investigation, we call the self-sufficient that which, taken even by itself, makes life desirable and wanting nothing at all; and this is what we mean by happiness.

Again, we think happiness the most desirable of all things, and that not merely as one good thing among others. If it were only that, the addition of the smallest more good would increase its desirableness; for the addition would make an increase of goods, and the greater of two goods is always the more desirable. Happiness is something final and self-sufficient and the end of all action.

Chapter 6 Perhaps, however, it seems commonplace to say that happiness is the supreme good; what is wanted is to define its nature a little more clearly. The best way of arriving at such a definition will probably be to ascertain the function of man. For, as with a flute player, a sculptor, or any artist, or in fact anybody who has a special function or activity, his goodness and excellence seem to lie in his function, so it would seem to be with man, if indeed he has a special function. Can it be said that, while a carpenter and a cobbler have special functions and activities, man, unlike them, is naturally functionless? Or, as the eye, the hand, the foot, and similarly each part of the body has a special function, so may man be regarded as having a special function apart from all these? What, then, can this function be? It is not life; for life is apparently something that man shares with plants; and we are looking for something peculiar to him. We must exclude therefore the life of nutrition and growth. There is next what may be called the life of sensation. But this too, apparently, is shared by man with horses, cattle, and all other animals. There remains what I may call the active life of the rational part of man's being. Now this rational part is twofold; one part is rational in the sense of being obedient to reason, and the other in the sense of possessing and exercising reason and intelligence. The active life too may be conceived of in two ways, either as a state of character, or as an activity; but we mean by it the life of activity, as this seems to be the truer form of the conception.

The function of man then is activity of soul in accordance with reason, or not apart from reason. Now, the function of a man of a certain kind, and of a man who is good of that kind—for example, of a harpist and a good harpist—are in our view the same in kind. This is true of all people of all kinds without exception, the superior excellence being only an addition to the function; for it is the function of a harpist to play the harp, and of a good harpist to play the harp well. This being so, if we define the function of man as a kind of life, and this life as an activity of the soul or a course of action in accordance with reason, and if the function of a good man is such activity of a good and noble kind, and if everything is well done when it is done in accordance with its proper excellence, it follows that the good of man is activity of soul in accordance with virtue, or, if there are more virtues than one, in accordance with the best and most complete virtue. But we must add the words "in a complete life." For as one swallow or one day does not make a spring, so one day or a short time does not make a man blessed or happy. . . .

Chapter 8 Goods have been divided into three classes: external goods as they are called, goods of the soul, and goods of the body. Of these three classes goods of the soul are considered goods in the strictest and truest sense. To the soul are ascribed spiritual actions and activities. Thus our definition must be a good one, at least according to this theory, which is both ancient and accepted by philosophers at the present time. It is correct too, inasmuch as we call certain actions and activities the end; for we put the end in some good of the soul and not in an external good. By a similar theory the happy man lives well and does well, and happiness, we have said, is in fact a kind of living and doing well. . . .

Chapter 10 The question is consequently raised whether happiness is something that can be learned or acquired by habit or training of some kind, or whether it comes by some divine dispensation, or even by chance.

Now if there is anything in the world that is a gift of the gods to men, it is reasonable to take happiness as a divine gift, and especially divine as it is the best of human things. This point, however, is perhaps more appropriate to another investigation than the present. But even if happiness is not sent by the gods but is the result of goodness and of learning or training of some kind, it is apparently one of the most divine things in the world; for that which is the prize and end of goodness would seem the best good and in its nature godlike and blessed. It may also be widely extended; for

all persons who are not morally deformed may share in it by a process of study and care. And if it is better that happiness should come in this way than by chance, we may reasonably suppose that it does so come, since the order of things in Nature is the best possible, as it is in art and in causation generally, and most of all in the highest kind of causation. And to leave what is greatest and noblest to chance would be altogether unworthy. The definition of happiness itself helps to clear up the question; for happiness we have defined as a kind of virtuous activity of the soul. . . .

It is reasonable then not to call an ox or a horse or any other animal happy; for none of them is capable of sharing in this activity. For the same reason no child can be happy, since the youth of a child keeps him for the time being from such activity; if a child is ever called happy, the ground of felicitation is his promise, rather than his actual performance. For happiness demands, as we said, a complete virtue and a complete life. And there are all sorts of changes and chances in life, and the most prosperous of men may in his old age fall into extreme calamities, as Priam did in the heroic legends. And a person who has experienced such chances and died a miserable death, nobody calls happy.

Chapter 13 Inasmuch as happiness is an activity of soul in accordance with perfect virtue, we must now consider virtue, as this will perhaps be the best way of studying happiness. . . . Clearly it is human virtue we have to consider; for the good of which we are in search is, as we said, human good, and the happiness, human happiness. By human virtue or excellence we mean not that of the body, but that of the soul, and by happiness we mean an activity of the soul.

There are some facts concerning the soul which are adequately stated in popular discourses, and these we may rightly accept. It is said, for example, that the soul has two parts, one irrational and the other rational. Whether these parts are separate like the parts of the body or like anything divisible, or whether they are theoretically distinct but in fact inseparable, like the convex and concave in the circumference of a circle, is of no importance to the present inquiry.

Of the irrational part of the soul one part is shared by man with all living things, and vegetative; I mean the part which is the cause of nutrition and growth. For we may assume such a faculty of the soul to exist in all young things that take food, even in embryos, and the same faculty to exist in things full grown, since it is more reasonable to suppose it is the same faculty than something different. Manifestly the virtue or excellence of this faculty is not peculiarly human but is shared by man with all living things; this part or faculty seems especially active in sleep, whereas goodness and badness never show so little as in sleep. Hence the saying that during half their lives there is no difference between the happy and the unhappy. And this is only natural; for sleep is an inactivity of the soul as regards its goodness or badness, except in so far as certain impulses affect it slightly and make the dreams of good men better than those of ordinary people. Enough, however, on this point; we shall now leave the faculty of nutrition, as it has by its nature no part in human goodness.

There is, we think, another natural element of the soul which is irrational and yet in a sense partakes of reason. For in continent and incontinent persons we praise their reason, and that part of their soul which possesses reason, because it counsels them aright and directs them to the best conduct. But we know there is in them also another element naturally opposed to reason that fights and contends against reason. Just as paralyzed parts of the body, when we try to move them to the right, pull in a contrary direction to the left, so it is with the soul; the impulses of incontinent people run counter to reason. But while in the body we see the part which pulls awry, in the soul we do not see it. We may, however, suppose with equal certainty that in the soul too there is something alien to reason, which opposes and thwarts it. The sense in which it is distinct from other things is unimportant. But it too partakes of reason, as we said; at all events, in a continent person it obeys reason, and in a temperate and brave man it is probably still more obedient, for in him it is absolutely harmonious with reason.

It appears then that the irrational part of the soul is twofold; for the vegetative faculty does not participate at all in reason, but the element of appetite and desire in general shares in it, in so far as it is submissive and obedient to reason. It is so in the sense in which we speak of "paying attention" to a father or to friends, but not in the sense in which we speak of "paying attention" to mathematics. All advice, reproof, and exhortation are witness that this irrational part of the soul is in a sense subject to influence by reason. And if we say that this part participates in reason, then as a part possessing reason, it will be twofold, one element possessing reason absolutely and in itself, the other listening to it as a child listens to its father.

Virtue too may be divided to correspond to this difference. For we call some virtues intellectual and others moral. Wisdom, intelligence, and prudence are intellectual; liberality and temperance moral. In describing a person's moral character we do not say that he is wise or intelligent but that he is gentle or temperate. A wise man, however, we praise for his mentality, and such mentality as deserves praise we call virtuous.

Book II

> Moral virtues can best be acquired by practice and habit. They imply a right attitude toward pleasures and pains. A good man deliberately chooses to do what is noble and right for its own sake. What is right in matters of moral conduct is usually a mean between two extremes.

Chapter 1 Virtue then is twofold, partly intellectual and partly moral, and intellectual virtue is originated and fostered mainly by teaching; it demands therefore experience and time. Moral virtue on the other hand is the outcome of habit, and accordingly its name, *ethike*, is derived by a slight variation from *ethos*, habit. From this fact it is clear that moral virtue is not implanted in us by nature; for nothing that exists by nature can be transformed by habit. Thus a stone, that naturally tends to fall downwards, cannot be habituated or trained to rise upwards, even if we tried to train it by throwing it up ten thousand times. Nor again can fire be trained to sink downwards, nor anything else that follows one natural law be habituated or trained to follow another. It is neither by nature then nor in defiance of nature that virtues grow in us. Nature gives us the capacity to receive them, and that capacity is perfected by habit.

Again, if we take the various natural powers which belong to us, we first possess the proper faculties and afterwards display the activities. It is obviously so with the senses. Not by seeing frequently or hearing frequently do we acquire the sense of seeing or hearing; on the contrary, because we have the senses we make use of them; we do not get them by making use of them. But the virtues we get by first practicing them, as we do in the arts. For it is by doing what we ought to do when we study the arts that we learn the arts themselves; we become builders by building and harpists by playing the harp. Similarly, it is by doing just acts that we become just, by doing temperate acts that we become temperate, by doing brave acts that we become brave. The experience of states confirms this statement, for it is by training in good habits that lawmakers make the citizens good. This is the object all lawmakers have at heart; if they do not succeed in it, they fail of their purpose; and it makes the distinction between a good constitution and a bad one.

Again, the causes and means by which any virtue is produced and destroyed are the same; and equally so in any part. For it is by playing the harp that both good and bad harpists are produced; and the case of builders and others is similar, for it is by building well that they become good builders and by building badly that they become bad builders. If it were not so, there would be no need of anybody to teach them; they would all be born good or bad in their several crafts. The case of the virtues is the same. It is by our actions in dealings between man and man that we become either just or unjust. It is by our actions in the face of danger and by our training ourselves to fear or to courage that we become either cowardly or courageous. It is much the same with our appetites and angry passions. People become temperate and gentle, others licentious and passionate, by behaving in one or the other way in particular circumstances. In a word, moral states are the results of activities like the states themselves. It is our duty therefore to keep a certain character in our activities, since our moral states depend on the differences in our activities. So the difference between one and another training in habits in our childhood is not a light matter, but important, or rather, all-important.

Chapter 2 Our present study is not, like other studies, purely theoretical in intention; for the object of our inquiry is not to know what virtue is but how to become good, and that is the sole benefit of it. We must, therefore, consider the right way of performing actions, for it is acts, as we have said, that determine the character of the resulting moral states.

That we should act in accordance with right reason is a common general principle, which may here be taken for granted. The nature of right reason, and its relation to the virtues generally, will be discussed later. But first of all it must be admitted that all reasoning on matters of conduct must be like a sketch in outline; it cannot be scientifically exact. We began by laying down the principle that the kind of reasoning demanded in any subject must be such as the subject matter itself allows; and questions of conduct and expediency no more admit of hard and fast rules than questions of health.

If this is true of general reasoning on ethics, still more true is it that scientific exactitude is impossible in treating of particular ethical cases. They do not fall under any art or law, but the actors themselves have always to take account of circumstances, as much as in medicine or navigation. Still, although such is the nature of our present argument, we must try to make the best of it.

The first point to be observed is that in the matters we are now considering deficiency and excess are both fatal. It is so, we see, in questions of health and strength. (We must judge of what we cannot see by the evidence of what we do see.) Too much or too little gymnastic exercise is fatal to strength. Similarly, too much or too little meat and drink is fatal to health, whereas a suitable amount produces, increases, and sustains it. It is the same with temperance, courage, and other moral virtues. A person who avoids and is afraid of everything and faces nothing becomes a coward; a person who is not afraid of anything but is ready to face everything becomes foolhardy. Similarly, he who enjoys every pleasure and abstains from none is licentious; he who refuses all pleasures, like a boor, is an insensible sort of person. For temperance and courage are destroyed by excess and deficiency but preserved by the mean.

Again, not only are the causes and agencies of production, increase, and destruction in moral states the same, but the field of their activity is the same also. It is so in other more obvious instances, as, for example, strength; for strength is produced by taking a great deal of food and undergoing a great deal of exertion, and it is the strong man who is able to take most food and undergo most exertion. So too with the virtues. By abstaining from pleasures we become temperate, and, when we have become temperate, we are best able to abstain from them. So again with courage; it is by training ourselves to despise and face terrifying things that we become brave, and when we have become brave, we shall be best able to face them.

The pleasure or pain which accompanies actions may be regarded as a test of a person's moral state. He who abstains from physical pleasures and feels pleasure in so doing is temperate; but he who feels pain at so doing is licentious. He who faces dangers with pleasure, or at least without pain, is brave; but he who feels pain at facing them is a coward. For moral virtue is concerned with pleasures and pains. It is pleasure which makes us do what is base, and pain which makes us abstain from doing what is noble. Hence the importance of having a certain training from very early days, as

Plato says, so that we may feel pleasure and pain at the right objects; for this is true education. . . .

Chapter 3 But we may be asked what we mean by saying that people must become just by doing what is just and temperate by doing what is temperate. For, it will be said, if they do what is just and temperate they are already just and temperate themselves, in the same way as, if they practice grammar and music, they are grammarians and musicians.

But is this true even in the case of the arts? For a person may speak grammatically either by chance or at the suggestion of somebody else; hence he will not be a grammarian unless he not only speaks grammatically but does so in a grammatical manner, that is, because of the grammatical knowledge which he possesses.

There is a point of difference too between the arts and the virtues. The productions of art have their excellence in themselves. It is enough then that, when they are produced, they themselves should possess a certain character. But acts in accordance with virtue are not justly or temperately performed simply because they are in themselves just or temperate. The doer at the time of performing them must satisfy certain conditions; in the first place, he must know what he is doing; secondly, he must deliberately choose to do it and do it for his own sake; and thirdly, he must do it as part of his own firm and immutable character. If it be a question of art, these conditions, except only the condition of knowledge, are not raised; but if it be a question of virtue, mere knowledge is of little or no avail; it is the other conditions, which are the results of frequently performing just and temperate acts, that are not slightly but all-important. Accordingly, deeds are called just and temperate when they are such as a just and temperate person would do; and a just and temperate person is not merely one who does these deeds but one who does them in the spirit of the just and the temperate.

It may fairly be said that a just man becomes just by doing what is just, and a temperate man becomes temperate by doing what is temperate, and if a man did not so act, he would not have much chance of becoming good. But most people, instead of acting, take refuge in theorizing; they imagine that they are philosophers and that philosophy will make them virtuous; in fact, they behave like people who listen attentively to their doctors but never do anything that their doctors tell them. But a healthy state of the soul will no more be produced by this kind of philosophizing than a healthy state of the body by this kind of medical treatment.

Chapter 4 We have next to consider the nature of virtue. Now, as the properties of the soul are three, namely, emotions, faculties, and moral states, it follows that virtue must be one of the three. By emotions I mean desire, anger, fear, pride, envy, joy, love, hatred, regret, ambition, pity—in a word, whatever feeling is attended by pleasure or pain. I call those faculties through which we are said to be capable of experiencing these emotions, for instance, capable of getting angry or being pained or feeling pity. And I call those moral states through which we are well or ill disposed in our emotions, ill disposed, for instance, in anger, if our anger be too violent or too feeble, and well disposed, if it be rightly moderate; and similarly in our other emotions.

Now neither the virtues nor the vices are emotions; for we are not called good or bad for our emotions but for our virtues or vices. We are not praised or blamed simply for being angry, but only for being angry in a certain way; but we are praised or blamed for our virtues or vices. Again, whereas we are angry or afraid without deliberate purpose, the virtues are matters of deliberate purpose, or require deliberate purpose. Moreover, we are said to be moved by our emotions, but by our virtues or vices we are not said to be moved but to have a certain disposition.

For these reasons the virtues are not faculties. For we are not called either good or bad, nor are we praised or blamed for having simple capacity for emotion. Also while Nature gives us our faculties, it is not Nature that makes us good or bad; but this point we have already discussed. If then the virtues are neither emotions nor faculties, all that remains is that they must be moral states.

Chapter 5 The nature of virtue has been now described in kind. But it is not enough to say merely that virtue is a moral state; we must also describe the character of that moral state.

We may assert then that every virtue or excellence puts into good condition that of which it is a virtue or excellence, and enables it to perform its work well. Thus excellence in the eye makes the eye good and its function good, for by excellence in the eye we see well. Similarly, excellence of the horse makes a horse excellent himself and good at racing, at carrying its rider and at facing the enemy. If then this rule is universally true, the virtue or excellence of a man will be such a moral state as makes a man good and able to perform his proper function well. How this will be the case we have already explained, but another way of making it clear will be to study the nature or character of virtue.

Now of everything, whether it be continuous or divisible, it is possible to take a greater, a smaller, or an equal amount, and this either in terms of the thing itself or in relation to ourselves, the equal being a mean between too much and too little. By the mean in terms of the thing itself, I understand that which is equally distinct from both its extremes, which is one and the same for every man. By the mean relatively to ourselves, I understand that which is neither too much nor too little for us; but this is not one nor the same for everybody. Thus if 10 be too much and 2 too little, we take 6 as a mean in terms of the thing itself; for 6 is as much greater than 2 as it is less than 10, and this is a mean in arithmetical proportion. But the mean considered relatively to ourselves may not be ascertained in that way. It does not follow that if 10 pounds of meat is too much and 2 too little for a man to eat, the trainer will order him 6 pounds, since this also may be too much or too little for him who is to take it; it will be too little, for example, for Milo but too much for a beginner in gymnastics. The same with running and wrestling; the right amount will vary with the individual. This being so, the skillful in any art avoids alike excess and deficiency; he seeks and chooses the mean, not the absolute mean, but the mean considered relatively to himself.

Every art then does its work well, if it regards the mean and judges the works it produces by the mean. For this reason we often say of successful works of art that it is impossible to take anything from them or to add anything to them, which implies that excess or deficiency is fatal to excellence but that the mean state ensures it. Good artists too, as we say, have an eye to the mean in their works. Now virtue, like Nature herself, is more accurate and better than any art; virtue, therefore, will aim at the mean. I speak of moral virtue, since it is moral virtue which is concerned with emotions and actions, and it is in these we have excess and deficiency and the mean. Thus it is possible to go too far, or not far enough in fear, pride, desire, anger, pity, and pleasure and pain generally, and the excess and the deficiency are alike wrong; but to feel these emotions at the right times, for the right objects, towards the right persons, for the right motives, and in the right manner, is the mean or the best good, which signifies virtue. Similarly, there may be excess, deficiency, or the mean, in acts. Virtue is concerned with both emotions and actions, wherein excess is an error and deficiency a fault, while the mean is successful and praised, and success and praise are both characteristics of virtue.

It appears then that virtue is a kind of mean because it aims at the mean.

On the other hand, there are many different ways of going wrong; for evil is in its nature infinite, to use the Pythagorean phrase, but good is finite and there is only one possible way of going right. So the former is easy and the latter is difficult; it is easy to miss the mark but difficult to hit it. And so by our reasoning excess and deficiency are characteristics of vice and the mean is a characteristic of virtue.

"For good is simple, evil manifold."

Chapter 6 Virtue then is a state of deliberate moral purpose, consisting in a mean relative to ourselves, the mean being determined by reason, or as a prudent man would determine it. It is a mean, firstly, as lying between two vices, the vice of excess on the one hand, the vice of deficiency on the other, and, secondly, because, whereas the vices either fall short of or go beyond what is right in emotion and action, virtue discovers and chooses the mean. Accordingly, virtue, if regarded in its essence or theoretical definition, is a mean, though, if regarded from the point of view of what is best and most excellent, it is an extreme.

But not every action or every emotion admits of a mean. There are some whose very name implies wickedness, as, for example, malice, shamelessness, and envy among the emotions, and adultery, theft, and murder among the actions. All these and others like them are marked as intrinsically wicked, not merely the excesses or deficiencies of them. It is never possible then to be right in them; they are always sinful. Right or wrong in such acts as adultery does not depend on our committing it with the right woman, at the right time, or in the right manner; on the contrary, it is wrong to do it at all. It would be equally false to suppose that there can be a mean or an excess or deficiency in unjust, cowardly or licentious conduct; for, if that were so, it would be a mean of excess and deficiency, an excess of excess and a deficiency of deficiency. But as in temperance and courage there can be no excess or deficiency, because the mean there is in a sense an extreme, so too in these other cases there cannot be a mean or an excess or a deficiency, but however the acts are done, they are wrong. For in general an excess or deficiency does not have a mean, nor a mean an excess or deficiency. . . .

Chapter 8 There are then three dispositions, two being vices, namely, excess and deficiency, and one virtue, which is the mean between them; and they are all in a sense mutually opposed. The extremes are opposed both to the mean and to each other, and the mean is opposed to the extremes. For as the equal if compared with the less is greater, but if compared with the greater is less, so the mean state, whether in emotion or action, if compared with deficiency is excessive, but if compared with excess is deficient. Thus the brave man appears foolhardy compared with the coward, but cowardly compared with the foolhardy. Similarly, the temperate man appears licentious compared with the insensible man but insensible compared with the licentious; and the liberal man appears extravagant compared with the stingy man but stingy compared with the spendthrift. The result is that the extremes each denounce the mean as belonging to the other extreme; the coward calls the brave man foolhardy, and the foolhardy man calls him cowardly; and so on in other cases.

But while there is mutual opposition between the extremes and the mean, there is greater opposition between the two extremes than between extreme and the mean; for they are further removed from each other than from the mean, as the great is further from the small and the small from the great than either from the equal. Again, while some extremes show some likeness to the mean, as foolhardiness to courage and extravagance to liberality, there is the greatest possible dissimilarity between extremes. But things furthest removed from each other are called opposites; hence the further things are removed, the greater is the opposition between them.

In some cases it is deficiency and in others excess which is more opposed to the mean. Thus it is not foolhardiness, an excess, but cowardice, a deficiency, which is more opposed to courage, nor is it insensibility, a deficiency, but licentiousness, an excess, which is more opposed to temperance. There are two reasons why this should be so. One lies in the nature of the matter itself; for when one of two extremes is nearer and more like the mean, it is not this extreme but its opposite that we chiefly contrast with the mean. For instance, as foolhardiness seems more like and nearer to courage than cowardice, it is cowardice that we chiefly contrast with courage; for things further removed from the mean seem to be more opposite to it. This reason lies in the nature of the matter itself; there is a second which lies in our own nature. The things to which we ourselves are naturally more inclined we think more opposed to the mean. Thus we are ourselves naturally more inclined to pleasures than to their opposites, and are more prone therefore to self-indulgence than to moderation. Accordingly we speak of those things in which we are more likely to run to

great lengths as more opposed to the mean. Hence licentiousness, which is an excess, seems more opposed to temperance than insensibility.

Chapter 9 We have now sufficiently shown that moral virtue is a mean, and in what sense it is so; that it is a mean as lying between two vices, a vice of excess on the one side and a vice of deficiency on the other, and as aiming at the mean in emotion and action.

That is why it is so hard to be good; for it is always hard to find the mean in anything; it is not everyone but only a man of science who can find the mean or center of a circle. So too anybody can get angry—that is easy—and anybody can give or spend money, but to give it to the right person, to give the right amount of it, at the right time, for the right cause and in the right way, this is not what anybody can do, nor is it easy. That is why goodness is rare and praiseworthy and noble. One then who aims at a mean must begin by departing from the extreme that is more contrary to the mean; he must act in the spirit of Calypso's advice,

"Far from this spray and swell hold thou thy ship,"

for of the two extremes one is more wrong than the other. As it is difficult to hit the mean exactly, we should take the second best course, as the saying is, and choose the lesser of two evils. This we shall best do in the way described, that is, steering clear of the evil which is further from the mean. We must also note the weaknesses to which we are ourselves particularly prone, since different natures tend in different ways; and we may ascertain what our tendency is by observing our feelings of pleasure and pain. Then we must drag ourselves away towards the opposite extreme; for by pulling ourselves as far as possible from what is wrong we shall arrive at the mean, as we do when we pull a crooked stick straight.

In all cases we must especially be on our guard against the pleasant, or pleasure, for we are not impartial judges of pleasure. Hence our attitude towards pleasure must be like that of the elders of the people in the *Iliad* towards Helen, and we must constantly apply the words they use; for if we dismiss pleasure as they dismissed Helen, we shall be less likely to go wrong. By action of this kind, to put it summarily, we shall best succeed in hitting the mean.

Undoubtedly this is a difficult task, especially in individual cases. It is not easy to determine the right manner, objects, occasion and duration of anger. Sometimes we praise people who are deficient in anger, and call them gentle, and at other times we praise people who exhibit a fierce temper as high spirited. It is not however a man who deviates a little from goodness, but one who deviates a great deal, whether on the side of excess or of deficiency, that is blamed; for he is sure to call attention to himself. It is not easy to decide in theory how far and to what extent a man may go before he becomes blameworthy, but neither is it easy

to define in theory anything else in the region of the senses; such things depend on circumstances, and our judgment of them depends on our perception.

So much then is plain, that the mean is everywhere praiseworthy, but that we ought to aim at one time towards an excess and at another towards a deficiency; for thus we shall most easily hit the mean, or in other words reach excellence.

---

6. *Secular Morality and Sacred Obligation*

Louis Dupré

Louis Dupré argues that religion and morality are not two separate spheres, as is often argued, but are, in fact, deeply interrelated. According to Dupré, whether the unbeliever acknowledges it or not, religion undergirds the moral life in three distinct ways. First, the vision of faith transforms the very notion of what one takes to be the good. Second, the person motivated by religion develops new understandings of moral values that may, over time, be more widely adopted by the community. Finally, Dupré insists that only religion can offer a way to understand and endure the inevitable experience of moral failure.

Unity of Religion and Morality

Before discussing religion and morality as two entirely distinct subjects, we ought to remind ourselves of their original unity. In an archaic society this unity is taken for granted. In Emile Durkheim's words:

> It has been said that primitive peoples had no morality. That was an historical error. There is no people without its morality. However, the morality of undeveloped societies is not ours. What characterizes them is that they are essentially religious. By that, I mean that the most numerous and important duties are not the duties of man toward other men, but of man toward his gods.[1]

From William J. O'Brien (ed.), *Riding Time Like a River* (Washington, DC: Georgetown University Press, 1993), pp. 47–57. Reprinted by permission of Georgetown University Press.

Morality as a separate branch of learning that deals with obligations distinct from rituals, customs, class, or tribal orders, never existed in most societies. *Ethics,* as its etymology indicates, originally referred to what people actually do, because they feel that they ought to do it for whatever reason. Within that same universal perspective, virtue (*arete* for Plato and Aristotle) still means "excellence" in any field. Aristotle (followed by Saint Thomas) ranks intellectual virtues on a par with moral ones. For him, the term "ethical" certainly does not have the purely deontological meaning that we have come to attach to it.

MacIntyre translates *ethikos* as "pertaining to character" and that is how it made its way into the Latin *moralis*.[2] The idea of a secular "morality" comprehending duties that apply to atheists and believers does not seem to have been current before the later part of the seventeenth century. The French philosopher Pierre Bayle may well have been the first to defend it in principle.

Limiting the discussion to our own tradition we find that three of antiquity's major philosophers set up different moral models all of which served Christians in elaborating a morality intrinsically dependent on their religion. The first model appears in Plato, the second in Aristotle, the third in Stoic philosophy. For Plato, the idea of the Good, by its very beauty, attracts and inspires the highest and noblest part of the soul. The purpose of life is to approach that ideal with all our powers until it takes full possession of us. Iris Murdoch put it well:

> One might say that true morality is a sort of mysticism, having its source in an austere and unconsoled love of the Good. When Plato wants to explain good, he uses the image of the sun. The moral pilgrim emerges from the cave and begins to see the real world in the light of the sun, and, last of all, is able to look at the sun itself.[3]

This vision certainly differs from Kant's understanding of morality.

Plato's vision passed, almost unchanged, to Augustine, the most influential Latin Father. Through him, it became the model of a divine attraction that lifts the mind beyond all finite desires, toward a divine ideal. In Augustine's "irrequietum est cor nostrum donec requiescat in te Domine" still resounds the voice of Plato's Eros. But he strengthens the appeal of the Good by identifying it with a Person.

With Aristotle we enter, of course, a wholly different world, yet not as different as we tend to think. In his early *Protreptikos,* Aristotle echoed the language of his master: "Who has even once contemplated the divine must wonder whether anything is great and durable in human reality." The norm of action, if we may believe the *Eudemian Ethics* to reflect Aristotle's own theory, consists in the contemplation of God. There are perhaps two moral ideals in the *Nicomachean Ethics,* and it is by no means clear how they are related. Is the tenth book, which presents contemplation as the supreme good, fully compatible with the rest of the work, which promotes more active and political virtues? At any rate, Aristotle's *theoria* consists of intellectual activity, not of devotional contemplation. The religious act of surrender to God has little to do with it.

In the main part of the *Nicomachean Ethics,* perfection consists in what we would probably call self-actualization. Since the highest human capacity is reason, it is by actualizing reason that a person reaches the highest perfection. Happiness, the subjective and agreeable awareness of this objective state of well-being, follows from it. The idea of a moral *obligation,* as Stoics or Christians understood it, appears to be absent. In fact, human action is not measured by any transcendent norm, but by experience alone.

Despite this apparently "secular" view, Aristotle's theory served as a basis for a second model of a religiously inspired morality. As interpreted by St. Thomas, the pursuit of personal perfection and happiness implies in fact the quest for an absolute Good: finite goodness partakes of the total good of a divine absolute. We detect a Platonic slant in this reading of Aristotelian ethics. Nevertheless, the accent on *personal* perfection sufficiently distinguishes it from Plato's *ec-static* ideal to justify considering it a different model.

The third classical model emerges with the Stoa: it includes a transcendent obligation. Nothing illustrates it more directly than the following fragment from Epictetus's *Diatribes,* describing how the good person ought to be able to address God at the moment of death:

> The faculties which I received from you to enable me to understand your governance and to follow it, these I have not neglected; I have not dishonored You as far as in me lay. Behold how I have dealt with my senses, behold how I have dealt with my preconceptions. Have I ever blamed You? . . . For that You begot me I am grateful; for what You have given I am grateful also. The length of time for which I have had the use of Your gifts is enough for me. Take them back again and assign them to what place You will, for they were all yours, and You gave them to me.[4]

Here the religious connotation is overt, and Christian writers found in the Stoic concept a direct support for their position that the moral obligation derives, in fact, from a divine command. It initiated a long line of religious interpretations of the concept of duty that culminate in Newman's declaration that the voice of conscience is the voice of God. Since the idea of obligation dominates ethics in the modern age, most of the controversy centers around this third model. It is from that perspective that in the next section I shall consider the question: Does morality depend on religion?

Loss of Religion and Moral Decline

At least in the past, each society possessed its own code of behavior, and since religion in archaic and traditional societies was all-comprehensive, that code reflected the dominant religious vision. It is to be expected, then, that any decline of the founding religion will entail a decline of its specific code of morals. But does such a decline mean more than a *temporary* crisis, caused by the transition from one code to another? Certain accepted values suffer from it. But as the secular observer might say, to rid a society of its exclusive religious code is a major step forward in the direction of a universal morality. Is the particularity of each religion and of the moral code it introduces not the main source of dissent, unrest, and war in the world?

The believer will, of course, retort that the loss of religion signifies a substantial moral decline. Since the person's obligation to God forms an essential part of moral life, to abolish religious duties results in a truncated, incomplete moral code. But to an outsider, such an argument begs the question. It merely states that a religiously conceived morality requires a religious foundation. If we assume, as many of our contemporaries do, that public morality ought to be religiously neutral in a manner that enables people, despite ideological differences, to observe rules of justice and even of charity toward one another, the argument loses much of its power. Is it fair to call those who do not share our religious beliefs immoral? Fairness aside, to do so in a pluralistic society can only deepen our divisions and weaken the chance of an agreement on basic moral principles. Thus I shall take my stand on that neutral domain. If the case for a religious foundation cannot be made here, it will fail to convince those who are not yet a priori convinced. If we abandon this religiously neutral position, the common ground for a moral discussion vanishes altogether.

Another issue related to an intrinsically religious view of morality needs to be clarified. If indeed, as we have assumed, much of our moral code has a religious origin, then, is not the agnostic in a Christian culture in fact living off religious capital? He certainly appears to be spending what he has not earned! If we all did so, the moral capital would gradually become depleted, for lack of new religious input. Standards would fall and inspiration dry up. But this objection also, though historically correct about the religious origins of morality, misses the point of the contemporary argument. The question concerns not origins—many

agnostics would happily concede that we owe the precept to love our neighbor to the Sermon on the Mount—but whether generally acceptable moral norms, *in whatever way introduced,* can or cannot be sustained in a religiously neutral climate. Do they possess enough *substance* to maintain themselves without a religious authority? If not, they are not worth preserving. But if they do and continue to be accepted by nonbelievers, the moral content no longer needs the original religious support. The language of morals may in that respect be misleading. Religious believers tend to read more in it than is there. As the British philosopher W.G. MacLagen put it:

> It seems to me quite untrue to say, for instance, that the *substance* of our thought when we speak of the brotherhood of man necessarily presupposes a conviction of the fatherhood of God, although it may be the case that this language would not naturally, or even could not properly, be used in the *expression* of our thought except in association with such a conviction.[5]

This brings us to the heart of the matter: Does the moral obligation presuppose *One* who obliges? We know how in his three *Critiques* Kant consistently denied that the presence of a moral imperative provided a proof of the existence of a divine lawgiver. Even in his later *Religion Within the Limits of Reason Alone,* Kant is unambiguous: "For its own sake morality does not need religion at all . . . ; by virtue of pure practical reason it is self-sufficient."[6] In his *Opus Posthumum,* however, he appears to relent when asserting that the religious perception of all duties, in which he had claimed the essence of religion to consist, is not given *subsequently* to our perception of them as duties, but *in* and *with* the perception itself. "The categorical imperative of the command of duty is grounded in the idea of an *imperantis,* who is all-powerful and holds universal sway. This is the idea of God."[7]

The moral obligation would thereby become intrinsically religious and, as Norman Kemp Smith concluded, the categorical imperative, then, "leads directly to God, and affords surety of his reality."[8] One may, of course, dismiss this single observation which contradicts all that Kant had maintained through a lifetime of reflection, as the scribbling of a scholar in his doting years. But an impressive number of other thinkers—in the full vigor of their intellectual life—have lent support to Kant's conclusion. Thus, Hans

Küng in *Does God Exist?* claims that no notion derived from human nature or from reason alone can ever be absolute. "Why should I observe these norms unconditionally? Why should I observe them even when they are completely at variance with my interests?"[9]

An absolute obligation can come only from an absolute Being. Similarly, Edouard Le Roy, Bergson's great disciple, wrote "Il y a un Absolu au fond de l'exigence morale: le reconnaître c'est affirmer Dieu déjà, de quelque nom qu'on le homme et quelque imparfaitement qu'on le conçoive."[10] Le Roy follows Kant in denying that the moral obligation is "deduced" from the religious affirmative: the two are perceived simultaneously. For English-speaking Christians, the idea of a religious foundation of morality is strongly connected with the name of John Henry Newman who described the voice of conscience as an authoritative "dictate" which threatens and promises, rewards and chastises, reminding us "that there is One to whom we are responsible, before whom we are ashamed, whose claims upon us we fear."[11]

Impressive testimonies, and in some respect irrefutable, to any person who accepts the moral imperative as absolute! But must the imperative necessarily be interpreted as "the voice of *God*"? If we mean by that term the God (personal or superpersonal) of monotheist believers, the absoluteness of the imperative appears not necessarily to imply a specifically religious determination of the absolute. I tend to agree with Karl Jaspers's assessment:

> Although in conscience I am confronted with transcendence, I do not hear the transcendent or listen to it as a voice from another world. The voice of conscience is not God's voice. In the voice of conscience the Deity remains silent. . . .[12]

Jaspers's denial may be too categorical. For there is a sense in which obligation undeniably confronts us as divine in origin. To one who already believes, conscience and its inexplicably absolute imperative is likely to be perceived as derived from such a divine source. That was Kant's own position in *Religion Within the Limits of Reason Alone* and that, I strongly suspect, was Newman's true insight—since elsewhere he declares himself incapable of erecting an irrefutable proof of God's existence. Even religious believers who remain skeptical about a direct identification of God with the moral obligation will accept that God sanctions the voice of conscience. This insight undoubtedly adds another dimension, even to a self-discovered morality. But that religious dimension of morality, reserved to the believer, in no way forecloses the possibility of a religiously neutral domain of morality.

A too easy identification of morality with religion may well lead to religiously questionable conclusions, as appears in the now fashionable notion of value. Many well-intentioned believers refer to God as the supreme value, or as the One who preestablishes the values humans ought to pursue. But the modern term value has a highly subjective connotation. It refers primarily to what *we* "value." In thus regarding the human subject as its essential source, we submit God to that subject's projective activity—precisely what Feuerbach declared all religious activity to be. If religion actualizes the person's relation to the absolute, it cannot be a value at all, even though it may *influence* his or her value judgments.

Nor should we consider God to be the One who preestablishes values. To do so, Sartre pointed out, undermines the essential creativity of human freedom. Freedom must do more than ratify preexisting values: it must invent them, imagine them, create them. Freedom can tolerate a great deal of conditioning and restraint. It is always forced to operate within a situation that it has not chosen. But to have its goals and values divinely established would destroy its very essence. God is the *foundation* of value-*creating* activity, not the One who defines values.

A *Religious Inspiration for Moral Striving*

The conclusions of the preceding discussion have turned out to be somewhat negative. It appears that a common morality requires no religious support for meeting our ordinary obligations, even though, all would agree, a religious inspiration may enhance our motivation for doing so. But to view the matter only in that light presents less than the whole picture. For a fuller vision we ought to change the perspective and ask ourselves the question: What happens when religion becomes the inspiring source of a person's moral endeavor? Does it contribute any significant element that, without its impact, would be missing even in a "common" morality? I shall devote this final section to that question. My answer consists of three parts. First, a religious vision transforms the very notion of what is good. Second, the religiously motivated person continues to invent new values that may later become generally accepted. Third and finally, only religion teaches how to live with moral failure, a failure that marks all human striving.

1. Mature religion creates a particular *ethos*, more comprehensive and open than a closed societal *ethos* can be, even if society attempts to remain above ideological divisions. All morality remains contextual: either its boundaries are defined by principles dominant in a particular society or it transcends the society within which it exists through a more universal but never purely abstract source of inspiration and sanction, such as a religious community. We may easily find examples of both instances. In his remarkable study, *A Theory of Justice* (1972), John Rawls laid down a fundamental principle of social ethics that by its ideological blindness and its mathematically strict norm of equality would impose itself, he hoped, on all unprejudiced parties. Despite his impressive achievement, it did not take critics long to point out that what he was describing as an impartial, humane, and universalizable goal presented in fact the social ideal of the liberal, educated segment of U.S. society. This ideal remains praiseworthy, but it is less than the conclusion of an argument based exclusively on pure reason.

Yet once we have recognized the inevitable conditioning of our moral striving, the question returns: Which context is likely to guarantee the greatest openness of our morality? I would think, with Bergson, that ideally it is the one inspired by the attitude most open to transcendence. I have qualified my answer by the words "ideally" and "open" to avoid identifying its realization with each and every religious normatization of human behavior. We have already conceded that religion may in fact be one of the most divisive factors, even in modern society. We might add that it often violates the elementary principles of a common morality.

Obviously, the rule of religion as a universalizing factor calls for important distinctions. Henri Bergson in *The Two Sources of Morality and Religion* distinguishes a "closed" morality, usually driven by a "closed" religion, from an "open" morality inspired by an "open" religion. A closed morality serves the particular interests of the group by protecting it against those of others, at whatever price. A closed religion hardens this attitude, and secular moralists are right in preferring to such a tribal particularization a religiously neutral, universal respect for elementary human rights. But the morality inspired by an *open* religion raises its ideals not only beyond the group, but also beyond the limits

of the values that are more or less universally accepted in modernized societies. In the eyes of such a religiously inspired person, many of these "universal" principles appear inadequate to satisfy the high ideals to which he or she feels called.

The difference in "valuation" dawned on me in a very concrete way some years ago when a woman who had adopted a child was shortly afterwards approached by the same maternity nurse who had been instrumental in the original transaction with a request that she adopt another, still unborn infant. Rather surprised by the request, the woman firmly declined. Three weeks later the nurse contacted her friend again to express her relief that she had not committed herself to the proposed adoption. The infant had been born anencephalic. Its totally undeveloped brain would prevent it from ever sitting up, speaking, or even feeding itself. At that point, the woman said, "In that case, I'll take it." One may interpret her motives for this heroic deed in any number of ways. To me, it clearly meant one thing: to care for a human being that could not care for itself was, from her religious perspective, a *good* thing—not a sacrifice, certainly not an obligation, not even a deliberate act of virtue, but a recognition that caring for helpless life is intrinsically desirable and *therefore* also emotionally satisfactory.

The current vociferous debate over abortion is not likely to result in any kind of lasting agreement, because what one party considers bad, the other holds to be intrinsically good, namely, the preservation of initial human life under highly adverse circumstances. (This religious "openness" is, of course, lacking in some pro-life groups using tribal tactics to enforce their position.) In this dilemma as in some others, secular moralists may regard as foolish or even immoral, in any case not to be imposed as a universal principle, what religiously inspired people consider universally normative. The religious perspective, or absence thereof, fundamentally changes the value coefficient. An open religion extends the range of responsibility by broadening that of value and love.

2. Most important, however, in the development of ethical thought has been the role of the religious imagination. If we have refined our moral sensitivity over the years, that refinement is largely the result of the inventive power of religious women and men who were not even primarily concerned about morality. The concrete realization of moral law requires the imagination to *invent* values that never existed.

A purely philosophical study of ethical principles and of their prudential application to individual cases in casuistics is indispensable. But the logic of ethics analyzes, discusses, and applies *existing* rules. Saints invent new rules: they subject to moral responsibility what before was morally neutral territory—neither moral nor immoral. Most denizens of an enlightened society agree that we ought to be kind to others. But does that rule not defeat its purpose when it leads a person to lay down his life for an unknown who may contribute less to society that he or she does, or to devote one's time and energy to the incurable, or to prefer a life of serious hardship to terminating a pregnancy? The remarkable thing about those whom we consider "saints"—those whom the church defines as persons of heroic virtue—is that their outstanding deeds are not demanded by common morality at all. A great deal has been written about the "ethics" of the gospel. Yet what strikes one at first reading is how few concrete *obligations* the gospel introduces and how, instead, it insists on a change of attitude. What we would call "counsels" appear to outweigh strict commandments. "If you want to be perfect, go and sell all you have . . ." They are ideals of a wholly different kind, challenging the person to what surpasses self-achievement—and to what *therefore* must be gratuitous.

Did Francis of Assisi commit a "moral" act when he embraced the leper, or when he gave up his present and future possessions? Gestures such as those, in some respects questionable and in all respects "useless," are in themselves, at best, morally "neutral." Yet Francis transformed them into symbols of a higher moral demand. Must we call Mother Teresa surpassingly "moral," because of what she does for dying paupers? Somehow the term seems strangely inappropriate to describe one so little concerned about established rules. From a utilitarian perspective there appears to be little in favor of the choice of her beneficiaries. If she wanted to augment the general well-being of the human race, is it not a waste of generous energy to pick the dying up from the street, rather than to improve the lot of the living? Clearly, her endeavors move beyond the established into new territory. The amazing achievement of those irresponsible mystical "inventors" is, however, that they, despite an apparent lack of "moral" concern, raise the general moral sensitivity. Others, observing them, are first surprised, then become attracted to follow them. Some of what began as the gratuitous action of a single individual becomes incorporated into our moral *patrimonium* and the

exception becomes part of the common ideal. If my analysis is at all right, we cannot but paradoxically conclude that only those not particularly concerned about morality are capable of transforming it. It takes a transcendent vision (which, until now, has almost always been a religious one) to advance moral attitudes beyond the constraints of the past toward a more inclusive future. Writers of textbooks on ethics have rarely raised moral standards, though they have occasionally lowered them.

3. Finally, religion's most significant but least appreciated contribution to moral striving may well consist in assisting us in dealing with failure. Unfortunately all moral endeavor results in some failure. Our high ideals and lofty desires soon yield to "the reality principle" of everydayness. Our goals have not been met and we gradually become convinced that they will probably never be met. Confronting the wall of our moral limitations we cannot escape feeling discouraged by our lack of accomplishment and even more by the inability to learn from our failures.

At this low point, as Kierkegaard pointed out, the ethical enterprise itself grinds to a halt. Morality provides no rules, at least no helpful ones, for coping with its own undoing. Precisely at this moment of failure religion steps in, empowering the individual to salvage his integrity from even the most lamentable defeat. Religion, especially the Christian one, enables me to *accept* my failing self, while at the same time repudiating the moral failure. Where moral reason ceases to justify me, repentance subjects me to a judgment beyond the moral order, at once more demanding and more forgiving.

To the religious person, the moral judgment over his or her conduct is not the ultimate one. Even one willing to die for a moral cause refuses to take ethical rules with *ultimate* seriousness. Such an attitude may appear shocking to the moral humanist for whom the moral judgment is indeed decisive. To the average believer, religion may not bring the higher moral standard, the greater perfection, the ethical innovation, but it may yield what is perhaps even more needed for continuing to live his or her life with dignity, namely, the comforting certainty that sins will be forgiven. Forgiveness may seem a rather dubious contribution to moral striving. It would be, if religion did not work on both sides of the moral scale: inspiring heroism at the top and consolation at the bottom. Both are equally essential, as Chesterton understood: "If a thing is worth doing, it is worth doing poorly."

Endnotes

1. Emile Durkheim, *Moral Education* (New York: Free Press of Glencoe, 1961), 6.

2. Alasdair MacIntyre, *After Virtue,* 2d ed. (Notre Dame, Indiana: University of Notre Dame Press, 1984), 38–39. On the "extended" view of morality, see Anthony Cua, "Hsun Tzu's Theory of Argumentation" in *Review of Metaphysics* 36(4): 869–876.

3. Iris Murdoch, *The Sovereignty of Good* (London: Routledge & Kegan Paul, 1970), 92.

4. Epictetus, *Arrian Discourses,* Loeb Classical Library edition, trans. W.A. Oldfather (New York: G.P. Putnam's Sons, 1926), 4.10.

5. W.G. MacLagen, *The Theological Frontier of Ethics* (New York: Macmillan, 1961), 25.

6. Immanuel Kant, *Religion Within the Limits of Reason Alone,* Preface to the First Edition, trans. Theodore M. Greene and Hoyt H. Hudson (LaSalle, Illinois: Open Court, 1934; reissued Harper & Brothers, 1960), 3.

7. Erich Adickes: *Kant's Opus Posthumum* (Berlin, 1920), 808.

8. Norman Kemp Smith, *A Commentary to Kant's Critique of Pure Reason,* 2d ed. (London: Macmillan & Company, Inc., 1923), 638.

9. Hans Küng, *Does God Exist?* trans. Edward Quinn (New York: Doubleday, 1980), 578.

10. Edouard Le Roy: "Le problème de Dieu" in *Revue de Metaphysique et de Morale* (1907). Republished in *Le problème de Dieu* (Paris: Cahiers de la Quinzaine, 19:11 [1929]), 202.

11. John Henry Newman, *A Grammar of Assent* (New York: Doubleday-Image, 1955), 101.

12. Karl Jaspers, *Philosophie* II (Berlin: J. Springer, 1932), 272. (My translation.)

7. *The Deep Structure*

RONALD M. GREEN

Ronald Green analyzes the deep structure of religious belief and develops three pivotal dimensions of its relationship to the nature and practice of moral reasoning. As Green explains, all religions provide instruction in the "moral point of view," which entails a recognition that discipline and self-restraint are necessary for a flourishing personal life, along with the requirement that one treat others with impartial concern for their well-being. In addition, in the face of the difficulties posed by its call to self-transcendence, religion reminds its adherents of the reality of moral retribution, a claim that encourages willingness to make the personal sacrifices required in the moral realm. Finally, Green claims that religion also universally offers an awareness of the inevitability of human wrongdoing and the reassurance, through notions of grace and forgiveness, that there are measures of our personal worth that transcend our moral performance.

Religion's deep structure has three essential elements: first, a method of moral reasoning involving "the moral point of view"; second, a set of beliefs affirming the reality of moral retribution; and third, a series of "trans-

moral" beliefs that suspend moral judgment and retribution when this is needed to overcome moral paralysis and despair. Whatever their surface differences, religions contain these elements. They point their adherents to the method of moral reasoning. They try to assure them that governing one's life by this method is not ultimately self-destructive, that the righteous are rewarded. And, in response to the kind of self-condemnation that inevitably accompanies sensitive moral striving, they are prepared to ease their insistence on judgment and retribution by holding out the promise of a redemption not based entirely on one's deeds.

That this structure contains elements so tensely related to one another—for example, the insistence on retribution and the qualified suspension of retribution—tells us that religious reasoning is complex. In fact, anyone unwilling to tolerate complexity should not undertake the study of religious belief. Religions seek to make reasoned conduct possible in a world that sometimes defies reason, and this effort often pushes them to the limits of human thought. Sometimes religions must resist the claims of experience or make assertions that defy common sense. And sometimes they must even qualify their own beliefs when these yield conclusions that threaten the ultimate rational purposes they have in mind. But none of this means that religions are illogical. Because they are grounded in reason, religions characteristically make painstaking efforts to guarantee the coherency and consistency of their beliefs. Thus, it is paradox, not overt self-contradiction, that characterizes religious thinking.

"The Moral Point of View"

Mention of paradox is an appropriate way of beginning a discussion of the deep structure of religious reasoning, since this structure has its origin in a familiar paradox of the moral life: that self-denial and self-restraint are conditions of human happiness and self-fulfillment. On a purely individual level, this truth impresses itself on us as we mature and learn that the attainment of our most important purposes in life requires self-discipline and the willingness to defer immediate gratification. The genuinely rational person, we know, does not pursue every satisfaction that comes along, but can arrange life's goals in a more or less coherent plan and act on this plan even if it means passing up immediate rewards.

What is true for the individual's personal existence is also true for social and collective life. Human society is predicated on our individual capacity for self-sacrifice and self-restraint. We can imagine a single life based on the impulsive pursuit of pleasure, and we can hypothesize a society whose members take every opportunity to pursue their own interests. But both possibilities eventually produce conflict and anarchy, and neither represents the fullest expression of reason. Only when the individual is prepared to subordinate parts to a whole in mat-

ters of personal choice, and self to society in matters that affect others, are conditions established for the harmonious and coherent pursuit of individual ends. The social side of this paradoxical truth is expressed in a hard-won lesson of constitutional democracy: the restraint on arbitrary conduct represented by a firm system of law is the best guarantee of individual freedom. Superficially regarded, law and freedom may seem opposed, but an understanding of the deeper logic of moral life shows they are not.

Three centuries ago, this understanding was expressed by the philosopher Immanuel Kant in a brief treatise on ethics entitled *Foundations of the Metaphysics of Morals*. Few books on ethics have been more widely read than this, and few have been more deeply misunderstood. Part of the blame rests with Kant's poor expression and misleading illustrations, but part of the problem also stems from the difficulty of Kant's pioneering effort to develop systematically the paradoxical truths underlying moral life. Repeatedly, for example, Kant rejects ethics based on "happiness" or the pursuit of any specific human satisfactions (including the satisfactions produced by sympathetic feeling for others). In their place, he sets an ethic based on "duty" and strict adherence to the moral law. These denials that happiness or sympathy have a place in ethics made Kant appear inhuman and led to characterizations of him as a dour misanthrope. In fact, Kant's point is the same as the one made above: happiness or personal satisfaction in any form cannot be people's most basic consideration in making decisions as social beings. For if it were, the result would be anarchy, and in the end, no one's happiness would be served. Instead, Kant argued that private pursuits and desires must always be subordinated to a rule of law whose moral expression he termed "the categorical imperative."

What exactly Kant meant by this imperative is among the most contested issues in moral philosophy. Kant himself had a definite idea of the rule or principle he had in mind. He believed it to be based strictly on reason and, as such, known a priori by all human beings. He believed that it furnished a decisive test of proposed courses of action (what he called "maxims"), enabling us to distinguish right from wrong. And he also believed that this one imperative provided a rational basis for all the more specific moral rules we usually respect (such as those prohibiting lying or cheating). Throughout his writings, Kant gave this imperative several different formulations, the most important of which is "Act only according to that maxim by which you can at the same time will that it should become a universal law."[1]

This imperative is usually viewed as involving a procedure of "universalization" or "generalization." If I propose to undertake some action, such as making a promise I do not intend to keep, I must be prepared to allow others to act this way toward me. "What is sauce for the goose is sauce for the gander." Understood in this way, the categorical imperative seems to be a basic rule of reason. It requires simple consistency and prohibits our doing things we would not want others to do if they were in our position.

Unfortunately, as prevalent as it is, this reading of the categorical imperative has serious problems. Most troublesome, I believe, is the problem posed by someone prepared to do immoral things who would gladly permit others to do the same. For example, a person suffering a terminal disease and able to embezzle funds that will help make his or her last days comfortable might willingly condone others acting the same. Yet we do not ordinarily think that these circumstances and this willingness justify theft. Nor do we think that persons with suicidal or self-destructive tendencies (like some mass murderers) should be allowed to kill or injure others so long as they are willing to put up with mistreatment themselves. Yet that is what the common interpretation of the categorical imperative seems to suggest.[2]

We cannot sort out here all the arguments and counterarguments produced by Kant's ethical theory, but I am convinced that in discussing the categorical imperative, Kant had more in mind than a simple rule of generalization. I believe he was developing something that recent moral philosophers have come to term "the moral point of view." This involves a perspective of radical impartiality or "omnipartiality" before the choices and issues facing us as moral agents. It asks us to choose as though we might be any of the people affected by our conduct. This moral point of view allows self-serving, reasoned choice but always from a standpoint of impartiality. As such, it includes the generalization rule, since what one wills in such circumstances will ordinarily be conduct permissible for the other people one must imagine oneself to be. But it adds to this the requirement that we assess our conduct not just from the egocentric perspective of our own situation but also from the standpoint of the others we might affect. In Kantian terms, what one wills must be capable of becoming "universal law" not only because it must *apply* to all other persons but also because it is something they might "vote for" or accept—a law *for*, *of*, and *by* everyone.[3]

A contrast with the simpler rule of generalization in cases just mentioned illustrates the importance of this understanding. We saw that the ill-fated embezzler, with little to lose by others' doing the same, might willingly generalize the proposed conduct. But if this person had to regard embezzlement from the viewpoint of all the others it might affect and if others' approval had to be taken into account, the conclusion would be quite different. Then this individual would have to consider the point of view of victims of embezzlement and of survivors in a world where theft and embezzlement had become commonplace. Similarly, however despairing and violent some might be and however willing to relinquish their own lives should they fall victim to the homicide they would permit, it is not enough that they consider this matter from their own perspective. Additionally, they must take into account the viewpoint and interests of all the others they would affect. But surely most people would not want their lives subject to such aberrant and deadly desires. Impartial reasoning about either of these choices appears to furnish overwhelming reasons against them.

Understood in terms of the impartial "moral point of view," the categorical imperative seems to do one of the things Kant says it does: it provides a reasonable and effective test of moral policies. Of course, showing this to be true for every type of choice is the work of a separate book on ethics. But this kind of work is being done. Various contemporary moral philosophers have shown convincingly that when it is strenuously applied, this point of view yields moral judgments consistent with many of our firmest moral intuitions and, more important, it helps us think about new and perplexing choices.[4] The work of these philosophers also indicates that this point of view underlies and justifies many of the ordinary moral rules we respect. However much particular persons might be willing to inflict injury on others, to lie, to steal, or to break solemn promises, none of these practices is likely to be advocated by individuals who must take into account the interests of the many other persons this conduct adversely affects. As Kant believed, therefore, this method of impartial reasoning provides us with a more basic rational justification of our intuitive moral beliefs.

This brief account of the method of moral reasoning leaves many questions unanswered. For example, even if matters are looked at impartially, there will always be conflicts of interest. How are these to be adjudicated? One answer is that a principle of "majority rule" should prevail. Reasoning impartially, one should act in a way that would be acceptable to *most* of the persons whose interests one must consider. In fact, as utilitarian theorists perceived, this will be a sound procedure in many instances of choice.[5] But there will also be instances where it is reasonable to forgo gain for a majority to avoid experiencing serious injury as a member of some minority. This may be why we feel that many basic human rights should not be subject to majority rule and why we believe—against the utilitarians—that certain principles of right and justice should be respected even if they do not always benefit the majority. In any event, these problems of conflict are surmountable. Various general rules for decision are among the first things that impartial persons are called on to work out as they try to think through concrete cases of moral decision.[6]

A more serious objection to this approach is that it assumes human beings capable of reasoning impartially about matters that affect their personal interests. But in our post-Freudian, post-Marxist world, have we not learned too well that our perception of issues and problems is colored by our background, our experiences, and our interests? Can we really expect people to assume the viewpoint of others? Of course, no one can deny that it is extremely difficult to be impartial. We shall see that religious communities invest enormous effort in trying to encourage their adherents to adopt the moral point of view. Failures of impartiality also underlie the problems of sin and wrongdoing that religions seek to address. Nevertheless, this serious practical problem does not lessen the value of the moral point of view as a *standard* for measuring conduct or as an ideal *reference point* for adjudicating disputes. When we try to justify an action morally, we assume it to be one that anyone looking at things impartially and objectively would approve. We may delude ourselves about this, but the need to justify even selfish conduct in this way is an inescapable accompaniment of human reasoning, the homage, as La Rochefoucauld said, that vice offers to virtue. When individuals disagree over the morality of a particular course of conduct, they also appeal to one another's impartial judgment and seek to arouse even keener efforts at impartiality and objectivity. If these efforts fail, individuals or groups commonly resort to other, more impartial persons to help resolve their conflicts. This is the logic of impartial mediation in social disputes and of judges or juries in matters of civil and criminal law. In all these cases, impartiality remains imperfect. But it is the model of reasoned, moral settlement to which the human mind inclines.

Finally, there is the problem posed by the sheer diversity of moral teaching and belief. Recall Kant's claim that this method of moral reasoning is a priori and universal, something known by human beings regardless of their particular beliefs or circumstances. But how can any claim to moral universality be sustained in the face of the great variety of moral teachings that global communication has brought to our attention? In view of this diversity, it seems much more reasonable to accept ethical relativism, the position that moral teachings and beliefs are dependent on one's individual or cultural standpoint.

Ethical relativism undoubtedly remains an attractive and fashionable position in our day. Ironically, this may be partly due to its *moral* appeal: it seems to be a fair alternative to the kind of moral arrogance and cultural imperialism that has often characterized Western civilization. But apart from this appeal, the case for ethical relativism is not impressive. That cultures differ substantially in moral teaching is obvious; that these differences represent fundamentally different ways of thinking about moral choice is far less so. And this is what ethical relativists must prove.

If we consider the method of moral decision, this "moral point of view," or "categorical imperative," as a basic way of thinking that must always be applied in context, we can almost predict diversity in moral conclusions. What is rational for impartial persons to accept in one circumstance, may not be so in another. Classic cases from anthropological lore often taken as proof of ethical relativism merely illustrate the contextual nature of moral reasoning. For example, while most societies regard parricide as a terrible sin, there have been some—including certain Eskimo communities—that once required the killing or abandonment of elderly parents. Examined closely, these cultures displayed similar features: they existed on the edge of survival, counted on the mobility of all their members, and engaged in strenuous pursuits like hunting or fishing. In these societies there was little room for the physically dependent. Not surprisingly, therefore, generations of shared reflection on social norms led all the members of these societies to accept the abandonment of those who could no longer sustain themselves. That this represented an impartially defensible moral decision and one that was freely accepted by all members of these communities was shown by the fact that the elderly regarded such abandonment as an honorable conclusion to their lives, as a duty owed to them that offspring dared not neglect.[7]

What has been true in these extreme cases is also true in other complex areas of moral choice. The sexual realm, for example, reveals a wide variety of different norms and rules across cultural lines. Those of us accustomed by Western religious teaching to regard sexual conduct as almost synonymous with morality may take this as evidence for the utter relativity of morals. However, if we remember that moral reasoning is not reducible to any set of rules but is a basic method of thinking about choices and making decisions, then we must expect this variability of norms. For the fundamental rational considerations underlying the regulation of sexual behavior, considerations such as the ordering of sexual opportunity, the protection of the weak from sexual abuse, and the proper socialization and care of the young can be achieved in a variety of ways. Which specific institutions and norms are selected will depend on the contexts in which these choices are made. Many tribal societies, for example, have found forms of polygamy and (to a lesser extent) polyandry a suitable response to these basic considerations, while other societies facing different circumstances have stressed more or less qualified forms of monogamy. Indeed, as social conditions have changed, cultures have often moved from one specific set of sexual values to another. (Most Western societies, for example, have moved from polygamy to monogamy and now, as aspirations for "personal fulfillment" grow and as the material well-being of women and children becomes less dependent on life-long family stability, these societies seem to be moving toward greater tolerance of serial "monogamy" and nonmarried parenting.)

This same variability of norms is also seen in the realm of supererogatory conduct. Supererogation is that side of the moral life that goes above and beyond the call of duty. For example, while it is usually regarded as obligatory to refrain from injuring other persons, whether or not one should go out of one's way to help others is a matter of supererogation. To this realm belong most of the altruistic, charitable, and self-sacrificial ideals of a society. Obviously, what constitutes "saintly" or "noble" behavior is a matter of dispute even within homogeneous cultures. Most persons would agree that killing is wrong, but just how much risk an individual should take to save another's life can be strenuously debated.[8] But if this is so within cultures, how much more is it likely to be true across cultural lines? We should not be surprised, therefore, to find wide differences in supererogatory ideals among human cultures. Indeed, we shall see that these differences are marked in the religious domain, because supererogation is a special interest of religious communities. This is the sphere in which religions often develop their own unique moral appeal. But these differences (though sustained by seemingly equal conviction on all sides) are not evidence for ethical relativism. In comparing religious ethics, we must look to their basic modes of reasoning and to their basic moral norms, and here we see wide agreement among religions, no matter what their ultimate beliefs or supererogatory teachings. For example, Judaism, Buddhism, and Christianity differ enormously in their respective visions of salvation and they also sharply disagree about the nature of the saintly life. But not one of these traditions permits wanton killing, cheating, or abuse of other persons.

One last point on this matter of moral diversity: Ethical relativists sometimes advance as evidence for their view the fact that conduct between human social groups violates even the most basic norms of our own culture. All over the world, people will deceive, injure, or kill "outsiders" with impunity, often in the belief that this is the "right" thing to do. Centuries ago, Thomas Aquinas, in a classic discussion of the universality of moral norms, attributed this behavior not to the relativity of values but to human beings' "evil persuasions" and "vicious customs."[9] Although Aquinas's words are strong, his point is well taken. Often, human moral community breaks down at cultural or political boundaries and what prevails between communities is a lawless state of violence and aggression. Within each community, moral rules, principles, and ways of thinking prevail. Outside the boundary, a morally lawless realm exists, and strangers are fair game for abuse or mistreatment. Sometimes they are also regarded as evil foes, against whom any form of preemptive self-defense is justified.

Whether they occur on the intertribal or international level, these attitudes are unfortunate. They constitute one of the great problems facing human civilization. But while they may result in part from value differences between human cultures and the tensions they cause, these attitudes are not proof of ethical relativism. What they attest to is either the breakdown of human moral imagination or wanton selfishness and aggression—what Aquinas termed "evil persuasions" and "vicious customs." That human communities often will not treat one another morally almost goes without saying. This reflects the difficulty of being moral and the fact that group life often compounds individual egoism.[10] What the relativist must show, however, is that in their internal standards and principles, including those by which they are sometimes led to "defend" themselves against others, communities fundamentally differ. But neither evidence nor common sense supports this view.

In the chapters ahead, we shall see that this universal structure of moral decision making is a key element of the deep structure of religious thought. Whatever their specific teachings, religions agree on the basic rules of morality. All prohibit wanton killing or injury of other persons (although many permit legitimate self-defense); all condemn deception and the breaking of solemn promises. On the positive side, all require giving some minimum of aid to those in need; all require reparation for wrongs committed; and all ask some expression of gratitude for assistance received. So prevalent are these rules across a variety of religious and cultural traditions that C. S. Lewis once called them "platitudes" of practical reason.[11] More important than these rules, however, is the fact that religions also seek to encourage their adherents to adopt "the moral point of view." Sometimes they take separate paths to this goal. Theistic religions commonly approach the matter very differently from mystical traditions. But despite these differences, the goal of impartiality—the ideal of transcending one's own immediate desires to make choices from a social point of view—is widely shared across religious cultures. Promoting this ideal is among the most important contributions religions make to the moral life.

"Why Should I Be Moral?": The Problem of Moral Retribution and the Justification of Morality

That religions devote so much effort to encouraging their adherents to think and act from the moral point of view partly reflects the difficulty of the task. The kind of self-transcendence that morality requires poses a special problem. Not only is it hard to think and act morally (this follows from the fact that every instance of moral decision requires a measure of self-denial), but a far deeper problem arises at the heart of reasoned reflection about morality: in crucial moments of moral choice, it is simply not rationally compelling that one should be moral. Good arguments can be arrayed both for and against moral choice: for and against adopting the moral point of view. In the context of moral decision, therefore,

human reason is at odds with itself and finds itself unable to order a dispute in its own house. Ultimately, this specific conceptual problem leads reason into the realm of religious thought and to the second component of the deep structure of religious reasoning: insistence on the reality of moral retribution.

We can better understand this problem and the ways religions respond to it if we keep in mind the precise mental exercise moral reasoning involves. At the moment of moral choice, each of us is required to regard all the interests lying before us in an impartial or, more precisely, "omnipartial" way. We must allow our own interests no pride of place and we must weigh these evenhandedly alongside those of all the other persons we affect. In some instances, reasoning from the moral point of view may lead us to advocate conduct markedly against our own interests. For example, as a small electronics manufacturer, I may know that I could never impartially agree to waste-disposal practices that endanger water supplies and people's health, but I may also know that halting these practices may jeopardize my firm's financial survival. To think and act morally in this case is to risk my entire welfare and the welfare of some people for whom I care very much (members of my family, my employees). Instances of this sort could by multiplied on the individual or group level. Whether it involves only modest loss or, as in some cases, risk to our very lives and happiness, a willingness to face sacrifice is the essence of morality.

Why, then, should we think and reason morally? When our happiness is on the line, why should we be willing to sacrifice it to the common good? These questions invoke many answers, almost all of which have been offered at one time or another in the course of human thinking about this problem. But closely regarded, most of these answers are inadequate, and the issue remains unresolved. What we have here, in effect, is a conflict between two equally important and equally viable exercises of reason. On the one hand, there is what is termed "prudential" reason: self-serving rationality exercised in the name of personal happiness. On the other hand, there is moral reason, which involves the same self-serving rational choice but now exercised from an impartial point of view. The great similarity between these forms of reason and their common practical goal of human welfare makes it easy to confuse them in justificatory arguments. But individuals sincerely involved in moral choice can detect such confusions and recognize the inadequacy of answers based on them.

For example, in trying to answer these questions, we could point to some of the considerations previously mentioned regarding the general rationality of morality. We can say that the willingness to subordinate private pursuits to moral regulation is the condition of happiness: that a society that allowed unchecked egoism would not be a secure or fulfilling place to live. But while morality is generally conducive to personal happiness, can we commend it to persons whose happiness and welfare are jeopardized by the moral alternative? They will not be misled by linguistic confusions; they may concede that morality yields "happiness," but they want to know why they should decisively forfeit their own happiness when it is in peril.

Again, we can ask individuals torn between these two rational standpoints to regard the conflict impartially. Ordinarily, this is how we reason in conflicts. If I am caught between two desires, I try momentarily to distance myself from each of them to make a "more objective" choice. Or if two persons are in dispute, we ask them to distance themselves from the issues and to look at them impartially (often summoning an impartial mediator to help). Impartial reasoning is our most basic instrument for thinking about conflict. But obviously, this crucial instrument is not available in the case we are now considering. Persons caught between prudential and moral reason cannot be encouraged to look at matters impartially, to distance themselves from their private concerns and to look at matters as would another person affected by their choice. For this is the standpoint of moral reason, and the question before us now is why anyone should bother to look at things this way. In other words, in this acute conflict between moral and prudential reasoning, our very means of rationally ordering disputes breaks down. There is no "third" or higher use of reason that can settle the dispute, and every effort to commend more strenuous impartiality is biased in the direction of moral reason.[12]

As obvious as this is, it is amazing how often philosophers and others have believed that persons could be rationally encouraged to be moral by pointing them to a more impartial assessment of the issues or by commending to them the "general superiority" of moral norms.[13] Certainly moral norms are superior to lesser considerations. Certainly they take priority over private interests. But where does this superiority come from, and why is it so compelling? We might reply, Because one who looked at matters impartially would agree that moral norms should have this priority. From an impartial standpoint, anything less is self-defeating and rationally unacceptable. We cannot live securely in a world where people fail to respect the moral law this way. But, again, can we really commend this kind of impartial assessment to persons who question why they should be impartial at all? The priority of moral norms makes sense to those who are willing to be impartial and moral. But our questions is, Why one should reason this way in the first place if it is seriously disadvantageous to do so?[14]

We may concede that there is no point in trying to commend morality to one who questions its worth. Since moral reasoning is one ultimate form of rational justification, it cannot in itself be justified. Some thinkers admit this and do not see it as a problem. They argue that one either is or is not moral. The matter rests on choice and nothing more can be said.[15] Presumably, they believe this is a problem only in relation to those who have chosen to be immoral, since these people cannot rationally be persuaded to alter their views. But this oversimplifies the difficulty. For even those who wish to be moral face a dilemma. On the one hand, they know there are good reasons for giving priority to morality, but, on the other hand, they are pulled by powerful prudential considerations in the form of all their natural desires, including the vital concerns they have for particular persons (family or friends). How can those torn by these conflicting attractions adopt the moral point of view without feeling that they are being in some ways irrational, that they are running counter to important dictates of prudential reason that ought to be respected? Can they silence this other voice of reason that counsels self-regard?

The moral life thus poses a painful dilemma for any rational being. On the one hand, moral reason does not speak with absolute authority: One can be rational and immoral, even if being so involves neglecting an important dimension of reason: morality. Or one can be moral, but even the most morally committed individual must know that this can involve violating another dimension of human reason: prudence. How then is it possible to act rationally at all without doing violence to some facet of our rational life?

Religious belief enters at precisely this point. We can think of religion as the effort by a rational being to act in a fully rational manner. I put matters this way because religion is often associated with the subjective, emotional side of human life, something apart from or opposed to reason. Of course religion has nonrational aspects as well. Any system of religious belief, as a full expression of human capacities, will relate to the affective and even aesthetic dimensions of human experience. But religion is also, and perhaps centrally, a rational enterprise. It is human reason's effort to resolve its own internal dispute and to make possible coherent rational choice.

How is this done? Obviously not by justifying immoral doing and willing. Human reason can never tolerate a subordination of the moral law, since this law, or method of reasoning, is a firm and essential part of our rational structure and is the condition of social life. Neither can reason deny the apparent discrepancy between morality and prudence. Moral commitment appears to entail self-sacrifice. But what a rational person can affirm, and what religions insist, is that this discrepancy is only apparent, not ultimate. Although the individual may appear to run terrible risks in choosing to be moral, these risks are not the last word on the matter. Beyond sacrifice lie possibilities of fulfillment directly proportional to moral effort. Moral retribution is certain. The righteous are rewarded. Those who risk their lives shall gain them.

In the chapter ahead, we will look at some of the subtle and profound ways that religions sustain this claim. Those of us raised in a Western culture are familiar with retributive ideas like heaven, hell, or a future "Kingdom of God," where moral judgment is supposed to take place. These ideas are so firmly embedded in our religious consciousness that we imagine them to be the only ways of thinking about the problem. Nevertheless, religious thought shows surprising creativity and plasticity. The anthropologist Claude Lévi-Strauss maintains that when confronting cultural possibilities, the human mind and human cultures often proceed by filling available "conceptual" boxes on the map of logical possibilities.[16] This is true as well where doctrines of retribution are concerned. In the chapters ahead we will see just a few of the different possibilities that religious traditions have developed. Overall, however, it is less important to explore all possible retributive concepts than to be aware of the underlying logic, the deep structure, that produces them.

I have stressed how this aspect of religious reasoning arises out of a conflict within reason between reason's prudential and moral employments. This conflict, I have said, points the way to a set of religious beliefs supporting the possibility of ultimate moral retribution. The discovery of these foundational ideas is not new. More than two centuries ago, Kant, pursuing a line of thought revealed by his own insightful analysis of the moral law, developed these ideas into what is sometimes called the "moral proof" of God's existence.[17] In fact, this is an unfortunate appellation (even

if Kant sometimes used it himself). Kant understood that he was not proving anything to one who rejected belief in God or a commitment to morality. Rather, he was developing the rational assumptions of those who had already made a commitment to morality and sought to justify this rationally to themselves and to others. Religious beliefs associated with this issue, therefore, are best thought of as *expressions* of a prior commitment to rationality and morality, as the concrete articulations of a series of deep valuations, especially the valuation of rationality itself. This means that religion is an important part of what it means to be a rational human being. It also suggests why religion is a universal and abiding aspect of human experience.

Sin and Its Transcendence

The third element in the deep structure of religious reasoning comes to our attention in two ways. In the course of religious development, this element usually makes its appearance after the breakdown of earlier retributive hopes. It comes to the fore as the effort to make salvation possible in a world where earlier moral confidences have been shaken. But while historically manifested this way, this element also has a place within the basic structure of moral and religious reason. It stems from a genuine rational difficulty that historical religious experience only emphasizes and makes clear.

We can easily trace the appearance of this element in the history of religious traditions, especially those traditions whose course of development is recorded in writing. In the earliest stages of development, religions characteristically affirm the reality of retribution in concrete, this-worldly terms: righteousness finds its reward in this world. The hope of upright persons is to end life surrounded by wealth and progeny, to "come to [the] grave in ripe old age" (Job 5.26). Though the wicked may flourish for a time and the righteous may suffer, there is confidence that more just rewards will soon follow. Religion itself, therefore, reinforces the conviction that the world is ruled by a moral geometry.

Such hopes are usually dashed by experience. No matter how upright the individual or community may be, no matter how attentive individuals are to their religious and moral duties, they suffer. Within the logic of religious belief, this situation demands explanation. Suffering may be viewed as a "trial" or "test" to which the righteous are put before their final, eschatological reward, but another explanation always at hand is that suffering results from sin. Indeed, the more a tradition has insisted on the firmness of retribution, the more it has emphasized the "moral geometry," the more likely it is to equate suffering with sin. Within this thought-world, therefore, the character of the moral and religious problem is changed. No longer is the question simply how the righteous can receive their due reward. Sin is now brought into focus, and because it is seen under penetrating gaze to involve even the most committed persons, the question becomes how one can transcend the penalties attached to wrongdoing, how one who necessarily sins can ever attain salvation. This means that as religious thought develops, the insistence on retribution, though never relinquished, becomes supplemented by teachings that point the way beyond the world of moral reward and punishment. In theistic religious systems, themes of grace and divine mercy appear. In nontheistic systems the hope becomes one of "liberation" to a state beyond our distinctions of good and evil.[18]

But the historical fact of persistent suffering is not the only thing driving this development. At the level of reasoned reflection, this response to experience is supported by close analysis of the moral life. A sense of the omnipresence and inescapability of sin is a concomitant to intense moral striving, and historical religious experience only makes this clear.

We can better understand this if we recall what we said in considering the question of why one should be moral: No one is rationally compelled to be moral. Morality ultimately rests on free choice. This is true not only because moral reason presumes our freedom from physical or psychological determination and our ability to make impartially reasoned choices[19] but, more important, because we are not rationally required to reason morally. Between the two rational perspectives of morality and prudence, we stand utterly undetermined. This truth is picked up by traditional Western religious literature in the observation that human wrongdoing, when it occurs, is not merely the result of a lost struggle between reason and desire, but involves the full complicity of reason.[20] And it has been given expression in our day in the existentialists' emphasis on the primacy of human freedom over reason in matters of moral choice.[21]

Our radical freedom to choose morality or immorality is not in itself the source of an awareness of sin. To this must be added an understanding of the rigor and ideality of the moral demand. To regard ourselves as upright persons, moral reasoning requires that we give unwavering and unexceptional priority to moral willing. Morality is universal not only in the sense that it applies to all persons but also in the sense that it applies to every instant of choosing. If I wish to be moral, I must make a commitment to pass every proposed future action before the bar of impartial reason and to act only in ways that can meet this test. Furthermore, if I am to judge myself to be a moral person, I must be reasonably confident of my own commitment to think and act this way. To doubt the sincerity of my commitment is to call into question my moral worth.

Superficially regarded, this demand may seem too rigorous. Certainly, persons who choose *never* to test their maxims by the method of moral decision cannot be regarded as morally upright. But is it not possible, now and then, to fail to be obedient to the moral law and still be a "good" person? Furthermore, cannot individuals, facing their future realistically, choose obedience to the moral law in *most instances,* while reserving the right on desperate occasions to protect their own interests? Can we not be *mostly* good? And are not mostly good persons better than those who choose never to be good at all?

Once again, I am indebted to Kant for a reply to these difficult questions. Addressing this problem in his *Religion within the Limits of Reason Alone,*[22] Kant considers the possibility that there might be an intermediate position between unwavering obedience to the moral law and systematic disobedience. But he asks us to consider the governing conditions of this intermediate position. If pure self-regard is the principle motive of the amoral or immoral person, what is my motive if I choose to allow myself *occasionally* to violate the moral law? Presumably, I say to myself "I will reason impartially and morally unless it proves seriously disadvantageous for me to do so." But if this is how I think, is it not true that self-interest is really my highest motivating consideration? It serves, after all, as the final reference in each instance of moral choice and it resolves every serious clash between morality and self-interest. True, one who reserves the right *occasionally* to violate the moral law may have a higher threshold of respect for morality's demands than the crassly immoral person, but this individual still gives self-interest a decisive role in choice. Furthermore, since those who reason this way reserve the right to determine how great the inconvenience must be before they abandon morality, there is no guarantee they will be morally better in practice than amoral or immoral persons, who may be led to act morally in most instances out of enlightened self-interest. In both analytical and in genuinely human terms, in other words, Kant's discussion leads us to see that there really is no intermediate position between moral and immoral willing.[23]

These two insights, the radical nature of the moral demand and our absolutely undetermined freedom to be moral or immoral, work together like jaws of a vise to produce the specific problem that gives rise to religious reasoning's third component: an awareness of the depth and intractability of human wrongdoing, and the need for suspension of moral self-judgment. In moments of honest moral insight, we know ourselves to be called to total moral commitment, but the awareness of our rational freedom to choose otherwise and the powerful attractions of self-interest work together to produce a sense that we may not be up to this demand. As a result, we can never confidently assert our own moral goodness. Furthermore, the fact that in past moments of free choice each of us has invariably neglected the priority due the moral law must convince us that wrongdoing is a recurrent possibility for our willing. Remorse for these past defections from morality thus combines with an honest estimate of their meaning for our future conduct to produce a pervasive sense of moral inadequacy. True, a shallow conscience can evade these facts. We can deny the meaning of our past, relax the rigorous demand of the moral law and perhaps conclude that we are of estimable character. But anyone with a sensitive conscience who is rightly disturbed by past failures must be driven to an awareness of the vast difference between the kind of willing that morality demands and the kind that he or she is able to offer. Indeed, the more sensitive our consciences are on this matter and the more we perceive the possibly deep corruption at the core of our being, the more likely we are to regard ourselves as among the worst of persons, hypocrites who conceal inner selfishness by an outward display of good conduct. We meet here, then, another moral paradox and one that is frequently emphasized by religious traditions: those who think themselves good rarely are. The best persons, the relative saints in our midst, are those who know themselves to be sinners.[24]

Granting this difficulty in the moral life, how can it be overcome? How can morally committed individuals surmount their own sense of moral inadequacy and their corresponding conviction that within a world of strict retribution, a world in which they already have chosen to believe, they merit only condemnation or punishment? If our worth were exclusively measured in terms of the moral judgments we must make about ourselves, there would be no escape from this terrible dilemma. We might carry on with a sense of futility, convinced that our moral striving will only provide further opportunities for wrongdoing, or we might cease trying altogether and expose ourselves directly to the charge of abandoning moral responsibility. Either way, we stand perilously close to moral paralysis and despair.

Here again religious beliefs enter to play a key role in facilitating moral commitment. Just as a belief in retribution eases the apparently insuperable opposition between prudence and morality, so religious beliefs can make it rational to renew our dedication to moral effort even as we realize the difficulty of this task and the failures that loom before us. In their general form the relevant beliefs involve the conviction that our self-imposed moral judgments are not a complete measure of our worth, nor the final determinant of our personal destiny. Ordinarily, these self-judgments must be authoritative for us. But in facing the seeming futility of efforts to attain moral worth, rational persons may allowably entertain the possible reality of a source or standard of judgment that somehow takes into account our moral frailties and confession of sinfulness. This source of judgment is "beyond morality" in the sense that it is not constrained to judge us as we must judge ourselves. It is also "beyond morality" in the positive sense of serving as the ultimate ground of the standards and of the retributive order we accept. The confidence that this supremely authoritative reality governs the evaluative and retributive process frees us from unsparing self-condemnation and despair over the repeated failures of our moral efforts, and it helps us rationally to renew our commitment to the moral conduct our reason otherwise demands.

Religiously expressed, this idea assumes some of the forms mentioned in connection with religious traditions' efforts to confront the fact of sin. In theistic traditions, this idea underlies the important themes of divine grace and forgiveness. Although God upholds morality, he is ultimately not constrained by it, and he is able to suspend punishment and redeem sinners. In some Asian traditions, where retribution is effected by the natural-moral law of karma, we find the belief that the highest levels of spritiual attainment transcend the world of karmic retribution altogether. The Chāndogya Upanishad characteristically describes this as a state "beyond merit and demerit," where evil deeds do not "stain" but depart from the self "even as water rolls off the smooth leaves of the lotus."[25]

These themes admittedly pose some of the most acute problems for religious thought. Superficially regarded, they appear to contradict the very insistence on morality and moral retribution that religions sustain. But this is usually not the case. While sophisticated religious thought permits a subordination of our rational moral standards and a suspension of just retribution, it does so within the framework of a more comprehensive moral vision. For example, although divine forgiveness appears to run counter to justice, this is usually so only with respect to the punitive aspects of the moral code. However, because God is not regarded as motivated by selfishness or weakness, his suspension of punishment is not a morally impermissible evasion of responsibility, as it would be for us, but is an expression of the "higher justice" that seeks to make possible others' moral renewal. Similarly, traditions that point to a domain beyond good and evil do not devalue the lower realm of moral causality ruled by karma. They view it as a necessary preparatory stage for those who aspire to liberation, and they usually insist that the realm beyond karma is open only to those who have first conquered selfish thoughts and impulses. In both theistic and nontheistic traditions, in other words, the higher reality "beyond morality" serves to fulfill and complete, not undermine, moral striving.

Be this as it may, whenever religions develop these themes, they also tend to spawn antinomian, "lawless" responses to their teaching, because some persons are mistakenly led to believe that the ultimate goal of the religion really lies beyond morality in a life free of moral restraints. These conclusions are natural, but as soon as they are voiced, they are repudiated by religious thinkers. Some of St. Paul's less acute readers may have thought that his diatribe against "the Law" and his emphasis on grace meant that Christians were freed from the requirement of moral obedience, that it was allowable "to continue in sin that grace may abound" (Rom. 6.1). But Paul responded to these conclusions with a horrified "By no means!" Similarly, some Hindus and some followers of the Buddha took the teaching that the spiritual adept is "beyond morality" to the antinomian conclusions of Tantra. But these were usually regarded as heretical responses. Against this, it was asserted that genuine enlightenment presupposed and culminated in a life of pure moral commitment, of genuine egolessness and sincere compassion.

The paradoxical aspect of this third element of religious reasoning, this seeming subordination of morality and suspension of retribution side by side with impassioned moral exhortations, illustrates how important it is to approach religious thought with an understanding of the deep structure beneath it. In some ways, the teachings of a religious tradition are like an ocean archipelago. Protruding above the surface, they appear to be a series of disconnected ideas with little relationship to one another. Seeing these surface atolls of thought as part of a deeper structure, however, makes their interconnections and logic more apparent, and allows us to identify and explain the presence of similar surface patterns in a wide variety of traditions.

One further illustration may help make this last point clearer. Paralleling these religious affirmations of both retribution and the suspension of retribution is a related tendency in religious thinking to insist on the reward for righteousness while urging believers not to strive for reward. In the Christian Gospels, for example, we find a puzzling alternation between the encouragement of heedless, self-sacrificial love for others and blatant promises of blessing for the righteous. Rabbinic teaching shows the same alternation, on the one hand admonishing the pious not to be like servants "who serve the master on condition of receiving a gift" while, on the other hand, encouraging them never to doubt the reality of reward.[26] In the Eastern traditions, the stress on the importance of liberation from samsara, the world of karmically conditioned becoming, goes hand in hand with an insistence on the certainty of karmic retribution for those within samsara.

These alternations have sometimes puzzled students of comparative religion and comparative ethics. Is Christian ethics "teleological" and "eudaemonistic" in the sense that it is oriented to the "goal" (*telos*) of happiness (*eudaimonia*) or is it "deontological" in its stress on duty and obligation without regard to any welfare produced?[27] Is it an ethic of self-sacrifice or of reward? The answer, of course, is that it is all these things. Reflecting the tense underlying structure of religious reasoning, Christian thinking stresses both the primacy of moral obligation *and* the benefits produced by moral conduct. It commands selflessness but promises ultimate happiness for self and others. To further complicate matters, Christian thinking (along with that of other major traditions) takes pains to see that the rewards it insists on do not become dominating considerations in the spiritual life. This reflects our deep moral conviction that truly righteous persons should aim at righteousness itself, not the praise or benefits it may reap.[28] Indeed, this issue constitutes a further reason (beyond that produced by the problem of despair over sin) why those at the highest reaches of spirituality are said to go beyond considerations of merit or demerit. In the rarified air of high spirituality, one has no regard for one's own moral worth and any reward this may produce, yet one acts compassionately on others' behalf. Naturally, all this must seem confusing and contradictory to the logically inclined beginning student of religion.[29] But when viewed in terms of the basic tensions within the moral life and the "deep structure" these produce, religious thinking appears coherent, rational, and morally sensitive.

It is one thing to say that religions are morally inclined at their deepest levels and another thing to demonstrate, tradition by tradition, belief by belief, that this is true. Counterevidence is easy to produce: the mutual hostility between traditions, the bouts of intolerance and holy war, the excesses of spirituality that can lead to worldly indifference and neglect.[30] Some of these excesses stem from religions' complexity, the fact that they seek to lead their adherents through a demanding program of moral perfection whose content and meaning is not always clear even to the better minds within the tradition. Other excesses stem from believers' convictions that their tradition alone guarantees the prospect of human righteousness. This can lead to the misguided conviction that these beliefs must be imposed on others. In the intensely moral domain of religious life, the old truism holds that the corruption of the best is sometimes the worst. Yet these difficulties and excesses should not dissuade us from the task of trying to discern and understand the deep moral intentionality underlying religious thought.

The chapters ahead exemplify this task. Across a variety of traditions widely separated in space and time, we will be looking at the ways in which these three elements of the deep structure find expression. In forms that may sometimes surprise us, and by paths that are often strikingly different, we shall see that religions strive in their teachings and in their practices to lead their adherents to a spontaneous and selfless but reasonable commitment to the moral point of view.

Endnotes

1. *Grundlegung zur Metaphysik der Sitten,* p. 421; *Foundations of the Metaphysics of Morals,* tr. Lewis White Beck (Indianapolis: Bobbs-Merrill, 1969), p. 39.

2. Kant mentions this problem in criticizing the "negative golden rule" (*Grundlegung,* p. 430; *Foundations,* p. 48 n. 14).

3. For a fuller discussion of these matters see John Rawls, *A Theory of Justice* (Cambridge: Harvard University Press, 1971), sec. 40 ("The Kantian Interpretation of Justice as Fairness") and "Kantian Constructivism in Moral Theory. The Dewey Lectures 1980" *Journal of Philosophy* 77 (1980); 515–572, Also, Thomas Hill, "The Kingdom of Ends," in *Proceedings of the Third International Kant Congress* (Dordrecht: D. Reidel, 1972), 307–315.

4. See, for example, David Richards, *A Theory of Reasons for Action* (Oxford: Clarendon Press, 1971); Bernard Gert, *The Moral Rules* (New York: Harper & Row, 1970) and Rawls, *Theory of Justice.* For sensitive applications of this procedure to new areas of choice, see Sissela Bok, *Lying* (New York: Pantheon Books, 1978) and *Secrets* (New York: Pantheon Books, 1982). A Rawlsian procedure is applied to the difficult issue of paternalism by Karen M. Tait and Gerald Winslow in their article, "Beyond Consent: The Ethics of Decision Making in Emergency Medicine," in *Medical Ethics,* ed. Nathalie Abrams and Michael Buckner (Cambridge: MIT Press, 1983), pp. 285–289.

5. This is perhaps the appeal of the utilitarian formula advanced by John Stuart Mill requiring us to promote "the greatest amount of happiness altogether" (see *Utilitarianism,* ch. 2). One serious problem with utilitarianism, however, is that it confuses what is a subordinate decision rule for certain instances of moral choice with the supreme principle of morality, which requires impartial rational choice.

6. Rawls, for example, provides an argument for the appropriateness of a "maximin" decision rule where the choice of basic and enduring principles for a social order is concerned, but he acknowledges that this rule is not appropriate for all cases of rational or moral choice (*Theory of Justice,* sec. 26).

7. For a series of discussions of the issue of ethical relativism, see John Ladd, ed., *Ethical Relativism* (Belmont, Calif.: Wadsworth, 1973).

8. This aspect of morality is discussed in David Heyd, *Supererogation* (New York: Cambridge University Press, 1982). Also, J.O. Urmson, "Saints and Heroes," in *Essays in Moral Philosophy,* ed. A.I. Melden (Seattle: University of Washington Press, 1958), pp. 198–216.

9. "Treatise on the Law," *Summa Theologiae,* pts. 1a–2ae, ques. 95, art. 6.

10. This idea is insightfully developed by Reinhold Niebuhr in his classic study *Moral Man and Immoral Society* (New York: Charles Scribner's Sons, 1932).

11. *The Abolition of Man* (New York: Macmillan, 1947), p. 28.

12. A similar point is made by Basil Mitchell in his *Morality: Religious and Secular* (Oxford: Clarendon Press, 1980), p. 141.

13. For an example of this kind of misleading argument see Kurt Baier, *The Moral Point of View* (Ithaca, N.Y.: Cornell University Press, 1958), ch. 12. Baier's discussion is criticized by

Kal Nielsen in his article, "Why Should I Be Moral?" *Methodos* 15 (1963): 275–306.

14. Kant similarly criticizes the effort to answer this question by appeal to the satisfactions created by heeding one's conscience. Rejecting the Stoic effort to ground moral obedience in these satisfactions, he remarks in the *Critique of Practical Reason,* "A man, if he is virtuous, will certainly not enjoy his life without being conscious of his righteousness in each action, however favorable fortune may be to him in the physical circumstances of life; but can one make him virtuous before he has so high an estimation of the moral worth of his existence merely by commending to him the contentment of spirit which will arise from the consciousness of righteousness for which he as yet has no sense?" (tr. Lewis White Beck [Indianapolis: Bobbs-Merrill, 1956,]), p. 120.

15. Stephen Toulmin, in *An Examination of the Place of Reason in Ethics* (Cambridge: Cambridge University Press, 1960), ch. 14, seems to hold this view.

16. Claude Lévi-Strauss, "The Structural Study of Myth," in *Structural Anthropology,* tr. Claire Jacobson and Brooke Grundfest (New York: Basic Books, 1963), pp. 217ff.

17. Although Kant's characteristic moral understanding of religion was already evident in the *Critique of Pure Reason,* the full outlines of Kant's view are made apparent only his later writings on religion, especially the *Critique of Practical Reason, Religion within the Limits of Reason Alone,* and the *Critique of Judgment.*

18. In theistic systems, doctrines of grace not only offer an escape from suffering for those conscientious individuals who have come to question their own righteousness, but these doctrines also have the incidental effect of explaining the continuing flourishing of the wicked, which can be attributed to God's mercy and to his willingness to suffer human sin. See, for example, *The Midrash on Psalms,* William G. Braude, tr. (New Haven: Yale University Press, 1959), pp. 423f. (Ps. 37:3).

19. This is the point of Kant's famous argument for freedom of the will in the *Critique of Practical Reason* and of his claim there that "freedom and unconditional practical law reciprocally imply each other" (*Practical Reason,* p. 29).

20. This understanding is forcefully expressed within the Pauline tradition of Christian thought. See, for example, Augustine's discussion in his *Confessions* (bk. 8, especially ch. 9) of the conflict within the human intellect and will.

21. As important as their stress on freedom is, existentialist writers sometimes carry this insistence so far that they overlook the valid role of reason in the choice of normative rules for conduct. This is true, for example, of Jean Paul Sartre's discussion of norms in his classic essay "Existentialism is a Humanism," in *Existentialism from Dostoevsky to Sartre,* ed. Walter Kaufman (New York: New American Library, 1975), pp. 345–369. Although he criticizes normative theories of ethics, including Kant's, Sartre clearly presumes certain standards

of right and wrong conduct, and the problematical cases he presents as undermining normative theories are simply very difficult instances of moral decision on any theoretical account.

22. Tr. Theodore M. Green and Hoyt H. Hudson (New York: Harper & Row, 1960), pp. 17–20.

23. Kierkegaard utilizes this essentially Kantian understanding of the unyielding "ideality" of ethics to develop his defense of the Christian doctrine of original sin in *The Concept of Anxiety,* tr. Reidar Thomte (Princeton: Princeton University Press, 1980), pp. 16f.

24. This understanding, too, is a staple of the Pauline-Lutheran tradition. But it is perhaps Kierkegaard who most insightfully perceives the paradox involved here. In the *Concluding Unscientific Postscript* he develops this idea in terms of the peculiar "catch" to guilt that makes professions of innocence amount to self-denunciation (tr. David Swenson [Princeton: Princeton University Press, 1941], p. 471).

25. 4.14.3.

26. *Aboth,* tr. J. Israelstam, pt. 4, vol, 8 of *The Babylonian Talmud,* ed. Isidore Epstein (London: Soncino, 1935), pp. 28, 44, 56–57.

27. David Little and Sumner B. Twiss express some puzzlement over the promises of reward of punishment alongside more formalistic appeals to God's will in the Gospel of Matthew. They end by dismissing the importance of these considerations in the gospel but they fail to identify the deeper logic that leads to their presence in the first place. See their *Comparative Religious Ethics* (San Francisco: Harper & Row, 1978), pp. 204f.

28. This sometimes characterized as a "double-bind" problem in the realm of moral desert. For discussions of this, see Joel Fienberg, *Doing and Deserving: Essays in the Theory of Responsibility* (Princeton: Princeton University Press, 1970), ch. 4. Also, Steven A. Edwards, "The Inward Turn: Justice and Responsibility in the Religious Ethics of Aquinas" (Ph.D. diss., Stanford University, 1981), pp. 48–53, 160–174.

29. It sometimes confuses advanced students, too. In the effort to understand Paul's shifts between moral exhortation and denials of the importance of moral striving, for example, the great biblical scholar Albert Schweitzer was led to conclude that Paul's seeming contradictions only made sense in terms of nonrational, mystical states experienced by the apostle (*The Mysticism of Paul the Apostle,* tr. W. Montgomery [London: Adam and Charles Black, 1931]).

30. Jeffrey Stout, in his *Flight from Autonomy,* criticizes the approach I am outlining here on the grounds that it cannot explain, among other things, some scholastic Christians' approval of the use of violence against heretics ([Notre Dame, Ind.: University of Notre Dame Press. 1981], pp. 226ff.). This single counterexample is an important one, but a systematic critique of the view I present requires more than one or two counterexamples. Furthermore, the examples adduced must

not be eccentric but must represent the major moral and religious tendencies of a tradition. Christian advocacy of the use of force for exclusively religious purposes, whether in war or internal repression, is a position that was contested by many generations of Christian writers and was eventually abandoned by most Christian communities. Good discussions

of this tradition of thought include Roland Bainton, *Christian Attitudes toward War and Peace* (New York: Abingdon Press, 1960); Frederick H. Russell, *The Just War in the Middle Ages* (New York: Cambridge University Press, 1975) and James T. Johnson, *Just War Tradition and the Restraint of War* (Princeton: Princeton University Press, 1981).

8. *Woman's Place in Man's Life Cycle*

Carol Gilligan

Citing extensive work in the social sciences, particularly in social psychology, Carol Gilligan demonstrates that in the areas of relationships and issues of dependency, women and men simply do not experience the world in same manner. The implications of this research are wide ranging, especially insofar as they undermine attempts to invoke the objectivity of the moral life or to promote ethical theories that characterize the world through the perspectives of men. If women are more prone to focus on the need to protect and restore relationships, and men are more prone to insist on issues of autonomy and requirements of justice, then ethical theories that assume a universal, rational point of origin mistakenly privilege the male point of view and are seriously compromised.

In the second act of *The Cherry Orchard,* Lopahin, a young merchant, describes his life of hard work and success. Failing to convince Madame Ranevskaya to cut down the cherry orchard to save her estate, he will go on in the next act to buy it himself. He is the self-made man who, in purchasing the estate where his father and grandfather were slaves, seeks to eradicate the "awkward, unhappy life" of the past, replacing the cherry orchard with summer cottages where coming generations "will see a new life." In elaborating this developmental vision, he reveals the image of man that underlies and supports his activity: "At times when I can't go to sleep, I think: Lord, thou gavest us immense forests, unbounded fields and the widest horizons, and living in the midst of them we should indeed be giants"—at which point, Madame Ranevskaya interrupts him, saying, "You feel the need for giants—They are good only in fairy tales, anywhere else they only frighten us."

Conceptions of the human life cycle represent attempts to order and make coherent the unfolding experiences and perceptions, the changing wishes and realities of everyday life. But the nature of such conceptions depends in part on the position of the observer. The brief excerpt from Chekhov's play suggests that when the observer is a woman, the perspective may be of a different sort. Different judgments of the image of man as giant imply different ideas about human development, different ways of imagining the human condition, different notions of what is of value in life.

At a time when efforts are being made to eradicate discrimination between the sexes in the search for social equality and justice, the differences between the sexes are being rediscovered in the social sciences. This discovery occurs when theories formerly considered to be sexually neutral in their scientific objectivity are found instead to reflect a consistent observational and evaluative bias. Then the presumed neutrality of science, like that of language itself, gives way to the recognition that the categories of knowledge are human constructions. The fascination with point of view that has informed the fiction of the twentieth century and the corresponding recognition of the relativity of judgment infuse our scientific understanding as well when we begin to notice how accustomed we have become to seeing life through men's eyes.

A recent discovery of this sort pertains to the apparently innocent classic *The Elements of Style* by William Strunk and E. B. White. The Supreme Court ruling on the subject of discrimination in classroom texts led one teacher of English to notice that the elementary rules of English usage were being taught through examples which counterposed the birth of Napoleon, the writings of Coleridge, and statements such as "He was an interesting talker. A man who had traveled all over the world and lived in half a dozen countries," with "Well, Susan, this is a fine mess you are in" or, less drastically, "He saw a woman, accompanied by two children, walking slowly down the road."

Psychological theorists have fallen as innocently as Strunk and White into the same observational bias. Implicitly adopting the male life as the norm, they have tried to fashion women out of a masculine cloth. It all goes back, of course, to Adam and Eve—a story which shows, among other things, that if you make a woman out of a man, you are bound to get into trouble. In the life cycle, as in the Garden of Eden, the woman has been the deviant.

The penchant of developmental theorists to project a masculine image, and one that appears frightening to women, goes back at least to Freud (1905), who built his theory of psychosexual development around the experiences of the male child that culminate in the Oedipus complex. In the 1920s, Freud struggled to resolve the contradictions posed for his theory by the differences in female anatomy and the different configuration of the young girl's early family relationships. After trying to fit women into his masculine conception, seeing them as envying that which they missed, he came instead to acknowledge, in the strength and persistence of women's pre-Oedipal attachments to their mothers, a developmental difference. He considered this difference in women's development to be responsible for what he saw as women's developmental failure.

Having tied the formation of the superego or conscience to castration anxiety, Freud considered women to be deprived by nature of the impetus for a clear-cut Oedipal resolution. Consequently, women's superego—the heir to the Oedipus complex—was compromised: it was never "so inexorable, so impersonal, so independent of its emotional origins as we require it to be in

men." From this observation of difference, that "for women the level of what is ethically normal is different from what it is in men," Freud concluded that women "show less sense of justice than men, that they are less ready to submit to the great exigencies of life, that they are more often influenced in their judgements by feelings of affection or hostility" (1925, pp. 257–258).

Thus a problem in theory became cast as a problem in women's development, and the problem in women's development was located in their experience of relationships. Nancy Chodorow (1974), attempting to account for "the reproduction within each generation of certain general and nearly universal differences that characterize masculine and feminine personality and roles," attributes these differences between the sexes not to anatomy but rather to "the fact that women, universally, are largely responsible for early child care." Because this early social environment differs for and is experienced differently by male and female children, basic sex differences recur in personality development. As a result, "in any given society, feminine personality comes to define itself in relation and connection to other people more than masculine personality does" (pp. 43–44).

In her analysis, Chodorow relies primarily on Robert Stoller's studies which indicate that gender identity, the unchanging core of personality formation, is "with rare exception firmly and irreversibly established for both sexes by the time a child is around three." Given that for both sexes the primary caretaker in the first three years of life is typically female, the interpersonal dynamics of gender identity formation are different for boys and girls. Female identity formation takes place in a context of ongoing relationship since "mothers tend to experience their daughters as more like, and continuous with, themselves." Correspondingly, girls, in identifying themselves as female, experience themselves as like their mothers, thus fusing the experience of attachment with the process of identity formation. In contrast, "mothers experience their sons as a male opposite," and boys, in defining themselves as masculine, separate their mothers from themselves, thus curtailing "their primary love and sense of empathic tie." Consequently, male development entails a "more emphatic individuation and a more defensive firming of experienced ego boundaries." For boys, but not girls, "issues of differentiation have become intertwined with sexual issues" (1978, pp. 150, 166–167).

Writing against the masculine bias of psychoanalytic theory, Chodorow argues that the existence of sex differences in the early experiences of individuation and relationship "does not mean that women have 'weaker' ego boundaries than men or are more prone to psychosis." It means instead that "girls emerge from this period with a basis for 'empathy' built into their primary definition of self in a way that boys do not." Chodorow thus replaces Freud's negative and derivative description of female psychology with a positive and direct account of her own: "Girls emerge with a stronger basis for experiencing another's needs or feelings as one's own (or of thinking that one is so experiencing another's needs and feelings). Furthermore, girls do not define themselves in terms of the denial of preoedipal relational modes to the same extent as do boys. Therefore, regression to these modes tends not to feel as much a basic threat to their ego. From very early, then, because they are parented by a person of the same gender . . . girls come to experience themselves as less differentiated than boys, as more continuous with and related to the external object-world, and as differently oriented to their inner object-world as well" (p. 167).

Consequently, relationships, and particularly issues of dependency are experienced differently by women and men. For boys and men, separation and individuation are critically tied to gender identity since separation from the mother is essential for the development of masculinity. For girls and women, issues of femininity or feminine identity do not depend on the achievement of separation from the mother or on the progress of individuation. Since masculinity is defined through separation while femininity is defined through attachment, male gender identity is threatened by intimacy while female gender identity is threatened by separation. Thus males tend to have difficulty with relationships, while females tend to have problems with individuation. The quality of embeddedness in social interaction and personal relationships that characterizes women's lives in contrast to men's, however, becomes not only a descriptive difference but also a developmental liability when the milestones of childhood and adolescent development in the psychological literature are markers of increasing separation. Women's failure to separate then becomes by definition a failure to develop.

The sex differences in personality formation that Chodorow describes in early childhood appear during the middle childhood years in studies of children's games. Children's games are considered by George Herbert Mead (1934) and Jean Piaget (1932) as the crucible of social development during the school years. In

games, children learn to take the role of the other and come to see themselves through another's eyes. In games, they learn respect for rules and come to understand the ways rules can be made and changed.

Janet Lever (1976), considering the peer group to be the agent of socialization during the elementary school years and play to be a major activity of socialization at that time, set out to discover whether there are sex differences in the games that children play. Studying 181 fifth-grade, white, middle-class children, ages ten and eleven, she observed the organization and structure of their playtime activities. She watched the children as they played at school during recess and in physical education class, and in addition kept diaries of their accounts as to how they spent their out-of-school time. From this study, Lever reports sex differences: boys play out-of-doors more often than girls do; boys play more often in large and age-heterogeneous groups; they play competitive games more often, and their games last longer than girls' games. The last is in some ways the most interesting finding. Boys' games appeared to last longer not only because they required a higher level of skill and were thus less likely to become boring, but also because, when disputes arose in the course of a game, boys were able to resolve the disputes more effectively than girls: "During the course of this study, boys were seen quarrelling all the time, but not once was a game terminated because of a quarrel and no game was interrupted for more than seven minutes. In the gravest debates, the final word was always, to 'repeat the play,' generally followed by a chorus of 'cheater's proof'" (p. 482). In fact, it seemed that the boys enjoyed the legal debates as much as they did the game itself, and even marginal players of lesser size or skill participated equally in these recurrent squabbles. In contrast, the eruption of disputes among girls tended to end the game.

Thus Lever extends and corroborates the observations of Piaget in his study of the rules of the game, where he finds boys becoming through childhood increasingly fascinated with the legal elaboration of rules and the development of fair procedures for adjudicating conflicts, a fascination that, he notes, does not hold for girls. Girls, Piaget observes, have a more "pragmatic" attitude toward rules, "regarding a rule as good as long as the game repaid it" (p. 83). Girls are more tolerant in their attitudes toward rules, more willing to make exceptions, and more easily reconciled to innovations. As a result, the legal sense, which Piaget considers essential to moral development, "is far less developed in little girls than in boys" (p. 77).

The bias that leads Piaget to equate male development with child development also colors Lever's work. The assumption that shapes her discussion of results is that the male model is the better one since it fits the requirements for modern corporate success. In contrast, the sensitivity and care for the feelings of others that girls develop through their play have little market value and can even impede professional success. Lever implies that, given the realities of adult life, if a girl does not want to be left dependent on men, she will have to learn to play like a boy.

To Piaget's argument that children learn the respect for rules necessary for moral development by playing rule-bound games, Lawrence Kohlberg (1969) adds that these lessons are most effectively learned through the opportunities for role-taking that arise in the course of resolving disputes. Consequently, the moral lessons inherent in girls' play appear to be fewer than in boys'. Traditional girls' games like jump rope and hopscotch are turn-taking games, where competition is indirect since one person's success does not necessarily signify another's failure. Consequently, disputes requiring adjudication are less likely to occur. In fact, most of the girls whom Lever interviewed claimed that when a quarrel broke out, they ended the game. Rather than elaborating a system of rules for resolving disputes, girls subordinated the continuation of the game to the continuation of relationships.

Lever concludes that from the games they play, boys learn both the independence and the organizational skills necessary for coordinating the activities of large and diverse groups of people. By participating in controlled and socially approved competitive situations, they learn to deal with competition in a relatively forthright manner—to play with their enemies and to compete with their friends—all in accordance with the rules of the game. In contrast, girls' play tends to occur in smaller, more intimate groups, often the best-friend dyad, and in private places. This play replicates the social pattern of primary human relationships in that its organization is more cooperative. Thus, it points less, in Mead's terms, toward learning to take the role of "the generalized other," less toward the abstraction of human relationships. But it fosters the development of the empathy and sensitivity necessary for taking the role of "the particular other" and points more toward knowing the other as different from the self.

The sex differences in personality formation in early childhood that Chodorow derives from her analysis of the mother-child relationship are thus extended by Lever's observations of sex differences in the play activities of middle childhood. Together these accounts suggest that boys and girls arrive at puberty with a different interpersonal orientation and a different range of social experiences. Yet, since adolescence is considered a crucial time for separation, the period of "the second individuation process" (Blos, 1967), female development has appeared most divergent and thus most problematic at this time.

"Puberty," Freud says, "which brings about so great an accession of libido in boys, is marked in girls by a fresh wave of *repression*," necessary for the transformation of the young girl's "masculine sexuality" into the specifically feminine sexuality of her adulthood (1905, pp. 220–221). Freud posits this transformation on the girl's acknowledgment and acceptance of "the fact of her castration" (1931, p. 229). To the girl, Freud explains, puberty brings a new awareness of "the wound to her narcissism" and leads her to develop, "like a scar, a sense of inferiority" (1925, p. 253). Since in Erik Erikson's expansion of Freud's psychoanalytic account, adolescence is the time when development hinges on identity, the girl arrives at this juncture either psychologically at risk or with a different agenda.

The problem that female adolescence presents for theorists of human development is apparent in Erikson's scheme. Erikson (1950) charts eight stages of psychosocial development, of which adolescence is the fifth. The task at this stage is to forge a coherent sense of self, to verify an identity that can span the discontinuity of puberty and make possible the adult capacity to love and work. The preparation for the successful resolution of the adolescent identity crisis is delineated in Erikson's description of the crises that characterize the preceding four stages. Although the initial crisis in infancy of "trust versus mistrust" anchors development in the experience of relationship, the task then clearly becomes one of individuation. Erikson's second stage centers on the crisis of "autonomy versus shame and doubt," which marks the walking child's emerging sense of separateness and agency. From there, development goes on through the crisis of "initiative versus guilt," successful resolution of which represents a further move in the direction of autonomy. Next, following the inevitable disappointment of the magical wishes of the Oedipal period, children realize that to compete with their parents, they must first join them and learn to do what they do so well. Thus in the middle childhood years, development turns on the crisis of "industry versus inferiority," as the demonstration of competence becomes critical to the child's developing self-esteem. This is the time when children strive to learn and master the technology of their culture, in order to recognize themselves and to be recognized by others as capable of becoming adults. Next comes adolescence, the celebration of the autonomous, initiating, industrious self through the forging of an identity based on an ideology that can support and justify adult commitments. But about whom is Erikson talking?

Once again it turns out to be the male child. For the female, Erikson (1968) says, the sequence is a bit different. She holds her identity in abeyance as she prepares to attract the man by whose name she will be known, by whose status she will be defined, the man who will rescue her from emptiness and loneliness by filling "the inner space." While for men, identity precedes intimacy and generativity in the optimal cycle of human separation and attachment, for women these tasks seem instead to be fused. Intimacy goes along with identity, as the female comes to know herself as she is known, through her relationships with others.

Yet despite Erikson's observation of sex differences, his chart of life-cycle stages remains unchanged: identity continues to precede intimacy as male experience continues to define his life-cycle conception. But in this male life cycle there is little preparation for the intimacy of the first adult stage. Only the initial stage of trust versus mistrust suggests the type of mutuality that Erikson means by intimacy and generativity and Freud means by genitality. The rest is separateness, with the result that development itself comes to be identified with separation, and attachments appear to be developmental impediments, as is repeatedly the case in the assessment of women.

Erikson's description of male identity as forged in relation to the world and of female identity as awakened in a relationship of intimacy with another person is hardly new. In the fairy tales that Bruno Bettelheim (1976) describes an identical portrayal appears. The dynamics of male adolescence are illustrated archetypically by the conflict between father and son in "The Three Languages." Here a son, considered hopelessly stupid by his father, is given one last chance at education and sent for a year to study with a master. But when he returns, all he has learned is "what the dogs bark." After two further attempts of this sort, the father gives up in disgust and orders his servants to take the child into the forest and kill him. But the servants, those perpetual rescuers of disowned and abandoned children, take pity on the child and decide simply to leave him in the forest. From there, his wanderings take him to a land beset by furious dogs whose

barking permits nobody to rest and who periodically devour one of the inhabitants. Now it turns out that our hero has learned just the right thing: he can talk with the dogs and is able to quiet them, thus restoring peace to the land. Since the other knowledge he acquires serves him equally well, he emerges triumphant from his adolescent confrontation with his father, a giant of the life-cycle conception.

In contrast, the dynamics of female adolescence are depicted through the telling of a very different story. In the world of the fairy tale, the girl's first bleeding is followed by a period of intense passivity in which nothing seems to be happening. Yet in the deep sleeps of Snow White and Sleeping Beauty, Bettelheim sees that inner concentration which he considers to be the necessary counterpart to the activity of adventure. Since the adolescent heroines awake from their sleep, not to conquer the world, but to marry the prince, their identity is inwardly and interpersonally defined. For women, in Bettelheim's as in Erikson's account, identity and intimacy are intricately conjoined. The sex differences depicted in the world of fairy tales, like the fantasy of the woman warrior in Maxine Hong Kingston's (1977) recent autobiographical novel which echoes the old stories of Troilus and Cressida and Tancred and Chlorinda, indicate repeatedly that active adventure is a male activity, and that if a woman is to embark on such endeavors, she must at least dress like a man.

These observations about sex difference support the conclusion reached by David McClelland (1975) that "sex role turns out to be one of the most important determinants of human behavior; psychologists have found sex differences in their studies from the moment they started doing empirical research." But since it is difficult to say "different" without saying "better" or "worse," since there is a tendency to construct a single scale of measurement, and since that scale has generally been derived from and standardized on the basis of men's interpretations of research data drawn predominantly or exclusively from studies of males, psychologists "have tended to regard male behavior as the 'norm' and female behavior as some kind of deviation from that norm" (p. 81). Thus, when women do not conform to the standards of psychological expectation, the conclusion has generally been that something is wrong with the women.

What Matina Horner (1972) found to be wrong with women was the anxiety they showed about competitive achievement. From the beginning, research on human motivation using the Thematic Apperception Test (TAT) was plagued by evidence of sex differences which appeared to confuse and complicate data analysis. The TAT presents for interpretation an ambiguous cue—a picture about which a story is to be written or a segment of a story that is to be completed. Such stories, in reflecting projective imagination, are considered by psychologists to reveal the ways in which people construe what they perceive, that is, the concepts and interpretations they bring to their experience and thus presumably the kind of sense that they make of their lives. Prior to Horner's work it was clear that women made a different kind of sense than men of situations of competitive achievement, that in some way they saw the situations differently or the situations aroused in them some different response.

On the basis of his studies of men, McClelland divided the concept of achievement motivation into what appeared to be its two logical components, a motive to approach success ("hope success") and a motive to avoid failure ("fear failure"). From her studies of women, Horner identified as a third category the unlikely motivation to avoid success ("fear success"). Women appeared to have a problem with competitive achievement, and that problem seemed to emanate from a perceived conflict between femininity and success, the dilemma of the female adolescent who struggles to integrate her feminine aspirations and the identifications of her early childhood with the more masculine competence she has acquired at school. From her analysis of women's completions of a story that began, "after first term finals, Anne finds herself at the top of her medical school class," and from her observation of women's performance in competitive achievement situations, Horner reports that, "when success is likely or possible, threatened by the negative consequences they expect to follow success, young women become anxious and their positive achievement strivings become thwarted" (p. 171). She concludes that this fear "exists because for most women, the anticipation of success in competitive achievement activity, especially against men, produces anticipation of certain negative consequences, for example, threat of social rejection and loss of femininity" (1968, p. 125).

Such conflicts about success, however, may be viewed in a different light. Georgia Sassen (1980) suggests that the conflicts expressed by the women might instead indicate "a heightened perception of the 'other side' of competitive success, that is, the great emotional costs at which success achieved through competition is often gained—an understanding which, though confused, indicates some underlying sense that something is rotten in the state in which success is

defined as having better grades than everyone else" (p. 15). Sassen points out that Horner found success anxiety to be present in women only when achievement was directly competitive, that is, when one person's success was at the expense of another's failure.

In his elaboration of the identity crisis, Erikson (1968) cites the life of George Bernard Shaw to illustrate the young person's sense of being co-opted prematurely by success in a career he cannot wholeheartedly endorse. Shaw at seventy, reflecting upon his life, described his crisis at the age of twenty as having been caused not by the lack of success or the absence of recognition, but by too much of both: "I made good in spite of myself, and found, to my dismay, that Business, instead of expelling me as the worthless imposter I was, was fastening upon me with no intention of letting me go. Behold me, therefore, in my twentieth year, with a business training, in an occupation which I detested as cordially as any sane person lets himself detest anything he cannot escape from. In March 1876 I broke loose" (p. 143). At this point Shaw settled down to study and write as he pleased. Hardly interpreted as evidence of neurotic anxiety about achievement and competition, Shaw's refusal suggests to Erikson "the extraordinary workings of an extraordinary personality [coming] to the fore" (p. 144).

We might on these grounds begin to ask, not why women have conflicts about competitive success, but why men show such readiness to adopt and celebrate a rather narrow vision of success. Remembering Piaget's observation, corroborated by Lever, that boys in their games are more concerned with rules while girls are more concerned with relationships, often at the expense of the game itself—and given Chodorow's conclusion that men's social orientation is positional while women's is personal—we begin to understand why, when "Anne" becomes "John" in Horner's tale of competitive success and the story is completed by men, fear of success tends to disappear. John is considered to have played by the rules and won. He has the *right* to feel good about his success. Confirmed in the sense of his own identity as separate from those who, compared to him, are less competent, his positional sense of self is affirmed. For Anne, it is possible that the position she could obtain by being at the top of her medical school class may not, in fact, be what she wants.

"It is obvious," Virginia Woolf says, "that the values of women differ very often from the values which have been made by the other sex" (1929, p. 76). Yet, she adds, "it is the masculine values that prevail." As a result, women come to question the normality of their feelings and to alter their judgments in deference to the opinion of others. In the nineteenth century novels written by women, Woolf sees at work "a mind which was slightly pulled from the straight and made to alter its clear vision in deference to external authority." The same deference to the values and opinions of others can be seen in the judgments of twentieth century women. The difficulty women experience in finding or speaking publicly in their own voices emerges repeatedly in the form of qualification and self-doubt, but also in intimations of a divided judgment, a public assessment and private assessment which are fundamentally at odds.

Yet the deference and confusion that Woolf criticizes in women derive from the values she sees as their strength. Women's deference is rooted not only in their social subordination but also in the substance of their moral concern. Sensitivity to the needs of others and the assumption of responsibility for taking care lead women to attend to voices other than their own and to include in their judgment other points of view. Women's moral weakness, manifest in an apparent diffusion and confusion of judgment, is thus inseparable from women's moral strength, an overriding concern with relationships and responsibilities. The reluctance to judge may itself be indicative of the care and concern for others that infuse the psychology of women's development and are responsible for what is generally seen as problematic in its nature.

Thus women not only define themselves in a context of human relationship but also judge themselves in terms of their ability to care. Women's place in man's life cycle has been that of nurturer, caretaker, and helpmate, the weaver of those networks of relationships on which she in turn relies. But while women have thus taken care of men, men have, in their theories of psychological development, as in their economic arrangements, tended to assume or devalue that care. When the focus on individuation and individual achievement extends into adulthood and maturity is equated with personal autonomy, concern with relationships appears as a weakness of women rather than as a human strength (Miller, 1976).

The discrepancy between womanhood and adulthood is nowhere more evident than in the studies on sex-role stereotypes reported by Broverman, Vogel, Broverman, Clarkson, and Rosenkrantz (1972). The repeated finding of these studies is that the qualities deemed necessary for adulthood—the capacity for autonomous thinking, clear decision-making, and

responsible action—are those associated with masculinity and considered undesirable as attributes of the feminine self. The stereotypes suggest a splitting of love and work that relegates expressive capacities to women while placing instrumental abilities in the masculine domain. Yet looked at from a different perspective, these stereotypes reflect a conception of adulthood that is itself out of balance, favoring the separateness of the individual self over connection to others, and leaning more toward an autonomous life of work than toward the interdependence of love and care.

The discovery now being celebrated by men in mid-life of the importance of intimacy, relationships, and care is something that women have known from the beginning. However, because that knowledge in women has been considered "intuitive" or "instinctive," a function of anatomy coupled with destiny, psychologists have neglected to describe its development. In my research, I have found that women's moral development centers on the elaboration of that knowledge and thus delineates a critical line of psychological development in the lives of both of the sexes. The subject of moral development not only provides the final illustration of the reiterative pattern in the observation and assessment of sex differences in the literature on human development, but also indicates more particularly why the nature and significance of women's development has been for so long obscured and shrouded in mystery.

The criticism that Freud makes of women's sense of justice, seeing it as compromised in its refusal of blind impartiality, reappears not only in the work of Piaget but also in that of Kohlberg. While in Piaget's account (1932) of the moral judgment of the child, girls are an aside, a curiosity to whom he devotes four brief entries in an index that omits "boys" altogether because "the child" is assumed to be male, in the research from which Kohlberg derives his theory, females simply do not exist. Kohlberg's (1958, 1981) six stages that describe the development of moral judgment from childhood to adulthood are based empirically on a study of eighty-four boys whose development Kohlberg has followed for a period of over twenty years. Although Kohlberg claims universality for his stage sequence, those groups not included in his original sample rarely reach his higher stages (Edwards, 1975; Holstein, 1976; Simpson, 1974). Prominent among those who thus appear to be deficient in moral development when measured by Kohlberg's scale are women, whose judgments seem to exemplify the third stage of his six-stage sequence.

At this stage morality is conceived in interpersonal terms and goodness is equated with helping and pleasing others. This conception of goodness is considered by Kohlberg and Kramer (1969) to be functional in the lives of mature women insofar as their lives take place in the home. Kohlberg and Kramer imply that only if women enter the traditional arena of male activity will they recognize the inadequacy of this moral perspective and progress like men toward higher stages where relationships are subordinated to rules (stage four) and rules to universal principles of justice (stages five and six).

Yet herein lies a paradox, for the very traits that traditionally have defined the "goodness" of women, their care for and sensitivity to the needs of others, are those that mark them as deficient in moral development. In this version of moral development, however, the conception of maturity is derived from the study of men's lives and reflects the importance of individuation in their development. Piaget (1970), challenging the common impression that a developmental theory is built like a pyramid from its base in infancy, points out that a conception of development instead hangs from its vertex of maturity, the point toward which progress is traced. Thus, a change in the definition of maturity does not simply alter the description of the highest stage but recasts the understanding of development, changing the entire account.

When one begins with the study of women and derives developmental constructs from their lives, the outline of a moral conception different from that described by Freud, Piaget, or Kohlberg begins to emerge and informs a different description of development. In this conception, the moral problem arises from conflicting responsibilities rather than from competing rights and requires for its resolution a mode of thinking that is contextual and narrative rather than formal and abstract. This conception of morality as concerned with the activity of care centers moral development around the understanding of responsibility and relationships, just as the conception of morality as fairness ties moral development to the understanding of rights and rules.

This different construction of the moral problem by women may be seen as the critical reason for their failure to develop within the constraints of Kohlberg's system. Regarding all constructions of responsibility as evidence of a conventional moral understanding, Kohlberg defines the highest stages of moral development as deriving from a reflective understanding of human rights. That the morality of rights differs from the morality of responsibility in its emphasis on separation rather than connection, in its consideration of the individual rather than the relationship as primary, is illustrated by two responses to interview questions about the nature of morality. The first comes from a twenty-five-year-old man, one of the participants in Kohlberg's study:

> [*What does the word morality mean to you?*] Nobody in the world knows the answer. I think it is recognizing the right of the individual, the rights of other individuals, not interfering with those rights. Act as fairly as you would have them treat you. I think it is basically to preserve the human being's right to existence. I think that is the most important. Secondly, the human being's right to do as he pleases, again without interfering with somebody else's rights.
>
> [*How have your views on morality changed since the last interview?*] I think I am more aware of an individual's rights now. I used to be looking at it strictly from my point of view, just for me. Now I think I am more aware of what the individual has a right to.

Kohlberg (1973) cites this man's response as illustrative of the principled conception of human rights that exemplifies his fifth and sixth stages. Commenting on the response, Kohlberg says: "Moving to a perspective outside of that of his society, he identifies morality with justice (fairness, rights, the Golden Rule), with recognition of the rights of others as these are defined naturally or intrinscially. The human's being right to do as he pleases without interfering with somebody else's rights is a formula defining rights prior to social legislation" (pp. 29–30).

The second response comes from a woman who participated in the rights and responsibilities study. She also was twenty-five and, at the time, a third-year law student:

> [*Is there really some correct solution to moral problems, or is everybody's opinion equally right?*] No, I don't think everybody's opinion is equally right. I think that in some situations there may be opinions that are equally valid, and one could conscientiously adopt one of several courses of action. But there are other situations in which I think there are right and wrong answers, that sort of inhere in the nature of existence, of all individuals here who need to live with each other

to live. We need to depend on each other, and hopefully it is not only a physical need but a need of fulfillment in ourselves, that a person's life is enriched by cooperating with other people and striving to live in harmony with everybody else, and to that end, there are right and wrong, there are things which promote that end and that move away from it, and in that way it is possible to choose in certain cases among different courses of action that obviously promote or harm that goal.

[*Is there a time in the past when you would have thought about these things differently?*] Oh, yeah, I think that I went through a time when I thought that things were pretty relative, that I can't tell you what to do and you can't tell me what to do, because you've got your conscience and I've got mine.

[*When was that?*] When I was in high school. I guess that it just sort of dawned on me that my own ideas changed, and because my own judgment changed, I felt I couldn't judge another person's judgment. But now I think even when it is only the person himself who is going to be affected, I say it is wrong to the extent it doesn't cohere with what I know about human nature and what I know about you, and just from what I think is true about the operation of the universe, I could say I think you are making a mistake.

[*What led you to change, do you think?*] Just seeing more of life, just recognizing that there are an awful lot of things that are common among people. There are certain things that you come to learn promote a better life and better relationships and more personal fulfillment than other things that in general tend to do the opposite, and the things that promote these things, you would call morally right.

This response also represents a personal reconstruction of morality following a period of questioning and doubt, but the reconstruction of moral understanding is based not on the primacy and universality of individual rights, but rather on what she describes as a "very strong sense of being responsible to the world." Within this construction, the moral dilemma changes from how to exercise one's rights without interfering with the rights of others to how "to lead a moral life which includes obligations to myself and my family and people in general." The problem then

becomes one of limiting responsibilities without abandoning moral concern. When asked to describe herself, this woman says that she values "having other people that I am tied to, and also having people that I am responsible to. I have a very strong sense of being responsible to the world, that I can't just live for my enjoyment, but just the fact of being in the world gives me an obligation to do what I can to make the world a better place to live in, no matter how small a scale that may be on." Thus while Kohlberg's subject worries about people interfering with each other's rights, this woman worries about "the possibility of omission, of your not helping others when you could help them."

The issue that this woman raises is addressed by Jane Loevinger's fifth "autonomous" stage of ego development, where autonomy, placed in a context of relationships, is defined as modulating an excessive sense of responsibility through the recognition that other people have responsibility for their own destiny. The autonomous stage in Loevinger's account (1970) witnesses a relinquishing of moral dichotomies and their replacement with "a feeling for the complexity and multifaceted character of real people and real situations" (p. 6). Whereas the rights conception of morality that informs Kohlberg's principled level (stages five and six) is geared to arriving at an objectively fair or just resolution to moral dilemmas upon which all rational persons could agree, the responsibility conception focuses instead on the limitations of any particular resolution and describes the conflicts that remain.

Thus it becomes clear why a morality of rights and noninterference may appear frightening to women in its potential justification of indifference and unconcern. At the same time, it becomes clear why, from a male perspective, a morality of responsibility appears inconclusive and diffuse, given its insistent contextual relativism. Women's moral judgments thus elucidate the pattern observed in the description of the developmental differences between the sexes, but they also provide an alternative conception of maturity by which these differences can be assessed and their implications traced. The psychology of women that has consistently been described as distinctive in its greater orientation toward relationships and interdependence implies a more contextual mode of judgment and a different moral understanding. Given the differences in women's conceptions of self and morality, women bring to the life cycle a different point of view and order human experience in terms of different priorities.

The myth of Demeter and Persephone, which McClelland (1975) cites as exemplifying the feminine attitude toward power, was associated with the Eleusinian Mysteries celebrated in ancient Greece for over two thousand years. As told in the Homeric *Hymn to Demeter*, the story of Persephone indicates the strengths of interdependence, building up resources and giving, that McClelland found in his research on power motivation to characterize the mature feminine style. Although, McClelland says, "it is fashionable to conclude that no one knows what went on in the Mysteries, it is known that they were probably the most important religious ceremonies, even partly on the historical record, which were organized by and for women, especially at the onset before men by means of the cult of Dionysos began to take them over." Thus McClelland regards the myth as "a special presentation of feminine psychology" (p. 96). It is, as well, a life-cycle story par excellence.

Persephone, the daughter of Demeter, while playing in a meadow with her girlfriends, sees a beautiful narcissus which she runs to pick. As she does so, the earth opens and she is snatched away by Hades, who takes her to his underworld kingdom. Demeter, goddess of the earth, so mourns the loss of her daughter that she refuses to allow anything to grow. The crops that sustain life on earth shrivel up, killing men and animals alike, until Zeus takes pity on man's suffering and persuades his brother to return Persephone to her mother. But before she leaves, Persephone eats some pomegranate seeds, which ensures that she will spend part of every year with Hades in the underworld.

The elusive mystery of women's development lies in its recognition of the continuing importance of attachment in the human life cycle. Woman's place in man's life cycle is to protect this recognition while the developmental litany intones the celebration of separation, autonomy, individuation, and natural rights. The myth of Persephone speaks directly to the distortion in this view by reminding us that narcissism leads to death, that the fertility of the earth is in some mysterious way tied to the continuation of the mother-daughter relationship, and that the life cycle itself arises from an alternation between the world of women and that of men. Only when life-cycle theorists divide their attention and begin to live with women as they have lived with men will their vision encompass the experience of both sexes and their theories become correspondingly more fertile.

9. From System to Story: An Alternative Pattern for Rationality in Ethics

Stanley Hauerwas with David B. Burrell

Criticizing the impersonal rationality that characterizes the standard accounts of ethics represented by Kant and Mill, Stanley Hauerwas and David Burrell argue that our ethical perspectives are inevitably dependent on our narrative context. As they explain, notions of character and moral vision only take on meaning in particular traditional or communal narratives and that many of our moral disagreements are, at the core, best understood as involving what they call "rival histories of explanation." The convictions and way of life exhibited in the Christian narrative, they argue, have a distinctive and compelling moral significance.

1. Narrative, Ethics and Theology

In the interest of securing a rational foundation for morality, contemporary ethical theory has ignored or rejected the significance of narrative for ethical reflection. It is our contention that this has been a profound mistake resulting in a distorted account of moral experience. Furthermore, the attempt to portray practical reason independent of narrative contexts has made it difficult to assess the value which convictions characteristic of Christians or Jews might have for moral existence. As a result, we have lost sight of the ways these traditions might help us deal with the moral issues raised by modern science and medicine.[1]

We will develop two independent but interrelated theses in order to illustrate and substantiate these claims. First, we will try to establish the significance of narrative for ethical reflection. By the phrase, "the significance of narrative," we mean to call attention to three points:[2] (1) that character and moral notions only take on meaning in a narrative; (2) that narrative and explanation stand in an intimate relationship, and therefore moral disagreements involve rival histories of explanation; and (3) that the standard account of moral objectivity is the obverse of existentialist ethics, since the latter assumes that the failure to secure moral objectivity implies that all moral judgments must be subjective or arbitrary. Ironically, by restricting the

meaning of "rationality" the standard account has unwarrantedly expanded the realm of the irrational. This has led some to the mistaken idea that the only way to be free from the tyranny and manipulative aspect of "reason" is to flee into the "irrational." By showing the way narrative can function as a form of rationality we hope to demonstrate that these represent false alternatives.

Second, we will try to show how the convictions displayed in the Christian story have moral significance. We will call particular attention to the manner in which story teaches us to know and do what is right under definite conditions. For at least one indication of the moral truthfulness of a particular narrative is the way it enables us to recognize the limits of our engagements and yet continue to pursue them.

2. The Standard Account of Moral Rationality

At least partly under the inspiration of the scientific ideal of objectivity,[3] contemporary ethical theory has tried to secure for moral judgments an objectivity that would free such judgments from the subjective beliefs, wants and stories of the agent who makes them. Just as science tries to insure objectivity by adhering to an explicitly disinterested method, so ethical theory tried to show that moral judgments, insofar as they can be considered true, must be the result of an impersonal rationality. Thus moral judgments, whatever else they may involve, must at least be nonegoistic in the sense that they involve no special pleading from the agent's particular history, community identification or otherwise particular point of view to establish their truthfulness.

Thus the hallmark of contemporary ethical theory, whether in a Kantian or utilitarian mode, has been to free moral behavior from the arbitrary and contingent nature of the agent's beliefs, dispositions and character. Just as science strives to free the experiment from the experimenter, so ethically, if we are to avoid unchecked subjectivism or relativism, it is thought that the moral life must be freed from the peculiarities of agents caught in the limits of their particular histories. Ethical rationality assumes it must take the form of science if it is to have any claim to being objective.[4]

There is an interesting parallel to this development in modern medical theory. Eric Cassell has located a tension between the explanation of a disease proper to science and the diagnosis a clinician makes for a particular patient.[5] The latter is well-described by Tolstoy in *War and Peace:*

> Doctors came to see Natasha, both separately and in consultation. They said a great deal in French, in German, and in Latin. They criticised one another, and prescribed the most diverse remedies for all the diseases they were familiar with. But it never occurred to one of them to make the simple reflection that they could not understand the disease from which Natasha was suffering, as no single disease can be fully understood in a living person; for every living person has his complaints unknown to medicine— not a disease of the lungs, of the kidneys, of the skin, of the heart, and so on, as described in medical books, but a disease that consists of one out of the innumerable combinations of ailments of those organs.[6]

The scientific form of rationality is represented by B. F. Skinner's commentary on this quote. Skinner suggests that Tolstoy was justified in calling every sickness a unique event during his day, but uniqueness no longer stands in the way of the development of the science of medicine since we can now supply the necessary general principles of explanation. Thus happily, according to Skinner, "the intuitive wisdom of the old-style diagnostician has been largely replaced by the analytic procedures of the clinic, just as a scientific analysis of behavior will eventually replace the personal interpretation of unique instances."[7]

Even if we were competent to do so, it would not be relevant to our argument to try to determine whether Tolstoy or Skinner, or some combination of both, describes the kind of explanation most appropriate to medical diagnosis (though our hunch lies with Tolstoy). Rather it is our contention that the tendency of modern ethical theory to find a functional equivalent to Skinner's "scientific analysis" has distorted the nature of practical reason. Ethical objectivity cannot be secured by retreating from narrative, but only by being anchored in those narratives that best direct us toward the good.

Many have tried to free the objectivity of moral reason from narrative by arguing that there are basic moral principles, procedures or points of view to which a person is logically or conceptually committed when engaged in moral action or judgment. This logical feature has been associated with such titles as the categorical imperative, the ideal observer, universalizability or more recently, the original position. Each of these in its own way assumes that reasons, if they are to be morally justified, must take the form of judgments that can and must be made from anyone's point of view.[8] All of the views assume that "objectivity" will be attained in the moral life only by freeing moral judgments from the "subjective" story of the agent.

This tradition has been criticized for the formal nature of its account of moral rationality, i.e., it seems to secure the objectivity of moral judgment exactly by vacating the moral life of all substantive content. Such criticism fails to appreciate, however, that these accounts of moral rationality are attempts to secure a "thin" theory of the moral life in order to provide an account of moral duty that is not subject to any community or tradition. Such theories are not meant to tell us how to be good in relation to some ideal, but rather to insure that what we owe to others as strangers, not as friends or sharers in a tradition, is nonarbitrary.

What I am morally obligated to do is not what derives from being a father, or a son, or an American, or a teacher, or a doctor, or a Christian, but what follows from my being a person constituted by reason. To be sure all these other roles or relations may involve behavior that is good to do, but such behavior cannot be required except as it can be based upon or construed as appropriate to rationality itself. This is usually done by translating such role-dependent obligations as relations of promise-keeping that are universalizable. (Of course, what cannot be given are any moral reasons why I should become a husband, father, teacher, doctor or Christian in the first place.)

It is our contention, however, that the standard account of moral rationality distorts the nature of the moral life by: (1) placing an unwarranted emphasis on particular decisions or quandaries; (2) by failing to account for the significance of moral notions and how they work to provide us skills of perception; and (3) by separating the agent from his interests. We will briefly spell out each of these criticisms and suggest how each stems in part from the way standard accounts avoid acknowledging the narrative character of moral existence.

2.1 Decisions, Character and Narrative

In his article, "Quandary Ethics," Edmund Pincoffs has called attention to the way contemporary ethics concentrates on problems—situations in which it is hard to know what to do—as paradigmatic concerns for moral analysis.[9] On such a model, ethics becomes a decision procedure for resolving conflict-of-choice situations. This model assumes that no one faces an ethical issue until they find themselves in a quandary: should I or should I not have an abortion, etc. Thus the moral life appears to be concerned primarily with "hard decisions."

This picture of the moral life is not accidental, given the standard account of moral rationality. For the assumption that most of our moral concerns are "problems" suggests that ethics can be construed as a rational science that evaluates alternative "solutions." Moral decisions should be based on rationally derived principles that are not relative to any one set of convictions. Ethics becomes a branch of decision theory. Like many of the so-called policy sciences, ethics becomes committed to those descriptions of the moral life that will prove relevant to its mode of analysis, that is, one which sees the moral life consisting of dilemmas open to rational "solutions."

By concentrating on "decisions" about "problems," this kind of ethical analysis gives the impression that judgments can be justified apart from the agent who finds himself or herself in the situation. What matters is not that David Burrell or Stanley Hauerwas confronts a certain quandary, but that anyone may or can confront X or Y. The only intentions or reasons for our behavior that are morally interesting are those that anyone might have. So in considering the question of abortion, questions like Why did the pregnancy occur? What kind of community do you live in? What do you believe about the place of children? may be psychologically interesting but cannot be allowed to enter into the justification of the decision. For such matters are

bound to vary from one agent to another. The "personal" can only be morally significant to the extent that it can be translated into the "impersonal."

(Though it is not central to our case, one of the implications of the standard account of rationality is its conservative force. Ethical choice is always making do in the societal framework we inherit, because it is only in such a framework that we are able to have a problem at all. But often the precise problem at issue cannot arise or be articulated given the limits of our society or culture. We suspect that this ineptness betrays a commitment of contemporary ethical theory to political liberalism: one can concentrate on the justification of moral decisions because one accepts the surrounding social order with its moral categories. In this sense modern ethical theory is functionally like modern pluralist democratic theory: it can afford to be concerned with incremental social change, to celebrate "issue" politics, because it assumes the underlying social structures are just.)[10]

By restricting rationality to choices between alternative courses of action, the various normative theories formed in accordance with the standard account have difficulty explaining the moral necessity to choose between lesser evils.[11] Since rational choice is also our moral duty, it must also be a good duty. Otherwise one would be obliged rationally to do what is morally a lesser evil. There is no place for moral tragedy; whatever is morally obligatory must be good, even though the consequences may be less than happy. We may subjectively regret what we had to do, but it cannot be a moral regret. The fact that modern deontological and teleological theories assume that the lesser evil cannot be a moral duty witnesses to their common commitment to the standard view of moral rationality.

The problem of the lesser evil usually refers to tragic choices externally imposed, e.g., the necessity of killing civilians in order to halt the manufacture of weapons. Yet the language of "necessity" is often misleading, for part of the "necessity" is the character of the actors, whether they be individuals or nations. Because moral philosophy under the influence of the standard account has thought it impossible to discuss what kind of character we should have—that, after all, is the result of the accident of birth and psychological conditioning—it has been assumed that moral deliberation must accept the limits of the decision required by his or her character. At best, "character" can be discussed in terms of "moral education"; but since the "moral" in education is determined by the standard account, it does not get us very far in addressing what kind of people we ought to be.

As a result, the standard account simply ignores the fact that most of the convictions that charge us morally are like the air we breathe—we never notice them. We never notice them precisely because they form us not to describe the world in certain ways and not to make certain matters subject to decision. Thus we assume that it is wrong to kill children without good reason. Or even more strongly we assume that it is our duty to provide children (and others who cannot protect themselves) with care that we do not need to give to the stranger. These are not matters that we need to articulate or decide about; their force lies rather in their not being subject to decision. And morally we must have the kind of character that keeps us from subjecting them to decision.

(What makes "medical ethics" so difficult is the penchant of medical care to force decisions that seem to call into question aspects of our life that we assumed not to be matters of decision, e.g., should we provide medical care for children who are born with major disabilities such as meningomyelocele.[12] In this respect, the current interest in "medical ethics" does not simply represent a response to issues arising in modern medicine, but also reflects the penchant of the standard account to respond to dilemmas.)

Another way to make this point is that the standard account, by concentrating on decision, fails to deal adequately with the formation of a moral self, i.e., the virtues and character we think it important for moral agents to acquire. But the kind of decisions we confront, indeed the very way we describe a situation, is a function of the kind of character we have. And character is not acquired through decisions, though it may be confirmed and qualified there; rather, it is acquired through the beliefs and dispositions we have come to possess.

But from the perspective of the standard account, beliefs and dispositions cannot be subject to rational deliberation and formation.[13] Positions based on the standard account do not claim that our dispositions, or our character, are irrelevant to how we act morally. But these aspects of our self are rational only as they enter into a moral decision. It is our contention, however, that it is character, inasmuch as it is displayed by a narrative, that provides the context necessary to pose the terms of a decision, or to determine whether a decision should be made at all.[14]

We cannot account for our moral life solely by the decisions we make; we also need the narrative that

forms us to have one kind of character rather than another. These narratives are not arbitrarily acquired, although they will embody many factors we might consider "contingent." As our stories, however, they will determine what kind of moral considerations—that is, what reasons—will count at all. Hence these narratives must be included in any account of moral rationality that does not unwarrantedly exclude large aspects of our moral existence, i.e., moral character.[15]

The standard account cannot help but view a narrative account as a retreat from moral objectivity. For if the individual agent's intentions and motives—in short, the narrative embodied in his or her character—are to have systematic significance for moral judgment, then it seems that we will have to give preference to the agent's interpretation of what he has done. So the dreaded first person singular, which the standard account was meant to purge from moral argument, would be reintroduced. To recall the force of 'I', however, does not imply that we would propose "because I want to" as a moral reason. The fact is that the first person singular is seldom the assertion of the solitary 'I,' but rather the narrative of that I. It is exactly the category of narrative that helps us to see that we are not forced to choose between some universal standpoint and the subjectivistic appeals to our own experience. For our experiences always come in the form of narratives that can be checked against themselves as well as against others' experiences. I cannot make my behavior mean anything I want it to mean, for I have learned to understand my life from the stories I have learned from others.

The language the agent uses to describe his behavior, to himself and to others, is not uniquely his; it is *ours*, just as the notions we use have meanings that can be checked for appropriate or inappropriate use. But what allows us to check the truthfulness of these accounts of our behavior are the narratives in which our moral notions gain their paradigm uses. An agent cannot make his behavior mean anything he wants, since at the very least it must make sense within his own story, as well as be compatible with the narrative embodied in the language he uses. All our notions are narrative-dependent, including the notion of rationality.

2.2 Moral Notions, Language and Narrative

We can show how our very notion of rationality depends on narrative by noting how the standard account tends to ignore the significance and meaning of moral notions. For the standard account pictures our world as a *given* about which we need to make decisions. So terms like 'murder', 'stealing', 'abortion', although admitted to be evaluative, are nonetheless regarded as descriptive. However, as Julius Kovesi has persuasively argued, our moral notions are not descriptive in the sense that 'yellow' is, but rather describe only as we have purposes for such descriptions.[16] Moral notions, in other words, like many of our non-moral notions (though we are not nearly so sure as the standard account how this distinction should be made) do not merely describe our activity; they also form it. Marx's claim that the point of philosophy should be not to analyze the world but to change it, is not only a directive to ethicists but also an astute observation about the way our grammar displays the moral direction of our lives. For the notions that form our moral perceptions involve skills that require narratives, that is, accounts of their institutional contexts and purposes, which we must know if we are to know how to employ them correctly. In other words, these notions are more like skills of perception which we must learn how to use properly.

The standard account's attempt to separate our moral notions from their narrative context, by trying to ground or derive their meaning from rationality in itself, has made it difficult to explain why moral controversies are so irresolvable. The standard account, for example, encourages us to assume that the pro- and anti-abortion advocates mean the same thing by the word 'abortion'. So it is assumed that the moral disagreement between these two sides must involve a basic moral principle such as "all life is sacred," or be a matter of fact such as whether the fetus is considered a human life. But this kind of analysis fails to see that the issue is not one of principle or fact, but one of perception determined by a history of interpretation.

Pro- and anti-abortion advocates do not communicate on the notion "abortion," since each group holds a different story about the purpose of the notion. At least so far as "abortion" is concerned, they live in conceptually different worlds. This fact does not prohibit discussion. But if it takes place, it cannot begin with the simple question of whether abortion is right or wrong. It is rather more like an argument between a member of the PLO and an Israeli about whether an attack on a village is unjustified terrorism. They both know the same "facts" but the issue turns on the story each holds, and within which those "facts" are known.

The advocates of the standard account try to train us to ignore the dependence of the meaning and use of notions on their narrative contexts, by providing a normative theory for the derivation and justification of basic moral notions. But to be narrative-dependent is not the same as being theory-dependent, at least in the way that a utilitarian or deontological position would have us think. What makes abortion right or wrong is not its capacity to work for or against the greatest good of the greatest number in a certain subclass. What sets the context for one's moral judgment is rather the stories we hold about the place of children in our lives, or the connection one deems ought or ought not to hold between sexuality and procreation, or some other such account. Deontological or utilitarian theories that try to free moral notions from their dependence on examples and the narratives that display them prove to be too monochromatic to account for the variety of our notions and the histories on which they are dependent.

There can be no normative theory of the moral life that is sufficient to capture the rich texture of the many moral notions we inherit. What we actually possess are various and sometimes conflicting stories that provide us with the skills to use certain moral notions. What we need to develop is the reflective capacity to analyze those stories, so that we better understand how they function. It is not theory-building that develops such a capacity so much as close attention to the ways our distinctive communities tell their stories. Furthermore, an analysis of this sort carries us to the point of assessing the worth these moral notions have for directing our life projects and shaping our stories.

The standard account's project to supply a theory of basic moral principles from which all other principles and actions can be justified or derived represents an attempt to make the moral life take on the characteristics of a system. But it is profoundly misleading to think that a rational explanation needs to be given for holding rational beliefs,[17] for to attempt to provide such an account assumes that rationality itself does not depend on narrative. What must be faced, however, is that our lives are not and cannot be subject to such an account, for the consistency necessary for governing our lives is more a matter of integrity than one of principle. The narratives that provide the pattern of integrity cannot be based on principle, nor are they engaging ways of talking about principles. Rather, such narratives are the ones which allow us to determine how our behavior "fits" within our ongoing pattern.[18] To be sure, fittingness cannot have the necessitating form desired by those who want the moral life to have the "firmness" of some sciences, but it can exhibit the rationality of a good story.

2.3 Rationality, Alienation and the Self

The standard account also has the distressing effect of making alienation the central moral virtue. We are moral exactly to the extent that we learn to view our desires, interests and passions as if they could belong to anyone. The moral point of view, whether it is construed in a deontological or teleological manner, requires that we view our own projects and life as if we were outside observers. This can perhaps be seen most vividly in utilitarianism (and interestingly in Rawls' account of the original position) as the utilitarian invites us to assume that perspective toward our projects which will produce the best consequences for anyone's life plan. So the standard account obligates us to regard our life as an observer would.

But paradoxically, what makes our projects valuable to us (as Bernard Williams has argued) is that they are ours. As soon as we take the perspective of the standard account we accept the odd position of viewing our stories as if they were anyone's or at least capable of being lived out by anyone. Thus we are required to alienate ourselves from the projects that make us interested in being anything at all.

The alienation involved in the standard account manifests itself in the different ways the self is understood by modern ethical theory. The self is often pictured as consisting of reason and desire, with the primary function of reason being to control desire. It is further assumed that desire or passion can give no clues to the nature of the good, for the good can only be determined in accordance with "reason." Thus the standard account places us in the odd position of excluding pleasure as an integral aspect of doing the good. The good cannot be the satisfaction of desire, since the morality of reason requires a sharp distinction between universal rules of conduct and the "contingent" appetites of individuals.

Not only are we taught to view our desires in contrast to our reason, but the standard account also separates our present from our past. Morally, the self represents a collection of discontinuous decisions bound together only in the measure they approximate the moral point of view. Our moral capacity thus depends exactly on our ability to view our past in discontinuity with our present. The past is a limit, as it can only prevent us from embodying more fully the new opportunities always guaranteed by the moral point of view. Thus our moral potentiality depends on our being able to alienate ourselves from our past in order to grasp the timelessness of the rationality offered by the standard account.[19]

(In theological terms the alienation of the self is a necessary consequence of sinful pretensions. When the self tries to be more than it was meant to be, it becomes alienated from itself and all its relations are disordered. The view of rationality offered by the standard account is pretentious exactly as it encourages us to try to free ourselves from history. In effect, it offers us the possibility of being like God. Ironically enough, however, this is not the God of the Jews and the Christians since, as we shall see, that God does not will himself to be free from history.)

In fairness, the alienation recommended by the standard account is motivated by the interest of securing moral truthfulness. But it mistakenly assumes that truthfulness is possible only if we judge ourselves and others from the position of complete (or as complete as possible) disinterest. Even if it were possible to assume such a stance, however, it would not provide us with the conditions for truthfulness. For morally there is no neutral story that insures the truthfulness of our particular stories. Moreover, any ethical theory that is sufficiently abstract and universal to claim neutrality would not be able to form character. For it would have deprived itself of the notions and convictions which are the necessary conditions for character. Far from assuring truthfulness, a species of rationality which prizes objectivity to the neglect of particular stories distorts moral reasoning by the way it omits the stories of character formation. If truthfulness (and the self-lessness characteristic of moral behavior) is to be found, it will have to occur in and through the stories that tie the contingencies of our life together.

It is not our intention to call into question the significance of disinterestedness for the moral life, but rather to deny that recent accounts of "universality" or the "moral point of view" provide adequate basis for such disinterest. For genuine disinterest reflects a noninterest in the self occasioned by the lure of a greater good or a more beautiful object than we can create or will into existence.[20] In this sense we are not able to choose to conform to the moral point of view, for it is a gift. But as a gift it depends on our self being formed by a narrative that provides the conditions for developing the disinterest required for moral behavior.

2.4 The Standard Account's Story

None of the criticisms above constitutes a decisive objection to the standard account, but taken together they indicate that the standard account is seriously inadequate as a description of our moral existence.

How then are we to account for the continued dominance of the standard account for contemporary ethical theory? If our analysis has been right, the explanation should be found in the narrative that provides an apparent cogency for the standard account in spite of its internal and external difficulties.[21]

But it is difficult to identify any one narrative that sets the context for the standard account. For it is not one but many narratives that sustain its plausibility. The form of some of these stories is of recent origin, but we suspect that the basic story underlying the standard account is of more ancient lineage, namely, humankind's quest for certainty in a world of contingency.

It seems inappropriate to attribute such a grand story to the standard account, since one of its attractions is its humility; it does not pretend to address matters of the human condition, for it is only a method. As a method it does not promise truth, only clarity.

Yet the process of acculturating ourselves and others in the use of this method requires a systematic disparaging of narrative. For by teaching us to prefer a "principle" or a "rational" description (just as science prefers a statistical description) to a narrative description, the standard account not only fails to account for the significance of narrative but also sets obstacles to any therapy designed to bring that tendency to light. It thus fails to provide us with the critical skills to know the limits of the narrative which currently has us in its grasp.

The reason for this lack of critical perspective lies in the narrative born of the Enlightenment. The plot was given in capsule by Auguste Comte: first came religion in the form of stories, then philosophy in the form of metaphysical analysis, and then science with its exact methods.[22] The story he tells in outline is set within another elaborated by Hegel, to show us how each of these ages supplanted the other as a refinement in the progressive development of reason. So stories are prescientific, according to the story legitimizing the age which calls itself scientific. Yet if one overlooks that budding contradiction, or fails to spell it out because everyone knows that stories are out of favor anyway, then the subterfuge has been worked and the exit blocked off.

Henceforth, any careful or respectable analysis, especially if it is moral in intent, will strike directly for the problem, leaving the rest for journalists who titillate or novelists who entertain. Serious folk, intent on improving the human condition, will have no time for that (except maybe after hours), for they must focus all available talent and resources on solving the problems in front of them. We all recognize the crude polarities

acting here, and know how effectively they function as blinders. It is sufficient for our interests to call attention only to the capacity stories hold for eliciting critical awareness, and how an awareness of story enhances that approach known as scientific by awakening it to its presuppositions. Hence, we have argued for a renewed awareness of stories as an analytic tool, and one especially adopted to our moral existence, since stories are designed to effect critical awareness as well as describe a state of affairs.

By calling attention to the narrative context of the standard account, we are not proposing a wholesale rejection of that account or of the theories formed under its inspiration. In fact, the efforts expended on developing contrasting ethical theories (like utilitarianism or formalism) have become part of our legacy, and offer a useful way to introduce one to ethical reasoning. Furthermore, the manner of proceeding which we associate with the standard account embodies concerns which any substantive moral narrative must respect: a high regard for public discourse, the demand that we be able to offer reasons for acting at once cogent and appropriate, and a way to develop critical skills of discrimination and judgment. Finally, any morality depends on a capacity to generate and to articulate moral principles that can set boundaries for proper behavior and guide our conduct.

Our emphasis on narrative need not militate against any of these distinctive concerns. Our difficulty rather lies with the way the standard account attempts to express and to ground these concerns in a manner of accounting which is narrative-free. So we are given the impression that moral principles offer the actual ground for conduct, while in fact they present abstractions whose significance continues to depend on original narrative contexts. Abstractions play useful roles in reasoning, but a continual failure to identify them as abstractions becomes systematically misleading: a concern for rationality thereby degenerates into a form of rationalism.

Our criticism of the standard account has focused on the anomalies which result from that rationalism. We have tried to show how the hegemony of the standard account in ethics has in fact ignored or distorted significant aspects of moral experience. We do not wish to gainsay the importance of rationality for ethics; only to expose a pretentious form of rationalism. Though the point can be made in different ways, it is no accident that the stories which form the lives of Jews and Christians make them peculiarly sensitive to any account which demands that human existence fit a rational framework. The legitimate human concern for rationality is framed by a range of powers of quite another order. It is this larger contingent context which narrative is designed to order in the only manner available to us.

In this way, we offer a substantive explication of narrative as a constructive alternative to the standard account. Our penchant has been to rely upon the standard account as though it were the only lifeboat in a sea of subjective reactions and reductive explanations. To question it would be tantamount to exposing the leaks in the only bark remaining to us. In harkening to the narrative context for action, we are trying to direct attention to an alternative boat available to us. This one cannot provide the security promised by the other, but in return it contains instructions designed to equip us with the skills required to negotiate the dangers of the open sea.

3. *Stories and Reasons for Acting*

Ethics deals explicitly with reasons for acting. The trick lies in turning reasons into a form proper to acting. The normal form for reasoning requires propositions to be linked so as to display how the conclusion follows quite naturally. The very skills which allow us to form statements lead us to draw other statements from them as conclusions. The same Aristotle who perfected this art, however, also reminded us that practical syllogisms must conclude in an action rather than another proposition.[23] As syllogisms, they will display the form proper to reasoning, yet they must do so in a way that issues in action.

This difference reflects the fact that practical wisdom cannot claim to be a science, since it must deal with particular courses of action (rather than recurrent patterns); nor can it call itself an art, since "action and making are different kinds of thing." The alternative Aristotle settles for is "a true and reasoned . . . capacity to act with regard to the things that are good or bad for man" (*N. Ethics*, 1140b5). We have suggested that stories in fact help us all to develop that capacity as a reasoned capacity. This section will focus on the narrative form as a form of rationality; the following section will show how the act of discriminating among stories develops skills for judging truly what is "good or bad for man." Using Aristotle's discriminations as a point of reference is meant to indicate that our thesis could be regarded as a development of his; in fact, we would be pleased to find it judged to be so.

(Our argument put in traditional terms is that the moral life must be grounded in the "nature" of man. However, that "nature" is not "rationality" itself, but the necessity of having a narrative to give our life coherence. The truthfulness of our moral life cannot be secured by claims of "rationality" in itself but rather by the narrative that forms our need to recognize the many claims on our lives without trying to subject them to a false unity of coherence.)

3.1 *Narrative Form as Rational Discourse*

There are many kinds of stories, and little agreement on how to separate them into kinds. We distinguish short stories from novels, while acknowledging the short novel as well. We recognize that some stories offer with a particular lucidity patterns or plots which recur in countless other stories. We call these more archetypal stories "myths," and often use them as a shorthand for referring to a typical tangle or dilemma which persons find themselves facing, whether in a story or in real life. That feature common to all stories which gives them their peculiar aptitude for illuminating real-life situations is their narrative structure.

Experts will want to anatomize narrative as well, of course, but for our purposes let it be the connected description of action and of suffering which moves to a point. The point need not be detachable from the narrative itself; in fact, we think a story better that does not issue in a determinate *moral*. The "point" we call attention to here has to do with that form of connectedness which characterizes a novel. It is not the mere material connection of happenings to one individual, but the connected unfolding that we call *plot*. Difficult as this is to characterize—independently of displaying it in a good story!—we can nonetheless identify it as a connection among elements (actions, events, situations) which is neither one of logical consequence nor one of mere sequence. The connection seems rather designed to move our understanding of a situation forward by developing or unfolding it. We have described this movement as gathering to a point. Like implication, it seeks to make explicit what would otherwise remain implicit; unlike implication, the rules of development are not those of logic but stem from some more mysterious source.

The rules of development are not logical rules because narrative connects contingent events. The intelligibility which plot affords is not a necessary one, because the events connected do not exhibit recurrent patterns. Narrative is not required to be explanatory, then, in the sense in which a scientific theory must show necessary connections among occurrences. What we demand of a narrative is that it display how occurrences are actions. Intentional behavior is purposeful but not necessary. We are not possessed of the theoretical capacities to predict what will happen on the basis of what has occurred. Thus a narrative moves us on to answer the question that dogs us: what happened next? It cannot answer that question by arbitrary statement, for our inquiring minds are already involved in the process. Yet the question is a genuine one precisely because we lack the capacity for sure prediction.

It is the intentional nature of human action which evokes a narrative account. We act for an end, yet our actions affect a field of forces in ways that may be characteristic yet remain unpredictable. So we can ask, What would follow from our hiring Jones?, as though certain events might be deduced from his coming on board. Yet we also know that whatever follows will not do so deductively, but rather as a plot unfolds. Nevertheless, we are right in inquiring into what might *follow from* our hiring him, since we must act responsibly. By structuring a plausible response to the question, And what happened next?, narrative offers just the intelligibility we need for acting properly.

3.2 *What the Narrative Unfolds*

But what makes a narrative plausible? The field of a story is actions (either deeds or dreams) or their opposite, sufferings. In either case, what action or passion is seen to unfold is something we call "character." *Character*, of course, is not a theoretical notion, but merely the name we give to the cumulative source of human actions. Stories themselves attempt to probe that source and discover its inner structure by trying to display how human actions and passions connect with one another to develop a character. As we follow the story, we gain some insight into recurrent connecting patterns, and also some ability to assess them. We learn to recognize different configurations and to rank some characters better than others.

Gradually, then, the characters (or ways of unifying actions) that we can recognize offer patterns for predicting recurring ways of acting. Expectations are set up, and the way an individual or others deal with those expectations shows us some of the capacities of the human spirit. In this way, character can assume the role of an analytic tool even though it is not itself an explanatory notion. Character is neither explanatory in origin nor in use, for it cannot be formulated prior to

nor independently of the narrative which develops it. Yet it can play an illuminating or analytic role by calling attention to what is going on in a narrative as the plot unfolds: a character is being developed. Moreover, this character, as it develops, serves as a relative baseline for further developing itself or other characters, as we measure subsequent actions and responses against those anticipated by the character already developed. In this way, character plays an analytic role by offering a baseline for further development. That the baseline itself will shift represents one more way of distinguishing narrative development from logical implication.

We may consider the set of expectations associated with a developing character as a "language," a systematic set of connections between actions which offers a setting or syntax for subsequent responses. Since character cannot be presented independently of the story or stories that develop it, however, the connection between a syntactical system and use, or the way in which a language embodies a form of life, becomes crystal clear. By attending to character, stories will display this fact to us without any need for philosophical reminders.

Similarly, we will see how actions, like expressions, accomplish what they do as part of a traditional repertoire. What a narrative must do is to set out the antecedent actions in such a way as to clarify how the resulting pattern becomes a tradition. In this way, we will see why certain actions prove effective and others fail, much as some expressions succeed in saying what they mean while others cannot. Some forms of story, like the three-generation Victorian novel, are expressly designed to display how a grammar for actions develops, by adopting a deliberately historical (even explicitly generational) structure. Lawrence's *Rainbow,* for example, shows how the shaping habits of speech and personal interaction are altered over three generations in response to industrial development. As he skilfully displays this alteration in grammar over against a traditional syntax, we can grasp something of the capacities latent in us as human beings. In articulating the characters, Lawrence succeeds in making explicit some reaches of the human spirit as yet unexplored.

Stories, then, certainly offer more than entertainment. What they do offer, however, cannot be formulated independently of our appreciating the story, so seeking entertainment is less distracting than looking for a moral. The reason lies with the narrative structure, whose plot cannot be abstracted without banality, yet whose unity does depend on its having a point. Hence it is appropriate to speak of a plot, to call attention to the ordering peculiar to narrative. It is that ordering, that capacity to unfold or develop character, and thus offer insight into the human conditions, which recommends narrative as a form of rationality especially appropriate to ethics.

3.3 How a Narrative Unfolds

If a narrative becomes plausible as it succeeds in displaying a believable character, we may still ask how *that* achievement offers us an intelligibility appropriate to discriminating among courses of action. Using Aristotle's language, how can stories assist in the formation of a practical wisdom? How can stories themselves develop a capacity for judging among alternatives? And further, how does discriminating among stories make that capacity even keener? Since reading stories for more than mere entertainment is usually described as "appreciating" them, some skills for assessing among them are already implied in one's appreciating any single story.

We often find ourselves quite unable, however, to specify the grounds for preferring one story to another. Critics, of course, develop a language for doing this, trying to formulate our normally inchoate criteria. Yet these criteria themselves are notoriously ambiguous. They must be rendered in utterly analogous terms, like 'unity', 'wholeness', 'consistency', 'integrity', etc. So we cannot hope to grasp the criteria without a paradigm instance, yet how present an exemplary instance without telling a story?[24] So criticism can only conceive itself as disciplining our native capacity to appreciate a good story.

A complete account of the way narrative functions, then, would be a narrative recounting how one came to judge certain stories better than others. Since this narrative would have to be autobiographical, we would have a vantage for judgment beyond the intrinsic merit of the narrative itself, in the perceived character of its author. If stories are designed to display how one might create and relate to a world and so offer us a paradigm for adopting a similar posture, this autobiographical story would have to show how a person's current manner of relating himself to the world itself represents a posture towards alternative stances. The narrative will have to recount why—and do so in the fashion proper to narrative—one stance comes after another, preferably by improving upon it.[25]

Augustine's *Confessions* offer just such an account by showing how Augustine's many relationships, all patterned on available stories, were gradually relativized to one overriding and ordering relationship

with God revealing himself in Jesus. Augustine's life story is the story of that process of ordering.

3.4 Augustine's Confessions: A Narrative Assessment of Life Stories

Writing ten years after the decisive moment in the garden, Augustine sees that event as culminating a quest shaped by two questions: How to account for evil? How to conceive of God? That quest was also dogged by demands much more immediate than questions, of course. These needs were symbolically ordered in the experience recounted in Book 9, and monitored sense by sense, passion by passion, in Book 10. What interests us here, however, is the step-wise manner in which Augustine relates himself relating to the shaping questions: How explain evil? How conceive divinity?

The pear-tree story allows him to telegraph to the reader how he was able to discriminate one question from the other early on, even though the skills developed to respond to one would help him meet the other. For his own action, reflected upon, allowed him to glimpse an evil deed as wanton or pointless (2.4–10). From the perspective displayed by the *Confessions,* he formulates clearly an intimation which guided his earlier quest: what makes an action evil is not so much a reason as the lack of one. So we would be misled to attribute evil to the creator who orders all things, since ordering and giving reasons belong together.

By separating in this way the query into the source of evil from the attempt to conceive divinity, Augustine took a categorical step. That is, he was learning how to slip from the grip in which Manichean teaching held him, as he came to realize that nothing could properly explain the presence of evil in the world. Nothing, that is, short of a quality of human freedom which allowed us to act for no reason at all. Since explanations offer reasons, and evil turns on the lack of reasons, some form other than a causal explanation must be called for. The only form which can exhibit an action without pretending to explain it is the very one he adopted for the book itself: narrative. So Augustine took his first decisive step towards responding to the shaping questions by eschewing the pretense of explanation in favor of a reflective story.

Categorical discriminations are not usually made all at once, of course, If we are set to turn up an explanation, we will ordinarily keep trying to find a satisfactory one. We cannot give up the enterprise of looking for an explanation unless our very horizon shifts. (It is just such a horizon shift or paradigm change which we identify as a categorical discrimination.) Yet horizons form the stable background for inquiry, so normally we cannot allow them to shift. In Augustine's case, as in many, it only occurred to him to seek elsewhere after repeated attempts at explaining proved fruitless. Furthermore, the specific way in which the Manichean scheme failed to explain the presence of evil also suggested why seeking an explanation was itself a fruitless tack.

To be sure, the Manichean accounts to which Augustine alludes strike us as altogether too crude to qualify as explanations. In fact, it sounds odd to identify his rejection of Manichean teachings with the explicit adoption of a story-form, since it is their schemes which sound to us like "stories." The confusion is understandable enough, of course; it is the very one this essay addresses: stories are fanciful, while explanations are what offer intelligibility. Yet fanciful as they appear to us, the Manichean schemes are explanatory in form. They postulate causes for behavior in the form of diverse combinations of "particles" of light or darkness. The nature of the particles is less relevant, of course, than the explanatory pretense.

What first struck Augustine was the scheme's inability to explain diverse kinds of behavior coherently (5.10, 7.1–6). What he came to realize, however, was that *any* explanatory scheme would in principle undermine a person's ability to repent because it would remove whatever capacity we might have for assuming responsibility for our own actions (6.5, 7.12–13, 8.10). This capacity to assume responsibility would not always suffice to accomplish what we (or at least a part of us) desire (8.8–9); but such a capacity is logically necessary if we are to claim our actions as our own—and so receive praise or blame for them. If our contrary actions could be explained by contrary substances within us, then we would not be able to own them. And if we cannot own our actions, then we have no self to speak of. So the incoherence of the explanations offered led Augustine to see how the very quest for explanation itself failed to cohere with the larger life project belonging to every person.

As the narrative of Augustine's own life project displays, this deliberate shift away from the explanatory modes of the Manichees or the astrologers led to adopting a form which would also help him better to conceive divinity. If evil is senseless, we cannot attribute it to the one who creates with order and reason. If we commit evil deeds, we must be able to own up to them, to confess them, if we want to open ourselves to a change of heart. And the more we examine that self

which can act responsibly—in accomplishing deeds or in judging among opinions—the more we come into possession of a language for articulating divinity. It was a language of inwardness, as practiced by the Platonists of his day (7.10). It assumed a scheme of powers of the soul, but made its point by transcendental argument: if we are to make the discriminations we do, we must do so by virtue of an innate light or power (7.17). This way of articulating the power by which we act responsibly, then, becomes the model for expressing divinity. The path which led away from seeking an explanation for evil offers some promise for responding to the second question as well.

Augustine must take one more step, however, lest he forfeit the larger lesson of his struggle with the Manichees, and simply substitute a Platonist explanatory scheme for theirs.[26] They appeal to formal facts by way of transcendental argument. His life, however, was framed by facts of another kind: of rights and wrongs dealt to others (6.15); of an order to which he now aspired to conform, but which he found himself unable to accomplish (8.11). What he misses in the Platonists' book is "the mien of the true love of God. They make no mention of the tears of confession" (7.21). He can read there "of the Word, God . . . but not read in them that 'the Word was made flesh and came to dwell among us' (John 1:14)" (7.9). While they speak persuasively of the conditions for acting and judging aright, they do not tell us how to do what we find ourselves unable to do: to set our hearts aright.

The key to that feat Augustine finds not in the books of the Platonists, but in the gospels. Or better, he finds it in allowing the stories of the gospels to shape his story. The moment of permission, as he records it, is preceded by stories of others allowing the same to happen to them, recounting how they did it and what allowing it to happen did to them. The effect of these stories is to insinuate a shift in grammar tantamount to the shift from explanation to narrative, though quite in line with that earlier shift. Since we think of stories as relating accomplishments, Augustine must use these stories together with his own to show us another way of conceiving them.

It is not a new way, for it consciously imitates the biblical manner of displaying God's great deeds in behalf of his people. Without ceasing to be the story of Israel, the tales of the Bible present the story of God. Similarly, without ceasing to be autobiography, Augustine's *Confessions* offer an account of God's way with him. The language of will and of struggle is replaced by that of the heart: "As I came to the end of the sentence, it was as though the light of confidence flooded into my heart and all the darkness of doubt was dispelled" (8.12). Yet the transformation is not a piece of magic; the narrative testifies to that. And his narrative will give final testimony to the transformation of that moment in the measure that it conforms to the life story of the "Word made flesh," So the answer to his shaping questions is finally received rather than formulated, and that reception is displayed in the narrative we have analyzed.

4. *Truthfulness as Veracity and Faithfulness*

The second step which Augustine relates is not a categorial one. It no longer has to do with finding the proper form for rendering a life project intelligible. The narrative Augustine tells shows us how he was moved to accept the gospel story by allowing it to shape his own. In more conventional terms, this second step moves beyond philosophical therapy to a judgment of truth. That is why recognizable arguments surround the first step, but not this one. Assent involves more subtle movements than clarification— notably assent of this sort, which is not an assent *to* evidence but an assent *of* faith. Yet we will grasp its peculiar warrants better if we see how it moves along the same lines as the categorial discrimination.

Accepting a story as normative by allowing it to shape one's own story in effect reinforces the categorial preference for story over explanation as a vehicle of understanding. Augustine adumbrates the way one step leads into the other towards the beginning of Book 6:

> From now on I began to prefer the Catholic teaching. The Church demanded that certain things should be believed even though they could not be proved. . . . I thought that the Church was entirely honest in this and far less pretentious than the Manichees, who laughed at people who took things on faith, made rash promises of scientific knowledge, and then put forward a whole system of preposterous inventions which they expected their followers to believe on trust because they could not be proved. (6.5)

The chapter continues in a similar vein, echoing many contemporary critiques of modern rationalist pretensions.

4.1 *Criteria for Judging among Stories*

The studied preference for story over explanation, then, moves one into a neighborhood more amenable to what thirteenth-century theologians called an "assent of faith," and in doing so, helps us develop a set of criteria for judging among stories. Books 8, 9, and 10 of the *Confessions* record the ways in which this capacity for discriminating among stories is developed. It is less a matter of weighing arguments than of displaying how adopting different stories will lead us to become different sorts of persons. The test of each story is the sort of person it shapes. When examples of diverse types are offered to us for our acceptance, the choices we make display in turn our own grasp of the *humanum*. Aristotle presumed we could not fail to recognize a just man, but also knew he would come in different guises (*N. Ethics* 1097b6–1098b7).

The criteria for judging among stories, then, will most probably not pass an impartial inspection. For the powers of recognition cannot be divorced from one's own capacity to recognize the good for humankind. This observation need not amount to a counsel of despair, however. It is simply a reminder that on matters of judgment we consult more readily with some persons than others, because we recognize them to be in a better position to weigh matters sensibly. Any account of that "position" would have to be autobiographical, of course. But it is not an account we count on; it is simply our recognition of the person's integrity.

Should we want to characterize the story which gives such coherence to a person's life, however, it would doubtless prove helpful to contrast it with alternatives. The task is a difficult one, however, either for oneself or for another. For we cannot always identify the paths we have taken; Augustine continued to be engaged in mapping out the paths he was actually traversing at the very time of composing the *Confessions* (*vide* Book 10). Yet we can certainly formulate a list of working criteria, provided we realize that any such list cannot pretend to completeness nor achieve unambiguous expression.

Any story which we adopt, or allow to adopt us, will have to display:

1. power to release us from destructure alternatives;
2. ways of seeing through current distortions;
3. room to keep us from having to resort to violence;
4. a sense for the tragic: how meaning transcends power.

It is inaccurate, of course, to list these criteria as features which a story must display. For they envisage rather the effect which stories might be expected to have on those who allow them to shape their lives. The fact that stories are meant to be read, however, forces one to speak of them as relational facts. So we cannot help regarding a story as something which (when well-constructed) will help us develop certain skills of perception and understanding. This perspective corresponds exactly to the primary function of narratives by contrast with explanatory schemes: to relate us to the world, including our plans for modifying it. Those plans have consequences of their own, but their shape as well as their execution depends on the expectations we entertain for planning.

Those expectations become a part of the plans themselves, but they can be articulated independently. And when they are, they take the form of stories, notably of heroes. Thus the process of industrialization becomes the story of tycoons, as the technology we know embodies a myth of man's dominating and transforming the earth. Not that industrial processes are themselves stories, or technological expertise a myth. In fact, we are witnessing today many attempts to turn those processes and that expertise to different ends by yoking them to a different outlook. Stories of these experiments suggest new ways of using some of the skills we have developed, and illustrate the role of narrative in helping us to formulate and to practice new perspectives.[27]

Stories, then, help us, as we hold them, to relate to our world and our destiny: the origins and goals of our lives, as they embody in narrative form specific ways of acting out that relatedness. So in allowing ourselves to adopt and be adopted by a particular story, we are in fact assuming a set of practices which will shape the ways we relate to our world and destiny. Lest this sound too instrumental, we should remind ourselves that the world is not simply waiting to be seen, but that language and institutions train us to regard it in certain ways.[28] The criteria listed above assume this fact; let us consider them in greater detail.

4.2 *Testing the Criteria*

Stories which (2) offer ways to see through current distortions can also (1) empower us to free ourselves from destructive alternatives. For we can learn how to see a current ideology as a distortion by watching what it can do to people who let it shape their story. The seduction of Manichean doctrine for Augustine and his contemporaries lay precisely in its offering itself as a *story* for humankind—much as current problem-solving techniques will invariably also be packaged as a set of practices leading to personal fulfillment. So Augustine's subsequent discrimination between explanation and story first required an accurate identification of Manichean teaching as explanatory pretense in the guise of a story.

To judge an alternative course to be destructive, of course, requires some experience of its effects on those who practice the skills it embodies. It is the precise role of narrative to offer us a way of experiencing those effects without experimenting with our own lives as well. The verisimilitude of the story, along with its assessable literary structure, will allow us to ascertain whether we can trust it as a vehicle of insight, or whether we are being misled. In the absence of narratives, recommendations for adopting a set of practices can only present themselves as a form of propaganda, and be judged accordingly.[29] Only narrative can allow us to take the measure of a scheme for human improvement, granting that we possess the usual skills for discriminating among narratives as well.

The last two criteria also go together: (3) providing room to keep us from having to resort to violence, and (4) offering a sense for the tragic: how meaning transcends power. We can watch these criteria operate if we contrast the story characteristic to Christians and Jews with one of the prevailing presumptions of contemporary culture: that we can count on technique to offer eventual relief from the human condition. This conviction is reflected in the penchant of consequential ethical theories not only to equate doing one's duty with the greatest good for all, but also to presume that meeting our obligations will provide the satisfaction we seek. Surely current medical practice is confirmed by the conviction that harnessing more human energies into preventing and curing disease will increasingly free our lives from tragic dilemmas.[30] Indeed, science as a moral enterprise has provided what Ernest Becker has called an anthropodicy, as it holds out the possibility that our increased knowledge serves human progress toward the creation of a new human ideal, namely, to create a mankind free of suffering.[31]

But this particular ethos has belied the fact that medicine, at least as characterized by its moral commitment to the individual patient, is a tragic profession. For to attend to one in distress often means many others cannot be helped. Or to save a child born retarded may well destroy the child's family and cause unnecessary burdens on society. But the doctor is pledged to care for each patient because medicine does not aim at some ideal moral good, but to care for the needs of the patient whom the doctor finds before him. Because we do not know how to regard medicine as a tragic profession, we tend of course to confuse caring with curing. The story which accompanies technology—of setting nature aright—results in the clinical anomalies to which we are subjecting others and ourselves in order to avoid the limits of our existence.[32]

The practice of medicine under the conditions of finitude offers an intense paradigm of the moral life. For the moral task is to learn to continue to do the right, to care for this immediate patient, even when we have no assurance that it will be the successful thing to do. To live morally, in other words, we need a substantive story that will sustain moral activity in a finite and limited world. Classically, the name we give such stories is tragedy. When a culture loses touch with the tragic, as ours clearly has done, we must redescribe our failures in acceptable terms. Yet to do so *ipso facto* traps us in self-deceiving accounts of what we have done.[33] Thus our stories quickly acquire the characteristics of a policy, especially as they are reinforced by our need to find self-justifying reasons for our new-found necessities.

This tactic becomes especially troublesome as the policy itself assumes the form of a central story that gives our individual and collective lives coherence. This story then becomes indispensable to us, as it provides us with a place to be. Phrases like "current medical practice," "standard hospital policy," or even "professional ethics," embody exemplary stories which guide the way we use the means at hand to care for patients. Since we fail to regard them as stories, however, but must see them as a set of principles, the establishment must set itself to secure them against competing views. If the disadvantaged regard this as a form of institutional violence, they are certainly correct.

Such violence need not take the form of physical coercion, of course. But we can detect it in re-descriptions which countenance coercion. So, for example, an abortion at times may be a morally necessary, but sorrowful, occurrence. But our desire for righteousness quickly invites us to turn what is morally unavoidable into a self-deceiving policy, e.g., the fetus, after all, is just another piece of flesh. It takes no mean skill, certainly, to know how to hold onto a description that acknowledges significant life, while remaining open to judging that it may have to be destroyed. Yet medical practice and human integrity cannot settle for less. Situations like these suggest, however, that we do not

lie because we are evil, but because we wish to be good or preserve what good we already embody.[34]

We do not wish to claim that the stories with which Christians and Jews identify are the only stories that offer skills for truthfulness in the moral life. We only want to identify them as ways to countenance a posture of locating and doing the good which must be done, even if it does not lead to human progress. Rather than encourage us to assume that the moral life can be freed from the tragedies that come from living in a limited and sinful world, these stories demand that we be faithful to God as we believe he has been faithful to us through his covenant with Israel and (for Christians) in the cross of Christ.[35]

4.3 A Canonical Story

Religious faith, on this account, comes to accepting a certain set of stories as canonical. We come to regard them not only as meeting the criteria sketched above, along with others we may develop, but find them offering ways of clarifying and expanding our sense of the criteria themselves. In short, we discover our human self more effectively through these stories, and so use them in judging the adequacy of alternative schemes for humankind.

In this formal sense, one is tempted to wonder whether everyone does not accept a set of stories as canonical. To identify those stories would be to discover the shape one's basic convictions take. To be unable to do so would either mark a factual incapacity or an utterly fragmented self. Current discussion of "polytheism" leads one to ask whether indiscriminate pluralism represents a real psychic possibility for a contemporary person.[36] In our terms, arguing against the need for a canonical story amounts to questioning "why be good?" Just as we do not require ethics to answer that question, so we need not demand a perspicuously canonical story. But we can point to the endemic tendency of men and women to allow certain stories to assume that role, just as ethicists remind us of the assessments we do in fact count on to live our lives.

Endnotes

1. For example, James Gustafson ends his recent Marquette Lecture, "The Contributions of Theology to Medical Ethics," by saying "For most persons involved in medical care and practice, the contribution of theology is likely to be of minimal importance, for the moral principles and values needed

can be justified without reference to God, and the attitudes that religious beliefs ground can be grounded in other ways. From the standpoint of immediate practicality, the contribution of theology is not great, either in its extent or in its importance" (p. 94). While we have no wish to challenge this as a descriptive statement of what pertains today, we think we can show that even though "moral principles can be justified without reference to God," how they are accounted for still makes a difference for the meaning of the principle and how it works to form institutions and ways of life that may have practical importance. To be sure, Christians may have common moral convictions with non-Christians, but it seems unwise to separate a moral conviction from the story that forms its context of interpretation. Moreover, a stance such as Gustafson's would seem to assume that medicine as it is currently formed is the way it ought to be. In this respect, we at least want to leave open the possibility of a more reformist if not radical stance.

2. We wish to thank Professor MacIntyre for helping us clarify these issues. As will be obvious to anyone acquainted with his work, we are deeply influenced by his argument that the "conflict over how morality is to be defined is itself a moral conflict. Different and rival definitions cannot be defended apart from defending different and rival sets of moral principles." "How To Identify Ethical Principles," unpublished paper prepared for the National Commission for the Protection of Human Subjects of Biomedical and Behavioral Research, p. 8.

3. The search for ethical objectivity, of course, is also a response to the social and political diversity of our day. Thus the search for a "foundation" for ethics involves the attempt to secure rational agreement short of violence. The attraction of the ideal of science for ethicists may be due partly to science appearing to be the last form of universal culture we have left. Of course, this strategy comes to grief on the diversity of activity and disciplines that constitute what we generally call science. For example, see Ernest Becker's reflection on this in his *This Structure of Evil* (New York: Braziller, 1968). The desire for "objectivity" in ethics, moreover, is part of the irrepressible human desire to think that what we have done or had to do is the right thing to do. The quest for certainty, both intellectually and morally, is the need to secure our righteousness in an ambiguous world.

4. We do not mean to claim the actual practice of science involves this sense of objectivity. Indeed we are very sympathetic with Toulmin's analysis of science, not as a tight and coherent logical system, but "as a conceptual aggregate, or 'population', within which there are—at most—localized pockets of logical systematicity." *Human Understanding*, (Princeton: Princeton University Press, 1972), p. 128. It is exactly his stress on necessity of understanding the history of the development of a discipline in order to understand its sense of "rationality" that we feel must be recovered in science as well as, though with different significance, in ethics. As he suggests, "In science as much as in ethics the historical

and cultural diversity of our concepts gives rise to intractable problems, only so long as we continue to think of 'rationality' as a character of particular systems of propositions or concepts, rather than in terms of the procedures by which men change from one set of concepts and beliefs to another" (p. 478). Rather, what must be seen is that rationality "is an attribute, not of logical or conceptual systems as such, but of the human activities or enterprises of which particular sets of concepts are the temporary cross-sections" (p. 133).

5. Eric Cassell, "Preliminary Exploration of Thinking in Medicine," *Ethics in Science and Medicine*, 2, 1 (1975), 1–12. MacIntyre and Gorovitz's "Toward a Theory of Medical Error" also obviously bears on this issue. See it in H. T. Englehardt and D. Callahan (eds.), *Science, Ethics and Medicine*, (Hastings-on-Hudson: Hastings Center Publication, 1976).

6. Quoted by B. F. Skinner in *Science and Human Behavior* (New York: Macmillan, 1953), pp. 18–19. Eric Cassell's, "Illness and Disease," *Hastings Center Report*, 6, 2 (April, 1976). 27–37, is extremely interesting in this respect. It is his contention that we as yet have failed to appreciate the obvious fact that doctors do not treat diseases but patients who have diseases.

7. Skinner, p. 19. In the light of Skinner's claim it is interesting to reflect on John Wisdom's observation in *Paradox and Discovery* (New York: Philosophical Library, 1965). "It is, I believe, extremely difficult to breed lions. But there was at one time at the Dublin zoo a keeper by the name of Mr. Flood who bred many lion cubs without losing one. Asked the secret of his success, Mr. Flood replied, 'Understanding lions.' Asked in what consists the understanding of lions, he replied, 'Every lion is different.' It is not to be thought that Mr. Flood, in seeking to understand an individual lion, did not bring to bear his great experience with other lions. Only he remained free to see each lion for itself' (p. 138). We are indebted to Professor Ed Erde for the Tolstoy and Wisdom quotes.

8. We are aware that this judgment would need to be qualified if each of these positions were considered in detail. Yet we think that this does characterize a tendency that these positions share. For each position is attempting to establish what Frankena calls the "institution of morality," that is, to show that morality is an institution that stands on its own, separate from other human activities such as politics, religion, etiquette. (We suspect connected with this attempt to establish the independence of ethics is the desire to give ethics a disciplinary character like that of the sciences. For an excellent discussion of ethics as a "quasi-discipline" see Toulmin, *Human Understanding*, pp. 406–411) The language of obligation tends to become central for these interpretations of the moral life as they trade on our feeling that we ought to do our duty irrespective of how it affects of relates to our other interests and activities. Obligation and rationality are thus interpreted in interdependent terms as it is assumed that an ethics of obligation can provide the standpoint needed to establish the independence of moral discourse from all the

relativities of interests, institutions and commitments save one, the interests of being rational. That is, the moral life, at least as it involves only those obligations that we owe one another apart from any special relationships, needs no further grounding apart from our common rationality. It should be obvious that our criticisms of this approach have much in common with such thinkers as Foot, MacIntyre, Toulmin and Hampshire. For a critique of the emphasis on obligation to the exclusion of virtue in contemporary accounts of the moral life see Hauerwas, "Obligation and Virtue Once More," *Journal of Religious Ethics,* 3, 1 (Spring, 1975), 27–44 (and included in this book), and the response and critique by Frankena in the same issue.

9. *Mind,* 80 (1971), 552–571. For similar criticism, see Hauerwas, *Vision and Virtue: Essay in Christian Ethical Reflection* (Notre Dame, Ind.: Fides, 1974).

10. To our mind one of the most disastrous aspects of the standard account of rationality is the resulting divorce of ethical reflection from political theory. It may be objected that the works of Rawls and Nozick are impressive counters to such a claim. However, it is interesting to note that the political theory they generate exists in a high level of abstraction from the actual workings of the modern state. It is only when ethicists turn their attention to C. B. MacPherson's challenge to the liberal democratic assumptions that Rawls and Nozick presuppose that they will address question that are basic. For liberal political theory and the objectivist's account of moral rationality share the assumption that morally and politically we are strangers to one another. Thus any common life can only be built on our willingness to qualify our self-interest in order to increase our long-term satisfaction. From this perspective the standard account can be viewed as an attempt to secure a basis for rational politics for a society that shares no interests beyond each individual increasing his chance for survival. It is our hunch that historically the disputes and disagreements in ethical theory such as that between Rawls and Hare will appear as scholastic debates within a liberal framework. For the disputants agree on far more than they disagree. For MacPherson's critique of these assumptions see his *Democratic Theory* (Oxford: Clarendon Press, 1973). For a radical critique of liberal democracy both in terms of the liberal understanding of rationality and the self similar to our own, see Roberto Unger's. *Knowledge and Politics* (New York: Free Press, 1975).

11. For a critique of this assumption see Michael Walzer, "Political Action: The Problem of Dirty Hand," *Philosophy and Public Affairs,* 2, 2 (Winter, 1973), 160–180. He is responding to Hare's "Rules of War and Moral Reasoning," *Philosophy and Public Affairs,* 1, 2 (Winter, 1972), 161–181. Hare argued that though one might wrongly think he was faced with a moral dilemma this could not be the case if a course of action suggested itself that was moral. See also John Ladd's very useful discussion of this issue in his "Are Science and Ethics Compatible?" in Engelhardt and Callahan (eds.), *Science, Ethics and Medicine.* This is also the issue that lies behind the theory of double effect in Roman Catholic moral theology though it is

seldom explicitly discussed in these terms. For example, see Richard McCormick's, *Ambiguity in Moral Choice* (Marquette Theology Lectures: Marquette University, 1973). See Hauerwas, "Natural Law, Tragedy, and Theological Ethics," for a different perspective.

For a fascinating study of the problem of moral evil in terms of the economic category of scarcity, see Vivian Walsh, *Scarcity and Evil* (Englewood Cliffs: Prentice-Hall, 1961). Ms. Walsh argues that we are often mistaken in trying to ascribe responsibility for actions that are the result of scarcity even when the scarcity is not the result of the "external" limits but in the person doing the action. What we often must do is the lesser good because of our own limits, but we must learn to know it is a lesser good without implying that we are morally blameworthy. Even though we are sympathetic with Ms. Walsh's analysis, we think the concept of character provides a way to suggest what is an inappropriate "scarcity" for anyone to lack in their character given the form of their engagements. Albert Speer lacked political sense that became morally blameworthy because of his political involvement, but that does not mean morally there is no way to indicate that his character should have provided him with the skills to know what kind of politics he was involved with. In classical terms the concept of character gives the means to assess in what ways we are blameworthy or praiseworthy for what we have omitted as for what we have "done."

12. For a discussion of these issues see Hauerwas, "The Demands and Limits of Care: Ethical Reflections on the Moral Dilemma of Neonatal Intensive Care."

13. It is not just Prichard that argues in this way but, as Henry Veatch suggests, Kant is the primary inspiration behind those that would make interest, desires and beliefs, in principle, unjustifiable, This, of course, relates to the matter discussed in note 4, as Kant wanted to provide a basis for morality not dependent on any theological or anthropological assumption—except that of man's rational capacity. That is why Kant's principle of universalizability, which has so often been misinterpreted, applies only to men as rational beings and not to just all human beings. As Veatch points out in this latter case, "the maxim of one's action would be based on a regard simply for certain desires and likings characteristic of human nature—albeit desires that all human beings happen to share in. But any mere desire of inclination or liking or sentiment of approbation, even if it be shared by the entire human race, would still not be universalizable in the relevant sense, simply because it was something characteristic of and peculiar to human kind, and hence not truly universal." "Justification of Moral Principles," *Review of Metaphysics,* 29, 2 (December, 1975). 225.

14. For example, witness this exchange between Lucy and Linus as Lucy walks by while Linus is preparing a snowball for launching.

LUCY: Life is full of Choices.

You may choose, if you so wish to throw that snowball at me.

You may also choose, if you so wish not to throw that snowball at me.
Now, if you choose to throw that snowball at me I will pound you right into the ground.
If you choose not to throw that snowball at me, your head will be spared.

LINUS: (*Throwing the snowball to the ground*) Life is full of choices, but you never get any.

15. For a more extended analysis of the concept of character, see Hauerwas *Character and the Christian Life: A Study in Theological Ethics* (San Antonio: Trinity University Press, 1975). For a similar critique of the Kantian inspired moral philosophy see Bernard Williams, "Person, Character, and Morality," in Amelie Rorty (ed.), *The Identities of Persons,* (Berkeley: University of California Press, 1976), pp. 197–215.

16. Julius Kovesi, *Moral Notions* (New York: Humanities Press, 1967), and Hauerwas, *Vision and Virue,* pp. 11–29. For a detailed account of how the meaning of a word depends on its history, see Raymond Williams, *Keywords* (New York: Oxford, 1976).

17. For example, R. S. Downie and Elizabeth Telfer attempt to argue that "the ordinary rules and judgments of social morality presuppose respect for persons as their ultimate ground . . . [and] that the area of private of self-referring morality also presupposes respect for persons at its ultimate ground." *Respect for Persons* (New York: Schocken, 1970), p. 9. They interpret respect for persons in a Kantian fashion of respecting the claim another rational capacity—that is, capable of self-determining and rule-governing behavior—can demand. It never seems to occur to them that the "ordinary rules of social morality" or "self-referring morality" may not need an "ultimate ground." Moreover, they have a good deal of trouble explaining why we owe respect to children or "idiots" on such grounds. They simply assert that there "are sufficient resemblances between them and persons" to justify extending respect to them (p. 35). For a different perspective on this issue, see Hauerwas; "The Retarded and the Criteria for the Human." It is Downie and Telfer's contention that "respect for persons" is the basis of such Christian notions as agape. It is certainly true that much of what a "respect for persons" ethic represents has been assumed by Christian morality, but we think that it is misleading to assume that the story that informs the latter can be translated into the former. One of the places to see this is how each construes the relationship between obligation and supererogation. The Christian ethic of charity necessarily makes obligatory what a follower of "respect for persons," can see only as supererogation. For an analysis of agape in terms of equal regard, see Gene Outka, *Agape: An Ethical Analysis* (New Haven: Yale University Press, 1972).

18. For a account of the moral life that makes :"fittingness" central, see H. R. Neibuhr, *The Responsible Self* (New York: Harper and Row, 1963).

19. It would take us too far afield to explore this point further, but surely it is Kant who stands behind this understanding of the self. It is impossible to document this, but it is at least worthwhile calling attention to two passages form *Religion Within the Limits of Reason Alone,* translated by Theodore Green (New York: Harper, 1960), "In the search for the rational origins of evil action, every such action must be regarded as though the individual had fallen into it directly from a state of innocence. For whatever his previous deportment may have been, whatever natural causes may have been influencing him, and whatever these causes were to be found within or outside him, his action is yet free and determined by none of these causes; hence it can and must always be judged as an original use of his will. . . . Hence we cannot inquire into the temporal origins of this deed, but solely into its rational origin, if we are thereby to determine and, whereby possible, to elucidate the propensity, if it exists, i.e., the general subjective ground of the adoption of transgression into our maxim" (p. 36). In case it is objected that Kant is only dealing with moral evil, consider "To reconcile the concept of freedom with the ideal of Good as a *necessary* Being raises no difficulty at all: for freedom consists not in the contingency of the act, i.e., not in indeterminism, but rather is absolute spontaneity. Such spontaneity is endangered only by predeterminism, where the determining ground of the act is in *antecedent time,* with the result that, the act being now no longer in my power but in the hands of nature, I am irresistibly determined; but since in God no temporal sequence is thinkable, this difficulty vanishes" (p. 45). It is, of course, the possibility of the moral law that Kant thinks gives men the possibility to be like God—timeless. It is not a far distance from Kant to the existentialist in this respect. Of course it is true that the Kantian outlook, as Williams suggests, makes less of an abstraction of the individual than utilitarianism. But the question arises "of whether the honourable instincts of Kantianism to defend the individuality of individuals against the agglomerative indifference of Utilitarianism can in fact be effective granted the impoverished and abstract character of persons as moral agents which the Kantian view seems to impose. . . . It is a real question, whether the conception of the individual provided by the Kantian theories is in fact enough for others who, while equally rejecting Utilitarianism, want to allow more room than Kantianism can allow for the importance of individual character and personal relations in moral experience." Bernard Williams, "Persons, Character, and Morality," in A. Rorty (ed.) *The Identities of Persons,* pp. 200–201.

20. For this point and much else that is involved in this paper, see Iris Murdoch, *The Sovereignty of the Good Over Other Concepts* (Cambridge: Cambridge University Press, 1967).

21. We have not based our criticism of the standard account on the debates between those who share its presuppositions. It is, of course, true that as yet so single theory of that standard account has proved to be persuasive to those who share its presuppositions. We still find Kant the single most satisfying statement of the program implied by the standard account.

22. Ernest Becker, however, argues that Comte has been misunderstood as his purpose was not to free science from morality but to call attention to what kind of moral activity science involved. Thus Becker suggests, "Comte's Positivism, in sum, solved the problem of science and morals by using science to support a man-based morality. With all the force at his command he showed that life is a moral problem, and science only a tool whose unity would serve the large unity of life, Like de Maistre and de Bonald, and like Carlyle in England, he looked approvingly on the Middle Ages. But he did not pine nostalgically for their institutions; he saw the Middle Ages as possessing what man needed most, and has since lost: a critical, unitary world view by which to judge right and wrong, good and bad, by which to subordinate personal desire to social interest. But instead of basing this knowledge on theological fiat, man could now settle in firmly on science. In this way, the Enlightenment could achieve what the Middle Ages almost possessed; but it could do this on a much sounder footing than could ever have been possible during the earlier time, namely, it could achieve the subordination of politics to morality on a scientific rather than on a theological basis. Social order and social harmony would be a call of the new day, and human progress could then be progress in social feeling, community, and love—all of it based on the superordinate science of man in society, serving man, elevating humanity." *The Structure of Evil,* p. 50.

In this respect, consider Simone Weil's observation that "The criticism of religion is always, as Marx said, the condition for all progress; but what Marx and the Marxists have not clearly seen it that, in our day, everything that is most retrograde in the spirit of religion has taken refuge, above all, in science itself. A science like ours, essentially closed to the layman, and therefore to scientists themselves, because each is layman outside his narrow specialism, is the proper theology of an ever increasingly bureaucratic society."

23. Cf. G. E. M. Anscombe, "Thought and Action in Aristotle," in R. Bambrough (ed.), *New Essays on Plato and Aristotle* (New York: 1965), pp. 151–152. See also Hauerwas, *Character and the Christian Life,* Chapter II.

24. For an account of the way analogous terms can be used once they are effectively linked to a paradigm instance, cf. Burrell, *Analogy and Philosophical Language* (New Haven and London: Yale University Press, 1973).

25. It may of course happen that one cannot sustain a particular relationship and "fails." Again, the way he deals with that becomes a story. Stories often seem better the more they overturn conventional assessments and challenge settled attitudes.

26. Peter Brown shows how this choice represented an existential decision as well. The *Platonici* formed an identifiable group of noble humanists, and as such offered a viable alternative to Christianity. While they were not formed into a church, their common aspirations could well be imagined to constitute a community of like-minded persons. See, *Augustine of Hippo* (Berkeley: University of California Press, 1967).

27. This is the point of Peter Winch's oft-cited analysis: "Understanding a Primitive Society," reprinted in Bryan R. Wilson (ed.), *Rationality* (Oxford, 1970).

28. For further elaboration of this, see Iris Murdoch, *The Sovereignty of the Good Over Other Concepts.*

29. Cf. James Cameron's efforts to offer perspective to current writing on the "sexual revolution," in *New York Review of Books,* 23 (May 13, 1976), 19–28.

30. MacIntyre's argument in "Towards a Theory of Medical Error," that medicine must necessarily deal with explanations of individuals only makes this claim more poignant. For the attempt to claim that the only errors in medicine were those characteristic of a science of universals was necessary if medicine was to make good its claim to be the means to free mankind of the limits of disease. To recognize that medical explanation and prediction is subject to the same limits as explanation and prediction of individuals will require a radical reorientation of the story that morally supports and directs medical care.

31. Becker, *The Structure of Evil,* p. 18. "The central problem posed by the Newtonian revolution was not long in making itself felt. This was the momentous new problem; it is still ours today—I mean of course the problem of a new theodicy. If the new nature was so regular and beautiful, then why was there evil in the human world? Man needs a new theodicy, but this time he could not put the burden on God. Man had to settle for a new limited explanation, an anthropodicy which would cover only those evils that allow for human remedy." Science naturally presented itself as the "remedy."

32. It is tempting to try to make, as many have, the ethic of "respect for persons" sufficient as a moral basis for medical care. (Cf. Paul Ramsey's *The Patient as Person.*) But if, as we suggest, medicine is necessarily involved in tragic choices, a more substantive story than that is needed to sustain and give direction to medical care. Without such a story we will be tempted to make technology serve as a substitute as it allows us to delay further decisions of life and death that we must make in one or another arena. For a critique of the way "person" is being used as a regulative moral notion in medical ethics, see Hauerwas, "Must a Patient Be a 'Person' To Be a Patient, or My Uncle Charlie is Not Much of a Person But He Is Still my Uncle Charlie."

33. For an analysis of the concept of self-deception, see Burrell and Hauerwas, "Self-Deception and Autobiography: Theological and Ethical Reflections in Speer's *Inside the Third Reich.*"

34. Jules Henry's analysis of the phenomenon of "sham" is perhaps the most graphic depiction of this. He says,

> Children in our culture cannot avoid sham, for adults cannot escape depression, hostility and so on. Since sham consists in one person's withholding information, while implying that the other person should act as if he had it all; since sham consists also in giving false information while

expecting the other person to act as if the information were true; since sham consists in deriving advantage from withholding or giving information—and since, on the whole, our culture is sham-wise, it might seem that the main problem for the mental health of children is to familiarize them with the edges of sham. Yet, if we were to do that, they would be "shot" for Albee is right. Our main problem, then, is to tell them the world lies but they should act as if it told the truth. But this, too, is impossible, for if one acted as if all sham were truth he might not be shot, but he certainly would lose all his money and marry the wrong person though he would have lots of friends. What then is the main problem; or rather, what does mankind do? People do not like children who lack innocence, for they hold the mirror up to adults. If children could not be deceived, they would threaten adults beyond toleration, they would never be orderly in elementary school and they clearly could not be taught the rot-gut dished out to them as truth. Personally I do not know what to do; and I anticipate a geometric increase in madness, for sham is at the basis of schizophrenia and murder itself (*On Sham, Vulnerability, and Other Forms of Self-Destruction* [New York: Vintage Books, 1973], pp. 123–124).

See also his *Pathways to Madness* (New York: Vintage Books, 1971), pp. 99–187.

35. For a fuller development of the issues in this last section see Hauerwas, "Natural Law, Tragedy, and Theological Ethics." Moreover, for a perspective similar to this see Ernest Becker, *The Denial of Death* (New York; Free Press, 1975). In a broad sense Becker suggests man's situation is tragic because, "Man has a symbolic identity that brings him sharply out of nature. He is a symbolic self, a creature with a name, a life history. He is a creator with a mind that soars to speculate about atoms and infinity, who can place himself imaginatively at a point in space and contemplate bemusedly his own planet . . . yet at the same time man is a worm and food for worms. This is the paradox: He is out of nature and hopeless in it; he is dual, up in the stars and yet housed in a heart-pumping, breath-grasping body that once belonged to a fish. Man literally is split in two; he has awareness of his own splendid uniqueness in that he sticks out of nature with a towering majesty, and yet he goes back into the ground a few feet in order blindly to rot and disappear forever. It is a terrifying dilemma to be in and to have to live with" (p. 26).

36. In his *Revisioning Psychology* (New York: Harper & Row, 1975), chapter 1, James Hillman questions whether psychic integration has not been conceive in too "monotheistic" a manner. His discussion is flawed by failing to see how an analogical "reference to one" offers a feasible way of mediating between an ideal which is too confining and a *laissez faire* program which jettisons ideals altogether.

10. A *Conversation Worth Having:*
Hauerwas and Gustafson on Substance in Theological Ethics

TERRENCE P. REYNOLDS

Terrence Reynolds argues that the ongoing debate between communitarians and universalists in Christian ethics is largely misplaced. Focusing on the sharp exchange of accusations between Stanley Hauerwas and James Gustafson, he insists that both thinkers can accurately be identified as Troeltschian historicists, operating out of shared methodological assumptions. Reynolds suggests that when this significant commonality is understood, the real issues that divide them can be exposed and a more fruitful conversation can ensue on the genuine areas of disagreement: their differing convictions, experiences, and, perhaps, their different pragmatic assessments of the performance of the Christian tradition.

In her 1998 presidential address to the Society of Christian Ethics, Lisa Cahill examined the contemporary debate between communitarians and universalists in Christian ethics. She argued that the debate is misplaced and that the focus of the discussion should be relocated (Cahill 1998, 6). Finding value in both positions, she affirmed the communitarian insight that there is a particularity to Christian witness and experience, as well as the insight of the universalists, who seek "some foundations or essentials in human moral experience to provide a common ground for social justice" (Cahill 1998, 6). In order to advance the conversation, Cahill defended the notion that there are some universally agreed-upon moral principles, but she did so in a historically nuanced manner. She also acknowledged openly the difficulties inherent in sustaining a common concern for the well-being of others across widely variegated interest groups. In what follows, I intend to build on Cahill's reshaping of the contours of the communitarian/universalist debate by focusing on the misdirected exchange between Stanley Hauerwas and James Gustafson and by offering suggestions for a more fruitful discussion.

Hauerwas himself, some years ago, took note of the confusions at work in the debate. In the introduction to Why Narrative? he complained, with co-editor L. Gregory Jones, that too much "of the contemporary discussion about narrative, particularly

within theology and ethics, has been beset by a poor understanding of what is at stake" and that proponents and opponents "talk past each other" on the issues, leaving interested onlookers perplexed and bemused (Hauerwas and Jones 1989, 5). In my view, this phenomenon is richly displayed in the extended exchanges between Hauerwas and Gustafson. Raising the specter of "Wittgensteinian fideism," Gustafson has suggested that Hauerwas's narrativist loyalties generate a truncated, sectarian ethic, incapable of useful dialogue with other ethical perspectives (Gustafson 1985, 85–86).[1] In response, Hauerwas has complained that Gustafson too quickly relinquishes the particularity of the Christian story in his quest for foundational dialogue and common moral principles. As he puts it, "Why doesn't Gustafson simply say that what is needed is a morality in which all people can agree?" (Hauerwas 1988, 16). The two ethicists are, as Hauerwas suggests, in "considerable disagreement" (Hauerwas 1988, 2).

---

[1]Bruce Marshall has identified three conversations in which contemporary Christian theology is continually engaged: conversation "with the ecumenical Christian community at large and the claims of the other segments of that community and other theologians about the shape Christian belief and practice ought to take; with the claims to goodness and truth . . . alive in their cultures; and with other religious traditions and the comprehensive ways of ordering life and understanding reality which they propose" (Marshall 1980, 1). It is from these multiple conversations that Gustafson thinks Hauerwas withdraws.

From *Journal of Religious Ethics*, Vol. 28, No. 3, pp. 395–421.
© 2000 Journal of Religious Ethics, Inc.

In the sections that follow, I will first examine in more detail the exchange of accusations between Hauerwas and Gustafson. Then, I will analyze their methodological approaches, suggesting that both can be understood as Troeltschian historicists and thereby essentially innocent of the charges leveled by each at the other. However, as I will indicate, while they are Troeltschian historicists, they are "historicists with a difference,"[2] and this possibly intractable difference, located at the level of presupposition and belief, complicates any possibility of discussion between them, despite the commonality that I hope to establish. More is at stake here than the question of whether productive conversation would be possible between these two particular scholars; their disagreement seems to me to be emblematic of the dialogical problem that all historicists face once we acknowledge the degree to which our rational arguments are grounded in prerational, experientially and socially formed commitments. Yet at the same time that appreciation of the contextual character of knowledge makes genuine exchange across boundaries of belief seem more problematic, it also makes it seem more essential. Thus, I would like to use reflection on the rift between Hauerwas and Gustafson as a vehicle for exploring, in the last section, how a conversation across these boundaries might proceed and what it might hope to achieve. In such a conversation, it is of first importance that the debate be properly focused; thus, a good deal of the following discussion of the quarrel between Gustafson and Hauerwas will be devoted to exposing the caricatures that have so far been at work in the their exchanges and to correcting what I regard as a basic confusion of method with substance. Then, with the help of David Tracy and John Hick, I hope to suggest a direction for a more candid conversation, offering some broad rules, as it were, for conversations between historicists with divergent convictions.

While I am hopeful that the suggestions I make will be helpful for all conversations that must be conducted across such boundaries, I have not selected the example of Hauerwas and Gustafson at random. The substantive and performative issues that divide these two eminent Christian theologians are issues that are of great importance for the Christian community as a whole, and they

are far more worthy of continued discussion than are the rather wearisome debates that artificially set "ahistorical foundations" against "walled-off conceptual schemes."

1. *Sectarianism Versus Moral Esperanto: A False Dichotomy*

In his 1985 address to the Catholic Theological Society of America, Gustafson characterizes the work of Hauerwas, George Lindbeck, Paul Holmer, and others as representative of "The Sectarian Temptation." He explains that the present age of pluralism in ethics and theology has left Christianity a "beleaguered religion," confronted on all sides by criticism and conflicting interpretive traditions (Gustafson 1985, 83). These turbulent times present the believing community with two dangerous alternatives. If the church seeks aggiornamento with the surrounding social order, it runs the risk of undermining its own historic continuity and the uniqueness of the Christian community. The opposite response, equally regrettable, involves a conservative retreat into the historic tradition, where moral and theological certainty can be retained. Gustafson thinks that ethicists like Hauerwas have succumbed to this latter temptation and have withdrawn from those engagements in which Christian beliefs could be challenged and Christian practices examined (Gustafson 1985, 84–86).

Gustafson's principal concern is that Hauerwas takes an uncontroversial sociological fact—namely, that we are products of communal narratives that shape our characters and our interpretations of the world—and elevates that fact to the level of the normative. For Hauerwas, it seems, Christians should be so shaped and should resist outside influences that call that conditioning into question. Gustafson wonders why this "turn to the normative" takes place. He suggests that Hauerwas requires the believer to remain faithful to the biblical narrative even at the cost of ignoring contrary evidence from other sources of human knowledge of God and God's purposes (Gustafson 1985, 88). Gustafson also expresses surprise that Hauerwas, though he affirms the unavoidable relativity of history, nevertheless clings tenaciously to the absoluteness of the biblical narrative. Gustafson thinks that historicist Christians would want to provide warrants for their faith in the face of competing interpretive narratives; instead, Hauerwas appears content to "isolate" the

---

[2]I wish to thank Lisa Cahill for this fortuitous phrase, which is so useful to my project of establishing unexpected commonalities between the work of Hauerwas and Gustafson while affirming that their disagreement, when rightly formulated, deservedly commands our attention.

believing community and "sustain the historical identity of the Christian tradition virtually for its own sake" (Gustafson 1985, 89).[3]

The problem is exacerbated for Gustafson by Hauerwas's seemingly uncritical acceptance of the biblical narrative. Even a strong, Barthian version of revelation, which Gustafson would find problematic for other reasons, would at least provide a justification or warrant for the elevated status of the narrative in the community, but since Hauerwas offers no such Barthian justification, Gustafson thinks he leaves the tradition supported only by its own self-assertion. Without a clear statement of what justifies the choice of a particular text as communally normative, the dangers of sectarianism are considerable (Gustafson 1985, 87). Gustafson thinks that Lindbeck, Holmer, and Hauerwas all erect a "cultural-linguistic" wall between the world of the Bible and that of other texts, thereby rejecting the dialogical interaction necessary to arrive at meaningful warrants for belief.

According to Gustafson, this creates three sectarian confusions. The first is the illusion of the church's sociological separation from the larger culture of which it is a part. Echoing H. Richard Niebuhr, Gustafson argues that such a thoroughgoing isolation has never existed in the history of the Christian community; believers, even if socialized into a distinctive biblical "form of life," remain related to other patterns of life and meaning, which they encounter on a daily basis.

Second, sectarianism mistakenly assumes that religious ways of knowing are so "radically distinct" from other ways of knowing that Christianity becomes "a separate cultural-linguistic enterprise" (Gustafson 1985, 92). Gustafson agrees that there are differences between religious and scientific ways of knowing, but he thinks that the similarities and the degree of overlap are sufficient to allow for extensive "correction and revision" across discourses (1985, 92).[4]

Finally, Hauerwas's church seems to drop out of all constructive theological dialogue and become "a modern and trivial form of gnosticism" (Gustafson 1985, 91). God becomes a "tribal" deity, available to only a small remnant of persons in the course of history, and even worse, Christian theology and ethics become more concerned about "maintaining fidelity to the biblical narratives about Jesus" than about providing any external justification for that fidelity (Gustafson 1985, 92, 93).[5] These difficulties, in combination, create an ethic that Gustafson calls "classically sectarian" (1985, 88).

Hauerwas responds that he has been misunderstood, a fact that does not surprise him since Gustafson "continues to presuppose the dominant philosophical and theological intellectual habits of the last hundred years" (Hauerwas 1988, 2).[6] According to Hauerwas, it is Gustafson's mistaken retention of confidence in the commonalities of reason that causes him to view widespread moral disagreement as a confusion to be rectified: "In such a world the emphasis of Christian ethics on the significance of the qualifier 'Christian' appears to many to capitulate to the chaos. We need instead, they say, to reformulate a universal morality that is able to bring order to our fragmentary world, securing peace between and in ourselves" (Hauerwas 1983, 6). While Hauerwas agrees that the current age is marked by ethical diversity, he is less troubled by it than Gustafson and less prone to think it correctable. If an insistence on the distinctiveness of Christian knowing and acting, together with a refusal to open the faith to alien warrants for justification, constitutes a "temptation," Hauerwas suggests that this "temptation" ought not to be resisted (Hauerwas 1988, 7).

In fact, Hauerwas thinks Gustafson has departed from the distinctive Christian narrative, seeking to overcome diversity and ambiguity by cultivating tradition spanning methods of moral justification. Where Gustafson believes that Hauerwas has fallen into the trap of sectarianism, Hauerwas believes that Gustafson is seeking an illusory "autonomous knowledge of

---

[3]Hauerwas would respond that he does offer reasons for his faith. I would suggest that his reasons, however, are of limited value to others outside the cultural-linguistic grammar that shapes his convictions.

[4]Although this sort of provisionality and openness to correction is common among historicists, the historicist need not, it seems to me, always hold positions provisionally. One could imagine a historicist who is genuinely convinced that the performative record of her or his interpretive scheme is such that it requires no revision.

[5]Of course, the more one is committed to the now common view that justification takes place within systems of discourse, the less sympathetic one will be to this criticism and the less one will be disposed to consider Hauerwas's failure in this regard to be a "sectarian" fault.

[6]As will become apparent in what follows, I regard as caricatures Hauerwas's descriptions of Gustafson as seeking a "universal" ethic.

autonomous nature" in order to make possible a common morality (Hauerwas 1988, 17).[7]

Although he regards Gustafson's approach as misguided and preordained to failure, Hauerwas is, nonetheless, clearly stung by the charge of sectarianism, and he responds to it carefully. He insists that he has neither "tried to justify Christian belief by making Christian convictions immune from other modes of knowledge" nor argued, as a fideist would, "that religious convictions are or should be treated as an internally consistent language-game that is self-validating" (Hauerwas 1988, 9–10). He does, however, insist that diversity among communities of discourse creates a rich complexity of incompatible moral narratives. In contrast to the true sectarian, he has, he argues, consistently engaged in ongoing conversations with liberal society and other religious traditions. Ultimately, the Christian story will prove itself advantageous to liberal society when the community of faith is set apart by its performance as a "community of virtue" (1988, 7).[8] Hauerwas concludes with this challenge to Gustafson: "Show me where I am wrong about God, Jesus, the limits of liberalism, the nature of the virtues, or the doctrine of the church—but do not shortcut that task by calling me a sectarian" (1988, 8).

These, then, are the terms in which the two men themselves have framed their disagreement, each accusing the other of faults that are essentially methodological. Gustafson holds Hauerwas guilty of an obstinate narrowness in his definition of theological resources and a foolish indifference to the challenges to faith propelled by modern habits of critical intelligence; Hauerwas holds Gustafson guilty of an unchastened Enlightenment rationalism that supposes a little hard thinking will yield universal moral norms that all reasonable people will be able to endorse, a kind of moral Esperanto. Their clash has had the quality of a defining moment for contemporary Christian ethics, which is now often mapped on a field defined by the coordinates of sectarianism and rationalist universalism. While people may argue about whether Hauerwas is really a sectarian despite his answer to Gustafson and about whether Gustafson is actually as much a secular rationalist as Hauerwas says he is, people do not usually question the coordinates that orient the discussion. It is my intention to show that the coordinates themselves are wrongly placed, that this quarrel has been framed according to a false and pernicious dichotomy, and that the issues that are at stake are, in fact, substantive, not methodological.

2. *Gustafson's Theocentric Ethics*

In his two-volume Ethics from a Theocentric Perspective, Gustafson begins with the historicist assumption, following the trajectory from Ernst Troeltsch through H. Richard Niebuhr, that all substantive moral and theological claims are related to particular contingent settings. Knowing what we do of history, we cannot responsibly assert universal foundations for ethics.[9] Gustafson is very clear about this, leaving no room for misinterpretation: "Whatever might be said about theology and ethics necessarily refers to human experiences. Indeed, there is no way in which a certain kind of anthropocentrism can be avoided. . . . There is

---

[7]See, also, Yoder 1988, 75. Yoder's critique of Gustafson follows a similar pattern: "Universality is for Gustafson a goal or an 'aspiration' to be approached by 'striving' and by 'overcoming' the boundaries of our communities. While saying elsewhere that all truth is particularly perceived and formulated, he seems here [in Ethics from a Theocentric Perspective] to believe that there are procedures for moving toward universality through some process of dilution, sifting, or abstraction." Gustafson's hope, says Yoder, is that one can discover in the "wider public arena" a "set of reasonable people who will agree to a departicularized set of affirmations." Yoder treats this possibility with a disdain similar to that of Hauerwas.

[8]Here, it is fair to ask Hauerwas about the criteria by which the performance of the community is measured. Certainly, Gustafson's appraisal of the performative record of the tradition would not accord with that of Hauerwas.

[9]See Kaufman 1988, 14–15, for this description of Gustafson's project: "Although, as he says repeatedly, his position is rooted in the piety of the Reformed theological tradition, Gustafson does not regard his position as grounded simply on a religious confessionalism. Rather, his dominant concern—that the pervasive anthropocentrism of our religious traditions and moral theories has become increasingly untenable—grows largely, I think, out of contemporary scientific knowledge of the bases of human life and contemporary ecological consciousness of the interconnectedness of all forms of life. . . . it is no longer reasonable to think of humans as the apex and center of God's creation. Ethics . . . must now be done in a way that is continually sensitive to our situatedness in the natural order." I take it that Gustafson's willingness to subject the tradition to the scrutiny of scientific theories of the origin of life and to other less anthropocentric interpretive models is based on his pragmatic judgment that the biblical narratives have become less defensible in the face of our shared experience. Hauerwas disagrees.

no avoiding the truism that man is the knower, and that the known comes through human experiences of one or many sorts" (Gustafson 1981, 1:115–16).[10]

However, Gustafson's heightened awareness of our epistemic limitations does not lead him to embrace relativism, skepticism, or nihilism. Though it is a given that we have no unmediated access to uninterpreted reality, his claims are intended to refer to the real. Nor do the facts of our sociotemporal contingency undermine his confidence in the value of his ethical project. Instead, Gustafson embraces our historical particularities as a platform for dialogue and seeks creatively to overcome them as much as possible. He openly acknowledges his own commitment to the Calvinist tradition, but also subjects it to critical scrutiny. In the light of criteria of coherence, experiential warrants, and performance, he finds this tradition seriously lacking, and he adapts it accordingly. Our knowledge of biological sciences and the obviously misshapen anthropocentrism of our received religious texts have made it impossible to ground moral judgments solely on the tradition's received concepts and categories. Although he has modified his own tradition considerably, Gustafson continues to ground his ethical project in the Christian theistic question, "What is God enabling and requiring us to be and to do?" (Gustafson 1981, 2:1).

Assuming a divine reality, Gustafson examines the question of how one discerns the intentions of God for the moral life. To repeat, he is not seeking some foundational, transhistorical rationality as a basis for moral discourse, yet he believes that ongoing conversation among conflicting moral narratives can uncover significant overlap among their views of human requisites and flourishing. In the absence of universal reason or a final, authoritative revelation, he pursues the moral truth of God's purpose for the creation by employing pragmatic criteria of consistency, coherence, and effective performance over time (James 1897/1956, 19–24).[11] Gustafson himself has agreed that

"the affinities between my work and pragmatism . . . are clearly there" (Gustafson 1988a, 244).[12]

To be shaped by a tradition, however, is not necessarily to be confined to it; meaningful conversation, criticism, explanation, translation, and, perhaps at times, even accommodation and agreement can occur between various dimensions of human knowledge and between religious traditions and forms of life. Obviously, one unavoidably begins within an interpretive tradition, theistic or otherwise, but that is a condition of, rather than an obstacle to, dialogue with others. Thus, when Gustafson consents to the affiliation of his work with American pragmatism, he means to call attention to the ways in which he has adapted his Calvinist interpretive scheme to the intellectual and spiritual challenges of the biological sciences, to various humanist objections to the received tradition (including the objection to its pervasive anthropocentrism), and to a more holistic understanding of the interconnectedness of all of life (see Kaufman 1988, 14, 15).

To pursue the issue further, what directions can one discover in human experience to assist in the informing and appropriate reshaping of one's tradition?

---

[10]Gustafson adds, "There is no avoiding the truism that man is the measurer: language, concepts, percepts, qualifications, theories, and tests of truth and adequacy are all human activities, and thus aspects of human experience" (Gustafson 1981, 1:116).

[11]My understanding of pragmatism has been heavily influenced by William James, the empiricist philosopher who attributed to it the following characteristics: (1) a conviction, based on our will, that there is truth and that it is worthy of our pursuit, (2) an imperative to seek the truth, and to do so

persistently, but with humility and a willingness to risk error, (3) a habit of continually consulting our unfolding experience for ongoing confirmation or disconfirmation of our hypotheses, and (4) a willingness to balance our eagerness for verification with an "equally keen nervousness" not to be deceived. I fully recognize the many forms pragmatism has adopted, and I use the term somewhat gingerly. Nevertheless, I think it is characteristic of pragmatism to hold that a hypothesis or interpretive scheme stakes a tentative claim to truth when it coherently and consistently appears to "perform" well over time. By "performance," I mean to suggest James's notion that the body of available evidence continues to confirm the view in question. This position is further developed by Niebuhr's discussion of "progressive validation" in The Meaning of Revelation. As Niebuhr explains: "In our conceptual knowledge we move back and forth from reason to experience and from experience back to reason. And in that dialectic of the mind our concepts are enriched, clarified and corrected no less than our experience is illuminated and directed. We do not easily change first principles but we discover more fully what they mean" (Niebuhr 1941, 99–100). When interpretive schemes withstand the rigors of this dialectic, they can be said to have "performed" well, to have been validated.

[12]See Reeder 1988, 122–26, for a discussion of the pragmatic character of Gustafson's work; and see Gustafson 1988b, 209, for Gustafson's endorsement of "the aptness of Reeder's classification of my work as pragmatic."

Gustafson begins with the assumption that God wills the best for the entire creation, sentient and nonsentient alike (Gustafson 1981, 1:271).[13] Thus, one should seek to determine what would bring about the overall good of the whole, not simply the good of humankind, for it is the good of the whole that would most closely approximate the intentions of the divine. I should add that there is no reason why this concern for the greater good of the "creation" could not be shared by those without theistic assumptions. In fact, Gustafson assumes that he will find ready conversation partners among nontheistic ethicists.

How, then, is one to determine the course of action likely to enhance the overall well-being of the whole? For Gustafson, the principles and values that will guide Christians are discerned in various Christian communities, and they coalesce, over time and through dialogue, with the understandings of the creation developed in other traditions of interpretation. Engaging in a rich conversation across communities of discourse and employing the knowledge attained through the physical and social sciences can help direct Christians toward an answer to Gustafson's overarching inquiry into the purposes of God (Gustafson 1981, 2:1). Blueprints for action, however, are far from established; the process of arriving at moral judgments remains a creative affair.[14] What all this suggests is that Gustafson follows a modest, pragmatic quest for moral truth. Emerging patterns of flourishing that arise from our social experience should be explored, but must remain objects of ongoing conversation and critique.

Finally, Gustafson's pragmatism permits a certain fluidity in moral judgments. There is no foundational epistemic principle to which one can appeal to order these varieties of goods and values. The discernment of moral courses of action is largely shaped, as Hauerwas would agree, in communities of discourse. In light of the sciences and other forms of knowledge about human and nonhuman life, one can give reasons for acting the way one does, but there remains an element of interpretive judgment at work in Gustafson's ethic. And this acknowledgment of the role of interpretive judgment leaves room for the development of the quality of one's discernment. I take it that an awareness of the limits of one's discernment is the source of a humility in ethics that characterizes Gustafson's and the pragmatist's search for moral truth.

If I have fairly sketched Gustafson's project, then Hauerwas is wrong to suggest that Gustafson is seeking a universal ethic. Gustafson does not seek universal "foundations" for justification, and he is as well aware as Hauerwas of the historical contingency of our judgments. However, whereas Hauerwas finds in historical contingency a license for treasuring, preserving, and renewing the historically given "story" that gives distinctive identity to a particular community, Gustafson finds in historical contingency a warrant for adapting the Christian narrative in consequence of engagement in the give-and-take of moral conversation with other communities. He believes that, over time, this process should edge us closer to a shared sense of the divine intention for human and nonhuman good as intimated in the creation. In short, he brings both theistic convictions and an earnest pragmatism to the realm of ethics.

Gustafson can be said to be "guilty" of "seeking a morality in which all can agree" (Hauerwas 1988, 16) insofar as he makes truth claims that he believes to be universally applicable, though not universally knowable—but this "guilt" is shared by Hauerwas. Gustafson also thinks that there are significant warrants or standards of reason recognized by all, and he therefore envisions the possibility of large-scale moral agreement based on overlapping views of human requisites and flourishing. His differences with Hauerwas here are, in my view, quantitative rather than qualitative in that he and Hauerwas part company dramatically over the degree to which the received Christian story directs us to truthful living. The complaint that Gustafson aspires to move toward universality is true, in these limited respects, but strikes me as a charge that could be effectively leveled at all who take part in the pragmatic conversation.

---

[13]One of Gustafson's central pragmatic concerns with the Christian tradition is its anthropocentrism. He explains, "My argument radically qualifies the traditional Christian claim that the ultimate power seeks the human good as its central focus of activity. 'Goodness' or 'value' are not terms that refer to some entity or entities in and of themselves. It is always appropriate to ask, Good for whom?"

[14]See Reeder 1988, 129, for this description of the process: "The good of all should be considered, but which principles of distribution we should adopt is neither revealed by God directly nor known through human resources. 'Discernment' involves a discrimination of the values involved in a case, and then an 'intuition,' which, I believe, means a decision to rank and distribute goods in a certain way in certain circumstances."

I should add that Gustafson's approach does not, in my view, constitute a methodological denial of the particularity of the Christian story—or of any story that stands up to the dual tests of coherence and performance. Obviously, Gustafson himself has rejected much of the biblical narrative,[15] but he has done so out of the substantive conviction that the tradition has not met the performative tests to which he has subjected it. On pragmatic grounds, he has refused to grant privileged status to the narratives to which Hauerwas remains attached. Hauerwas may be correct in suggesting that Gustafson gives away too much of the tradition; that is a question I leave to confessional settings to determine. However, in theory, one is not left with the false dichotomy, presented by Hauerwas, that one either "relativizes" Christianity or adheres unwaveringly to one's tradition. One can hold to the truth of the Christian narrative, in whole or in part, while engaging in ongoing dialogue over its merits without thereby relativizing it. The alternatives are certainly not limited to theological absolutism or relativism. A modest pragmatism can retain theological realism and ontological truth claims without requiring a withdrawal from moral dialogue.[16]

3. *Hauerwas on Biblical Narrative*

Having argued that Gustafson is innocent of seeking a universally justifiable ethic, I now turn to the question of whether Hauerwas is aptly described as sectarian. To answer this question, one must examine his views on the nature and authority of the biblical narrative, and his understanding of the meaning, truth, and justification of theological and ethical claims.

For the most part, Hauerwas seems to share Gustafson's commitment to pragmatism, although his hyperbole at times makes him seem vulnerable to Gustafson's critique. Hauerwas often speaks of the necessity of subjecting the biblical narrative to public

tests of performance. When he argues from this perspective, his "thick" account of the Christian story is methodologically compatible with Gustafson's "thin" theistic version, and their different "narratives" are equally open to the dialogue inherent in the pragmatic search for truth. The two simply enter the conversation from different substantive ends of the theological spectrum, one remaining faithful to the received tradition and the other retaining only a limited version of it. There is no reason, in principle, why one could not cling to a more complete version of the "stories of Jesus" and continue publicly to defend the interpretive coherence and performative success of the Christian faith. Pragmatism does not impose limits on the nature of one's background beliefs; rather, it requires that those beliefs be open to critical assessment across communities of interpretation. As Hauerwas indicates, "the question of truthfulness of our theological convictions is most appropriately raised by asking how through our language and character they form and display our practical affairs" (Hauerwas 1977, 9). The truth of the theological convictions intrinsic to the biblical narrative is tied not to their correspondence to "metaphysical or ontological schemes" (Hauerwas 1977, 9), but to the sort of lives they produce. This should not imply a vicious relativism or subjectivism, for "there are 'criteria' of moral truthfulness, though such criteria can never be independent of a substantive narrative" (Hauerwas 1977, 9). The question to be put to competing narratives, then, is not whether they correspond to the real itself, but rather, "which narrative gives us the ability to form our existence" most appropriately and truthfully (Hauerwas 1977, 12). Hauerwas, unlike Gustafson, has experienced the Christian narrative as a performative masterpiece and is unconvinced by arguments to the contrary.

Hauerwas agrees with Gustafson that we always argue out of perspectival context and that our perceptions are largely determined by "a history of interpretation" (Hauerwas 1977, 22). He also, at least implicitly, opens the Christian story to interactive criticism by tracing the way it differs from alternative interpretive accounts, particularly that of contemporary liberal culture, but because he thinks the narrative is so performatively successful, he is less willing to alter it in light of these differences. He sees no reason to compromise a performative masterpiece in order to find common ground with other less successful and less truthful interpretive schemas. Again, Hauerwas would seem to echo Gustafson in describing the process of discussion and discernment through which

---

[15]Jeffrey Stout has aptly captured the ambiguity of Gustafson's relationship with Scripture and tradition: "He speaks eloquently on behalf of his tradition, especially that strand of Calvinist piety in which the sense of dependence on God figures most centrally, although he forcibly denounces elements of the tradition that either conflict with the themes he deems most central or that cannot be given sufficient experiential warrant" (Stout 1988, 167).

[16]For a similar argument made with reference to the work of Sallie McFague, see Reynolds 1995.

our moral judgments take shape. Affirming elements of the thought of Stuart Hampshire and William Frankena, Hauerwas adds the following:

> . . . the unity and consistency of a "way of life" cannot be derived from abstractly posited "rationality," but rather is learned "from observation, direct experience, and from psychology and history.". . . our ability to offer public reasons for our behavior is fundamental to the moral life. But it is not clear that such reasons only work within the context of an abstractly constructed ethics of obligation [Hauerwas 1977, 52, emphasis added].

Hauerwas describes the church as a community fundamentally dedicated to the perpetuation of the Christian story: "the church's primary mission is to be a community that keeps alive the language and narrative necessary to form lives in a truthful manner" (Hauerwas 1977, 11). The church's purpose is to proclaim the achievement of the linguistic universe of Scripture in fostering virtue. Still, witness and conversion are intended to reach persons outside the church and must rely on some shared sense of the good, or of human flourishing, to make communication possible.[17]

With respect to Gustafson's question as to how the "true" or "normative" interpretive community is to be discerned, Hauerwas returns again to the persuasive power of performance as demonstrated by truthful communities: "The Scriptures are exhibited in communities that are capable of pointing to holy lives through which we rightly see the reality that has made the Scriptures possible" (Hauerwas 1977, 39). Moral truths are discovered through the performative assessment of the practices displayed by those living a particular narrative.

The process of justifying a preference for one narrative, and the lives it forms, over others is a complex one. Hauerwas attempts to offer assistance, but, at the same time, he acknowledges the limitations that loyalty to one narrative places on public dialogue. "The test of each story," he argues, "is the sort of person it shapes" (Hauerwas 1977, 35). I think Hauerwas is suggesting

here that overlaps and "translations" are possible to the extent that the way of life shaped by the Christian narrative has a certain public, performative effect on others who may be drawn to it. Translation is certainly difficult, as Lindbeck has argued in The Nature of Doctrine, but there is a sense of the good to which many are attracted.[18] One can also offer warrants for the interpretive and performative success of the biblical narratives in forming truthful character, but these warrants cannot be entirely public in nature.

Of course, matters are further complicated by the fact that the evaluation of the moral quality of persons is also shaped by narrative communities themselves, creating an apparent circularity. Hauerwas recognizes this dilemma, but it is not clear that he solves it. He admits that the criteria for adjudicating between conflicting stories "will most probably not pass an impartial inspection," because one's powers of discernment "cannot be divorced from one's own capacity to recognize the good for humankind" (Hauerwas 1977, 35). Hauerwas attempts to provide guidelines for assessing competing narratives:

> Any story which we adopt, or allow to adopt us, will have to display: (1) power to release us from destructive alternatives; (2) ways of seeing through current distortions; (3) room to keep us from having to resort to violence; (4) a sense for the tragic: how meaning transcends power. It is inaccurate, of course, to list these criteria as features which a story must display. For they envisage rather the effect which stories might be expected to have on those who allow them to shape their lives [Hauerwas 1977, 35–36].

Assessment of any narrative's superiority or inferiority to another would therefore entail: (1) an extended conversation between representatives of the communities formed by the divergent stories, (2) critical dialogue inside each community as well as with the "outside" traditions, and (3) ongoing attention to the level of performative success achieved by both narratives in their interaction with the world they seek to understand. Hauerwas, I take it, is a willing participant in the conversation between conflicting moral narratives, but he participates in a more limited fashion than

---

[17]If Hauerwas's ethics as best understood as an exercise in evangelization, as Jonathan R. Wilson has rightly suggested (Wilson 1995, 155), some expectations about the possibility of translation, overlap, and persuasion must be at work if the activity of evangelization is to make any sense.

---

[18]Lindbeck argues that converts were "first attracted by the Christian community and form of life" it embodied, not by the doctrines it professed (Lindbeck 1984, 132).

Gustafson does—or perhaps it would be more accurate to say that his participation has a different stance and quality. This is not because Hauerwas is immured within the walls of a closed community; it is because Hauerwas, apparently out of his own personal experience, begins with an existentially grounded belief that the interpretive framework of the Christian faith has been pragmatically effective for himself, that it has the power to be equally effective for others, and that it ought therefore to be defended in these conversations rather than adjusted or departicularized.

In a recent critique of Hauerwas published in this journal, Christopher Beem has followed Gustafson in claiming that while Hauerwas "does not view dialogue between narratives as useless. . . . the prospects associated with any such attempt appear hopelessly insufficient to the contemporary moral task" (Beem 1995, 126). Obviously, Beem's sense of the "contemporary moral task" is not shared by Hauerwas, nor do I see, on pragmatic grounds, why it should be. Hauerwas sees no point in diluting the transcendent core of the Christian faith and its truthfulness, and he appropriately, in my view, indicates why he has no interest in following Beem's directions: "Beem faults me for not providing an epistemology or theory of rationality that will allow us (I assume by 'us' he means 'we' liberal Americans) to 'develop a shared substantive conception of the good that transcends [our] metaphysical differences.' To which I am tempted to say, 'Oh my, I am so sorry'" (Hauerwas 1995, 146). If Hauerwas is correctly seen as a pragmatist, convinced of the truthfulness of the Christian narrative, his unwillingness to compromise that truth would be justifiable.

In essence, Hauerwas seems to echo Lindbeck in suggesting that Scripture is "paradigmatic" for the Christian community and "is thus able to absorb the universe" and not be absorbed by it (Lindbeck 1984, 117). If this is so, then how can genuine conversation take place? Is the tradition truly improvable or malleable from without, or are suggested linguistic or conceptual changes best understood as threats to the semiotic universe of the Bible? When Hauerwas asks Gustafson to show him where he is wrong about God, Jesus, and the church, one wonders how that would be possible. On what basis could Gustafson meaningfully criticize Hauerwas, having set aside as unworkable so much of the narrative tradition out of which Hauerwas speaks?

Here, the question of sectarianism resurfaces and must be faced. According to Lindbeck, Christian sectarianism, in a sociological sense, occurs when the church maintains its distinctive set of beliefs and practices in such a way as to be a "creative minority in the society from which it deviates, serving as a perpetual witness on behalf of the poor and the oppressed in the name of the Kingdom of God" (Lindbeck 1971, 232). It seems beyond dispute that, in this sociological sense, Hauerwas is "sectarian," as accused, and that he is proud of it. Hauerwas would endorse without hesitation Lindbeck's concluding words in The Nature of Doctrine that "some younger theologians . . . in a post-traditional and postliberal mode" are renewing "the ancient practice of absorbing the universe into the biblical world. May their tribe increase" (Lindbeck 1984, 135). Hauerwas's extensive critique of the liberal society surrounding the Christian church speaks eloquently to the sociological separation of the believing community.

According to Lindbeck, Christian sectarianism can also be understood in another different sense. What he calls theological sectarianism occurs when a small group of believers insist that they are the only true church and separate themselves off from dialogue with other Christians. Is Hauerwas also guilty of this more serious form of sectarianism, the form which prompts Gustafson's critique and against which Hauerwas reacts? Insofar as his project can be understood as an exercise in pragmatism, I think he is innocent. Certainly, holding to a "thicker" set of well-entrenched beliefs is not problematic as long as some conversation with the surrounding culture can be carried out. Hauerwas believes—and argues—that the Christian tradition has proven itself a classic in outperforming the competition in its formation of "truthful" lives. His voluminous argumentation on behalf of the Christian moral perspective clearly suggests that he thinks some form of persuasion is possible across traditions. I think that Hauerwas is clearly taking part in a pragmatic discussion of moral judgments and their implications and that he consistently, if only implicitly, appeals to some shared sense of the human good when he asserts so vigorously the superiority of the Christian way of life. If this is what it means to be sectarian, then Gustafson's charge is a weak one, and Hauerwas should readily plead guilty.

If I am correct, Hauerwas has merely refused to acquiesce to the critiques of the tradition leveled by Gustafson. From the point of view of Hauerwas, Gustafson's suggestion that the tradition has failed interpretively is based on a caricature of the narrative's performance and an application of alien criteria of assessment to the tradition. Properly understood and lived, the narratives of the church have far more to offer the liberalism of the current day than liberalism has to offer the church.

4. *Toward a Meaningful Conversation*

As we have seen, Hauerwas labels Gustafson a rational universalist and says he lacks all historical perspective, while Gustafson, for his part, treats Hauerwas as a communitarian who has so historicized Christianity as to become imprisoned in a self-enclosed sect. However, this debate is fundamentally misplaced. And it is misplaced because, as careful study of their positions abundantly shows, they are both Troeltschian historicists—Christian ethicists who take historical particularity seriously but are attempting to preserve and make accessible to non-Christians (liberal secularists or rational intellectuals) the essential meaning of Christian faith and practice. Unlike Troeltsch, neither is a relativist. Gustafson is a "rational universalist" insofar as he is willing to subject religious truth claims about God and reality to scientific and experiential criteria of assessment that he thinks are more or less universally recognizable, though he realizes that different cultural perspectives will always bias the results. This latter element represents the Troeltschian dimension of his thinking. Hauerwas is a "communitarian fideist" insofar as he believes that the God known in faith is knowable only in the Christian community; in fact, the community of belonging absolutely defines one's knowledge of God, which is Hauerwas's concession to Troeltsch. Unlike Troeltsch, however, Hauerwas thinks that knowledge of God is not just a historical construction, since the absolute God is present in a unique way in the life and practice of that historical community. Hauerwas does not, therefore, lose interest in larger social issues, but he does not expect or envision a public conversion to the insights of Christian morality. To read their exchanges with insufficient subtlety on the matter of their historicist premises is to miss the point entirely amidst the hyperbole, and to look at either through the lens the other provides is to focus on distorted characterizations of their disagreement rather than its cause. Since their quarrel is so often interpreted as a disagreement between dangerous historicist particularism and possibly more dangerous rational hubris, one might expect the discovery of their shared historicist premises to provide grounds for dissolving the quarrel. Of course, it does nothing of the kind. Historicists they may be, but, as I said at the beginning, they are clearly historicists with a difference.

Because nearly all of us are now, to greater or lesser degrees, historicists, we are no longer struggling to secure or to discredit historicism; rather, we are struggling to resolve the problems historicism has thrust upon us. Gustafson and Hauerwas genuinely disagree about truth; about the role of Scripture and reason in shaping moral sentiments, moral judgments, and forms of moral justification; and about the nature of God. These are the things about which historicists are bound to disagree. And this is what makes their conversation a conversation worth having—and worth having in a straightforward and productive way. If we focus on their real, substantive disagreement and not on some counterfeit that is partly of their own making and partly the work of their partisan commentators, we can at least see what meaningful form this crucial conversation might take. The paradox of this endeavor (and the reason it is so prone to derailment) is that the very differences that make the conversation so potentially illuminating also make it exceptionally difficult to conduct.

The debate between Gustafson and Hauerwas is significantly complicated by the fact that the opposing convictions at work are virtually incommensurable. Hauerwas is committed to the God of Scripture; Gustafson is not. In a different context, Stanley Fish has proposed that argument between persons holding different substantive convictions invariably produces different forms of reasoning. This does not mean that one or the other reasons improperly or inadequately (if the reasoning were flawed, the issues would be simply methodological). The two simply reason differently. In a passage that aptly applies to Hauerwas and Gustafson's conversation, Fish explains:

> The difference between a believer and a nonbeliever is not that one reasons and the other doesn't, but that one reasons from a first premise the other denies; and from this difference flow others that make the fact that both are reasoning a sign not of commonality but of its absence. . . . while two persons proceeding within opposing faiths might perform identical operations of logi-

cal entailment, they will end up in completely different places because it is from different (substantive) places that they begin [Fish 1996, 35].[19]

If this is so, for Hauerwas to accuse Gustafson of accommodating himself to too broad a range of perspectives is to overlook the fact that Gustafson's substantive convictions leave him little choice. Since Gustafson rejects substantial elements of the scriptural narrative's version of the divine, his conception of the real and its implications for ethics must be derived from other resources. Hauerwas looks solely to the narratives because they continue to "work" for him, to perform with such interpretive success that he is virtually closed to new substantive convictions. Neither is willing to adopt the method of the other because each believes that his bedrock convictions are, in fact, true and thereby preclude extensive methodological compromise.

Is Gustafson, then, seeking a more commonly agreed-upon ethic? Of course. What would one expect, given his worldview? Is he methodologically at fault for doing so? Only if one believes that he is substantively at fault for not believing otherwise, which drives us back to the foundational issue. And is Hauerwas obstinately proclaiming Christian truth to a pagan nation? Of course. What would one expect, given his worldview? Is he methodologically at fault for doing so? Only if one believes that he is substantively at fault for not seeing the faults of the narrative—which, again, drives us back to the foundational issue: if we accept the historicist belief in the perspectival character and social inflection of all knowledge claims, how can people converse, or reason together, if they do not share the same presuppositions?

4.1 The Methodization of Substance

The first point to be made—and I hope the foregoing analysis has helped to make this clear—is that reciprocal polemical attack, with each seizing on the most exaggerated claims of the other, is counterproductive and does not constitute genuine intellectual engagement. Not only does it defeat the search for possible common ground and heighten the conflict, but it also

feeds a tendency to displace the real origin of complaint, treating a dispute about the adequacy of presuppositions as if it were a dispute about right reasoning.

In the case of Hauerwas and Gustafson, what ought to be a debate about substantive issues has been displaced to a debate about method. However misleading this may be, it is not at all surprising that it should happen. If, as Nicholas Wolterstorff has argued, one's worldview, interpretive scheme, or beliefs about the real function as a control over the theories one is willing to accept (Wolterstorff 1984, 16–17), then methods in theology and ethics, while noticeably different, are, in fact, symptomatic of more fundamental, substantive discrepancies. Method is deeply interrelated with conviction since it is clear that we cannot seriously entertain thoughts that are rendered implausible to us by our core beliefs. As a result, methodological debates sometimes have a certain comedic air about them; their very heatedness betrays the substantive intractability beneath the surface that goes largely unnoticed. When historicists engage in ethical conversation, they ought to have a heightened awareness of the critical influence of substantive convictions on their methodological choices.

The illusion that appears to be at work in the conversation between Gustafson and Hauerwas is that if they debate issues of method with sufficient rigor, they may be able largely to resolve their differences. Why else would Gustafson lecture Hauerwas about his dependence on Scripture, or Hauerwas chide Gustafson for his openness to other sources of moral authority? What makes this a fanciful strategy is the nostalgic assumption on which it appears to be based, namely, that these matters can be "objectively" discussed and adjudicated when, in fact, they cannot. Absent the requisite linguistic framework, neither is capable of experiencing the world as the other does. Barring a substantive conversion experience, a horizon shift, or the wholesale appropriation of a compatible interpretive grammar by one or the other, Hauerwas and Gustafson can endlessly debate methodology to little avail.

4.2 Addressing Conflicts at the Point at Which They Arise

The second point to be made is surely that any such conversation, if it is to be of any worth, must address the conflict at its true level: at the substantive level of beliefs that are being taken for granted on both sides. Once the proper level has been achieved, I would think

---

[19]This is not to suggest, of course, that Gustafson is a "non-believer" and Hauerwas a "believer." The point is that their respective Christian commitments are deeply dissimilar.

that a polemical tone would be justified only if each believed that the substantive convictions and performative record defended by the other were incontrovertibly opposed to human flourishing. If there is to be conversation between parties whose presuppositions conflict, each participant must be genuinely open to the presumption that the perspective of the other is at least rationally plausible and worthy of serious discussion.

The heatedness of the exchanges between Gustafson and Hauerwas sometimes suggests that in their case this might, in fact, be too much to ask. Nevertheless, it seems difficult to imagine that Gustafson could fail to acknowledge the performative track record of the narrative ethical tradition or that Hauerwas could reject entirely the ethical plausibility of a nuanced theism like Gustafson's. Such tolerance would not mean that each could not hold to the truth of his own convictions and the falsity of the other's, but a conversation that fails to take note of these substantive and ethical differences is doomed to pointlessness.

But is it not equally pointless if we do take these differences seriously? It seems beyond dispute that Gustafson, though a product of Calvinist roots, has discarded many of the substantive details and authorities of that tradition. He has been persuaded that a broader conversation with a wider range of traditions and with the natural sciences will be more conducive to the discovery of moral truth. I leave the question of why he has been so persuaded for another time. Because Gustafson believes that the void left by the failure of traditional Christian language in ethical practice needs filling, he is open to a broader range of interpretive possibilities than is Hauerwas. Hauerwas continues to believe that other interpretive schemes can be absorbed, and improved upon, by the linguistic universe of the biblical narratives. Given the substantive gulf that divides them, is there any realistic hope for meaningful conversation? Why bother to talk with someone whose foundational commitments, whose fundamental faith, differs from one's own?

4.3 The Discovery of Common Ground

Different as Gustafson and Hauerwas may be, they both think of themselves as Christians, and they are both generally regarded as Christians. So while their debates arise from profound substantive disagreements, they at least imagine that they share the same fundamental form of life. So there is, in their case, a special and urgent reason for trying to discern not only how they differ, but also what they share.

Gustafson and Hauerwas disagree about human requisites and flourishing, about warrants for belief and practice, about the performative success of the Christian tradition, about how God is known, about whether the Christian witness to God is subject to (or immune to) external tests, and, finally, about whether God's truth is knowable, at least in its moral dimensions, to outsiders. Part of a useful conversation would include discovering areas in which they actually come together pragmatically on certain dimensions of morality, even while disagreeing on the basic issues I have listed. I readily grant that the tests by which one could assess such competing religious interpretive schemes are ambiguous and disputed, but a conversation on such pragmatic grounds would at least focus on the genuine issues at stake and offer the possibility of a more useful exchange.

4.4 The Origins and Validations of Beliefs

The question then arises concerning how a more useful exchange might be achieved. David Tracy, for example, contends that the "Enlightenment belief in a purely autonomous consciousness has been . . . torn apart" and that the only way to avoid reducing the self to "a purely passive carrier of whatever codes—familial, social, historical—have formed it" is to take the risk of engaging in interpretive dialogue (Tracy 1987, 16). Such conversation, for Tracy, refers to "the exploration of possibilities in search for truth," and it should seek imaginatively to see possibility in the different views of the other (Tracy 1987, 20). To be successful, such conversations between divergent communities must follow particular guidelines:

> Conversation is a game with some hard rules: say only what you mean; say it as accurately as you can; listen to and respect what the other says, however different or other; be willing to correct or defend your opinions if challenged by the conversation partner; be willing to argue if necessary, to confront if demanded, to endure necessary conflict, to change your mind if the evidence suggests it [Tracy 1987, 19].[20]

---

[20]Arguments, which may arise as a moment within a conversation, involve response to challenges to one's interpretations or perspectives. Arguments, too, should follow particular guidelines, as Tracy explains: ". . . all argument assumes the following conditions: respect for the sincerity of the other; that all conversation partners are, in principle, equals; saying what one means and meaning what one says; a willingness to

Once the participants in a conversation acknowledge the divergence of the nonfoundational premises that undergird their work, both should also acknowledge that they therefore lack universally agreed-upon criteria of justification to differentiate true from false claims. Since their conflict arises not from faults of reasoning but from divergent presuppositions, resolution, which would involve conversion, is not likely. Each can, however, hope to understand the interpretive and performative rationale that supports the position of the other; at best, the conversation might lead, as Cahill suggests, to some limited, agreed-upon orientation toward the common good.

To begin, Hauerwas should ask Gustafson (and be prepared to listen) for a detailed account of why he discarded those aspects of the tradition that Hauerwas continues to affirm. Gustafson, in turn, could offer an unavoidably personal, yet challenging, explanation of why he came to regard those aspects of the tradition as irredeemably flawed. This sketch would entail a look at data or experiences that, for him, undermined the interpretive success of the biblical narratives and ultimately required their large-scale dismissal. It would also entail a defense of the warrants that Gustafson brings to the task of moral discernment. Gustafson could also indicate his uneasiness with the apparent circularity at work in Hauerwas's warrants for belief. Such an account would be autobiographical, not entirely unfamiliar, and, one suspects, altogether unconvincing to Hauerwas. Still, even if unpersuaded, Hauerwas might nonetheless take note of the gravity and the seriousness of Gustafson's critique of, among other things, the tradition's anthropocentrism, its absolutism, and its habit of orienting the life of the church to the past rather than the future. Gustafson's penetrating assessment of the failures of the received tradition could not casually be dismissed. Next, Hauerwas would be asked to indicate how he has overcome these critical challenges as he continues conscientiously to endorse the narratives. He could offer his rationale for rejecting the more "liberal" tradition espoused by Gustafson, along with its more broadly based warrants for belief, and he could defend the performative record of the received tradition. His account would also be lengthy, autobiographical, and, in all likelihood, unconvincing to Gustafson.

Yet it seems that this account of a possible conversation between these two Christian theologians only brings us back to where we began. If it can be predicted that these substantive explanations will fail to persuade, then what conceivable value would be found in them?

First, both thinkers would be obliged to respond to a forceful and rich rejection of the performative record and heuristic power of their substantive beliefs, as well as the warrants that they employ in testing their moral judgments. This would, at least, focus their debate on genuine issues (such as the requisites for human flourishing) about which some degree of agreement might be discovered, and on their warrants for their convictions, which would necessarily move the conversation from personal conviction to shareable evidence. This alone would foster a fuller measure of understanding—but what is the value of understanding a position that you maintain is substantively wrong?

4.5 *John Hick's account*

Would any additional results be possible? To answer this critical question, I want to rely on John Hick's analysis of what he terms "experiencing-as." Hick explains that the cognitive processes by which persons find themselves aware of natural, moral, and religious realities share a "basic epistemological pattern" (Hick 1978, 97). According to Hick, persons are incapable of meaningful existence in an undifferentiated environment that is "totally insignificant" to them. Without the exercise of some form of perceptual or cognitive discernment by which we interpret our world and endow it with meaning, we would endure a subhuman form of existence. It is through the application of language or concepts to our perceptions that we are able to endow objects or situations with significance and thereby to experience them "as" something distinctive.[21] If we were without "signifying" objects and situations—that is, if we were unable to differentiate among objects and events and interpret their purpose in relation to ourselves—we would be unable to func-

---

weigh all relevant evidence, including one's warrants and backings; a willingness to abide by the rules of validity, coherence, and especially possible contradictions between my theories and my actual performance" (Tracy 1987, 26).

[21]David Tracy echoes Hick on the significance of language: "We understand in and through language. We do not invent our own private languages and then find a way to translate our communications to others. We find ourselves understanding in and through particular and public languages" (Tracy 1987, 49).

tion as persons. Hick defines "significance" as "that fundamental and all-pervasive characteristic of our conscious experience which de facto constitutes it for us the experience of a 'world' and not of a mere empty void or churning chaos" (Hick 1978, 98).

At the most basic level, Hick endorses the Kantian thesis that a mental framework of orientation and categorization structures our experience with a minimal level of orderliness. However, our interpretive abilities take us much further. Language, according to Hick, plays a crucial role in the creation of distinctively human experience. In order to experience a pen "as" a pen, for example, one requires a familiarity with the concept in question. Others, "seeing" the same object but lacking the concept, would be unable to interpret the object's meaning or apply to it the same "significance." It follows that such persons would thereby be unable to relate themselves to the function of a pen and would be uncertain how to use it. Experience, therefore, is potentially multilayered, as levels of interpretive subtlety enable different persons to experience varying degrees of significance. If Hick is correct, our experiences of the world, therefore, will be very different, despite the fact that the same things present themselves to our eyes.

According to Hick, an analogous interpretive process occurs at the moral and religious levels. The differential appropriation of moral language, exquisitely nuanced or dismayingly threadbare, makes possible an extraordinary range of moral experience. Some, better trained, so to speak, in the grammar of morality, can experience a broader range of situations as having moral "significance." Moreover, they enjoy a heightened sensitivity to the demands of the moral life and of their own moral shortcomings. The morally "illiterate," on the other hand, experience moral obligation sporadically (if at all) and without the richness made possible by a more sophisticated moral vocabulary.

If Hick's analysis is trustworthy, persons who are well versed in the language of neighbor love, the requirements of justice, fairness, and duty, the subtleties of selflessness, and the like presumably experience the world they inhabit as awash in moral significance. It seems inconceivable that the same can be said for the morally uninitiated. Both in degree and in kind, the moral language that we appropriate and imaginatively employ shapes our moral sensitivities and, by extension, the significance of our moral experience. Substantive convictions, transmitted through cultural-linguistic circumstances, are a given for all of us. Though they are not impervious to change, as gains and losses of faith attest, the influence of these grammars is considerable.

Naturally, moral development is continuous, and other ways of seeing or experiencing the world regularly collide with our own. Vocabularies grow; terms once employed no longer seem as fitting as before; or other grammars may seem to empower speakers to greater eloquence and interpretive coherence. If Hick's premises are reliable, when such changes occur in our interpretive grammar, concomitant changes will follow in the nature of our experience. We will begin to see things differently or to experience events in ways that had previously eluded us. I would suggest that no one is immune to this interplay with other grammars of interpretation; historicism, again, assures us that diversities of perspective and colliding interpretations are a part of the human condition.

4.6 Expanding the Horizon of Experience

Hick provides us with a model of conversation that recognizes radical differences at the presuppositional level but, unlike other models, supposes that there can be changes and adjustments short of sudden and complete conversions. It seems to me that two things follow from this suggestive analysis.

First, Hick's approach suggests that any conceptual system is most open to change precisely where it is least successful as an interpretive schema. When persons are convinced that their interpretive scheme is a masterpiece, capable of absorbing and giving sense to the multiplicity of experience, they will, of course, have little interest in appropriating alternative linguistic terminology. In broad, pragmatic terms, if one's ethical system is working well, one is not prone to revise it. However, I take it that no one would persist in holding to an interpretive scheme that had failed performatively. A perceived interpretive inadequacy would lead one more readily to "try on" linguistic variations; one might say that the planks in one's interpretive raft are replaced only when leaks are detected.

The even more radical implication of Hick's analysis is that when people with disparate beliefs converse about the differences between their beliefs, the very fact of imaginative dwelling in the beliefs they do not share will necessarily alter their own conceptual repetoire.

Even while remaining unconverted, each will be opened to a broadened range of experiences, each will begin to be able to see things that were not seen before.[22] The believer may well be able to fold these emergent realities into her or his existing conceptual schema—in which case, that interpretive framework will be considerably enriched. On the other hand, the believer may not be able to fold these emergent realities into her or his existing framework, in which case, it may become more urgent for the believer to consider alternative belief systems that can account for these dimensions of experience.

This, it seems to me, is the means by which it is possible to move forward toward some degree of resolution of the conflicts that have their roots, not in the failure of reason or logic, but in different convictions, different experiences, and, often, different forms of life.

---

[22]Allow me an example. A woman explains to an unconvinced male acquaintance the unpleasantries she experiences in a sexist social system. The man hears what he takes to be exaggerated tales of perceived slights and sexual impositions; his friend, he thinks, lives in an imagined world, uninformed by the "reality" that the behavior she describes is far less common than she believes. From the woman's perspective, one might say he "doesn't get it" at all. If the two argue over the "facts" or the "methods" by which they assess the data, they are likely to hit an impasse because the "facts" are shaped by their widely divergent interpretive convictions. There is no objective method through which the man can "experience" what the woman "experiences." He can no more apply a feminist grammar to his social experience than he can an alien religious grammar to his faith life. If, however, the man listens sympathetically rather than critically, if he genuinely tries to grasp the experience of a respected friend, he may, in fact, develop an empathetic willingness to consider the possibility that her linguistic pattern provides some measure of interpretive accuracy. The coherence and consistency of her account, buttressed by her personal credibility, assist him in appreciating the plausibility of her interpretive narrative. Further, the man may find himself able, on occasion, imaginatively to apply the interpretive "grammar" of his friend to experiences in his own life. Seeing a female colleague ill treated by a male, he may realize that the interpretive scheme of his friend comes alive or "works" for him in this situation. The experience may now take on an entirely different "significance" for him because he has been enabled to see what he could not previously see. To use Hick's terminology, he may be able to experience this moment morally "as" a form of harassment or objectification, whereas he had previously lacked the linguistic capacity to do so. This involves a linguistic conversion of sorts, but unless the plausibility of an alternative interpretive scheme is persuasively presented, or, one might say, "proclaimed," the possibility of applying new language and evoking a different experience would be eliminated.

References

Beckley, Harlan R., and Charles M. Swezey, eds. 1988 James M. Gustafson's Theocentric Ethics. Atlanta, Ga.: Mercer University Press.

Beem, Christopher 1995 "American Liberalism and the Christian Church: Stanley Hauerwas vs. Martin Luther King Jr." Journal of Religious Ethics 23.1 (Spring): 119–33.

Cahill, Lisa Sowle 1998 "Community versus Universals: A Misplaced Debate in Christian Ethics." The Annual of the Society of Christian Ethics 18:3–12.

Fish, Stanley 1996 "Stanley Fish Replies to Richard John Neuhaus." First Things 60 (February): 35–40.

Gustafson, James M. 1981 Ethics from a Theocentric Perspective. 2 vols. Chicago: University of Chicago Press.

—— 1985 "The Sectarian Temptation: Reflections on Theology, the Church, and the University." Proceedings of the Catholic Theological Society 40:83–94.

—— 1988a "Afterword." See Beckley and Swezey 1988, 241–54.

—— 1988b "Response." See Beckley and Swezey 1988, 201–24.

Hauerwas, Stanley 1977 Truthfulness and Tragedy. With Richard Bondi and David B. Burrell. Notre Dame, Ind.: University of Notre Dame Press.

—— 1983 The Peaceable Kingdom. Notre Dame, Ind.: University of Notre Dame Press.

—— 1988 Christian Existence Today. Durham, N.C.: The Labyrinth Press.

—— 1995 "Remembering Martin Luther King Jr. Remembering: A Response to Christopher Beem." Journal of Religious Ethics 23.1 (Spring): 135–48.

Hauerwas, Stanley, and L. Gregory Jones 1989 "Introduction." In Why Narrative? edited by Stanley Hauerwas and L. Gregory Jones, 1–18. Grand Rapids, Mich.: Wm. B. Eerdmans.

Hick, John 1978 Faith and Knowledge. Glasgow, Scotland: William Collins Sons and Co.

James, William 1956 "The Will to Believe." 1897. In The Will to Believe and Other Essays in Popular Philosophy, 1–31. New York: Dover Publications.

Kaufman, Gordon 1988 "How Is God to Be Understood in a Theocentric Ethics?" See Beckley and Swezey 1988, 13–37.

Lindbeck, George 1971 "The Sectarian Future of the Church." In The God Experience, edited by Joseph P. Whelen, 226–43. New York: Newman Press.

—— 1984 The Nature of Doctrine. Philadelphia, Pa.: Westminster Press.

Marshall, Bruce D., ed. 1980 Theology and Dialogue. Notre Dame, Ind.: University of Notre Dame Press.

Niebuhr, H. Richard 1941 The Meaning of Revelation. New York: Macmillan Co.

Reeder, John P., Jr. 1988 "The Dependence of Ethics." See Beckley and Swezey 1988, 119–41.

Reynolds, Terrence 1995 "Two McFagues: Meaning, Truth, and Justification in Models of God." Modern Theology 11.3 (July): 289–314.

Stout, Jeffrey 1988 Ethics after Babel: The Languages of Morals and Their Discontents. Boston: Beacon Press.

Tracy, David 1987 Plurality and Ambiguity. San Francisco: Harper and Row.

Wilson, Jonathan R. 1995 "From Theology of Culture to Theological Ethics: The Hartt-Hauerwas Connection." Journal of Religious Ethics 23.1 (Spring): 149–64.

Wolterstorff, Nicholas 1984 Reason within the Bounds of Religion. Grand Rapids, Mich.: Wm. B. Eerdmans.

Yoder, John Howard 1988 "Theological Revision and the Burden of Particular Identity." See Beckley and Swezey 1988, 63–94.

Part 2
Sexual Ethics

11. *Humanae Vitae*

Pope Paul VI

In *Humanae Vitae* (1968), Pope Paul VI claims that natural sex, as established by God and understood by reason, is limited to acts that are both unitive and procreative. He limits such sex acts to heterosexual, genital, noncontraceptive acts open to the possibility of procreation and carried out within the lifelong institution of marriage. Other sexual acts, both inside and outside the boundaries of marriage, are disordered, contrary to the will of God, and diminishing to the partners involved.

To the venerable Patriarchs, Archbishops and other local ordinaries in peace and communion with the Apostolic See, to priests, the faithful and to all men of good will.

Venerable brothers and beloved sons:

The Transmission of Life

1. The most serious duty of transmitting human life, for which married persons are the free and responsible collaborators of God the Creator, has always been a source of great joys to them, even if sometimes accompanied by not a few difficulties and by distress.

At all times the fulfillment of this duty has posed grave problems to the conscience of married persons, but, with the recent evolution of society, changes have taken place that give rise to new questions which the Church could not ignore, having to do with a matter which so closely touches upon the life and happiness of men.

New Aspects of the Problem and Competency of the Magisterium

New Formulation of the Problem

2. The changes which have taken place are in fact noteworthy and of varied kinds. In the first place, there is the rapid demographic development. Fear is shown by many that world population is growing more rapidly than the available resources, with growing distress to

The encyclical *Humanae Vitae* was issued July 29, 1968, at Rome. This official translation was prepared by the National Catholic News Service.

many families and developing countries, so that the temptation for authorities to counter this danger with radical measures is great. Moreover, working and housing conditions, as well as increased exigencies both in the economic field and in that of education, often make the proper education of a large number of children difficult today. A change is also seen both in the manner of considering the person of woman and her place in society, and in the value to be attributed to conjugal love in marriage, and also in the appreciation to be made of the meaning of conjugal acts in relation to that love.

Finally and above all, man has made stupendous progress in the domination and rational organization of the forces of nature, such that he tends to extend this domination to his own total being: to the body, to psychical life, to social life and even to the laws which regulate the transmission of life.

3. This new state of things gives rise to new questions. Granted the conditions of life today, and granted the meaning which conjugal relations have with respect to the harmony between husband and wife and to their mutual fidelity, would not a revision of the ethical norms, in force up to now, seem to be advisable, especially when it is considered that they cannot be observed without sacrifices, sometimes heroic sacrifices?

And again: by extending to this field the application of the so-called "principle of totality," could it not be admitted that the intention of a less abundant but more rationalized fecundity might transform a materially sterilizing intervention into a licit and wise control of birth? Could it not be admitted, that is, that the finality of procreation pertains to the ensemble of conjugal life, rather than to its single acts? It is also asked whether, in view of the increased sense of responsibility of modern man, the moment has not come for him to entrust to his reason and his will, rather than to the biological rhythms of this organism, the task of regulating birth.

Competency of the Magisterium

4. Such questions required from the teaching authority of the Church a new and deeper reflection upon the principles of the moral teaching on marriage: a teaching founded on the natural law, illuminated and enriched by divine revelation.

No believer will wish to deny that the teaching authority of the Church is competent to interpret even the natural moral law. It is, in fact, indisputable, as our predecessors have many times declared,[1] that Jesus Christ, when communicating to Peter and to the Apostles His divine authority and sending them to

teach all nations His commandments,[2] constituted them as guardians and authentic interpreters of all the moral law, not only, that is, of the law of the Gospel, but also of the natural law, which is also an expression of the will of God, the faithful fulfillment of which is equally necessary for salvation.[3]

Conformable to this mission of hers, the Church has always provided—and even more amply in recent times—a coherent teaching concerning both the nature of marriage and the correct use of conjugal rights and the duties of husband and wife.[4]

Special Studies

5. The consciousness of that same mission induced us to confirm and enlarge the study commission which our predecessor Pope John XXIII of happy memory had instituted in March, 1963. That commission which included, besides several experts in the various pertinent disciplines, also married couples, had as its scope the gathering of opinions on the new questions regarding conjugal life, and in particular on the regulation of births, and of furnishing suitable elements of information so that the magisterium could give an adequate reply to the expectation not only of the faithful, but also of world opinion.[5]

The work of these experts, as well as the successive judgments and counsels spontaneously forwarded by or expressly requested from a good number of our brothers in the episcopate, have permitted us to measure exactly all the aspects of this complex matter. Hence with all our heart we express to each of them our lively gratitude.

Reply of the Magisterium

6. The conclusions at which the commission arrived could not, nevertheless, be considered by us as definitive, nor dispense us from a personal examination of this serious question; and this also because, within the commission itself, no full concordance of judgments concerning the moral norms to be proposed had been reached, and above all because certain criteria of solutions had emerged which departed from the moral teaching of marriage proposed with constant firmness by the teaching authority of the Church.

Therefore, having attentively sifted the documentation laid before us, after mature reflection and assiduous prayers, we now intend, by virtue of the mandate entrusted to us by Christ, to give our reply to these grave questions.

Doctrinal Principles

A Total Vision of Man

7. The problem of birth, like every other problem regarding human life, is to be considered, beyond partial perspectives—whether of the biological or psychological, demographic or sociological orders—in the light of an integral vision of man and of his vocation, not only his natural and earthly, but also his supernatural and eternal vocation. And since, in the attempts to justify artificial methods of birth control, many have appealed to the demands both of conjugal love and of "responsible parenthood," it is good to state very precisely the true concept of these two great realities of married life, referring principally to what was recently set forth in this regard, and in a highly authoritative form, by the Second Vatican Council in its pastoral constitution *Gaudium et Spes*.

Conjugal Love

8. Conjugal love reveals its true nature and nobility, when it is considered in its supreme origin, God, who is love,[6] "the Father, from whom every family in heaven and on earth is named."[7]

Marriage is not, then, the effect of chance or the product of evolution of unconscious natural forces; it is the wise institution of the Creator to realize in mankind His design of love. By means of the reciprocal personal gift of self, proper and exclusive to them, husband and wife tend towards the communion of their beings in view of mutual personal perfection, to collaborate with God in the generation and education of new lives.

For baptized persons, moreover, marriage invests the dignity of a sacramental sign of grace, inasmuch as it represents the union of Christ and of the Church.

Its Characteristics

9. Under this light, there clearly appear the characteristic marks and demands of conjugal love, and it is of supreme importance to have an exact idea of these.

This love is first of all fully human, that is to say, of the senses and of the spirit at the same time. It is not, then, a simple transport of instinct and sentiment, but also, and principally, an act of the free will, intended to endure and to grow by means of the joys and sorrows of daily life, in such a way that husband and wife become only one heart and only one soul, and together attain their human perfection.

Then, this love is total, that is to say, it is a very special form of personal friendship, in which husband and wife generously share everything, without undue reservations or selfish calculations. Whoever truly loves his marriage partner loves not only for what he receives, but for the partner's self, rejoicing that he can enrich his partner with the gift of himself.

Again, this love is faithful and exclusive until death. Thus in fact, do bride and groom conceive it to be on the day when they freely and in full awareness assume the duty of the marriage bond. A fidelity, this, which can sometimes be difficult, but is always possible, always noble and meritorious, as no one can deny. The example of so many married persons down through the centuries shows, not only that fidelity is according to the nature of marriage, but also that it is a source of profound and lasting happiness and finally, this love is fecund for it is not exhausted by the communion between husband and wife, but is destined to continue, raising up new lives, "Marriage and conjugal love are by their nature ordained toward the begetting and educating of children. Children are really the supreme gift of marriage and contribute very substantially to the welfare of their parents."[8]

Responsible Parenthood

10. Hence conjugal love requires in husband and wife an awareness of their mission of "responsible parenthood," which today is rightly much insisted upon, and which also must be exactly understood. Consequently it is to be considered under different aspects which are legitimate and connected with one another.

In relation to the biological processes, responsible parenthood means the knowledge and respect of their functions; human intellect discovers in the power of giving life biological laws which are part of the human person.[9]

In relation to the tendencies of instinct or passion, responsible parenthood means that necessary dominion which reason and will must exercise over them.

In relation to physical, economic, psychological and social conditions, responsible parenthood is exercised, either by the deliberate and generous decision to raise a large family, or by the decision, made for grave motives and with due respect for the moral law, to avoid for the time being, or even for an indeterminate period, a new birth.

Responsible parenthood also and above all implies a more profound relationship to the objective moral order established by God, of which a right conscience is the faithful interpreter. The responsible exercise of parenthood implies, therefore, that husband and wife recognize fully their own duties towards God, towards themselves, towards the family and towards society, in a correct hierarchy of values.

In the task of transmitting life, therefore, they are not free to proceed completely at will, as if they could determine in a wholly autonomous way the honest path to follow; but they must conform their activity to the creative intention of God, expressed in the very nature of marriage and of its acts, and manifested by the constant teaching of the Church.[10]

Respect for the Nature and Purpose of the Marriage Act

11. These acts, by which husband and wife are united in chaste intimacy, and by means of which human life is transmitted, are, as the council recalled, "noble and worthy,"[11] and they do not cease to be lawful if, for causes independent of the will of husband and wife, they are foreseen to be infecund, since they always remain ordained towards expressing and consolidating their union. In fact, as experience bears witness, not every conjugal act is followed by a new life. God has widely disposed natural laws and rhythms of fecundity which, of themselves, cause a separation in the succession of births. Nonetheless the Church, calling men back to the observance of the norms of the natural law, as interpreted by their constant doctrine, teaches that each and every marriage act (*quilibet matrimonii usus*) must remain open to the transmission of life.[12]

Two Inseparable Aspects: Union and Procreation

12. That teaching, often set forth by the magisterium, is founded upon the inseparable connection, willed by God and unable to be broken by man on his own initiative, between the two meanings of the conjugal act: the unitive meaning and the procreative meaning. Indeed, by its intimate structure, the conjugal act, while most closely uniting husband and wife, empowers them to generate new lives, according to laws inscribed in the very being of man and of woman. By safeguarding both these essential aspects, unitive and procreative, the conjugal act preserves in its fullness the sense of true mutual love and its ordination towards man's

most high calling to parenthood. We believe that the men of our day are particularly capable of seizing the deeply reasonable and human character of this fundamental principle.

Faithfulness to God's Design

13. It is in fact justly observed that a conjugal act imposed upon one's partner without regard for his or her condition and lawful desires is not a true act of love, and therefore denies an exigency of right moral order in the relationships between husband and wife. Hence, one who reflects well must also recognize that a reciprocal act of love, which jeopardizes the responsibility to transmit life which God the Creator, according to particular laws, inserted therein is in contradiction with the design constitutive of marriage, and with the will of the Author of life. To use this divine gift destroying, even if only partially, its meaning and its purpose is to contradict the nature both of man and of woman and of their most intimate relationship, and therefore, it is to contradict also the plan of God and His will. On the other hand, to make use of the gift of conjugal love while respecting the laws of the generative process means to acknowledge oneself not to be the arbiter of the sources of human life, but rather the minister of the design established by the Creator. In fact, just as man does not have unlimited dominion over his body in general, so also, with particular reason, he has no such dominion over his generative faculties as such, because of their intrinsic ordination towards raising up life, of which God is the principle. "Human life is sacred," Pope John XXIII recalled; "from its very inception it reveals the creating hand of God."[13]

Illicit Ways of Regulating Birth

14. In conformity with these landmarks in the human and Christian vision of marriage, we must once again declare that the direct interruption of the generative process already begun, and, above all, directly willed and procured abortion, even if for therapeutic reasons, are to be absolutely excluded as licit means of regulating birth.[14]

Equally to be excluded, as the teaching authority of the Church has frequently declared, is direct sterilization, whether perpetual or temporary, whether of the man or of the woman.[15] Similarly excluded is every action which, either in anticipation of the conjugal act, or in its accomplishment, or in the deveopment of its natural consequences, proposes, whether as an end or as a means, to render procreation impossible.[16]

To justify conjugal acts made intentionally infecund, one cannot invoke as valid reasons the lesser evil, or the fact that such acts would constitute a whole together with the fecund acts already performed or to follow later, and hence would share in one and the same moral goodness. In truth, if it is sometimes licit to tolerate a lesser evil in order to avoid a greater evil or to promote a greater good[17] it is not licit, even for the gravest reasons, to do evil so that good may follow therefrom,[18] that is, to make into the object of a positive act of the will something which is intrinsically disordered, and hence unworthy of the human person, even when the intention is to safeguard or promote individual, family, or social wellbeing. Consequently it is an error to think that a conjugal act which is deliberately made infecund and so is intrinsically dishonest could be made honest and right by the ensemble of a fecund conjugal life.

Licitness of Therapeutic Means

15. The Church, on the contrary, does not at all consider illicit the use of those therapeutic means truly necessary to cure diseases of the organism, even if an impediment to procreation, which may be foreseen, should result therefrom, provided such impediment is not, for whatever motive, directly willed.[19]

Licitness of Recourse to Infecund Periods

16. To this teaching of the Church on conjugal morals, the objection is made today, as we observed earlier, that it is the prerogative of the human intellect to dominate the energies offered by irrational nature and to orientate them towards an end conformable to the good of man. Now, some may ask: in the present case, is it not reasonable in many circumstances to have recourse to artificial birth control if, thereby, we secure the harmony and peace of the family, and better conditions for the education of the children already born? To this question it is necessary to reply with clarity: the Church is the first to praise and recommend the intervention of intelligence in a function which so closely associates the rational creature with his Creator; but she affirms that this must be done with respect for the order established by God.

If, then, there are serious motives to space out births, which derive from the physical or psychological condition of husband and wife, or from external conditions, the Church teaches that it is then licit to take into account the natural rhythms immanent in the generative functions, for the use of marriage in the infecund periods only, and in this way to regulate birth without offending the moral principles which have been recalled earlier.[20]

The Church is consistent with herself when she considers recourse to the infecund periods to be licit, while at the same time condemning, as being always illicit, the use of means directly contrary to fecundation, even if such use is inspired by reasons which may appear honest and serious. In reality, there are essential differences between the two cases; in the former, the married couple make legitimate use of a natural disposition; in the latter, they impede the development of natural processes. It is true that, in the one and the other case, the married couple are in agreement in the positive will of avoiding children for plausible reasons, seeking the certainty that offspring will not arrive; but it is also true that only in the former case are they able to renounce the use of marriage in the fecund periods when, for just motives, procreation is not desirable, while making use of it during infecund periods to manifest their affection and to safeguard their mutual fidelity. By so doing, they give proof of a truly and integrally honest love.

Grave Consequences of Methods of Artificial Birth Control

17. Upright men can even better convince themselves of the solid grounds on which the teaching of the Church in this field is based, if they care to reflect upon the consequences of methods of artificial birth control. Let them consider, first of all, how wide and easy a road would thus be opened up towards conjugal infidelity and the general lowering of morality. Not much experience is needed in order to know human weakness, and to understand that men—especially the young, who are so vulnerable on this point—have need of encouragement to be faithful to the moral law, so that they must not be offered some easy means of eluding its observance. It is also to be feared that the man, growing used to the employment of anticonceptive practices, may finally lose respect for the woman and, no longer caring for her physical and psychological equilibrium, may come to the point of considering her as a mere instrument of selfish enjoyment, and no longer as his respected and beloved companion.

Let it be considered also that a dangerous weapon would thus be placed in the hands of those public authorities who take no heed of moral exigencies. Who could blame a government for applying to the solution of the problems of the community those means acknowledged to be licit for married couples in the solution of a family problem? Who will stop rulers from favoring, from even imposing upon their peoples, if they were to consider it necessary, the method of contraception which they judge to be most efficacious? In such a way men, wishing to avoid individual, family, or social difficulties encountered in the observance of the divine law, would reach the point of placing at the mercy of the intervention of public authorities the most personal and most reserved sector of conjugal intimacy.

Consequently, if the mission of generating life is not to be exposed to the arbitrary will of men, one must necessarily recognize unsurmountable limits to the possibility of man's domination over his own body and its functions; limits which no man, whether a private individual or one invested with authority, may licitly surpass. And such limits cannot be determined otherwise than by the respect due to the integrity of the human organism and its functions, according to the principles recalled earlier, and also according to the correct understanding of the "principle of totality" illustrated by our predecessor Pope Pius XII.[21]

The Church Guarantor of True Human Values

18. It can be foreseen that this teaching will perhaps not be easily received by all: Too numerous are those voices—amplified by the modern means of propaganda—which are contrary to the voice of the Church. To tell the truth, the Church is not surprised to be made, like her divine founder, a "sign of contradiction,"[22] yet she does not because of this cease to proclaim with humble firmness the entire moral law, both natural and evangelical. Of such laws the Church was not the author, nor consequently can she be their arbiter; she is only their depositary and their interpreter, without ever being able to declare to be licit that which is not so by reason of its intimate and unchangeable opposition to the true good of man.

In defending conjugal morals in their integral wholeness, the Church knows that she contributes towards the establishment of a truly human civilization; she engages man not to abdicate from his own responsibility in order to rely on technical means; by that very fact she defends the dignity of man and wife. Faithful to both the teaching and the example of the

Saviour, she shows herself to be the sincere and disinterested friend of men, whom she wishes to help, even during their earthly sojourn, "to share as sons in the life of the living God, the Father of all men."[23]

Pastoral Directives

The Church Mater et Magistra

19. Our words would not be an adequate expression of the thought and solicitude of the Church, mother and teacher of all peoples, if, after having recalled men to the observance and respect of the divine law regarding matrimony, we did not strengthen them in the path of honest regulation of birth, even amid the difficult conditions which today afflict families and peoples. The Church, in fact, cannot have a different conduct towards men than that of the Redeemer: She knows their weaknesses, has compassion on the crowd, receives sinners; but she cannot renounce the teaching of the law which is, in reality, that law proper to a human life restored to its original truth and conducted by the spirit of God.[24]

Possibility of Observing the Divine Law

20. The teaching of the Church on the regulation of birth, which promulgates the divine law, will easily appear to many to be difficult or even impossible of actuation. And indeed, like all great beneficent realities, it demands serious engagement and much effort, individual, family, and social effort. More than that, it would not be practicable without the help of God, who upholds and strengthens the good will of men. Yet, to anyone who reflects well, it cannot but be clear that such efforts ennoble man and are beneficial to the human community.

Mastery of Self

21. The honest practice of regulation of birth demands first of all that husband and wife acquire and possess solid convictions concerning the true values of life and of the family, and that they tend towards securing perfect self-mastery. To dominate instinct by means of one's reason and free will undoubtedly requires ascetical practices, so that the affective manifestations of conjugal life may observe the correct order, in particular with regard to the observance of periodic continence. Yet this discipline which is proper to the purity

of married couples, far from harming conjugal love, rather confers on it a higher human value. It demands continual effort yet, thanks to its beneficent influence, husband and wife fully develop their personalities, being enriched with spiritual values. Such discipline bestows upon family life fruits of serenity and peace, and facilitates the solution of other problems; it favors attention for one's partner, helps both parties to drive out selfishness, the enemy of true love; and deepens their sense of responsibility. By its means, parents acquire the capacity of having a deeper and more efficacious influence in the education of their offspring; little children and youths grow up with a just appraisal of human values, and in the serene and harmonious development of their spiritual and sensitive faculties.

Creating an Atmosphere Favorable to Chastity

22. On this occasion, we wish to draw the attention of educators, and of all who perform duties of responsibility in regard to the common good of human society, to the need of creating an atmosphere favorable to education in chastity, that is, to the triumph of healthy liberty over license by means of respect for the moral order.

Everything in the modern media of social communications which leads to sense excitation and unbridled habits, as well as every form of pornography and licentious performances, must arouse the frank and unanimous reaction of all those who are solicitous for the progress of civilization and the defense of the common good of the human spirit. Vainly would one seek to justify such depravation with the pretext of artistic or scientific exigencies,[25] or to deduce an argument from the freedom allowed in this sector by the public authorities.

Appeal to Public Authorities

23. To Rulers, who are those principally responsible for the common good, and who can do so much to safeguard moral customs, we say: Do not allow the morality of your peoples to be degraded; do not permit that by legal means practices contrary to the natural and divine law be introduced into that fundamental cell, the family. Quite other is the way in which public authorities can and must contribute to the solution of the demographic problem: namely the way of a provident policy for the family, of a wise education of peoples in respect of moral law and the liberty of citizens.

We are well aware of the serious difficulties experienced by public authorities in this regard, especially in the developing countries. To their legitimate preoccupations we devoted our encyclical letter *Populorum Progressio*. But with our predecessor Pope John XXIII, we repeat: No solution to these difficulties is acceptable "which does violence to man's essential dignity" and is based only on an utterly materialistic conception of man himself and of his life. The only possible solution to this question is one which envisages the social and economic progress both of individuals and of the whole of human society, and which respects and promotes of true human values.[26] Neither can one, without grave injustice, consider divine providence to be responsible for what depends, instead, on a lack of wisdom in government, on an insufficient sense of social justice, on selfish monopolization, or again on blameworthy indolence in confronting the efforts and the sacrifices necessary to ensure the raising of living standards of a people and of all its sons.[27]

May all responsible public authorities—as some are already doing so laudably—generously revive their efforts. And may mutual aid between all the members of the great human family never cease to grow. This is an almost limitless field which thus opens up to the activity of the great international organizations.

To Men of Science

24. We wish now to express our encouragement to men of science, who "can considerably advance the welfare of marriage and the family, along with peace of conscience, if by pooling their efforts they labor to explain more thoroughly the various conditions favoring a proper regulation of births."[28] It is particularly desirable that, according to the wish already expressed by Pope Pius XII, medical science succeed in providing a sufficiently secure basis for a regulation of birth, founded on the observance of natural rhythms.[29] In this way, scientists and especially Catholic scientists will contribute to demonstrate in actual fact that, as the Church teaches, "a true contradiction cannot exist between the divine laws pertaining to the transmission of life and those pertaining to the fostering of authentic conjugal love."[30]

To Christian Husbands and Wives

25. And now our words more directly address our own children, particularly those whom God calls to serve

Him in marriage. The Church, while teaching imprescriptible demands of the divine law, announces the tidings of salvation, and by means of the sacraments opens up the paths of grace, which makes man a new creature, capable of corresponding with love and true freedom to the design of his Creator and Saviour, and of finding the yoke of Christ to be sweet.[31]

Christian married couples, then, docile to her voice, must remember that their Christian vocation, which began at baptism, is further specified and reinforced by the sacrament of matrimony. By it husband and wife are strengthened and as it were consecrated for the faithful accomplishment of their proper duties, for the carrying out of their proper vocation even to perfection, and the Christian witness which is proper to them before the whole world.[32] To them the Lord entrusts the task of making visible to men the holiness and sweetness of the law which unites the mutual love of husband and wife with their cooperation with the love of God, the author of human life.

We do not at all intend to hide the sometimes serious difficulties inherent in the life of Christian married persons; for them as for everyone else, "the gate is narrow and the way is hard, that leads to life."[33] But the hope of that life must illuminate their way, as with courage they strive to live with wisdom, justice and piety in this present time,[34] knowing that the figure of this world passes away.[35]

Let married couples, then, face up to the efforts needed, supported by the faith and hope which "do not disappoint . . . because God's love has been poured into our hearts through the Holy Spirit, who has been given to us."[36] Let them implore divine assistance by persevering prayer; above all, let them draw from the source of grace and charity in the Eucharist. And if sin should still keep its hold over them, let them not be discouraged, but rather have recourse with humble perseverance to the mercy of God, which is poured forth in the sacrament of Penance. In this way they will be enabled to achieve the fullness of conjugal life described by the Apostle: "husbands, love your wives, as Christ loved the Church . . . husbands should love their wives as their own bodies. He who loves his wife loves himself. For no man ever hates his own flesh, but nourishes and cherishes it, as Christ does the Church . . . this is a great mystery, and I mean in reference to Christ and the Church. However, let each one of you love his wife as himself, and let the wife see that she respects her husband."[37]

Apostolate in Homes

26. Among the fruits which ripen forth from a generous effort of fidelity to the divine law, one of the most precious is that married couples themselves not infrequently feel the desire to communicate their experience to others. Thus there comes to be included in the vast pattern of the vocation of the laity a new and most noteworthy form of the apostolate of like to like; it is married couples themselves who become apostles and guides to other married couples. This is assuredly, among so many forms of apostolate, one of those which seem most opportune today.[38]

To Doctors and Medical Personnel

27. We hold those physicians and medical personnel in the highest esteem who, in the exercise of their profession, value above every human interest the superior demands of their Christian vocation. Let them persevere, therefore, in promoting on every occasion the discovery of solutions inspired by faith and right reason, let them strive to arouse this conviction and this respect in their associates. Let them also consider as their proper professional duty the task of acquiring all the knowledge needed in this delicate sector, so as to be able to give those married persons who consult them wise counsel and healthy direction, such as they have a right to expect.

To Priests

28. Beloved priest sons, by vocation you are the counselors and spiritual guides of individual persons and of families. We now turn to you with confidence. Your first task—especially in the case of those who teach moral theology—is to expound the Church's teaching on marriage without ambiguity. Be the first to give, in the exercise of your ministry, the example of loyal internal and external obedience to the teaching authority of the Church. That obedience, as you know well, obliges not only because of the reasons adduced, but rather because of the light of the Holy Spirit, which is given in a particular way to the pastors of the Church in order that they may illustrate the truth.[39] You know, too, that it is of the utmost importance, for peace of consciences and for the unity of the Christian people, that in the field of morals as well as in that of dogma, all should attend to the magisterium of the

Church, and all should speak the same language. Hence, with all our heart we renew to you the heartfelt plea of the great Apostle Paul: "I appeal to you, brethren, by the name of Our Lord Jesus Christ, that all of you agree and that there be no dissensions among you, but that you be united in the same mind and the same judgment."[40]

29. To diminish in no way the saving teaching of Christ constitutes an eminent form of charity for souls. But this must ever be accompanied by patience and goodness, such as the Lord himself gave example of in dealing with men. Having come not to condemn but to save,[41] he was indeed intransigent with evil, but merciful towards individuals.

In their difficulties, many married couples always find, in the words and in the heart of a priest, the echo of the voice and the love of the Redeemer.

Speak out confidently, beloved sons, with the conviction that the Spirit of God, while assisting the Magisterium in propounding doctrine, enlightens internally the hearts of the faithful, and invites them to give their assent. Teach married couples the necessary way of prayer, and prepare them to have recourse frequently and with faith to the sacraments of the Eucharist and Penance, without ever allowing themselves to be disheartened by their weakness.

To Bishops

30. Beloved and venerable brothers in the episcopate, with whom we most intimately share the solicitude of the spiritual good of the people of God, at the conclusion of this encyclical our reverent and affectionate thoughts turn to you. To all of you we extend an urgent invitation. At the head of the priests, your collaborators, and of your faithful, work ardently and incessantly for the safeguarding and the holiness of marriage, so that it may always be lived in its entire human and Christian fullness. Consider this mission as one of your most urgent responsibilities at the present time. As you know, it implies concerted pastoral action in all the fields of human activity, economic, cultural and social; for, in fact, only a simultaneous improvement in these various sectors will make it possible to render the life of parents and of children within their families not only tolerable, but easier and more joyous, to render the living together in human society more fraternal and peaceful, in faithfulness to God's design for the world.

Final Appeal

31. Venerable brothers, most beloved sons, and all men of good will, great indeed is the work of education, of progress and of love to which we call you, upon the foundation of the Church's teaching, of which the successor of Peter is, together with his brothers in the episcopate, the depositary and interpreter. Truly a great work, as we are deeply convinced, both for the world and for the Church, since man cannot find true happiness—towards which he aspires with all his being—other than in respect of the laws written by God in his very nature, laws which he must observe with intelligence and love. Upon this work, and upon all of you, and especially upon married couples, we invoke the abundant graces of the God of holiness and mercy, and in pledge thereof we impart to you all our apostolic blessing.

Given at Rome, from St. Peter's, this 25th day of July, feast of St. James the Apostle, in the year 1968, the sixth of our pontificate.

Endnotes

1. Cf. Pius IX, encyc. *Qui Pluribus,* November 9, 1846; in *PII IX P. M. Acta,* I, pp. 9–10; St. Pius X, encyc. *Singulari Quadam,* Sept. 24, 1912; in *AAS* IV (1912), p. 658; Pius XI, encyc. *Casti Connubii,* Dec. 31, 1930; in *AAS* XXI (1930), pp. 579–81; Pius XXI, allocution *Magnificate Dominum* to the episcopate of the Catholic world, Nov. 2, 1954; in *AAS* XLVI (1954), 671–72; John XXIII, encyc. *Mater et Magistra,* May 15, 1961; in *AAS* LIII (1961), p. 457.

2. Cf. Matthew 28:18–19.

3. Cf. Matthew 7:21.

4. Cf. *Catechismus Romanus Concilii Tridentini,* part 2, chap. 8, Leo XIII, encyc. *Arcanum,* Feb. 19, 1880; in *Acta Leonis XIII,* II (1881), pp. 26–29; Pius XI, encyc. *Divini Illius Magistri,* Dec. 31, 1929, in *AAS* XXII (1930), pp. 58–61; encyc. *Casti Connubii,* in *AAS* XXII (1930), pp. 545–46; Pius XII, alloc. to the Italian medicobiological union of St. Luke, Nov. 12, 1944, in *Discorsi e Radiomessaggi,* 6, pp. 191–92; to the Italian Catholic union of midwives, Oct. 29, 1951, in *AAS* XLIII (1951), pp. 857–59; to the seventh Congress of the International Society of Haematology, Sept. 12, 1958, in *AAS* L (1958), pp. 734–35; John XXIII, encyc. *Mater et Magistra,* in *AAS* LIII (1961), pp. 446–47; *Codex Iuris Canonici,* Canon 1067; Can. 1968, S 1, Can. 1066 S 1–2; II Vatican Council, Pastoral Constitution, *Gaudium et Spes,* nos. 47–52.

5. Cf. Paul VI, allocution to the Sacred College, June 23, 1964, in *AAS* LVI (1964), p. 588; to the Commission for Study of Problems of Population, Family and Birth, March 27, 1965,

in *AAS* LVII (1965), p. 388; to the National Congress of the Italian Society of Obstetrics and Gynecology, Oct. 29, 1966, in *AAS* LVIII (1966), p. 1168.

6. Cf. I John 4:8.

7. Cf. Ephesians 3:15.

8. Cf. Pastoral Const. *Gaudium et Spes,* no. 50.

9. Cf. St. Thomas, *Summa Theologica,* I-II, q. 94, art. 2.

10. Cf. Pastoral Const. *Gaudium et Spes,* nos. 50, 51.

11. Ibid., no. 49.

12. Cf. Pius XI, encyc. *Casti Connubii,* in *AAS* XXII (1930), p. 560; Pius XII, in *AAS* XLIII (1951), p. 843.

13. Cf. John XXIII, encyc. *Mater et Magistra,* in *AAS* LIII (1961), p. 447.

14. Cf. *Catechismus Romanus Concilii Tridentini,* part 2, chap. 8; Pius XI, encyc. *Casti Connubii,* in *AAS* XXII (1930); pp. S62–64; Pius XII, *Discorsi e Radiomessaggi,* VI (1944), pp. 191–92; *AAS* XLIII (1951), pp. 842–43; pp. 857–59; John XXIII, encyc. *Pacem in Terris,* Apr. 11, 1963, in *AAS* LV (1963), pp. 259–60; *Gaudium et Spes.* no. 51.

15. Cf. Pius XI, encyc. *Casti Connubii,* in *AAS* XXII (1930), p. 565; decree of the Holy Office, Feb. 22, 1940, in *AAS* L (1958), pp. 734–35.

16. Cf. *Catechismus Romanus Concilii Tridentini,* part 2, chap. 8; Pius XI, encyc. *Casti Connubii,* in *AAS* XXII (1930), pp. 559-61; Pius XII, *AAS* XLIII (1951), p. 843; *AAS* L (1958), pp. 734-35; John XXIII, encyc. *Mater et Magistra,* in *AAS* LIII (1961), p. 447.

17. Cf. Pius XII, alloc. to the National Congress of the Union of Catholic Jurists, Dec. 6, 1953, in *AAS* XLV (1953), 798–99.

18. Cf. Romans 3:8.

19. Cf. Pius XII, alloc. to Congress of the Italian Association of Urology, Oct. 8, 1953, in *AAS* XLV (1953), pp. 674–75; *AAS* L (1958), pp. 734–35.

20. Cf. Pius XII, *AAS* XLIII (1951), p. 846.

21. Cf. *AAS* XLV (1953), pp. 674–75; *AAS* XLVIII (1956), pp. 461–62.

22. Cf. Luke 2:34.

23. Cf. Paul VI, encyc. *Populorum Progressio,* March 26, 1967, no. 21.

24. Cf. Romans 8.

25. Cf. II Vatican Council, decree *Inter Mirifica, On the Instruments of Social Communication,* nos. 6–7.

26. Cf. encyc. *Mater et Magistra,* in *AAS* LIII (1961), p. 447.

27. Cf. encyc. *Populorum Progressio,* nos. 48–55.

28. Cf. Pastoral Const. *Gaudium et Spes,* no. 52.

29. Cf. *AAS* XLIII (1951), p. 859.

30. Cf. Pastoral Const. *Gaudium et Spes,* no. 51.

31. Cf. Matthew 11:30.

32. Cf. Pastoral Const. *Gaudium et Spes,* no. 48; II Vatican Council, Dogmatic Const. *Lumen Gentium,* no. 35.

33. Matthew 7:14; cf. Hebrews 11:12.

34. Cf. Titus 2:12.

35. Cf. I Corinthians 7:31.

36. Cf. Romans 5:5.

37. Ephesians 5:25, 28–29, 32–33.

38. Cf. Dogmatic Const. *Lumen Gentium,* nos. 35 and 41; Pastoral Const. *Gaudium et Spes,* nos. 48–49; II Vatican Council, Decree *Apostolicam Actuositatem,* no. 11.

39. Cf. Dogmatic Const. *Lumen Gentium,* no. 25.

40. Cf. I Corinthians 1:10.

41. Cf. John 3:17.

12. *The Homosexual Movement*

THE RAMSEY COLLOQUIUM*

The members of the Ramsey Colloquium, a group of Jewish and Christian scholars of the Institute for Religion and Public Life, argue that the movement toward extending civil rights to homosexuals represents a larger cultural shift that proposes sweeping changes in our social practices, morality, religious convictions, and law. They trace this movement to the sexual revolution of the 1960s and 1970s, during which the place of sex in human relations was trivialized, exaggerated, and distorted. Along with the growing insistence that sexual practices are no more than lifestyle choices and matters of personal preference, permissive abortion, easy divorce, adultery, and the promotion of the gay and lesbian movement have all followed as a result. The Ramsey Colloquium claims that restraint, discipline, and respect for the power of sexual expression are not repressive notions and that the heterosexual norm has endured because it is truly natural and fosters our relationships with children, other adults, and God himself.

The New Thing

Homosexual behavior is a phenomenon with a long history to which there have have been various cultural and moral responses. But today in our public life there is something new, a *novum,* which demands our attention and deserved a careful moral response.

The new thing is a movement that variously presents itself as an appeal for compassion, as an extension

---

*Hadley Arkes, Amherst College; Matthew Berke, *First Things;* Gerard Bradley, Notre Dame Law School; Rabbi David Dalin, University of Hartford; Ernest Fortin, Boston College; Jorge Garcia, Rutgers University; Rabbi Marc Gellman, Hebrew Union College; Robert George, Princeton University; The Rev. Hugh Haffenreffer, Emanuel Lutheran Church Hartford, Conn.; John Hittinger, College of Saint Francis; Russell Hittinger, Catholic University of America; Robert Jenson, St. Olaf College; Gilbert Meilaender, Oberlin College; Jerry Muller, Catholic University of America; Fr. Richard John Neuhaus, Institute on Religion and Public Life; Rabbi David Novak, University of Virginia; James Nuechterlein, *First Things;* Max Stackhouse, Princeton Theological Seminary; Philip Turner, Berkeley Divinity School (Yale University) George Weigel, Ethics and Public Policy Center; Robert Wilken, University of Virginia.

From *First Things: A Monthly Journal of Religion and Public Life.* No. 41, March 1994. FIRST THINGS is a monthly journal published in New York City by the Institute of Religion and Public Life. Reprinted by permission.

of civil rights to minorities, and as a cultural revolution. The last of these seems to us the best description of the phenomenon indeed, that is what its most assertive and passionate defenders say it is. The *Nation,* for example, asserts (May 3, 1993): "All the crosscurrents of present day liberation struggles are subsumed in the gay struggle. The gay moment is in some ways similar to the moment that other communities have experienced in the nation's past, but it is also something more, because sexual identity is in crisis throughout the population, and gay people—at once the most conspicuous.

It is a testimony to the perduring role of religion in American life that many within the gay and lesbian movement seek the blessing of religious institutions. The movement correctly perceives that attaining such formal approbation—through, for example, the content and style of seminary education and the ordination of practicing homosexuals—will give it an effective hold upon the primary institutions of moral legitimation in our popular culture. The movement also correctly perceives that our churches and synagogues have typically been inarticulate and unpersuasive in offering reasons for withholding the blessing that is sought.

One reason for the discomfort of religious leaders in the face of this new movement is the past and continuing failure to offer supportive and knowledgeable pastoral care to persons coping with the problems of their homosexuality. Without condoning homogenital acts, it is necessary to recognize that many such persons are, with fear and trembling, seeking as best they can to live lives pleasing to God and in service to others. Confronted by the vexing ambiguities of eros in human life, religious communities should be better equipped to support people in their struggle, recognizing that we all fall short of the vocation to holiness of life.

The sexual revolution is motored by presuppositions that can and ought to be effectively challenged. Perhaps the key presupposition of the revolution is that human health and flourishing require that sexual desire, understood as a "need," be acted upon and satisfied. Any discipline of denial or restraint has been popularly depicted as unhealthy and dehumanizing. We insist, however, that it is dehumanizing to define ourselves, or our personhood as male and female, by our desires alone. Nor does it seem plausible to suggest that what millennia of human experience have taught us to regard as self-command should now be dismissed as mere repression.

At the same time that the place of sex has been grotesquely exaggerated by the sexual revolution, it has also been trivialized. The mysteries of human sexuality are commonly reduced to matters of recreation or taste, not unlike one's preferences in diet, dress, or sport. This peculiar mix of the exaggerated and the trivialized makes it possible for the gay and lesbian movement to demand, simultaneously, a respect for what is claimed to be most importantly and constitutively true of homosexuals, and tolerance for what is, after all, simply a difference in "lifestyle."

It is important to recognize the linkages among the component parts of the sexual revolution. Permissive abortion, widespread adultery, easy divorce, radical feminism, and the gay and lesbian movement have not by accident appeared at the same historical moment. They have in common a declared desire for liberation from constraint—especially constraints associated with an allegedly repressed culture and religious tradition. They also have in common the presuppositions that the body is little more than an instrument for the fulfillment of desire, and that the fulfillment of desire is the essence of the self. On biblical and philosophical grounds, we reject this radical dualism between the self and the body. Our bodies have their own dignity, bear their own truths, and are participant in our personhood in a fundamental way.

This constellation of movements, of which the gay movement is part, rests upon an anthropological doctrine of the autonomous self. With respect to abortion and the socialization of sexuality, this anthropology has gone a long way toward entrenching itself in the jurisprudence of our society as well as in popular habits of mind and behavior. We believe it is a false doctrine that leads neither to individual flourishing nor to social well-being.

The Heterosexual Norm

Marriage and the family—husband, wife, and children, joined by public recognition and legal bond—are the most effective institutions for the rearing of children, the directing of sexual passion, and human flourishing in community. Not all marriages and families "work," but it is unwise to let pathology and failure, rather than a vision of what is normative and ideal, guide us in the development of social policy.

Of course many today doubt that we can speak of what is normatively human. The claim that all social institutions and patterns of behavior are social constructions that we may, if we wish, alter without harm to ourselves is a proposal even more radical in origin and implication than the sexual revolution. That the institutions of marriage and family are culturally conditioned and subject to change and development no one should doubt, but such recognition should not undermine our ability to discern patterns of community that best serve human well-being, Judaism and Christianity did not invent the heterosexual norm, but these faith traditions affirm that norm and can open our eyes to see in it important truths about human life.

Fundamental to human life in society is the creation of humankind as male and female, which is typically and paradigmatically expressed in the marriage of a man and a woman who form a union of persons in which two become one flesh—a union which, in the biblical tradition, is the foundation of all human community. In faithful marriage, three important elements of human life are made manifest and given support.

1. *Human society extends over time; it has a history.* It does so because, through the mysterious participation of our procreative powers in God's own creative work, we transmit life to those who will succeed us. We become a people with a shared history over time and with a common stake in that history. Only the heterosexual norm gives full expression to the commitment to time and history evident in having and caring for children.

2. *Human society requires that we learn to value difference within community.* In the complementarity of male and female we find the paradigmatic instance of this truth. Of course, persons may complement each other in many different ways, but the complementarity of male

and female is grounded in, and fully embraces, our bodies and their structure. It does not sever the meaning of the person from bodily life, as if human beings were simply desire, reason, or will. The complementarity of male and female invites us to learn to accept and affirm the natural world from which we are too often alienated.

Moreover, in the creative complementarity of male and female we are directed toward community with those unlike us. In the community between male and female, we do not and cannot see in each other mere reflections of ourselves. In learning to appreciate this most basic difference, and in forming a marital bond, we take both difference and community seriously. (And ultimately, we begin to be prepared for communion with God, in Whom we never find simply a reflection of ourselves.)

3. Human society requires the direction and restraint of many impulses. Few of those impulses are more powerful or unpredictable than sexual desire. Throughout history societies have taken particular care to socialize sexuality toward marriage and the family. Marriage is a place where, in a singular manner, our waywardness begins to be healed and our fear of commitment overcome, where we may learn to place another person's needs rather than our own desires at the center of life.

Thus, reflection on the heterosexual norm directs our attention to certain social necessities: the continuation of human life, the place of difference within community, the redirection of our tendency to place our own desires first. These necessities cannot be supported by rational calculations of self-interest alone; they require commitments that go well beyond the demands of personal satisfaction. Having and rearing children is among the most difficult of human projects. Men and women need all the support they can get to maintain stable marriages in which the next generation can flourish. Even marriages that do not give rise to children exist in accord with, rather than in opposition to, this heterosexual norm. To depict marriage as simply one of several alternative "lifestyles" is seriously to undermine the normative vision required for social well-being.

There are legitimate and honorable forms of love other than marriage. Indeed, one of the goods at stake in today's disputes is a long-honored tradition of friendship between men and men, women and women, women and men. In the current climate of sexualizing and politicizing all intense interpersonal relationships, the place of sexually chaste friendship and of religiously motivated celibacy is gravely jeopardized. In our cultural moment of narrow-eyed prurience, the single life of chastity has come under the shadow of

suspicion and is no longer credible to many people. Indeed, the nonsatisfaction of sexual "needs" is widely viewed as a form of deviance.

In this context it becomes imperative to affirm the reality and beauty of sexually chaste relationships of deep affectional intensity. We do not accept the notion that self-command is an unhealthy form of repression on the part of single people, whether their inclination be heterosexual or homosexual. Put differently, the choice is not limited to heterosexual marriage on the one hand, or relationships involving homogenital sex on the other.

The Claims of the Movement

We turn our attention now to a few of the important public claims made by gay and lesbian advocates (even as we recognize that the movement is not monolithic). As we noted earlier, there is an important distinction between those who wish to "mainstream" homosexual life and those who aim at restructuring culture. This is roughly the distinction between those who seek integration and those who seek revolution. Although these different streams of the movement need to be distinguished, a few claims are so frequently encountered that they require attention.

Many gays argue that they have no choice, that they could not be otherwise than they are. Such an assertion can take a variety of forms—for example, that "being gay is natural for me" or even that "God made me this way."

We cannot settle the dispute about the roots—genetic or environmental—of homosexual orientation. When some scientific evidence suggests a genetic predisposition for homosexual orientation, the case is not significantly different from evidence of predispositions toward other traits—for example, alcoholism or violence. In each instance we must still ask whether such a predisposition should be acted upon or whether it should be resisted. Whether or not a homosexual orientation can be changed—and it is important to recognize that there are responsible authorities on both sides of this question—we affirm the obligation of pastors and therapists to assist those who recognize the value of chaste living to resist the impulse to act on their desire for homogenital gratification.

The Kinsey data, which suggested that 10 percent of males are homosexual, have now been convincingly discredited. Current research suggests that the percentage of males whose sexual desires and behavior are exclusively homosexual is as low as 1 percent or 2 percent in developed societies. In any case, the statistical frequency of an act or desire does not determine its moral status. Racial discrimination and child abuse occur frequently in society, but that does not make them "natural" in the moral sense. What is in accord with human nature is behavior appropriate to what we are meant to be—appropriate to what God created and calls us to be.

In a fallen creation, many quite common attitudes and behaviors must be straightforwardly designated as sin. Although we are equal before God, we are not born equal in terms of our strengths and weaknesses, our tendencies and dispositions, our nature and nurture. We cannot utterly change the hand we have been dealt by inheritance and family circumstances, but we are responsible for how we play that hand. Inclination and temptation are not sinful, although they surely result from humanity's fallen condition. Sin occurs in the joining of the will, freely and knowingly, to an act or way of life that is contrary to God's purpose. Religious communities in particular must lovingly support all the faithful in their struggle against temptation, while at the same time insisting that precisely for their sake we must describe as sinful the homogenital and extramarital heterosexual behavior to which some are drawn.

Many in our society—both straight and gay—also contend that what people do sexually is entirely a private matter and no one's business but their own. The form this claim takes is often puzzling to many people—and rightly so. For what were once considered private acts are now highly publicized, while, for the same acts, public privilege is claimed because they are private. What is confusedly at work here is an extreme individualism, a claim for autonomy so extreme that it must undercut the common good.

To be sure, there should in our society be a wide zone for private behavior, including behavior that most Americans would deem wrong. Some of us oppose anti-sodomy statutes. In a society premised upon limited government there are realms of behavior that ought to be beyond the supervision of the state. In addition to the way sexual wrongdoing harms character, however, there are often other harms involved. We have in mind the alarming rates of sexual promiscuity, depression, and suicide and the ominous presence of AIDS within the homosexual subculture. No one can doubt that these are reasons for public concern. Another legitimate reason for public concern is the harm done to the social order when policies are advanced that would increase the incidence of the gay lifestyle and undermine the normative character of marriage and family life.

Since there are good reasons to support the heterosexual norm, since it has been developed with great difficulty, and since it can be maintained only if it is cared for and supported, we cannot be indifferent to attacks upon it. The social norms by which sexual behavior is inculcated and controlled are of urgent importance for families and for the society as a whole. Advocates of the gay and lesbian movement have the responsibility to set forth publicly their alternative proposals. This must mean more than calling for liberation from established standards. They must clarify for all of us how sexual mores are to be inculcated in the young, who are particularly vulnerable to seduction and solicitation. Public anxiety about homosexuality is preeminently a concern about the vulnerabilities of the young. This, we are persuaded, is a legitimate and urgent public concern.

Gay and lesbian advocates sometimes claim that they are asking for no more than an end to discrimination, drawing an analogy with the earlier civil rights movement that sought justice for black Americans. The analogy is unconvincing and misleading. Differences of race are in accord with—not contrary to—our nature, and such differences do not provide justification for behavior otherwise unacceptable. It is sometimes claimed that homosexuals want only a recognition of their status, not necessarily of their behavior. But in this case the distinction between status and behavior does not hold. The public declaration of status ("coming out of the closet") is a declaration of intended behavior.

Certain discriminations are necessary within society; it is not too much to say that civilization itself depends on the making of such distinctions (between, finally, right and wrong). In our public life, some discrimination is in order—when, for example, in education and programs involving young people the intent is to prevent predatory behavior that can take place under the guise of supporting young people in their anxieties about their "sexual identity." It is necessary to discriminate between relationships. Gay and lesbian "domestic partnerships," for example, should not be socially recognized as the moral equivalent of marriage. We note again that marriage and the family are institutions necessary for our continued social well-being and, in an individualistic society that tends to liberation from all constraint, they are fragile institutions in need of careful and continuing support.

Conclusion

We do not doubt that many gays and lesbians—perhaps especially those who seek the blessing of our religious communities—believe that theirs is the only form of love, understood as affection and erotic satisfaction, of which they are capable. Nor do we doubt that they have found in such relationships something of great personal significance, since even a distorted love retains traces of love's grandeur. Where there is love in morally disordered relationships we do not censure the love. We censure the form in which that love seeks expression. To those who say that this disordered behavior is so much at the core of their being that the person cannot be (and should not be) distinguished from the behavior; we can only respond that we earnestly hope they are wrong.

We are well aware that this declaration will be dismissed by some as a display of "homophobia," but such dismissals have become unpersuasive and have ceased to intimidate. Indeed, we do not think it a bad thing that people should experience a reflexive recoil from what is wrong. To achieve such a recoil is precisely the point of moral education of the young. What we have tried to do here is to bring this reflexive and often pre-articulate recoil to reasonable expression.

Our society is, we fear, progressing precisely in the manner given poetic expression by Alexander Pope:

> Vice is a monster of so frightful mien,
> As to be hated needs but to be seen;
> Yet seen too oft, familiar with her face,
> We first endure, then pity, then embrace.

To endure (tolerance), to pity (compassion), to embrace (affirmation): that is the sequence of change in attitude and judgment that has been advanced by the gay and lesbian movement with notable success. We expect that this success will encounter certain limits and that what is truly natural will reassert itself, but this may not happen before more damage is done to innumerable individuals and to our common life.

Perhaps some of this damage can be prevented. For most people marriage and family is the most important project in their lives. For it they have made sacrifices beyond numbering; they want to be succeeded in an ongoing, shared history by children and grandchildren; they want to transmit to their children the beliefs that have claimed their hearts and minds. They should be supported in that attempt. To that end, we have tried to set forth our view and the reasons that inform it. Whatever the inadequacies of this declaration, we hope it will be useful to others. The gay and lesbian movement, and the dramatic changes in sexual attitudes and behavior of which that movement is part, have unloosed a great moral agitation in our culture. Our hope is that this statement will contribute to turning that agitation into, civil conversation about the kind of people we are and hope to be.

13. *Why Homosexuality Is Abnormal**

Michael Levin

In this essay, Michael Levin argues that the practice of homosexuality is undesirable, although he insists that he does not regard the behavior as either immoral or sinful. Instead, he claims that homosexuality is abnormal on what he calls "mechanical" grounds, meaning that the behavior requires a misuse of body parts, and that such regular misuse is likely to lead to personal unhappiness. Citing a number of illustrations from science as well as nature in which a distortion of intended function has proven damaging, Levin concludes that it may well be in society's best interests to protect its children from the possible acceptance or even approval of such a harmful way of life. Legislation, therefore, that grants privileges to homosexuals should not be approved because no empirical evidence has been discovered that overturns our longstanding convictions about its disvalue.

Introduction

This paper defends the view that homosexuality is abnormal and hence undesirable—not because it is immoral or sinful, or because it weakens society or hampers evolutionary development, but for a purely mechanical reason. It is a misuse of bodily parts. Clear empirical sense attaches to the idea of *the use* of such bodily parts as genitals, the idea that they are *for* something, and consequently to the idea of their misuse. I argue on grounds involving natural selection that misuse of bodily parts can with high probability be connected to unhappiness. I regard these matters as prolegomena to such policy issues as the rights of homosexuals, the rights of those desiring not to associate with homosexuals, and legislation concerning homosexuality, issues which I shall not discuss systematically

here. However, I do in the last section draw a seemingly evident corollary from my view that homosexuality is abnormal and likely to lead to unhappiness.

I have confined myself to male homosexuality for brevity's sake, but I believe that much of what I say applies *mutatis mutandis* to lesbianism. There may well be significant differences between the two: the data of Bell and Weinberg, for example, support the popular idea that sex *per se* is less important to women and in particular lesbians than it is to men. On the other hand, lesbians are generally denied motherhood, which seems more important to women than is fatherhood—normally denied homosexual males—to men. . . . Overall, it is reasonable to expect general innate gender differences to explain the major differences between male homosexuals and lesbians.

Despite the publicity currently enjoyed by the claim that one's "sexual preference" is nobody's business but one's own, the intuition that there is something unnatural about homosexuality remains vital. The erect penis fits the vagina, and fits it better than any other natural orifice; penis and vagina seem made for each other. This intuition ultimately derives from, or is another way of capturing, the idea that the penis is not *for* inserting into the anus of another man—that so using the penis is not the way it is *supposed,* even *intended,* to be used. Such intuitions may appear to rest on an outmoded teleological view of nature, but recent work in the logic of functional ascription shows how they may be explicated, and justified, in suitably naturalistic terms. . . . Furthermore, when we understand the

*Arthur Caplan, R. M. Hare, Michael Slote, Ed Erwin, Steven Goldberg, Ed Sagarin, Charles Winnick, Robert Gary, Thomas Nagel, David Benfield, Michael Green, and my wife, Margarita, all commented helpfully on earlier drafts of this paper, one of which was read to the New York chapter of the Society for Philosophy and Public Policy. My definition of naturalness agrees to some extent with Gary's (1978), and I have benefited from seeing an unpublished paper by Michael Ruse.

sense in which homosexual acts involve a misuse of genitalia, we will see why such misuse is bad and not to be encouraged. . . . Clearly, the general idea that homosexuality is a pathological violation of nature's intent is not shunned by scientists. Here is Gadpille (1972):

> The view of cultural relativity seems to be without justification. Cultural judgment is collective human caprice, and whether it accepts or rejects homosexuality is irrelevant. Biological intent . . . is to differentiate male and female both physiologically and psychologically in such a manner as to insure species survival, which can be served only through heterosexual union.

Gadpille refers to homosexuality as "an abiological maladaptation." The novelty of the present paper is to link adaptiveness and normality via the notion of happiness.

But before turning to these issues, I want to make four preliminary remarks. The first concerns the explicitness of my language in the foregoing paragraph and the rest of this paper. Explicit mention of bodily parts and the frank description of sexual acts are necessary to keep the phenomenon under discussion in clear focus. Euphemistic vagary about "sexual orientation" or "the gay lifestyle" encourage one to slide over homosexuality without having to face or even acknowledge what it really is. Such talk encourages one to treat "sexual preference" as if it were akin to preference among flavors of ice cream. Since unusual taste in ice cream is neither right nor wrong, this usage suggests, why should unusual taste in sex be regarded as objectionable? Opposed to this usage is the unblinkable fact that the sexual preferences in question are such acts as mutual fellation. Is one man's taste for pistachio ice cream really just like another man's taste for fellation? Unwillingness to call this particular spade a spade allows delicacy to award the field by default to the view that homosexuality is normal. Anyway, such delicacy is misplaced in a day when "the love that dare not speak its name" is shouting its name from the rooftops.[1]

My second, related, point concerns the length of the present paper, which has a general and a specific cause. The general cause is that advocates of an unpopular position—as mine is, at least in intellectual circles—assume the burden of proof. My view is the one that needs defending, my presuppositions the ones not widely shared. I would not have entertained so many implausible and digressive objections had not so many competent philosophers urged them on me with great seriousness. Some of these objections even generate a dialectic among themselves. For example, I have to defend my view on two sociobiological fronts—against the view that what is innate is polymorphous sexuality shaped by culture, and against the incompatible view that not only are the details of sexual behavior innate, but homosexuality is one such behavior, and hence "normal."

The third point is this. The chain of intuitions I discussed earlier has other links, links connected to the conclusion that homosexuality is bad. They go something like this: Homosexual acts involve the use of the genitals for what they aren't for, and it is a *bad* or at least *unwise* thing to use a part of your body for what it isn't for. Calling homosexual acts "unnatural" is intended to sum up this entire line of reasoning. "Unnatural" carries disapprobative connotations, and any explication of it should capture this. One can, stipulatively or by observing the ordinary usage of biologists, coin an evaluatively neutral use for "normal," or "proper function," or any cognate thereof. One might for example take the normal use of an organ to be what the organ is used for 95 percent of the time. But there is a normative dimension to the concept of abnormality that all such explications miss. To have anything to do with our intuitions—even if designed to demonstrate them groundless—an explication of "abnormal" must capture the analytic truth that the abnormality of a practice is a reason for avoiding it. If our ordinary concept of normality turns out to be ill-formed, so that various acts are at worst "abnormal" in some nonevaluative sense, this will simply mean that, as we ordinarily use the expression, *nothing is abnormal.* (Not that anyone really believes this—people who deny that cacophagia or necrophilia is abnormal do so only to maintain the appearance of consistency.). . .

On "Function" and Its Cognates

To bring into relief the point of the idea that homosexuality involves a misuse of bodily parts, I will begin with an uncontroversial case of misuse, a case in which the clarity of our intuitions is not obscured by the conviction that they are untrustworthy. Mr. Jones pulls all his teeth and strings them around his neck because he thinks his teeth look nice as a necklace. He takes puréed liquids supplemented by intravenous solutions for nourishment. It is surely natural to say that Jones is misusing his teeth, that he is not using them for what they are for, that indeed the way he is using them is incompatible with what they are for. Pedants might argue that Jones's teeth are no longer part of him and hence that he is not misusing any bodily parts. To them I offer Mr. Smith, who likes to play "Old MacDonald" on his teeth. So devoted is he to this amusement, in fact, that he never uses his teeth for chewing—like Jones, he takes nourishment intravenously. Now, not only do we find it perfectly plain that Smith and Jones are misusing their teeth, we predict a dim future for them on purely physiological grounds; we expect the muscles of Jones's jaw that are used for—that *are* for—chewing to lose their tone, and we expect this to affect Jones's gums. Those parts of Jones's digestive tract that are for processing solids will also suffer from disuse. The net result will be deteriorating health and perhaps a shortened life. Nor is this all. Human beings enjoy chewing. Not only has natural selection selected in muscles for chewing and favored creatures with such muscles, it has selected in a tendency to find the use of those muscles reinforcing. Creatures who do not enjoy using such parts of their bodies as deteriorate with disuse will tend to be selected out. Jones, product of natural selection that he is, descended from creatures who at least tended to enjoy the use of such parts. Competitors who didn't simply had fewer descendants. So we expect Jones sooner or later to experience vague yearnings to chew something, just as we find people who take no exercise to experience a general listlessness. Even waiving for now my apparent reification of the evolutionary process, let me emphasize how little anyone is tempted to say "each to his own" about Jones or to regard Jones's disposition of his teeth as simply a deviation from a statistical norm. This sort of case is my paradigm when discussing homosexuality. . . .

Applications to Homosexuality

The application of this general picture to homosexuality should be obvious. There can be no reasonable doubt that one of the functions of the penis is to introduce semen into the vagina. It does this, and it has been selected in because it does this. . . . Nature has consequently made this use of the penis rewarding. It is clear enough that any proto-human males who found unrewarding the insertion of penis into vagina have left no descendants. In particular, proto-human males who enjoyed inserting their penises into each other's anuses have left no descendants. This is why homosexuality is abnormal, and why its abnormality

counts prudentially against it. Homosexuality is likely to cause unhappiness because it leaves unfulfilled an innate and innately rewarding desire. And should the reader's environmentalism threaten to get the upper hand, let me remind him again of an unproblematic case. Lack of exercise is bad and even abnormal not only because it is unhealthy but also because one feels poorly without regular exercise. Nature made exercise rewarding because, until recently, we had to exercise to survive. Creatures who found running after game unrewarding were eliminated. Laziness leaves unreaped the rewards nature has planted in exercise, even if the lazy man cannot tell this introspectively. If this is a correct description of the place of exercise in human life, it is by the same token a correct description of the place of heterosexuality.

It hardly needs saying, but perhaps I should say it anyway, that this argument concerns tendencies and probabilities. Generalizations about human affairs being notoriously "true by and large and for the most part" only, saying that homosexuals are bound to be less happy than heterosexuals must be understood as short for "Not coincidentally, a larger proportion of homosexuals will be unhappy than a corresponding selection of the heterosexual population." There are, after all, genuinely jolly fat men. To say that laziness leads to adverse affective consequences means that, because of our evolutionary history, the odds are relatively good that a man who takes no exercise will suffer adverse affective consequences. Obviously, some people will get away with misusing their bodily parts. Thus, when evaluating the empirical evidence that bears on this account, it will be pointless to cite cases of well-adjusted homosexuals. I do not say they are nonexistent; my claim is that, of biological necessity, they are rare. . . .

Utilitarians must take the present evolutionary scenario seriously. The utilitarian attitude toward homosexuality usually runs something like this: even if homosexuality is in some sense unnatural, as a matter of brute fact homosexuals take pleasure in sexual contact with members of the same sex. As long as they don't hurt anyone else, homosexuality is as great a good as heterosexuality. But the matter cannot end here. Not even a utilitarian doctor would have words of praise for a degenerative disease that happened to foster a certain kind of pleasure (as sore muscles uniquely conduce to the pleasure of stretching them). A utilitarian doctor would presumably try just as zealously to cure diseases that feel good as less pleasant degenerative diseases. A pleasure causally connected with great distress cannot be treated as just another pleasure to be toted up on the felicific scoreboard. Utilitarians have to reckon with the inevitable consequences of pain-causing pleasure.

Similar remarks apply to the question of whether homosexuality is a "disease." A widely quoted pronouncement of the American Psychiatric Association runs:

> Surely the time has come for psychiatry to give up the archaic practice of classifying the millions of men and women who accept or prefer homosexual object choices as being, by virtue of that fact alone, mentally ill. The fact that their alternative life-style happens to be out of favor with current cultural conventions must not be a basis in itself for a diagnosis.

Apart from some question-begging turns of phrase, this is right. One's taste for mutual anal intercourse is nothing "in itself" for one's psychiatrist to worry about, any more than a life of indolence is anything "in itself" for one's doctor to worry about. In fact, in itself there is nothing wrong with a broken arm or an occluded artery. The fact that my right ulna is now in two pieces is just a fact of nature, not a "basis for diagnosis." But this condition is a matter for medical science anyway, because it will lead to pain. Permitted to persist, my fracture will provoke increasingly punishing states. So if homosexuality is a reliable sign of present or future misery, it is beside the point that homosexuality is not "by virtue of that fact alone" a mental illness. High rates of drug addiction, divorce, and illegitimacy are in themselves no basis for diagnosing social pathology. They support this diagnosis because of what else they signify about a society which exhibits them. Part of the problem here is the presence of germs in paradigm diseases, and the lack of a germ for homosexuality (or psychosis). I myself am fairly sure that a suitably general and germ-free definition of "disease" can be extruded from the general notion of "function" . . ., but however that may be, whether homosexuality is a disease is a largely verbal issue. If homosexuality is a self-punishing maladaptation, it hardly matters what it is called.

Evidence and Further Clarification

I have argued that homosexuality is "abnormal" in both a descriptive and a normative sense because—for evolutionary reasons—homosexuals are bound to be unhappy. In Kantian terms, . . . it is possible for homosexuality to be unnatural even if it violates no cosmic purpose or such purposes as we retrospectively impose on nature. What is the evidence for my view? For one thing, by emphasizing homosexual unhappiness, my view explains a ubiquitous fact in a simple way. The fact is the universally acknowledged unhappiness of homosexuals. Even the staunchest defenders of homosexuality admit that, as of now, homosexuals are not happy. (Writers even in the very recent past, like Lord Devlin, could not really believe that anyone could publicly advocate homosexuality as intrinsically good: see Devlin, p. 87.). . .

The usual environmentalist explanation for homosexuals' unhappiness is the misunderstanding, contempt, and abuse that society heaps on them. But this not only leaves unexplained why society has this attitude, it sins against parsimony by explaining a nearly universal phenomenon in terms of variable circumstances that have, by coincidence, the same upshot. Parsimony urges that we seek the explanation of homosexual unhappiness in the nature of homosexuality itself, as my explanation does. Having to "stay in the closet" may be a great strain, but it does not account for all the miseries that writers on homosexuality say is the homosexual's lot.

Incorporating unhappiness into the present evolutionary picture also smooths a bothersome ad-hocness in some otherwise appealing analyses of abnormality. Many writers define abnormality as compulsiveness. On this conception, homosexuality is abnormal because it is an autonomy-obstructing compulsion. Such an analysis is obviously open to the question, What if an autonomous homosexual comes along? To that, writers like van den Haag point out that homosexuality is, in fact, highly correlated with compulsiveness. The trouble here is that the definition in question sheds no light on why abnormal, compulsive, traits are such. The present account not only provides a criterion for abnormality, it encapsulates an explanation of *why* behavior abnormal by its lights is indeed compulsive and bound to lead to unhappiness.

One crucial test of my account is its prediction that homosexuals will continue to be unhappy even if people altogether abandon their "prejudice" against homosexuality. This prediction, that homosexuality being unnatural homosexuals will still find their behavior self-punishing, coheres with available evidence. It is consistent with the failure of other oppressed groups, such as American Negroes and European Jews, to become warped in the direction of "cruising," sado-masochism, and other practices common in homosexual life (see McCracken, 1979). It is consistent as well with the admission by even so sympathetic an observer of homosexuality as Rechy (1977) that the immediate cause of homosexual unhappiness is a taste for promiscuity, anonymous encounters, and humiliation. It is hard to see how such tastes are related to the dim view society takes of them. Such a relation would be plausible only if homosexuals courted multiple anonymous encounters *faute de mieux,* longing all the while to settle down to some sort of domesticity. But, again, Europeans abhorred Jews for centuries, but this did not create in Jews a special weakness for anonymous, promiscuous sex. Whatever drives a man away from women, to be fellated by as many different men as possible, seems independent of what society thinks of such behavior. It is this behavior that occasions misery, and we may expect the misery of homosexuals to continue.

In a 1974 study, Weinberg and Williams found no difference in the distress experienced by homosexuals in Denmark and the Netherlands, and in the U.S., where they found public tolerance of homosexuality to be lower. This would confirm rather strikingly that homosexual unhappiness is endogenous, unless one says that Weinberg's and Williams's indices for public tolerance and distress—chiefly homosexuals' self-reports of "unhappiness" and "lack of faith in others"—are unreliable. Such complaints, however, push the social causation theory toward untestability. Weinberg and Williams themselves cleave to the hypothesis that homosexual unhappiness is entirely a reaction to society's attitudes, and suggest that a condition of homosexual happiness is positive endorsement by the surrounding society. It is hard to imagine a more flagrantly *ad hoc* hypothesis. Neither a Catholic living among Protestants nor a copywriter working on the great American novel in his off hours asks more of society than tolerance in order to be happy in his pursuits.

It is interesting to reflect on a natural experiment that has gotten under way in the decade since the Weinberg-Williams study. A remarkable change in public opinion, if not private sentiment, has occurred in America. For whatever reason—the prodding of homosexual activists, the desire not to seem like a fuddy-duddy—various organs of opinion are now hard at work providing a "positive image" for homosexuals. Judges allow homosexuals to adopt their lovers. The Unitarian Church now performs homosexual marriages. Hollywood produces highly sanitized movies like *Making Love* and *Personal Best* about homosexuality. Macmillan strongly urges its authors to show little boys using cosmetics. Homosexuals no

longer fear revealing themselves, as is shown by the prevalence of the "clone look." Certain products run advertising obviously directed at the homosexual market. On the societal reaction theory, there ought to be an enormous rise in homosexual happiness. I know of no systematic study to determine if this is so, but anecdotal evidence suggests it may not be. The homosexual press has been just as strident in denouncing pro-homosexual movies as in denouncing Doris Day movies. Especially virulent venereal diseases have very recently appeared in homosexual communities, evidently spread in epidemic proportions by unabating homosexual promiscuity. One selling point for a presumably serious "gay rights" rally in Washington, D.C., was an "all-night disco train" from New York to Washington. What is perhaps most salient is that, even if the changed public mood results in decreased homosexual unhappiness, the question remains of why homosexuals in the recent past, who suffered greatly for being homosexuals, persisted in being homosexuals.

But does not my position also predict—contrary to fact—that any sexual activity not aimed at procreation or at least sexual intercourse leads to unhappiness? First, I am not sure this conclusion is contrary to the facts properly understood. It is universally recognized that, for humans and the higher animals, sex is more than the insertion of the penis into the vagina. Foreplay is necessary to prepare the female and, to a lesser extent, the male. Ethologists have studied the elaborate mating rituals of even relatively simple animals. Sexual intercourse must therefore be understood to include the kisses and caresses that necessarily precede copulation, behaviors that nature has made rewarding. What my view does predict is that exclusive preoccupation with behaviors normally preparatory for intercourse is highly correlated with unhappiness. And, so far as I know, psychologists do agree that such preoccupation or "fixation" with, e.g., cunnilingus, is associated with personality traits independently recognized as disorders. In this sense, sexual intercourse really is virtually necessary for well-being. Only if one is antecedently convinced that "nothing is more natural than anything else" will one confound foreplay as a prelude to intercourse with "foreplay" that leads nowhere at all. One might speculate on the evolutionary advantages of foreplay, at least for humans: by increasing the intensity and complexity of the pleasures of intercourse, it binds the partners more firmly and makes them more fit for child-rearing. In fact, such analyses of sexual perversion as Nagel's (1969), which correctly focus on the interruption of mutuality as central to perversion, go wrong by ignoring the evolutionary role and built-in rewards of mutuality. They fail to explain why the interruption of mutuality is disturbing.

It should also be clear that my argument permits gradations in abnormality. Behavior is the more abnormal, and the less likely to be rewarding, the more its emission tends to extinguish a genetic cohort that practices it. The less likely a behavior is to get selected out, the less abnormal it is. Those of our ancestors who found certain aspects of foreplay reinforcing might have managed to reproduce themselves sufficiently to implant this strain in us. There might be an equilibrium between intercourse and such not directly reproductive behavior. It is not required that any behavior not directly linked to heterosexual intercourse lead to maximum dissatisfaction. But the existence of these gradations provides no entering wedge for homosexuality. As no behavior is more likely to get selected out than rewarding homosexuality—except perhaps an innate tendency to suicide at the onset of puberty—it is extremely unlikely that homosexuality can now be unconditionally reinforcing in humans to any extent.

Nor does my position predict, again contrary to fact, that celibate priests will be unhappy. My view is compatible with the existence of happy celibates who deny themselves as part of a higher calling which yields compensating satisfactions. Indeed, the very fact that one needs to explain how the priesthood can compensate for the lack of family means that people do regard heterosexual mating as the natural or "inertial" state of human relations. The comparison between priests and homosexuals is in any case inapt. Priests do not simply give up sexual activity without ill effect; they give it up for a reason. Homosexuals have hardly given up the use of their sexual organs for a higher calling or anything else. Homosexuals continue to use them, but, unlike priests, they use them for what they are not for.

I have encountered the thought that by my lights female heterosexuality must be abnormal, since according to feminism women have been unhappy down the ages. The datum is questionable, to say the least. Feminists have offered no documentation whatever for this extravagant claim; their evidence is usually the unhappiness of the feminist in question and her circle of friends. Such attempts to prove female discontent in past centuries as Greer's (1979) are transparently anachronistic projections of contemporary feminist discontent onto inappropriate historical objects. An objection from a similar source runs that my argument, suitably extended, implies the natural-ness and hence rewardingness of traditional monogamous marriage. Once again, instead of seeing this as a *reductio*, I am inclined to take the supposed absurdity as a truth that nicely fits my theory. It is not a theoretical contention but an observable fact that women enjoy motherhood, that failure to bear and care for children breeds unhappiness in women, and that the role of "primary caretaker" is much more important for women than men. However, there is no need to be dogmatic. This conception of the family is in extreme disrepute in contemporary America. Many women work and many marriages last less than a decade. Here we have another natural experiment about what people find reinforcing. My view predicts that women will on the whole become unhappier if current trends continue. Let us see.

Not directly bearing on the issue of happiness, but still empirically pertinent, is animal homosexuality. I mentioned earlier that the overwhelmingly heterosexual tendencies of animals in all but such artificial and genetically irrelevant environs as zoos cast doubt on sheer polymorphous sexuality as a sufficiently adaptive strategy. By the same token, it renders implausible the claim in Masters and Johnson (1979) that human beings are born with only a general sex drive, and that the objects of the sex drive are *entirely* learned. If this were so, who teaches male tigers to mate with female tigers? Who teaches male primates to mate with female primates? In any case, the only evidence Masters and Johnson cite is the entirely unsurprising physiological similarity between heterosexual and homosexual response. Plainly, the inability of the penile nerve endings to tell what is rubbing them has nothing to do with the innateness of the sexual object. The inability of a robin to tell twigs from clever plastic lookalikes is consistent with an innate nest-building instinct.

The work of Beach (1976) is occasionally cited (e.g., in Wilson, 1978) to document the existence of animal homosexuality and to support the contention that homosexuality has some adaptive purpose, but Beach in fact notes certain important disanalogies between mammalian homosexual behavior in the wild and human homosexuality. Citing a principle of "stimulus-response complementarity," he remarks that a male chimpanzee will mount another male if the latter emits such characteristically female behavior as display of nether parts. Male homosexual humans, on the other hand, are attracted to maleness. More significantly, the male chimpanzee's mounting is unaccompanied by erection, thrusting or, presumably, intromission. Beach suggests that this display-mounting sequence may be multipurpose in nature, signalling submission and dominance when it occurs between males. In the same vein, Barash (1979: 60) cites male-male rape in *Xylocanis maculipennis,* but here the rapist's sperm is deposited in the rape victim's storage organs. This is a smart evolutionary move . . . but it is not comparable in its effects to homosexuality in humans. . . .

On Policy Issues

Homosexuality is intrinsically bad only in a prudential sense. It makes for unhappiness. However, this does not exempt homosexuality from the larger categories of ethics—rights, duties, liabilities. Deontic categories apply to acts which increase or decrease happiness or expose the helpless to the risk of unhappiness.

If homosexuality is unnatural, legislation which raises the odds that a given child will become homosexual raises the odds that he will be unhappy. The only gap in the syllogism is whether legislation which legitimates, endorses, or protects homosexuality does increase the chances that a child will become homosexual. If so, such legislation is *prima facie* objectionable. The question is not whether homosexual elementary school teachers will molest their charges. Prohomosexual legislation might increase the incidence of homosexuality in subtler ways. If it does, and if the protection of children is a fundamental obligation of society, legislation which legitimates homosexuality is a dereliction of duty. I am reluctant to deploy the language of "children's rights," which usually serves as one more excuse to interfere with the prerogatives of parents. But we do have obligations to our children, and one of them is to protect them from harm. If, as some have suggested, children have a right to protection from a religious education, they surely have a right to protection from homosexuality. So protecting them limits somebody else's freedom, but we are often willing to protect quite obscure children's rights at the expense of the freedom of others. There is a movement to ban TV commercials for sugar-coated cereals, to protect children from the relatively trivial harm of tooth decay. Such a ban would restrict the freedom of advertisers, and restrict it even though the last clear chance of avoiding the harm, and thus the responsibility, lies with the parents who control the TV set. I cannot see how one can consistently support such legislation and also urge homosexual rights, which risk much graver damage to children in exchange for increased freedom for homosexuals. (If homosexual behavior is largely compulsive, it is falsifying the issue to present it as balancing risks to children against the freedom of homosexuals.) The right of a homosexual to work for the Fire Department is not a negligible good. Neither is fostering a legal atmosphere in which as many people as possible grow up heterosexual.

It is commonly asserted that legislation granting homosexuals the privilege or right to be firemen endorses not homosexuality, but an expanded conception of human liberation. It is conjectural how sincerely this can be said in a legal order that forbids employers to hire whom they please and demands hours of paperwork for an interstate shipment of hamburger. But in any case legislation "legalizing homosexuality" cannot be neutral because passing it would have an inexpungeable speech-act dimension. Society cannot grant unaccustomed rights and privileges to homosexuals while remaining neutral about the value of homosexuality. Working from the assumption that society rests on the family and its consequences, the Judaeo-Christian tradition has deemed homosexuality a sin and withheld many privileges from homosexuals. Whether or not such denial was right, for our society to grant these privileges to homosexuals *now* would amount to declaring that it has rethought the matter and decided that homosexuality is not as bad as it had previously supposed. And unless such rethinking is a direct response to new empirical findings about homosexuality, it can only be a revaluing. Someone who suddenly accepts a policy he has previously opposed is open to the same interpretation: he has come to think better of the policy. And if he embraces the policy while knowing that this interpretation will be put on his behavior, and if he knows that others know that he knows they will so interpret it, he is acquiescing in this interpretation. He can be held to have intended, meant, this interpretation. A society that grants privileges to homosexuals while recognizing that, in the light of generally known history, this act can be interpreted as a positive reevaluation of homosexuality, is signalling that it now thinks homosexuality is all right. Many commentators in the popular press have observed that homosexuals, unlike members of racial minorities, can always "stay in the closet" when applying for jobs. What homosexual rights activists really want, therefore, is not access to jobs but legitimation of their homosexuality. Since this is known, giving them what they want will be seen as conceding their claim to legitimacy. And since legislators know their actions will support this interpretation, and know that their constituencies know they know this, the Gricean effect or symbolic meaning of passing anti-discrimination ordinances is to declare homosexuality legitimate (see Will, 1977).

Legislation permitting frisbees in the park does not imply approval of frisbees for the simple reason that frisbees are new; there is no tradition of banning them from parks. The legislature's action in permitting frisbees is not interpretable, known to be interpretable, and so on, as the reversal of long-standing disapproval. It is because these Gricean conditions are met in the case of abortion that legislation—or rather judicial fiat—permitting abortions and mandating their public funding are widely interpreted as tacit approval. Up to now, society has deemed homosexuality so harmful that restricting it outweighs putative homosexual rights. If society reverses itself, it will in effect be deciding that homosexuality is not as bad as it once thought.

Endnotes

1. "Sexual preference" typifies the obfuscatory language in which the homosexuality debate is often couched. "Preference" suggests that sexual tastes are voluntarily chosen, whereas it is a commonplace that one cannot decide what to find sexually stimulating. True, we talk of "preferences" among flavors of ice cream even though one cannot choose what flavor of ice cream to like; such talk is probably a carry-over from the voluntariness of *ordering* ice cream. "Sexual preference" does not even sustain this analogy, however, since sex is a forced choice for everyone except avowed celibates, and especially for the relatively large number of homosexuals who cruise regularly.

2. Nagel attempts to meet these counterexamples in effect by accepting such consequences of the classical analysis as that the beat of the heart is sometimes for diagnosis. The only reply to this sort of defense is that this is *not* what people mean. Met with such a reply, many philosophers feel impelled to say, "Well, it ought to be what you mean." This invitation to change the subject is attractive or relevant only if we haven't meant anything the first time around. If a coherent thought can be found behind our initial words which maximizes coherence with all hypothetical usages, it is *that*

thought we were expressing and whose articulation was the aim of the analytic exercise.

Bibliography

Barash, D. *The Whispering Within.* New York: Harper & Row, 1979.

Beach, F. "Cross-Species Comparisons and the Human Heritage." *Archives of Sexual Behavior* 5 (1976): 469–85.

Bell, A., and M. Weinberg. *Homosexualities.* New York: Simon and Schuster, 1978.

Devlin, P. *The Enforcement of Morals.* Oxford: Oxford University Press, 1965.

Gadpille, W. "Research into the Physiology of Maleness and Femaleness: Its Contribution to the Etiology and Psychodynamics of Homosexuality." *Archives of General Psychiatry* (1972): 193–206.

Gary, R. "Sex and Sexual Perversion." *Journal of Philosophy* 74 (1978): 189–99.

Greer, G. *The Obstacle Race.* New York: Farrar, Strauss & Giroux, 1979.

Masters, W. and V. Johnson. *Homosexuality in Perspective.* Boston: Little, Brown and Company, 1979.

McCracken, S. "Replies to Correspondents." *Commentary,* April 1979.

Mossner, E. *The Life of David Hume,* 1st. ed. New York: Nelson & Sons, 1954.

Nagel, E. "Teleology Revisited." *Journal of Philosophy* 74 (1977): 261–301.

_____. "Sexual Perversion." *Journal of Philosophy* 66 (1969): 5–17. This discussion can be found elsewhere in the present volume.

Rechy, J. *The Sexual Outlaw.* New York: Grove Press, 1977.

Weinberg, M., and C. Williams. *Male Homosexuals: Their Problems and Adaptations.* Oxford: Oxford University Press, 1974.

Will, G. "How Far Out of the Closet?" *Newsweek,* 30 May 1977, p. 92.

Wilson, E. *Sociobiology: The New Synthesis.* Cambridge, Mass.: Harvard University Press, 1975.

_____. *On Human Nature.* Cambridge, Mass.: Harvard University Press, 1978.

14. *Toward a New Theology of Sexuality*

Judith Plaskow

Judith Plaskow argues that traditional Jewish attitudes toward sexuality have emphasized the legality of the sexual union and focused on the patriarchal possession and control that have characterized such unions. From her perspective, these attitudes must be overcome by a richer appreciation of the positive and unfettered experience of women's sexuality. Freed from the traditional patriarchal paradigm, women will have available to them a fuller and more liberating experience of embodied sexuality.

Feminist reconceptualization of the energy/control model of sexuality and affirmation of the profound connection between sexuality and spirituality provide directions for rethinking the ambivalent attitudes toward sexuality within Judaism. Acceptance and avowal of a link between sex and spirit is, as I argued earlier, by no means foreign to Jewish experience. In the mysteries of the marriage bed on Sabbath night; in the sanctity of the Song of Songs; for mysticism, in the very nature and dynamics of the Godhead, sexual expression is an image of and path to the holy.[1] Yet again and again in theology and practice, Judaism turns away from and undermines this acknowledged connection by defining sexuality in terms of patriarchal possession and control. Where women's sexuality is seen as an object to be possessed, and sexuality itself is perceived as an impulse that can take possession of the self, the central issues surrounding sexuality will necessarily be issues of control: Who has the right to control a particular woman's sexuality in what situation? How can a man control his own sexual impulses, given the constant bombardment of female temptation? How can the law control women and the relations between men and women so that the danger of illicit sexual relations (relations with a woman whose sexuality is owned by some other man) is minimized? All these questions make perfect sense as related aspects of a patriarchal system, but they are inimical to the mutuality, openness, and vulnerability in sexual relations that tie sexuality to the sacred.

Recognizing then that the role of women's sexuality in the institution of the family, the rules surrounding the relations of the sexes, and the energy/control paradigm of sexuality are all connected pieces of a patriarchal understanding of sexuality, the question becomes: What would it mean to develop a model of sexuality that is freed from this framework? How can we think about sexuality in a way that springs from and honors the experience of women? How can we develop a positive feminist discourse about sexuality in a Jewish context?

In line with the fundamental feminist insight that sexuality is socially constructed, a Jewish feminist understanding of sexuality begins with the insistence that what goes on in the bedroom can never be isolated from the wider cultural context of which the bedroom is part.[2] The inequalities of the family are prepared for by, and render plausible, larger social inequalities, and the task of eradicating sexual inequality is part of the wider feminist project of ending hierarchical separation as a model for communal life.[3] Thus a Jewish feminist approach to sexuality must take sexual mutuality as a task for the whole of life and not just for Friday evening, fitting its commitment to sexual equality into its broader vision of a society based on mutuality and respect for difference.

It is striking that one of the profoundest images of freedom and mutuality in sexual relations that the Jewish tradition has to offer is at the same time its central image of the connection between sexuality and spirituality. Unlike the Garden of Eden, where Eve and Adam are ashamed of their nakedness and women's subordination is the punishment for sin, the Garden of the Song of Songs is a place of sensual delight and sexual equality. Unabashed by their desire, the man and woman of these poems delight in their own embodiment and the beauty surrounding them, each seeking the other out to inaugurate their meetings, each rejoicing in the love without dominion that is also the love of God.[4] Since this book offers a vision of delight that is easier to achieve in a sacred garden than in the midst of the demands of daily living, it is perhaps no criticism of the institution of marriage that the couple in the Song of Songs is not married. Yet the picture of mutuality, and the sacredness of mutuality, offered by this book stand in fundamental tension with the structures of marriage as Judaism defines them. When the central rituals of marriage and divorce celebrate or enact the male acquisition and relinquishment of female sexuality, what are the supports and resources for the true reciprocity of intimate exchange that marks the holiness of *Shir Hashirim* (Song of Songs)? Despite the efforts of the tradition to legislate concern for women's sexual needs, the achievement of mutuality in the marriage bed is extremely difficult in the absence of justice for women in those institutions that legitimate and surround it.

A central task, then, of the feminist reconstruction of Jewish attitudes toward sexuality is the radical transformation of the institutional, legal framework within which sexual relations are supposed to take place. Insofar as Judaism maintains its interest in the establishment of enduring relationships both as a source of adult companionship and development and as a context for raising and educating children, these relationships will be entered into and dissolved by mutual initiative and consent. "Marriage" will not be about the transfer of women or the sanctification of potential disorder through the firm establishment of women in the patriarchal family, but the decision of two adults—any two adults—to make their lives together, lives that include the sharing of sexuality. Although, in the modern West, it is generally assumed that such a commitment is a central meaning of marriage, this assumption is contradicted by a religious (and secular) legal system that outlaws homosexual marriage and institutionalizes inequality in its basic definitions of marriage and divorce.

This redefinition of the legal framework of marriage, which accords with the feminist refusal to sanctify any hierarchical relationship, is also based on the important principle that sexuality is not something we can acquire or possess in another. We are each the possessor of our own sexuality—in Adrienne Rich's phrase, the "presiding genius" of our own bodies. The sharing of sexuality with another is something that should happen only by mutual consent, a consent that is not a blanket permission, but that is continually renewed in the actual rhythms of particular relation-

ships. This principle, simple as it seems, challenges both the fundamental assumptions of Jewish marriage law and the Jewish understanding of what women's sexuality is "about." It defines as immoral legal regulations concerning the possession, control, and exchange of women's sexuality, and disputes the perspective that a woman's sexuality is her contribution to the family rather than the expression of her own embodiment.

But if one firm principle for feminist thinking about sexuality is that no one can possess the sexuality of another, it is equally the case that from a feminist perspective, sexuality is not something that pertains only or primarily to the self. Indeed, our sexuality is fundamentally about moving out beyond ourselves. As ethicist James Nelson puts it,

> The mystery of sexuality is the mystery of
> the human need to reach out for the physical
> and spiritual embrace of others. Sexuality
> thus expressés God's intention that people
> find authentic humanness not in isolation
> but in relationship.[5]

Our capacity for intimacy, for sharing, for touch is rooted in our early relations with others; and throughout our lives, we seek genuine connection, longing for at least some relationship(s) that can touch the core of our being. The connecting, communicative nature of sexuality is not something we can experience or look for only in sexual encounters narrowly defined, but in all real relationships in our lives. We live in the world as sexual beings. As Audre Lorde argues, our sexuality is a current that flows through all activities that are important to us, in which we invest our selves. True intellectual exchange, common work, shared experience are laced with sexual energy that animates and enlivens them. The bonds of community are erotic bonds. The power that is generated by real community, that gives us access to a greater power that grounds and embraces us, is in part the power of our own sexual, life energy that flows through community and enlarges and seals it. We are all, women and men, embodied, sexual persons who respond sexually to the women and men among whom we live.

This erotic nature of community is by no means lost on Judaism; indeed, it is the subject of profound ambivalence in both the midrash and law. The story I described earlier in which the rabbis blind rather than kill the imprisoned *yetzer hara* concedes the vital role of the sexual impulse in the creation and maintenance of the world. A similar ambivalence underlies the extensive rabbinic legislation enforcing the separation of the sexes, legislation that tries to protect against the feelings it recognizes, even as it acknowledges the sexual power of community and the continuity of sexuality with other feelings. If the energy of community is erotic, there are no guarantees that eroticism will stay within prescribed legal boundaries rather than breaking out and disrupting communal sanctity. The strict "fence around the law" felt necessary when it comes to sexual behavior is itself testimony to the power of sexuality.

It is tempting for a feminist account of sexuality to deny the disruptive power of the erotic, and to depict the fear of it in rabbinic thought as simply misplaced. But it is truer to experience to acknowledge the power of sexuality to overturn rules and threaten boundaries. Then feminists can embrace this power as a significant ally. There is no question that the empowerment that comes from owning the erotic in our lives can disturb community and undermine familiar structures. On the level of sexual behavior, if we allow ourselves to perceive and acknowledge sexual feelings, there is always the danger we may act on them, and they may not correspond to group concensus about whom we may desire and when. The potentially disruptive effects of sexual feelings exist for communities with stringent sexual ethics that carefully restrict permitted behavior, but also for those with more open boundaries. Starhawk, in discussing the dynamics of political action and other small resistance and countercultural groups, formulates three pessimistic laws of group dynamics: (1) Sexual involvement in small groups is bound to cause problems. (2) "In any small group in which people are involved, sooner or later they will be involved sexually. (3) Small groups tend to break up."[6] Not only the values of a group can be trampled upon by unlooked-for sexual connections but—given the feelings of fear, vulnerability, pain, and anger that can accompany the birth and demise of relationships— sexual liaisons can threaten a group's ability to function cohesively as a community.

When the erotic is understood not simply as sexual feeling in the narrow sense but as our fundamental life energy, the owning of this power in our lives is even more threatening to established structures. In Audre Lorde's terms, if we allow the eroticism to become a lens through which we evaluate all aspects of our existence, we can no longer "settle for the convenient, the shoddy, the conventionally expected, nor the merely safe."[7] Having glimpsed the possibility of genuine satisfaction in work we've done, we are less likely to

settle for work that is alienating and meaningless. Having experienced the power and legitimacy of our own sexual desire, we are less likely to subscribe to a system that closely and absolutely prescribes and proscribes the channels of that desire. Having experienced our capacity for creative and joyful action, we are less likely to accept hierarchical power relationships that deny or restrict our ability to bring that creativity and joy to more and more aspects of our lives. It may be that the ability of women to live within the patriarchal family and the larger patriarchal structures that govern Jewish life depends on our suppression of the erotic, on our numbing ourselves to the sources of vision and power that fuel meaningful resistance. It may also be that the ability of Jews to live unobtrusively as a minority in a hostile culture has depended on blocking sources of personal power that might lead to resistance that feels foolish or frightening. Obviously, from a patriarchal perspective, then—or the perspective of any hierarchical system—erotic empowerment is dangerous. That is why, in Lorde's words, "We are taught to separate the erotic demand from most vital areas of our lives other than sex,"[8] and that is why we are also taught to restrain our sexuality, so that it too fits the parameters of hierarchical control that govern the rest of our lives.

From a feminist perspective, however, the power and danger of the erotic are not reasons to fear and suppress it but to nurture it as a profound personal and communal resource in the struggle for change. When "we begin to demand from ourselves and from our life-pursuits that they feel in accordance with that joy which we know ourselves to be capable of," we carry with us an inner knowledge of the kind of world we are seeking to create.[9] If we repress this knowledge because it also makes us sexually alive, then we repress the clarity and creative energy that is the basis of our capacity to envision and work toward a more just social order.

It is in relation to this understanding of the power of the erotic that feminist insistence on seeing sexuality as part of a continuum of body/life energy is a particularly crucial corrective to rabbinic attitudes toward sexual control. As I have argued, the rabbis recognized the connection between the sexual impulse and human creativity. "The bigger the man, the bigger the *yetzer*," they said, and advised, "Hold him [the *yetzer hara*] off with the left hand and draw him nigh with the right."[10] Yet at the same time they acknowledged the role of sexuality as an ingredient in all activity, they apparently believed one could learn the fear of a woman's little finger without damaging the larger capacity to act and to feel. To love God with all the heart meant to love God with the good *and evil* impulses, and yet it was imagined one could rein in the so-called evil impulse without diminishing the love of God.[11] If we take sexuality seriously, however, as an expression of our embodiment that cannot be disconnected from our wider ability to interact feelingly with the world, then to learn fear and shame of our own bodies and those of others—even when these feelings are intermixed with other conflicting attitudes—is to learn suspicion of feeling as a basic way of knowing and valuing the world. We should not expect, then, to be able to block out our sexual feelings without blocking out the longing for social relations rooted in mutuality rather than hierarchy, without blocking out the anger that warns us that something is amiss in our present social arrangements, without blocking and distorting the fullness of our love for God.[12]

I am not arguing here for free sex or for more sexual expression, quantitatively speaking. I am arguing for living dangerously, for choosing to take responsibility for working through the possible consequences of sexual feelings rather than repressing sexual feeling and thus feeling more generally. I am arguing that our capacity to transform Judaism and the world is rooted in our capacity to be alive to the pain and anger that is caused by relationships of domination, and to the joy that awaits us on the other side. I am arguing that to be alive is to be sexually alive, and that in suppressing one sort of vitality, we suppress the other.

I mentioned above Starhawk's three laws of group dynamics that acknowledge the potential disruptiveness of sex to the creation of community. On the basis of more experience, she adds a fourth: A group that has survived one breakup between members is more likely to survive subsequent ones, and may experience a deepened sense of trust and safety because of what it has been through.[13] This fourth law points to the possibility that even the disruptions caused by sexuality can be a source of power if we refuse to look away from the feelings they evoke in us, maintaining our commitment to the building of community in full cognizance of its erotic bonds.

The question becomes, then: Can we affirm our sexuality as the gift it is, making it sacred not by cordoning off pieces of it, but by increasing our awareness of the ways in which it connects us to all things? Can we stop evicting our sexuality from the synagogue, hiding it behind a *mechitzah* or praying with our heads, and instead bring it in, offering it to God in the experience of full spiritual/physical connection?[14] Dare we trust our capacity for joy—knowing it is related to our sexuality—to point the direction toward new and different ways of structuring communal life?

While I am suggesting that the implications of a changed conception of sexuality go well beyond the sexual sphere, it is also the case that they shape that sphere. The ability to feel deeply in the whole of our lives affects what we want and are willing to accept in the bedroom, just as what we experience in the bedroom prepares us for mutuality or domination in the rest of our lives. A new understanding of sexuality and a transformed institutional context for sexual relationships will have significant impact on personal sexual norms. If the traditional models and categories for understanding sexuality are no longer morally acceptable from a feminist perspective, but sexuality is fundamentally about relationships with others, what values might govern sexual behavior for modern Jews?

It should be clear from all I have said thus far that rejection of the traditional energy/control model of sexuality and of ownership as a category for understanding sexual exchange is by no means synonymous with a sexual ethic of "anything goes." On the contrary, I would argue—and the current move back toward sexual repression supports this—that the obsession with sexuality in U.S. culture for the last twenty years, the pressures toward early sexual activity for women and men, the expectation that sex could compensate for dissatisfactions in every other area of life, all reflect a reversal of traditional paradigms that does not succeed in moving beyond them. If the Jewish tradition says sex is a powerful impulse that needs to be controlled, certain strains in modern culture say it is healthier to act out our impulses. If the tradition says men may have affairs but women may not, certain strains in modern culture give women "permission" to be promiscuous on male terms. If the tradition says sex has a place in life, but it must not be allowed to take over, modern culture offers sex as a panacea for all that ails us. But when sex is understood as a particular impulse that we act out instead of control, the result is an alienated sexuality that can never rescue us from the alienation in the rest of our lives. If greater genital expression were really the solution to our social miseries, says Beverly Harrison, we would expect ours to be the happiest society around. In fact, however, since, in Audre Lorde's terms, our "erotic comings-together. . . are almost always characterized by a simultaneous looking away," sexual encounters often leave us feeling used and abused rather than renewed and connected.[15]

To see sexuality as an aspect of our life energy, as part of a continuum with other ways of relating to the world and other people, is to insist that the norms of mutuality, respect for difference, and joint empowerment that characterize the larger feminist vision of community apply also—indeed especially—to the area of sexuality. If, in our general communal life, we seek to be present with each other in such a way that we can touch the greater power of being in which all communities dwell, how much more should this be true in those relationships which are potentially the most open, intimate, and vulnerable in our lives? The Song of Songs, because it unifies sensuality, spirituality, and profound mutuality, may offer us the finest Jewish vision of what our sexual relationships can be, a vision that at the same time points to the transformation of our common life. Beverly Harrison places the unification of these elements in a feminist framework:

> A feminist moral theology requires that we ground our new ethics of sexuality in a "spirituality of sensuality.". . . Sexuality is indispensable to our spirituality because it is a power of communication, most especially a power to give and receive powerful meaning—love and respect or contempt and disdain. . . . The moral norm for sexual communication in a feminist ethic is radical mutuality—the simultaneous acknowledgment of vulnerability to the need of the other, the recognition of one's own power to give and receive pleasure and to call forth another's power of relation and to express one's own.[16]

It is important to note that this "spirituality of sensuality" and mutuality specifies and intensifies for sexual ethics what are also broader norms for interaction with the world.

The unification of sexuality and spirituality is a sometime gift, a measure of the possible, rather than the reality of everyday. What keeps this unification alive as a recurring possibility is the exercise of respect, responsibility, and honesty—commensurate with the nature and depth of the particular relationship—as basic values in any sexual relationship. In terms of concrete life choices, I believe that radical mutuality is most fully possible in the context of an ongoing, committed relationship in which sexual expression is one dimension of a shared life. Traditional insistence that sex be limited to heterosexual marriage might find its echo in support for and celebration of long-term partnerships as the richest setting for negotiating and living out the meanings of mutuality, responsibility, and honesty amidst the dis-

tractions, problems, and pleasures of daily life. Such partnerships are not, however, a choice for all adults who want them, and not all adults would choose them, given the possibility. To respond within a feminist framework to the realities of different life decisions and at the same time affirm the value of sexual well-being as an aspect of our total well-being, we need to apply certain fundamental values to a range of sexual choices and styles. While honesty, responsibility, and respect are goods that pertain to any relationship, the concrete meaning of these values will vary considerably depending on the duration and significance of the connection involved. In one relationship, honesty may mean complete and open sharing of feelings and experiences; in another, clarity about intent for that encounter. In the context of a committed partnership, responsibility may signify lifelong presence, trust, and exchange; in a brief encounter, discussion of birth control, AIDS, and safe sex. At its fullest, respect may mean regard for another as a total person; at a minimum, absence of pressure or coercion, and a commitment, in Lorde's terms, not to "look away" as we come together. If we need to look away, then we should walk away: The same choices about whether and how to act on our feelings that pertain to any area of moral decision making are open to us in relation to our sexuality.

The same norms that apply to heterosexual relationships also apply to gay and lesbian relationships.[17] Indeed, I have formulated them with both in mind. There are many issues that might be considered in reevaluating traditional Jewish rejection of homosexuality.[18] But the central issue in the context of a feminist reconceptualization of sexuality is the relationship between homosexual choice and the continuity between sexual energy and embodied life energy. If we see sexuality as part of what enables us to reach out beyond ourselves, and thus as a fundamental ingredient in our spirituality, then the issue of homosexuality must be placed in a somewhat different framework from those in which it is most often discussed. The question of the morality of homosexuality becomes one not of halakhah or the right to privacy or freedom of choice, but the affirmation of the value to the individual and society of each of us being able to find that place within ourselves where sexuality and spirituality come together.[19] It is possible that some or many of us for whom the connections between sexuality and deeper sources of personal and spiritual power emerge most richly, or only, with those of the same sex could choose to lead heterosexual lives for the sake of conformity to halakhah or wider social pressures and values. But this choice would then violate the deeper vision offered by the Jewish tradition that sexuality can be a medium for the experience and reunification of God.[20] Historically, this vision has been expressed entirely in heterosexual terms. The reality is that for some Jews, however, it is realized only in relationships between two men or two women. Thus what calls itself the Jewish path to holiness in sexual relations is for some a cutting off of holiness—a sacrifice that comes at high cost for both the individual and community. Homosexuality, then, does not necessarily represent a rejection of Jewish values but the choice of certain Jewish values over others—where these conflict with each other, the choice of the possibility of holiness over control and law.

Potential acceptance of gays and lesbians by the Jewish community raises the issue of children—for Judaism a primary warrant for sexual relations, and the facade that prejudice often hides behind in rejecting homosexuality as a Jewish choice. Again to place this issue in the context of a feminist paradigm for understanding sexuality, procreation is a dimension of our sexuality, just as sexuality itself is a dimension of our embodied personhood. If sexuality allows us to reach out to others, having children is a way of reaching out beyond our own generation, affirming the biological continuity of life and the continuity of Jewish community and communal values. Insofar as Jewish communities have an important stake in the rearing of Jewish children, it is in their interest to structure communal institutions to support in concrete ways all Jews who choose to have children, including increasing numbers of lesbians and gay men.[21] But, just as Judaism has always recognized that procreation does not exhaust the meaning of sexuality, so having children does not exhaust the ways in which Jews can contribute to future generations.[22] Recognizing the continuities between sexuality and personal empowerment strengthens the conviction of the inherent value of sexuality as an expression of our personhood and of our connection with and love for others. The sense of integrity and self-worth that a loving sexual relationship can foster enhances the capacity to make a commitment to the future, whether this takes the form of bearing and raising children or nurturing communal continuity in other ways.

Lastly, but underlying all that I have said, sexuality as an aspect of our life energy and power connects us with God as the sustaining source of energy and power in the universe. In reaching out to another sexually with the total self, the boundaries between self and other can dissolve and we may feel ourselves united with larger currents of energy and sustenance, is also the case, however, that even in ordinary, daily reaching out to others, we reach toward the God who is present in connection, in the web of relation with a wider world. On the one hand, the wholeness, the "all-embracing quality of sexual expression" that includes body, mind, and feeling, is for many people the closest we can come in this life to experiencing the embracing wholeness of God.[23] On the other hand, the everyday bonds of community are also erotic bonds through which we touch the God of community, creating a place where the divine presence can rest. Feminist metaphors that name God not simply as female but sexual female—beautiful, filled with vitality, womb, birthgiver—seek to give imagistic expression and the continuity between our own sexual energy and the great currents that nourish and renew it. Feminist images name female sexuality as powerful and legitimate and name sexuality as part of the image of God. They tell us that sexuality is not primarily a moral danger (though, of course, it can be that but a source of energy and power that, schooled in the value of respect and mutuality, can lead us to the related, and therefore sexual, God.

Endnotes

1. Green, "A Contemporary Approach," 98.

2. Harrison, "Sexuality and Social Policy," 83–114; Ruby Rich, "Feminism and Sexuality in the 1980s," *Feminist Studies* 12 (Fall 1986): 549–58.

3. See Mariana Valverde's insistence that the eroticization of equality is a central task of feminism, *Sex, Power, and Pleasure* (Toronto; The Women's Press, 1985), 43.

4. Nelson, *Between Two Gardens,* 7; Phyllis Trible, *God and the Rhetoric of Sexuality* (Philadelphia: Fortress Press, 1978). chapter 5; Arthur Waskow *Godwrestling* (New York: Schocken Books, 1978), chapter 6.

5. Nelson, *Between Two Gardens,* 6.

6. Starhawk, *Truth or Dare: Encounters with Power, Authority, and Mystery* (San Francisco: Harper & Row, 1987), 153.

7. Lorde, "Uses of the Erotic," 57.

8. *Ibid.,* 55. Compare Starhawk, *Dreaming the Dark,* 141.

9. Lorde, "Uses of the Erotic," 57; compare Starhawk, *Dreaming the Dark,* 141.

10. Epstein, *Sex Laws and Customs,* 14.

11. Gordis, *Love and Sex,* 106.

12. Harrison, "The Power of Anger," 13–14; Lillian Smith, *Killers of the Dream* (New York and London: W. W. Norton, The Norton Library, 1978), 81–85.

13. Starhawk, *Truth or Dare,* 153.

14. See, for example, Waskow, *Godwrestling*, 59; Nelson, *Between Two Gardens*, 3–4.

15. Harrison, "Sexuality and Social Policy," 85; Lorde, "Uses of the Erotic," 59.

16. Harrison, "Misogyny and Homophobia," 149–50.

17. For a clear statement of this principle, see James Nelson, *Embodiment: An Approach to Sexuality and Christian Theology* (Minneapolis, MN: Augsburg Publishing House, 1978), 126 and chapter 8; and Artson, "Judaism and Homosexuality," 92–93.

18. The best consideration of this issue in a Jewish context that I am aware of is Artson, "Judaism and Homosexuality," 52–54, 92–93. See also Hershel Matt. "Sin, Crime, Sickness or Alternative Life Style? A Jewish Approach to Homosexuality," *Judaism* 27 (Winter 1978): 13–24 and Arthur Waskow; "Down

to Earth Judaism," 48–49, 88–89, *Twice Blessed: On Being Lesbian, Gay, and Jewish,* Christie Balka and Andy Rose, eds. (Boston: Beacon Press, 1989) appeared too late to be considered here.

19. I am grateful to Denni Liebowitz for putting the issue in this way; conversation, fall 1983.

20. Compare Waskow, "Down-to-Earth Judaism," 88.

21. Martha Ackelsberg, "Families and the Jewish Community; A Feminist Perspective," *Response* 14 (Spring 1983): 15–16.

22. Feldman, *Marital Relations,* chapters 2, 4, 5; Martha Ackelsberg, "Family or community?" *Sh'ma* 17/330 (March 20, 1987); 76–78.

23. Green, "A Contemporary Approach," 98.

15. *The Case for Gay Marriage*

Richard D. Mohr

Arguing that the nature and meaning of marriage should be reconceived, Richard Mohr claims that gay marriages ought to be legalized. As he explains, marriage, like knowledge, is a common good that benefits both individuals and the society as a whole; the broadening of that good to more persons will not diminish its good for others. Gayness, he concludes, is a deeply relational property and one that needs and deserves social support and nurture.

Introduction: Marital Stories

The climax of Harvey Fierstein's 1979 play, *Torch Song Trilogy,* is a dialogue—well, shouting match—between mother and son about traditional marriage and its gay variant. As is frequently the case, the nature and function of an institution flashes forth only when the institution breaks down or is dissolved—here by the death of Arnold's lover.

Arnold: [I'm] widowing . . .

Ma: Wait, wait, wait, wait, wait. Are you trying to compare my marriage with you and Alan? Your father and I were married for

thirty-five years, had two children and a wonderful life together. You have the nerve to compare yourself to that?. . .

What loss did you have? . . . Where do you come to compare that to a marriage of thirty-five years? . . .

It took me two months until I could sleep in our bed alone, a year to learn to say "I" instead of "we." Are you going to tell me you were "widowing"? How dare you!

Arnold: You're right, Ma. How dare I. I couldn't possibly know how it feels to pack someone's clothes in plastic bags and watch the garbage-pickers carry them away. Or what it feels like to forget and set his place at the table. How about the food that rots in the refrigerator because you forgot how to shop for one? How dare I? Right, Ma? How dare I?

This article originally appeared in the *Notre Dame Journal of Law, Ethics & Public Policy* 9, no. 1 (1995). © Richard D. Mohr, 1995. Reprinted with permission from the author.

Ma: May God strike me dead! Whatever I did to my mother to deserve a child speaking to me this way. The disrespect!

Arnold: Listen, Ma, you had it easy. You have thirty-five years to remember, I have five. You had your children and friends to comfort you, I had me! My friends didn't want to hear about it. They said "What're you gripin' about? At least you had a lover." 'Cause everybody knows that queers don't feel nothin'. How dare I say I loved him? You had it easy, Ma. You lost your husband in a nice clean hospital, I lost mine out there. They killed him there on the street. Twenty-three years old, laying dead on the street. Killed by a bunch of kids with baseball bats. Children. Children taught by people like you. 'Cause everybody knows that queers don't matter! Queers don't love! And those that do deserve what they get![1]

In its representation both of the day-to-day nature of gay relationships and of the injustices which beset these relationships because they are not socially, let alone legally, acknowledged as marriages, Fierstein's moving fictional account has its roots deep in the real life experience of lesbian and gay couples. Consider three true-life stories of gay couples:

Years of domesticity have made Brian and Ed familiar figures in the archipelago of middle-aged, middle-class couples who make up my village's permanent gay male community. Ed drives a city bus. Brian is a lineman for the power company—or rather he was until a freak accident set aflame the cherry-picker atop which he worked. He tried to escape by leaping to a nearby tree, but lost his grip and landed on his head. Eventually, it became clear that Brian would be permanently brain-damaged. After a few awkward weeks in the hospital, Brian's parents refused to let Ed visit anymore. Eventually they moved Brian to their village and home, where Ed was not allowed.

A similar case garnered national attention. In Minnesota, Karen Thompson fought a seven-year legal battle to gain guardianship of her lover, Sharon Kowalski. Sharon was damaged of body and mind in a 1983 car accident, after which Sharon's parents barred Karen for years from seeing her.[2] Although the Minnesota tragedy made headlines, the causes of such occurrences are everyday stuff in gay and lesbian lives. In both Sharon and Karen's and Brian and Ed's cases, if the government had through marriage allowed the members of each couple to be next-of-kin for each other, the stories would have had different endings—ones in keeping with our cultural belief that in the first instance those to whom we as adults entrust our tendency in crisis are people we choose, our spouses, who love us because of who we are, not people who are thrust upon us by the luck of the draw and who may love us only in spite of who we are.[3]

On their walk back from their neighborhood bar to the Victorian which, over the years, they had lovingly restored, Warren and Mark stopped along San Francisco's Polk Street to pick up milk for breakfast and for Sebastian, their geriatric cat. Just for kicks, some wealthy teens from the Valley drove into town to "bust some fags." Warren dipped into a convenience store, while Mark had a smoke outside. As Mark turned to acknowledge Warren's return, he was hit across the back of the head with a baseball bat. Mark's blood and vomit splashed across Warren's face. In 1987, a California appellate court held that under no circumstance can a relationship between two homosexuals—however emotionally significant, stable, and exclusive—be legally considered a "close relationship," and so Warren was barred from bringing any suit against the bashers for negligently causing emotional distress.[4]

Gay and lesbian couples are living together as married people do, even though they are legally barred from getting married. The legally aggravated injustices contained in the stories above suggest both that this bar deserves a close examination and that the law, if it aims at promoting justice, will have to be attentive and responsive to the ways couples actually live their lives rather than, as at present, preemptively and ignorantly determining which relationships are to be acknowledged and even created by it. America stands at a point where legal tradition is largely a hindrance to understanding what the law should be.

In this article, I advocate the legalization of gay marriage.[5] My analysis does not in the main proceed by appeal to the concept of equality; in particular, nothing will turn on distinctive features of equal protection doctrine. Rather, the analysis is substantive and turns on understanding the nature and meaning of marriage itself.

To count as a marriage, a relation must fulfill certain normative conditions. Marriage is norm-dependent. In the first half of the article, I examine this aspect of marriage. First, in Part II-A, I examine the going social and legal definitions of marriage and find them all wanting. I then in Part II-B tender a substantive, nonstipulative definition of marriage that is centered and analytically based on the norms which inform the way people actually live as couples. I go on to show that gay couples in fact meet this definition.

But marriage is also norm-invoking: when a relation is determined to be a marital one, that property, in turn, has normative consequences. In particular, it invokes a certain understanding of the relation of marriage to government. And so, Part III of this article examines, along several dimensions, various normative consequences and legal reforms that are suggested by the values that inform marriage. Along the way, I suggest that the lived experience of gay couples not only shows them as fulfilling the norms of marriage but can even indicate ways of improving marital law for everyone. The article concludes in Part IV with an examination of the social, religious, and legal reforms that are under way toward the recognition and support of gay marital relationships. Part of the chore of plumping for radical legal reform is to show that the reform is in fact possible—and that it does not cause the skies to fall.

II. *Definitions of Marriage: Its Normative Content*

A. *Definitional Failures*

Social and Legal Attempts to Define Marriage Usually in religious, ethical, and legal thinking, issues are settled with reference to a thing's goodness. Yet oddly, the debate over gay marriage has focused not on whether the thing is good but on whether the thing can even exist. Those opposing gay marriage say that the very definition of marriage rules out the possibility that gay couples can be viewed as married.[6]

If one asks the average Jo(e) on the street what marriage is, the person generally just gets tongue-tied. Try it. The meaning of marriage is somehow supposed to be so obvious, so entrenched and ramified in daily life, that it is never in need of articulation.

Standard dictionaries, which track and make coherent common usages of terms, are unhelpfully circular. Most commonly, dictionaries define marriage in terms of spouses, spouses in terms of husband and wife, and husband and wife in terms of marriage.[7] In consequence, the various definitions do no work in explaining what marriage is and so simply end up assuming or stipulating that marriage must be between people of different sexes.

Legal definitions of marriage fare no better. Many state laws only speak of spouses or partners and do not

actually make explicit that people must be of different sexes to marry.[8] During the early 1970s and again in the early 1980s, gays directly challenged these laws in four states, claiming that in accordance with common law tradition, whatever is not prohibited must be allowed, and that if these laws were judicially construed to require different-sex partners, then the laws constituted unconstitutional sex or sexual-orientation discrimination.[9] Gays lost all these cases, which the courts treated in dismissive, but revealing, fashion.[10]

The courts would first claim that the silence of the law notwithstanding, marriage automatically entails gender difference. The best known of these rulings is the 1974 case *Singer* v. *Hara,* which upheld Washington's refusal to grant a marriage license to two males. The case defined marriage as "the legal union of one man and one woman" as husband and wife.[11] This definition has become *the* legal definition of marriage, since it has been taken up into the standard law dictionary, *Black's Sixth Edition,* where the case is the only citation given in the section on marriage.[12]

Yet, the *Singer* definition tells us nothing whatever of the content of marriage. First, the qualification "as husband and wife" is simply circular. Since "husband" and "wife" mean people who are in a marriage with each other, the definition, as far as these terms go, presupposes the very thing to be defined. So what is left is that marriage is "the legal union of one man and one woman." Now, if the term "legal" here simply means "not illegal," then notice that a kiss after the prom can fit its bill: "the legal union of one man and one woman." We are told nothing of what "the union" is that is supposed to be the heart of marriage. The formulation of the definition serves no function other than to exclude from marriage—whatever it is—the people whom America views as destroyers of the American family, same-sex couples and polygamists: *"one* man and *one* woman." Like the ordinary dictionary definitions, the legal definition does no explanatory work.[13]

Nevertheless, the courts take this definition, turn around, and say that since this is what marriage *means,* gender discrimination and sexual-orientation discrimination is built right into the institution of marriage; therefore, since marriage itself is permitted, so, too, must be barring same-sex couples from it. Discrimination against gays, they hold, is not an illegitimate discrimination in marriage, indeed it is necessary to the very institution: No one would be married if gays were, for then marriage wouldn't be marriage. It took a gay case to reveal what marriage is, but the case reveals it, at least as legally understood, to be nothing but an empty space, delimited only by what it excludes—gay couples. And so the case has all the marks of being profoundly prejudicial in its legal treatment of gays.

Gender in Marital Law If we shift from considering the legal definition of marriage to the legal practices of marriage, are there differences of gender that insinuate themselves into marriage, so that botched definitions aside, marriage does after all require that its pairings be of the male-female variety? There used to be major gender-based legal differences in marriage, but these have all been found to be unjust and have gradually been eliminated through either legislative or judicial means. For example, a husband used to have an obligation to take care of his wife's material needs without his wife (no matter how wealthy) having any corresponding obligation to look after her husband (however poor). Now both spouses are mutually and equally obliged.[14] At one time a husband could sell his wife's property without her consent; the wife had no independent power to make contracts. But these laws have not generally been in force since the middle of the last century and are now unconstitutional.[15] It used to be that a husband *by definition* could not rape his wife—one could as well rape oneself, the reasoning went. Now, while laws governing sexual relations between husbands and wives are not identical to those governing relations between (heterosexual) strangers, they are nearly so, and such differences as remain are in any case cast in gender-neutral terms.[16] Wives are legally protected from ongoing sexual abuse from husbands—whatever the nonlegal reality.

Now that gender distinctions have all but vanished from the legal *content* of marriage, there is no basis for the requirement that the legal form of marriage unite members of different sexes. The legal definition of marriage—"union of one man and one woman"—though doggedly enforced in the courts, is a dead husk that has been cast off by marriage as a living legal institution.[17]

Babies in Marital Law Perhaps sensing the shakiness of an argument that rests solely on a stipulative definition of little or no content, the courts have tried to supplement the supposedly obvious requirement for gender disparity in access to marriage with appeal to reproduction. By assuming that procreation and rearing of children is essential to married life, the courts have implicitly given marriage a functional definition designed to eliminate lesbians and gay men from the

ranks of the marriageable.[18] "As we all know" (the courts self-congratulatorily declare), lesbians are "constitutionally incapable" of bearing children by other lesbians, and gay men are incapable of siring children by other gay men.

But the legally acknowledged institution of marriage in fact does not track this functional definition. All states allow people who are over sixty to marry each other, with all the rights and obligations marriage entails, even though biological reality dictates that such marriages will be sterile. In Hawaii, the statute that requires women to prove immunity against rubella as a condition for getting a marriage license exempts women "who, by reason of age or other medically determined condition are not and never will be physically able to conceive children."[19] In 1984, Hawaii also amended its marriage statute to delete a requirement that "neither of the parties is impotent or physically incapable of entering into the marriage state."[20] This statutory latitude belies any claim that the narrow purpose of marriage is to promote and protect propagation.[21]

The functional definition is too broad as well. If the function of marriage is only to bear and raise children in a family context, then the state should have no objection to the legal recognition of polygamous marriages. Male-focused polygamous families have been efficient bearers of children; and the economies of scale afforded by polygamous families also make them efficient in the rearing of children.[22] So given the actual scope of legal marriage, reproduction and child rearing cannot be its purpose or primary justification.

This finding is further confirmed if we look at the rights and obligations of marriage, which exist independently of whether a marriage generates children and which frequently are not even instrumental to childbearing and rearing. While mutual material support might be viewed as guarding (indirectly) the interests of children, other marital rights, such as the immunity against compelled testimony from a spouse, can hardly be grounded in child-related purposes. Indeed, this immunity is waived when relations with one's own children are what is at legal stake, as in cases of alleged child abuse.[23]

The assumption that childrearing is a function uniquely tethered to the institution of heterosexual marriage also collides with an important but little acknowledged social reality. Many lesbian and gay male couples already are raising families in which children are the blessings of adoption, artificial insemination, surrogacy, or prior marriages. The country is experiencing something approaching a gay and lesbian baby boom.[24] Many more gays would like to raise or foster children. A 1988 study by the American Bar Association found that eight to ten million children are currently being raised in three million gay and lesbian households.[25] This statistic, in turn, suggests that around six percent of the U.S. population is made up of gay and lesbian families with children.[26] We might well ask what conceivable purpose can be served for these children by barring to their gay and lesbian parents the mutual cohesion, emotional security, and economic benefits that are ideally promoted by legal marriage.[27]

Marriage as a Creature of the State If the desperate judicial and social attempts to restrict marriage and its benefits to heterosexual parents are conceptually disingenuous, unjust, and socially inefficient, the question arises: What is left of marriage? Given the emptiness of its standard justifications, should marriage as a legal institution simply be abolished? Ought we simply to abandon the legal institution in favor of a family policy that simply and directly looks after the interests of children, leaving all other possible familial relations on the same legal footing as commercial transactions?

Not quite; but to see what is left and worth saving, we need to take a closer look at the social realities of marriage. Currently, state-sanctioned marriage operates as a legal institution that defines and creates social relations. The law creates the status of husband and wife; it is not a reflection of or response to spousal relations that exist independently of law. This notion that the law "defines and creates social relations" can be clarified by looking at another aspect of family law, one which ordinary people might well find surprising, even shocking. If Paul consensually sires a boy and raises the boy in the way a parent does, then we are strongly inclined to think that he is the boy's father in every morally relevant sense. And we expect the law to reflect this moral status of the father. But the law does not see things this way; it does not reflect and respond to moral reality. For if it turns out that at the time of the boy's birth, his mother was legally married not to Paul but to Fred, the boy is declared by law to be Fred's son, and Paul is, legally speaking, a stranger to the boy. If the mother subsequently leaves Paul and denies him access to the child, Paul has no right at all even to explore legally the possibility that he might have some legislated rights to visit the boy—or so the Supreme Court declared in 1989.[28] Here the law defines and creates the relation of father and son—which frequently, but only by legal accident, happens to accord with the moral reality and lived experience of father and son.

Similarly, in the eyes of the law, marriage is not a social form that exists independently of the law and which marriage law echoes and manages. Rather, marriage is entirely a creature of the law—or as Hawaii's Supreme Court recently put it: "Marriage is a state-conferred legal partnership status."[29]

If we want to see what's left in the box of marriage, we need to abandon this model of legal marriage as constitutive of a status, and rather look at marriage as a form of living and repository of norms independent of law, a moral reality that might well be helped or hindered, but not constituted by the law.[30] Further, current legal marriage, at least as conceptualized by judges, with its definitional entanglements with gender and procreation, is likely to distract us from perceiving lived moral reality.

B. Marriage Defined

What is marriage? Marriage is intimacy given substance in the medium of everyday life, the day-to-day. Marriage is the fused intersection of love's sanctity and necessity's demand.

Not all loves or intimate relations count or should count as marriages. Culturally, we are disinclined to think of "great loves" as marriages. Antony and Cleopatra, Tristan and Isolde, Catherine and Heathcliff— these are loves that burn gloriously but too intensely ever to be manifested in a medium of breakfasts and tire changes. Nor are Americans inclined to consider as real marriages arranged marriages between heads of state who never see each other, for again the relations do not grow in the earth of day-to-day living.

Friendships, too, are intimate relations that we do not consider marital relations. Intimate relations are ones that acquire the character they have—that are unique—because of what the individuals in the relation bring to and make of it; the relation is a distinctive product of their separate individualities. Thus, intimate relations differ markedly from public or commercial transactions. For instance, there is nothing distinctive about your sales clerk that bears on the meaning of your buying a pair of socks from him. The clerk is just carrying out a role, one that from the buyer's perspective nearly anyone could have carried out. But while friendships are star cases of intimate relationships, we do not count them as marriages; for while a person might count on a friend in a pinch to take her to the hospital, friendly relations do not usually manifest themselves through such necessities of life. Friendships are for the sake of fun, and tend to break down when put to other uses. Friendships do not count as marriages, for they do not develop in the medium of necessity's demand.

On the other hand, neither do we count roommates who regularly cook, clean, tend to household chores and share household finances as married, even though they "share the common necessities of life." This expression is the typical phrase used to define the threshold requirement for being considered "domestic partners" in towns that have registration programs for domestic partners.[31] Neither would we even consider as married two people who were roommates and even blended their finances if that is all their relationship comprised. Sharing the day-to-day is, at best, an ingredient of marriage.

Marriage requires the presence and blending of both necessity and intimacy. Life's necessities are a mixed fortune: on the one hand, they frequently are drag, dross, and cussedness, yet on the other hand, they can constitute opportunity, abidingness, and prospect for nurture. They are the field across which, the medium through which, and the ground from which the intimacies which we consider marital flourish, blossom, and come to fruition.

III. *The Normative and Legal Consequence of Marriage*

A. *The Legal Rights and Benefits of Marriage*

This required blend of intimacy and everyday living explains much of the legal content of marriage. For example, the required blend means that for the relationship to work, there must be a presumption of trust between partners; and, in turn, when the relationship *is* working, there will be a transparency in the flow of information between partners—they will know virtually everything about each other. This pairing of trust and transparency constitutes the moral ground for the common law right against compelled testimony between spouses, and explains why this same immunity is not extended to (mere) friends.[32]

The remaining vast array of legal rights and benefits of marriage fit equally well this matrix of love and necessity—chiefly by promoting the patient tendency that such life requires (by providing for privacy, nurture, support, persistence) and by protecting against the occasions when necessity is cussed rather than opportune, especially when life is marked by crisis, illness, and destruction.[33]

First and foremost, state-recognized marriage changes strangers-at-law into next-of-kin with all the rights which this status entails. These rights include: the right to enter hospitals, jails and other places restricted to "immediate family"; the right to obtain "family" health insurance and bereavement leave; the right to live in neighborhoods zoned "single family only"; and the right to make medical decisions in the event a partner is injured or incapacitated.

Both from the partners themselves and from the state, marriage provides a variety of material supports which ameliorate, to a degree, necessity's unfriendly intervals. Marriage requires mutual support between spouses. It provides income tax advantages, including deductions, credits, improved rates, and exemptions. It provides for enhanced public assistance in times of need. It governs the equitable control, division, acquisition, and disposition of community property. At death it guarantees rights of inheritance in the absence of wills—a right of special benefit to the poor, who frequently die intestate. For the wealthy, marriage virtually eliminates inheritance taxes between spouses, since spouses as of 1981 can make unlimited untaxed gifts to each other even at death.[34] For all, it exempts property from attachments resulting from one partner's debts. It confers a right to bring a wrongful death suit. And it confers the right to receive survivor's benefits.

Several marital benefits promote a couple's staying together in the face of changed circumstances. Included in the benefits are the right to collect unemployment benefits if one partner quits her job to move with her partner to a new location because the partner has obtained a new job there, and the right to obtain residency status for a noncitizen partner. Currently lesbians and gay men are denied all of these rights in consequence of being barred access to legal marriage, even though these rights and benefits are as relevant to committed gay relationships as to heterosexual marriages.

B. *The Structuring of Lesbian and Gay Relationships*

The portraits of gay and lesbian committed relationships that emerge from ethnographic studies suggest that in the way they typically arrange their lives, gay and lesbian couples fulfill in an exemplary manner the definition of marriage developed here.[35]

In gay relationships, the ways in which the day-to-day demands of necessity are typically fulfilled are themselves vehicles for the development of intimacy. It is true that gay and lesbian relationships generally divide duties between the partners—this is the efficient thing to do, the very first among the economies of scale that coupledom affords. But the division of duties is in the first instance a matter of personal preference and joint planning, in which decisions are made in part with an eye to who is better at doing any given task and who has free time—say, for ironing or coping with car dealerships. But adjustments are made in cases where one person is better at most things, or even everything. In these cases, the relation is made less efficient for the sake of equality between partners, who willingly end up doing things they would rather not do. Such joint decisions are made not from a sense of traditionally assigned duty and role, but from each partner's impulse to help out, a willingness to sacrifice, and a commitment to equality.[36] In these ways, both the development of intimacy through choice and the proper valuing of love are interwoven in the day-to-day activities of gay couples. Choice improves intimacy. Choice makes sacrifices meaningful. Choice gives love its proper weight.

C. Weddings and Licensing Considered

If this analysis of the nature of marriage is correct, then misguided is the requirement, found in most states, that beyond securing from government a marriage license, the couple, in order to be certifiably married, must also undergo a ceremony of solemnization, either in a church or before a justice of the peace.[37] For people are mistaken to think that the sacred valuing of love is something that can be imported from the outside, in public ceremonies invoking praise from God or community.[38] Even wedding vows can smack of cheap moral credit, since they are words, not actions. The sacred valuing of love must come from within and realize itself over time through little sacrifices in day-to-day existence. In this way, intimacy takes on weight and shine, the ordinary becomes the vehicle of the extraordinary, and the development of the marital relation becomes a mirror reflecting eternity. It is more proper to think of weddings with their ceremonial trappings and invocations as bon voyages than as a social institution which, echoing the legal institution of marriage, defines and confers marital status. In a gay marriage, the sanctifications that descend instantly through custom and ritual in many heterosexual marriages descend gradually over and through time—and in a way they are better for it. For the sacred values and loyal intimacies contained in such a marriage are a product of the relation itself; they are truly the couple's own.

The model of marriage advanced here is highly compatible with, indeed it recommends, what has been, until recently, by far the most usual form of marriage in Western civilization, namely, common-law marriage—in which there is no marriage license or solemnization. Currently only about one-fourth of the states legally acknowledge common-law marriages, but over the largest stretches of Western civilization, legally certifiable marriage was an arrangement limited almost exclusively to the wealthy, the noble—in short, the few.[39]

In a common-law arrangement, the marriage is at some point, as the need arises, culturally and legally acknowledged in retrospect as having existed all along. It is important to remember that as matter of law, the standard requirement of living together seven years is entirely evidentiary and not at all constitutive of the relation as a marriage.[40] So, for example, a child born in the third year of a common-law marriage is legitimate from the moment of its birth and need not wait four years as Mom and Dad log seven years together. The marriage was there in substance all along. The social and legal custom of acknowledging common-law marriage gives an adequately robust recognition to marriage as a lived arrangement and as a repository of values.

The securing of a marriage license is something the state may well want to encourage as a useful device in the administration of the legal benefits of marriage. But the licensing should not be seen as what legally constitutes the marriage when questions arise over whether the marriage in fact exists (say, in paternity, custody, or inheritance disputes). In turn, it is completely legitimate for the state to terminate marital benefits if in fact the couple gets a license but is not fulfilling the definition of marriage as a living arrangement. The state already investigates such cases of fraud when marriage licenses are secured simply to acquire an enhanced immigration status for one of the licensees.[41] Indeed, that immigration fraud through marriage licenses is even conceptually possible is a tacit recognition that marriage *simpliciter* is marriage as a lived arrangement, while legally certified marriage is and should be viewed as epiphenomenal or derivative—and not vice versa.

D. The Relation between Love and Justice

If intimate or private relations of a certain quality provide the content of marriage, what can the law and public policy provide to marriage? Why do we need legal marriage at all? Folk wisdom has it that both love and justice are blind. But they are blind in different ways, ways which reveal possible conflicts and tensions between love and justice in practice.[42]

Justice is blind—blindfolded—so that it may be a system of neutral, impersonal, impartial rules, a governance by laws, not by idiosyncratic, biased, or self-interested persons. Principles of justice in the modern era have been confected chiefly with an eye to relations at arm's length and apply paradigmatically to competitions conducted between conflicting interests in the face of scarce resources. Equal respect is the central concern of justice.[43]

Love is blind—(as the song goes) blinded by the light—because the lover is stutteringly bedazzled by the beloved. In love, we overlook failings in those whom we cherish. And the beloved's happiness, not the beloved's respect, is love's central concern.

Within the family, we agree that the distribution of goods should be a matter of feeling, care, concern, and sacrifice rather than one conducted by appeal to impartial and impersonal principles of equity. Indeed, if the impersonal principles of justice are constantly in the foreground of familial relations, intimacy is destroyed. If every decision in a family requires a judicial-like determination that each member got an equal share, then the care, concern, and love that are a family's breath and spirit are dead. Justice should not be front and center in family life.

But love may lead to intolerable injustices, even as a spinoff effect of one of its main virtues. In the blindness of love, people will love even those who beat them and humiliate them. Conversely, aggressors in these cases will feel more free to aggress against a family member than a stranger exactly because the family is the realm of love rather than of civic respect. Some of these humiliations are even occasioned by the distinctive opportunities afforded by traditional family life—in particular, society's misguided notion that everything that occurs behind the family's four walls is private, and so beyond legitimate inquiry.

Conflicts between love and justice can be relieved if we view marriage as a legal institution that allows for appeals to justice when they are needed. Justice should not be the motivation for loving relations, but neither should love and family exist beyond the reach of justice. Justice needs to be a reliable background and foundation for family life. Therefore, legal marriage should be viewed as a nurturing ground for social marriage, and not (as now) as that which legally defines and creates marriage and so tends to preclude legal examination of it.

E. The Contribution of Minorities to Family Law Reform

Marriage law should be a conduit for justice in moments of crisis—in financial collapse, in illness, at death—to guard against exploitation both in general and in the distinctive forms that marriage allows.

And, indeed, family law reform has generally been moving in this direction. State-defined marriage is an evolving institution, not an eternal verity. As noted, inequitable distributions of power by gender have been all but eliminated as a legally enforced part of marriage.[44] People at the margins of society have frequently provided the beacon for reform in family law. Already by the 1930s, black American culture no longer stigmatized children born out of wedlock, though whites continued to do so.[45] In 1968, the Supreme Court belatedly came to realize that punitively burdening innocent children is profoundly unjust, and subsequently, through a series of some thirty Supreme Court cases, illegitimacy has all but vanished as a condition legally affecting children born out of wedlock.[46] Further, black Americans provided to the mainstream the model of the extended family with its major virtue of a certain amount of open texture and play in the joints. In 1977, this virtue, too, was given constitutional status when the Supreme Court struck down zoning laws that discriminated against extended, typically black, families.[47]

Currently society and its discriminatory impulse make gay coupling very difficult. It is hard for people to live together as couples without having their sexual orientation perceived in the public realm, which in turn targets them for discrimination. Sharing a life in hiding is even more constricting than life in a nuclear family. Members of nongay couples are here asked to imagine what it would take to erase every trace of their own sexual orientation for even one week. Still, despite oppressive odds, gays have shown an amazing tendency to nest.[48] And those lesbian and gay male couples who have persevered show that the structure of more usual couplings is not a matter of destiny, but of personal responsibility. The so-called basic unit of society turns out not to be a unique immutable atom; it can adopt different parts, and be adapted to different needs.

F. Gay Couples As Models of Family Life

Gay life, like black culture, might even provide models and materials for rethinking family life and improving family law. I will now chart some ways in which this might be so—in particular drawing on the distinctive experiences and ideals of gay male couples.[49]

Take sex. Traditionally, a commitment to monogamy—to the extent that it was not simply an adjunct of property law, a vehicle for guaranteeing property rights and succession—was the chief mode of sacrifice imposed upon or adopted by married couples as a means of showing their sacred valuing of their relation. But gay men have realized that while couples may choose to restrict sexual activity in order to show their love for each other, it is not necessary for this purpose; there are many other ways to manifest and ritualize commitment. And so monogamy (it appears) is not an essential component of love and marriage. The authors of *The Male Couple* found that:

> [T]he majority of [gay male] couples, and *all* of the couples together for longer than five years, were not continuously sexually exclusive with each other. Although many had long periods of sexual exclusivity, it was not the ongoing expectation for most. We found that gay men *expect* mutual emotional dependability with their partners [but also believe] that relationship fidelity transcends concerns about sexuality and exclusivity.[50]

Both because marital sacrifices must be voluntary to be meaningful and because sexual exclusivity is not essential to marital commitment, the law should not impose monogamy on married couples. And, indeed, half the states have decriminalized adultery.[51]

Other improvements that take their cue from gay male couplings might include a recognition that marriages evolve over time. *The Male Couple* distinguishes six stages that couples typically pass through: blending (year one), nesting (years two and three), maintaining (years four and five), building (years six though ten), releasing (years eleven through twenty), and renewing (beyond twenty years).[52] Relations initially submerge individuality, and emphasize equality between partners, though the equality usually at first takes the form of complementarity rather than similarity.[53] With the passage of years individuality reemerges. Infatuation gives way to collaboration. The development of a foundational trust between the partners and a blending of finances and possessions, interestingly enough, occurs much later in the relationship—typically after ten years.[54] While the most important factor in keeping men together over the first ten years is finding compatibility, the most important factor for the second decade is a casting off of possessiveness, even as the men's

lives become more entwined materially and by the traditions and rituals they have established.

The fact that relations evolve makes the top-down model of legal marriage as creator of relations particularly inappropriate for human life. Currently at law, the only recognition that marriages change and gather moral weight with time, is the vesting of one spouse's (typically the wife's) interests in the other's Social Security benefits after ten years of marriage.[55] More needs to be explored along these lines. For example, one spouse's guaranteed share of the other's inheritance might rise with the logging of years, rather than being the same traditionally fixed, one-third share, both on day one of the marriage and at its fiftieth anniversary.[56] Men's relations also suggest, however, that the emphasis that has been put on purely material concerns, like blended finances, as the marks of a relation in domestic partnership legislation and in a number of gay family law cases is misguided and fails to understand the dynamics and content of gay relations.[57]

In gay male relations, the relation itself frequently is experienced as a third element or "partner" over and above the two men.[58] This third element frequently has a physical embodiment in a home, business, joint avocation, or companion animal, but also frequently consists of joint charitable, civil, political, or religious work. The third-element of the relation both provides a focus for the partners and relieves some of the confining centrifugal pressures frequently found in small families. Whether this might have legal implications deserves exploration—it certainly provides a useful model for small heterosexual families.

All longterm gay male relationships, *The Male Couple* reports, devise their own special ways of making the relations satisfying: "Their styles of relationship were developed without the aid of visible role models available to heterosexual couples."[59] This strongly suggests that legal marriage ought not to enforce any tight matrix of obligations on couples if their longterm happiness is part of the laws' stake. Rather the law ought to provide a ground in which relations can grow and change and even recognize their own endings.

IV. *Conclusion: Religious and Legal Reforms Afoot*

Given the nature of marriage and the nature of gay relations, it is time for the law to let them merge. And, indeed, there have been some general legal, social, and cultural shifts in the direction of acknowledging and supporting gay marriages. On January 1, 1995, gay marriages [became] legal in Sweden; they [became] legal in Denmark in 1989 and Norway in 1993.[60]

In 1993, Hawaii's Supreme Court ruled that Hawaii's marriage laws, which the court interpreted as requiring spouses to be of different sex presumptively violate Hawaii's Equal Rights Amendment, which bars sex discrimination. The court ruled that the laws could only be upheld on remand if shown to be necessary to further a compelling state interest.[61] The court preemptively found illegitimate the two standard justifications that have been used in other jurisdictions to claim state interests in restricting marriage to different-sex couples—namely, appeals to the very definition of marriage and procreation.[62] It looks promising, then, that the court will strike down the ban on same-sex marriages. And if one is married in Hawaii, one is married everywhere—thanks both to common-law tradition and to the U.S. Constitution's full faith and credit clause.[63]

As a matter of general cultural perception, recognitions of same-sex domestic partnerships are baby steps toward the legalization of gay marriage. A number of prestigious universities (including Harvard, Columbia, Stanford, the University of Chicago, and the University of Iowa) and prestigious corporations (including AT&T, Bank of America, Levi Strauss and Company, Lotus Development Corp., Apple Computer, Inc., Warner Brothers, MCA/Universal Inc., the *New York Times* and *Time* magazine) have extended to their employees' same-sex partners domestic partnership benefits, which include many of the privileges extended to their employees' heterosexual spouses.[64] These benefits typically include health insurance. Approximately thirty municipalities, beginning with Berkeley in 1984 and including San Francisco, Seattle, and New York City, have done the same, establishing in some cases a system of civic registrations for same-sex couples.[65]

In June 1994, Vermont became the first state to extend health insurance coverage to the same-sex partners of its state workers.[66] In August 1994, the California legislature passed a bill to establish a registry of domestic partners for both mixed-sex and same-sex couples and gave the partners three legal rights: (1) access to each other when one of them is hospitalized; (2) the use of California's short form will to designate each other as primary beneficiaries, and, most importantly; (3) the establishment of one's partner as conservator if one is incapacitated.[67] On September 11, Governor Pete Wilson vetoed the legislation, issuing a

veto message that failed even to acknowledge the bill's impact on the lives of California's gay couples.[68]

In 1984, the General Assembly of the Unitarian-Universalist Association voted to "affirm the growing practice of some of its ministers in conducting services of union of gay and lesbian couples and urges member societies to support their ministers in this important aspect of our movement's ministry to the gay and lesbian community."[69]

In October 1993, the General Assembly of the Union of American Hebrew Congregations—which is the federation of U.S. and Canadian Reform synagogues—adopted a resolution calling for the legal and social recognition and support of gay domestic partners.[70]

Mainline Protestant denominations have ceased full-scale attacks on gay and lesbian relationships and are struggling with the issue of blessing them.[71] In June 1994, the General Assembly of the Presbyterian Church (U.S.A.) came within a few votes of permitting ministers to bless same-sex unions.[72] Also in June 1994, a draft proposal by the Episcopal bishops, after describing homosexuality as an orientation of "a significant minority of persons" that "cannot usually be reversed," went on to say that sexual relationships work best within the context of a committed life-long union: "We believe this is as true for homosexual relationships as for heterosexual relationships and that such relationships need and should receive the pastoral care of the church."[73] In October 1993, a draft report by a national Lutheran study group on sexuality had called for the blessing and even legal acknowledgment of loving gay relationships.[74]

These actions addressing the material dimensions of gay relationships through domestic partnership legislation and the spiritual dimensions of gay relationships through holy union ceremonies constitute true moral progress if they are steps toward the full legal and religious recognition of gay marriages. They are morally suspect, though, if they simply end up establishing and then entrenching a system of gay relations as separate but equal to heterosexual ones. To move from a position of no gay blessings and privileges to a structure of separate blessings and privileges is to traverse only the moral ground from the Supreme Court's 1857 *Dred Scott* ruling upholding the form of white supremacy under which blacks could not marry at all—slavery—to its 1896 *Plessy* v. *Ferguson* ruling upholding the reign of white supremacy that allowed blacks to marry blacks but not to marry whites.[75]

Whether domestic partnership legislation is a stepping-stone or a distracting impediment to gay marriage cannot be known categorically. Whether it is one or the other depends on a number of factors: the specific content of the legislation, the social circumstances of its passage, and the likely social consequences of its passage. I conjecture that states will take the route of domestic partnership legislation until they find out that a "separate but equal" structuring of gay and nongay relationships is hopelessly unwieldy. Then states will resort to the benefits of simplicity and recognize gay marriages straight out.

If the analysis of marriage in this article is correct, then marriage, like knowledge, is a common good, one which any number of people can share without its diminution for any one of the sharers. So heterosexuals have nothing to lose from the institutionalization of gay marriage. And the legalization of gay marriage is a moral advance over mere civil rights legislation. For civil rights legislation tends to treat gayness as though it were a property, like having an eye color or wearing an earring, which one could have in isolation from all other people. But gay marriage is an acknowledgement that gayness, like loving and caring, is a relational property, a connection between persons, a human bonding, one in need of tendance and social concern.

Endnotes

1. Harvey Fierstein, *Torch Song Trilogy* (New York: Villard Books, 1983; c. 1979), pp. 144–46.

2. See Karen Thompson and Julie Andrzejewski, *Why Can't Sharon Kowalski Come Home?* (San Francisco: Spinsters/Aunt Lute, 1988).

3. Eventually, Thompson did get guardianship of Kowalski, but only after Kowalski's parents withdrew from the field of battle. A Minnesota appeals court held that "this choice [of guardianship] is further supported by the fact that Thompson and Sharon are a family of affinity, which ought to be accorded respect." In re Guardianship of Kowalski, 478 N.W.2d 790, 796 (Minn. 1991).

4. *Coon v. Joseph,* 237 Cal. Rptr. 873, 877–78 (Cal. Ct. App. 1987).

5. As a subsidiary matter, I also advocate domestic partnership legislation to the extent that such legislation is a determinate step toward the realization of gay legal marriage and not a distraction from or new hurdle to this goal. See below, Part IV.

6. See, e.g., *Adams v. Howerton*, 486 F. Supp. 1119, 1123 (C.D. Cal. 1980) (holding that under the immigration and Nationality Act a gay man could not be considered an "immediate relative" of another with whom he had lived for years and had had a marriage ceremony). "Thus there has been for centuries a combination of scriptural and canonical teaching

under which a 'marriage' between persons of the same sex was unthinkable and, by definition, impossible." Id.

Similarly, in 1991, Hawaii's Director of the Department of Health argued before Hawaii's Supreme Court: "The right of persons of the same sex to marry one another does not exist because marriage, by definition and usage, means a special relationship between a man and a woman." *Baehr v. Lewin* 852 P.2d 44, 61 (Haw. 1993).

7. *The Concise Oxford Dictionary* (3d ed., 1964), pp. 594, 746, 1241, 1478, 1493, for example, offers the following definitions:

"Marriage: relation between married persons, wedlock."
"Married: united in wedlock."
"Wedlock: the married state."
"Spouse: husband or wife."
"Husband: man joined to woman by marriage."
"Wife: married woman esp. in relation to her husband."

8. For example, "Kentucky statutes do not specifically prohibit marriage between persons of the same sex, nor do they authorize the issuance of a marriage license to such persons." *Jones v. Hallahan,* 501 S.W.2d 588, 589 (Ky. 1973). One of the very first gay marriage cases—one from Minnesota—also dealt with a state statute that failed to expressly prohibit same-sex marriages. *Baker v. Nelson,* 191 N.W.2d 185 (Minn. 1971), appeal dismissed, 409 U.S. 810 (1972).

9. *De Santo v. Barnsicy,* 476 A.2d 952 (Pa. 1984) (two persons of the same sex cannot contract a common-law marriage notwithstanding the state's recognition of common-law marriages between persons of different sexes); *Singer v. Hara,* 522 P.2d 1187 (Wash. 1974); *Jones,* 501 S.W.2d at 588; *Baker,* 191 N.W.2d at 185.

10. Other cases that, in one way or another, have held that gays cannot marry are *Adams,* 486 F. Supp. at 1119; Succession of Bascot, 502 So. 2d 1118, 1127–30 (La. 1987) (holding that a man cannot be a "concubine" of another man); *Slayton v. Texas,* 633 S.W.2d 934, 937 (Tex. 1982) (stating that same-sex marriage is impossible in Texas); *Jennings v. Jennings,* 315 A.2d 816, 820 n.7 (Md. 1974) (explaining that "Maryland does not recognize a marriage between persons of the same sex"); *Dean v. District of Columbia,* No. CA 90-13892, slip op. at 18–21 (D.C. Super. Ct. Dec. 30, 1991) (invoking passages from Genesis, Deuteronomy, Matthew, and Ephesians to hold that "societal recognition that it takes a man and a woman to form a marital relationship is older than Christianity itself"); in re Estate of Cooper, 564 N.Y.S.2d 684, 687 (N.Y. Sup. Ct. 1990) (refusing to "elevat[e] homosexual unions to the same level achieved by the marriage of two people of the opposite sex"); *Anonymous v. Anonymous,* 325 N.Y.S.2d 499, 500 (N.Y., Sup. CL. 1971) (stating that "[m]arriage is and always has been a contract between a man and a woman").

11. *Singer,* 522 P.2d at 1193.

12. *Black's Law Dictionary* (6th ed. 1990), p. 972.

13. Even the highly analytical historian John Boswell, in his recent book on the history of gay marriage, fares no better in

coming up with a definition of marriage: "It is my understanding that most modern speakers of English understand the term 'marriage' to refer to what the partners expect to be a permanent and exclusive union between two people, which would produce legitimate children if they chose to have children, and which creates mutual rights and responsibilities, legal, economic, and moral." John Boswell, *Same-Sex Unions in Premodern Europe* (New York: Villard Books, 1994), p. 10; cf. Boswell, p. 190. But if one asks "what partners?" "what union?" "what rights?" and "what responsibilities?" I fear the answer in each instance must be "marital ones," in which case the definition goes around in the same small circle as the law. And legitimate children just are children of a marriage, so that component of the definition is circular as well.

14. Harry D. Krause, *Family Law in a Nutshell,* 2d ed. (St. Paul, Minn.: West Publishing Co., 1986), p. 92 (hereinafter *Family Law*).

15. Ibid., pp. 96–103. See, e.g., *Kirchberg* v. *Feenstra,* 450 U.S. 455 (1981) (invalidated Louisiana's community property statute that gave the husband, as the family's "head and master," the unilateral right to dispose of property jointly owned with his wife without her consent).

16. *Family Law,* pp. 127–29.

17. "However unpleasant, outmoded or unnecessary, whatever sex discrimination remains in family law is trivial in comparison with the inequality of spouses that result from family facts, from the traditional role division which places the husband into the money-earner role and the wife into the home where she acquires neither property nor marketable skills." *Family Law,* p. 146.

18. See *Singer* v. *Hara,* 522 P.2d 1187, 1195 (Wash. 1974).

19. *Baehr* v. *Lewin,* 852 P.2d 44, 50 n.7 (Haw. 1993) (quoting Haw. Rev. Stat. §572–7[a] [Supp. 1992]).

20. Id. at 48 n.1 (quoting Haw. Rev. Stat. 580–21 [1985]).

21. Id. at 48.

22. See Dirk Johnson, "Polygarnists Emerge from Secrecy, Seeking Not Just Peace, But Respect," *New York Times,* April 9, 1991, p. A22.

23. *Family Law,* p. 131.

24. See, e.g., Susan Chira, "Gay and Lesbian Parents Grow More Visible," *New York Times,* September 30, 1993, p. A1; Daniel Coleman, "Gay Parents Called No Disadvantage," *New York Times,* December 2, 1992, p. B7; "Homosexuality Does Not Make Parent Unfit, Court Rules," *New York Times,* June 22, 1994, p. A8.

25. Editors of the *Harvard Law Review, Sexual Orientation and the Law* 119 (1990).

26. Craig R. Dean, "Legalize Gay Marriage," *New York Times,* September 28, 1991 §I, p. 19.

27. Andrew Sullivan, "Here Comes the Groom: A (Conservative) Case for Gay Marriage," *New Republic,* August 1989, p. 22.

28. *Michael H.* v. *Gerald D., 491* U.S. 110 (1989).

29. *Baehr* v. *Lewin,* 852 P.2d 44, 58 (Haw. 1993).

30. The Supreme Court's three "right to marry" cases implicitly acknowledge that marriage is a social reality and repository of norms, indeed of rights, independent of statutory law, since the right to marry is a substantive liberty right which overrides, trumps, and voids statutory marital law. *Loving* v. *Virginia,* 388 U.S. 1, 12 (1967) (voiding laws barring blacks and whites from marrying each other); *Zablocki* v. *Redhail,* 434 U.S. 374 (1978) (voiding law barring child support scofflaws from marrying); *Turner* v. *Safley,* 482 U.S. 78, 94–99 (1987) (voiding regulation barring prisoners from marrying).

31. See, e.g., City of Berkeley, California, Domestic Partnership Policy, Statement of General Policy, December 4, 1984, quoted in Harry D. Krause, *Family Law: Cases, Comments and Questions,* 3rd ed. (1990), p. 159.

32. See *Family Law,* pp. 131–32.

33. *Baehr* 852 P.2d at 59 (catalogues the most salient rights and benefits that are contingent upon marital status). The benefits discussed in this section are drawn from this case and from a catalogue of marital privileges given in a 1993 Georgia Supreme Court case, *Van Dyck* v. *Van Dyck,* 425 S.E.2d 853 (Ga. 1993) (Sears-Collins, J., concurring) (holding that a state law authorizing cutoff of alimony payments to a former spouse who enters into a voluntary cohabitation does not apply when the cohabitation in question is a lesbian one). See also 1 Hayden Curry and Denis Clifford, *A Legal Guide for Lesbian and Gay Couples,* R. Leonard, ed., 6th ed. (Berkeley, Calif.: Nole Press, 1991), p. 2.

34. *Family Law,* p. 107.

35. See Alan P. Bell and Martin S. Weinberg, *Homosexualities: A Study of Diversity among Men and Women* (New York: Simon and Schuster, 1978); Philip Blumstein and Pepper Schwartz, *American Couples: Money, Work, Sex* (New York: Morrow, 1983); David McWhirter and Andrew M. Mattison, *The Male Couple: How Relationships Develop* (Englewood Cliffs, N.J.: Prentice-Hall, 1984); Suzanne Sherman, *Lesbian and Gay Marriages: Private Commitments, Public Ceremonies* (Philadelphia: Temple University Press, 1992); Kath Weston, *Families We Choose: Lesbians, Gays, Kinship* (New York: Columbia University Press, 1991).

36. See Weston, *Families We Choose,* pp. 149–50.

37. *Family Law,* pp. 47–48.

38. On sacred values, see generally Douglas MacLean, "Social Values and the Distribution of Risk," in *Values at Risk,* Douglas MacLean, ed. (Totowa, N.J.: Rowman & Allanheld, 1986), pp. 85–93.

39. *Family Law,* p. 50. For a review of the literature on the vagaries of marriage as an institution, see Lawrence Stone, "Sex in the West: The Strange History of Human Sexuality," *New Republic,* July 8, 1985, pp. 25–37. See also Boswell, *Same-Sex Unions in Premodern Europe,* pp. 32–33, 35.

40. *Family Law,* p. 49.

41. Ibid. p. 47.

42. This section draws on some ideas in Claudia Mills and Douglas MacLean, "Love and Justice," *QQ: Report from the Institute for Philosophy and Public Policy,* Fall 1989, pp. 12–15.

43. For a classic statement of this position, see Ronald Dworkin, *Taking Rights Seriously* (Cambridge, Mass.: Harvard University Press, 1978), pp. 180–83, 272–78.

44. Ibid., 1944; text accompanying notes 14–17.

45. Gunnar Myrdal, *An American Dilemma* (New York: Harper & Row, 1944; 1962), p. 935.

46. *Family Law,* pp. 154–55.

47. *Moore* v. *City of East Cleveland, Ohio,* 431 U.S. 494 (1977).

48. Ibid., note 35 (studies of gay couples).

49. Lesbian legal theorists have generally supposed marriage too sexist an institution to be salvaged, and lesbian moral theorists also have found traditional forms of coupling highly suspect. Some recommend communal arrangements as the ideal for lesbians. Others have proposed that lovers should not even live together. See Paula L. Ettelbrick, "Since When Is Marriage a Path to Liberation?" *OUT/LOOK,* Fall 1989, pp. 9, 14–17; Nancy D. Polikoff, "We Will Get What We Ask For: Why Legalizing Gay and Lesbian Marriage Will Not 'Dismantle Legal Structure of Gender in Every Marriage,'" *Virginia Law Review* 79 (1993): 1535; Sarah Lucia Hoagland, *Lesbian Ethics: Toward New Value* (1988); Claudia Card, *Lesbian Choices* (1994).

50. McWhirter and Mattison, *The Male Couple,* p. 285.

51. *Family Law,* p. 130.

52. McWhirter and Mattison, *The Male Couple,* pp. 15–17.

53. Ibid., pp. 31–33.

54. Ibid., pp. 104–105.

55. *Family Law,* pp. 369, 386.

56. Ibid., p. 104.

57. I am thinking in particular of the 1989 case *Braschi* v. *Stahl,* 543 N.E.2d 49 (N.Y. 1989), in which New York's highest court ruled that two men who had been living together for years with blended finances—whom the court called "unmarried lifetime partners"—qualified as "family members" for the purposes of New York's law governing succession rights on apartment leases. At the time, this was considered the most progressive gay family law case of record. And in one regard the case was progressive. It proposed that the concept "family" should be given an operational definition: if it waddles, flaps, and quacks like a family, then it is a family. But then the case went on to dwell almost exclusively on the material and monetary side of life, so much so that in the end it appeared almost to be a case promoting property fights rather than familial relations. And, indeed, this case has had no progeny.

Two years later, the same court abandoned any effort to define family relationships operationally or functionally and held that a lesbian had no rights at all to visit a daughter whom she had jointly reared with the girl's biological mother. *Alison D.* v. *Virginia M.,* 572 N.E.2d 27 (N.Y. 1991). Here only biology mattered. The same court held later that year that grandparents do have a right to visit their grandchildren even over the objections of both parents. In re *Emanuel S.,* 577 N.E.2d 77 (N.Y 1991). Clearly much work remains to be done in bringing law into accord with what families and marriages functionally are and operationally do. Mere reference to the material circumstances of marriage will not do that work.

58. McWhirter and Mattison, *The Male Couple,* p. 285.

59. Ibid., p. 286.

60. "A Swede Deal for Couples," *Advocate,* July 12, 1994, p. 16.

61. *Baehr* v. *Lewin,* 852 P.2d 44, 60–68 (Haw. 1993). Subsequently, Hawaii's legislature voted that marriages in Hawaii must have mixed-sex partners; but since the court had already evaluated this condition in its constitutional analysis of Hawaii's laws, the legislature's vote seems to be a case of moral grandstanding and political posturing. "Hawaii Legislature Blocks Gay Marriage," *New York Times,* April 27, 1994, at A18.

62. *Baehr,* 852 P.2d at 48 n.1, 61 (Haw. 1993).

63. "Full Faith and Credit shall be given in each State to the public Acts, Records, and judicial Proceedings of every other State." U.S. Const. art. IV, § 1.

Gay marriage is also gradually coming into law through the back door of same-sex second parent adoptions. At least six states have allowed the lesbian partner of a woman with a child to adopt—become the second mother of—the child. But if Heather has at law two moms, what is the relation between her two parents? Strangers at law? Surely not. "Court Grants Parental Rights to Mother of Lesbian Lover," *New York Times,* September 12, 1993, § 1, p. 42.

64. "Two Universities Give Gay Partners Same Benefits as Married Couples," *New York Times,* December 24, 1992, p. A10; "Domestic Partnership Benefits Found Not to Increase Employer Costs," *Windy City Times,* June 4, 1992, p. 9; *Frontiers* (Los Angeles), October 7, 1994, p. 16.

65. "Workers' Partners Get Benefit of Health Plan," *New York Times,* October 31, 1993, § 1, p. 40.

66. "Vermont Union Wins Benefits for Partners," *New York Times,* June 13, 1994, p. A12. In some jurisdictions, including Vermont, such benefits are also extended to unmarried but cohabiting heterosexual couples.

67. "Senate Passes Historic Domestic Partners Bill," *Frontiers* (Los Angeles), September 9, 1994, p. 17.

68. "Domestic Partner Bill Vetoed in California," *New York Times,* September 13, 1994, p. A6; see *Frontiers* (Los Angeles), October 7, 1994, p. 36.

69. Paul H. Landen, "Unitarian-Universalist Views on Issues in Human Sexuality" (unpublished Ph.D. thesis, Michigan State University, 1992), p. 134.

70. General Assembly, Union of American Hebrew Congregations, Recognition for Lesbian and Gay Partnerships (October 21–25, 1993).

71. See William N. Eskridge Jr., "A History of Same-Sex Marriage," *Virginia Law Review* 79 (1993): 1419, 1497–1502.

72. "Presbyterians Try to Resolve Long Dispute," *New York Times,* June 17, 1994, p. A9.

73. "Episcopal Draft on Sexuality Tries to Take a Middle Course," *New York Times,* June 26, 1994, § 1, p. 9.

74. "Lutherans to Decide Whether to Sanction Homosexual Unions," *New York Times,* October 21, 1993, p. A1; "Lutheran Church Stalled in Drafting Sex Statement," *New York Times,* November 26, 1993, p. A14.

In marked contrast, the Catholic Church has dug in its heels on the issue. In February 1994, Pope John Paul II issued a hundred-page "Letter to Families." Among other things, the letter sent a message to Catholics to refrain from supporting the notion of gay and lesbian marriages, calling such unions "a serious threat to the family and society" and viewing them

as "inappropriately conferring an institutional value on deviant behavior." The pope's own definition of marriage, however, seems to be as circular in its exclusion of gays as those definitions explored above (See above Part II, A.1): "Marriage . . . is constituted by the covenant whereby a man and a woman establish between themselves a partnership for their whole life." "Pope Calls Gay Marriage Threat to Family," *New York Times,* February 23, 1994, p. A2. The complete English language text of the Letter is published in *Origins: CNS Documentary Service* 23:37 (March 3, 1994): 637–59.

75. *Dred Scott* v. *Sandford,* 60 U.S. (19 How.) 393 (1857); *Plessy* v. *Ferguson,* 163 U.S. 537 (1896). In 1883, the Supreme Court in a cursory opinion had upheld against constitutional challenge anti-miscegenation laws. *Pace* v. *Alabama,* 106 U.S. 583 (1883). These laws were finally struck down in 1967. *Loving* v. *Virginia,* 388 U.S. 1 (1967).

16. *Is Adultery Immoral?*

RICHARD A. WASSERSTROM

Examining the phenomenon of marital infidelity, Richard Wasserstrom argues that the practice of adultery is ordinarily thought to be blameworthy because it invariably involves deceit and a breaking of trust. He suggests, however, that in a more open and honest relationship, one in which love and sexual intimacy were properly distinguished, one could, in fact, enjoy sexual experiences with partners other than one's spouse without the necessity of deception. In such instances, adultery might no longer be morally problematic.

Many discussions of the enforcement of morality by the law take as illustrative of the problem under consideration the regulation of various types of sexual behavior by the criminal law. It was, for example, the Wolfenden Report's recommendations concerning homosexuality and prostitution that led Lord Devlin to compose his now famous lecture, "The Enforcement of Morals." And that lecture in turn provoked important philosophical responses from H.L.A. Hart, Ronald Dworkin, and others.

Much, if not all, of the recent philosophical literature on the enforcement of morals appears to take for granted the immorality of the sexual behavior in question. The focus of discussion, at least, is whether such things as homosexuality, prostitution, and adultery ought to be made illegal even if they are immoral, and not whether they are immoral.

I propose in this paper to think about the latter, more neglected topic, that of sexual morality, and to do so in the following fashion. I shall consider just one kind of behavior that is often taken to be a case of sexual immorality—adultery. I am interested in pursuing at least two questions. First, I want to explore the question of in what respects adulterous behavior falls within the domain of morality at all: For this surely is one of the puzzles one encounters when considering the topic of sexual morality. It is often hard to see on what grounds much of the behavior is deemed to be either moral or immoral, for example, private homosexual behavior between consenting adults. I have purposely selected adultery because it seems a more plausible candidate for moral assessment than many other kinds of sexual behavior.

The second question I want to examine is that of what is to be said about adultery, without being especially concerned to stay within the area of morality. I shall endeavor, in other words, to identify and to assess a number of major arguments that might be advanced against adultery. I believe that they are the chief arguments that would be given in support of the view that adultery is immoral, but I think they are worth considering even if some of them turn out to be nonmoral arguments and considerations.

A number of the issues involved seem to me to be complicated and difficult. In a number of places I have at best indicated where further philosophical exploration is required without having successfully conducted the exploration myself. The paper may very well be more useful as an illustration of how one might begin to think about the subject of sexual morality than as an elucidation of important truths about the topic.

Before I turn to the arguments themselves there are two preliminary points that require some clarification. Throughout the paper I shall refer to the immorality of such things as breaking a promise, deceiving someone, etc. In a very rough way, I mean by this that there is something morally wrong that is done in doing the action in question. I mean that the action is, in a strong sense of *"prima facie," prima facie* wrong or unjustified. I do not mean that it may never be right or justifiable to do the action; just that the fact that it is an action of this description always does count against the rightness of the action. I leave entirely open the question of what it is that makes actions of this kind immoral in this sense of "immoral."

The second preliminary point concerns what is meant or implied by the concept of adultery. I mean by "adultery" any case of extramarital sex, and I want to explore the arguments for and against extramarital sex, undertaken in a variety of morally relevant situations. Someone might claim that the concept of adultery is conceptually connected with the concept of immorality, and that to characterize behavior as adulterous is already to characterize it as immoral or unjustified in the sense described above. There may be something to this. Hence the importance of making it clear that I want to talk about extramarital sexual relations. If they are always immoral, this is something that must be shown by argument. If the concept of adultery does in some sense entail or imply immorality, I want to ask whether that connection is a rationally based one. If not all cases of extramarital sex are immoral (again, in the sense described above), then the concept of adultery should either be weakened accordingly or restricted to those classes of extramarital sex for which the predication of immorality is warranted.

One argument for the immorality of adultery might go something like this: what makes adultery immoral is that it involves the breaking of a promise, and what makes adultery seriously wrong is that it involves the breaking of an important promise. For, so the argument might continue, one of the things the two parties promise each other when they get married is that they will abstain from sexual relationships with third persons. Because of this promise both spouses quite reasonably entertain the expectation that the other will behave in conformity with it. Hence, when one of the parties has sexual intercourse with a third person he or she breaks that promise about sexual relationships which was made when the marriage was entered into, and defeats the reasonable expectations of exclusivity entertained by the spouse.

In many cases the immorality involved in breaching the promise relating to extramarital sex may be a good deal more serious than that involved in the breach of other promises. This is so because adherence to this promise may be of much greater importance to the parties than is adherence to many of the other promises given or received by them in their lifetime. The breaking of this promise may be much more hurtful and painful than is typically the case.

Why is this so? To begin with, it may have been difficult for the nonadulterous spouse to have kept the promise. Hence that spouse may feel the unfairness of having restrained himself or herself in the absence of reciprocal restraint having been exercised by the adulterous spouse. In addition, the spouse may perceive the breaking of the promise as an indication of a kind of indifference on the part of the adulterous spouse. If you really cared about me and my feelings—the spouse might say—you would not have done this to me. And third, and related to the above, the spouse may see the act of sexual intercourse with another as a sign of affection for the other person and as an additional rejection of the nonadulterous spouse as the one who is loved by the adulterous spouse. It is not just that the adulterous spouse does not take the feelings of the spouse sufficiently into account, the adulterous spouse also indicates through the act of adultery affection for someone other than the spouse. I will return to these points later. For the present, it is sufficient to note that a set of arguments can be developed in support of the proposition that certain kinds of adultery are wrong just because they involve that breach of a serious promise which, among other things, leads to the intentional infliction of substantial pain by one spouse upon the other.

Another argument for the immorality of adultery focuses not on the existence of a promise of sexual exclusivity but on the connection between adultery and deception. According to this argument, adultery involves deception. And because deception is wrong, so is adultery.

Although it is certainly not obviously so, I shall simply assume in this paper that deception is always immoral. Thus the crucial issue for my purposes is the asserted connection between extramarital sex and deception. Is is plausible to maintain, as this argument does, that adultery always does involve deception and is on that basis to be condemned?

The most obvious person on whom deceptions might be practiced is the nonparticipating spouse; and the most obvious thing about which the nonparticipating spouse can be deceived is the existence of the adulterous act. One clear case of deception is that of lying. Instead of saying that the afternoon was spent in bed with *A,* the adulterous spouse asserts that it was spent in the library with *B,* or on the golf course with *C.*

There can also be deception even when no lies are told. Suppose, for instance, that a person has sexual intercourse with someone other than his or her spouse and just does not tell the spouse about it. Is that deception? It may not be a case of lying if, for example, the spouse is never asked by the other about the situation. Still, we might say, it is surely deceptive because of the promises that were exchanged at marriage. As we saw earlier, these promises provide a foundation for the reasonable belief that neither spouse will engage in sexual relationships with any other persons. Hence the failure to bring the fact of extramarital sex to the attention of the other spouse deceives that spouse about the present state of the marital relationship.

Adultery, in other words, can involve both active and passive deception. An adulterous spouse may just keep silent or, as is often the fact, the spouse may engage in an increasingly complex way of life devoted to the concealment of the facts from the nonparticipating spouse. Lies, half-truths, clandestine meetings, and the like may become a central feature of the adulterous

spouse's existence. These are things that can and do happen, and when they do they make the case against adultery an easy one. Still neither active nor passive deception is inevitably a feature of an extramarital relationship.

It is possible, though, that a more subtle but pervasive kind of deceptiveness is a feature of adultery. It comes about because of the connection in our culture between sexual intimacy and certain feelings of love and affection. The point can be made indirectly at first by seeing that one way in which we can, in our culture, mark off our close friends from our mere acquaintances is through the kinds of intimacies that we are prepared to share with them. I may, for instance, be willing to reveal my very private thoughts and emotions to my closest friends or to my wife, but to no one else. My sharing of these intimate facts about myself is from one perspective a way of making a gift to those who mean the most to me. Revealing these things and sharing them with those who mean the most to me is one means by which I create, maintain, and confirm those interpersonal relationships that are of most importance to me.

Now in our culture, it might be claimed, sexual intimacy is one of the chief currencies through which gifts of this sort are exchanged. One way to tell someone—particularly someone of the opposite sex—that you have feelings of affection and love for them is by allowing to them or sharing with them sexual behaviors that one doesn't share with the rest of the world. This way of measuring affection was certainly very much a part of the culture in which I matured. It worked something like this. If you were a girl, you showed how much you liked someone by the degree of sexual intimacy you would allow. If you liked a boy only a little, you never did more than kiss—and even the kiss was not passionate. If you liked the boy a lot and if your feeling was reciprocated, necking, and possibly petting, was permissible. If the attachment was still stronger and you thought it might even become a permanent relationship, the sexual activity was correspondingly more intense and more intimate, although whether it would ever lead to sexual intercourse depended on whether the parties (and particularly the girl) accepted fully the prohibition on nonmarital sex. The situation for the boy was related, but not exactly the same. The assumption was that males did not naturally link sex with affection in the way in which females did. However, since women did, males had to take this into account. That is to say, because a woman would permit sexual intimacies only if she had feelings of affection for the male and only if those feelings were reciprocated, the male had to have and express those feelings, too, before sexual intimacies of any sort would occur.

The result was that the importance of a correlation between sexual intimacy and feelings of love and affection was taught by the culture and assimilated by those growing up in the culture. The scale of possible positive feelings toward persons of the other sex ran from casual liking at the one end to the love that was deemed essential to and characteristic of marriage at the other. The scale of possible sexual behavior ran from brief, passionless kissing or hand-holding at the one end to sexual intercourse at the other. And the correlation between the two scales was quite precise. As a result, any act of sexual intimacy carried substantial meaning with it, and no act of sexual intimacy was simply a pleasurable set of bodily sensations. Many such acts were, of course, more pleasurable to the participants because they were a way of saying what the participants' feelings were. And sometimes they were less pleasurable for the same reason. The point is, however, that in any event sexual activity was much more than mere bodily enjoyment. It was not like eating a good meal, listening to good music, lying in the sun, or getting a pleasant back rub. It was behavior that meant a great deal concerning one's feelings for persons of the opposite sex in whom one was most interested and with whom one was most involved. It was among the most authoritative ways in which one could communicate to another the nature and degree of one's affection.

If this sketch is even roughly right, then several things become somewhat clearer. To begin with, a possible rationale for many of the rules of conventional sexual morality can be developed. If, for example, sexual intercourse is associated with the kind of affection and commitment to another that is regarded as characteristic of the marriage relationship, then it is natural that sexual intercourse should be thought properly to take place between persons who are married to each other. And if it is thought that this kind of affection and commitment is only to be found within the marriage relationship, then it is not surprising that sexual intercourse should only be thought to be proper within marriage.

Related to what has just been said is the idea that sexual intercourse ought to be restricted to those who are married to each other as a means by which to confirm the very special feelings that the spouses have for each other. Because the culture teaches that sexual intercourse means that the strongest of all feelings for each other are shared by the lovers, it is natural that persons who are married to each other should be able to say this to each other in this way. Revealing and confirming verbally that these feelings are present is one thing that helps to sustain the relationship; engaging in sexual intercourse is another.

In addition, this account would help to provide a framework within which to make sense of the notion that some sex is better than other sex. As I indicated earlier, the fact that sexual intimacy can be meaningful in the sense described tends to make it also the case that sexual intercourse can sometimes be more enjoyable than at other times. On this view, sexual intercourse will typically be more enjoyable where the strong feelings of affection are present than it will be where it is merely "mechanical." This is so in part because people enjoy being loved, especially by those whom they love. Just as we like to hear words of affection, so we like to receive affectionate behavior. And the meaning enhances the independently pleasurable behavior.

More to the point, moreover, an additional rationale for the prohibition on extramarital sex can now be developed. For given this way of viewing the sexual world, extramarital sex will almost always involve deception of a deeper sort. If the adulterous spouse does not in fact have the appropriate feelings of affection for the extramarital partner, then the adulterous spouse is deceiving that person about the presence of such feelings. If, on the other hand, the adulterous spouse does have the corresponding feelings for the extramarital partner but not toward the nonparticipating spouse, the adulterous spouse is very probably deceiving the nonparticipating spouse about the presence of such feelings toward that spouse. Indeed, it might be argued, whenever there is no longer love between the two persons who are married to each other, there is deception just because being married implies both to the participants and to the world that such a bond exists. Deception is inevitable, the argument might conclude, because the feelings of affection that ought to accompany any act of sexual intercourse can only be held toward one other person at any given time in one's life. And if this is so, then the adulterous spouse always deceives either the partner in adultery or the nonparticipating spouse about the existence of such feelings. Thus extramarital sex involves deception of this sort and is for this reason immoral even if no deception vis-à-vis the occurrence of the act of adultery takes place.

What might be said in response to the foregoing arguments? The first thing that might be said is that the account of the connection between sexual intimacy and feelings of affection is inaccurate. Not inaccurate in the sense that no one thinks of things that way, but in the sense that there is substantially more divergence of opinion than that account suggests. For example, the view I have delineated may describe reasonably accurately the concept of the sexual world in which I grew up, but it does not capture the sexual *weltanschauung* of today's youth at all. Thus, whether or not adultery implies deception in respect to feelings depends very much on the persons who are involved and the way they look at the "meaning" of sexual intimacy.

Second, the argument leaves to be answered the question of whether it is desirable for sexual intimacy to carry the sorts of messages described above. For those persons for whom sex does have these implications, there are special feelings and sensibilities that must be taken into account. But it is another question entirely whether any valuable end—moral or otherwise—is served by investing sexual behavior with such significance. That is something that must be shown and not just assumed. It might, for instance, be the case that substantially more good than harm would come from a kind of demystification of sexual behavior: one that would encourage the enjoyment of sex more for its own sake and one that would reject the centrality both of the association of sex with love and of love with only one other person.

I regard these as two of the more difficult, unresolved issues that our culture faces today in respect to thinking sensibly about the attitudes toward sex and love that we should try to develop in ourselves and in our children. Much of the contemporary literature that advocates sexual liberation of one sort or another embraces one or the other of two different views about the relationship between sex and love.

One view holds that sex should be separated from love and affection. To be sure sex is probably better when the partners genuinely like and enjoy each other. But sex is basically an intensive, exciting sensuous activity that can be enjoyed in a variety of suitable settings with a variety of suitable partners. The situation in respect to sexual pleasure is not different from that of the person who knows and appreciates fine food and who can have a very satisfying meal in any number of good restaurants with any number of congenial companions. One question that must be settled here is whether sex can be so demystified: another, more important question is whether it would be desirable to do so. What would we gain and what might we lose if we all lived in a world in which an act of sexual intercourse was no more or less significant or enjoyable than having a delicious meal in a nice setting with a good friend? The answer to this question lies beyond the scope of this paper.

The second view seeks to drive the wedge in a different place. It is not the link between sex and love that needs to be broken; rather, on this view, it is the connection between love and exclusivity that ought to be severed. For a number of the reasons already given, it is desirable, so this argument goes, that sexual intimacy continue to be reserved to and shared with only those for whom one has very great affection. The mistake lies in thinking that any "normal" adult will only have those feelings toward one other adult during his or her lifetime—or even at any time in his or her life. It is the concept of adult love, not ideas about sex, that, on this view, needs demystification. What are thought to be both unrealistic and unfortunate are the notions of exclusivity and possessiveness that attach to the dominant conception of love between adults in our and other cultures. Parents of four, five, six, or even ten children can certainly claim and sometimes claim correctly that they love all of their children, that they love them all equally, and that it is simply untrue to their feelings to insist that the numbers involved diminish either the quantity or the quality of their love. If this is an idea that is readily understandable in the case of parents and children, there is no necessary reason why it is an impossible or undesirable ideal in the case of adults. To be sure, there is probably a limit to the number of intimate "primary" relationships that any person can maintain at any given time without the quality of the relationship being affected. But one adult ought surely be able to love two, three, or even six other adults at any time without that love being different in kind or degree from that of the traditional, monogamous, lifetime marriage. And as between the individuals in these relationships, whether within a marriage or without, sexual intimacy is fitting and good.

The issues raised by a position such as this one are also surely worth exploring in detail and with care. Is there something to be called "sexual love" which is different from parental love or the nonsexual love of close friends? Is there something about love in general that links it naturally and appropriately with feelings of exclusivity and possession? Or is there something about sexual love, whatever that may be, that makes these feelings especially fitting here? Once again the issues are conceptual, empirical, and normative all at once: What is love? How could it be different? Would it be a good thing or a bad thing if it were different?

Suppose, though, that having delineated these problems we were now to pass them by. Suppose, moreover, we were to be persuaded to the possibility and the desirability of weakening substantially either the links between sex and love or the links between sexual love and exclusivity. Would it not then be the case that adultery could be free from all of the morally objectionable features described so far? To be more specific, let us imagine that a husband and wife have what is today sometimes characterized as an "open marriage." Suppose, that is, that they have agreed in advance that extramarital sex is—under certain circumstances—acceptable behavior for each to engage in. Suppose, that as a result there is no impulse to deceive each other about the occurrence or nature of any such relationships, and that no deception in fact occurs. Suppose, too, that there is no deception in respect to the feelings involved between the adulterous spouse and the extramarital partner. And suppose, finally, that one or the other or both of the spouses then have sexual intercourse in circumstances consistent with these understandings. Under this description, so the argument might conclude, adultery is simply not immoral. At a minimum, adultery cannot very plausibly be condemned either on the ground that it involves deception or on the ground that it requires the breaking of a promise.

At least two responses are worth considering. One calls attention to the connection between marriage and adultery; the other looks to more instrumental arguments for the immorality of adultery. Both issues deserve further exploration.

One way to deal with the case of the "open marriage" is to question whether the two persons involved are still properly to be described as being married to each other. Part of the meaning of what it is for two persons to be married to each other, so this argument would go, is to have committed oneself to have sexual relationships only with one's spouse. Of course, it would be added, we know that that commitment is not always honored. We know that persons who are married to each other often do commit adultery. But there is a difference between being willing to make a commitment to marital fidelity, even though one may fail to honor that commitment, and not making the commitment at all. Whatever the relationship may be between the two individuals in the case described above, the absence of any commitment to sexual exclusivity requires the conclusion that their relationship is not a marital one. For a commitment to sexual exclusivity is a necessary although not a sufficient condition for the existence of a marriage.

Although there may be something to this suggestion, as it is stated it is too strong to be acceptable. To begin with, I think it is very doubtful that there are many, if any, *necessary* conditions for marriage; but even if there are, a commitment to sexual exclusivity is not such a condition.

To see that this is so, consider what might be taken to be some of the essential characteristics of a marriage. We might be tempted to propose that the concept of marriage requires the following: a formal ceremony of some sort in which mutual obligations are undertaken between two persons of the opposite sex; the capacity on the part of the persons involved to have sexual intercourse with each other; the willingness to have sexual intercourse only with each other; and feelings of love and affection between the two persons. The problem is that we can imagine relationships that are clearly marital and yet lack one or more of these features. For example, in our own society, it is possible for two persons to be married without going through a formal ceremony, as in the commonlaw marriages recognized in some jurisdictions. It is also possible for two persons to get married even though one or both lacks the capacity to engage in sexual intercourse. Thus, two very elderly persons who have neither the desire nor the ability to have intercourse can, nonetheless, get married, as can persons whose sexual organs have been injured so that intercourse is not possible. And we certainly know of marriages in which love was not present at the time of the marriage, as, for instance, in marriages of state and marriages of convenience.

Counterexamples not satisfying the condition relating to the abstention from extramarital sex are even more easily produced. We certainly know of societies and cultures in which polygamy and polyandry are practiced, and we have no difficulty in recognizing these relationships as cases of marriages. It might be objected, though, that these are not counterexamples because they are plural marriages rather than marriages in which sex is permitted with someone other than with one of the persons to whom one is married. But we also know of societies in which it is permissible for married persons to have sexual relationships with persons to whom they were not married; for example, temple prostitutes, concubines, and homosexual lovers. And even if we knew of no such societies, the conceptual claim would still, I submit, not be well taken. For suppose all of the other indicia of marriage were present: suppose the two persons were of the opposite sex, suppose they participated in a formal ceremony in which they understood themselves voluntarily to be entering into a relationship with each other in which substantial mutual commitments were assumed. If all these conditions were satisfied, we would not be in any doubt about whether or not the two persons were married even though they had not taken on a commitment of sexual exclusivity and even though they had expressly agreed that extramarital sexual intercourse was a permissible behavior for each to engage in.

A commitment to sexual exclusivity is neither a necessary nor a sufficient condition for the existence of a marriage. It does, nonetheless, have this much to do with the nature of marriage: like the other indicia enumerated above, its presence tends to establish the existence of a marriage. Thus, in the absence of a formal ceremony of any sort, an explicit commitment to sexual exclusivity would count in favor of regarding the two persons as married. The conceptual role of the commitment to sexual exclusivity can, perhaps, be brought out through the following example. Suppose we found a tribe which had a practice in which all the other indicia of marriage were present but in which the two parties were *prohibited* ever from having sexual intercourse with each other. Moreover, suppose that sexual intercourse with others was clearly permitted. In such a case we would, I think, reject the idea that the two were married to each other and we would describe their relationship in other terms, for example, as some kind of formalized, special friendship relation— a kind of heterosexual "blood-brother" bond.

Compare that case with the following. Suppose again that the tribe had a practice in which all of the other indicia of marriage were present, but instead of a prohibition on sexual intercourse between the persons in the relationship there was no rule at all. Sexual intercourse was permissible with the person with whom one had this ceremonial relationship, but it was no more or less permissible than with a number of other persons to whom one was not so related (for instance, all consenting adults of the opposite sex). Although we might be in doubt as to whether we ought to describe the persons as married to each other, we would probably conclude that they were married and that they simply were members of a tribe whose views about sex were quite different from our own.

What all of this shows is that *a prohibition* on sexual intercourse between the two persons involved in a relationship is conceptually incompatible with the claim that the two of them are married. The *permissibility* of intramarital sex is a necessary part of the idea of marriage. But no such incompatibility follows simply from the added permissibility of extramarital sex.

These arguments do not, of course, exhaust the arguments for the prohibition on extramarital sexual relations. The remaining argument that I wish to

consider—as I indicated earlier—is a more instrumental one. It seeks to justify the prohibition by virtue of the role that it plays in the development and maintenance of nuclear families. The argument, or set of arguments, might, I believe, go something like this.

Consider first a farfetched nonsexual example. Suppose a society were organized so that after some suitable age—say, 18, 19, or 20—persons were forbidden to eat anything but bread and water with anyone but their spouse. Persons might still choose in such a society not to get married. Good food just might not be very important to them because they have underdeveloped taste buds. Or good food might be bad for them because there is something wrong with their digestive system. Or good food might be important to them, but they might decide that the enjoyment of good food would get in the way of the attainment of other things that were more important. But most persons would, I think, be led to favor marriage in part because they preferred a richer, more varied, diet to one of bread and water. And they might remain married because the family was the only legitimate setting within which good food was obtainable. If it is important to have society organized so that persons will both get married and stay married, such an arrangement would be well suited to the preservation of the family, and the prohibitions relating to food consumption could be understood as fulfilling that function.

It is obvious that one of the more powerful human desires is the desire for sexual gratification. The desire is a natural one, like hunger and thirst, in the sense that it need not be learned in order to be present within us and operative upon us. But there is in addition much that we do learn about what the act of sexual intercourse is like. Once we experience sexual intercourse ourselves—and in particular once we experience orgasm—we discover that it is among the most intensive, short-term pleasures of the body.

Because this is so, it is easy to see how the prohibition upon extramarital sex helps to hold marriage together. At least during that period of life when the enjoyment of sexual intercourse is one of the desirable bodily pleasures, persons will wish to enjoy those pleasures. If one consequence of being married is that one is prohibited from having sexual intercourse with anyone but one's spouse, then the spouses in a marriage are in a position to provide an important source of pleasure for each other that is unavailable to them elsewhere in the society.

The point emerges still more clearly if this rule of sexual morality is seen as of a piece with the other rules of sexual morality. When this prohibition is coupled, for example, with the prohibition on nonmarital sexual intercourse, we are presented with the inducement both to get married and to stay married. For if sexual intercourse is only legitimate within marriage, then persons seeking that gratification which is a feature of sexual intercourse are furnished explicit social directions for its attainment; namely marriage.

Nor, to continue the argument, is it necessary to focus exclusively on the bodily enjoyment that is involved. Orgasm may be a significant part of what there is to sexual intercourse, but it is not the whole of it. We need only recall the earlier discussion of the meaning that sexual intimacy has in our own culture to begin to see some of the more intricate ways in which sexual exclusivity may be connected with the establishment and maintenance of marriage as the primary heterosexual, love relationship. Adultery is wrong, in other words, because a prohibition on extramarital sex is a way to help maintain the institutions of marriage and the nuclear family.

Now I am frankly not sure what we are to say about an argument such as this one. What I am convinced of is that, like the arguments discussed earlier, this one also reveals something of the difficulty and complexity of the issues that are involved. So, what I want now to do—in the brief and final portion of this paper—is to try to delineate with reasonable precision what I take several of the fundamental, unresolved issues to be.

The first is whether this last argument is an argument for the *immorality* of extramarital sexual intercourse. What does seem clear is that there are differences between this argument and the ones considered earlier. The earlier arguments condemned adulterous behavior because it was behavior that involved breaking of a promise, taking unfair advantage, or deceiving another. To the degree to which the prohibition on extramarital sex can be supported by arguments which invoke considerations such as these, there is little question but that violations of the prohibition are properly regarded as immoral. And such a claim could be defended on one or both of two distinct grounds. The first is that things like promise-breaking and deception are just wrong. The second is that adultery involving promise-breaking or deception is wrong because it involves the straightforward infliction of harm on another human being—typically the nonadulterous spouse—who has a strong claim not to have that harm so inflicted.

The argument that connects the prohibition on extramarital sex with the maintenance and preservation of the institution of marriage is an argument for the instrumental value of the prohibition. To some degree this counts, I think, against regarding all violations of the prohibition as obvious cases of immorality. This is so partly because hypothetical imperatives are less clearly within the domain of morality than are categorical ones, and even more because instrumental prohibitions are within the domain of morality only if the end they serve or the way they serve it is itself within the domain of morality.

What this should help us see, I think, is the fact that the argument that connects the prohibition on adultery with the preservation of marriage is at best seriously incomplete. Before we ought to be convinced by it, we ought to have reasons for believing that marriage is a morally desirable and just social institution. And this is not quite as easy or obvious a task as it may seem to be. For the concept of marriage is, as we have seen, both a loosely structured and a complicated one. There may be all sorts of intimate, interpersonal relationships which will resemble but not be identical with the typical marriage relationship presupposed by the traditional sexual morality. There may be a number of distinguishable sexual and loving arrangements which can all legitimately claim to be called *marriages*. The prohibitions of the traditional sexual morality may be effective ways to maintain some marriages and ineffective ways to promote and preserve others. The prohibitions of the traditional sexual morality may make good psychological sense if certain psychological theories are true, and they may be purveyors of immense psychological mischief if other psychological theories are true. The prohibitions of the traditional sexual morality may seem obviously correct if sexual intimacy carries the meaning that the dominant culture has often ascribed to it, and they may seem equally bizarre when sex is viewed through the perspective of the counterculture. Irrespective of whether instrumental arguments of this sort are properly deemed moral arguments, they ought not to fully convince anyone until questions like these are answered.

17. Sexual Perversion

Thomas Nagel

In this essay, Thomas Nagel offers a theory of natural and unnatural sex based on Jean Paul Sartre's notion of "double reciprocal incarnation." As Nagel explains, such a model requires that there be a free, mutual attraction and reciprocity of desire between persons and that sexual acts carried out in the absence of such reciprocity be considered incomplete or coercive. Nagel's approach seems to include under the heading of "natural sex" a broader range of sexual activities than would be acceptable to Kant or Pope Paul VI.

There is something to be learned about sex from the fact that we possess a concept of sexual perversion. I wish to examine the concept, defending it against the charge of unintelligibility and trying to say exactly what about human sexuality qualifies it to admit of perversions. But let me make some preliminary comments about the problem before embarking on its solution.

Some people do not believe that the notion of sexual perversion makes sense, and even those who do, disagree over its application. Nevertheless, I think it will be widely conceded that if the concept is viable at all, it must meet certain general conditions. First, if there are any sexual perversions, they will have to be sexual desires or practices that can be plausibly described as in some sense unnatural, though the explanation of this natural/unnatural distinction is, of course, the main problem. Second, certain practices, such as shoe fetishism, bestiality, and sadism will be perversions if anything is; other practices, such as unadorned sexual intercourse, will not be; and about still others there is controversy. Third, if there are perversions, they will be unnatural sexual *inclinations* rather than merely unnatural practices adopted not from inclination but for other reasons. I realize that this is at variance with the view, maintained by some Roman Catholics, that contraception is a sexual perversion. But although contraception may qualify as a deliberate perversion of the sexual and reproductive functions, it cannot be significantly described as a *sexual* perversion. A sexual perversion must reveal itself in conduct that expresses an unnatural *sexual* preference.

And although there might be a form of fetishism focused on the employment of contraceptive devices, that is not the usual explanation for their use.

I wish to declare at the outset my belief that the connection between sex and reproduction has no bearing on sexual perversion. The latter is a concept of psychological, not physiological interest, and it is a concept that we do not apply to the lower animals, let alone to plants, all of which have reproductive functions that can go astray in various ways (think, for example, of seedless oranges). Insofar as we are prepared to regard higher animals as perverted, it is because of their psychological, not their anatomical similarity to humans. Furthermore, we do not regard as a perversion every deviation from the reproductive function of sex in humans: sterility, miscarriage, contraception, abortion.

Another matter that I believe has no bearing on the concept of sexual perversion is social disapprobation or custom. Anyone inclined to think that in each society the perversions are those sexual practices of which the community disapproves should consider all of the societies that have frowned upon adultery and fornication. These have not been regarded as unnatural practices, but have been thought objectionable in other ways. What is regarded as unnatural admittedly varies from culture to culture, but the classification is not a pure expression of disapproval or distaste. In fact it is often regarded as a *ground* for disapproval, and that suggests that the classification has an independent content.

I am going to attempt a psychological account of sexual perversion, which will depend on a specific psychological theory of sexual desire and human sexual interactions. To approach this solution I wish first to

This article is reprinted from the *Journal of Philosophy* 66, no. 1 (January 16, 1969), with the permission of the publisher and author.

consider a contrary position, one that provides a basis for skepticism about the existence of any sexual perversions at all, and perhaps about the very significance of the term. The skeptical argument runs as follows:

Sexual desire is simply one of the appetites, like hunger and thirst. As such it may have various objects, some more common than others perhaps, but none in any sense "natural." An appetite is identified as sexual by means of the organs and erogenous zones in which its satisfaction can be to some extent localized, and the special sensory pleasures that form the core of that satisfaction. This enables us to recognize widely divergent goals, activities, and desires as sexual, since it is conceivable in principle that anything should produce sexual pleasure and that a nondeliberate, sexually charged desire for it should arise (as a result of conditioning, if nothing else). We may fail to empathize with some of these desires, and some of them, like sadism, may be objectionable on extraneous grounds, but once we have observed that they meet the criteria for being sexual, there is nothing more to be said on *that* score. Either they are sexual or they are not: sexuality does not admit of imperfection, or perversion, or any other such qualification—it is not that sort of affection.

This is probably the received radical position. It suggests that the cost of defending a psychological account may be to deny that sexual desire is an appetite. But insofar as that line of defense is plausible, it should make us suspicious of the simple picture of appetites on which the skepticism depends. Perhaps the standard appetites, like hunger, cannot be classed as pure appetites in that sense either, at least in their human versions.

Let us approach the matter by asking whether we can imagine anything that would qualify as a gastronomical perversion. Hunger and eating are importantly like sex in that they serve a biological function and also play a significant role in our inner lives. It is noteworthy that there is little temptation to describe as perverted an appetite for substances that are not nourishing. We should probably not consider someone's appetites as perverted if he liked to eat paper, sand, wood, or cotton. Those are merely rather odd and very unhealthy tastes: they lack the psychological complexity that we expect of perversions. (Coprophilia, being already a sexual perversion, may be disregarded.) If, on the other hand, someone liked to eat cookbooks or magazines with pictures of food in them, and preferred these to ordinary food—or if when hungry he sought satisfaction by fondling a napkin or ashtray from his favorite restaurant—then the concept of perversion might seem appropriate (in fact it would be

natural to describe this as a case of gastronomical fetishism). It would be natural to describe as gastronomically perverted someone who could eat only by having food forced down his throat through a funnel, or only if the meal were a living animal. What helps in such cases is the peculiarity of the desire itself, rather than the inappropriateness of its object to the biological function that the desire serves. Even an appetite, it would seem, can have perversions if in addition to its biological function it has a significant psychological structure.

In the case of hunger, psychological complexity is provided by the activities that give it expression. Hunger is not merely a disturbing sensation that can be quelled by eating; it is an attitude toward edible portions of the external world, a desire to relate to them in rather special ways. The method of ingestion— chewing, savoring, swallowing, appreciating the texture and smell—is an important component of the relation, as is the passivity and controllability of the food (the only animals we eat live are helpless mollusks). Our relation to food depends also on our size: we do not live upon it or burrow into it like aphids or worms. Some of these features are more central than others, but any adequate phenomenology of eating would have to treat it as a relation to the external world and a way of appropriating bits of that world, with characteristic affection. Displacements or serious restrictions of the desire to eat could then be described as perversions, if they undermined the direct relation between man and food that is the natural expression of hunger. This explains why it is easy to imagine gastronomical fetishism, voyeurism, exhibitionism, or even gastronomical sadism and masochism. Indeed, some of these perversions are fairly common.

If we can imagine perversions of an appetite like hunger, it should be possible to make sense of the concept of sexual perversion. I do not wish to imply that sexual desire is an appetite—only that being an appetite is no bar to admitting of perversions. Like hunger, sexual desire has as its characteristic object a certain relation with something in the external world; only in this case it is usually a person rather than an omelet, and the relation is considerably more complicated. This added complication allows scope for correspondingly complicated perversions.

The fact that sexual desire is a feeling about other persons may tempt us to take a pious view of its psychological content. There are those who believe that sexual desire is properly the expression of some other attitude, like love, and that when it occurs by itself it is incomplete and unhealthy—or at any rate subhuman. (The extreme Platonic version of such a view is that sexual practices are all vain attempts to express something they cannot in principle achieve: this makes them all perversions, in a sense.) I do not believe that any such view is correct. Sexual desire is complicated enough without having to be linked to anything else as a condition for phenomenological analysis. It cannot be denied that sex may serve various functions—economic, social, altruistic—but it also has its own content as a relation between persons, and it is only by analyzing that relation that we can understand the conditions of sexual perversion.

It is very important that the object of sexual attraction is a particular individual, who transcends the properties that make him attractive. When different persons are attracted to a single person for different reasons—eyes, hair, figure, laugh, intelligence—we feel that the object of their desire is nevertheless the same, namely, that person. There is even an inclination to feel that this is so if the lovers have different sexual aims, if they include both men and women, for example. Different specific attractive characteristics seem to provide enabling conditions for the operation of a single basic feeling, and the different aims all provide expressions of it. We approach the sexual attitude toward the person through the features that we find attractive, but these features are not the objects of that attitude.

This is very different from the case of an omelet. Various people may desire it for different reasons, one for its fluffiness, another for its mushrooms, another for its unique combination of aroma and visual aspect; yet we do not enshrine the transcendental omelet as the true common object of their affections. Instead we might say that several desires have accidentally converged on the same object: any omelet with the crucial characteristics would do as well. It is not similarly true that any person with the same flesh distribution and way of smoking can be substituted as object for a particular sexual desire that has been elicited by those characteristics. It may be that they will arouse attraction whenever they recur, but it will be a new sexual attraction with a new particular object, not merely a transfer of the old desire to someone else. (I believe this is true even in cases where the new object is unconsciously identified with a former one.)

The importance of this point will emerge when we see how complex a psychological interchange constitutes the natural development of sexual attraction. This would be incomprehensible if its object were not a particular person, but rather a person of a certain *kind.* Attraction is only the beginning, and fulfillment does not consist merely of behavior and contact expressing this attraction, but involves much more.

The best discussion of these matters that I have seen is in part three of Sartre's *Being and Nothingness.*[1] Since it has influenced my own views, I shall say a few things about it now. Sartre's treatment of sexual desire and of love, hate, sadism, masochism, and further attitudes toward others depends on a general theory of consciousness and the body that we can neither expound nor assume here. He does not discuss perversion, partly because he regards sexual desire as one form of the perpetual attempt of an embodied consciousness to come to terms with the existence of others, an attempt that is as doomed to fail in this form as it is in any of the others, which include sadism and masochism (if not certain of the more impersonal deviations) as well as several nonsexual attitudes. According to Sartre, all attempts to incorporate the other into my world as another subject, that is, to apprehend him as at once an object for me and a subject for whom I am an object, are unstable and doomed to collapse into one or the other of the two aspects. Either I reduce him entirely to an object, in which case his subjectivity escapes the possession or appropriation I can extend to that object; or I become merely an object for him, in which case I am no longer in a position to appropriate his subjectivity. Moreover, neither of these aspects is stable: each is continually in danger of giving way to the other. This has the consequence that there can be no such thing as a *successful* sexual relation, since the deep aim of sexual desire cannot in principle be accomplished. It seems likely, therefore, that this view will not permit a basic distinction between successful, or complete, and unsuccessful, or incomplete, sex and therefore cannot admit the concept of perversion.

I do not adopt this aspect of the theory, nor many of its metaphysical underpinnings. What interests me is Sartre's picture of the attempt. He says that the type of possession that is the object of sexual desire is carried out by "a double reciprocal incarnation" and that this is accomplished, typically in the form of a caress, in the following way: "I make myself flesh in order to impel the Other to realize *for herself* and *for me* her own flesh, and my caresses cause my flesh to be born for me in so far as it is for the Other *flesh causing her to be born as flesh.*"[2] The incarnation in question is described variously as a clogging or troubling of consciousness, which is inundated by the flesh in which it is embodied.

The view I am going to suggest—I hope in less obscure language—is related to Sartre's, but differs in allowing sexuality to achieve its goal on occasion and thus in providing the concept of perversion with a foothold.

Sexual desire involves a kind of perception, but not merely a single perception of its object, for in the paradigm case of mutual desire there is a complex system of superimposed mutual perceptions—not only perceptions of the sexual object, but perceptions of oneself. Moreover, sexual awareness of another involves considerable self-awareness to begin with—more than is involved in ordinary sensory perception. The experience is felt as an assault on oneself by the view (or touch, or whatever) of the sexual object.

Let us consider a case in which the elements can be separated. For clarity we will restrict ourselves initially to the somewhat artificial case of desire at a distance. Suppose a man and a woman, whom we may call Romeo and Juliet, are at opposite ends of a cocktail lounge with many mirrors on its walls, permitting unobserved observation and even mutual unobserved observation. Each of them is sipping a martini and studying other people in the mirrors. At some point Romeo notices Juliet. He is moved, somehow, by the softness of her hair and the diffidence with which she sips her martini, and this arouses him sexually. Let us say that X *senses* Y whenever X regards Y with sexual desire. (Y need not be a person, and X's apprehension of Y can be visual, tactile, olfactory, and so on, or purely imaginary. In the present example we shall concentrate on vision.) So Romeo senses Juliet, rather than merely noticing her. At this stage he is aroused by an unaroused object; so he is more in the sexual grip of his body than she of hers.

Let us suppose, however, that Juliet now senses Romeo in another mirror on the opposite wall, though neither of them yet knows that he is seen by the other (the mirror angles provide three-quarter views). Romeo then begins to notice in Juliet the subtle signs of sexual arousal: heavy-lidded stare, dilating pupils, a faint flush. This of course renders her much more bodily, and he not only notices but senses this as well. His arousal is nevertheless still solitary. But now, cleverly calculating the line of her stare without actually looking her in the eyes, he realizes that it is directed at him through the mirror on the opposite wall. That is, he notices, and moreover senses, Juliet sensing him. This is definitely a new development, for it gives him a sense of embodiment, not only through his own reactions, but also through the eyes and reactions of another. Moreover, it is separable from the initial sensing of Juliet, for sexual arousal might begin with a person's sensing that he is sensed and being assailed by the perception of the other person's desire rather than merely by the perception of the person.

But there is a further step. Let us suppose that Juliet, who is a little slower than Romeo, now senses that he senses her. This puts Romeo in a position to notice, and be aroused by, her arousal at being sensed by him. He senses that she senses that he senses her. This is still another level of arousal, for he becomes conscious of his sexuality through his awareness of its effect on her and of her awareness that this effect is due to him. Once she takes the same step and senses that he senses her sensing him, it becomes difficult to state, let alone imagine, further iterations, though they may be logically distinct. If both are alone, they will presumably turn to look at each other directly, and the proceedings will continue on another plane. Physical contact and intercourse are perfectly natural extensions of this complicated visual exchange, and mutual touch can involve all the complexities of awareness present in the visual case, but with a far greater range of subtlety and acuteness.

Ordinarily, of course, things happen in a less orderly fashion—sometimes in a great rush—but I believe that some version of this overlapping system of distinct sexual perceptions and interactions is the basic framework of any full-fledged sexual relation and that relations involving only part of the complex are significantly incomplete. The account is only schematic, as it must be to achieve generality. Every real sexual act will be psychologically far more specific and detailed, in ways that depend not only on the physical techniques employed and on anatomical details but also on countless features of the participants' conceptions of themselves and of each other, which become embodied in the act. (It is a familiar enough fact, for example, that people often take their social roles and the social roles of their partners to bed with them.)

The general schema is important, however, and the proliferation of levels of mutual awareness it involves is an example of a type of complexity that typifies human interactions. Consider aggression, for example. If I am angry with someone, I want to make him feel it, either to produce self-reproach by getting him to see himself through the eyes of my anger and to dislike what he sees, or to produce reciprocal anger or fear by getting him to perceive my anger as a threat or attack. What I want will depend on the details of my anger, but in either case it will involve a desire that the object of that anger be aroused. This accomplishment constitutes the fulfillment of my emotion through domination of the object's feelings.

Another example of such reflexive mutual recognition is to be found in the phenomenon of meaning, which appears to involve an intention to produce a belief or other effect in another by bringing about his recognition of one's intention to produce that effect. (That result is due to H.P. Grice,[3] whose position I shall not attempt to reproduce in detail.) Sex has a related structure: it involves a desire that one's partner be aroused by the recognition of one's desire that he or she be aroused.

It is not easy to define the basic types of awareness and arousal of which these complexes are composed, and that remains a lacuna in this discussion. I believe that the object of awareness is the same in one's own case as it is in one's sexual awareness of another, although the two awarenesses will not be the same, the difference being as great as that between feeling angry and experiencing the anger of another. All stages of sexual perception are varieties of identification of a person with his body. What is perceived is one's own or another's *subjection* to or *immersion* in his body, a phenomenon that has been recognized with loathing by St. Paul and St. Augustine, both of whom regarded "the law of sin which is in my members" as a grave threat to the dominion of the holy will.[4] In sexual desire and its expression the blending of involuntary response with deliberate control is extremely important. For Augustine, the revolution launched against him by his body is symbolized by erection and the other involuntary physical components of arousal. Sartre too stresses the fact that the penis is not a prehensile organ. But mere involuntariness characterizes other bodily processes as well. In sexual desire the involuntary responses are combined with submission to spontaneous impulses: not only one's pulse and secretions but one's actions are taken over by the body; ideally, deliberate control is needed only to guide the expression of those impulses. This is to some extent also true of an appetite like hunger, but the takeover there is more localized, less pervasive, less extreme. One's whole body does not become saturated with hunger as it can with desire. But the most characteristic feature of a specifically sexual immersion in the body is its ability to fit into the complex of mutual perceptions that we have described. Hunger leads to spontaneous interactions with food; sexual desire leads to spontaneous interactions with other persons, whose bodies are asserting their sovereignty in the same way, producing involuntary reactions and spontaneous impulses in *them*. These reactions are perceived, and the perception of them is perceived, and that perception is in turn perceived; at each step the domination of the person by his body is reinforced, and the sexual partner becomes more possessible by physical contact, penetration, and envelopment.

Desire is therefore not merely the perception of a preexisting embodiment that in turn enhances the original subject's sense of himself. This explains why it is important that the partner be aroused, and not merely aroused, but aroused by the awareness of one's desire. It also explains the sense in which desire has unity and possession as its object: physical possession must eventuate in creation of the sexual object in the image of one's desire, and not merely in the object's recognition of that desire or in his or her own private arousal. (This may reveal a male bias. I shall say something about that later.)

To return, finally, to the topic of perversion: I believe that various familiar deviations constitute truncated or incomplete versions of the complete configuration and may therefore be regarded as perversions of the central impulse.

In particular, narcissistic practices and intercourse with animals, infants, and inanimate objects seem to be stuck at some primitive version of the first stage. If the object is not alive, the experience is reduced entirely to an awareness of one's own sexual embodiment. Small children and animals permit awareness of the embodiment of the other, but present obstacles to reciprocity, to the recognition by the sexual object of the subject's desire as the source of his (the object's) sexual self-awareness.

Sadism concentrates on the evocation of passive self-awareness in others, but the sadist's engagement is itself active and requires a retention of deliberate control that impedes awareness of himself as a bodily subject of passion in the required sense. The victim must recognize him as the source of his own sexual passivity, but only as the active source. De Sade claimed that the object of sexual desire was to evoke involuntary responses from one's partner, especially audible ones. The infliction of pain is no doubt the most efficient way to accomplish this, but it requires a certain abrogation of one's own exposed spontaneity. All this, incidentally, helps to explain why it is tempting to regard as sadistic an excessive preoccupation with sexual technique, which does not permit one to abandon the role of agent at any stage of the sexual act. Ideally one should be able to surmount one's technique at some point.

A masochist on the other hand imposes the same disability on his partner as the sadist imposes on himself. The masochist cannot find a satisfactory embodiment as the object of another's sexual desire but only as the object of his control. He is passive not in relation to his partner's passion but in relation to his nonpassive agency. In addition, the subjection to one's body characteristic of pain and physical restraints is of a very different kind from that of sexual excitement: pain causes people to contract rather than dissolve.

Both of these disorders have to do with the second stage, which involves the awareness of oneself as an object of desire. In straightforward sadism and masochism other attentions are substituted for desire as a source of the object's self-awareness. But it is also possible for nothing of that sort to be substituted, as in the case of a masochist who is satisfied with self-inflicted pain or of a sadist who does not insist on playing a role in the suffering that arouses him. Greater difficulties of classification are presented by three other categories of sexual activity: elaborations of the sexual act, intercourse of more than two persons, and homosexuality.

If we apply our model to the various forms that may be taken by two-party heterosexual intercourse, none of them seem clearly to qualify as perversions. Hardly anyone can be found these days to inveigh against oral-genital contact, and the merits of buggery are urged by such respectable figures as D. H. Lawrence and Norman Mailer. There may be something vaguely sadistic about the latter technique (in Mailer's writings it seems to be a method of introducing an element of rape), but it is not obvious that this has to be so. In general, it would appear that any bodily contact between a man and a woman that gives them sexual pleasure is a possible vehicle for the system of multilevel interpersonal awareness that I have claimed is the basic psychological content of sexual interaction. Thus a liberal platitude about sex is upheld.

About multiple combinations the least that can be said is that they are bound to be complicated. If one considers how difficult it is to carry on two conversations simultaneously, one may appreciate the problems of multiple simultaneous interpersonal perception that can arise in even a small-scale orgy. It may be inevitable that some of the component relations should degenerate into mutual epidermal stimulation by participants otherwise isolated from each other. There may also be a tendency toward voyeurism and exhibitionism, both of which are incomplete relations. The exhibitionist wishes to display his desire without needing to be desired in return; he may even fear the sexual attentions of others. A voyeur, on the other hand, need not require any recognition at all by his object, certainly not a recognition of the voyeur's arousal.

It is not clear whether homosexuality is a perversion if that is measured by the standard of the described configuration, but it seems unlikely. For such a classification would have to depend on the possibility of extracting from the system a distinction between male and female sexuality; and much that has been said so far applies equally to men and women. Moreover, it would have to be maintained that there was a natural tie between the type of sexuality and the sex of the body and that two sexualities of the same type could not interact properly.

Certainly there is much support for an aggressive-passive distinction between male and female sexuality. In our culture the male's arousal tends to initiate the perceptual exchange; he usually makes the sexual approach, largely controls the course of the act, and of course penetrates whereas the woman receives. When two men or two women engage in intercourse they cannot both adhere to these sexual roles. The question is how essential the roles are to an adequate sexual relation. One relevant observation is that a good deal of deviation from these roles occurs in heterosexual intercourse. Women can be sexually aggressive and men passive, and temporary reversals of role are not uncommon in heterosexual exchanges of reasonable length. If such conditions are set aside, it may be urged that there is something irreducibly perverted in attraction to a body anatomically like one's own. But alarming as some people in our culture may find such attraction, it remains psychologically unilluminating to class it as perverted. Certainly if homosexuality is a perversion, it is so in a very different sense from that in which shoe-fetishism is a perversion, for some version of the full range of interpersonal perceptions seems perfectly possible between two persons of the same sex.

In any case, even if the proposed model is correct, it remains implausible to describe as perverted every deviation from it. For example, if the partners in heterosexual intercourse indulge in private heterosexual fantasies, that obscures the recognition of the real partner and so, on the theory, constitutes a defective sexual relation. It is not, however, generally regarded as a perversion. Such examples suggest that a simple dichotomy between perverted and unperverted sex is too crude to organize the phenomena adequately.

I shall close with some remarks about the relation of perversion to good, bad, and morality. The concept of perversion can hardly fail to be evaluative in some sense, for it appears to involve the notion of an ideal or at least adequate sexuality that the perversions in some way fail to achieve. So, if the concept is viable, the judgment that a person or practice or desire is perverted will constitute a sexual evaluation, implying that better sex, or a better specimen of sex, is possible. This in itself is a very weak claim since the evaluation might be in a dimension that is of little interest to us. (Though, if my account is correct, that will not be true.)

Whether it is a moral evaluation, however, is another question entirely, one whose answer would require more understanding of both morality and perversion than can be deployed here. Moral evaluation of acts and of persons is a rather special and very complicated matter and by no means are all of our evaluations of persons and their activities moral evaluations. We make judgments about people's beauty or health or intelligence that are evaluative without being moral. Assessments of their sexuality may be similar in that respect.

Furthermore, moral issues aside, it is not clear that unperverted sex is necessarily *preferable* to the perversions. It may be that sex that receives the highest marks for perfection *as sex* is less enjoyable than certain perversions, and if enjoyment is considered very important, that might outweigh considerations of sexual perfection in determining rational preference.

That raises the question of the relation between the evaluative content of judgments of perversion and the rather common *general* distinction between good and bad sex. The latter distinction is usually confined to sexual acts, and it would seem, within limits, to cut across the other: even someone who believed, for example, that homosexuality was a perversion could admit a distinction between better and worse homosexual sex, and might even allow that good homosexual sex could be better *sex* than not very good unperverted sex. If this is correct, it supports the position—if judgments of perversion are viable at all—that they represent only one aspect of the possible evaluation of sex, even *qua sex*. Moreover it is not the only important aspect: certainly sexual deficiencies that evidently do not constitute perversions can be the object of great concern.

Finally, even if perverted sex is to that extent not so good as it might be, bad sex is generally better than none at all. This should not be controversial: it seems to hold for other important matters, like food, music, literature, and society. In the end, one must choose from among the available alternatives, whether their availability depends on the environment or on one's own constitution. And the alternatives have to be fairly grim before it becomes rational to opt for nothing.

Endnotes

1. Trans. Hazel E. Barnes (New York: Philosophical Library, 1956).

2. Ibid., p. 391. Sartre's italics.

3. "Meaning," *Philosophical Review* 66, no. 3 (July 1957): 377–88.

4. See Romans 7:23, and the *Confessions,* Book 8, v.

Part 3

Abortion

18. *An Almost Absolute Value in History*

JOHN T. NOONAN, JR.

John T. Noonan, Jr., argues from biology that the conceptus is, indeed, a separate living being, with its own distinctive genetic code. Though heavily dependent on the mother, it is clearly human, the first moment in the continuum of human life from its beginning to its end. Because we grant moral standing to human beings regardless of their age, their physical or mental condition, or their social status, a fetus should be protected from abortion as a full-fledged member of the human community. For Noonan, exceptions to the protective rule can only occur when the mother's very life is jeopardized by the pregnancy.

The most fundamental question involved in the long history of thought on abortion is: How do you determine the humanity of a being? To phrase the question that way is to put in comprehensive humanistic terms what the theologians either dealt with as an explicitly theological question under the heading of "ensoulment" or dealt with implicitly in their treatment of abortion. The Christian position as it originated did not depend on a narrow theological or philosophical concept. It had no relation to theories of infant baptism.[1] It appealed to no special theory of instantaneous ensoulment. It took the world's view on ensoulment as that view changed from Aristotle to Zacchia. There was, indeed, theological influence affecting the theory of ensoulment finally adopted, and, of course, ensoulment itself was a theological concept, so that the position was always explained in theological terms. But the theological notion of ensoulment could easily be translated into humanistic language by substituting "human" for "rational soul"; the problem of knowing when a man is a man is common to theology and humanism.

[1]According to Glanville Williams (*The Sanctity of Human Life supra* n. 169, at 193), "The historical reason for the Catholic objection to abortion is the same as for the Christian Church's historical opposition to infanticide: the horror of bringing about the death of an unbaptized child." This statement is made without any citation of evidence. As has been seen, desire to administer baptism could, in the Middle Ages, even be urged as a reason for procuring an abortion. It is highly regrettable that the American Law Institute was apparently misled by Williams' account and repeated after him the same baseless statement. See American Law Institute, *Model Penal Code: Tentative Draft No. 9* (1959), p. 148, n. 12.

If one steps outside the specific categories used by the theologians, the answer they gave can be analyzed as a refusal to discriminate among human beings on the basis of their varying potentialities. Once conceived, the being was recognized as man because he had man's potential. The criterion for humanity, thus, was simple and all-embracing: if you are conceived by human parents, you are human.

The strength of this position may be tested by a review of some of the other distinctions offered in the contemporary controversy over legalizing abortion. Perhaps the most popular distinction is in terms of viability. Before an age of so many months, the fetus is not viable, that is, it cannot be removed from the mother's womb and live apart from her. To that extent, the life of the fetus is absolutely dependent on the life of the mother. This dependence is made the basis of denying recognition to its humanity.

There are difficulties with this distinction. One is that the perfection of artificial incubation may make the fetus viable at any time: it may be removed and artificially sustained. Experiments with animals already show that such a procedure is possible.[2] This hypothetical extreme case relates to an actual difficulty: there is considerable elasticity to the idea of viability. Mere length of life is not an exact measure. The viability of the fetus depends on the extent of its anatomical and functional development.[3] The weight and length of the fetus are better guides to the state of its development than age, but weight and length vary.[4] Moreover, different racial groups have different ages at which their fetuses are viable. Some evidence, for example, suggests that Negro fetuses mature more quickly than white fetuses.[5] If viability is the norm, the standard would vary with race and with many individual circumstances.

The most important objection to this approach is that dependence is not ended by viability. The fetus is still absolutely dependent on someone's care in order to continue existence; indeed a child of one or three or even five years of age is absolutely dependent on another's care for existence; uncared for, the older fetus or the younger child will die as surely as the early fetus detached from the mother. The unsubstantial lessening in dependence at viability does not seem to signify any special acquisition of humanity.

A second distinction has been attempted in terms of experience. A being who has had experience, has lived and suffered, who possesses memories, is more human than one who has not. Humanity depends on formation by experience. The fetus is thus "unformed" in the most basic human sense.[6]

This distinction is not serviceable for the embryo which is already experiencing and reacting. The embryo is responsive to touch after eight weeks[7] and at least at that point is experiencing. At an earlier stage the zygote is certainly alive and responding to its environment.[8] The distinction may also be challenged by the rare case where aphasia has erased adult memory: has it erased humanity? More fundamentally, this distinction leaves even the older fetus or the younger child to be treated as an unformed inhuman thing. Finally, it is not clear why experience as such confers humanity. It could be argued that certain central experiences such as loving or learning are necessary to make a man human. But then human beings who have failed to love or to learn might be excluded from the class called man.

A third distinction is made by appeal to the sentiments of adults. If a fetus dies, the grief of the parents is not the grief they would have for a living child. The fetus is an unnamed "it" till birth, and is not perceived as personality until at least the fourth month of existence when movements in the womb manifest a vigorous presence demanding joyful recognition by the parents.

Yet feeling is notoriously an unsure guide to the humanity of others. Many groups of humans have had difficulty in feeling that persons of another tongue, color, religion, sex, are as human as they. Apart from reactions to alien groups, we mourn the loss of a ten-year-old boy more than the loss of his one-day-old brother or his 99-year-old grandfather. The difference felt and the grief expressed vary with the potentialities

---

[2]E.g., R. L. Brinster and J. L. Thomson, "Development of Eight-Cell Mouse Embryos in Vitro," 42 *Experimental Cell Research* 308 (1966).

[3]J. Edgar Morison, *Fetal and Neonatal Pathology* 99–100 (1963).

[4]Peter Gruenwald, "Growth of the Human Fetus," 94 *American Journal of Obstetrics and Gynecology* 1112 (1966).

[5]Morison, *Fetal and Neonatal Pathology supra* n. 175, at 101.

[6]This line of thought was advanced by some participants at the International Conference on Abortion sponsored by the Harvard Divinity School in cooperation with the Joseph P. Kennedy, Jr., Foundation in Washington, D.C., Sept. 8–10, 1967.

[7]Frank D. Allan, *Essentials of Human Embryology* 165 (1960).

[8]Frederick J. Gottlieb, *Developmental Genetics* 28 (1966).

extinguished, or the experience wiped out; they do not seem to point to any substantial difference in the humanity of baby, boy, or grandfather.

Distinctions are also made in terms of sensation by the parents. The embryo is felt within the womb only after about the fourth month.[9] The embryo is seen only at birth. What can be neither seen nor felt is different from what is tangible. If the fetus cannot be seen or touched at all, it cannot be perceived as man.

Yet experience shows that sight is even more untrustworthy than feeling in determining humanity. By sight, color became an appropriate index for saying who was a man, and the evil of racial discrimination was given foundation. Nor can touch provide the test; a being confined by sickness, "out of touch" with others, does not thereby seem to lose his humanity. To the extent that touch still has appeal as a criterion, it appears to be a survival of the old English idea of "quickening"—a possible mistranslation of the Latin *animatus* used in the canon law.[10] To that extent touch as a criterion seems to be dependent on the Aristotelian notion of ensoulment, and to fail when this notion is discarded.

Finally, a distinction is sought in social visibility. The fetus is not socially perceived as human. It cannot communicate with others. Thus, both subjectively and objectively, it is not a member of society. As moral rules are rules for the behavior of members of society to each other, they cannot be made for behavior toward what is not yet a member. Excluded from the society of men, the fetus is excluded from the humanity of men.[11]

By force of the argument from the consequences, this distinction is to be rejected. It is more subtle than that founded on an appeal to physical sensation, but it is equally dangerous in its implications. If humanity depends on social recognition, individuals or whole groups may be dehumanized by being denied any status in their society. Such a fate is fictionally portrayed in *1984* and has actually been the lot of many men in many societies. In the Roman empire, for example, condemnation to slavery meant the practical denial of most human rights; in the Chinese Communist world, landlords have been classified as enemies of the people and so treated as nonpersons by the state. Humanity does not depend on social recognition, though often the failure of society to recognize the prisoner, the alien, the heterodox as human has led to the destruction of human beings. Anyone conceived by a man and a woman is human. Recognition of this condition by society follows a real event in the objective order, however imperfect and halting the recognition. Any attempt to limit humanity to exclude some group runs the risk of furnishing authority and precedent for excluding other groups in the name of the consciousness or perception of the controlling group in the society.

A philosopher may reject the appeal to the humanity of the fetus because he views "humanity" as a secular view of the soul and because he doubts the existence of anything real and objective which can be identified as humanity.[12] One answer to such a philosopher is to ask how he reasons about moral questions without supposing that there is a sense in which he and the others of whom he speaks are human. Whatever group is taken as the society which determines who may be killed is thereby taken as human. A second answer is to ask if he does not believe that there is a right and wrong way of deciding moral questions. If there is such a difference, experience may be appealed to: to decide who is human on the basis of the sentiment of a given society has led to consequences which rational men would characterize as monstrous.[13]

The rejection of the attempted distinctions based on viability and visibility, experience and feeling, may be buttressed by the following considerations: Moral judgments often rest on distinctions, but if the

---

[9]Allan, *Essentials of Human Embryology supra* n. 179, at 165.

[10]See David W. Louisell and John T. Noonan, Jr., "Constitutional Balance," *infra*.

[11]Another line of thought advanced at the Conference mentioned in n. 178. Thomas Aquinas gave an analogous reason against baptizing a fetus in the womb: "As long as it exists in the womb of the mother, it cannot be subject to the operation of the ministers of the Church as it is not known to men" (*In sententias Petri Lombardi* 4.6 1.1.2).

[12]Compare John O'Connor, "Humanity and Abortion," 12 *Natural Law Forum* 128-130 (1968), with John T. Noonan, Jr. "Deciding Who Is Human," 12 *Natural Law Forum* 134–138.

[13]A famous passage of Montesquieu reads:

"Ceux dont il s'agit sont noirs depuis les pieds jusqu'à la tête; et ils ont le nez si écrasé qu'il est presque impossible de les plaindre.

"On ne peut se mettre dans l'esprit que Dieu qui est un être très-sage, ait mis une âme, surtout une âme bonne, dans un corps tout noir.

"Il est si naturel de penser que c'est la couleur qui constitue l'essence de l'humanité, que les peuples d'Asie, qui font des eunuques, privent toujours les noirs du rapport qu'ils ont avec nous d'une façon plus marquée." *Montesquieu, De l'esprit des lois*, in *Oeuvres Complètes* book 15, chap. 5 (Paris, 1843).

distinctions are not to appear arbitrary fiat, they should relate to some real difference in probabilities. There is a kind of continuity in all life, but the earlier stages of the elements of human life possess tiny probabilities of development. Consider for example, the spermatozoa in any normal ejaculate: There are about 200,000,000 in any single ejaculate, of which one has a chance of developing into a zygote.[14] Consider the oocytes which may become ova: there are 100,000 to 1,000,000 oocytes in a female infant, of which a maximum of 390 are ovulated.[15] But once spermatozoon and ovum meet and the conceptus is formed, such studies as have been made show that roughly in only 20 percent of the cases will spontaneous abortion occur.[16] In other words, the chances are about 4 out of 5 that this new being will develop. At this stage in the life of the being there is a sharp shift in probabilities, an immense jump in potentialities. To make a distinction between the rights of spermatozoa and the rights of the fertilized ovum is to respond to an enormous shift in possibilities. For about twenty days after conception the egg may split to form twins or combine with another egg to form a chimera, but the probability of either event happening is very small.

It may be asked, What does a change in biological probabilities have to do with establishing humanity? The argument from probabilities is not aimed at establishing humanity but at establishing an objective discontinuity which may be taken into account in moral discourse. As life itself is a matter of probabilities, as most moral reasoning is an estimate of probabilities, so it seems in accord with the structure of reality and the nature of moral thought to found a moral judgment on the change in probabilities at conception. The appeal to probabilities is the most commensensical of arguments, to a greater or smaller degree all of us base our actions on probabilities, and in morals, as in law, prudence and negligence are often measured by the account one has taken of the probabilities. If the chance is 200,000,000 to 1 that the movement in the bushes into which you shoot is a man's, I doubt if many persons would hold you careless in shooting; but if the chances are 4 out of 5 that the movement is a human being's, few would acquit you of blame. Would the argument be different if only one out of ten children conceived came to term? Of course this argument would be different. This argument is an appeal

to probabilities that actually exist, not to any and all states of affairs which may be imagined.

The probabilities as they do exist do not show the humanity of the embryo in the sense of a demonstration in logic any more than the probabilities of the movement in the bush being a man demonstrate beyond all doubt that the being is a man. The appeal is a "buttressing" consideration, showing the plausibility of the standard adopted. The argument focuses on the decisional factor in any moral judgment and assumes that part of the business of a moralist is drawing lines. One evidence of the nonarbitrary character of the line drawn is the difference of probabilities on either side of it. If a spermatozoon is destroyed, one destroys a being which had a chance of far less than 1 in 200 million of developing into a reasoning being, possessed of the genetic code, a heart and other organs, and capable of pain. If a fetus is destroyed, one destroys a being already possessed of the genetic code, organs, and sensitivity to pain, and one which had an 80 percent chance of developing further into a baby outside the womb who, in time, would reason.

The positive argument for conception as the decisive moment of humanization is that at conception the new being receives the genetic code.[17] It is this genetic information which determines his characteristics, which is the biological carrier of the possibility of human wisdom, which makes him a self-evolving being. A being with a human genetic code is man.

This review of current controversy over the humanity of the fetus emphasizes what a fundamental question the theologians resolved in asserting the inviolability of the fetus. To regard the fetus as possessed of equal rights with other humans was not, however, to decide every case where abortion might be employed. It did decide the case where the argument was that the fetus should be aborted for its own good. To say a being was human was to say it had a destiny to decide for itself which could not be taken from it by another man's decision. But human beings with equal rights often come in conflict with each other, and some decision must be made as whose claims are to prevail. Cases of conflict involving the fetus are different only in two respects: the total inability of the fetus to speak for itself and the fact that the right of the fetus regularly at stake is the right to life itself.

The approach taken by the theologians to these conflicts was articulated in terms of "direct" and "indirect." Again, to look at what they were doing from

[14]J. S. Baxter, *Frazer's Manual of Embryology* 5 (1963).

[15]Gregory Pincus, *The Control of Fertility* 197 (1965).

[16]*Idem.* Apparently there is some small variation by region.

[17]Gottleib, *Developmental Genetics supra* n. 180, at 17.

outside their categories, they may be said to have been drawing lines or "balancing values." "Direct" and "indirect" are spatial metaphors; "line-drawing" is another. "To weigh" or "to balance" values is a metaphor of a more complicated mathematical sort hinting at the process which goes on in moral judgments. All the metaphors suggest that, in the moral judgments made, comparisons were necessary, that no value completely controlled. The principle of double effect was no doctrine fallen from heaven, but a method of analysis appropriate where two relative values were being compared. In Catholic moral theology, as it developed, life even of the innocent was not taken as an absolute. Judgments on acts affecting life issued from a process of weighing. In the weighing, the fetus was always given a value greater than zero, always a value separate and independent from its parents. This valuation was crucial and fundamental in all Christian thought on the subject and marked it off from any approach which considered that only the parents' interests needed to be considered.

Even with the fetus weighed as human, one interest could be weighed as equal or superior: that of the mother in her own life. The casuists between 1450 and 1895 were willing to weigh this interest as superior. Since 1895, that interest was given decisive weight only in the two special cases of the cancerous uterus and the ectopic pregnancy. In both of these cases the fetus itself had little chance of survival even if the abortion were not performed. As the balance was once struck in favor of the mother whenever her life was endangered, it

could be so struck again. The balance reached between 1895 and 1930 attempted prudentially and pastorally to forestall a multitude of exceptions for interests less than life.

The perception of the humanity of the fetus and the weighing of fetal rights against other human rights constituted the work of the moral analysts. But what spirit animated their abstract judgments? For the Christian community it was the injunction of Scripture to love your neighbor as yourself. The fetus as human was a neighbor; his life had parity with one's own. The commandment gave life to what otherwise would have been only rational calculation.

The commandment could be put in humanistic as well as theological terms: Do not injure your fellow man without reason. In these terms, once the humanity of the fetus is perceived, abortion is never right except in self-defense. When life must be taken to save life, reason alone cannot say that a mother must prefer a child's life to her own. With this exception, now of great rarity, abortion violates the rational humanist tenet of the equality of human lives.

For Christians the commandment to love had received a special imprint in that the exemplar proposed of love was the love of the Lord for his disciples. In the light given by this example, self-sacrifice carried to the point of death seemed in the extreme situations not without meaning. In the less extreme cases, preference for one's own interests to the life of another seemed to express cruelty or selfishness irreconcilable with the demands of love.

19. *Our Bodies, Our Souls*

NAOMI WOLF

Writing from a feminist perspective, Naomi Wolf supports a woman's right to choose but takes pro-choice advocates to task for not taking with sufficient seriousness the personhood of the fetus and the lived experience of women who have undergone abortions. As Wolf explains, the rhetoric of pro-choice advocates tends to demean the humanness of the fetus as well as the profundity of the choice made by women choosing abortion. Referring to the fetus as biological "material" or "a mass of dependent protoplasm" minimizes the importance of the fetus and mischaracterizes the moral tragedy experienced by women when they choose to end their pregnancies. She argues that there is a life-altering moral choice involved in abortion, one well captured by notions of sin and forgiveness, and that pro-choice feminists would be more honest about the experience of women if they characterized abortion as the profound, life-and-death moral choice that it is.

I had an abortion when I was a single mother and my daughter was 2 years old. I would do it again. But you know how in the Greek myths when you kill a relative you are pursued by furies? For months, it was as if baby furies were pursuing me.

These are not the words of a benighted, superstition-ridden teenager lost in America's cultural backwaters. They are the words of a Cornell-educated, urban-dwelling, Democratic-voting 40-year-old cardiologist—I'll call her Clare. Clare is exactly the kind of person for whom being pro-choice is an unshakeable conviction. If there were a core constituent of the movement to secure abortion rights, Clare would be it. And yet: her words are exactly the words to which the pro-choice movement is not listening.

At its best, feminism defends its moral high ground by being simply faithful to the truth: to women's real-life experiences. But, to its own ethical and political detriment, the pro-choice movement has relinquished the moral frame around the issue of abortion. It has ceded the language of right and wrong to abortion foes. The movement's abandonment of what Americans have always, and rightly, demanded of their movements—an ethical core—and its reliance instead on a political rhetoric in which the fetus means nothing are proving fatal.

From Naomi Wolf, "Our Bodies, Our Souls," which appeared in the *New Republic*, October 16, 1995.

The effects of this abandonment can be measured in two ways. First of all, such a position causes us to lose political ground. By refusing to look at abortion within a moral framework, we lose the millions of Americans who want to support abortion as a legal right but still need to condemn it as a moral iniquity. Their ethical allegiances are then addressed by the pro-life movement, which is willing to speak about good and evil.

But we are also in danger of losing something more important than votes; we stand in jeopardy of losing what can only be called our souls. Clinging to a rhetoric about abortion in which there is no life and no death, we entangle our beliefs in a series of self-delusions, fibs and evasions. And we risk becoming precisely what our critics charge us with being: callous, selfish and casually destructive men and women who share a cheapened view of human life.

In the following pages, I will argue for a radical shift in the pro-choice movement's rhetoric and consciousness about abortion: I will maintain that we need to contextualize the fight to defend abortion rights within a moral framework that admits that the death of a fetus is a real death; that there are degrees of culpability, judgment and responsibility involved in the decision to abort a pregnancy; that the best understanding of feminism involves holding women as well as men to the responsibilities that are inseparable from their rights; and that we need to be strong enough to acknowledge that this country's high rate of abortion—which ends more than a quarter of all pregnancies—can only be rightly understood as what Dr. Henry Foster was brave enough to call it: "a failure."

Any doubt that our current pro-choice rhetoric leads to disaster should be dispelled by the famous recent defection of the woman who had been Jane Roe. What happened to Norma McCorvey? To judge by her characterization in the elite media and by some prominent pro-choice feminists, nothing very important. Her change of heart about abortion was relentlessly "explained away" as having everything to do with the girlish motivations of insecurity, fickleness and the need for attention, and little to do with any actual moral agency.

This dismissive (and, not incidentally, sexist and classist) interpretation was so highly colored by subjective impressions offered up by the very institutions that define objectivity that it bore all the hallmarks of an exculpatory cultural myth: poor Norma—she just needed stroking. She was never very stable, the old dear—first she was a chess-piece for the pro-choice movement ("just some anonymous person who suddenly emerges," in the words of one NOW member) and then a codependent of the Bible-thumpers. Low self-esteem, a history of substance abuse, ignorance— these and other personal weaknesses explained her turnaround.

To me, the first commandment of real feminism is: when in doubt, listen to women. What if we were to truly, respectfully listen to this woman who began her political life as, in her words, just "some little old Texas girl who got in trouble"? We would have to hear this: perhaps Norma McCorvey actually had a revelation that she could no longer live as the symbol of a belief system she increasingly repudiated.

Norma McCorvey should be seen as an object lesson for the pro-choice movement—a call to us to search our souls and take another, humbler look at how we go about what we are doing. For McCorvey is in fact an American Everywoman: she is the lost middle of the abortion debate, the woman whose allegiance we forfeit by our refusal to use a darker and sterner and more honest moral rhetoric.

McCorvey is more astute than her critics; she seems to understand better than the pro-choice activists she worked with just what the woman-in-the-middle believes: "I believe in the woman's right to choose. I'm like a lot of people. I'm in the mushy middle," she said. McCorvey still supports abortion rights through the first trimester—but is horrified by the brutality of abortion as it manifests more

obviously further into a pregnancy. She does not respect the black-and-white ideology on either side and insists on referring instead, as I understand her explanation, to her conscience. What McCorvey and other Americans want and deserve is an abortion-rights movement willing publicly to mourn the evil— necessary evil though it may be—that is abortion. We must have a movement that acts with moral accountability and without euphemism.

With the pro-choice rhetoric we use now, we incur three destructive consequences—two ethical, one strategic: hardness of heart, lying and political failure.

Because of the implications of a Constitution that defines rights according to the legal idea of "a person," the abortion debate has tended to focus on the question of "personhood" of the fetus. Many pro-choice advocates developed a language to assert that the fetus isn't a person, and this, over the years, has developed into a lexicon of dehumanization. Laura Kaplan's *The Story of Jane,* an important forthcoming account of a pre-*Roe* underground abortion service, inadvertently sheds light on the origins of some of this rhetoric: service staffers referred to the fetus—well into the fourth month—as "material" (as in "the amount of material that had to be removed. . ."). The activists felt exhilaration at learning to perform abortions themselves instead of relying on male doctors: "When [a staffer] removed the speculum and said, 'There, all done,' the room exploded in excitement." In an era when women were dying of illegal abortions, this was the understandable exhilaration of an underground resistance movement.

Unfortunately, though, this cool and congratulatory rhetoric lingers into a very different present. In one woman's account of her chemical abortion, in the January/February 1994 issue of *Mother Jones,* for example, the doctor says, "By Sunday you won't see on the monitor *what we call the heartbeat*" (my italics). The author of the article, D. Redman, explains that one of the drugs the doctor administered would "end the growth of the fetal tissue." And we all remember Dr. Joycelyn Elders's remark, hailed by some as refreshingly frank and pro-woman, but which I found remarkably brutal: that. "We really need to get over this love affair with the fetus. . . ."

How did we arrive at this point? In the early 1970s, Second Wave feminism adopted this rhetoric in response to the reigning ideology in which motherhood was invoked as an excuse to deny women legal and social equality. In a climate in which women risked being defined as mere vessels while their fetuses were given "personhood" at their expense, it made sense that women's advocates would fight back by depersonalizing the fetus.

The feminist complaint about the pro-life movement's dehumanization of the pregnant woman in relation to the humanized fetus is familiar and often quite valid: pro-choice commentators note that the pro-life film *The Silent Scream* portrayed the woman as "a vessel"; Ellen Frankfort's *Vaginal Politics,* the influential feminist text, complained that the fetus is treated like an astronaut in a spaceship.

But, say what you will, pregnancy confounds Western philosophy's idea of the autonomous self: the pregnant woman is in fact both a person in her body and a vessel. Rather than seeing both beings as alive and interdependent—seeing life within life—and acknowledging that sometimes; nonetheless, the woman must choose her life over the fetus's, Second Wave feminists reacted to the dehumanization of women by dehumanizing the creatures within them. In the death-struggle to wrest what Simone de Beauvoir called transcendence out of biological immanence, some feminists developed a rhetoric that defined the unwanted fetus as at best valueless; at worst an adversary, a "mass of dependent protoplasm."

Yet that has left us with a bitter legacy. For when we defend abortion rights by emptying the act of moral gravity we find ourselves cultivating a hardness of heart.

Having become pregnant through her partner's and her own failure to use a condom, Redman remarks that her friend Judith, who has been trying to find a child to adopt, begs her to carry the pregnancy to term. Judith offers Redman almost every condition a birth-mother could want: "'Let me have the baby,'" she quotes her friend pleading. "'You could visit her anytime, and if you ever wanted her back, I promise I would let her go.'" Redman does not mention considering this possibility. Thinking, rather, about the difficulty of keeping the child—"My time consumed by the tedious, daily activities that I've always done my best to avoid. Three meals a day. Unwashed laundry. . ."—she schedules her chemical abortion.

The procedure is experimental, and the author feels "almost heroic," thinking of how she is blazing a trail for other women. After the abortion process is underway, the story reaches its perverse epiphany: Redman is on a Women's Day march when the blood from the abortion first appears. She exults at this: "'Our bodies, our lives, our right to decide.'. . . My life feels luxuriant with possibility. For one precious moment, I believe that we have the power to dismantle this system. I finish the march, borne along by the women. . . ." As for the pleading Judith, with everything she was ready to offer a child, and the phantom baby? They are both off-stage, silent in this chilling drama of "feminist" triumphalism.

And why should we expect otherwise? In this essay, the fetus (as the author writes, "the now-inert material from my womb") is little more than a form of speech: a vehicle to assert the author's identity and autonomy.

The pro-life warning about the potential of widespread abortion to degrade reverence for life does have a nugget of truth: a free-market rhetoric about abortion can, indeed, contribute to the eerie situation we are now facing, wherein the culture seems increasingly to see babies not as creatures to whom parents devote their lives but as accoutrements to enhance parental quality of life. Day by day, babies seem to have less value in themselves, in a matrix of the sacred, than they do as products with a value dictated by a market economy.

Stories surface regularly about "worthless" babies left naked on gratings or casually dropped out of windows, while "valuable," genetically correct babies are created at vast expense and with intricate medical assistance for infertile couples. If we fail to treat abortion with grief and reverence, we risk forgetting that, when it comes to the children we choose to bear, we are here to serve them—whomever they are; they are not here to serve us.

Too often our rhetoric leads us to tell untruths. What Norma McCorvey wants, it seems, is for abortion-rights advocates to face, really face, what we are doing: "Have you ever seen a second-trimester abortion?" she asks. "It's a baby. It's got a face and a body, and they put him in a freezer and a little container."

Well, so it does; and so they do.

The pro-choice movement often treats with contempt the pro-lifers' practice of holding up to our faces their disturbing graphics. We revile their placards showing an enlarged scene of the aftermath of a D & C abortion; we are disgusted by their lapel pins with the little feet, crafted in gold, of a 10-week-old fetus; we mock the sensationalism of *The Silent Scream.* We look with pity and horror at someone who would brandish a fetus in formaldehyde—and we are quick to say that they are lying: "Those are stillbirths, anyway," we tell ourselves.

To many pro-choice advocates, the imagery is revolting propaganda. There is a sense among us, let us be frank, that the gruesomeness of the imagery *belongs* to the pro-lifers; that it emerges from the dark, frightening minds of fanatics; that it represents the violence of imaginations that would, given half a chance, turn our world into a scary, repressive place. "People like us" see such material as the pornography of the pro-life movement.

But feminism at its best is based on what is simply true. While pro-lifers have not been beyond dishonesty, distortion and the doctoring of images (preferring, for example, to highlight the results of very late, very rare abortions), many of those photographs are in fact photographs of actual D & Cs; those footprints are in fact the footprints of a 10-week-old fetus; the pro-life slogan, "Abortion stops a beating heart," is incontrovertibly true. While images of violent fetal death work magnificently for pro-lifers as political polemic, the pictures are not polemical in themselves: they are biological facts. We know this.

Since abortion became legal nearly a quarter-century ago, the fields of embryology and perinatology have been revolutionized—but the prochoice view of the contested fetus has remained static. This has led to a bizarre bifurcation in the way we who are pro-choice tend to think about wanted as opposed to unwanted fetuses; the unwanted ones are still seen in schematic black-and-white drawings while the wanted ones have metamorphosed into vivid and moving color. Even while Elders spoke of our need to "get over" our love affair with the unwelcome fetus, an entire growth industry—Mozart for your belly; framed sonogram photos; home fetal-heartbeat stethoscopes—is devoted to sparking fetal love affairs in other circumstances, and aimed especially at the hearts of overscheduled yuppies. If we avidly cultivate love for the ones we bring to term, and "get over" our love for the ones we don't, do we not risk developing a hydroponic view of babies—and turn them into a product we can cull for our convenience?

Any happy couple with a wanted pregnancy and a copy of *What to Expect When You're Expecting* can see the cute, detailed drawings of the fetus whom the book's owner presumably is not going to abort, and can read the excited descriptions of what that fetus can do and feel, month by month. Anyone who has had a sonogram during pregnancy knows perfectly well that the 4-month-old fetus responds to outside stimulus— "Let's get him to look this way," the technician will say, poking gently at the belly of a delighted mother-to-be. *The Well Baby Book,* the kind of whole-grain, holistic guide to pregnancy and childbirth that would find its audience among the very demographic that is most solidly pro-choice, reminds us that: "Increasing knowledge is increasing the awe and respect we have for the unborn baby and is causing us to regard the unborn baby as a real person long before birth. . . ."

So, what will it be: "Wanted fetuses are charming, complex, REM-dreaming little beings whose profile on the sonogram looks just like Daddy, but unwanted ones are mere "uterine material"? How can we charge that it is vile and repulsive for pro-lifers to brandish vile and repulsive images if the images are real? To insist that the truth is in poor taste is the very height of hypocrisy. Besides, if these images *are* often the facts of the matter, and if we then claim that it is offensive for pro-choice women to be confronted by them, then we are making the judgment that women are too inherently weak to face a truth about which they have to make a grave decision. This view of women is unworthy of feminism. Free women must be strong women, too; and strong women, presumably, do not seek to cloak their most important decisions in euphemism.

Other lies are not lies to others, but to ourselves. An abortion-clinic doctor, Elizabeth Karlin, who wrote a recent "Hers" column in *The New York Times,* declared that "There is only one reason I've ever heard for having an abortion: the desire to be a good mother."

While that may well be true for many poor and working-class women—and indeed research shows that poor women are three times more likely to have abortions than are better-off women—the elite, who are the most vociferous in their morally unambiguous pro-choice language, should know perfectly well how untrue that statement often is in their own lives. All abortions occupy a spectrum, from full lack of alternatives to full moral accountability. Karlin and many other pro-choice activists try to situate all women equally at the extreme endpoint of that spectrum, and it just isn't so. Many women, including middle-class women, do have abortions because, as one such woman put it, "They have a notion of what a good mother is and don't feel they can be that kind of mother at this phase of their lives." In many cases, that is still a morally defensible place on the spectrum; but it is not the place of absolute absolution that Dr. Karlin claims it to be. It is, rather, a place of moral struggle, of self-interest mixed with selflessness, of wished-for good intermingled with necessary evil.

Other abortions occupy places on the spectrum that are far more culpable. Of the abortions I know of, these were some of the reasons: to find out if the woman could get pregnant; to force a boy or man to take a relationship more seriously; and, again and again, to enact a rite of passage for affluent teenage girls. In my high school, the abortion drama was used to test a boyfriend's character. Seeing if he would accompany the girl to the operation or, better yet, come up with the money for the abortion could almost have been the 1970s Bay Area equivalent of the '50s fraternity pin.

The affluent teenage couples who conceive because they can and then erase the consequences—and the affluent men and women who choose abortion because they were careless or in a hurry or didn't like the feel of latex—are not the moral equivalent of the impoverished mother who responsibly, even selflessly, acknowledges she already has too many mouths to feed. Feminist rights include feminist responsibilities; the right to obtain an abortion brings with it the responsibility to contracept. Fifty-seven percent of unintended pregnancies come about because the parents used no contraception at all. Those millions certainly include women and men too poor to buy contraception, girls and boys too young and ill-informed to know where to get it, and countless instances of marital rape, coerced sex, incest and couplings in which the man refused to let the woman use protection.

But they also include millions of college students, professional men and women, and middle and upper-middle-class people (11 percent of abortions are obtained by people in households with incomes of higher than $50,000)—who have no excuse whatsoever for their carelessness. "There is only one reason I've ever heard for having an abortion: the desire to be a good mother"—this is a falsehood that condescends to women struggling to be true agents of their own souls, even as it dishonors through hypocrisy the terminations that are the writer's subject.

Not to judge other men and women without judging myself, I know this assertion to be false from my own experience. Once, I made the choice to take a morning-after pill. The heavily pregnant doctor looked at me, as she dispensed it, as if I were the scum of the earth.

If what was going on in my mind had been mostly about the well-being of the possible baby, that pill would never have been swallowed. For that potential baby, brought to term, would have had two sets of loving middle-income grandparents, an adult mother with an education and even, as I discovered later, the beginning of diaper money for its first two years of life

(the graduate fellowship I was on forbade marriage but, frozen in time before women were its beneficiaries, said nothing about unwed motherhood). Because of the baby's skin color, even if I chose not to rear the child, a roster of eager adoptive parents awaited him or her. If I had been thinking only or even primarily about the baby's life, I would have had to decide to bring the pregnancy, had there been one, to term.

No: there were two columns in my mind—"Me" and "Baby"—and the first won out. And what was in it looked something like this: unwelcome intensity in the relationship with the father; desire to continue to "develop as a person" before "real" parenthood; wish to encounter my eventual life partner without the off-putting encumbrance of a child; resistance to curtailing the nature of the time remaining to me in Europe. Essentially, this column came down to: I am not done being responsive only to myself yet.

At even the possibility that the cosmos was calling my name, I cowered and stepped aside. I was not so unlike those young louts who father children and run from the specter of responsibility. Except that my refusal to be involved with this potential creature was as definitive as a refusal can be.

Stepping aside in this way is analogous to draft evasion; there are good and altruistic reasons to evade the draft, and then there are self-preserving reasons. In that moment, feminism came to one of its logical if less-than-inspiring moments of fruition: I chose to sidestep biology; I acted—and was free to act—as if I were in control of my destiny, the way men more often than women have let themselves act. I chose myself on my own terms over a possible someone else, for self-absorbed reasons. But "to be a better mother"? "*Dulce et decorum est*. . ."? Nonsense.

Now, freedom means that women must be free to choose self or to choose selfishly. Certainly for a woman with fewer economic and social choices than I had—for instance, a woman struggling to finish her higher education, without which she would have little hope of a life worthy of her talents—there can indeed be an *obligation* to choose self. And the defense of some level of abortion rights as fundamental to women's integrity and equality has been made fully by others, including, quite effectively, Ruth Bader Ginsberg. There is no easy way to deny the powerful argument that a woman's equality in society must give her some irreducible rights unique to her biology, including the right to take the life within her life.

But we don't have to lie to ourselves about what we are doing at such a moment. Let us at least look with clarity at what that means and not whitewash self-interest with the language of self-sacrifice. The landscape of many such decisions looks more like Marin County than Verdun. Let us certainly not be fools enough to present such spiritually limited moments to the world with a flourish of pride, pretending that we are somehow pioneers and heroines and even martyrs to have snatched the self, with its aims and pleasures, from the pressure of biology.

That decision was not my finest moment. The least I can do, in honor of the being that might have been, is simply to know that.

Using amoral rhetoric, we weaken ourselves politically because we lose the center. To draw an inexact parallel, many people support the choice to limit the medical prolongation of life. But, if a movement arose that spoke of our "getting over our love affair" with the terminally ill, those same people would recoil into a vociferous interventionist position as a way to assert their moral values. We would be impoverished by a rhetoric about the end of life that speaks of the ill and the dying as if they were meaningless and of doing away with them as if it were a bracing demonstration of our personal independence.

Similarly, many people support necessary acts of warfare (Catholics for a Free Choice makes the analogy between abortion rights and such warfare). There are legal mechanisms that allow us to bring into the world the evil of war. But imagine how quickly public opinion would turn against a president who waged war while asserting that our sons and daughters were nothing but cannon fodder. Grief and respect are the proper tones for all discussions about choosing to endanger or destroy a manifestation of life.

War is legal; it is sometimes even necessary. Letting the dying die in peace is often legal and sometimes even necessary. Abortion should be legal; it is sometimes even necessary. Sometimes the mother must be able to decide that the fetus, in its full humanity, must die. But it is never right or necessary to minimize the value of the lives involved or the sacrifice incurred in letting them go. Only if we uphold abortion rights within a matrix of individual conscience atonement and responsibility can we both correct the logical and ethical absurdity in our position—and consolidate the support of the center.

Many others, of course, have wrestled with this issue: Camille Paglia, who has criticized the "convoluted casuistry" of some pro-choice language; Roger Rosenblatt, who has urged us to permit but discourage abortion; Laurence Tribe, who has noted that we place the fetus in shadow in order to advance the pro-choice argument. But we have yet to make room for this conversation at the table of mainstream feminism.

And we can't wait much longer. Historical changes—from the imminent availability of cheap chemical abortifacients to the ascendancy of the religious right to Norma McCorvey's defection—make the need for a new abortion-rights language all the more pressing.

In a time of retrenchment, how can I be so sure that a more honest and moral rhetoric about abortion will consolidate rather than scuttle abortion rights? Look at what Americans themselves say. When a recent *Newsweek* poll asked about support for abortion using the rare phrasing, "It's a matter between a woman, her doctor, her family, her conscience and her God," a remarkable 72 percent of the respondents called that formulation "about right." This represents a gain of thirty points over the abortion-rights support registered in the latest Gallup poll, which asked about abortion without using the words "God" or "conscience." When participants in the Gallup poll were asked if they supported abortion "under any circumstances" only 32 percent agreed; only 9 percent more supported it under "most" circumstances. Clearly, abortion rights are safest when we are willing to submit them to a morality beyond just our bodies and our selves.

But how, one might ask, can I square a recognition of the humanity of the fetus, and the moral gravity of destroying it, with a pro-choice position? The answer can only be found in the context of a paradigm abandoned by the left and misused by the right: the paradigm of sin and redemption.

It was when I was four months pregnant, sick as a dog, and in the middle of an argument, that I realized I could no longer tolerate the fetus-is-nothing paradigm of the pro-choice movement. I was being interrogated by a conservative, and the subject of abortion rights came up. "You're four months pregnant," he said. "Are you going to tell me that's not a baby you're carrying?"

The accepted pro-choice response at such a moment in the conversation is to evade: to move as swiftly as possible to a discussion of "privacy" and "difficult personal decisions" and "choice." Had I not been so nauseated and so cranky and so weighed down with the physical gravity of what was going on inside me, I might not have told what is the truth for me. "Of course it's a baby," I snapped. And went rashly on: "And if I found myself in circumstances in which I had to make the terrible decision to end this life, then that would be between myself and God."

Startlingly to me, two things happened: the conservative was quiet; I had said something that actually made sense to him. And I felt the great relief that is the grace of long-delayed honesty.

Now, the G-word is certainly a problematic element to introduce into the debate. And yet "God" or "soul"—or, if you are secular and prefer it, "conscience"—is precisely what is missing from pro-choice discourse. There is a crucial difference between "myself and my God" or "my conscience"—terms that imply moral accountability—and "myself and my doctor," the phrasing that Justice Harry Blackmun's wording in *Roe* ("inherently, and primarily, a medical decision") has tended to promote in the pro-choice movement. And that's not even to mention "between myself and myself" (Elders: "It's not anybody's business if I went for an abortion"), which implies just the relativistic relationship to abortion that our critics accuse us of sustaining.

The language we use to make our case limits the way we let ourselves think about abortion. As a result of the precedents in *Roe* (including *Criswold* v. *Connecticut* and *Eisenstadt* v. *Baird*), which based a woman's right to an abortion on the Ninth and Fourteenth Amendments' implied right to personal privacy, other unhelpful terms are also current in our discourse. Pro-choice advocates tend to cast an abortion as "an intensely personal decision." To which we can say, No: one's choice of *carpeting* is an intensely personal decision. One's struggles with a life-and-death issue must be understood as a matter of personal conscience. There is a world of difference between the two, and it's the difference a moral frame makes.

Stephen L. Carter has pointed out that spiritual discussion has been robbed of a place in American public life. As a consequence we tend—often disastrously—to use legislation to work out right and wrong. That puts many in the position of having to advocate against abortion rights in order to proclaim their conviction that our high rate of avoidable abortion (one of the highest in developed countries, five times that of the Netherlands, for example) is a social evil; and, conversely, many must pretend that abortion is not a transgression of any kind if we wish to champion abortion rights. We have no ground on which to say that abortion is a necessary evil that should be faced and opposed in the realm of conscience and action and even soul; yet remain legal.

But American society is struggling to find its way forward to a discourse of right and wrong that binds together a common ethic for the secular and the religious. When we do that, we create a moral discourse that can exist in its own right independent of legislation, and we can find ground to stand upon.

Norma McCorvey explained what happened to her in terms of good and evil: she woke in the middle of the night and felt a presence pushing violently down on her. "I denounce you, Satan," she announced. This way of talking about evil is one of the chief class divisions in America: working-class people talk about Satan, and those whom Paul Fussell calls "the X group"—those who run the country—talk instead about neurotic guilt. While the elite scoff at research that shows that most Americans maintain a belief in the embodiment of evil—"the devil"—they miss something profound about the human need to make moral order out of chaos. After all, the only real difference between the experience described by Clare, the Cornell-educated pro-choicer, and McCorvey, the uneducated ex-alcoholic, is a classical allusion.

There is a hunger for a moral framework that we pro-choicers must reckon with. In the Karlin "Hers" column, the author announced proudly that pregnant women are asked by the counselor in the office, "So, how long have you been pro-choice?" Dr. Karlin writes that "Laughter and the answer, 'About ten minutes,' is the healthiest response. 'I still don't believe in abortion,' some women say, unaware that refusal to take responsibility for the decision means that I won't do the procedure."

How is this "feminist" ideological coercion any different from the worst of pro-life shaming and coercion? The women who come to a clinic that is truly feminist—that respects women—are entitled not only to their abortions but also to their sense of sin.

To use the term "sin" in this context does not necessarily mean, as Dr. Karlin believes, that a woman thinks she must go to hell because she is having an abortion. It may mean that she thinks she must face the realization that she has fallen short of who she should be; and that she needs to ask forgiveness for that, and atone for it. As I understand such a woman's response, she *is* trying to take responsibility for the decision.

We on the left tend to twitch with discomfort at that word "sin." Too often we have become religiously illiterate, and so we deeply misunderstand the word. But in all of the great religious traditions, our recognition of sin, and then our atonement for it, brings on God's compassion and our redemption. In many faiths, justice is linked, as it is in medieval Judaism and in Buddhism, to compassion. From Yom Kippur and the Ash Wednesday-to-Easter cycle to the Hindu idea of karma, the individual's confrontation with her or his own culpability is the first step toward ways to create and receive more light.

How could one live with a conscious view that abortion is an evil and still be pro-choice? Through acts of redemption, or what the Jewish mystical tradition calls *tikkun;* or "mending." Laurence Tribe, in *Abortion: The Clash of Absolutes,* notes that "Memorial services for the souls of aborted fetuses are fairly common in contemporary Japan," where abortions are both legal and readily available. Shinto doctrine holds that women should make offerings to the fetus to help it rest in peace; Buddhists once erected statues of the spirit guardian of children to honor aborted fetuses (called "water children" or "unseeing children"). If one believes that abortion is killing and yet is still pro-choice, one could try to use contraception for every single sex act; if one had to undergo an abortion, one could then work to provide contraception, or jobs, or other choices to young girls; one could give money to programs that provide prenatal care to poor women; if one is a mother or father, one can remember the aborted child every time one is tempted to be less than loving—and give renewed love to the living child. And so on: *tikkun.*

But when you insist, as the "Hers" column writer did, on stripping people of their sense of sin, they react with a wholesale backing-away into a rigid morality that reimposes order: hence, the ascendancy of the religious right.

Just look at the ill-fated nomination of Dr. Henry Foster for Surgeon General. The Republicans said "abortion," and the discussion was over. The Democrats, had they worked out a moral framework for progressivism, could have responded: "Yes: our abortion rate is a terrible social evil. Here is a man who can help put a moral framework around the chaos of a million and a half abortions a year. He can bring that rate of evil down. And whichever senator among you has ever prevented an unplanned pregnancy—and Dr. Foster has—let him ask the first question."

Who gets blamed for our abortion rate? The ancient Hebrews had a ritual of sending a "scapegoat" into the desert with the community's sins projected upon it. Abortion doctors are our contemporary scapegoats. The pro-lifers obviously scapegoat them in one way: if pro-lifers did to women what they do to abortion doctors—harassed and targeted them in their homes and workplaces—public opinion would rapidly turn against them; for the movement would soon find itself harassing the teachers and waitresses, housewives and younger sisters of their own communities. The pro-life movement would have to address the often all-too-pressing good reasons that lead good people to abort. That would be intolerable, a tactical defeat for the pro-life movement, and as sure to lose it "the mushy middle" as the pro-choice movement's tendency toward rhetorical coldness loses it the same constituency.

But pro-choicers, too, scapegoat the doctors and clinic workers. By resisting a moral framework in which to view abortion we who are pro-abortion-rights leave the doctors in the front lines; with blood on their hands: the blood of the repeat abortions—at least 43 percent of the total; the suburban summer country-club rite-of-passage abortions; the "I don't know what came over me, it was such good Chardonnay" abortions; as well as the blood of the desperate and the unpreventable and accidental and the medically necessary and the violently conceived abortions. This is blood that the doctors and clinic workers often see clearly, and that they heroically rinse and cause to flow and rinse again. And they take all our sins, the pro-choice as well as the pro-life among us, upon themselves.

And we who are pro-choice compound their isolation by declaring that that blood is not there.

As the world changes and women, however incrementally, become more free and more powerful, the language in which we phrase the goals of feminism must change as well. As a result of the bad old days before the Second Wave of feminism, we tend to understand abortion as a desperately needed exit from near-total male control of our reproductive lives. This scenario posits an unambiguous chain of power and powerlessness in which men control women and women, in order to survive, must have unquestioned control over fetuses. It is this worldview, all too real in its initial conceptualization, that has led to the dread among many pro-choice women of departing from a model of woman-equals-human-life, fetus-equals-not-much.

This model of reality may have been necessary in an unrelenting patriarchy. But today, in what should be, as women continue to consolidate political power, a patriarchy crumbling in spite of itself, it can become obsolete.

Now: try to imagine real gender equality. Actually, try to imagine an America that is female-dominated, since a true working democracy in this country would reflect our 54–46 voting advantage.

Now imagine such a democracy, in which women would be valued so very highly, as a world that is accepting and responsible about human sexuality; in which there is no coerced sex without serious jailtime; in which there are affordable, safe contraceptives available for the taking in every public health building; in which there is economic parity for women—and basic economic subsistence for every baby born; and in which every young American woman knows about and understands her natural desire as a treasure to cherish, and responsibly, when the time is right, on her own terms, to share.

In such a world, in which the idea of gender as a barrier has become a dusty artifact, we would probably use a very different language about what would be—then—the rare and doubtless traumatic event of abortion. That language would probably call upon respect and responsibility, grief and mourning. In that world we might well describe the unborn and the never-to-be-born with the honest words of life.

And in that world, passionate feminists might well hold candlelight vigils at abortion clinics, standing shoulder to shoulder with the doctors who work there, commemorating and saying goodbye to the dead.

20. Abortion: Why the Arguments Fail

Stanley Hauerwas

Stanley Hauerwas, ~~writi~~ ... tinctive perspective of the Christian narrative ... has been mistakenly conducted on the basis ... ns, rights, obligations, and the like that are l... view. Hauerwas argues that larger issue ... under God, reproduction, families, and childr... t often remain unaddressed. The result of the... rtion debate is ill conceived and produces ... sofar as it fails to address the deeper issues ...

P. 188 – 198

Have the Arguments Failed?

Essays on the morality of abortion, whether they be anti or pro, have begun to take on a ritualistic form. Each side knows the arguments and counterarguments well, but they continue to go through the motions. Neither side seems to have much hope of convincing the other, but just as in some rituals we continue to repeat words and actions though we no longer know why, in like manner we continue to repeat arguments about why abortion is right, wrong, or indifferent. It is almost as though we assume that the repetition of the arguments

From Stanley Hauerwas, *A Community of Character* (Notre Dame, IN: University of Notre Dame Press, 1986), pp. 212–229. Reprinted with permission from the University of Notre Dame Press.

will magically break the moral and political impasse concerning the status of abortion in our society.

The intractability of the debate frustrates us and our frustration gives way to shrillness. Having tried to develop good philosophical, theological, legal, and social arguments we find our opponents still unconvinced. In the heat of political exchange, both sides resort to rhetoric designed to make their opponents appear stupid or immoral. Thus we are besieged by slogans affirming the "right to life" or that every woman has the "right over her body"; or it seems we must choose between being "pro-life" or "pro-choice." Some, concluding that there is no hope of conducting the public debate in a manner befitting the moral nuances of the abortion issue, have withdrawn from the field of battle.

Yet before anyone beats too hasty a retreat it is worth considering why the arguments seem to have failed and why we have been left with little alternative to the oversimplifications of the public debate. There may be a moral lesson to be learned from the intractable character of the debate that is as important as the morality of abortion itself. And I suspect it offers a particularly important lesson for Christians. It is my contention that Christian opposition to abortion on demand has failed because, by attempting to meet the moral challenge within the limits of public polity, we have failed to exhibit our deepest convictions that make our rejection of abortion intelligible. We have failed then in our first political task because we accepted uncritically an account of "the moral question of abortion" determined by a politics foreign to the polity appropriate to Christian convictions. We have not understood, as Christians, how easily we have presumed that the presuppositions of our "liberal" cultural ethos are "Christian." As a result, our temptation has been to blame the intractability of the abortion controversy on what appears to us as the moral blindness or immorality of pro-abortionists. We fail to see how much of the problem lies in the way we share with the pro-abortion advocates the moral presumptions of our culture.

As Christians we have assumed that we were morally and politically required to express our opposition to abortion in terms acceptable in a pluralist society. To be sure, we did this with depth of conviction, as we assumed those terms were the ones which should inform our understanding of the moral injustice involved in abortion. Hence we could claim that our opposition to abortion was not based on our special theological convictions, but rather founded on the profoundest presumptions of Western culture. All agree murder is wrong; all agree life is sacred; all agree that each individual deserves the protection of law; such surely are the hallmarks of our civilization.

Yet we discovered that not everyone agrees about when human life begins. This, we have supposed, is the point of dispute. And no matter how earnestly we tried to document genetically that human life begins at conception, we found many accepting Justice Blackmun's claim that the unborn are not "persons in the whole sense."[1] Philosophically we are told that our assumption that the fetus has moral status confuses the moral sense of being "human" or a "person" with the genetic,[2] and that we have to understand how the intelligibility of the notion of being a human or of being a person is anchored in our civilization's deepest moral values.[3]

Indeed even as strong an anti-abortion advocate as John Noonan has recently suggested that the issue of when human life begins is part of the public contro-

versy that cannot be settled. "It depends on assumptions and judgments about what human beings are and about what human beings should do for one another. These convictions and conclusions are not easily reached by argument. They rest on particular perspectives that are bound to the whole personality and can shift only with a reorientation of the person."[4] But if that is true, then surely we Christians have already lost the battle by letting the enemy determine the terrain on which the battle must be fought.

If the issue is limited to the determination of when human life begins, we cannot prevail, given the moral presuppositions of our culture. When the debate is so limited, it has already been uncritically shaped by the political considerations of our culture, the "moral" has already been determined by the "political," and the very convictions that make us Christian simply never come up. Indeed we have made a virtue of this, since some allege that appeals to religious convictions invalidate our views for the formulation of public policy.[5] As a result the Christian prohibition of abortion appears as an irrational prejudice of religious people who cannot argue it on a secular, rational basis.

But if Noonan is right that the convictions about human life rest on a perspective that is bound up with the "whole personality," then it seems that we Christians must make clear what we take such a "personality" to involve. For the Christian prohibition of abortion is a correlative to being a particular kind of people with a particular set and configuration of virtues. Yet we have tried to form our moral arguments against abortion within the moral framework of a liberal culture, as though the issue could be abstracted from the kind of people we should be. How the moral description and evaluation of abortion depends on more profound assumptions about the kind of people we ought to be was thus not even recognized by ourselves, much less by those who do not share our convictions. As a result Christian arguments about abortion have failed. They have not merely failed to convince, but have failed to suggest the kind of "reorientation" necessary if we are to be the kind of people and society that make abortion unthinkable.

Of course it may be objected that the arguments have not failed. The fact that not everyone agrees that abortion is immoral and the failure to pass a constitutional amendment are of themselves no indication that the anti-abortion arguments have been invalid. Even at the political level there is still good reason to think that all is not lost, for there are political and legal strategies that are just beginning to have an effect on reversing our society's current abortion stance.[6] Yet even if such strategies succeed, our success may still be a form of failure if we "win" without changing the presuppositions of the debate.

To understand why this is the case it is necessary to look more generally at the obstacle to moral agreement in our society. Only from such a perspective can we appreciate why the Christian stance concerning abortion may be a far more fundamental challenge to our society's moral presuppositions than even the most radical anti-abortionists have considered.

Abortion in a Liberal Society

According to Alasdair MacIntyre there is nothing peculiar about the failure of our society to reach a moral consensus concerning the appropriate manner to deal with abortion. Indeed the very character of debate in a liberal, secular, pluralist culture like ours shows that there is no rational method for resolving most significant matters of moral dispute. Any rational method for resolving moral disagreements requires a shared tradition that embodies assumptions about the nature of man and our true end.[7] But it is exactly the presumption of liberalism that a just society can be sustained by freeing the individual from all tradition.[8]

MacIntyre illustrates his argument by calling attention to three different positions concerning abortion:

A: Everybody has certain rights over their own person, including their own body. It follows from the nature of these rights that at the stage when the embryo is essentially part of the mother's body, the mother has a right to make her uncoerced decision on whether she will have an abortion or not. Therefore each pregnant woman ought to decide and ought to be allowed to decide for herself what she will do in the light of her own moral views.

B: I cannot, if I will to be alive, consistently will that my mother should have had an abortion when she was pregnant with me, except if it had been certain that the embryo was dead or gravely damaged. But if I cannot consistently will this in my own case, how can I consistently deny to others the right to life I claim for myself? I would break the so-called Golden Rule unless I denied that a mother has in general a right to abortion. I am not of course thereby committed to the view that abortion ought to be legally prohibited.

C: Murder is wrong, prohibited by natural and divine law. Murder is the taking of innocent life. An embryo is an identifiable individual, differing from a new-born infant only in being at an earlier stage on the long road to adult capacities. If infanticide is murder, as it is, then abortion is murder. So abortion is not only morally wrong, but ought to be legally prohibited.[9]

MacIntyre suggests the interesting thing about these arguments is that each of the protagonists reaches his conclusion by valid forms of inferences, yet there is no agreement about which premises are the right starting points. And in our culture there is no generally agreed upon procedure for weighing the merits of the rival premises. Each of the above positions represents fragments of moral systems that exist in uneasy relation to one another. Thus position A, premised as "an understanding of rights which owes something to Locke and something to Jefferson is counterposed to a universalibility argument whose debt is first to Kant and then to the gospels and both to an appeal to the moral law as conceived by Hooker, More, and Aquinas."[10]

The fact that these are "fragments" of past moral positions is particularly important. For as fragments they have been torn from the social and intellectual contexts in which they gained their original intelligibility and from which they derive such force and validity as they continue to possess. But since they now exist *only* as fragments, we do not know how to weigh one set of premises against another. We do not know what validity to grant to each in isolation from those presuppositions that sustained their original intelligibility.

To understand the roots of our dilemma, MacIntyre argues that we must look to the moral presuppositions on which our society was founded. For in spite of the appeal to self-evident truths about equality and rights to life, liberty, and the pursuit of happiness, there was the attempt to provide some cogent philosophical basis for these "truths." The difficulty, however, begins when appeals such as Jefferson's to Aristotle and Locke fail to acknowledge these to be mutually antagonistic positions. We are thus a society that may be in the unhappy position of being founded upon a moral contradiction.

The contradiction, in its most dramatic form, involves the impossibility of reconciling classical and modern views of man. Thus as MacIntyre points out:

the central preoccupation of both ancient and medieval communities was characteristically: how may men together realize the true human good? The central preoccupation of modern men is and has been characteristically: how may we prevent men interfering with each other as each of us goes about our own concerns? The classical view begins with the community of the *polis* and with the individual viewed as having no moral identity apart from the communities of kinship and citizenship; the modern view begins with the concept of a collection of individuals and the problem of how out of and by individuals social institutions can be constructed.[11]

The attempt to answer the last question has been the primary preoccupation of social theorists since the seventeenth century, and their answers to it are not always coherent with one another.

In the face of this disagreement the political consensus has been that the most nearly just social arrangement is one which requires no commitment to any good except the protection of each individual to pursue his or her interests fairly. Thus John Rawls describes the way we ought to envisage the terms of an original contract between individuals on which a just society can be founded as one where they "do not share a conception of the good by reference to which the fruition of their powers or even the satisfaction of their desires can be evaluated. They do not have an agreed criterion of perfection that can be used as a principle for choosing between institutions. To acknowledge any such standard would be, in effect, to accept a principle that might lead to a lesser religious or other liberty."[12]

Such a view can no longer provide a place for the classical perspective's insistence on the development of virtuous people. From the classical perspective judgments about virtues and goods are interdependent, since the good is known only by observing how a virtuous man embodies it. But in the absence of any shared conception of the good, judgments about virtues and judgments about goods are logically independent of one another. Thus it becomes a political necessity, anchored in our society's profoundest moral convictions, that an issue such as abortion be considered on grounds independent of the kind of persons we would like to encourage in our society. The morality of the "act" of abortion must be considered separately from the "agent," for to take the character of the agent into account offends the basic moral and political consensus of our society.

We should be hesitant to criticize the moral achievement of political liberalism too quickly. By making the moral purpose of government the securing of the equal right of all individuals to pursue their happiness as they understand it, liberalism was able to secure political peace in a morally pluralistic and fragmentary society. Its deepest advantage is to remove from the political arena all issues that might be too deeply divisive of the citizenry.[13] The ideal of liberalism is thus to make government neutral on the very subjects that matter most to people, precisely *because* they matter most.

Of course our society has never acted with complete consistency on the principle of neutrality. Thus, we ended slavery, and polygamy was outlawed. And, more recently, the modern welfare function of the state appears to require that certain beliefs about what is good for people be the basis of public policy. But it can still be claimed that the state leaves to individuals and groups the power to determine what private vision of happiness to pursue. "Hence governmental programs to assure full employment, to guarantee equal opportunity to enter the professions, to give everyone as much education as he wants, etc., imply no communal understanding of the good which is to be imposed on all. These programs aim only at establishing the conditions that enable everyone to pursue his own good as he understands it."[14]

One of the ironies, however, is that the liberal state so conceived has worked only because its citizens continued to assume that the classical conception still held some validity for the regulation of their lives. Thus even though the virtues could not be encouraged as a "public" matter, they were still thought important as a private concern and of indirect benefit for our public life. Religion and the family institutions appropriate for the training of virtue were encouraged on the assumption they were necessary to sustain a polity based on the overriding status of the individual.

Thus, as Francis Canavan has argued,

Liberal democracy has worked as well as it has and as long as it has because it has been able to trade on something that it did not create and which it tends on the whole to undermine. That is the moral tradition that prevailed among the greater part of the people. It is not necessary to pretend that most Americans in the past kept the Ten Commandments, certainly not that they kept them all the time. It is enough that by and large Americans agreed that there were Ten Commandments and that in principle they ought to be kept. The pluralist solution of withdrawing certain areas of life from legal control worked precisely because American pluralism was not all that pronounced. In consequence, many important areas of life were not withdrawn from the reach of law and public policy and were governed by a quasi-official public ethos.[15]

But in our day the moral consensus has disintegrated in a number of significant respects: we no longer have agreement on the value of human life, or on such basic social institutions as marriage and the family, or for that matter on the meaning of being human.

At this point, it is doubtful whether the typical response of the liberal pluralist society is any longer adequate, that is, to take the dangerously controversial matters out of politics and relegate them to the conscience of individuals. For this way of eliminating controversy in fact does much more. Intentionally or not, it contributes to a reshaping of basic social institutions and a revision of the moral beliefs of multitudes of individuals beyond those directly concerned. It turns into a process by which one ethos, with its reflection in law and public policy, is replaced by another. Liberal pluralism then becomes a sort of confidence game in which, in the guise of showing respect for individual rights, we are in reality asked to consent to a new kind of society based on a new set of beliefs and values.[16]

Perhaps this is nowhere better seen than in the phenomenon that Noonan has called the "masks" of liberty. By masks he means the linguistic conventions that are developing to redescribe the object and means of injustice.[17] Language such as child, baby, and killing have to be avoided, for if such language is used it will require a break with the moral culture we assume we wish to preserve.[18] "If all that has happened may fairly be described as 'termination of a pregnancy' with 'fetal wastage' the outcome, abortion may be accepted without break with the larger moral culture. If, however, such a description is a mask, if the life of an unborn child is being taken, it is difficult to reconcile the acceptance of abortion with the overarching prohibition against the taking of life."[19]

Thus we attempt to change our language so our commitment to greater individual liberty concerning abortion will not contradict our traditional views about what kind of people we should be to deserve to be free. The reason that our arguments concerning abortion are bound to fail is that we cannot resolve the morally antithetical traditions that form our society and our Christian ambitions for ourselves. Attempting

to resolve the issue as though the act of abortion could be separated from our conviction about character has been a futile attempt to settle a substantive moral issue on "objective" or procedural grounds acceptable to a liberal culture.

Thus Justice Blackmun's opinion, while no doubt out of harmony with the majority of opinion concerning abortion in America, may actually be in accordance with our deepest views if we apply them more consistently. An indication, perhaps, that we are better off as a people if we fail to think and act consistently! For the underlying presupposition of *Roe v. Wade* is consistent liberalism in assuming that the only entity with political standing is the individual. And individuals are understood to consist of characteristics sufficient to make him or her a "person." Of course, as Noonan points out, a liberalism so consistently applied also challenges some of our presumptions about the family,[20] but that may be but another price we have to pay in order to be "free."

Noonan has located the paradox of Justice Blackmun's opinion:

> To invalidate the state abortion statutes it was necessary for him not only to ignore the unborn child but to recognize a liberty anterior to the state in the carrier of the child. The invocation of liberty which was the very heart of his opinion was the invocation of a standard superior to enacted law. His radical use of "higher law" was only disguised by his claim that something in the Constitution supplied the standard by which the state laws on abortion were invalid. The ultimate basis of his decision was nothing in the Constitution but rather his readings of the natural law liberties of an individual.[21]

Blackmun has based his opinion on the most cherished moral presumption of our society: freedom of the individual.[22] Ironically, in the absence of a tradition, the ideal of a society constituted by individuals free of all tradition remains the sole moral basis we have for settling issues of moral significance.

Christians and Abortion: The Philosophical Issues

I showed above how in attempting to form their arguments against abortion in a manner that could be translated into public policy, Christians have accepted the moral limits imposed by our liberal heritage. As a result the reasons that Christians qua Christians should oppose abortion have not become a matter of public record. It should be noted that this was not just a strategic policy, but it also witnesses to our standing conviction of a profound commonality between Christianity and liberalism. Christians have assumed that the liberal commitment to the individual carried with it the prohibition of abortion. Yet what they have found is that the "individual" whom liberalism has an interest in protecting does not, either conceptually or normatively (though perhaps legally), necessarily include the fetus.

Such a discovery is shocking in itself; worse, it seems to leave Christians without further appeal. For we must admit that the fact and way abortion became a matter of moral controversy caught us by surprise and unprepared. We were prepared to argue about whether certain kinds of abortion might or might not be legally prohibited or permitted, but that we would be required to argue whether abortion as an institution is moral, amoral, or immoral was simply unthinkable. As Christians we knew generally that we were against abortion, but we were not clear why. We assumed it surely had to do with our prohibition against the taking of life, and we assumed that that was surely all that needed to be said.

There is nothing unusual about the Christian failure to know why abortion is to be prohibited. Most significant moral prohibitions do not need to be constantly justified or rethought. They are simply part and parcel of the way we are. When asked why we do or do not engage in a particular form of activity we often find that it makes perfectly good sense to say "Christians just do or do not do that kind of thing." And we think that we have given a moral reason. But it is moral because it appeals to "what we are," to what kind of people we think we should be; yet liberalism wishes to exclude such contentions from moral consideration in the interest of securing cooperation in a morally pluralistic society. Liberalism seeks a philosophical account of morality that can ground the rightness or wrongness of particular actions or behavior in a "theory" divorced from any substantive commitments about what kind of people we are or should be—except perhaps to the extent that we should be rational or fair.[23] However, as Stuart Hampshire has argued, such theories falsify the way in which moral injunctions function, such as those about life-taking, sexual relations, relations between parents and children, truth-telling. The meaning and unity between such injunctions cannot be easily inferred from the axioms of a theory. Rather,

taken together, a full set of such injunctions, prohibiting types of conduct in types of circumstance, describes in rough and indeterminate outline, an attainable and recognizable way of life, aspired to, respected and admired: or at least the minimum general features of a respectworthy way of life. And a way of life is not identified and characterized by one distinct purpose, such as in the increase of general happiness, or even by a set of such distinct purposes. The connection between the injunctions, the connection upon which a reasonable man reflects, is to be found in the coherence of a single way of life, distinguished by the characteristic virtues and vices recognized within it.[24]

Of course ways of life are complicated matters marked out by many details of style and manner. Moreover the "connectedness" of any set of injunctions often has the character, not of "rational" necessity, but rather of a "reasonableness" that derives from the history of a community's moral experience and wisdom. Such a community may well have prohibitions that have an almost absolute character, such as the Christian prohibition of abortion, but such prohibitions need not be categorical, in the Kantian sense, nor based on principles of rationality. Rather they are judgments of unconditioned necessity,

> in the sense that they imply that what must be done is not necessary because it is a means to some independently valued end, but because the action is a necessary part of a way of life and ideal of conduct. The necessity resides in the nature of the action itself, as specified in the fully explicit moral judgment. The principal and proximate grounds for claiming that the action must, or must not, be performed are to be found in the characterization of the action offered within the prescription; and if the argument is pressed further, first a virtue or vice, and then a whole way of life will have to be described.[25]

But I am suggesting that this is exactly what we as Christians failed to do when it came to explaining why abortion is to be avoided. We failed to show, for ourselves or others, why abortion is an affront to our most basic convictions about what makes life meaningful and worthwhile. We tried to argue in terms of the "facts" or on the basis of "principles" and thus failed to make intelligible why such "facts" or "principles" were relevant in the first place. We have spent our time arguing abstractly about when human life does or does not begin.[26] As a result, we have failed to challenge the basic presuppositions that force the debate to hinge on such abstractions.

Hampshire suggests that the best means to avoid the kind of abstract thinking encouraged by moral theories given birth by liberalism is to tell stories. For

> telling stories, with the facts taken from experience and not filtered and at second hand, imposes some principles of selection. In telling the story one has to select the facts and probabilities which, taken together, constitute the situation confronting the agent. Gradually, and by accumulation of examples, belief that the features of the particular case, indefinite in number, are not easily divided into the morally relevant and morally irrelevant will be underlined by the mere process of storytelling. One cannot establish conclusively by argument in general terms the general conclusion that the morally relevant features of situations encountered cannot be circumscribed. One can only appeal to actual examples and call the mind back to personal experience, which will probably include occasions when the particular circumstances of the case modified what would have been the expected and principled decisions, and for reasons which do not themselves enter into any recognized principle.[27]

In a like manner I am suggesting that if Christians are to make their moral and political convictions concerning abortion intelligible we must show how the meaning and prohibition of abortion is correlative to the stories of God and his people that form our basic conviction. We must indicate why it is that the Christian way of life forms people in a manner that makes abortion unthinkable. Ironically it is only when we have done this that we will have the basis for suggesting why the fetus should be regarded as but another of God's children.

For as Roger Wertheimer has shown, arguments concerning the status of the fetus's humanity are not factual arguments at all, but actually moral claims requiring the training of imagination and perception. Wertheimer suggests that the argument over the status of the fetus is a

> paradigm of what Wittgenstein had in mind when he spoke of the possibility of two people agreeing on the application of a rule for

a long period, and then, suddenly and quite inexplicably, diverging in what they call going on in the same way. This possibility led him to insist that linguistic communication presupposes not only agreement in definitions, but also agreement in judgments, in what he called forms of life—something that seems lacking in the case at hand (i.e., the fetus). Apparently, the conclusion to draw is that it is not true that the fetus is a human being, but it is not false either. Without agreement in judgments, without a common response to the pertinent data, the assertion that the fetus is a human being cannot be assigned a genuine truth value.[28]

Wertheimer suggests that there seems to be no "natural" response, no clear forms of life, which provide the basis for why the fetus should be regarded one way rather than another. Thus failure to respect the fetus is not analogous to failure to respect blacks or Jews, since we share forms of life, common responses with them that make the denial of their humanity unintelligible. Thus the forms of life that lead some to believe and treat blacks and Jews as less than human can be shown to be perverse by appeal to obvious factual counterclaims based on our common experiences.

Wertheimer may be right that the case for respect for blacks and Jews is more immediately obvious than the case for the fetus, but I hope to show that the Christian form of life provides powerful reasons why the fetus should be regarded with respect and care. Moreover such respect is as profoundly "natural" as our current belief that blacks and Jews have moral status. What we must understand is that all "natural" relations are "historical" insofar as the natural is but what we have come to accept as "second nature."[29] The recognition of blacks and Jews was no less dependent on a history than the recognition of the status of the fetus. Both are the result of the experience of communities which are formed by substantive convictions of the significance of being open to new life. Because such an "openness" has become so "natural," and often so perverted, we have forgotten what profound moral commitments support and are embodied in the simple and everyday desire and expectation of new life that appears among us through and after pregnancy. Such a desire is obviously not peculiar to Christians, but by attending more directly to the Christian form of life I hope to show why and how the Christian desire for children makes it imperative that the fetus be regarded with respect and care.

Christians and Abortion: The Narrative Context

If my analysis has been correct we should now have a better hold on why arguments concerning abortion have failed in our society. At one level I have tried to show they must fail given the moral presuppositions and language offered by our liberal ethos. But I have also tried to suggest that failure at this level is but an indication of a deeper failure for Christians. Christians have failed their social order by accepting too easily the terms of argument concerning abortion offered by our society. If we are to serve our society well, and on our own terms, our first task must be to address ourselves by articulating for Christians why abortion can never be regarded as morally indifferent for us. Only by doing this can we witness to our society what kind of people and what kind of society is required if abortion is to be excluded.

Such a suggestion may sound extremely odd, since it seems to ask that we reinvent the wheel. Surely that is not the case, for both anti- and pro-abortion advocates know that, rightly or wrongly, Christians have had their minds made up about abortion from the beginning. It is certainly true that Christians, drawing on their Jewish roots, have condemned abortion from earliest days.[30] Yet this condemnation does not come from nowhere; it is a correlative of a way of life that must be constantly renewed and rethought. The task of each new generation of Christians is to rediscover that way of life and why prohibitions such as that against abortion are critical reminders of what kind of life it is that they are called to lead. The Christian way of life, though often lived simply, is no simple matter but involves a complex set of convictions that are constantly being reinterpreted as our understanding of one aspect of the tradition illuminates another. What we must do is show how this process makes a difference for our understanding of the prohibition of abortion.

It is important, furthermore, to distinguish my argument in this respect from those who make the often unfair criticism that the church must rethink its position on abortion because it allows the taking of life in other contexts. Though I do not wish to deny that Christians have often been inconsistent, especially in practice, about the protection and taking of life, there is nothing conceptually inconsistent about the prohibition of abortion as the unjust taking of life and the permissibility of just war and capital punishment. My call for the church to rethink her understanding of abortion involves the more fundamental concern that the church understand why abortion is incompatible with a community whose constitution is nothing less than the story of God's promise to mankind through the calling of Israel and the life of Jesus.

Such a discussion must be both theological and political. One cannot be separated from the other. Our beliefs about God are political, as they form the kind of community that makes the prohibition of abortion intelligible. But the discussion is also political, as it must be done in such a manner that Christians listen and learn from one another concerning their different understanding of what is at stake in abortion. Only by proceeding in this way can we be a paradigm, and perhaps even a witness, to our society of what a genuine moral discussion might look like.

I do not mean to imply that such discussion has been missing entirely in recent Christian history. Yet I think it is fair to say that we have not paid sufficient attention to how Christians as Christians should think about abortion.[31] Indeed I suspect many are not even sure what a call for this kind of discussion entails. Therefore I will try to suggest the kind of theological concerns that any discussion of abortion by Christians should involve.

To begin with, the first question is not, "Why do Christians think abortion is wrong?" To begin there already presupposes that we know and understand what abortion is. Rather, if we are to understand why Christians assume that by naming abortion they have already said something significant, we have to begin still a step back. We have to ask what it is about the kind of community, and corresponding world, that Christians create that makes them single out abortion in such a way as to exclude it.

For we must remember that "abortion" is not a description of a particular kind of behavior; rather it is a word that teaches us to see a singular kind of behavior from a particular community's moral perspective. The removal of the fetus from the mother's uterus before term can be called an "interruption of pregnancy," the child can be called "fetal matter," and the mother can be called a "patient." But from the Christian perspective, to see the situation in that way changes the self and the community in a decisive way. The Christian insistence on the term "abortion" is a way to remind them that what happens in the removal of the fetus from the mother in order to destroy it strikes at the heart of their community. From this perspective the attempt of Christians to be a community where the term "abortion" remains morally intelligible is a political act.

In this respect the pro-abortionists have always been at a disadvantage.[32] For they have had to carry out the argument in a language created by the moral presuppositions of the Jewish and Christian communities. "Abortion" still carries the connotation that this is not a good thing. Thus to be "pro-abortion" seems to put one in an embarrassing position of recommending a less than good thing. It is not without reason, therefore, that pro-abortion advocates seek to redescribe both the object and act of abortion. We must remind them, however, that by doing so they not only change the description of the act, they also change themselves.

Christians insist on the significance of such a change by refusing to live in a world devoid of abortion as a moral description—a world which admittedly may, as a result, involve deep tragedy. There can be no doubt that the insistence that unjust termination of pregnancy be called "abortion" has to do with our respect for life, but that is surely too simple. Jews and Christians are taught to respect life, not as an end in itself, but as a gift created by God. Thus life is respected because all life serves God in its way. Respect for human life is but a form of our respect for all life.

But note that just as no particular life can claim highest value, except as it exists for the love and service of God, neither can human life be thought to have absolute value. The Christian prohibition against taking life rests not on the assumption that human life has overriding value, but on the conviction that it is not ours to take. The Christian prohibition of abortion derives not from any assumption of the inherent value of life, but rather from the understanding that as God's creatures we have no basis to claim sovereignty over life.

And we cannot forget that this creator is also our redeemer. The life that lies in the womb is also a life that has come under the lordship of Jesus Christ. As Karl Barth has said,

> this child is a man for whose life the Son of God has died, for whose unavoidable part in the guilt of all humanity and future individual guilt He has already paid the price. The true light of the world shines already in the darkness of the mother's womb. And yet they want to kill him deliberately because certain reasons which have nothing to do with the child himself favor the view that he had better not be born! Is there any emergency which can justify this? It must surely be clear to us that until the question is put in all its gravity a serious discussion of the

problem cannot even begin, let alone lead to serious results.[33]

The temptation, in this secular age, is to ignore this kind of rhetorical flourish on the assumption that all it really amounts to is that Christians also believe in the value or sacredness of life. But from the perspective of Christian convictions about life as the locus of God's creating and redeeming purpose, claims of life's "value" or "sacredness" are but empty abstractions. The value of life is God's value and our commitment to protect it is a form of our worship of God as a good creator and a trustworthy redeemer. Our question is not "When does life begin?" but "Who is its true sovereign?" The creation and meaningfulness of the term "abortion" gain intelligibility from our conviction that God, not man, is creator and redeemer, and thus, the Lord of life. The Christian respect for life is first of all a statement, not about life, but about God.[34]

Yet the way of life of Christians involves more than the conviction of God's creating and redeeming purposes. We also believe that God has created and called us to be a people whose task it is to manifest and witness to his providential care of our existence. Thus to be a Christian is not just to hold certain beliefs, but it is to be part of a historic community that has the task of maintaining faithful continuity with our forebears. To be a Christian is to be part of a people who live through memory, since we only know how to face and create our future by striving to be as faithful and courageous as our forebears. The necessity of memory for our continued existence is but a form of our worship of our God, who wills to be known through the lives of his followers.

Christians are thus a people who have an immense stake in history. We look neither to escape nor to transcend history. Rather we are determined to live within history, hopefully living faithful to the memory of our founder. There is no conviction, therefore, more significant for Christians than our insistence on having children. For children are our anchors in history, our pledge and witness that the Lord we serve is the Lord, not only of our community, but of all history. The family is, therefore, symbolically central for the meaning of the existence of the Christian people.

From a Christian perspective children represent our continuing commitment to live as a historic people.[35] In the Christian community children are, for those who are called to be married, a duty. For the vocation of marriage in part derives its intelligibility from a couple's willingness to be open to new life. Indeed that is part of the test of the validity of their unity as one worthy to be called "love" in the Christian sense. It must necessarily be open to creation of another.

The Christian community's openness to new life and our conviction of the sovereignty of God over that life are but two sides of the same conviction. Christians believe that we have the time in this existence to care for new life, especially as such life is dependent and vulnerable, because it is not our task to rule this world or to "make our mark on history." We can thus take the time to live in history as God's people who have nothing more important to do than to have and care for children. For it is the Christian claim that knowledge and love of God is fostered by service to the neighbor, especially the most helpless, as in fact that is where we find the kind of Kingdom our God would have us serve.

It is the Christian belief, nurtured by the command of Jesus, that we must learn to love one another, that we become more nearly what we were meant to be through the recognition and love of those we did not "choose" to love. Children, the weak, the ill, the dispossessed provide a particularly intense occasion for such love, as they are beings we cannot control. We must love them for what they are rather than what we want or wish them to be, and as a result we discover that we are capable of love. The existence of such love is not unique or limited to Christians. Indeed that is why we have the confidence that our Christian convictions on these matters might ring true even for those who do not share our convictions. The difference between the Christian and the non-Christian is only that what is a possibility for the non-Christian is a duty for the Christian.

But the Christian duty to welcome new life is a joyful duty, as it derives from our very being as God's people. Moreover correlative to the language of duty is the language of gift. Because children are a duty they can also be regarded as gift, for duty teaches us to accept and welcome a child into the world, not as something that is "ours," but as a gift which comes from another.[36] As a result Christians need not resort to destructive and self-deceiving claims about the qualities they need to have, or the conditions of the world necessary to have children. Perhaps more worrisome than the moral implications of the claim "no unwanted child ought ever to be born," are the ominous assumptions about what is required for one to "want" to have a child.

Christians are thus trained to be the kind of people who are ready to receive and welcome children into the world. For they see children as a sign of the trustworthiness of God's creation and his unwillingness to abandon the world to the powers of darkness.

The Christian prohibition of abortion is but the negative side of their positive commitment to welcome new life into their community: life that they know must challenge and perhaps even change their own interpretation of their tradition, but also life without which the tradition has no means to grow.

It is, of course, true that children will often be conceived and born under less than ideal conditions, but the church lives as a community which assumes that we live in an age which is always dangerous. That we live in such a time is all the more reason we must be the kind of community that can receive children into our midst. Just as we need to be virtuous, not because virtue pays but because we cannot afford to be without virtue where it does not pay, so we must learn how to be people open to new life. We can neither protect them from that suffering nor deny them the joy of participating in the adventure of God's Kingdom.

For Christians, therefore, there can be no question of whether the fetus is or is not a "human being." That way of putting the matter is far too abstract and formal. Rather, because of the kind of community we are, we see in the fetus nothing less than God's continuing creation that is destined in hope to be another citizen of his Kingdom. The question of when human life begins is of little interest to such a people, since their hope is that life will and does continue to begin time after time.[37]

This is the form of life that brings significance to our interaction with the fetus. Our history is the basis for our "natural" sympathies, which have been trained to look forward to the joy and challenge of new life. Wertheimer may well be right that there is no corresponding "natural" welcome for life in our society that would make intelligible the recognition of the fetus as having moral status. Yet I suspect that the expectation of parents, and in particular of women, for the birth of their children remains a powerful form of life that continues to exert a force on everyone. Such an "expectation," however, in the absence of more substantive convictions about parenting, too easily becomes a destructive necessity that distorts the experience of being a parent and a child. Particularly repugnant is the assumption that women are thus primarily defined by the role of "mother," for then we forget that the role of being a parent, even for the childless, is a responsibility for everyone in the Christian community.

Nor should it be thought that the Christian commitment to welcome new life into the world stems from a sentimental fondness for babies. Rather, for Christians the having of children is one of their most significant political acts. From the world's perspective the birth of a child represents but another drain on our material and psychological resources. Children, after all, take up much of our energy that could be spent on making the world a better place and our society more just. But from the Christian perspective the birth of a child represents nothing less than our commitment that God will not have this world "bettered" by destroying life. That is why there is no more profound political act for Christians than taking the time for children. It is but an indication that God, not man, rules this existence, and we have been graciously invited to have a part in God's adventure and his Kingdom through the simple action of having children.

Christians and Abortion: The Immediate Political Task

To some it may seem that I have argued Christians right out of the current controversy, for my argument has made appeal to religious convictions that are inadmissible in the court of our public ethos. But it has certainly not been my intention to make it implausible for Christians to continue to work in the public arena for the protection of all children; nor do I think that this implication follows from the position I have developed. Of course, Christians should prefer to live in societies that provide protection for children. And Christians should certainly wish to encourage those "natural" sentiments that would provide a basis for having and protecting children.

Moreover Christians must be concerned to develop forms of care and support, the absence of which seem to make abortion such a necessity in our society. In particular Christians should, in their own communities, make clear that the role of parent is one we all share. Thus the woman who is pregnant and carrying the child need not be the one to raise it. We must be a people who stand ready to receive and care for any child, not just as if it were one of ours, but because in fact each is one of ours.

But as Christians we must not confuse our political and moral strategies designed to get the best possible care for children in our society with the substance of our convictions. Nor should we hide the latter in the interest of securing the former. For when that is done we abandon our society to its own limits. And then our arguments fall silent in the most regrettable manner, for we forget that our most fundamental political task is to be and to point to that truth which we believe to be the necessary basis for any life-enhancing and just society.

In particular, I think that we will be wise as Christians to state our opposition to abortion in a manner that makes clear our broader concerns for the kind of people we ought to be to welcome children into the world. Therefore, rather than concentrating our energies on whether the fetus is or is not a "person," we would be better advised by example and then argument to make clear why we should hope it is a child. We must show that such a hope involves more than just the question of the status of the fetus, but indeed is the very reason why being a part of God's creation is such an extraordinary and interesting adventure.

Endnotes

1. Roe v. Wade, 410 U.S. 113.

2. For example see Mary Anne Warren, "On the Moral and Legal Status of Abortion," in *Contemporary Issues in Bioethics,* ed. I. Beauchamp and L. Walters (Encino: Dickenson Publishing Co., 1978), pp. 222–225. Warren's argument in this respect is common in current philosophical literature. Perhaps the most celebrated form of it is Michael Tooley's article, "Abortion and Infanticide," in *The Rights and Wrongs of Abortion*, ed. M. Cohen, T. Nagel, and T. Scanlon (Princeton, N.J.: Princeton University Press, 1974), pp. 52–84.

3. Thus Warren argues that "the moral community consists of all and only *people,* rather than all and only human beings," and the characteristics of the former she takes to be consciousness, reasoning, self-motivated activity, the capacity to communicate whatever the means, and presence of self-concepts, pp. 223–224. For an extremely interesting article dealing with the ambiguity of deciding whether a class of beings are human see Edmund Pincoffs, "Membership Decisions and the Limits of Moral Obligation," in *Abortion: New Directions for Policy Studies*, ed. E. Manier, W. Liu, and D. Solomon (Notre Dame, Ind.: University of Notre Dame Press, 1977), pp. 31–49. I have argued elsewhere against the significance of "person" as a moral ascription, but it is hard to deny its significance in a society such as ours. For the idea of "person" embodies our attempt to recognize that everyone has a moral status prior to any role they might assume. It therefore represents the profound egalitarian commitment of our culture. The difficulty, of course, is that the notion of being a "person" seems to carry with it psychological implications that simply exclude certain beings from being treated with respect. See my *Truthfulness and Tragedy* (Notre Dame, Ind.: University of Notre Dame Press, 1977), pp. 127–132, 157–163.

4. John Noonan *A Private Choice: Abortion in America in the Seventies* (New York: The Free Press, 1979), pp. 2–3. In his earlier essay, "An Almost Absolute Value in History," Noonan had argued that conception is the decisive moment of humanization because "at conception the being receives

the genetic code. It is this genetic information which determines his characteristics, which is the biological carrier of the possibility of human wisdom, which makes him a self-evolving being. A being with a human genetic code is man." In John T. Noonan, ed., *The Morality of Abortion* (Cambridge, Mass.: Harvard University Press, 1970), pp. 1–59. Noonan obviously no longer regards such empirical claims as decisive for establishing the moral status of the fetus, though they may certainly be sufficient for claiming that the fetus is a human being. Underlying the issue of the relation between the moral and descriptive status of the fetus may be the larger assumption that the distinction between facts and values, or better, how values include factual claims, makes sense. Thus the claim that the anti-abortionist is confusing a "moral" claim with a "factual" claim may involve the unwarranted assumption that such "facts" are not moral.

5. Thus Roger Wertheimer suggests that the anti-abortionist "realizes that, unless he uses religious premises, premises inadmissible in the court of common morality, he has no way of categorically condemning the killing of a fetus except by arguing that a fetus is a person." "Understanding the Abortion Argument," in *The Rights and Wrongs of Abortion,* p. 37. But, as we shall see, the assumption that there is a common morality with an agreed upon content can hardly be accepted in our society. Moreover, I hope to show that theological convictions play quite a different role than Wertheimer and many others seem to assume. For there is no theological means to determine when life begins. Indeed, a Christian understanding of the morality of abortion should make such a question irrelevant.

6. Noonan has made a strong case, for example, for a constitutional amendment that would not prohibit states from protecting unborn life if it is the will of their legislatures. Such an amendment would at least provide the possibility of a more refined moral debate on this issue in our society. Moreover it might result in laws that do not have the negative effect on other institutions, such as the family, that the current abortion ruling seems to involve: See Noonan; *A Private Choice,* pp. 178–188.

7. Alasdair MacIntyre, "How Virtues Become Vices," in *Evaluation and Explanation in Biomedical Sciences,* ed. Engelhardt and Spicker (Dordrecht: Reidel: 1974), p. 104.

8. Ironically the anti-traditional stance of liberalism results in self-deception, since liberalism is only intelligible in the light of its history. It is, of course, true that liberalism is an extremely complex phenomenon that is not easily characterized even by the most sophisticated forms of political theory. I associate liberalism, however, with the political philosophy of Rawls and Nozick, the political science of Dahl, and the economics of neo-capitalism. There often appear to be deep disagreements between the advocates of liberalism in America, but such disagreements are finally arguments between brothers.

9. Alasdair MacIntyre, "How to Identify Ethical Principles," *The Belmont Report: Ethical Principles and Guidelines for the Protection of Human Subjects of Research,* I (Washington, D.C.:

DHEW Publication No. (OS) 78-0013, 1978), article 10, pp. 9–10. For an extremely able development of this argument, see Philip Devine, *The Ethics of Homicide* (Ithaca, N.Y.: Cornell University Press, 1978). Devine argues "that acts of homicide are prima facie seriously wrong because they are acts of homicide, and not for any supposedly more fundamental reason, such as that they tend to produce disutility or are unjust or unkind, and that this prima facie wrongness cannot be overridden by merely utilitarian considerations," p. 11. He correctly refuses to try to give a further theoretical account for why unjustified homicide is wrong, since such an account necessarily has the effect of qualifying the prohibition.

10. MacIntyre, "How to Identify Ethical Principles," p. 10. Garry Wills' recent study of Jefferson certainly requires a reconsideration of Jefferson's position vis-à-vis Locke. Wills makes clear that Jefferson's position owes more to the communitarian strains of the Scottish Common Sense philosophers, such as Hutcheson, than had been suspected. An indication of the power of Locke and the general liberal-contractarian tradition in America is that, in spite of what Jefferson's own views might have been, they were simply interpreted through the eyes of Locke. See Garry Wills, *Inventing America: Jefferson's Declaration of Independence* (Garden City, N.Y.: Doubleday, 1978).

11. MacIntyre, "How to Identify Ethical Principles," p. 22. This change in perspective also makes clear why so many attempt to form all moral arguments in the language of "right." "Rights" become our way to protect ourselves from one another.

12. John Rawls, *A Theory of Justice* (Cambridge, Mass.: Harvard University Press, 1971), p. 327. One of the difficulties with Rawls' assumption that the meaning of justice can be separated from a conception of the good is that he ends up endorsing an understanding of the good to which he would object on other grounds. For, in spite of Rawls' richer view of the relation of individual and community in the last sections of *A Theory of Justice,* methodologically his position does not exclude the economic man enshrined in liberal theory.

13. Francis Canavan, "The Dilemma of Liberal Pluralism," *The Human Life Review* 5/3 (Summer 1979), p. 7. The social and political experience of the American people has often contained more profound moral commitments than our commitment to liberal ideology could express. As a result we have often been unable to give some of our most significant achievements political standing.

14. Ibid., p. 9.

15. Ibid., p. 14.

16. Ibid., p. 15.

17. Noonan, *A Private Choice,* pp. 153–169.

18. It is interesting, however, that women undergoing abortion often continue to describe the fetus as a baby or child. See, for example, Linda Bird Francke, *The Ambivalence of Abortion* (New York: Random House, 1978).

19. Noonan, *A Private Choice,* p. 175. Warren's attempt to deny that her arguments imply infanticide are interesting in this respect. She says that it would be wrong to kill a newborn infant, "because even if its parents do not want it and would not suffer from its destruction, there are other people who would like to have it, and would in all probability, be deprived of a great deal of pleasure by its destruction. Thus, infanticide is wrong for reasons analogous to those which make it wrong to wantonly destroy natural resources, or great works of art: Secondly, most people, at least in this country, value infants and would much prefer that they be preserved, even if foster parents are not immediately available," p. 227. Warren seems to feel no difficulty in making the prohibition against infanticide depend on whether someone might want a child. Moreover she is rigorously consistent and clear that if an "unwanted or defective infant is born into a society which cannot afford and/or is not willing to care for it, then its destruction is permissible," p. 227. It does not seem to occur to her that we ought to be the kind of society, no matter what our material appetites, that is able to receive children, even retarded children, into our midst. Her argument is a clear example, therefore, of the assumption that the rightness or wrongness of acts can be abstracted from the kind of people we ought to be.

20. Noonan, *A Private Choice,* pp. 90–96.

21. Ibid., p. 17.

22. The abortion decisions of the current Supreme Court can in some ways be interpreted as further extensions of the arguments of the laissez faire capitalist, only now they are being applied to issues of personal morality. Just as those earlier decisions that enshrined for a time such views as the law of the land regarding the regulation of business distorted the law, so do these recent decisions. Indeed there has always been an uneasy tension between our legal tradition and the ideology of liberalism. It may well be, however, that as liberalism has become an increasingly self-fulling prophecy in so many other aspects of our life, so it will ultimately transform our legal tradition.

23. It is my contention that current ethical theory involves an attempt to write about "morality" in a manner required by a liberal society. The very assumption that "ethics" can be a "discipline" separate from political theory and economics seems to me to be an indication of the power of liberalism over our imagination. Such moral philosophies attempt to provide highly formal accounts of the conditions of moral argument and judgment separate from the beliefs of actual agents. One cannot help but admire their attempt to find a way to make moral argument work between people who share no common values, but they fail to see that such accounts too easily become ideologies for the status quo.

24. Stuart Hampshire, "Morality and Pessimism," in *Public and Private Morality* ed. Hamphire (Cambridge: Cambridge University Press, 1978), p. 11.

25. Ibid., p. 13.

26. Ironically, Christians have often tried to construct their arguments by using moral theories, especially the more deontological theories, that make rationality the basis for any moral claim. Though these theories often provide powerful accounts for why everyone deserves a minimum of respect, by their very structure they exclude the fetus from their account.

27. Stuart Hampshire, "Public and Private Morality," in *Public and Private Morality,* pp. 38–39.

28. Wertheimer, p. 42. See Wertheimer's fine article, "Philosophy on Humanity," in *Abortion: New Directions for Policy Studies* (Notre Dame: University of Notre Dame Press, 1977), pp. 117–136.

29. I suspect that Wertheimer would not deny this point as he is not using "nature" in a theory-laden sense but simply means by it "what is common." Thus whereas we have many everyday experiences with blacks, we do not "bump into" the fetus in the same manner. Yet as I will argue below, there are powerful forms of life which are unintelligible apart from the existence of the fetus.

30. See for example John Connery's excellent history of moral reflection on the subject, *Abortion: The Development of the Roman Catholic Perspective* (Chicago: Loyola University Press, 1977).

31. In a sense, Christian discussion of abortion has been too "ethical" and insufficiently theological. In effect we became the victim of our own highly refined casuistry on the subject and failed to rethink the theological context that made the casuistry intelligible in the first place. Thus consideration of whether certain acts of abortion might be permissible were abstracted from the community's narrative that made the prohibition of abortion intelligible. No community can or should avoid casuistical reflection, but it should always remember that the function of casuistry is to help the community save its language and judgments from distortion through analogical comparisons. And control of the analogies ultimately depends on paradigms rooted in the community's experience as interpreted through its central narratives.

32. There is a broader issue involved here, which can only be mentioned. For just as liberalism has often "worked" only because it could continue to count on forms of life that it did not support and even worked against, so current ethical theory has often seemed intelligible because it continued to be able to rely on moral language and descriptions for which it can give little basis. Thus contemporary ethical theory tends to concentrate on questions of decision and justification and avoids issues of how we learn to see and describe our experience morally.

33. Karl Barth, *Church Dogmatics,* III/4, trans. MacKay, et al. (Edinburgh: T. and T. Clark, 1961), p. 416.

34. There is nothing about this claim that requires that all abortions are to be prohibited. Indeed, when abortions may be permitted will depend on the experience and discussion of a community formed by the conviction of God's sovereignty over life. The broad theological claims I am developing here cannot determine concrete cases, though they can determine how abortion as a practice can and should be understood and evaluated.

35. In his *The Culture of Narcissism* (New York: Norton, 1978), Christopher Lasch suggests that a people's sense of historical time and their attitudes toward children are closely interrelated. Thus "the narcissistic personality reflects among other things a drastic shift in our sense of historical time. Narcissism emerges as the typical form of character structure in a society that has lost interest in the future. Psychiatrists who tell parents not to live through their offspring; married couples who postpone or reject parenthood, often for good practical reasons; social reformers who urge zero population growth, all testify to a pervasive uneasiness about reproduction—to widespread doubts, indeed, about whether our society should reproduce itself at all. Under these conditions, the thought of our eventual suppression and death becomes utterly insupportable and gives rise to attempts to abolish old age and to extend life indefinitely. When men find themselves incapable of taking an interest in earthly life after their own death, they wish for eternal youth; for the same reason they no longer care to reproduce themselves. When the prospect of being superseded becomes intolerable, parenthood itself, which guarantees that it will happen, appears almost as a form of self-destruction," p. 211.

36. For a fuller presentation of this theme see my *Truthfulness and Tragedy*, pp. 147–156.

37. The issue of when life begins will of course come up in considering hard cases. Connery, for example, provides a good overview of the history of such reflection in his book. Yet just as hard cases make bad law, so hard cases can distort our moral reflection if, in the process of our reflection on them, we forget the more positive commitments that make the casuistry intelligible. It is noteworthy, however, as Connery makes clear, that the question of when life begins has always been a side issue for Christian casuistry. Rather, the concern has been whether the taking of the life of the fetus under particular circumstances is analogous to other situations where it is unavoidable or permissible that life be taken.

21.   A *Defense of Abortion*

Judith Jarvis Thomson

Judith Jarvis Thomson, though an advocate of abortion rights, grants for argument's sake the conservative premise that the fetus is a full-fledged member of the moral community with a right to life. But she goes on to argue that such an assumption does not serve to rule out abortions in cases in which the mother's life is in danger, in cases of rape, or in cases of pregnancy caused by unintended, failed contraception. The rights of the mother in these cases may well override the right to life granted to the fetus.

Most opposition to abortion relies on the premise that the fetus is a human being, a person, from the moment of conception. The premise is argued for, but, as I think, not well. Take, for example, the most common argument. We are asked to notice that the development

From Judith Jarvis Thomson, "A Defense of Abortion," *Philosophy & Public Affairs*, 1, no. 1 (Fall 1971). Reprinted with permission from Blackwell Publishing Ltd. Ms. Thomson acknowledges her indebtness to James Thomson for discussion, criticism, and many helpful suggestions.

of a human being from conception through birth into childhood is continuous; then it is said that to draw a line, to choose a point in this development and say "before this point the thing is not a person, after this point it is a person" is to make an arbitrary choice, a choice for which in the nature of things no good reason can be given. It is concluded that the fetus is, or anyway that we had better say it is, a person from the moment of conception. But this conclusion does not follow. Similar things might be said about the development of an acorn into an oak tree, and it does not follow that acorns are oak trees, or that we had better say they are. Arguments of this form are sometimes called "slippery slope arguments"—the phrase is perhaps self-explanatory—and it is dismaying that opponents of abortion rely on them so heavily and uncritically.

I am inclined to agree, however, that the prospects for "drawing a line" in the development of the fetus look dim. I am inclined to think also that we shall probably have to agree that the fetus has already become a human person well before birth. Indeed, it comes as a surprise when one first learns how early in its life it begins to acquire human characteristics. By the tenth week, for example, it already has a face, arms and legs, fingers and toes; it has internal organs, and brain activity is detectable.[1] On the other hand, I think that the premise is false, that the fetus is not a person from the moment of conception. A newly fertilized ovum, a newly implanted clump of cells, is no more a person than an acorn is an oak tree. But I shall not discuss any of this. For it seems to me to be of great interest to ask what happens if, for the sake of argument, we allow the premise. How, precisely, are we supposed to get from there to the conclusion that abortion is morally impermissible? Opponents of abortion commonly spend most of their time establishing that the fetus is a person, and hardly any time explaining the step from there to the impermissibility of abortion. Perhaps they think the step too simple and obvious to require much comment. Or perhaps instead they are simply being economical in argument. Many of those who defend abortion rely on the premise that the fetus is not a person, but only a bit of tissue that will become a person at birth; and why pay out more arguments than you have to? Whatever the explanation, I suggest that the step they take is neither easy nor obvious, that it calls for closer examination than it is commonly given, and that when we do give it this closer examination we shall feel inclined to reject it.

I propose, then, that we grant that the fetus is a person from the moment of conception. How does the argument go from here? Something like this, I take it. Every person has a right to life. So the fetus has a right to life. No doubt the mother has a right to decide what shall happen in and to her body; everyone would grant that. But surely a person's right to life is stronger and more stringent than the mother's right to decide what happens in and to her body, and so outweighs it. So the fetus may not be killed; an abortion may not be performed.

It sounds plausible. But now let me ask you to imagine this. You wake up in the morning and find yourself back to back in bed with an unconscious violinist. A famous unconscious violinist. He has been found to have a fatal kidney ailment, and the Society of Music Lovers has canvassed all the available medical records and found that you alone have the right blood type to help. They have therefore kidnapped you, and last night the violinist's circulatory system was plugged into yours, so that your kidneys can be used to extract poisons from his blood as well as your own. The director of the hospital now tells you, "Look, we're sorry the Society of Music Lovers did this to you—we would never have permitted it if we had known. But still, they did it, and the violinist now is plugged into you. To unplug you would be to kill him. But never mind, it's only for nine months. By then he will have recovered from his ailment, and can safely be unplugged from you." Is it morally incumbent on you to accede to this situation? No doubt it would be very nice of you if you did, a great kindness. But do you *have* to accede to it? What if it were not nine months, but nine years? Or lo... of the hospital says, ...ow got to stay in bed, ...u, for the rest of your ...ersons have a right to ...nted you have a right ...your body, but a per... ...right to decide what ...you cannot ever be ...ou would regard this ...ggests that something really is wrong with that plausible-sounding argument I mentioned a moment ago.

In this case, of course, you were kidnapped; you didn't volunteer for the operation that plugged the violinist into your kidneys. Can those who oppose abortion on the ground I mentioned make an exception for a pregnancy due to rape? Certainly. They can say that persons have a right to life only if they didn't come into existence because of rape; or they can say that all persons have a right to life, but that some have less of a right to life than others, in particular, that those who came into existence because of rape have less. But these statements have a rather unpleasant sound. Surely the question of whether you have a right to life at all, or how much of it you have, shouldn't turn on the question of whether or not you are the product of a rape. And in fact the people who oppose abortion on the ground I mentioned do not make this distinction, and hence do not make an exception in the case of rape.

Nor do they make an exception for a case in which the mother has to spend the nine months of her pregnancy in bed. They would agree that would be a great pity, and hard on the mother; but all the same, all persons have a right to life, the fetus is a person, and so on. I suspect, in fact, that they would not make an exception for a case in which, miraculously enough, the pregnancy went on for nine years, or even the rest of the mother's life.

Some won't even make an exception for a case in which continuation of the pregnancy is likely to shorten the mother's life; they regard abortion as impermissible even to save the mother's life. Such cases are nowadays very rare, and many opponents of abortion do not accept this extreme view. All the same, it is a good place to begin: A number of points of interest come out in respect to it.

1. Let us call the view that abortion is impermissible even to save the mother's life "the extreme view." I want to suggest first that it does not issue from the argument I mentioned earlier without the addition of some fairly powerful premises. Suppose a woman has become pregnant, and now learns that she has a cardiac condition such that she will die if she carries the baby to term. What may be done for her? The fetus, being a person, has a right to life, but as the mother is a person too, so has she a right to life. Presumably they have an equal right to life. How is it supposed to come out that an abortion may not be performed? If mother and child have an equal right to life, shouldn't we perhaps flip a coin? Or should we add to the mother's right to life her right to decide what happens in and to her body, which everybody seems to be ready to grant—the sum of her rights now outweighing the fetus' right to life?

The most familiar argument here is the following. We are told that performing the abortion would be directly killing[2] the child, whereas doing nothing would not be killing the mother, but only letting her die. Moreover, in killing the child, one would be killing an innocent person, for the child has committed no crime, and is not aiming at his mother's death. And then there are a variety of ways in which this might be continued. (1) But as directly killing an innocent person is always and absolutely impermissible, an abortion may not be performed. Or, (2) as directly killing an innocent person is murder, and murder is always and absolutely impermissible, an abortion may not be performed.[3] Or, (3) as one's duty to refrain from directly killing an innocent person is more stringent than one's duty to keep a person from dying, an abortion may not be performed. Or, (4) if one's only options are directly killing an innocent person or letting a person die, one must prefer letting the person die, and thus an abortion may not be performed.[4]

Some people seem to have thought that these are not further premises which must be added if the conclusion is to be reached, but that they follow from the very fact that an innocent person has a right to life.[5] But this seems to me to be a mistake, and perhaps the simplest way to show this is to bring out that while we must certainly grant that innocent persons have a right to life, the theses in (1) through (4) are all false. Take (2), for example. If directly killing an innocent person is murder, and thus is impermissible, then the mother's directly killing the innocent person inside her is murder, and thus is impermissible. But it cannot seriously be thought to be murder if the mother performs an abortion on herself to save her life. It cannot seriously be said that she *must* refrain, that she *must* sit passively by and wait for her death. Let us look again at the case of you and the violinist. There you are, in bed with the violinist, and the director of the hospital says to you, "It's all most distressing, and I deeply sympathize, but you see this is putting an additional strain on your kidneys, and you'll be dead within the month. But you *have* to stay where you are all the same. Because unplugging you would be directly killing an innocent violinist, and that's murder, and that's impermissible." If anything in the world is true, it is that you do not commit murder, you do not do what is impermissible, if you reach around to your back and unplug yourself from that violinist to save your life.

The main focus of attention in writings on abortion has been on what a third party may or may not do in answer to a request from a women for an abortion. This is in a way understandable. Things being as they are, there isn't much a woman can safely do to abort herself. So the question asked is what a third party may do, and what the mother may do, if it is mentioned at all, is deduced, almost as an afterthought, from what it is concluded that third parties may do. But it seems to me that to treat the matter in this way is to refuse to grant to the mother that very status of person which is so firmly insisted on for the fetus. For we cannot simply read off what a person may do from what a third party may do. Suppose you find yourself trapped in a tiny house with a growing child. I mean a very tiny house, and a rapidly growing child—you are already up against the wall of the house and in a few minutes you'll be crushed to death. The child on the other hand won't be crushed to death; if nothing is done to stop him from growing he'll be hurt, but in the end he'll simply burst open the house and walk out a free man. Now I could well understand it if a bystander were to say, "There's nothing we can do for you. We cannot choose between your life and his, we cannot be the ones to decide who is to live, we cannot intervene." But it cannot be concluded that you too can do nothing, that you cannot attack it to save your life. However innocent the child may be, you do not have to wait passively while it crushes you to death. Perhaps a pregnant woman is vaguely felt to have the status of house, to which we don't allow the right of self-defense. But if the woman houses the child, it should be remembered that she is a person who houses it.

I should perhaps stop to say explicitly that I am not claiming that people have a right to do anything whatever to save their lives. I think, rather, that there are drastic limits to the right of self-defense. If someone threatens you with death unless you torture someone else to death, I think you have not the right, even to save your life, to do so. But the case under consideration here is very different. In our case there are only two people involved, one whose life is threatened, and one who threatens it. Both are innocent: The one who is threatened is not threatened because of any fault, the one who threatens does not threaten because of any fault. For this reason we may feel that we bystanders cannot intervene. But the person threatened can.

In sum, a woman surely can defend her life against the threat to it posed by the unborn child, even if doing so involves its death. And this shows not merely that the theses in (1) through (4) are false; it shows also that the extreme view of abortion is false, and so we need not canvass any other possible ways of arriving at it from the argument I mentioned at the outset.

2. The extreme view could of course be weakened to say that while abortion is permissible to save the mother's life, it may not be performed by a third party, but only by the mother herself. But this cannot be right either. For what we have to keep in mind is that the mother and the unborn child are not like two tenants in a small house which has, by an unfortunate mistake, been rented to both: The mother *owns* the house. The fact that she does adds to the offensiveness of deducing that the mother can do nothing from the supposition that third parties can do nothing. But it does more than this: It casts a bright light on the supposition that third parties can do nothing. Certainly it lets us see that a third party who says "I cannot choose between you" is fooling himself if he thinks this is impartiality. If Jones has found and fastened on a certain coat, which he needs to keep him from freezing, but which Smith also needs to keep him from freezing, then it is not impartiality that says "I cannot choose between you" when Smith owns the coat. Women have said again and again "This body is *my* body!" and they have reason to feel

angry, reason to feel that it has been like shouting into the wind. Smith, after all, is hardly likely to bless us if we say to him, "Of course it's your coat, anybody would grant that it is. But no one may choose between you and Jones who is to have it."

We should really ask what it is that says "no one may choose" in the face of the fact that the body that houses the child is the mother's body. It may be simply a failure to appreciate this fact. But it may be something more interesting, namely the sense that one has a right to refuse to lay hands on people, even where it would be just and fair to do so, even where justice seems to require that somebody do so. Thus justice might call for somebody to get Smith's coat back from Jones, and yet you have a right to refuse to be the one to lay hands on Jones, a right to refuse to do physical violence to him. This, I think, must be granted. But then what should be said is not "no one may choose," but only "*I* cannot choose," and indeed not even this, but "*I* will not *act*," leaving it open that somebody else can or should, and in particular that anyone in a position of authority, with the job of securing people's rights, both can and should. So this is no difficulty. I have not been arguing that any given third party must accede to the mother's request that he perform an abortion to save her life, but only that he may.

I suppose that in some views of human life the mother's body is only on loan to her, the loan not being one which gives her any prior claim to it. One who held this view might well think it impartiality to say "I cannot choose." But I shall simply ignore this possibility. My own view is that if a human being has any just, prior claim to anything at all, he has a just, prior claim to his own body. And perhaps this needn't be argued for here anyway, since, as I mentioned, the arguments against abortion we are looking at do grant that the woman has a right to decide what happens in and to her body.

But although they do grant it, I have tried to show that they do not take seriously what is done in granting it. I suggest the same thing will reappear even more clearly when we turn away from cases in which the mother's life is at stake, and attend, as I propose we now do, to the vastly more common cases in which a woman wants an abortion for some less weighty reason than preserving her own life.

3. Where the mother's life is not at stake, the argument I mentioned at the outset seems to have a much stronger pull. "Everyone has a right to life, so the unborn person has a right to life." And isn't the child's right to life weightier than anything other than the mother's own right to life, which she might put forward as ground for an abortion?

This argument treats the right to life as if it were unproblematic. It is not, and this seems to me to be precisely the source of the mistake.

For we should now, at long last, ask what it comes to, to have a right to life. In some views having a right to life includes having a right to be given at least the bare minimum one needs for continued life. But suppose that what in fact *is* the bare minimum a man needs for continued life is something he has no right at all to be given? If I am sick unto death, and the only thing that will save my life is the touch of Henry Fonda's cool hand on my fevered brow, then all the same, I have no right to be given the touch of Henry Fonda's cool hand on my fevered brow. It would be frightfully nice of him to fly in from the West Coast to provide it. It would be less nice, though no doubt well meant, if my friends flew out to the West Coast and carried Henry Fonda back with them. But I have no right at all against anybody that he should do this for me. Or again, to return to the story I told earlier, the fact that for continued life that violinist needs the continued use of your kidneys does not establish that he has a right to be given the continued use of your kidneys. He certainly has no right against you that *you* should give him continued use of your kidneys. For nobody has any right to use your kidneys unless you give him such a right; and nobody has the right against you that you shall give him this right—if you do allow him to go on using your kidneys, this is a kindness on your part, and not something he can claim from you as his due. Nor has he any right against anybody else that *they* should give him continued use of your kidneys. Certainly he had no right against the Society of Music Lovers that they should plug him into you in the first place. And if you now start to unplug yourself, having learned that you will otherwise have to spend nine years in bed with him, there is nobody in the world who must try to prevent you, in order to see to it that he is given something he has a right to be given.

Some people are rather stricter about the right to life. In their view, it does not include the right to be given anything, but amounts to, and only to, the right not to be killed by anybody. But here a related difficulty arises. If everybody is to refrain from killing that violinist, then everybody must refrain from doing a great many different sorts of things. Everybody must refrain from slitting his throat, everybody must refrain from shooting him—and everybody must refrain from unplugging you from him. But does he have a right against everybody that they shall refrain from unplugging you from him? To refrain from doing this is to

allow him to continue to use your kidneys. It could be argued that he has a right against us that *we* should allow him to continue to use your kidneys. That is, while he had no right against us that we should give him the use of your kidneys, it might be argued that he anyway has a right against us that we shall not now intervene and deprive him of the use of your kidneys. I shall come back to third-party interventions later. But certainly the violinist has no right against you that *you* shall allow him to continue to use your kidneys. As I said, if you do allow him to use them, it is a kindness on your part, and not something you owe him.

The difficulty I point to here is not peculiar to the right of life. It reappears in connection with all the other natural rights; and it is something which an adequate account of rights must deal with. For present purposes it is enough just to draw attention to it. But I would stress that I am not arguing that people do not have a right to life—quite to the contrary, it seems to me that the primary control we must place on the acceptability of an account of rights is that it should turn out in that account to be a truth that all persons have a right to life. I am arguing only that having a right to life does not guarantee having either a right to be given the use of or a right to be allowed continued use of another person's body—even if one needs it for life itself. So the right to life will not serve the opponents of abortion in the very simple and clear way in which they seem to have thought it would.

4. There is another way to bring out the difficulty. In the most ordinary sort of case, to deprive someone of what he has a right to is to treat him unjustly. Suppose a boy and his small brother are jointly given a box of chocolates for Christmas. If the older boy takes the box and refuses to give his brother any of the chocolates, he is unjust to him, for the brother has been given a right to half of them. But suppose that, having learned that otherwise it means nine years in bed with that violinist, you unplug yourself from him. You surely are not being unjust to him, for you gave him no right to use your kidneys, and no one else can have given him any such right. But we have to notice that in unplugging yourself, you are killing him; and violinists, like everybody else, have a right to life, and thus in the view we were considering just now, the right not to be killed. So here you do what he supposedly has a right you shall not do, but you do not act unjustly to him in doing it.

The emendation which may be made at this point is this: The right to life consists not in the right not to be killed, but rather in the right not to be killed unjustly. This runs a risk of circularity, but never mind: It would enable us to square the fact that the violinist has a right to life with the fact that you do not act unjustly toward him in unplugging yourself, thereby killing him. For if you do not kill him unjustly, you do not violate his right to life, and so it is no wonder you do him no injustice.

But if this emendation is accepted, the gap in the argument against abortion stares us plainly in the face: It is by no means enough to show that the fetus is a person, and to remind us that all persons have a right to life—we need to be shown also that killing the fetus violates its right to life, i.e., that abortion is unjust killing. And is it?

I suppose we may take it as a datum that in the case of pregnancy due to rape the mother has not given the unborn person a right to the use of her body for food and shelter. Indeed, in what pregnancy should it be supposed that the mother has given the unborn person such a right? It is not as if there were unborn persons drifting about the world, to whom a woman who wants a child says "I invite you in."

But it might be argued that there are other ways one can have acquired a right to the use of another person's body than by having been invited to use it by that person. Suppose a woman voluntarily indulges in intercourse, knowing of the chance it will issue in pregnancy, and then she does become pregnant; is she not in part responsible for the presence, in fact the very existence, of the unborn person inside? No doubt she did not invite it in. But doesn't her partial responsibility for its being there itself give it a right to the use of her body?[6] If so, then her aborting it would be more like the boy's taking away the chocolates, and less like your unplugging yourself from the violinist—doing so would be depriving it of what it does have a right to, and thus would be doing it an injustice.

And then, too, it might be asked whether or not she can kill it even to her own life: If she voluntarily called it into existence, how can she now kill it, even in self-defense?

The first thing to be said about this is that it is something new. Opponents of abortion have been so concerned to make out the independence of the fetus, in order to establish that it has a right to life, just as its mother does, that they have tended to overlook the possible support they might gain from making out that the fetus is *dependent* on the mother, in order to establish that she has a special kind of responsibility for it, a responsibility that gives it rights against her which are not possessed by any independent person—such as an ailing violinist who is a stranger to her.

On the other hand, this argument would give the unborn person a right to its mother's body only if her pregnancy resulted from a voluntary act, undertaken in full knowledge of the chance a pregnancy might result from it. It would leave out entirely the unborn person whose existence is due to rape. Pending the availability of some further argument, then, we would be left with the conclusion that unborn persons whose existence is due to rape have no right to the use of their mothers' bodies, and thus that aborting them is not depriving them of anything they have a right to and hence is not unjust killing.

And we should also notice that it is not at all plain that this argument really does go even as far as it purports to. For there are cases and cases, and the details make a difference. If the room is stuffy, and I therefore open a window to air it, and a burglar climbs in, it would be absurd to say, "Ah, now he can stay, she's given him a right to the use of her house—for she is partially responsible for his presence there, having voluntarily done what enabled him to get in, in full knowledge that there are such things as burglars, and that burglars burgle." It would be still more absurd to say this if I had had bars installed outside my windows, precisely to prevent burglars from getting in, and a burglar got in only because of a defect in the bars. It remains equally absurd if we imagine it is not a burglar who climbs in, but an innocent person who blunders or falls in. Again, suppose it were like this: Peopleseeds drift about in the air like pollen, and if you open your windows, one may drift in and take root in your carpets or upholstery. You don't want children, so you fix up your windows with fine mesh screens, the very best you can buy. As can happen, however, and on very, very rare occasions does happen, one of the screens is defective; and a seed drifts in and takes root. Does the personplant who now develops have a right to the use of your house? Surely not—despite the fact that you voluntarily opened your windows, you knowingly kept carpets and upholstered furniture, and you knew that screens were sometimes defective. Someone may argue that you are responsible for its rooting, that it does have a right to your house, because after all you *could* have lived out your life with bare floors and furniture, or with sealed windows and doors. But this won't do—for by the same token anyone can avoid a pregnancy due to rape by having a hysterectomy, or anyway by never leaving home without a (reliable!) army.

It seems to me that the argument we are looking at can establish at most that there are *some* cases in which the unborn person has a right to the use of its mother's body, and therefore *some* cases in which abortion is unjust killing. There is room for much discussion and argument as to precisely which, if any. But I think we should sidestep this issue and leave it open, for at any rate the argument certainly does not establish that all abortion is unjust killing.

5. There is room for yet another argument here, however. We surely must grant that there may be cases in which it would be morally indecent to detach a person from your body at the cost of his life. Suppose you learn that what the violinist needs is not nine years of your life, but only one hour: All you need do to save his life is spend one hour in that bed with him. Suppose also that letting him use your kidneys for that one hour would not affect your health in the slightest. Admittedly you were kidnapped. Admittedly you did not give anyone permission to plug him into you. Nevertheless it seems to me plain you *ought* to allow him to use your kidneys for that hour—it would be indecent to refuse.

Again, suppose pregnancy lasted only an hour, and constituted no threat to life or death [sic]. And suppose that a woman becomes pregnant as a result of rape. Admittedly she did not voluntarily do anything to bring about the existence of a child. Admittedly she did nothing at all which would give the unborn person a right to the use of her body. All the same it might well be said, as in the newly emended violinist story, that she *ought* to allow it to remain for that hour—that it would be indecent in her to refuse.

Now some people are inclined to use the term "right" in such a way that it follows from the fact that you ought to allow a person to use your body for the hour he needs, that he has a right to use your body for the hour he needs, even though he has not been given that right by any person or act. They may say that it follows also that if you refuse, you act unjustly toward him. This use of the term is perhaps so common that it cannot be called wrong; nevertheless it seems to me to be an unfortunate loosening of what we would better to keep a tight rein on. Suppose that box of chocolates I mentioned earlier had not been given to both boys jointly, but was given only to the older boy. There he sits, stolidly eating his way through the box, his small brother watching enviously. Here we are likely to say "You ought not to be so mean. You ought to give your brother some of those chocolates." My own view is that it just does not follow from the truth of this that the brother has any right to any of the chocolates. If the boy refuses to give his brother any, he is greedy, stingy, callous—but not unjust. I suppose that the people I

have in mind will say it does follow that the brother has a right to some of the chocolates, and thus that the boy does act unjustly if he refuses to give his brother any. But the effect of saying this is to obscure what we should keep distinct, namely the difference between the boy's refusal in this case and the boy's refusal in the earlier case, in which the box was given to both boys jointly, and in which the small brother thus had what was from any point of view clear title to half.

A further objection to so using the term "right" that from the fact that A ought to do a thing for B, it follows that B has a right against A that A do it for him, is that it is going to make the question of whether or not a man has a right to a thing turn on how easy it is to provide him with it; and this seems not merely unfortunate, but morally unacceptable. Take the case of Henry Fonda again. I said earlier that I had no right to the touch of his cool hand on my fevered brow, even though I needed it to save my life. I said it would be frightfully nice of him to fly in from the West Coast to provide me with it, but that I had no right against him that he should do so. But suppose he isn't on the West Coast. Suppose he has only to walk across the room, place a hand briefly on my brow—and lo, my life is saved. Then surely he ought to do it, it would be indecent to refuse. Is it to be said, "Ah, well, it follows that in this case she has a right to the touch of his hand on her brow, and so it would be an unjustice in him to refuse"? So that I have a right to it when it is easy for him to provide it, though no right when it's hard? It's rather a shocking idea that anyone's rights should fade away and disappear as it gets harder and harder to accord them to him.

So my own view is that even though you ought to let the violinist use your kidneys for the one hour he needs, we should not conclude that he has a right to do so—we should say that if you refuse, you are, like the boy who owns all the chocolates and will give none away, self-centered and callous, indecent in fact, but not unjust. And similarly, that even supposing a case in which a woman pregnant due to rape ought to allow the unborn person to use her body for the hour he needs, we should not conclude that he has a right to do so; we should conclude that she is self-centered, callous, indecent, but not unjust, if she refuses. The complaints are no less grave; they are just different. However, there is no need to insist on this point. If anyone does wish to deduce "he has a right" from "you ought," then all the same he must surely grant that there are cases in which it is not morally required of you that you allow that violinist to use your kidneys, and in which he does not have a right to use them, and in which you do not do him an injustice if you refuse. And so also for mother and unborn child. Except in such cases as the unborn person has a right to demand it—and we were leaving open the possibility that there may be such cases—nobody is morally *required* to make large sacrifices, of health, of all other interests and concerns, of all other duties and commitments, for nine years, or even for nine months, in order to keep another person alive.

6. We have in fact to distinguish between the two kinds of Samaritan: the Good Samaritan and what we might call the Minimally Decent Samaritan. The story of the Good Samaritan, you will remember, goes like this:

> A certain man went down from Jerusalem to Jericho, and fell among thieves, which stripped him of his raiment, and wounded him, and departed, leaving him half dead.
>
> And by chance there came down a certain priest that way; and when he saw him, he passed by on the other side.
>
> And likewise a Levite, when he was at the place, came and looked on him, and passed by on the other side.
>
> But a certain Samaritan, as he journeyed, came where he was; and when he saw him he had compassion on him.
>
> And went to him, and bound up his wounds, pouring in oil and wine, and set him on his own beast, and brought him to an inn, and took care of him.
>
> And on the morrow, when he departed, he took out two pence, and gave them to the host, and said unto him, "Take care of him; and whatsoever thou spendest more, when I come again, I will repay thee."
>
> (Luke 10:30–35)

The Good Samaritan went out of his way, at some cost to himself, to help one in need of it. We are not told what the options were, that is, whether or not the priest and the Levite could have helped by doing less than the Good Samaritan did, but assuming they could have, then the fact they did nothing at all shows they were not even Minimally Decent Samaritans, not because they were not Samaritans, but because they were not even minimally decent.

These things are a matter of degree, of course, but there is a difference, and it comes out perhaps most clearly in the story of Kitty Genovese, who, as you will remember, was murdered while thirty-eight people watched or listened, and did nothing at all to help her. A Good Samaritan would have rushed out to give direct assistance against the murderer. Or perhaps we had better allow that it would have been a Splendid Samaritan who did this, on the ground that it would have involved a risk of death for himself. But the thirty-eight not only did not do this, they did not even trouble to pick up a phone to call the police. Minimally Decent Samaritanism would call for doing at least that, and their not having done it was monstrous.

After telling the story of the Good Samaritan, Jesus said, "Go, and do thou likewise." Perhaps he meant that we are morally required to act as the Good Samaritan did. Perhaps he was urging people to do more than is morally required of them. At all events it seems plain that it was not morally required of any of the thirty-eight that he rush out to give direct assistance at the risk of his own life, and that it is not morally required of anyone that he give long stretches of his life—nine years or nine months—to sustaining the life of a person who has no special right (we were leaving open the possibility of this) to demand it.

Indeed, with one rather striking class of exceptions, no one in any country in the world is *legally* required to do anywhere near as much as this for anyone else. The class of exceptions is obvious. My main concern here is not the state of the law in respect to abortion, but it is worth drawing attention to the fact that in no state in this country is any man compelled by law to be even a Minimally Decent Samaritan to any person; there is no law under which charges could be brought against the thirty-eight who stood by while Kitty Genovese died. By contrast, in most states in this country women are compelled by law to be not merely Minimally Decent Samaritans, but Good Samaritans to unborn persons inside them. This doesn't by itself settle anything one way or the other, because it may well be argued that there should be laws in this country—as there are in many European countries—compelling at least Minimally Decent Samaritanism.[7] But it does show that there is a gross injustice in the existing state of the law. And it shows also that the groups currently working against liberalization of abortion laws, in fact working toward having it declared unconstitutional for a state to permit abortion, had better start working for the adoption of Good Samaritan laws generally, or earn the charge that they are acting in bad faith.

I should think, myself, that Minimally Decent Samaritan laws would be one thing, Good Samaritan laws quite another, and in fact highly improper. But we are not here concerned with the law. What we should ask is not whether anybody should be compelled by law to be a Good Samaritan, but whether we must accede to a situation in which somebody is being compelled—by nature, perhaps—to be a Good Samaritan. We have, in other words, to look now at third-party interventions. I have been arguing that no person is morally required to make large sacrifices to sustain the life of another who has no right to demand them, and this even where the sacrifices do not include life itself; we are not morally required to be Good Samaritans or anyway Very Good Samaritans to one another. But what if a man cannot extricate himself from such a situation? What if he appeals to us to extricate him? It seems to me plain that there are cases in which we can, cases in which a Good Samaritan would extricate him. There you are, you were kidnapped, and nine years in bed with that violinist lie ahead of you. You have your own life to lead. You are sorry, but you simply cannot see giving up so much of your life to the sustaining of his. You cannot extricate yourself, and ask us to do so. I should have thought that—in light of his having no right to the use of your body—it was obvious that we do not have to accede to your being forced to give up so much. We can do what you ask. There is no injustice to the violinist in our doing so.

7. Following the lead of the opponents of abortion, I have throughout been speaking of the fetus merely as a person, and what I have been asking is whether or not the argument we began with, which proceeds only from the fetus' being a person, really does establish its conclusion. I have argued that it does not.

But of course there are arguments and arguments, and it may be said that I have simply fastened on the wrong one. It may be said that what is important is not merely the fact that the fetus is a person, but that it is a person for whom the woman has a special kind of responsibility issuing from the fact that she is its mother. And it might be argued that all my analogies are therefore irrelevant—for you do not have that special kind of responsibility for that violinist, Henry Fonda does not have that special kind of responsibility for me. And our attention might be drawn to the fact that men and women both *are* compelled by law to provide support for their children.

I have in effect dealt (briefly) with this argument in section 4 above; but a (still briefer) recapitulation now may be in order. Surely we do not have any such "special responsibility" for a person unless we have assumed it, explicitly or implicitly. If a set of parents do not try to prevent pregnancy do not obtain an abor-

tion, but rather take it home with them, then they have assumed responsibility for it, they have given it rights, and they cannot *now* withdraw support from it at the cost of its life because they now find it difficult to go on providing for it. But if they have taken all reasonable precautions against having a child, they do not simply by virtue of their biological relationship to the child who comes into existence have a special responsibility for it. They may wish to assume responsibility for it, or they may not wish to. And I am suggesting that if assuming responsibility for it would require large sacrifices, then they may refuse. A Good Samaritan would not refuse—or anyway, a Splendid Samaritan, if the sacrifices that had to be made were enormous. But then so would a Good Samaritan assume responsibility for that violinist; so would Henry Fonda, if he is a Good Samaritan, fly in from the West Coast and assume responsibility for me.

8. My argument will be found unsatisfactory on two counts by many of those who want to regard abortion as morally permissible. First, while I do argue that abortion is not impermissible, I do not argue that it is always permissible. There may well be cases in which carrying the child to term requires only Minimally Decent Samaritanism of the mother, and this is a standard we must not fall below. I am inclined to think it a merit of my account precisely that it does *not* give a general yes or a general no. It allows for and supports our sense that, for example, a sick and desperately frightened fourteen-year-old schoolgirl, pregnant due to rape, may of *course* choose abortion, and that any law which rules this out is an insane law. And it also allows for and supports our sense that in other cases resort to abortion is even positively indecent. It would be indecent in the woman to request an abortion, and indecent in a doctor to perform it, if she is in her seventh month, and wants the abortion just to avoid the nuisance of postponing a trip abroad. The very fact that the arguments I have been drawing attention to treat all cases of abortion, or even all cases of abortion in which the mother's life is not at stake, as morally on a par ought to have made them suspect at the outset.

Secondly, while I am arguing for the permissibility of abortion in some cases, I am not arguing for the right to secure the death of the unborn child. It is easy to confuse these two things in that up to a certain point in the life of the fetus it is not able to survive outside the mother's body; hence removing it from her body guarantees its death. But they are importantly different. I have argued that you are not morally required to spend nine months in bed, sustaining the life of that violinist; but to say this is by no means to say that if, when you unplug yourself, there is a miracle and he survives, you then have a right to turn around and slit his throat. You may detach yourself even if this costs him his life; you have no right to be guaranteed his death, by some other means, if unplugging yourself does not kill him. There are some people who will feel dissatisfied by this feature of my argument. A woman may be utterly devastated by the thought of a child, a bit of herself, put out for adoption and never seen or heard of again. She may therefore want not merely that the child be detached from her, but more, that it die. Some opponents of abortion are inclined to regard this as beneath contempt—thereby showing insensitivity to what is surely a powerful source of despair. All the same, I agree that the desire for the child's death is not one which anybody may gratify, should it turn out to be possible to detach the child alive.

At this place, however, it should be remembered that we have only been pretending throughout that the fetus is a human being from the moment of conception. A very early abortion is surely not the killing of a person, and so is not dealt with by anything I have said here.

Endnotes

1. Daniel Callahan, *Abortion: Law, Choice and Morality* (New York, 1970), p. 373. This book gives a fascinating survey of the available information on abortion. The Jewish tradition in David M. Feldman, *Birth Control in Jewish Law* (New York, 1963), part 5; the Catholic tradition in John T. Noonan, Jr., "An Almost Absolute Value in History," in *The Morality of Abortion*, ed. John T. Noonan, Jr. (Cambridge, Mass., 1970).

2. The term "direct" in the arguments I refer to is a technical one. Roughly, what is meant by "direct killing" is either killing as an end in itself, or killing as a means to some end, for example, the end of saving someone else's life. See note 5 on this page, for an example of its use.

3. Cf. *Encyclical Letter of Pope Pius XI on Christian Marriage*, St. Paul Editions (Boston, n.d.), p. 32: "However much we may pity the mother whose health and even life is gravely imperiled in the performance of the duty allotted to her by nature, nevertheless what could ever be a sufficient reason for excusing in any way the direct murder of the innocent? This is precisely what we are dealing with here." Noonan (*The Morality of Abortion*, p. 43) reads this as follows: "What cause can ever avail to excuse in any way the direct killing of the innocent? For it is a question of that."

4. The thesis in (4) is in an interesting way weaker than those in (1), (2), and (3): They rule out abortion even in cases in which both mother *and* child will die if the abortion is not performed. By contrast, one who held the view expressed in (4) could consistently say that one needn't prefer letting two persons die to killing one.

5. Cf. the following passage from Plus XII, *Address to the Italian Catholic Society of Midwives*: "The baby in the maternal breast has the right to life immediately from God.—Hence there is no man, no human authority, no science, no medical, eugenic, social, economic or moral 'indication' which can establish or grant a valid juridical ground for a direct deliberate disposition of an innocent human life, that is a disposition which looks to its destruction either as an end or as a means to another end perhaps in itself not illicit.—The baby, still not born, is a man in the same degree and for the same reason as the mother" (quoted in Noonan, *The Morality of Abortion*, p. 45).

6. The need for a discussion of this argument was brought home to me by members of the Society for Ethical and Legal Philosophy, to whom this paper was originally presented.

7. For a discussion of the difficulties involved, and a survey of the European experience with such laws, see *The Good Samaritan and the Law*, ed. James M. Ratcliffe (New York, 1966).

22. Who Shall Count as a Human Being?
A Treacherous Question in the Abortion Discussion

Sissela Bok

Sissela Bok examines the issue of fetal humanness in some detail because she acknowledges that the concept of humanity is "indispensable" to the central arguments against abortion. Bok questions the assumptions upon which humanness is ascribed to the fetus early in the pregnancy and argues for a developmental notion of humanness that makes early-term abortions permissible but later-term abortions, from mid-pregnancy onward, morally problematic.

> "The temptation to introduce premature ultimates — Beauty in Aesthetics, the Mind and its faculties in Psychology, Life in Physiology, are representative examples — is especially great for believers in Abstract Entities. The objection to such Ultimates is that they bring an investigation to a dead end too suddenly."
>
> I.A. RICHARDS
> *Principles of Literary Criticism*, p. 40.

In discussions of abortion policy, the premature ultimate is 'humanity.' Does the fetus possess 'humanity'? How does one go about deciding whether a living being possesses it? And what rights go with such possession? These and similar questions have arisen beginning with the earliest speculations about human origins and characteristics. They are still thought central to the abortion debate. I propose to show in this paper that they cannot help us come to grips with the problem of abortion; indeed that they obfuscate all discussion in this domain and lend themselves to dangerous interpretations precisely because of their obscurity.

The concept of 'humanity' is indispensable to two main arguments against abortion. The first defines the fetus as a human being and then concludes that abortion must be murder since it is generally considered murder to take the life of a human being. The second argument is designed to speak to those who do not believe that fetuses are human and cannot share,

From Robert L. Perkins (ed.), *Abortion: Pro and Con* (Cambridge, MA: Schenkman Publishing Company, 1974), pp. 91–105. Reprinted with permission from Schenkman Books.

therefore, the conclusion that abortion is murder. It stresses, not the inherent wrong in individual acts of abortion, but rather the fearful consequences flowing from a *social acceptance* of abortion. According to this argument, it is impossible to draw a line in the period of prenatal development when humanity can be said to begin. There will therefore be no way to stop at early abortions, since they cannot be distinguished from later and yet later abortions; eventually society may even come to permit infanticide and the taking of lives generally. We are all at risk, according to such an argument, once we allow abortions to take place.

An analysis of these two arguments will show the ways in which the concept of 'humanity' operates as a premature ultimate.[1] I propose to substitute for this vague concept an inquiry into the commonly shared principles concerning the protection of life. These principles help to define workable rules for abortions and make it possible to draw a clear line between abortion, on the one hand, and the taking of life in infanticide, euthanasia, and genocide, on the other.

A. Humanity A long tradition of religious and philosophical and legal thought has approached the problem of abortion by trying to determine whether there is human life before birth, and, if so, when it *becomes* human. If human life is present from conception on, according to this tradition, it must be protected as such from that moment. And if the embryo becomes human at some point during the pregnancy, then that is the point at which the protection should set in.

John Noonan[2] generalizes the predominant Catholic view as follows:

> "Once conceived, the being was recognized
> as a man because he had man's potential.
> The criterion for humanity, then, was simple
> and all-embracing: If you are conceived by
> human parents, you are human."

Similarly, no less than ten resolutions had been introduced in Congress in the three months following the U.S. Supreme Court's decisions on abortion.[3] These resolutions call for a constitutional amendment providing that

> "neither the United States, nor any state shall
> deprive any human being, *from the moment
> of conception,* of life without the due process
> of law. . ."

Others have held that the moment when *implantation* of the fertilized egg occurs, 6-7 days after conception, is more significant from the point of view of individual humanity than conception itself. This view permits them to allow the intrauterine device and the 'morning after pill' as not taking human life, merely interfering with implantation. Whether or not one considers such distinctions to be theoretically possible, however, modern contraceptive developments are making them increasingly difficult to draw in practice.

Another widely shared approach to establishing humanity is that of stressing the time when the embryo first begins to *look human.* A photo of the first cell having divided in half clearly does not depict what most people mean when they use the expression 'human being.' Even the four-week embryo does not look human in this sense, whereas the six-week-old one begins to do so. Recent techniques of depicting the embryo and the fetus have remarkably increased our awareness of this early stage; this new 'seeing' of life before birth may come to increase the psychological recoil from aborting those who already look human — thus adding a psychological factor to the medical and other factors already influencing the trend to earlier and earlier abortions.

Another dividing line, once more having to do with perceiving the fetus, is held to occur when the mother can feel the fetus moving. *Quickening*—when these moments are first felt—has traditionally represented an important distinction; in some legal traditions, such as that of the common law, abortion was permitted before quickening, but considered a misdemeanor afterwards, until the more restrictive 19th century legislation was established. It is certain that the first-felt movements of the fetus represent an awe-inspiring change for the mother, comparable perhaps, in some primitive sense, to a 'coming to life' or the being she carries.

Yet another distinction occurs when the fetus is considered *viable.* According to this view, once the fetus is capable of living independently of its mother, it must be regarded as a human being and protected as such. The U.S. Supreme Court decisions on abortion established viability as the "compelling" point for the state's "important and legitimate interest in potential life," while eschewing the question of when 'life' or 'human life' begins.[4]

A set of later distinctions cluster around the process of birth itself. This is the moment when life begins, according to certain religious traditions, and the point at which 'persons' are fully recognized in the law, according to the Supreme Court.[5] The first breaths taken by newborn babies have been invested with symbolic meaning since the earliest gropings toward understanding what it means to be alive and human. And the rituals of acceptance of babies or children have often defined humanity to the point where the baby could be killed if it were not named or declared accepted by the elders of the community or by the head of the household.

In the positions here examined, and in the abortion debate generally, a number of concepts are at times used as if they were interchangeable. 'Humanity,' 'human life,' 'life,' are such concepts, as are 'man,' 'person,' 'human being,' or 'human individual.' In particular, those who hold that humanity begins at conception or at implantation often have the tendency to say that at that time a human being or a person or a man exists as well, whereas others find it impossible to equate them.

Each of these terms can, in addition, be used in different senses which overlap but are not interchangeable. For instance, humanity and human life, in one sense, are possessed by every cell in our bodies. Many cells have the full genetic makeup required for asexual reproduction—so called cloning—of a human being. Yet clearly this is not the sense of those words intended when the protection of humanity or human life is advocated. Such protection would press the reverence for human life to the mad extreme of ruling out haircuts and considering mosquito bites murder.

It may be argued, however, that for most cells which have the potential of cloning to form a human being, extraordinarily complex measures would be required which are not as yet perfected beyond the animal stage. Is there, then, a difference, from the point of view of human potential, between these cells and egg cells or sperm cells? And is there still another difference in potential between the egg cell before and after conception? While there is a statistical difference in the *likelihood* of their developing into a human being, it does not seem possible to draw a clear line where humanity definitely begins.

The different views as to when humanity begins are little dependent upon factual information. Rather, these views are representative of different world-views, often of a religious nature involving deeply held commitments with moral consequences. There is no disagreement as to what we now know about life and its development before and after conception; differences arise only about the names and moral consequences we attach to the changes in this development and the distinctions we consider important. Just as there is no point at which Achilles can be pinpointed as catching up with the tortoise, though everyone knows he does, so everyone is aware of the distance traveled, in terms of humanity, from before conception to birth, though there is no one point at which humanity can be agreed upon as setting in. Our efforts to pinpoint and to define reflect the urgency with which we reach for abstract labels and absolute certainty in facts and in nature; and the resulting confusion and puzzlement are close to what Wittgenstein described, in *Philosophical Investigations,* as the "bewitchment of our intelligence by means of language."

Even if some see the fertilized egg as possessing humanity and as being "a man" in the words used by Noonan, however, it would be quite unthinkable to act upon all the consequences of such a view. It would be necessary to undertake a monumental struggle against all spontaneous abortions—known as miscarriages—often of severely malformed embryos expelled by the mother's body. This struggle would appear increasingly misguided as we learn more about how to preserve early prenatal life. Those who could not be saved would have to be buried in the same way as dead infants. Those who engaged in abortion would have to be prosecuted for murder. Extraordinary practical complexities would arise with respect to detection of early abortion, and to the question of whether the use of abortifacients in the first few days after conception should also count as murder. In view of these inconsistencies, it seems likely that this view of humanity, like so many others, has been adopted for limited purposes having to do with the prohibition of induced abortion, rather than from a real belief in the full human rights of the first few cells after conception.

A related reason why there are so many views and definitions is that they have been sought for such different *purposes.* I indicated above that many of the views about humanity developed in the abortion dispute seem to have been worked out for one such purpose: that of defending a preconceived position on abortion, with little concern for the other consequences flowing from that particular view. But there have been so many other efforts to define humanity and to arrive at the essence of what it means to be human—to distinguish men from angels and demons, plants and animals, witches and robots. The most powerful one has been the urge to know about the human species and to trace the biological or divine origins and the essential characteristics of mankind. It is magnificently set forth beginning with the very earliest writings in philosophy and poetry; in fact, this consciousness of oneself and wonder at one's condition has often been thought one of the essential distinctions between men and animals.

A separate purpose, both giving strength to and flowing from these efforts to describe and to understand humanity, has been that of seeking to define what a *good* human being is—to delineate human aspirations. What ought fully human beings be like, and how should they differ from and grow beyond their immature, less perfect, sick or criminal fellow men? Who can teach such growth—St. Francis or Nietzsche, Buddha or Erasmus? And what kind of families and societies give support and provide models for growth?

Finally, definitions of humanity have been sought in order to try to set limits to the protection of life. At what level of developing humanity can and ought lives to receive protection? And who, among those many labelled less than human at different times in history—slaves, enemies in war, women, children, the retarded—should be denied such protection?

Of these three purposes for defining 'humanity,' the first is classificatory and descriptive in the first hand (though it gives rise to normative considerations). It has roots in religious and metaphysical thought, and has branched out into biological and archeological and anthropological research. But the latter two, so often confused with the first, are primarily *normative* or prescriptive. They seek to set norms or guidelines for who is fully human and who is at least minimally human—so human as to be entitled to the protection of life. For the sake of these normative purposes, definitions of 'humanity' established elsewhere have been sought in order to determine action—and all too often the action has been devastating for those excluded.

It is crucial to ask at this point why the descriptive and the normative definitions have been thought to coincide; why it has been taken for granted that the line between human and non-human or not-yet-human is identical with that distinguishing those who may be killed from those who are to be protected.

One or both of two fundamental assumptions are made by those who base the protection of life upon the possession of 'humanity.' The first is that human beings are not only different from, but *superior to* all other living matter. This is the assumption which changes the definition of humanity into an evaluative one. It lies at the root of Western religious and social thought, from the Bible and the Aristotelian concept of the "ladder of nature" all the way to Teilhard de Chardin's view of mankind as close to the intended summit and consummation of the development of living beings.

The second assumption holds that the superiority of human beings somehow justifies their using what is non-human as they see fit, dominating it, even killing it when they wish to. St. Augustine, in *The City of God*,[6] expresses both of these anthropocentric assumptions when he holds that the injunction "Thou shalt not kill" does not apply to killing animals and plants, since, having no faculty of reason,

> "therefore by the altogether righteous ordinance of the Creator both their life and death are a matter subordinate to our needs."

Neither of these assumptions is self-evident. And the results of acting upon them, upon the bidding to subdue the earth, to subordinate living matter to human needs, are no longer seen by all to be beneficial. The ancient certainties about man's preordained place in the universe are faltering. The supposition that only human beings have rights is no longer regarded as beyond question.[7]

Not only, therefore, can the line between human and non-human not be drawn empirically so as to permit normative conclusions: the very enterprise of *basing* normative conclusions on such distinctions can no longer be taken for granted. Despite these difficulties,

many still try to employ definitions of 'humanity' to do just that. And herein lies by far the most important reason for abandoning such efforts: the monumental misuse of the concept of 'humanity' in so many practices of discrimination and atrocity throughout history. Slavery, witchhunts, and wars have all been justified by their perpetrators on the ground that they thought their victims to be less than fully human. The insane and the criminal have for long periods been deprived of the most basic necessities for similar reasons, and excluded from society. A theologian, Dr. Joseph Fletcher, has even suggested as recently as last year that someone who has an I.Q. below 40 is "questionably a person" and that those below the 20-mark are not persons at all.[8] He adds that:

> "This has bearing, obviously, on decision-making in gynecology, obstetrics, and pediatrics, as well as in general surgery and medicine."

Here, a criterion for 'personhood' is taken as a guideline for action which could have sinister and far-reaching effects. Even when entered upon with the best of intentions, and in the most guarded manner, the enterprise of basing the protection of human life upon such criteria and definitions is dangerous. To question someone's humanity or personhood is a first step to mistreatment and killing.

We must abandon, therefore, this quest for a definition of humanity capable of showing us who has a right to live. We must seek, instead, common principles for the protection of life that reflect a clear understanding of the harm that comes from the taking of life. Why do we hold life to be sacred? Why does it require protection beyond that given to anything else? The question seems unnecessary at first glance—surely most people share what has been called "the elemental sensation of vitality and the elemental fear of its extinction," and what Hume called "our horrors at annihilation."[9] Many think of this elemental sensation as incapable of further analysis. They view any attempt to say *why* we hold life sacred as an instrumentalist, utilitarian rocking of the boat which may loosen this fundamental respect for life. Yet a failure to scrutinize this respect, to ask what it protects and what it ought to protect, lies at the root not only of the confusion about abortion, but of the persistent vagueness and consequent abuse of the notion of the respect for life. The result is that everyone, including those who authorize or perform the most brutal killings in war, can protest their belief in life's sacredness. I shall therefore list the most important reasons which underlie the elemental sense of the sacredness of life. Having done so, these reasons can be considered as they apply or do not apply to the embryo and the fetus.

B. Reasons for Protecting Life

1. Killing is viewed as the greatest of all dangers *for the victim.*
   - The knowledge that there is a threat to life causes intense anguish and apprehension.
   - The actual taking of life can cause great suffering.
   - The continued experience of life, once begun, is considered so valuable, so unique, so absorbing, that no one who has this experience should be unjustly deprived of it. And depriving someone of this experience means that all else of value to him will be lost.

2. Killing is brutalizing and criminalizing *for the killer.* It is a threat to others and destructive to the person engaging therein.

3. Killing often causes *the family of the victim and others* to experience grief and loss. They may have been tied to the dead person by affection or economic dependence; they may have given of themselves in the relationship, so that its severance causes deep suffering.

4. All of society, as a result, has a stake in the protection of life. Permitting killing to take place sets patterns for victims, killers, and survivors that are threatening and ultimately harmful to all.

These are neutral principles governing the protection of life. They are shared by most human beings reflecting upon the possibility of dying at the hands of others. It is clear that these principles, if applied in the absence of the confusing terminology of 'humanity,' would rule out the kinds of killing perpetrated by conquerors, witch-hunters, slave-holders, and Nazis. Their victims feared death and suffered; they grieved for their dead; and the societies permitting such killing were brutalized and degraded.

Turning now to abortion once more, how do these principles apply to the taking of the lives of embryos and fetuses?

C. Reasons to Protect Life in the Prenatal Period Consider the very earliest cell formations soon after conception. Clearly the reasons for protecting human life fail to apply here:

This group of cells cannot feel the anguish or pain connected with death, nor can it fear death. Its experiencing of life has not yet begun; it is not yet conscious of the interruption of life nor of the loss of anything it has come to value in life, nor is it tied by bonds of affection to others. If the abortion is desired by both parents, it will cause no grief such as that which accompanies the death of a child. Almost no human care and emotion and resources have been invested in it. Nor is such an early abortion brutalizing for the person voluntarily performing it, or a threat to other members of the society where it takes place.

Some may argue that one can conceive of other deaths with those factors absent, which nevertheless would be murder. Take the killing of a hermit in his sleep by someone who instantly commits suicide. Here there is no anxiety or fear of the killing on the part of the victim, no pain in dying, no mourning by family or friends (to whom the hermit has, in leaving them for ever, already in a sense 'died'), no awareness by others that a wrong has been done; and the possible brutalization of the murderer has been made harmless to others through his suicide. Speculate further that the bodies are never found. Yet we would still call the act one of murder. The reason we would do so is inherent in the act itself and depends on the fact that his life was taken and that he was denied the chance to continue to experience it.

How does this deprivation differ from abortion in the first few days of pregnancy? I find that I cannot use words like 'deprive,' 'deny,' 'take away,' and 'harm' when it comes to the group of cells, whereas I have no difficulty in using them for the hermit. These words require, if not a person conscious of his loss, at least someone who at a prior time has developed enough to be or have been conscious thereof. Because there is no semblance of human form, no conscious life or capability to live independently, no knowledge of death, no sense of pain, one cannot use such words meaningfully to describe early abortion.

In addition, whereas it is possible to frame a rule permitting abortion which will cause no anxiety on the part of others covered by the rule—other embryos or fetuses—it is not possible to frame such a rule permitting the killing of hermits without threatening other *hermits.* All hermits would have to fear for their lives if there were a rule saying that hermits can be killed if they are alone and asleep and if the agent commits suicide.

The reasons, then, for the protection of lives are minimal in very early abortions. At the same time, many of these reasons are clearly present with respect

to *infanticide,* most important among them the brutalization of those participating in the act and the resultant danger for all who are felt to be undesirable by
their families or by others. This is not to say that acts
of infanticide have not taken place in our society;
indeed, as late as the 19th century, newborns were frequently killed, either directly or by giving them into
the care of institutions such as foundling hospitals,
where the death rate could be as high as 90% in the
first year of life.[10] A few primitive societies, at the edge
of extinction, without other means to limit families,
still practice infanticide. But I believe that the *public
acceptance* of infanticide in all other societies is
unthinkable, given the advent of modern methods of
contraception and early abortion and of institutions to
which parents can give their children, assured of their
survival and of the high likelihood that they will be
adopted and cared for by a family.

D. Dividing Lines If, therefore, very early abortion
does not violate these principles of protection for life,
but infanticide does, we are confronted with a new
kind of continuum in the place of that between less
human and more human: that of the growth in
strength, as the fetus develops during the prenatal
period, of these principles, these reasons for protecting life. In this second continuum, it would be as difficult as in the first to draw a line based upon
objective factors. Since most abortions can be performed earlier or later during pregnancy, it would be
preferable to encourage early abortions rather than
late ones and to draw a line before the second half of
the pregnancy, permitting later abortions only on a
clear showing of need. For this purpose, the two concepts of *quickening* and *viability*—so unsatisfactory in
determining when humanity begins—can provide
such limits.

Before quickening, the reasons to protect life are,
as has been shown, negligible, perhaps absent altogether. During this period, therefore, abortion could
be permitted upon request. Alternatively, the end of
the first trimester could be employed as such a limit,
as is the case in a number of countries.

Between quickening and viability, when the operation is a more difficult one medically and more traumatic for parents and medical personnel, it would not
seem unreasonable to hold that special reasons justifying the abortion should be required in order to coun-
terbalance this resistance: reasons not known earlier,
such as the severe malformation of the fetus. After

viability, finally, all abortions save the rare ones required
to save the life of the mother,[11] should be prohibited,
because the reasons to *protect* life may now be thought
to be partially present; even though the viable fetus
cannot fear death or suffer consciously therefrom, the
effects on those participating in the event, and thus on
society indirectly, could be serious. This is especially
so because of the need, mentioned above, for a protection against infanticide. In the unlikely event, however, that the mother should wish to be separated from
the fetus at such a late stage,[12] the procedure ought to
be delayed until it can be one of premature birth, not
one of harming the fetus in an abortive process.

Medically, however, the definition of 'viability' is
difficult. It varies from one fetus to another. At one
stage in pregnancy, a certain number of babies, if born,
will be viable. At a later stage, the percentage will be
greater. Viability also depends greatly on the state of
our knowledge concerning the support of life after
birth and on the nature of the support itself. Support
can be given much earlier in a modern hospital than in
a rural village, or in a clinic geared to doing abortions
only. It may some day even be the case that almost any
human life will be considered viable before birth, once
artificial wombs are perfected.

As technological progress pushes back the time
when the fetus can be helped to survive independently
of the mother, a question will arise as to whether the
cut-off point marked by viability ought also to be
pushed back. Should abortion then be prohibited
much earlier than is now the case, because the medical
meaning of 'viability' will have changed, or should we
continue to rely on the conventional meaning of the
word for the distinction between lawful and unlawful
abortion?

In order to answer this question it is necessary to
look once more at the reasons for which 'viability' was
thought to be a good dividing line in the first place. Is
viability important because the baby can survive outside of the mother? Or because this chance of survival
comes at a time in fetal development when the *reasons*
to protect life have grown strong enough to prohibit
abortion? At present, the two coincide, but in the
future, they may come to diverge increasingly.

If the time comes when an embryo *could* be kept
alive without its mother and thus be 'viable' in one
sense of the word, the *reasons* for protecting life from
the point of view of victims, agents, relatives and society would still be absent; it seems right, therefore,
to tie the obligatory protection of life to the present

conventional definition of 'viability' and to set a socially agreed upon time in pregnancy after which abortion should be prohibited.

To sum up, the justifications a mother has for not wishing to give birth can operate up to a certain point in pregnancy; after that point, the reasons society has for protecting life become sufficiently weighty so as to prohibit late abortions and infanticide.

E. The Slippery Slope Some argue, however, that such views of abortion could lead, if widely followed, to great dangers for society. This second major argument against abortion appears to set aside the question of when the fetus becomes human. It focuses, rather, on the risks for society—for the newborn, the handicapped, and the aged—which may stem from allowing abortions; it evokes the age-old fear of the slippery slope.[13] Because there are no sharp transitions in the period of fetal development, this argument holds, it would be unreasonable to permit abortion at one time in pregnancy and prohibit it shortly thereafter; in addition, it would be impossible to enforce such prohibitions. Later and later abortions may therefore be allowed, and there will be risks of slipping towards infanticide, euthanasia, even genocide.

The assumption made here is that once we admit reasons for justifying early abortions—reasons such as rape, incest, or maternal illness—nothing will prevent people from acting upon these very same reasons later in pregnancy or even after birth. If abortion is permissible at four weeks of pregnancy, then why not at four weeks and one day, four weeks and two days, and so on until birth and beyond? The reason that this argument possesses superficial plausibility has to do, once more with the concept of 'humanity'. Since all agree that the newborn infant is a human being, and since there are no ways of drawing clear lines before birth in the development of this human being, there appears to be no clear way of saying that the fetus is *not* human. On the assumption that humanity is the *only* criterion, there can then be a slippage from abortion to infanticide, with no clear dividing line between the two. Once more, then, 'humanity' turns out to be at stake. It is the concept providing the "slipperiness" to the slope—the dimension along which no distinctions can be made which make sense and are enforceable.

Once again, here, 'humanity' operates as a premature ultimate, bringing discussion to a dead end too soon. For the discontinuity which is not found in fetal development can be established by society, and indeed

has been so established in modern societies permitting abortion. The argument that the reasons *for* aborting may still be declared to exist at childbirth completely ignores the reasons advanced *against* killing. These reasons grow in strength during pregnancy. Sympathy for the victim, grief on the part of those aware of the loss, recoil on the part of those who would do the killing, and a sense of social catastrophe would accompany the acceptance of infanticide by a contemporary democracy.

But, it may be asked, how can one know that these reasons would prevail? How can one be sure that the discontinuity will be respected by most, and that there will not be pressure to move closer and closer to an acceptance of infanticide?

The best way to answer such a question is to see whether that kind of development has actually taken place in one or more of the societies which permit abortion. To the best of my knowledge, the societies which have permitted abortion for considerable lengths of time have not experienced any tendency to infanticide. The infant mortality statistics of Sweden and Denmark, for example, are extremely low, and the protection and care given to all living children, including those born with special handicaps, is exemplary.[14] It is true that facts cannot satisfy those who want a *logical* demonstration that dangerous developments cannot under any circumstances come about. But the burden of proof rests upon them to show *some* evidence of such developments taking place before opposing a policy which will mean so much to women and their families, and also to show why it would not be possible to stop any such development *after* it begins to take place.

The fear of slipping from abortion towards infanticide, therefore, while superficially plausible, does not seem to be supported by the available evidence, so long as a cut-off time in pregnancy is established, either by law or in medical practice, after which all fetuses are protected against killing.[15]

I have sketched an approach to seeking community norms for abortion and tried to show the difficulties and dangers in using considerations of 'humanity' to set such norms. Needless to say, *individual* choices for or against abortion will have to be more complex and influenced by religious and moral considerations.[16] Every effort must be made to show that abortion is a last resort. It presents difficulties not present in contraception, yet it is sometimes the only way out of a great dilemma.

Endnotes

1. The focus in this paper is on abortion as a problem of social policy. Decisions made by individuals must take other factors into consideration. See S. Bok, "Ethical Problems of Abortion," *Hastings Studies*, January 1974; first prepared for the Harvard Interfaculty Seminar on Children, chaired by Nathan B. Talbot. The results and findings of this seminar will be published by Little, Brown, and Company (Boston) and entitled *Raising Children in Modern Urban America: Problems and Prospective Solutions.*

2. John Noonan, Jr., "An Almost Absolute Value in History," in John Noonan, Jr., ed., *The Morality of Abortion*, p. 51, Harvard University Press, Cambridge, Massachusetts. For a thorough discussion of this and other views concerning the beginnings of human life, see Daniel Callahan, *Abortion: Law, Choice and Morality*, New York: the Macmillan Company, 1970.

3. "How the Constitution is Amended," p. 56, *Family Planning/Population Reporter*, Vol. 2, no. 3.

4. Roe v. Wade, *The United States Law Week*, 41, pp. 4227, 4229.

5. *Ibid.*, p. 4227. For a discussion of this and other positions taken in the 1973 Supreme Court abortion decisions see L. Tribe, Foreword, *Harvard Law Review*, Vol. 87, Nov. 1973, pp. 1–54.

6. Augustine, *The City of God against the Pagans*, Book I, Ch. XX, Cambridge: Harvard University Press, 1957.

7. Christopher D. Stone, "Should Trees Have Standing? Toward Legal Rights for Natural Objects," *Southern California Law Review*, Vol. 45, 450–501, provides an interesting analysis of the extension of rights to those not previously considered persons, such as children, and a discussion of possible future extensions to natural objects.

8. Joseph Fletcher, "Indicators of Humanhood: A Tentative Profile of Man," *The Hastings Center Report*, Vol. 2, no. 5, pp. 1–4.

9. Edward Shils, "The Sanctity of Life," in D. H. Labby, ed., p. 12, *Life or Death: Ethics and Options*, Seattle: University of Washington Press, 1968. David Hume, *Essay on Immortality*.

10. William Langer, "Checks on Population Growth: 1750–1850," *Scientific American*, Vol. 226, no. 2, 1972.

11. Every effort must be made by physicians and others to construe the Supreme Court's statement (*supra*) "If the State is interested in protecting fetal life after viability, it may go so far as to proscribe abortion during that period except when it is necessary to preserve the life or health of the mother" to concern, in effect, only the life or threat to life of the mother. See Alan Stone, "Abortion and the Supreme Court: What Now?" *Modern Medicine*, April 30, 1973, pp. 33–37, for a discussion of this question and what it means for physicians.

12. For an insightful discussion of this dilemma, see Judith Thomson, "A Defense of Abortion," *Philosophy and Public Policy*, Vol. 1, no. 1, pp. 47-66. My conclusions are set forth in detail in "Ethical Problems of Abortion," (footnote 1).

13. See S. Bok, "The Leading Edge of the Wedge," *The Hastings Center Report*, pp. 9-11, Vol. 1, no. 3, 1971.

14. Moreover, Nazi Germany, which is frequently cited as a warning of what is to come once abortion becomes lawful, had very strict laws prohibiting abortion. In 1943, Hitler's regime made the existing penalties for women having abortions and for those performing them even more severe by removing the limit on imprisonment and by including the possibility of hard labor for "especially serious cases." See *Reichsgezetzblatt*, 1926, Teil I, Nr. 28, par. 218, and 1943, Teil I, Art. I, "Angriffe auf Ehe, Familie, und Mutterschaft."

15. Another type of line-drawing and slippery slope problem is that which would exist if abortions, once permissible, came to be coercively obtained in the case of mothers thought unable to bring up children, or in cases where deformed children were expected. To outlaw abortions out of a fear that involuntary abortions would take place, however, would be the wrong response to such a danger, just as outlawing voluntary divorces, operations, and adoptions on the grounds that they might lead to involuntary divorces, operations, and adoptions, would be. The battle against coercion must be fought at all times, with respect to many social options, but this is no reason to prohibit the options themselves.

16. See "Ethical Problems of Abortion" (footnote 1).

23.   Roe v. Wade: A Study in Male Ideology

CATHARINE MACKINNON

Exposing the patriarchal assumptions at work in the *Roe v. Wade* U.S. Supreme Court decision of 1973, Catharine MacKinnon argues that the abortion ruling leaves undisturbed the social arrangements wherein sex is understood in male terms. By appealing to a woman's right to privacy, *Roe v. Wade* guarantees to women the right to engage in sex the way men do, "without consequences," and removes from women the one legitimized excuse they possessed for refusing to engage in sex. As an exercise in ideological suppression, the decision privatizes, and hence secures from public consideration, feminists' concerns about battery, marital rape, women's exploited labor, and even their autonomy and self-definition; it also protects and enforces male supremacy.

In a society where women entered sexual intercourse willingly, where adequate contraception was a genuine social priority, there would be no "abortion issue." . . . Abortion is violence. . . . It is the offspring, and will continue to be the accuser of a more pervasive and prevalent violence, the violence of rapism.

ADRIENNE RICH
Of Woman Born

This is a two-part feminist critique of *Roe v. Wade.* First I will situate abortion and the abortion right in the experience of women. The argument is that abortion is inextricable from sexuality, assuming that the feminist analysis of sexuality is our analysis of gender inequality.[1] I will then criticize the doctrinal choice to pursue the abortion right under the law of privacy. The argument is that privacy doctrine reaffirms what the feminist critique of sexuality criticizes: the public/private split. The political and ideological meaning of privacy as a legal doctrine is connected with the concrete consequences of the public/private split for the lives of women. This analysis makes *Harris v. McRae,* in which public funding for abortions was held not required, appear consistent with the larger meaning of *Roe.*[2]

I will neglect two important explorations, which I bracket now. The first is, What are babies to men? On

one level, men respond to women's right to abort as if confronting the possibility of their own potential nonexistence—at *women's* hands, no less. On another level, men's issues of potency, of continuity as a compensation for mortality, of the thrust to embody themselves or their own image in the world, underlie their relation to babies (as well as to most everything else). To overlook these meanings of abortion to men as men is to overlook political and strategic as well as fundamental theoretical issues, and is to misassess where much of the opposition to abortion is coming from. The second issue I bracket is one that, unlike the first, has been discussed extensively in the abortion debate: the moral rightness of abortion itself. My stance is that the abortion choice should be available and must be *women's,* but not because the fetus is not a form of life. In the usual argument, the abortion decision is made contingent on whether the fetus is a form of life. I cannot follow that. Why should not women make life or death decisions? This returns us to the first bracketed issue.

The issues I will explore have largely not been discussed in the terms I will use. What has happened instead, I think, is that women's embattled need to survive in a world hostile to our survival has precluded our exploring these issues as I am about to. That is, the perspective from which we have addressed abortion has been shaped and constrained by the very situation that the abortion issue requires us to address. We have not been able to risk thinking about these issues on our own terms because the terms have not been ours, either in sex, in life in general, or in court. The attempt to grasp women's situation on our own terms, from our own point of view, defines the feminist impulse. If doing that is risky, our situation also makes it risky not to. So, first feminism, then law.

Most women who seek abortions became pregnant while having sexual intercourse with men. Most did not mean or wish to conceive. In contrast to this fact of women's experience, the abortion debate has centered on separating control over sexuality from control over reproduction, and on separating both from gender. Liberals have supported the availability of the abortion choice as if the woman just happened on the fetus.[3] The political Right imagines that the intercourse which precedes conception is usually voluntary, only to urge abstinence, as if sex were up to women. At the same time, the Right defends male authority, specifically including a wife's duty to submit to sex. Continuing with this logic, many opponents of state funding of abortions, such as supporters of some versions of the Hyde Amendment, would permit funding of abortions when pregnancy results from rape or incest.[4] Thus, they make exceptions for those special occasions during which they presume women did not control sex. From all this I deduce that abortion's proponents and opponents share a tacit assumption that women significantly do control sex.

Feminist investigations suggest otherwise. Sexual intercourse, the most common cause of pregnancy, cannot simply be presumed co-equally determined. Feminism has found that women feel compelled to preserve the appearance—which, acted upon, becomes the reality—of male direction of sexual expression, as if it is male initiative itself that we want: it is that which turns us on. Men enforce this. It is much of what men want in a woman. It is what pornography eroticizes and prostitutes provide. Rape—that is, intercourse with force that is recognized as force—is adjudicated not according to the power of force that the man wields, but according to indices of intimacy between the parties. The more intimate you are with your accused rapist, the less likely a court is to find that what happened to you was rape. Often indices of intimacy

include intercourse itself. If "no" can be taken as "yes," how free can "yes" be?

Under these conditions, women often do not use birth control because of its social meaning, a meaning we did not create. Using contraception means acknowledging and planning and taking direction of intercourse, accepting one's sexual availability, and appearing nonspontaneous. It means appearing available to male incursions. A good user of contraception is a bad girl. She can be presumed sexually available and, among other consequences, raped with relative impunity. (If you think this isn't true, you should consider rape cases in which the fact that a woman had a diaphragm in is taken as an indication that what happened to her was intercourse, not rape. "Why did you have your diaphragm in?") From studies of abortion clinics, women who repeatedly seek abortions (and now I'm looking at the repeat offenders high on the list of the Right's villains, their best case for opposing abortion as female irresponsibility),[5] when asked why, say something like, "The sex just happened." Like every night for two and a half years. I wonder if a woman can be presumed to control access to her sexuality if she feels unable to interrupt intercourse to insert a diaphragm; or worse, cannot even want to, aware that she risks a pregnancy she knows she does not want. Do you think she would stop the man for any other reason, such as, for instance, the real taboo—lack of desire? If not, how is sex, hence its consequences, meaningfully voluntary for women? Norms of sexual rhythm and romance that are felt to be interrupted by women's needs are constructed against women's interests. Sex doesn't look a whole lot like freedom when it appears normatively less costly for women to risk an undesired, often painful, traumatic, dangerous, sometimes illegal, and potentially life-threatening procedure, than it is to protect oneself in advance. Yet abortion policy has never been explicitly approached in the context of how women get pregnant; that is, as a consequence of intercourse under conditions of gender inequality; that is, as an issue of forced sex.

Now we come to the law. In 1973, *Roe v. Wade* found that a statute that made criminal all abortions except those to save the life of the mother violated the constitutional right to privacy.[6] The privacy right had been previously created as a constitutional principle in a case that decriminalized the prescription and use of contraceptives.[7] Note that courts use the privacy rubric to connect contraception with abortion in a way that parallels what I just did under the sexuality rubric. In *Roe,* that right to privacy was found "broad enough to encompass a woman's decision whether or not to terminate her pregnancy." In 1977, three justices observed, "In the abortion context, we have held that the right to privacy shields the woman from undue state intrusion in and external scrutiny of her very personal choice."[8] In 1981, the Supreme Court in *Harris v. McRae* decided that this right to privacy did not mean that federal Medicaid programs had to cover medically necessary abortions. According to the Court, the privacy of the woman's choice was not unconstitutionally burdened by the government supporting her decision to continue, but not her decision to end, a conception. In support of this conclusion, the Supreme Court stated that "although the government may not place obstacles in the path of a woman's exercise of her freedom of choice, it need not remove those not of its own creation."[9] It is apparently a very short step from that which the government has a duty *not* to intervene in, to that which it has *no* duty to intervene in.

If regarded as the outer edge of the limitations on government, I think the idea of privacy embodies a tension between precluding public exposure or governmental intrusion on the one hand, and autonomy in the sense of protecting personal self-action on the other. This is a tension, not just two facets of one whole right. This tension is resolved in the liberal state by identifying the threshold of the state with its permissible extent of penetration (a term I use advisedly) into a domain that is considered free by definition: the private sphere. By this move the state secures what has been termed "an inviolable personality" by insuring what has been called "autonomy or control over the intimacies of personal identity."[10] The state does this by centering its self-restraint on body and home, especially bedroom. By staying out of marriage and the family, prominently meaning sexuality—that is to say, heterosexuality—from contraception through pornography to the abortion decision, the law of privacy proposes to guarantee individual bodily integrity, personal exercise of moral intelligence, and freedom of intimacy.[11] What it actually does is translate traditional social values into the rhetoric of individual rights as a means of subordinating those rights to specific social imperatives.[12] In feminist terms, I am arguing that the logic of *Roe* consummated in *Harris* translates the ideology of the private sphere into the individual woman's legal right to privacy as a means of subordinating women's collective needs to the imperatives of male supremacy.

This is my retrospective on *Roe v. Wade:* reproduction is sexual, men control sexuality, and the state

supports the interest of men as a group. *Roe* does not contradict this. So why was abortion legalized; why were women even imagined to have such a right as privacy? It is not an accusation of bad faith to answer that the interests of men as a social group converge with the definition of justice embodied in law in what I call the male point of view. The way the male point of view constructs a social event or legal need will be the way that social event or legal need is framed by state policy. For example, to the extent possession is the point of sex, illegal rape will be sex with a woman who is not yours unless the act makes her yours. If part of the kick of pornography involves eroticizing the putatively prohibited, illegal pornography—obscenity—will be prohibited enough to keep pornography desirable without ever making it truly illegitimate or unavailable. If, from the male standpoint, male is the implicit definition of human, maleness will be the implicit standard by which sex equality is measured in discrimination law. In parallel terms, abortion's availability frames, and is framed by, the conditions under which men, worked out between themselves, will grant legitimacy to women to control the reproductive consequences of intercourse.

Since Freud, the social problem posed by sexuality has been perceived as the problem of the innate desire for sexual pleasure being repressed by the constraints of civilization. Inequality arises as an issue in this context only in women's repressive socialization to passivity and coolness (so-called frigidity), in women's so-called desexualization, and in the disparate consequences of biology, that is, pregnancy. Who defines what is sexual, what sexuality therefore is, to whom what stimuli are erotic and why, and who defines the conditions under which sexuality is expressed—these issues are not even available for consideration. "Civilization's" answer to these questions instead fuses women's reproductivity with our attributed sexuality in its definition of what a woman is. We are defined as women by the uses to which men put us. In this context it becomes clear why the struggle for reproductive freedom has never included a woman's right to refuse sex. In this notion of sexual liberation, the equality issue has been framed as a struggle for women to have sex with men on the same terms as men: without consequences. In this sense the abortion right has been sought as freedom from the unequal reproductive consequences of sexual expression, with sexuality defined as centered on heterosexual genital intercourse. It has been as if biological organisms, rather than social relations, reproduce the species. But if your concern is not how more people can get more sex, if instead your concern is who defines sexuality—hence pleasure and violation—then the abortion right is situated within a very different problematic: the social and political problematic of the inequality of the sexes. As Susan Sontag said, "Sex itself is not liberating for women. Neither is more sex. . . . The question is, what sexuality shall women be liberated to enjoy?"[13] To be able to address this requires rethinking the problem of sexuality, from the repression of drives by civilization to the oppression of women by men.

Arguments for abortion under the rubric of feminism have rested upon the right to control one's own body—gender neutral. I think that argument has been appealing for the same reasons it is inadequate: Socially, women's bodies have not been ours; we have not controlled their meanings and destinies. Feminists tried to assert that control without risking the pursuit of the idea that something more might be at stake than our bodies, something closer to a net of relations in which we are (at present unescapedly) gendered.[14] Some feminists have noticed that our right to decide has become merged with an overwhelmingly male profession's right not to have his professional judgment second-guessed by the government.[15] But most abortion advocates argue in rigidly and rigorously gender-neutral terms.

Thus, for instance, because Judith Jarvis Thomson's celebrated abducted violinist had no obligation to be somebody else's life support system, women have no obligation to support a fetus.[16] Never mind that no woman who needs an abortion—no woman period—is valued, no potential a woman's life might hold is cherished, like a gender-neutral famous violinist's unencumbered possibilities. Not to mention that in that hypothetical, the underlying parallel to rape—the origin in force, in abduction, that gives the hypothetical its weight while confining its application to instances in which force is recognized as force—is seldom interrogated in the abortion context for its applicability to the normal case. And abortion policy is to apply to the normal case. So we need to talk about sex, specifically about intercourse in relation to rape in relation to conception. By avoiding this issue in the abortion context liberal feminists have obscured the unequal basis on which they are attempting to construct our personhood.

The meaning of abortion in the context of a sexual critique of gender inequality is its promise to women of sex with men on the same terms as promised to men—that is, "without consequences." Under conditions in which women do not control access to our sexuality, this facilitates women's heterosexual availability. In other words, under conditions of gender inequality, sexual liberation in this sense does not free women, it frees male sexual aggression. The availability of abortion thus removes the one remaining legitimized reason that women have had for refusing sex besides the headache. As Andrea Dworkin puts it, analyzing male ideology on abortion: "Getting laid was at stake."[17] The Playboy Foundation has supported abortion rights from day one; it continues to, even with shrinking disposable funds, on a level of priority comparable to its opposition to censorship.

Privacy doctrine is an ideal vehicle for this process. The democratic liberal ideal of the private holds that, so long as the public does not interfere, autonomous individuals interact freely and equally. Conceptually, this private is hermetic. It *means* that which is inaccessible to, unaccountable to, unconstructed by anything beyond itself. By definition, it is not part of or conditioned by anything systematic or outside of it. It is personal, intimate, autonomous, particular, individual, the original source and final outpost of the self, gender neutral. It is, in short, defined by everything that feminism reveals women have never been allowed to be or to have, and everything that women have been equated with and defined in terms of *men's* ability to have. It contradicts the liberal definition of the private to complain in public of inequality within it. In this view, no act of the state contributes to—hence should properly participate in—shaping its internal alignments or distributing its internal forces. Its inviolability by the state, framed as an individual right, presupposes that it is not already an arm of the state. In this scheme, intimacy is implicitly thought to guarantee symmetry of power. Injuries arise in violating the private sphere, not within and by and because of it.

In private, consent tends to be presumed. It is true that a showing of coercion voids this presumption. But the problem is getting anything private to be perceived as coercive. Why one would allow force in private—the "why doesn't she leave" question raised to battered women—is a question given its urgency by the social meaning of the private as a sphere of choice. But for women the measure of the intimacy has been the measure of the oppression. This is why feminism has had to explode the private. This is why feminism has seen the personal as the political. The private is public for those for whom the personal is political. In this sense, there is no private, either normatively or empirically. Feminism confronts the fact that women have no privacy to lose or to guarantee. We are not inviolable. Our sexuality is not only violable, it is—hence, we are—seen *in* and *as* our violation. To confront the fact that we have no privacy is to confront the intimate degradation of women as the public order.

In this light, a right to privacy looks like an injury got up as a gift. Freedom from public intervention coexists uneasily with any right which requires social preconditions to be meaningfully delivered. For example, if inequality is socially pervasive and enforced, equality will require intervention, not abdication, to be meaningful. But the right to privacy is not thought to require social change. It is not even thought to require any social preconditions, other than nonintervention by the public. The point for the abortion cases is not that indigency—which was the specific barrier to effective choice in *McRae*—is well within the public power to remedy, nor that the state is hardly exempt in issues of the distribution of wealth. The point is rather that *Roe v. Wade* presumes that government nonintervention into the private sphere promotes a woman's freedom of choice. When the alternative is jail, there is much to be said for this argument. But the *McRae* result sustains the meaning of privacy in *Roe:* women are guaranteed by the public no more than what we can get in private—that is, what we can extract through our intimate associations with men. Women with privileges get rights.

So women got abortion as a private privilege, not as a public right. We got control over reproduction that is controlled by "a man or The Man," an individual man or the doctors or the government. Abortion was not decriminalized, it was legalized. In *Roe,* the government set the stage for the conditions under which women gain access to this right. Virtually every ounce of control that women won out of legalization has gone directly into the hands of men—husbands, doctors, or fathers—or is now in the process of attempting to be reclaimed through regulation.[18] This, surely, must be what is meant by reform.

It is not inconsistent, then, that framed as a privacy right a woman's decision to abort would have no claim on public support and would genuinely not be seen as burdened by that deprivation. Privacy conceived as a right from public intervention and disclosure is the opposite of the relief that *McRae* sought for welfare women. State intervention would have provided a choice women did *not* have in private. The women in *McRae,* women whose sexual refusal has

counted for particularly little, needed something to make their privacy effective.[19] The logic of the court's response resembles the logic by which women are supposed to consent to sex. Preclude the alternatives, then call the sole remaining option "her choice." The point is that the alternatives are precluded *prior to* the reach of the chosen legal doctrine. They are precluded by conditions of sex, race, and class—the very conditions the privacy frame not only leaves tacit, but which it exists to *guarantee.*

When the law of privacy restricts intrusions into intimacy, it bars change in control over that intimacy. The existing distribution of power and resources within the private sphere will be precisely what the law of privacy exists to protect. Just as pornography is legally protected as individual freedom of expression—without questioning whose freedom and whose expression and at whose expense—abstract privacy protects abstract autonomy, without inquiring into whose freedom of action is being sanctioned, at whose expense. It is probably not coincidence that the very things feminism regards as central to the subjection of women—the very place, the body; the very relations, heterosexual; the very activities, intercourse and reproduction; and the very feelings, intimate—form the core of privacy doctrine's coverage. From this perspective, the legal concept of privacy can and has shielded the place of battery, marital rape, and women's exploited labor; has preserved the central institutions whereby women are *deprived* of identity, autonomy, control and self-definition; and has protected the primary activity through which male supremacy is expressed and enforced.

To fail to recognize the meaning of the private in the ideology and reality of women's subordination by seeking protection behind a right *to* that privacy is to cut women off from collective verification and state support in the same act. I think this has a lot to do with why we can't organize women on the abortion issue. When women are segregated in private, separated from each other, one at a time, a right *to* that privacy isolates us at once from each other and from public recourse. This right to privacy is a right of men "to be let alone" to oppress women one at a time.[20] It embodies and reflects the private sphere's existing definition of womanhood. This instance of liberalism—applied to women as if we *are* persons, gender neutral—reinforces the division between public and private that is *not* gender neutral. It is at once an ideological division that lies about women's shared experience and mystifies the unity among the spheres of women's violation. It is a very material division that keeps the private beyond public redress and depoliticizes women's subjection within it. It keeps some men out of the bedrooms of other men.

Endnotes

1. See my article, "Feminism, Marxism, Method and the State," *Signs* 8 (1983): 635–58.

2. This is not to suggest that the decision should have gone the other way, or to propose individual hearings to determine coercion prior to allowing abortions. Nor is it to criticize Justice Blackmun, author of the majority opinion in *Roe*, who probably saw legalizing abortion as a way to help women out of a desperate situation, which it has done.

3. D. H. Regan, "Rewriting *Roe v. Wade.*" *77 Michigan Law Review* 1569 (1979), in which the Good Samaritan happens in the fetus.

4. As of 1973, ten states that made abortion a crime had exceptions for rape and incest; at least three had exceptions for rape only. Many of these exceptions were based on Model Penal Code Section 230.3 (Proposed Official Draft 1962), quoted in *Doe v. Bolton*, 410 U.S. 179, 205-7, App. B (1973), permitting abortion, *inter alia*, in cases of "rape, incest, or other felonious intercourse." References to states with incest and rape exceptions can be found in *Roe v. Wade*, 410 U.S. 113 n.37 (1973). Some versions of the Hyde Amendment, which prohibits use of public money to fund abortions, have contained exceptions for cases of rape or incest. All require immediate reporting of the incident.

5. Kristin Luker, *Taking Chances: Abortion and the Decision Not to Contracept* (Berkeley and Los Angeles; University of California Press, 1976).

6. *Roe v. Wade*, 410 U.S. 113 (1973).

7. *Griswold v. Connecticut*, 381 U.S. 479 (1965).

8. *Eisenstadt v. Baird*, 405 U.S. 438 (1972).

9. *Harris v. McRae*, 448 U.S. 297 (1980).

10. T. Gerety, "Redefining Privacy," *Harvard Civil Rights Civil Liberties Law Review* 12 (1977): 233-96, at 236.

11. Kenneth I. Karst, "The Freedom of Intimate Association," *Yale Law Journal* 89 (1980): 624; "Developments—The Family," *Harvard Law Review* 93 (1980): 1157–1383; *Doe v. Commonwealth Atty,* 403 F. Supp. 1199 (E.D. Va. 1975), *aff'd without opinion*, 425 U.S. 901 (1976) but cf. *People v. Onofre*, 51 N.Y.2d 476 (1980), *cert. denied* 451 U.S. 987 (1981).

12. Tom Grey, "Eros, Civilization and the Burger Court," *Law and Contemporary Problems* 43 (1980): 83.

13. Susan Sontag, "The Third World of Women," *Partisan Review* 40 (1973): 188.

14. See Adrienne Rich, *Of Women Born: Motherhood As Experience and Institution* (New York: Bantam Books, 1977), ch. 3, "The Kingdom of the Fathers," esp. pp. 47, 48: "The child that I carry for nine months can be defined *neither* as me or as not-me" (emphasis in the original).

15. Kristin Booth Glen, "Abortion in the Courts: A Lay Women's Historical Guide to the New Disaster Area," *Feminist Studies* 4 (1978): 1.

16. Judith Jarvis Thomson, "A Defense of Abortion," *Philosophy and Public Affairs* 1 (1971): 47-66.

17. Andrea Dworkin, *Right Wing Women* (New York: Perigee, 1983). You must read this book. See also Friedrich Engels arguing on removing private housekeeping into social industry, *Origin of the Family, Private Property and the State* (New York: International Publishers, 1942).

18. *H. L. v. Matheson*, 450 U.S. 398 (1981); *Poe v. Gerstein; Bellotti v. Baird*, 443 U.S. 622 (1979); but cf. *Planned Parenthood of Central Missouri v. Danforth*, 428 U.S. 52 (1976).

19. See Dworkin, *Right Wing Women*, pp. 98-99.

20. S. Warren and L. Brandeis, "The Right to Privacy," *Harvard Law Review* 4 (1890); 190, p. 205; but note that the right of privacy under some *state* constitutions has been held to *include* funding for abortions: *Committee to Defend Reproductive Rights v. Meyers*, 29 Cal. 3d 252 (1981); *Moe v. Society of Admin. and Finance*, 417 N.E.2d 387 (Mass. 1981).

24. Judaism and the Justification of Abortion for Nonmedical Reasons

Sandra B. Lubarsky

Sandra B. Lubarsky assesses the justification for abortion found in biblical and Talmudic sources. Lubarsky's inquiry leads her to conclude that there are no *Halakic* statements that oppose abortion; in fact, these materials clearly indicate that fetal life has little independent value, that only a monetary recompense was required for the destruction of fetal life, and that the mother's life was always thought to possess greater value than the potential life of the fetus. She argues that extra-*Halakic* sources have undergirded rabbinic opposition to abortion except in those cases when the life or health of the mother is in serious jeopardy. Lubarsky concludes that a proper reading of *Halakic* sources suggests that Judaism can support abortion on other, nonmedical grounds without denying its tragic and life-affirming dimensions.

All rabbis see the need for justifying abortion, and almost all have found the sole justification in the preservation of the mother's life or health. Yet, there is no clearcut prohibition against abortion in biblical or talmudic sources and no *halakic* reason to limit abortion to those circumstances described as "medically indicated." Why, in the absence of any *Halakic* prohibition, do so many rabbis decide against abortion unless it is necessary to a woman's physical well-being? What is the basis of this Jewish stance against abortion other than for medical reasons?

The answer involves a discussion of the status of extra-*Halakic* philosophical and theological principles in rabbinic decision making. In general, the rabbis do not find that the legal action guides given in *halakic* literature sufficiently address the issue of abortion. The legal status of abortion is clear: the killing of an embryo is not murder. But what of the moral implications of abortion? As R. Jacob Emden put it in his Glosses to the Talmud, "Who would *permit* killing an embryo without reason, even if there be no death penalty for it?"[1] Abortion may not be a capital offense, but it is still morally reprehensible. Within Jewish circles, the discussion about abortion is a discussion about sufficient moral justification for an act that is not legally culpable.

Though agreement among rabbis as to what constitutes *sufficient reason* for abortion falls short of

unanimity, it does not fall short by much. In the greatest number of decisions made by members of both the "lenient" and the "stringent" schools, abortion has been permitted on medical grounds only.[2] By "medically advised" abortion I mean the traditional "therapeutic" abortion, that is, abortion for the purpose of preserving the life of the mother, a definition that was often broadened to include any severe threat to the mother's physical health, and less often included a threat to the mother's mental health. By "non-medically advised" abortion I mean abortion that is justified by ecological, sociological, economic, emotional, or intellectual reasons. These reasons may be predicated upon such current concerns as pollution, overpopulation, and male and female liberation. One way to account for the rabbis' conservative attitude—the attitude that permits only medically advised abortion, in the face of a more permissive *halakhah*—is to seek a set of premises that is common to the rabbis and predisposes them to a more restrictive view of abortion. Because the rabbis hold to these premises, they find themselves uncomfortable with the *legal* position on abortion and attempt to mitigate the influence of that position.

In the first section of this essay I will give support for my assertions about the method of rabbinic decision making. The second section will be a very brief overview of the biblical and Talmudic passages that address abortion. In the third section, I will consider the six theological and philosophical assumptions which I believe form the implicit foundation for rabbinic decisions on abortion. In the last section, I will

From Sandra Lubarsky, " Judaism and The Justification of Abortion for Nonmedical Reasons," *Journal of Reform Judaism* 31(1984): 1–13.

argue against the validity of some of these assumptions and for a reinterpretation of others.

Extralegal Elements in Rabbinic Decision Making

The rabbinic decision-making process as it pertains to the issue of abortion is an inductive one, that is, the rabbis enter the discussion with certain preestablished ethical perspectives which they then seek to validate by invoking corroborative texts and rulings. This assertion is in direct opposition to that made by J. David Bleich, who contends that "definitive *pesak* [is] derived from fundamental principles,"[3] rabbinic decisions on abortion are reached through a deductive process. I base my assertion on the debate engendered by Maimonides' discussion of abortion in terms of "pursuer" and "pursued."

Maimonides' discussion is as follows:

> This, too, is a [negative] commandment: Not to take pity on the life of a pursuer. Therefore the Sages ruled that when the woman has difficulty in giving birth, one may dismember the child in her womb—either with drugs or by surgery—*because he is like a pursuer seeking to kill her.* Once his head has emerged, he may not be touched, for we do not set aside one life for another; *this is the natural course of the world.*[4]

Maimonides' postulate that the fetus can be destroyed because it is a pursuer of the mother has been variously interpreted as an additional requirement for abortion, as an independent criterion, as a more specific and hence more rigorous requirement, and as a more specific and hence more lenient requirement for abortion. For example, R. Hayyim Soloveitchik renders the strict reading that only when the fetus is a pursuer can its life be forfeited.[5] R. Isaac Lampronti follows this with the notion that dire physical distress arising from nonfetal causes (for example, diabetes), but complicated by pregnancy, is not a valid reason for abortion. Abortion is justifiable only if the "pursuer" fetus is *directly* responsible for the threat to the mother's life.[6] The justification for abortion is made even more rigorous by R. Ezekiel Landau, who maintains that although the status of the fetus is inferior to that of the mother (as established by *halakhah* and upheld by Rashi), the justification for abortion *must be augmented* by Maimonides' "pursuer" argument. That the fetus is inferior to the mother

is insufficient; it must also be "like a pursuer seeking to kill her" if abortion is to be authorized.[7] More lenient positions are held by Rabbis Isaac Schorr and Jacob Schorr, who hold that Maimonides' formulation serves to reinforce the right of feticide, and by R. Moshe Zweig of Antwerp, who believes that the pursuer argument changes the status of therapeutic abortion from permitted to required.[8]

There is, in short, no single interpretation of Maimonides' ruling. That the pursuer argument can be used both to justify abortion and to limit it strictly suggests that interpretive decisions are based not on "pertinent sources"[9] but rather on preconceived ethical stances. The underpinnings of these ethical positions are extralegal philosophical and theological ideas.

Overview of Biblical and Talmudic Sources on Abortion

There are no biblical or Talmudic statements directly opposed to abortion. Indeed, in the one place in which abortion is explicitly dealt with, one finds outright support for medical abortion:

> If a woman has [life-threatening] difficulty in childbirth, one dismembers the embryo within her, limb by limb, because her life takes precedence over its life. (Mishna, Oholot 7:6)[10]

There are other passages which, although they do not address the matter of abortion per se, suggest that a fetus is not considered to be a person:

> If men strive, and wound a pregnant woman so that her fruit be expelled, but no harm befall [her], then shall he [the assailant] be fined as her husband assesses, and the matter placed before the judges. But if harm befall [her], then "shalt thou give life for life . . ." (Exod. 21:22–23)
>
> [In the case of] a woman [convicted of a capital crime] who goes forth to be executed [and who, after the verdict was returned, is found to be pregnant], we do not wait for her to give birth. (Mishnah, Arakhin I, 4 [7a])

In the first case, feticide is not murder because the fetus does not have the status of a self-sufficient human being. Capital compensation is not required, only monetary. In the second case, punishment of the woman that results in the fetus's death is not murder because the fetus has no status distinct from any other part of her body. While the fetus is in utero, it is not an independent entity. It is a part of the mother like her thigh or her limb.[11] In both cases it is clear that the death of a fetus is not murder. Prior to being born, the life within a pregnant woman is not a human life.

In the above passages, the fetus is accorded little value because of its status as a dependent and undifferentiated being. There are, however, Talmudic statements which presuppose that the fetus has some intrinsic value. For example, it is required that the Sabbath be broken in order to remove a fetus from a woman who has died during labor.[12] Though the fetus's viability is yet doubtful, it is sufficiently valuable that the Sabbath laws must be set aside in order to save it. There is debate between the authorities as to whether the Sabbath should be violated to save a fetus that has not attained the transitional status of a *gufa acharina* (a separate, though not wholly independent, body), that is, a fetus that has not reached the birthing stage. Nevertheless, all authorities agree that at some point in its development, the life of the fetus is of such worth as to require the violation of the Sabbath laws. Though not a person, the embryo participates in life and for this reason is awarded some degree of value.

The assumptions undergirding the legal action guides on abortion may be summarized as follows: (a) Human fetal life has little independent value. It is certainly not "sacred." (b) The value that it has is far inferior to the value of a fully viable human being, so much so that only monetary recompense must be made for the destruction of fetal life, whereas capital recompense is made for the destruction of a person's life. (c) An existing human being has greater worth than a *potential* human being, that is, the mother is of greater value than the fetus, so that "medically advised" abortion— abortion when the mother's life is endangered—is not only permitted, but is required. The question of abortion, then, is not a question of "whose blood is redder," nor is it a matter of "setting one life against another." The legal tradition makes it clear, first, that human fetal life is not equivalent in value to fully formed, self-supportive human life and, second, that "medically advised" abortion is required.

Philosophical and/or Theological Assumptions

There are at least six assumptions that are evident in the thinking of most Jews (and non-Jewish Westerners) who are opposed to a policy of abortion which, like the Supreme Court ruling of 1973, allows for both medically advised abortion and abortion for other than medical reasons within the first three months of a pregnancy. Of course, not all six of the assumptions listed below are held by every Jewish thinker who opposes "nonmedically advised" abortion. Still these six notions have a centrality and popularity that justify our consideration of them. The assumptions are these:

1. With the exception of God, human life is valued over every other kind of life.
2. In almost all cases, an increase in human life amounts to an increase in value.
3. All humans are of equal worth from God's perspective.
4. God is unchanging, or, at least, God's essence is unchanging.
5. The mental or psychological aspect of human life is (somehow) less basic than the physical aspect.
6. Existing human life has precedence over potential human life.

Assumption 1 Except for God, nothing is more valuable than human life. Murder and adultery are sins because they undermine the value of human life, but the greatest sin of all is idolatry because it places something above God. Most Jews do not deny that value can be located outside the divine and human realms— all that God created was called "good"—but only God is more valuable than human life, which was given dominion over the earth. The death of an animal *may* be a genuine loss, the death of a plant, less so, but the death of a human being is always a loss. There is a reverence for all life, but especially for human life.

Assumption 2 If human life is intrinsically valuable, then an increase of human life leads to an increase of value in the world. What requires justification is the taking of a human life or the intentional delay or absence of procreational activity, that is, contraception. There is a sense that abortion and/or neglect of the duty of procreation can be said to "diminish God's image."

Quality of human life is linked to quantity of human life. Except in times of famine, an increase in population has been preferred to an increase in material comfort. Qualitative increase in any other sense that numerical increase is seen as a secondary, though not unimportant, value.

A corollary to the notion that quantitative increase is of primary importance is the idea that the principal activity in life is reproductive activity. And in the post-Holocaust world, the increase of human life, especially Jewish life, takes on new significance. There are few Jews who would doubt that an increase in the Jewish population is an increase of value in the world.

Assumption 3 From God's vantage point, all humans are of equal value. Some are wise, some are foolish, some rich, some poor, some strong, some weak, but none is more valuable in God's eyes than the next. God is just, which means that God discriminates between the good and the bad, but God's judgment of each individual is made in light of the Divine's ideals for humanity and not in light of other individuals.

Assumption 4 God in Godself is changeless. What God has revealed and what God has decided are as true today as they were in the time of Moses. The Jewish God of history—the divine may intervene in the course of human events—but God will not reinvent the terms of history itself. If God said, "Be fruitful and multiply," that command is as appropriate to our time as it is to any other time. The value system of the historical structure stands firm.

Assumption 5 This assumption addresses the implicit belief that the mental or psychological aspect of human existence is dependent upon the physical aspect of human existence and, therefore, that the physical aspect is more fundamental. If a pregnancy threatens the physical existence of a woman, an abortion is always in order; if a pregnancy threatens the psychological well-being of a woman, abortion may be permitted, but is not required. The primary concern is with the woman's continued physical existence, not with her happiness or peace of mind. Mental health is at best secondary to physical health and at worst, epiphenomenal.

Assumption 6 Present life is more valuable than future life. A pregnant woman's life is more valuable than the life of a fetus, because her life is actual and its human life (note the qualification "human") is only potential. Similarly, though less obviously, a woman's life *now,* or the life of any person now, is more valuable than what it potentially might be in the future. At each moment the present is actual, the future only potential. In the case of pregnancy, both types of actual-potential distinctions are relevant, for a pregnant woman is both who she actually is and who she potentially could be, while the fetus within her is actually alive as a fetus and potentially alive as a person.

Reassessment of the Philosophical and/or Theological Assumptions

It is my contention that the biblical and talmudic evaluations of human fetal life—that, at least in the early stages of pregnancy, a fetus is not a *human* life, and that while it has great *potential* value, it has only minimal *actual* value—makes for a position that upholds abortion for both medically advised and other than medically advised reasons. The fact that most rabbis believe that only medically advised abortion is justified (and abortion for economic, sociological, ecological, or intellectual reasons is not justified—even though abortion as presented in authoritative Jewish sources was not restricted to any one set of justifications) is evidence that an extra-*Halakic* conviction set is operating in the decision-making process. It is my belief that the rabbis depend to a large extent on these extra-*Halakic* presuppositions when formulating their position on abortion. The purpose of this final section is to examine some of the ways in which these six philosophical and/or theological assumptions mitigate the justification of non-medically advised abortion and to consider some of the consequences such exclusion has in the contemporary world.[13]

Assumptions 1, 2, and 3

The first three assumptions of the extra-*Halakic* conviction set are so closely interconnected that it is useful to address them jointly. These three assumptions are: (1) With the exception of God, human life is valued over every other kind of life; (2) in almost all cases, an increase in human life amounts to an increase in value; and (3) all humans are of equal worth from God's perspective.

The two questions under consideration are: (a) "How does an interpretation of these notions lead to a justification of only medically advised abortion?" (b) "is this the only legitimate interpretation at which one may arrive within the Jewish tradition?"

The first question can be restated as, "Why are abortions for other than medical reasons not permitted?" Part of the answer lies in the anthropocentrism of the first two assumptions. In Judaism, human life is held to be superior to nonhuman life because only humans are created in God's image and only they are endowed with souls. Nonhuman life has intrinsic value, but in rabbinic tradition its intrinsic value is generally subordinated to its instrumental value, that is, the value it has *for* human beings. There is a reverence for life in general in Judaism, but there is a particular reverence for human life, and often this comes to mean that human life is "absolutely" valuable (subject, of course, to God's will). By "absolutely" valuable the rabbis mean both that human life is superior to nonhuman life (Assumption 1) and that one human life cannot be weighed against another insofar as human life per se is absolutely valuable (Assumption 3). Two consequences of this anthropocentrism are the neither ecological concerns nor (oddly enough) sociological concerns are accepted as legitimate justifications for abortion. The reason that ecological concerns are not treated with any seriousness is because of a philosophy of nature that is anthropocentrically dualistic—humanity is distinct from and superior to nonhuman nature. The reason that sociological considerations are not judged legitimate is because of a philosophy of human nature that is absolutistic.

A worldview that, in fact (if not in principle), separates the human realm from the nonhuman realm is a distorted worldview.[14] We come to see ourselves as related only externally to the nonhuman world so that we think of ourselves as the only real *subjects* in a world of objects. The relationship that subjects and objects have is one-directional—the lower species contribute to the life of the higher species but not vice versa—and the essential mutuality, interdependence, and internal relatedness of all beings is denied. It then makes sense to limit the justifications for abortion to human concerns alone. In such a world, it is only the robbing of potential (and actual) human life that must be justified.

In the statement "Whatever the Holy One created in His universe, He created for His Glory," "His Glory" has been interpreted to mean humanity.[15] Here is conspicuous and unnecessary anthropocentrism; it is quite fair to the text to understand "His Glory" as referring to God, and not to humanity. When it is understood in this way, the intrinsic value of nonhuman life is recalled; it, too, is a direct glorification of God. From an ecological perspective (which includes humanity), life itself is robbery, for the living depend on the dead to sustain them. Because life feeds on life, "the robber requires justification."[16] Human life requires some sort of justification for the sacrifice it demands from other forms of life. The taking of any life, human or nonhuman, must be justified. Abortion, then, becomes an issue that cannot be considered apart from ecological issues.

A philosophy that recognizes that all beings have some degree of intrinsic value is very different from a philosophy in which only human beings have intrinsic value or a philosophy in which all beings are equally valuable. The first worldview requires that some kind of hierarchy of value be established. The rabbinic belief that every individual is of immeasurable worth in God's sight, that is, that human life per se is absolutely valuable, stands against the calculation of life presumed by a hierarchy of value. The rabbis have been unwilling to "set one life against another," to judge the "redness" of one person's blood over another's. In fact, however, there is a hierarchy at work in rabbinic evaluations, most obviously in the qualitative differences made between human and nonhuman life, between humankind and God, and between actual and potential persons. The distinction between humans and nonhumans is discussed above. The second distinction, between humanity and divinity, is made clear in the discussion of those situations in which human life is not worth living. Under conditions that lead to idolatry, adultery, or murder, the absolute value of human life is shattered. By divine command, human life in those instances is to be forfeited. Thirdly, in the discussion of abortion, it is affirmed that the fetus is less than a person; though it is life, it is not at the level of human life and hence is of lesser value.[17] There is, then, a calculus of lie embedded in Jewish tradition so that a discussion of hierarchy of value is not without precedent.

That calculus is, I believe, based on the measure of *experience*—on the unique, purposeful moments of existence that distinguish one form of life from another. There is no equality of value between a fetus and a person because the experiences that define their existences are radically unequal—the fetus's experience lacks the richness, intentionality, and consciousness of a person's experience. We can affirm the intrinsic value of a fetus, an infant, and an adult, without also having to affirm an equality of value for them. And since we can do this, it is unreasonable to limit abortion to those instances in which a threat to the mother's health is present. Abortion may then be justified for other than medical reasons. Abortion may be judged to be beneficial to the mother's experience as a whole, including her intellectual, moral, emotional, and physical health and her sociological and ecological milieu.

Assumption 4

This is the assumption that God is unchanging, or, at least, the divine essence is unchanging. But if experience is worthwhile, if it counts for us, then it must also count for God. The biblical roots of this thesis are exemplified in the concept of a God of History. A God who is truly involved in the world is a God who is felt by others and who feels the experiences of others. To be affected by our relations with others is to be *internally related.* In the model of internal relations, an entity is what it is in relation to the environment. It is an abstraction, then, to talk about an entity without reference to its environment.[18]

What God does is influenced to some degree by what kind of world God participates in. If the world is an unpopulated one, God may work to increase the richness of experience by urging the creation to reproduce at a higher level. If the world is an overpopulated one, God may work to increase the richness of experience by urging the creatures to reduce their rates of reproduction and to increase their enjoyment in other ways. God is a deontologist only insofar as God *always* works to bring about good in the cosmos. God's purpose is to elicit intensity of experience, not to achieve one final experience. And the ways in which God works are never decided independently of the situation. Hence, God may not always act so as to increase the human population, although God will always act in such a way as to encourage richness of experience. To say that abortion always "diminishes God's image" is to undermine God's ability to be responsive.

Assumption 5

Both the mental and physical aspects of human beings are affirmed in Jewish tradition. Indeed, it is because we are not merely material beings that God can influence us in noncoercive ways. But there is an overwhelming tendency in the tradition to emphasize the physical aspects over the mental aspects, so much so that the mental is often understood to be an epiphenomenon of the physical. This tendency is very apparent in rabbinic discussions of abortion.

It is an issue of debate among the rabbis as to whether a threat to mental health is a justifiable cause for abortion. Many agree that it is, but a good many of these hold that it is so only when mental instability is a threat to physical health, for example, when suicide threatens. The permit for abortion is less likely to be granted when the mother's mental instability appears not to be reflected in self-damaging physical behavior.

Even when the mother's mental health is considered in an abortion decision, there is no evidence that "mentality" is understood to include anything other than "emotional health." The intellectual aspect of a woman's mental life is not considered. "Considerations of physical hazard and fundamental welfare of existing children are admissible" as justifications for abortion, and occasionally a woman's emotional well-being alone is admitted. However, a woman's intellectual life is never discussed as a possible reason for abortion, and it can be surmised that such an argument would fall under the category of "self-indulgence or convenience."[19]

Not to take a woman's mental life, in all its aspects, seriously is to deny women what has been permitted to men: the assumption of interiority and, thereby, of individuality. Not to accord significance to the mental aspects of her life—significance that at least equals and ought to surpass the physical aspects of her life—is not to accord her the freedom and creativity that is given to men. In this kind of Judaism, women bear children, not witness. So long as mentality is subservient to physicality in the discussion about abortion, or any issue concerning women, the tendency will be to perceive women as being less than fully human.

Assumption 6

The assumption that existing human life has precedence over potential human life is the basis for many of the more "lenient" rulings on abortion. "The judge can rule only on the evidence before his eye," and in many cases it was ruled that "her pain comes first," that is, that abortion on the basis of her physical and sometimes emotional pain is justified.[20]

This logic is commendable because it recognizes the difference between the value of potential life and the value of actual life; or, to put it differently, it recognizes that a fetus is potentially very valuable, but *actually* only somewhat valuable. When the actual life of the mother is weighed against the actual life of the fetus qua fetus, the mother's concerns (at least her physical and sometimes mental concerns) are given precedence. The health of an actually existing child also is granted precedence, in one responsum, over the life of the actually existing fetus. And finally, greater weight is given to the life of the actual fetus over the life of the future fetus; abortion on the grounds that the fetus is probably developing in a defective way such that the future child's life will be less than normal is not permitted.[21]

However, always to grant precedence to the present over the future—to existing human life over potential life—is to ignore the pull of the future upon the present moment. Our actions and God's actions in the present are partially influenced by our anticipations of the future. The danger in focusing almost exclusively on the present is the danger of becoming almost entirely centered on the momentary self. Shortsightedness and self-centeredness are obstacles in the way of transcendence. Our survival—and beyond that, peace—depends upon our ability to respond to the present in light of the possibilities that may become actualities.

The concept of sacrifice is an important corrective to the view that potential life is always less valuable than actual life. In sacrifice, one gives up a present actuality in order to enable the possible actualization of present potentialities. The possible is given greater weight than the actual. There are cases in which the value of potential life—the intrinsic value of future humans which may be actualized if these future humans become actual humans—is greater than the value of actually existing life. And those cases include not just that potential value the fetus harbors, but that potential which is completely unactualized (i.e., the value of potential fetuses) and that potential which is part of the future life of those who are already persons, for example, the existing mother's future, the existing family's future, the future of the population at large, and so forth.

Conclusion

The purpose of this essay has been to illuminate some of the extra-*Halakic* assumptions that undergird the rabbinic responsa on abortion and to show that these assumptions are not demanded by tradition. There are biblical and Talmudic precedents for correcting anthropocentrism with ecocentrism, absolutism with a hierarchy of values, philosophical materialism with dipolarity, conservatism with "sacred discontent,"[22] and sexism with egalitarianism.[23] When these correctives are assumed, Judaism becomes a worldview that recognizes that all life—human, nonhuman, and divine—is interdependent and mutually responsive. Hence, a decision about abortion is a decision that must be made in light of both actual and potential human, nonhuman, and divine life. All decisions involve judgments of values, and if those judgments are to be made with the subtlety that an ecological and dipolar worldview demands, they will be decisions based on concrete units of experience rather than on abstractions of life. When the Jewish sources are thus considered, it becomes clear that Judaism not only permits abortions for medical reasons, but also supports abortion for nonmedical reasons. More importantly, Judaism can uphold such positions without denying either the tragedy of abortion—"What might have been and was not"—or the life-affirming aspects of abortion—"What can be."[24]

Endnotes

1. *Hagahot Ya'avetz* to Nida 44b.

2. See David Feldman, *Birth Control in Jewish Law* (New York: New York University Press, 1968), (chapters 14 and 15, for his thorough discussion of the positions represented on the one hand by R. Untermann and on the other by R. Uziel.

3. J. David Bleich, "Abortion in Halakic Literature," *Tradition,* vol. 6, no. 4 (Winter 1968), p. 73.

4. *Yad, Hilkhot Rotseach Ushemirat Nefesh,* 1, 9, quoted in Feldman, op. cit., p. 276.

5. R. Hayyim Soloveitchik, *Chiddushei R. Chayim Halevi* (1936), quoted in Feldman, *op. cit.,* pp. 279, 281.

6. R. Isaac Lampronti, *Pachad Yitschak,* s.v. *nefalim,* quoted in Feldman, op. cit., p. 282.

7. R. Ezekiel Landau, Responsa *Noda Biyehuda,* Second Series, H.M., no. 59, quoted in Feldman, op. cit., p. 278.

8. R. Isaac Schorr, Responsa *Koach Shor,* no. 20.; R. Jacob Schorr, Responsa *Ge-onim Batra-ei,* no. 45; R. Moshe Zweig, *No-am,* VII (1964), especially pp. 49-53, quoted in Feldman, op. cit., pp. 277-83.

9. Bleich, op. cit., p. 73.

10. The passage continues: "Once its head (or 'its greater part') has emerged, it may not be touched, for we do not set aside one life for another."

11. E.g., Bab. Talmud, Hulin 58, "The fetus is the thigh of its mother," and Gittin 23b, "The fetus is regarded as one of her limbs."

12. Bab. Talmud, Arakhin 7a.

13. I make the following evaluation from a Whiteheadian-Hartshornean perspective. The Whiteheadian, or process, metaphysics is not, I believe, in conflict with the thrust of our basic Jewish insights and may be used to place these insights within an appropriate ontology. Central to the process schema are such notions as the internality of relations, the primacy of experience, the gradation of values, the dipolar (mental-physical) nature of every experience, and a sympathetic and mutable God. These are notions that are applied in the discussion which follows.

14. This is true from both a biblical and a Whiteheadian perspective.

15. Avot 6:2. This interpretation is given by A. Cohen in *Everyman's Talmud* (New York: Schocken Books, 1978), pp. 67ff.

16. Alfred North Whitehead, *Process and Reality,* corrected edition, ed. David R. Griffin (New York: The Free Press, 1978), p. 105.

17. Also pertinent here is the mishnaic ruling that "A man takes precedence over a woman when it comes to saving a life and to restoring something lost" (M. Horayot 3.7).

18. Formally referred to by Whitehead as "the fallacy of simple location."

19. Feldman, op. cit., p. 53.

20. *Ibid.,* pp. 292, 294.

21. *Ibid.,* p. 292.

22. See Herbert N. Schneidau, *Sacred Discontent* (Baton Rouge: Louisiana State University Press, 1976).

23. See Cynthia Ozick, "Notes toward Finding the Right Question," in *On Being a Jewish Feminist,* ed. Susannah Heschel (New York: Schocken Books, 1983), pp. 120–51.

24. Alfred North Whitehead, *Adventures of Ideas* (New York: The Free Press, 1933), p. 286.

Part 4

Just War and Pacifism

25. Moral Judgment in Time of War

Michael Walzer

Michael Walzer engages the judgment of the realists that war possesses no moral limits and argues instead that useful moral distinctions remain available, even in times of war, that enable us to recognize and later prosecute criminal behavior. There are grounds for going to war (*jus ad bellum*) and criteria for fighting wars justly (*jus in bello*) that clearly acknowledge war as brutal and regrettable, but still a rule-governed activity.

When you resorted to force as the arbiter of human difficulty, you didn't know where you were going. . . . If you got deeper and deeper, there was just no limit except what was imposed by the limitations of force itself. (Dwight Eisenhower, at a press conference, January 12, 1955)

I have said to these young men that they make too much of American brutality. The Viet Cong is equally brutal. Whether one is among the battling Pakistanis and Indians, or in Watts, or in warfare anywhere, the law of violence is such that each side becomes equally vicious. To try to distinguish which is more vicious is to fail to recognize the logic of war. (Bayard Rustin, in *Civil Disobedience*, an occasional paper of the Center for the Study of Democratic Institutions, 1966)

From opposite sides of the spectrum of American politics, Eisenhower and Rustin suggest the same general theory of moral judgment in wartime. They both suggest that only one judgment is possible. War itself (Rustin is a pacifist), or some particular war, can be called just or unjust. But apparently nothing whatsoever can be said about morality *in* war, about justice or injustice in the midst of the strife, because the "logic of war" imposes brutality equally on all participants. Once war begins, there are no moral limits, only practical ones, only the "limitations of force itself" and of the "law of violence." This is a very common American view and one sufficiently serious to warrant careful refutation. I want to argue that it is profoundly wrong and that what the old lawyers called *jus in bello* (justice in war) is at least as important as *jus ad bellum* (the justice of war). War is indeed ugly, but there are degrees of ugliness and

From Michael Walzer, "Moral Judgment in Time of War," *Dissent*, vol. 14, no. 3 (1967), pp. 284–292. Reprinted with permission from Dissent Magazine.

humane men must, as always, be concerned with degrees. As we watch the continued escalation of the war in Vietnam, this truth is driven home with especial force. Surely there is a point at which the means employed for the sake of this or that political goal come into conflict with a more general human purpose: the maintenance of moral standards and the survival of some sort of international society. At that point, political arguments against the use of such means are overshadowed, or ought to be, by moral arguments. At that point, war is not merely ugly, but criminal.

There are limits to what can be done in wartime, even by men convinced that they are pursuing justice. These limits are never easy to specify, and it may be that they need to be newly specified for every war. It may be that morality in war is a discretionary morality. But that does not absolve us from making judgments. It only requires that we be undogmatic, pay close attention to the facts, and struggle to grasp, as best we can, the anguish of each concrete decision.

There is an immediate improbability about Rustin's statement which is worth noting at the outset. If brutality is something that can be measured and apportioned, as he seems to suggest, then there are an infinite number of possible apportionments, and it is extremely unlikely that equality will ever be attained. In every war, the likelihood is that one side is more brutal than the other, though often the differences are too small to matter much, even to the most scrupulous of moralists. But in the case of Vietnam, where the destructive powers of the two protagonists are so radically unequal, a casual insistence on equal brutality cannot satisfy even the least scrupulous of moralists.

But perhaps what Rustin means is that each side is as brutal as it can be, given its relative power. Brutality stops only when force is limited or when it encounters superior force. That is presumably also Eisenhower's meaning. But then what the two men are talking about is, so to speak, the logic of intentions and not of behavior. Even here, however, they are probably not right. In many wars it is possible to say that different degrees of brutality are intended by the different sides. Sometimes these different intentions are an inherent part of different strategies, sometimes of different military situations. It is fairly obvious, for example, that armies fighting in friendly territory are likely to intend less brutality—whatever the limits of their power—than armies fighting amidst a hostile population. Insofar as wars are territorially limited (most wars are), one side probably has to be more brutal than the other. There are moral as well as strategic disadvantages to fighting wars in other peoples' countries.

Even if there is an identity of brutal intentions, however, it does not follow that the judgments we make of the two sides should be the same. Military decisions are guided by a kind of reciprocity: one side must do, or thinks it must do, whatever the other side does. In every war, however, there exist agreements, mostly informal, which rule out certain actions. Such agreements are usually enforced by mutual deterrence, though self-restraint also plays a part. Sometimes mutual deterrence doesn't work; perhaps one side is so strong that it need not fear retaliation from the other, whatever it does. Then self-restraint may break down also, and the agreements will be violated. After all, it might be said, the purpose of soldiers is to escape reciprocity, to inflict more damage on the enemy than he can inflict on them. Soldiers can never be blamed for taking advantage of superior strength. But that is not so, for there are many different ways of taking advantage of one's strength. In every case where superiority is attained and the war escalated beyond some previously established set of limits, a hard judgment has to be made. If the escalation breaks down limits useful not merely to the enemy, but to humanity generally, if precedents are established which make it likely that future wars will be more brutal than they would otherwise be, the initiating party can and must be condemned. This is so even if it can plausibly be said (for it can always be *said*) that the other side would have done the same if it could. Men are guilty of the crimes they commit, not the ones they are said to have wished to commit.

When we speak of brutality in wartime, we do not usually mean the killing of enemy combatants. So long as the fighting is actually in progress, virtually anything can be done to combatants—within limits set by such conventions as the ban on the use of poison gas. They have every reason to expect the worst and presumably are trained to defend themselves. It is their business to kill others until they are themselves killed. That is a brutal business when compared to peacetime pursuits; nevertheless, it involves behavior which is appropriate in time of war. Brutality most often begins with the killing of prisoners and non-combatants.

In the case of prisoners, the line between legitimate and illegitimate behavior is fairly easy to draw, in part because the condition which makes a man a prisoner is fairly easy to specify. A prisoner is an ex-combatant, helplessly in the hands of his enemies. He is entitled (according to explicit international agreements) to benevolent quarantine for the duration of the war. There has been a tendency in recent years to deny the quarantine and maintain a state of warfare, a struggle for the minds of the prisoners, even in the prison camps themselves. This is indeed a struggle limited only by the nature of available force: confessions and conversions cannot be won by killing prisoners. Virtually every form of violence short of murder, however, has been used. (See "The Destruction of Conscience in Vietnam" by Marshall Sahlins, *Dissent,* January-February 1966, for a description of ideological warfare against Vietcong prisoners; the theories behind this warfare and the methods employed in it seem to have been adapted from the Chinese Communists.) All this is criminal brutality. There is surely nothing in the "logic of war" that requires it.

With regard to non-combatants, the theoretical problems are much more difficult. This is so for a great number of reasons, several of which have been brought forward in recent months as justifications for American actions in Vietnam. First of all, modern military technology makes it very difficult to limit the damage one inflicts to enemy soldiers alone or even military installations. Even if a decision is made not to wage a full-scale campaign of terror against civilian populations, civilians are bound to be hurt and killed by what are called necessary efforts to prevent the production and transportation of military supplies. The function of the word "necessary" in arguments of this sort is worth examining. It serves to foreclose the very possibility of moral protest. Bombing is legitimate in war, the argument goes, whenever it is necessary to victory (or stalemate, or attrition, or whatever purpose is being pursued). Military necessity cannot justify wanton destruction; at the same time, moral principles cannot invalidate necessary destruction. In effect, necessity is the only standard, and the trained officers and strategists of the armed forces are the only competent judges. They solemnly conclude that civilian deaths are part of the inevitable ugliness of war.

They are sometimes right; but the argument does not hold in every case. It does not hold, for example, against all efforts to limit the geographic areas within which military judgments can apply. Rearward areas are not always subject to the same political jurisdiction as are the armies at the front. In the past, serious attempts have been made to recognize different degrees of neutrality for such areas and to admit the possibility of benevolent neutrality short of war—the kind of position the U.S. adopted vis-a-vis Great Britain in 1940 and 1941. We would have said at the time that despite the supplies we were providing for the British, German bombing of American factories would not have been morally justified (that is, it would have constituted aggression). The same principle applies with even greater force, I should think, to "little wars" where limitation of the struggle is much more likely than in big ones. Thus the U.S. participated informally in efforts to prevent the French from bombing Morocco and Tunisia during the Algerian war (February 1958), despite the constructions which French strategists, perhaps quite reasonably, put upon the notion of military necessity. Limits of this sort are very precarious and need to be re-examined in every case. Exceptions are always possible. Allowance might be made for the interdiction of supplies, for example, if it could be carried out with sufficient precision or at the very borders of the battle area. And, of course, a point may be reached when assistance from some ostensibly neutral country passes over into active participation: then the limits have been broken by the other side, and the soldiers must do what they can. Until then, however, decisions are moral and political as well as military, and all of us are involved.

In one sense, however, that is always true, for there are limits to the arguments that can be made from military necessity even after the disappearance of every distinction between battleground and hinterland. The distinction between civilian and soldier still stands, and among civilians that between partial participants in the business of war (workers in munitions factories) and virtual non-participants. In the past, systematic terror bombing of urban residential areas has been defended in the name of military necessity—and it has been carried out, as it probably will be again, even when the defense was none too good. But I find it very difficult even to conceive of circumstances in which such a defense could be good enough to warrant the denial and eradication of these distinctions. For the bar against the systematic slaughter of civilians is of such immense benefit to mankind that it could only be broken by a country absolutely certain not only that the immediate gains would be enormous, but that the shattered limit would never again be of any use. That is why wars to end war (or to end aggression, subversion, or anything else) are potentially so much more brutal than wars fought for realistic and limited objectives. They encourage men to think that *this time anything goes,* for there will never be another time. But there is always another time, and so *jus in bello* is always of crucial importance.

The second argument currently being made relies on the character of guerrilla warfare. By the special use they make of the civilian population, it is said, the guerrillas themselves destroy all conventional distinctions. But it has to be added that guerrillas do this only when they are successful in winning popular support. Failure clearly destroys no distinctions at all. It leaves the guerrillas isolated and subject to attacks which will be horrifying to non-combatants only if the attackers are wantonly careless and cruel. Limited success is a different matter. It can open the way for anything from endemic banditry to actual civil war, with the local authorities never certain just who or how many their enemies are: never certain, either, what actions against the population might be justified. The problems faced by foreign troops fighting local guerrillas are different again: their very presence is generally enough to extend the limits of guerrilla success in such a way that the foreigners must assume that all natives are at least potential enemies. Foreigners fighting local guerrillas are likely to find themselves driven to justify, or rather to attempt to justify, virtually every conceivable action against a hostile population–until they reach that climactic brutality summed up in the orders issued by General Okamura, Japanese commander in the struggle against Communist guerrillas in North China during World War II: "Kill all! Burn all! Destroy all!"

At this point, the questions of morality in war and of the morality of a particular war come together. Any war that requires the methods of General Okamura, or anything approaching them, is itself immoral, however exalted the purposes in the name of which it is being fought. It is simply not the case that every war requires such methods or that violence has some inherent logic which imposes this ultimate brutality on every combatant. The violence of the guerrillas themselves, for example, takes a very different form. But any effort to destroy a guerrilla movement which has won some substantial degree of popular support is almost certain to involve the indiscriminate slaughter of civilians, the shelling and bombing of inhabited villages (it may even require the development of atrocious "anti-personnel" weapons), the burning of homes, the forced transfer of populations, the establishment of civilian internment camps, and so on. It is no use saying that the guerrillas bring all this on themselves, or on their own people, by not wearing uniforms and fighting set battles. Strangely enough, men seem to prefer to wear uniforms and fight set battles when they can. They fight as guerrillas only when they lack the material resources to fight as soldiers.

Guerrilla warfare is a means the weak have invented for fighting the strong. It is not for that reason automatically justifiable: the weak have no monopoly on morality. Nevertheless, it must be recognized that guerrilla warfare is effective, in part, precisely because of the moral onus it imposes on the strong. The popularity of the guerrillas (they are not always popular) forces their powerful enemies either to give up the fight or accept responsibility for actions universally condemned by the moral opinion of mankind. I see no reason not to admit that it is almost always better to give up the fight.

Guerrilla warfare is brutal on both sides, though the brutality of the guerrillas is likely to be inhibited by their need to maintain support among the population. The terror campaigns of even moderately successful guerrillas tend to be more discriminating than those of the authorities, partly because the guerrillas have better sources of information, but also because their enemies are forced by their positions to make themselves visible. Under the circumstances, attacks on local magistrates probably constitute legitimate warfare. Such men have consciously joined one side in a civil dispute and presumably know the risks their choice entails. They are, for all practical purposes, combatants. On the other hand, the arbitrary selection of hostages from unfriendly villages, the murder of suspects and "class enemies," the public administration of atrocious punishments—all fairly common guerrilla practices—are illegitimate actions, inadequately justified by some underground version of the theory of military necessity. Brutality of this sort must be balanced against the brutality of the authorities or the foreigners.

Let us assume that in a particular case the balance favors the guerrillas. It still might be said that this provides no basis for a final judgment. For what if the guerrillas advocate the establishment of a tyrannical regime, while the foreign troops are defending democracy? I cannot think of any historical case in which these two conditions are met, but they are possible conditions and need to be discussed. The view is common enough that the side fighting a just war has greater latitude in choosing means than does the side fighting an unjust war. After all, war is not a game; crucial issues are being decided; sticking to the rules may well be less important than winning. But this is a very unstable position, since both sides always claim to be fighting a just war and so might argue that the limits don't apply to them. The real issue, then, is not whether the justice of one's cause legitimizes this or that act of unlimited violence, but whether one's own conviction as to the justice of one's cause does so. The very least that can be said is that most often it doesn't. The maintenance of some internal limits of war-making is almost certainly more important than the military or political objectives of either side. Once again, however, exceptions are always possible. One would have to be morally obtuse to insist that near-certainty is certainty itself. All that can finally be said is that there is an extraordinarily powerful prima facie case for *jus in bello*.

I do not mean to deny the possibility of justifying some degree of wartime brutality by reference to the purposes of the fighting. War is never an end in itself, and so it either can never be justified or it can be justified only by reference to ends outside itself. The resort to war is at best a desperate wager that things will be better, men happier or more free, when it is over than they would be if it were never fought. There are times, it seems to me, when that wager is morally acceptable. Then we fight, and since we hope to finish fighting as soon as possible, and since we are convinced that our cause is just, we resort to these means that seem to promise victory. Yet ends, we all know, do not justify *any* means, both because ends are contingent and uncertain (the results of the war depend in large part upon the ways in which it is fought), and because there are other ends in the world besides the ones we have most recently chosen. Unlimited violence, whatever its immediate effects, compromises everyone's future: for some it is a final solution, for others a warning of things to come.

Obviously, judgments of relative brutality are not the only basis of our political choices. We also pay attention to the purposes that brutality serves or supposedly serves; we may even choose, not necessarily rightly, greater brutality for the sake of greater purposes. So a man may decide that he wants to fight alongside soldiers who burn peasant villages, because he approves of their long-term goals or fears the consequences of their defeat. I have only tried to suggest that such choices ought to be worrying (that they do not simply trap us in the inexorable logic of war) and that they have their moral limits: there come moments when the sheer criminality of the means adopted by one side or another overwhelms and annuls all righteous intentions. One further point should be made: even short of such moments, our political choices do not free us from the business of judging. We judge our comrades and our enemies, in the name of ourselves, our comrades and our enemies. "I have to take part in

the struggle, not to humanize it," Jean Paul Sartre has said. That seems to me precisely wrong. If one must take sides, it is not in order to escape having to impose limits on oneself and one's comrades, but (in part) in order to do so effectively.

The same argument holds, I think, in those interior moments of war, when officers in the field sometimes face the most difficult and agonizing choices. They, above all, have a clear responsibility to uphold the limits. But it may be the case that only some act of brutality against the enemy will save the lives of the soldiers under their command, to whom they have an even clearer responsibility. Prisoners are sometimes killed, for example, because there seems no other way to guarantee their helplessness and protect one's own men. Whatever one thinks of such acts, when they are literally *incidents,* they are at least understandable. And when the exigencies of each incident are taken into account, they are possibly justifiable: here the end may justify the means. But it is something else again when brutality becomes a settled policy. Then it is probably true that officers ought to disobey, or at least to protest, the commands which follow from that policy (and which are unrelated to the exigencies of some particular situation). They ought to do so even if they still approve of the ends for which the war is being fought. Protest and disobedience are now the necessary consequences of their judgments, the only way they have to "humanize" the struggle.

Even if the lives of one's own troops are spared by a policy of unlimited violence, and even if more lives are spared than are lost on the other side, the policy is not justified. Morality in war is not settled by any single measure; it is a matter of long-term agreements and precedents as much or more than of immediate arithmetic. Here the rigorous "law of violence" comes into conflict with what are more loosely called the "laws" of international society. With regard to these laws soldiers must keep two facts in mind: that war is only a temporary rupture in international society and that it is a recurrent rupture. For both these reasons, it ought never to be a total rupture.

It is never the case that wartime actions are limited only by the force available to one side or to the other. Not that such limits are no limits at all; the second is especially effective. Fear of the enemy often has a wonderfully moralizing effect. We must all pray that we never find ourselves at war with an utterly powerless country, deprived of every retaliatory capacity. Still, many wars will be fought between states of radically unequal strength. In such cases, more than in other types of war, it is enormously important that the moral opinion of neutral nations and of all mankind be mobilized to uphold those precarious barriers, distinctions and limits which stand between conventional warfare, ugly as it is, and criminal brutality. Rather than accept the "logic of war" we must judge every military act by another logic.

It is, to be sure, disturbing to see a few men seize upon this other logic and make it the basis for hysterical and self-righteous denunciation. Moral judgment, like moral choice, is highly vulnerable to distortion. Both can become occasions for the shrill expression of personal malaise. The tensions and ambiguities implicit in the very idea of *morality in the midst of war* are all too easy to ignore. And then moral judgments are made in bad faith. But it is, I think, only another kind of bad faith to refuse altogether to total up the gruesome balance, to apply one's moral reason even to the business of war. Let us judge with due hesitation, judge without certainty; and then defend our judgments with all the passion we can command.

---

26. *Threats, Values, and Defense: Does the Defense of Values by Force Remain a Moral Possibility?*

James Turner Johnson

James Turner Johnson devotes careful attention to the importance of *jus ad bellum* considerations in establishing the justification for war and *jus in bello* considerations as a basis for determining its limitations. Because there are, indeed, times when the protection and preservation of values may call for the use of force, Johnson defends these distinctions and insists that they should not be discarded but rather consciously scrutinized for moral guidance, either when war appears as a possible option or when participation in war has become a reality.

The Just War Tradition

Two deep and broad streams of moral reflection on war run through Western history. These streams have their thematic origin in a single fundamental question: Is it ever morally allowable to employ force in the protection and preservation of values? The moral tradition of pacifism has resulted from a negative response to this question, given in various ways under various historical

From "Threats, Values, and Defense: Does the Defense of Values by Force Remain a Moral Possibility?" by James Turner Johnson, *Parameters* (Spring 1985). Reprinted with permission from Parameters and the author.

circumstances. A positive answer, given in ways no less conditioned by historical circumstances yet with a similar depth of underlying consistency and wholeness, has produced the other moral tradition on force and violence, which it is both convenient and proper to call by a familiar name: *just war tradition*. We should note two characteristic facts about this tradition.

First, it is a moral response to the question of value and force that is not only historically deep but is a product of reflection and action across the whole breadth of this culture's experience. It is not a moral doctrine in the narrow sense, reflecting the attitudes only of those sectors of the culture, like religion, often conceived as having a specialized function of moralizing cut off from the rest of human existence. To be sure, this tradition has often found expression in church law and theological reflection; yet it also appears in codifications and theories of international law, in military manuals on how rightly to conduct war, and—as Michael Walzer has shown in *Just and Unjust Wars*—in the judgments and reactions of common people.[1] In short, this tradition encapsulates something of how we in this culture respond morally to the question of protection of value by force. It is not the only response—pacifist rejection of force parallels it through history—but it is a fundamental one, revealing how we characteristically think about morality and war and defining the terms for our reflections in new or changing circumstances.

The second characteristic fact about just war tradition is that it preserves not one but two kinds of moral response to the question of value and force: limitation always accompanies justification. The response that says, yes, here are some conditions in which it is morally right to use force to protect value, goes on to set limits to what may rightly be done toward that end. This second element in the response is determined by the nature of the value or values to be protected; thus the need for limitation is built into the need to protect value as a necessary correlate. This means in general that unlimited or even disproportionately large amounts of force are not what is justified when the use of force to protect values is itself justified. Just war tradition, as recognized by such contemporary commentators as Paul Ramsey, William V. O'Brien, and Walzer, is a moral tradition of justifiable and limited war.[2] What has come to be known as the *jus ad bellum* has to do with the question of justification; that of limitation is addressed by the *jus in bello*. These are interconnected areas, but the priority, logical as well as historical, is with the former: only after the fundamental question is answered about the moral justification of employing force to protect values does the second question, about the morally requisite limits governing the use of that force, arise in turn. Problems arising in the *jus in bello* context may cause us to want to reflect further about the nature of the values we hold, the threat against them, and the means we may use to defend them; yet such further reflection means only that we must again enter the arena of the "war decision," the *jus ad bellum*.[3]

It is often claimed that the development of nuclear weapons has made this traditional way of thinking about morality and war obsolete and irrelevant.[4] From what I have said, it should be clear that I think this is not the case. Indeed, my claim is that we naturally think in the same terms that are encountered in the tradition, whether we want to or not. A pacifist critic like James Douglass employs one part of the tradition to reject the whole of it.[5] No sooner has another critic, Stanley Hoffmann, rejected it than he reinvents it point by point.[6] Such phenomena should be instructive. We would do well not to repudiate this tradition of moral reflection from the past; to do so merely isolates us from the wisdom of others surely no less morally or intellectually acute than we—others who in their own historical contexts have faced problems analogous to our own about whether and how to employ force in the defense of values. It is thus better to use this tradition consciously—trying to learn from it and with it, even in the nuclear age—than to forget it and subsequently have to reinvent it.

Defense of Values by Force as a Moral Possibility

To protect and preserve values is the only justifying cause for the use of force that is admitted in Western moral tradition. Classically, the use of force in response to a threat to values was justified in four ways: to protect the innocent, to recover something wrongly taken, to punish evil, and to defend against a wrongful attack in progress. Let us look briefly at each of these and inquire what we may derive from them in our present context.

Defense of the innocent is an idea that can be traced at least as far as Augustine in Christian thought.[7] It also has a history in military traditions back through the code of chivalry into the customs of premedieval Germanic societies.[8] By itself it implies an interventionist model of the justified use of military force and, more broadly, of national power. This not only flies in the face of much contemporary moralizing but also challenges such neoisolationists as Laurence Beilenson who argue for a retreat from foreign involvement by this country and the creation of a new "fortress America."[9] It is also at odds with the individualistic ethics fostered domestically in our society with the demise of close ties of community, an ethic that implies "not getting involved" perhaps even in extreme cases like mugging or rape.[10] Granted that it is extremely dangerous to throw military power around in a world that has the capability of destroying itself by global war; granted also that national *hubris*, if unrestrained, could use defense of others as an unwarranted excuse for a new round of imperialistic conquests;[11] there still, I submit, remain in the contemporary world cases in which limited and proportionate use of force may be the appropriate means to preserve the value referred to in the phrase "defense of the innocent." The case of Grenada was not morally the same as that of Afghanistan; intervention in Hungary by the West at the time of the 1956 uprising would not have been the moral equivalent of the Soviet invasion that did in fact occur; intervention in Uganda by neighboring Tanzania to depose Idi Amin and put an end to his bloodthirsty and self-aggrandizing rule was not the same as would have been an invasion aimed simply at increasing Tanzanian territory. Clearly, not every case where the rights of innocent persons need to be protected should become an occasion for military intervention; the case of Hungary offers a clear instance when following out this line of implication from just war tradition to the exclusion of other considerations would have led to the wrong decision. But my point is that the moral distinctions assumed by the classical formulation of just war tradition still remain, and the necessity to tread warily (which was no less an obligation in any previous age of human history) does not remove either the moral outrage that comes from violation of the innocent,[12] the obligation to prevent or stop such violation if at all possible,[13] or the possibility that among all the means available, military ones may be the best.

The recovery of something wrongly taken is a necessary counterpart to the idea of defense against aggression in progress.[14] If such after-the-fact reaction were not allowed, the result would be that expansion or other aggressive acts would, if speedy and effective, be tacitly accepted. There must be, of course, some consistent and agreed-on means of identifying what belongs to one society or one polity and what to another; but even in the absence of complete consensus on this, it is not necessary to reduce everything to a matter of different ideological or national perspective, so that what is one's own is simply whatever one says is one's own. The Falklands conflict provides an instructive contemporary example of the relevance of such reflection. The Argentine claim to the islands was not without some merit, but this was hardly of sufficient value to justify military invasion and occupation against the will of the inhabitants. The principle of self-determination, often cited to protect weak nations against military and other forms of aggression by stronger ones, though not the only meaningful principle here, was certainly violated by Argentina's action.

If only defense against an aggression in progress were justified, then Britain and the British inhabitants of the islands would have had no recourse, after the failure of the intensively pursued negotiations, but to accept the newly established status quo of Argentine military rule. The allowance of after-the-fact use of force to regain something wrongly taken is the source of moral justification for Britain's military actions in the Falklands war.

The punishment of evil is, in my judgment, the least useful of the classic formulations of just cause in the present context.[15] One reason for this is the prevalence of ideological divisions in the contemporary world. This line of justification for the use of force to protect value is all too easily changed into a justification for ideological warfare by one's own "forces of light" against the "forces of darkness" with their different ideological beliefs. This problem is not as acute among the superpowers as it once was, although it still exists and might still be fanned back to its former heat; more pressing immediate instances are to be found in the conflicts of the Middle East and Northern Ireland. Yet classically the punishment of differences of *belief* was not what was implied by this idea of just cause; what was to be punished was the kind of *action* identified in the other three kinds of justifying cause.[16]

What is unique to this concept of punishment taken alone is that it implicitly allows going beyond what these other concepts justify to further action aimed at insuring that the same thing does not happen again. Because such an allowance can easily be pushed too far, we should be cautious in citing this reason to justify force for the protection of value in the present age. Nuclear deterrence depends on the threat of punishment above all else; yet the use of current types of strategic nuclear weapons kept for deterrence purposes could itself threaten the very values such use would ostensibly seek to preserve. This is, of course, the heart of the nuclear dilemma, and I will return to it later. For now, my only point is that the justification of force as punishment for wrong done must not be allowed to become isolated from the general question of the protection of value or from the other justifying moral reasons for the use of force to protect value. Yet even with this caveat, if the goal of permitted military action is, as another part of just war tradition insists, the end of peace, then it is not proper to rule out the morality of punishment entirely.

If we had begun with twentieth-century international law and some other aspects of contemporary moral, political, and legal thought, we would have started with the justification of *defense against aggression in progress*—and perhaps got no further.[17] By keeping this classic idea of justifying cause for the use of force until last, I mean to symbolize that this idea is not as fundamental over the whole history of Western moral reflection on war as it has become in contemporary thought. Indeed, when we set this justification for the use of force alongside the others just identified and discussed, we discover that the right of self-defense is not in fact a moral absolute. One may oneself be in the wrong in a particular conflict. Rather than to exalt one's own righteousness and well-being over that of others, the better moral course is to deflate somewhat this allowance of self-defense to more appropriate proportions alongside the other *jus ad bellum* provisions.

In short, self-defense is not an absolute right, and the means of self-defense may therefore not be unlimited; there are other values to consider than the integrity of the self or one's own national polity. It is this consideration from just war tradition that points to the wrongness of schemes of national defense based on a threat of catastrophic annihilation, even if that threat is mutual. The irony of the present situation is that the very legal and moral efforts that attempt to restrict the incidence of the use of force by allowing only its defensive use—I am thinking of the Kellogg-Briand Pact of 1928 and Article 2 of the United Nations Charter, as well as current ostensibly moral arguments that the more terrible the deterrent threat, the less likelihood there will be of war—have the effect of insuring that should war come, despite these efforts, it will be of the most immoral and value-destructive kind attainable through military technology. That is, concentrating solely on the rightness of defense against aggression, though admittedly a moral justification for the use of force, has led us to think of strategic nuclear deterrence by threat of catastrophe as morally right, while ruling out lesser levels of force as possible responses to threats to value, even when these latter are more justifiable from the broader perspectives of just war tradition.[18]

In short, we would do well to remember what many in our present debate have either forgotten or systematically ignored: that circumstances may come into being in human history in which the use of force, at appropriate levels and discriminatingly directed, may be the morally preferable means for the protection and preservation of values. In forgetting or ignoring this, sometimes in the name of ostensibly moral considerations, those who would reject such a use of force are in fact choosing a less moral course than the one historically given form in the tradition that says that just war must also be limited war.

The Question of Values

May values ever be defended by forceful means? Answering this question requires us to think, first, about the nature of the values to be protected and the interrelation among values. We do this normally not by reflection but by affirmation. Hence the following from John Stuart Mill:

> War is an ugly thing, but not the ugliest of things. The decayed and degraded state of moral and patriotic feeling which thinks nothing *worth* a war, is worse. . . . A man who has nothing which he cares about more than he does about his personal safety is a miserable creature who has no chance of being free, unless made and kept so by the existing of better men than himself.[19]

Mill in this context alludes to the values from which he speaks, but the salient fact about this statement is his ranking of relative values. He does not deny the value of personal safety; yet it is not for him the *highest* value. He does not deny the ugliness of war; he only affirms that in the ranking of priorities it is not the *worst* evil. Mill was, of course, a utilitarian in ethics; yet such priority ranking of values is not a feature unique to utilitarianism and to be dismissed by all nonutilitarians. Such ranking is indeed a features of *any* ethic, for the service of one value often conflicts with the service of another, and there must be some way of deciding among them. Consider the following from Erasmus, a figure who was anything but a utilitarian:

> Think . . . of all the crimes that are committed with war as a pretext, while "good lawes fall silent amid the clash of arms"—all the instances of sack and sacrilege, rape, and other shameful acts, such as one hesitates even to name. And even when the war is over, this moral corruption is bound to linger for many years. Now assess for me the cost—a cost so great that, even if you win the war, you will lose much more than you gain. Indeed, what realm . . . can be weighed against the life, the blood, of so many thousand men?[20]

This passage is replete with priority ranking of values. Erasmus begins by identifying war rhetorically with criminal activity, thus locating it at the bottom of the value scale. He then turns explicitly to proportional counting of relative costs: "even if you win the war, you will lose much more than you gain"; "what realm . . . can be weighed against the life, the blood, of so many thousand men?" Such comparative weighting of goods is as central to the ethics of Erasmian humanism as it is to Mill's utilitarianism; indeed, it appears as a core feature of moral argument as such. Ultimately, there is no way to get to the truth or falsity of various perceptions of value. This is why, finally, there can be no real argument between absolute pacifists, who reject all possibility of the use of force to protect value, and those who accept some possibility of such use of force.[21] But this is not a problem in most of the current defense debate, which is a debate over ranking of values among persons who weight their values as differently as do Mill and Erasmus.

Recognizing values where they exist and sorting them according to priorities where there are conflicts among them is the function of moral agency, an art learned in one's community of moral discourse.[22] Without going into a full theory of moral agency, which is far beyond the scope of this chapter, the most we can say here is that affirmations like those of Mill and Erasmus allow us to glimpse the structure of relative values held by each participant in a moral debate and to relate those structures of value both to a larger normative conception of common life and to our own personal rankings of value. For our present purposes this is enough.

One interesting thing about Erasmus and Mill on war is how contemporary they sound; by thinking about them, we may learn something about ourselves. Erasmus counted costs both great and small in his rejection of war. A glimpse of the latter appears elsewhere in the letter quoted earlier, where he complains that preparations for war have dried up the sources of patronage on which he depended for support.[23] This was purely personal injury, but the complaint is not unlike contemporary arguments against military spending as subtracting from resources available for feeding the hungry, healing the sick and—in direct continuity with Erasmus—supporting humanistic scholarship. The value ranking is obvious.

The real meat of Erasmus' objection to war is found, however, in his idealistic vision of world community, which he conceived as both good in itself beyond the goods of any national community and achievable by the right kind of human cooperative interaction.[24] Again, this way of thinking has parallels in current debate, where rejection of force to protect values associated with the nation-state is coupled to a new vision of world order in which the nation-state system has no place.[25] The preservation of peace among nations, both in Erasmus and in contemporary debate, appears as the highest instrumental value, on which the maintenance of all other values depends. This is a different sort of reasoning from that of the pacifism of absolute principle; even the latter, however, may engage in priority ranking, as in these words of Mennonite theologian John Howard Yoder: "'Thou shalt not kill' . . . is an absolute . . . immeasurably more human, more personalistic, more genuinely responsible than the competitive absolute, 'Thou shalt not let Uncle Sam down' or 'Thou shalt fight for freedom' or 'Never give up the ship.'"[26] What we may note here is the tendency to diminish rhetorically the values being downgraded; similarly, Erasmus in all his works against war represents war-making as nothing more than the result of frivolous and misguided rivalry among sovereigns. War, Yoder and Erasmus alike suggest, may never be anything more than frivolous and misguided; the possibility that it might be an instrumental means of protecting value is dismissed out of hand. Contemporary examples of such reasoning abound, centering around the dismissal of any form of military preparedness as "militarism" and rejection of "war-fighting" strategic planning as opposed to deterrence strategy.[27]

The influence of Erasmian humanistic pacifism on contemporary debate runs deep, and I cannot here chart its full extent, but one more example of this presence must be noted for what it is. Erasmus rejects war as the *summum malum,* assimilating it to criminality; in contemporary debate the counterpart is the assimilation of all war to the evil of catastrophic nuclear holocaust. Erasmus cites "sack, sacrilege, and rape"; Jonathan Schell, in the idiom of our own age, cites "the biologic effects of ultraviolet radiation with emphasis on the skin,"[28] while piling up evidence of "the likely consequences of a holocaust for the earth"[29]—as if anyone had to be reminded that a holocaust is, by definition, evil.

It should be clear that Erasmus, Schell, and Yoder are simply moving in a different sphere from Mill and the main line of just war thinking (which I also share). It is simply impossible, given the assimilation of war to criminality and holocaust, for Erasmus and Schell to share Mill's judgment that "[w]ar is an ugly thing, but not the ugliest of things." No more could Yoder, for whom the use of force is trivialized into the maxim, "Never give up the ship," or those who, like Erasmus, regard war as the result of frivolous self-assertion by political leaders or, in the current phrase, "militarism." Between these and the position represented by Mill there would seem to be an impassible gulf. Yet it is possible at least to see across that gulf, if not to bridge or remove it. And from the perspective of just war tradition, there is something fundamentally wrong with the perception of value found on the other side.

First, although there is no need to deny the charm of an idealistic vision of world community, such a conception of an ideal that is not yet a reality (and may never become one) should not subtract from the quite genuine value to be found in the nation-state system or, more particularly, in a national community like our own. Historically, the roots of the nation-state system lie in the need to organize human affairs so as to minimize conflict while preserving the unique cultural identities of different peoples. It can be argued plausibly that it still fulfills these functions—imperfectly, to be sure, but with nothing better currently at hand. Likewise, the personal security, justice, freedom, and domestic peace provided in a liberal democratic nation-state like the United States are not to be dismissed lightly by reference to a utopian vision in which these and other values would all be present in greater measure. We must always, as moral beings, measure reality against our ideals; yet to reject the penultimate goods secured by the real because they do not measure up to the ultimate goods envisioned in the ideal is to ensure the loss of even the penultimate goods that we now enjoy. The ultimate would certainly be better; yet in the meantime, we have the obligation to hold as fast as possible to the value at hand, even though doing so must inevitably incur costs. A positive response to the original just war question recognizes this, as did Mill; Erasmus and his contemporary idealistic descendants did not.

Second, if force is to be used to protect values, it is not trivia that are to be protected but values of fundamental worth. Mill's allusion to the value of "being free" is on a quite different level from Yoder's maxim, "Never give up the ship," or Erasmus' collapsing of all reasons for war into the venality of princes. Equally, I believe, not to be reduced to the trivial or frivolous is Walzer's perception, expressed throughout *Just and Unjust Wars,* that the justification for fighting lies in the recognition of evil and revulsion against it.[30] Walzer's negative way of putting the matter is important for

another reason: it reminds us that we do not have to be able to give an extensive and comprehensive listing of all values that may be protected and in what ranking in order to know *that there are* such values; they will be apparent when they are violated or threatened with violation.

Third, knowing that some wars have resulted from the aggressively self-assertive characters of rulers does not mean that war may never be anything else. It is doubtful that Erasmus was right even about the rulers of his own time. In our own age we must surely make a distinction between, for example, the war made by Hitler and that made by Churchill; nor is it particularly useful to reduce the rise and fall of relations between the United States and the Soviet Union to the personalities of a Carter and a Brezhnev, Gorbachev and a Reagan. A manichaean dismissal of everything military as "militaristic" is also an uncalled for reductionism that makes military preparedness itself an evil, not an instrument for good or ill in ways to be determined by human choices.

Finally, neither in Erasmus' time nor in our own is it right to represent war as the irreducible *summum malum.* I have already suggested why I think Erasmus was wrong in making this claim; more important for our current context is the wrongness of assimilating all contemporary war to catastrophic nuclear war. Let us dwell on this for a moment.

Who could want a nuclear holocaust? Yet the effort to avoid such a catastrophe is not itself justification for rejection of the possibility that lower levels of force may justifiably be employed to protect value. This is, nonetheless, the clear import of the argument when limited conventional war is collapsed into limited nuclear war by reference to the threat of escalation and when nuclear war of any extent is collapsed into catastrophic holocaust on a global scale.[31] Such an argument has the effect of making any contemporary advocate of the use of force to protect values an advocate instead of the total destruction of humankind or even of all life on earth. It should hardly need to be said that such rhetorical hyperbole is unjustified; no one who argues from just war tradition, with its strong emphasis on counting the costs and estimating the probability of success of any projected military action, should be represented as guilty of befriending the idea of nuclear holocaust.

Yet this collapsing of categories is also wrong historically. War in the nuclear age has not been global catastrophe but a continuation of conventional warfare limited in one or several ways—by geography, goals, targets, means. This arena of contemporary limited warfare is one in which traditional moral categories for judging war are very much at home, as such different writers as William V. O'Brien and Michael Walzer have, in their respective ways, both recognized. The issue, then, is not of the prohibition of all means of defense in the nuclear age, because the assimilation of all contemporary war to the *summum malum* of nuclear holocaust is invalid; it is, rather, the perennial question of when and how force may be used for the defense of values.[32] We will return to this question later.

The Problem of Threats to Values

For there to be a need to defend values, there must be a threat to those values. To anyone with a modicum of objectivity, however, it must be apparent that in the current defense debate there is no agreement about the nature of the threat, and so there can be little hope of agreement about the means of preserving values in the face of the menace identified. Speaking broadly, I find in the present debate three distinct identifications of the threat to values that must be met. For some, there is no danger worth mentioning beyond that of nuclear holocaust, which is defined as threatening everything that is of value. For others the principal challenge to the values that matter for them is the arms race as such, with its diversion of resources to military ends and a perceived transformation of values toward those of militarism. Finally, a third perspective identifies the principal threat to values in the rivalry between the United States and the Soviet Union, West and East, two different and competing social, economic, political, and moral systems. This last is the most easily identifiable in terms of traditional interstate political analysis and in terms of just war tradition. All three perspectives have many forms and are somewhat fluid, so that in painting them with broad strokes of the brush I cannot render the inner details of each. Yet the broadly painted pictures of these different perspectives are themselves interesting morally, and it is on these that I will focus in this brief context.

Let us begin by exploring what is distinctive about each of the first two positions I have identified. These clearly overlap, but their emphases are importantly different, as are their respective histories and implicit value commitments. One way of recognizing this quickly is by noting that the anti–nuclear-holocaust position can be expressed in a commitment to increased military spending for a strengthened deterrent, quite contrary to the anti–arms race position, which finds typical expression in the nuclear freeze movement and support for disarmament programs. Similarly, part of the historical case for tactical and theater nuclear weapons has been that they cost less to provide than equivalent conventional forces, thus tending to free economic and manpower resources for nonmilitary purposes; yet many from the anti–nuclear-holocaust position view such war-fighting weapons as inherently destabilizing and dangerously likely to lead to catastrophic nuclear war.[33] Within the anti–nuclear-holocaust position, opposition to the arms race and military spending is but an instrumentality, whereas within the anti–arms race position opposition to nuclear arms is only an instrumentality. When there is convergence between these two positions (as there has been in the most recent stage of the defense debate), it is a mixed marriage that is as likely to end in divorce as in conversion of one or both partners.

These two positions also have different historical and ideological roots. The anti–nuclear-holocaust position is, of course, a product of the nuclear age and specifically of the period in which the United States and the Soviet Union have practiced strategic nuclear deterrence against each other. It is thus the child of nuclear deterrence theory and finds a characteristic expression in one such theory, the deterrence-only position. Clearly, however, there has been a transformation of values from parent to offspring. Thus when Philip Green wrote *Deadly Logic* in the mid-1960s, he cited "resistence of Communism" as the fundamental "ethical root of deterrence theory,"[34] but the ethical root of the contemporary deterrence-only position is the perception of *nuclear warfare,* not the menace to values posed by a totalitarian political system, as the evil to be avoided by the possession of a nuclear deterrent.[35]

The historical roots of the anti–arms race position are at least a century old; they lie in opposition to the increasing practice in nineteenth-century European states of sustaining a standing army built up by universal or nearly universal conscription, and in opposition to the social and economic costs of sustaining such armies. Religious groups have been the chief enunciators of this position and they are so today. A direct line runs between the *Postulata* on war prepared for Vatican Council I in 1870, which deplored the "intolerable burden" of defense spending and the social costs of "huge standing and conscript armies,"[36] and the 1983 pastoral of the U.S. Catholic bishops with its deploring of the "economic distortion of priorities" due to the "billions readily spent for destructive instruments,"[37] or, to take a Protestant example, the 1980 statement on the arms race by the Reformed Church in America decrying "the devastating social and personal consequences of the arms race."[38] Two ethical roots of this position are visible in the sources cited: an opposition to war and weapons as contrary to the biblical vision of peace, and an identification with the needs of the poor as best expressing Christian conformity to Christ. Both themes have secular counterparts in contemporary debate, and the first obviously parallels the utopian vision of Erasmian humanism.

If nuclear holocaust is the danger against which values must be protected, then deterrence theory is one rational response, but so would be general nuclear disarmament. If the arms race itself is the menace to values that must be defended against, then a freeze on military expenditures followed by a general scaling down of military establishments is the clear implication. Both these perspectives on the contemporary threat to values incorporate truths about the present historical situation; both are rooted in important perceptions of moral value; each offers, in its own way, a response to the problem of threat to values as it perceives that threat. Yet neither of these perspectives is really about the question with which we began this chapter, the fundamental question that is the root of our moral tradition on war: When and how may force justifiably be employed for the defense of values? Rather than approaching seriously the problem of possible moral justification of force, each of these perspectives has, in its own way, *defined that possibility out of existence* in the search for a general rejection of the use of force as a moral option in the contemporary age. The reason is that neither of these perspectives is able to comprehend the possibility of significant threats to value alongside the one on which each of them is fixed.

The problem, however, is that what is thus ignored does not for this reason cease to exist. International rivalries persist, as they did in the prenuclear era; ideologies and realistic perceptions of national interest continue to influence the actions of nations, and these actions are often played out through projections of force. Terrorism, civil war, and international war continue to be plain realities of our present era, and there is no reason to suppose either that aggression will no longer take place in human history or that it can effectively be opposed by means other than military ones.[39] Indeed, prospective victims of aggression today might reflect with Clausewitz: "The aggressor is always peace-loving; he would prefer to take over our country unopposed."[40] The just war perspective, the third perspective in the contemporary debate, views the problem of threats to value in this light, in continuity with the main line of statecraft over history, and conceives the problem of defense against such threats also in terms continuous with that historical experience.

Let it be clear: the rivalry between the Soviet Union and the United States is not the only source of danger to American values; yet it would be blindness to wish away the existence of this rivalry, which is rooted in more than common possession of mutual annihilative power; more than competing ideologies; more than national interest; more than global competition for friends, allies, and trading partners—and yet in all of these. And this rivalry is more than simply a product of adverse perceptions; it is real. Where it takes military form, as for example most unambiguously along the NATO-Warsaw Pact border, thinking about the menace to values must go beyond efforts to avoid catastrophic nuclear war and to end the arms race to include efforts to define and mount a credible, effective, and moral defense against the particular military threat manifest there.

At the same time, however, potential military defense of values is not limited to this confrontation or to the global East-West rivalry; it may be a matter of attempting to secure a weak Third World nation against the power of a nearby predator, of deterring or responding to terrorist attacks, or of maintaining the traffic of oil tankers through the Strait of Hormuz. All these possible uses of force involve the defense of value; all are, in general terms, the kind of resort to force regarded as justified in just war tradition. This third perspective on the threat to values, then, is the one I wish to address in my concluding section.

The Problem of Defense against Threats to Value

I wish now to return to a reflection with which this chapter began—that in general the nature of values to be protected and the threats against them are such that unlimited or even disproportionate amounts of force are not what is justified when the use of force to defend values is justified. When defense of values by force appears to require transgressing the boundaries set by the *jus in bello* concepts of proportionality and discrimination, this necessitates that we look again to see whether this is an occasion when the defense of values by force is morally justified. The answer may be no; yet it may also be yes, and this is the possibility I wish to explore in this section.

In fact there are two directions of thought, not one, that lead toward a renewal of the justification of value protection by force in such a situation. The first drives toward restructuring the application of force and beyond that to creating new kinds of force capabilities suited to limited application in the defense of value. The second leads into the far more dangerous consideration of whether values may ever be protected by means that themselves violate important values. I will discuss these in turn.

Clausewitz in his time understood well the difference between "absolute war"—war pushed to the limits of the destructive capacities of the belligerents—and "real" wars carried on by less than absolute means for limited purposes as an extension of politics. In the twentieth century many others have forgotten or ignored this difference.[41] Typically, the values threatened by war are less than ultimate, and so the threat; it is wrong to defend these values against such challenges by totalistic means disproportionate to both the values to be defended and the evil that menaces them. When we add that total war implies also the indiscriminate targeting of noncombatants, a violation of the fundamental idea of protection of the innocent, the indictment of such use of force in response to threats against values grows yet more damning.

Nevertheless, the problem of limitation of force in contemporary warfare is different from that which existed earlier. Today limitation must be accomplished first and foremost by human choice; in previous ages such limitation was also a product of the nature of weapons available, the restraints imposed by the seasons of the year, and the economic and social bases on which war was waged. Limitation in the use of force was relatively easy when the means were battle-axes or smooth-bore muskets, when three-quarters of the year was closed to military actions, and when soldiers were themselves units of economic production who could not be in arms year round. Today the problem is more complex: the structuring of force capabilities to defend against possible menaces to value must at the same time provide an effective deterrent and an effective means of active defense while still honoring the moral identity manifest in the society or culture in which the threatened values are known and maintained. Among the recent nuclear strategies that did

not meet this dual test is massive retaliation, conceived as a strategy for use, since it allowed so-called brush-fire wars to erupt unchecked and threatened disproportionate and indiscriminate nuclear devastation as a response to aggression on a much lower scale. Nor does contemporary mutual assured destruction doctrine, for reasons already given. But the issue is not simply one of the disproportionateness of nuclear arms. The same moral problems exist, for example, with the strategic conventional air strikes against population centers of World War II. Similarly, in the context of current history one of the most acute problems is how to frame a moral response against terrorist activity without oneself being forced into the characteristic patterns of terrorism.

Though complicated, this problem is not insoluble. If the use of force is justified in response to threats against value, but the only means of force available are such that they contravene important values themselves, then the preferred moral alternative is the development of different means of force. If tactical and theater nuclear weapons are judged too destructive to use or deemed too likely to result in escalation to all-out nuclear war if employed, then the moral choice is to devise nonnuclear defenses to replace them and to pay the costs, economic and social, of such defenses.[42] If the strategic nuclear deterrent is deemed immoral to employ, then the right response is not to engage in the self-deception of deterrence-only reasoning but to explore possible means of defense against nuclear strikes that would not require a preemptive first strike by this nation or a possibly indiscriminate and disproportionate punitive second strike.[43] The justification of using force to defend value certainly means, as I have said earlier, more than *defense* in its narrow sense, the warding off of attacks in progress; yet it certainly also means at least that, and to claim the moral high ground for a rejection of steps toward creating such defense is simply to twist moral reasoning out of shape.

Finally, however, there remains the possibility that values must be protected and preserved by force, and by force that itself contravenes at least some of the values it intends to protect and preserve. This is the possibility that, at the extreme, has been called "supreme emergency,"[44] and only at this extreme is it a morally unique case. Must one fight honorably and die, even knowing that one's ultimate moral values will thus die also? Or may one sin for the moment in order to defeat the evil that threatens, hoping for time to repent later and making the commitment to pass on undiluted to future generations the values that have been transgressed in the emergency?[45] Some of the lines of argument already advanced bear on this dilemma. I have suggested that ideological claims ought not to be inflated to the point of seeming to justify unlimited warfare; I have argued against disproportionate and indiscriminate warfare as morally evil in themselves; and I have suggested that part of the trouble in responding to an immoral form of warfare like terrorism is that in making such a response one's own humanity may be diminished to the level of that of the terrorist. In short, I tend to be dubious of supreme-emergency claims and am inclined to hold the moral line for preservation of value in the means chosen as well as in the decision to offer a defense. Even so there remains a possibility of a genuine supreme-emergency situation. What is to be said about this?

First, it is not a newly recognized kind of situation. In the early Middle Ages Christian soldiers were required to do penance after participating in war because of the possibility that they might have acted sinfully in that war, killing perhaps out of malice toward the enemy rather than with a feeling of regretful duty in the service of justice. Here we encounter a case in which the possibility is admitted that protection of values may involve violation of values. When in the sixteenth century Vitoria considered what might be done in a just war, he allowed that a militarily necessary storming of a city could be undertaken even though this would inevitably result in violations of the rights of noncombatants in the city.[46] Such historical evidence suggests a moral acceptance of the possibility of preserving value by wrong means; yet this evidence also implies the limits on that acceptance.

Second, the transgression of value in the service of value must be approached through the general recognition that value conflicts are the stuff with which human moral agency has to deal. Every moral system provides means for handling such conflicts, and that a genuine supreme emergency might come to exist is by definition such a conflict, in which higher values must in the last analysis be favored over lower ones. The values constituting the *jus ad bellum*, having priority over those of the *jus in bello*, would on my reasoning have to be honored in such a case, even at some expense to the latter.

I have thus brought this discussion to the brink of morally admissible possibility so that we might look over and see what lies below. The view is not a pretty one. Having seen it, though, we may the more

purposefully return to the other line of implication sketched before: the development of military capabilities suited to our moral commitments. We may still yearn—and work—for a world without war, for an end to the menace of catastrophic nuclear war, for an end to the arms race; yet with such military capabilities we would be the better prepared to meet morally the threats to value that may be expected to be inevitable so long as these ideals are not achieved.

Endnotes

1. Michael Walzer, *Just and Unjust Wars* (New York: Basic Books, 1977).

2. See Paul Ramsey, *War and the Christian Conscience* (Durham, N. C.: Duke University Press, 1961), and *The Just War* (New York: Charles Scribner's Sons, 1968); William V. O'Brien, *The Conduct of Just and Limited War* (New York: Praeger, 1981).

3. The term is O'Brien's and is meant by him to emphasize the difference in order of priority between the *jus ad bellum* and the *jus in bello*, which has to do with war-fighting once the initial decision to make war has been made. See O'Brien, *Just and Limited War*, esp. chaps. 1–3.

4. Cf. Stanley Hoffmann, *Duties beyond Borders* (Syracuse, N.Y.: Syracuse University Press, 1981), pp. 46–55, and James Douglass, *The Non-Violent Cross* (New York: Macmillan, 1968).

5. Cf. Ramsey's criticism in *The Just War*, pp. 259–278.

6. Hoffmann, *Duties*, p. 59ff.

7. For an example of such tracing in contemporary argument, see Ramsey, *War and the Christian Conscience*, pp. 34–37.

8. For discussion, see James Turner Johnson, *Just War Tradition and the Restraint of War* (Princeton, N.J.: Princeton University Press, 1981), pp. 131–150.

9. See Laurence Beilenson, *Survival and Peace in the Nuclear Age* (Chicago: Regnery and Company, 1980).

10. On the loss of community and its implications, see James Sellers, *Warming Fires* (New York: Seabury Press, 1975), and Thomas Luckmann, *The Invisible Religion* (New York: Macmillan, 1967).

11. This is a familiar theme in the thought of Reinhold Niebuhr. Cf. his *Christianity and Power Politics* (New York: Charles Scribner's Sons, 1940), and *The Structure of Nations and Empires* (New York: Charles Scribner's Sons, 1959).

12. Cf. Walzer, *Just and Unjust Wars*, pp. 133–135.

13. Cf. Ramsey, *The Just War*, pp. 141–147.

14. This concept, taken over from Roman law by Augustine and Isidore of Seville, was central to the definition of just war given in medieval canon law. See *Corpus Juris Canonici*, Pars Prior, *Decretum Magistri Gratiani*, Pars Secunda, Causa XXIII, Quaest. II, Can. II.

15. This is another *jus ad bellum* criterion that came from Roman law through Augustine into church law; see ibid. But it had a more central place in the thought of Thomas Aquinas, who connected it to the words of Paul in Romans 13:4: "[The prince] is the minister of God to execute his vengeance against the evildoer." See Thomas Aquinas, *Summa Theologica*, II/II, Quaest. XL, Art. 1.

16. I make this judgment cognizant of the minority tradition in Christian just war theory from Augustine forward that allowed some forms of war for religion; in Augustine's words, repeated for canon law by Gratian, "The enemies of the church are to be coerced even by war" (*Decretum Magistri Gratiani*, Quaest. VIII, Can. XL VIII). In fact, however, efforts to justify wars in Western cultural history, even those clearly involving some benefit or detriment to religion, have generally been justified by appeal to the other reasons already given: protection of the innocent, retaking of something lost, punishment of evil. For discussion of this issue of religious war—and by extension ideological war—see James Turner Johnson, *Ideology, Reason, and the Limitation of War* (Princeton, N.J.: Princeton University Press, 1975), chaps. I–III.

17. See ibid., pp. 266–270.

18. An early version of this kind of argument undergirded massive retaliation strategy, which Robert W. Tucker in *The Just War* (Baltimore, Md.: The Johns Hopkins Press, 1960) regards as an expression of a general American moral attitude justifying all-out responses to injustice received rather than limited uses of force proportionate to harm done to U.S. interests. But suppose that this opposition to limited warfare is retained while all-out retaliation is itself denied as immoral (although the use of deterrence as a *threat* continues to be accepted); then the argument changes shape, though its fundamentals remain. Such a new version of the moral argument for deterrence and against limited warfare can be found in the 1983 Pastoral Letter of the U.S. Catholic bishops. (See National Conference of Catholic Bishops, *The Challenge of Peace* (Washington, D.C.: United States Catholic Conference, 1983). The purpose of deterrence, as defined here, is "only to prevent the *use* of nuclear weapons by others" (par. 188, emphasis in original). "War-fighting strategies," including even *planning* for fighting nuclear war at a limited level over a protracted period, are explicitly rejected (pars. 184, 188, 189). The reason is the prudential judgment that limited nuclear warfare can be expected to escalate to "mass destruction" (pars. 151–61, 184). Although this suggests heavier reliance on conventional weapons (par. 155), even a conventional war "could escalate to the nuclear level" (par. 156). Although the resultant position is not *explicitly* a deterrence-only one, it is difficult to find in the pessimism toward limited war and war-fighting strategies expressed in the bishops' letter any room for limited and proportionate responses to limited levels of harm done, such as the traditional *jus in bello* implies.

19. John Stuart Mill, "The Contest in America," in John Stuart Mill, *Dissertations and Discussions* (Boston: William V. Spencer,

1867), pp. 208–209. The full text of the passage in question, written to oppose England's siding with the Confederacy in the American Civil War, is as follows:

> War is an ugly thing, but not the ugliest of things: the decayed and degraded state of moral and patriotic feeling which thinks nothing *worth* a war, is worse. When a people are used as mere human instruments for firing cannon or thrusting bayonets, in the service and for the selfish purposes of a master, such war degrades a people. A war to protect other human beings against tyrannical injustice; a war to give victory to their own ideas of right and good, and which is their own war, carried on for an honest purpose by their own free choice—is often the means of their regeneration. A man who has nothing which he cares about more than he does about his personal safety is a miserable creature who has no chance of being free, unless made and kept so by the existing of better men than himself. As long as justice and injustice have not terminated their ever renewing fight for ascendancy in the affairs of mankind, human beings must be willing, when need is, to do battle for the one against the other.

20. Desiderius Erasmus, Letter to Antoon van Bergen, Abbot of St. Bertin, dated London, 14 March 1514; number 288 in *The Correspondence of Erasmus, Letters 142 to 297*, trans. R.A.B. Minors and D.F.S. Thomson, annotated by Wallace K. Ferguson (Toronto and Buffalo: University of Toronto Press, 1975), lines 47–63.

21. That is, for such pacifists the rejection of force has itself become a value, or it is necessarily implied by some other value (for example, Christian love in some forms of religious pacifism); in either case it is unassailable from outside the moral system in which this value is held. Other forms of pacifism, of course, reach their judgment against the use of force by argument based not on the evil of force as such but on the harm to some higher good that the use of force may entail. The contemporary position sometimes called *just-war pacifism*, which is based on a prudential calculation of proportionality, is such a form of pacifism.

22. See, further, James Turner Johnson "On Keeping Faith: The Uses of History for Religious Ethics," *Journal of Religious Ethics* 7, no. 1(Spring 1979):98–116.

23. Erasmus, Letter, 14 March 1514, lines 17–24.

24. See, further, Roland H. Bainton, *Christian Attitudes toward War and Peace* (New York and Nashville: Abingdon Press, 1960), p. 131, and Lester K. Born, *The Education of a Christian Prince by Desiderius Erasmus* (New York: Octagon Books, 1965), pp. 1–26.

25. See, for example, Richard A. Falk, *A Study of Future Worlds* (New York: Macmillan/The Free Press, 1975).

26. John Howard Yoder, *Nevertheless* (Scottdale, Penna., and Kitchener, Ont.: Herald Press, 1976), p. 33.

27. Condemnation of "militarism" has become a common feature of the public policy statements of many Protestant denominations. See, for example, the statements by The Christian Church (Disciples of Christ) and the Reformed Church in America in Robert Heyer, ed., *Nuclear Disarmament* (New York and Ramsey, N.J.: Paulist Press, 1982), pp. 245–246, 251–252, 267. A prominent example of condemnation of war-fighting strategic planning is the U.S. Catholic bishops' pastoral; see National Conference of Catholic Bishops, *The Challenge of Peace,* paragraphs 184–190. Such thinking is far more like the traditional pacifism represented by Yoder and Erasmus than it is like the reasoning of just war tradition.

28. Jonathan Schell, *The Fate of the Earth* (New York: Avon Books, 1982), p. 85.

29. Ibid., p. 78.

30. See, for example, the discussions of noncombatant immunity found in Walzer, chaps. 8–10. Despite the criticisms I have earlier directed at the U.S. Catholic bishops' letter, it clearly embodies an understanding that the values that might be endangered by an enemy are not trivial; they include "those key values of justice, freedom and independence which are necessary for personal dignity and national integrity" (National Conference of Catholic Bishops, *The Challenge of Peace,* paragraph 175).

31. See, for example, Louis Rene Beres, *Mimicking Sisyphus* (Lexington, Mass.: Lexington Books, D. C. Heath and Company, 1983), pp. 15–24; cf. the argument of the U.S. Catholic bishops, note 18.

32. O'Brien, *Just and Limited War,* chap. 1.

33. Cf. National Conference of Catholic Bishops, *The Challenge of Peace,* pars. 188, 190.

34. Philip Green, *Deadly Logic* (New York: Schocken Books, 1968), pp. 249–51.

35. Cf. National Conference of Catholic Bishops, *The Challenge of Peace,* pars. 175, 188. This document, on my reading, is only a whisker away from the deterrence-only position on nuclear weapons; that whisker is the ambiguity maintained in the threat of strategic nuclear retaliation, specifically in the possible difference between "declaratory policy" and "action policy" (par. 164). Paragraph 148 denies counterpopulation retaliation; paragraph 184 repeats this and also undercuts the possibility of counterforce strategic retaliation. These themes recur elsewhere in section II of the document as well. Is the "conditional acceptance of nuclear deterrence" (par. 198) in this Pastoral Letter then anything more than a "conditional acceptance" of the *possession* of such weapons (not making any distinctions among types, purposes, or relative destructive power, but treating all nuclear weapons the same), and does not the "no first use" position taken in the letter (par. 150 and *passim*) in practical terms collapse into a policy of "no use at all"?

36. See John Eppstein, *The Catholic Tradition of the Law of Nations* (Washington, D.C.: Catholic Association for International Peace, 1935), p. 132.

37. National Conference of Catholic Bishops, *The Challenge of Peace,* par. 134.

38. Heyer, *Nuclear Disarmament,* p. 266.

39. Cf. Walzer, *Just and Unjust Wars,* pp. 329–335.

40. Carl von Clausewitz, *On War,* ed. and trans. Michael Howard and Peter Paret (Princeton, N.J.: Princeton University Press, 1976), p. 370.

41. See, for example, Paul Fussell's argument in *The Great War and Modern Memory* (New York and London: Oxford University Press, 1975), passim, that modern war is inevitably totalistic, chaotic, beyond human control, and disproportionately destructive of values.

42. Cf. National Conference of Catholic Bishops, *The Challenge of Peace,* pars. 155, 215–16.

43. See, further, Sam Cohen, "Rethinking Strategic Defense," in Robert W. Poole, Jr., ed., *Defending a Free Society* (Lexington, Mass.: Lexington Books, D.C. Heath and Company, 1984), pp. 99–122.

44. Walzer, *Just and Unjust Wars,* chap. 16.

45. See, further, my discussion of Walzer on this matter in *Just War Tradition,* pp. 24–28.

46. Franciscus de Vitoria, *De Jure Belli,* section 37, in Franciscus de Vitoria, *De Indis et De Jure Belli Relectiones,* ed. Ernest Nys (Washington, D.C.: Carnegie Institute, 1917). Vitoria makes clear, however, that he thought few wars meet the test of an unambiguous conflict of justice against injustice.

27. The Tradition and the Real World

John Howard Yoder

John Howard Yoder, advocating for nonviolence, examines the just war tradition in detail, assessing its strengths and shortcomings. The tradition is essentially well intentioned, insofar as it is based on a presumption against war and seeks, when necessary, to extend moral categories into the arena of combat. Having developed from earlier Christian sources such as St. Augustine and St. Thomas Aquinas, it provides strict criteria on the basis of which the decision to enter into war may be justified. But Yoder points out that the tradition is only credible if its criteria actually impose effective limitations on war making. He goes on to argue that, in fact, the tradition does not represent the mainstream of Christian thought on the issues it addresses and that it has been so riddled with exceptions in its development that it no longer can be said to offer the meaningful restraints it intends.

As we near the end of the conversation with the just-war tradition, we can tie a few threads together. The following observations about the terrain we have covered will not constitute a final judgment on the validity of the just-war tradition, but they may help the reader to test some preliminary experience-based conclusions about its status as classical consensus.

The Scale Keeps Sliding

The reader will already be aware that the just-war tradition as a whole is more complicated than it sounded at first. It has numerous necessary sub-themes, and its terms presuppose prior definitions, many of them debatable, without which the system cannot work. More important, though, its fundamental logic is ambivalent. The just-war tradition says that war is generally deplorable and is always in need of being limited—and that there are ways to limit it. These ways, it is held, are relevant and effective, so that those who (regretfully) have recourse to lethal violence can be assured that what they are doing is not murder.

The credibility of this statement, morally and logically, is tied to the degree to which the defined criteria actually impose effective restraints. Beneath the basic concession—that some exceptions will have to be made to the general rule of the wrongness of killing—we come upon a still "lower" level of exceptions to the need for exceptional justifications. The different arguments to which we now turn will be seen to carry different weights for different persons, and they proceed on different levels. Yet their cumulative impact is to decrease the credibility of the tradition and the applicability of the limits initially stated.

Lowering the Hurdles

Any set of rules, obviously, will tend to favor the interests of those who wrote it. As technology changes, rules will be written to favor those parties whose strength was greatest in terms of the older technology.[1] Two examples are obvious in recent strategic history.

a) The earlier rules defined those who have the right to be considered soldiers (rather than as bandits or common criminals) by their wearing a uniform (or other visible, distinguishing sign) and carrying their

From John Howard Yoder, *When War Is Unjust* (Maryknoll, N.Y.: Orbis Books, 1996), pp. 50–70. Reprinted by permission of the Estate of John Howard Yoder.

[1]This is argued with special force in Chris af Jochnick and Roger Norman, "Legitimation of Violence: A Critical History of the Laws of War," *Harvard International Law Review* 35 (1994): 49–85; and Jochnick and Norman, "The Legitimation of Violence: A Critical Analysis of the Gulf War," *Harvard International Law Review* 35 (1994): 387ff.

arms in the open. Modern times have seen an escalation of the importance of irregular or guerrilla forces (called terrorists by their enemies and freedom fighters by their friends), whose operation would be rendered impossible by obeying those earlier rules. So we need new rules, which permit guerrilla war, in order to regulate it. United Nations negotiations since 1949 have begun to make such changes.[2]

b) The earlier rules for submarine warfare, derived from those for surface naval combat, forbade torpedoing a ship without confirming that it was in fact armed. To do that, the submarine would have to surface, which made it vulnerable, sacrificing the entire advantage of being a submarine, especially in the face of the British ruse of secretly arming what looked like merchant vessels. It was thus no surprise that the Germans disregarded this rule during World War II.

The victorious Allies, stronger on the surface and weaker undersea, reaffirmed the old rules in new treaties written in the 1920s, but they were again disregarded in World War II *on both sides.* In the Nuremberg trials Allied submarine commanders testified in defense of German commanders accused of ignoring these rules, saying that Allied submarines had disregarded them too.[3]

These two examples illustrate the principle that rules are more likely to be kept if they are less demanding and more realistic. One therefore consents to sacrifice one part of the values which the original rules safeguarded in the hope of avoiding complete lawlessness. In the interest of maintaining restraint in a minimal way, one agrees to relax the particular restraints that would really have made it more difficult to continue hostilities and to win. It is thought better to have a few modest rules that both sides can afford

to keep rather than more demanding requirements that will not be respected.

Going farther in this same direction, William V. O'Brien has argued that the principle of noncombatant immunity can no longer be effectively respected.[4] Instead of continuing to affirm it abstractly but undercutting its meaning by the use of arguments of necessity and double effect, it would be more appropriate to declare it a dead letter and to concentrate on building up those other restraints that are still realistic.

As we already noted briefly, George Orwell, the British journalist better known for the novels *Animal Farm* and *1984,* was saying something similar during World War II. Once one has resolved to accept war at all, it is better to get it over with quickly, by whatever means, rather than let it be strung out and the total destructiveness increased by placing artificial limits on the use of one's best weapons. When the enemy's troops are draftees, they may be morally just as innocent as the aged. Why should a war be better which kills only healthy young people?[5]

Necessity

The classic just-war tradition said that the means used in war should be "necessary and proportionate." That rejected wanton or vengeful destruction and any damage not directly functional toward the goal of winning the war. Necessity was thus a supplemental criterion operative *within* the limits set by the other rules. It was classically so defined by Francis Lieber in 1863,[6] and it was so defined in the U.S. Army Field Manual 27–10 of 1956:

---

[2]Increasing numbers of younger nations, now represented in the United Nations commissions which rewrite the rules, look back to origins in irregular warfare. Robert E. Rodes, Jr., proposes an updated body of *in bello* law to make fighting fair possible in such circumstances ("On Clandestine Warfare," *Washington and Lee Law Review* 39/2 [Spring 1982], 333–72). There is parallel material in Michael Howard, *Restraints on War* (New York: Oxford University Press, 1979), 33ff. and 135ff.

[3]The literature is strikingly devoid of attention to the phenomenon of the "dead letter," i.e., a law all parties tacitly agree need not be obeyed and infractions of which will not be punished. During World War II, that is what submarine commanders on both sides thought of these rules, and the tribunal agreed.

[4]William V. O'Brien, *War and/or Survival* (Garden City: Doubleday, 1969), 248ff. He argues that to insist firmly on noncombatant immunity is tantamount to pacifism. While constantly restated as an ideal, noncombatant immunity has been losing ground since Napoleon. To be honest in the nuclear age, we should drop that hurdle. Later, O'Brien argues further that noncombatant immunity cannot be and has never been respected, because by definition discrimination is contradictory to self-defense (*The Conduct of Just and Limited War* [New York: Praeger Publishers 1981], 44ff.). This is certainly an exaggeration.

[5]George Orwell, "As I Please."

[6]See Lieber, "General Orders No. 100" (1863), in Friedman, 158–85.

The prohibitory effect of the law of war is not minimized by "military necessity" which has been defined as that principle which justifies *those measures not forbidden* by international law which are indispensable for securing the complete submission of the enemy as soon as possible. Military necessity has been generally rejected as a defense for acts forbidden by the customary and conventional laws of war (inasmuch as the latter have been developed and framed with consideration for the concept of military necessity).

Yet increasingly the ordinary use of necessity in the popular mind has become the opposite. It has come to mean a claimed justification for breaking one or another of the rules if one "really has to." "Really having to" depends, of course, on a judgment concerning the particular value that is at stake at the time. It may mean a captain's not wanting to jeopardize his troop's lives "unnecessarily"; a general not wanting to risk the outcome of a particular battle; or a statesman not wanting to prolong, or to lose, "unnecessarily," a war.

The practical effect of this shift is to reduce necessity to utility, providing *carte blanche* for any destruction that is not purely wanton, wasteful, or vengeful.[7] Yet this fact is not openly avowed; phrases like "only if it is *really* necessary" preserve the illusion that there is still a limit. One claims not to have descended to the level where "anything goes."

Political philosopher Michael Walzer, whose *Just and Unjust Wars* has done much to enhance the seriousness of discourse in this field, has proposed a yet more complex version of the necessity argument, namely, the notion of *supreme emergency*, which authorizes overriding the normal restraints of law and morality, but only if in fact all of civilization is at stake. How does one measure that? Taking off from the ancient maxim, Let justice be done even if the heavens fall, Walzer claims justification for an exception, *"but only if the heavens are (really) about to fall"* (emphasis added).[8]

They Did It First

This theme also characterizes a long spectrum of degrees of infraction. The minimum is a specific act of reprisal overtly identified as a breach of the usual rules and as intended to punish the adversary for an infraction and prevent its recurrence.[9] This calls for a renewed application, on the new lower level, of the notions of proportion and discrimination. There needs to be a way to communicate with enemies (for example, through the Red Cross) so that they know:

- that we will do to them what they do to us;
- that the act is not a gratuitous escalation but a targeted reprisal, from which it follows.
- that we will stop doing it if they do.

Thus the (stated) intention of the single infraction is to restore respect for the rules; the retaliatory infringement must go no farther than the original offense did.

A more sweeping loosening of the rules results if one gives more weight to the dimension of contract thinking that obtained in the development of the international conventions. What those treaties forbid, in detail, is not wrong primarily morally or intrinsically. Its wrongness is defined by the treaty, conventionally, because two parties, in the interest of both, have agreed to fight fairly, and that fairness is defined by those rules. If, however, the other side breaks the rules, "the deal is off" and we are no longer bound by them either. If they have made military use of vehicles marked with a red cross, the immunity of the wounded has thereby been sacrificed.[10] We claim that we are still more moral than they, but we descend to fight them on their terms.

They Are Unworthy

The identity of the adversaries whose rights the just-war tradition protects is not fully clear in the tradition. On the one hand, it would seem natural that since all the values we talk about needing to respect are those of our enemies, it would hardly be fitting to distinguish between those enemies to whom we do and

---

[7]See Wasserstrom, "The Laws of War" and Taylor, "War Crimes," in Wakin, *War, Morality, and the Military Profession,* 2d ed. (Boulder, Col.: Westview, 1986), 394ff., 400ff., 375ff.; and Walzer, *Just and Unjust Wars,* 254, 144ff.

[8]Walzer, *Just and Unjust Wars,* 230–31. How one determines this Walzer does not say. Since the heavens' falling is a metaphor, there is no simple explanation of what "(really)" means.

[9]Ibid., 207ff.

[10]In the 1991 Gulf War allied military spokesmen claimed that the killing of civilians in Baghdad was justified by the fact that Saddam Hussein should not have permitted civilians to take shelter in buildings the allies considered military targets.

those to whom we do not owe such restraint. Yet as the tradition evolved and was applied, there often has been such differentiation, denying that *all* adversaries have the same rights. This fact should be no surprise. Just-war standards are then thought of as something like the good manners that should exist among the citizens of civil society. Warfare that respects the rules is then something like a court trial or a duel. The medieval limitations against illicit weapons or tactics forbade their use only against Christians, assuming that against the infidel the standards could be lower. Thus the conceptual wedge between the just war, properly so-called, and the holy war alternative begins to exist as a wedge between two kinds of adversaries as well. The infidel (or the barbarian), being beyond the pale of civility, did not possess even those rights the just-war tradition protected.

In modern times the notion remains that adversaries can put themselves "beyond the pale" and forfeit their right to be fought against fairly. Sometimes this can be argued on the grounds that the adversary was not a party to the treaty that defined the rules. The Afrikaner nations that faced the British in the Boer war had claimed independence for years, but they had not been represented at the drafting of The Hague conventions; so the British, fighting to force them back into the Empire, could claim that they did not count as a legitimate war-making authority. Thus the British could treat them as common brigands. The British developed new inhuman forms of conflict—the concentration camp and scorched earth—partly under the pretext that the enemy did not exist as a people. A parallel argument has raged more recently in Northern Ireland, Algeria, Latin America, and South Africa over whether insurrectionists when captured should be treated as political prisoners or as common criminals.

Before 1939 Japan had not signed some of the international conventions on the treatment of prisoners of war, partly because of the conviction that Japanese soldiers would not be taken prisoner. Thus it could not be demanded of Japan with force of law that Allied prisoners of war in the Asian theater during World War II be cared for under those rules.

Perhaps more often, one or more of the parties are declared to be "beyond the pale" not because of a document they did not sign, but because they broke the rule first, and thereby qualified themselves as outlaws rather than as combatants. The right to be fought against according to the laws of war would then, the argument goes, be revocable.

The escalation of the evil we allow ourselves to commit on the ground of the special evil incarnate in the adversary has often seemed convincing, especially when exacerbated by ideological and/or racial overtones. The Turks had that image in the late Middle Ages (and still do for Armenians and Greeks), Nazism had it in the mid-twentieth century, and communism had it until recently.

Though generally critical of what he called the logic of the "sliding scale," Michael Walzer was open, as we saw, to arguing for a specific "supreme emergency" in favor of the massive bombing of German cities, because a Nazi victory—qualitatively different from most losses in most wars—would have meant the end of certain basic values of world civilization.[11] I mentioned this before as a special form of the necessity argument, but for it to be convincing one must have made some previous global judgments about Nazism and civilization.

Here again we observe a shift from intrinsic morality to contract thinking. According to this notion we are not obligated to honor the dignity of the enemy noncombatant population because they are human, but only because their government has made and keeps a commitment to carry on the combat according to our rules. If their rulers deny our basic value system, the enemies (not only the rulers but the populations) forfeit the privilege of our respect. It was, in sum, a privilege that we, being morally superior, had bestowed upon them. Or it was a conditional right they had earned by meeting us on our terrain, rather than an intrinsic right by virtue of their humanity. "Savages" and "outlaws" have no intrinsic rights.[12] Thus the worse the enemy's cause, the more room we may have to break the rules.

Situationism

Many of the common-sense responses that arise in the effort to move just-war thought beyond the first phases of superficial realism take the shape of anti-intellectual

---

[11] Walzer, *Just and Unjust Wars*, 253ff.

[12] Soon after the bombing of Hiroshima, President Truman made much of the fact that Japan had treacherously attacked Pearl Harbor and had not treated war prisoners humanely. Both accusations were true, but neither of those crimes was committed by the people of Hiroshima, and neither of them suspended the adhesion of the United States to The Hague treaties, which forbade that kind of attack. Truman's first announcements had in fact claimed that Hiroshima was a military base.

or anti-structural reasoning. "In a combat situation there is not time for complicated calculation of possibilities."[13] "When the lives of my men are at stake, philosophy is not very convincing." The normal penchant of the selfish heart and the lazy mind for such excuses is precisely why we need to have rules and to think about them before the crisis.[14] It is precisely because there is little time and the stakes may be great that decision-makers need reminders of the fundamental rights of other parties in the conflict, rights which remain binding even in the midst of unavoidable conflict. Precisely because abstract analysis is not easy under fire, the limits of our entitlement to destroy our fellow humans' lives and property need to be formulated and rehearsed ahead of time, to protect ourselves as well as others against our (partially, but not infinitely) justified self-interest.

Systematizing Moral Thought

Whereas some of the least morally worthy adjustments, like those just described, use ordinary debating language, or even anti-academic "realism" appeals, and whereas some of them claim the superior authority of the lay person against the more complex work of the specialist, there is one line of argument which claims deep roots in the tradition of moral theologians. The doctrine of double effect claims a long history, offering to throw light on especially difficult choices in which competing or coinciding values cannot be separated from one another, so that in order to ward off one evil it seems that one must accept another. Thus the case one makes for needing to break one rule can be interpreted as part of a larger rule-governed process of adjudication.

Moral theologians are far from agreeing on the precise interpretation and justification of this pattern of argument, but there is agreement on its basic outlines.[15] One must be able to show that:

a) The evil which happens (the secondary effect of the action) is less than the evil which is prevented;

b) The evil which happens, though it is the outcome of the entire set of situations and events, is not itself the actual cause of the good results (or one would be directly doing evil for the sake of good, which is not permitted);

c) The evil which happens is not willed or intended;

d) The actual deed, which both triggers the unintended evil byproduct and is indispensable to the primary intended good, is not in itself intrinsically wrong.

It cannot be our agenda here to review the appropriateness of double-effect reasoning as a whole, as a mode of moral argument.[16] I note only that it constitutes a powerful intellectual apparatus contributing to the downward drift, while still claiming to hold the line somewhere. Some argue that the just-war theory as a whole represents a case of double-effect reasoning, where the killing of enemies is the regrettable and unintended result of the intrinsically good defense of national values. Others, however, would use double-effect argument on the next lower level: the evil one regretfully accepts for the sake of a higher good is not the killing itself, or war itself, but the fact that one pursues one's war goals in infraction of one or another of the just-war criteria.[17] Thus one can discuss, for instance, the acceptance of noncombatant casualties or the misuse of Red Cross protection, as a lesser evil, not intended but regretfully accepted as a part of the price for a higher good. It is not easy for the critic who wants to be fair to know where the line runs between careful casuistic good faith and plain cynical abuse.

This Far and No Farther?

The earliest firm landmark in the development of what came to be called nuclear pacifism was a study process convened by the Study Department of the World Council of Churches following its 1954

---

[13]Sometimes in the ethical parlance of the last two generations "situation ethics" meant simply that one must take account of every element of a setting to be able to decide morally. Here it may mean a stronger case: "The heat of battle" may count as a reason to be less careful.

[14]John Courtney Murray, S.J., "Remarks on the Moral Problem of War," *Theological Studies* 20 (1959), 40–61.

[15]A landmark treatment of the theme is *Doing Evil to Achieve Good*, ed. Richard C. McCormick, S.J., and Paul Ramsey (Chicago: Loyola University Press, 1978). Walzer also reviews the theme (*Just and Unjust Wars*, 152–59).

[16]Some would argue that all four criteria can be redefined as proportional reasoning about the values at stake in a decision. Critics of the system challenge the definitions of each of the terms. Can one deny intending the foreseeable results of one's acts? Does the intrinsic-evil category include anything that it would be costly to renounce doing?

[17]This is what Walzer assumes when he digests and reformulates the argument (*Just and Unjust Wars*, 152–59).

Evanston Assembly. A group of fourteen men, all of them from the North Atlantic world, worked for several sessions on the theme "Christians and the Prevention of War in an Atomic Age." Of the fourteen commission members (in addition to Study Department staff), only three could in any way be described as pacifists.

Their report was far ahead of what any Christian bodies in any national or denominational framework were to think for another decade. Their conclusion about the use of nuclear weapons was:

> Although there are differences of opinion on many points, we are agreed on one point. This is that Christians should openly declare that the all-out use of these weapons should never be resorted to. Moreover, that Christians must oppose all policies which give evidence of leading to all-out war. Finally, if all-out war should occur, Christians should urge a cease-fire, if necessary on the enemy's terms, and resort to non-violent resistance.[18]

This wording was logically irreproachable, in fact inevitable, as an application of the ordinary meaning of the just-war tradition, but it was so threatening politically that the study process was terminated. Yet the logic was clear, and it has never been refuted on its own terrain. If it is not possible to prosecute a war with moral and civil legitimacy, then the only alternative is not to prosecute it. The only remaining path is to pursue by other means the purpose which can no longer be legitimately achieved militarily.

Sue for Peace?

This has led us to the crudest form of the credibility question. Is there a point at which it would be morally and legally obligatory to surrender rather than wrongfully to go on with a war? Does the doctrine imply that? On the level of common sense and the lay meaning of the just-war tradition, it certainly did and must imply the possibility that the wrongness

of a particular battle, weapon, or tactic is so clear that it must be rejected, even at the cost of important sacrifice. This possible negation is a part of the dignity of the tradition. The negation applies most dramatically and globally when one recognizes that *if* the only way to defend a just cause is by a fundamentally wrong means, *then* it is mandatory to surrender and to seek to pursue further the defense of one's valid interests through means other than the belligerent defense of natural sovereignty. If this has not been recognized, and plans befitting such an insight have not been made, that is because the just-war heritage has itself not been clearly understood by those claiming to hold to it.

The clearest statement to the effect that the just-war tradition has not been applied by the major political actors in recent Western experience has come not from pacifists but from the most qualified interpreters of that tradition. Paul Ramsey, the preeminent Protestant author in the field, made this very point:

> The test is whether we are willing to limit ends and means in warfare and yet sustain the burden of this evil necessity, whether we as a people are willing, if war comes, to *accept defeat when our fighters cannot win the hoped-for victory* rather than venture more and exact more than the nature of just endurable warfare requires, whether we can mount the resources for action with at most small effect and plan surrender when none is possible [emphasis added].[19]

Another witness is John Courtney Murray, S.J., author of numerous writings in the field, clearly the most qualified Roman Catholic voice of his generation. Murray explained widespread distrust for the doctrine on the grounds of its long disuse:

> That is, it has not been made the basis for a sound critique of public policies and as a means for the formation of a right public opinion. The classic example, of course, was the policy of "unconditional surrender" during the last war. This policy clearly violated the requirement of the "right intention" that has always been a principle in the traditional doctrine of war. Yet no sustained criticism

---

[18]Quoted here from the 1957 original. The point is less clear in the toned-down version *Christians and the Prevention of War in an Atomic Age,* ed. Robert. S. Bilheimer and Thomas Taylor (London: SCM Press, 1961). This passage is not included in the excerpt from the same report in Donald Durnbaugh, ed., *On Earth Peace* (Elgin, Penn.: Brethren Press, 1978), 185.

[19] Paul Ramsey, *War and Christian Conscience* (Durham, N.C.: Duke University Press, 1961), 151f.

was made of the policy by Catholic spokes-men. Nor was a substantial effort made to clarify by moral judgment the thickening mood of savage violence that made possible the atrocities of Hiroshima and Nagasaki. I think it is true that the traditional doctrine was irrelevant during World War II. This is no argument against the traditional doctrine. The Ten Commandments do not lose their imperative relevance by reason of the fact that they are violated. But there is place for an indictment of all of us who failed to make the tradition relevant.[20]

Murray not only let the doctrine speak honestly to condemn what the political authorities of his nation had done, but he also drew the honest and logical conclusion that if the tradition is to be respected, it must set a limit to what a nation is willing to do in order to win. This must mean concretely defining the point at which it is morally imperative to sue for peace.

> On grounds of the moral principle of proportion the doctrine supports the grave recommendation of the greatest theorist of war in modern times, von Clausewitz: "We must therefore familiarize ourselves with the thought of an honorable defeat." . . . "Losing," said von Clausewitz, "is a function of winning," thus stating in his own military idiom the moral calculus described by traditional moral doctrine. The moralist agrees with the military theorist that the essence of a military situation is uncertainty. And when he requires, with Pius XII, a solid probability of success as a moral ground for a legitimate use of arms, he must reckon with the possibility of failure and be prepared to accept it. But this is a moral decision, worthy of a man and of a civilized nation. It is a free, morally motivated, and responsible act, and therefore it inflicts no stigma of dishonor.[21]

Murray was no defeatist and no pacifist. He insisted that surrender is not the first but the last possibility. The just-war tradition assumes that there can be justifiable ways to wage war, even in modern times. Yet Murray had the integrity to insist that the entire argument is sustainable only if and in so far as those who hold to it do in fact set a limit beyond which they would abandon the military defense of their goals. That may never mean the annihilation of the enemy, nor need it (in the case of a war which may justifiably be waged) demand one's own surrender.

> Surrender may be morally tolerable; but it is not to be tolerated save on a reasonable calculus of proportionate moral costs. In contrast, annihilation is on every count morally intolerable; it is to be averted at all costs.[22]

It is thus undeniable that for some nonpacifists a mandatory cease-fire point is dictated by loyalty to the just-war tradition.[23]

The simplest functional definition of the just-war tradition "with teeth" is that one would rather sue for peace than commit certain legally or morally illicit belligerent acts. *If the only way not to lose a war is to commit a war crime, it is morally right to lose that war.* If that is intended seriously, there will be moral teaching and technical contingency planning in preparation for that extreme eventuality. If that possibility is not affirmed by someone, that person or community has not yet faced the basic moral issue, and we do not yet know that it will not use the notion of necessity arbitrarily.

Category Slide

One of the most frequent ways of undercutting the critical potential of the just-war tradition is to narrow attention to only one or the other of the criteria. Robert Tucker has in fact identified as a specifically American temptation the idea that only the criterion of just cause really matters.[24] This describes both 1914 and 1939. We try to stay out of a war until it is very clear to us that we know whom to blame. Then we want to plunge in and fight without restraint, to win

---

[20]Murray, "Remarks on the Moral Problem of War," 53–54.

[21]Ibid., 55. I have not been able to locate these particular phrases in Clausewitz, but there is no doubt that Murray has the thought of Clausewitz right. The criterion of "probable success" mentioned by Murray is a traditional one. Murray refers specifically to Pius XII only because he had been reviewing recent papal statements earlier in the article.

[22]Ibid., 56.

[23]See John Howard Yoder, "Surrender: A Moral Imperative," *Review of Politics* 48 (Fall 1986), 576ff.

[24]Robert W. Tucker, *The Just War: A Study in Contemporary American Doctrine* (Baltimore: Johns Hopkins University Press, 1960), esp. 11ff. President Bush reasoned publicly in this mode concerning the Gulf War.

at all costs. To say it technically, considerations of *jus ad bellum* are given such weight that, once satisfied, they threaten to override the restraints of *jus in bello*. If the cause that is at stake is great enough, some of the ordinary restraints may be disregarded in order to win soon and decisively.[25] It may be a weakness of the entire just-war tradition that it permits such selective application.

It is also possible to avoid considering all the criteria by looking in the other direction. Many contemporaries say that since the rise of theologies of revolution it is no longer possible to ask the question of just authority, or that since the rise of the notion of national sovereignty it is no longer possible to ask about just cause (since every nation is judge in its own case). Thus we are reduced to being able to ask only the questions of discrimination—proportion and immunity. We can ask only the most formal questions, since for the others no one has the authority to answer.[26]

In a backhanded way this argument has some value. It keeps people from saying that since their own cause is just, they need not be restrained by the rules *in bello*. Restraints *in bello* have to remain in effect against us, assuming our cause is just, as protection for our adversaries' natural rights, even if their cause is unjust. That does not mean, however, that Christian moral responsibility can avoid the questions of moral evaluation on the levels of authority and cause merely by saying that all the parties to the conflict are biased. It is precisely for situations in which people are biased that we need the appeal to common ("natural") criteria. It is precisely because people are biased that we have wars that need to be restrained. The multiple rooting of Christian moral thought—in the thought of the ages, in the goals of rational critical discourse, and in the awareness of world community—should enable asking the hard questions, including the debatable issues of authority and cause, even if the other parties to the conflict are not willing to face them.

Meta-Morality

Thus far we have been proceeding on the basis of the ordinary understanding of the just-war tradition as intended to provide moral guidance for decision-makers in government and in combat. The "sliding" we have documented in many forms was articulated in "realistic" terms used to justify exceptions and to explain trade-offs on that level. There is however a more philosophical or academic level on which the binding authority of the rules can be challenged. James Childress[27] argues that what he calls a "substantive" just-war tradition, which could give concrete guidance or impose precise demands, is impossible in a pluralistic world with competing theories of value. In a pluralistic world people will never agree on what is a just government or a just cause. Therefore there can never be a clear *no* to an unjust war in our modern, pluralistic world. Yet Childress holds that the tradition is nevertheless usable. As a formal theory it provides a common language with which to debate.

There have been dozens of variants within just-war thought in the past. No one can deny Childress the freedom to create yet another. Yet in the measure in which he takes that freedom, he forsakes the claim to be interpreting a classical moral tradition. That the classical tradition (moral and legal) includes the possibility of concrete normative negative answers, regarding the admissibility of specific belligerent acts, has always, especially in our pluralistic modern times, been evidenced by:

- The prosecution of war crimes;
- The founding of one nation's claims to just cause and reprisal in the objective wrongness of offenses committed by the other side;
- The possibility of surrender in the just-war thought of John Courtney Murray, Paul Ramsey, and the World Council of Churches commission[28];

---

[25]Another way to characterize this pattern would be that it uses just-war thinking *ad bellum* and then becomes "realist." The language of just war is thereby co-opted but has no restraining power once the threshold is crossed.

[26]Thus Ramsey argued that since we can never agree about legitimate authority or just cause, we can only regulate means.

---

[27]This is James Childress's point about the limited validity of the whole system, and Paul Ramsey's on our inability to judge just cause objectively. James Childress, "Just War Criteria," in Thomas A. Shannon, ed., *War or Peace* (Maryknoll, N.Y.: Orbis Books, 1980), 151ff. Also in James Childress, *Moral Responsibility in Conflicts: Essays on Nonviolence, War, and Conscience* (Baton Rouge: LSU Press, 1982). The essay is reprinted frequently in anthologies.

[28]See, for example, Ramsey, *War and Christian Conscience.* Childress would not deny that these figures largely merit the credit for restoring the viability of just-war reasoning in this century.

- The possibilities of civil disobedience, disobedience to unjust orders, and selective conscientious objection.

In favor of Childress's relativism it is still possible to appeal to other differences, lay or sophisticated, perhaps between the citizen and the politician, or between the idealist and the realist. It can be argued that some restraint is always better than none, even if the rules are never *fully* respected. It may be better for the enemy population if we respect only some of the just-war restraints than if we respected none of them. But what I am asking about here is not about the greater or lesser disutility, for victims, of this or that way of being killed. I am concerned for the moral claims being made for the killers. In some respects the hypocritical claim to be exercising real restraint, when in fact there is none, may do more harm than outright honest "realism."[29] All such arguments in favor of relativism belong to the unavoidable complexity of public moral discourse; I have no intention to avoid them. My point is that in most cases they diminish rather than heighten the capacity of just-war thought to provide effective moral guidance.

By now the reader will have discerned the drift of our culture. The person who is concerned to give a fair hearing, open-mindedly and critically, to the claim that the just-war tradition is a usable structure of moral accountability was first told that the just-war tradition agrees that war is an evil. Only under the circumstances stated by the criteria evolved over centuries can participation in that evil be justified, on the grounds that (as the application of the criteria serves to verify or falsify) it is less than the evil it prevents. Those criteria are supposed to guarantee that there is no *carte blanche*; there are some things one would never do, even for a just cause.

But then when we ask about the firmness with which the criteria apply, we discover that they keep sliding farther down the scale. With each concession the claim is renewed that this still does not mean that "anything goes." Indeed,

- The double-effect argument is still subject to criteria;
- Reprisals are still subject to proportionality;

- Relaxing some rules is done in order to safeguard the idea of law as such;
- The rules will never be met, but if we keep talking about them the infractions will not be as bad as if we don't;
- We have no common notion of what compliance would mean, or what must never happen, but at least we have a common vocabulary.

The slippery slope pattern is obvious.

Retreats or Routs?

Does the tradition lay a reliable foundation for common discussion and possible common decision about admissible levels of damage that political imperatives may oblige responsible decision makers to accept without becoming immoral? What seems on closer scrutiny actually to be going on is a series of what we are told are strategic retreats, but they turn out not to be that. A strategic retreat is a sober decision to take some loss, stepping back to a line which may be more firmly defended. That is what *seems* at first to be happening when someone begins the discussion saying that concessions will need to be made (just this once), but only in cases of last resort, self-defense, and so on. That sounds like a line that would be easier to defend than the prohibition of all killing. But when it comes to defending that line, we discover that other reasons are being alleged for stepping back still farther:

- The law will not be respected if we make it too demanding;
- We cannot be expected to stand by all the niceties of the law if the enemy does not;
- Sometimes the best defense may be a preemptive aggression, when the enemy's threat is the moral equivalent of an actual attack.

What had been presented as a line that could be defended now has several degrees of concessions to whatever recourse the most pessimistic picture of the conflict enables someone to claim is necessary. What claimed to be a firm structure for moral discernment has turned spongy. What claimed (in contrast to the intrinsic values served by pacifism or the holy war) to be a toolkit of resources for fine-tuned discrimination turns out in most of the cases we can find in the literature to have been special pleading.

In short, when we give the just-war system a chance to prove its integrity, to prove that a strategic

---

[29]In the 1991 Gulf War the coalition forces' publicity made much of their careful respect for *some* of the just-war restraints. There was no recognition of those rules which were not respected. See below, pages 93f., for the lessons some draw from the Gulf War.

retreat was authentically that by being able more effectively to hold the new lower line, it does not deliver.

Counter to the standard history,[30] the just-war position is not the one which has been taken practically by most Christians since Constantine. Most Christians (baptized people) in most wars since pacifism was forsaken have died and killed in the light of thought patterns derived from the crusade or the national-interest pattern. Some have sought to cover and interpret this activity with the rhetoric of the just-war heritage; others have not bothered. The just-war tradition remains prominent as a consensus of the stated best insights of a spiritual and intellectual elite, who used that language as a tool for moral leverage on sovereigns for whom the language of the gospel carried no conviction. Thus just-war rhetoric and consistent pacifism are on the same side of most debates. When honest, both will reject most wars, most causes, and most strategies being prepared and implemented.

How then did the notion that the just-war tradition is the mainstream position remain alive at all? Certainly it is not only that people were misled as to the power of theologians to get a hearing. Certainly there have been both ideal visions and real models of Christian statesmanship and civil heroism. There have been people who, in the exercise of public responsibility, saved or created nations, kept the blood-thirstiness of war from getting out of control, and made some kind of peace through limited power, with restraint, wisdom, and magnanimity. The closer one comes to the domestic model, where restrained violence is like that of the police officer, the more applicable, by analogy, is the just-war language, and the more credible is its claim to be providing real guidance. Those persons who incarnate domestic order and who succeed in imposing social peace from positions of power may have more to do with making believable the idea of subjecting violence to restraint than do actual experiences in war between nations.

---

[30]For example, *The Challenge of Peace* (Washington, D.C.: U.S. Catholic Conference, 1983).

The Faith Was Often Different

Not only was the just-war tradition not really in charge in history, but it was not dominant in spirituality. When a history of thought is based on the writings of a magisterial elite, then it is the just-war tradition which we must report. But how many people like that were there, and how many more drew spiritual sustenance from them?

If, on the other hand, we were to ask how through the centuries most people—who were at the same time somehow authentic Christian believers and lived their lives of faith with some explicit sincerity—thought about war, then we should have to report that their lives were sincerely burdened, not nourished, by the just-war grid. Their lives were nourished, not by the summas of the academicians, but by the lives of the saints. Most of the saints were tacitly nonviolent. Most of the martyr-saints were expressly nonviolent. The rejection of violent self-defense or of service in the armies of Caesar was sometimes the reason for which the saint was martyred. The lives of the saints are told to incite the hearer to trust God for his or her surviving and prospering. Even those saints (like Francis) who lived in the midst of war and the few who were soldiers were not Machiavellian. They cultivated a worldview marked by trusting God for survival, a willingness to suffer rather than to sin, and an absence of any cynical utilitarianism in their definition of the path of obedience. The penitent and the pilgrim were normally, naturally defenseless. The stories of the saints abound in tales of miraculous deliverance from the threats of bandits and brigands.

It is a source of deep historical confusion to identify the history of Christian morality as a whole with the record of the thought of academic moralists, where just-war thought in Christendom has been located. Such academic formulations may, in some cultures, make a major contribution to how people will actually make decisions in the future, *if* local preachers or confessors take their cues from the professor. But in other traditions, where the instrument of enforcement that the confessional provides is not used, the relation between the academic articulation and the real life of the community is more like that of the froth to the beer.

28. *Love, Law, and Civil Disobedience*

MARTIN LUTHER KING, JR.

In this selection, Martin Luther King, Jr., discusses his commitment to nonviolence as an approach to social change. Basing his convictions on the premise that God is on the side of justice and truth, King calls for his followers to rise above the inclination for vengeance and to love their enemy as they seek to overcome the evil systems that they have created. In the end, one's purpose is to manifest the will of God by winning over one's adversaries without humiliating them, and only nonviolent resistance makes possible the achievement of these two ends.

Members of the Fellowship of the Concerned, of the Southern Regional Council, I need not pause to say how very delighted I am to be here today, and to have the opportunity of being a little part of this very significant gathering. I certainly want to express my personal appreciation to Mrs. Tilly and the members of the Committee, for giving me this opportunity. I would also like to express just a personal word of thanks and appreciation for your vital witness in this period of transition which we are facing in our Southland, and in the nation, and I am sure that as a result of this genuine concern, and your significant work in communities all across the South, we have a better South today and I am sure will have a better South tomorrow with your continued endeavor and I do want to express my personal gratitude and appreciation to you of the Fellowship of the Concerned for your significant work and for your forthright witness.

Now, I have been asked to talk about the philosophy behind the student movement. There can be no gainsaying of the fact that we confront a crisis in race relations in the United States. This crisis has been precipitated on the one hand by the determined resistance of reactionary forces in the South to the Supreme Court's decision in 1954 outlawing segregation in the public schools. And we know that at times this resistance has risen to ominous proportions. At times we find the legislative halls of the South ringing loud with such words

as interposition and nullification. And all of these forces have developed into massive resistance. But we must also say that the crisis has been precipitated on the other hand by the determination of hundreds and thousands and millions of Negro people to achieve freedom and human dignity. If the Negro stayed in his place and accepted discrimination and segregation, there would be no crisis. But the Negro has a new sense of dignity, a new self-respect and new determination. He has reevaluated his own intrinsic worth. Now this new sense of dignity on the part of the Negro grows out of the same longing for freedom and human dignity on the part of the oppressed people all over the world; for we see it in Africa, we see it in Asia, and we see it all over the world. Now we must say that this struggle for freedom will not come to an automatic halt, for history reveals to us that once oppressed people rise up against that oppression, there is no stopping point short of full freedom. On the other hand, history reveals to us that those who oppose the movement for freedom are those who are in privileged positions who very seldom give up their privileges without strong resistance. And they very seldom do it voluntarily. So the sense of struggle will continue. The question is how will the struggle be waged.

Now there are three ways that oppressed people have generally dealt with their oppression. One way is the method of acquiescence, the method of surrender; that is, the individuals will somehow adjust themselves to oppression, they adjust themselves to discrimination or to segregation or colonialism or what have you. The other method that has been used in history is that of rising up against the oppressor with corroding hatred and physical violence. Now of course we know about this method in Western civilization because in a sense it has been the hallmark of its

From Martin Luther King, Jr., "Law, Love, and Civil Disobedience," published in *New South* (December 1961): 3ff. Reprinted by arrangement with the Estate of Martin Luther King, Jr., c/o Writers House as agent for the proprietor, New York, NY. Copyright 1961 Martin Luther King, Jr., copyright renewed 1989 Coretta Scott King.

grandeur, and the inseparable twin of western materialism. But there is a weakness in this method because it ends up creating many more social problems than it solves. And I am convinced that if the Negro succumbs to the temptation of using violence in his struggle for freedom and justice, unborn generations will be the recipients of a long and desolate night of bitterness. And our chief legacy to the future will be an endless reign of meaningless chaos.

But there is another way, namely the way of nonviolent resistance. This method was popularized in our generation by a little man from India, whose name was Mohandas K. Gandhi. He used this method in a magnificent way to free his people from the economic exploitation and the political domination inflicted upon them by a foreign power.

This has been the method used by the student movement in the South and all over the United States. And naturally whenever I talk about the student movement I cannot be totally objective. I have to be somewhat subjective because of my great admiration for what the students have done. For in a real sense they have taken our deep groans and passionate yearnings for freedom, and filtered them in their own tender souls, and fashioned them into a creative protest which is an epic known all over our nation. As a result of their disciplined, nonviolent, yet courageous struggle, they have been able to do wonders in the South, and in our nation. But this movement does have an underlying philosophy, it has certain ideas that are attached to it, it has certain philosophical precepts. These are the things that I would like to discuss for the few moments left.

I would say that the first point or the first principle in the movement is the idea that means must be as pure as the end. This movement is based on the philosophy that ends and means must cohere. Now this has been one of the long struggles in history, the whole idea of means and ends. Great philosophers have grappled with it, and sometimes they have emerged with the idea, from Machiavelli on down, that the end justifies the means. There is a great system of thought in our world today, known as communism. And I think that with all of the weakness and tragedies of communism, we find its greatest tragedy right here, that it goes under the philosophy that the end justifies the means that are used in the process. So we can read or we can hear the Lenins say that lying, deceit, or violence, that many of these things justify the ends of the classless society.

This is where the student movement and the nonviolent movement that is taking place in our nation would break with communism and any other system that would argue that the end justifies the means. For in the long run, we must see that the end represents the means in process and the ideal in the making. In other words, we cannot believe, or we cannot go with the idea that the end justifies the means because the end is preexistent in the means. So the idea of nonviolent resistance, the philosophy of nonviolent resistance, is the philosophy which says that the means must be as pure as the end, that in the long run of history, immoral destructive means cannot bring about moral and constructive ends.

There is another thing about this philosophy, this method of nonviolence which is followed by the student movement. It says that those who adhere to or follow this philosophy must follow a consistent principle of noninjury. They must consistently refuse to inflict injury upon another. Sometimes you will read the literature of the student movement and see that, as they are getting ready for the sit-in or stand-in, they will read something like this, "If you are hit do not hit back, if you are cursed do not curse back." This is the whole idea, that the individual who is engaged in a nonviolent struggle must never inflict injury upon another. Now this has an external aspect and it has an internal one. From the external point of view it means that the individuals involved must avoid external physical violence. So they don't have guns, they don't retaliate with physical violence. If they are hit in the process, they avoid external physical violence at every point. But it also means that they avoid internal violence of spirit. This is why the love ethic stands so high in the student movement. We have a great deal of talk about love and nonviolence in this whole thrust.

Now when the students talk about love, certainly they are not talking about emotional bosh, they are not talking about merely a sentimental outpouring; they're talking something much deeper, and I always have to stop and try to define the meaning of love in this context. The Greek language comes to our aid in trying to deal with this. There are three words in the Greek language for love; one is the word *eros*. This is a beautiful type of love, it is an aesthetic love. Plato talks about it a great deal in his Dialogue, the yearning of the soul for the realm of the divine. It has come to us to be a sort of romantic love, and so in a sense we have read about it and experienced it. We've read about it in all the beauties of literature. I guess in a sense Edgar Allan Poe was talking about *eros* when he talked about his beautiful Annabelle Lee, with the love surrounded by the halo of eternity. In a sense Shakespeare was talking about *eros* when he said "Love is not love which alters when it alteration finds, or bends with the remover to remove;

O'no! It is an ever fixed mark that looks on tempests and is never shaken, it is the star to every wandering bark." (You know, I remember that because I used to quote it to this little lady when we were courting; that's *eros*.) The Greek language talks about *philia* which was another level of love. It is an intimate affection between personal friends, it is a reciprocal love. On this level you love because you are loved. It is friendship.

Then the Greek language comes out with another word which is called the *agape*. *Agape* is more than romantic love, *agape* is more than friendship. *Agape* is understanding, creative, redemptive, good will to all men. It is an overflowing love which seeks nothing in return. Theologians would say that it is the love of God operating in the human heart. So that when one rises to love on this level, he loves men not because he likes them, not because their ways appeal to him, but he loves every man because God loves him. And he rises to the point of loving the person who does an evil deed while hating the deed that the person does. I think this is what Jesus meant when he said "love your enemies." I'm very happy that he didn't say like your enemies, because it is pretty difficult to like some people. Like is sentimental, and it is pretty difficult to like someone bombing your home; it is pretty difficult to like somebody threatening your children; it is difficult to like congressmen who spend all of their time trying to defeat civil rights. But Jesus says love them, and love is greater than like. Love is understanding, redemptive, creative, good will for all men. And it is this idea, it is this whole ethic of love which is the idea standing at the basis of the student movement.

There is something else: that one seeks to defeat the unjust system, rather than individuals who are caught in that system. And that one goes on believing that somehow this is the important thing, to get rid of the evil system and not the individual who happens to be misguided, who happens to be misled, who was taught wrong. The thing to do is to get rid of the system and thereby create a moral balance within society.

Another thing that stands at the center of this movement is another idea: that suffering can be a most creative and powerful social force. Suffering has certain moral attributes involved, but it can be a powerful and creative social force. Now, it is very interesting at this point to notice that both violence and nonviolence agree that suffering can be a very powerful social force. But there is this difference: violence says that suffering can be a powerful social force by inflicting the suffering on somebody else: so this is what we do in war, this is what we do in the whole violent thrust of the violent movement. It believes that you achieve some end by inflicting suffering on another. The nonviolent say that suffering becomes a powerful social force when you willingly accept that violence on yourself, so that self-suffering stands at the center of the nonviolent movement and the individuals involved are able to suffer in a creative manner, feeling that unearned suffering is redemptive, and that suffering may serve to transform the social situation.

Another thing in this movement is the idea that there is within human nature an amazing potential for goodness. There is within human nature something that can respond to goodness. I know somebody's liable to say that this is an unrealistic movement if it goes on believing that all people are good. Well, I didn't say that. I think the students are realistic enough to believe that there is a strange dichotomy of disturbing dualism within human nature. Many of the great philosophers and thinkers through the ages have seen this. It caused Ovid the Latin poet to say, "I see and approve the better things of life, but the evil things I do." It caused even Saint Augustine to say. "Lord, make me pure, but not yet." So that is in human nature. Plato, centuries ago said that the human personality is like a charioteer with two headstrong horses, each wanting to go in different directions, so that within our own individual lives we see this conflict and certainly when we come to the collective life of man, we see a strange badness. But in spite of this there is something in human nature that can respond to goodness. So that man is neither innately good nor is he innately bad; he has potentialities for both. So in this sense, Carlyle was right when he said that, "there are depths in man which go down to the lowest hell, and heights which reach the highest heaven, for are not both heaven and hell made out of him, everlasting miracle and mystery that he is?" Man has the capacity to be good, man has the capacity to be evil.

And so the nonviolent resister never lets this idea go, that there is something within human nature than can respond to goodness. So that a Jesus of Nazareth or a Mohandas Gandhi can appeal to human beings and appeal to that element of goodness within them, and a Hitler can appeal to the element of evil within them. But we must never forget that there is something within human nature that can respond to goodness, that man is not totally depraved; to put it in theological terms, the image of God is never totally gone. And so the individuals who believe in this movement and who believe in nonviolence and our struggle in the South, somehow believe that even the worst segra-tionist can become an integrationist. Now sometimes it is hard to believe that this is what this movement says, and it believes it firmly, that there is something within human nature that can be changed, and this stands at the top of the whole philosophy of the student movement and the philosophy of nonviolence.

It says something else. It says that it is as much a moral obligation to refuse to cooperate with evil as it is to cooperate with good. Noncooperation with evil is as much a moral obligation as the cooperation with good. So that the student movement is willing to stand up courageously on the idea of civil disobedience. Now I think this is the part of the student movement that is probably misunderstood more than anything else. And it is a difficult aspect, because on the one hand the students would say, and I would say, and all the people who believe in civil rights would say, obey the Supreme Court's decision of 1954 and at the same time, we would disobey certain laws that exist on the statutes of the South today.

This brings in the whole question of how can you be logically consistent when you advocate obeying some laws and disobeying other laws. Well, I think one would have to see the whole meaning of this movement at this point by seeing that the students recognize that there are two types of laws. There are just laws and there are unjust laws. And they would be the first to say obey the just laws, they would be the first to say that men and women have a moral obligation to obey just and right laws. And they would go on to say that we must see that there are unjust laws. Now the question comes into being, what is the difference, and who determines the difference, what is the difference between a just and an unjust law?

Well, a just law is a law that squares with a moral law. It is a law that squares with that which is right, so that any law that uplifts human personality is a just law. Whereas that law which is out of harmony with the moral is a law which does not square with the moral law of the universe. It does not square with the law of God, so for that reason it is unjust and any law that degrades the human personality is an unjust law.

Well, somebody says that does not mean anything to me; first, I don't believe in these abstract things called moral laws and I'm not too religious, so I don't believe in the law of God; you have to get a little more concrete, and more practical. What do you mean when you say that a law is unjust, and a law is just? Well, I would go on to say in more concrete terms that an unjust law is a code that the majority inflicts on the minority that is not binding on itself. So that this becomes difference made legal. Another thing that we can say is that an unjust

law is a code which the majority inflicts upon the minority, which that minority had no part in enacting or creating, because that minority had no right to vote in many instances, so that the legislative bodies that made these laws were not democratically elected. Who could ever say that the legislative body of Mississippi was democratically elected, or the legislative body of Alabama was democratically elected, or the legislative body even of Georgia has been democratically elected, when there are people in Terrell County and in other counties because of the color of their skin who cannot vote? They confront reprisals and threats and all of that; so that an unjust law is a law that individuals did not have a part in creating or enacting because they were denied the right to vote.

Now the same token of just law would be just the opposite. A just law becomes saneness made legal. It is a code that the majority, who happen to believe in that code, compel the minority, who don't believe in it, to follow, because they are willing to follow it themselves, so it is saneness made legal. Therefore the individuals who stand up on the basis of civil disobedience realize that they are following something that says that there are just laws and there are unjust laws. Now, they are not anarchists. They believe that there are laws which must be followed; they do not seek to defy the law, they do not seek to evade the law. For many individuals who would call themselves segregationists and who would hold on to segregation at any cost seek to defy the law, they seek to evade the law, and their process can lead on into anarchy. They seek in the final analysis to follow a way of uncivil disobedience, not civil disobedience. And I submit that the individual who disobeys the law, whose conscience tells him it is unjust and who is willing to accept the penalty by staying in jail until that law is altered, is expressing at the moment the very highest respect for law.

This is what the students have followed in their movement. Of course there is nothing new about this; they feel that they are in good company and rightly so. We go back and read the Apology and the Crito, and you see Socrates practicing civil disobedience. And to a degree academic freedom is a reality today because Socrates practiced civil disobedience. The early Christians practiced civil disobedience in a superb manner, to a point where they were willing to be thrown to the lions. They were willing to face all kinds of suffering in order to stand up for what they knew was right even though they knew it was against the laws of the Roman Empire.

We could come up to our own day and we see it in many instances. We must never forget that everything that Hitler did in Germany was "legal." It was illegal to aid and comfort a Jew, in the days of Hitler's Germany. But I believe that if I had the same attitude then as I have now I would publicly aid and comfort my Jewish brothers in Germany if Hitler were alive today calling this an illegal process. If I lived in South Africa today in the midst of the white supremacy law in South Africa, I would join Chief Luthuli and others in saying break these unjust laws. And even let us come up to America. Our nation in a sense came into being through a massive act of civil disobedience for the Boston Tea Party was nothing but a massive act of civil disobedience. Those who stood up against the slave laws, the abolitionists, by and large practiced civil disobedience. So I think these students are in good company, and they feel that by practicing civil disobedience they are in line with men and women through the ages who have stood up for something that is morally right.

Now there are one or two other things that I want to say about this student movement, moving out of the philosophy of nonviolence, something about what it is a revolt against. On the one hand it is a revolt against the negative peace that has encompassed the South for many years. I remember when I was in Montgomery, Alabama, one of the white citizens came to me one day and said—and I think he was very sincere about this— that in Montgomery for all of these years we have been such a peaceful community, we have had so much harmony in race relations and then you people have started this movement and boycott, and it has done so much to disturb race relations, and we just don't love the Negro like we used to love them, because you have destroyed the harmony and the peace that we once had in race relations. And I said to him, in the best way I could say and I tried to say it in nonviolent terms, we have never had peace in Montgomery, Alabama, we have never had peace in the South. We have had a negative peace, which is merely the absence of tension; we've had a negative peace in which the Negro patiently accepted his situation and his plight, but we've never had true peace, we've never had positive peace, and what we're seeking now is to develop this positive peace. For we must come to see that peace is not merely the absence of some negative force, it is the presence of a positive force. True peace is not merely the absence of tension, but it is the presence of justice and brotherhood. I think this is what Jesus meant when he said, "I come not to bring peace but a sword." Now Jesus didn't mean he came to start war, to bring a physical sword, and he didn't

mean, I come not to bring positive peace. But I think what Jesus was saying in substance was this, that I come not to bring an old negative peace, which makes for stagnant passivity and deadening complacency, I come to bring something different, and whenever I come, a conflict is precipitated, between the old and the new, whenever I come a struggle takes place between justice and injustice, between the forces of light and the forces of darkness. I come not to bring a negative peace, but a positive peace, which is brotherhood, which is justice, which is the Kingdom of God.

And I think this is what we are seeking to do today, and this movement is a revolt against a negative peace and a struggle to bring into being a positive peace, which makes for true brotherhood, true integration, true person-to-person relationships. This movement is also revolt against what is often called tokenism. Here again many people do not understand this, they feel that in this struggle the Negro will be satisfied with tokens of integration, just a few students and a few schools here and there and a few doors open here and there. But this isn't the meaning of the movement and I think that honesty impels me to admit it everywhere I have an opportunity, that the Negro's aim is to bring about complete integration in American life. And he has come to see that token integration is little more than token democracy, which ends up with many new evasive schemes and it ends up with new discrimination, covered up with such niceties of complexity. It is very interesting to discover that the movement has thrived in many communities that had token integration. So this reveals that the movement is based on a principle that integration must become real and complete, not just token integration.

It is also a revolt against what I often call the myth of time. We hear this quite often, that only time can solve this problem. That if we will only be patient, and only pray—which we must do, we must be patient and we must pray—but there are those who say just do these things and wait for time, and time will solve the problem. Well the people who argue this do not themselves realize that time is neutral, that it can be used constructively or destructively. At points the people of ill will, the segregationists, have used time much more effectively than the people of good will. So individuals in the struggle must come to realize that it is necessary to aid time, that without this kind of aid, time itself will be come an ally of the insurgent and primitive forces of social stagnation. Therefore, this movement is a revolt against the myth of time.

There is a final thing that I would like to say to you, this movement is a movement based on faith in the future. It is a movement based on a philosophy, the possibility of the future bringing into being something real and meaningful. It is a movement based on hope. I think this is very important. The students have developed a theme song for their movement, maybe you've heard it. It goes something like this, "We shall overcome, deep in my heart, I do believe, we shall overcome," and then they go on to say another verse, "We are not afraid, we are not afraid today, deep in my heart I do believe, we shall overcome." So it is out of this deep faith in the future that they are able to move out and adjourn the councils of despair, and to bring new light in the dark chambers of pessimism. I can remember the times that we've been together, I remember that night in Montgomery, Alabama, when we had stayed up all night discussing the Freedom Rides, and that morning came to see that it was necessary to go on with the Freedom Rides, that we would not in all good conscience call an end to the Freedom Rides at that point. And I remember the first group got ready to leave, to take a bus for Jackson, Mississippi, we all joined hands and started singing together. "We shall overcome, we shall overcome." And something within me said, now how is it that these students can sing this, they are going down to Mississippi, they are going to face hostile and jeering mobs, and yet they could sing, "We shall overcome." They may even face physical death, and yet they could sing, "We shall overcome." Most of them realized that they would be thrown into jail, and yet they could sing, "We shall overcome, we are not afraid." Then something caused me to see at that moment the real meaning of the movement. That students had faith in

the future. That the movement was based on hope, that this movement had something within it that says somehow even though the arc of the moral universe is long, it bends toward justice. And I think this should be a challenge to all others who are struggling to transform the dangling discords of our Southland into a beautiful symphony of brotherhood. There is something in this student movement which says to us, that we shall overcome. Before the victory is won some may have to get scarred up, but we shall overcome. Before the victory of brotherhood is achieved, some will maybe face physical death, but we shall overcome. Before the victory is won, some will lose jobs, some will be called communists, and reds, merely because they believe in brotherhood, some will be dismissed as dangerous rabblerousers and agitators merely because they're standing up for what is right, but we shall overcome. That is the basis of this movement, and as I like to say, there is something in this universe that justifies Carlyle in saying no lie can live forever. We shall overcome because there is something in this universe which justifies William Cullen Bryant in saying truth crushed to earth shall rise again. We shall overcome because there is something in this universe that justifies James Russell Lowell in saying, truth forever on the scaffold, wrong forever on the throne. Yet that scaffold sways the future and behind the dim unknown standeth God within the shadows keeping watch above His own. With this faith in the future, with this determined struggle, we will be able to emerge from the bleak and desolate midnight of man's inhumanity to man, into the bright and glittering daybreak of freedom and justice. Thank you.

29. New Testament Reflections on Peace and Nuclear Arms

SANDRA M. SCHNEIDERS

Sandra M. Schneiders considers the pastoral letter of the American bishops on "The Challenge of Peace" and commends it for its insights into the need for, and process of, peace making. Nonetheless, she criticizes the biblical section of the pastoral for its failure to integrate scriptural materials properly into the core reasoning of the document. She argues that the centrality of the biblical mandate for peace, the love command, the preferential option for the poor proclaimed in the Gospels, the ministry of reconciliation entrusted to the Christian community, and the willingness to overturn conventional thinking in the name of Christ all strongly proclaim against contemporary defense policy.

With so many others, Catholics and non-Catholics alike, I rejoiced at the prophetic witness the bishops gave to the possibility of peace and the moral leadership they provided for those who are working to bring it about.[1] The pastoral is a major contribution to reflection and incentive to action on the most pressing issue of our time. Nevertheless, I have to conclude that the weakest element of the letter is the section on scripture. The biblical section in the final document is a major improvement over the corresponding sections in the first and second drafts. It evokes the biblical message with greater fullness and shows better the relationship between the Old and New Testaments. However, the major weakness, namely, the failure to integrate the biblical material into the central reasoning of the document, remains.

This weakness is not peculiar to this pastoral. The pastoral merely exemplifies a problem which is becoming more evident as Catholics try to make their relatively recently recovered sense of the centrality of scripture function in their reflection on contemporary issues. The problem is that we lack an adequate hermeneutical theory to ground our use of biblical material in relationship to contemporary problems. As a result, we tend to "invoke" scripture at the outset of a reasoning process whose real dynamics are derived from moral theology, papal social teaching, theology, or elsewhere. What I will try to do in this essay is to demonstrate a more integral use of biblical material, not as an introduction to other kinds of reasoning but as the substance of the argument.

From Philip Murnion (ed.), *Catholics and Nuclear War* (New York: Crossroads/Herder & Herder, 1984), pp. 91–105. Reprinted by permission of the author.

First, I will outline briefly the theoretical framework for the biblical reflection; second, I will briefly summarize the theological-ecclesial context of the reflections; third, I will discuss at some length five aspects of the New Testament vision of Christian discipleship which bear upon the questions of peace and nuclear arms.

Theoretical Framework

To begin, I want to mention, in order to repudiate them, two approaches to New Testament material which are unreliable as contributions to pastoral reflection. Then I will examine two legitimate approaches to New Testament material and the kinds of contributions each can make to the effort to find Christian responses to questions and problems which could not have occurred to the first-century authors who composed the New Testament texts.

The first illegitimate approach, biblical fundamentalism, is not historically characteristic of Roman Catholics but has recently achieved a disturbing prominence in certain conservative Catholic circles. Fundamentalism might be defined as literalism in interpretation based on an untenable theological doctrine that each word of the Bible is divinely dictated and thus must be regarded as not subject to error. Its basic theological error is its rejection of the incarnational character of divine revelation which entails that God's word is mediated through historical human understanding and speech.[2]

This theological error leads directly to the methodological position of rejecting the methods and conclusions of historical criticism[3] and treating the biblical texts as timeless formulations, in an unchanging language, of eternal truths. Although often motivated by a genuine desire to hear God's word without guile, that is, without possible distortion by human scientific interventions in the interpretative process, fundamentalism results in a type of reading which is sometimes merely simplistic but often enough completely erroneous. This type of interpretation becomes particularly dangerous when used to deal with issues of such extraordinary complexity as nuclear war.

The second illegitimate approach is closely related to fundamentalism and is historically much more characteristic of Roman Catholic theology. It is still sometimes operative even in official documents and is descriptively referred to as "prooftexting." Prooftexting could be defined as the use of isolated texts out of context to substantiate conclusions derived from extrabiblical premises, for example, from moral theology or papal teaching. Although the positions finally taken may be quite valid, the use of scripture to support it is not, because the text in question has been read outside the literary context which controls its meaning.

The faulty theological position which underlies prooftexting involves a misunderstanding of the complex nature of the biblical witness to divine revelation. Scripture is understood as a kind of collection of aphorisms or detachable citations which have meaning independently of their literary and canonical context and which can be applied, like proverbs, as universal truths unaffected by the historical conditions in which they were written.

What fundamentalism and prooftexting have in common is their reading of scripture out of context. A valid approach to the sacred text demands that it be read and used as a canonical whole, a theologically complex and pluriform unity in which time-conditioned human understanding and expression is the medium of divine, ever-actual revelation. The final pastoral, in its reading of scripture, is happily free of both fundamentalism (which is a frequent trap of both "hawks" and "doves") and prooftexting (which is a frequent weakness in official ecclesiastical documents).

Let us turn now to two legitimate approaches to biblical material which, although both useful, make different kinds of contributions in the pastoral sphere. The first, classical historical criticism, is the approach of the majority of recognized Roman Catholic and nonfundamentalist Protestant scholars. It seems to be the underlying approach of the pastoral.

Historical criticism assigns to the biblical scholar as his or her primary (although not necessarily exclusive) task the critical exegesis of specific passages such as the Sermon on the Mount as a whole (Mt. 5–7) or a subsection such as the Beatitudes (Mt. 5:3–11), in order to discern the literal sense of the text, that is, the sense intended by the sacred author.[4] Such exegesis, carried out by rigorously critical methods, provides both historical and theological data. This material can then, in a subsequent and independent operation, be applied to pastoral or theological problems.[5]

A growing number of biblical scholars, while fully accepting the methodological soundness and the absolute indispensability of historical critical exegesis as the basis of any valid interpretation, are finding themselves increasingly uncomfortable with the separation of what the Bible meant in its own time (which inevitably appears to be its only *real* meaning) from what the Bible means today (which inevitably appears to be a kind of extraneous and non-necessary "application" rather than a real meaning) and are seeking a more integrated approach to the meaning of texts based on a more dynamic understanding of the reality of "meaning."[6]

Basic to this hermeneutical approach, or approach to the meaning of texts, is an understanding of the text not as a collection of words that can have but one meaning, which can be stated in a finite number of correct propositions and which is imbedded in the text in a permanent and unchanging way,[7] but as an experience which has the power to transform us in the encounter between the text and the interpreter. Thus every experience of genuine understanding, although subject to the controls and norms of historical and literary analysis, is potentially new and always somewhat different from its predecessors because the mind which encounters the ancient text is a contemporary mind bringing to the text new questions and a new context of understanding.[8] In other words, rather than applying an ancient meaning which, in itself, is limited by its first-century context, to a contemporary question such as the nuclear arms race, the scholar who adopts this approach interprets the text as always speaking to and in the present because of the transcendent and ever-active power which can be found in all classical texts and a fortiori in the scriptures which are our primary witness to divine revelation.[9]

It is within the framework of a contemporary hermeneutical theory of biblical interpretation that I will attempt to draw from the New Testament some light on the issue of nuclear arms.

Theological-Ecclesial Context

The theological-ecclesial context within which the following reflections will be situated is woven of four theological strands articulated, though not originated, by Vatican Council II.

The first strand is the understanding, especially evident in the Pastoral Constitution on the Church in the Modern World,[10] of how Christian ideals operate in our theological efforts to make moral judgments. There seems to be a move away from moral reasoning based on a somewhat static theology that uses God's creation as the framework. In such a theology Christ is seen primarily as eternal Logos, or wisdom of God, who expresses an unchanging natural law from which we can deduce what is acceptable human behavior. The transition is toward a more dynamic approach to moral reasoning rooted in a theology of salvation in which Jesus, the resurrected Lord, is seen as the primary expression of a new humanity, drawing individuals and the race toward the fullness of human existence, according to a developing understanding of natural law.[11]

The prophetic ministry of the historical Jesus, comprised of his authoritative teaching and his martyr's death, has come to play a much larger role than abstract moral principles in our efforts to understand the meaning of discipleship in the contemporary world. This is largely responsible for the post-conciliar tendency to view discipleship as self-transcending love of God and neighbor defined by the dynamic model of divine love embodied in the crucified and risen Jesus rather than in terms of minimal requirements for salvation. Thus, the Christian vocation emerges clearly not as the minimum required of a human being by nature but as the maximum made possible by our sharing in divine life. It is on this basis that I will argue below that it is not a theory of just war, however morally sound, but the gospel imperative to make peace even at the cost of ultimate self-sacrifice that must guide our response to the question of nuclear arms.

The second strand in the theological-ecclesial context is the conciliar reemphasis on the integral role that reading the "signs of the times" must play in our discerning what Christian discipleship means in our day. We are not called merely to apply timeless and unchanging norms to changed conditions but to allow our own hearts and consciences to be the theater in which occurs the encounter between the unsearchable riches of divine revelation and the arresting realities of our contemporary human experience. In fact, only in this encounter do we experience the potentiality of sacred scripture to be divine revelation for us.

It seems to have been, at least in part, such an encounter between the word of God and the realities of twentieth-century existence which led the participants at Vatican II, contemplating the incredibly destructive capacity of nuclear weapons, to declare that they felt compelled not to refurbish old views or doctrines but to "undertake an evaluation of war with an entirely new attitude."[12]

The third strand in the theological-ecclesial context is the renewed theology of the church. As we see in the council's Dogmatic Constitution on the Church[13] there is a discernible tendency away from a static understanding of the church as a perfect and superior society which proposes the minimal demands of natural morality to the state which is considered as a perfect but inferior society, and toward a dynamic conception of the church as the people of God called to be in the world as sign, herald, and agent of the reign of God.[14] It is from this perspective that I will argue that violence, prepared for, threatened, intended, or used can never function as a Christian option, can never be given a place, however grudging, within our preaching as a church even though it might, at times, be the justifiable option of an individual Christian.

Finally, and as a consequence of the preceding three developments, there has emerged a powerful sense of the Christian vocation not as a second and/or private identity nor simply as a religious motive for ordinary good citizenship, but as a prophetic responsibility to transform the world in liberty, justice, and peace.

My own work on the New Testament leads me to affirm, and to operate within, this understanding of the Christian vocation as a distinctive call, not contrary to our human vocation but only clear to us in the light of the self-transcending act of reconciliation on Calvary. In short, the context of theology and church within which we should draw on the scriptures is one that sees the human encounter with Christ as a continually developing reality. It is one that sees discipleship as a demanding conversion of heart and the church as a people calling the world to the quality of God's reign. It is a context which calls the Christian to transform the world.

The New Testament Contribution to the Question of Peace and Nuclear Arms

There are numerous possible approaches to the New Testament data which bear upon the questions with which we are concerned. I will explore five aspects of the New Testament message which seem to me particularly important for reflection on peace and nuclear arms. In line with the observations in the preceding section I will try to show not what could conceivably be justified as consonant with New Testament demands, but what the Christian vocation as presented in the Gospels seems to call us to in the face of the incessant build-up of nuclear arms in our country and abroad. In other words, I will attempt to bring the inner dynamics of Christian discipleship into dialogue with the inner dynamics of the current situation in order to expose the challenge that the former addresses to the latter. In what follows I shall, first, look briefly at the Christian mandate to make peace; second, and in somewhat greater detail, explore the radicality of the Christian love commandment; third, examine the ministry of reconciliation as the concrete locus of peacemaking and Christian love; fourth, look at Jesus' preferential option for the poor in relation to military spending. Finally, I shall make some suggestions about the bearing of the Gospel's "reversal dynamic" on the practical question of political realism in the present situation.

The Christian Vocation to Peace

The Sermon on the Mount (Mt. 5–7; cf. Lk. 6:17–49), and especially the Beatitudes, is recognized by most scholars as a kind of Christian *Magna Carta,* an aphoristic description of the Christian vocation. Only one of the beatitudes has as its reward the ultimate gift of becoming a child of God. "Blessed are the peacemakers, for they shall be called children of God" (Mt. 5:9).

The New Testament notion of peace is rooted in that marvelously comprehensive Old Testament conception of *shalom.* Peace, in the biblical perspective, is not simply the absence of conflict but is that plenitude of life which involves length of days in fullness of strength, covenantal unity within the community and with God, freedom from fear of enemies or calamity, and the immortality achieved through one's descendents when one is finally gathered to one's ancestors.[15]

In John's Gospel the essential gift flowing from the resurrection of Jesus is that peace which the world cannot give (Jn. 14:27 and 20:19). And as John Donahue shows in great detail,[16] it is particularly Luke's Gospel and the Acts of the Apostles which present both the vocation of Jesus and that of the New Testament community as a vocation to preach the "good news of peace" (Acts 10:36). The letters of Paul contain frequent exhortations to the new Christian communities to build, foster, protect, and cherish peace among themselves and with their neighbors (e.g., 2 Cor. 12:11–12 and elsewhere).

We are called by the Gospel not merely to avoid aggression or conflict but to actively announce and bring about peace. If this peace is fullness of life as God's community living together in freedom from fear, and if the condition of both the possibility and realization of justice is such peace (cf. Jas. 3:18), it seems that we must raise serious questions about preparation for war even when such preparation is undertaken as a way of preventing war. The philosophy which regards preparedness for and willingness to engage in war as the best safeguard of peace is radically opposed to the Gospel of Christ. This opposition must create a dilemma for the Christian in regard to deterrence policies based on a balance of terror.

Probably, the most difficult question with which the bishops wrestled in the writing of the pastoral was the question of deterrence, the possession of massive arsenals of nuclear weapons as an incentive to the enemy not to declare war. It seems to me that there are two aspects of the gospel vocation to be peacemakers which challenge the possession of nuclear weapons, even for purposes of deterrence. The first has to do with fear and the second with intention.

Biblical *shalom* involves, in an integral way, freedom from fear. Fear, widespread and constant, is one of the most devastating direct results of the stockpiling of nuclear weapons. We are holding ourselves and all of our sisters and brothers in a web of terror. It is difficult not to raise the question of whether the manufacture and stockpiling of this lethal potential is not so contrary to our Christian vocation to make peace, to establish the conditions of fullness of life in freedom from fear, as to be intolerable as a Christian option for any reason whatsoever.

The second perspective from which deterrence seems questionable in the light of the gospel vocation to make peace has to do with intention. Since the atomic explosion at Hiroshima in 1945 the popes and the episcopal magisterium have insisted repeatedly that the use of nuclear weapons and even the threat or intention to use them are strictly immoral. The pastoral takes the same position. But it is extremely difficult to see what real deterrent force the mere possession of nuclear weapons, if one is publicly committed not to use them under any circumstances, really has. The possession of nuclear weapons as a deterrent seems to imply the willingness to use them if provoked. The United States government has made it perfectly clear that it rules out neither retaliation nor first strike. There is a terrible logic in this position if one intends to be realistic about deterrence. But this only raises again the question of whether the moral acceptability of possession of nuclear weapons is not more academic than morally realistic.

The Christian Love Commandment

All four Gospels, but particularly the Gospel of John, present the command to love one's fellow human beings as the very heart of the lifestyle Jesus sought to establish among his disciples. This commandment is rooted in the second great commandment of the Mosaic law (cf. Dt. 6:5 and Lv. 19:18): to love one's neighbor as oneself. But Jesus' presentation of it goes well beyond the Old Testament injunction in two important ways.

First, Jesus *universalized* the command which bound the Israelites to love the members of their own people with whom they were united by ethnic and religious bonds and who had not forfeited their right to that love by infidelity to the covenant obligations. Jesus commands his disciples to love even those who are not members of their own community: "If you love those who love you, what reward have you? . . . And if you salute only your brothers and sisters, what more are you doing than others?" (Mt. 5:46–47; cf. also Lk. 6:32–34) He even commands them to love their enemies, not just the anonymous collective enemy such as the Samaritans (cf. Lk. 10:29–37) but the personal enemy who was actually persecuting them (Mt. 5:44; cf. Lk. 6:27). The specific motive of this astounding love, like that of making peace, is "so that you may be children of your Father who is in heaven" (Mt. 5:45; cf. Lk. 6:35). Our vocation to become children of God is intimately bound up with our capacity and obligation to seek unity among ourselves.

Second, Jesus *intensified* the love command. Not only are his disciples to love universally; they are actually to refrain even from resisting evil done against them and positively to return good for evil, praying for their persecutors, and willingly accepting further harm rather than do harm to protect or avenge themselves (cf. Mt. 5:38–42; Lk. 6:27–31). In John's Gospel this love of the enemy is given its final development as the command of universal love in imitation of Jesus' love for us. Furthermore, the Christian's love of others implies the willingness to lay down one's life for those one loves, even as Jesus laid down his life for us (Jn. 15:12–13). No one may remain "enemy" for those who have accepted the love of God in Jesus.

It is in the Gospel of John, in the last discourses, especially chapters 13 and 15, that we have the fullest and most original presentation of the Christian love command. According to the Fourth Gospel the relations among Christians are rooted in the fact that they are all God's children. Jesus came to give power to become children of God to those who believed in him (Jn. 1:12). By sharing in Jesus' own filiation through the gift of the Spirit his disciples become his brothers and sisters (Jn. 20:17) and brothers and sisters of one another. But Jesus, at the Last Supper, both by word and gesture, indicated that the full development of this sibling relationship is friendship. He no longer calls his disciples servants but friends because he has chosen them and because he has, in a certain real way, abolished their natural inferiority to him, made them his equals, by sharing with them everything he had received from his Father (cf. Jn. 15:12–17).

The relationship of friendship, a relationship of equality, mutuality, complete sharing of material and spiritual goods, which Jesus establishes between himself and his disciples must, he says, be the model of their relationships among themselves. They are to love one another as he has loved them (Jn. 15:12). Indeed, this is, in the Fourth Gospel, the single identifying mark of the Christian (Jn. 13:34–35) and the means by which they will draw all other people to participate in the saving revelation of Jesus: "That they may be one even as we [Jesus and the Father] are one, I in them and thou in me, that they may become perfectly one, so that the world may know that thou hast sent me" (Jn. 17:22–23).

The ultimate expression of this love of friendship is the willingness to lay down one's life for one's friends. To love as Jesus has loved us is not only not to injure the other but actually to choose the other's life over our own if the choice comes to that. Jesus chose to die rather than to kill (cf. Jn. 18:36), and he made his death not an unwilling submission to violence but the free preference to suffer violence rather than to inflict it (cf. Jn. 19:11) in order to validate beyond any possibility of doubt his offer of divine friendship.

Of all the conclusions we might draw from these reflections on the nature of the Christian love command I would suggest only two at this point. First, if the distinctive character of Christian love is friendship and the very essence of friendship is equality and mutual total self-gift, then all relations of superiority/inferiority are out of place among Christians. How can we, as Christians, cooperate in building a national defense policy whose intention is to establish and maintain not only superiority over our adversaries but dominance carried to the point of absolute world supremacy?

My second conclusion has to do with the universality of the love command in the Gospel. As Christians we cannot regard others as our enemies because we must love our enemies, thus making them our friends. We are actually called to prefer the life of our friend to our own. How, then, can we support a defense policy which generates and aggravates mistrust between nations and relies on felt hostility toward the "enemy" to keep the "national will" strong? It is precisely the conflict in the Christian conscience between the call to take up arms against enemy regimes and the obligation that such action implies of killing real people whom one must, as a Christian, love as Jesus has loved us that has made Christian conscientious objection an increasingly frequent phenomenon among people whose devotion to the values of democracy cannot be doubted.

The Ministry of Reconciliation

We are called to make peace in a world enmeshed in animosity, to love universally in a world structured by mutual fear and hatred. It is this conflicting reality which, it seems to me, establishes the ministry of reconciliation as the primary practical expression of a Christian stance in a violent world.

Paul presents Jesus as the expression of God's reconciling action among us. "God was in Christ reconciling the world to himself" (2 Cor. 5:19) and the one "who through Christ reconciled us to himself . . . gave us the ministry of reconciliation" (2 Cor. 5:18).

In the Gospels Jesus is presented as giving numerous concrete injunctions concerning the task of overcoming division between ourselves and others. We are to bless those who curse us, pray for those who abuse us, offer the other cheek to the one who strikes us, give our coat to the one who steals our cloak, and refrain from reclaiming the goods that have been taken from us (Lk. 6:27–30). Virtually all reputable scripture scholars recognize that these injunctions cannot be made a literal code for the handling of interpersonal conflicts. They represent, in the form of concrete examples, the real ideal of Christian reconciliation. Yet, the Christian's attitude and desire is not to "even the score" but to dissolve enmity, to soften hatred with love, and to make it possible for the one who is doing the evil to stop doing it without fear of being destroyed. The cycle of violence cannot be broken by retaliation but only by forgiveness.

Jesus' demand that his disciples renounce retaliation as a means of achieving justice has historically been one of the most unrealizable of ideals, whether at the individual or at the societal level. He consistently struggled against injustice toward himself and others. He did not stand idly by wishing for the conversion of those who constituted themselves his enemies. He defended himself against those who sought to entrap him, escaped physically when he could, and protected his outcast friends against the cleverness of the self-righteous defenders of morality. Nevertheless, what we see very clearly in Jesus' own behavior is his refusal, even under the most unjust attack and extreme provocation, to resort to retaliation or the threat of retaliation. Because Jesus would not use violence he could not threaten violence.

One of the most encouraging and original sections of the pastoral is Part III, "The Promotion of Peace: Proposals and Policies." It clearly points out the numerous possibilities open to us for the pursuit of peace without recourse to war or the threat of war. At the heart of these proposals is a constant concern with reconciliation. Peoples must come to know each other so that they can trust one another. Nations must commit themselves to the building and honoring of international institutions and procedures for the resolution of conflicts. The art of peacemaking must be studied and taught. Retaliation and the threat of retaliation can never achieve peace and must finally be renounced in favor of the constant effort at reconciliation to which the Gospel calls us.

Preferential Option for the Poor

Throughout the Gospel we are confronted with Jesus' self-definition as the physician sent to the sick (cf. Mt. 9:12), the savior sent to sinners (Mt. 9:12–13), the divine shepherd of God sent to the lost sheep (cf. Lk. 15:3–7), the long-awaited messiah anointed to preach good news to the poor (Lk. 4:18). Jesus is born in poverty to a mother who celebrates Yahweh's historical choice of the lowly, the hungry, and the downtrodden (cf. Lk. 1:47–55). He chooses to associate with the poor and the sinners (Mt. 9:11; Lk. 7:34 and elsewhere), and finally dies, stripped even of his clothes (Jn. 19:23–24), in utter destitution. Jesus' choice of solidarity with the poor is perhaps the most unmistakable characteristic of his life among us.

As the Statement of the Holy See to the United Nations in 1976 so graphically stated, the overproduction of military devices is an act of aggression against the poor "for even when they are not used, by their cost alone, armaments kill the poor by causing them to starve." If, as bearers of the name of Christ, we must embody Jesus' own preferential option for the poor, it is hard to see how we can tolerate, much less endorse, our government's clear preferential option for military spending at the cost of daily increasing unemployment, hunger, disease, and social unrest here and abroad.

Although the pastoral devotes less space to this issue than one might wish, stressing the need for a more equitable world order if peace is to be established rather than the gospel imperative of solidarity with the poor, it is nonetheless strong and insistent on our obligation to order our economic priorities according to the Gospel.

The "Reversal Dynamic" of the Gospel

Surely anyone reading the above arguments, and especially the questioning of the possession of nuclear weapons for purposes of deterrence, will raise the issue of political realism, the issue raised repeatedly by the Reagan administration as the process surrounding the pastoral developed.

The question comes down to the rather simple dilemma: as long as the Soviet Union is armed with nuclear weapons do we have any choice but to maintain a superior arsenal for defense and deterrence? On the basis of the Gospel I would answer: yes, we do have a choice. The mystery of Jesus' resurrection is the grounds for the Christian defiance of death. For us, death is not the ultimate tragedy (cf. Mt. 10:28) and thus not something which must be avoided at any cost. Security, much less invulnerability, is therefore not the ultimate value for us who are challenged to be willing to lose our life in order to find it (Mt. 10:39), to fall to the ground and die in order to bear fruit (Jn. 12:24–25). Our Judeo-Christian heritage says nothing if not that power is made perfect in infirmity (2 Cor. 12:5–10), that God can and does use the weak to confound the strong (1 Cor. 1:26–31). Like the Israelites who had to learn not to trust in horses or chariots (cf. Ps. 20:7–8) and Jesus who refused to summon the legions of heaven (Mt. 26:53) or the forces of earth (Lk. 22:51) to his defense, can we not, in faith, lay down our arms?

To some this is undoubtedly a counsel of madness if not despair. But even from a human point of view it might be possible to argue the Christian position. Even the current administration has admitted that a nuclear war would mean disaster for victors and vanquished alike. The medical and scientific communities are in agreement that there will be no victors in a nuclear exchange. Our weapons, as defense, are useless, and their stockpiling daily increases the chance of their accidental or deliberate use.

But, as the pastoral points out so well, to say that we have no military defense is not to say that we have no defense at all. It does say that we must rechannel our efforts from military build-up into the building of international agencies of conflict resolution, engagement in mutually respectful and honest negotiations, and the solution of the problem of unjust distribution of resources which underlies so much of the world's

tension. To lay down our arms is not to abandon defense, but to abandon useless and, quite possibly, immoral posturing. And it would place all the burden of world opinion on any nation which remained armed or threatened to use arms. I would want to argue that no use of nuclear weapons, either by firing or by threat, and thus probably also by possession, is moral or effective. We have nothing to gain by keeping them and everything, literally, to lose.

Yet, the basic issue is not whether this is a reasonable strategy. The Gospel's peacemaking mandate, its love command, the ministry of reconciliation which it entrusts to the Christian community, the preferential option for the poor to which it calls us, and the reversal dynamic inaugurated by the resurrection of Jesus which it proclaims are not just the requirements of human nature or the conclusions of enlightened rationality. They are a new wine which must burst the wineskins of the ancient dynamics of competition and conflict, aggression and hatred, retaliation, the oppression of the poor and the weak by the rich and powerful, and the search for unlimited human security and national supremacy upon which our current defense policy is based. In other words, the Gospel's contribution to our reflection on war and peace is neither accidental nor purely exhortatory. It is substantive and structural. The question is whether the dynamics of Christian discipleship are reconcilable with the dynamics of national policy in the area of defense. If the answer is no, then those who call themselves Christians have hard choices to make. One of the most encouraging signs of the maturity and commitment of Christians in our time is that increasing numbers of Christians are making those choices and making it clear that the source of their convictions and their actions is the Gospel they profess.

Endnotes

1. In January of 1982 I gave the substance of this essay as testimony before the bishops' committee which drafted *The Challenge of Peace*. In the present version I have tried to place my original reflections on this subject in relation to the final document.

2. See R. E. Brown, "The Human Word of the Almighty God," *The Critical Meaning of the Bible* (New York/Ramsey: Paulist, 1981), pp. 1–22.

3. Cf. A. Richardson, "The Rise of Modern Biblical Scholarship and Recent Discussion of the Authority of the Bible," *The Cambridge History of the Bible*, vol. 3, ed. S. L. Greeslade (Cambridge: At the University Press, 1963), pp. 294–338, esp. pp. 306–11, on this point.

4. Pope Pius XII, *Divino Affiante Spiritu,* in H. Denziger and C. Bannwart, eds., *Enchiridion Symbolorum,* rev. A. Schonmetzer, 32nd ed. (Freiburg: Herder, 1963), no. 3826.

5. For a good example of this approach, see R. E. Brown, "What the Biblical Word Meant and What It Means," *The Critical Meaning of the Bible,* pp. 23–44, and "An Example: Rethinking the Episcopate of the New Testament Churches," ibid., pp. 124–46.

6. For a fuller explanation of this position see my articles "From Exegesis to Hermeneutics: The Problem of the Contemporary Meaning of Scripture," *Horizons* 8 (Spring 1981). 23–39; "The Paschal Imagination: Objectivity and Subjectivity in New Testament Interpretation," *Theological Studies* 43 (March 1982): 52–68.

7. J. L. McKenzie gave classic expression to this more static conception of meaning in 1958 in "Problems of Hermeneutics in Roman Catholic Exegesis," *Journal of Biblical Literature* 77 (1958): 199. The position he expressed then is still operative in much of the exegetical work being done today.

8. This position takes much more seriously the role of pre-understanding and effective historical consciousness in the hermeneutical process than does the more classical historical-critical approach which has more faith in the ability of the interpreter to step out of his or her own historical setting and enter the ancient world which was the context of the text. See H.-G. Gadamer, *Truth and Method* (New York: Crossroad, 1975), pp. 235–74.

9. This notion of the surplus of meaning in classical texts is supported by the philosophical work of Gadamer, *Truth and Method,* esp. pp. 258–67, and P. Ricoeur, *Interpretation Theory: Discourse and the Surplus of Meaning* (Fort Worth: Texas Christian University Press, 1976), esp. pp. 43–44 and chap. 3, "Metaphor and Symbol," pp. 45–60. D. Tracy (*The Analogical Imagination: Christian Imagination and the Culture of Pluralism* [New York: Crossroad, 1981]) has explored extensively the notion of "classic text" as a theological category.

10. Available in *Renewing the Earth: Catholic Documents on Peace, Justice and Liberation,* ed. D. J. O'Brien and T. A. Shannon (Garden City: Image, 1977), pp. 171–284.

11. I am indebted to my colleague Drew Christiansen, S.J., for his help on this section.

12. *Gaudium et Spes,* no. 80.

13. Available in *The Documents of Vatican II,* ed. and trans. W. M. Abbott and J. Gallagher (New York: Guild, 1966), pp. 14–101.

14. This ecclesiology is lucidly developed by R. P. McBrien in *Church: The Continuing Quest* (Paramus/New York: Newman, 1970), esp. chap. 4, pp. 67–85, and in *Catholicism* (Minneapolis: Winston, 1981), Part IV, esp. pp. 691–729.

15. See J. Pedersen, *Israel: Its Life and Culture,* vol. 1 (Copenhagen: Brannen Og Korch, 1926), pp. 311–17.

16. J. Donahue, "The Good News of Peace," *The Way* 22 (April 1982):88–99.

30. Reflections on War and Political Discourse: Realism, Just War, and Feminism in a Nuclear Age

JEAN BETHKE ELSHTAIN

Casting a critical eye on both the realist and just war traditions, Jean Bethke Elshtain suggests that both are grounded upon unjustifiable male/female role expectations. She criticizes what she calls "equal opportunity or integrationist" feminism for essentially endorsing the central role of the military in the social realm and the gender assumptions on which it is built and also for seeking only to be given equal access to it. In the face of nuclear realities, however, old assumptions must be replaced with new ones, and a more "robust" notion of the just female citizen must be fostered. Building upon the thoughts of Hannah Arendt, Elshtain offers the possibility of constructing new narratives that redefine the nature of war and political life and that move away from the dynamisms of vengeance and fear toward a vision of human life in which deeper flourishing may begin to occur.

How did we get from Machiavelli to MAD, to Mutual Assured Destruction? The tradition of realism that dominates our thinking about international relations not only presumes but requires a move "from . . . to" in ways I shall take up in the first part of this article as I examine realism's givens in light of feminist questions. In part two, I assay the most important historic contender against realism's discursive hegemony, just war theory, with similar questions in mind. Because the central markers of realist and just war thinking are well-known to readers of this journal, I shall concentrate on rethinking the too-thinkable—exposing the presumptions that get wheeled into place when the matter at hand is collective violence. As the argument in parts one and two unfolds, feminism as a critical lever gives way to contemporary feminisms as articulated positions. I note the ways in which feminist thinking on war and politics may get stuck within received discursive forms, reproducing presumptions that deepen rather than challenge the present order.[1] I conclude with an interpretation of Hannah Arendt's *On Violence,* a text with animating symbols and images that suggest an alternative discourse.

Realism's bracing promise is to spring politics free from the constraints of moral judgment and limitation, thereby assuring its autonomy as historic force and discursive subject matter, and to offer a picture of the world of people and states as they really are rather than as we might yearn for them to be. We have all marked this story and its designated prototypical events and spokespersons. The genealogy of realism as international relations, although acknowledging antecedents, gets down to serious business with Machiavelli, moving on to theorists of sovereignty and apologists for *raison d'état,* and culminating, in its early modern forms, with Hobbes's *Leviathan* before continuing the trek into the present. The contemporary realist locates himself inside a potent, well-honed tradition. Realist thinkers exude the confidence of those whose narrative long ago "won the war." Realism's hegemony means that alternatives to realism are evaluated from the standpoint of realism, cast into a bin labeled idealism that, for the realist, is more or less synonymous with dangerous if well-intentioned naiveté.[2]

But is the realist throne that secure? We are familiar with what modern realism presumes: a world of sovereign states as preposited ontological entities, each seeking either to enhance or to secure its own power. State sovereignty is the motor that moves the realist system as well as its (nearly) immutable object. Struggle is endemic to the system and force is the court of last resort. It cannot be otherwise, for states exist in a condition of anarchy in relation to one another. Wars will and must occur because there is nothing to prevent them. On one level, then, realism is a theory pitched to structural imperatives that are said to bear on all actors

From Jean Bethke Elshtain, "Reflections on War and Political Discourse," *Political Theory,* Vol. 13, No. 1 (February 1985), pp. 39–57. Copyright © 1985 by Sage Publications, Inc. Reprinted by permission of Sage Publications, Inc.

in the international arena. No state, argues the realist, can reasonably or responsibly entertain the hope that through actions it takes, or refrains from taking, it may transform the wider context. Given that context, conflict is inevitable. There is nothing to prevent wars. The only logical solution to this unhappy state of affairs is a unitary international order to remedy international chaos.[3] Alas, what is logically unassailable is practically unattainable given the realist refrain: a world of sovereign and suspicious states.

Historic realism involves a way of thinking—a set of presumptions about the human condition that secretes images of men and women and the parts they play in the human drama; and, as well, a potent rhetoric. Whether in its uncompromising Hobbesian version or the less remorseless Machiavellian narrative, realism exaggerates certain features of the human condition and downgrades or ignores others.[4] Interpreting foundational realist texts from a vantage point informed by feminist concerns, one is struck by the suppression and denial of female images and female-linked imperatives, hence alert to the restricted and oversimplifying terms through which realism constitutes symbolism and narrative roles more generally.

For example, Hobbes describes a world of hostile monads whose relations are dominated by fear, force, and instrumental calculation. Yet (and almost simplemindedly) we know this to be anthropologically false. From the simplest tribal beginnings to the most complex social forms, women have had to tend to infants—no matter what the men were up to—if life was to go on in any sustained manner. That important features of the human condition are expunged from Hobbes's universe suggests that his realism is a dramatic distortion rather than a scientific depiction of the human condition at rock bottom. To acknowledge this by insisting that the state of nature is an analytic fiction fails to address the concerns I raise here. Fictions are also truths and what gets left out is often as important as what is put in and assumed.

To be sure, the contemporary realist is unlikely to endorse a full constellation of Hobbesian presumptions. He might reject Hobbes's vision of the state of nature, and his depiction of social relations, as dire and excessive. It is likely, however, that he would continue to affirm the wider conclusions Hobbes drew by analogy from the miserable condition of human beings in the state of nature to the unrelenting fears and suspicions of states in their relations to one another. Yet it seems plausible that if Hobbes omitted central features of human existence internal to civil societies

and families, perhaps he is guilty of similar one-sidedness in his characterization of the world of states. To take up this latter possibility is to treat Hobbes's realism as problematic, not paradigmatic.

Machiavelli goes down more smoothly in large part because we have internalized so much of his legacy already. We all know the story. Human beings are inconstant and trustworthy only in their untrustworthiness. Political action cannot be judged by the standards of Christian morality. Civic virtue requires troops "well disciplined and trained" in times of peace in order to prepare for war: This is a "necessity," a law of history.[5] *Si vis pacem, para bellum*, a lesson successive generations (or so the story goes) must learn, though some tragically learn it too late, others in the nick of time.

Machiavelli's narrative revolves around a public-private split in and through which women are constituted, variously, as mirrors to male war-making (a kind of civic cheerleader) or as a collective "other," embodying the softer values and virtues out of place within, and subversive of, *realpolitik*.[6] Immunized from political action, the realist female may honor the Penates but she cannot embark on a project to bring her values to bear on the civic life of her society. J.G.A. Pocock calls Machiavelli's "militarization of citizenship" a potent legacy that subverts (even for some feminists, as I argue below) consideration of alternatives that do not bind civic and martial virtue together. Military preparedness, in this narrative, becomes the sine qua non of a viable polity. Although women cannot embody armed civic virtue, a task for the man, they are sometimes drawn into the realist picture more sharply as occasions for war (we must fight to protect her), as goads to action, as designated weepers over the tragedies war trails in its wake, or, in our own time, as male prototypes mobilized to meet dwindling "manpower" needs for the armed forces.[7]

Rethinking realism using feminist questions defamiliarizes its central categories: the male homme de guerre retains his preeminent role, to be sure, but we recognize explicitly the ways in which his soldierly virilization is linked to the realist woman's privatization, and so on. But matters are never quite so simple. There are variants of modern feminist argumentation indebted to realist discourse in its Hobbesian and Machiavellian modes respectively.[8]

Hardline feminist realists, for example, endorse a Hobbesian social ontology and construe politics as a battleground, the continuation of war by warlike means. They advise women to learn to "fight dirty." Making generous use of military metaphors (Who is the Enemy? Where is he located?), Hobbesian feminists declare politics and political theory inevitably a "paradigm case of the Oppressor and the Oppressed."[9] There is tough talk about sex-war, shock troops, and the need for women to be integrated into the extant power structure construed as the aggregate of all those who defend law and order, wear uniforms, or carry guns for a living—"the national guard . . . state troopers . . . sheriffs." Women are enjoined to prepare for combat as the only way to end their "colonization."[10]

Such feminist realists share with their Hobbesian forefather a self-reproducing discourse of fear, suspicion, anticipated violence, and force to check-mate force. Their discussions are peppered with worst-case scenarios and proclamations of supreme emergency that reaffirm the bleakest images of "the enemy" and pump up the will to power of combatants. Possibilities for reciprocity between men and women, or for a politics not reducible to who controls or coerces whom, are denied in much the same way Hobbes eliminates space for any noninstrumental human relations.

This hard-line position is less important, however, than the modified realism, more Machiavellian in its claims and categories, expressed in a 1981 legal brief filed by the National Organization for Women as part of a challenge to all-male military registration.[11] Beginning with the claim that compulsory, universal military service is central to the concept of citizenship in a democracy, NOW buttresses an ideal of armed civic virtue. If women are to gain "first-class citizenship" they, too, must have the right to fight. Laws excluding women from draft registration and combat duty perpetuate "archaic notions" of women's capabilities; moreover, "devastating long-term psychological and political repercussions" are visited upon women given their exclusion from the military of their country.[12]

NOW's brand of equal opportunity or integrationist feminism here loses a critical edge, functioning instead to reinforce "the military as an institution and militarism as an ideology" by perpetuating "the notion that the military is so central to the entire social order that it is only when women gain access to its core that they can hope to fulfill their hopes and aspirations."[13] In its deep structure, NOW's legal narrative is a leap out of the female/private side of the public/private divide basic to Machiavellian realism and straight into the arms of the hegemonic male whose sex-linked activities are valorized thereby. Paradoxically, NOW's repudiation of "archaic notions of women's role"

becomes a tribute to "archaic notions of men's role." Because of the indebtedness of their discourse to presumptions geared historically against women and the values to which they are symbolically if problematically linked, feminist realism, whether in its Hobbesian or less extreme "armed civic virtue" forms, fails to provide a sustained challenge to the Western narrative of war and politics. Ironically, female-linked symbolism is once again suppressed or depreciated, this time under a feminist imprimatur as a male-dominant ideal—the "dirty fighter" or the "citizen-warrior" is urged on everyone.

Just Wars as Modified Realism

In a world organized along the lines of the realist narrative, there are no easy ways out. There is, however, an alternative tradition to which we in the West have sometimes repaired either to challenge or to chasten the imperatives realism claims merely to describe and denies having in any sense wrought.

Just war theory grows out of a complex genealogy, beginning with the pacifism and withdrawal from the world of early Christian communities through later compromises with the world as Christianity took institutional form. The Christian saviour was a "prince of peace" and the New Testament Jesus deconstructs the powerful metaphor of the warrior central to Old Testament narrative. He enjoins Peter to sheath his sword; he devirilizes the image of manhood; he tells his followers to go as sheep among wolves and to offer their lives, if need be, but never to take the life of another in violence. From the beginning, Christian narrative presents a pacific ontology, finding in the "paths of peace" the most natural as well as the most desirable way of being. Violence must justify itself before the court of nonviolence.

Classic just war doctrine, however, is by no means a pacifist discourse.[14] St. Augustine's *The City of God*, for example, distinguishes between legitimate and illegitimate use of collective violence. Augustine denounces the *Pax Romana* as a false peace kept in place by evil means and indicts Roman imperialist wars as paradigmatic instances of unjust war. But he defends, with regret, the possibility that a war may be just if it is waged in defense of a common good and to protect the innocent from certain destruction. As elaborated over the centuries, non-combatant immunity gained a secure niche as the most important of *jus in bello* rules, responding to unjust aggression is the central *jus ad bellum.* Just war thinking requires that moral considerations enter into all determinations of collective violence, not as a post hoc gloss but as a serious ground for making political judgments.

In common with realism, just war argument secretes a broader worldview, including a vision of domestic politics. Augustine, for example, sees human being as innately social. It follows that all ways of life are laced through with moral rules and restrictions that provide a web of social order not wholly dependent on external force to keep itself intact. Augustine's household, unlike Machiavelli's private sphere, is "the beginning or element of the city" and domestic peace bears a relation to "civic peace."[15] The sexes are viewed as playing complementary roles rather than as segregated into two separate normative systems governed by wholly different standards of judgment depending upon whether one is a public man or a private woman.

Just war discourse, like realism, has a long and continuing history; it is a gerrymandered edifice scarred by social transformation and moral crisis. A specific strength embedded in its ontology of peace is the vantage point it affords with reference to social arrangements, one from which its adherents frequently assess what the world calls peace and find it wanting. From Augustine's thunderings against the *Pax Romana* to John Paul II's characterization of our present armed-to-the-teeth peace as the continuation of war by other means—not war's opposite but one of the forms war takes in the modern world—just war thinking has, from time to time, offered a critical discursive edge.[16]

My criticisms of just war are directed to two central concerns: One flows directly from just war teaching; the other involves less explicit filiations. I begin with the latter, with cultural images of males and females rooted, at least in part, in just war discourse. Over time, Augustine's moral householders (with husbands cast as just, meaning neither absolute nor arbitrary heads) gave way to a discourse that more sharply divided males and females, their honored activities, and their symbolic force. Men were constituted as just Christian warriors, fighters, and defenders of righteous causes. Women, unevenly and variously depending upon social location, got solidified into a culturally sanctioned vision of virtuous, nonviolent womanhood that I call the "beautiful soul," drawing upon Hegel's *Phenomenology.*

The tale is by no means simple but, by the late eighteenth century, "absolute distinctions between men and women in regard to violence" had come to prevail.[17] The female beautiful soul is pictured as fru-gal, self-sacrificing, and, at times, delicate. Although many women empowered themselves to think and to act on the basis of this ideal of female virtue, the symbol easily slides into sentimentalism. To "preserve the purity of its heart," writes Hegel, the beautiful soul must flee "from contact with the actual world."[18] In matters of war and peace, the female beautiful soul cannot put a stop to suffering, cannot effectively fight the mortal wounding of sons, brothers, husbands, fathers. She continues the long tradition of women as weepers, occasions for war, and keepers of the flame of nonwarlike values.

The just warrior is a complex construction, an amalgam of Old Testament, chivalric, and civic republican traditions. He is a character we recognize in all the statues on all those commons and greens of small New England towns: the citizen-warrior who died to preserve the Union and to free the slaves. Natalie Zemon Davis shows that the image of warlike manliness in the later Middle Ages and through the seventeenth century was but one male ideal among many, having to compete, for example, with the priest and other religious men who foreswore use of their "sexual instrument" and were forbidden to shed blood. However, "male physical force could sometimes be moralized" and "thus could provide the foundation for an ideal of warlike manliness."[19] This moralization of collective male violence held sway and continues to exert a powerful fascination and to inspire respect.

But the times have outstripped beautiful souls and just warriors alike; the beautiful soul can no longer be protected in her virtuous privacy. Her world, and her children, are vulnerable in the face of nuclear realities. Similarly, the just warrior, fighting fair and square by the rules of the game, is a vision enveloped in the heady mist of an earlier time. War is more and more a matter of remote control. The contemporary face of battle is anomic and impersonal, a technological nightmare, as weapons technology obliterates any distinction between night and day, between the "front" and the "rear." Decades before laser weapons, however, the reality of battle had undermined the ideal of the warrior, World War I constituted the foot-soldier as cannon-fodder. In the first day of the Battle of the Somme, July 1, 1916, 110,000 British men got out of the trenches and began to walk forward along a thirteen-mile front. They had no visible enemy to fight; they wore number tags hung around their necks; 60,000 were dead by the end of the day.

A just war requires agents to carry out its purposes. But if the warrior no longer serves as an avatar of justice, how is war itself to claim this imprimatur? If the present human condition can be described as the continuation of war by other means, a false peace, how can human agents legitimate their aims in the waging of a real war rather than the maintenance of a bogus peace? Does it make sense any longer to construe war as a coherent entity at all? These questions take me to my criticisms of just war argument in our time.

Just war discourse from its inception recognized the rights of political entities to self-defense. The moral requirements for waging war have also remained essentially unchanged from the fourth century to the present. Over time, of course, much has changed including the nature of political bodies, the context of international life, and the totalistic deadliness of weapons. Faced with historic transformations of such awesome magnitude, just war thinkers seek valiantly to apply the appropriate rules to cover increasingly horrific situations. All agree that violence is regrettable, tragic, and to be avoided devoutly. But much slips through the cracks when one gets down to hard cases.

For example, in Michael Walzer's *Just and Unjust Wars*, the most lucid modern treatment of the topic by a nontheologian, queries concerning past practice (the British decision to engage in saturation bombing of German cities during World War II) and present policy (nuclear deterrence theory) are assessed on consequentialist criteria that frequently override the deontological formulae of classic just war teaching (though it, too, required projections of consequence in certain situations). For example, Walzer justifies, with regret, British saturation bombing of German cities in light of the Nazi threat and given the predictable outcome should Britain fall to Germany. Present threat and future danger override *jus in bello* rules.[20] By declaring Nazism an "immeasurable evil," Walzer foreordains his judgment: "Immeasurable" is an absolute and the "determinate crime" of terror bombing is clearly a lesser evil—it must be the way the issues get framed.

By continually adjusting to the realities of total war, just war discourse is hard to distinguish from modified realism. I noted the example from World War II above in part because Walzer proclaims the present moment one of continuing "supreme emergency," analogous to the Nazi peril. If what we've got is supreme emergency, what we need—nuclear deterrence—is inexorable. Once again, Walzer regrets his own conclusion. Deterrence is a "bad way" of "coping" with supreme emergency but "there may well be no other that is practical in a world of sovereign and suspicious states. We threaten evil in order not to do it."[21]

Despite the impressive and determined efforts of Walzer, the U.S. Catholic Bishops, and others, the just war frame is stretched to the breaking point as it can no longer provide a coherent picture of its discursive object—war in any conventional sense. Take, for example, Walzer's discussion of American use of the atomic bombs on Hiroshima and Nagasaki, unjustifiable, he argues, within a just war frame. He goes on to ask: "How did the people of Hiroshima forfeit their rights?"[22] The language of rights and their forfeiture is impoverished in this context, inadequate to describe what happened on those dreadful days. The shakiness of just war discourse, then, is forced upon us by "the nature of the modern state combined with the nature of modern total war."[23] In a twilight zone of false peace, with war deeply rooted inside the infrastructure of the modern state, the discourses of just war and realism link up to confront jointly the seemingly intractable present. I return to this matter in part three.

Few feminist writers on war and peace take up just war discourse explicitly. There is, however, feminist theorizing that may aptly be situated inside the broader frames of beautiful souls and just warriors as features of inherited discourse. The strongest contemporary feminist statement of a beautiful soul position involves celebrations of a "female principle" as ontologically given and superior to its dark opposite, masculinism. (The male "other" in this vision is not a just warrior but a dangerous beast.) The evils of the social world are traced in a free-flowing conduit from masculinism to environmental destruction, nuclear energy, wars, militarism, and states. In utopian evocations of "cultural feminism," women are enjoined to create separate communities to free themselves from the male surround and to create a "space" based on the values they embrace. An essentially Manichean vision, the discourse of feminism's beautiful souls contrasts images of "caring" and "connected" females in opposition to "callous" and "disconnected" males. Deepening sex segregation, the separatist branch of cultural feminism draws upon, yet much exaggerates received understandings of the beautiful soul.[24]

A second feminist vision indebted implicitly to the wider discursive universe of which just war thinking is a part features a down-to-earth female subject, a soul less beautiful than virtuous in ways that locate her as a social actor. She shares just war's insistence that politics must come under moral scrutiny. Rejecting the hard-line gendered epistemology and metaphysic of an absolute beautiful soul, she nonetheless insists that ways of knowing flow from ways of being in the world and that hers have vitality and validity in ways private and public. The professed ends of feminists in this loosely fitting frame locate the woman as a moral educator and a political actor. She is concerned with "mothering," whether or not she is a biological mother, in the sense of protecting society's most vulnerable members without patronizing them. She thinks in terms of human dignity as well as social justice and fairness. She also forges links between "maternal thinking" and pacifist or nonviolent theories of conflict without presuming that it is possible to translate easily particular maternal imperatives into a public good.[25]

The pitfalls of this feminism are linked to its intrinsic strengths. By insisting that women are in and of the social world, its framers draw explicit attention to the context within which their constituted subjects act. But this wider surround not only derogates maternal women, it bombards them with simplistic formulae that equate "being nice" with "doing good." Even as stereotypic maternalisms exert pressure to sentimentalize, competing feminisms are often sharply repudiating, finding in any evocation of "maternal thinking" a trap and a delusion. A more robust concept of the just (female) as citizen is needed to shore up this disclosure, a matter I take up below.

Rescuing *Politics* from *War*: Hannah Arendt's Hope

Hannah Arendt's attempt to rescue politics from war deepens an important insight of just war theory— underdeveloped in the theory itself—by insisting that the problem lies not only in the compulsions of international relations but in that ordering of modern, technological society just war thinkers call a "false" or "armed" peace. Dulled by the accretion of tropes, truths, necessities, and concepts that help us talk ourselves into war, situated inside a world of armed peace, Norman Mailer's claim in 1948 that "the ultimate purpose" of modern society is continuation of the army by other means seems exaggerated but not altogether far-fetched.[26] Michel Foucault, too, argues that 'politics' (the single quotes are his) "has been conceived as a continuation, if not exactly and directly of war, at least of the military model as a fundamental means of preventing civil disorder. Politics . . . sought to implement the mechanism of the perfect army, of the disciplined mass, of the docile, useful troop," and so on.[27]

In an over-coordinated social world, violence may promise a release from inner emptiness or a temporary escape from overplanned pointlessness. Paradoxically, on this view, the routinization of everyday life, much at odds with a heroic or warrior society, nevertheless feeds rather than sates a deeper will to warfare as the prospect of escape from "impersonality, monotony, standardization," the chance to take and to share risks, to act rather than to persist in predetermined behavior.[28] That promise, however, is itself a victim of our armed peace. War technology devirilizes war fighting. The fighter exists for, and is eclipsed by, his weapons and an awesome nuclear arsenal.

More problematic than the inadequacies of just war doctrine in light of social mimesis of military order, however, is the discourse of "disassociation" evident in contemporary rationalist, scientized realism. Such realists portray themselves as clear-sighted, unsentimental analysts describing the world as it is. At present, hundreds of think tanks, universities, and government bureaucracies support the efforts of "scientifically minded brain trusters" who should be criticized, argues Arendt, not because they are thinking the unthinkable, but rather because "they do not *think* at all."[29] The danger is this: a world of self-confirming theorems invites fantasies of control over events that we do not have. The scientization of rationalist realism eclipses the strengths classical realists could claim, including awareness of the intractability of events and a recognition that relations between and among states are necessarily alienated. Through abstracted models and logic, hyper-rationalism reduces states and their relations to games that can be simulated. Consider the following depiction of Western Europe by a strategic analyst: "Western Europe amounts geographically to a peninsula projecting out from the Eurasian landmass from which large continents of military force can emerge on relatively short notice to invade the peninsula."[30] Western Europe, reduced to an undifferentiated, manageable piece of territory, becomes (theoretically) expendable or indiscriminately usable for our strategic planning.

Modern thinkers of the abstracted unthinkable are not alone in doing violence to complex realities. "If truth is the main casualty in war, ambiguity is another," notes Paul Fussell, and one of the legacies of war is a "habit of simple distinction, simplification, and opposition."[31] Mobilized language, wartime's rhetoric of "binary deadlock," may persist and do much of our thinking for us. The absorption of politics by the language and imperatives of war becomes a permanent rhetorical condition.[32] J. Glenn Gray reminds us that one basic task of a state at war is to portray the enemy in terms as absolute and abstract as possible in order to distinguish as sharply as possible the act of killing from the act of murder. It is always *the enemy,* a "pseudo-concrete universal." This moral absolutism is constituted through language: there is no other way to do it. We are invited to hate without limit and told we are good citizens for doing so.

At one time war fighting often served, paradoxically, to deconstruct war rhetoric as soldiers rediscovered concreteness and particularity in tragic and terrifying ways. For example, Eric Maria Remarque's protagonist in *All Quiet on the Western Front* bayonets a frightened French soldier who, seeking refuge, has leapt into the trench beside him. Four agonizing hours later the Frenchman dies and when he has died, Remarque's hero, his capacity to perceive and to judge concretely restored, speaks to the man he has killed: "Comrade, I did not want to kill you. . . . But you were only an idea to me before, an abstraction that lived in my mind and called forth its appropriate response. It was that abstraction I stabbed."[33] Grey, similarly, observes that the abstract bloodthirstiness expressed by civilians furthest removed from war fighting was often in contrast to the thinking of front-line soldiers whose moral absolutism dissolved once they met "the enemy" face to face.[34] Because it is now possible for us to destroy the enemy without ever seeing him or her, abstract hatreds are less likely to rub against concrete friction.

If realism's modern offspring invites dangerous disassociations, an alternative discourse should be one less available for such purposes even as it offers a compelling orientation to the systemic imperatives at work in a world of "sovereign and suspicious states." Too often alternatives to "thinking war" reproduce problematic features of the discourse they oppose, for example, by insisting that we love (rather than hate) abstract collectives. But "the human race" is a pseudo-concrete universal much like "the enemy." Pitched at a level of abstract universals, the discourse of "the victims" falls apart if one moves to specify connections between its grand vision and political exigencies. Also, an alternative discourse must problematize war narratives with their teleological assurance of triumphant endings and their prototypical figurations of fighting men and weeping women, even as it acknowledges the attraction of the narrative.[35] Admitting rather than denying what Grey calls "the communal enthusiasm and ecstasies of war," we are invited to ask if we might not enlist our energies in some other way. Peace discourse that denies the violent undercurrents and possibilities in everyday life and in each one of us, perhaps by projecting that violence outward into oth-ers ("masculinism") is but the opposite side of the hard-line realist coin.

Hannah Arendt's *On Violence* responds to these concerns by exposing our acceptance of politics as war by other means. Arendt asks what historic transformations and discursive practices made possible a consensus "among political theorists from Left to Right . . . that violence is nothing more than the most flagrant manifestation of power?"[36] (The violence Arendt has in mind is that of groups or collectives, not individual outrage culminating in a single violent act; Melville's *Billy Budd* is her example.) Her answer is multiple: teleological constructions of historic inevitability (known to us as Progress); theories of absolute power tied to the emergence of the nation-state; the Old Testament tradition of God's Commandments that fed command-obedience conceptions of law in Judaeo-Christian discourse; the infusion of biologism into political discourse, particularly the notion that destruction is a law of nature and violence a "life promoting force" through which men purge the old and rotten. All these "time-honored opinions have become dangerous." Locked into dangerously self-confirming ways of thinking, embracing "progress" as a standard of evaluation, we manage to convince ourselves that goodwill comes out of horrendous things; that somehow, in history, the end does justify the means. Both classical liberals and their Marxist adversaries share this discursive terrain, Arendt argues, though she is especially critical of "great trust in the dialectical 'power of negation'" that soothes its adherents into believing that evil "is but a temporary manifestation of a still-hidden good."

By conflating the crude instrumentalism of violence with power, defined by Arendt as the human ability to act in concert and to begin anew, we guarantee further loss of space within which authentic empowerment is possible. In this way violence nullifies power and stymies political being. One important step away from the instrumentalism of violence and toward the possibility of politics is to resist the reduction of politics to domination. Arendt evokes no image of isolated heroism here; rather, she underscores the ways in which centralized orders dry up power and political possibility. If we recognize the terms through and means by which this happens, we are less susceptible to unreflective mobilization and more open to finding and creating public space in the current order. As citizens through their actions break repetitive cycles of behavior, power as the "true opposite" of violence reveals itself.

Arendt's discourse constitutes its subjects as citizens: neither victims nor warriors. She paints no rosy picture of her rescue effort. Just as Grey argues that the will to war is deepened by the emptiness of a false peace, Arendt believes that the greater a society's bureaucratization, the greater will be secret fantasies of destruction. She repudiates grandiose aims and claims, refusing to dictate what politics should do or accomplish instrumentally, for that would undermine her exposé of the future oriented teleologies on which violence and progress feed. To the extent that we see what she is doing and let it work on us, her symbolic alternative for political being offers a plenary jolt to our reigning political metaphors and categories—state of nature, sovereignty, statism, bureaucratization, contractualism, nationalist triumphalism, and so on. If we remain entrapped in this cluster of potent typifications, each of them suffused with violent evocations or built on fears of violence, we will face only more, and deadlier, of what we've already got. Contrastingly, Arendt locates as central a powerful but pacific image that engenders hope, the human capacity that sustains political being.

Evidence of hopelessness is all around us. The majority of young people say they do not believe there will be a future of any sort. We shake our heads in dismay, failing to see that our social arrangements produce hopelessness and require it to hold themselves intact. But the ontological possibility for hope is always present, rooted, ultimately, in "the fact of natality." Arendt's metaphor, most fully elaborated in the following passage from *The Human Condition*, is worth quoting in full:

> The miracle that saves the world, the realm of human affairs, from its normal, "natural" ruin is ultimately the fact of natality, in which the faculty of action is ontologically rooted. It is, in other words, the birth of new human beings and the new beginning, the action they are capable of by being born. *Only the full experience of this capacity can bestow upon human affairs faith and hope, those two essential characteristics of human existence* . . . that found perhaps their most glorious and most succinct expression in the new words with which the Gospels accounted their "glad tiding": 'A Child has been born unto us.'[37]

The infant, like all beginnings, is vulnerable. We must nurture that beginning, not knowing and not being able to control the "end" of the story.

Arendt's evocation of natal imagery through its most dramatic Ur-narrative is not offered as an abstraction to be endorsed abstractly. Rather, she invites us to restore long atrophied dispositions of commemoration and awe; birth, she declares, is a "miracle," a beginning that renews and irreversibly alters the world. Hers is a fragile yet haunting figuration that stirs recognition of our own vulnerable beginnings and our necessary dependency on others. Placed alongside the reality of human beginnings, many accounts of political beginnings construed as the actions of male hordes or contractualists seem parodic in part because of the massive denial (of "the female") on which they depend. A "full experience" of the "capacity" rooted in birth helps us to keep before our mind's eye the living reality of singularities' differences, and individualities rather than a human mass as objects of possible control or manipulation.[38]

By offering an alternative genealogy that problematizes collective violence and visions of triumph, Arendt devirilizes discourse, not in favor of feminization (for the feminized and masculinized emerged in tandem and both embody dangerous distortions), but politicalization, constituting her male and female objects as citizens who share alike the "faculty of action."[39] At this juncture, Arendt's discourse makes contact with that feminism I characterized as a modified vision of the beautiful soul. Her bracing ideal of the citizen adds political robustness to a feminist picture of women drawn to action from their sense of being and their epistemic and social location. Arendt's citizen, for example, may act from her maternal thinking but not as a mother—an important distinction that could help to chasten sentimentalism or claims of moral superiority.

But war is the central concern of this essay. Does Arendt's discourse offer a specifiable orientation toward international relations? Her discourse shifts the ground on which we stand when we think about states and their relations. We become skeptical about the forms and the claims of the sovereign state; we deflate fantasies of control inspired by the reigning teleology of progress; we recognize the (phony) parity painted by a picture of equally "sovereign states" and are thereby alert to the many forms hegemony can take. Additionally, Arendt grants "forgiveness" a central political role as the only way human beings have to break remorseless cycles of vengeance. She embraces an "ascesis," a refraining or withholding that allows refusal to bring one's force to bear to surface as a strength not a weakness.

Take the dilemma of the nuclear arms race that seems to have a life and dynamic of its own. From an Arendtian perspective, we see current arms control efforts for what they are—the arms race under another name negotiated by a bevy of experts with a vested interest in keeping the race alive so they can "control" it. On the other hand, her recognition of the limiting conditions internal to the international political order precludes a leap into utopian fantasies of world order or total disarmament. For neither the arms control option (as currently defined) nor calls for immediate disarmament are bold—the first because it is a way of doing business as usual; the second because it covertly sustains business as usual by proclaiming "solutions" that lie outside the reach of possibility.

Instead, Arendt's perspective invites us—as a strong and dominant nation of awesome potential force—to take unilateral initiatives in order to break symbolically the cycle of vengeance and fear signified by our nuclear arsenals. Just as action from an individual or group may disrupt the automisms of everyday life, action from a single state may send shock waves that reverberate throughout the system. Arendt cannot be pegged as either a "systems dominance" nor "sub-systems dominance" thinker—a form of argumentation with which she has no patience in any case. She recognizes systemic imperatives yet sees space for potentially effective change from "individual (state) action." The war system is so deeply rooted that to begin to dismantle it in its current and highly dangerous form requires bold strokes.

At this juncture, intimations of an alternative genealogy emerge. Freeman Dyson suggests the *Odyssey* or the theme of homecoming rather than the *Iliad* or the theme of remorseless force as a dominant Ur-political myth if we break the deadlock of victims versus warriors. Socrates, Jesus of Nazareth, and Nietzsche, in some of his teachings, emerge as articulators of the prototypical virtues of restraint and refusal to bring all one's power to bear. For it was Nietzsche, from his disillusionment, who proclaimed the only way out of "armed peace" to be a people, distinguished by their wars and victories who, from strength, not weakness, "break the sword" thereby giving peace a chance. "Rather perish than hate and fear," he wrote, "and twice rather perish than make oneself hated and feared."[40] Historic feminist thinkers and movements who rejected politics as force take center stage rather than being relegated to the periphery in this alternative story.

To take up war-as-discourse compels us to recognize the powerful sway of received narratives and reminds us that the concepts through which we think about war, peace, and politics get repeated endlessly, shaping debates, constraining consideration of alternatives, often reassuring us that things cannot really be much different than they are. As we nod an automatic yes when we hear the truism (though we may despair of the truth it tells) that "there have always been wars," we acknowledge tacitly that "there have always been war stories," for wars are deeded to us as texts. We cannot identify "war itself" as an entity apart from a powerful literary tradition that includes poems, epics, myths, official histories, first-person accounts, as well as the articulated theories I have discussed. War and the discourse of war are imbricated, part and parcel of political reality. Contesting the discursive terrain that identifies and gives meaning to what we take these realities to be does not mean one grants a self-subsisting, unwarranted autonomy to discourse; rather, it implies a recognition of the ways in which received doctrines, "war stories," may lull our critical faculties to sleep, blinding us to possibilities that lie within our reach.

Endnotes

1. A full elaboration of the major theoretical frames of contemporary feminism as political discourse appears in Jean Bethke Elshtain, *Public Man, Private Woman: Women in Social and Political Thought* (Princeton: Princeton University Press, 1981), Chap. 5.

2. This was one of the things I learned in graduate school.

3. Interestingly, Hannah Arendt, in *On Violence*, seems to endorse this view. Yet she qualifies it and, as I argue in the final section of this article, finally undermines the ground on which such claims are based.

4. I am drawing on portions of *Public Man, Private Woman* for this discussion.

5. Niccolo Machiavelli, *The Prince and the Discourses* (New York: Modern Library, 1950), p. 61.

6. Ibid., p. 503. My views on Machiavelli are not widely shared, especially by those theorists who evoke his name as a father of civic republicanism. Nevertheless, I believe there is textual warrant for my claims. Women, or woman, also gets cast as a symbolic nemesis in portions of Machiavelli's discourse, but I do not take up that theme here.

7. Nancy Huston, "Tales of War and Tears of Women," *Women's Studies International Forum* 5 no. 3/4 (1982), pp. 271–282, wonderfully evokes women's supporting roles in war narrative.

8. It should be noted that many realists of the "old school" express skepticism concerning the modern hyperrationalized realism I discuss later on.

9. Ti-Grace Atkinson, "Theories of Radical Feminism," *Notes from the Second Year: Women's Liberation*, ed. Shulamith Firestone (n.p., 1970), p. 37.

10. Susan Brownmiller, *Against Our Will: Men, Women and Rape* (New York: Simon and Schuster, 1975), p. 388.

11. My point here is not to argue either the fairness or the constitutionality of the all-male draft but to examine the kinds of arguments NOW brought to bear in the case. It should also be noted that there was division inside NOW on this matter.

12. The brief is available from the NOW Legal Defense and Educational Fund, 132 West 42nd Street, New York, NY 10036.

13. Cynthia Enloe, *Does Khaki Become YOU? The Militarisation of Women's Lives* (London: Pluto Press, 1983), pp. 16–17.

14. The 1983 Pastoral Letter of the U.S. Bishops on War and Peace restored the pacifist tradition to a place of importance, however. The pastoral is printed in full in *Origins* (May 19, 1983), pp. 1–32.

15. Henry Paolucci, ed., *The Political Writings of St. Augustine* (Chicago: Henry Regnery, 1967), p. 151.

16. John Paul II, "On Pilgrimage: The UN Address" *Origins* 9, no. 42, pp. 675–680.

17. Natalie Zemon Davis, "Men, Women, and Violence: Some Reflections on Equality" *Smith Alumnae Quarterly* (April, 1972), p. 15.

18. G.W.F. Hegel, *The Phenomenology of Spirit*, trans. A. V. Miller (Oxford: Clarendon Press, 1977), pp. 399–400.

19. Davis, "Men, Women and Violence," p. 13.

20. Michael Walzer, *Just and Unjust Wars* (New York: Basic Books, 1977), pp. 251–263. A different view of the process is found in Freeman Dyson's *Disturbing the Universe* (New York: Harper Colophon, 1979). Dyson served in the "Operational Research Section" of British Bomber Command during the war, calculating probabilities for bombing raids without much of a "feeling of personal responsibility. None of us ever saw the people we killed. None of us particularly cared" (p. 30). But his reflections after the fact are mordant. He writes: "I began to look backward and to ask myself how it happened that I got involved in this crazy game of murder. Since the beginning of the war I had been retreating step by step from one moral position to another, until at the end I had no moral position at all" (pp. 30–31).

21. Walzer, *Just and Unjust Wars*, p. 274.

22. Ibid., p. 264.

23. Gordon Zahn, *Another Part of the War. The Camp Simon Story* (Amherst, MA: University of Massachusetts Press, 1979), p. 251.

24. The separatist literature is vast but the strongest statement of its theory remains Mary Daly's works, including *Gyn/Ecology: The Metaethics of Radical Feminism* (Boston: Beacon Press, 1979). A softer version in which men may be redeemable is Helen Caldicott, *Missile Envy* (New York: William Morrow, 1984).

25. This perspective has past and present elaborations. See, for example, Jane Addams, *The Long Road of Women's Memory* (New York: Macmillan, 1916) and Sara Ruddick,

"Maternal Thinking," which appears most recently in Joyce Trebilcot, ed., *Mothering: Essays in Feminist Theory* (Totowa, NJ: Rowman and Allanheld, 1984), p. 213–230. I have evoked Ruddick's formulation in several of my essays. The strengths and weaknesses of "maternal thinking" as a basis for political action are described in historic depth by Amy Swerdlow in her forthcoming work on the Mothers Strike for Peace.

26. Cited in Paul Fussell, *The Great War and Modern Memory* (Oxford: Oxford University Press, 1975): 320.

27. Michel Foucault, *Discipline and Punish* (New York: Vintage Books, 1979), pp. 168–169.

28. J. Glenn Gray, *The Warriors: Reflections on Men in Battle* (New York: Harper Colophon, 1970), p. 224.

29. Arendt, *On Violence*, p. 12.

30. Cited in E. P. Thompson, *Beyond the Cold War* (New York: Pantheon, 1982), p. 10.

31. Fussell, *Great War and Modern Memory*, p. 79.

32. See Fussell's discussion in *Great War and Modern Memory*, p. 108.

33. Eric Maria Remarque, *All Quiet on the Western Front* (New York: Fawcett, 1975), p. 195.

34. Gray, *The Warriors*, p. 135.

35. Huston's "Tales of War, Tears of Women" reminds us of the antiquity and pervasiveness of this narrative in Western history.

36. Arendt, *On Violence*, p. 35.

37. Hannah Arendt, *The Human Condition* (Chicago: University of Chicago Press, 1958), p. 247.

38. Arendt, *On Violence*, p. 81.

39. Arendt makes no gender-based distinction in this faculty though some commentators have argued—I am one of them— that the way she construes social arrangements contains its own built-in, unacceptable restrictions on action for particular groups and classes. I am not as persuaded of the thorough soundness of this criticism as I once was. The most complete treatment of a strategic doctrine based on neither "warrior" nor "victim" thinking, but drawing from each, is Freeman Dyson's recent *Weapons and Hope* (New York: Basic Books, 1984).

40. Grey cites in full the paragraph from Nietzsche's *The Wanderer and His Shadow* in which he repudiates the corruptions that flow from being hated and feared, pp. 225–26. To be sure, one could count twenty declarations by Nietzsche in praise of war for every one condemning it but even in such passages an ironic ambivalence may be at work. A genealogy that locates Jesus and Nietzsche on the "same side" is provocative and I cannot make a full argument here. But see René Girard, "The Extinction of Social Order," *Salmagundi* (Spring-Summer, 1984), pp. 204–237 for a discussion of the Gospel deconstruction of mimetic (violent) rivalries and the mechanism of the scapegoat on which rests the "false transcendence" of violent systems.

31.   A *Critique of Pacifism*

JAN NARVESON

Jan Narveson describes various forms of pacifism and then attacks the logical coherence of the version he finds most morally significant. In essence, pacifism insists that persons have a fundamental right not to be attacked and that a violation of that right constitutes a serious moral harm. At the same time, pacifists argue that one may not engage in violent self-defense. Narveson maintains that it is logically inconsistent that a person possess a right not to be attacked but at the same time lack the moral authority to defend that right.

Several different doctrines have been called "pacifism," and it is impossible to say anything cogent about it without saying which of them one has in mind. I must begin by making it clear, then, that I am limiting the discussion of pacifism to a rather narrow band of doctrines, further distinctions among which will be brought out below. By "pacifism," I do *not* mean the theory that violence is evil. With appropriate restrictions, this is a view that every person with any pretensions to morality doubtless holds. Nobody thinks that we have a right to inflict pain wantonly on other people. The pacifist goes a very long step further. *His* belief is not only that violence is evil but also that it is morally wrong to use force to resist, punish, or prevent violence. This further step makes pacifism a radical moral doctrine. What I shall try to establish below is that it is in fact more than merely radical—it is actually incoherent because it is self-contradictory in its fundamental intent. I shall also suggest that several moral attitudes and psychological views which have tended to be associated with pacifism as I have defined it do not have any necessary connection with that doctrine. Most proponents of pacifism, I shall argue, have tended to confuse these different things, and that confusion is probably what accounts for such popularity as pacifism has had.

It is next in order to point out that the pacifistic attitude is a matter of degree, and this in two respects. In the first place, there is the question: How much violence should not be resisted, and what degree of force is one not entitled to use in resisting, punishing, or preventing it? Answers to this question will make a lot of difference. For example, everyone would agree that

there are limits to the kind and degree of force with which a particular degree of violence is to be met: we do not have a right to kill someone for rapping us on the ribs, for example, and yet there is no tendency toward pacifism in this. We might go further and maintain, for example, that capital punishment, even for the crime of murder, is unjustified without doing so on pacifist grounds. Again, the pacifist should say just what sort of reaction constitutes a forcible or violent one. If somebody attacks me with his fists and I pin his arms to his body with wrestling holds which restrict him but cause him no pain, is that all right in the pacifist's book? And again, many nonpacifists could consistently maintain that we should avoid, to the extent that it is possible, inflicting a like pain on those who attempt to inflict pain on us. It is unnecessary to be a pacifist merely in order to deny the moral soundness of the principle, "an eye for an eye and a tooth for a tooth." We need a clarification, then, from the pacifist as to just how far he is and is not willing to go. But this need should already make us pause, for surely the pacifist cannot draw these lines in a merely arbitrary manner. It is his reasons for drawing the ones he does that count, and these are what I propose to discuss below.

The second matter of degree in respect of which the pacifist must specify his doctrine concerns the question: Who ought not to resist violence with force? For example, there are pacifists who would only claim that they themselves ought not to. Others would say that only pacifists ought not to, or that all persons of a certain type, where the type is not specified in terms of belief or non-belief in pacifism, ought not to resist violence with force. And finally, there are those who hold that everyone ought not to do so. We shall see that considerations about this second variable doom some forms of pacifism to contradiction.

My general program will be to show that (1) only the doctrine that everyone ought not to resist violence with force is of philosophical interest among those doctrines known as "pacifism"; (2) that doctrine, if advanced as a moral doctrine, is logically untenable; and (3) the reasons for the popularity of pacifism rest on failure to see exactly what the doctrine is. The things which pacifism wishes to accomplish, insofar as they are worth accomplishing, can be managed on the basis of quite ordinary and conservative moral principles.

Let us begin by being precise about the kind of moral force the principle of pacifism is intended to have. One good way to do this is to consider what it is intended to deny. What would non-pacifists, which I suppose includes most people, say of a man who followed Christ's suggestion and when unaccountably slapped, simply turned the other cheek? They might say that such a man is either a fool or a saint. Or they might say, "It's all very well for him to do that, but it's not for me"; or they might simply shrug their shoulders and say, "Well, it takes all kinds, doesn't it?" But they would *not* say that a man who did that ought to be punished in some way; they would not even say that he had done anything wrong. In fact, as I have mentioned, they would more likely than not find something admirable about it. The point, then, is this: The non-pacifist does *not* say that it is your *duty* to resist violence with force. The non-pacifist is merely saying that there's nothing wrong with doing so, that one has every right to do so if he is so inclined. Whether we wish to add that a person would be foolish or silly to do so is quite another question, one on which the non-pacifist does not *need* to take any particular position.

Consequently, a genuine pacifist cannot merely say that we may, if we wish, prefer not to resist violence with force. Nor can he merely say that there is something admirable or saintly about not doing so, for, as pointed out above, the non-pacifist could perfectly well agree with that. He must say, instead, that, for whatever class of people he thinks it applies to, there is something positively wrong about meeting violence with force. He must say that, insofar as the people to whom his principle applies resort to force, they are committing a breach of moral duty—a very serious thing to say. Just how serious, we shall ere long see.

Next, we must understand what the implications of holding pacifism as a moral principle are, and the first such implication requiring our attention concerns the matter of the size of the class of people to which it is supposed to apply. It will be of interest to discuss two of the four possibilities previously listed, I think. The first is that in which the pacifist says that only pacifists have the duty of pacifism. Let us see what this amounts to.

If we say that the principle of pacifism is the principle that all and only pacifists have a duty of not opposing violence with force, we get into a very odd situation. For suppose we ask ourselves, "Very well, which people are the pacifists then?" The answer will have to be "All those people who believe that pacifists have the duty not to meet violence with force." But surely one could believe that a certain class of people, whom we shall call "pacifists," have the duty not to meet violence with force without believing that one ought not, oneself, to meet violence with force. That is to say, the "principle" that pacifists ought to avoid meeting violence with force is circular: It presupposes that one already knows who the pacifists are. Yet this is precisely what that statement of the principle is supposed to answer! We are supposed to be able to say that anybody who believes that principle is a pacifist; yet, as we have seen, a person could very well believe that a certain class of people called "pacifists" ought not to meet violence with force without believing that he himself ought not to meet violence with force. Thus everyone could be a "pacifist" in the sense of believing that statement and yet no one believes that he *himself* (or anyone in particular) ought to avoid meeting violence with force. Consequently, pacifism cannot be specified in that way. A pacifist must be a person who believes either that he himself (at least) ought not to meet force with force or that some larger class of persons, perhaps everyone, ought not to meet force with force. He would then be believing something definite, and we are then in a position to ask why.

Incidentally, it is worth mentioning that when people say things such as "Only pacifists have the duty of pacifism," "Only Catholics have the duties of Catholicism," and, in general, "Only *X*-ists have the duties of *X*-ism" they probably are falling into a trap which catches a good many people. It is, namely, the mistake of supposing that what it *is* to have a certain duty is to *believe* that you have a certain duty. The untenability of this is parallel to the untenability of the previously mentioned attempt to say what pacifism is. For, if having a duty is believing that you have a certain duty, the question arises, "*What* does such a person believe?" The answer that must be given if we follow this analysis would then be, "He believes that he believes that he has a certain duty"; and so on, *ad infinitum*.

On the other hand, one might believe that having a duty does not consist in believing that one has and yet believe that only those people really have the duty who believe that they have it. But in that case, we would, being conscientious, perhaps want to ask the question, "Well, *ought* I to believe that I have that duty, or oughtn't I?" If you say that the answer is "Yes," the reason cannot be that you already do believe it, for you are asking whether you *should*. On the other hand, the answer "No" or "It doesn't make any difference—it's up to you," implies that there is really no reason for doing the thing in question at all. In short, asking whether I ought to believe that I have a duty to do *x* is equivalent to asking whether I should *do x*. A person might very well believe that he ought to do *x* but be wrong. It might be the case that he really ought *not* to do *x*; in that case the fact that he believes he ought to do *x*, far from being a reason why he ought to do it, is a reason for us to point out his error. It also, of course, presupposes that he has some reason other than his belief for thinking it is his duty to do *x*.

Having cleared this red herring out of the way, we must consider the view of those who believe that they themselves have a duty of pacifism and ask ourselves the question: What general kind of reason must a person have for supposing a certain type of act to be *his* duty, in a moral sense? Now, one answer he might give is that pacifism as such is a duty, that is, that meeting violence with force is, as such, wrong. In that case, however, what he thinks is not merely that *he* has this duty, but that *everyone* has this duty.

Now he might object, "Well, but no; I don't mean that everyone has it. For instance, if a man is defending, not himself, but *other* people, such as his wife and children, then he has a right to meet violence with force." Now this, of course, would be a very important qualification to his principle and one of a kind which we will be discussing in a moment. Meanwhile, however, we may point out that he evidently still thinks that, if it weren't for certain more important duties, everyone would have a duty to avoid meeting violence with force. In other words, he then believes that, other things being equal, one ought not to meet violence with force. He believes, to put it yet another way, that if one does meet violence with force, one must have a special excuse or justification of a moral kind; then he may want to give some account of just which excuses and justifications would do. Nevertheless, he is now holding a general principle.

Suppose, however, he holds that no one *else* has this duty of pacifism, that only he himself ought not to meet force with force, although it is quite all right for others to do so. Now if this is what our man feels, we may continue to call him a "pacifist," in a somewhat attenuated sense, but he is then no longer holding pacifism as a *moral* principle or, indeed, as a principle at all.[1] For now his disinclination for violence is essentially just a matter of taste. I like pistachio ice cream, but I wouldn't dream of saying that other people have a duty to eat it; similarly, this man just doesn't *like* to meet force, although he wouldn't dream of insisting that others act as he does. And this is a secondary sense of "pacifism," first, because pacifism has always been advocated on moral grounds and, second, because non-pacifists can easily have this same feeling. A person might very well feel squeamish, for example, about using force, even in self-defense, or he might not be able to bring himself to use it even if he wants to. But none of these has anything to do with asserting pacifism to be a duty. Moreover, a mere attitude could hardly license a man to refuse military service if it were required of him, or to join ban-the-bomb crusades, and so forth. (I fear, however, that such attitudes have sometimes caused people to do those things.)

And, in turn, it is similarly impossible to claim that your support of pacifism is a moral one if your position is that a certain selection of people, but no one else, ought not to meet force with force, even though you are unprepared to offer any reason whatever for this selection. Suppose, for example, that you hold that only the Arapahoes, or only the Chinese, or only people more than six feet high have this "duty." If such were the case, and no reasons offered at all, we could only conclude that you had a very peculiar attitude toward the Arapahoes, or whatever, but we would hardly want to say that you had a moral principle. Your "principle" amounts to saying that these particular individuals happen to have the duty of pacifism just because they are the individuals they are, and this, as Bentham would say, is the "negation of all principle." Of course, if you meant that somehow the property of being over six feet tall *makes* it your duty not to use violence, then you have a principle, all right, but a very queer one indeed unless you can give some further reasons. Again, it would not be possible to distinguish this from a sheer attitude.

Pacifism, then, must be the principle that the use of force to meet force is wrong *as such*, that is, that nobody may do so unless he has a special justification.

There is another way in which one might advocate a sort of "pacifism," however, which we must also dispose of before getting to the main point. One might argue that pacifism is desirable as a tactic: that, as a matter of fact, some good end, such as the reduction of violence itself, is to be achieved by "turning the other cheek." For example, if it were the case that turning the other cheek caused the offender to break down and repent, then that would be a very good reason for behaving "pacifistically." If unilateral disarmament causes the other side to disarm, then certainly unilateral disarmament would be a desirable policy. But note that its desirability, if this is the argument, is due to the fact that peace is desirable, a moral position which anybody can take, pacifist or no, plus the purely contingent fact that this policy causes the other side to disarm, that is, it brings about peace.

And of course, that's the catch. If one attempts to support pacifism, because of its probable effects, then one's position depends on what the effects are. Determining what they are is a purely empirical matter, and, consequently, one could not possibly be a pacifist as a matter of pure principle if his reasons for supporting pacifism are merely tactical. One must, in this case, submit one's opinions to the governance of fact.

It is not part of my intention to discuss matters of fact, as such, but it is worthwhile to point out that the general history of the human race certainly offers no support for the supposition that turning the other cheek always produces good effects on the aggressor. Some aggressors, such as the Nazis, were apparently just "egged on" by the "pacifist" attitude of their victims. Some of the S.S. men apparently became curious to see just how much torture the victim would put up with before he began to resist. Furthermore, there is the possibility that, while pacifism might work against some people (one might cite the British, against whom pacifism in India was apparently rather successful—but the British are comparatively nice people), it might fail against others (e.g., the Nazis).

A further point about holding pacifism to be desirable as a tactic is that this could not easily support the position that pacifism is a *duty*. The question whether we have no *right* to fight back can hardly be settled by noting that not to fight back might cause the aggressor to stop fighting. To prove that a policy is a desirable one because it works is not to prove that it is *obligatory* to follow it. We surely need considerations a good deal less tenuous than this to prove such a momentous contention as that we have no *right* to resist.

It appears, then, that to hold the pacifist position as a genuine, full-blooded moral principle is to hold that nobody has a right to fight back when attacked, that fighting back is inherently evil, as such. It means that we are all mistaken in supposing that we have a right of self-protection. And, of course, this is an extreme and extraordinary position in any case. It appears to mean, for instance, that we have no right to punish criminals, that all of our machinery of criminal justice is, in fact, unjust. Robbers, murderers, rapists, and miscellaneous delinquents ought, on this theory, to be let loose.

Now, the pacifist's first move, upon hearing this, will be to claim that he has been misrepresented. He might say that it is only one's *self* that one has no right to defend, and that one may legitimately fight in order to defend other people. This qualification cannot be made by those pacifists who qualify as conscientious objectors, of course, for the latter are refusing to defend their fellow citizens and not merely themselves. But this is comparatively trivial when we contemplate the next objection to this amended version of the theory. Let us now ask ourselves what it is about attacks on *other* people which could possibly justify *us* in defending them, while we are not justified in defending ourselves? It cannot be the mere fact that they are other people than ourselves, for, of course, everyone is a different person from everyone else, and if such a consideration could ever of itself justify anything at all it could also justify anything whatever. That mere difference of person, as such, is of no moral importance, is a presupposition of anything that can possibly pretend to be a moral theory.

Instead of such idle nonsense, then, the pacifist would have to mention some specific characteristic which every *other* person has which we lack and which justifies us in defending them. But this, alas, is impossible, for, while there may be some interesting difference between *me* on the one hand and everyone else on the other, the pacifist is not merely addressing himself to me. On the contrary, as we have seen, he has to address himself to everyone. He is claiming that each person has no right to defend himself, although he does have a right to defend other people. And, therefore, what is needed is a characteristic which distinguishes *each* person from everyone else, and not just *me* from everyone else—which is plainly self-contradictory.

Again, then, the pacifist must retreat in order to avoid talking nonsense. His next move might be to say that we have a right to defend all those who are not able to defend themselves. Big, grown-up men who are able to defend themselves ought not to do so, but they ought to defend mere helpless children who are unable to defend themselves.

This last, very queer theory could give rise to some amusing logical gymnastics. For instance, what about groups of people? If a group of people who cannot defend themselves singly can defend themselves together, then when it has grown to that size ought it to stop defending itself? If so, then every time a person *can* defend someone else, he would form with the person being defended a "defensive unit" which was able to defend itself, and thus would by this very presence debar himself from making the defense. At this rate, no one will ever get defended, it seems: The defenseless people by definition cannot defend themselves, while those who can defend them would enable the group consisting of the defenders and the defended to defend themselves, and hence they would be obliged not to do so.

Such reflections, however, are merely curious shadows of a much more fundamental and serious logical problem. This arises when we begin to ask: But why should even defenseless people be defended? If resisting violence is inherently evil, then how can it suddenly become permissible when we use it on behalf of other people? The fact that they are defenseless cannot possibly account for this, for it follows from the theory in question, that everyone ought to put himself in the position of people who are defenseless by refusing to defend himself. This type of pacifist, in short, is using the very characteristic (namely, being in a state of not defending oneself) which he wishes to encourage in others as a reason for denying it in the case of those who already have it (namely, the defenseless). This is surely inconsistent.

To attempt to be consistent, at least, the pacifist is forced to accept the characterization of him at which we tentatively arrived. He must say that no one ought ever to be defended against attack. The right of self-defense can be denied coherently only if the right of defense, in general, is denied. This in itself is an important conclusion.

It must be borne in mind, by the way, that I have not said anything to take exception to the man who simply does not wish to defend himself. So long as he does not attempt to make his pacifism into a principle, one cannot accuse him of any inconsistency, however much one might wish to say that he is foolish or eccentric. It is solely with moral principles that I am concerned here.

We now come to the last and most fundamental problem of all. If we ask ourselves what the point of pacifism is, what gets it going, so to speak, the answer is, of course, obvious enough: opposition to violence.

The pacifist is generally thought of as the man who is so much opposed to violence that he will not even use it to defend himself or anyone else. And it is precisely this characterization which I wish to show is morally inconsistent.

To begin with, we may note something which at first glance may seem merely to be a matter of fact, albeit one which should worry the pacifist, in our latest characterization of him. I refer to the commonplace observation that, generally speaking, we measure a man's degree of opposition to something by the amount of effort he is willing to put forth against it. A man could hardly be said to be dead set against something if he is not willing to lift a finger to keep it from going on. A person who claims to be completely opposed to something yet does nothing to prevent it would ordinarily be said to be a hypocrite.

As facts, however, we cannot make too much of these. The pacifist could claim to be willing to go to any length, short of violence, to prevent violence. He might, for instance, stand out in the cold all day long handing out leaflets (as I have known some to do), and this would surely argue for the sincerity of his beliefs.

But would it really?

Let us ask ourselves, one final time, what we are claiming when we claim that violence is morally wrong and unjust. We are, in the first place, claiming that a person *has no right* to indulge in it, as such (meaning that he has no right to indulge in it, *unless* he has an overriding justification). But what do we mean when we say that he has no right to indulge in it? Violence, of the type we are considering, is a two-termed affair: one does violence *to* somebody, one cannot simply "do violence." It might be oneself, of course, but we are not primarily interested in those cases, for what makes it wrong to commit violence is that it harms the people to whom it is done. To say that it is wrong is to say that those to whom it is done have a right *not* to have it done to them. (This must again be qualified by pointing out that this is so only if they have done nothing to merit having that right abridged.)

Yet what could that right to their own security, which people have, possibly consist in if not a right at least to be protected from whatever violence might be offered them? But lest the reader think that this is a gratuitous assumption, note carefully the reason why having a right involves having a right to be defended from breaches of that right. It is because the prevention of infractions of that right is precisely what one has a right to when one has a right at all. A right just *is* a status justifying preventive action. To say that you have a right to X but that no one has any justification whatever for preventing people from depriving you of it, is self-contradictory. If you claim a right to X, then to describe some action as an act of depriving you of X, is logically to imply that its absence is one of the things that you have a right to.

Thus far it does not follow logically that we have a right to use force in our own or anyone's defense. What does follow logically is that one has a right to whatever may be necessary to prevent infringements of his right. One might at first suppose that the universe *could* be so constructed that it is never necessary to use force to prevent people who are bent on getting something from getting it.

Yet even this is not so, for when we speak of "force" in the sense in which pacifism is concerned with it, we do not mean merely physical "force." To call an action a use of force is not merely to make a reference to the laws of mechanics. On the contrary, it is to describe whatever is being done as being a means to the infliction on somebody of something (ordinarily physical) which he does not want done to him; and the same is true for "force" in the sense in which it applies to war, assault and battery, and the like.

The proper contrary of "force" in this connection is "rational persuasion." Naturally, one way there *might* be of getting somebody not to do something he has no right to do is to convince him he ought not to do it or that it is not in his interest to do it. But it is inconsistent, I suggest, to argue that rational persuasion is the only morally permissible method of preventing violence. A pragmatic reason for this is easy enough to point to: Violent people are too busy being violent to be reasonable. We cannot engage in rational persuasion unless the enemy is willing to sit down and talk; but what if he isn't? One cannot contend that every human being can be persuaded to sit down and talk before he strikes, for this is not something we can determine just by reasoning; it is a question of observation. But these points are not strictly relevant anyway, for our question is not the empirical question of whether there is some handy way which can always be used to get a person to sit down and discuss moral philosophy when he is about to murder you. Our question is: *If* force is the only way to prevent violence in a given case, is its use justified *in that case?* This is a purely moral question which we can discuss without any special reference to matters of fact. And, moreover, it is precisely this question which we should have to discuss with the would-be violator. The point is that if a person can be rationally persuaded that he ought not to engage in violence, then precisely what he would be rationally persuaded of if we were to succeed would be the proposition that the use of force is justifiable to prevent him from doing so. For note that if we were to argue that only rational persuasion is permissible as a means of preventing him, we would have to face the question: Do we mean *attempted* rational persuasion, or *successful* rational persuasion, that is, rational persuasion which really does succeed in preventing him from acting? Attempted rational persuasion might fail (if only because the opponent is unreasonable), and then what? To argue that we have a right to use rational persuasion which also succeeds (i.e., we have a right to its success as well as to its use) is to imply that we have a right to prevent him from performing the act. But this, in turn, means that, if attempts at rational persuasion fail, we have a right to the use of force. Thus what we have a right to, if we ever have a *right* to anything, is not merely the use of rational persuasion to keep people from depriving you of the thing to which you have the right. We do indeed have a right to that, but we also have a right to anything else that might be necessary (other things being equal) to prevent the deprivation from occurring. And it is a logical truth, not merely a contingent one, that what *might* be necessary is *force*. (If merely saying something could miraculously deprive someone of the ability to carry through a course of action, then those speech-acts would be called a type of force, if a very mysterious one. And we could properly begin to oppose their use for precisely the same reasons as we now oppose violence.)

What this all adds up to, then, is that *if* we have any rights at all, we have a right to use force to prevent the deprivation of the thing to which we are said to have a right. But the pacifist, of *all* people, is the one most concerned to insist that we do have some rights, namely, the right not to have violence done to us. This is logically implied in asserting it to be a duty on everyone's part to avoid violence. And this is why the pacifist's position is self-contradictory. In saying that violence is wrong, one is at the same time saying that people have a right to its prevention, by force if necessary. Whether and to what extent it may be necessary is a question of fact, but, since it is a question of fact only, the moral right to use force on some possible occasions is established.[2]

We now have an answer to the question. How much force does a given threat of violence justify for preventive purposes? The answer, in a word, is "Enough." That the answer is this simple may at first sight seem implausible. One might suppose that some elaborate equation between the aggressive and the preventive force is needed: the punishment be proportionate to the crime. But this is a misunderstanding. In the first place, prevention and punishment are not the same, even if punishment is thought to be directed mainly toward prevention. The punishment of a particular crime logically cannot prevent *that* instance of the crime, since it presupposes that it has already been performed; and punishment need not involve the use of any violence at all, although law-enforcement officers in some places have a nasty tendency to assume the contrary. But preventive force is another matter. If a man threatens to kill me, it is desirable, of course, for me to try to prevent this by the use of the least amount of force sufficient to do the job. But I am justified even in killing him *if* necessary. This much, I suppose, is obvious to most people. But suppose his threat is much smaller: suppose that he is merely pestering me, which is a very mild form of aggression indeed. Would I be justified in killing him to prevent this, under any circumstances whatever?

Suppose that I call the police and they take out a warrant against him, and suppose that when the police come, he puts up a struggle. He pulls a knife or a gun, let us say, and the police shoot him in the ensuing battle. Has my right to the prevention of his annoying me extended to killing him? Well, not exactly, since the immediate threat in response to which he is killed is a threat to the lives of the policemen. Yet my annoyer may never have contemplated real violence. It is an unfortunate case of unpremeditated escalation. But this is precisely what makes the contention that one is justified in using enough force to do the job, whatever amount that may be, to prevent action which violates a right less alarming than at first sight it seems. For it is difficult to envisage a reason why extreme force is needed to prevent mild threats from realization except by way of escalation, and escalation automatically justifies increased use of preventive force.

The existence of laws, police, courts, and more or less civilized modes of behavior on the part of most of the populace naturally affects the answer to the question of how much force is necessary. One of the purposes of a legal system of justice is surely to make the use of force by individuals very much less necessary than it would otherwise be. If we try to think back to a "state of nature" situation, we shall have less difficulty envisaging the need for large amounts of force to prevent small threats of violence. Here Hobbes's contention that in such a state every man has a right to the

life of every other becomes understandable. He was, I suggest, relying on the same principle as I have argued for here: that one has a right to use as much force as necessary to defend one's rights, which include the right of safety of person.

And needless to say, my arguments here do not give us any reason to modify the obviously vital principle that if force should be necessary, then one must use the least amount of it compatible with maintaining the rights of those being protected. There is, for example, no excuse for sending armed troops against unarmed students to contain protest marches and demonstrations.

I have said that the duty to avoid violence is only a duty, other things being equal. We might arrive at the same conclusion as we have above by asking the question: Which "other things" might count as being *un*equal? The answer to this is that whatever else they may be, the purpose of preventing violence from being done is necessarily one of these justifying conditions. That the use of force is never justified to prevent initial violence being done to one logically implies that there is nothing wrong with initial violence. We cannot characterize it as being wrong if preventive violence is not simultaneously being characterized as justifiable.

We often think of pacifists as being gentle and idealistic souls, which in its way is true enough. What I have been concerned to show is that they are also confused. If they attempt to formulate their position using our standard concepts of rights, their position involves a contradiction: Violence is wrong, *and* it is wrong to resist it. But the right to resist is precisely what having a right of person is, if it is anything at all.

Could the position be reformulated with a less "commital" concept of rights? I do not think so. It has been suggested[3] that the pacifist need not talk in terms of this "kind" of rights. He can affirm, according to this suggestion, simply that neither the aggressors nor the defenders "have" rights to what they do, that to affirm their not having them is simply to be against the use of force, without this entailing the readiness to use force if necessary to protect the said rights. But this will not do, I believe. For I have not maintained that having a right, or believing that one has a right, entails a *readiness* to defend that right. One has a perfect right not to resist violence to oneself if one is so inclined. But our question has been whether self-defense is justifiable, and not whether one's belief that violence is wrong entails a willingness or readiness to use it. My contention has been that such a belief does entail the justifiability of using it. If one came upon a community in which no sort of violence was ever resisted and it was claimed in that community that the non-resistance was a matter of conscience, we should have to conclude, I think, not that this was a community of saints, but rather that this community lacked the concept of justice—or perhaps that their nervous systems were oddly different from ours.

The true test of the pacifist comes, of course, when he is called upon to assist in the protection of the *safety of other persons* and not just of himself. For while he is, as I have said, surely entitled to be pacific about *his own person* if he is so inclined, he is not entitled to be so about the safety of others. It is here that the test of principles comes out. People have a tendency to brand conscientious objectors as cowards or traitors, but this is not quite fair. They are acting as if they were cowards or traitors, but claiming to do so on principle. It is not surprising if a community should fail to understand such "principles," for the test of adherence to a principle is willingness to act on it, and the appropriate action, if one believes a

certain thing to be grossly wrong, is to take steps to prevent or resist it. Thus people who assess conscientious objection as cowardice or worse are taking an understandable step: from an intuitive feeling that the pacifist does not really believe what he is saying they infer that his actions (or inaction) must be due to cowardice. What I am suggesting is that this is not correct: The actions are due, not to cowardice, but to confusion.

Endnotes

1. Compare, for example, K. Baier, *The Moral Point of View* (Ithaca: Cornell University Press, 1958), p. 191.

2. This basic argument may be compared with a view of Kant's, to be found in the *Rechtslehre*, translated under the title *Metaphysical Elements of Justice* by J. Ladd, Library of Liberal Arts, pp. 35–36 (Introduction, D).

3. I owe this suggestion to my colleague, Leslie Armour.

Part 5

Euthanasia and Physician-Assisted Suicide

32. Euthanasia and Christian Vision

GILBERT MEILAENDER

Gilbert Meilaender defends the position that Christian faith precludes the direct taking of innocent life. Though Christians are obliged to provide compassionate care for the dying, they must not conclude that their wish that the suffering cease justifies direct killing as a means to that humane end. For the believer, some choices are simply beyond our domain of moral authority under God, and the taking of an innocent human life, however noble the motives, is never permissible.

Every teacher has probably experienced, along with countless frustrations, moments in the classroom when something was said with perfect lucidity. I still recall one such moment three years ago when I was teaching a seminar dealing with ethical issues in death and dying. Knowing how difficult it can be to get students to consider these problems from within religious perspectives, I decided to force the issue at the outset by assigning as the first reading parts of those magnificent sections from Volume III/4 of Karl Barth's *Church Dogmatics* in which he discusses "Respect for Life" and "The Protection of Life." I gave the students little warning in advance, preferring to let the vigor and bombast of Barth's style have whatever effect it might.

Reprinted by permission of the publisher from "Euthanasia and Christian Vision," *Thought 57,* December 1982 (New York: Fordham University Press, 1982), pp. 465–75. Copyright © 1982 by Gilbert Meilaender.

The students, I must say in retrospect, probably thought more kindly of Barth (who had, after all, only written these sections) than of their teacher (who had assigned them to be read). But they good-naturedly went about doing the assignment, and our seminar had a worthwhile discussion—with students criticizing Barth and, even, sometimes defending him. However, neither criticism nor defense was really my goal. It was understanding—understanding of death and dying within a perspective steeped in centuries of Christian life and thought—that I was seeking. And at one moment, even in a moment of criticism, we achieved that understanding.

One young woman in the class, seeking to explain why Barth puzzled her so, put it quite simply: "What I really don't like about him is that he seems to think our lives are not our own." To which, after a moment of awed silence, I could only respond: "If you begin to see that about Barth, even if it gets under your skin and offends you deeply, then indeed you have begun to understand what he is saying."

In his discussion of "The Protection of Life," and in fact, within his specific discussion of euthanasia, Barth notes many of the difficult questions we might raise which seem to nudge us in the direction of approving euthanasia in certain tormenting cases. And then, rejecting these "tempting questions," he responds with his own typical flair. "All honour to the well-meaning humanitarianism of underlying motive! But that derivation is obviously from another book than that which we have thus far consulted."[1] In this brief essay I want to think about euthanasia not from the perspective of any "well-meaning humanitarianism" but from within the parameters of Christian belief—though, as we will see, one of the most important things to note is that, within those parameters, only what is consonant with Christian belief can be truly humane.[2]

The Paradigm Case

Determining what really qualified as euthanasia is no easy matter. Need the person "euthanatized" be suffering terribly? Or, at least, be near death? Suppose the person simply feels life is no longer worth living in a particular condition which may be deeply dissatisfying though not filled with suffering? Suppose the person's life is filled with suffering or seemingly devoid of meaning but he is unable to request euthanasia (because of a comatose condition, senility, etc.)? Or suppose the person is suffering greatly but steadfastly says he does not want to die? Suppose the "euthanizer's" motive is not mercy but despair at the continued burden of caring for the person—will that qualify?

The list of questions needing clarification is endless once we start down this path. But I intend to get off the path at once by taking as our focus of attention a kind of paradigm case of what must surely count as euthanasia. If we can understand why *this* is morally wrong, much else will fall into place. James Rachels has suggested that "the clearest possible case of euthanasia" would be one having the following five features:[3]

1. The person is deliberately killed.
2. The person would have died soon anyway.
3. The person was suffering terrible pain.
4. The person asked to be killed.
5. The motive of the killing was mercy—to provide the person with as good a death as possible under the circumstances.

Such a case is not simply "assisted suicide," since the case requires the presence of great suffering, the imminence of death in any case, and a motive of mercy. Furthermore, considering this sort of case sets aside arguments about voluntary and involuntary euthanasia and gives focus to our discussion.[4] If this case of voluntary euthanasia is permissible, other cases may also be (or may not). If this case is itself morally wrong, we are less likely to be able to argue for euthanasia in nonvoluntary and involuntary circumstances.

Aim and Result

One way of arguing that the paradigm case of euthanasia is morally permissible (perhaps even obligatory) is to claim that it does not differ in morally relevant ways from other acts which most of us approve. Consider a patient whose death is imminent, who is suffering terribly, and who may suddenly stop breathing and require resuscitation. We may think it best not to resuscitate such a person but simply to let him die. What could be the morally significant difference between such a "letting die" and simply giving this person a lethal injection which would have ended his life (and suffering) just as quickly? If it is morally right not to prolong his dying when he ceases breathing for a few moments, why is it morally wrong to kill him quickly and painlessly? Each act responds to the fact that death is imminent and recognizes that—terrible suffering calls for relief. And the result in each case is the same: death.

In order to appreciate the important difference between these possibilities we must distinguish what we *aim* at in our action from the *result* of the action. Or, to paraphrase Charles Fried, we must distinguish between those actions which we invest with the personal involvement of purpose and those which merely "run through" our person.[5] This is a distinction which moral reflection can scarcely get along without. For example, if we fail to distinguish between aim and result we will be unable to see any difference between the self-sacrifice of a martyr and the suicide of a person weary of life. The result is the same for each: death. But the aim or purpose is quite different. Whereas the suicide aims at his death, the martyr aims at faithfulness to God (or loyalty of some other sort). Both martyr and suicide recognize in advance that the result of their choice and act will be death. But the martyr does not aim at death.

This distinction between aim and result is also helpful in explaining the moral difference between euthanatizing a suffering person near death and simply letting such a person die. Suppose this patient were to stop breathing, we were to reject the possibility of resuscitation, and then the person were suddenly to begin breathing again. Would we, simply because we had been willing to let this patient die, now proceed to smother him so that he would indeed die? Hardly. And the fact that we would not indicates that we did not *aim* at his death (in rejecting resuscitation), though his death could have been one *result* of what we did aim at (namely, proper care for him in his dying). By contrast, if we euthanatized such a person by giving him a lethal injection, we would indeed aim at his death; we would invest the act of aiming at his death with the personal involvement of our purpose.

A rejoinder: It is possible to grant the distinction between aim and result while still claiming that euthanasia in our paradigm case would be permissible (or obligatory). It may be true that there is a difference between allowing a patient to die and aiming at someone's death. But if the suffering of the dying person is truly intense and the person requests death, on what grounds could we refuse to assist him? If we refuse on the grounds that it would be wrong for us to aim at his death (which will certainly result soon anyway after more terrible suffering), are we not saying that we are unwilling to do him a great good if doing it requires that we dirty our hands in any way? To put the matter this way makes it seem that our real concern is with our own moral rectitude, not with the needs of the sufferer. It seems that we are so concerned about ourselves that in our eagerness to narrow the scope of our moral responsibility we have lost sight of the need and imperative to offer care.

This is, it should be obvious, what ethicists call a *consequentialist* rejoinder. It suggests that the good results (relieving the suffering) are sufficiently weighty to make the aim (of killing) morally permissible or obligatory. And, as far as I can tell, this rejoinder has become increasingly persuasive to large numbers of people.

Consequentialism may be described as that moral theory that holds that from the fact that some state of affairs *ought to be* it follows that we *ought to do* whatever is necessary to bring about that state of affairs. And, although teleological theories of morality are very ancient, consequentialism as a full-blown moral theory is traceable largely to Bentham and Mill in the late 18th and early 19th centuries. To remember this is instructive, since it is not implausible to suggest that

such a moral theory would be most persuasive when Christendom had, in large measure, ceased to be Christian. Those who know themselves as creatures— not Creator—will recognize limits even upon their obligation to do good. As creatures we are to do all the good we can, but this means all the good we "morally can"—all the good we can within certain limits. It may be that the Creator *ought to do* whatever is necessary to bring about states of affairs which *ought to be,* but we stand under no such godlike imperative.[6]

One of the best ways to understand the remarkable appeal today of consequentialism as a moral theory is to see it as an ethic for those who (a) remain morally serious but (b) have ceased to believe in a God whose providential care will ultimately bring about whatever ought to be the case. If God is not there to accomplish what ought to be the case, we are the most likely candidates to shoulder the burden of that responsibility.[7] Conversely, it may be that we can make sense of distinguishing between two acts whose *result* is the same but whose *aim* is different only if we believe that our responsibilities (as creatures) are limited— that the responsibility for achieving certain results has been taken out of our hands (or, better, never given us in the first place). It ought to be the case that dying people not suffer terribly (indeed, that they not die). But, at least for Christians, it does not follow from that "ought to be" that we "ought to do" whatever is necessary—even euthanasia—to relieve them of that suffering.[8]

We are now in a position to see something important about the argument which claims that euthanasia (in the paradigm case) is permissible because it does not differ morally from cases of "letting die" which most of us approve. This argument often begins in a failure to distinguish aim and result; however, it is, as we have seen, difficult for moral theory to get along without this distinction. Seeing this, we recognize that the argument really becomes a claim that if the results are sufficiently good, any aim necessary to achieve them is permissible. And precisely at this turn in the argument, it may be difficult to keep "religion" and "morality" in those neat and separate compartments we have fashioned for them. At this point one steeped in Christian thought and committed to Christian life may wish to say with Barth: All honor to the well-meaning humanitarianism—and it is well-meaning. But the derivation—fit only for those who would, even if reluctantly, be "like God"—is obviously "derived from another book" than that which Christians are wont to consult.

Aim and Motive

If the distinction between aim and result makes it difficult to justify euthanasia in the paradigm case, another
distinction may be more useful. We might suggest that
the act of euthanizing be redescribed in terms of the
motive of mercy. We could describe the act not as killing
but as relieving suffering. Or, rather than engaging in
such wholesale redescription of the act, we might simply
argue that our moral evaluation of the act cannot depend
solely on its *aim* but must also consider its *motive.*

Consider the following illustration.[9] A condemned
prisoner is in his cell only minutes before his scheduled
execution. As he sits in fear and anguish, certain of his
doom, another man who has managed to sneak into the
prison shoots and kills him. This man is either (a) the
father of children murdered by the prisoner, or (b) a
close friend of the prisoner. In case (a) he shoots because
he will not be satisfied simply to have the man executed.
He desires that his own hand should bring about the
prisoner's death. In case (b) the friend shoots because he
wishes to spare his friend the terror and anguish of those
last minutes, to deliver him from the indignity of the
sheer animal fright he is undergoing.

Would it be proper to describe the father's act in
(a) as an act of killing and the friend's in (b) as an act
of relieving suffering? Although many people may be
tempted to do so, it muddies rather than clarifies our
analysis. If anything is clear in these cases, it is that
both the vengeful father and the compassionate friend
aim to kill though their *motives* are very different. Only
by refusing to redescribe the aim of the act in terms of
its motive do we keep the moral issue clearly before
us. That issue is whether our moral evaluation of the
act should depend solely on the agent's *aim* or whether
that evaluation must also include the *motive.*

That the motive makes *some* difference almost
everyone would agree. Few of us would be content to
analyze the two cases simply as instances of "aiming to
kill" without considering the quite different motives.
The important question, however, is whether the praiseworthy motive of relieving suffering should so dominate our moral reflection that it leads us to term the act
"right." I want to suggest that it should not, at least not
within the parameters of Christian belief.

One might think that Christian emphasis on the
overriding importance of love as a motive would suggest that whatever was done out of love was right.
And, to be sure, Christians will often talk this way.
Such talk, however, must be done against the background assumptions of Christian anthropology. Apart

from that background of meaning we may doubt
whether we have really understood the motive of love
correctly. We need therefore to sketch in the background against which we can properly understand
what loving care for a suffering person should be.[10]

Barth writes that human life "must always be
regarded as a divine act of trust."[11] This means that all
human life is "surrounded by a particular solemnity,"
which, if recognized, will lead us to "treat it with
respect." At the same time, however, "life is no second
God, and therefore the respect due to it cannot rival
the reverence owed to God." One who knows this will
seek to live life "within its appointed limits." Recognizing our life as a trust, we will be moved not by an
"absolute will to live" but a will to live within these
limits. Hence, when we understand ourselves as creatures, we will both value God's gift of life and recognize that the Giver himself constitutes the limit
beyond which we ought not value the gift. "Temporal
life is certainly not the highest of all goods. Just
because it belongs to God, man may be forbidden to
will its continuation at all costs." And at the same time,
"if life is not the highest possession, then it is at least
the highest and all-inclusive price" which human
beings can pay. In short, life is a great good, but not the
greatest (which is fidelity to God).

Death, the final enemy of life, must also be understood dialectically. The human mind can take and has
quite naturally taken two equally plausible attitudes
toward death.[12] We can regard death as of no consequence, heeding the Epicurean maxim that while we
are alive death is not yet here, and when death is here
we are no more. Thus the human being, in a majestic
transcendence of the limits of earthly life, might seek
to soar beyond the limits of finitude and find his good
elsewhere. If death is of no consequence, we may seek
it in exchange for some important good. Equally natural to the human mind is a seemingly opposite view—
that death is the *summum malum*, the greatest evil to be
avoided at all costs. Such a view, finding good only in
earthly life, can find none in suffering and death.

The Christian mind, however, transcending what is
"natural" and correcting it in light of the book it is accustomed to consult, has refused to take either of these
quite plausible directions. Understood within the biblical narrative, death is an ambivalent phenomenon—too
ambivalent to be seen only as the greatest of all evils, or
as indifferent. Since the world narrated by the Bible
begins in God and moves toward God, earthly life is his
trust to be sustained faithfully and his gift to be valued
and cared for. When life is seen from this perspective,

we cannot say that death and suffering are of no conse-quence; on the contrary, we can even say with Barth that the human task in the face of suffering and death is not to accept but to offer "final resistance."[13] It is just as true, however, that death could never be the greatest evil. That title must be reserved for disobedience to and dis-belief in God—a refusal to live within our appointed limits. So we can also repeat with Barth that "life is no second God."[14] We remember, after all, that Jesus goes to the cross in the name of obedience to his Father. We need not glorify or seek suffering, but we must be struck by the fact that a human being who is a willing sufferer stands squarely in the center of Christian piety. Jesus bears his suffering not because it is desirable but because the Father allots it to him within the limits of his earthly life. Death is—there is no way to put the matter simply—a great evil which God can turn to his good purposes. It is an evil which must ordinarily be resisted but which must also at some point be acknowledged. We can and ought to acknowledge what we do not and ought not seek. George Orwell, himself an "outsider," nicely summarized these background assumptions of Christian anthropology:

> The Christian attitude towards death is not that it is something to be welcomed, or that it is something to be met with stoical indiffer-ence, or that it is something to be avoided as long as possible; but that it is something pro-foundly tragic which has to be gone through with. A Christian, I suppose, if he were offered the chance of everlasting life on this earth would refuse it, but he would still feel that death is profoundly sad.[15]

This vision of the world, and of the meaning of life and death, has within Christendom given guidance to those reflecting on human suffering and dying. That moral guidance has amounted to the twofold proposi-tion that, though we might properly cease to oppose death while aiming at other choiceworthy goods in life (hence, the possibility of martyrdom), we ought never aim at death as either our end or our means.

Against this background of belief we can better understand what *love* and *care* must be within a world construed in Christian terms. In *this* world no action which deliberately hastens death can be called "love." Not because the euthanizer need have any evil motive. Indeed, as the case of the compassionate friend makes clear, the one who hastens death may seem to have a praiseworthy motive. Rather, such action cannot be loving because it cannot be part of the meaning of

commitment to the well-being of another human being within the appointed limits of earthly life. The benevo-lence of the euthanizer is enough like love to give us pause, to tempt us to call it love. And *perhaps* it may even be the closest those who feel themselves to bear full responsibility for relief of suffering and produc-tion of good in our world can come to love. But it is not the creaturely love which Christians praise, a love which can sometimes do no more than suffer as best we can with the sufferer.

Christian Love Enacted and Inculcated

Against this background—a background which pours meaning into words like "love" and "care"—we can contemplate the kind of case often considered in discus-sions of euthanasia.[16] A person may be in severe pain, certain to die within only a few days. Most of us would agree that further "lifesaving" treatment were not in order for such a person, that they would do no more than prolong his dying. Why, one may ask, do we not subject such a patient to useless treatments? Because, we reply, he is in agony and it would be wrong to pro-long that agony needlessly. But now, if we face the facts honestly, we will admit that it takes this patient longer to die—and prolongs his suffering—if we simply with-hold treatment than if we euthanize him. Hence, there seems to be a contradiction within our reasoning. The motive for withholding treatment was a humanitarian one: relief of suffering. But in refusing to take the next step and euthanize the patient we prolong his suffering and, thereby, belie our original motive. Hence the con-clusion follows, quite contrary to the moral guidance embedded in the Christian vision of the world: Either we should keep this person alive as long as possible (and not pretend that our motive is the relief of suffer-ing), or we should be willing to euthanize him.

The argument gets much of its force from the seeming simplicity of the dilemma, but that simplicity is misleading. For, at least for Christian vision, the fun-damental imperative is not "minimize suffering" but "maximize love and care." In that Christian world, in which death and suffering are great evils but not the greatest evil, love can never include in its meaning hastening a fellow human being toward (the evil of) death, nor can it mean a refusal to acknowledge death when it comes (as an evil but not the greatest evil). We can only know what the imperative "maximize love" means if we understand it against the background assumptions which make intelligible for Christians words like "love" and "care." The Christian mind has certainly not recommended that we seek suffering or call it an unqualified good, but it is an evil which, when endured faithfully, can be redemptive. William May has noted how parents in our time think that love for their children means, above all else, protecting those children from suffering. "As conscientious parents, they operate as though the powers that are decisive in the universe could not possibly do anything in and through the suffering of their children. . . . They take upon themselves the responsibilities of a savior-figure. . . ."[17] May sees clearly that "minimize suffering" and "maximize love" are not identical imperatives and do not offer the same direction for human action. Perhaps the direction they give may often be the same, but at times—especially when we consider what it is proper to do for the irretrievably dying—we will discover how sharply they may differ.

I suggested above that we should not redescribe the *aim* of an act in terms of its *motive*. (We should not say that an act of killing a suffering person was simply an act of relieving suffering. We should say rather that we aimed at the death of the person in order to relieve his suffering. This keeps the moral issue more clearly before us.) But by now it will be evident that I have in fact gone some way toward redescribing the *motive* of the act in terms of its *aim*. (If the act is aimed at hastening the death of the suffering person, we should not see it as motivated by love.) Is this any better? The answer, I think, is "it depends."

It would not be better, it might even be worse, if my purpose were to deny any humanitarian motive to the person tempted to euthanize a sufferer. Few people would find such a denial persuasive, and because we would not we are tempted to turn in the opposite direction and describe the act's aim in terms of its motive. We *do* recognize a difference between the vengeful father and the compassionate friend even though both aim to kill the condemned prisoner, and we want our moral judgments to be sufficiently nuanced to take account of these differences. The simple truth is that our evaluation of the act (described in terms of motive) often fall apart. In a world broken by sin and its consequences this should perhaps come as no surprise. Christians believe that we sinners—all of us—are not whole, and many of the stubborn problems of systematic ethical reflection testify to the truth of that belief. It is our lack of wholeness which is displayed in our inability to arrive at one judgment (or even one description) "whole and entire" of a single act. We find ourselves in a world in which people may sometimes seem to aim at doing evil

from the best of motives (and think they must do so). And then we are tempted to elide aim and motive and call that evil at which they aim "good."

No amount of ethical reflection can heal this rift in our nature. From that predicament we will have to look for a deliverance greater than ethics can offer. However, here and now, in our broken world, we do better to take the aim of an act as our guiding light in describing and evaluating the act—and then evaluate the motive in light of this aim. This is better because moral reflection is not primarily a tool for fixing guilt and responsibility (in which case motive comes to the fore). It is, first and foremost, one of the ways in which we train ourselves and others to see the world rightly. We would be wrong to assert that no euthanizer has or can have a humanitarian motive. But if we want not so much to fix praise or blame but to teach the meaning of the word "love," we are not wrong to say that love could never euthanize. In the Christian world this is true. And in that world we know the right name for our own tendency to call those other, seemingly humanitarian, motives "love." The name for that tendency is *temptation*. We are being tempted to be "like God" when we toy with the possibility of defining our love—and the meaning of humanity—apart from the appointed limits of human life.

To redescribe the motive in terms of the act's aim, to attempt to *inculcate* a vision of the world in which love could never euthanize, is therefore not only permissible but necessary for Christians. It is the only proper way to respond to the supposed dilemmas we are confronted with by reasoning which brackets Christian background assumptions from the outset. The Christian moral stance which emerges here is not a club with which to beat over the head those who disagree. It does not provide a superior vantage point from which to deny them any humanitarian motive in the ordinary sense. But it *is* a vision of what "humanity" and "humanitarian motives" should be. We may therefore say of those who disagree: "All honour to the well-meaning humanitarianism of underlying motive! But the derivation is obviously from another book than that which we have thus far consulted."

Endnotes

1. Karl Barth, *Church Dogmatics*, Vol. III/4, ed. G. W. Bromiley and T. F. Torrance (Edinburgh: T&T Clark, 1961), p. 425.

2. I will be exploring some of the *moral* issues involved in euthanasia without taking up *legal* problems which also arise.

I do not assume any answer to the question, Should what is morally wrong be legally prohibited?

3. James Rachels, "Euthanasia," *Matters of Life and Death: New Introductory Essays in Moral Philosophy,* ed. Tom Regan (New York: Random House, 1980), p. 29.

4. Nonvoluntary euthanasia occurs when the person euthanized is in a condition which makes it impossible for him to express a wish (e.g., senile, comatose). Involuntary euthanasia occurs when the person euthanized expresses a desire *not* to be killed but is nevertheless euthanized.

5. Charles Fried, *Right and Wrong* (Cambridge, Mass.: Harvard University Press, 1978), p. 27.

6. Cf. Joseph Butler, Dissertation "On the Nature of Virtue," appended to *The Analogy of Religion Natural and Revealed.* Morley's Universal Library edition (London: George Routledge & Sons, 1884), p. 301: "The fact then appears to be, that we are constituted so as to condemn falsehood, unprovoked violence, injustice, and to approve of benevolence to some preferably to others abstracted from all consideration, which conduct is likely to produce an overbalance of happiness or misery; and therefore, were the Author of Nature to propose nothing to Himself as an end but the production of happiness, were His moral character merely that of benevolence; yet ours is not so." In other words, though the Creator may be a consequentialist, creatures are not! For a contrary view, see Peter Geach, *The Virtues* (Cambridge: Cambridge University Press, 1977), pp. 95ff.

7. Whether this enlargement of the scope of our responsibility really works is another matter. Being responsible for everything may, for human beings, come quite close to being responsible for nothing. Charles Fried comments: "If, as consequentialism holds, we were indeed equally morally responsible for an infinite radiation of concentric circles originating from the center point of some action, then while it might look as if we were enlarging the scope of human responsibility and thus the significance of personality, the enlargement would be greater than we could support. . . . Total undifferentiated responsibility is the correlative of the morally overwhelming, undifferentiated plasma of happiness or pleasure" (*Right and Wrong,* pp. 34f.).

8. It is a hard, perhaps unanswerable, question whether there might ever be exceptions to this general standard for Christian conduct which I have enunciated. There might be a circumstance in which the pain of the sufferer was so terrible and unconquerable that one would want to consider an exception. To grant this possibility is not really to undermine the principle, since, as Charles Fried has noted, the "catastrophic" is a distinct moral concept, identifying an extreme situation in which the usual rules of morality do not apply (Right and Wrong, p. 10). We would be quite mistaken to build the whole of our morality on the basis of the

catastrophic; in fact, it would then become the norm rather than the exception. One possible way to deal with such extreme circumstances without simply lapsing into consequentialism is to reason in a way analogous to Michael Walzer's reasoning about the rules of war in *Just and Unjust Wars* (New York: Basic Books, Inc., 1977). Walzer maintains the rules of war are binding even when they put us at a disadvantage, even when they may cost us victory. But he grants that there might be "extreme emergencies" in which we could break the rules; namely, when doing so was (a) morally necessary (i.e., the opponent was so evil—a Hitler—that it was morally imperative to defeat him) and (b) strategically necessary (no other way than violating the rules of war was available for defeating this opponent). Reasoning in an analogous way we might wonder whether the rule prohibiting euthanasia could be violated if (a) the suffering was so unbearable that the sufferer lost all capacity to bear that suffering with any sense of moral purpose or faithfulness to God; and (b) the pain was truly unconquerable. Whether such extreme circumstances ever occur is a question whose answer I cannot give. And even if such circumstances are possible, I remain uncertain about the force of this "thought experiment," which is offered tentatively.

9. This illustration is "inspired" by a different set of hypothetical cases offered by Paul Ramsey in "Some Rejoinders," *The Journal of Religious Ethics* 4 (Fall 1976): 204.

10. In what follows I draw upon my own formulations in two previous articles: "The Distinction Between Killing and Allowing to Die," *Theological Studies* 37 (September 1976): 467–70 and "Lutheran Theology and Bioethics: A Juxtaposition," *SPC Journal* 3 (1980): 25–30.

11. The passages cited in this paragraph may be found scattered throughout pages 336–42 and pages 401–2 of Vol. III/4 of *Church Dogmatics.*

12. For what follows cf. C. S. Lewis, *Miracles* (New York: Macmillan, 1947), pp. 129ff, and Paul Ramsey, *The Patient as Person* (New Haven and London: Yale University Press, 1970), pp. 144ff.

13. *Church Dogmatics,* III/4, p. 368.

14. Ibid., p. 342.

15. George Orwell, "The Meaning of a Poem," *My Country Right or Left,* 1940–1943. Volume II of *The Collected Essays, Journalism and Letters of George Orwell,* ed. Sonia Orwell and Ian Angus (New York: Harcourt Brace Jovanovich, 1968), p. 133.

16. For a strong statement of such a case see James Rachels, "Active and Passive Euthanasia," *New England Journal of Medicine* 292 (1975): 78–80.

17. William May, "The Metaphysical Plight of the Family," *Death Inside Out,* ed. Peter Steinfels and Robert M. Veatch (New York: Harper & Row, 1974), p. 51.

33. *Objections to the Institutionalization of Euthanasia*

Stephen G. Potts

Stephen G. Potts takes issue with the movement toward legalizing active euthanasia on a variety of grounds, including its impact on research and the development of curative treatment, its diminution of patient hope for cure, the difficulties of oversight and regulation, the danger of abuse and the extension of voluntary euthanasia toward nonvoluntary, the increase of various psychological pressures on both patients and physicians, and the long-term negative cost-benefit impact on health care. In addition, Potts fears that an institutionalized right to die may mistakenly evolve, in many cases, into a social expectation that patients have a duty to die.

[I am opposed] to any attempt to institutionalise euthanasia . . . because the risks of such institutionalisation are so grave as to outweigh the very real suffering of those who might benefit from it.

Risks of Institutionalisation

Among the potential effects of a legalised practice of euthanasia are the following:

1. Reduced Pressure to Improve Curative or Symptomatic Treatment If euthanasia had been legal forty years ago, it is quite possible that there would be no hospice movement today. The improvement in terminal care is a direct result of attempts made to minimise suffering. If that suffering had been extinguished by extinguishing the patients who bore it, then we may never have known the advances in the control of pain, nausea, breathlessness and other terminal symptoms that the last twenty years have seen.

Some diseases that were terminal a few decades ago are now routinely cured by newly developed treatments. Earlier acceptance of euthanasia might well have undercut the urgency of the research efforts which led to the discovery of those treatments. If we accept euthanasia now, we may well delay by decades the discovery of effective treatments for those diseases that are now terminal.

2. Abandonment of Hope Every doctor can tell stories of patients expected to die within days who surprise everyone with their extraordinary recoveries. Every doctor has experienced the wonderful embarrassment of being proven wrong in their pessimistic prognosis. To make euthanasia a legitimate option as soon as the prognosis is pessimistic enough is to reduce the probability of such extraordinary recoveries from low to zero.

3. Increased Fear of Hospitals and Doctors Despite all the efforts at health education, it seems there will always be a transference of the patient's fear of illness from the illness to the doctors and hospitals who treat it. This fear is still very real and leads to large numbers of late presentations of illness that might have been cured if only the patients had sought help earlier. To institutionalise euthanasia, however carefully, would undoubtedly magnify all the latent fear of doctors and hospitals harbored by the public. The inevitable result would be a rise in late presentations and, therefore, preventable deaths.

4. Difficulties of Oversight and Regulation [Proposals to legalise euthanasia typically] list sets of precautions designed to prevent abuses. They acknowledge that such abuses are a possibility. I am far from convinced that the precautions are sufficient to prevent either those abuses that have been foreseen or those that may arise after passage of the law. The history of legal "loopholes" is not a cheering one: Abuses might arise when the patient is wealthy and an inheritance is at stake, when the doctor has made mistakes in diagnosis and treatment and hopes to avoid detection, when

From Stephen G. Potts, "Looking for the Exit Door: Killing and Caring in Modern Medicine," *Houston Law Review* 25 (1988), pp. 504–511. Reprinted with permission from the Houston Law Review.

insurance coverage for treatment costs is about to expire, and in a host of other circumstances.

5. Pressure on the Patient [Proposals to legalise euthanasia typically] seek to limit the influence of the patient's family on the decision, again acknowledging the risks posed by such influence. Families have all kinds of subtle ways, conscious and unconscious, of putting pressure on a patient to request euthanasia and relieve them of the financial and social burden of care. Many patients already feel guilty for imposing burdens on those who care for them, even when the families are happy to bear that burden. To provide an avenue for the discharge of that guilt in a request for euthanasia is to risk putting to death a great many patients who do not wish to die.

6. Conflict with Aims of Medicine The pro-euthanasia movement cheerfully hands the dirty work of the actual killing to the doctors who, by and large, neither seek nor welcome the responsibility. There is little examination of the psychological stresses imposed on those whose training and professional outlook are geared to the saving of lives by asking them to start taking lives on a regular basis. Euthanasia advocates seem very confident that doctors can be relied on to make the enormous efforts sometimes necessary to save some lives, while at the same time assenting to requests to take other lives. Such confidence reflects, perhaps, a high opinion of doctors' psychic robustness, but it is a confidence seriously undermined by the shocking rates of depression, suicide, alcoholism, drug addiction, and marital discord consistently recorded among this group.

7. Dangers of Societal Acceptance It must never be forgotten that doctors, nurses, and hospital administrators have personal lives, homes, and families, or that they are something more than just doctors, nurses, or hospital administrators. They are *citizens* and a significant part of the society around them. I am very worried about what the institutionalisation of euthanasia will do to society, in general, and, particularly, how much it will further erode our attachment to the sixth commandment. ["Thou shalt not kill."] How will we regard murderers? What will we say to the terrorist who justifies killing as a means to his political end when we ourselves justify killing as a means to a humanitarian end? I do not know and I daresay the euthanasia advocates do not either, but I worry about it and they appear not to. They need to justify their complacency.

8. The Slippery Slope How long after acceptance of voluntary euthanasia will we hear the calls for nonvoluntary euthanasia? There are thousands of comatose or demented patients sustained by little more than good nursing care. They are an enormous financial and social burden. How soon will the advocates of euthanasia be arguing that we should "assist them in dying"—for, after all, they won't mind, will they?

How soon after *that* will we hear the calls for involuntary euthanasia, the disposal of the burdensome, the unproductive, the polluters of the gene pool? We must never forget the way the Nazi euthanasia programme made this progression in a few short years. "Oh, but they were barbarians," you say, and so they were, but not at the outset.

If developments in terminal care can be represented by a progression from the CURE mode of medical care to the CARE mode, enacting voluntary euthanasia legislation would permit a further progression to the KILL mode. The slippery slope argument represents the fear that, if this step is taken, then it will be difficult to avoid a further progression to the CULL mode, as illustrated:

CURE The central aim of medicine
CARE The central aim of terminal care once patients are beyond cure
KILL The aim of the proponents of euthanasia for those patients beyond cure and not helped by care
CULL The feared result of weakening the prohibition on euthanasia

I do not know how easy these moves will be to resist once voluntary euthanasia is accepted, but I have seen little evidence that the modern euthanasia advocates care about resisting them or even worry that they might be possible.

9. Costs and Benefits. Perhaps the most disturbing risk of all is posed by the growing concern over medical costs. Euthanasia is, after all, a very cheap service. The cost of a dose of barbiturates and curare and the few hours in a hospital bed that it takes them to act is minute compared to the massive bills incurred by many patients in the last weeks and months of their lives. Already in Britain, there is a serious underprovision of expensive therapies like renal dialysis and intensive care, with the result that many otherwise preventable deaths occur. Legalising euthanasia would save substantial financial resources which could be diverted to more "useful" treatments. These economic concerns already exert pressure to accept euthanasia, and, if accepted, they will inevitably tend to enlarge the category of patients for whom euthanasia is permitted.

Each of these objections could, and should, be expanded and pressed harder. I do not propose to do so now, for it is sufficient for my purposes to list them as *risks*, not inevitabilities. Several elements go into our judgment of the severity of a risk: the *probability* that the harm in question will arise (the odds), the *severity* of the harm in question (the stakes), and the ease with which the harm in question can be corrected (the *reversibility*). The institutionalisation of euthanasia is such a radical departure from anything that has gone before in Western society that we simply cannot judge the probability of any or all of the listed consequences. Nor can we rule any of them out. There must, however, be agreement that the severity of each of the harms listed is enough to give serious cause for concern, and the severity of all the harms together is enough to horrify. Furthermore, many of the potential harms seem likely to prove very difficult, if not impossible, to reverse by reinstituting a ban on euthanasia.

Weighing The Risks

For all these reasons, the burden of proof *must* lie with those who would have us gamble by legalising euthanasia. They should demonstrate beyond reasonable doubt that the dangers listed will not arise, just as chemical companies proposing to introduce a new drug are required to demonstrate that it is safe as well as beneficial. Thus far, the proponents of euthanasia have relied exclusively on the compassion they arouse with tales of torment mercifully cut short by death, and have made little or no attempt to shoulder the burden of proving that legalising euthanasia is safe. Until they make such an attempt and carry it off successfully, their proposed legislation must be rejected outright.

The Right to Die and the Duty to Kill

The nature of my arguments should have made it clear by now that I object, not so much to individual acts of euthanasia, but to institutionalising it as a practice. All the pro-euthanasia arguments turn on the individual case of the patient in pain, suffering at the center of an intolerable existence. They exert powerful calls on our compassion, and appeal to our pity; therefore, we assent too readily when it is claimed that such patients have a *"right to die"* as an escape from torment. So long as the right to die means no more than the right to refuse life-prolonging treatment and the right to rational suicide, I agree. The advocates of euthanasia want to go much further than this though. They want to extend the right to die to encompass the right to receive assistance in suicide and, beyond that, the right to be killed. Here, the focus shifts from the patient to the agent, and from the killed to the killer, but, the argument begins to break down because our compassion does not extend this far.

If it is true that there is a right to be assisted in suicide or a right to be killed, then it follows that someone, somewhere, has a *duty* to provide the assistance or to do the killing. When we look at the proposed legislation, it is very clear upon whom the advocates of euthanasia would place this duty: the doctor. It would be the doctor's job to provide the pills and the doctor's job to give the lethal injection. The regulation of euthanasia is meant to prevent anyone, other than the doctor, from doing it. Such regulation would ensure that the doctor does it with the proper precautions and consultations, and would give the doctor security from legal sanctions for doing it. The emotive appeal of euthanasia is undeniably powerful; but it lasts only so long as we can avoid thinking about who has to do the killing, and where, and when, and how. Proposals to institutionalise euthanasia force us to think hard about these things, and the chill that their contemplation generates is deep enough to freeze any proponent's ardor. . . .

[One final objection to the institutionalisation of euthanasia] relates to another set out above (#5. Pressure on the patient). The objection turns on the concern that many requests for euthanasia will not be truly voluntary because of pressure on the patient or the patient's fear of becoming a burden. There is a significant risk that legalising voluntary euthanasia out of respect for the *right* to die will generate many requests for euthanasia out of a perceived *duty* to die. . . .

34. *Ask Your Ancestors and They Will Tell You**

Rabbi Daniel A. Roberts

Rabbi Daniel A. Roberts describes how looking more deeply into his own religious tradition for guidance on matters of living and dying changed his perspective dramatically on the issue of active euthanasia. Once a staunch advocate of euthanasia on the grounds of personal autonomy and overall utility, Roberts discovered in the Hebrew Bible and rabbinic literature that dying well involves more than the avoidance of pain; instead, it entails a recognition of the finitude of life itself. Human dignity is enhanced, therefore, not by asking others to participate in our death or by committing suicide, but by our sharing the reality of a loved one facing the close of life. The tradition to which Roberts directs our attention guides us to see that death with dignity means allowing our loved ones to die in the knowledge that they have been loved until the end and that those who cared for them most are at their side, not needlessly extending their lives but minimizing their pain and assuring them that they will not be forsaken as their life draws to an end.

The arguments of Dr. Jack Kevorkian, Derrick Humphery, and others have captivated the imagination and fear of the public. We have been sucked into believing that doctors and hospitals are conspiring to keep our loved ones alive in order to milk our pocketbooks and that to die with dignity we need "assisted suicide" or active euthanasia. Today, almost everyone who goes into a hospital or a nursing home is required to sign a "living will" indicating what level of care they would like to receive and at what point care should be stopped.

I, too, was one of those who was drawn into the idea that if I could no longer be a vibrant and active human being, my family should turn off the machines. I did not want my loved ones to keep me alive by artificial means. I feared becoming an economic burden to them, and I certainly detested the concept of lying in a hospital bed in a vegetative state. In fact, I once wrote my sons an impassioned plea requesting that should the time come that there was no chance of my returning to a full and active life, they should disconnect me from life-sustaining machines. I was an advocate and a devotee of this philosophy.

Of course, the questions I never answered for them were: When would that moment be? Which person or persons would decide that there was no chance of my returning to a full and active life? What did being a full and active human being really mean to me? I left my loved ones to their own recognizance and definitions. Would I be kept alive longer than I should be because they had some kind of unrealistic hope that I would return to good health? Would they pull the plug too quickly because they were worried that my lingering would eat into their inheritance? Would they let me remain connected to machines because psychologically they could not handle my dying? Would they want me out of the way because they were angry that I was taking so long to die?

Like many others, I had fallen victim to the "new" and the "logical" without carefully investigating what ancient resources tell us about care of the dying. We are certainly not the first civilization to wrestle with assisted suicide and/or deciding when an individual is no longer economically viable to society. We know of communities whose norm was to send their aged out onto a mountain or an iceberg to die. Why did the writers of the Bible and the Talmud[1] choose to prohibit such actions? Why not

*An exploration of Jewish texts from ancient to modern on the holiness of life, ethical dilemmas, and how life and death decisions are made.

From John Morgan (ed.), *Ethical Issues in the Care of the Dying and Bereaved Aged* (Amityville, NY: Baywood Publishing Company, 1996). Reprinted with permission from Baywood Press.

[1]A commentary on the Bible.

allow those who were a liability to the community to go off into the wilderness to die? The answers to such questions are found in our ancestors' concepts of living and dying.

We start our journey at the beginning. The Book of Genesis tells us that in the beginning, when God created man, He did so "in His own image" [1]. The idea that every human being was created in God's image was as much a revolutionary idea as the oneness of God or resting on the Sabbath. A different ideology had begun in which taking another's life was a violation of God's command. Other civilizations sacrificed children to their gods, but in Genesis 22, when God restrains Abraham from sacrificing Isaac, we learn that God neither wants nor needs us to do this. We deduce from this story that *any* human sacrifice is prohibited.

"You shall be holy as I, the Lord your God am holy" [2] is mandated in the Book of Leviticus. That is, we are to live a life of holiness. Say the rabbis, "To save a single human life is to save the whole world. To destroy a life is to destroy the whole world" [3]. The object of life in the ancient world of the Bible was to strive for holiness by distinguishing between the holy and the profane. This was the ideology behind *kashrut* (kosher dietary laws): "to make a difference between the unclean and the clean,[2] and between the living things that may be eaten and the living things that may not be eaten" [4].

Life was so precious in the eyes of the rabbis that every prohibition concerning the Sabbath, *kashrut*, or the holidays could be broken in order to save a life. For instance, although Jewish law traditionally forbids driving on the Sabbath, a Jew who refuses to drive a very sick person to the hospital on the Sabbath would violate Jewish law. It is interesting to note that prohibitions against murder, idolatry, or perverse sexuality are maintained—these exceptions reveal that although life *is* precious, the highest value is not always placed on it [5].

We read, "It is forbidden to strike another person, even if that person gives you permission to do so, because one has absolutely no authority over one's own body as to allow it to be struck" [6]. From this and other related sources it can be concluded that Jewish law would neither allow Shylock to collect the pound of flesh, nor Antonius to offer it, in as much as Antonius did not own his flesh in the first place. Our life and limb are entrusted to us by God, and we are

forbidden to neglect or misappropriate them any more so than can we abuse any other property entrusted to us for safekeeping. It is because God, and God alone, can give us life and limb that God alone may take them.

The medieval Christian thinker, St. Thomas Aquinas, expresses a similar view in *Summa Theologica*:

> It is altogether unlawful to kill oneself, for three reasons:
>
> **a.** Because everything naturally loves itself, the result being that naturally everything keeps itself in being. . . . Wherefore suicide is contrary to the inclination of nature.
>
> **b.** Because every man is part of a community and so, as such, he belongs to the community. Hence by killing himself, he injures the community.
>
> **c.** Because life is God's gift to man, and is subject to His power, Who kills and makes to live. Hence whoever takes his own life, sins against God, even as he who kills another's slave, sins against that slave's master. . . . For it belongs to God alone to pronounce sentence of death and life, according to Deuteronomy 32:39: "I will kill and I will make to live" (quoted in Cytron and Schwartz [6]).

The yardstick which the ancient Hebrews used to measure an action (including, of course, the treatment of the ill or infirm) was whether or not it promoted or profaned holiness. Rabbi Abraham Joshua Heschel writes:

> The test of a people is how it behaves toward the old. It is easy to love children. Even tyrants and dictators make a point of being fond of children. But the affection and care for the old, the incurable, the helpless are the true gold mines of a culture. . . .
>
> In our own days, a new type of fear has evolved in the hearts of men: the fear of medical bills. In the spirit of the principle that reverence for the old takes precedence over reverence for God, we are compelled to confess that a nation should be ready to sell, if necessary, the treasures from its art collection and the sacred objects from its houses of worship in order to help one sick man. . . . Is there anything as holy, as urgent, as noble, as the effort of the whole nation to provide medical care for the old?. . . .

---

[2]"Unclean and clean" are euphemisms for animals fit and forbidden for sacrifice.

The aged may be described as a person *who does not dream anymore*, devoid of ambition, and living in fear of losing his status. Regarding himself as a person who has outlived his usefulness, he feels as if he had to apologize for being alive [7, pp. 72–73].

What do we wish to accomplish in the current debate over assisted suicides? In the future, will the sick and the infirm, once diagnosed with cancer, Alzheimer's disease, or some other "fatal" disease, feel the need to apologize for being alive? Will they be made to feel that it is *incumbent* upon them to instruct others not to take heroic measures to prolong their lives? Are we to suggest a new norm: that when people become economic burdens to their families or the medical community we should encourage them to engage in assisted suicide?

In the seventeenth century, Rabbi Gur Aryeh HaLevi wrote, "It is natural for old people to be despised by the general population when they can no longer function as they once did, but sit idle and have no purpose. The commandment, 'Honor your father and your mother,' was given specifically for such a situation" [8]. The reader will note that the command is not to love one's parents, only to honor them. According to the Talmud, "A father endows his son with blessings of beauty, strength, riches, wisdom and length of years. . . . And just as the father endows the son with five things, so, too, is the son obliged in five things: to feed him and give drink, to clothe him, put on his shoes for him and lead him" [9]. The great philosopher Maimonides further elaborates, "But if the condition of the parent has grown worse, and the son is no longer able to endure the strain, he may leave his father or mother, go elsewhere, and delegate others to give to the parents proper care" [10]. Thus, realizing that it would be impossible to command people to love their parents, the rabbis understood that they could preserve the dignity of parents by ensuring that their children were *respectful* through their responsibility to financially sustain their parents. We deduce that it would be a violation of the commandment to honor one's parents to suggest that the life-prolonging machines be disconnected in order to preserve the capital of a parent as an inheritance.

Ultimately, underlying all questions concerning assisted suicides and/or the removal of life support is the issue of what meaning can be derived from sustaining a person's life as long as we can. Then we must ask if there are other meanings to the concept of ending life with "dignity."

The Psalmist long ago gave us insight into the great fears of the elderly, or for that matter, anyone terminally ill, when he wrote, "Do not cast me off in old age; when my strength fails do not forsake me" [11]. The fears of dying alone, of being cast off—in pain, incapacitated, and warehoused—are so great these days that people are willing to leave this world early to avoid these fears. Suicides of older adults are on the rise. Everyone has heard of older couples who have made a pact to commit joint suicide, and members of their families who have found them in each other's arms in the back seat of their car with the motor still running. Suicide among the elderly is a very serious problem and our society has not paid much attention to this phenomenon.

Consider how many of the readers of this chapter have parents or grandparents who live in another city or state. As much as you feel torn and troubled about becoming ill and needing care, and are concerned about how your family will provide it, *your* parents equally feel isolated and alone and fret as to who will take care of them. In our individualistic society of individualism, parents worry about becoming an economic and psychological burden to their children. Assisted suicides and "pulling the plug" become more and more plausible options.

Another underlying fear rages within our souls. Within our psyche there is an innate will to live. I have watched cancer patients racked with pain continue to get up each day even though the opportunity to commit suicide is available to them. Why, I ask myself, do they fight every day for life? I would suggest that in part it is their innate desire to live and in part because they still have hope. The power of hope has kept many alive. Nietzsche suggests that "He who has a why to live can bear with almost any how" (quoted by Gordon Allport in Preface to Frankl [12, p. 12]). What greater fear could the dying have but that their heirs, either not wanting to bear the burdens of care any longer or anxious to acquire their estate, will allow them to die "before their time." The thought races through the mind of the dying that his/her guardians, under pressure to preserve estates, might not take the aggressive actions required to continue life. Leon Kass in his article, "Death with Dignity and the Sanctity of Life," reminds us:

> There is nothing of human dignity in the
> process of dying itself—only in the way
> we face it: At its best, death with complete
> dignity will always be compromised by the

extinction of dignified humanity; it is, I suspect, a death-denying culture's anger about dying and mortality that expresses itself in the partly oxymoronic and unreasonable demand for dignity in death . . . insofar as we seek better health and longer life, insofar as we turn to doctors to help us get better, we necessarily and voluntarily compromise our dignity: Being a patient rather than an agent is, humanly speaking, undignified. All people, especially the old, willingly, if unknowingly, accept a whole stable of indignities simply by seeking medical assistance [13, p. 132].

The lesson to be learned from death is not that we should try to exit life as painlessly as possible; rather, dying is about how we cope with the knowledge that there is an end to life. The basic tenet of religion is to teach people how to cope, how to face life's tragedies, how to have hope in spite of a darkened vision of the world, and how to still treat others as human beings even as they lie on their death beds. Kass continues:

. . . a dignified human life is not just a lonely project against an inevitable death, but a life whose meaning is entwined in human relationships. We must stress again the importance for a death with dignity—as for a life with dignity—of dignified human intercourse with all those around us. Who we are to ourselves is largely inseparable from who we are to and for others; thus our own exercise of dignified humanity will depend crucially on continuing to receive respectful treatment from others. The manner in which we are addressed, what is said to us or in our presence, how our bodies are tended to or our feelings regarded— in all these ways, our dignity in dying can be nourished and sustained. Dying people are all too easily reduced ahead of time to "thinghood" by those who cannot bear to deal with the suffering or disability of those they love. Objectification and detachment are understandable defenses. Yet this withdrawal of contact, affection, and care is probably the greatest single cause of the dehumanization of dying. Death with dignity requires absolutely that the survivors treat the human being at all times as if full god-like-ness remains, up to the very end [13, p. 135].

Referring to the above in a footnote, Kass cites comments from New York attorney John F. Cannon:

If a person who is dying has ceased to be an agent and has been "attached to catheters, respirators, and suction tubes [that] hide the human countenance" or has "been swept off the stage and been abandoned by the rest of the cast," he can still respond virtuously to his awful predicament (in the former case, only if he is aware of it), and if he so responds, he can be said to have "lost" his dignity only in the sense that others have refused to grant it to him. He is no less "worthy" a person, but what he is "worthy of" has been withheld, or worse. Dignity, in other words, is something that is simultaneously earned and conferred.

From this perspective, to argue that assisted suicide or active euthanasia is a means to the end of "death with dignity" is to make the absurd claim that if I cannot maintain a "dignified attitude and conduct in the face of [my own] death," or if I manage to do that but it turns out to be too much to ask others to accord me the dignity my virtuous conduct deserves, killing me is somehow a way to let me die *with my dignity;* in the case of a loved one who is dying, it is to claim that if he is hopelessly racked by fear, pain and self-pity, or if the degree of courage he shows in the face of death merits more compassion and affection for him that I can bear to give, his *dignity,* and mine, will somehow be advanced by killing him [13, pp. 144–145].

Does asking others to participate in our death, or creating legal means for people to commit suicide, *really* advance human dignity? Is not dignity heightened more through people's actions on their death beds as they face death?

In defense of Kevorkian and others, some might cite Maimonides, who holds that one who ends the life of one whose disease is estimated by doctors to end in death within twelve months (a *terefah*) is not liable. Although this person cannot be tried by the courts, the rabbis assert that he will be tried by the heavenly tribunal. How could this be, especially when we will see further on that one is culpable if one even moves a person on his death bed? Rabbi Maurice Lamm, in a paper delivered at the First National Conference on Hospice for the Jewish Community explains, "It must be made clear, that the prohibition of fatally injuring a *terefah* is not a simple prohibition of murder, but a prohibition of fatal wounding through *chavalah*, a destructively intended injury. If the fatality was a consequence of an injury for constructive purposes, such as healing or relieving, it would not be considered *chavalah*" [14].

Joseph Caro in his influential code of law entitled *Shulhan Aruch* ("A Set Table"), completed in approximately 1564, instructs us how we are to act in the presence of a person whose death appears to be imminent (a *goses*[3]):

> A *goses* is to be considered alive in all respects. One does not tie his jaw, anoint him, purge him, stop up his orifices, remove his pillow, nor place him on sand, floor, or ground. One does not place a plate on his belly, nor a bit of salt. The announcement [of death] is not made, nor flute players and mourners hired. And one does not close his eyes until he has died. Anyone who closes another's eyes at the moment the *nefesh* (soul) is leaving has shed blood. One does not tear one's clothing, remove one's shoes, give a eulogy, or bring a casket into the house where the dying person is located until the person has died [15].

In other words, making plans for the funeral of a person while she/he is on the death bed would be a violation of Jewish law, for conceivably it could take away the dying's last vestige of hope. Bernie Siegel, in *Love, Medicine and Miracles* [16] and *Peace, Love and Healing* [17], demonstrates that as long as people have hope, they can extend the length and quality of their lives. What are the hopes that we can give a person in his last moments? "One could hope for less pain. . . . one could hope for the happiness of mate and children, for the family's continuation of the values that one taught" [15].

Is it proper to remove obstacles impeding death? Moses Isserles in a commentary to the *Shulhan Aruch* passage above, wrote:

> Thus, it is forbidden to accelerate a person's death. For example, one may not remove the pillow or mattress of a person who has been a *goses* for a long time and is unable to expire, on the grounds that some claim that the feath-

ers of certain birds can be the cause of this condition. Likewise, such a person is not to be moved, and it is forbidden to put the keys to the house under the head of a person in this state in order to cause the person to expire. However, if something is present which is preventing the *nefesh* from leaving, e.g., the sound of pounding near the house as is made by a woodcutter, for instance, or if there is salt on the person's tongue,[4] and these things are preventing the *nefesh* from leaving, it may be removed inasmuch as this does not constitute an act in and of itself beyond removal of the impediment [18].

As we can see from above, one prolongs living but not dying. There is a fine line between actively causing another's death and the passive euthanasia that allows us to comfort the dying and not aggressively work to prevent their death. The distinction rests upon our own philosophy of dying. If we are comfortable allowing our beloved to slip peacefully into the next world then we can assist them in dying. That is, we can assure them that we will do everything to alleviate their fears: we will not allow them to die alone,[5] we will relieve their pain to the best of our abilities even if it means administering addictive drugs, and we will not cause their death before their time. Yet, neither will we do anything heroic that would delay their anguish. In addition, it would be important not only to tell them of our feelings for them, and that we will miss them, but that even while they are on their death bed, the manner in which they handle this sacred moment will be a learning experience for us as a model for our own dying moments. Victor Frankl, the famed logotherapist and author of *Man's Search for Meaning,* put it well:

> We must never forget that we may also find meaning in life even when confronted with a hopeless situation, when facing a fate that cannot be changed. . . . for what then matters is to bear witness to the uniquely human potential at its best, which is to transform a personal tragedy into a triumph [12].

---

[3]A time span of no longer than three days. This in contrast to a *terefah,* one whose disease is estimated by doctors to end in death within twelve months.

[4]"Salt on his tongue." A belief that salt on a dying person's tongue slowed down the dying process probably originated in the observation that salt's power to preserve various foods might also work to preserve life as well.

[5]When a person is in his last moments one is to bring a *minyan* (a religious quorum) to his bedside so that he dies with people around him.

Even on one's deathbed it is important and meaningful to know that one is having an impact on another's life. That is the true definition of dignity in death.

In the Talmud it is written, "Respect an old man who lost his learning: remember that the fragments of the tablets broken by Moses were preserved alongside the new" [19]. It is our sacred trust to care for both the old and the new, to make both feel as if they were holy, for indeed from the very beginning both were created in God's image.

Norman Cousins summarizes the care we must give to the dying most eloquently in *The Anatomy of an Illness:*

> Death is not the ultimate tragedy of life. The ultimate tragedy is de-personalization—dying in an alien and sterile area, separated from the spiritual nourishment that comes from being able to reach out to a loving hand, separated from a desire to experience the things that make life worth living [20].

The concept of death with dignity must be conceived differently: as allowing our beloved to die with the knowledge that we will be with them, that we will minimize their pain, that we will not take heroic measures to extend their life beyond their allotted time, nor will we do anything to shorten it as long as there is hope. This would then truly be death with dignity and with love.

References

1. *Genesis,* 1:27, 9:6.

2. *Leviticus,* 19:2.

3. *Sanhedrin, 37a.*

4. *Leviticus,* 11:47.

5. *Talmud,* Yoma, 85b.

6. B. Cytron and E. Schwartz, *When Life is in the Balance: Life and Death Decisions in the Light of the Jewish Tradition,* United Synagogue of America, Department of Youth Activities, New York, 1986.

7. A. J. Heschel, *The Insecurity of Freedom,* Schocken Books, New York, 1972.

8. G. A. HaLevi, (17th century), Commentary on the Fifth Commandment, in *Voices of Wisdom: Jewish Ideals and Ethics for Everyday Living,* F. Klagsbrun (ed.), Pantheon Books, New York, 1980.

9. *Talmud,* Mishna Eduyot, 2:9.

10. Maimonides, Laws Concerning Rebels, *Maimonides' Code,* Ch. 6, Section 10.

11. *Psalms 71:9.*

12. V. Frankl, *Man's Search for Meaning,* Washington Square Press, New York, 1969.

13. L. R. Kass, Death with Dignity and the Sanctity of Life, in *A Time to be Born and a Time to Die,* B. Kogan (ed.), Aldine de Gruyter, New York, 1991.

14. M. Lamm, *The Fundamental Jewishness of Jewish Hospice,* paper delivered at the First National Conference on Hospice for the Jewish Community, June 13, 1984.

15. J. Caro, *Shulhan Aruch, Yoreh De'ah* 339, 2, 1564.

16. B. Siegel, *Love, Medicine and Miracles,* Harper & Row, New York, 1986.

17. B. Siegel, *Peace, Love and Healing,* Harper & Row, New York, 1989.

18. M. Isserles, *Mapah to Shulhan Aruch, Yoreh De'ah* 339.

19. *Berakhot, 8b.*

20. N. Cousins, *Anatomy of an Illness,* Norton, New York, 1979.

35.   A "Natural Law" Reconsideration of Euthanasia

LISA SOWLE CAHILL

Lisa Sowle Cahill, drawing on elements in the Roman Catholic moral tradition, focuses her attention on the notion of totality and arrives at a conclusion that permits the active taking of life only in the most extreme of circumstances. Cahill explains that full, embodied humanness entails not only a physical dimension, but also a spiritual dimension, which she defines as our capacity to relate to others in love. In the face of imminent death and the complete and irremedial loss of that dimension of our humanness, a moment may arrive at which the taking of the patient's physical life, though a last resort, may be morally justified as a good for the whole person without diminishing our personal and communal respect for the sanctity of life.

Respect for the value of human life and care for its preservation in a state of physical well-being have traditionally motivated the practice of medicine in Western societies. Because of the relatively recent but very rapid advancement of medical technology, it has become commonplace to observe that the proper affirmation of that respect and the adequate fulfillment of that care are perplexing ethical issues. It is often no easy matter for the physician to determine how best to honor his obligation "to render service to humanity with full respect for the dignity of man."[1]

Some of the moral uncertainty which surrounds our current perceptions of the relation of the sick to the healthy (especially to members of the health care professions) and to alternative courses of treatment, might be alleviated by careful reflection upon the meaning of "the sanctity of life" and its implications for action. Difficult questions about life and death ought to be considered in light of the totality of the human person to whom this principle has reference. Biological life is said to be "sacred" because it is a fundamental condition of human meaning. But physical existence is not an *absolute* value for the human person. What are some conflict situations in which other values are foremost? What kinds of acts are compatible both with respect for life and with the recognition that it is not an absolute? Ought direct euthanasia or "mercy-killing" always to

be excluded from such acts, even in cases of severe terminal suffering or permanent unconsciousness?

The conviction that human life has a value and commands respect not comparable to that of lower forms of life can be expressed variously and rests upon a broad base of support from diverse ethical traditions. The Judaeo-Christian communities have endorsed the principle of the sanctity of life because it is consistent with a religious belief in a God who creates and preserves human life, and Who imposes a moral obligation of life to life, consisting in its preservation and protection. The Roman Catholic tradition of Christianity in particular has attempted in the realm of medical ethics to supply this rather abstract principle with appropriate moral content. Only God has full "dominion" or right of control over human life; man's dominion over his own life is limited. "God is the creator and master of human life and no one may take it without His authorization."[2] Although religious belief in a Divine Maker Who loves and sustains personal life provides a strong warrant for respect, the principle of the sanctity of life can also be defended on philosophical grounds, by an appeal to common human experience. Many an atheistic or agnostic humanist would agree that since life is the fundamental and irreplaceable condition of the experience of all human values, it is a basic, or *the* basic, value and must not be destroyed without grave cause.[3]

In Catholic medical-moral theology, the principle of the sanctity of life has been affirmed not only because it is compatible with biblical anthropologies, but because it is part of the natural moral law. As such,

From *Linacre Quarterly*, Vol. 44 (February 1977), pp. 47–63. Reprinted with permission from the Linacre Institute.

it indicates a universal ethical obligation, known to all men and women, not to Christians only. In the natural law moral theology of Catholicism, the principle has been given two primary expressions, one negative and one positive. First, we may consider the negative prohibition of the violation or destruction of life, patterned on Thomas Aquinas's arguments against murder.[4] It is often formulated as, "It is always wrong directly to kill an innocent human being."[5] This has been the basis for the Church's stance against abortion (as murder) and euthanasia (as suicide or murder or both).[6] Second, we have the positive affirmation of respect for the integrity of human personhood, also rooted in Aquinas.[7] It is called "the principle of totality," the standard medical formulation of which proclaims the proper subordination of an organ to the good of the body as part to whole. This affirmation of the value of life has provided a framework within which to justify surgical mutilation of the body (e.g., excision of a diseased organ) in order to further its total well-being.[8] The intention of the principle of totality is to respect and safeguard the integrity and welfare of the whole human being.

The referent of the principle of totality has usually been the life of the human individual considered as a physical organism. However, it can be argued that the fullest meaning of this principle, as it is actually used by Catholic theologians writing on medical ethics, includes the subordination of the physical aspect of man to the whole "person" which also includes his spiritual aspect.

During his pontificate, Pius XII addressed himself repeatedly to contemporary problems of ethics confronting the medical professions. These teachings are significant both because they are expressions of "natural law" thinking about medical morality and because they were promulgated as authoritative (although not infallible) for members of the Catholic Church. The principle of totality is frequently used in Pius's analyses of the medical-moral issue of which he speaks, and it is his formulations of that principle which are most often invoked by Catholic theologians. Pius XII delivered a now well-known speech on medical research to the First International Congress of the Histopathology of the Nervous System convened in Rome on September 13, 1952. Therein he declared that since "the parts exist for the whole," it is true of any physical entity that "the whole is a determining factor for the part and can dispose of it in its own interest."[9] Therefore, "the patient can allow the individual parts to be destroyed or mutilated when and to the extent necessary for the good of his being as a whole."[10]

Consideration of the principle of totality in its abstract version leads us to ask whether the "totality" of a person's "being as a whole" can be adequately defined in terms of the "physical organism" here mentioned by Pope Pius XII. On the contrary, Catholic teaching does in fact provide a strong basis for describing human personhood as a totality which is essentially constituted by the integration of both physical and *spiritual* aspects. The Pope himself states in his encyclical *The Mystical Body of Christ* that "the whole of man" is not "encompassed within the organism of our mortal body."[11] Perhaps his most forthright statement on the matter is given in an address to the International College of Psychoneuropharmacology on September 9, 1958. Speaking of medical experimentation, the Pope affirmed that "there must be added to the subordination of the individual organs to the organism and its end the subordination of the organism itself to the spiritual end of the person."[12]

An expanded and perhaps more technical version of the Pope's view of human personhood is given in a 1958 address to a Congress of the International Association of Applied Psychology. The self is explicitly described as a "totality" having "parts." Says Pius, "We define personality as 'the psychosomatic unity of man in so far as it is determined and governed by the soul'. . . ."[13] Thus in an address to the International Union Against Cancer, in 1956, the Pope feels constrained to warn that "before anything else, the doctor should consider the whole man, in the unity of his person, that is to say, not merely his physical condition but his psychological state as well as his spiritual and moral ideals and his place in society."[14] The question to be asked is whether Pius's strong concern for the "whole man" is consistent with his absolute prohibition of euthanasia.[15] If the body is a "part" of the total person, are there any circumstances in which it may, through a direct act, be sacrificed for the good of the whole? This problem will bear reflection which goes beyond the past prohibitions of such acts.

Considering Life and Death

It is certainly essential to a Thomistic version of Roman Catholic moral theology to consider human life and death in view of the final end of the human person. Consequently, it would seem most inconsistent for any theologian who ostensibly stands within that tradition to interpret moral dilemmas according to a principle of human "totality" which neglects not only man's supernatural goal, but his natural goal of mature integration of body and spirit. It is this total human nature which contemporary Catholic theologians want to give its proper due in considerations of medical ethics. This concern is related specifically to the practice of medicine in the current *Ethical and Religious Directives for Catholic Health Facilities*, which maintains that a Catholic hospital has a "responsibility to seek and protect the total good of its patients." This good is not just a physical one. "The total good of the patient, which includes his higher spiritual as well as his bodily welfare, is the primary concern of those entrusted with the management of a Catholic health facility."[16] Kieran Nolan, a priest and theologian involved in pastoral care of the sick, reminds us that if euthanasia is to be morally acceptable, it must be a sign of "the deep Christian respect for the integrity of the individual."[17] According to the positive sense of the sanctity of life principle, the good of the totality of an individual's human personhood must be foremost in all deliberations about his welfare and the obligations of others to him in his living and his dying. As Nolan significantly puts it, "The Christian concern must be to provide for human survival and not for mere biological preservation."[18]

Why is it that the protection of biological life is usually considered to be an essential factor in respect for the whole human person? Both the negative and the positive versions of the sanctity of life principle express an insight into the human "right" to life and the concomitant human "duty" to protect it. An individual is not to be unjustly deprived of his life, and, furthermore, his total personal well-being is to be promoted. These insights are based on the judgment that life is the fundamental condition of all other human values and is therefore to be preserved itself insofar as it can ground those values. The foremost human value is the love of God achieved at least in part through love of other persons. This Christian view of the meaning of life as the condition of personal love has been given consistent expression in the context of Catholic medical ethics. Pius XII, in "The Prolongation of Life," mentions the ultimacy of a "higher, more important good," the good of love for God, over bodily life.[19] Thomas J. O'Donnell, S.J., observes that life as a "relative good" is valuable because it is a context for other values which contribute to the "absolute good," man's pursuit in charity of his supernatural end, God.[20] Recently, Richard A. McCormick, S.J., has employed a very similar line of argument in discussing the life prospects of defective newborn children. He states that

life is to be preserved only insofar as it can ground the highest human good of loving relationships with other persons. A meaningful life is one in which the individual has relational consciousness and is free from physical pain or suffering so severe that the sheer effort to survive distracts the person from the primary human good, love.[21]

Because the Christian affirms the transcendence of full human personhood over sheer biological existence, life is for him never an *absolute* value, a value to be salvaged at all costs. Sometimes continued life does not constitute a good for a certain individual because it cannot offer him the conditions of meaningful personal existence. Sometimes the continued life of an individual is incompatible with the preservation of other values which also claim protection. In such instances, the Christian does not deny that human life is a value to be respected. However, he realizes that under the finite and sinful conditions of historical moral choice, he is called upon responsibly to mediate between conflicting values and the rights and duties which are devolved from them. Occasions of moral choice do not always involve clear-cut issues and alternatives neatly organized into a hierarchy of ethical preferability.[22] While this does not remove from us the obligation to choose, it does forestall false confidence in the finality of particular moral judgments and in the ability of the moral agent to avoid responsibility for the undesirable consequences of a difficult moral choice. At times, decisions about life and death necessitate arbitration among competing values which cannot all be actualized in a given instance.

Classical examples of ethical dilemmas in which this reality must be acknowledged are war, self-defense, and capital punishment. In these three cases, the "right to life" of one individual conflicts with the right of another individual, or even of the community, to life itself, or to the pursuit of goods still more valuable than life, for which life may be sacrificed. If we recall the standard prohibition of killing, we will observe that each instance can be exempted from the range of the prohibition because the object of the act of direct killing can be said in some sense not to be "innocent."[23]

Even the lives of the innocent, however, are not absolutely inviolable goods. In consistence with its concern for the "total good" of the person, the Catholic moral tradition affirms that preservation of the life of even the just man is sometimes not the highest value to be maintained in a situation of conflict. It is clear, however, that in the past only indirect killing of the innocent has been considered to be justifiable. For instance, the martyr may allow his physical welfare to be negated in order to testify to the highest good of love for God in Christ. Here the individual permits (but does not directly cause) his own death in order to protect a greater value. The frequent distinction in medical ethics between "ordinary" means of life support (as mandatory) and "extraordinary" means (as elective) is given similar warrants. Death may be permitted (or "indirectly caused") by withholding treatments which do not serve the best interests of the patient. According to the current definition, a means is not obligatory if it is difficult to maintain or use, *or if it will probably not offer much benefit to the patient in terms of either quality or duration of life.* A treatment need not be used if it will not restore an individual's life to a state in which it can support the development of life's highest (spiritual) goods or which will prevent it from furnishing such support in the future.[24] On the other hand, a human life is indeed worth prolonging if it can provide an opportunity to enjoy forgetfulness of self in love of others. Personal relations are those for the sake of which life is to be sustained.

Direct/Indirect Causes of Death

When an innocent person is involved, an act of killing falls outside the sphere of efficacy of the sanctity of life prohibition if it may be described as "indirect."[25] The martyr neither wills nor directly causes his own death; it is an undesired consequence of his steadfast faith commitment. Similarly, to omit to provide extraordinary life support to a patient is not to directly cause his death, but to permit it to occur as a result of disease. The decision is made in light of the judgment that the active pursuit of life's continuation is not consistent with concern for and protection of the total welfare of that person. His right to life and the physician's concomitant duty to preserve it must, in this particular instance of conflict, be subordinated to his "right to die." Life for him no longer provides the sufficient conditions for the fruitful development of loving relationships, both with other humans, and through them, with God. When extraordinary or ultimately useless treatments are not used, recognition is given to the patient's right to be freed from physical and spiritual deterioration and suffering and to the physician's duty to care for his patient's physical wellbeing within the larger context of human personhood. This is not to say that the patient no longer has a right to life or that he

may be deprived of his life against his will or for the good of any other person or of society. Both the right to life and the right to death must be subsumed under the promotion of the welfare of the whole human person himself. In situations where the values of life and of death conflict, the patient or his proxy may prefer to exercise voluntarily the right to die as most appropriate to the patient's own total well-being.

"Respect" may be shown to a person both by acting in ways which express esteem for his or her dignity and by not acting in ways which express contempt for or indifference to his or her dignity. What does "respect for life" as an ethical principle now mean, demand, require in choices about death in medical practice? There is consensus in theological ethics (though perhaps not always in medicine) that respect for life does not always entail its indefinite prolongation. Sometimes respect is most adequately conveyed by a refusal to intervene or to continue intervention in the progress of the human organism toward biological death. This is the main argument of Pius XII in "The Prolongation of Life"; it is not a new one in Christian or philosophical ethics.

The "hard question" remains and at this juncture unrelentingly confronts us: Can respect ever mean *direct* intervention to end the life of a patient? (We now move from the consideration of the morality of an act of omission to that of one of commission, to use the technical language of moral theology.) It is clear that the magisterial Roman Catholic rejoinder to this specific question has been negative.[26] Life-sustaining treatments may be omitted, but death may not be hastened directly. It must now be asked whether this position in fact meets the test of consistency with other values explicitly upheld and protected by the Church, such as the value of the dignity and welfare of the whole human person.

It will be recalled that the sanctity of life principle in Catholic theology has been given two ethically normative expressions. Its prohibitive form supplies warrants for condemning voluntary euthanasia. Its affirmative form supplies warrants for respecting and promoting the integrity of the individual. But can both of these conclusions from the more generally valid principle of respect for life be observed together in every particular situation? Can the obligation not to cause death directly and the obligation to respect the goods and proper goals of human personhood ever be in conflict? If a conflict should arise in medical practice, which obligation should be given preference on the basis that it best fulfills the grounding principle of life's sanctity?

Let us consider a possible case, one which is very frequently mentioned in discussion of euthanasia because it appropriately frames decision-making about causing death in a context of personal agony, both for the performer and the recipient of the act. A patient with terminal cancer is in "the dying process."[27] The best medical judgment offers a prognosis of only a few days' life. He is undergoing extreme personal suffering, involving both physical and "spiritual" aspects. Bodily pain is intimately related to mental stress, to one's total outlook on life and to one's ability to make the most of biological existence as the condition for fully human meaning, centered on personal relationships. The physical pain of our patient cannot be effectively alleviated by the use of analgesics (this may be either because of the nature of his particular disease, or because of the state of medical practice in the locale in which he is receiving treatment). The integrity and maturity of personality which he has acquired as the goal of his lifetime thus far is slipping rapidly away as he endures the demoralizing experience of physical and mental deterioration. He acknowledges that the life which was once a good to him is now approaching its conclusion. He is reconciled to death and perhaps hopes for peace or joy in an existence beyond death. He requests that his physician hasten his progress toward death and out of his unbearable suffering. He asks that this be done not only out of mercy, but out of respect for his claim to freedom from severe threats to his personal integrity and to the achievement without undue delay of the appropriate goal of this now dying life.

The first objections which will be raised against a physician's compliance with this request will be directed at the very possibility of describing a case in these terms. Some will argue that there is always chance of a wrong diagnosis; examples are recounted of "miracle recoveries" in which an unexplained remission ensued upon the diagnosis of a "hopeless case" of cancer. Anyone who reflects upon human moral experience must grant the fallibility of all creaturely decision-making. Human persons must act, nonetheless, on the basis of strong probabilities, acknowledging that while outside possibilities do exist, they do not provide a reasonable basis for action in the face of far more persuasive evidence.

Other Objections

Others may object that no human being ever has a true desire to die and, with the assistance of a supportive medical team and family, will cherish even the last few hours of his or her existence. Elisabeth Kübler-Ross, M.D., has offered plentiful evidence on the basis of clinical experience that terminal patients are able to achieve acceptance of and readiness for death.[28] When this information is combined with an appreciation of the fact that critical suffering cannot in all circumstances be alleviated, one is able to envision more readily a patient who desires death after he has realistically assessed his prospects for human fulfillment during the short span left to him. Although most patients may be able to live meaningfully even during terminal illness, this does not negate the responsibility to consider the situation of the one who is not able to do so.

The moral character of such a case, admittedly exceptional in medical practice, may be examined in terms of the two expressions of the sanctity of life principle. The first furnishes the traditional prohibition, which describes voluntary euthanasia as a direct act to kill a man (oneself or another) who is "innocent."[29] If one views the moral act through the lens of this principle, the only legitimate killing is that in which either the term "direct" does not apply to the act, or the term "innocent" does not apply to the object of euthanasia.[30] This is certainly not to say that a dying patient is "guilty." The real question to be considered is whether the context of innocence and guilt is an appropriate one within which to ponder the moral character of voluntary euthanasia.

How ought we to interpret the negative phrasing of the natural law command to protect the individual's right to life? In Thomas, the adjective "innocent" refers primarily to the man who is "righteous" in the sense that he has *not forfeited* his right to life so that he may be deprived of it by lawful authority. To have lost one's innocence means to have injured the common good.[31] Thus the command not to kill the innocent seems fundamentally to be a prohibition against the deprivation of another's life against his will, unless that other has somehow forfeited his right to protection. The phrasing of this prohibition envisions correlative exceptions such as war, capital punishment, and self-defense. The terms of the prohibition make an awkward context within which to approach suicide and euthanasia, where the "innocent" person is willing.[32]

More importantly, since in the latter cases the argument is made that death is in the better interests of the person, the language of "innocence" vs. guilt, forfeiture, and deprivation is not really applicable. The "innocent" man is one whose rights, among them the "right to life," must be respected. What about another right also belonging to the "righteous man" leading a God-oriented moral life, the "right to death"? Sometimes this right contravenes the importance of the first right. When this is so, it makes little sense to apply the word "innocent" out of its original context of forfeiture and punishment. The individual may be "innocent" in the sense of "legally or morally blameless," but what is the moral relevance of this fact?

It can be granted that the dying individual is innocent. However, it is the duty of those who care for and about him to consider that with which he has a right to be provided, as well as that of which he has a right not to be deprived. There may exist a positive duty to support his desire to die, *if* no conflict exists with other overriding rights and duties. The central problems are deciding, first, whether the duty to sustain life or the duty to end life is in the concrete case more important, and second, what are the morally legitimate means of upholding the predominant right. In care of the sick, the obligation to prolong life is foremost *until* that point at which an individual's life no longer offers to him or her the opportunity to nurture relationships as life's central endeavor. It has traditionally been granted that "hopeless cases" have, in such circumstances, a right to die which it may be the duty of others to support by withholding or withdrawing extraordinary means of treatment. Can the right to die ever justify direct killing? Does a terminal patient have a right to death which in some cases entails a duty on the part of those entrusted with his care to hasten positively its arrival?

Principle of Life's Sanctity

This brings the discussion to the affirmative expression of the principle of life's sanctity. What does it mean to respect and protect the life of a dying person? First, Kieran Nolan has remarked that a patient in the last phases of a terminal illness may be said to be oriented toward death as the appropriate goal of his existence, just as the healthy are appropriately oriented toward continued life.[33] Death is also the natural end of the biological organism. Although the death of a human as a personal being is not a good in itself, it still may be understood as a mediate and necessary goal of the Christian in his hope for eternal life in God. Secondly, the terminal patient who may be a candidate for euthanasia is one who is suffering both physically and spiritually or even "morally" in the sense of proximity to sin. In the first place, personal integration is threatened with degeneration. Physical pain, accompanied

by mental exhaustion or sedation, often makes it difficult to sustain a vital concern for the needs of loved family members and friends. Furthermore, as Pius XII has stated, "suffering can also furnish occasion for new faults."[34] Nolan concurs that prolonged physical and mental torment can conduce to rebellion against God or despair.

Death for the Christian is never an unambiguous good, but it is sometimes a lesser evil than the evil of suffering, and is for the Christian a good in a limited but positive sense.[35] If in the light of these considerations, it is agreed that death is a good for a particular suffering and dying patient here and now, and if death will not follow quickly if treatment is ended, then can voluntary euthanasia ever constitute a legitimate moral option? From the evidence thus far (evidence which must be verified in every case from consideration of the situation of a particular individual), it would seem so. Life is not a value to be preserved absolutely. Sometimes it must yield to greater values. If death is for this person the better alternative, there exists sufficient reason for causing it.[36] Deliberately caused death is not so great an evil that it can never be outweighed by greater goods.

The usual and most well-founded argument against voluntary euthanasia in even exceptional cases is made in terms of social consequences. It is not based on the alleged immorality of the individual act. The act itself may be conceded to result in desirable consequences for the patient, consequences which it would, in fact, be the responsibility of others to hasten directly, were it not for the evil long-range effects of such an act. However, it is argued that it is wrong to commit any act which, while good in itself, would lead to eventual consequences whose evil character would be disproportionate to the initial good. This venerable rejoinder is called the "wedge argument," a contemporary proponent of which is Richard McCormick.[37]

McCormick agrees with those who are convinced that "the direct causing of death involves dangers, especially for the living, not associated with conservative procedures. . . ."[38] Thus he gives a "prudential validity" to a rule against euthanasia of a "virtually exceptionless" sort. Direct killing as a premoral evil would be justified were there sufficient reason, but the reasons in favor of euthanasia in concrete cases are outbalanced by the reasons against instituting euthanasia as a general practice. McCormick believes that an immediate act, perhaps morally justifiable "in itself," is to be refrained from because of consequences such as an attitudinal decrease in mercy and sensitivity on the part of the hospital staff, or the ambiguities inherent in the procedures of ascertaining consent, etc.

This argument is a forceful one, but it need not signal the end of the discussion. Although McCormick has enumerated real dangers, he has not eradicated the problem with which any proposed wedge argument must deal, i.e., whether the long-term effects of an act ought to have the same moral importance as the immediate effects of an act. In cases where the latter are very certain and unavoidable, the former may be relatively uncertain because further moral choices (by others who share responsibility) will have to intervene in order either to actualize or to prevent the anticipated danger.

Traditional Catholic morals have held that it is always wrong to cause a moral evil in order to achieve a moral good or to prevent another moral evil even if it is greater. We also have a responsibility to try to avoid even that moral evil for which we are not directly responsible. Some ethicists have suggested that, at least in some cases, to refuse to hasten the death of a grossly suffering terminal patient is to permit, if not cause, in extreme cases, a moral evil—the despair of the dying man or woman.[39] Even in less severe cases, there is frequently present the clear spiritual, or personal, evil of mental enervation and distress, and of inability to escape the circle of suffering which encloses and limits all efforts to transcend oneself in concern for others. This is not moral evil in the sense of sin, but it is a clear disvalue for the whole human person as composed of both body and "spirit." It is a violation of the purpose and meaning of human existence.

Aquinas distinguishes between a certain and an uncertain moral evil; there exists a greater responsibility to avoid the former than the latter.[40] In the case of euthanasia, there are two possible dangers of moral evil, that to the patient if the act is not performed, and that to future generations if it is performed. In addition, there is the more realistic threat to personality, or fully personal spirit, not to mention the physical evil of bodily degeneration. Does the avoidance of an uncertain future evil actually constitute a proportionate reason for permitting a present evil, which, while of much narrower scope, is of much greater certainty? Is the failure to avoid an immediate moral evil, such as a loss of faith in the ultimate meaning of life, *or even* excruciating and prolonged spiritual and physical evil, such as conscious suffering or unconscious degeneration, sufficiently justified by the "proportionate reason" of avoidance of the danger (not the certainty) of future moral evil? In fact, this future evil seems more than the present one to be described most accurately

as "permitted" rather than "caused." This is to say that our moral responsibility for the attitudes toward death of future physicians, etc., is more indirect than is our responsibility for the total personal distress (moral, mental, and physical) of our neighbor suffering here and now and immediately dependent upon our care.

I believe the usual criticism of the wedge argument has force against its use in the condemnation of euthanasia. The opposing contention is that each act must be judged right or wrong primarily *in itself* and only secondarily in its relation to other acts. "In itself" does indeed include effects, and it is admittedly difficult to draw a line around the more "immediate" ones. But the range of effects of an act cannot be extended indefinitely or the very meaning of a discrete "occasion of moral choice" is dissipated to the point of disappearance.

In addition, the social effects of the wedge will more likely be cut short where there is a standard by which to differentiate the first case from other similar but morally distinct cases.[41] The stipulation that a candidate for euthanasia be "in the dying process" is such a standard, and a relatively clear one, though its application is not in every case entirely unambiguous. There is a marked difference between euthanasia for those dying and in pain and euthanasia for the sick but not dying, for the socially useless, for the insane, etc., which can be judged by a relatively objective standard. Where such a criterion is available we must at least say that the "future danger" becomes more "uncertain." Another standard is the one McCormick offers as a justification for permitting death to occur, that of relational consciousness. Such a standard might apply also to the patient with a grossly damaged neocortex, whose vital functions are still maintained spontaneously by the brainstem. The prolonged and meaningless physical deterioration of a permanently comatose individual can be construed as an insult to his or her total personhood. In such a case, as well as that of the dying person, euthanasia may present a viable moral option. Once a patient is in the terminal stage of a fatal illness or is permanently comatose, it may become evident that his or her life is past the point of possible restoration to a quality which would support significant pursuit of the highest human values.

Christian Respect for Life

This discussion of moral responsibilities of and toward the dying does not represent a comprehensive grasp of the problem but rather an indication of appropriate ways to think about it. Through a consideration of Christian respect for the sanctity of human life, which is ultimately a concern for the good of the total person, I have tried to indicate that some relatively limited number of cases may constitute an arena of moral choice about euthanasia.[42] Life can fail to constitute a sufficient condition for the fulfillment of human value in either the presence of gross suffering or the absence of consciousness. These circumstances are predictably permanent if one is in the dying process or is irretrievably brain-damaged. It is at this point that the prospect of a choice about euthanasia arises. Such choices would involve only terminal or comatose patients for whom it is impossible to continue to pursue those human values for which the Creator intended life to serve as the condition. Every such choice must be informed by an authoritative respect for the dignity of human life as God's image and by the intent to protect that dignity. It is essential to remember that no such choices can be free from ambiguity, since death is never an unambiguous good. In particular, it is necessary to repudiate any attempt to define circumstances in which there always exists a moral obligation to perform an act of euthanasia. There is no definable "class" of patients for whom euthanasia is the only morally responsible alternative.

Most importantly, it must be made clear that there weighs on the community of fellow human beings, of which the dying patient is a member, the obligation to exhaust every resource in an effort to make the last phase of that patient's life positively meaningful. This obligation especially impinges upon the Christian, if love is in any sense to be taken as normative for conduct. At least it must be conceded that euthanasia ought always to be a final resort, not an option to be considered before all others have been explored. It goes without saying that such a stipulation ensures that authentic candidates for euthanasia will be few. We may say with confidence that euthanasia would be morally wrong where it is an act which deprives an individual of a real opportunity to live within self-offering relationships to others. In such a case, euthanasia would not be in the best interest of the patient, since life could be of further value *to him* or *her.*

In general, euthanasia is to be avoided or rejected on the basis of what is commonly termed "the sanctity of life principle." Human life has an inherent claim to respect. In certain circumstances, however, other considerations come into play which may influence persons to manifest respect by causing death. Life may cease, in some sense, to be a "good." It may inhibit or prevent the pursuit of human values instead of providing conditions conducive to their fulfillment. In addition, the continuation and development of a personal life history may lose considerable weight as a real alternative among others if terminal illness promises to critically abbreviate the life in question. A positive "choice" to end life in such a case is not a choice of significant continuation of life or of death but a choice of immediate death or of a wait for impending death. In such situations, the positive value of death may gain the ascendancy over the negative value, although both are always co-present. It must be said that euthanasia may not be justified because death is ever a value, right, or goal which can clearly cancel out the value of life. It must be said that euthanasia is never justified because the obligation of the living to the dying, or of the individual to attempt to live meaningfully, is ever ended.

In the resolution of these conflicts of value, the overriding concern must be the good of the patient himself or herself, who is the primary subject concerned. When conditions preclude the patient's voluntary selection of an option, that selection must be made on the basis of his or her own benefit and inferred interests. If these interests are assessed on the basis of a Christian anthropology which views the human being as a body-soul entity, then the primary consideration in life and death decisions in medical practice will be the good of the whole human person, not simply the perpetuation of physical existence.[43] Since the distinctive and controlling element of human nature is the personal self or spirit, then according to the principle of totality, the body which is a "part" may in some cases be sacrificed for the good of the "whole" body-soul entity. Even direct intervention as a final option will not necessarily entail diminishing communal protectiveness toward human life's sanctity, if death is encompassed reluctantly and with a profound (and Christian) reverence for the personal existence within which it is an event.

Endnotes

1. A.M.A., "Principles of Medical Ethics," *Journal of the American Medical Association,* 226 (1973), 137.

2. Kelly, Gerald, S.J., *Medico-Moral Problems* (St. Louis, 1958), p. 62.

3. For an extended discussion of the sanctity of life principle as a basis of consensus in matters of life and death, see Daniel Callahan, "The Sanctity of Life," *Updating Life and Death,* ed. Donald R. Cutler (Boston, 1968), pp. 181–250.

4. Aquinas, Thomas, *Summa Theologica*, II-II. Q 64, especially article 6.

5. *Cf.*, Kelly, pp. 62, 117.

6. *Cf.*, *Ethical and Religious Directives for Catholic Health Facilities* (St. Louis, 1971), Directives 10, 11, 28, 29.

7. Aquinas, *Summa*, I. Q 61, a5; II-II. Q 64. a 2, 5, 6, Q 65; I-II. Q 17. a 4, Q 2. a 8; and *Summa Contra Gentiles*, Book 3, Chapter 112.

8. Kelly, "The Morality of Mutilation," *Theological Studies*, 17 (1956), 322–344; *Medico-Moral Problems*, pp. 8–11, 246–248; "Pope Pius XII and the principle of Totality," *Theological Studies*, 16 (1955), 373–396. *Cf.*, *Ethical and Religious Directives for Catholic Health Facilities*, Directives 4, 5, 6, 33.

9. Pope Pius XII, "Moral Limits of Medical Research," *The Major Addresses of Pope Pius XII*, ed. Vincent A. Yzermans (St. Paul, 1961), I, 233.

10. *Ibid.*, p. 228.

11. Pope Pius XII, *The Mystical Body of Christ* (New York, 1943), p. 36.

12. Pope Pius XII, "Tranquilizers and Christian Morals," *The Pope Speaks*, 5 (1958), 8–9.

13. Pope Pius XII, "Applied Psychology," *The Pope Speaks*, 5 (1958), 10.

14. Pope Pius XII, "Cancer: A Medical and Social Problem," *The Pope Speaks*, 3 (1957), 48.

15. Pope Pius XII, *The Mystical Body of Christ*, p. 55; and "Anesthesia: Three Moral Questions," Address to a Symposium of the Italian Society of Anesthesiologists (1957), *The Pope Speaks*, 4 (1957), 48.

16. *Ethical and Religious Directives for Catholic Health Facilities*, pp. 3. 1.

17. Nolan, Kieran, O.S.B., "The Problem of Care for the Dying," *Absolutes in Moral Theology?*, ed. Charles Curran (Washington, D.C., 1968), p. 249.

18. *Ibid.*, p. 249.

19. Pope Pius XII, "The Prolongation of Life," An Address to an International Congress of Anesthesiologists (1957), *The Pope Speaks*, 4 (1958), 396.

20. O'Donnell, Thomas J., S.J., *Morals in Medicine* (Westminster, Maryland, 1959), pp. 71–72.

21. McCormick, Richard A., S.J., "To Save or Let Die," *America*, 30 (1975), 6–10.

22. *Cf.*, Karl Rahner, *The Christian of the Future* (West Germany, 1967), pp. 42–44, 62–63; McCormick, *Ambiguity in Moral Choice*, The 1973 Pere Marquette Theology Lecture (Milwaukee, 1973), p. 106.

23. *Cf.*, Aquinas, *Summa*, II-II. Q 40, Q 64. An individual may be killed who presents a grave *material* danger, even if he is not *morally* guilty of an intended offense against the rights of another. Examples are the killing of enemy soldiers in war and the killing of an insane person who threatens one's life.

24. Kelly, "The Duty of Using Artificial Means of Preserving Life," *Theological Studies*, 11 (1950). 204; Pope Pius XII, "The Prolongation of Life," p. 396; McCormick, "To Save or Let Die," p. 9. Such would be the theological justification for refusing or withdrawing treatments such as a respirator from patients whom responsible medical prognosis designates as "hopeless." The well-publicized case of Karen Ann Quinlan recently decided before the New Jersey Supreme Court is a case in point. Legal ramifications aside, Pius's address provides more than ample ethical justification for allowing death to occur by removing life-sustaining equipment. In general, "ordinary" means of life support (obligatory) are those which can be obtained and used without excessive expense, inconvenience, or difficulty or repugnance for the patient, and which offer a reasonable hope of benefit to his or her total condition.

25. Thomistic natural law morality uses the language of direct and indirect acts to define the degree of responsibility which the agent has for a particular moral act. Since a fully human act is one performed in the use of reason and free will, the agent is not fully responsible for any act to which he does not fully consent. For a standard definition of "indirect effect," see Kelly, *Medico-Moral Problems*, pp. 13–14.

26. *Cf.*, the prohibition of euthanasia by the Congregation of the Holy Office, December, 1940, cited in full by Kelly, *Medico-Moral Problems*, pp. 116–117.

27. Cavanagh, John R., M.D., describes the "dying process" as "the time in the course of an irreversible illness when treatment will no longer influence it. Death is inevitable." "Bene Mori: The Right of the Patient to Die with Dignity," *Linacre Quarterly*, 30 (1963), 65.

28. Kübler-Ross, Elisabeth, *On Death and Dying* (New York, 1969), *Questions about Death and Dying* (New York, 1974), and ed., *Death: The Final Stage of Growth* (Englewood Cliffs, New Jersey, 1975).

29. *Cf.*, Kelly, *Medico-Moral Problems*, pp. 117–118.

30. A case can also be made for the inapplicability of the word "direct." Space does not allow me to pursue that argument at length here. I will mention only that Aquinas defends killing in self-defense because, even though the act is directly willed and performed, the intention of the agent does not terminate in the death for its own sake, but in self-protection. Similarly, an act of euthanasia is "indirectly" intended (although directly performed) in that its final object is not the death of the patient for itself but for the sake of his protection from suffering.

31. Aquinas, *Summa*, II-II. Q 64. a 2, 6.

32. Direct voluntary euthanasia for the terminal patient is a subclass of suicide, but differs from suicide in general in that the end of the person's lifespan is imminent because of reasons beyond human control.

33. Nolan, p. 256.

34. Pope Pius XII, "Anesthesia: Three Moral Questions," p. 46.

35. Thomas Aquinas prohibits suicide in order to avoid suffering because he sees death as "the ultimate and most fearsome evil of this life" (II-II. Q 64, a 5. r. obj. 3). I cannot agree with this and do not think it is consistent with Thomas's own anthropology. St. Thomas states many times that a properly ordered view of human nature places the good of the spiritual aspect of man over that of the physical. Spiritual evils far outweigh bodily ones, even when the latter include death. (*Cf., Summa,* II-II. Q 25. a 7, 12, Q 26. a 4; *Summa Contra Gentiles,* Chapter 121.)

36. Aquinas has stated that "evil must not be done that good may come" (II-II. Q 64. a 5. r. obj. 3). But this is only true when the good violated by the "evil" act is equal to or greater than the good pursued. In *Ambiguity in Moral Choice* (p. 55), Richard McCormick has suggested that death may be caused directly for sufficient reason, since death is a physical and therefore a "premoral" evil. Life may be overriden by other goods. The only sort of evil which may never be directly caused is the spiritual and moral evil of sin. (McCormick himself does not find "proportionate reason" to justify euthanasia, not because causing death is an evil which outweighs all goods, but because he envisions disastrous social consequences of a policy of euthanasia.)

37. McCormick, "The New Medicine and Morality," *Theology Digest,* 21 (1973), 308–321. For a classical use of the "wedge argument" against euthanasia, see Joseph V. Sullivan, S.J., *The Morality of Mercy Killing* (Westminster, Maryland, 1950), pp. 54–55.

38. McCormick, "The New Medicine and Morality," p. 319.

39. Nolan, p. 257; Antony Flew, "The Principle of Euthanasia," *Euthanasia and the Right to Death,* ed. A. B. Downing (Los Angeles, 1970), p. 33; Joseph Fletcher, *Morals and Medicine* (Boston, 1954), p. 175; *cf.,* Daniel Maguire, *Death by Choice* (New York, 1974), p. 155; Pope Pius XII, "Anesthesia: Three Moral Questions," p. 46.

40. Aquinas, *Summa,* II-II. Q 64. a 5.

41. This is important, since the telling point in arguments for and against euthanasia (e.g., the present author in contrast to McCormick) is whether one believes that the future danger is so probable and so serious that it outweighs harm done or permitted in the present instance, or whether it in fact represents the "lesser evil." Such an estimation is more a product of moral insight into human nature and moral responsibility than of rational deduction with probative force. We can only hope to persuade the opposition, not dismantle it!

42. Of course, the practical medical and legal circumstances of such choices remain to be specified, an important task not easily to be accomplished.

43. Religious faith is not a necessary precondition for arguing that the total human person is more than physical existence. An atheist or agnostic might agree that human life has a spiritual dimension which transcends the body Even if the spirit is believed to die with the body, it may be the key element in one's concept of human dignity. Thus when living becomes destructive to personal integrity, one may have a right to die.

36. Active and Passive Euthanasia

JAMES RACHELS

In this essay, James Rachels argues that the distinction between killing and letting die, so regularly employed in discussions of active versus passive euthanasia, is a faulty one. As he points out, the American Medical Association supported the distinction in 1973 when it endorsed the withdrawal of unnecessary, extraordinary care for the prolonging of life when death was imminent, but refused to sanction the intentional and direct termination of life under similar circumstances. Rachels insists, however, that in both cases physicians aim to bring the patient's life to an end for humane reasons. He concludes, therefore, that the distinction between active and passive euthanasia lies only in the method employed by the physician and that when this distinction fails to be morally useful, active euthanasia may be seen as the preferable option for end-of-life care because it more effectively achieves the end in view.

The distinction between active and passive euthanasia is thought to be crucial for medical ethics. The idea is that it is permissible, at least in some cases, to withhold treatment and allow a patient to die, but it is never permissible to take any direct action designed to kill the patient. This doctrine seems to be accepted by most doctors, and it is endorsed in a statement adopted by the House of Delegates of the American Medical Association on December 4, 1973:

> The intentional termination of the life of one human being by another—mercy killing—is contrary to that for which the medical profession stands and is contrary to the policy of the American Medical Association.

> The cessation of the employment of extraordinary means to prolong the life of the body when there is irrefutable evidence that biological death is imminent is the decision of the patient and or his immediate family. The advice and judgment of the physician should be freely available to the patient and or his immediate family.

However, a strong case can be made against this doctrine. In what follows I will set out some of the relevant arguments, and urge doctors to reconsider their views on this matter.

To begin with a familiar type of situation, a patient who is dying of incurable cancer of the throat is in terrible pain, which can no longer be satisfactorily alleviated. He is certain to die within a few days, even if present treatment is continued, but he does not want to go on living for those days since the pain is unbearable. So he asks the doctor for an end to it, and his family joins in the request.

Suppose the doctor agrees to withhold treatment, as the conventional doctrine says he may. The justification for his doing so is that the patient is in terrible agony, and since he is going to die anyway, it would be wrong to prolong his suffering needlessly. But now notice this. If one simply withholds treatment it may take the patient longer to die, and so he may suffer more than he would if more direct action were taken and a lethal injection given. This fact provides strong reason for thinking that, once the initial decision not to prolong his agony has been made, active euthanasia is actually preferable to passive euthanasia, rather than the reverse. To say otherwise is to endorse the option that leads to more suffering rather than less, and is contrary to the humanitarian impulse that prompts the decision not to prolong his life in the first place.

Part of my point is that the process of being "allowed to die" can be relatively slow and painful, whereas being given a lethal injection is relatively quick

From *The New England Journal of Medicine*, vol. 292, no. 2, January 9, 1975, pp. 78–80. Copyright © 1975 Massachusetts Medical Society. All rights reserved. Reprinted by permission of the Massachusetts Medical Society.

and painless. Let me give a different sort of example. In the United States about one in 600 babies is born with Down's syndrome. Most of these babies are otherwise healthy—that is, with only the usual pediatric care, they will proceed to an otherwise normal infancy. Some, however, are born with congenital defects such as intestinal obstructions that require operations if they are to live. Sometimes, the parents and the doctor will decide not to operate, and let the infant die. Anthony Shaw describes what happens then.

> . . . When surgery is denied (the doctor) must try to keep the infant from suffering while natural forces sap the baby's life away. As a surgeon whose natural inclination is to use the scalpel to fight off death, standing by and watching a salvageable baby die is the most emotionally exhausting experience I know. It is easy at a conference, in a theoretical discussion, to decide that such infants should be allowed to die. It is altogether different to stand by in the nursery and watch as dehydration and infection wither a tiny being over hours and days. This is a terrible ordeal for me and the hospital staff—much more so than for the parents who never set foot in the nursery.[1]

I can understand why some people are opposed to all euthanasia, and insist that such infants must be allowed to live. I think I can also understand why other people favor destroying these babies quickly and painlessly. But why should anyone favor letting "dehydration and infection wither a tiny being over hours and days?" The doctrine that says that a baby may be allowed to dehydrate and wither, but may not be given an injection that would end its life without suffering, seems so patently cruel as to require no further refutation. The strong language is not intended to offend, but only to put the point in the clearest possible way.

My second argument is that the conventional doctrine leads to decisions concerning life and death made on irrelevant grounds.

Consider again the case of the infants with Down's syndrome who need operations for congenital defects unrelated to the syndrome to live. Sometimes, there is no operation, and the baby dies, but when there is no such defect, the baby lives on. Now, an operation such as that to remove an intestinal obstruction is not prohibitively difficult. The reason why such operations are not performed in these cases is, clearly, that the child

has Down's syndrome and the parents and doctor judge that because of that fact it is better for the child to die.

But notice that this situation is absurd, no matter what view one takes of the lives and potentials of such babies. If the life of such an infant is worth preserving, what does it matter if it needs a simple operation? Or, if one thinks it better that such a baby should not live on, what difference does it make that it happens to have an unobstructed intestinal tract? In either case, the matter of life and death is being decided on irrelevant grounds. It is the Down's syndrome, and not the intestines, that is the issue. The matter should be decided, if at all, on that basis, and not be allowed to depend on the essentially irrelevant question of whether the intestinal tract is blocked.

What makes this situation possible, of course, is the idea that when there is an intestinal blockage, one can "let the baby die," but when there is no such defect there is nothing that can be done, for one must not "kill" it. The fact that this idea leads to such results as deciding life or death on irrelevant grounds is another good reason why the doctrine should be rejected.

One reason why so many people think that there is an important moral difference between active and passive euthanasia is that they think killing someone is morally worse than letting someone die. But is it? Is killing, in itself, worse than letting die? To investigate this issue, two cases may be considered that are exactly alike except that one involves killing whereas the other involves letting someone die. Then, it can be asked whether this difference makes any difference to the moral assessments. It is important that the cases be exactly alike, except for this one difference, since otherwise one cannot be confident that it is this difference and not some other that accounts for any variation in the assessments of the two cases. So, let us consider this pair of cases:

In the first, Smith stands to gain a large inheritance if anything should happen to his six-year-old cousin. One evening while the child is taking his bath, Smith sneaks into the bathroom and drowns the child, and then arranges things so that it will look like an accident.

In the second, Jones also stands to gain if anything should happen to his six-year-old cousin. Like Smith, Jones sneaks in planning to drown the child in his bath. However, just as he enters the bathroom Jones sees the child slip and hit his head, and fall face down in the water. Jones is delighted; he stands by, ready to push the child's head back under if it is necessary, but it is not necessary. With only a little thrashing about, the child drowns all by himself, "accidentally," as Jones watches and does nothing.

Now Smith killed the child, whereas Jones "merely" let the child die. That is the only difference between them. Did either man behave better, from a moral point of view? If the difference between killing and letting die were in itself a morally important matter, one should say that Jones's behavior was less reprehensible than Smith's. But does one really want to say that? I think not. In the first place, both men acted from the same motive, personal gain, and both had exactly the same end in view when they acted. It may be inferred from Smith's conduct that he is a bad man, although that judgment may be withdrawn or modified if certain further facts are learned about him—for example, that he is mentally deranged. But would not the very same thing be inferred about Jones from his conduct? And would not the same further considerations also be relevant to any modification of this judgment? Moreover, suppose Jones pleaded, in his own defense, "After all, I didn't do anything except just stand there and watch the child drown. I didn't kill him; I only let him die." Again, if letting die were in itself less bad than killing, this defense should have at least some weight. But it does not. Such a "defense" can only be regarded as a grotesque perversion of moral reasoning. Morally speaking, it is no defense at all.

Now it may be pointed out, quite properly, that the cases of euthanasia with which doctors are concerned are not like this at all. They do not involve personal gain or the destruction of normal healthy children. Doctors are concerned only with cases in which the patient's life is of no further use to him, or in which the patient's life has become or will soon become a terrible burden. However, the point is the same in these cases: the bare difference between killing and letting die does not, in itself, make a moral difference. If a doctor lets a patient die, for humane reasons, he is in the same moral position as if he had given the patient a lethal injection for humane reasons. If his decision was wrong—if, for example, the patient's illness was in fact curable—the decision would be equally regrettable no matter which method was used to carry it out. And if the doctor's decision was the right one, the method used is not in itself important.

The AMA policy statement isolates the crucial issue very well; the crucial issue is "the intentional termination of the life of one human being by another." But after identifying this issue, and forbidding "mercy killing," the statement goes on to deny that the cessation of treatment is the intentional termination of a life.

This is where the mistake comes in, for what is the cessation of treatment, in these circumstances, if it is not "the intentional termination of the life of one human being by another?" Of course it is exactly that, and if it were not, there would be no point to it.

Many people will find this judgment hard to accept. One reason, I think, is that it is very easy to conflate the question of whether killing is, in itself, worse than letting die, with the very different question of whether most actual cases of killing are more reprehensible than most actual cases of letting die. Most actual cases of killing are clearly terrible (think, for example, of all the murders reported in the newspapers), and one hears of such cases every day. On the other hand, one hardly ever hears of a case of letting die, except for the actions of doctors who are motivated by humanitarian reasons. So one learns to think of killing in a much worse light than of letting die. But this does not mean that there is something about killing that makes it in itself worse than letting die, for it is not the bare difference between killing and letting die that makes the difference in these cases. Rather, the other factors—the murderer's motive of personal gain, for example, contrasted with the doctor's humanitarian motivation—account for different reactions to the different cases.

I have argued that killing is not in itself any worse than letting die; if my contention is right, it follows that active euthanasia is not any worse than passive euthanasia. What arguments can be given on the other side? The most common, I believe, is the following:

"The important difference between active and passive euthanasia is that, in passive euthanasia, the doctor does not do anything to bring about the patient's death. The doctor does nothing, and the patient dies of whatever ills already afflict him. In active euthanasia, however, the doctor does something to bring about the patient's death: he kills him. The doctor who gives the patient with cancer a lethal injection has himself caused his patient's death; whereas if he merely ceases treatment, the cancer is the cause of death."

A number of points need to be made here. The first is that it is not exactly correct to say that in passive euthanasia the doctor does nothing, for he does do one thing that is very important: he lets the patient die. "Letting someone die" is certainly different, in some respects, from other types of action—mainly in that it is a kind of action that one may perform by way of not performing certain other actions. For example, one may let a patient die by way of not giving medication, just as one may insult someone by way of not shaking his hand. But for any purpose of moral assessment, it is a type of action nonetheless. The decision to let a patient die is subject to moral appraisal in the same way that a decision to kill him would be subject to moral appraisal: it may be assessed as wise or unwise, compassionate or sadistic, right or wrong. If a doctor deliberately let a patient die who was suffering from a routinely curable illness, the doctor would certainly be to blame for what he had done, just as he would be to blame if he had needlessly killed the patient. Charges against him would then be appropriate. If so, it would be no defense at all for him to insist that he didn't "do anything." He would have done something very serious indeed, for he let his patient die.

Fixing the cause of death may be very important from a legal point of view, for it may determine whether criminal charges are brought against the doctor. But I do not think that this notion can be used to show a moral difference between active and passive euthanasia. The reason why it is considered bad to be the cause of someone's death is that death is regarded as a great evil—and so it is. However, if it has been decided that euthanasia—even passive euthanasia—is desirable in a given case, it has also been decided that in this instance death is no greater an evil than the patient's continued existence. And if this is true, the usual reason for not wanting to be the cause of someone's death simply does not apply.

Finally, doctors may think that all of this is only of academic interest—the sort of thing that philosophers may worry about but that has no practical bearing on their own work. After all, doctors must be concerned about the legal consequences of what they do, and active euthanasia is clearly forbidden by the law. But even so, doctors should also be concerned with the fact that the law is forcing upon them a moral doctrine that may well be indefensible, and has a considerable effect on their practices. Of course, most doctors are not now in the position of being coerced in this matter, for they do not regard themselves as merely going along with what the law requires. Rather, in statements such as the AMA policy statement that I have quoted, they are endorsing this doctrine as a central point of medical ethics. In that statement, active euthanasia is condemned not merely as illegal but as "contrary to that for which the medical profession stands," whereas passive euthanasia is approved. However, the preceding considerations suggest that there is really no moral difference between the two, considered in themselves (there may be important moral differences in some cases in their *consequences,* but, as I pointed out, these differences may make active euthanasia, and not passive euthanasia, the morally preferable option). So, whereas doctors may have to discriminate between active and passive euthanasia to satisfy the law, they should not do any more than that. In particular, they should not give the distinction any added authority and weight by writing it into official statements of medical ethics.

Endnotes

1. Shaw A.: 'Doctor, Do We Have a Choice?' *The New York Times Magazine,* January 30, 1972, p. 54.

37. Is There a Duty to Die?

John Hardwig

John Hardwig suggests that American culture has fostered the notion that persons possess unfettered autonomy and that this right to self-determination has been assumed to apply to the areas of life and death. More and more, it has been argued that persons have a right to choose to extend their lives as much as humanly possible or to end their lives at their own discretion. On the contrary, Hardwig insists that persons may, in some circumstances, have a moral requirement or duty that they consent to die for the sake of others. Hardwig lists a number of cost-benefit considerations that might impose the duty to die on an individual and argues that the recognition of such factors may serve to enhance, rather than to diminish, the meaning of one's life.

When Richard Lamm made the statement that old people have a duty to die, it was generally shouted down or ridiculed. The whole idea is just too preposterous to entertain. Or too threatening. In tact, a fairly common argument against legalizing physician-assisted suicide is that if it were legal, some people might somehow get the idea that they have a duty to die. These people could only be the victims of twisted moral reasoning or vicious social pressure. It goes without saying that there is no duty to die.

But for me the question is real and very important. I feel strongly that I may very well some day have a duty to die. I do not believe that I am idiosyncratic, morbid, mentally ill, or morally perverse in thinking this. I think many of us will eventually face precisely this duty. But I am first of all concerned with my own duty. I write partly to clarify my own convictions and to prepare myself. Ending my life might be a very difficult thing for me to do.

This notion of a duty to die raises all sorts of interesting theoretical and metaethical questions. I intend to try to avoid most of them because I hope my argument will be persuasive to those holding a wide variety of ethical views. Also, although the claim that there is a duty to die would ultimately require theoretical underpinning, the discussion needs to begin on the normative level. As is appropriate to my attempt to steer clear of

theoretical commitments, I will use "duty," "obligation," and "responsibility" interchangeably, in a pre-theoretical or preanalytic sense.[1]

Circumstances and a Duty to Die

Do many of us really believe that no one ever has a duty to die? I suspect not. I think most of us probably believe that there is such a duty, but it is very uncommon. Consider Captain Oates, a member of Admiral Scott's expedition to the South Pole. Oates became too ill to continue. If the rest of the team stayed with him, they would all perish. After this had become clear, Oates left his tent one night, walked out into a raging blizzard, and was never seen again.[2] That may have been a heroic thing to do, but we might be able to agree that it was also no more than his duty. It would have been wrong for him to urge—or even to allow—the rest to stay and care for him.

This is a very unusual circumstance—a "lifeboat case"—and lifeboat cases make for bad ethics. But I expect that most of us would also agree that there have been cultures in which what we would call a duty to die has been fairly common. These are relatively poor, technologically simple, had especially nomadic cultures. In such societies, everyone knows that if you manage to live long enough, you will eventually become old and debilitated. Then you will need to take steps to end your life. The old people in these societies regularly did precisely that. Their cultures prepared and supported them in doing so.

From *The Hastings Center Report*, 27, no. 2 (March 13, 1997), pp. 34–42. Reprinted with permission from The Hastings Center and the author.

Those cultures could be dismissed as irrelevant to contemporary bioethics; their circumstances are so different from ours. But if that is our response, it is instructive. It suggests that we assume a duty to die is irrelevant to us because our wealth and technological sophistication have purchased exemption for us . . . except under very unusual circumstances like Captain Oates's.

But have wealth and technology really exempted us? Or are they, on the contrary, about to make a duty to die common again? We like to think of modern medicine as all triumph with no dark side. Our medicine saves many lives and enables most of us to live longer. That is wonderful, indeed. We are all glad to have access to this medicine. But our medicine also delivers most of us over to chronic illnesses and it enables many of us to survive longer than we can take care of ourselves, longer than we know what to do with ourselves, longer than we even are ourselves.

The costs—and these are not merely monetary of prolonging our lives when we are no longer able to care for ourselves—are often staggering. If further medical advances wipe out many of today's "killer diseases"—cancers, heart attacks, strokes, ALS, AIDS, and the rest—then one day most of us will survive long enough to become demented or debilitated. These developments could generate a fairly widespread duty to die. A fairly common duty to die might turn out to be only the dark side of our life-prolonging medicine and the uses we choose to make of it.

Let me be clear, I certainly believe that there is a duty to refuse life-prolonging medical treatment and also a duty to complete advance directives refusing life-prolonging treatment. But a duty to die can go well beyond that. There can be a duty to die before one's illnesses would cause death, even if treated only with palliative measures. In fact, there may be a fairly common responsibility to end one's life in the absence of any terminal illness at all. Finally, there can be a duty to die when one would prefer to live. Granted, many of the conditions that can generate a duty to die also seriously undermine the quality of life. Some prefer not to live under such conditions. But even those who want to live can face a duty to die. These will clearly be the most controversial and troubling cases; I will, accordingly, focus my reflections on them.

The Individualistic Fantasy

Because a duty to die seems such a real possibility to me, I wonder why contemporary bioethics has dismissed it without serious consideration. I believe that most bioethics still shares in one of our deeply embedded American dreams: the individualistic fantasy. This fantasy leads us to imagine that lives are separate and unconnected, or that they could be so if we chose. If lives were unconnected, things that happened in my life would not or need not affect others. And if others were not (much) affected by my life, I would have no duty to consider the impact of my decisions on others. I would then be free morally to live my life however I please, choosing whatever life and death I prefer for myself. The way I live would be nobody's business but my own. I certainly would have no duty to die if I preferred to live.

Within a health care context, the individualistic fantasy leads us to assume that the patient is the only one affected by decisions about her medical treatment. If only the patient were affected, the relevant questions when making treatment decisions would be precisely those we ask: What will benefit the patient? Who can best decide that? The pivotal issue would always be simply whether the patient wants to live like this and whether she would consider herself better off dead.[3] "Whose life is it, anyway?" we ask rhetorically.

But this is morally obtuse. We are not a race of hermits. Illness and death do not come only to those who are all alone. Nor is it much better to think in terms of the bald dichotomy between "the interests of the patient" and "the interests of society" (or a third-party payer), as if we were isolated individuals connected only to "society" in the abstract or to the other, faceless members of our health maintenance organization.

Most of us are affiliated with particular others and most deeply, with family and loved ones. Families and loved ones are bound together by ties of care and affection, by legal relations and obligations, by inhabiting shared spaces and living units, by interlocking finances and economic prospects, by common projects and also commitments to support the different life projects of other family members, by shared histories, by ties of loyalty. This life together of family and loved ones is what defines and sustains us; it is what gives meaning to most of our lives. We would not have it any other way. We would not want to be all alone, especially when we are seriously ill, as we age, and when we are dying.

But the fact of deeply interwoven lives debars us from making exclusively self-regarding decisions, as the decisions of one member of a family may dramatically affect the lives of all the rest. The impact of my decisions upon my family and loved ones is the source of many of my strongest obligations and also the most plausible and likeliest basis of a duty to die. "Society," after all, is only very marginally affected by how I live, or by whether I live or die.

A Burden to My Loved Ones

Many older people report that their one remaining goal in life is not to be a burden to their loved ones. Young people feel this, too: when I ask my undergraduate students to think about whether their death could come too late, one of their very first responses always is, "Yes, when I become a burden to my family or loved ones." Tragically, there are situations in which my loved ones would be much better off—all things considered, the loss of a loved one notwithstanding—if I were dead.

The lives of our loved ones can be seriously compromised by caring for us. The burdens of providing care or even just supervision twenty-four hours a day, seven days a week are often overwhelming.[4] When this kind of caregiving goes on for years, it leaves the caregiver exhausted, with no time for herself or life of her own. Ultimately, even her health is often destroyed. But it can also be emotionally devastating simply to live with a spouse who is increasingly distant, uncommunicative, unresponsive, foreign, and unreachable. Other family members' needs often go unmet as the caring capacity of the family is exceeded. Social life and friendships evaporate, as there is no opportunity to go out to see friends and the home is no longer a place suitable for having friends in.

We must also acknowledge that the lives of our loved ones can be devastated just by having to pay for health care for us. One part of the recent SUPPORT study documented the financial aspects of caring for a dying member of a family. Only those who had illnesses severe enough to give them less than a 50 percent chance to live six more months were included in this study. When these patients survived their initial hospitalization and were discharged about one-third required considerable caregiving from their families; in 20 percent of cases a family member had to quit work or make some other major lifestyle change; almost one-third of these families lost all of their savings; and just under 30 percent lost a major source of income.[5]

If talking about money sounds venal or trivial, remember that much more than money is normally at stake here. When someone has to quit work, she may well lose her career. Savings decimated late in life cannot be recouped in the few remaining years of employability, so the loss compromises the quality of the rest of the caregiver's life. For a young person, the chance to go to college may be lost to the attempt to pay debts due to an illness in the family, and this decisively shapes an entire life.

A serious illness in a family is a misfortune. It is usually nobody's fault; no one is responsible for it. But we face choices about how we will respond to this misfortune. That's where the responsibility comes in and fault can arise. Those of us with families and loved ones always have a duty not to make selfish or self-centered decisions about our lives. We have a responsibility to try to protect the lives of loved ones from serious threats or greatly impoverished quality, certainly an obligation not to make choices that will jeopardize or seriously compromise their futures. Often, it would be wrong to do just what we want or just what is best for ourselves; we should choose in light of what is best for all concerned. That is our duty in sickness as well as in health. It is out of these responsibilities that a duty to die can develop.

I am not advocating a crass, quasi-economic conception of burdens and benefits, nor a shallow, hedonistic view of life. Given a suitably rich understanding of benefits, family members sometimes do benefit from suffering through the long illness of a loved one. Caring for the sick or aged can foster growth, even as it makes daily life immeasurably harder and the prospects for the future much bleaker. Chronic illness or a drawn-out death can also pull a family together, making the care for each other stronger and more evident. If my loved ones are truly benefiting from coping with my illness or debility, I have no duty to die based on burdens to them.

But it would be irresponsible to blithely assume that this always happens, that it will happen in my family, or that it will be the fault of my family if they cannot manage to turn my illness into a positive experience. Perhaps the opposite is more common: a hospital chaplain once told me that he could not think of a single case in which a family was strengthened or brought together by what happened at the hospital.

Our families and loved ones also have obligations, of course—they have the responsibility to stand by us and support us through debilitating illness and death. They must be prepared to make significant sacrifices to respond to an illness in the family. I am far from denying that. Most of us are aware of this responsibility and most families meet it rather well. In fact, families deliver more than 80 percent of the long-term care in this country, almost always at great personal cost. Most of us who are a part of a family can expect to be sustained in our time of need by family members and those who love us.

But most discussions of an illness in the family sound as if responsibility were a one-way street. It is not, of course. When we become seriously ill or debilitated, we, too, may have to make sacrifices. To think that my loved ones must bear whatever burdens my illness, debility, or dying process might impose upon them is to reduce them to means to my well-being. And that would be immoral. Family solidarity, altruism, bearing the burden of a loved one's misfortune, and loyalty are all important virtues of families, as well. But they are all also two-way streets.

Objections to a Duty to Die

To my mind, the most serious objections to the idea of a duty to die lie in the effects on my loved ones of ending my life. But to most others, the important objections have little or nothing to do with family and loved ones. Perhaps the most common objections are: (1) there is a higher duty that always takes precedence over a duty to die; (2) a duty to end one's own life would be incompatible with a recognition of human dignity or the intrinsic value of a person; and (3) seriously ill, debilitated, or dying people are already bearing the harshest burdens and so it would be wrong to ask them to bear the additional burden of ending their own lives.

These are all important objections; all deserve a thorough discussion. Here I will only be able to suggest some moral counterweights—ideas that might provide the basis for an argument that these objections do not always preclude a duty to die.

An example of the first line of argument would be the claim that a duty to God, the giver of life, forbids that anyone take her own life. It could be argued that this duty always supersedes whatever obligations we might have to our families. But what convinces us that we always have such a religious duty in the first place? And what guarantees that it always supersedes our obligations to try to protect our loved ones?

Certainly, the view that death is the ultimate evil cannot be squared with Christian theology. It does not reflect the actions of Jesus or those of his early followers. Nor is it clear that the belief that life is sacred requires that we never take it. There are other theological possibilities.[6] In any case, most of us—bioethicists, physicians, and patients alike—do not subscribe to the view that we have an obligation to preserve human life as long as possible. But if not, surely we ought to agree that I may legitimately end my life for other-regarding reasons, not just for self-regarding reasons.

Secondly, religious considerations aside, the claim could be made that an obligation to end one's own life would be incompatible with human dignity or would embody a failure to recognize the intrinsic value of a person. But I do not see that in thinking I had a duty to die I would necessarily be failing to respect myself or to appreciate my dignity or worth. Nor would I necessarily be failing to respect you in thinking that you had a similar duty. There is surely also a sense in which we fail to respect ourselves if in the face of illness or death, we stoop to choosing just what is best for ourselves. Indeed, Kant held that the very core of human dignity is the ability to act on a self-imposed moral law, regardless of whether it is in our interest to do so.[7] We shall return to the notion of human dignity.

A third objection appeals to the relative weight of burdens and thus, ultimately, to considerations of fairness or justice. The burdens that an illness creates for the family could not possibly be great enough to justify an obligation to end one's life—the sacrifice of life itself would be a far greater burden than any involved in caring for a chronically ill family member.

But is this true? Consider the following case:

An 87-year-old woman was dying of congestive heart failure. Her APACHE score predicted that she had less than a 50 percent chance to live for another six months. She was lucid, assertive, and terrified of death. She very much wanted to live and kept opting for rehospitalization and the most aggressive life-prolonging treatment possible. That treatment successfully prolonged her life (though with increasing debility) for nearly two years. Her 55-year-old daughter was her only remaining family, her caregiver, and the main source of her financial support. The daughter duly cared for her mother. But before her mother died, her illness had cost the daughter all of her savings, her home, her job, and her career.

This is by no means an uncommon sort of case. Thousands of similar cases occur each year. Now, ask yourself which is the greater burden:

a. To lose a 50 percent chance of six more months of life at age 87?
b. To lose all your savings, your home, and your career at age 55?

Which burden would you prefer to bear? Do we really believe the former is the greater burden? Would even the dying mother say that (a) is the greater burden? Or has she been encouraged to believe that the burdens of (b) are somehow morally irrelevant to her choices?

I think most of us would quickly agree that (b) is a greater burden. That is the evil we would more hope to avoid in our lives. If we are tempted to say that the mother's disease and impending death are the greater evil, I believe it is because we are taking a "slice of time" perspective rather than a "lifetime perspective."[8] But surely the lifetime perspective is the appropriate perspective when weighing burdens. If (b) is the greater burden, then we must admit that we have been promulgating an ethic that advocates imposing greater burdens on some people in order to provide smaller benefits for others just because they are ill and thus gain our professional attention and advocacy.

A whole range of cases like this one could easily be generated. In some, the answer about which burden is greater will not be clear. But in many it is. Death or ending your own life is simply not the greatest evil or the greatest burden.

This point does not depend on a utilitarian calculus. Even if death were the greatest burden (thus disposing of any simple utilitarian argument), serious questions would remain about the moral justifiability of choosing to impose crushing burdens on loved ones in order to avoid having to bear this burden oneself. The fact that I suffer greater burdens than others in my family does not license me simply to choose what I want for myself, nor does it necessarily release me from a responsibility to try to protect the quality of their lives.

I can readily imagine that, through cowardice, rationalization, or failure of resolve, I will fail in this obligation to protect my loved ones. If so, I think I would need to be excused or forgiven for what I did. But I cannot imagine it would be morally permissible for me to ruin the rest of my partner's life to sustain mine or to cut off my sons' careers, impoverish them, or compromise the quality of their children's lives simply because I wish to live a little longer. This is what leads me to believe in a duty to die.

Who Has a Duty to Die?

Suppose, then, that there can be a duty to die. Who has a duty to die? And when? To my mind, these are the right questions, the questions we should be asking. Many of us may one day badly need answers to just these questions.

But I cannot supply answers here, for two reasons. In the first place, answers will have to be very particular and contextual. Our concrete duties are often situated, defined in part by the myriad details of our circumstances, histories, and relationships. Though there may be principles that apply to a wide range of cases and some cases that yield pretty straightforward answers, there will also be many situations in which it is very difficult to discern whether one has a duty to die. If nothing else, it will often be very difficult to predict how one's family will bear up under the weight of the burdens that a protracted illness would impose on them. Momentous decisions will often have to be made under conditions of great uncertainty.

Second and perhaps even more importantly, I believe that those of us with family and loved ones should not define our duties unilaterally, especially not a decision about a duty to die. It would be isolating and distancing for me to decide without consulting them what is too much of a burden for my loved ones to bear. That way of deciding about my moral duties is not only atomistic; it also treats my family and loved ones paternalistically. They must be allowed to speak for themselves about the burdens my life imposes on them and how they feel about bearing those burdens.

Some may object that it would be wrong to put a loved one in a position of having to say, in effect, "You should end your life because caring for you is too hard on me and the rest of the family." Not only will it be almost impossible to say something like that to someone you love, it will carry with it a heavy load of guilt. On this view, you should decide by yourself whether you have a duty to die and approach your loved ones only after you have made up your mind to say goodbye to them. Your family could then try to change your mind, but the tremendous weight of moral decision would be lifted from their shoulders.

Perhaps so. But I believe in family decisions. Important decisions for those whose lives are interwoven should be made together, in a family discussion. Granted, a conversation about whether I have a duty to die would be a tremendously difficult conversation. The temptations to be dishonest could be enormous. Nevertheless, if I am contemplating a duty to die, my family and I should, if possible, have just such an agonizing discussion. It will act as a check on the information, perceptions, and reasoning of all of us. But even more importantly, it affirms our connectedness at a critical juncture in our lives and our life together. Honest talk about difficult matters almost always strengthens relationships.

However, many families seem unable to talk about death at all, much less a duty to die. Certainly most families could not have this discussion all at once, in one sitting. It might well take a number of discussions to be able to approach this topic. But even if talking about death is impossible, there are always behavioral clues—about your caregiver's tiredness, physical condition, health, prevailing mood, anxiety, financial concerns, outlook, overall well-being, and so on. And families unable to talk about death can often talk about how the caregiver is feeling, about finances, about tensions within the family resulting from the illness, about concerns for the future. Deciding whether you have a duty to die based on these behavioral clues and conversation about them honors your relationships better than deciding on your own about how burdensome you and your care must be.

I cannot say when someone has a duty to die. Still, I can suggest a few features of one's illness, history, and circumstances that make it more likely that one has a duty to die. I present them here without much elaboration or explanation.

1. A duty to die is more likely when continuing to live will impose significant burdens—emotional burdens, extensive caregiving, destruction of life plans, and, yes, financial hardship—on your family and loved ones. This is the fundamental insight underlying a duty to die.

2. A duty to die becomes greater as you grow older. As we age, we will be giving up less by giving up our lives, if only because we will sacrifice fewer remaining years of life and a smaller portion of our life plans. After all, it's not as if we would be immortal and live forever if we could just manage to avoid a duty to die. To have reached the age of, say, seventy-five or eighty years without being ready to die is itself a moral failing, the sign of a life out of touch with life's basic realities.[9]

3. A duty to die is more likely when you have already lived a full and rich life. You have already had a full share of the good things life offers.

4. There is greater duty to die if your loved ones' lives have already been difficult or impoverished, if they have had only a small share of the good things that life has to offer (especially if through no fault of their own).

5. A duty to die is more likely when your loved ones have already made great contributions—

perhaps even sacrifices—to make your life a good one. Especially if you have not made similar sacrifices for their well-being or for the well-being of other members of your family.

6. To the extent that you can make a good adjustment to your illness or handicapping condition, there is less likely to be a duty to die. A good adjustment means that smaller sacrifices will be required of loved ones and there is more compensating interaction for them. Still, we must also recognize that some diseases—Alzheimer's or Huntington's chorea—will eventually take their toll on your loved ones no matter how courageously, resolutely, even cheerfully you manage to face those illnesses.

7. There is less likely to be a duty to die if you can still make significant contributions to the lives of others, especially your family. The burdens to family members are not only or even primarily financial, neither are the contributions to them. However, the old and those who have terminal illnesses must also bear in mind that the loss their family members will feel when they die cannot be avoided, only postponed.

8. A duty to die is more likely when the part of you that is loved will soon be gone or seriously compromised. Or when you soon will no longer be capable of giving love. Part of the horror of cementing disease is that it destroys the capacity to nurture and sustain relationships, taking away a person's agency and the emotions that bind her to others.

9. There is a greater duty to die to the extent that you have lived a relatively lavish lifestyle instead of saving for illness or old age. Like most upper middle-class Americans, I could easily have saved more. It is a greater wrong to come to your family for assistance if your need is the result of having chosen leisure or a spendthrift lifestyle. I may eventually have to face the moral consequences of decisions I am now making.

These, then, are some of the considerations that give shape and definition to the duty to die. If we can agree that these considerations are all relevant, we can see that the correct course of action will often be difficult to discern. A decision about when I should end my life will sometimes prove to be every bit as difficult as the decision about whether I want treatment for myself.

Can the Incompetent Have a Duty to Die?

Severe mental deterioration springs readily to mind as one of the situations in which I believe I could have a duty to die. But can incompetent people have duties at all? We can have moral duties we do not recognize or acknowledge, including duties that we never recognized. But can we have duties we are unable to recognize? Duties when we are unable to understand the concept of morality at all? If so, do others have a moral obligation to help us carry out this duty? These are extremely difficult theoretical questions. The reach of moral agency is severely strained by mental incompetence.

I am tempted to simply bypass the entire question by saying that I am talking only about competent persons. But the idea of a duty to die clearly raises the specter of one person claiming that another—who cannot speak for herself—has such a duty. So I need to say that I can make no sense of the claim that someone has a duty to die if the person has never been able to understand moral obligation at all. To my mind, only those who were formerly capable of making moral decisions could have such a duty.

But the case of formerly competent persons is almost as troubling. Perhaps we should simply stipulate that no incompetent person can have a duty to die, not even if she affirmed belief in such a duty in an advance directive. If we take the view that formerly competent people may have such a duty, we should surely exercise extreme caution when claiming a formerly competent person would have acknowledged a duty to die or that any formerly competent person has an unacknowledged duty to die. Moral dangers loom regardless of which way we decide to resolve such issues.

But for me personally, very urgent practical matters turn on their resolution. If a formerly competent person can no longer have a duty to die (or if other people are not likely to help her carry out this duty), I believe that may obligation may be to die while I am still competent, before I become unable to make and carry out that decision for myself. Surely it would be irresponsible to evade my moral duties by temporizing until I escape into incompetence. And so I must die sooner than I otherwise would have to. On the other hand, if I could count on others to end my life after I become incompetent, I might be able to fulfill my responsibilities while also living out all my competent or semi-competent days. Given our society's reluctance to permit physicians, let alone family members, to perform aid-in-dying, I believe I may well have a duty to end my life when I can see mental incapacity on the horizon.

There is also the very real problem of sudden incompetence—due to a serious stroke or automobile accident, for example. For me, that is the real nightmare. If I suddenly become incompetent, I will fall into the hands of a medical-legal system that will conscientiously disregard my moral beliefs and do what is best for me, regardless of the consequences for my loved ones. And that is not at all what I would have wanted!

Social Policies and a Duty to Die

The claim that there is a duty to die will seem to some a misplaced response to social negligence. If our society were providing for the debilitated, the chronically ill, and the elderly as it should be, there would be only very rare cases of a duty to die. On this view, I am asking the sick and debilitated to step in and accept responsibility because society is derelict in its responsibility to provide for the incapacitated.

This much is surely true: there are a number of social policies we could pursue that would dramatically reduce the incidence of such a duty. Most obviously, we could decide to pay for facilities that provided excellent long-term care (not just health care!) for all chronically ill, debilitated, mentally ill, or demented people in this country. We probably could still afford to do this. If we did, sick, debilitated, and dying people might still be morally required to make sacrifices for their families. I might, for example, have a duty to forgo personal care by a family member who knows me and really does care for me. But these sacrifices would only rarely include the sacrifice of life itself. The duty to die would then be virtually eliminated.

I cannot claim to know whether in some abstract sense a society like ours should provide care for all who are chronically ill or debilitated. But the fact is that we Americans seem to be unwilling to pay for this kind of long-term care, except for ourselves and our own. In fact, we are moving in precisely the opposite direction—we are trying to shift the burdens of caring for the seriously and chronically ill onto families in order to save costs for our health care system. As we shift the burdens of care onto families, we also dramatically increase the number of Americans who will have a duty to die.

I must not, then, live my life and make my plans on the assumption that social institutions will protect my family from my infirmity and debility. To do so would be irresponsible. More likely, it will be up to me to protect my loved ones.

A Duty to Die and the Meaning of Life

A duty to die seems very harsh, and often it would be. It is one of the tragedies of our lives that someone who wants very much to live can nevertheless have a duty to die. It is both tragic and ironic that it is precisely the very real good of family and loved ones that gives rise to this duty. Indeed, the genuine love, closeness, and supportiveness of family members is a major source of this duty: we could not be such a burden if they did not care for us. Finally, there is deep irony in the fact that the very successes of our life-prolonging medicine help to create a widespread duty to die. We do not live in such a happy world that we can avoid such tragedies and ironies. We ought not to close our eyes to this reality or pretend that it just doesn't exist. We ought not to minimize the tragedy in any way.

And yet, a duty to die will not always be as harsh as we might assume. If I love my family, I will want to protect them and their lives. I will want not to make choices that compromise their futures. Indeed, I can easily imagine that I might want to avoid compromising their lives more than I would want anything else. I must also admit that I am not necessarily giving up so much in giving up my life: the conditions that give rise to a duty to die would usually already have compromised the quality of the life I am required to end. In any case, I personally must confess that at age fifty-six, I have already lived a very good life, albeit not yet nearly as long a life as I would like to have.

We fear death too much. Our fear of death has led to a massive assault on it. We still crave after virtually any life-prolonging technology that we might conceivably be able to produce. We still too often feel morally impelled to prolong life—virtually any form of life— as long as possible. As if the best death is the one that can be put off longest.

We do not even ask about meaning in death, so busy are we with trying to postpone it. But we will not conquer death by one day developing a technology so magnificent that no one will have to die. Nor can we conquer death by postponing it ever longer. We can conquer death only by finding meaning in it.

Although the existence of a duty to die does not hinge on this, recognizing such a duty would go some way toward recovering meaning in death. Paradoxically, it would restore dignity to those who are seriously ill or dying. It would also reaffirm the connections required to give life (and death) meaning. I close now with a few words about both of these points.

First, recognizing a duty to die affirms my agency and also my moral agency. I can still do things that make an important difference in the lives of my loved ones. Moreover, the fact that I still have responsibilities keeps me within the community of moral agents. My illness or debility has not reduced me to a mere moral patient (to use the language of the philosophers). Though it may not be the whole story, surely Kant was onto something important when he claimed that human dignity rests on the capacity for moral agency within a community of those who respect the demands of morality.

By contrast, surely there is something deeply insulting in a medicine and an ethic that would ask only what I want (or would have wanted) when I become ill. To treat me as if I had no moral responsibilities when I am ill or debilitated implies that my condition has rendered me morally incompetent. Only small children,[7] the demented or insane, and those totally lacking in the capacity to act are free from moral duties. There is dignity, then, and a kind of meaning in moral agency, even as it forces extremely difficult decisions upon us.

Second, recovering meaning in death requires an affirmation of connections. If I end my life to spare the futures of my loved ones, I testify in my death that I am connected to them. It is because I love and care for precisely these people (and I know they care for me) that I wish not to be such a burden to them. By contrast, a life in which I am free to choose whatever I want for myself is a life unconnected to others. A bioethics that would treat me as if I had no serious moral responsibilities does what it can to marginalize, weaken, or even destroy my connections with others.

But life without connection is meaningless. The individualistic fantasy, though occasionally liberating, is deeply destructive. When life is good and vitality seems unending, life itself and life lived for yourself may seem quite sufficient. But if not life, certainly death without connection is meaningless. If you are only for yourself, all you have to care about as your life draws to a close is yourself and your life. Everything you care about will then perish in your death. And that—the end of everything you care about—is precisely the total collapse of meaning. We can, then, find meaning in death only through a sense of connection with something that will survive our death.

This need not be connections with other people. Some people are deeply tied to land (for example, the family farm), to nature, or to a transcendent reality. But for most of us, the connections that sustain us are to other people. In the full bloom of life, we are connected to others in many ways—through work, profession, neighborhood, country, shared faith and worship, common leisure pursuits, friendship. Even the guru meditating in isolation on his mountain top is connected to a long tradition of people united by the same religious quest.

But as we age or when we become chronically ill, connections with other people usually become much more restricted. Often, only ties with family and close friends remain and remain important to us. Moreover, for many of us, other connections just don't go deep enough. As Paul Tsongas has reminded us, "When it comes time to die, no one says, 'I wish I had spent more time at the office.'"

If I am correct, death is so difficult for us partly because our sense of community is so weak. Death seems to wipe out everything when we can't fit it into the lives of those who live on. A death motivated by the desire to spare the futures of my loved ones might well be a better death for me than the one I would get as a result of opting to continue my life as long as there is any pleasure in it for me. Pleasure is nice, but it is meaning that matters.

I don't know about others, but these reflections have helped me. I am now more at peace about facing a duty to die. Ending my life if my duty required might still be difficult. But for me, a far greater horror would be dying all alone or stealing the futures of my loved ones in order to buy a little more time for myself. I hope that if the time comes when I have a duty to die, I will recognize it, encourage my loved ones to recognize it, too, and carry it out bravely.

Acknowledgments

I wish to thank Mary English, Hilde Nelson, Jim Bennett, Tom Townsend, the members of the Philosophy Department at East Tennessee State University, and anonymous reviewers of the *Report* for many helpful comments on earlier versions of this paper. In this paper, I draw on material in John Hardwig, "Dying at the Right Time; Reflections on (Un)Assisted Suicide" in *Practical Ethics*, edited by H. LaFollette (London: Blackwell, 1996), with permission.

Endnotes

1. Given the importance of relationships in my thinking, "responsibility"—rooted as it is in "respond"—would perhaps be the most appropriate word. Nevertheless, I often use "duty" despite its legalistic overtones, because Lamm's famous statement has given the expression "duty to die" a certain familiarity. But I intend no implication that there is a law that grounds this duty, nor that someone has a right corresponding to it.

2. For a discussion of the Oates case, see Tom L. Beauchamp, "What Is Suicide?" in *Ethical Issues in Death and Dying*, edited by Tom L. Beauchamp and Seymour Perlin (Englewood Cliffs, NJ: Prentice-Hall, 1978).

3. Most bioethicists advocate a "patient-centered ethics"—an ethics which claims only the patients' interests should be considered in making medical treatment decisions. Most health care professionals have been trained to accept this ethic and to see themselves as patient advocates. For arguments that a patient-centered ethics should be replaced by a family-centered ethics, see John Hardwig, "What About the Family?" *Hastings Center Report* 20, no. 2 (1990): 5–10; Hilde L. Nelson and James L. Nelson, *The Patient in the Family* (New York: Routledge, 1995).

4. A good account of the burdens of caregiving can be found in Elaine Brody, *Women in the Middle: Their Parent-Care Years* (New York: Springer, 1990). Perhaps the best article-length account of these burdens is Daniel Callahan, "Families as Caregivers; the Limits of Morality" in *Aging and Ethics: Philosophical Problems in Gerontology*, edited by Nancy Jecker (Totowa, NJ: Humana Press, 1991).

5. Kenneth E. Covinsky et al., "The Impact of Serious Illness on Patients' Families," *Journal of the American Medical Association* 272 (1994): 1839–1844.

6. Larry Churchill, for example, believes that Christian ethics takes us far beyond my present position: "Christian doctrines of stewardship prohibit the extension of one's own life at a great cost to the neighbor. . . . And such a gesture should not appear to us a sacrifice, but as the ordinary virtue entailed by a just, social conscience." Larry Churchill, *Rationing Health Care in America* (South Bend, IN: Notre Dame University Press, 1988), p. 112.

7. Kant, as is well known, was opposed to suicide. But he was arguing against taking your life out of self-interested motives. It is not clear that Kant would or we should consider taking your life out of a sense of duty to be wrong. See Hilde L. Nelson, "Death with Kantian Dignity," *Journal of Clinical Ethics* 7 (1996): 215–221.

8. Obviously, I owe this distinction to Norman Daniels. Norman Daniels, *Am I My Parents' Keeper? An Essay on Justice Between the Young and the Old* (New York: Oxford University Press, 1988). Just as obviously, Daniels is not committed to my use of it here.

9. Daniel Callahan, The *Troubled Dream of Life* (New York: Simon & Schuster, 1993).

38. A Non-Consequentialist Argument for Active Euthanasia

Baruch A. Brody

Arguing from a Kantian perspective, Baruch Brody examines cases of euthanasia
in which the agent benevolently takes the life of the dying for the benefit, and
with the consent, of the patient. Brody argues that such cases of voluntary euthanasia can be morally justified, for the agent has deprived the patient of nothing to which he or she any longer has a right, having consented to his or her own
death. Brody also considers a range of cases in which patients are no longer capable of giving consent to their own death, though they have authoriized the
taking of their life in advance if certain conditions came to be realized. Again, in
this type of case, Brody indicates that active euthanasia is morally justified because patients voluntarily waived the right to their own lives.

I

An act of euthanasia is one in which one person (I shall
refer to him as A) kills another person (B) for the benefit of the second person, who does actually benefit
from being killed. This definition emphasizes two features of acts of euthanasia. The first is that they involve
one person killing another. It is, of course, this feature
that raises serious doubts about the moral permissibility of such acts. The second is that they involve A's acting from benevolent motives and in so doing benefitting
B. It is this feature (a mixture of subjective and objective factors) that suggests that such acts may be morally permissible.

Let us look more carefully at each of these features. The first feature distinguishes acts of euthanasia
from suicides, on one hand, and mere omissions to
save others, on the other hand. Suicides are not acts of
euthanasia because they do not involve killings of others. More importantly, omissions are not (usually) acts
of euthanasia because they do not (usually) involve
killings. Therefore, the question of the moral permissibility of one must be distinguished from the question
of the moral permissibility of the other. This is an
important point. In a recent, much-publicized case in
Maine in which parents refused to authorize an operation needed to save the life of their seriously deformed
child, much of the public discussion was marred by a

From M. Kohl (ed.), *Beneficient Euthanasia* (Buffalo, NY:
Prometheus Press, 1975), pp. 161–165. Reprinted with permission from the author.

failure to distinguish the omission of medical efforts to
save a life from an act of euthanasia.

There are those who challenge this second distinction, who maintain that it is a distinction without
a difference. According to them there is no morally relevant difference between A's killing B and A's failure to
save B. Thus, Joseph Fletcher writes: "What, morally,
is the difference between doing nothing to keep the
patient alive and giving a fatal dose of a painkilling or
other lethal drug? The intention is the same either
way. A decision not to keep a patient alive is as
morally deliberate as a decision to end a life."
Fletcher's arguments are very weak. That both decisions are morally deliberate does not entail that there
are no morally relevant differences between them.
And the same is true of the fact that the two actions
are performed in order to accomplish the same result
(this is, presumably, what Fletcher means when he
says that "the intention is the same either way"); after
all, the means chosen, as well as the end pursued,
count in the moral evaluation of an action. More
importantly, Fletcher's position seems untenable for
two reasons. First, it seems that we have an equally
strong obligation not to kill anyone, but the existence
and strength of our obligation to save others depends,
to a considerable degree, upon our relationship to that
person. Fletcher would, I am sure, agree that a father
has a greater obligation to save his starving child than
to save a starving stranger who lives thousands of
miles away. Second, there are many things that would
relieve us from our obligation to save another but that
would not relieve us from our obligation not to kill

another. Thus, if someone threatens to take my life (a limb, or my life's savings) unless I refrain from saving you, that seems to relieve me of my obligation to save you; but if he threatens to take my life (a limb, or my life's-savings) unless I kill you, then it would seem as though I still have an obligation not to kill you. So, on two counts, we have a distinction that does make a difference.

All of this is perfectly compatible with a realization that the boundary between killing someone and failing to save him is not always precise. Has one killed someone or has one merely refrained from continuing to save him when one turns off the life-supporting machine that is keeping him alive? My point is that one can distinguish clear-cut cases of killing from clear-cut cases of failure to save and that the moral considerations relevant to an evaluation of the one act are not necessarily relevant to an evaluation of the other act.

So much for the first feature of euthanasia cases. We turn now to the second feature: that A is killing B for the benefit of B and B does actually benefit from being killed. Before commenting on this point, let me add that if B consents to A's killing him or requests that A kill him, we have a case of voluntary euthanasia.

In such cases of voluntary euthanasia, there are three different factors that might justify A's killing B: A's benevolent motives, B's gain, and B's consent or request. Proponents of voluntary euthanasia have to be clear on the precise weight that they ascribe to each of these features. To be sure, if we have a case in which B is suffering from the terminal stages of an incurable disease and would be better off dead, in which B requests that A kill him, and in which A does so to save B from his terrible suffering, all of these factors are present, and the proponents of voluntary euthanasia need not decide which is most important. But there are obviously cases in which these differences become important. (1) Suppose that A kills B, in the above case, to gain a legacy. Is A's act permissible if done for a bad motive, or does A's motive turn his act into an act of murder? (2) Suppose that A kills B, in the above case, but B has never requested or consented to euthanasia and is now incapable of doing so. Is A's act permissible because of his motives in performing it and because of its benefits, or does the lack of consent turn A's act into an act of murder? (3) Suppose that A kills B, in the above case, but because of special circumstances the act results in a loss to B. Is A's act permissible because of his motives and B's consent, or does the resulting harm to B turn A's act into an act of murder?

This point can also be put as follows: Proponents of euthanasia have to decide which of the three factors, or which disjunction(s) of them, is (are) necessary for A's act to be permissible and which of these three factors, or which conjunction(s) of them, is (are) sufficient for A's act to be permissible. Their decision on this point will determine whether they are proposing euthanasia, voluntary euthanasia, or killing for benevolent motives.

I will be arguing only for voluntary euthanasia, since I will only be arguing that B's consent or request justifies A's killing him. I will also try to show that there are cases in which, by extension, euthanasia is permissible even if it has not been consented to or requested. For reasons that will emerge below, I will treat A's motives and the benefit to B as neither necessary nor sufficient.

My argument will be based upon certain assumptions about killing and about the right to life. These are: (1) A's killing B is wrong—when it is wrong—only because it involves A's wrongfully depriving B of that life to which, in those cases, B has a right; (2) there should be laws prohibiting A's killing B only because of the law's function of protecting our possession of that to which we have a right. I shall try to show that these assumptions lead to the conclusion that voluntary euthanasia is permissible and should be legalized. Without entering into a full-fledged defense of these assumptions, I shall defend them against some standard objections. In any case, since these assumptions are both plausible and widely believed, I think that the assertion that they lead to these consequences will be of interest.

II

Let us begin by considering a case in which B requests that A kill him. Can A do so without wrongfully depriving B of something to which he has a right? In order to answer this question, we must first remind ourselves of an elementary point concerning the possession of rights.

Suppose that B has the right to some property. Normally, this entails that A has a duty to refrain from taking the property away from B and that A would act wrongly (unless there were special circumstances) if he took it away from B. But now suppose that B consents to A's taking it. Then, although A has no duty to do so (unless there are special circumstances), A does not wrongfully deprive B of the property if he does take it away. Although A is depriving B of that to which B has a right, A is not doing so wrongfully, because of B's consent.

This point can be generalized. If A takes from B something to which B has a right, then A has not wrongfully deprived B of that thing if B consents to A's doing so. Notice that this claim is weaker than the claim that A has wrongfully deprived B of the thing in question only if B positively wants it; A will have wrongfully deprived B of that to which he has a right, even if B does not positively want the thing in question, so long as B does not actually consent to A's taking it.

This general principle about rights leads to an argument for the moral permissibility of voluntary euthanasia. According to assumption 1, A's killing B is wrong only when it involves A's wrongfully depriving B of that life to which B has a right. But in cases of voluntary euthanasia, B consents to A's taking his life. Therefore, by our general principle about rights, A has not wrongfully deprived B of that life to which he has a right. So, by assumption 1, A's killing B is not wrong when it is an act of voluntary euthanasia.

But does our general principle about rights hold in all cases? Consider a person's right to be free: Is it permissible for A to deprive B of that right by enslaving him even if B consents to A's doing so? If not, doesn't this show that there are some rights that a person can be wrongfully deprived of even when he consents to the deprivation? Perhaps the right to life is another example of such a right.

I do not find this objection convincing. That it is wrong for A to enslave B does not entail that A has wrongfully deprived B of that freedom to which he has a right. It may be wrong for other, independent reasons, most notably because it may be wrong for us to treat another person as a thing to be used. Moreover, even if one insists that A has wrongfully deprived B of his right to freedom, the case is not like the case of euthanasia because, unlike the case of euthanasia, the person deprived of his right goes on existing without that right. In short, then, it is not clear that the right to freedom does serve as a counter-example to our principle, and in any event, it is significantly different from the right to life; I am therefore inclined to treat the right to life analogously to all other rights.

There are three points about our argument that should be noted: (1) this argument is also an argument for the moral permissibility of suicide. After all, if B kills himself, then he has consented to his being killed, and he has therefore done nothing wrong. Indeed, from the perspective of this argument, there is no sig-nificant difference between suicide and voluntary euthanasia; (2) the question of A's motive and the benefit to B is irrelevant: our argument shows that A's act is permissible as long as B consents. Consent is a sufficient condition and neither benevolent motives nor beneficial consequences are necessary conditions; (3) there are limitations on our argument, growing out of general limitations upon the efficacy of consent. There are, after all, cases in which B's consent does not count, cases in which A wrongfully deprives B of that to which B has a right even though B consents. These include, among others, cases in which B (because of his youth or insanity) is incompetent to consent and cases in which B's consent is obtained by duress or fraud. It would be wrong, therefore, for A to kill B despite B's consent if B is incompetent or if his consent is obtained by fraud or duress. But one must not overemphasize this last point. There are those who claim that by consenting to being killed B has shown that he is incompetent and that his consent does not count. This claim should be accepted only if one also accepts the claim that consenting to being killed is so irrational in all circumstances that anyone so consenting could do so only by virtue of mental incompetence. But this last claim seems implausible; it would be hard to show that so consenting is always irrational. We must therefore reject the view that anyone who consents to being killed has thereby shown that he is incompetent to consent.

I have argued for voluntary euthanasia on the grounds of B's consent. There is, however, an additional, and perhaps more significant, point to consider. B also requested that A kill him, and this seems to provide another basis for the permissibility of A's killing B, namely, that A is acting as B's agent. After all, if it is permissible—and I have argued that it is—for B to kill himself, why should not it also be permissible for his agent, A, to do it? This argument rests upon the assumption that if it is permissible for B to do something, then it is also permissible for B to appoint A as his agent to perform the action in question and it is also permissible for A to perform that action. But this assumption is incorrect. If, for example, B is a judge, then it is permissible for B, in certain circumstances, to sentence a criminal, but it is not permissible for B to appoint an agent to do so. Or, while it is permissible for B to have intercourse with his or her spouse (providing that the spouse has consented), it hardly follows that it is permissible for A to do so as B's agent. Still, our argument can be saved. After all, in these cases, B's privileges result from the permission of someone else (society, the spouse), and that permission has been granted only to B personally. But since B's right to kill himself does not derive from the permission of others, our general principle about agency holds.

We have so far considered the case in which B both consents to A's killing him and requests that A kill him. This is the paradigm case of voluntary euthanasia. But there are other, more perplexing, cases to consider. One is that in which B is no longer competent to consent and/or request (for example, if he is doped with pain-killing drugs), but in which, at some earlier time, he requested that A kill him if certain conditions—the ones that actually do obtain now—were to exist. In short, this is the case of euthanasia arranged for in advance. Is this also a case of permissible voluntary euthanasia?

Those who emphasize the importance of A's benevolent motives and the benefit to B would not find such cases perplexing. They would say that it is still permissible for A to kill B, even when B does not consent, so long as B benefits and A has benevolent motives. They would concede that our earlier argument showed that neither factor was necessary to justify A's killing B; but, they would claim, either (or, perhaps, just both) is sufficient.

I find this argument, with its supposition about what is sufficient to justify A's killing B, problematic. Suppose that A kills B for B's benefit, it is beneficial for B, but B objects. Or suppose that B does not object because he cannot; but would object if he could. Would we say in such cases that it is permissible for A to kill B? And if we would not, then we must reject the view that even A's benevolent motives joined with the benefit to B is sufficient to justify A's killing B, so this argument collapses.

It must be conceded that the case we are considering—euthanasia arranged for in advance—is different because B has previously consented to, and authorized, A's killing him. But this suggests that we

consider that factor, and leave aside for now A's motives and the consequences for B. Does B's previous action suffice to justify A's killing him?

There are two lines of argument for concluding that it does: (1) one's privilege to waive one's right, to consent to others' taking what is yours, is not limited to doing so at the actual time in question; one can, and often does, consent in advance and conditionally. Similarly, one can, and often does, appoint agents in advance and conditionally. So, concludes this argument, as long as B does not revoke his earlier conditional consent and/or request, there is no morally significant difference between the paradigm case of voluntary euthanasia and the extended case of euthanasia arranged for in advance; (2) what justifies A's killing B in such cases is the consent that B would now give, and the request that B would now make, if he could. All that B's previous arrangements do is to serve as evidence as to what B would do now.

There are two difficulties with this second hypothetical approach. Practically speaking, it is hard to be sure what B would do now, even in light of his previous actions, since people do change their minds. Theoretically speaking, it rests upon a stronger, and perhaps more dubious, principle than any we have employed until now, namely, that if A takes from B something to which B has a right, then A has not wrongfully deprived B of that thing if B would consent if he could. On the other hand, this approach might allow more cases of permissible euthanasia if B's hypothetical consent were evidenced by something other than his earlier consent and/or request.

In conclusion, then, considerations of consent and agency, independent of any considerations of motives and benefit, seem sufficient to justify, on the assumptions outlined in section one, voluntary euthanasia, both in the paradigm case and in the extended case of consent in advance. They may even do so in cases in which B has never consented.

Part 6

Capital Punishment

39. What Do Murderers Deserve?
The Death Penalty in Civilized Societies

DAVID GELERNTER

David Gelernter argues that capital punishment is morally justified as a statement that murder is communally understood to be absolutely evil and intolerable. The exercise of the death penalty is not a pronouncement on the value of life; rather, it is a profound indication of the community's stance on the crime of murder. In an age in which the willingness to insist that some actions are simply evil is eroding, there is a resulting uneasiness with the application of the death penalty. For Gelernter, however, capital punishment is justified as an exercise in social catharsis, a means by which a society can remind itself that the taking of innocent life is beyond the moral pale, and will not be tolerated.

No civilized nation ever takes the death penalty for granted; two recent cases force us to consider it yet again. A Texas woman, Karla Faye Tucker, murdered two people with a pickaxe, was said to have repented in prison, and was put to death. A Montana man, Theodore Kaczynski, murdered three people with mail bombs, did not repent, and struck a bargain with the Justice Department. He pleaded guilty and will not be executed. (He also attempted to murder others and succeeded in wounding some, myself included.) Why did we execute the penitent and spare the impenitent?

From Lawrence M. Hinman (ed.), *Contemporary Moral Issues: Diversity and Consensus,* 2nd Edition, © 2000. Reprinted by permission of Pearson Education, Inc., Upper Saddle River, NJ.

However we answer this question, we surely have a duty to ask it.

And we ask it—I do, anyway—with a sinking feeling, because in modern America, moral upside-downness is a specialty of the house. To eliminate race prejudice we discriminate by race. We promote the cultural assimilation of immigrant children by denying them schooling in English. We throw honest citizens in jail for child abuse, relying on testimony so phony any child could see through it. Orgasm studies are okay in public high schools but the Ten Commandments are not. We make a point of admiring manly women and womanly men. None of which has anything to do with capital punishment directly, but it all obliges us to approach any question about morality in modern

America in the larger context of this country's desperate confusion about elementary distinctions.

Why execute murderers? To deter? To avenge? Supporters of the death penalty often give the first answer, opponents the second. But neither can be the whole truth. If our main goal were deterring crime, we would insist on public executions—which are not on the political agenda, and not an item that many Americans are interested in promoting. If our main goal were vengeance, we would allow the grieving parties to decide the murderer's fate; if the victim had no family or friends to feel vengeful on his behalf; we would call the whole thing off.

In fact, we execute murderers in order to make a communal proclamation: that murder is intolerable. A deliberate murderer embodies evil so terrible that it defiles the community. Thus the late social philosopher Robert Nisbet: "Until a catharsis has been effected through trial, through the finding of guilt and then punishment, the community is anxious, fearful, apprehensive, and above all, contaminated."

Individual citizens have a right and sometimes a duty to speak. A community has the right, too, and sometimes the duty. The community certifies births and deaths, creates marriages, educates children, fights invaders. In laws, deeds, and ceremonies it lays down the boundary lines of civilized life, lines that are constantly getting scuffed and needing renewal.

When a murder takes place, the community is obliged, whether it feels like it or not, to clear its throat and step up to the microphone. Every murder demands a communal response. Among possible responses, the death penalty is uniquely powerful because it is permanent and can never be retracted or overturned. An execution forces the community to assume forever the burden of moral certainty; it is a form of absolute speech that allows no waffling or equivocation. Deliberate murder, the community announces, is absolutely evil and absolutely intolerable, period.

Of course, we could make the same point less emphatically if we wanted to—for example, by locking up murderers for life (as we sometimes do). The question then becomes: is the death penalty overdoing it? Should we make a less forceful proclamation instead?

The answer might be yes if we were a community in which murder was a shocking anomaly and thus in effect a solved problem. But we are not. Our big cities are full of murderers at large. "One can guesstimate," writes the criminologist and political scientist John J. Dilulio, Jr., "that we are nearing or may already have passed the day when 500,000 murderers, convicted and undetected, are living in American society."

Dilulio's statistics show an approach to murder so casual as to be depraved. We are reverting to a pre-civilized state of nature. Our natural bent in the face of murder is not to avenge the crime but to shrug it off, except in those rare cases when our own near and dear are involved. (And even then, it depends.)

This is an old story. Cain murders Abel and is brought in for questioning: where is Abel, your brother? The suspect's response: how should I know? "What am I, my brother's keeper?" It is one of the very first statements attributed to mankind in the Bible; voiced here by an interested party, it nonetheless expresses a powerful and universal inclination. Why mess in other people's problems? And murder is always, in the most immediate sense, someone else's problem, because the injured party is dead.

Murder in primitive societies called for a private settling of scores. The community as a whole stayed out of it. For murder to count, as it does in the Bible, as a crime not merely against one man but against the whole community and against God—that was a moral triumph that is still basic to our integrity, and that is never to be taken for granted. By executing murderers, the community reaffirms this moral understanding by restating the truth that absolute evil exists and must be punished.

Granted (some people say), the death penalty is a communal proclamation; it is nevertheless an incoherent one. If our goal is to affirm that human life is more precious than anything else, how can we make such a declaration by destroying life?

But declaring that human life is more precious than anything else is not our goal in imposing the death penalty. Nor is the proposition true. The founding fathers pledged their lives (and fortunes and sacred honor) to the cause of freedom; Americans have traditionally believed that some things are more precious than life. ("Living in a sanitary age, we are getting so we place too high a value on human life—which rightfully must always come second to human ideas." Thus E.B. White in 1938, pondering the Munich pact ensuring "peace in our time" between the Western powers and Hitler.) The point of capital punishment is not to pronounce on life in general but on the crime of murder.

Which is not to say that the sanctity of human life does not enter the picture. Taking a life, says the Talmud (in the course of discussing Cain and Abel), is equivalent to destroying a whole world. The rabbis used this statement to make a double point: to tell us why murder is the gravest of crimes, and to warn against false testimony in a murder trial. But to believe in the sanctity of human life does not mean, and the Talmud does not say it means, that capital punishment is ruled out.

A newer objection grows out of the seemingly random way in which we apply capital punishment. The death penalty might be a reasonable communal proclamation in principle, some critics say, but it has become so garbled in practice that it has lost all significance and ought to be dropped. Dilulio writes that "the ratio of persons murdered to persons executed for murder from 1977 to 1996 was in the ballpark of 1,000 to 1"; the death penalty has become in his view "arbitrary and capricious," a "state lottery" that is "unjust both as a matter of Judeo-Christian ethics and as a matter of American citizenship."

We can grant that, on the whole, we are doing a disgracefully bad job of administering the death penalty. After all, we are divided and confused on the issue. The community at large is strongly in favor of capital punishment; the cultural elite is strongly against it. Our attempts to speak with assurance as a community come out sounding in consequence like a man who is fighting off a choke-hold as he talks. But a community as cavalier about murder as we are has no right to back down. That we are botching things does not entitle us to give up.

Opponents of capital punishment tend to describe it as a surrender to our emotions—to grief, rage, fear, blood lust. For most supporters of the death penalty, this is exactly false. Even when we resolve in principle to go ahead, we have to steel ourselves. Many of us would find it hard to kill a dog, much less a man. Endorsing capital punishment means not that we yield to our emotions but that we overcome them. (Immanuel Kant, the great advocate of the death penalty precisely on moral grounds, makes this point in his reply to the anti-capital-punishment reformer Cesare Beccaria—accusing Beccaria of being "moved by sympathetic sentimentality and an affectation of humanitarianism.") If we favor executing murderers it is not because we want to but because, however much we do not want to, we consider ourselves obliged to.

Many Americans, of course, no longer feel that obligation. The death penalty is hard for us as a community above all because of our moral evasiveness. For at least a generation, we have urged one another to switch off our moral faculties. "Don't be judgmental!" We have said it so many times, we are starting to believe it.

The death penalty is a proclamation about absolute evil, but many of us are no longer sure that evil even exists. We define evil out of existence by calling it "illness"—a tendency Aldous Huxley anticipated in his novel *Brave New World* (1932) and Robert Nisbet wrote about in 1982: "America has lost the villain, the evil one, who has now become one of the sick,

the disturbed. . . . America has lost the moral value of guilt, lost it to the sickroom."

Our refusal to look evil in the face is no casual notion; it is a powerful drive. Thus we have (for example) the terrorist Theodore Kaczynski, who planned and carried out a hugely complex campaign of violence with a clear goal in mind. It was the goal most terrorists have: to get famous and not die. He wanted public attention for his ideas about technology; he figured he could get it by attacking people with bombs.

He was right. His plan succeeded. It is hard to imagine a more compelling proof of mental competence than this planning and carrying out over decades of a complex, rational strategy. (Evil, yes; irrational, no; they are different things.) The man himself has said repeatedly that he is perfectly sane, knew what he was doing, and is proud of it.

To call such a man insane seems to me like deliberate perversity. But many people do. Some of them insist that his thoughts about technology constitute "delusions," though every terrorist holds strong beliefs that are wrong, and many nonterrorists do, too. Some insist that sending bombs through the mail is ipso facto proof of insanity—as if the twentieth century had not taught us that there is no limit to the bestiality of which sane men are capable.

Where does this perversity come from? I said earlier that the community at large favors the death penalty, but intellectuals and the cultural elite tend to oppose it. This is not (I think) because they abhor killing more than other people do, but because the death penalty represents absolute speech from a position of moral certainty, and doubt is the black-lung disease of the intelligentsia—an occupational hazard now inflicted on the culture as a whole.

American intellectuals have long differed from the broader community—particularly on religion, crime and punishment, education, family, the sexes, race relations, American history, taxes and public spending, the size and scope of government, art, the environment, and the military. (Otherwise, I suppose, they and the public have been in perfect accord.) But not until the late 60s and 70s were intellectuals finally in a position to act on their convictions. Whereupon they attacked the community's moral certainties with the enthusiasm of guard dogs leaping at throats.* The result is an American community smitten with the disease of intellectual doubt—or, in this case, self-doubt.

---

*I have written about this before in "How the Intellectuals Took Over (And What to Do About It)," *Commentary,* March 1997.

The failure of our schools is a consequence of our self-doubt, of our inability to tell children that learning is not fun and they are required to master certain topics whether they want to or not. The tortured history of modern American race relations grows out of our self-doubt: we passed a civil rights act in 1964, then lost confidence immediately in our ability to make a race-blind society work; racial preferences codify our refusal to believe in our own good faith. During the late stages of the cold war, many Americans laughed at the idea that the American way was morally superior or the Soviet Union was an "evil empire"; some are still laughing. Within their own community and the American community at large, doubting intellectuals have taken refuge (as doubters often do) in bullying, to the point where many of us are now so uncomfortable at the prospect of confronting evil that we turn away and change the subject.

Returning then to the penitent woman and the impenitent man: the Karla Faye Tucker case is the harder of the two. We are told that she repented of the vicious murders she committed. If that is true, we would still have had no business forgiving her, or forgiving any murderer. As Dennis Prager has written apropos this case, only the victim is entitled to forgive, and the victim is silent. But showing mercy to penitents is part of our religious tradition, and I cannot imagine renouncing it categorically.

Why was Cain not put to death, but condemned instead to wander the earth forever? Among the answers given by the rabbis in the Midrash is that he repented. The moral category of repentance is so important, they said, that it was created before the world itself. I would therefore consider myself morally obligated to think long and hard before executing a penitent. But a true penitent would have to have renounced (as Karla Faye Tucker did) all legal attempts to overturn the original conviction. If every legal avenue has been tried and has failed, the penitence window is closed. Of course, this still leaves the difficult problem of telling counterfeit penitence from the real thing, but everything associated with capital punishment is difficult.

As for Kaczynski, the prosecutors who accepted the murderer's plea bargain say they got the best outcome they could, under the circumstances, and I believe them. But I also regard this failure to execute a cold-blooded impenitent terrorist murderer as a tragic abdication of moral responsibility. The tragedy lies in what, under our confused system, the prosecutors felt compelled to do. The community was called on to speak unambiguously. It flubbed its lines, shrugged its shoulders, and walked away.

Which brings me back to our moral condition as a community. I can describe our plight better in artistic than in philosophical terms. The most vivid illustrations I know of self-doubt and its consequences are the paintings and sculptures of Alberto Giacometti (who died in 1966). Giacometti was an artist of great integrity; he was consumed by intellectual and moral self-doubt, which he set down faithfully. His sculpted figures show elongated, shriveled human beings who seem corroded by acid, eaten-up to the bone, hurt and weakened past fragility nearly to death. They are painful to look at. And they are natural emblems of modern America. We ought to stick one on top of the Capitol and think it over.

In executing murderers, we declare that deliberate murder is absolutely evil and absolutely intolerable. This is a painfully difficult proclamation for a self-doubting community to make. But we dare not stop trying. Communities may exist in which capital punishment is no longer the necessary response to deliberate murder. America today is not one of them.

40. On Deterrence and the Death Penalty

ERNEST VAN DEN HAAG

Ernest Van Den Haag shares David Gelernter's support for the death penalty, but for quite different reasons. From Van Den Haag's perspective, a society's collective response to wrongdoing helps shape the conscience of its citizens. As a result, the voice of a forceful external authority on murder will help create a strong psychological disincentive to carry out such acts, and also serve as a deterrent when swift punishment is carried out against offenders. Arguing on utilitarian grounds, Van Den Haag thinks that criminals calculate the risks and benefits of their behaviors and that, whether or not deterrence can be statistically proven, the realization that murder will be met with the severest of penalties will produce long-term social benefits that justify the maintenance of the death penalty.

I

If rehabilitation and the protection of society from unrehabilitated offenders were the only purposes of legal punishment, the death penalty could be abolished: It cannot attain the first end, and is not needed for the second. No case for the death penalty can be made unless "doing justice" or "deterring others" is among our penal aims.[1] Each of these purposes can justify capital punishment by itself; opponents, therefore, must show that neither actually does, while proponents can rest their case on either.

Although the argument from justice is intellectually more interesting, and, in my view, decisive enough, utilitarian arguments have more appeal: The claim that capital punishment is useless because it does not deter others is most persuasive. I shall, therefore, focus on this claim. Lest the argument be thought to be unduly narrow, I shall show, nonetheless, that some claims of injustice rest on premises which the claimants reject when arguments for capital punishment are derived therefrom; while other claims of injustice have no independent standing: Their weight depends on the weight given to deterrence.

Reprinted by special permission of Northwestern University School of Law, *The Journal of Criminal Law, Criminology, and Police Science*, Vol. 60, No. 2.

II

Capital punishment is regarded as unjust because it may lead to the execution of innocents, or because the guilty poor (or disadvantaged) are more likely to be executed than the guilty rich.

Regardless of merit, these claims are relevant only if "doing justice" is one purpose of punishment. Unless one regards it as good, or, at least, better, that the guilty be punished rather than the innocent, and that the equally guilty be punished equally,[2] unless, that is, one wants penalties to be just, one cannot object to them because they are not. However, if one does include justice among the purposes of punishment, it becomes possible to justify any one punishment—even death—on grounds of justice. Yet, those who object to the death penalty because of its alleged injustice usually deny not only the merits, or the sufficiency, of specific arguments based on justice, but the propriety of justice as an argument: They exclude "doing justice" as a purpose of legal punishment. If justice is not a purpose of penalties, injustice cannot be an objection to the death penalty, or to any other; if it is, justice cannot be ruled out as an argument for any penalty.

Consider the claim of injustice on its merits now. A convicted man may be found to have been innocent; if he was executed, the penalty cannot be reversed. Except for fines, penalties never can be reversed. Time spent in prison cannot be returned. However, a prison sentence may be remitted once the prisoner serving it is found innocent; and he can be compensated for the time served (although compensation ordinarily cannot repair the harm). Thus, though (nearly) all penalties are irreversible, the death penalty, unlike others, is irrevocable as well.

Despite all precautions, errors will occur in judicial proceedings: The innocent may be found guilty,[3] or the guilty rich may more easily escape conviction, or receive lesser penalties than the guilty poor. However, these injustices do not reside in the penalties inflicted but in their maldistribution. It is not the penalty—whether death or prison—which is unjust when inflicted on the innocent, but its imposition on the innocent. Inequity between poor and rich also involves distribution, not the penalty distributed.[4] Thus injustice is not an objection to the death penalty but to the distributive process—the trial. Trials are more likely to be fair when life is at stake—the death penalty is probably less often unjustly inflicted than others. It requires special consideration not because it is more, or more often, unjust than other penalties, but because it is always irrevocable.

Can any amount of deterrence justify the possibility of irrevocable injustice? Surely injustice is unjustifiable in each actual individual case; it must be objected to whenever it occurs. But we are concerned here with the process that may produce injustice, and with the penalty that would make it irrevocable—not with the actual individual cases produced, but with the general rules which may produce them. To consider objections to a general rule (the provision of any penalties by law) we must compare the likely net result of alternative rules and select the rule (or penalty) likely to produce the least injustice. For however one defines justice, to support it cannot mean less than to favor the least injustice. If the death of innocents because of judicial error is unjust, so is the death of innocents by murder. If some murders could be avoided by a penalty conceivably more deterrent than others—such as the death penalty—then the question becomes: Which penalty will minimize the number of innocents killed (by crime and by punishment)? It follows that the irrevocable injustice sometimes inflicted by the death penalty would not significantly militate against it, if capital punishment deters enough murders to reduce the total number of innocents killed so that fewer are lost than would be lost without it.

In general, the possibility of injustice argues against penalization of any kind only if the expected usefulness of penalization is less important than the probable harm (particularly to innocents) and the probable inequities. The possibility of injustice argues against the death penalty only inasmuch as the added usefulness (deterrence) expected from irrevocability is thought less important than the added harm. (Were my argument specifically concerned with justice, I could compare the injustice inflicted by the courts with the injustice—outside the courts—avoided by the judicial process. *I.e.,* "important" here may be used to include everything to which importance is attached.)

We must briefly examine now the general use and effectiveness of deterrence to decide whether the death penalty could add enough deterrence to be warranted.

III

Does any punishment "deter others" at all? Doubts have been thrown on this effect because it is thought to depend on the incorrect rationalistic psychology of some of its 18th- and 19th-century proponents. Actually deterrence does not depend on rational calculation, on rationality or even on capacity for it; nor do arguments for it depend on rationalistic psychology. Deterrence depends on the likelihood and on the regularity—not on the rationality—of human responses to danger; and further on the possibility of reinforcing internal controls by vicarious external experiences.

Responsiveness to danger is generally found in human behavior; the danger can, but need not, come from the law or from society; nor need it be explicitly verbalized. Unless intent on suicide, people do not jump from high mountain cliffs, however tempted to fly through the air; and they take precautions against falling. The mere risk of injury often restrains us from doing what is otherwise attractive; we refrain even when we have no direct experience, and usually without explicit computation of probabilities, let alone conscious weighing of expected pleasure against possible pain. One abstains from dangerous acts because of vague, inchoate, habitual and, above all, preconscious fears. Risks and rewards are more often felt than calculated; one abstains without accounting to oneself, because "it isn't done," or because one literally does not conceive of the action one refrains from. Animals as well refrain from painful or injurious experiences presumably without calculation; and the threat of punishment can be used to regulate their conduct.

Unlike natural dangers, legal threats are constructed deliberately by legislators to restrain actions which may impair the social order. Thus legislation transforms social into individual dangers. Most people further transform external into internal danger: They acquire a sense of moral obligation, a conscience, which threatens them, should they do what is wrong. Arising originally from the external authority of rulers and rules, conscience is internalized and becomes independent of external forces. However, conscience is constantly reinforced in those whom it controls by the coercive imposition of external authority on recalcitrants and on those who have not acquired it. Most people refrain from offenses because they feel an obligation to behave lawfully. But this obligation would scarcely be felt if those who do not feel or follow it were not to suffer punishment.

Although the legislators may calculate their threats and the responses to be produced, the effectiveness of the threats neither requires nor depends on calculations by those responding. The predictor (or producer) of effects must calculate; those whose responses are predicted (or produced) need not. Hence, although legislation (and legislators) should be rational, subjects, to be deterred as intended, need not be: They need only be responsive.

Punishments deter those who have not violated the law for the same reasons—and in the same degrees (apart from internalization: moral obligation) as do natural dangers. Often natural dangers—all dangers not deliberately created by legislation (*e.g.,* injury of the criminal inflicted by the crime victim) are insufficient. Thus, the fear of injury (natural danger) does not suffice to control city traffic; it must be reinforced by the legal punishment meted out to those who violate the rules. These punishments keep most people observing the regulations. However, where (in the absence of natural danger) the threatened punishment is so light that the advantage of violating rules tends to exceed the disadvantage of being punished (divided by the risk), the rule is violated (*i.e.,* parking fines are too light). In this case the feeling of obligation tends to vanish as well. Elsewhere punishment deters.

To be sure, not everybody responds to threatened punishment. Non-responsive persons may be (a) self-destructive or (b) incapable of responding to threats, or even of grasping them. Increases in the size, or certainty, of penalties would not affect these two groups. A third group (c) might respond to more certain or more severe penalties.[5] If the punishment threatened for burglary, robbery, or rape were a $5 fine in North Carolina, and 5 years in prison in South Carolina, I have no doubt that the North Carolina treasury would become quite opulent until vigilante justice would provide the deterrence not provided by law. Whether to increase penalties (or improve enforcement) depends

on the importance of the rule to society, the size and likely reaction of the group that did not respond before, and the acceptance of the added punishment and enforcement required to deter it. Observation would have to locate the points—likely to differ in different times and places—at which diminishing, zero, and negative returns set in. There is no reason to believe that all present and future offenders belong to the *a priori* non-responsive groups, or that all penalties have reached the point of diminishing, let alone zero returns.

IV

Even though its effectiveness seems obvious, punishment as a deterrent has fallen into disrepute. Some ideas which help explain this progressive heedlessness were uttered by Lester Pearson, then Prime Minister of Canada, when, in opposing the death penalty, he proposed that instead "the state seek to eradicate the causes of crime—slums, ghettos and personality disorders."[6]

"Slums, ghettos, and personality disorders" have not been shown, singly or collectively, to be "the causes" of crime.

(1) The crime rate in the slums is indeed higher than elsewhere; but so is the death rate in hospitals. Slums are no more "causes" of crime than hospitals are of death; they are locations of crime, as hospitals are of death. Slums and hospitals attract people selectively; neither is the "cause" of the condition (disease in hospitals, poverty in slums) that leads to the selective attraction.

As for poverty which draws people into slums, and, sometimes, into crime, any relative disadvantage may lead to ambition, frustration, resentment and, if insufficiently restrained, to crime. Not all relative disadvantages can be eliminated; indeed very few can be, and their elimination increases the resentment generated by the remaining ones; not even relative poverty can be removed altogether. (Absolute poverty—whatever that may be—hardly affects crime.) However, though contributory, relative disadvantages are not a necessary or suffcient cause of crime: Most poor people do not commit crimes, and some rich people do. Hence, "eradication of poverty" would, at most, remove one (doubtful) cause of crime.

In the United States, the decline of poverty has not been associated with a reduction of crime. Poverty measured in dollars of constant purchasing power, according to present government standards and statistics, was the condition of ½ of all our families in 1920; of ⅕ in 1962; and less than ⅙ in 1966. In 1967, 5.3 million families out of 49.8 million were poor—⅛ of all families in the United States. If crime has been reduced in a similar manner, it is a well-kept secret.

Those who regard poverty as a cause of crime often draw a wrong inference from a true proposition: The rich will not commit certain crimes—Rockefeller never riots; nor does he steal. (He mugs, but only on T.V.) Yet while wealth may be the cause of not committing (certain) crimes, it does not follow that poverty (absence of wealth) is the cause of committing them. Water extinguishes or prevents fire; but its absence is not the cause of fire. Thus, if poverty could be abolished, if everybody had all "necessities" (I don't pretend to know what this would mean), crime would remain, for, in the words of Aristotle, "the greatest crimes are committed not for the sake of basic necessities but for the sake of superfluities." Superfluities cannot be provided by the government; they would be what the government does not provide.

(2) Negro ghettos have a high, Chinese ghettos have a low crime rate. Ethnic separation, voluntary or forced, obviously has little to do with crime; I can think of no reason why it should.[7]

(3) I cannot see how the state could "eradicate" personality disorders even if all causes and cures were known and available. (They are not.) Further, the known incidence of personality disorders within the prison population does not exceed the known incidence outside—though our knowledge of both is tenuous. Nor are personality disorders necessary or sufficient causes for criminal offenses, unless these be identified by means of (moral, not clinical) definition with personality disorders. In this case, Mr. Pearson would have proposed to "eradicate" crime by eradicating crime—certainly a sound, but not a helpful idea.

Mr. Pearson's views are part as well of the mental furniture of the former U.S. Attorney General Ramsey Clark; who told a congressional committee that ". . . only the elimination of the causes of crime can make a significant and lasting difference in the incidence of crime." Uncharitably interpreted, Mr. Clark revealed that only the elimination of causes eliminates effects—a sleazy cliché and wrong to boot. Given the benefit of the doubt, Mr. Clark probably meant that the causes of crime are social; and that therefore crime can be reduced "only" by non-penal (social) measures.

This view suggests a fireman who declines fire-fighting apparatus by pointing out that "in the long run only the elimination of the causes" of fire "can make a significant and lasting difference in the incidence" of fire, and that fire-fighting equipment does not eliminate "the causes"—except that such a fireman would probably not rise to fire chief. Actually, whether fires are checked depends on equipment and on the efforts of the firemen using it no less than on the presence of "the causes": inflammable materials. So with crimes. Laws, courts and police actions are no less important in restraining them than "the causes" are in impelling them. If firemen (or attorney generals) pass the buck and refuse to use the means available, we may all be burned while waiting for "the long run" and "the elimination of the causes."

Whether any activity—be it lawful or unlawful—takes place depends on whether the desire for it, or for whatever is to be secured by it, is stronger than the desire to avoid the costs involved. Accordingly people work, attend college, commit crimes, go to the movies—or refrain from any of these activities. Attendance at a theatre may be high because the show is entertaining and because the price of admission is low. Obviously the attendance depends on both—on the combination of expected gratification and cost. The wish, motive or impulse for doing anything—the experienced, or expected, gratification—is the cause of doing it; the wish to avoid the cost is the cause of not doing it. One is no more and no less "cause" than the other. (Common speech supports this use of "cause" no less than logic: "Why did you go to Jamaica?" "*Because* it is such a beautiful place." "Why didn't you go to Jamaica?" "*Because* it is too expensive."—"Why do you buy this?" "*Because* it is so cheap." "Why don't you buy that?" "*Because* it is too expensive.") Penalties (costs) are causes of lawfulness, or (if too low or uncertain) of unlawfulness, of crime. People do commit crimes because, given their conditions, the desire for the satisfaction sought prevails. They refrain if the desire to avoid the cost prevails. Given the desire, low cost (penalty) causes the action, and high cost restraint. Given the cost, desire becomes the causal variable. Neither is intrinsically more causal than the other. The crime rate increases if the cost is reduced or the desire raised. It can be decreased by raising the cost or by reducing the desire.

The cost of crime is more easily and swiftly changed than the conditions producing the inclination to it. Further, the costs are very largely within the power of the government to change, whereas the conditions producing propensity to crime are often only indirectly affected by government action, and some are altogether beyond the control of the government. Our unilateral emphasis on these conditions and our undue neglect of costs may contribute to an unnecessarily high crime rate.

V

The foregoing suggests the question posed by the death penalty: Is the deterrence added (return) sufficiently above zero to warrant irrevocability (or other, less clear, disadvantages)? The question is not only whether the penalty deters, but whether it deters more than alternatives and whether the difference exceeds the cost of irrevocability. (I shall assume that the alternative is actual life imprisonment so as to exclude the complication produced by the release of the unrehabilitated.)

In some fairly infrequent but important circumstances the death penalty is the only possible deterrent. Thus, in case of acute *coups d'état,* or of acute substantial attempts to overthrow the government, prospective rebels would altogether discount the threat of any prison sentence. They would not be deterred because they believe the swift victory of the revolution will invalidate a prison sentence and turn it into an advantage. Execution would be the only deterrent because, unlike prison sentences, it cannot be revoked by victorious rebels. The same reasoning applies to deterring spies or traitors in wartime. Finally, men who, by virtue of past acts, are already serving, or are threatened, by a life sentence could be deterred from further offenses only by the threat of the death penalty.[8]

What about criminals who do not fall into any of these (often ignored) classes? Prof. Thorsten Sellin has made a careful study of the available statistics: He concluded that they do not yield evidence for the deterring effect of the death penalty.[9] Somewhat surprisingly, Prof. Sellin seems to think that this lack of evidence for deterrence is evidence for the lack of deterrence. It is not. It means that deterrence has not been demonstrated statistically—not that non-deterrence has been.

It is entirely possible; indeed likely (as Prof. Sellin appears willing to concede), that the statistics used; though the best available, are nonetheless too slender a reed to rest conclusions on. They indicate that the homicide rate does not vary greatly between similar areas with or without the death penalty, and in the same area before and after abolition. However, the similar areas are not similar enough; the periods are not long enough; many social differences and changes, other than the abolition of the death penalty, may account for the variation (or lack of it) in homicide rates with and without, before and after abolition; some of these social differences and changes are likely to have affected homicide rates. I am unaware of any statistical analysis which adjusts for such changes and differences. And logically, it is quite consistent with the postulated deterrent effect of capital punishment that there be less homicide after abolition: With retention there might have been still less.

Homicide rates do not depend exclusively on penalties any more than do other crime rates. A number of conditions which influence the propensity to crime, demographic, economic or general social changes or differences—even such matters as changes of the divorce laws or of the cotton price—may influence the homicide rate. Therefore variation or constancy cannot be attributed to variations or constancy of the penalties, unless we know that no other factor influencing the homicide rate has changed. Usually we don't. To believe the death penalty deterrent does not require one to believe that the death penalty, or any other, is the only or the decisive causal variable; this would be as absurd as the converse mistake that "social causes" are the only or always the decisive factor. To favor capital punishment, the efficacy of neither variable need be denied. It is enough to affirm that the severity of the penalty may influence some potential criminals, and that the added severity of the death penalty adds to deterrence or may do so. It is quite possible that such a deterrent effect may be offset (or intensified) by non-penal factors which affect propensity; its presence or absence therefore may be hard, and perhaps impossible to demonstrate.

Contrary to what Prof. Sellin *et al.* seem to presume, I doubt that offenders are aware of the absence or presence of the death penalty state by state or period by period. Such unawareness argues against the assumption of a calculating murderer. However, unawareness does not argue against the death penalty if by deterrence we mean a preconscious, general response to a severe, but not necessarily specifically and explicitly apprehended, or calculated threat. A constant homicide rate, despite abolition, may occur because of unawareness and not because of lack of deterrence. People remain deterred for a lengthy interval by the severity of the penalty in the past, or by the severity of penalties used in similar circumstances nearby.

I do not argue for a version of deterrence which would require me to believe that an individual shuns murder while in North Dakota, because of the death penalty, and merrily goes to it in South Dakota since it has been abolished there; or that he will start the murderous career from which he had hitherto refrained, after abolition, I hold that the generalized threat of the death penalty may be a deterrent, and the more so, the more generally applied. Deterrence will not cease in the particular areas of abolition or at the particular times of abolition. Rather, general deterrence will be somewhat weakened, through local (partial) abolition. Even such weakening will be hard to detect owing to changes in many offsetting, or reinforcing, factors.

For all of these reasons, I doubt that the presence or absence of a deterrent effect of the death penalty is likely to be demonstrable by statistical means. The statistics presented by Prof. Sellin *et al.* show only that there is no statistical proof for the deterrent effect of the death penalty. But they do not show that there is no deterrent effect. Not to demonstrate presence of the effect is not the same as to demonstrate its absence; certainly not when there are plausible explanations for the non-demonstrability of the effect.

It is on our uncertainty that the case for deterrence must rest.[10]

VI

If we do not know whether the death penalty will deter others, we are confronted with two uncertainties. If we impose the death penalty, and achieve no deterrent effect thereby, the life of a convicted murderer has been expended in vain (from a deterrent viewpoint). There is a net loss. If we impose the death sentence and thereby deter some future murderers, we spared the lives of some future victims (the prospective murderers gain too; they are spared punishment because they were deterred). In this case, the death penalty has led to a net gain, unless the life of a convicted murderer is valued more highly than that of the unknown victim, or victims (and the non-imprisonment of the deterred non-murderer).

The calculation can be turned around, of course. The absence of the death penalty may harm no one and therefore produce a gain—the life of the convicted murderer. Or it may kill future victims of murderers who could have been deterred, and thus produce a loss—their life.

To be sure, we must risk something certain—the death (or life) of the convicted man, for something uncertain—the death (or life) of the victims of murderers who may be deterred. This is in the nature of uncertainty—when we invest, or gamble, we risk the money we have for an uncertain gain. Many human actions, most commitments—including marriage and crime—share this characteristic with the deterrent purpose of any penalization, and with its rehabilitative purpose (and even with the protective).

More proof is demanded for the deterrent effect of the death penalty than is demanded for the deterrent effect of other penalties. This is not justified by the absence of other utilitarian purposes such as protection and rehabilitation; they involve no less uncertainty than deterrence.[11]

Irrevocability may support a demand for some reason to expect more deterrence than revocable penalties might produce, but not a demand for more proof of deterrence, as has been pointed out above. The reason for expecting more deterrence lies in the greater severity, the terrifying effect inherent in finality. Since it seems more important to spare victims than to spare murderers, the burden of proving that the greater severity inherent in irrevocability adds nothing to deterrence lies on those who oppose capital punishment. Proponents of the death penalty need show only that there is no more uncertainty about it than about greater severity in general.

The demand that the death penalty be proved more deterrent than alternatives cannot be satisfied any more than the demand that six years in prison be proved to be more deterrent than three. But the uncertainty which confronts us favors the death penalty as long as by imposing it we might save future victims of murder. This effect is as plausible as the general idea that penalties have deterring effects which increase with their severity. Though we have no proof of the positive deterrence of the penalty, we also have no proof of zero or negative effectiveness. I believe we have no right to risk additional future victims of murder for the sake of sparing convicted murderers; on the contrary, our moral obligation is to risk the possible ineffectiveness of executions. However rationalized, the opposite view appears to be motivated by the simple fact that executions are more subjected to social control than murder. However, this applies to all penalties and does not argue for the abolition of any.

Endnotes

1. Social solidarity of "community feeling" (here to be ignored) might be dealt with as a form of deterrence.

2. Certainly a major meaning of *suum cuique tribue.*

3. I am not concerned here with the converse injustice, *which I regard as no less grave.*

4. Such inequity, though likely, has not been demonstrated. Note that, since there are more poor than rich, there are likely to be more guilty poor; and, if poverty contributes to crime, the proportion of the poor who are criminals also should be higher than of the rich.

5. I neglect those motivated by civil disobedience or, generally, moral or political passion. Deterring them depends less on penalties than on the moral support they receive, though

penalties play a role. I also neglect those who may belong to all three groups listed, some successively, some even simultaneously, such as drug addicts. Finally, I must altogether omit the far-from-negligible role that problems of apprehension and conviction play in deterrence—beyond saying that, by reducing the government's ability to apprehend and convict, courts are able to reduce the risks of offenders.

6. I quote from the *New York Times* (November 24, 1967, p. 22). The actual psychological and other factors which bear on the disrepute—as distinguished from the rationalizations—cannot be examined here.

7. Mixed areas, incidentally, have higher crime rates than segregated ones (see, e.g., R. Ross and E. van den Haag, *The Fabric of Society* (New York: Harcourt, Brace & Co., 1957), pp. 102–4. Because slums are bad (morally) and crime is, many people seem to reason that "slums spawn crime"—which confuses some sort of moral with a causal relation.

8. Cautious revolutionaries, uncertain of final victory, might be impressed by prison sentences—but not in the acute stage, when faith in victory is high. And one can increase even the severity of a life sentence in prison. Finally, harsh punishment of rebels can intensify rebellious impulses. These points, though they qualify it, hardly impair the force of the argument.

9. Sellin considered mainly homicide statistics. His work may be found in his *Capital Punishment* (New York: Harper & Row, 1967); or, most conveniently, in H. A. Bedau, *The Death Penalty in America* (Garden City, N.Y.: Doubleday & Co., 1964), which also offers other material, mainly against the death penalty.

10. In view of the strong emotions aroused (itself an indication of effectiveness to me: Might not murderers be as upset over the death penalty as those who wish to spare them?) and because I believe penalties must reflect community feeling to be effective, I oppose mandatory death sentences and favor optional, and perhaps binding, recommendations by juries after their finding of guilt. The opposite course risks the non-conviction of guilty defendants by juries who do not want to see them executed.

11. Rehabilitation or protection are of minor importance in our actual penal system (though not in our theory). We confine many people who do not need rehabilitation and against whom we do not need protection (e.g., the exasperated husband who killed his wife); we release many unrehabilitated offenders against whom protection is needed. Certainly rehabilitation and protection are not, and deterrence is, the main actual function of legal punishment if we disregard non-utilitarian ones.

41. *Christian Ethics and Capital Punishment: A Reflection*

ALEXANDER WILLIAMS, JR.

Assessing the issue of the death penalty from a distinctively Christian perspective, Alexander Williams, Jr., examines the central arguments for and against the practice and then considers scriptural references to capital punishment from both the Hebrew Bible and Christian New Testament. After a brief analysis of these texts, Williams concludes that Christians are called upon to focus on love and compassion, to de-emphasize thoughts of retribution, and to search for fairness and humanness in all deliberations concerning criminal matters. At the same time, the biblical texts do not preclude capital punishment and the Christian is called upon by God to deliver justice in a fair and even-handed manner. In conclusion, Williams argues that a Christian can support the application of the death penalty as an appropriate social response to murders accompanied by aggravating circumstances.

Never will the time be more opportune than now for serious reflection and discussion of capital punishment and Christian ethics. The United States of

From *The Journal of Religious Thought,* Summer/Fall 1992, pp. 59–77.

America now holds the dubious distinction of being the world's leader in the area of homicides. General interest in the death penalty has never been greater than it is today as we witness the vicious killings of individuals by fellow human beings in almost every urban community in America. According to a Senate

Judiciary Committee report recently released, it has been projected that more than 23,220 people will be murdered in 1990—about 2,000 more than in 1989 and higher than the national record of 23,040 murders in 1980.[1] Senator Joseph R. Biden, Jr. (D-Del.), the Committee chairman, commented during the hearing: "The nation is faced with an immediate peril and the situation is doomed to get worse unless we take action today." He called for an "all-fronts assault on the drug epidemic" as well as swift House passage of a Senate-passed crime bill that would ban domestically manu-factured assault weapons and impose the death penalty for thirty-four federal offenses.[2]

Franz Bockle and Jacques Pohier, in their book *The Death Penalty and Torture*,[3] identify two major factors that affect the public's current assessment of capital punishment. First, they point out the extraordinary emphasis placed upon crimes by the media and partic-ularly the audiovisual media. Under the section enti-tled "The Part Played By the Media," they state:

> It is particularly striking how many newspa-pers, for example, nowadays regard it as their special responsibility to give a full ac-count of the facts of a crime, to conduct an inquiry in parallel with that of the police and in this way to involve their readers in their pursuit of the criminal. These newspapers reached perhaps several hundred thousand people. Information on the television, on the other hand, reaches millions, even tens of millions. The crime that is in the limelight at any given time is repeated in the newspapers and on the screen again and again, described in all its details and subjected to a great deal of comments, so that the readers, viewers and listeners' attention is captured and re-tained. Oftentimes, the media almost always fastens onto what is of secondary importance and neglects the essential aspects of a case; the reader is often given thrilling publica-tions and revelations and information which has often the ability to broadcast the seeds of fear in the minds and hearts of many of the viewers and listeners.[4]

Second, it is suggested that many public officials take a less than honest approach to the question of capital punishment. The authors boldly assert that

> Unscrupulous politicians have a stake in ex-ploiting uninformed public opinion while conscientious legislators are threatened with loss of election for being permissive and soft on crime if they do not join in the enactment of the death penalty statutes.[5]

Undoubtedly, then, there are few issues in American justice that spark passion like the death penalty. In fact, many would deny that the death penalty is a criminal justice issue at all, but instead is one of basic human rights. Indeed, there are emotional arguments both in support of and against the death penalty. It is of little consequence that the thirty-seven states that execute criminals differ in the various meth-ods of execution. Whether the approach is by shoot-ing, hanging, electrocution, gassing, or lethal injection, personal feelings are not affected. On the one hand, there are those who argue that capital punishment is wrong on the theory that life is too sacred to be taken by anyone, even by the State for what would appear to be good reason. On the other hand, those who favor the death penalty will shake their heads, wondering why we should value the murderer's life when he did not value that of his victim. As with many of life's most fundamental moral questions, there seems to be no middle ground for compromise concerning the death penalty. Similar to the abortion debate, each side engages in politics of confrontation rather than reconciliation.

The religious community is clearly obligated to enter this great moral issue of our time. As indicated by Richard Niebuhr in his book *Christ and Culture*,[6] we as Christians are not isolated from civilization but are part and parcel of society and everything included in society. Christ, according to Niebuhr's fifth motif, con-verts and transforms culture, and as such all human issues must get direction and invigoration from Christ and those of us (Christians) who profess to subscribe to the ideals of Christ.[7]

This article reflects on the religious and ethical considerations in determining the approach for the Christian on the question of capital punishment. To

---

[1] "Murder Rate Surges Toward U.S. Record," *Washington Post*, August 1, 1990.

[2] Ibid.

[3] Franz Bockle and Jacques Pohier, *The Death Penalty and Torture* (New York: The Seabury Press, 1979).

[4] Ibid., 87.

[5] Ibid., 38.

[6] H. Richard Niebuhr, *Christ and Culture* (New York: Har-per & Row, 1951).

[7] Ibid., 45.

begin with, it is necessary to articulate and examine the arguments advanced in favor of capital punishment as well as those in opposition to the death penalty. Following that exposition, some of the biblical references in both the Old and New Testaments will be set forth in order to review the basis upon which many Christians and many churches cite authority for their position. Finally, several observations and factors will be pinpointed that should critically shape and influence the guidelines and paradigms that can determine the appropriate position of the Christian on capital punishment. Following the development of the Christian approach to the issue is the inevitable conclusion of one personally involved in decisions of capital punishment.

Arguments in Favor of Capital Punishment

It has been said that "The right of administering punishment is the right of the sovereign as the supreme power to inflict pain upon a subject on account of a crime committed by him."[8] This statement is at the foundation of all arguments favoring capital punishment.

The proponents of capital punishment vigorously support the imposition of death as a punishment for heinous offenses. First, they raise the question as to why law-abiding citizens have to suffer at the hands of law breakers. Inasmuch as the public is outraged and disgusted with violence perpetrated against innocent victims and citizens, it is perfectly legitimate for the State to express this anger and vent this outrage by imposing capital punishment. Second, it logically follows that retribution and vengeance should be, and have long been, valid purposes of the criminal justice system. If private acts of vengeance (recent trends in New York suggest that private citizens are now seeking vengeance on their own) and vigilante groups are to be suppressed, citizens must have some assurance that the State will seek retribution on behalf of its citizens.

Third, capital punishment serves as a general deterrent to others who will come to realize what will happen to them if they engage in this kind of violent behavior.

The argument here is that although there is no empirical data to verify the role of deterrence, those who claim that it does not deter have the burden to prove their position. It is further insisted that those with that burden cannot themselves prove that it does not deter. Moreover, as the proponents posit, the death penalty serves as a special deterrent. It is beyond dispute that the execution of the offender is the most effective and certain method by which the offender is incapacitated or prevented from perpetrating additional crimes against society.

Fourth, the proponents of the death penalty argue that the majority of people in this country support capital punishment and America has always followed the democratic notion of the majority and consensus as a principle of operation. In support of this argument they point out that approximately thirty-seven state legislatures, representing most of the people in this country, have enacted legislation to impose capital punishment. Candidates for political office campaign on that issue and are elected over those who do not so favor (remember President Bush versus Governor Dukakis in 1988).

Fifth, proponents insist that biblical text supports capital punishment, and, in fact, during the medieval period even the Church recognized the right of the State to execute for the common good. *Lex talionis*, the Law of Retribution, they claim, has long been the basis upon which the State is authorized to protect and defend the common good by using violent means to repel the vicious.

The retributive aspect of the proponents' position has been often repeated by any number of authors. The proponents believe that most of these murderers never express regret for the heinous crimes they commit, nor do they feel the slightest sympathy for the victim or their families. The proponents approve of the Supreme Court's recent attempts to streamline, curtail, and quicken the appeal mechanisms in order that the criminal justice system can become better balanced toward providing more justice to victims rather than always focusing on expanding the rights for criminal defendants.

Arguments Against Capital Punishment

Championed by the likes of recently retired Justice William Brennan of the United States Supreme Court, the opponents of capital punishment raise equally forceful arguments. They first argue that the death penalty

---

[8]Michael E. Endres, *The Morality of Capital Punishment: Equal Justice Under the Law?* (Mystic, Conn.: Twenty-Third Publications, 1985), 103.

serves no legitimate utility, and, in fact, they assert, it has demonstrably failed to accomplish its stated objectives. Modern scholars and theologians commencing with the eighteenth century have long rejected retribution as a valid aim of the criminal justice system. They have seriously challenged the right of the State to execute. With respect to deterrence, they claim that with over 20,000 homicides committed each year, and only 300 convicted murders receiving the death penalty, it is clear that the death penalty does not deter. In fact, they suggest that drug dealers are more aware of the death penalty on the streets (for selling bad drugs, or not paying for drugs, or invading another's territory) than the State's imposed capital punishment. Consequently, they posit, when you successfully assail the only two purposes advanced as support for capital punishment (retribution and deterrence), any other purposes can be achieved by other punitive measures. For example, protection of society can be achieved by incarcerating dangerous individuals for the rest of their lives. Moreover, a life without parole sentence can also serve to deter and can address rehabilitation as a goal, which capital punishment cannot.

Second, they argue that notwithstanding the Supreme Court's opinion in *Gregg v. Georgia*,[9] the evolving standards of decency have not reached a point where society as a whole condones State executions. They reject the notion of the majority on the theory that the majority has frequently been wrong throughout history. (The historical majority favored slavery, favored the separate but equal doctrine until 1954, used to sanction ill treatment for women, and used to cut off a person's hands for being convicted as a thief.) They argue that capital punishment is barbaric and very cruel and unusual in the sense that if we don't abuse the rapist, don't burn down the house of the arsonist, don't beat up the robber or the one who assaults, and don't cut off the hand of the thief, why should we kill the killer?

Third, the opponents argue that capital punishment is arbitrarily and capriciously inflicted as a punishment. It is beyond real debate that the underclass, the poor, and the black in the country disproportionately are the hardest hit and most often the target of capital punishment. Those without money to hire private attorneys and those not the favorite of police, prosecutors, judges, and governors are seen as the victims of discriminatory application of the death penalty. While no effort is being made to cast aspersions on public defender agencies, the reality is that

inadequate funding and staffing problems give rise to shortcomings in the quality of representation with respect to the resources of the government.

There has also been statistical evidence established with reference to the discrimination of African Americans. The opponents of capital punishment cite the Baldus study[10] presented by a black defendant who was convicted and sentenced to die in Georgia for the robbery and murder of a white police officer. In the majority opinion by Supreme Court Justice Powell, which held that the Baldus study did not establish that Georgia's capital punishment scheme violated the Equal Protection clause, the Court, nevertheless, referenced the study in detail:

> In support of his claim, McCleskey proffered a statistical study performed by Professors David C. Baldus, George Woodworth, and Charles Pulaski [the Baldus study] that purports to show a disparity in the imposition of the death sentence in Georgia based on the race of the murder victim and, to a lesser extent, the race of the defendant. The Baldus study is actually two sophisticated statistical studies that examine over 2,000 murder cases that occurred in Georgia during the 1970s. The raw numbers collected by Professor Baldus indicate that defendants charged with killing white persons received the death penalty in 11% of the cases, but defendants charged with killing blacks received the death penalty in only 1% of the cases. The raw numbers also indicate a reverse racial disparity according to the race of the defendant: 4% of the black defendants received the death penalty, as opposed to 7% of the white defendants.[11]

Fourth, capital punishment, as a punitive measure, is final and irreversible, which the opponents advance as the strongest reason for rejecting the death penalty.

---

[9]*Gregg v. Georgia*, 428 U.S. 153 (1976).

[10]Statistical study performed by Professors David C. Baldus, George Woodworth, and Charles Pulski purporting to show a disparity in the imposition of the death sentence in Georgia based on race.

[11]Baldus's 230-variable model divided cases into eight different ranges, according to the estimated aggravation level of the offense. Baldus argued in his testimony to the District Court that the effects of racial bias were most striking in the mid-range cases. "[W]hen the cases become tremendously aggravated so that everybody would agree that if we're going to have a death sentence, these are the cases that should get it, the race effects go away. It's only in the mid-range of cases

There have been mistakes in convictions throughout history, and the death penalty precludes the opportunity to rectify a miscarriage of justice. Hugo Bedau, in his treatise *The Death Penalty in America*, emphatically asserts that the innocent have been executed and that there is no system of criminal jurisprudence that has on the whole provided safeguards against the conviction and possible execution of an innocent man.[12]

Fifth, similar to assertions by the proponents, there is ample authority in the scripture replete with suggestion for compassion, condonation, and remorse as well as for retribution, which the opponents dismiss as primitive and animalistic.

Sixth, the opponents stress the fiscal impact and argue that the $1,000,000 amount per execution (which includes the entire legal process) is too costly and the sum should be placed elsewhere to meet the State's pressing demands on the treasury from its citizens.

Last, the death penalty, many observers have claimed, has made securing convictions more difficult and has often resulted in the acquittal of obviously guilty defendants. In other words, unpunished criminals are walking the streets because juries won't convict them of capital crimes knowing that they would get mandatory death. In short, many are satisfied that mandatory capital punishment does indeed have a deterrent effect: It deters jurors from convicting probably guilty men.[13] To recap, it is the sacredness of life, the criminal as a victim, and the discriminatory application of the death penalty that undergird the basic position of the opponents to capital punishment.

Religion and the Biblical Basis

Theological arguments both for and against the death penalty rely heavily on scriptural text.[14] Emphatically, the proponents who employ scriptural text argue that capital punishment is justified or even mandated by the scriptures, whereas the opponents assert that the text unequivocally rejects capital punishment under all circumstances.

The bottom line is that even though many people occasionally invoke God to buttress their particular viewpoint, it is the "picking and choosing" of what they find morally acceptable out of the Bible that casts doubts on the issue of justice and morality.[15] Regardless of one's viewpoint, there is always ample authority and scriptural text that can be cited in support of a position. Yet for every passage cited by the proponents of capital punishment, there is a corresponding citation to the contrary. Most of the citations, unfortunately, rarely convince scholars and theologians, inasmuch as most of the cited authority is taken out of its historical context and has not been adequately studied for its contemporary application.

The Old Testament

The proponents of capital punishment vigorously advance the various passages of the Old Testament to support their position favoring capital punishment. To cite a few examples:

> Leviticus 24:17—"He who kills a man shall be put to death."

> Genesis 4:15—"Then the Lord said to him, "Not so! If any one slays Cain, vengeance shall be taken on him sevenfold."

> Exodus 21:12—"Whoever strikes a man so that he dies shall be put to death."

> Genesis 9:6—"Whoever sheds the blood of man, by man shall his blood be shed."

> Exodus 21:23–24—"If any harm follows, then you shall give life for life, eye for eye, tooth for tooth, hand for hand, foot for foot, burn for burn, wound for wound, stripe for stripe."

> Numbers 35:30—"If any one kills a person, the murderer shall be put to death on the evidence of witnesses."

> Deuteronomy 19:21—"Your eye shall not pity, it shall be life for life, eye for eye, tooth for tooth, hand for hand, foot for foot."

---

where the decision makers have a real choice as to what to do. If there's room for the exercise of discretion, then the [racial] factors begin to play a role." Under this model, Baldus found that 14.4 percent of the black-victim mid-range cases received the death penalty, and 34.4 percent of the white-victim cases received the death penalty. According to Baldus, the facts of McCleskey's case placed it within the mid-range.

[12]Hugo Adam Bedau, *The Death Penalty in America* (Chicago: Aldine Publishing Company, 1964), 189.

[13]Hugo Adam Bedau, *Capital Punishment in the United States* (New York: AMS Press, 1975), 49.

[14]Endres, *The Morality of Capital Punishment*, 25.

[15]Howard E. Kiefer and Milton K. Munitz, *Ethics and Social Justice* (Albany: State University of New York Press, 1968), 53.

Isaiah 59:18—"According to their deeds, so will he repay, wrath to his adversaries, requital to his enemies."

In citing such Old Testament passages as authority for the imposition of capital punishment, these proponents appear to overlook other seemingly contradictory Old Testament text. They fail to explain or resolve conflicting passages such as

Exodus 20:13—"Thou (you) shall not kill."

Deuteronomy 5:17—"Thou (you) shall not kill."

Ezekiel 33:11—"Say to them, As I live, says the Lord God, I have no pleasure in the death of the wicked, but that the wicked turn back from your evil ways; for why will you die, O house of Israel."

There is a serious problem with taking particular passages from the Old Testament as authority for contemporary applications. For one thing, too many people view much of the Old Testament as mandating retributive punishment. The other point is that the historical Israel frequently invoked capital punishment because, as a primitive society, it had no prisons, no incarceration, no concept of rehabilitation, and hence no alternative to execution of violent individuals.[16] Gerald Austin McHugh, in his book *Christian Faith and Criminal Justice,* concluded that it is a common error to regard the God of the Old Testament as a wrathful God,[17] who punishes for the sake of vengeance.

In sum, though there are numerous passages in the Old Testament implying a retributive and vengeful tone in God's word, it is pure folly to cite such text as unequivocal authority for either the justification or condemnation of capital punishment.

The New Testament

Likewise, there are those who cite scripture in the New Testament in support of their opposition to the death penalty. The opponents of capital punishment argue that the New Testament has its spiritual foundation in elements of forgiveness, love, redemption, and compassion. Despite Matthew 5:17, where Christ was reported to have said "Think not that I have come to abolish the law and the prophets; I have come not to abolish them, but to fulfill them," the opponents of capital punishment turn to numerous teachings of Jesus for their direction and advice. To cite a few examples, the following is indicative of what they posit is the clear love message of Jesus Christ:

Matthew 5:33–39—"You have heard that it was said, An eye for an eye and a tooth for a tooth, but I say to you, Do not resist one who is evil. But if any one strikes you on the right cheek, turn to him the other also."

Matthew 5:43–44—"You have heard that it was said, You shall love your neighbor and hate your enemy. But I say to you, love your enemies, and pray for those who persecute you."

Luke 6:37—"Judge not, and you will not be judged; condemn not, and you will not be condemned, forgive, and you will be forgiven."

Luke 6:41—"Why do you look at the speck in your brother's eye, but pay no attention to the log in your own?"

Romans 12:19—"Beloved, never avenge yourselves, but leave it to the wrath of God; for it is written, vengeance is mine, I will repay, says the Lord."

Just as with the Old Testament passages, Christians are nevertheless divided on the issue and many are still searching for the Christian position. In "Should Christians Trumpet the Resurrection of the Death Penalty?" Bob Hutchinson mentions the perplexity of Christians:

When Christ was confronted by a lynch mob preparing to stone a woman to death for adultery, he asked, "Who among you is without sin?" (John 8:7). But when Peter attempted to leap to Christ's defense in the Garden of Gethsemane, he said, "Those who live by the sword will die by the sword" (Matthew 26:52). Was this merely a simple statement of fact . . . or was it an implicit sanction of capital punishment? What would Christ have done if, instead of bringing a woman before him accused of adultery, the community had brought a man who regularly slit the throats of little boys?[18]

---

[16]Robert Conuse, "The Bible and Capital Punishment," *Blueprint For Social Justice* (December 1982): 3.

[17]Gerald Austin McHugh, *Christian Faith and Criminal Justice. Toward a Christian Response to Crime and Punishment* (New York: Paulist Press, 1978), 91.

[18]Bob Hutchinson, "Should Christians Trumpet the Resurrection of the Death Penalty?" *Salt* (4 June 1984): 9.

The New Testament, fortunately, gives us some insight on the question of capital punishment. It is preposterous to accept all of the mercy, love, and redemptive teaching of Christ for general contemporary application, but there is guidance and instruction in several events of the New Testament. In "A Protestant's View of the Death Penalty,"[19] Charles S. Milligan describes three events that, though not dealing explicitly with capital punishment, nevertheless relate to it:

> One is that of the woman taken in adultery, whose guilt was not questioned, and who should have been executed according to a legalistic application of the law. It is of interest not only that Jesus brought about her release, but that the legalists threw him into the situation to entrap him. There would have been no point in questioning Jesus about the execution had he not impressed them as the sort of person who might disapprove of capital punishment (John 8:1–11). A second event is Paul's effort to save the life of the escaped slave, Onesimus, who under Roman law was liable to execution (Philemon). The third event is the crucifixion: the supreme case in which malice, cruelty, and injustice combined forces so that even those who found no crime in this man participated in and gave consent to his execution.[20]

To those three events I would add the stoning of Stephen as reported in the Book of the Acts of the Apostles.[21] It is almost shear irony that, as stated by Franz Bockle and Jacques Pohier in *Death Penalty and Torture*,[22] "The Christian religion derives its very existence from the death of a man who was unjustly, and indeed, arbitrarily and capriciously, hung from the gibbet of the cross."[23] And so there are instructions and guidelines. But to this must be added caution and circumspection.

The conclusion is inescapable. While the relevant passages in the New Testament have questionable modern application in difficult times such as those today, they do provide reasonable guidelines for Christian action. A careful and critical review of New Testament scripture does require of Christians (1) an emphasis on love and compassion; (2) a deemphasis, but perhaps not a rejection, of retribution; and (3) a search for humanness and fairness during all deliberations of criminal justice.

What Do the Churches Say on Capital Punishment?

Generally, with the exception of African American Protestants, the religious community (a part of the American majority who favor capital punishment) has taken a position of support for capital punishment. There are some who disagree and argue that the Christian position should be against capital punishment.

The general African American religious and church community (although there are signs this may be changing) pretty much still adhere to its pre-*Gregg v. Georgia*[24] position. The traditional and lingering statement of the American Baptist Convention serves as today's protocol for many churches and denominations:

1. Because the Christian believes in the inherent worth of human personality and in the unceasing availability of God's mercy, forgiveness, and redemptive power, and
2. Because the Christian wholeheartedly supports the emphasis in modern penology upon the process of creative, redemptive rehabilitation, rather than on punitive and primitive retribution, and
3. Because the deterrent effects of capital punishment are not supported by available evidence, and
4. Because the death penalty tends to brutalize the human spirit and the society which condones it, and
5. Because human agencies of legal justice are fallible, permitting the possibility of the executing of the innocent.

We, therefore, recommend the abolition of capital punishment and the reevaluation of the parole system relative to such cases.[25]

---

[19]Cited in Bedau, *The Death Penalty in America*, 175.

[20]Ibid., 176–177.

[21]Acts 6–7; specifically for stoning see Acts 7:57–60.

[22]Bockle and Pohier, *The Death Penalty and Torture*, section on Theological Reflections.

[23]Ibid., 35.

[24]*Gregg v. Georgia*, 428 U.S. 153 (1976) (U.S. Supreme Court case upholding the validity and constitutionality of the Georgia capital punishment statutory scheme).

[25]American Baptist Convention, Statement on Capital Punishment. Adopted Rochester, New York, June 7, 1960.

It is not *what* churches are saying on capital punishment that is at issue. The problem is what they are *not* saying. They have failed to provide the clear reflection and direction for Christians that is needed. Neither has the church set the tone for assessment and resolution of the issue. Like many of the other great issues of our time (AIDS, abortion, affirmative action, gay rights, etc.), capital punishment and its appropriateness or inappropriateness in the context of today's world has remained seriously unaddressed by society's moral leader: the church. The time has now come for the church to enter the debate and address the theological and ethical arguments raised by the proponents and opponents of capital punishment. Anything less is a disservice of great magnitude.

Developing Ethical and Christian Paradigms

On the dawn of the twenty-first century, there have come to the forefront great emotional issues that have bifurcated much of society. Issues such as abortion, homosexuality, drug testing and its effect on loss of privacy, affirmative action, political activism of the church, homelessness, and legalization of drugs all require serious debate, reflection, and clear direction. K. E. Goodpaster and K. M. Sayre in *Ethics and Problems of the 21st Century*[26] discuss these moral issues.

Ample recognition, of course, must be granted for the differences of opinions where people are concerned. This is a very diverse society now and people differ as to the means and manner of resolving society's conflicts. Though it is important that our sense of democracy and the notion of the "majority rule" continue to be elements in the deliberations regarding moral conflicts, the church must not blindly accept the will of the majority. Fairness and justice oftentimes starts with one individual who has challenged a situation on one occasion. In an article by Sidney Hook, "In Defense of Justice," we are told:

> The cry for justice, heard throughout the ages, when clear, has always been a cry for the elimination of specific inequities in specific histori-

cal contexts. It is a demand for equality of treatment or consideration or opportunity in some specific respect in which it is currently being denied. It never dreams of contending or establishing that no conceivable relevant differences are present that would affect the justice of its demand.[27]

The call for justice commences with a dispute and blossoms into a position adopted by many. In the absence of clear guidelines by moral and ethical leaders, there is very little to repudiate the will of the majority.

The religious community and the churches in particular must be urged to speak. For African Americans, who have long been heavily affected by capital punishment in terms of their disproportionate exposure to the penalty, guidance from the Bible and the church is imperative. Many African Americans are very unclear as to the position of the church on capital punishment and accordingly seek church guidance. Enoch H. Oglesby, in *Ethics and Theology from the Other Side: Sounds of Moral Struggle,* depicts the importance of the Bible and the black church as a source of moral guidance:

> In the black christian community, the scheme or orientational topology attempts to partially describe the dynamic patterns of interaction between the "biblical and communal," the black spirituals and the black preacher as sources and resources of ethical and moral guidance in black community life. At the practical level, the Bible for blacks has always served as a central source, as well as normative resource for the christian moral life. In the life of the black christian community, the Bible is perceived, not simply as a book, but *The Book,* wherein the oppressed meet God in their suffering and toil; and this almighty God is perceived to give not only freedom but residual moral guidance to the children of dark skin. So then, the "biblical" is a central moral paradigm for right living. For black Christians, it is both a normative source and practical resource.[28]

---

[26]K. E. Goodpaster and K. M. Sayre, *Ethics and Problems of the 21st Century.* (Notre Dame, Ind.: University of Notre Dame Press, 1979).

[27]In Kiefer and Munitz, *Ethics and Social Justice,* 79.

[28]Enoch H. Oglesby, *Ethics and Theology from the Other Side: Sounds of Moral Struggle* (Lanham, Md.: University Press of America, 1979), 29–30.

Developing Christian Paradigms

In developing Christian paradigms with reference to capital punishment, several observations can be made. First, there is clear indication that a significant number of people view the criminal justice system as inequitable and ineffective. Sociologists, penologists, and other professionals admit that many of the theories for punishment such as deterrence and retribution have questionable utility. Many judges and other persons who are part of the criminal justice system are frustrated because of the lack of resources and expertise available to deal with the sociological and psychological issues that must be addressed as part of the overall solution to violent criminal activity. Second, elected and other public officials are also less than candid, with many of them "hustling" in the sense that they must say the right thing in order to get elected and reelected.

The time has come for the religious community to help develop workable rules and paradigms to approach capital punishment and other issues. These new paradigms must "provide uniform justice based on realistic concepts of human and civil rights, morality and acceptable social norms."[29] As we move toward Christian paradigms, it is imperative that we understand that strict adherence to the Old Testament concept of *lex talionis* as justification for supporting capital punishment is as unacceptable as the blind implementation of New Testament principles of love, compassion, and forgiveness.

Guidelines for the development of such paradigms should involve the following factors:

1. The Christian must clearly recognize that dangerous criminals roam our society on a daily basis, a situation that is inimical to our health, safety, and life.

2. Christians must clearly recognize that the society through the mechanism of the state has an absolute right to protect itself from such vicious and dangerous individuals.

3. Christians must face the fact that the criminal justice system has points of unfairness that must be addressed. The disproportionality of blacks on death row is of grave concern, as is the possibility of verdicts involving erroneous convictions.

4. There must be some degree of compassion for persons who are the defendants and accused persons in the criminal justice system; however, the nature of this compassion and love deserves clarity in the sense that it should focus on fairness and the elimination of oppressive conditions for the inmate or defendant.

5. Christians must understand that on the dawn of the twenty-first century, the idea of forgiveness as a part and parcel of the criminal justice system is now archaic and of little consequence.

6. We may have visions and anticipations that someday we will live in a utopia that is as close to God's kingdom as possible, but the reality of life is that today no such condition exists. The best thing that we can do as Christians is to anticipate that great day of joy, peace, and the absence of conflict.

A Functional Approach

What is the purpose of religion? What is the purpose and function of the Bible? What is the utility of capital punishment? A reflection on the overall purposes of the Bible, religion, and capital punishment encompasses what is termed the functional approach to resolving the issue.

A functional approach to the question of capital punishment first requires the elimination of emotion in assessing the issue and then, second, incorporating the six aforesaid paradigms in reaching a clear approach to the issue. A functional approach also requires that after focusing on the various purposes of the Bible, religion, and capital punishment, those purposes then be read harmoniously together in connection with arriving at a reasonable position. In other words, the design of taking a functional approach to deciding the issue is to make every effort to construe the various purposes as complementing and supplementing each other and not as necessarily clashing or conflicting.

Being uniquely involved in the issue of capital punishment, I take a functional approach to resolving the issue of capital punishment. As the elected State's Attorney for Prince George's County, Maryland,[30] I recognize that the amount of discretion exercised in

---

[29]Lou Torok, *Straight Talk from Prison. A Convict Reflects on Youth, Crime and Society* (New York: Human Science Press, 1974), 125.

[30]Elected in November 1986 as the first African American ever elected as Chief Prosecutor in Prince George's County, Maryland, a suburban jurisdiction in the Washington-Metropolitan area with a population of 700,000 people.

connection with capital punishment is awesome. In our American system of criminal jurisprudence, the prosecutor has a key role in deciding when to seek the death penalty and against whom. Unless the prosecutor (State's Attorney) in the exercise of his or her discretion notifies the accused that he or she intends to seek the death penalty, neither the judge nor the jury would ever have an opportunity to have an impact on such a case. Accordingly, the prosecutor is obligated to possess clear direction and insight in discharging his or her ethical consideration of this issue.

The issue of capital punishment is a difficult one for the Christian. Words in the scripture, such as "die," "death," "vengeance," "kill," "murder," "life for a life," and "blood," have meanings and usage that vary according to one's philosophy or interpretation. What does the phrase in John 8:7 "Those who live by the sword will die by the sword" denote? Does the phrase "The wages of sin are death" authorize the death penalty? It appears that both the proponents and opponents of capital punishment may find a phrase or passage to support their position. That is the beauty of the Bible—it is such a flexible and resilient document that it has lasted through many years and is able to be applied today.

There is nothing substantive in the Bible that unequivocally precludes the imposition of capital punishment. If the people of God can accept a self-defense killing or killing in the course of war and defending freedom, then there is nothing so shocking or barbaric about the death penalty as a means of punishment. The Christian must seek to assure fairness in the process. A Christian must subscribe to love ethics, which historically has embodied kindness, forgiveness, forbearance, and redemption. Love ethics must, however, be expanded to include resistance to violence even if it results in the taking of life. Christians may continue to love the vicious criminal, but we need not love violence and oppression, which must at times be forcefully prevented.

The world is not a perfect place. There are some areas of imperfections. Similarly, the criminal justice system has some deficiencies. We must work to cure the shortcomings, such as disproportion in sentencing, and do the best that, as Christians, we can do under very difficult and emotional circumstances. Those in the criminal justice system must seek to promote fairness and compassion wherever they can possibly make a difference. Beyond that, of course, Christians must assume that the majority of citizens struggle to enact just, fair, and well-reasoned rules of law that must be followed in order to maintain the moral order.[31]

As a Christian who happens to be the elected State's Attorney for Prince George's County, Maryland, I support the death penalty and intend to execute it as part of my sworn duty. The Maryland legislature saw fit to impose a penalty of death in appropriate capital cases, and the Court of Appeals of Maryland and the United States' Supreme Court have determined it to be legal and within the boundaries of the state and federal constitutions.

Traditionally, juries in Prince George's County have expressed a reluctance to impose the death penalty in every capital case. However, it is my view that carefully selected cases setting forth strong, aggravating, and heinous factors warrant being presented as capital cases for consideration and decision by juries. It is my duty, however, as State's Attorney to ensure that a reasonable, fair, and consistent death penalty policy is in place. Accordingly, I have established and implemented a policy pertaining to the procedure to be used in filing notices of intent to seek the death penalty. Each aggravated murder will be reviewed by myself and my executive staff, which consists of two deputies and four division chiefs. Following a full discussion and a recommendation from the executive staff, I shall make the final decisions whether to file a notice of intent to seek the death penalty. Factors to be considered in making this determination include any aggravating or mitigating circumstances, any past criminal history of the accused, the youth of the accused, and the general and specific background of the accused.

In sum, those individuals who have a part in the capital punishment process must make certain that unfairness and unreasonableness be eliminated from the process. Ethical considerations of this nature must be instilled by those who have an opportunity to make

---

[31]Pending before the House recently was the Comprehensive Crime Control Act of 1990 (HR-5269). Under the "Racially discriminatory capital sentencing" Chapter of HR-5269 (Chapter 177), this congressional bill had it been enacted stated generally that if the percentage of any particular race on death row exceeds that race in the general population, execution of members of that race is prohibited. Exceptions are if the prosecutor can prove by clear and convincing evidence that nonracial factors explain the higher percentage of members on death row or that the sentence being challenged does not fall within a racially discriminatory pattern.

such an impact. Only with this kind of ethical reflection and ethical search does the functional approach receive its imprimatur of legitimacy.

Application of the Functional Approach

On October 13, 1989, Damon Bowie and James Edmonds armed with handguns entered Stoney's Restaurant located in Prince George's County, Maryland. Once inside the restaurant and after having the money handed over to him, Damon Bowie executed two employees, Kevin Brian Shelby and Arnold James Batson, on his way out of the restaurant. Shelby and Batson died as a result of close-range shootings while they were lying down on the floor in compliance with Bowie's instructions. Two other persons were also shot by Bowie, but survived. Damon Bowie and others were indicted on thirty-five counts ranging from murder in the first degree to conspiracy to commit robbery with a deadly weapon.

On July 9, 1990, the Prince George's County State's Attorney, Alexander Williams, Jr., pursuant to policies and guidelines established by the State's Attorney,[32] and after extensive debate and reflection by the State's Attorney and his top assistants, filed a notice of the State's intent to seek the sentence of death against Damon Bowie, who at trial was alleged to be the shooter in this matter. The trial commenced on August 27, 1990, and lasted five days. A jury deliberated for about four hours before handing down a guilty verdict on 20 counts, including the murders of Arnold Batson, a black male, and Kevin Shelby, a white male. About two months later, the same jury, consisting of four black males, one Asian male, three white females, two white males, and two black females, reconvened to pronounce sentencing. Under the Maryland Code, a defendant may be given the death penalty if certain aggravating circumstances exist (for example, committing murder while engaging in a crime of violence, to wit, armed robbery). Although the jury found that there were certain mitigating factors, such as the defendant's age and his troubled childhood, they determined that the aggravating circumstances outweighed the mitigating circumstances. Finding that Damon Bowie was, in fact, the shooter in this incident in which two or more persons were killed, and that the murder occurred while he was attempting

to commit a robbery, the jury pronounced a sentence of death after deliberating for six hours.[33]

During my first term as the elected State's Attorney, I had 15 opportunities to file notices of intent to seek the death penalty based on the presence of certain statutory aggravating circumstances. All but one of those fifteen cases involved young black male defendants. In four of those cases, I applied the functional approach and decided to request that the jury return a death sentence.[34] The case of Damon Bowie was one of those cases. My decision to seek the death penalty in that case reflects my overall position as supportive of capital punishment and also illustrates the process upon which that pro-capital punishment point of view is based. Let me be more specific:

First, and from a biblical standpoint, the scripture, in my view, does not preclude capital punishment. God mandates that human beings treat each other in a fair, just, and righteous manner. This means to me that criminal laws and punishment are to be applied evenly, humanely, and fairly to all. Second, I believe that God has directed that my role in this process is to be on the inside of the criminal justice system where certain critical and fair judgments are to be made. Third, I understand and recognize the politics involved in being on the inside as an elected public servant. The political reality of this role is that I am charged with carrying out the letter and spirit of the law while representing all of the citizens, who expect integrity and impartiality on behalf of all. In order to remain on the inside and maintain this key role of administering justice, it is imperative that I enforce capital punishment, which has been declared legally and constitutionally appropriate. My political health and further interest in politics demands that I find some circumstance warranting my requesting capital punishment in a county experiencing record homicide rates for the past four years. Therefore, I candidly admit that politics and public opinion play a part in this decision.

Fourth, I personally believe that retribution is an appropriate criterion for seeking capital punishment. Having spoken to many families of murdered victims, I am thoroughly convinced that a portion of their grief,

---

[32]Policy and Procedure for Review of Potential Death Penalty Cases (May 1990), Appendix.

[33]On appeal the verdict and sentence was reversed and remanded for a new trial due to error attributed to the trial judge.

[34]Prince George's County juries agreed with the State's Attorney in 75 percent of those cases, thereby returning verdicts of death in three of those cases.

suffering, and resentment is curtailed and eased once they receive assurance that the State is seeking vengeance by requesting capital punishment. Last, I believe that capital punishment is appropriate where a reasonable procedure is put in place that substantially minimizes the arbitrariness, caprice, and unfairness that has been an inherent part of the history of America where African Americans have been accused of murdering whites.

Under procedures that I have put in place since becoming State's Attorney,[35] every effort is made to obtain consistency of treatment and fair play. In the Damon Bowie case, the decision to seek the death penalty was made without reservation and in compliance with my established policy. The debate and deliberation with my staff prior to deciding to file was thorough and spirited. I determined that Mr. Bowie executed at close range two innocent victims who were lying on the floor as ordered in a completely helpless and defenseless position. One murdered victim was white and the other murdered victim was black. The jury that convicted Bowie and sentenced him to death consisted of six African Americans, one Asian-American, and five whites. In view of other aggravating factors, such as a third victim being shot in the face (he is disabled with a severely deformed face) who miraculously lived despite being left for dead, my decision was a correct and ethical one. The

---

[35]Policy on Death Penalty Cases, Appendix.

community rightfully demanded that I seek the death penalty and a jury of an even number of whites and blacks confirmed my opinion and decision.

In short, then, my ultimate position of pro-capital punishment is based upon a myriad of factors. Some of those factors are religious in the sense that I believe God expects us to participate in delivering justice. Other reasons include my personal feeling that capital punishment has a legitimate utility as a punishment, and also my recognition that politics and public opinion play a significant (though not a controlling) role in determining whether a chief law enforcement officer remains in office. This last statement, however, should not be taken out of context. If the majority of citizens through their elected representatives enact a criminal law that is judicially upheld by the courts as legal, then the elected prosecutor ought to reasonably and fairly enforce that law or expect to voluntarily or involuntarily (politically) prepare to leave public service.

Conclusion

As a debatable moral issue, the views relating to the death penalty are varied and stimulating. Despite the deep-seated feelings on both sides, we Christians cannot run from the debate. The bottom line is to approach the issue with reason, respect for both positions, and resolute determination to arrive at a Christian position of fairness and reasonableness.

42. Is *the Death Penalty Irrevocable?*

Michael Davis

Michael Davis pays particular attention to the claim that the death penalty ought
to be discontinued because it is irrevocable in a way that imprisonment is not.
Opponents of capital punishment insist that fallible human beings should not use
a penalty that cannot be corrected because errors are inevitable; because capital
punishment is irrevocable and life imprisonment is not, we should rely instead
on life imprisonment in crimes of murder. Davis argues that the argument is flawed
because it fails to appreciate the character of imprisonment itself as well as the
relative and not absolute differences between life imprisonment and capital
punishment. In the end, Davis refuses to argue for or against the death penalty,
but he suggests that the debate would be much clarified if arguments based on
irrevocability were moderated.

It is sometimes argued that we should abolish the
death penalty (in part at least) because the death
penalty is irrevocable in a way imprisonment is not.
Human beings are fallible, it is said, and fallible beings
should not use a penalty which in effect assumes their
infallibility. Let us call this "the argument from irrevocability."

The argument from irrevocability is treated with
respect both by philosophers and by people with more
practical concerns. Thus Burton Leiser (who favors the
death penalty) is quite willing to admit:

> The death penalty is irrevocable. Although it
> is true that years spent in prison can never be
> returned to a man who was wrongly convict-
> ed, he at least has the opportunity of starting
> over; with the compensation he ought to re-
> ceive from those who wrongfully deprived
> him of those years, he should be able to enjoy
> whatever remains to him. But a person who
> has been executed cannot be brought back if
> he is later found to have been innocent of the
> crime for which he was convicted. Such mis-
> takes cannot be rectified. Mistakes have oc-
> curred. Innocent men have been executed.
> Those who support the death penalty must
> be prepared to live with the fact. . . .[1]

U.S. Supreme Court Justice Brennan (who opposes
the death penalty) makes a similar point in the much-
discussed *Furman* v. *Georgia:*

> Death is truly an awesome punishment. . . .
> The contrast with the plight of a person pun-
> ished by imprisonment is evident. An individ-
> ual in prison does not lose "the right to have
> rights." A prisoner retains, for example, the
> constitutional right . . . of access to the courts.
> His punishment is not irrevocable. Apart from
> the common charge, grounded upon the recog-
> nition of human fallibility, that the punish-
> ment of death must inevitably be inflicted
> upon innocent men, we know that death has
> been the lot of men whose convictions were
> unconstitutionally secured in view of later,
> retroactively applied, holdings of this court . . .
> [Yet] the finality of death precludes relief.[2]

Brennan does not, of course, make exactly the same
argument as Leiser does. Brennan's concern is the
legal consequences of death's irrevocability (for example, loss of "the right to have rights") while Leiser's is
primarily the nonlegal consequences (for example,
lack of "the opportunity to start over").

The arguments are, however, sufficiently alike to
be represented as a single argument from irrevocability having this form:

1. Fallible beings should not, all else equal, use a
    penalty not permitting correction of error if

there is an alternative penalty permitting correction of error.

2. We are fallible beings.

   (So, we should not, all else equal, use a penalty not permitting correction of error if there is an alternative penalty permitting correction of error.)

3. An irrevocable penalty (and only an irrevocable penalty) does not permit correction of error.

4. The death penalty is irrevocable.

5. Imprisonment is an alternative to the death penalty.

6. Imprisonment is not irrevocable.

7. All else is equal (between imprisonment and death). So, we should not use the death penalty.

Many people find this argument compelling. Of those who do not, most (like Leiser) argue that premise 7 is false. Imprisonment and death are (they say) not equal with respect to deterrence, incapacitation, humaneness, or the like. Their arguments are not so much objections to the argument from irrevocability as to other arguments against the death penalty. While I have some sympathy with such objections, my concern here is with premises 3, 4, and 6. What I shall argue is that those three premises cannot, without question-begging, highly dubious assumptions, or equivocation, all be made true at once. The argument from irrevocability is not good even if all else *is* equal. This objection, if sustained, would constitute a complete refutation of the argument from irrevocability.

I proceed in this way. First, I consider those non-legal senses of "irrevocability" supposed to make the premises true. Next, I do the same for the legal senses. Last, I consider several alternatives to "irrevocability" that might charitably be allowed to be what those using the argument "really" mean if they do not mean what they say. While the argument from irrevocability makes a good point, putting that point in terms of irrevocability seems to be a mistake.

Nonlegal Revocability

There is, as Leiser points out, one obvious sense in which death certainly is an irrevocable penalty. Once a convict has been hanged, electrocuted, gassed, or otherwise put to death, he cannot be given back his life. Death is final and irreversible. A dead man cannot be returned to the condition he was in before he was put to death. When you're dead, you're dead.

Let us call the sort of revocability that would allow us to put a person subject to a penalty back in the exact condition he would have been in had he not been subject to that penalty, "absolute revocability." Clearly the death penalty is not absolutely revocable. But as Leiser readily admits, neither is imprisonment. The years in prison cannot be returned. Each day behind bars "scants our mortal lot." So, absolute revocability cannot be what the argument from irrevocability assumes.

Absolute revocability is one sort of nonlegal revocability. There is another, what we may call "substantial revocability." Considerations of substantial revocability yield this defense of premises 3, 4, and 6: While we cannot return a single day of imprisonment served, we can, as Leiser says, give the prisoner a chance to "start over," compensate him, or otherwise put him in a condition more or less *equivalent* to what he would have been in had he not been imprisoned. We can substantially undo imprisonment. But we cannot (Leiser implies) do the same for a dead man. We cannot give a dead man the chance to start life over, compensate him, or otherwise put him in a condition more or less equivalent to what he would have been in had he not been executed. The death penalty is not substantially revocable. Hence, the death penalty is irrevocable in a way imprisonment is not.

How are we to understand this defense of premises 3, 4, and 6? One way to understand it is as an argument from definition. The death penalty is, by definition, a penalty excluding all possibility of the executed starting life over (just as imprisonment is, by definition, a penalty that excludes giving the prisoner a chance to live at liberty any day served in prison). If we define "irrevocability" as (roughly) "not permitting compensation during one's lifetime," the argument from irrevocability is sound. The death penalty would not permit (substantial) revocation because (but only because) the death penalty makes compensation during one's lifetime impossible (while imprisonment does not). But, so understood, this defense of premises 3, 4, and 6 would invite an embarrassing question. Why should revoking be limited to compensation during one's lifetime? Without an argument to show that giving the convict a chance to start life over is the *necessary* mode of correcting error, the definitional version of the argument from irrevocability would beg the question.

We cannot defend defining "irrevocability" as "not permitting compensation during one's lifetime" by pointing to the meaning of words. Ordinary usage does not require us to consider the liberty lost by a day served in prison as any less irrevocably lost than a day of life lost by execution. Any defense of that definition must give us a reason to use "irrevocable" in a sense narrower than the word's ordinary meaning allows.

There is such an argument. The argument assumes that death is the end of all. Death completes one's biography, terminates one's interests, and so makes compensation impossible by making it impossible for anything more to happen to one. The argument has some appeal. But the appeal is fatally limited. The argument requires that we identify our biography with our life. The argument should appeal only to those who make such an identification. For the rest of us—those who plant trees in the shade of which we shall never sit, who buy life insurance our children will collect, who hope to have a decent burial, or who would like to be remembered fondly after we die—death does not seem the end of all. The death that will put us beyond all joy and suffering will not put us beyond all benefit or harm. Our interests exceed bodily survival. Our biography could have a happy ending even if we died sad.

The argument for defining "irrevocability" as "not permitting compensation during one's lifetime" should, I said, appeal only to those who identify our biography with our life. But in fact its appeal is wider. Even many who do not think their own joy and suffering is all that matters are likely to gloss "When you're dead, you're dead" as "When consciousness permanently ceases, one ceases to exist." The difference between any number of days left to live and none to live seems a qualitative difference beyond all dispute and above all price. Imprisonment takes a certain part of life. The death penalty takes all of it. Taking all rather than part may (it seems) be what makes the death penalty irrevocable in a way that imprisonment is not.

Is it? I think not. The death penalty may be a more severe punishment than imprisonment (in part at least) because the death penalty takes the whole of life rather than a part. The difference between the death penalty and even life imprisonment is indeed qualitative, not just quantitative (though perhaps only because taking someone's life deprives him of certain options even life imprisonment does not).[3] But the question here is not why the death penalty is a more severe punishment than even life imprisonment. The question is whether it is irrevocable in a way imprisonment is not. The gloss given above on the truism "When you're dead, you're dead" cannot, I believe, support the argument from irrevocability. It cannot both because its equation of consciousness with existence is dubious and because the connection between the death penalty and death is not quite what appeal to that gloss requires.

We do, of course, tend to equate consciousness with life (just as we tend to equate life with all we are). The permanently comatose seem to many to be "as good as dead," a haunting likeness rather than the person known before. Talk of afterlife without survival of memory seems no more than death by another name. The river Lethe is almost as frightening as the grave. Even sleep, if dreamless, can afterward seem outside life, a temporary death. Yet, we are not consistent about such things. We seldom *treat* the permanently comatose as if already dead (for example, by burying them alive or probating their will). We recognize the rationality of traditions that find attractive the prospect of afterlife without survival of memory. And so on. While we would like to have a clear border between when we are and when we are not, our practice reveals a vast region of disputed claims.

The death penalty itself lies closer to the middle of that disputed region than to the dark country beyond. The irrevocability of death itself seems to be (more or less) a conceptual truth. If you're not permanently dead, you're not really dead at all. If you're also not alive, you're something for which we have no common term because we have no common use for one. ("In limbo," "undead," or the like is about as good as we can do.) The irrevocability of the death penalty seems, in contrast, a mere matter of fact. We can easily imagine a world in which someone executed today might be reviewed (or, perhaps, reconstituted) tomorrow (or next year or decade) if a court so ordered, his memories, personality, and so on intact even if much or all of his body had to be replaced by a copy. In such a world, we might not be willing to say that the executed person, now revived, had been dead at all. We might want to reserve the word "dead" for those whose execution has become "final." Or perhaps we might instead distinguish between the "provisionally dead" and the "finally dead."

However that may be, in such a world the death penalty would remain pretty much what it is now. The execution would look like an execution today. The physical state of the executee would be just what it is now both before and after execution. If no one did anything thereafter to "revive" him, the effect of execution would be just what it is now. If no one did anything thereafter to "revive" him, the effect of execution would be that he was put to death. He would have been put to death even though it might not be correct to say that he was dead (or, at least, "really dead") until the power to revive him had been lost too.

In such a world, the death penalty would be somewhat less objectionable than it is in this one. But the difference is not dramatic. The death penalty would be no more absolutely revocable in that world than in this one. Neither the suffering endured in waiting for execution, nor the experience of execution itself, nor even the time spent "dead" could be undone. Only the "being dead" could be interrupted. Such a death penalty would, I think, have much the same power to deter that it does now, having that power because death (while it lasts) would in such a world deprive the person executed of just what it deprives him of in this world.

If what I have just said seems more or less right, the qualitative difference between even life imprisonment and the death penalty cannot be attributed to the one penalty permitting compensation during one's lifetime while the other does not.

So, if the argument from irrevocability requires assuming that death is the end of all, it is an argument far harder to defend than its defenders seem to suppose. Because its defenders do not seem to be a philosophical clique organized around a special view of death (for example, the reduction of all benefit and burden to joy and suffering), we should not. I think, understand the argument from irrevocability as assuming such a controversial view.

But, if we reject that understanding of the argument, we must understand the argument as indifferent to the mode of compensation. That a punishment permits compensation during one's lifetime will be a consideration but not necessarily the decisive consideration. Not the mode of compensation is important, but compensating one way or another, that is, somehow or other putting the person punished into something like the condition he would have been in had he not been imprisoned or put to death. The motivation for this way of understanding the argument is plainly moral. We should, we think, make up as best we can for any wrong we do another. If monetary compensation will do that, we can (it seems) still substantially revoke the sentence. If we can do it some other way, all well and good. Only if there is no way to put the convict in something like the condition he would have been in had he not been punished is the punishment not substantially revocable. Only then would we owe the convict a "debt" we cannot pay. So, if imprisonment is substantially revocable while the death penalty is not, imprisonment must (given this understanding of the argument) permit making up for the wrong done while the death penalty does not. Let us see.

Suppose we release someone from prison after he has served a sentence of just one day. Surely, if it is possible to put someone in substantially the condition he would have been in had he not been imprisoned, it

should be possible to do it in this case. How would we revoke our ex-prisoner's imprisonment? We could, of course, get him back his old job (without loss of status for the day missed), pay him for his day in prison, and do whatever else we can. Have we now substantially undone that day in prison? There is an important respect in which we have. We have done all we could to make it up to him (and what we have done is far from negligible). There is, however, also an important respect in which we may not have substantially undone that day in prison. That day remains one on which our ex-prisoner did not do what he would otherwise have done and suffered much he would not otherwise have suffered, a day both he and others may never forget. He might well feel that any compensation within our power is too small for that. "Whatever you do," he might say truthfully, "you can't make up to me for that day."

Whether we agree with our ex-prisoner will depend in part on what we take to be the criterion of substantial revocability. Our discussion so far suggests two. If the criterion of revocability is that the convict's condition really be more or less what it was before, then even imprisonment is not always substantially revocable. The prisoner can*not* "start life over." He can at best "start fresh," a dark abyss between the day he entered prison and the day he left. He has a chance to enjoy what remains of his life, nothing more. If, however, the criterion of substantial revocability is either that we do all in our power to compensate the convict (and what we do is far from negligible) or that we do enough so that he would say, "That would make it worth it," then it is sometimes in our power substantially to revoke imprisonment.

But, what is true of imprisonment given such criteria of substantial revocability is true of the death penalty too. The death penalty does not prevent us from doing all in our power to compensate the person executed. The death penalty simply circumscribes what we can do more than imprisonment does. What it leaves within our power is far from negligible. We cannot give the dead man back his old job, but we can pay him for what he lost in wages, benefits, and the like. Any money would, of course, have to go to his estate rather than to him personally. We cannot give him a chance to enjoy life again, but we can arrange his affairs so that they turn out much as they would have had he not been executed. He may not be able to regain his self-respect, but we can posthumously assure him the respect of others. The situation of the dead man is remarkably like that of our ex-prisoner. While some people might feel nothing could repay them for being put to death (just as some might feel that way about being imprisoned for even a day), certainly there is some amount of compensation great enough so that some people (in prospect, of course) would say, "Well, that would make it worth it." So, it seems that if compensation can substantially revoke imprisonment, it can as well (though perhaps not as often) substantially revoke death. Premises 4 and 6 cannot both be true if "irrevocable" means "substantially irrevocable."

Legal Irrevocability

But, it might be thought, all this really misses the point. The point is, as Brennan suggests, that the death penalty cannot be revoked *in law* while a sentence of imprisonment can. Once a man is hanged, his sentence is eternal. He can no longer appeal. Even new evidence cannot change the verdict. His case is closed. His legal situation is (it seems) entirely different from that of a prisoner who can still appeal. A prisoner can always be released before his sentence is complete. In a sense, his case is never closed. If that is the difference between the death penalty and imprisonment, it is certainly a big one. But is that the difference?

I think not. In one way, a death sentence is just as revocable in law as is a sentence of imprisonment. Until the death sentence is executed, carrying out the sentence may be interrupted and the condemned man released. He can be released after being sent to death row, after being marched to the gallows, and even after having the noose slipped around his neck. The death penalty takes time to carry out. The death sentence, like any other sentence, names a *process* as well as an *outcome*. The process of putting someone to death can be interrupted just as the process of serving ten years in prison can.

But interruptibility may not be what those invoking the argument from irrevocability have in mind. They may be thinking of the *outcome* of the death penalty, not the process of putting someone to death. That would not be surprising. The death sentence ends so dramatically that we easily forget the process leading up to it. We even use "execution" to refer only to the last step in executing a sentence of death, as if that were all there were to a sentence of death (and as if we did not also execute sentences of imprisonment). In contrast, a sentence of imprisonment does not end dramatically. What drama there is in it is in the passage of time. We tend to forget the outcome, the last day of imprisonment differing little from the first except for a handshake and the opening of a gate. So, if we are to consider whether the sentence of death, once executed, is irrevocable in a way imprisonment is not, we must

be careful to compare outcome of the death penalty with outcome of imprisonment.

What happens if we compare those two outcomes? Once a prisoner has served his full term, there is a legal sense in which his sentence is irrevocable just as a sentence of death, once carried out, is irrevocable. A sentence of imprisonment, once carried out, cannot be legally undone. The question of imprisonment is, by itself, moot (though the related questions of compensation, clearing the record, and the like are not). *Habeas corpus* is now impossible.

There is, however, also a legal sense in which imprisonment is still revocable. The former prisoner can still be exonerated. He can still formally regain the status he had before conviction. He can still sue for compensation. But, of course, in this sense, the death penalty is also revocable. There is nothing about being dead to prevent exoneration. Tim Evans was exonerated after his execution (though no doubt he took no pleasure in that). There is still in the U.S. an active movement to have Sacco and Vanzetti exonerated some sixty years after their execution. Execution did not close their case. Should they eventually be exonerated, they might perhaps (through a relative) sue for wrongful death. Our legal relations with a person need not end with his death. If a legal system denies the dead even "the right to have rights" (which few do), that is a failing of the particular legal system needing correction, not a fact about the death penalty justifying its abolition. The death penalty is no more necessarily legally irrevocable than imprisonment is.

It may still seem that I have missed the point. After all (it might be said), we have only so many years to live, say, seventy. If two men are convicted of murder and one gets the death penalty while the other gets life imprisonment, is it not obvious that the one executed will, once executed, not be a possible object of a certain form of revocation while the one serving the life sentence will be? If, for example, both "murderers" were sentenced on the same day and at the same age, say, twenty, and both were also later exonerated, say, twenty years later, could we not return to the lifer his last thirty years while the dead man could not have even those years returned to him? Is that not (it might be asked) an important difference and just the difference the argument from irrevocability plainly rests on?

This difference is, I think, what the argument from irrevocability rests on. What I have denied is that it is enough to make the argument from irrevocability a good argument. Indeed, I believe I have already explained why this difference cannot make it a good argument during discussion of the "nonlegal" version of the argument. But perhaps this is the place for a brief recapitulation.

The difference pointed to is either conceptual or practical. The conceptual difference would have to be that the death penalty takes a life (more or less) all at once while life imprisonment takes a life a day at a time. The death penalty, once executed, wipes out the account from which a partial "refund" might be made. Life imprisonment preserves that account (though the balance becomes ever smaller) for the natural life of the prisoner. Insofar as any defense of the argument from irrevocability rests on this conceptual difference, it seems to rest on a mistake. Nothing in the concept of the death penalty seems to make the death penalty irrevocable in this sense. As noted in the previous section, we can easily *imagine* "reviving" or "reconstituting" the dead should we discover a mistake. The concept of the death penalty does not preclude full refund of life (provided life is measured simply in so many days alive). The problem with such refunds is technological, not logical.

The practical interpretation of the objection we are now considering would have to be that we cannot in fact revive the dead though we can in fact release the living from prison. I agree that this is a significant difference. I deny only that it is enough to establish that the death penalty is irrevocable in a way life imprisonment is not. We can indeed release a prisoner before his term is up. But we cannot really refund the life he *would* have had remaining had he not gone to prison. Prison has not only irrevocably taken the life he would have lived during the years he was imprisoned; it has also irrevocably changed the life he has remaining. We should not make too much of the mere fact of walking about, doing day labor, or falling asleep in a dingy room just because there are no bars or guards. For some people, perhaps for most people, the chance to live the last twenty years out of prison may not (by itself) seem a substantial contribution to their welfare. The twenty years in prison, years during which friends and relatives have become strangers, skills have atrophied, and the world he knew has disappeared, may make a prisoner feel (quite rightly) that what is being "given back" is not the life that was taken from him initially but something worth infinitely less. My criticism of the argument from irrevocability has emphasized *compensation* because I find it difficult to understand how letting a prisoner out of prison before his term is up makes a full *refund* of even the years he has yet to serve. There is, I agree, an argument against the death penalty here. All I claim is that that argument cannot turn on the death penalty's being irrevocable in a sense in which imprisonment is importantly different.

Alternatives to Revocability

There are at least three ways the death penalty differs from imprisonment which might be confused with irrevocability. Let us now consider these alternatives to see whether they would provide a way of saving the argument from irrevocability without drastically changing it.

Completeness. A punishment is complete if it takes from a person all that he has, leaving no possibility of further punishment. The death penalty is often treated as if it were a complete penalty. For example, Justice Brennan says that the death penalty deprives one even of the "the right to have rights." Of course, as I have shown, the death penalty is not a complete penalty. Even the dead can (and often do) have rights. But the death penalty is certainly a *more* complete penalty than imprisonment. The death penalty takes more than imprisonment does. That is why the death penalty is a more severe penalty than imprisonment. Does relative completeness then provide a way of saving the argument from irrevocability? I think not. We cannot substitute relative completeness for irrevocability without making premise 3 false. It just is not true that the more complete a penalty, the less it permits the correction of error.

Duration. A sentence of death is ordinarily executed more quickly than a sentence of (long) imprisonment. That difference in relative duration makes a difference in what can be done if an error is discovered within a certain period after sentence is passed. If a sentence of death is ordinarily executed within a year after sentencing, then after that year what we can do to compensate for any error we make is suddenly and sharply reduced. The same is not true of a sentence of imprisonment. Whatever reduction in options for compensation goes on while a prisoner serves his term (and there certainly is some), is much more gradual and spread over a much longer period (assuming a long term of imprisonment). A prisoner serving a life sentence can be freed any time during his natural life, but the condemned man cannot be freed after his natural life is cut short by execution of sentence.

Substituting duration for irrevocability has much to be said for it. Appeal to relative duration does not commit the fallacy of comparing the death penalty's outcome with imprisonment's process. The comparison is between duration of processes. The appeal rests upon a general fact about the death penalty. Even in a country like the U.S. where the time between sentence of death and execution can be many years, the alternative sentence of imprisonment is likely to be longer.

The substitution of duration for irrevocability is, however, not without its costs. The substitution would require a substantial rewriting of the argument from irrevocability. The distinction between the death penalty and imprisonment would not be that one permits correction of error while the other does not, but that one permits more to be done to correct error than the other does. Premise 1″ would have to be rewritten to read:

> 1′. Fallible beings should not, all else equal, use a penalty permitting them to do less to correct error if there is an alternative penalty permitting them to do more to correct error.

The other premises would have to be rewritten accordingly. (For example, premise 3 would have to say that an irrevocable penalty is one that does not permit doing as much to correct error as some alternative does.) The resulting argument would, I think, not be open to the objections made here to the argument from irrevocability (and explains much of its appeal). But the new argument would also lack much of the force of the old one (and might require use of fines and similar reversible penalties instead of imprisonment more often than we do). Because everything would now be a matter of degree, showing all else not to be equal would be much easier. Because conditions vary so much from place to place, the new argument would also be less likely to provide a general argument for abolition. The argument from relative duration, though worth more consideration than I can give it here, is, I think, clearly not a mere restatement of the argument from irrevocability.

Contingent noncompensation. The argument of this paper is largely "conceptual," that is, dependent upon certain relatively general facts about this world (and worlds very much like this one). The conceptual nature of this paper may suggest that the "real" argument from irrevocability is not conceptual but "statistical" or "contingent." For example, much of what I said relied on the relatively weak claim that we can substantially compensate *some* people we put to death. That claim is consistent with the contingent claim that we can probably substantially compensate more people for mistaken imprisonment than for mistaken execution of a sentence of death. The "real" argument from irrevocability may then seem to rest upon something like that contingent claim. Premise 3 might be rewritten to read something like:

> 3″. An irrevocable penalty (and only an irrevocable penalty) makes substantial compensation for error less probable than imprisonment does.

Other premises would remain as they are, but the resulting argument would beg the question. Premise 3″ in effect defines "irrevocability" in terms making imprisonment the zero point. The definition is arbitrary. Why should a mere difference of degree (probability of compensation) be turned into the qualitative difference between revocability and irrevocability? Why is the natural zero point not fine rather than imprisonment. The arbitrariness can, of course, be avoided by rewriting premise 1 rather than premise 3. For example, premise 1 might be rewritten to read:

> 1″. Fallible beings should not, all else equal, use a penalty making correction of error less probable than the alternative penalties do.

Other premises would have to be rewritten accordingly. But the result would be, as it was for duration, an argument that is clearly not a mere restatement of the argument from irrevocability.

Other alternatives? The death penalty is, of course, less variable than imprisonment, has more irreversible effects than imprisonment, and so on. There certainly are differences between death and imprisonment. Nothing I have said here should be taken to deny that. All that I have argued is that irrevocability is not one of those differences and so no argument founded on that difference can be good. Given the number of other arguments against the death penalty, the loss of this one should not decide the controversy between abolitionists and retentionists. But it might simplify things a bit.[4]

Endnotes

1. Burton M. Leiser, *Liberty, Justice, and Morals,* 2nd ed. (New York Macmillan Publishing Co., Inc., 1979), p. 251.

2. Furman v. Georgia, 408, U.S. 238, 92 S.Ct. 276 (1972), 290–291.

3. If this statement seems controversial, see my "Death, Deterrence, and the Method of Common Sense," *Social Theory and Practice* 7 (1981) 145–77, where I argue that death is an order of magnitude more severe than imprisonment (no matter how severe imprisonment happens to be). That paper also reveals that until recently I too uncritically accepted the argument from irrevocability. See pp. 159–60.

4. I should like to thank my colleagues Michael Gorr, Clark Zumbach, and Mark Strasser for helpful comments on previous versions of this paper.

43. *Instrument of Justice or Tool of Vengeance?*

Matthew L. Stephens

In his essay, Matthew L. Stephens examines four questions: "(1) Is capital punishment evenly applied to all cases of murder? (2) Will those charged in a capital
punishment case have both the best lawyers and defense available to them? (3) Is
the cost of carrying out the death penalty worth the money spent to execute one
person? and (4) Is capital punishment a deterrent to murder?" Stephens argues
that the death penalty is found wanting with respect to all four of these questions.
As a result, he concludes that capital punishment does not work as a deterrent,
cannot be reversed when mistakenly applied, is arbitrary in its application and
racist in its result, and should be eliminated.

There are many moral dilemmas that face The United
Methodist Church and the United States. None of the
crises that loom on the horizon are as representative of
all forms of injustice and immorality as the death
penalty. It is wrong for many reasons. I will attempt to
look at only a few of those reasons, yet, I encourage the
reader to continue to search for anything that justifies
the taking of human life in the name of justice.

When we look at capital punishment as an instrument of the administration of justice, we must ask: (1)
Is capital punishment evenly applied to all cases of
murder? (2) Will those charged in a capital punishment case have both the best lawyers and defense
available to them? (3) Is the cost of carrying out the
death penalty worth the money spent to execute one
person? and (4) Is capital punishment a deterrent to
murder? After all, the latter is ultimately the question
our society must answer. If it works, we must carry it
out; if it doesn't, it is a ghastly and irrevocable error.

Applying the Death Penalty

In the United States, we experience the tragedy of over
20,000 homicides each year. These statistics are constantly increasing due to the devastating effects of

Used by permission from *Christian Social Action;* copyright
1990 by the General Board of Church and Society of the United
Methodist Church. Matthew L. Stephens is a chaplain at
Lebanon Correctional Institute in Ohio's prison system, and
pastor of Ninth Street United Methodist Church in Coving-
ton, Kentucky.

drugs, racism and poverty. Yet, we choose, as a society,
only 200, (or 1 percent of all murderers) to receive the
ultimate punishment of death. When one looks at the
criteria for selecting this nominal fraction of all murderers, the real issues come to light. Who are these
people? What is their economic and racial background? What are their legal resources and representation? What is their intellectual capacity?

The facts are clear. Those on death row are the
poorest of the poor. They are disproportionately "people of color": African American (40.7 percent), Hispanic
(5.72 percent), Native American (1.49 percent) and
Asian (0.61 percent), as compared to European/
Caucasian. This means approximately 50 percent of all
death row inmates are people of color in a society in
which all of these populations constitute significant
minorities.

Additionally, it is estimated that over one-third of
all death row inmates are mentally retarded (with IQ's
of less than 70), and that nearly half are functionally
illiterate.

It is these poor and oppressed children of God
who become the victims of our society's anger and
need for revenge. The death penalty is clearly *not*
equally applied under the law, or under the more significant mandate of moral, ethical and spiritual values
of a nation founded on these principles.

In a society that champions human rights and
individual dignity in all of our creeds, we are far
behind the rest of the so-called "civilized" western
world in showing compassion to the poor and
oppressed of our country. There are only two countries
that still engage the death penalty as justice: South

Africa and the United States. Recently, the South African government officially put a "hold" on death sentences and executions.

There is overwhelming evidence that race is the single most important factor in choosing those who will be sentenced to death. Of the more than 3,000 people executed since 1930, nearly half were people of color. Eighty-five percent of those executed since 1977, when new death penalty statutes were passed, were punished for crimes against white victims. This is true despite the fact that the homicide rate for people of color is roughly 50 percent higher than that of the majority community.

Take, for example, the state of Ohio where 342 people have been executed since 1884. Of this number, only one white man was executed for killing a black person. In 1989, there were 100 people on death row in Ohio: 51 black men, 45 white men and 4 black women. Ohio has not executed anyone since the state reinstituted the death penalty, but the first execution will probably take place soon. Keep in mind that the minimum age for death sentencing in Ohio is 18.

Consider the historic case of Willie Jasper Darden, executed March 15, 1988 in Florida's electric chair. He was 54 years old. Willie Darden was sentenced to death for the murder of a furniture store owner in Lakeland, Florida. Darden proclaimed his innocence from the moment of his arrest until the moment of his execution, over 14 years later. Significant doubt of Darden's guilt remains.

Willie Darden was tried by an all-white jury in Inverness, Florida, a county with a history of racial segregation and oppression. The prosecutor's opening remarks in the trial demonstrate the racial implications of this case:

> "... The testimony is going to show, I think very shortly, when the trial starts, that the victims in this case were white. And of course, Mr. Darden, the defendant, is black. Can each of you tell me you can try Mr. Darden as if he was white?"

Throughout the trial, the prosecutor characterized Darden as subhuman, saying such things as, "Willie Darden is an animal who should be placed on a leash." The U.S. Supreme Court sharply criticized this misconduct, but refused to find that it unfairly influenced the trial.

In the face of evidence that those who kill whites in Florida are nearly five times more likely to be sentenced to death than those who kill blacks, the prosecution of Willie Darden becomes the story of a man who may well have been innocent, but whose protestations were overshadowed by the color of his victim and himself.

Finally, consider the case of Delbert Tibbs who went from Chicago Theological Seminary to Florida's death row. Luckily, he did not "graduate" from either. Deciding to take some time off from his studies, he hitchhiked across country. "White boys could drop out to 'find themselves'," says Tibbs, "but nobody ever heard of a black man needing to do the same thing." His journey ended abruptly when, being in the wrong place at the wrong time, he was arrested and later convicted for the rape of a 16-year-old girl and the murder of her boyfriend in 1974. He was sentenced to death.

It was only with the assistance of the National Council of Churches Defense Fund attorneys that on appeal, his conviction was overturned on the grounds that it was not supported by the weight of the evidence. However, he was never said to be innocent of the crime. In spite of a US Supreme Court decision that he could be retried, the state decided not to reopen the case on the grounds that the police investigation of the crime was tainted from the start. The original prosecutor said, "If there is a retrial, I will appear as a witness for Mr. Tibbs." Today, Delbert Tibbs devotes his life to his family and to anti–death penalty work across the nation and around the world.

It is more than clear that race is the single most contributing factor to one being dealt the death penalty. In combination with poverty, lack of adequate legal representation and the drive of society for vengeance, people of color are the common victims of this catharsis of hate and cycle of violence.

Quality of Legal Representation

The quality of legal representation of indigent defendants in capital cases is of widespread concern. Most capital defendants cannot afford to pay for their own counsel and are represented by court-appointed lawyers in private practice, or by public defenders. Many times they are given inexperienced counsel, ill-equipped to handle such cases and working with severely limited resources. Many public defenders' offices are overextended with caseloads and cannot devote the time necessary to defend a capital case.

In rural areas, lawyers handling capital cases have little or no experience in criminal law; many are ignorant of the special issues relating to capital punishment. A recent study found that capital defendants in Texas with court-appointed lawyers were more than twice as likely to receive death sentences than those who retained counsel. The trial lawyers of a number of executed prisoners were found to have spent very little time preparing the case for trial. Often, they failed to interview potentially important witnesses or to raise mitigating factors at the proper times.

A good example of this problem is the case of John Young, a black man executed in Georgia. He was convicted in 1976 of murdering three elderly people while under the influence of drugs. He was 18 years old. His trial lawyer was disbarred from legal practice within days after the trial and left the state of Georgia.

When the lawyer learned of the execution, he came forward and submitted an affidavit to the court in which he admitted spending hardly any time preparing for the case, due to personal problems. He admitted he did not investigate his client's background or raise any mitigating circumstances at the sentencing stage of the trial that might have influenced the jury's decision. These circumstances included the fact that at the age of three, John Young had seen his mother murdered while he was lying in bed with her. He later was placed with an alcoholic relative who turned him out on the street to survive at an early age.

The US District Court and the Court of Appeals ruled that they could not consider the lawyer's affidavit as new evidence because it should have been presented earlier. John Young died because of inadequate defense counsel. (Reference: Amnesty International "USA: The Death Penalty Briefing")

The Cost of Capital Punishment

Certainly there is the moral cost of taking a life, to make up for the taking of another life. There is no real way to replace one life with the death of another. Yet when capital punishment is the choice of the courts, this is exactly what has been decided.

The moral issue here is: Do we have the right to kill, or is that the right of God only? This does not excuse one who takes the life of another. That is clearly wrong. They will have to answer to the vengeance of their God. We do have the right to demand restitution and protection in the form of taking away the freedom of that individual found guilty of taking a life.

Taking freedom from individuals who kill others has also been shown to be less costly than executing

them through our court system. The current debate on sidestepping a lengthy appeal process is nothing more than a rationale to expedite the death sentence while saving money.

In 1972, the Supreme Court of the United States, in *Furman vs. Georgia* held that "arbitrary and capricious" application of capital punishment violated the Eighth Amendment prohibition against cruel and unusual punishment. This means that a defendant has to be prosecuted and convicted in a way that is extraordinarily righteous and free of any kind of prejudice.

This "super" due process requirement has made the prosecutions of capital cases enormously expensive. In a recent University of California at Davis Law Review article, Margaret Garey calculated that it costs a minimum of $500,000 to complete a capital case in California. It costs approximately $30,000 per year to house an inmate in the California system.

Between August of 1977 and December of 1985, only 10 percent (190 of 1,847 cases) resulted in the death sentence. Data from New York State suggests that if it adopted capital punishment, the cost would be $1,828,000 per capital trial. Assuming even a 0.75 percent failure rate, it would cost about $7.3 million to sentence one person to death in New York, compared with $4.5 million ($500,000 × 0.90 percent rate) to sentence one person to death in California. (Reference: "Price of Executions is Just Too High," Richard Moran and Joseph Ellis, *Wall Street Journal*, 1986.)

Cost effectiveness is a weak argument when talking about the value of human life. However, even when put on such a shallow rationale as cost-analysis, the death penalty does not hold up.

It has cost the state of Florida $57 million to execute 18 men. It is estimated that this is six times the cost of life imprisonment. A report from the *Miami Herald* said that keeping a prisoner in jail for life would cost the state $515,964 based on a 40-year life span in prison. It would cost $3.17 million for each execution. The newspaper broke the cost of execution down to show $36,000 to $116,700 for trial and sentencing; $69,480 to $160,000 for mandatory state review, which is not required in non-capital trials; $274,820 to $1 million for additional appeals; $37,600 to $312,000 for jail costs, and $845,000 for the actual execution.

These figures should make us ask ourselves: Is the need for our vengeance worth all this money when the possibility that we still convict and execute the wrong person exists? What really guides our conscience—the money or the moral issue of state murder and street murder? Whatever side moves us, we must see that the cost of capital punishment is too high. (Reference: "The Cost of the Death Penalty," Illinois Coalition Against the Death Penalty.)

Deterrent to Murder?

Since capital punishment has been reinstated as a legal sentence of the law, there is no proof that shows murder has declined in any of the states in which it is being used. In fact, some states show an increase in violent crimes.

People who favor the death penalty often believe it helps reduce the number of violent crimes. This may be true if the person who considers homicide would make a rational decision in anticipation of the consequences. This rarely happens because most homicides happen in the "heat of passion," anger, and under the influence of drugs or alcohol.

Studies show that murder rates in states with capital punishment, such as Illinois, differ little from the states that do not have capital punishment, such as Michigan. In 1975, the year before Canada abolished the death penalty, the homicide rate was 3.09 per 100,000 persons. In 1986, that rate was down to 2.19 per 100,000 persons, the lowest in 15 years. In some states, the use of capital punishment increased the crime rate. In New York, between 1903 and 1963, executions were followed by a slight rise in the state's homicide rate.

The recent cry for the death penalty in our country comes more from the need for revenge than for justice. The "get tough" attitude of the law enforcement community and our "kinder and gentler" government telling the nation that killing offenders will stop the rise of violence, is paradoxical. Could it be that violence begets violence? Could it be that as long as the state is killing, we are sending a message that killing is the way to solve problems?

With all of the various factors we have considered, it is clear, even to the casual observer, that the death penalty does not work. It cannot be taken back, and it is arbitrary in its application and racist in its result. People of faith must take a stand. We must choose the day when we will transform instead of kill, when we will "do justice and love mercy and walk humbly with our God" instead of perpetuating a system that is evil, barbaric, costly and ineffective. Let us pray for forgiveness. Let us be transformed as the people of God, a nation of hope. Let us know the healing truth that sets us free in Jesus our Christ.

44. *Punishment of the* Innocent

MICHAEL L. RADELET, HUGO ADAM BEDAU, AND CONSTANCE E. PUTNAM

Michael L. Radelet, Hugo Adam Bedau, and Constance E. Putnam focus on the arrest, trial, conviction, and ultimate execution of James Adams for a crime he may not have committed. Evidence not presented at the trial would likely have raised serious doubts in the minds of the jurors had it been made available, but once Adams had been executed his attorneys naturally turned their attention to the defense of other convicts on Death Row. Radelet, Bedau, and Putnam do not insist on Adams's innocence, but they indicate that some two dozen other cases can be documented in which it seems likely that the wrong person was convicted of murder, sentenced to death, and executed, a finding that suggests the unfairness and irreversibility of capital punishment.

At about half past eight on the evening of Monday, October 23, 1989, the telephone rang at Officer Gary McLaughlin's desk. He picked it up immediately, answering, "State Police, Boston." From the other end of the line he heard a man's voice: "My wife's been shot. I've been shot." Thus began a thirteen-minute, life-or-death conversation between Officer McLaughlin and the caller.

McLaughlin quickly learned that the man on the line, using a car phone as he sat behind the steering wheel, was Charles Stuart. Half an hour earlier Stuart and his wife, Carole, had been at Brigham and Women's Hospital attending a birthing clinic. Carole DiMaiti Stuart was pregnant with their first child. Now, slumped down on the seat next to her husband, she bled profusely; a bullet had been fired point-blank into her face. Stuart himself had been shot in the stomach. Minutes later a patrol car arrived, and the young couple was on its way to the hospital emergency room.

When the police arrived at the crime scene, so did the media. Starting with the eleven o'clock news on television that night, the media flooded the country with stories and pictures of the crime and its victims. For several days the nation's attention was fixed on their fate. Carole Stuart died, as did the couple's

From *In Spite of Innocence: Erroneous Convictions in Capital Cases*, by Michael L. Radelet, Hugo Adam Bedau, and Constance E. Putnam. Copyright 1992 by Michael L. Radelet, Hugo Adam Bedau, and Constance E. Putnam. Reprinted with permission from Northeastern University Press, Boston.

premature child delivered by Caesarean section. For countless Americans, the brutal attack on a young couple about to become parents—attractive, white, professional, still in their twenties—was a nightmare suddenly made real.

Right behind the police and the news media came the politicians. In 1989 Massachusetts was one of fourteen states in the nation that did not punish any kind of murder with the death penalty. The day after Carole Stuart's death, the chairman of the Massachusetts State GOP, Raymond Shamie, flanked by his party's gubernatorial candidates, held a news conference at the State House urging speedy enactment of death penalty legislation. Representative John H. Flood, a Democrat seeking his party's nomination for governor, filed a death penalty bill in the legislature. Attorney General Francis X. Bellotti, also a Democrat and a rival for the gubernatorial nomination, said he would himself willingly pull the switch of the electric chair on the killer. At Carole Stuart's funeral, a thousand people—led by Governor Michael Dukakis—paid their last respects.

Under considerable public pressure to solve the crime, the police promptly began their search for the murderer. Charles Stuart, out of danger and recovering from his stomach wound, was able to provide some help. He described the gunman as 6 feet tall, black, and about thirty years old. Not much, but still something for the police to go on. The next day Stuart elaborated on his description of the killer, and the police circulated the information. So did the Boston papers. By Wednesday evening, two days after the crime, Police Commissioner Francis Roache could report to the media that Stuart's description, along with fingerprint evidence from his automobile, was yielding good leads. "We have reduced our list of suspects to a chosen few," he said.

The police concentrated their attention on the Mission Hill district near the hospital. Mission Hill is on the border between the Fenway—part of Boston's middle-class, still-fashionable Back Bay—and Roxbury, where some of the city's poorest neighborhoods are found. Not normally a setting for street violence of the sort found in Boston's less well-integrated areas, Mission Hill was soon overrun with law-enforcement officers. Residents felt besieged as platoons of police swept through the area, looking for the black killer. Search efforts were concentrated on the public-housing projects in the district, home mainly to blacks and other minorities.

On November 10, two weeks after the Stuart murder, police in the Boston suburb of Burlington arrested Willie Bennett on a traffic offense. Less than three days later, he was arraigned by the authorities in Brookline—a mile or so from the Mission Hill district where the Stuart murder had occurred—for armed robbery of a video store. Bennett, who had a previous criminal record, was thirty-nine years old and black. Just after Christmas, the Boston police showed a photograph of Bennett to Charles Stuart; they also arranged a line-up with Bennett in it for Stuart to review. He promptly fingered Bennett as the man who looked "most like" the killer of his wife. Thus, within six weeks of the crime, it appeared the police had their man. The newspapers applauded and turned to other stories.

Shortly thereafter, the case was suddenly turned inside out. On the morning of January 5, 1990, readers of the *Boston Globe* were stunned when they saw bold headlines: "STUART DIES IN JUMP OFF TOBIN BRIDGE AFTER POLICE ARE TOLD HE KILLED HIS WIFE." Incredible though it seemed, it was true. Apparently from well before the murder, Stuart had carefully woven a fabric of lies as he plotted the death of his pregnant wife. For reasons still not altogether clear, he, too, was dead, an apparent suicide.

The news that Stuart himself might have been the killer led Willie Bennett to say that his life had "been ruined and no one is willing to take responsibility." His anger and bitterness were understandable. Through an improbable pattern of bad luck, he had come very close to being indicted for a crime he had nothing to do with.

Why? Because he had an arrest record in other cases, including armed robbery. Because the police

were under intense pressure to solve the crime. Because Bennett more or less fit the description provided by a seemingly unimpeachable eyewitness to the crime. And, above all, because the public—clamoring for some way to express its indignation—found him a plausible target.

There seems to be no doubt about Willie Bennett's complete innocence. Fortunately, the truth—or enough of it—emerged in time to spare him not only a trial for murder but all of the possible undeserved consequences of such a trial. Bad as Bennett's ordeal was, the system did not come close to convicting him. And it is, of course, erroneous *conviction,* not merely wrongful *arrest,* that is the crucial threshold to undeserved punishment—whether years in prison or death in the execution chamber. Crossing that threshold from accusation and indictment to a guilty verdict is one of the gravest steps the system can take. Only two steps are more serious: actually sentencing the defendant to death, and carrying out the execution.

The Willie Bennett case marks one end of the spectrum on which miscarriages of justice in capital cases occur. The case of James Adams marks the other. On May 10, 1984, Adams was executed in Florida for murder. (As Adams was being executed in the electric chair in Florida State Prison and as death penalty opponents stood in silent vigil across the street, an unidentified man drove by in a pickup truck, and with a thumbs-up gesture shouted, "Fry the nigger!") No national publicity surrounded this case, which had stretched out over a decade. It had begun on the morning of November 12, 1973, with the murder of Edgar Brown in Ft. Pierce, Florida. Brown was found badly beaten, allegedly during the course of a robbery in his home. A 61-year-old rancher and former deputy sheriff, Brown died the next day. Adams was promptly arrested, tried, and convicted.

During the penalty phase of his trial, the State called only one witness, a Tennessee sheriff, who testified that Adams had escaped from prison there after conviction for rape. Adams's public defender called no witnesses, and the jury spent a mere five minutes deliberating over the sentence. Four months and three days after the crime, St. Lucie County Circuit Judge Wallace Sample, concurring with the jury's recommendation, sentenced James Adams to death.

Barely more than a week before the execution, Adam's appellate attorneys, led by West Palm Beach public defenders Richard Burr and Craig Barnard, filed with Governor Bob Graham their second request for execution clemency. In their application, the lawyers presented for the first time facts relating to Adams's background and the circumstances surrounding his conviction, asserting:

> We believe, as strongly as human beings can believe, that the life of James Adams is in your hands today solely because he is a poor black Southerner. . . . The outcome of Mr. Adams's every involvement in the criminal justice system since 1955 has been influenced by his race or by the race of the victims of his alleged crimes.

Adams's first encounter with the law had come in 1955 when he was convicted of assault and battery. In 1957 he and his brother were convicted of petit larceny (they had stolen a pig for their family's dinner table), and Adams was sentenced to one year in jail. He was not provided with counsel in connection with either of these two convictions. During his incarceration for stealing the pig, he was once beaten unconscious with a bat by a jailer and severely beaten on other occasions as well. He suffered dizzy spells, blackouts, and blurred vision as a result of these beatings, and he bore their marks until his death.

In October 1962, Adams was convicted of rape. The records of this conviction did not become available to the attorneys fighting for Adams's life until December 1983. No blacks had been included among the five hundred persons on the list from which jurors at his trial were selected. In addition, the white victim had repeatedly referred to her assailant as a "nigger." Despite the lack of any physical evidence of rape—it was simply her word against his—Adams was convicted. He was sentenced to ninety-nine years in prison.

Under decisions of the United States Supreme Court, Adams's first two convictions ought to have been ruled unconstitutional because he had been denied the assistance of counsel. Racial discrimination in the selection of the jury made the rape conviction also constitutionally defective. Nonetheless, all three convictions were cited by the prosecution as aggravating factors in the sentencing phase of Adams's Florida trial, and they no doubt played a role in the jury's decision to recommend a death sentence.

After Adams had served nine years of his prison sentence for rape, the Tennessee Board of Probation and Paroles found his behavior "exemplary" and recommended to the governor that his sentence be commuted to time served. The governor refused, on the ground that the district attorney who had prosecuted Adams objected. A year later, the Board of Probation and Paroles decided not to recommend release, because the district attorney still opposed such a move.

At the time, Adams was not being housed as one might think a convicted rapist would be: he was a "trusty" at a correctional facility for teenaged girls. As part of his job he had access to state-owned vehicles. When he was told that he would not be released until the prosecutor dropped his objections, Adams—heartbroken (he had done all he could to earn release)—drove off in one of the prison trucks. Ten months later he was arrested for murder in Florida.

The killer had entered Edgar Brown's unoccupied home on the morning of November 12, 1973. Sometime later Brown returned home, where he was attacked and beaten with a fireplace poker. Adams's car had been parked in the driveway, and it was seen traveling to and from the victim's home. One witness, Willie Orange, positively identified Adams as the driver of the car; a second witness, John Thompkins, "thought" Adams was the driver. The car was located later that day at a shop where it had been left for the repainting job Adams had been planning for months. Adams claimed his car had been driven that morning, at 10:00 or 10:15 A.M. (one half hour before the assault) by a friend, Vivian Nickerson, and another man, Kenneth Crowell. According to Adams, while they were off in his car—precisely at the time of the homicide—he was at the Nickerson home playing cards.

The victim, it was known, always carried between $700 and $1500 in cash; no cash was found in his wallet after the assault. When Adams was arrested, he had only $185 with him. He also had a credible explanation for the source of this money: His employer had recently lent him $200. The State offered no explanation of what it thought had happened to the other $500 to $1300 that Brown would have been carrying and that had in all likelihood been taken by his killer. One bill in Adams's possession had a dried patch of O-positive blood on it, consistent with the blood of the victim—and that of 45 percent of the rest of the population.

The one person who had a chance to identify the killer at Brown's home was Foy Hortman. He testified that he drove up to the house shortly after Brown had returned home and heard a woman shout from inside, "In the name of God, don't do it!" He then saw and briefly spoke with someone leaving the house, but failed to identify Adams as that person. More than that, he testified that the person he spoke with was blacker than Adams and, unlike Adams, had no mustache. On the day of the homicide, Hortman viewed a police lineup that included Adams and said he was positive that none of the men was the person he had seen leaving the Brown house. Nonetheless, at trial Hortman testified that Adams "may or may not have been" the person at the scene. (A logician would call that remark a tautology, but the jury appears to have been influenced by it.)

John Thompkins testified that he thought it was James Adams he had seen driving a car to the victim's home shortly before the homicide. "It had to be (Adams)," Thompkins said, "because he throwed up his hand at me, because everybody that passed there don't hardly wave at you unless you know him." Not a very precise or damning statement, yet the State relied heavily on it.

Willie Orange, on the other hand, did positively identify Adams as driving the car away from the Brown home. His was the sole testimony that placed Adams near the crime scene. Perhaps not so incidentally, it later turned out that Orange believed Adams was having an affair with his wife. During the clemency hearing, three witnesses were located who had heard Orange stating before the trial that he was going to testify against Adams because of this affair. One witness quoted Orange as saying before the trial, "I'm going to send him [Adams] because he's been going with my wife." A polygraph administered to Orange to support Adams's appeal for clemency in 1984, while hardly conclusive, indicated that Orange was being deceptive when he testified at the trial.

Vivian Nickerson, the person Adams said had access to his car at the time of the homicide, was fifteen years old. She was very large for her age and had a strikingly masculine appearance. In fact, she resembled James Adams, and her height, size, and complexion fit Hortman's eyewitness description better than Adams did. It is possible that she was the person Hortman saw leaving the victim's house. If she was, that would explain another loose end not tied up by the State's theory of the crime: Hers could have been the woman's voice Hortman testified he had heard coming from inside the house. Yet no photos of Vivian Nickerson were shown to Hortman, and he never saw her in a police line-up.

Interestingly enough, Nickerson was called by Adams to corroborate his alibi at trial. She was a reluctant witness, however, and ended up hurting his case. By claiming that he had not arrived at her house until 11:00 A.M., she undermined his testimony. In a pretrial deposition, given under oath, she had stated that Adams reached her house prior to 10:30 and that she had then borrowed his car. In other words, contrary to what she claimed during the trial, Nickerson when

deposed had said that Adams was at her house and that she was driving his car at the time of the crime. This inconsistency was by no means a minor one; unfortunately, Adams's defense counsel never confronted Nickerson with the contradiction.

The most significant blow to the State's case against Adams arose from evidence not presented at trial. En route to the hospital in an ambulance with her husband, Mrs. Brown found strands of hair clasped in his hand—hair presumably pulled from the head of his assailant. The State's crime laboratory compared these hairs with samples of Adams's hair and determined that although the hair was "very dark brown, Negroid, [and] curly," Adams was definitely not its source. This report, however, was not released until three days after Adams had been sentenced. Even then, when it could have been used to support a request for a new trial, it was not given to the defense attorneys.

In their 1984 clemency papers, Adams's attorneys succinctly stated their case as follows:

> In sum, had all of the evidence raising doubt about Mr. Adams's guilt been submitted to the jury, there would have been at least a reasonable doubt about Mr. Adams's guilt. The evidence would have shown that the only person who had an opportunity to observe the perpetrator was "positive" that Mr. Adams was not that person. The evidence would have shown that Willie Orange's identification of Mr. Adams as the person driving away from Brown's house was wholly unbelievable because of his stated motive to "get" James Adams. The evidence would have shown that a specimen of hair asserted by the investigating deputy to have been recovered from the hand of Mr. Brown in the ambulance after the assault against him could not have come from James Adams. . . . Had the jury been told about Vivian Nickerson's sworn testimony less than two months before James Adams's trial which unequivocally corroborated Mr. Adams's testimony that he was continuously at Ms. Nickerson's house from before the homicide until well after the homicide, the jury would have been more likely to suspect Vivian Nickerson as the perpetrator than James Adams.

No doubt due process of law failed rather badly in the Adams case, and these deficiencies played a critical role in his conviction and death sentence. But was Adams truly innocent? Did he deserve to be acquitted on the ground that he had no involvement in the murder of Edgar Brown, even though members of the trial jury—given the evidence before them—believed otherwise? Adams's postconviction attorneys, Burr and Barnard, thought so. We think so. But from the moment Adams was executed, it became virtually impossible to resolve the issue one way or the other. There is no legal forum in which the innocence of the dead can be officially confirmed, or even satisfactorily investigated. The court of public opinion—such as it is—is the only recourse, and James Adams was too obscure, too bereft of friends and supporters with time and money, to have his claim of innocence tested and vindicated posthumously in that forum.

Once Adams was dead, his attorneys had to turn their full attention to the plight of other death row clients. Time spent reinvestigating the circumstances of the Edgar Brown murder in the hope of vindicating the late James Adams was time denied to clients still alive but facing the electric chair. No newspaper editor or team of reporters, no investigative journalist, has seen fit (so far as we know) to reopen the Adams case. Instead, a giant question mark continues to haunt his execution, a question mark that will probably never be removed. A rare case? Perhaps, but not unique. We know of nearly two dozen cases in this century where the evidence similarly suggests that the wrong person was convicted of murder or rape, sentenced to death, and executed.

---

45. *The Death Penalty as a Symbolic Issue*

STEPHEN NATHANSON

Stephen Nathanson examines the symbolism at work in the debate over capital punishment, particularly the values that both proponents and opponents of the death penalty seek to affirm. He concludes that the abolition of the death penalty would not involve either cowardice or moral indifference, as some have suggested. Instead, the unwillingness of the state to execute the guilty would express a deep commitment to the inviolability of human dignity and would assist in minimizing the levels of permissible violence.

THE DEBATE ABOUT the morality of the death penalty is one of those recurring questions that seems to have a life of its own. Shifts in public opinion, actions by legislatures, or decisions by courts may sometimes appear to put the issue to rest, but somehow the debate retains its vigor. Why is this?

The first and perhaps most important reason is the obvious one that lives are at stake. Death penalty opponents cannot accept defeat because the operation of the death penalty means that people will die. Some of those who die ought not to be executed, even if

From Stephen Nathanson, A*n Eye For An Eye? The Morality of Punishing by Death* (Totowa, NJ: Rowman & Littlefield, 1987), pp. 131–146. Reprinted with permission from Rowman & Littlefield.

we accept the criteria of death penalty supporters. They may be innocent, or they may have acted wrongly but not from deep-seated malice or cruelty. To let the issue rest is to allow these errors to occur without challenge. Likewise, for death penalty supporters who believe that executions are a superior deterrent, it is the lives of potential victims that are at stake. They too cannot rest when public policy runs contrary to their views.

Second, because the stakes are high, people's feelings are deeply engaged by the issue, and they are motivated to continue the struggle. The taking of lives—whether by murder or by legal execution—is a "gut" issue, not in the sense that we cannot reason about it but rather in the sense that we are deeply affected by killings and feel strongly about the views we hold. Given the strong feelings aroused by the issue, neither side is willing to accept defeat.

Finally, the question whether we ought to punish by death is a question with great symbolic meaning. For people on both sides, whether we impose or refrain from imposing the death penalty seems to say something about our values, about the kind of people we are, about the nature of our society. The death penalty debate is in part a field on which we champion some of our most central social and ethical ideals. We think that retaining or abolishing the death penalty conveys an important message, and we want it to be the right message.

One might think that symbolic messages are even more difficult to reason about than the other questions we have considered, but there is no obvious reason why assessing these messages is beyond our ability. If they are an important component of the debate, we should try to confront them directly.

The Courage of Our Convictions

Commenting on the motivation of death penalty opponents, Ernest van den Haag has described opposition to executions as rooted in a kind of weakness of the will, an inability to overcome fears and doubts in order to act decisively in the face of evil. Describing those who oppose the death penalty, he writes:

> [T]hose who affect such a view do so because of a failure of nerve. They do not think themselves—and therefore anyone else—competent to decide questions of life and death. Aware of human frailty they shudder at the gravity of the decision and refuse to make it. The irrevocability of a verdict of death is contrary to the modern spirit that likes to pretend that nothing is ever definitive, that everything is open-ended, that doubts must always be entertained and revisions made. Such an attitude may be proper for inquiring philosophers and scientists. But not for the courts. They can evade decisions on life and death only by giving up their paramount duties: to do justice, to secure the lives of the citizens, and to vindicate the norms society holds inviolable.[1]

The rhetoric of this passage is powerful, as it draws its strength from a number of important ideals. Since no opponent of the death penalty would deny the value of doing justice, securing the lives of citizens,

and vindicating important social norms, van den Haag thinks that it can only be a kind of moral squeamishness that leads them to oppose the death penalty. They are unable to support doing the unpleasant, even when it is morally required.

If van den Haag is correct about what motivates opposition to the death penalty, then his analysis might have some force in discrediting the opposition. Although it is an ad *hominem* argument, it would be important if it could be shown that only this sort of motivation could lead to opposing the death penalty. This in itself is an implausible claim, however, and indeed, none of the specific charges he makes necessarily applies to death penalty opponents.

It is not true, for example, that death penalty opponents need think of themselves as being incompetent to make life-and-death decisions. Anyone who believes that it is morally permissible to kill in self-defense is willing to sanction a life-and-death decision. Moreover, anyone who believes that the right to kill to defend oneself or others implies the legitimacy of authorizing police officers to carry weapons and to use them when necessary is clearly willing to grant the making of life-and-death decisions to other people. Anyone who believes that there can be morally just participation in war is willing to make and allow precisely these decisions. All of these positions sanction the use of deadly force, and they are all compatible with opposition to the death penalty. Opponents of the death penalty need not deny the legitimacy or necessity of killing in defense of people's lives. They may grant this, while at the same time insisting that we exercise the strictest possible limitations on the taking of lives. Killing may be morally justified in many cases, but it is not justified as punishment.

It is important to see that killing itself has different meanings in different contexts. The execution of a person convicted of a crime is a violent act. Typically, it cuts short the life of the criminal against his will and with no regard for his interests or well-being. This is quite different from what happens in the case of a "mercy killing." Those who kill in this type of situation take someone's life in the belief that this accords with that person's best interests. Whatever the merits of the arguments for or against euthanasia, approval of this practice is consistent with opposition to the death penalty. Where a person favors euthanasia but opposes the death penalty, it is evident that his motivation is not an irrational fear of making life and death decisions.

So, the general disability that van den Haag claims to see in his opponents, the failure of nerve, is in no way a necessary trait in those who oppose the death penalty. One can be quite prepared to support some acts of killing and hence be as strong willed and courageous as van den Haag without thinking that punishing by death is morally legitimate.

The failure of nerve that van den Haag claims to find in death penalty opponents is linked in his mind with a tendency toward skepticism and an awareness of human frailty and fallibility. Here, there may be some justice to his claim, but the trait that he regards as a flaw is a virtue. Of course, we are frail and fallible in our judgments, and in the light of that, we ought to be most careful when we take actions with dire, irrevocable consequences. To take someone's life is a serious matter, and we ought not to do this lightly. This is not to say that we should never do it, but we want to limit such actions to the minimum, and where there is serious doubt, we may want to avoid such actions altogether.

In saying this, I do not mean that it is always wrong to kill under conditions of uncertainty. Faced with a situation in which one person appears intent on killing another without apparent justification, one might legitimately kill the first to save the apparent victim. The action might be justified even if (tragically) it turned out that one was mistaken about who was the victim and who the attacker. The circumstance leaves no time for inquiry and no alternative actions as options.

In the case of the death penalty, however, the victim's life is unfortunately beyond recovery, and imprisonment is sufficient to insure that the killer is no longer an active threat to other members of society. In this context, faced with our knowledge of our own fallibility in making both factual judgments and moral assessments, there is nothing improper in refraining from the more drastic action involved in punishing by death.

The kind of skepticism we are talking about here is not the abstract sort of philosophical doubt that one might acquire from reading Descartes' *Meditations* or Plato's early dialogues. The skepticism of death penalty opponents is rooted in the knowledge of the imperfections of our legal system, its history of error, misjudgment, and injustice. We know that while people may speak of seeking justice and making people's lives secure and while they may even conscientiously strive to achieve these goals, their actions and judgments are influenced by many factors. The result of their pursuit may be unnecessary deaths and widespread injustice. Given the facts of human history, skeptical worries about the correctness of the life-and-death decisions involved in punishing by death are quite legitimate.

By all means, let us be decisive when we can act to protect ourselves and others from victimization. But at the same time, let us be aware of our weaknesses and the defects of our institutions, and let us temper our actions and policies in the light of this knowledge. A bit of skepticism in this context is quite appropriate and need not reflect any moral or character weakness in opponents of the death penalty.

The Morality of Anger

The symbolic importance of the death penalty is strongly emphasized by Walter Berns in his defense of the death penalty. In discussing the symbolism of punishing by death, Berns stresses the moral significance of anger. He writes:

> If . . . men are not angry when someone else is robbed, raped, or murdered, the implication is that no moral community exists, because those men do not care for anyone other than themselves. Anger is an expression of that caring, and society needs men who care for one another. . . . [Anger] is the passion that can cause us to act for reasons having nothing to do with selfish or mean calculation; indeed, when educated, it can become a generous passion, the passion that protects the community or country by demanding punishment for its enemies.[2]

Berns wants to vindicate anger because he regards it as an expression of concern for others, and he fears that society is being undermined by a lack of other-directed concerns. He criticizes liberal political theory for what he sees as a capitulation to self interest. Anger shows that we are not simply self-interested individuals joined together in a marriage of convenience. Instead, we are a community of people who share common concerns and recognize common values.

Berns is certainly correct that anger may reveal important virtues in people, especially if a failure to be angry arises either from callousness or indifference. Nonetheless, whatever virtues are displayed by anger, everyone would agree that the actions that flow from anger must be controlled. The expression of anger needs to be limited by moral constraints, and the reasons for these constraints are moral and not simply pragmatic or self-interested.

A person whose family has been killed in an automobile accident caused by the carelessness of another driver may be angry enough to kill the driver. The anger shows the depth of the person's caring for other human beings, but it does not provide a justification for killing the driver. Virtually everyone would agree that execution for carelessness is too severe a response. While some negative response to destructive and harmful actions is appropriate, it does not follow that anything done in the name of righteous anger is morally right.

I know of no one who denies that anger and outrage are the appropriate responses to the murder of innocent human beings. Nor do I know of anyone who argues that murderers should not be punished at all. The question is whether punishing by death is morally required. That we may feel angry enough to kill someone does not imply that doing so would be morally legitimate.

So, one can sympathize and agree with much of Berns's message, but that message does nothing to support the appropriateness of using death as a punishment. To favor severe but lesser punishments is in no way to express indifference or callousness toward the deaths of murder victims. The anger and grief that we feel about these deaths do not give us a license to kill.

Indeed, at the level of symbolism, one would think that it was important to convey the message that strong feelings of anger or hatred do not by themselves justify the taking of life. In a society where the strength of one's passions became a justification for harming others (and not just a potential excuse or mitigating factor), those whom we care about would be more rather than less threatened. It would be a mistake to convey to people that killing in anger is a morally acceptable act.

Affirming the Moral Order

Berns is critical of liberal political theorists because they emphasize that government is a humanly created instrument. He believes that if people regard laws as conveniences for improving life, then they will not take them seriously enough. They will feel free to disobey the law when obedience is inconvenient. Part of the appeal of the death penalty for Berns is that it suggests that the law possesses a transcendent value. "Capital punishment," he writes,

> serves to remind us of the majesty of the moral order that is embodied in our law and of the terrible consequences of its breach. The law must not be understood to be merely statute that we enact or repeal at our will and obey or disobey at our convenience, especially not the criminal law. . . . The criminal law must be made awful, by which I mean, awe-inspiring. . . . It must remind us of the moral order by which alone we can live as human beings, and in our day the only punishment that can do this is capital punishment.[3]

For Berns, permitting the state to punish by death is a means of affirming the moral order and its embodiment in the law.

Berns is correct about one point here. The law must support the moral order in the sense that it must provide appropriate punishments for particular crimes. Morality is subverted when terrible crimes go unpunished or are punished very leniently, since these responses would suggest that the crimes are not really serious. One of the worst implications of the statistics that show fewer death sentences for murders of black victims is that this undermines the value of the lives of black citizens and sends a permissive signal to people about the killing of blacks.

In the same way, however, the disproportionate number of blacks who have been executed for killing whites seriously calls into question Berns's notion that the actual practice of the death penalty affirms the moral order. Berns's romantic vision of the death penalty cannot withstand confrontation with the actual practice of executions. The actual history of the death penalty is scarcely an ennobling spectacle.

Thinking about the actual practice of executions as opposed to a romanticized vision of what punishment might be leads to the most serious problem with Berns's view of the symbolism of executions. Berns wants to see the moral order reaffirmed, but he equates this order with the legal system. He does not want us to view the law "merely [as] statute that we enact or repeal at will." Yet, that is precisely what the law is. While the moral order does not shift with the votes of a legislature, the legal order does. All too frequently, the legal order itself runs quite counter to what morality would require. Berns does the cause of morality no service by offering a blanket sanctification of the law.

Surely Berns is correct in his view that the nature and content of the law is a serious matter, but it is doubtful that we need to kill people in order to convey that message. Moreover, by revering the law when it does not deserve reverence, we help to perpetuate injustice. A critical and sober view of the law may do more to affirm the moral order than an attitude of awe or exaggerated respect. The critic who sees the flaws of the legal system and wants to limit its powers may be as committed to the moral order as Berns and may indeed have a better way to make the legal system conform to the moral order.

There are, then, several flaws in Berns' argument. He nowhere shows that the death penalty is necessary to producing the right moral attitude toward the law. He ignores the reality of the death penalty and the messages that its actual—as opposed to its idealized—workings convey. Finally, he supports a reverential and uncritical view of the law that is not likely to help us to improve the legal order.

The Symbolism of Abolishing the Death Penalty

What is the symbolic message that we would convey by deciding to renounce the death penalty and to abolish its use?

I think that there are two primary messages. The first is the most frequently emphasized and is usually expressed in terms of the sanctity of human life, although I think we could better express it in terms of respect for human dignity. One way we express our respect for the dignity of human beings is by abstaining from depriving them of their lives, even if they have done terrible deeds. In defense of human well-being, we may punish people for their crimes, but we ought not to deprive them of everything, which is what the death penalty does.

If we take the life of a criminal, we convey the idea that by his deeds he has made himself worthless and totally without human value. I do not believe that we are in a position to affirm that of anyone. We may hate such a person and feel the deepest anger against him, but when he no longer poses a threat to anyone, we ought not to take his life.

But, one might ask, hasn't the murderer forfeited whatever rights he might have had to our respect? Hasn't he, by his deeds, given up any rights that he had to decent treatment? Aren't we morally free to kill him if we wish?

These questions express important doubts about the obligation to accord any respect to those who have acted so deplorably, but I do not think that they prove that any such forfeiture has occurred. Certainly, when people murder or commit other crimes, they do forfeit some of the rights that are possessed by the law-abiding. They lose a certain right to be left alone. It becomes permissible to bring them to trial and, if they

are convicted, to impose an appropriate—even a dreadful—punishment on them.

Nonetheless, they do not forfeit all their rights. It does not follow from the vileness of their actions that we can do anything whatsoever to them. This is part of the moral meaning of the constitutional ban on cruel and unusual punishments. No matter how terrible a person's deeds, we may not punish him in a cruel and unusual way. We may not torture him, for example. His right not to be tortured has not been forfeited. Why do these limits hold? Because this person remains a human being, and we think that there is something in him that we must continue to respect in spite of his terrible acts.

One way of seeing why those who murder still deserve some consideration and respect is by reflecting again on the idea of what it is to deserve something. In most contexts, we think that what people deserve depends on what they have done, intended, or tried to do. It depends on features that are qualities of individuals. The best person for the job deserves to be hired. The person who worked especially hard deserves our gratitude. We can call the concept that applies in these cases *personal* desert.

There is another kind of desert, however, that belongs to people by virtue of their humanity itself and does not depend on their individual efforts or achievements. I will call this impersonal kind of desert *human* desert. We appeal to this concept when we think that everyone deserves a certain level of treatment no matter what their individual qualities are. When the signers of the Declaration of Independence affirmed that people had inalienable rights to "life, liberty, and the pursuit of happiness," they were appealing to such an idea. These rights do not have to be earned by people. They are possessed "naturally," and everyone is bound to respect them.

According to the view that I am defending, people do not lose all of their rights when they commit terrible crimes. They still deserve some level of decent treatment simply because they remain living, functioning human beings. This level of moral desert need not be earned, and it cannot be forfeited. This view may sound controversial, but in fact everyone who believes that cruel and unusual punishment should be forbidden implicitly agrees with it. That is, they agree that even after someone has committed a terrible crime, we do not have the right to do anything whatsoever to him.

What I am suggesting is that by renouncing the use of death as a punishment, we express and reaffirm our belief in the inalienable, unforfeitable core of human dignity.

Why is this a worthwhile message to convey? It is worth conveying because this belief is both important and precarious. Throughout history, people have found innumerable reasons to degrade the humanity of one another. They have found qualities in others that they hated or feared, and even when they were not threatened by these people, they have sought to harm them, deprive them of their liberty, or take their lives from them. They have often felt that they had good reasons to do these things, and they have invoked divine commands, racial purity, and state security to support their deeds.

These actions and attitudes are not relics of the past. They remain an awful feature of the contemporary world. By renouncing the death penalty, we show our determination to accord at least minimal respect even to those whom we believe to be personally vile or morally vicious. This is, perhaps, why we speak of the *sanctity* of human life rather than its value or worth. That which is sacred remains, in some sense, untouchable, and its value is not dependent on its worth or usefulness to us. Kant expressed this ideal of respect in the famous second version of the Categorical Imperative: "So act as to treat humanity, whether in thine own person or in that of any other, in every case as an end withal, never as a means only."[4]

The Problem of Moral Monsters

One may feel attracted to this ideal and yet resist it by calling to mind people like Hitler or Stalin or their various henchmen, who were responsible for the deaths of millions of innocent people. Aren't such people beyond the pale? Haven't they forfeited *all* claims to even minimal decency so that it would be appropriate to execute them as punishment for their deeds? Doesn't the existence of such people show that the death penalty is legitimate?

These troubling questions raise important issues, and death penalty opponents might meet them in diverse ways. For myself, I am willing to say that even in these cases, so long as these people no longer pose an active threat to others, it would be best not to execute them. Moreover, though their deeds were terrible beyond words, I think it best that we not renounce our respect for their humanity.

One reason for refusing to execute such people is that we may be misled by thinking of them as solely and entirely responsible for the terrible policies carried out under their rule. In quite important ways, it is misleading to think of Hitler and Stalin or other comparable people as the doers of the terrible deeds we associate with them. Certainly, they were agents of death and destruction, but they could not have carried out their plans without the encouragement, the complicity, and the active assistance of vast numbers of people. Had others turned a deaf ear to Hitler's nationalistic, antisemitic ravings, there would have been no Nazi party. Had others refused to work within the Nazi and Soviet bureaucracies of death, there would have been neither Holocaust nor Gulag. It is in fact too comforting to personalize these evils and lay them at the footsteps of monsters. It is too comforting to think that only a special kind of monstrous person could bring about such evil. It is both more accurate and more frightening to realize what ordinary human beings are capable of. Without the assistance of many ordinary people, Hitler and Stalin would have been quite powerless to carry out their evil wishes.

It is important, too, to realize just how selective we are in our appraisals of historic figures. Looking back, for example, we think of Napoleon as one of the great men of history. In Paris, there is an imposing monument to him at Les Invalides. Yet, Napoleon was responsible for plunging Europe into almost twenty years of war. In his Russian campaign alone, over 400,000 French soldiers died. His actions led to untold numbers of casualties and deaths. Yet he is remembered by most as a heroic figure.

Coming closer to home, the Allied forces in World War II carried out a policy of continuous, deliberate bombings of German and Japanese cities that was designed to terrorize the civilian populations. Many thousands of people were killed by these raids. This effort culminated, of course, in the atomic bombings at Hiroshima and Nagasaki. Vast numbers of innocent people were victims of these campaigns. The names of Churchill and Truman, however, remain highly honored. We do not consider them monsters.

Nor do we think of the various presidents since Harry Truman as moral monsters, though each one has apparently been willing to launch nuclear bombs that would kill millions of innocent people in retaliation against an attack on the United States. Smiling young men in missile silos report on television that of course they would push the buttons if they were given the orders to do so. Thousands of other ordinary people earn their living by designing and making the components of nuclear weapons.

None of these people are monsters, and yet all contribute to an effort whose result could be the extermination of human life. In general, however, we are not horrified by them as we are by Hitler or Stalin. We find our own officials and our fellow citizens more human, easier to identify with. We take their justifications for their acts more seriously because we share their concerns. We do not think that our military and political officials must have lost every shred of humanity in order to be involved in these efforts. Yet, the destruction they declare themselves willing to produce dwarfs that which was done by Hitler and Stalin.

My point here is not that Hitler and Stalin were not evil people. Nor do I wish to deny that there are differences between them and other leaders. What I want to draw attention to is the selective nature of our moral vision. We are horrified by the destructive deeds and intentions of some world leaders, while we take those of other leaders quite in stride. Some evil deeds strike us as indicative of no humanity in a person, while others are oddly untroubling.

It would be worth exploring the criteria by which we judge people to be moral monsters and worth trying to see what one must do in order to lose all claims to human consideration. This might be a more difficult task than many think and might well have unwelcome consequences.

What I have been trying to suggest here is that when people focus on figures like Hitler or Stalin, they often want to exhibit examples of superhuman evil. Yet, this exhibition rests on a number of comforting illusions. I find it more telling to recognize the humanity of the motives that can lead to terrible actions and to see that these motivations are not limited to the few terrible figures we tend to pick out as exemplars of evil. The appeal to the existence of moral monsters to justify executions rests on too simple a conception of the roots of evil.

Not all opponents of the death penalty would agree with the views I have expressed about figures like Hitler and Stalin, and though I regard them as important points, they are not essential to meet the original objection. The objection we were considering offered Hitler and Stalin as examples of people who had acted so vilely that they had forfeited any right to decent treatment. In their cases, it could be argued, we need not worry about imposing death, and therefore, the death penalty can be legitimate.

While I have rejected this view, it would be possible for an opponent of the death penalty to agree with the premise of this argument and to concede that Hitler and Stalin might have gone so far that they no longer merited any consideration as human beings. One could even acknowledge that they should be executed.

All of this is consistent with opposition to the death penalty. Why? Because these cases are extraordinary and atypical. The death penalty controversy is concerned with the use of death as a punishment for murders that occur within society. It is advocated as a part of our ordinary criminal justice system. One could favor executing Hitler because of his extraordinary acts and still think that executions should play no regular role in the achievement of domestic order within a society.

From the perspective of this reply, the whole issue of moral monsters is a distraction that confuses the issue. If death penalty supporters were proposing executions only for extraordinary political criminals like Hitler and Stalin, these examples would be to the point. Since they are proposing executions for people whose deeds do not begin to approach the evil of these famous persons, death penalty supporters must make a different sort of case for their view. The specter of Hitler and Stalin does not help their case at all.

The Morality of Restraint

I have argued that the first symbolic meaning conveyed by a renunciation of the death penalty is that human dignity must be respected in every person. To execute a person for murder is to treat that person as if he were nothing but a murderer and to deprive him of everything that he has. Therefore, if we want to convey the appropriate message about human dignity, we will renounce the death penalty.

One might object that, in making this point, I am contradicting my earlier claim that killing in defense of oneself or others can be morally justified. If it is wrong to execute a person because this violates his dignity as a human being and deprives him of everything, it would seem to be equally wrong to kill this person as a means of defense. Defensive killing seems to violate these ideals in the same way that I claim punishing by death does. Isn't this inconsistent? Mustn't I either retreat to the absolute pacifist view or else allow that the death penalty is permissible?

In chapter 1, I argued that defensive killing is morally permissible. What I need to do now is to show that defensive killing is compatible with respect for human dignity. We can easily see that it is by recalling the central fact about killing to ward off an assault on one's own life. In this circumstance, someone will die.

The only question open is whether it will be the attacker or the intended victim. We cannot act in any way that shows the very same respect and concern for both the attacker and the intended victim. Although we have no wish to harm the attacker, this is the only way to save the innocent person who is being attacked. In this situation, assuming that there are no alternative means of preventing the attack from succeeding, it is permissible to kill the attacker.

What is crucial here is that the choice is forced on us. If we do not act, then one person will be destroyed. There is no way of showing equal concern for both attacker and victim, so we give preference to the intended victim and accept the morality of killing the attacker.

The case of punishing by death is entirely different. If this punishment will neither save the life of the victim nor prevent the deaths of other potential victims, then the decision to kill the murderer is avoidable. We can restrain ourselves without sacrificing the life or well-being of other people who are equally deserving of respect and consideration. In this situation, the restrained reaction is the morally right one.

In addition to providing an answer to the objection, this point provides us with the second important message conveyed by the renunciation of punishing by death. When we restrain ourselves and do not take the lives of those who kill, we communicate the importance of minimizing killing and other acts of violence. We reinforce the idea that violence is morally legitimate only as a defensive measure and should be curbed whenever possible.

We can see the point of this message by contrasting it with Walter Berns's emphasis on the morality of anger. Without discounting all that Berns says, it seems to me that the death penalty supports the morality of anger in an unacceptable way. It suggests that if someone's acts have provoked you to be very angry, then you may legitimately act violently against that person. The morality of restraint, on the other hand, requires that one control one's anger and allows one to attack another person only defensively. Anger by itself provides no justification for violence.

When the state has a murderer in its power and could execute him but does not, this conveys the idea that even though this person has done wrong and even though we may be angry, outraged, and indignant with him, we will nonetheless control ourselves in a way that he did not. We will not kill him, even though we could do so and even though we are angry and indignant. We will exercise restraint, sanctioning killing only when it serves a protective function.

Why should we do this? Partly out of a respect for human dignity. But also because we want the state to set an example of proper behavior. We do not want to encourage people to resort to violence to settle conflicts when there are other ways available. We want to avoid the cycle of violence that can come from retaliation and counter-retaliation. Violence is a contagion that arouses hatred and anger, and if unchecked, it simply leads to still more violence. The state can convey the message that the contagion must be stopped, and the most effective principle for stopping it is the idea that only defensive violence is justifiable. Since the death penalty is not an instance of defensive violence, it ought to be renounced.

We show our respect for life best by restraining ourselves and allowing murderers to live, rather than by following a policy of a life for a life. Respect for life and restraint of violence are aspects of the same ideal. The renunciation of the death penalty would symbolize our support of that ideal.

Conclusions

In this chapter, I have tried to interpret and evaluate several of the symbolic messages that our acceptance or renunciation of the death penalty might convey. I have tried to show that the abolition of punishing by death reflects neither cowardice nor moral indifference. Rather, it expresses a commitment to respect human dignity and to minimize the degree of permissible violence. These two tasks clearly go together. Where violence is not severely limited, human dignity is constantly violated, and human life becomes precarious.

Part 7

Environmental Ethics

46. Can and Ought We to Follow Nature?

Holmes Rolston III

In this essay, Holmes Rolston explores the meaning of Barry Commoner's third law of ecology, "Nature knows best." According to Rolston, there are four possible ways to interpret Commoner's call to follow nature: (1) in a homeostatic sense, (2) in an imitative ethical sense, (3) in an axiological sense, and (4) in a tutorial sense. Rolston critically analyzes these four possible approaches and argues that it is most reasonable for us to follow nature in the tutorial sense. He reminds us that in a wide variety of ways nature has much to teach us.

Introduction

"Nature knows best" is the third law of ecology according to Barry Commoner and the gravity of his claim is underlined by its ranking with the first two, that everything is interconnected and that nothing is ever destroyed, only recycled.[1] But this third law is curiously normative, not merely describing what nature does, but evaluating it, and implying that we ought to follow nature. Such following may ordinarily be more prudential than moral for Commoner, but for others, if not for him too, the deepest commands of nature reach the ethical level. Radcliffe Squires writes of Robinson Jeffers, "To direct man toward a moral self by means of the wise, the solemn lessons of Nature: that has been Jeffers' life work."[2]

But there are dissenting voices. We have for too long thought of "Mother Nature" as "sensitive, efficient, purposeful, and powerful," laments Frederick E. Smith, a Harvard professor of resources and ecology. She does not exist; nature is adrift. "This absence of 'goal' in the world systems is what makes the concept of Mother Nature dangerous. In the final analysis nothing is guiding the ship."[3] This, of course, exempts us from following nature—to the contrary, we must take control of our aimless ecosystem. And, again, if this is for Smith more a matter of prudence than of

---

From *Environmental Ethics*, 1 (1979): 7–30. Reprinted with permission from the publisher and the author.

[1]Barry Commoner, *The Closing Circle: Nature, Man & Technology* (New York: Alfred A. Knopf, 1972), p. 41.

[2]Radcliffe Squires, *The Loyalties of Robinson Jeffers* (Ann Arbor: University of Michigan Press, 1956), p. 134.

[3]Frederick E. Smith, "Scientific Problems and Progress in Solving the Environmental Crisis" (Address delivered at conference on "Environment, the Quest for Quality," Washington, D.C., February 19, 1970), pp. 3, 5.

morality, another earlier Harvard professor noted with intensity the moral indifference of nature. Coining a memorable phrase, William James called us to "the moral equivalent of war" in our human resistance to amoral nature:

> Visible nature is all plasticity and indifference,—a moral multiverse . . . and not a moral universe. To such a harlot we owe no allegiance; with her as a whole we can establish no moral communion; and we are free in our dealing with her several parts to obey or to destroy, and to follow no law but that of prudence in coming to terms with such of her particular features as will help us to our private ends.[4]

Those with a philosophical memory will see that the environmental debate reconnects with a long-standing problem in the ethics of nature, and recognize the two camps into which those before us have so often divided, the one setting human conduct morally and valuationally in essential discontinuity with our environment, the other finding continuity there. John Stuart Mill stands within one paradigm: "Conformity to nature has no connection whatever with right and wrong."[5] Ralph Waldo Emerson represents the other: "Right is conformity to the laws of nature so far as they are known to the human mind."[6] Sometimes old debates can be thrown into fresh perspective by more recent insights and discoveries. Of late, having become ecologically aware, can we say anything more about the question, "Can and ought we to follow nature?"

Much of the puzzle is in the way we use that grand word *nature* and here an analysis of our language is necessary. Still, it is not a sufficient answer to the question. The issue will finally turn on one's sensitivities to value, and to what degree this can be found in the environment we address. We shall try here to disentangle the phrase "follow nature," reaching in conclusion limited but crucial senses in which we both can and ought to follow nature. *Nature* is an absolutely indispensable English word, but there are few others

with such a tapestry of meanings. In this respect it is like other monumental words round which life turns to such a high degree that we often capitalize them—*Freedom, the Good, the Right, Beauty, Truth, God, my Country, Democracy, the Church*—words that demand an ethical response, words that we cannot altogether and at once keep in logical perspective, but can only attack piecemeal, always reasoning out of the personal backing of our responsive perceptual experience. Earlier and in the foreground, we will put "following nature" into logical focus. But, later on and in the background, we can only invite the reader to share our moral intuitions. In ethics, Aristotle remarked, "The decision rests with perception."[7]

Nature is whatever is, all in sum, and in that universal sense the word is quite unmanageable. Even the sense of the physical universe going back to the Greek *physis* is both too broad and too simple. We reach the meaning we need (which also recalls the sense of *physis*) if we refer to our complex earthen ecosphere—a biosphere resting on physical planetary circulations. Nature is most broadly whatever obeys natural laws, and that also includes astronomical nature. Used in this way the word has a contrast only in the supernatural realm, if such there is. But nevertheless we restrict the word to a global, not a cosmic sense, as our typical use of the word *nature* still retains the notion, coming from the Latin root *natus* and also present in *physis*, of a system giving birth to life. No one urges that we follow physicochemical nature—dead nature. What is invariably meant features that vital evolutionary or ecological movement we often capitalize as *Nature* and sometimes personify as *Mother Nature*.

In the present state of human knowledge we are not in any position to estimate the cosmic rarity or frequency of this motherhood on our planet. Perhaps it has regularly appeared wherever nature has been given proper opportunity to organize itself; if so, that would tell us a great deal about the tendency of nature. But it may be that all this vitality is but an eddy in the all-consuming stream of entropy. Although it seems that the stars serve as the necessary furnaces in which all the chemical elements except the very lightest are forged—elements foundational to any biosystem—we nevertheless know little about the contributions of astronomical nature to our local ecosystem. We draw many conclusions about universal nature based on our knowledge of physics and chemistry, but we are reluctant to do so

---

[4]William James, "The Moral Equivalent of War," in *Memories and Studies* (New York: Longmans, Green, and Co., 1911), pp. 267–96; "Is Life Worth Living?" in *The Will to Believe* (New York: Longmans, Green, and Co., 1896). pp. 43–44.

[5]John Stuart Mill, "Nature," in *Collected Works,* 19 vols. (Toronto: University of Toronto Press, 1963–77), 10:400.

[6]Ralph Waldo Emerson, *Journals* (Cambridge, Mass.: Riverside Press, 1910). 3:208.

[7]Aristotle *Nicomachean Ethics* 2. 8. 1109^{b}23.

with biology, for we do not like to project from only one known case. Furthermore, profound and mysterious though it is, astronomical nature is too simple. We know nature in its most sophisticated organization on Earth; so, we speak now only of that face of nature which has yielded our own flourishing organic community—eco-nature.

In what follows we distinguish seven senses in which we may follow nature—first, in general terms, an *absolute* sense; an *artifactual* sense, and a *relative* sense, and then, in more detail, four specific relative senses, a *homeostatic* sense, an *imitative ethical* sense, an *axiological* sense, and finally a *tutorial* sense. We answer our basic question, whether we can and ought to follow nature, in terms of each.

Following Nature in an Absolute Sense

Everything which conducts itself or is conducted in accordance with the laws of nature "follows nature" in a broad, elemental sense, and here it is sometimes asked whether human conduct does or ought to follow these laws. The human species has come into evolutionary nature lately and yet dramatically and with such upset that we are driven to ask whether persons are some sort of anomaly, literally apart from the laws that have hitherto regulated and otherwise still regulate natural events. No doubt our bodies have very largely the same biochemistries as the higher animals. But in our deliberative and rational powers, in our moral and spiritual sensitivities, we do not seem to run with the same mechanisms with which the coyotes and the chimpanzees so naturally run. These faculties seem to "free" us from natural determinisms; we transcend nature and escape her clutches.

Perhaps it is true that in their cultural life humans are not altogether subject to the laws of evolutionary nature. But we may immediately observe that humans are, in a still more basic sense, subject to the operation of these natural laws which we sometimes seem to exceed. If nature is defined as the aggregate of all physical, chemical, and biological processes, there is no reason why it should not *include* human agency. The human animal, as much as all the others, seems to be subject to all the natural laws that we have so far formulated. Although we live at a higher level of natural organization than any other animal, and even though we act as intelligent agents as perhaps no other animal can, there does not seem to be any law of

nature that we violate either in our biochemistry or in our psychology. It is, however, difficult to get clear on the logical connections, to say nothing of the psychosomatic connections, of agency with causation. In any case, insofar as we operate as agents on the world, we certainly do so by using rather than by exempting ourselves from laws of nature. No one has ever broken the laws of gravity, or those of electricity, nutrition, or psychology. All human conduct is natural inasmuch as the laws of nature operate in us and on us willy-nilly. We cannot help but follow nature, and advice to do so in this basic law-of-nature sense is idle and trivial even while some high-level questions about the role of human deliberation in nature remain open.

Following Nature in an Artifactual Sense

Still, within this necessary obedience to the laws of nature humans do have options through agentive capacities. Submit we must, but we may nevertheless sometimes choose our route of submission. Something remains "up to us." We alter the course of spontaneous nature. That forces us to a second extreme— asking whether, in what we may call an *artifactual* sense, we can follow nature. The feeling that deliberation exempts us from the way that nature otherwise runs suggests the possibility that all agentive conduct is unnatural. Here nature is defined as the aggregate of all physical, chemical, and biological processes *excluding* those of human agency. What we most commonly mean by a natural course of events lies not so much in a scientific claim about our submission to natural laws as it does in a contrast of the natural with the artificial, the artifactual. Nature runs automatically and, within her more active creatures, instinctively; but persons do things by design, which is different, and we for the most part have no trouble distinguishing the two kinds of events. A cabin which we encounter hiking through the woods is not natural, but the rocks, trees, and the stream that form its setting are. A warbler's nest or a beaver's skull are natural while a sign marking the way to a lake or an abandoned hiking boot are not. These things differ in their architecture. The one kind is merely caused. The other kind is there for reasons.

By this account no human has ever acted deliberately except to interfere in the spontaneous course of nature. All human *actions* are in this sense unnatural because they are artifactual, and the advice to follow nature is impossible. We could not do so if we tried, for in deliberately trying to do so we act unnaturally.[8]

Each extreme—the absolute and the artifactual—so strongly appeals to part of our usage of the word *nature* that some inquirers are stalled here and can go no further. Yet even Mill, whose celebrated essay on "Nature" begins with these as the only two options, continues to ask at length about following nature as though it is possible and optional, an inquiry which cannot arise in terms of either of the above senses of the phrase. Are there not some other intermediate and reasonably distinct senses in which we can follow nature?

Following Nature in a Relative Sense

There is a relative sense in which we may follow nature. Although always acting deliberately, we may conduct ourselves more or less continuously or receptively with nature as it is proceeding upon our entrance. Man is the animal with options who, when he acts, chooses just how natural or artificial his actions will be. All human agency proceeds in rough analogy with the sailing of a ship, which, if it had no skipper, would be driven with the natural wind. But the skipper may set the sails to move crosswind or even tack against the wind using the natural wind all the while. There are no unnatural energies. Our deliberative agency only manages to shift the direction of these natural forces, and it is that intervention which we call unnatural. But our interventions are variously disruptive, and, having admitted these senses in which they are all both natural and unnatural, we recognize further a range across which some are more and some are less natural.

Any parents who "plan" their children act unnaturally in the artifactual sense. Yet marriage, mating, and the rearing of children proceed with the laws of nature. In between, we debate just how natural or artificial birth control methods really are. Some moralists

and some medical persons dislike methods that greatly tamper with natural cycles. In contrast to the natural love of man and woman, homosexual conduct is unnatural, "queer," which is one of the strongest reasons why many condemn it. All childbirth is natural, all medically attended childbirth is unnatural, and in between we speak of natural childbirth as opposed to a more medically manipulative childbirth.

All landscaping is artificial. On the other hand, no landscaping violates the laws of nature. Some landscaping, which blends with natural contours and uses natural flora or introduced plants compatible with it, is considered natural; however, landscaping which involves bulldozing out half a hill and setting a building and artificial shrubbery against a scarred landscape is unnatural. All farming is unnatural, against spontaneous nature, but some farming practices fit in with the character of the soil and climate while others do not. Bluegrass does well in Kentucky and in the Midwest, but the Southern farmer is foolish to plant it; and who would plant cotton in New England? On millions of acres found on every continent our unnatural agricultural practices strain fragile semi-desert ecosystems with the fate of millions of persons at stake. Highly manipulative industrial agriculture seems increasingly unnatural with its hybrid "strains," herbicides and pesticides, monocultures, factory farming of chickens, and hormone lacing of beef cattle on feedlots. Some lakes are natural while others are manmade, but among the latter a pond with a relatively fixed shoreline which permits natural flora to flourish there seems more natural than a drawdown reservoir with barren edges.

All clothing is unnatural; only nudists go *au naturel*. We are usually oblivious to whether style and color have any connection with our environment, but still, when the issue arises, we may prefer "the natural look." The traditional Scots plaids come almost literally from the landscape; "earth tones" are in. The iridescent, gaudy colors of modern chemistry are unnatural. Some prefer furniture with a "natural finish" to having the wooden grain hidden beneath DuPont's latest exotic colors. We hardly object to trails for hikers in our natural areas, but if humans go there with motors and highways the wildness is spoiled. Even along interstate highways we prohibit billboards lest they pollute the countryside.

It is sometimes thought that with increasing amendation and repair of spontaneous nature the degree of unnaturalness is roughly the same as the degree of progress—the successful shift from nature to

---

[8]We take notice here of a common usage of *nature* in order to set it aside. The word is sometimes used in the sense of "not affected, spontaneous" and applied to conduct that is not studied or strained. Such conduct is not deliberated, not a result of intentional effort, and, hence, natural like the spontaneous course of non-deliberative nature. Notice that our senses of "follow" shift, although they all unfold from the basic sense of "going in the track of." The senses of "follow" which mean to replace or to succeed in a chronological or causal sequence are not used here.

culture. But our ecological perspective has forced us to wonder whether modern life has become increasingly out of kilter with its environment, lost to natural values that we ought to conserve. Big city life in a high rise apartment—to say nothing of the slum—as well as a day's work in a windowless, air-conditioned factory represent synthetic life filled with plastic everything from teeth to trees. They are foreign to the earthen element from which we were reared. We have lost touch with natural reality; life is, alas, artificial.

This relative sense of following nature has to do with the degree of alteration of our environment, with our appreciative incorporation of this environment into our life styles, and with our nearness to nature. But is it not natural for us to be cultured? Consider our hands, each composed of four dexterous fingers and an opposable thumb. Their natural homologues run back through the primates and even to the birds and reptiles. Consider our brain evolving for speech with the jaw released from prehensile functions, and our eyes moving round to frontal focus on hands that enable us to be agents in the world. What are we to say when we deliberately use this natural equipment? That we act unnaturally? Surely not more so than when we use our eyes and ears. Yet with the brain and hand what are we to do? To follow nature? To build a culture that opposes it? Or is there room for the pursuit of both?

With these questions in mind we now examine four specific relative senses of following nature.

Following Nature in a Homeostatic Sense

The ecological crisis has introduced us to what we may call the homeostatic sense of following nature: "You ought not to upset the stability of the ecosystem." Here human welfare and survival depend upon our following nature, but in a sense so basic and rudimentary that we wonder whether it is moral. Human conduct may run through a spectrum from what is minimally to what is maximally disruptive of natural cycles. In its primitive state the human race had only local and relatively inconsequential environmental impact, but technological humanity has at its option powers capable of massive environmental alteration. We use these clumsily and wrongly, partly out of ignorance, partly because of the erratic, unplanned growth of society, but significantly too because of our defiant refusal to participate in our environment, to accept it,

and to fit into it. Environmental rebels, we seek to exploit nature and become misfits. Our modern conduct is thus unnatural.

Ecology awakens us to these unnatural actions. Natural systems fluctuate dynamically and sometimes dramatically, but there is also a resilience and recuperative capacity built into them. Still, they may be pushed to the point of collapse. Ordinarily, if a species becomes too much of a misfit, it perishes while the system continues. But humankind may push the system to collapse, perish taking nearly everything else down with it, and thus wreck all. This danger is especially clear in the case of hundreds of soil/water/air interactions. What will supersonic jets or aerosol cans do to the ozone layer? Where does all the DDT go, or the strontium 90? What becomes of the pollutants from coal-fired generators, or from nuclear plants? Where we use natural chemicals, we sling them around in unnatural volumes allowing lead from gasoline, arsenic from pesticides, mercury from batteries, and nitrogen from fertilizers to find their way into places where they are more disruptive than most people imagine. Worse, so much of our chemistry is exotic, not biodegradable, unnatural in the sense that nature cannot break it down and recycle it, or does so very slowly. Every rock made underground can be eroded at the surface; every compound organically synthesized has some enzyme that will digest it, and so on. But our artificial products choke up the system. Alas, not only our technology, but our whole profiteering, capitalistic, industrial system may be "unnatural" in that it cheats by incurring an environmental debt that moves us ever onward toward reduced homeostasis.

Should we then behave naturally? Humans are the only animals with deliberate options and these options do enable us to command nature, the more so with the advance of science. This capacity to command nature is indeed a sort of escape from obeying nature, but of the sort that must remain in intimate contact with nature if the capacity is to continue. We can no more escape from nature than we can from human nature, than the mind can from the body, but we can bring all these increasingly under our deliberative control. Technology does not release us from natural dependencies; it only shifts the location and character of these, releasing us from some dependencies while immediately establishing new ones. A tree escapes above the soil pushing ever higher only by rooting ever more deeply. On the one hand, we are driven back to our original observation that we can never escape the laws of nature, but must obey them willy-nilly. The only sense in which we can ever break natural laws is to neglect to consider their implication for our welfare. We might even say that any creature acts unnaturally whose behavior is such that the laws of nature run to the detriment of that organism, and when that happens such an unnatural creature soon becomes extinct.

But then, on the other hand, we must not forget our second observation, that all our human actions are unnatural. According to this viewpoint, our successful actions relieve us from the need of following nature—in the sense of submitting to narrow natural constraints—by enlarging our sphere of deliberate options. Room for the homeostatic sense of following nature must be found somewhere between these extremes. The key point we need to consider seems to be that among our deliberate options some will help retain stability in the ecosystem and in our relationship to it while others will not. In this sense it seems perfectly straightforward to say that we may or may not follow nature, and that we both can and ought to do so. To follow nature means to choose a route of submission to nature that utilizes natural laws for our well-being.

It may be objected that the advice to *follow* nature has been subtly converted into the injunction to *study* nature—conduct with which no rational person will quárrel. According to this objection, *studying* nature has nothing to do with *following* nature. To the contrary, its purpose is to repair nature, to free us from conforming to its spontaneous course, by examining just how much alteration we can get by with. This objection has force, but its scope is too narrow, for we study nature to manipulate only parts of it, always within the larger picture of discovering our organic, earthen roots, the natural givens to which we have to submit and with which we have to work. We study cancer in order to eradicate it; we study diabetes in order to repair a natural breakdown in insulin production; but we study the laws of health in order to follow them. We study the causes of floods in order to prevent them, but we study the laws of ecosystemic health in order to follow them. Those who study nature find items they may alter, but they also discover that the larger courses of nature are always to be obeyed. This applies not only in the strong sense in which we have no option, but also in the weak optional sense of intelligently fitting ourselves into their pattern of operation; and in that sense we do study nature, in the end, in order to follow nature.

But is any of this moral? There are a great many ways in which morality readily combines with the injunction to find a life style compatible with our planetary ecosystemic health. The jet set who have insisted on flying in SSTs, should these planes prove to deplete the protective ozone in the atmosphere, would be acting immorally against their fellow humans, as would farmers who continue long-term poisoning of the soil with non-biodegradable pesticides in order to achieve short-term gains. But it is relatively easy to isolate out the *moral* ends here—respect for the welfare of others—and to see the natural means—conformity to the limitations of our ecosystem—as *nonmoral*.[9] So, we are forced to conclude that there is nothing moral about following nature in and of itself; our relations with nature are always technical or instrumental; and the moral element emerges only when our traffic with nature turns out to involve our inter-human relations. We establish no moral communion with nature, but only with other persons. It is not moral to repair a ship nor immoral to sink it except if it happens to be one that we and our fellow travelers are sailing in. We have reached then a homeostatic sense in which we both can and ought to follow nature only to find it submoral or premoral because the morality surrounding it can be separated off from it.

Following Nature in an Imitative Ethical Sense

It is difficult to propose that we ought to follow nature in an imitative ethical sense because our usual estimate—and here we vacillate—is that nature is either amoral or immoral. We call nature amoral because morality appears in humans alone and is not, and has never been, present on the natural scene. Human conduct may be moral or immoral, but the "conduct" of nature, if indeed it can be called that, is simply amoral. The moral dimension in human nature has no counterpart in mother nature. No being can be moral unless he is free deliberatively; something must be "up to him"; and nothing else in nature has sufficient mental competence to be moral. Mother nature simply unfolds in creatures their genetic programming, like the developing seed, and they respond to their environments driven like the leaf before the wind. Even if there are erratic, indeterminate elements in nature, these provide no moral options; they just happen. Biological and evolutionary processes are no more moral than the laws of gravity or electricity. Whether something

---

[9]See Holmes Rolston, III, "Is There an Ecological Ethic?" in *Ethics: An International Journal of Social, Political, and Legal Philosophy* 85 (1975): 93–109.

does or must happen has nothing to do with whether it ought to happen. Out of this estimate arises the basic cleavage that runs through the middle of the modern mind dividing every study into the realm of the *is* and the realm of the *ought*. No study of nature whether physical, biological, or even social can tell us what ought to happen, and following nature where it is possible and optional is something that is never in itself moral. Nature is blind to this dimension of reality. It is a moral nullity.

We immediately grant that there are no other moral agents in nature, whether orangutans, butterflies, wind, or rain; nor is nature as a whole a moral agent even when personified as "Mother Nature." We have no evidence that any natural species or forces do things deliberately, choosing the most moral route from less moral options. If anyone proposes that we "follow nature" in something like the ethical sense in which Christians "follow Jesus," or the Buddhists, Buddha, he has very much gone astray, and the blind does indeed lead the blind. Such a person ignores the emergent sphere of deliberative morality in humans for which there is no precedent in birds or field mice. In this sense, Mill is undoubtedly right when he protests that conformity to nature has no connection with right and wrong. There is no way to derive any of the familiar moral maxims from nature: *"One ought to keep promises," "Tell the truth," "Do to others as you would have them do to you." "Do not cause needless suffering."* There is no natural decalogue to endorse the Ten Comandments; nature tells us nothing about how we should be moral in this way, *even if* it should turn out that this is approximately the morality ingrained by natural selection in human nature.

But this does not end the matter, for there may nevertheless be some good or goods in nature with which we morally ought to conform even if these goods have not been produced by the process of deliberative options necessary to us if we are to be moral. The resolution of this form of our question will prove more difficult. Because nature has no moral agency, and because inter-human relations are clearly moral, it has been easy to suppose that there is nothing moral in our relations with nature. It has also been easy to conclude that morality is not "natural," but rather belongs to our "super-natural" nature. But to grant that morality appears with the emergence of human beings out of nonmoral nature does not settle the question whether we, who are moral, should follow nature.

When the issue of good in nature is raised, we are at once confronted with the counterclaim that the course of nature is bad—one which, if we were to follow it, would be immoral. Nature proceeds with an absolute recklessness that is not only indifferent to life, but results in senseless cruelty which is repugnant to our moral sensibilities. Life is wrested from her creatures by continual struggle, usually soon lost; and those "lucky" few who survive to maturity only face more extended suffering and eventual collapse in disease and death. With what indifference nature casts forth to slaughter ten thousand acorns, a thousand grasshoppers, a hundred minnows, and a dozen rabbits, so that one of each might survive. Things are no sooner sprouted, hatched, or born than they are attacked; life is unrelieved stress, until sooner or later, swiftly or by inches, fickle nature crushes out the life she gave, and the misery is finally over. All we can be sure of from the hands of nature is calamity. We are condemned to live by attacking other life. Nature is a gory blood bath; she permits life only in agony. The world's last word is what the Buddhists call *duhkha*, suffering. Few persons can read Mill's essay on "Nature" without being chastened in their zeal for following nature:

> In sober truth, nearly all the things which men are hanged or imprisoned for doing to one another, are nature's everyday performances.... Nature impales men, breaks them as if on the wheel, casts them to be devoured by wild beasts, burns them to death, crushes them with stones like the first Christian martyr, starves them with hunger, freezes them with cold, poisons them by the quick or slow venom of her exhalations, and has hundreds of other hideous deaths in reserve, such as the ingenious cruelty of a Nabis or a Domitian never surpassed.... A single hurricane destroys the hopes of a season; a flight of locusts, or an inundation, desolates a district.... Everything, in short, which the worst men commit either against life or property is perpetrated on a larger scale by natural agents.[10]

The Darwinian paradigm of nature in the nineteenth century strongly reinforced that of Mill. Nature became a kind of hellish jungle where only the fittest survive, and these but barely. The discovery of the genetic basis of Darwin's random mutations only added to the sense of nature's rudderless proceedings, law-like to be sure in the sense that natural selection conserves beneficial mutations, but still aimless since

---

[10]Mill. *Collected Works*, 10:385–86.

natural selection operates blindly over mutations which are mostly worthless, irrelevant, or detrimental. There seemed a kind of futility to it all, certainly nothing worthy of our moral imitation. This portrait of nature affected several generations of ethicists who frequently concluded that ethics had nothing to do with the laws of nature unless it was to alter and overcome our natural instincts and drives, lest we too behave "like beasts." The *is/ought* cleavage became entrenched in earlier twentieth-century philosophy in large part because of this nineteenth-century portrait of nature. G.L. Dickinson expresses with great force the protest of this period:

> I'm not much impressed by the argument you attribute to Nature, that if we don't agree with her we shall be knocked on the head. I, for instance, happen to object strongly to her whole procedure. I don't much believe in the harmony of the final consummation . . . and I am sensibly aware of the horrible discomfort of the intermediate stages, the pushing, kicking, trampling of the host, and the wounded and dead left behind on the march. Of all this I venture to disapprove; then comes Nature and says, "but you ought to approve!" I ask why, and she says, "Because the procedure is mine." I still demur, and she comes down on me with a threat—"Very good, approve or no, as you like; but if you don't approve you will be eliminated!" "By all means," I say, and cling to my old opinion with the more affection that I feel myself invested with something of the glory of a martyr. . . . In my humble opinion it's Nature, not I, that cuts a poor figure![11]

Here we have undoubtedly reached a moral sense of following nature, but one we cannot recommend. Virtually none of us, except perhaps ethical mavericks like Nietzsche, will recommend that this pushing, kicking, and trampling be taken as a moral model for inter-human conduct. So, offered this imitative ethical sense of following nature, we observe that nature is not a moral agent and therefore really cannot be followed, and secondly that there are elements in nature which, if we were to transfer them to inter-human conduct, would be immoral, and therefore ought not to be imitated. But does it follow that nature is therefore bad, a savage realm without natural goods? Is this ferocity and recklessness all that is to be said, or even the principal thing to be said, or can this be set in some different light?

Following Nature in an Axiological Sense

In order to develop an axiological sense in which human conduct may be natural, let us make a fresh start and postpone answering the question we have just posed until we can come at it from another side. Three environments—the urban, the rural, and the wild—provide three human pursuits—culture, agriculture, and nature. All three are vocations which ought to be followed and environments which are needed for our well-being. We are concerned for the moment with human activity collectively and will examine individual responsibility later. When Aristotle observed that "Man is by nature a political animal,"[12] he was speaking in terms of the Greek word *polis*, city-state, of which Athens is such a memorable example. Here *city* refers indiscriminately to village, town, and city. We are social animals and the story of civilization is largely the growth of our capacity for building a cultured state. We are both *Homo sapiens* and *Homo faber*; the brain and the hand combine in wisdom and in craft to construct the enormous world of artifacts which is our urban environment. All these products are unnatural in the sense that they are independent of nature's spontaneous production. It cannot, on the other hand, be unnatural for us to build cities, for, after all, nature has supplied us with the brain and the hand as well as the social propensities for community. Humans are the creatures whom nature did not specialize, but rather equipped with marvelous faculties for culture and craft. We ought to use them, both prudentially and morally, for is not wasted talent a sin? In this sense it is not unnatural for man to be urban even though, as soon as we do anything deliberately, we alter spontaneous nature. We reach the paradox that "Man is the animal for whom it is natural to be artificial."[13]

In culture we allow a discontinuity between human life and nature, but this discontinuity is still an extension out of the ultimate natural environment.

---

[11]Goldworthy Lowes Dickinson, *The Meaning of Good* (New York: McClure, Phillips and Co., 1907), p. 46.

[12]Aristotle *Politics* 1. 2. 1253[a]2.

[13]Lucius Garvin. *A Modern Introduction to Ethics* (Cambridge, Mass.: Houghton Mifflin, 1953), p. 378.

Nature releases us to develop our culture; here she offers no model; we are on our own; the mores of the human city are up to us, albeit judged by a culturing of those native endowments we call reason and conscience. The city is in some sense our *niche*; we belong there, and no one can achieve full humanity without it. Cultured human life is not possible in the unaltered wilderness; it is primitive and illiterate if it remains at a merely rural level. The city mentality provides us with literacy and advancement, whether through the market with its trade and industry, or through the library and laboratory, out of which so much of our knowledge of nature has come.

By the term *rural environment* we mean nature as domesticated for the life support of the human population, primarily the cultivated landscape, the field, the woodlot, the pasture, the groved road, the orchard, the ranch. The farm feeds the city, of course, and that may be taken as a metaphor for the whole support of society in soil, water, and air—for the organic circulations of the city in nature. The rural environment is the one in which humans meet nature in productive encounter, where we command nature by obeying her. Here there is a judiciously mixed sense of discontinuity and continuity: by human agency we adapt the natural course— yet we adopt it too; we alter nature—yet accept its climates and capacities. We both get into nature's orbit and bring nature into our orbit. We direct nature round to our goals; yet, if we are intelligent, we use only those disruptions that nature can absorb, those appropriate to the resilience of the ecosystem under cultivation. In the urban environment, no burden of proof rests on a person proposing an alteration whether or not the change is natural (so long as it does not spill over to disrupt rural or wild areas). But in the rural environment, a burden of proof does rest upon the proposer to show that the alteration will not deteriorate the ecosystem. Within our agricultural goals our preference is for those alterations that can be construed as "natural," those most congenial to the natural environment; and we prohibit those that disfigure it.

The rural environment is an end in itself as well as an instrument for the support of the city. It has beauty surpassing its utility. If we ask why there are gardens, we answer "for food," only to recall that there are also flower gardens. The English garden combines both the rose and the berry bush. Both the farm and the park belong in the pastures of the Shenandoah Valley, the blue grass farms of Kentucky, and the cornfields of Iowa, where there is a form of beauty not possible either in the city or in the wilderness. We love the green, green grass of home, the tree in the meadow, the forested knobs behind the church, and the walk down by the pond. We are deeply satisfied by the rural environment. Although we appreciate our modern freedom from the drudgery of the farm, many still cherish, within limits, experiences that can only be had in the country—sawing down an oak tree, shelling peas, drawing a bucket of water from a well.

The rural environment is, or ought to be, a place of *symbiosis* between humankind and nature, for we may sometimes improve a biosystem. The climax forest of an ecosystemic succession is usually not suited for the maximum number and kinds of fauna and flora, and this succession can be interrupted by agriculture with benefit to those natural species which prefer fields and edging. There are more deer in Virginia now than when the Indians inhabited its virtually unbroken forests, and that is probably true of cottontails, bobwhites, and meadowlarks. Suitable habitat for all but a few of the wildest creatures can be made consistent with the rural use of land. With pleasant results humans have added the elm and the oak to the British landscape, the Russian olive to the high plains, the eucalyptus to California, the floribunda rose to interstate highway roadsides, and the ring-necked pheasant to the prairies. In his idyllic love of nature, Emerson did not write of the wilderness so much as of the domestic New England countryside. When we sing "America the Beautiful," we sing largely of this gardened nature.

We may even speak of a micro-rural environment—an urban garden, a city park, an avenue of trees with squirrels and rabbits, a suburban fence row with cardinals and mockingbirds, a creekside path to a school. Anyone who flies over all but the worst of our Eastern cities will be impressed by how much nature is still there. We love something growing about us if only trees and lawns, and everyone would consider a city improved if it had more green space, more landscape left within it. We prefer our homes, bridges, streets, offices, and factories to be "in a natural setting." We want our cities graced with nature, and that alone suffices to undermine Mill's claim that "All praise of Civilization, or Art, or Contrivance, is so much dispraise of Nature."[14] The wood fire on the stone hearth or the gentle night rain on a tin roof recall for us this natural element; even our plastic trees vicariously return us to nature.

---

[14]Mill, *Collected Works*, 10:381.

Our requirements for wild nature are more difficult to specify than those for tamed nature, but nonetheless real. The scarcest environment we now have is wilderness, and, when we are threatened with its possible extinction, we are forced to think through our relationships to it. Do we preserve wild nature only as a potential resource for activity that humans may someday wish to undertake in terms of urban or rural nature? Or are there richer reasons, both moral and prudential, why we ought to maintain some of our environment in a primitive state?

It is beyond dispute that we enjoy wild places, that they fill a *recreational* need, but that word by which we typically designate this fulfillment seems a poor one until we notice a deeper etymology. Something about a herd of elk grazing beneath the vista of wind and sky, or an eroded sandstone mesa silhouetted against the evening horizon, *re-creates* us. We have loved our national parks almost to death, the more so because they are kept as close to spontaneous nature as is consistent with their being extensively visited. Worried about park overuse, we are now struggling to preserve as much wilderness area as possible; resolving to keep the human presence there is lower profile. We set aside the best first—the Yellowstone, the Grand Canyon, the High Sierra, the Great Smokies, the Everglades—but later found that there was really no kind of landscape for which we did not wish some preservation—the desert, the pine barrens, the grasslands, the wild rivers, the swamps, the oak-hickory forests. We began by preserving the buffaloes and lady-slippers, and soon became concerned for the toads and mosses. But why is it that sometimes we would rather look for a pasqueflower than see the latest Broadway hit?

Wild nature is a place of encounter where we go not to act on it, but to contemplate it, drawing ourselves into its order of being, not drawing it into our order of being. This accounts for our tendency to think of our relationship to wild nature as recreational, and therefore perhaps idle, since we do not do any work while there. We are at leisure there, often, of course, an active leisure, but not one that is economically productive. In this respect our attitude toward wilderness will inevitably be different from that of our grandfathers who for the most part went into it to reduce the wild to the rural and urban. Their success forces us to the question of the worth of the wild. But, when the answer has to be given in non-resource terms, it is not the kind or level of answer to which we are accustomed in questions about nature. For in important senses wild nature is not for us a commodity at all. Even when the answer is given in terms of some higher, noneconomic value, our philosophical apparatus for the analysis and appraisal of wild value is, frankly, very poorly developed for we have too much fallen into the opinion that the only values that there are, moral or artistic or whatever, are human values, values which we have selected or constructed, over which we have labored. Modern philosophical ethics has left us insensitive to the reception of nonhuman values.

We need wild nature in much the same way that we need the other things in life which we appreciate for their intrinsic rather than their instrumental worth, somewhat like we need music or art, philosophy or religion, literature or drama. But these are human activities, and our encounter with nature has the additional feature of being our sole contact with worth and beauty independent of human activity. We need friends not merely as our instruments, but for what they are in themselves, and, moving one order beyond this, we need wild nature precisely because it is a realm of values which are independent of us. Wild nature has a kind of integrity, and we are the poorer if we do not recognize it and enjoy it. That is why seeing an eagle or warbler, a climbing fern or a blue spruce is a stirring experience. The Matterhorn leaves us in awe, but so does the fall foliage on any New England hillside, or the rhododendron on Roan Mountain. Those who linger with nature find this integrity where it is not at first suspected, in the copperhead and the alligator, in the tarantula and the morel, in the wind-stunted banner spruce and the straggly box elder, in the stormy sea and the wintry tundra. Such genuine nature precedes and exceeds us despite all our dominion over it or our uniqueness within it, and its spontaneous value is the reason why contact with nature can be re-creating.

We are so indisposed to admit the possibility of wild value that the cautious naturalist, finding himself undeniably stimulated by his outings, will still be inclined to locate these values within himself—values which he believes he has somehow constructed or unfolded out of the raw materials of natural encounter. These encounters provide him with an account of why only some of nature has value for him. If he has successfully used it, it has value. The rest of nature, left unused, has no value, not yet at least. Wild nature, then, according to this account, serves only as an occasion of value; it triggers dormant human potential. Even such a naturalist, however, needs wild nature for the triggering of these values, and he will have to reckon with why nature has this capacity to occasion value, being necessary if insufficient for it. But what makes this account peculiarly unsatisfying is its persistent anthropocentrism and its artificiality in actual natural encounter. It takes considerable straining, even after studying philosophy, to accept the idea that the beauty of the sunset is only in the eye of the beholder. The sensitive naturalist is again and again surprised by nature, being converted to its values and delighted by it just because he has gone beyond his previous, narrowly human values. It is the autonomous otherness of the natural expressions of value that we learn to love, and that integrity becomes vain when this value secretly requires our composing.

This value is often artistic or aesthetic, and is invariably so if we examine a natural entity at the proper level of observation or in terms of its ecological setting. An ordinary rock in microsection is an extraordinary crystal mosaic. The humus from a rotting log supports an exquisite hemlock. But this value also has to do with the intelligibility of each of the natural members; and here natural science, especially ecology, has greatly helped us. This intelligibility often leads to a blending of the autonomy of each of the natural kinds creating a harmony in the earthen whole. A world in which there are many kinds of things, the simple related to the complex, is a valuable world, and especially so if all of them are intelligibly related. Everything has its *place,* and that justifies it. Natural value is further resident in the vitality of things, in their struggle and zest, and it is in this sense that we often speak of a reverence for life, lovely or not. Or should we say that we find all life beautiful, even when we sometimes must sacrifice it? We love the natural mixture of consistency and freedom; there is something about the word *wild* that goes well with the word *free,* whether it is the determined freedom of the wild river or the more spontaneous freedom of the hawk in the sky. In the splendor, sublimity, and mystery the very word *wild* is one of our value words. Simply put, we find *meanings* in wild things.

In this context we may offer yet another answer to our question. We may be said to follow that which is the object of our orienting interest, as when we follow sports, medicine, or law, or the latest news developments. Many scientists, perhaps all the "pure" ones, "follow nature" in that they find its study to be of consuming interest—intrinsically worthwhile—and those who are also naturalists go on in varying senses to say that they appreciate nature, find great satisfaction in it, and even love it. We follow what we "participate in," especially goals we take to be of value. This sense of "follow" is less than "ethical imitation," but it is significantly

more than the notion that our conduct toward nature is not moral. For we look to nature as a realm of natural value beyond mere natural facts, which, maintained in its integrity, we may and ought to encounter. The notion of "following" nature, in addition, is deeper than following art, music, or sports, in that, when encountering nature, we are led by it through sensitive study to the importation of nonhuman kinds of meaning. When I delight in the wild hawk in the wind-swept sky, that is not a value that I invent, but one that I discover. Nature has an autonomy which art does not have. We must follow nature to gain this meaning—in the sense of leaving it alone, letting it go its way. We take ourselves to it and listen for and to its natural forms of expression, drawn by a range and realm of values which are not of our own construction. We ought not to destroy this integrity, but rather preserve it and contemplate it, and in this sense our relations with nature are moral. Even G.E. Moore, who so much lamented the "naturalistic fallacy," by which we mistakenly move from a natural *is* to an ethical *ought,* still finds that appreciation of the existence of natural beauty is a good.[15] But morality is the science of the good; so, as soon as we move from a natural *is* to a natural *is good,* our relations with that natural good are moral. We follow what we love, and the love of an intrinsic good is always a moral relationship. We thus find it possible to establish that moral communion with nature which James thought impossible. In this axiological sense, we ought to follow nature, to make its value one among our goals; and, in so doing, our conduct is here guided by nature.

How far is this value so distributed that each individual is obligated to moral conduct towards nature? There is no person who ought not to be concerned with the preservation of natural goodness, if only because others undeniably do find values there. Nevertheless, we allow individuals to weigh their preferences, and there may be differing vocations, some seeking the social goods more than the natural ones. But a purely urban person is a one-dimensional person; only those who add the rural and the wild are three-dimensional persons. As for myself, I consider life morally atrophied when respect for and appreciation of the naturally wild is absent. No one has learned the full scope of what it means to be moral until he has learned to respect the integrity and worth of those things we call wild.

---

[15]George Edward Moore, *Principia Ethica* (Cambridge: Cambridge University Press, 1903), pp. 36–58, 188, 193, 195–98, 200, 206.

Following Nature in a Tutorial Sense

In positing a tutorial sense in which human conduct may follow nature, I admit that I can only give witness and invite the sharing of a gestalt, rather than provide a reasoned conceptual argument. I find I can increasingly "draw a moral" from reflecting over nature—that is, gain a lesson in living. Nature has a "leading capacity"; it prods thoughts that educate us, that lead us out (*educo*) to know who and where we are, and what our vocation is. Take what we call natural symbols—*light and fire, water or rock, morning and evening, life and death, waking and sleeping, the warmth of summer and the cold of winter, the flowers of spring and the fruits of fall, rain and rivers, seeds and growth, earth and sky.* How readily we put these material phenomena to "metaphorical" or "spiritual" use, as when we speak of life's "stormy weather," of strength of character "like a rock," of insecurity "like shifting sand," of the "dark cloud with the silver lining," or of our "roots" in a homeland. Like a river, life flows on with persistence in change. How marvelously Lanier could sing of the watery marshes of Glynn—and the darkey, of Old Man River! How profound are the psychological forces upon us of the grey and misty sky, the balmy spring day, the colors we call bright or somber, the quiet of a snowfall, the honking of a skein of wild geese, or the times of natural passage—birth, puberty, marriage, death! How the height of the mountains "elevates" us, and the depths of the sea stimulates "deep" thoughts within!

Folk wisdom is routinely cast in this natural idiom. The sage in Proverbs admonishes the sluggard to consider the ways of the ant and be wise. The farmer urges, "Work, for the night comes, when man's work is done." "Make hay while the sun shines." The Psalmist notices how much we are like grass which flourishes but is soon gone, and those who understand the "seasonal" character of life are the better able to rejoice in the turning of the seasons and to do everything well in its time. Jesus asks us, in our search for the goods of life, to note the natural beauty of the lilies of the field, which the affected glory of Solomon could not surpass, and he points out birds to us, who, although hardly lazy, are not anxious or worried about tomorrow. *"What you sow, you reap." "Into each life some rain must fall." "All sunshine makes a desert." "By their fruits shall you know them." "The early bird gets the worm." "Time and tide wait for no man." "The loveliest rose has yet its thorns." "The north wind made the Vikings." "The tree stands that bends with the wind." "White ants pick a carcass cleaner than a lion." "Every mile is two in*

winter." "If winter comes, can spring be far behind." It is no accident that our major religious seasons are naturally scheduled. Christmas comes at the winter solstice, Easter with the bursting forth of spring, and Thanksgiving with the harvest. Encounter with nature integrates me, protects me from pride, gives a sense of proportion and place, teaches me what to expect, and what to be content with, establishes other value than my own, and releases feelings in my spirit that I cherish and do not find elsewhere.

Living well is the catching of certain natural rhythms. Those so inclined can reduce a great deal of this to prudence, to the natural conditions of value; and we may be particularly prone to do this because nature gives us no ethical guidance in our inter-human affairs. But human conduct must also be an appropriate form of life toward our environment, toward what the world offers us. Some will call this mere efficiency, but for some of us it is a kind of wisdom for which prudence and efficiency are words that are too weak. For we do not merely accept the limits that nature thrusts upon us, but endorse an essential goodness, a sufficiency in the natural fabric of life which encompasses both our natural talents and the constitution of the world in which, with our natural equipment, we must conduct ourselves. What I call a larger moral virtue, excellence of character, comes in large part, although by no means in the whole, from this natural attunement; and here I find a natural ethic in the somewhat old-fashioned sense of a way of life—a life style that should "follow nature," that is, be properly sensitive to its flow through us and its bearing on our habits of life. A very significant portion of the *meaning* of life consists in our finding, expressing, and endorsing its naturalness. Otherwise, life lacks propriety.

We have enormous amounts of nature programmed into us. The protoplasm that flows within us has flowed naturally for over a billion years. Our internal human nature has evolved in response to external nature for a million years. Our genetic programming—which largely determines what we are, making each of us so alike and yet so different—is entirely natural. It is difficult to think that we do not possess a good natural fit in the wellspring of our behavior. Our cultural and our agentive life must be, and, so far as it is optional, ought to be consistent with that fit—freeing us no doubt for the cities we build, permitting our rural adaptations, and yet in the end further fitting us for life within our overarching natural environment. We are not, in the language of geographers, environmentally determined, for we have exciting options, and these increase with the advance of culture. But we are inescapably environmentally grounded as surely as we are mortal. This *is* the case, and hence our optional conduct *ought* to be commensurately natural; and, if we can transpose that from a grudging prudential *ought* to a glad moral *ought,* we shall be the happier and the wiser for finding our "place under the sun." Life moves, we are saying, not so much against nature as with it, and that remains true even of cultured human life which never really escapes its organic origins and surroundings. Our ethical life *ought* to maintain for us a good natural fit in both an efficient and a moral sense. This is what Emerson means when he commends moral conduct as conformity to the laws of nature. There is in this communion with nature an ethic for life, and that is why exposure to natural wildness is as necessary for a true education as the university.

Someone may complain, and perhaps fiercely, that in this ethic nature only serves as an occasion for the construction of human virtues; that the natural wisdom we have cited shows only the virtues that develop *in us* when we confront nature; and that thus there is no following of nature, but rather a resistance to it, a studied surmounting in which we succeed despite nature. But this anthropocentric account is too one-sided. Evolution and ecology have taught us that every kind of life is what it is not autonomously but because of a natural fit. We are what I call *environmental reciprocals* indebted to our environment for what we have become in ways which are as complementary as they are oppositional. Nature is, I think, not sufficient to produce all these virtues in us, and that allows for our own integrity and creativity—but nature is necessary for them. Admittedly, we must attain these virtues before we find and establish natural symbols for them—we must undergo the natural course in order to understand it—but I do not think that this ethical strength is merely and simply inside us. It is surely relational, at a minimum, arising out of the encounter between humans and nature. At the maximum, we are realizing and expressing in this strong and good life which we live something of the strength and goodness which nature has bequeathed us.

Nature is often enigmatic. Human life is complex. Each contains many times and seasons. The danger here is that any secretly desired conduct can somehow be construed as natural and found virtuous. Nature gives us little help concerning how we are to behave toward one another. In these matters we are free to do as we please, although nature has endowed us with reason and conscience out of which ethics may be constructed.

Especially suspicious are arguments which assign human roles to nature, as is sometimes done with women or blacks, for we easily confuse the natural with the culturally conventional.

There may also be cases where we learn what is bad from nature. In rare cases, we may unwisely elect to follow some process in nature which in itself is indefensible—as some say the bloodthirsty conduct of the weasel is. I do not wish to defend the course of nature in every particular, but most of these cases involve learning something bad—an ethic of selfishness, a dog-eat-dog attitude, or a might-makes-right life style—by inappropriately projecting into moral inter-human conduct, and thereby making bad what is quite appropriate at some lower, nonmoral level—for example, the principle of the survival of the fittest or the self-interest programmed into the lower life forms. We cannot assume that the way things work at lower, nonmoral levels is the way that they ought to work at human, moral levels, for the appearance of the capacity for moral deliberation makes a difference. This is what is correct about the *is-ought* distinction. Our moral conduct exceeds nature, and we must deliberate with an ethic based on reason and conscience which supplants instinct. It is our conduct or mores insofar as it fits us to our environment—our ethic of bearing toward the natural world, not toward other persons—that I refer to in the tutorial sense, and which I here defend. Moreover, I call this conduct moral too in the sense that it contributes to our wisdom and our excellence of character.

In catching these natural rhythms, we must judiciously blend what I call *natural resistance* and *natural conductance.* Part of nature opposes life, increases entropy, kills, rots, destroys. Human life, like all other life, must struggle against its environment, and I much admire the human conquest of nature. However, I take this dominion to be something to which we are naturally impelled and for which we are naturally well-equipped. Furthermore, this struggle can be resorbed into a natural conductance, for nature has both generated us and provided us with life support—and she has stimulated us into culture by her resistance. Nature is not all ferocity and indifference. She is also the bosom out of which we have come, and she remains our life partner, a realm of otherness for which we have the deepest need. I resist nature, and readily for my purposes amend and repair it. I fight disease and death, cold and hunger—and yet somehow come to feel that wildness is not only, not finally, the pressing night. Rather, that wildness with me and in me kindles fires against the night.

I am forced, of course, to concede that there are gaps in this account of nature. I do not find nature meaningful everywhere, or beautiful, or valuable, or educational; and I am moved to horror by malaria, intestinal parasites, and genetic deformities. My concept of the good is not coextensive with the natural, but it does greatly overlap it; and I find my estimates steadily enlarging that overlap. I even find myself stimulated positively in wrestling with nature's deceits. They stir me with a creative discontent, and, when I go nature one better, I often look back and reflect that nature wasn't half bad. I notice that my advanced life depends on nature's capacity to kill and to rot, and to make a recycling and pyramidal use of resources. Nature is not first and foremost the bringer of disease and death, but of life, and with that we touch the Latin root, *natus*. When nature slays, she takes only the life she gave as no murderer can; and she gathers even that life back to herself by reproduction and by re-enfolding organic resources and genetic materials, and produces new life out of it.

Environmental life, including human life, is nursed in struggle; and to me it is increasingly inconceivable that it could, or should, be otherwise. If nature is good, it must be both an assisting and a resisting reality. We cannot succeed unless it can defeat us. My reply, then, to G.L. Dickinson's lament over the kicking and pushing in nature is that, although I do not imitate it, certainly not in human ethics, I would not eliminate it if I could, not at least until I have come to see how life could be better stimulated, and nobler human character produced without it. Nature is a vast scene of birth and death, springtime and harvest, permanence and change, of budding, flowering, fruiting, and withering away, of processive unfolding, of pain and pleasure, of success and failure, of ugliness giving way to beauty and beauty to ugliness. From the contemplation of it we get a feeling for life's transient beauty sustained over chaos. There is as it were a music to it all, and not the least when in a minor key. Even the religious urges within us, though they may promise a hereafter, are likely to advise us that we must for now rest content with the world we have been given. Though we are required to spend our life in struggle, yet we are able to cherish the good earth and to accept the kind of universe in which we find ourselves. It is no coincidence that our ecological perspective often approaches a religious dimension in trying to help us see the beauty, integrity, and stability of nature within and behind its seeming indifference, ferocity, and evils.

Dickenson's portrait can give an account of only half of nature, natural resistance, and even that is an enigmatic account of human life set oddly, set for martyrdom, in a hostile world. He can give no account of natural conductance; indeed, he cannot even see it, and thus he has mistakenly taken the half for the whole. But the account which I am seeking contains both elements, and not merely as a nonsensical mixture of goods and evils—each is absurd in relation to the other. A world in which there is an absurd mixture of helps and hurts is little better than a world of steady hostility. Neither could tutor us. What one needs is a nature where the evils are tributary to the goods, or, in my language of philosophical ecology, where natural resistance is embraced within and made intelligible by natural conductance. It is not death, but life, including human life as it fits this planetary environment, which is the principal mystery that has come out of nature. For several billion years, the ongoing development and persistence of that life, culminating in human life, have been the principal features of eco-nature behind which the element of struggle must be contained as a subtheme. Our conduct morally ought to fit this natural conductance. Life follows nature because nature follows life.

I do endorse in principle, though not without reservations, the constitution of the ecosystem. I do not make any long-range claims about the invariable, absolute law of evolution, about who is guiding the ship, or about the overall record of cosmic nature. There is beauty, stability, and integrity in the evolutionary ecosystem that we happen to have. There is a natural, an earthen, trend to life, although we cannot know it as a universal law. We ought to preserve and to value this nature, if only because it is the only nature that we know in any complexity and detail. If and when we find ourselves in some other nature, of a sort in which we earthlings can still maintain our sanity, we can then revise our ethic appropriately. In the meantime, however, we can at least sometimes "seek nature's guidance" in a tutorial sense almost as one might seek guidance from the Bible, or Socrates, or Shakespeare, even though nature, of course, does not "write" or "speak." None of us lives to the fullest who does not study the natural order, and, more than that, none of us is wise who does not ultimately make his peace with it.

When Mill faces the prospect of an unending expansion of the urban and rural environments, his attitude toward nature shifts, and, rather surprisingly, we find him among the defenders of nature. Suppose, God forbid, he writes, that we were brought by our industry to some future "world with nothing left to the spontaneous activity of nature; with every rood of land brought into cultivation, which is capable of growing food for human beings; every flowery waste or natural pasture ploughed up, all quadrapeds or birds which are not domesticated for man's use exterminated as his rivals for food, every hedgerow or superfluous tree rooted out, and scarcely a place left where a wild shrub or flower could grow without being eradicated as a weed in the name of improved agriculture." Such a world without "natural beauty and grandeur," Mill asserts, "is not good for man." Wild nature "is the cradle of thoughts and aspirations which are not only good for the individual, but which society could ill do without."[16] Thus, in the end, we enlist even this celebrated opponent of our morally following nature among those who wish to follow nature in our axiological sense.

For a closing statement on the tutorial sense of following nature, however, we do better to consult a poet rather than an ecologist or an ethicist. "I came from the wilderness," remembers Carl Sandburg as he invites us to reflect on the wilderness—how it tries to hold on to us and how, in our tutorial sense, we ought not to be separated from it:

> There is an eagle in me and a mockingbird . . . and the eagle flies among the Rocky Mountains of my dreams and fights among the Sierra crags of what I want . . . and the mockingbird warbles in the early forenoon before the dew is gone, warbles in the underbrush of my Chattanoogas of hope, gushes over the blue Ozark foothills of my wishes—And I got the eagle and the mockingbird from the wilderness.[17]

---

[16]John Stuart Mill. *Principles of Political Economy,* in *Collected Works,* 3:756. Mill also records that reading Wordsworth's poetry reawoke in him a love of nature after his analytic bent of mind had caused a crisis in his mental history. See John Stuart Mill, *Autobiography* (Boston: Houghton Mifflin, 1969), pp. 88–90.

[17]Carl Sandburg, "Wilderness," in *Complete Poems* (New York: Harcourt, Brace, Jovanovich, 1970), p. 100. Ellipsis in original.

47. The Land Ethic

ALDO LEOPOLD

In this selection from his seminal book on environmental ethics, *A Sand County Almanac*, Aldo Leopold discusses our obligations to the world around us. His land ethic envisions an ethical community expanded well beyond the human to include soil, waters, plants, and animals. No longer should persons regard them-selves as conquerors of the natural world, privileged to use its resources as if they were mere property; instead, humans are to understand themselves as members of the natural community, with a vital connection to the land and charged with moral obligations to preserve and protect it. Ultimately, the adoption of such an ethic will reshape both our intellectual and emotional assessment of the world and will generate the same social approval for right actions and social disapproval of wrong actions toward the land that we have traditionally reserved only for our treatment of one another.

When godlike Odysseus returned from the wars in Troy, he hanged all on one rope a dozen slave-girls of his household whom he suspected of misbehavior during his absence.

This hanging involved no question of propriety. The girls were property. The disposal of property was then, as now, a matter of expediency, not of right or wrong.

Concepts of right and wrong were not lacking from Odysseus' Greece: witness the fidelity of his wife through the long years before at last his black-prowed galleys clove the wine-dark seas for home. The ethical structure of that day covered wives, but had not yet been extended to human chattels. During the three thousand years which have since elapsed, ethical criteria have been extended to many fields of conduct, with corresponding shrinkages in those judged by expedi-ency only.

The Ethical Sequence

This extension of ethics, so far studied only by philoso-phers, is actually a process in ecological evolution. Its sequences may be described in ecological as well as in

philosophical terms. An ethic, ecologically, is a limita-tion on freedom of action in the struggle for existence. An ethic, philosophically, is a differentiation of social from anti-social conduct. These are two definitions of one thing. The thing has its origin in the tendency of interde-pendent individuals or groups to evolve modes of coop-eration. The ecologist calls these symbioses. Politics and economics are advanced symbioses in which the original free-for-all competition has been replaced, in part, by cooperative mechanisms with an ethical content.

The complexity of cooperative mechanisms has increased with population density, and with the effi-ciency of tools. It was simpler, for example, to define the anti-social uses of sticks and stones in the days of the mastodons than of bullets and billboards in the age of motors.

The first ethics dealt with the relation between individuals; the Mosaic Decalogue is an example. Later accretions dealt with the relation between the individual and society. The Golden Rule tries to inte-grate the individual to society; democracy to integrate social organization to the individual.

There is as yet no ethic dealing with man's rela-tion to land and to the animals and plants which grow upon it. Land, like Odysseus's slave-girls, is still prop-erty. The land-relation is still strictly economic, entail-ing privileges but not obligations.

The extension of ethics to this third element in human environment is, if I read the evidence correctly, an evolutionary possibility and an ecological necessity.

It is the third step in a sequence. The first two have already been taken. Individual thinkers since the days of Ezekiel and Isaiah have asserted that the despoliation of land is not only inexpedient but wrong. Society, however, has not yet affirmed their belief. I regard the present conservation movement as the embryo of such an affirmation.

An ethic may be regarded as a mode of guidance for meeting ecological situations so new or intricate, or involving such deferred reactions, that the path of social expediency is not discernible to the average individual. Animal instincts are modes of guidance for the individual in meeting such situations. Ethics are possibly a kind of community instinct in-the-making.

The Community Concept

All ethics so far evolved rest upon a single premise: that the individual is a member of a community of interdependent parts. His instincts prompt him to compete for his place in the community, but his ethics prompt him also to cooperate (perhaps in order that there may be a place to compete for).

The land ethic simply enlarges the boundaries of the community to include soils, waters, plants, and animals, or collectively: the land.

This sounds simple: do we not already sing our love for and obligation to the land of the free and the home of the brave? Yes, but just what and whom do we love? Certainly not the soil, which we are sending helter-skelter downriver. Certainly not the waters, which we assume have no function except to turn turbines, float barges, and carry off sewage. Certainly not the plants, of which we exterminate whole communities without batting an eye. Certainly not the animals, of which we have already extirpated many of the largest and most beautiful species. A land ethic of course cannot prevent the alteration, management, and use of these "resources," but it does affirm their right to continued existence, and, at least in spots, their continued existence in a natural state.

In short, a land ethic changes the role of *Homo sapiens* from conqueror of the land-community to plain member and citizen of it. It implies respect for his fellow-members, and also respect for the community as such.

In human history, we have learned (I hope) that the conqueror role is eventually self-defeating. Why? Because it is implicit in such a role that the conqueror knows, *ex cathedra*, just what makes the community clock tick, and just what and who is valuable, and what and who is worthless, in community life. It always turns out that he knows neither, and this is why his conquests eventually defeat themselves.

In the biotic community, a parallel situation exists. Abraham knew exactly what the land was for: it was to drip milk and honey into Abraham's mouth. At the present moment, the assurance with which we regard this assumption is inverse to the degree of our education.

The ordinary citizen today assumes that science knows what makes the community clock tick; the scientist is equally sure that he does not. He knows that the biotic mechanism is so complex that its workings may never be fully understood.

That man is, in fact, only a member of a biotic team is shown by an ecological interpretation of history. Many historical events, hitherto explained solely in terms of human enterprise, were actually biotic interactions between people and land. The characteristics of the land determined the facts quite as potently as the characteristics of the men who lived on it.

Consider, for example, the settlement of the Mississippi valley. In the years following the Revolution, three groups were contending for its control: the native Indian, the French and English traders, and the American settlers. Historians wonder what would have happened if the English at Detroit had thrown a little more weight into the Indian side of those tipsy scales which decided the outcome of the colonial migration into the cane-lands of Kentucky. It is time now to ponder the fact that the cane-lands, when subjected to the particular mixture of forces represented by the cow, plow, fire, and axe of the pioneer, became bluegrass. What if the plant succession inherent in this dark and bloody ground had, under the impact of these forces, given us some worthless sedge shrub, or weed? Would Boone and Kenton have held out? Would there have been any overflow into Ohio, Indiana, Illinois, and Missouri? Any Louisiana Purchase? Any transcontinental union of new states? Any Civil War?

Kentucky was one sentence in the drama of history. We are commonly told what the human actors in this drama tried to do, but we are seldom told that their success, or the lack of it, hung in large degree on the reaction of particular soils to the impact of the particular forces exerted by their occupancy. In the case of Kentucky, we do not even know where the bluegrass came from—whether it is a native species, or a stowaway from Europe.

Contrast the cane-lands with what hindsight tells us about the Southwest, where the pioneers were equally brave, resourceful, and persevering. The impact of the occupancy here brought no bluegrass, or other plant fitted to withstand the bumps and buffetings of hard use. This region, when grazed by livestock, reverted through a series of more and more worthless grasses, shrubs, and weeds to a condition of unstable equilibrium. Each recession of plant types bred erosion; each increment to erosion bred a further recession of plants. The result today is a progressive and mutual deterioration, not only of plants and soils, but of the animal community subsisting thereon. The early settlers did not expect this: on the ciénegas of New Mexico some even cut ditches to hasten it. So subtle has been its progress that few residents of the region are aware of it. It is quite invisible to the tourist who finds this wrecked landscape colorful and charming (as indeed it is, but it bears scant resemblance to what it was in 1848).

This same landscape was "developed" once before, but with quite different results. The Pueblo Indians settled the Southwest in pre-Columbian times, but they happened *not* to be equipped with range livestock. Their civilization expired, but not because their land expired.

In India, regions devoid of any sod-forming grass have been settled, apparently without wrecking the land, by the simple expedient of carrying the grass to the cow, rather than vice versa. (Was this the result of some deep wisdom, or was it just good luck? I do not know.)

In short, the plant succession steered the course of history; the pioneer simply demonstrated, for good or ill, what successions inhered in the land. Is history taught in this spirit? It will be, once the concept of land as a community really penetrates our intellectual life.

The Ecological Conscience

Conservation is a state of harmony between men and land. Despite nearly a century of propaganda, conservation still proceeds at a snail's pace; progress still consists largely of letterhead pieties and convention oratory. On the back forty we still slip two steps backward for each forward stride.

The usual answer to this dilemma is "more conservation education." No one will debate this, but is it certain that only the *volume* of education needs stepping up? Is something lacking in the *content* as well?

It is difficult to give a fair summary of its content in brief form, but as I understand it, the content is substantially this: obey the law, vote right, join some organizations, and practice what conservation is profitable on your own land; the government will do the rest.

Is not this formula too easy to accomplish anything worthwhile? It defines no right or wrong, assigns no obligation, calls for no sacrifice, implies no change in the current philosophy of values. In respect of land-use, it urges only enlightened self-interest. Just how far will such education take us? An example will perhaps yield a partial answer.

By 1930 it had become clear to all except the ecologically blind that southwestern Wisconsin's topsoil was slipping seaward. In 1933 the farmers were told that if they would adopt certain remedial practices for five years, the public would donate CCC labor to install them, plus the necessary machinery and materials. The offer was widely accepted, but the practices were widely forgotten when the five-year contract period was up. The farmers continued only those practices that yielded an immediate and visible economic gain for themselves.

This led to the idea that maybe farmers would learn more quickly if they themselves wrote the rules. Accordingly the Wisconsin Legislature in 1937 passed the Soil Conservation District Law. This said to farmers, in effect: *We, the public, will furnish you free technical service and loan you specialized machinery, if you will write your own rules for land-use. Each county may write its own rules, and these will have the force of law.* Nearly all the counties promptly organized to accept the proffered help, but after a decade of operation, *no county has yet written a single rule.* There has been visible progress in such practices as strip-cropping, pasture renovation, and soil liming, but none in fencing woodlots against grazing, and none in excluding plow and cow from steep slopes. The farmers, in short, have selected those remedial practices which were profitable anyhow, and ignored those which were profitable to the community, but not clearly profitable to themselves.

When one asks why no rules have been written, one is told that the community is not yet ready to support them; education must precede rules. But the education actually in progress makes no mention of obligations to land over and above those dictated by self-interest. The net result is that we have more education but less soil, fewer healthy woods, and as many floods as in 1937.

The puzzling aspect of such situations is that the existence of obligations over and above self-interest is taken for granted in such rural community enterprise as the betterment of roads, schools, churches, and baseball teams. Their existence is not taken for granted, nor as yet seriously discussed, in bettering the behavior of the water that falls on the land, or in the preserving of the beauty or diversity of the farm landscape. Land-use ethics are still governed wholly by economic self-interest, just as social ethics were a century ago.

To sum up: we asked the farmer to do what he conveniently could to save his soil, and he has done just that, and only that. The farmer who clears the woods off a 75 percent slope, turns his cows into the clearing, and dumps its rainfall, rocks, and soil into the community creek, is still (if otherwise decent) a respected member of society. If he puts lime on his fields and plants his crops on contour, he is still entitled to all the privileges and emoluments of his Soil Conservation District. The District is a beautiful piece of social machinery, but it is coughing along on two cylinders because we have been too timid, and too anxious for quick success, to tell the farmer the true magnitude of his obligations. Obligations have no meaning without conscience, and the problem we face is the extension of the social conscience from people to land.

No important change in ethics was ever accomplished without an internal change in our intellectual emphasis, loyalties, affections, and convictions. The proof that conservation has not yet touched these foundations of conduct lies in the fact that philosophy and religion have not yet heard of it. In our attempt to make conservation easy, we have made it trivial.

Substitutes for a Land Ethic

When the logic of history hungers for bread and we hand out a stone, we are at pains to explain how much the stone resembles bread. I now describe some of the stones which serve in lieu of a land ethic.

One basic weakness in a conservation system based wholly on economic motives is that most members of the land community have no economic value. Wildflowers and songbirds are examples. Of the 22,000 higher plants and animals native to Wisconsin, it is doubtful whether more than 5 percent can be sold, fed, eaten, or otherwise put to economic use. Yet these creatures are members of the biotic community, and if (as I believe) its stability depends on its integrity, they are entitled to continuance.

When one of these non-economic categories is threatened, and if we happen to love it, we invent subterfuges to give it economic importance. At the beginning of the century songbirds were supposed to be disappearing. Ornithologists jumped to the rescue with some distinctly shaky evidence to the effect that insects would eat us up if birds failed to control them. The evidence had to be economic in order to be valid.

It is painful to read these circumlocutions today. We have no land ethic yet, but we have at least drawn nearer the point of admitting that birds should continue as a matter of biotic right, regardless of the presence or absence of economic advantage to us.

A parallel situation exists in respect of predatory mammals, raptorial birds, and fish-eating birds. Time was when biologists somewhat overworked the evidence that these creatures preserve the health of game by killing weaklings, or that they control rodents for the farmer, or that they prey only on "worthless" species. Here again, the evidence had to be economic in order to be valid. It is only in recent years that we hear the more honest argument that predators are members of the community, and that no special interest has the right to exterminate them for the sake of a benefit, real or fancied, to itself. Unfortunately this enlightened view is still in the talk stage. In the field the extermination of predators goes merrily on: witness the impending erasure of the timber wolf by fiat of Congress, the Conservation Bureaus, and many state legislatures.

Some species of trees have been "read out of the party" by economics-minded foresters because they grow too slowly, or have too low a sale value to pay as timber crops: white cedar, tamarack, cypress, beech, and hemlock are examples. In Europe, where forestry is ecologically more advanced, the non-commercial tree species are recognized as members of the native forest community, to be preserved as such, within reason. Moreover some (like beech) have been found to have a valuable function in building up soil fertility. The interdependence of the forest and its constituent tree species, ground flora, and fauna is taken for granted.

Lack of economic value is sometimes a character not only of species or groups, but of entire biotic communities: marshes, bogs, dunes, and "deserts" are examples. Our formula in such cases is to relegate their conservation to government as refuges, monuments, or parks. The difficulty is that these communities are usually interspersed with more valuable private lands; the government cannot possibly own or control such scattered parcels. The net effect is that we have relegated some of them to ultimate extinction over large areas. If the private owner were ecologically minded, he would be proud to be the custodian of a reasonable proportion of such areas, which add diversity and beauty to his farm and to his community.

In some instances, the assumed lack of profit in these "waste" areas has proved to be wrong, but only after most of them have been done away with. The present scramble to reflood muskrat marshes is a case in point.

There is a clear tendency in American conservation to relegate to government all necessary jobs that private landowners fail to perform. Government ownership, operation, subsidy, or regulation is now widely prevalent in forestry, range management, soil and watershed management, park and wilderness conservation, fisheries management, and migratory bird management, with more to come. Most of this growth in governmental conservation is proper and logical; some of it is inevitable. That I imply no disapproval of it is implicit in the fact that I have spent most of my life working for it. Nevertheless the question arises: What is the ultimate magnitude of the enterprise? Will the tax base carry its eventual ramifications? At what point will governmental conservation, like the mastodon, become handicapped by its own dimensions? The answer, if there is any, seems to be in a land ethic, or some other force which assigns more obligation to the private landowner.

Industrial landowners and users, especially lumbermen and stockmen, are inclined to wail long and loudly about the extension of government ownership and regulation to land, but (with notable exceptions) they show little disposition to develop the only visible alternative: the voluntary practice of conservation on their own lands.

When the private landowner is asked to perform some nonprofitable act for the good of the community, he today assents only with outstretched palm. If the act costs him cash this is fair and proper, but when it costs only forethought, open-mindedness, or time, the issue is at least debatable. The overwhelming growth of land-use subsidies in recent years must be ascribed, in large part, to the government's own agencies for conservation education: the land bureaus, the agricultural colleges, and the extension services. As far as I can detect, no ethical obligation toward land is taught in these institutions.

To sum up: a system of conservation based solely on economic self-interest is hopelessly lopsided. It tends to ignore, and thus eventually to eliminate, many elements in the land community that lack commercial value, but that are (as far as known) essential to its healthy functioning. It assumes, falsely, I think,

that the economic parts of the biotic clock will function without the uneconomic parts. It tends to relegate to government many functions eventually too large, too complex, or too widely dispersed to be performed by government.

An ethical obligation on the part of the private owner is the only visible remedy for these situations.

The Land Pyramid

An ethic to supplement and guide the economic relation to land presupposes the existence of some mental image of land as a biotic mechanism. We can be ethical only in relation to something we can see, feel, understand, love, or otherwise have faith in.

The image commonly employed in conservation education is "the balance of nature." For reasons too lengthy to detail here, this figure of speech fails to describe accurately what little we know about the land mechanism. A much truer image is the one employed in ecology: the biotic pyramid. I shall first sketch the pyramid as a symbol of land, and later develop some of its implications in terms of land-use.

Plants absorb energy from the sun. This energy flows through a circuit called the biota, which may be represented by a pyramid consisting of layers. The bottom layer is the soil. A plant layer rests on the soil, an insect layer on the plants, a bird and rodent layer on the insects, and so on up through various animal groups to the apex layer, which consists of the larger carnivores.

The species of a layer are alike not in where they came from, or in what they look like, but rather in what they eat. Each successive layer depends on those below it for food and often for other services, and each in turn furnishes food and services to those above. Proceeding upward, each successive layer decreases in numerical abundance. Thus, for every carnivore there are hundreds of his prey, thousands of their prey, millions of insects, uncountable plants. The pyramidal form of the system reflects this numerical progression from apex to base. Man shares an intermediate layer with the bears, raccoons, and squirrels which eat both meat and vegetables.

The lines of dependency for food and other services are called food chains. Thus soil-oak-deer-Indian is a chain that has now been largely converted to soil-corn-cow-farmer. Each species, including ourselves, is a link in many chains. The deer eats a hundred plants other than oak, and the cow a hundred plants other than corn. Both, then, are links in a hundred chains. The pyramid is a tangle of chains so complex as to seem disorderly, yet the stability of the system proves it to be a highly organized structure. Its functioning depends on the cooperation and competition of its diverse parts.

In the beginning, the pyramid of life was low and squat; the food chains short and simple. Evolution has added layer after layer, link after link. Man is one of thousands of accretions to the height and complexity of the pyramid. Science has given us many doubts, but it has given us at least one certainty: the trend of evolution is to elaborate and diversify the biota.

Land, then, is not merely soil; it is a fountain of energy flowing through a circuit of soils, plants, and animals. Food chains are the living channels which conduct energy upward; death and decay return it to the soil. The circuit is not closed; some energy is dissipated in decay, some is added by absorption from the air, some is stored in soils, peats, and long-lived forests; but it is a sustained circuit, like a slowly augmented revolving fund of life. There is always a net loss by downhill wash, but this is normally small and offset by the decay of rocks. It is deposited in the ocean and, in the course of geological time, raised to form new lands and new pyramids.

The velocity and character of the upward flow of energy depend on the complex structure of the plant and animal community, much as the upward flow of sap in a tree depends on its complex cellular organization. Without this complexity, normal circulation would presumably not occur. Structure means the characteristic numbers, as well as the characteristic kinds and functions, of the component species. This interdependence between the complex structure of the land and its smooth functioning as an energy unit is one of its basic attributes.

When a change occurs in one part of the circuit, many other parts must adjust themselves to it. Change does not necessarily obstruct or divert the flow of energy; evolution is a long series of self-induced changes, the net result of which has been to elaborate the flow mechanism and to lengthen the circuit. Evolutionary changes, however, are usually slow and local. Man's invention of tools has enabled him to make changes of unprecedented violence, rapidity, and scope.

One change is in the composition of floras and faunas. The larger predators are lopped off the apex of the pyramid; food chains, for the first time in history, become shorter rather than longer. Domesticated species from other lands are substituted for wild ones, and wild ones are moved to new habitats. In this worldwide pooling of faunas and floras, some species get out of bounds as pests and diseases, others are extinguished. Such effects are seldom intended or foreseen; they represent unpredicted and often untraceable readjustments in the structure. Agricultural science is largely a race between the emergence of new pests and the emergence of new techniques for their control.

Another change touches the flow of energy through plants and animals and its return to the soil. Fertility is the ability of soil to receive, store, and release energy. Agriculture, by overdrafts on the soil, or by too radical a substitution of domestic for native species in the superstructure, may derange the channels of flow or deplete storage. Soils depleted of their storage, or of the organic matter which anchors it, wash away faster than they form. This is erosion.

Waters, like soil, are part of the energy circuit. Industry, by polluting waters or obstructing them with dams, may exclude the plants and animals necessary to keep energy in circulation.

Transportation brings about another basic change: the plants or animals grown in one region are now consumed and returned to the soil in another. Transportation taps the energy stored in rocks, and in the air, and uses it elsewhere; thus we fertilize the garden with nitrogen gleaned by the guano birds from the fishes of seas on the other side of the Equator. Thus the formerly localized and self-contained circuits are pooled on a worldwide scale.

The process of altering the pyramid for human occupation releases stored energy, and this often gives rise, during the pioneering period, to a deceptive exuberance of plant and animal life, both wild and tame. These releases of biotic capital tend to becloud or postpone the penalties of violence.

This thumbnail sketch of land as an energy circuit conveys three basic ideas:

1. That land is not merely soil.
2. That the native plants and animals kept the energy circuit open; others may or may not.
3. That man-made changes are of a different order than evolutionary changes, and have effects more comprehensive than is intended or foreseen.

These ideas, collectively, raise two basic issues: Can the land adjust itself to the new order? Can the desired alterations be accomplished with less violence?

Biotas seem to differ in their capacity to sustain violent conversion. Western Europe, for example, carries a far different pyramid than Caesar found there. Some large animals are lost; swampy forests have become meadows or plowland; many new plants and animals are introduced, some of which escape as pests; the remaining natives are greatly changed in distribution and abundance. Yet the soil is still there and, with the help of imported nutrients, still fertile; the waters flow normally; the new structure seems to function and to persist. There is no visible stoppage or derangement of the circuit.

Western Europe, then, has a resistant biota. Its inner processes are tough, elastic, resistant to strain. No matter how violent the alterations, the pyramid, so far, has developed some new *modus vivendi* which preserves its habitability for man, and for most of the other natives.

Japan seems to present another instance of radical conversion without disorganization.

Most other civilized regions, and some as yet barely touched by civilization, display various stages of disorganization, varying from initial symptoms to advanced wastage. In Asia Minor and North Africa diagnosis is confused by climatic changes, which may have been either the cause or the effect of advanced wastage. In the United States the degree of disorganization varies locally; it is worst in the Southwest, the Ozarks, and parts of the South, and least in New England and the Northwest. Better land-uses may still arrest it in the less advanced regions. In parts of Mexico, South America, South Africa, and Australia a violent and accelerating wastage is in progress, but I cannot assess the prospects.

This almost world-wide display of disorganization in the land seems to be similar to disease in an animal, except that it never culminates in complete disorganization or death. The land recovers, but at some reduced level of complexity, and with a reduced carrying capacity for people, plants, and animals. Many biotas currently regarded as "lands of opportunity" are in fact already subsisting on exploitative agriculture, i.e., they have already exceeded their sustained carrying capacity. Most of South America is overpopulated in this sense.

In arid regions we attempt to offset the process of wastage by reclamation, but it is only too evident that the prospective longevity of reclamation projects is often short. In our own West, the best of them may not last a century.

The combined evidence of history and ecology seems to support one general deduction: the less violent the man-made changes, the greater the probability of successful readjustment in the pyramid. Violence, in turn, varies with human population density; a dense population requires a more violent conversion. In this respect, North America has a better chance for permanence than Europe, if she can contrive to limit her density.

This deduction runs counter to our current philosophy, which assumes that because a small increase in density enriched human life, that an indefinite increase will enrich it indefinitely. Ecology knows of no density relationship that holds for indefinitely wide limits. All gains from density are subject to a law of diminishing returns.

Whatever may be the equation for men and land, it is improbable that we as yet know all its terms. Recent discoveries in mineral and vitamin nutrition reveal unsuspected dependencies in the up-circuit: incredibly minute quantities of certain substances determine the value of soils to plants, of plants to animals. What of the down-circuit? What of the vanishing species, the preservation of which we now regard as an esthetic luxury? They helped build the soil; in what unsuspected ways may they be essential to its maintenance? Professor Weaver proposes that we use prairie flowers to reflocculate the wasting soils of the dust bowl; who knows for what purpose cranes and condors, otters and grizzlies may some day be used?

Land Health and the A-B Cleavage

A land ethic, then, reflects the existence of an ecological conscience, and this in turn reflects a conviction of individual responsibility for the health of the land. Health is the capacity of the land for self-renewal. Conservation is our effort to understand and preserve this capacity.

Conservationists are notorious for their dissensions. Superficially these seem to add up to mere confusion, but a more careful scrutiny reveals a single plane of cleavage common to many specialized fields. In each field one group (A) regards the land as soil and its function as commodity-production; another group (B) regards the land as a biota, and its function as something broader. How much broader is admittedly in a state of doubt and confusion.

In my own field, forestry, group A is quite content to grow trees like cabbages, with cellulose as the basic forest commodity. It feels no inhibition against violence; its ideology is agronomic. Group B, on the other hand, sees forestry as fundamentally different from agronomy because it employs natural species, and manages a natural environment rather than creating an artificial one. Group B prefers natural reproduction on principle. It worries on biotic as well as economic grounds about the loss of species like chestnut and the threatened loss of the white pines. It worries about a whole series of secondary forest functions: wildlife, recreation, watersheds, wilderness areas. To my mind, Group B feels the stirrings of an ecological conscience.

In the wildlife field, a parallel cleavage exists. For Group A the basic commodities are sport and meat; the yardsticks of production are ciphers of take in pheasants and trout. Artificial propagation is acceptable as a permanent as well as a temporary recourse—if its unit costs permit. Group B, on the other hand, worries about a whole series of biotic side-issues. What is the cost in predators of producing a game crop? Should we have further recourse to exotics? How can management restore the shrinking species, like prairie grouse, already hopeless as shootable game? How can management restore the threatened rarities, like trumpeter swan and whooping crane? Can management principles be extended to wildflowers? Here again it is clear to me that we have the same A-B cleavage as in forestry.

In the larger field of agriculture I am less competent to speak, but there seem to be somewhat parallel cleavages. Scientific agriculture was actively developing before ecology was born, hence a slower penetration of ecological concepts might be expected. Moreover the farmer, by the very nature of his techniques, must modify the biota more radically than the forester or the wildlife manager. Nevertheless, there are many discontents in agriculture which seem to add up to a new vision of "biotic farming."

Perhaps the most important of these is the new evidence that poundage or tonnage is no measure of the food-value of farm crops; the products of fertile soil may be qualitatively as well as quantitatively superior. We can bolster poundage from depleted soils by pouring on imported fertility, but we are not necessarily bolstering food-value. The possible ultimate ramifications of this idea are so immense that I must leave their exposition to abler pens.

The discontent that labels itself "organic farming," while bearing some of the earmarks of a cult, is nevertheless biotic in its direction, particularly in its insistence on the importance of soil flora and fauna.

The ecological fundamentals of agriculture are just as poorly known to the public as in other fields of land-use. For example, few educated people realize that the marvelous advances in technique made during recent decades are improvements in the pump, rather than the well. Acre for acre, they have barely sufficed to offset the sinking level of fertility.

In all of these cleavages, we see repeated the same basic paradoxes: man the conqueror *versus* man the biotic citizen; science the sharpener of his sword *versus* science the searchlight on his universe; land the slave and servant *versus* land the collective organism. Robinson's injunction to Tristram may well be applied, at this juncture, to *Homo sapiens* as a species in geological time:

> Whether you will or not
> You are a King, Tristram, for you are one
> Of the time-tested few that leave the world,
> When they are gone, not the same place it was.
> Mark what you leave.

The Outlook

It is inconceivable to me that an ethical relation to land can exist without love, respect, and admiration for land, and a high regard for its value. By value, I of course mean something far broader than mere economic value; I mean value in the philosophical sense.

Perhaps the most serious obstacle impeding the evolution of a land ethic is the fact that our educational and economic system is headed away from, rather than toward, an intense consciousness of land. Your true modern is separated from the land by many middlemen, and by innumerable physical gadgets. He has no vital relation to it; to him it is the space between cities on which crops grow. Turn him loose for a day on the land, and if the spot does not happen to be a golf links or a "scenic" area, he is bored stiff. If crops could be raised by hydroponics instead of farming, it would suit him very well. Synthetic substitutes for wood, leather, wool, and other natural land products suit him better than the originals. In short, land is something he has "outgrown."

Almost equally serious as an obstacle to a land ethic is the attitude of the farmer for whom the land is still an adversary, or a taskmaster that keeps him in slavery. Theoretically, the mechanization of farming ought to cut the farmer's chains, but whether it really does is debatable.

One of the requisites for an ecological comprehension of land is an understanding of ecology, and this is by no means co-extensive with "education"; in fact, much higher education seems deliberately to avoid eco-logical concepts. An understanding of ecology does not necessarily originate in courses bearing ecological labels; it is quite as likely to be labeled geography, botany, agronomy, history, or economics. This is as it should be, but whatever the label, ecological training is scarce.

The case for a land ethic would appear hopeless but for the minority which is in obvious revolt against these "modern" trends.

The "key-log" which must be moved to release the evolutionary process for an ethic is simply this: quit thinking about decent land-use as solely an economic problem. Examine each question in terms of what is ethically and esthetically right, as well as what is eco-nomically expedient. A thing is right when it tends to preserve the integrity, stability, and beauty of the biotic community. It is wrong when it tends otherwise.

It of course goes without saying that economic fea-sibility limits the tether of what can or cannot be done for land. It always has and it always will. The fallacy the economic determinists have tied around our collective neck, and which we now need to cast off, is the belief that economics determines *all* land-use. This is simply not true. An innumerable host of actions and attitudes, comprising perhaps the bulk of all land relations, is determined by the land-users' tastes and predilections, rather than by his purse. The bulk of all land relations hinges on investments of time, forethought, skill, and faith rather than on investments of cash. As a land-user thinketh, so is he.

I have purposely presented the land ethic as a prod-uct of social evolution because nothing so important as an ethic is ever "written." Only the most superficial stu-dent of history supposes that Moses "wrote" the Decalogue; it evolved in the minds of a thinking com-munity, and Moses wrote a tentative summary of it for a "seminar." I say tentative because evolution never stops.

The evolution of a land ethic is an intellectual as well as emotional process. Conservation is paved with good intentions which prove to be futile, or even dan-gerous, because they are devoid of critical understand-ing either of the land, or of economic land-use. I think it is a truism that as the ethical frontier advances from the individual to the community, its intellectual con-tent increases.

The mechanism of operation is the same for any ethic: social approbation for right actions: social disap-proval for wrong actions.

By and large, our present problem is one of attitudes and implements. We are remodeling the Alhambra with a steamshovel, and we are proud of our yardage. We shall hardly relinquish the shovel, which after all has many good points, but we are in need of gentler and more objective criteria for its successful use.

48. The Ethics of Respect for Nature

PAUL W. TAYLOR

Paul Taylor suggests that the notion of "respect for nature" plays a critical role in the emergence of environmental ethics. This grounding principle helps establish norms of conduct for the treatment of nature and justifies the moral requirement that all rational agents follow them. He further argues that relying upon a life-centered ethic instead of a human-centered ethic makes possible such a respect for nature and imposes on persons the duty to treat animals, plants, and ecosystems with moral seriousness.

Human-Centered and Life-Centered Systems of Environmental Ethics

In this paper I show how the taking of a certain ultimate moral attitude toward nature, which I call "respect for nature," has a central place in the foundations of a life-centered system of environmental ethics. I hold that a set of moral norms (both standards of character and rules of conduct) governing human treatment of the natural world is a rationally grounded set if and only if, first, commitment to those norms is a practical entailment of adopting the attitude of respect for nature as an ultimate moral attitude, and second, the adopting of that attitude on the part of all rational agents can itself be justified. When the basic characteristics of the attitude of respect for nature are made clear, it will be seen that a life-centered system of environmental ethics need not be holistic or organicist in its conception of the kinds of entities that are deemed the appropriate objects of moral concern and consideration. Nor does such a system require that the concepts of ecological homeostasis, equilibrium, and integrity provide us with normative principles from which could be derived (with the addition of factual knowledge) our obligations with regard to natural ecosystems. The "balance of nature" is not itself a moral norm, however important may be the role it plays in our general outlook on the natural world that underlies the attitude of respect for nature. I argue that finally it is the good (well-being, welfare) of individual

From *Environmental Ethics*, 3 (1981): 197–218. Reprinted with permission from the publisher and the author. Notes renumbered.

organisms, considered as entities having inherent worth, that determines our moral relations with the Earth's wild communities of life.

In designating the theory to be set forth as life-centered, I intend to contrast it with all anthropocentric views. According to the latter, human actions affecting the natural environment and its nonhuman inhabitants are right (or wrong) by either of two criteria: they have consequences which are favorable (or unfavorable) to human well-being, or they are consistent (or inconsistent) with the system of norms that protect and implement human rights. From this human-centered standpoint it is to humans and only to humans that all duties are ultimately owed. We may have responsibilities *with regard to* the natural ecosystems and biotic communities of our planet, but these responsibilities are in every case based on the contingent fact that our treatment of those ecosystems and communities of life can further the realization of human values and/or human rights. We have no obligation to promote or protect the good of nonhuman living things, independently of this contingent fact.

A life-centered system of environmental ethics is opposed to human-centered ones precisely on this point. From the perspective of a life-centered theory, we have prima facie moral obligations that are owed to wild plants and animals themselves as members of the Earth's biotic community. We are morally bound (other things being equal) to protect or promote their good for *their* sake. Our duties to respect the integrity of natural ecosystems, to preserve endangered species, and to avoid environmental pollution stem from the fact that these are ways in which we can help make it possible for wild species populations to achieve and maintain a healthy existence in a natural state. Such obligations are due those living things out of recognition of their inherent worth. They are entirely additional to and independent of the obligations we owe to our fellow humans. Although many of the actions that fulfill one set of obligations will also fulfill the other, two different grounds of obligation are involved. Their well-being, as well as human well-being, is something to be realized *as an end in itself*.

If we were to accept a life-centered theory of environmental ethics, a profound reordering of our moral universe would take place. We would begin to look at the whole of the Earth's biosphere in a new light. Our duties with respect to the "world" of nature would be seen as making prima facie claims upon us to be balanced against our duties with respect to the "world" of human civilization. We could no longer simply take the human point of view and consider the effects of our actions exclusively from the perspective of our own good.

The Good of a Being and the Concept of Inherent Worth

What would justify acceptance of a life-centered system of ethical principles? In order to answer this it is first necessary to make clear the fundamental moral attitude that underlies and makes intelligible the commitment to live by such a system. It is then necessary to examine the considerations that would justify any rational agent's adopting that moral attitude.

Two concepts are essential to the taking of a moral attitude of the sort in question. A being which does not "have" these concepts, that is, which is unable to grasp their meaning and conditions of applicability, cannot be said to have the attitude as part of its moral outlook. These concepts are, first, that of the good (well-being, welfare) of a living thing, and second, the idea of an entity possessing inherent worth. I examine each concept in turn.

(1) Every organism, species population, and community of life has a good of its own which moral agents can intentionally further or damage by their actions. To say that an entity has a good of its own is simply to say that, without reference to any *other* entity, it can be benefited or harmed. One can act in its overall interest or contrary to its overall interest, and environmental conditions can be good for it (advantageous to it) or bad for it (disadvantageous to it). What is good for an entity is what "does it good" in the sense of enhancing or preserving its life and well-being.

What is bad for an entity is something that is detrimental to its life and well-being.[1]

We can think of the good of an individual nonhuman organism as consisting in the full development of its biological powers. Its good is realized to the extent that it is strong and healthy. It possesses whatever capacities it needs for successfully coping with its environment and so preserving its existence throughout the various stages of the normal life cycle of its species. The good of a population or community of such individuals consists in the population or community maintaining itself from generation to generation as a coherent system of genetically and ecologically related organisms whose average good is at an optimum level for the given environment. (Here *average good* means that the degree of realization of the good of *individual organisms* in the population or community is, on average, greater than would be the case under any other ecologically functioning order of interrelations among those species populations in the given ecosystem.)

The idea of a being having a good of its own, as I understand it, does not entail that the being must have interests or take an interest in what affects its life for better or for worse. We can act in a being's interest or contrary to its interest without its being interested in what we are doing to it in the sense of wanting or not wanting us to do it. It may, indeed, be wholly unaware that favorable and unfavorable events are taking place in its life. I take it that trees, for example, have no knowledge or desires or feelings. Yet is undoubtedly the case that trees can be harmed or benefited by our actions. We can crush their roots by running a bulldozer too close to them. We can see to it that they get adequate nourishment and moisture by fertilizing and watering the soil around them. Thus we can help or hinder them in the realization of their good. It is the good of trees themselves that is thereby affected. We can similarly act so as to further the good of an entire tree population of a certain species (say, all the redwood trees in a California valley) or the good of a whole community of plant life in a given wilderness area, just as we can do harm to such a population or community.

When construed in this way, the concept of a being's good is not coextensive with sentience or the capacity for feeling pain. William Frankena has argued for a general theory of environmental ethics in which the ground of a creature's being worthy of moral consideration is its sentience. I have offered some criticisms of this view elsewhere, but the full refutation of such a position, it seems to me, finally depends on the positive reasons for accepting a life-centered theory of the kind I am defending in this essay.[2]

It should be noted further that I am leaving open the question of whether machines—in particular, those which are not only goal-directed, but also self-regulating—can properly be said to have a good of their own.[3] Since I am concerned only with human treatment of wild organisms, species populations, and communities of life as they occur in our planet's natural ecosystems, it is to those entities alone that the concept "having a good of its own" will here be applied. I am not denying that other living things, whose genetic origin and environmental conditions have been produced, controlled, and manipulated by humans for human ends, do have a good of their own in the same sense as do wild plants and animals. It is not my purpose in this essay, however, to set out or defend the principles that should guide our conduct with regard to their good. It is only insofar as their production and use by humans have good or ill effects upon natural ecosystems and their wild inhabitants that the ethics of respect for nature comes into play.

(2) The second concept essential to the moral attitude of respect for nature is the idea of inherent worth. We take that attitude toward wild living things (individuals, species populations, or whole biotic communities) when and only when we regard them as entities possessing inherent worth. Indeed, it is only because they are conceived in this way that moral agents can think of themselves as having validly binding duties, obligations, and responsibilities that are *owed* to them as their *due*. I am not at this juncture arguing why they *should* be so regarded; I consider it at length below. But so regarding them is a presupposition of our taking the attitude of respect toward them and accordingly understanding ourselves as bearing certain moral relations to them. This can be shown as follows:

What does it mean to regard an entity that has a good of its own as possessing inherent worth? Two general principles are involved: the principle of moral consideration and the principle of intrinsic value.

According to the principle of moral consideration, wild living things are deserving of the concern and consideration of all moral agents simply in virtue of their being members of the Earth's community of life. From the moral point of view their good must be taken into account whenever it is affected for better or worse by the conduct of rational agents. This holds no matter what species the creature belongs to. The good of each is to be accorded some value and so acknowledged as having some weight in the deliberations of all rational

agents. Of course, it may be necessary for such agents to act in ways contrary to the good of this or that particular organism or group of organisms in order to further the good of others, including the good of humans. But the principle of moral consideration prescribes that, with respect to each being an entity having its own good, every individual is deserving of consideration.

The principle of intrinsic value states that, regardless of what kind of entity it is in other respects, if it is a member of the Earth's community of life, the realization of its good is something *intrinsically* valuable. This means that its good is prima facie worthy of being preserved or promoted as an end in itself and for the sake of the entity whose good it is. Insofar as we regard any organism, species population, or life community as an entity having inherent worth, we believe that it must never be treated as if it were a mere object or thing whose entire value lies in being instrumental to the good of some other entity. The well-being of each is judged to have value in and of itself.

Combining these two principles, we can now define what it means for a living thing or group of living things to possess inherent worth. To say that it possesses inherent worth is to say that its good is deserving of the concern and consideration of all moral agents, and that the realization of its good has intrinsic value, to be pursued as an end in itself and for the sake of the entity whose good it is.

The duties owed to wild organisms, species populations, and communities of life in the Earth's natural ecosystems are grounded on their inherent worth. When rational, autonomous agents regard such entities as possessing inherent worth, they place intrinsic value on the realization of their good and so hold themselves responsible for performing actions that will have this effect and for refraining from actions having the contrary effect.

The Attitude of Respect for Nature

Why should moral agents regard wild living things in the natural world as possessing inherent worth? To answer this question we must first take into account the fact that, when rational, autonomous agents subscribe to the principles of moral consideration and intrinsic value and so conceive of wild living things as having that kind of worth, such agents are *adopting a certain ultimate moral attitude toward the natural world.* This is the attitude I call "respect for nature." It parallels the attitude of respect for persons in human ethics.

When we adopt the attitude of respect for persons as the proper (fitting, appropriate) attitude to take toward all persons as persons, we consider the fulfillment of the basic interests of each individual to have intrinsic value. We thereby make a moral commitment to live a certain kind of life in relation to other persons. We place ourselves under the direction of a system of standards and rules that we consider validly binding on all moral agents as such.[4]

Similarly, when we adopt the attitude of respect for nature as an ultimate moral attitude we make a commitment to live by certain normative principles. These principles constitute the rules of conduct and standards of character that are to govern our treatment of the natural world. This is, first, an *ultimate* commitment because it is not derived from any higher norm. The attitude of respect for nature is not grounded on some other, more general, or more fundamental attitude. It sets the total framework for our responsibilities toward the natural world. It can be justified, as I show below, but its justification cannot consist in referring to a more general attitude or a more basic normative principle.

Second, the commitment is a *moral* one because it is understood to be a disinterested matter of principle. It is this feature that distinguishes the attitude of respect for nature from the set of feelings and dispositions that comprise the love of nature. The latter stems from one's personal interest in and response to the natural world. Like the affectionate feelings we have toward certain individual human beings, one's love of nature is nothing more than the particular way one feels about the natural environment and its wild inhabitants. And just as our love for an individual person differs from our respect for all persons as such (whether we happen to love them or not), so love of nature differs from respect for nature. Respect for nature is an attitude we believe all moral agents ought to have simply as moral agents, regardless of whether or not they also love nature. Indeed, we have not truly taken the attitude of respect for nature ourselves unless we believe this. To put it in a Kantian way, to adopt the attitude of respect for nature is to take a stance that one wills it to be a universal law for all rational beings. It is to hold that stance categorically, as being validly applicable to every moral agent without exception, irrespective of whatever personal feelings toward nature such an agent might have or might lack.

Although the attitude of respect for nature is in this sense a disinterested and universalizable attitude, anyone who does adopt it has certain steady, more or less permanent dispositions. These dispositions, which are themselves to be considered disinterested and universalizable, comprise three interlocking sets: dispositions to seek certain ends, dispositions to carry on one's practical reasoning and deliberation in a certain way, and dispositions to have certain feelings. We may accordingly analyze the attitude of respect for nature into the following components. (a) The disposition to aim at, and to take steps to bring about, as final and disinterested ends, the promoting and protecting of the good of organisms, species populations, and life communities in natural ecosystems. (These ends are "final" in not being pursued as means to further ends. They are "disinterested" in being independent of the self-interest of the agent.) (b) The disposition to consider actions that tend to realize those ends to be prima facie obligatory *because* they have that tendency. (c) The disposition to experience positive and negative feelings toward states of affairs in the world *because* they are favorable or unfavorable to the good of organisms, species populations, and life communities in natural ecosystems.

The logical connection between the attitude of respect for nature and the duties of a life-centered system of environmental ethics can now be made clear. Insofar as one sincerely takes that attitude and so has the three sets of dispositions, one will at the same time be disposed to comply with certain rules of duty (such as nonmaleficence and noninterference) and with standards of character (such as fairness and benevolence) that determine the obligations and virtues of moral agents with regard to the Earth's wild living things. We can say that the actions one performs and the character traits one develops in fulfilling these moral requirements are the way one *expresses* or *embodies* the attitude in one's conduct and character. In his famous essay, "Justice as Fairness," John Rawls describes the rules of the duties of human morality (such as fidelity, gratitude, honesty, and justice) as "forms of conduct in which recognition of others as persons is manifested."[5] I hold that the rules of duty governing our treatment of the natural world and its inhabitants are forms of conduct in which the attitude of respect for nature is manifested.

The Justifiability of the Attitude of Respect for Nature

I return to the question posed earlier, which has not yet been answered: why *should* moral agents regard wild living things as possessing inherent worth? I now argue that the only way we can answer this question is by showing how adopting the attitude of respect for nature is justified for all moral agents. Let us suppose that we were able to establish that there are good reasons for adopting the attitude, reasons which are intersubjectively valid for every rational agent. If there are such reasons, they would justify anyone's having the three sets of dispositions mentioned above as constituting what it means to have the attitude. Since these include the disposition to promote or protect the good of wild living things as a disinterested and ultimate end, as well as the disposition to perform actions for the reason that they tend to realize that end, we see that such dispositions commit a person to the principles of moral consideration and intrinsic value. To be disposed to further, as an end in itself, the good of any entity in nature just because it is that kind of entity, is to be disposed to give consideration to *every* such entity and to place intrinsic value on the realization of its good. Insofar as we subscribe to these two principles we regard living things as possessing inherent worth. Subscribing to the principles is what it *means* to so regard them. To justify the attitude of respect for nature, then, is to justify commitment to these principles and thereby to justify regarding wild creatures as possessing inherent worth.

We must keep in mind that inherent worth is not some mysterious sort of objective property belonging to living things that can be discovered by empirical observation or scientific investigation. To ascribe inherent worth to an entity is not to describe it by citing some feature discernible by sense perception or inferable by inductive reasoning. Nor is there a logically necessary connection between the concept of a being having a good of its own and the concept of inherent worth. We do not contradict ourselves by asserting that an entity that has a good of its own lacks inherent worth. In order to show that such an entity "has" inherent worth we must give good reasons for ascribing that kind of value to it (placing that kind of value upon it, conceiving of it to be valuable in that way). Although it is humans (persons, valuers) who must do the valuing, for the ethics of respect for nature, the value so ascribed is not a human value. That is to say, it is not a value derived from considerations regarding human well-being or human rights. It is a value that is ascribed to nonhuman animals and plants themselves, independently of their relationship to what humans judge to be conducive to their own good.

Whatever reasons, then, justify our taking the attitude of respect for nature as defined above are also reasons that show why we *should* regard the living things of the natural world as possessing inherent worth. We saw earlier that, since the attitude is an ultimate one, it cannot be derived from a more fundamental attitude nor shown to be a special case of a more general one. On what sort of grounds, then, can it be established?

The attitude we take toward living things in the natural world depends on the way we look at them, on what kind of beings we conceive them to be, and on how we understand the relations we bear to them. Underlying and supporting our attitude is a certain *belief system* that constitutes a particular world view or outlook on nature and the place of human life in it. To give good reasons for adopting the attitude of respect for nature, then, we must first articulate the belief system which underlies and supports that attitude. If it appears that the belief system is internally coherent and well-ordered, and if, as far as we can now tell, it is consistent with all known scientific truths relevant to our knowledge of the object of the attitude (which in this case includes the whole set of the Earth's natural ecosystems and their communities of life), then there remains the task of indicating why scientifically informed and rational thinkers with a developed capacity of reality awareness can find it acceptable as a way of conceiving of the natural world and our place in it. To the extent we can do this we provide at least a reasonable argument for accepting the belief system and the ultimate moral attitude it supports.

I do not hold that such a belief system can be *proven* to be true, either inductively or deductively. As we shall see, not all of its components can be stated in the form of empirically verifiable propositions. Nor is its internal order governed by purely logical relationships. But the system as a whole, I contend, constitutes a coherent, unified, and rationally acceptable "picture" or "map" of a total world. By examining each of its main components and seeing how they fit together, we obtain a scientifically informed and well-ordered conception of nature and the place of humans in it.

This belief system underlying the attitude of respect for nature I call (for want of a better name) "the biocentric outlook on nature." Since it is not wholly analyzable into empirically confirmable assertions, it should not be thought of as simply a compendium of the biological sciences concerning our planet's ecosystems. It might best be described as a philosophical world view, to distinguish it from a scientific theory or explanatory system. However, one of its major tenets is the great lesson we have learned from the science of ecology: the interdependence of all living things in an organically unified order whose balance and stability are necessary conditions for the realization of the good of its constituent biotic communities.

Before turning to an account of the main components of the biocentric outlook, it is convenient here to set forth the overall structure of my theory of environmental ethics as it has now emerged. The ethics of respect for nature is made up of three basic elements: a belief system, an ultimate moral attitude, and a set of rules of duty and standards of character. These elements are connected with each other in the following manner. The belief system provides a certain outlook on nature which supports and makes intelligible an autonomous agent's adopting, as an ultimate moral attitude, the attitude of respect for nature. It supports and makes intelligible the attitude in the sense that, when an autonomous agent understands its moral relations to the natural world in terms of this outlook, it recognizes the attitude of respect to be the only *suitable* or *fitting* attitude to take toward all wild forms of life in the Earth's biosphere. Living things are now viewed as *the appropriate objects of the attitude of respect* and are accordingly regarded as entities possessing inherent worth. One then places intrinsic value on the promotion and protection of their good. As a consequence of this, one makes a moral commitment to abide by a set of rules of duty and to fulfill (as far as one can by one's own efforts) certain standards of good character. Given one's adoption of the attitude of respect, one makes that moral commitment because one considers those rules and standards to be validly binding on all moral agents. They are seen as embodying forms of conduct and character structures in which the attitude of respect for nature is manifested.

This three-part complex which internally orders the ethics of respect for nature is symmetrical with a theory of human ethics grounded on respect for persons. Such a theory includes, first, a conception of oneself and others as persons, that is, as centers of autonomous choice. Second, there is the attitude of respect for persons as persons. When this is adopted as an ultimate moral attitude it involves the disposition to treat every person as having inherent worth or "human dignity." Every human being, just in virtue of her or his humanity, is understood to be worthy of moral consideration, and intrinsic value is placed on the autonomy and well-being of each. This is what Kant meant by conceiving of persons as ends in themselves. Third, there is an ethical system of duties which are acknowledged to be owed by everyone to everyone. These duties are forms of conduct in which public recognition is given to each individual's inherent worth as a person.

This structural framework for a theory of human ethics is meant to leave open the issue of consequentialism (utilitarianism) versus nonconsequentialism (deontology). That issue concerns the particular kind of system of rules defining the duties of moral agents toward persons. Similarly, I am leaving open in this paper the question of what particular kind of system of rules defines our duties with respect to the natural world.

The Biocentric Outlook on Nature

The biocentric outlook on nature has four main components. (1) Humans are thought of as members of the Earth's community of life, holding that membership on the same terms as apply to all the nonhuman members. (2) The Earth's natural ecosystems as a totality are seen as a complex web of interconnected elements, with the sound biological functioning of each being dependent on the sound biological functioning of the others. (This is the component referred to above as the great lesson that the science of ecology has taught us.) (3) Each individual organism is conceived of as a teleological center of life, pursuing its own good in its own way. (4) Whether we are concerned with standards of merit or with the concept of inherent worth, the claim that humans by their very nature are superior to other species is a groundless claim and, in the light of elements (1), (2), and (3) above, must be rejected as nothing more than an irrational bias in our own favor. . . .

The Denial of Human Superiority

This fourth component of the biocentric outlook on nature is the single most important idea in establishing the justifiability of the attitude of respect for nature. Its central role is due to the special relationship it bears to the first three components of the outlook. This relationship will be brought out after the concept of human superiority is examined and analyzed.[6]

In what sense are humans alleged to be superior to other animals? We are different from them in having certain capacities that they lack. But why should these capacities be a mark of superiority? From what point of view are they judged to be signs of superiority and what sense of superiority is meant? After all, various nonhuman species have capacities that humans lack. There is the speed of a cheetah, the vision of an eagle, the agility of a monkey. Why should not these be taken as signs of *their* superiority over humans?

One answer that comes immediately to mind is that these capacities are not as *valuable* as the human capacities that are claimed to make us superior. Such uniquely human characteristics as rational thought, aesthetic creativity, autonomy and self-determination, and moral freedom, it might be held, have a higher value than the capacities found in other species. Yet we must ask: valuable to whom, and on what grounds?

The human characteristics mentioned are all valuable to humans. They are essential to the preservation and enrichment of our civilization and culture. Clearly it is from the human standpoint that they are being judged to be desirable and good. It is not difficult here to recognize a begging of the question. Humans are claiming human superiority from a strictly human point of view, that is, from a point of view in which the good of humans is taken as the standard of judgment. All we need to do is to look at the capacities of nonhuman animals (or plants, for that matter) from the standpoint of *their* good to find a contrary judgment of superiority. The speed of the cheetah, for example, is a sign of its superiority to humans when considered from the standpoint of the good of its species. If it were as slow a runner as a human, it would not be able to survive. And so for all the other abilities of nonhumans which further their good but which are lacking in humans. In each case the claim to human superiority would be rejected from a nonhuman standpoint.

When superiority assertions are interpreted in this way, they are based on judgments of *merit*. To judge the merits of a person or an organism one must apply grading or ranking standards to it. (As I show below, this distinguishes judgments of merit from judgments of inherent worth.) Empirical investigation then determines whether it has the "good-making properties" (merits) in virtue of which it fulfills the standards being applied. In the case of humans, merits may be either moral or nonmoral. We can judge one person to be better than (superior to) another from the moral point of view by applying certain standards to their character and conduct. Similarly, we can appeal to nonmoral criteria in judging someone to be an excellent piano player, a fair cook, a poor tennis player, and so on. Different social purposes and roles are implicit in the making of such judgments, providing the frame of reference for the choice of standards by which the nonmoral merits of people are determined. Ultimately such purposes and roles stem from a society's way of

life as a whole. Now a society's way of life may be thought of as the cultural form given to the realization of human values. Whether moral or nonmoral standards are being applied, then, all judgments of people's merits finally depend on human values. All are made from an exclusively human standpoint.

The question that naturally arises at this juncture is: why should standards that are based on human values be assumed to be the only valid criteria of merit and hence the only true signs of superiority? This question is especially pressing when humans are being judged superior in merit to nonhumans. It is true that a human being may be a better mathematician than a monkey, but the monkey may be a better tree climber than a human being. If we humans value mathematics more than tree climbing, that is because our conception of civilized life makes the development of mathematical ability more desirable than the ability to climb trees. But is it not unreasonable to judge nonhumans by the values of human civilization, rather than by values connected with what it is for a member of *that* species to live a good life? If all living things have a good of their own, it at least makes sense to judge the merits of nonhumans by standards derived from *their* good. To use only standards based on human values is already to commit oneself to holding that humans are superior to nonhumans, which is the point in question.

A further logical flaw arises in connection with the widely held conviction that humans are *morally* superior beings because they possess, while others lack, the capacities of a moral agent (free will, accountability, deliberation, judgment, practical reason). This view rests on a conceptual confusion. As far as moral standards are concerned, only beings that have the capacities of a moral agent can properly be judged to be *either* moral (morally good) *or* immoral (morally deficient). Moral standards are simply not applicable to beings that lack such capacities. Animals and plants cannot therefore be said to be morally inferior in merit to humans. Since the only beings that can have moral merits *or be deficient in such merits* are moral agents, it is conceptually incoherent to judge humans as superior to nonhumans on the ground that humans have moral capacities while nonhumans don't.

Up to this point I have been interpreting the claim that humans are superior to other living things as a grading or ranking judgment regarding their comparative merits. There is, however, another way of understanding the idea of human superiority. According to this interpretation, humans are superior to nonhumans not as regards their merits but as regards their inherent worth. Thus the claim of human superiority is to be understood as asserting that all humans, simply in virtue of their humanity, have *a greater inherent worth* than other living things.

The inherent worth of an entity does not depend on its merits.[7] To consider something as possessing inherent worth, we have seen, is to place intrinsic value on the realization of its good. This is done regardless of whatever particular merits it might have or might lack, as judged by a set of grading or ranking standards. In human affairs, we are all familiar with the principle that one's worth as a person does not vary with one's merits or lack of merits. The same can hold true of animals and plants. To regard such entities as possessing inherent worth entails disregarding their merits and deficiencies, whether they are being judged from a human standpoint or from the standpoint of their own species.

The idea of one entity having more merit than another, and so being superior to it in merit, makes perfectly good sense. Merit is a grading or ranking concept, and judgments of comparative merit are based on the different degrees to which things satisfy a given standard. But what can it mean to talk about one thing being superior to another in inherent worth? In order to get at what is being asserted in such a claim it is helpful first to look at the social origin of the concept of degrees of inherent worth.

The idea that humans can possess different degrees of inherent worth originated in societies having rigid class structures. Before the rise of modern democracies with their egalitarian outlook, one's membership in a hereditary class determined one's social status. People in the upper classes were looked up to, while those in the lower classes were looked down upon. In such a society one's social superiors and social inferiors were clearly defined and easily recognized.

Two aspects of these class-structured societies are especially relevant to the idea of degrees of inherent worth. First, those born into the upper classes were deemed more worthy of respect than those born into the lower orders. Second, the superior worth of upper class people had nothing to do with their merits nor did the inferior worth of those in the lower classes rest on their lack of merits. One's superiority or inferiority entirely derived from a social position one was born into. The modern concept of a meritocracy simply did not apply. One could not advance into a higher class by any sort of moral or nonmoral achievement. Similarly, an aristocrat held his title and all the privileges that went with it just because he was the eldest son of a titled nobleman. Unlike the bestowing of knighthood in contemporary Great Britain, one did not earn membership in the nobility by meritorious conduct.

We who live in modern democracies no longer believe in such hereditary social distinctions. Indeed, we would wholeheartedly condemn them on moral grounds as being fundamentally unjust. We have come to think of class systems as a paradigm of social injustice, it being a central principle of the democratic way of life that among humans there are no superiors and no inferiors. Thus we have rejected the whole conceptual framework in which people are judged to have different degrees of inherent worth. That idea is incompatible with our notion of human equality based on the doctrine that all humans, simply in virtue of their humanity, have the same inherent worth. (The belief in universal human rights is one form that this egalitarianism takes.)

The vast majority of people in modern democracies, however, do not maintain an egalitarian outlook when it comes to comparing human beings with other living things. Most people consider our own species to be superior to all other species and this superiority is understood to be a matter of inherent worth, not merit. There may exist thoroughly vicious and depraved humans who lack all merit. Yet because they are human they are thought to belong to a higher class of entities than any plant or animal. That one is born into the species *Homo sapiens* entitles one to have lordship over those who are one's inferiors, namely, those born into other species. The parallel with hereditary social classes is very close. Implicit in this view is a hierarchical conception of nature according to which an organism has a position of superiority or inferiority in the Earth's community of life simply on the basis of its genetic background. The "lower" orders of life are looked down upon and it is considered perfectly proper that they serve the interests of those belonging to the highest order, namely humans. The intrinsic value we place on the well-being of our fellow humans reflects our recognition of their rightful position as our equals. No such intrinsic value is to be placed on the good of other animals, unless we choose to do so out of fondness or affection for them. But their well-being imposes no moral requirement on us. In this respect there is an absolute difference in moral status between ourselves and them.

This is the structure of concepts and beliefs that people are committed to insofar as they regard humans to be superior in inherent worth to all other species. I now wish to argue that this structure of concepts and beliefs is completely groundless. If we accept the first three components of the biocentric outlook and from that perspective look at the major philosophical traditions which have supported that structure, we find it to be at bottom nothing more than the expression of an irrational bias in our own favor. The philosophical traditions themselves rest on very questionable assumptions or else simply beg the question. I briefly consider three of the main traditions to substantiate the point. These are classical Greek humanism, Cartesian dualism, and the Judeo-Christian concept of the Great Chain of Being.

The inherent superiority of humans over other species was implicit in the Greek definition of man as a rational animal. Our animal nature was identified with "brute" desires that need the order and restraint of reason to rule them (just as reason is the special virtue of those who rule in the ideal state). Rationality was then seen to be the key to our superiority over animals. It enables us to live on a higher plane and endows us with a nobility and worth that other creatures lack. This familiar way of comparing humans with other species is deeply ingrained in our Western philosophical outlook. The point to consider here is that this view does not actually provide an argument *for* human superiority but rather makes explicit the framework of thought that is implicitly used by those who think of humans as inherently superior to nonhumans. The Greeks who held that humans, in virtue of their rational capacities, have a kind of worth greater than that of any nonrational being, never looked at rationality as but one capacity of living things among many others. But when we consider rationality from the standpoint of the first three elements of the ecological outlook, we see that its value lies in its importance for *human* life. Other creatures achieve their species-specific good without the need of rationality, although they often make use of capacities that humans lack. So the humanistic outlook of classical Greek thought does not give us a neutral (nonquestion-begging) ground on which to construct a scale of degrees of inherent worth possessed by different species of living things.

The second tradition, centering on the Cartesian dualism of soul and body, also fails to justify the claim to human superiority. That superiority is supposed to derive from the fact that we have souls while animals do not. Animals are mere automata and lack the divine element that makes us spiritual beings. I won't go into the now familiar criticisms of this two-substance view. I only add the point that, even if humans are composed of an immaterial, unextended soul and a material, extended body, this in itself is not a reason to deem them of greater worth than entities that are only bodies. Why is a soul substance a thing that adds value to its possessor? Unless some theological reasoning is offered here (which many, including myself, would find unacceptable on epistemological grounds), no logical connection is evident. An immaterial something which thinks is better than a material something which does not think only if thinking itself has value, either intrinsically or instrumentally. Now it is intrinsically valuable to humans alone, who value it as an end in itself, and it is instrumentally valuable to those who benefit from it, namely humans.

For animals that neither enjoy thinking for its own sake nor need it for living the kind of life for which they are best adapted, it has no value. Even if "thinking" is broadened to include all forms of consciousness, there are still many living things that can do without it and yet live what is for their species a good life. The anthropocentricity underlying the claim to human superiority runs throughout Cartesian dualism.

A third major source of the idea of human superiority is the Judeo-Christian concept of the Great Chain of Being. Humans are superior to animals and plants because their Creator has given them a higher place on the chain. It begins with God at the top, and then moves to the angels, who are lower than God but higher than humans, then to humans, positioned between the angels and the beasts (partaking of the nature of both), and then on down to the lower levels occupied by nonhuman animals, plants, and finally inanimate objects. Humans, being "made in God's image," are inherently superior to animals and plants by virtue of their being closer (in their essential nature) to God.

The metaphysical and epistemological difficulties with this conception of a hierarchy of entities are, in my mind, insuperable. Without entering into this matter here, I only point out that if we are unwilling to accept the metaphysics of traditional Judaism and Christianity, we are again left without good reasons for holding to the claim of inherent human superiority.

The foregoing considerations (and others like them) leave us with but one ground for the assertion that a human being, regardless of merit, is a higher kind of entity than any other living thing. This is the mere fact of the genetic makeup of the species *Homo sapiens.* But this is surely irrational and arbitrary. Why should the arrangement of genes of a certain type be a mark of superior value, especially when this fact about an organism is taken by itself, unrelated to any other aspect of its life? We might just as well refer to any other genetic makeup as a ground of superior value. Clearly we are confronted here with a wholly arbitrary claim that can only be explained as an irrational bias in our own favor.

That the claim is nothing more than a deep-seated prejudice is brought home to us when we look at our relation to other species in the light of the first three elements of the biocentric outlook. Those elements taken conjointly give us a certain overall view of the natural world and of the place of humans in it. When we take this view we come to understand other living things, their environmental conditions, and their ecological relationships in such a way as to awake in us a deep sense of our kinship with them as fellow members of the Earth's community of life. Humans and nonhumans alike are viewed together as integral parts of one unified whole in which all living things are functionally interrelated. Finally, when our awareness focuses on the individual lives of plants and animals, each is seen to share with us the characteristic of being a teleological center of life striving to realize its own good in its own unique way.

As this entire belief system becomes part of the conceptual framework through which we understand and perceive the world, we come to see ourselves as bearing a certain moral relation to nonhuman forms of life. Our ethical role in nature takes on a new significance. We begin to look at other species as we look at ourselves, seeing them as beings which have a good they are striving to realize just as we have a good we are striving to realize. We accordingly develop the disposition to view the world from the standpoint of their good as well as from the standpoint of our own good. Now if the groundlessness of the claim that humans are inherently superior to other species were brought clearly before our minds, we would not remain intellectually neutral toward that claim but would reject it as being fundamentally at variance with our total world outlook. In the absence of any good reasons for holding it, the assertion of human superiority would then appear simply as the expression of an irrational and self-serving prejudice that favors one particular species over several million others.

Rejecting the motion of human superiority entails its positive counterpart: the doctrine of species impartiality.

One who accepts that doctrine regards all living things as possessing inherent worth—the *same* inherent worth, since no one species has been shown to be either "higher" or "lower" than any other. Now we saw earlier that, insofar as one thinks of a living thing as possessing inherent worth, one considers it to be the appropriate object of the attitude of respect and believes that attitude to be the only fitting or suitable one for all moral agents to take toward it.

Here, then, is the key to understanding how the attitude of respect is rooted in the biocentric outlook on nature. The basic connection is made through the denial of human superiority. Once we reject the claim that humans are superior either in merit or in worth to other living things, we are ready to adopt the attitude of respect. The denial of human superiority is itself the result of taking the perspective on nature built into the first three elements of the biocentric outlook.

Now the first three elements of the biocentric outlook, it seems clear, would be found acceptable to any rational and scientifically informed thinker who is fully "open" to the reality of the lives of nonhuman organisms. Without denying our distinctively human characteristics, such a thinker can acknowledge the fundamental respects in which we are members of the Earth's community of life and in which the biological conditions necessary for the realization of our human values are inextricably linked with the whole system of nature. In addition, the conception of individual living things as teleological centers of life simply articulates how a scientifically informed thinker comes to understand them as the result of increasingly careful and detailed observations. Thus, the biocentric outlook recommends itself as an acceptable system of concepts and beliefs to anyone who is clearminded, unbiased, and factually enlightened, and who has a developed capacity of reality awareness with regard to the lives of individual organisms. This, I submit, is as good a reason for making the moral commitment involved in adopting the attitude of respect for nature as any theory of environmental ethics could possibly have.

Moral Rights and the Matter of Competing Claims

I have not asserted anywhere in the foregoing account that animals or plants have moral rights. This omission was deliberate. I do not think that the reference class of the concept, bearer of moral rights, should be extended to include nonhuman living things. My reasons for taking this position, however, go beyond the scope of this paper. I believe I have been able to accomplish many of the same ends which those who ascribe rights to animals or plants wish to accomplish. There is no reason, moreover, why plants and animals, including whole species populations and life communities, cannot be accorded *legal* rights under my theory. To grant them legal protection could be interpreted as giving them legal entitlement to be protected, and this, in fact, would be a means by which a society that subscribed to the ethics of respect for nature could give public recognition to their inherent worth.

There remains the problem of competing claims, even when wild plants and animals are not thought of as bearers of moral rights. If we accept the biocentric outlook and accordingly adopt the attitude of respect for nature as our ultimate moral attitude, how do we resolve conflicts that arise from our respect for persons in the domain of human ethics and our respect for nature in the domain of environmental ethics? This is a question that cannot adequately be dealt with here. My main purpose in this paper has been to try to establish a base point from which we can start working toward a solution to the problem. I have shown why we cannot just begin with an initial presumption in favor of the interests of our own species. It is after all within our power as moral beings to place limits on human population and technology with the deliberate intention of sharing the Earth's bounty with other species. That such sharing is an ideal difficult to realize even in an approximate way does not take away its claim to our deepest moral commitment.

Endnotes

1. The conceptual links between an entity *having* a good, something being good *for* it, and events doing good *to* it are examined by G. H. Von Wright in *The Varieties of Goodness* (New York: Humanities Press, 1963), chaps. 3 and 5.

2. See W. K. Frankena, "Ethics and the Environment," in K. E. Goodpaster and K. M. Sayre, eds., *Ethics and Problems of the 21st Century* (Notre Dame, University of Notre Dame Press, 1979), pp. 3–20. I critically examine Frankena's views in "Frankena on Environmental Ethics," *Monist,* forthcoming.

3. In the light of considerations set forth in Daniel Dennett's *Brainstorms: Philosophical Essays on Mind and Psychology* (Montgomery, Vermont: Bradford Books, 1978), it is advisable to leave this question unsettled at this time. When machines are developed that function in the way our brains do, we may well come to deem them proper subjects of moral consideration.

4. I have analyzed the nature of this commitment of human ethics in "On Taking the Moral Point of View," *Midwest Studies in Philosophy,* vol. 3, *Studies in Ethical Theory* (1978), pp. 35–61.

5. John Rawls, "Justice As Fairness," *Philosophical Review* 67 (1958): 183.

6. My criticisms of the dogma of human superiority gain independent support from a carefully reasoned essay by R. and V. Routley showing the many logical weaknesses in arguments for human-centered theories of environmental ethics. R. and V. Routley, "Against the Inevitability of Human Chauvinism," in K. E. Goodpaster and K. M. Sayre, eds., *Ethics and Problems of the 21st Century* (Notre Dame: University of Notre Dame Press, 1979), pp. 36–59.

7. For this way of distinguishing between merit and inherent worth, I am indebted to Gregory Vlastos, "Justice and Equality," in R. Brandt, ed., *Social Justice* (Englewood Cliffs, N. J.: Prentice-Hall, 1962), pp. 31–72.

49.   The Planetary Environment: Challenge on Every Front

Larry L. Rasmussen

Larry Rasmussen opens his essay with the claim that we are in the midst of an environmental crisis brought about by human destruction of the fragile ecological balance of our planet. Building on the premise that we face global disaster if steps are not taken to address this crisis, Rasmussen examines in turn the political, economic, religious, and cultural obstacles that stand in the way of our successfully averting this tragedy. He closes with a challenge to face the daunting moral choices that lie ahead.

The economist John Maynard Keynes once remarked that "words ought to be a little wild, for they are the assault of thoughts upon the unthinking."[1] I am going to avoid wild words. . . . But there are some wild *facts* to be shared; it is those I intend to address.[2]

We more readily attend to "wild facts" these days because the impossible happens with stunning regularity. Like the figure in *Alice in Wonderland*, we normally scoff when we're asked to believe three impossible things before breakfast. But now as we twist the knob an eighth of an inch, to check the morning news before breakfast, three or more unbelievable things have already happened in some time zone somewhere in the world. . . .

There is great hope in these events. It seems that just as nature abhors a vacuum, so history resists a dead end. The Dark Ages gave way to the Renaissance, the religious wars to the Enlightenment, the Cold War to the eruption of peace in the direction of democracy. A-bombs and H-bombs have suddenly become massively irrelevant just at the time we claim we're too broke to house the homeless and just when we realize, in Senator Gore's sober analogy, that there is an ecological "Kristalnacht" happening around the globe.

The wild fact I want to address follows from this warning of an environmental Kristalnacht. The fact is stated by Gerald Barney: "For the first time in the history of creation, the life support systems of the Planet Earth are being destroyed by human activities."[3] He goes on: "Throughout history humans have caused locally significant damage to the environment, but never before have human numbers and actions combined to threaten the integrity of the entire planet. Human poverty and wealth are involved both as causes and consequences."[4] This is the wild fact against which I want to explore the challenges we face as planetary caretakers of the present and future, this wild fact that we have gone beyond even "locally significant damage" to threaten "the integrity of the entire planet."

Granted, the fragile state of the planetary environment is not a wild fact that stands by itself. Nothing stands by itself. Elements interact in ways that often aggravate one another—population growth and per capita consumption; use of resources and the pollution of the air, land, and water, plus difficulties of waste disposal and storage; poverty and desperate human need for the essentials of nutrition, shelter, income, and security. The list has the somber beat of a funeral dirge. The opening paragraph of the *Global 2000 Report* is now more alarmingly accurate than when it was written a decade ago:

Used by permission from *Theology and Public Policy* (Summer 1990); published by the Churches' Center for Theology and Public Policy, Washington, DC.

[1]The quotation from Keynes and the term I use later, "wild facts," are taken from the opening of the important volume by Herman E. Daly and John B. Cobb, Jr., *For the Common Good: Redirecting the Economy toward Community, the Environment, and a Sustainable Future* (Boston: Beacon Press, 1990), p.1.

[2]This article is adapted from an address prepared for the February, 1990, meeting of the Pacific Section of the Society of Christian Ethics and for an event at the University of Tulsa sponsored by the journal, *Christianity & Crisis*, and the Tulsa Metropolitan Ministries.

[3]Unpublished paper, dated 2/15/89, to the "Bishops, Executives, Chairs and Leaders of the Evangelical Lutheran Church in America," p. 1.

[4]*Ibid.*, p. 2.

Memo to the President: If present trends continue, the world in 2000 will be more crowded, more polluted, less stable ecologically, and more vulnerable to disruption than the world we live in now. Serious stresses involving population, resources, and environment are clearly visible ahead. Despite greater material output, the world's people will be poorer in many ways than they are today.[5]

Prestigious international studies since *Global 2000*—the Brandt report *North-South* (1980), its sequel *Common Crisis* (1983), the Palme report *Common Security* (1985), and the Bruntland report *Our Common Future* (1987)—only underline this message as a message to all presidents and add an exclamation point to get the attention of the rest of us. The respected *State of the World Report* issued by Worldwatch Institute for 1990 says the world has 40 years, more or less, to achieve an environmentally sustainable economy or it will slide into extended economic and physical decline.[6]

There is yet another important wild fact with which to reckon. On some matters absolutely essential to our survival, we cannot use the time-tested method of trial-and-error. Trial-and-error, whether used in the course of everyday socialization or in the course of sophisticated scientific experiments in the laboratory, is not an option *if* the planet itself is the laboratory. We dare not field test which scientists and which scenarios are right about nuclear winter. We dare not experiment to find the point at which the ozone shield is massively damaged for a thousand years. We dare not experiment to determine how few plant and animal species can support the health and nutritional needs of eight to ten billion people. We dare not test the consequences of humanly induced warming of the atmosphere in the range of 5 degrees. What do you do when you must abandon trial and error as a method because the consequences of failure are too staggering to contemplate and, in some cases, to survive? I guess you buy more computers and hope improved programs better reflect a reality you dare not directly test.

Educational institutions have an enormous challenge: to educate the public about the wild facts which now frame a new era in the planetary tale. Fortunately,

these institutions have at least one wild fact in their favor, namely: the world itself has become an issue of world consciousness. There is a growing awareness around the globe that humanity and the earth are facing a global environmental crisis. More and more people are realizing that radical changes are required if a massive and truly transnational catastrophe is to be averted. Thus, educators will meet a public eager for "saving" knowledge.

Such are the wild facts, then, summarized in Daly and Cobb's crisp, if bland, recognition that "[t]he scale of human activity relative to the biosphere has grown too large."[7] Assuming this point is sufficiently plausible to consider possible consequences, I go directly to four impressive challenges. These four are: the political challenge, the economic challenge, the religious challenge, and the cultural challenge.

The Political Challenge

The earth is demonstrably one. There is only one ozone shield; there is a single greenhouse affected atmosphere. But the world is clearly not one. It is politically vibrant, varied, chaotic, fragmented. While the greenhouse effect may be causing global warming, the White House effect to date has been relatively cool. John Sununu, the President's chief of staff, acknowledged he took a Presidential speech on global warming and lopped off the hard choices, saying that "some of the faceless bureaucrats on the environmental side" have been trying to "create a policy in this country that cuts off our use of coal, oil and natural gas." "I don't think that's what this country wants . . . I don't think America wants not to be able to use their automobiles."[8] He is certainly correct about automobiles, though he wildly exaggerated the message of the "faceless" environmental bureaucrats. They had not argued for a policy that "*cuts off* our use of coal, oil and natural gas." But whether we agree with Sununu or not, we can hardly fault him for assuming that his responsibility is to "America." He works for a particular nation-state and his responsibilities are circumscribed by it. Unfortunately, he is not only facing an undecided nation, the United States, on an unprecedented issue, possible serious global warming; he is also caught like

---

[5]Barney, G. O., Ed. and Study Director, *The Global 2000 Report to the President*, Volume I, published originally by the U.S. Government Printing Office (1980), republished by Seven Locks Press (Cabin John, MD), p. 1.

[6]"40-Year Countdown Is Seen for Environment," *The New York Times*, February 11, 1990, A48.

[7]Herman E. Daly and John B. Cobb, Jr., *For the Common Good*, p. 2.

[8]"Sununu Says He Revised Speech on Warming," *The New York Times*, February 5, 1990, A15.

the rest of us in the reality that the nation-state is, on some crises and issues, now too small to be the principal unit of government, while at the same time it seems too large for many local problems. The planetary environment requires the cooperation of nations on an unprecedented scale. It is difficult to see how that can happen without some selective surrendering of sovereignty, whether in the form of strengthened international institutions like the UN and the World Court, or in the form of treaties with a global reach—the Law of the Sea, for example, or Antarctica. Elliot Richardson is surely right that the world "cannot afford to rely on independent action by individual countries" and that "nothing will get done without an institutional mechanism to develop, institute and enforce regulations across national boundaries."[9]

Fortunately, movement has begun. The agreements to date on the regulation of chlorofluorocarbons represent unprecedented international cooperation in the number of nations signing on in such a short period of time—only to be followed up immediately with cries that even more nations must do far more. A more encompassing treaty must and probably will be secured rather soon. An international conference of some 160 sovereign nations is scheduled for Brazil in 1992. We can, I think, expect a revenging biosphere too fragile for the present habits of exuberant *Homo sapiens* to elicit transnational cooperation on a scale we have never before seen. At the same time, the nation-state, where it is not itself dissolving into smaller units still, remains the principal unit of political sovereignty; and the John Sununus will continue to answer to what they interpret as the will of what is in fact only a minuscule portion of the people affected by one-earth issues. In short, our current state is reminiscent of a line from Reinhold Niebuhr's *Children of Light and Children of Darkness*. It was written in 1944: "The world community, toward which all historical forces seem to be driving us, is [hu]mankind's final possibility and impossibility."[10] This is where we are presently poised politically in world community affairs. We are poised between possibility and impossibility, unprecedented cooperation and widespread chaos, new unities and new chaos, transnational loyalties and local conflicts. The political challenge is to enhance the possibility of world community in ways that do not further jeopardize the planet's physical environment and do not further increase the ranks of the impoverished and disenfranchised. No mean challenge! And this account is a privileged world account—"do not further jeopardize," "do not further increase" massive public suffering. That is essentially *status quo* policy and it is deadly for many, many people. So the political challenge is actually some manner of "conversion"—to hear the cry of the people and to hear the cry of the earth such as to change direction.

How grand is this political challenge? Some claim that "the global environment is in the process of becoming the new organizing principle in international relations."[11] Whether that is correct or not, it would be surprising if the international issues of the planetary environment did not occupy something of the same high place over the next forty years that the Cold War has over the last forty. Indeed, the scope could be even broader in that *both* East-West *and* North-South matters are increasingly forced by global ecology to search for a common framework of consideration. The alternative is to consign millions, maybe billions, to abject misery. We might do so. That would be to utterly fail to meet the political challenge. The challenge is to somehow manage *one-world* politics, in the face of *one-earth* issues. We have not really been here before. Are we ready for this challenge?

There is a justice issue here. Moral philosophers from the ancient Greeks to Martin Luther King, Jr. have insisted that the universe is one and that justice is, finally, indivisible. We are knit together in a single garment of destiny. But the wild facts never forced us to seriously test that ancient contention, much less make certain it happened. Are one-earth issues now forcing us, in a down-to-earth way, to test the age-old religious vision of the unity of creation and the indivisibility of justice? Are we now in a "do or die" dilemma in which we must address social justice and ecological justice simultaneously or we lose it all? In one of the severities of God, acid rain falls on the just and the unjust alike. Perpetrators and victims alike are done in. In a new manifestation of ancient moral wisdom, the poor have the rich by the neck this time. Not by open revolt, but simply by helping us run out of space for depositing the damage we do. Wherever the damage is deposited, it fouls a common nest. The poor foul the nest—deforestation, erosion, soil exhaustion,

[9]Elliot L. Richardson, "How To Fight Global Warming," *The New York Times,* February 7, 1990, A25.

[10]Reinhold Niebuhr, *The Children of Light and the Children of Darkness* (New York: Charles Scribner's Sons, 1944), p. 189.

[11]*The New York Times,* October 5, 1989.

population growth, acid rain. The rich foul a larger portion through the environmentally unsustainable habits of industrial and technological civilization—deforestation, soil exhaustion, falling water tables, toxic wastes, acid rain, insane per capita consumption, solid waste disposal, the burning of fossil fuels. This time the rich cannot further export the negative consequences of affluence; and this time the environmentally destructive ways of the desperate poor will ravage the planet as well. I am asking: what happens if justice truly is indivisible, not as a matter of pure religious vision, nor as a matter of mysticism, nor as a matter of wistful philosophical contention, but as a matter of the very down-to-earth existence of the polis and the planet? Such is the practical moral challenge of one-earth issues to one-world politics.

The challenge is heightened, not lessened, by the rush to democracy. "Democracy" is a sacred word on the lips of billions now. We should rejoice in that development. Yet, there is a far-reaching, troublesome issue. For how does democracy work? The answer is: through the registering of citizens' interests via their chosen representatives. The genius of democracy is to set the mighty power of individual and collective self-interest within a framework of accountability to a wider public good. But what is the time-span and the reach of people's interests? Do present citizens vote the interests of future generations together with their own and on a par with their own? Who in a democracy represents future generations and takes account of their claims to well-being? The answer does not actually matter, *unless* present choices mean forced future options. The answer does not matter, moreover, if there is a natural harmony of present desires with the conditions for sustainable life some generations hence. But that harmony cannot be assumed. Yet democracy either assumes that harmony, or else assumes unlimited resources for all for an indefinite future.

Let us trade a focus on the future for one on the present. On one-earth issues, who votes on those policies in this nation which impact the interests of those beyond these shores right now? Can democracy in nation-state form match the needs of a world with only one ozone shield, one atmosphere, one enormous but apparently singular hydrological system?

In short, how do we transform democracy to represent interests we do not experience as our own most important interests, when democracy itself commands us to represent our own pre-eminent interests? How do we extend democracy to encompass the interests of unborn generations and of neighbors around the world we will never see but whose destiny we shape and share for worse and better? And, it must be added, how do we extend democracy to encompass the welfare of our non-human neighbors, the flora and fauna, the soil, rocks, water, and air upon which we are totally and utterly dependent? These necessary extensions confront us with a mammoth, puzzling political challenge in a time when democracy has largely won the day ideologically. We must ask: is there such a thing as a "bio-democracy?" Is there a democracy for the unborn? If there is not, do we simply assume that acting in our own best interests in a world facing innumerable pressures and constraints will of itself redound to the welfare of future generations? If we do, we have a confidence which surpasses even God's own, since God seems intent upon weaning us from such an egocentric view. Or do we finally join the late 20th century hedonist and say, "Eat, drink, and be merry, for tomorrow *they* die." Democracy has won the day, but is it adequate to a world of expanded human consequences in contracted time and space? This is part of the political challenge.

The Economic Challenge

We cannot have infinite physical growth on a finite planet. This is a hard saying, and true. It is also true that we do not know yet how to generate sufficient wealth for mass well-being apart from the model of the industrial and technological age, namely, economic growth. What is further true is that we are now challenged to achieve an environmentally sustainable economy at the same time that we must meet the material needs of unprecedented numbers of people. The economic challenge, then, is a series of questions: How, in a bulging world which seemingly must rely on economic growth, do we respect the ecosphere's physical limits? How do we grow, yet halt the degradation and begin to repair the damage? How do we fashion a truly huge economy which is at the same time environmentally kinder and gentler? The dilemma is that we depend upon an economy which grows, grows, grows, while the ecosystem, *of which the economy is a subsystem*, does not grow. The economy is a subsystem of the ecosystem, and we have already overshot the optimal scale in the crucial relationship of economy to ecosphere. We respect a growth-driven economy, but we do not respect its most basic law of all, biospheric sustainability. The challenge is enormous, because the very engine which first lifted the masses from economic slavery, industrial and technological capitalism and socialism, is the same engine which delivered much of the ecocrisis. Furthermore, at the important level of theory, we have almost no developed economic theory which truly takes account of ecological constraints and requirements. We have met the challenge neither conceptually nor practically.[12]

Some do not think the challenge this radical. Indeed, some think it is no challenge at all. Rather, there is a simple convergence of good capitalist economic policy and good environmental policy. In the speech I referred to earlier, the one Sununu doctored for the President, Bush called for "a convergence between global environmental policy and global economic policy, where both perspectives benefit and neither is compromised." "[O]ur policies," he added, "must be consistent with economic growth and free-market principles in all countries." Such economics will "provide the resources for better protection of the environment."[13]

I am not a doomsayer; indeed, I am curiously optimistic. I emphatically disbelieve in the Reagan-Bush-Quayle Revolution, however. Extending the current course will not do, Bush's assurance to the contrary. The present economy is destructive of both nature and community. We need some alternative. It may come through capitalism of some sort. Capitalism has an impressive capacity to modify itself, sometimes dramatically. It can accommodate various cultural orientations, though by no means all. My point, however, is to pose the economic challenge of one-earth realities, and to note the need for a blessed alternative which does not entail either catastrophic economic dislocation (i.e., further dislocation) for human beings or catastrophic dislocation (i.e., further dislocation) for the rest of nature. The place to begin is with a simple question rarely asked: what, in the end, is economic activity ultimately for? The answer? The continuity of life. Let us begin to think from there, keeping in mind that the economy is a subsystem of the ecosystem.

The Religious Challenge

There is a religious resurgence underway. It is happening globally. It takes both traditional and non-traditional forms. It includes well-organized communities of faith

and wildly varied forms of individual expression. No one has mapped it well yet and the scene is in such flux that most any up-to-date map would be out-of-date by the time the ink dried. A recent report says California is a forest of "crosses and crystals," but I am sure that that simplification itself would offend many people in that religiously florid state.[14] Considering the breadth and variety entailed in current religious expression, I will restrict myself to some few comments which show the challenge of planetary environmental conditions to long-established world religions and, within this sphere, to Christianity in particular. I choose to comment on Christianity, not because Christianity is most important, but because I know it best and stand within it.

The reality of one-earth issues presses hard upon world religions. They all—Islam, Judaism, Christianity, Hinduism, Buddhism, Shintoism, Ba'hai—are being called urgently to embody their ancient claims of a global vision of human unity, of care for the earth, of a generosity toward all creatures great and small, of compassion for all that suffers, of seeing all things together in or before the divine, and of seeing all things as precious, indeed holy. Even world citizens who by their own testimony are utterly secular in orientation, and skeptical about religious belief, sound the trumpet. In January, 1990, the first of the national meetings sponsored by Global Forum (an international organization of world religious leaders and parliamentarians) took place in Moscow. Note the sponsors: the Politburo of the then-intact Communist Party, the Soviet Academy of Sciences, and the Russian Orthodox Church! It was another unbelievable thing before breakfast, another wild fact. Note next the call of one of the speakers, the popular professor of astronomy, Carl Sagan. Sagan said: "Efforts to safeguard and cherish the environment need to be infused with a vision of the sacred. I am personally skeptical about many aspects of revealed religion, but I am sure of the awe and reverence that the meticulously balanced nature of the global environment elicits in me." Sagan went on to make an appeal highly unusual for the scientific guild, namely, that clerics and other religious leaders join hands with the scientists. He and twenty-two other scientists, most of them world-renowned, wrote a statement. After it listed dangers to the global environment, it went on to say, almost matter-of-factly, "Problems of such magnitude, and solutions demanding so broad a perspective,

---

[12]This paragraph is paraphrased from a portion of a review I have written on the book by Herman Daly and John Cobb, *For the Common Good*. See "A World Out of Scale," *Christianity & Crisis*, Vol. 50, No. 7 (May 14, 1990), pp. 154-158.

[13]"Bush Asks Cautious Approach to Global Warming," *The New York Times*, February 6, 1990, A25.

[14]Russell Chandler, "Californians: Spiritual but not Conventional," *Progressions: A Lilly Endowment Occasional Report*, Vol. 2, Issue 1, p. 8.

must be recognized from the outset as having a religious as well as a scientific dimension."[15]

Thus is the challenge put to religious communities worldwide by scientists and by parliamentarians. They are certainly right that planetary environmental issues are a religious challenge. Religion is that dimension of our existence which insistently tries to see things whole and in relation to the sacred. Religion gives the transient and finite a sense of ultimacy, or a framework of ultimacy, within which to understand and cherish the fleeting and creaturely. Religion also engenders enduring commitment and forms or supports the most ardent convictions. Religion can be as demonic as it can be redemptive, to be sure. So beware the holy, for it destroys as well as saves. But *that* the deep need for an encompassing vision in which we understand ourselves anew in the cosmic scheme of things is a need that is deeply *religious,* on this the scientists are right without qualification. And *that* one-earth environmental issues carry with them matters of cosmic proportions and sense is also correct. The challenge *is* religious at heart.

I speak now of Christianity. It is a faith that remains largely anthropocentric in conception and practice. It has been dualistic on many fronts, including fateful separations of spirit and matter, mind and body, and humanity and (the rest of) nature. It has often encouraged an earth- and world-denying spirituality and, from its own Scriptures onward, has been deeply ambivalent about sensuality. It has, over the last couple of centuries, contributed to and adjusted itself to "modernity;" that is, Christianity has largely supported an industrial, technological, and urban world, and promoted economic growth and consumption. It has been male-minded in the Enlightenment and industrial-technological mode, and thus has been even more male-centered than human-centered. There have been elective affinities between the vaunted Protestant ethic and capitalism, and an American gospel of wealth has spread well beyond Protestantism.

In brief, in the massive and spreading civilization we call the modern world, a civilization which is in so many ways now dying by increments, Christianity has done little to nurture a *bio*-spiritual faith or find a way to rally its considerable legacy of asceticism in a manner that fiercely loves the earth in a simple way of life. Nevertheless, there is great ferment in Christianity now, partly in response to the cry of the earth and partly in response to the cry of the people in a world where Christianity has shifted from the religion of the rich to the faith of the poor, and in a world where women's voices are more insistent everywhere. This ferment has great resources in Christianity's teachings on creation, incarnation, stewardship, and the need for a restraining discipline upon the imperious ego. It has great resources by virtue of the fact Judaism is its elder and has always been less susceptible to debilitating dualisms and better attached to the sacred amidst the material, historical, and mundane. Judaism has not done much better with a shared, debilitating patriarchy, however. The general conclusion is this: like many of its co-religions, Christianity's promise and resources are great, but much that is basic must be recast in the faith itself. So just as environmental issues are themselves given to profoundly religious stirrings, the planetary environment itself also entails a profound challenge to religion.

The Cultural Challenge

The last challenge I address is cultural. In many ways, the others merge here, since culture always includes religious, economic, political, social, and moral dimensions. But I want to focus on the cultural assumptions of North American society in particular, and more specifically on the assumptions of dominant cultural strains. I will not discuss the cultural assumptions of the native peoples of this land or of the peoples brought as slaves. I list the assumptions of those who have lived a largely European-American cultural life. They are as follows.

- Nature has a virtually limitless storehouse of resources intended for human use.
- Humanity has the commission to control nature.
- Humanity has the right to use resources for an ongoing improvement in the material standard of living.
- The most effective way to assume the continuing elevation of material standards of living is through ongoing economic growth.
- The quality of life itself is furthered by an economic system directed to ever-expanding material abundance.
- The future is open, systematic material progress for the whole human race is possible, and through the careful use of human powers humanity can make history turn out right.

---

[15] "Sagan Urges Clerics to Join In an Effort To Save Globe," *The New York Times,* January 16, 1990.

- Human failures can be overcome through effective problem solving.
- Problem solving will be effective if reason and good will are present, and science and technology are developed and applied in a free environment.
- Science and technology are neutral means for serving human ends, and the things we create are under our control.
- Modern science and technology have helped achieve a superior civilization in the West.
- What can be scientifically known and technologically done should be known and done.
- The good life is one of productive labor and material well-being.
- The successful person is the achiever.
- Both social progress and individual interests are best served by competitive, achievement-oriented behavior.
- A work ethic is essential to human satisfaction and social progress.
- The diligent, hard-working, risk-taking, and educated will attain their goals.
- There is freedom in material abundance.
- When people have more, their freedom of choice is expanded and they can and will *be* more.[16]

Enough already! The whole list is but an echo of Carl Sandburg's poem, "Chicago," or an elaboration on the entry in a seventeenth century diary: "I'd rather face a thousand attacking Turks than one Calvinist bent on doing the will of God." Our culture has always been a little "bulldozer-Calvinist." Not that it is only Calvinist. The book, *Crosstown Sabbath,* narrates the experience of riding the 42nd St. crosstown bus in New York City. The fatigue on the faces of the riders is, the author writes, "Judeo-Christian." We are imitating the God of our civilization, the "Workaholic Supernal" who "assembled the world in Factory terms." "Before the Hebrews, no other people had a sabbath," Morton goes on, "No other people needed one."[17]

But returning to the list of cultural assumptions, some of them are no doubt good and some bad. The salient point, however, is none of them knows anything about *limits* of any kind. Thus, we are at a very serious loss when, as today, the earth strikes back. The state of the planetary environment poses a profound challenge to the dominant mores and the deep cultural layers of this society.

I close with what is more whimper than bang. It doesn't sum up. It doesn't issue an alter call. It only adds a note that comes with the kind of territory ethicists love to map. I want to slide the various challenges—economic, political, religious, and cultural—beneath a light which exposes them collectively as a *moral* challenge. To this end, I cite remarkable sentences from a newer head of state, President Vaclav Havel of Czechoslovakia, in a speech to a German audience on New Year's Day, 1990. Just before the punchline, he notes the sorry, even dangerous state of the environment in his homeland: "We have spoiled our land, rivers and forests, inherited from our ancestors, and we have, today, the worst environment in the whole of Europe. Adults die here earlier than in the majority of European countries. . . ." Then this:

> The worst of it all is that we live in a spoiled moral environment. We have become morally ill because we are used to saying one thing and thinking another. We have learned not to believe in anything, not to care about each other, to worry only about ourselves. The concepts of love, friendship, mercy, humility or forgiveness have lost their depths and dimension, and for many of us they represent only some sort of psychological curiosity or they appear as long-lost wanderers from faraway times, somewhat ludicrous in the era of computers and spaceships. . . .[18]

Perhaps we can modify a line from a President of our own nation and close with a moral challenge. The line is a little "hokey," perhaps. Try it anyway: "Ask not what your planet can do for you, but what you can do for your planet."

---

[16]This list is only slightly modified from the one in Bruce C. Birch and Larry L. Rasmussen, *The Predicament of the Prosperous* (Philadelphia: The Westminster Press, 1978), pp. 44–45.

[17]Frederic Morton, *Crosstown Sabbath: A Street Journey Through History* (New York: Grove Press, 1987), p. 31.

---

[18]"Excerpts From Speech By the Czech President," *The New York Times,* January 2, 1990, A13.

50. *People or Penguins*

WILLIAM F. BAXTER

William Baxter raises objections to several of the working assumptions of environmental ethicists, focusing in particular on the claims that some natural phenomena are intrinsically valuable and that we must move away from a person-centered ethic if we hope to address environmental concerns. Baxter can see no demonstrable intrinsic value in nature, and insists that its only value is related to the benefits it provides for persons. He supports a human-centered ethic and argues that even though persons are never to be used as means to an end, nature enjoys no such moral protection. The only set of environmental issues that should concern us morally relates to the question of how nature can best be utilized to serve human needs.

I start with the modest proposition that, in dealing with pollution, or indeed with any problem, it is helpful to know what one is attempting to accomplish. Agreement on how and whether to pursue a particular objective, such as pollution control, is not possible unless some more general objective has been identified and stated with reasonable precision. We talk loosely of having clean air and clean water, of preserving our wilderness areas, and so forth. But none of these is a sufficiently general objective: each is more accurately viewed as a means rather than as an end.

With regard to clean air, for example, one may ask, "how clean?" and "what does clean mean?" It is even reasonable to ask, "why have clean air?" Each of these questions is an implicit demand that a more general community goal be stated—a goal sufficiently general in its scope and enjoying sufficiently general assent among the community of actors that such "why" questions no longer seem admissible with respect to that goal.

If, for example, one states as a goal the proposition that "every person should be free to do whatever he wishes in contexts where his actions do not interfere with the interests of other human beings," the speaker is unlikely to be met with a response of "why." The goal may be criticized as uncertain in its implications or difficult to implement, but it is so basic a tenet of our

civilization—it reflects a cultural value so broadly shared, at least in the abstract—that the question "why" is seen as impertinent or imponderable or both.

I do not mean to suggest that everyone would agree with the "spheres of freedom" objective just stated. Still less do I mean to suggest that a society could subscribe to four or five such general objectives that would be adequate in their coverage to serve as testing criteria by which all other disagreements might be measured. One difficulty in the attempt to construct such a list is that each new goal added will conflict, in certain applications, with each prior goal listed; and thus each goal serves as a limited qualification on prior goals.

Without any expectation of obtaining unanimous consent to them, let me set forth four goals that I generally use as ultimate testing criteria in attempting to frame solutions to problems of human organization. My position regarding pollution stems from these four criteria. If the criteria appeal to you and any part of what appears hereafter does not, our disagreement will have a helpful focus: which of us is correct, analytically, in supposing that his position on pollution would better serve these general goals. If the criteria do not seem acceptable to you, then it is to be expected that our more particular judgments will differ, and the task will then be yours to identify the basic set of criteria upon which your particular judgments rest.

My criteria are as follows:

1. The spheres of freedom criterion stated above.
2. Waste is a bad thing. The dominant feature of human existence is scarcity—our available

resources, our aggregate labors, and our skill in employing both have always been, and will continue for some time to be, inadequate to yield to every man all the tangible and intangible satisfactions he would like to have. Hence, none of those resources, or labors, or skills, should be wasted—that is, employed so as to yield less than they might yield in human satisfactions.

3. Every human being should be regarded as an end rather than as a means to be used for the betterment of another. Each should be afforded dignity and regarded as having an absolute claim to an evenhanded application of such rules as the community may adopt for its governance.

4. Both the incentive and the opportunity to improve his share of satisfactions should be preserved to every individual. Preservation of incentive is dictated by the "no-waste" criterion and enjoins against the continuous, totally egalitarian redistribution of satisfactions, or wealth; but subject to that constraint, everyone should receive, by continuous redistribution if necessary, some minimal share of aggregate wealth so as to avoid a level of privation from which the opportunity to improve his situation becomes illusory.

The relationship of these highly general goals to the more specific environmental issues at hand may not be readily apparent, and I am not yet ready to demonstrate their pervasive implications. But let me give one indication of their implications. Recently scientists have informed us that use of DDT in food production is causing damage to the penguin population. For the present purposes let us accept that assertion as an indisputable scientific fact. The scientific fact is often asserted as if the correct implication—that we must stop agricultural use of DDT—followed from the mere statement of the fact of penguin damage. But plainly it does not follow if my criteria are employed.

My criteria are oriented to people, not penguins. Damage to penguins, or sugar pines, or geological marvels is, without more, simply irrelevant. One must go further, by my criteria, and say: Penguins are important because people enjoy seeing them walk about rocks; and furthermore, the well-being of people would be less impaired by halting use of DDT than by giving up penguins. In short, my observations about environmental problems will be people-oriented, as

are my criteria. I have no interest in preserving penguins for their own sake.

It may be said by way of objection to this position, that it is very selfish of people to act as if each person represented one unit of importance and nothing else was of any importance. It is undeniably selfish. Nevertheless I think it is the only tenable starting place for analysis for several reasons. First, no other position corresponds to the way most people really think and act—i.e., corresponds to reality.

Second, this attitude does not portend any massive destruction of nonhuman flora and fauna, for people depend on them in many obvious ways, and they will be preserved because and to the degree that humans do depend on them.

Third, what is good for humans is, in many respects, good for penguins and pine trees—clean air for example. So that humans are, in these respects, surrogates for plant and animal life.

Fourth, I do not know how we could administer any other system. Our decisions are either private or collective. Insofar as Mr. Jones is free to act privately, he may give such preferences as he wishes to other forms of life: he may feed birds in winter and do with less himself, and he may even decline to resist an advancing polar bear on the ground that the bear's appetite is more important than those portions of himself that the bear may choose to eat. In short my basic premise does not rule out private altruism to competing life-forms. It does rule out, however, Mr. Jones' inclination to feed Mr. Smith to the bear, however hungry the bear, however despicable Mr. Smith.

Insofar as we act collectively on the other hand, only humans can be afforded an opportunity to participate in the collective decisions. Penguins cannot vote now and are unlikely subjects for the franchise—pine trees more unlikely still. Again each individual is free to cast his vote so as to benefit sugar pines if that is his inclination. But many of the more extreme assertions that one hears from some conservationists amount to tacit assertions that they are specially appointed representatives of sugar pines, and hence that their preferences should be weighted more heavily than the preferences of other humans who do not enjoy equal rapport with "nature." The simplistic assertion that agricultural use of DDT must stop at once because it is harmful to penguins is of that type.

Fifth, if polar bears or pine trees or penguins, like men, are to be regarded as ends rather than means, if they are to count in our calculus of social organization, someone must tell me how much each one counts, and someone must tell me how these life-forms are to be permitted to express their preferences, for I do not know either answer. If the answer is that certain people are to hold their proxies, then I want to know how those proxy-holders are to be selected: self-appointment does not seem workable to me.

Sixth, and by way of summary of all the foregoing, let me point out that the set of environmental issues under discussion—although they raise very complex technical questions of how to achieve any objective—ultimately raise a normative question: what *ought* we to do. Questions of *ought* are unique to the human mind and world—they are meaningless as applied to a nonhuman situation.

I reject the proposition that we *ought* to respect the "balance of nature" or to "preserve the environment" unless the reason for doing so, express or implied, is the benefit of man.

I reject the idea that there is a "right" or "morally correct" state of nature to which we should return. The word "nature" has no normative connotation. Was it "right" or "wrong" for the earth's crust to heave in contortion and create mountains and seas? Was it "right" for the first amphibian to crawl up out of the primordial ooze? Was it "wrong" for plants to reproduce themselves and alter the atmospheric composition in favor of oxygen? For animals to alter the atmosphere in favor of carbon dioxide both by breathing oxygen and eating plants? No answers can be given to these questions because they are meaningless questions.

All this may seem obvious to the point of being tedious, but much of the present controversy over environment and pollution rests on tacit normative assumptions about just such nonnormative phenomena: that it is "wrong" to impair penguins with DDT, but not to slaughter cattle for prime rib roasts. That it is wrong to kill stands of sugar pines with industrial fumes, but not to cut sugar pines and build housing for the poor. Every man is entitled to his own preferred definition of Walden Pond, but there is no definition that has any moral superiority over another, except by reference to the selfish needs of the human race.

From the fact that there is no normative definition of the natural state, it follows that there is no normative definition of clean air or pure water—hence no definition of polluted air—or of pollution—except by reference to the needs of man. The "right" composition of the atmosphere is one which has some dust in it and some lead in it and some hydrogen sulfide in it—just those amounts that attend a sensibly organized society

thoughtfully and knowledgeably pursuing the greatest possible satisfaction for its human members.

The first and most fundamental step toward solution of our environmental problems is a clear recognition that our objective is not pure air or water but rather some optimal state of pollution. That step immediately suggests the question: How do we define and attain the level of pollution that will yield the maximum possible amount of human satisfaction?

Low levels of pollution contribute to human satisfaction but so do food and shelter and education and music. To attain ever lower levels of pollution, we must pay the cost of having less of these other things. I contrast that view of the cost of pollution control with the more popular statement that pollution control will "cost" very large numbers of dollars. The popular statement is true in some senses, false in others; sorting out the true and false senses is of some importance. The first step in that sorting process is to achieve a clear understanding of the difference between dollars and resources. Resources are the wealth of our nation; dollars are merely claim checks upon those resources. Resources are of vital importance; dollars are comparatively trivial.

Four categories of resources are sufficient for our purposes: At any given time a nation, or a planet if you prefer, has a stock of labor, of technological skill, of capital goods, and of natural resources (such as mineral deposits, timber, water, land, etc.). These resources can be used in various combinations to yield goods and services of all kinds—in some limited quantity. The quantity will be larger if they are combined efficiently, smaller if combined inefficiently. But in either event the resource stock is limited, the goods and services that they can be made to yield are limited; even the most efficient use of them will yield less than our population, in the aggregate, would like to have.

If one considers building a new dam, it is appropriate to say that it will be costly in the sense that it will require x hours of labor, y tons of steel and concrete, and z amount of capital goods. If these resources are devoted to the dam, then they cannot be used to build hospitals, fishing rods, schools, or electric can openers. That is the meaningful sense in which the dam is costly.

Quite apart from the very important question of how wisely we can combine our resources to produce goods and services, is the very different question of how they get distributed—who gets how many goods? Dollars constitute the claim checks which are distributed among people and which control their share of national output. Dollars are nearly valueless pieces of paper except to the extent that they do represent claim checks to some fraction of the output of goods and services. Viewed as claim checks, all the dollars outstanding during any period of time are worth, in the aggregate, the goods and services that are available to be claimed with them during that period—neither more nor less.

It is far easier to increase the supply of dollars than to increase the production of goods and services—printing dollars is easy. But printing more dollars doesn't help because each dollar then simply becomes a claim to fewer goods, i.e., becomes worth less.

The point is this: many people fall into error upon hearing the statement that the decision to build a dam, or to clean up a river, will cost $X million. It is regrettably easy to say: "It's only money. This is a wealthy country, and we have lots of money." But you cannot build a dam or clean a river with $X million—unless you also have a match, you can't even make a fire. One builds a dam or cleans a river by diverting labor and steel and trucks and factories from making one kind of goods to making another. The cost in dollars is merely a shorthand way of describing the extent of the diversion necessary. If we build a dam for $X million, then we must recognize that we will have $X million less housing and food and medical care and electric can openers as a result.

Similarly, the costs of controlling pollution are best expressed in terms of the other goods we will have to give up to do the job. This is not to say the job should not be done. Badly as we need more housing, more medical care, and more can openers, and more symphony orchestras, we could do with somewhat less of them, in my judgment at least, in exchange for somewhat cleaner air and rivers. But that is the nature of the trade-off, and analysis of the problem is advanced if that unpleasant reality is kept in mind.

Once the trade-off relationship is clearly perceived, it is possible to state in a very general way what the optimal level of pollution is. I would state it as follows:

People enjoy watching penguins. They enjoy relatively clean air and smog-free vistas. Their health is improved by relatively clean water and air. Each of these benefits is a type of good or service. As a society we would be well advised to give up one washing machine if the resources that would have gone into that washing machine can yield greater human satisfaction when diverted into pollution control. We should give up one hospital if the resources thereby freed would yield more human satisfaction when devoted to elimination of noise in our cities. And so on, trade-off by trade-off, we should divert our productive capacities from the production of existing goods and services to the production of a cleaner, quieter, more pastoral nation up to—and no further than—the point at which we value more highly the next washing machine or hospital that we would have to do without than we value the next unit of environmental improvement that the diverted resources would create.

Now this proposition seems to me unassailable but so general and abstract as to be unhelpful—at least unadministerable in the form stated. It assumes we can measure in some way the incremental units of human satisfaction yielded by very different types of goods. The proposition must remain a pious abstraction until I can explain how this measurement process can occur. In subsequent chapters I will attempt to show that we can do this—in some contexts with great precision and in other contexts only by rough approximation. But I insist that the proposition stated describes the result for which we should be striving—and again, that it is always useful to know what your target is even if your weapons are too crude to score a bull's eye.

51. A *Refutation* of *Environmental* Ethics

JANNA THOMPSON

Janna Thompson examines a central claim of environmental ethicists, that "natural entities and/or states of affairs are intrinsically valuable" and should, therefore, be the objects of our moral concern. Thompson claims that environmental ethicists do not consistently explain what entities or states of affairs qualify as possessing intrinsic value, or on what basis they ascribe such value, nor do they advocate with consistency what should be done to protect or enhance these natural goods. As a result, she concludes that environmental ethics, because it lacks a clear philosophical foundation, fails to qualify as an ethical system at all.

An environmental ethic holds that some entities in nature or in natural states of affairs are intrinsically valuable. I argue that proposals for an environmental ethic either fail to satisfy requirements which any ethical system must satisfy to be an ethic, or they fail to give us reason to suppose that the values they promote are intrinsic values. If my arguments are correct, then environmental ethics is not properly ethics at all.

In "The Shallow and the Deep, Long Range Ecology Movement" Arne Naess distinguishes between two responses to ecological degradation. The shallow response recommends that we be nice to nature so that nature will be nice for us. The deep ecological response, on the other hand, insists that a proper appreciation of nature leads to a recognition that "the equal right to live and blossom is an intuitively clear and obvious value axiom."[1]

Following Naess, a considerable number of philosophers and others have chosen the deep ecology path, and they have understood this to require the development of an ethic which values things in nature for their own sake. John Rodman expresses a common motivation for having such an ethic:

> I need only to stand in the midst of a clearcut forest, a stripmined hillside, a defoliated jungle, or a dammed canyon to feel uneasy with assumptions that could yield the conclusion that no human action can make any difference

From Lawrence M. Hinman (ed.), *Contemporary Moral Issues: Diversity and Consensus*, 2nd Edition, © 2000. Reprinted by permission of Pearson Education, Inc., Upper Saddle River, NJ.

to the welfare of anything but sentient animals.[2]

Val and Richard Routley in "Human Chauvinism and Environmental Ethics" argue that only a truly environmental ethic which regards natural systems or their properties as valuable in themselves can adequately express the standpoint of those who want to preserve wilderness and who abhor strip-mined hillsides and defoliated jungles.[3] More recently Holmes Rolston, III in *Environmental Ethics*[4] and Paul W. Taylor in *Respect for Nature*[5] have both argued for an ethic which recognizes value in nature.

An environmental ethic, as I understand it, is an ethic which holds that natural entities and/or states of affairs are intrinsically valuable, and thus deserve to be the object of our moral concern. What exactly it means to say that something is intrinsically valuable depends on the account given of what values are and where they come from.[6] At a minimum, however, those who find intrinsic value in nature are claiming two things: first, that things and states which are of value are valuable for what they are in themselves and not because of their relations to us (and in particular, not because they provide us with pleasure and satisfaction). Second, the intrinsic value which these states of nature have is objective in the sense that its existence is not a matter of individual taste or personal preference. Any rational, morally sensitive person ought to be able to recognize that it is there. This means, of course, that those who claim that intrinsic value exists in nature must provide some criteria for identifying what is of value and some reasons for believing that the things and states in question are valuable.

In general, an ethic is supposed to tell us two things: (1) what states of affairs, things, and properties are intrinsically desirable or valuable (as opposed to what is valuable as a means to an end); and (2) what we should do or not do in order to promote, protect, or bring into existence that which is of intrinsic value. Given that an ethic is supposed to tell us these things, it must satisfy the following formal requirements in order to count as an ethic at all:

(1) The requirement of consistency. If a thing or state of affairs is thought to be intrinsically valuable, then all things that are like it in relevant respects must also be judged to have intrinsic value. On the other hand, if something is thought not to have intrinsic value, then all things that are like that thing in relevant respects must be regarded as not having intrinsic value. Supporters of animal liberation and environmental ethics have made heavy use of the consistency requirement in their condemnations of "human chauvinism." They argue, for example, that if human beings are regarded as being intrinsically valuable, and if some animals are like human beings in all respects that seem relevant, then a consistent ethic must regard these animals as valuable. If animals are not regarded as being valuable, then those human beings that are like animals in relevant respects (babies, children, the mentally retarded) must be judged by a consistent ethic not to have intrinsic value.[7]

The requirement of consistency presupposes that the ethic in question has provided us with an account of what differences and similarities are relevant and why. If that ethic is to have any claim to being objective, then that account must not seem arbitrary. In other words, if something is thought to be of value and another thing is not, then there must be reason for believing that the differences between them justify making that judgment, and if two things are regarded to be of equal value then the similarities they have must be such so that this judgment can reasonably be made.

(2) The requirement of non-vacuity. The criteria for determining what things or states of affairs are intrinsically valuable must not be such so that it turns out that every thing and every state of affairs counts as equally valuable. The reason why this requirement must be satisfied should be clear. An ethic is supposed to tell us what we ought or ought not to do; however, it cannot do so if it turns out that all things and states of affairs are equally valuable, for if they are, then there is no reason to do one thing rather than another, to bring about one state of affairs rather than another.

(3) The decidability requirement. The criteria of value which an ethic offers must be such that in most cases it is possible to determine what counts as valuable and what does not. Probably all ethical systems will have problems with borderline cases. For example, an ethic which regards sentient creatures as objects of moral concern and their well-being as something that we should promote may have difficulties determining what counts as a sentient creature and what the well-being of a particular creature consists of. Nevertheless, in general it is usually clear what satisfies the criteria and what does not. A more serious difficulty arises if the criteria leave us in doubt in most cases. If this happens, then we do not simply have a problem within an ethic, but a problem regarding something as an ethic in the first place.[8] The reason for having a decidability requirement is much the same as the reason for requiring non-vacuity. If an ethic is to make prescriptions, then we have to have a good idea of what we are supposed to be promoting and avoiding. If an ethic can't tell us this, if it leaves us uncertain in too many cases about what things or states of affairs are valuable and which are more valuable than others, then its claim to be an ethic is brought into question.

My claim is that proposals for an environmental ethic either fail to satisfy one or more of these formal criteria or fail to give us reason to suppose that the values they promote are intrinsic values. It should be noted that my objection to environmental ethics is not that its ideas about what is valuable are implausible, or that rational, morally sensitive people should not value what environmental ethicists tell them to value. Rather, if my arguments are correct, what is called environmental ethics is not properly ethics at all.

What can go wrong with environmental ethics is illustrated by an argument presented by Paul Taylor in *Respect for Nature*. The argument is meant to establish that there is no good reason for thinking that sentient creatures alone have intrinsic value (*inherent worth*), indeed, that there is no reason to deny that nonsentient creatures—plants, lower animals—have less intrinsic value than sentient creatures. Human beings, Taylor admits, have properties that many living things do not have—e.g., intelligence—and some philosophers, most notoriously Descartes, have believed that human beings are distinguished from all other creatures by the possession of mind. Apart from the question of whether other creatures do not have minds, however, there is no reason in nature why we should regard the qualities that human beings happen to have as making them more valuable than living creatures that do not have these qualities—no reason why creatures who can think or feel should be regarded as more valuable than plants and other nonsentient creatures.[9]

A natural response to this argument is to ask, "Why stop here?" Why should we regard rocks, rivers, volcanoes, molecules as being of less value simply because they happen to lack the properties associated with life? Why indeed should we say that anything is more valuable than any other thing? The argument Taylor uses to overthrow human chauvinism seems to undermine the very possibility of an ethic. We might conclude that if we leave it up to nature to tell us what we should or should not value, that we get no answer—that we can only find nature to be valuable insofar as natural states of affairs are related to us: to our interests and concerns, or more generally the interests and concerns of sentient creatures. This is in fact the position I hold, but to establish it requires much more argument, for environmental ethicists do think that they can give us criteria for discovering objective value in nature, criteria which do not set us on the slippery slope into inconsistency, vacuity, or undecidability.

There are two ways in which environmental ethicists have tried to establish their thesis that there are intrinsic values in nature. The first is to argue by analogy. Taylor (and sometimes Rolston) does this. Let us assume that human individuals are intrinsically valuable and that it is desirable that their well-being be promoted. The reason we think that this is so (the argument goes) is that human individuals have interests, preferences, purposes—a good that can be frustrated or furthered. But if this is our criterion for having value, then in all consistency we must recognize that since some animals also have interests, preferences, and purposes, they too should count as having intrinsic value. Plants, nonsentient creatures, may not have interests in a true sense, but they do have a good (unlike a rock). "Once we come to understand the life cycle of a butterfly," Taylor says, "and know the environmental conditions it needs to survive in a healthy state, we have no difficulty speaking about what is beneficial to it and what might be harmful to it."[10] The same can be said about bacteria or plants. Furthermore, the good that a butterfly and a blue gum have is a good of their own. Unlike machines, the good of which is determined by human purposes, we can say what is good for a natural organism without reference to any other entity. Thus, we can understand how nonsentient

organisms can be candidates for having intrinsic value, and once we come to appreciate their nature and the role that they play in environmental systems, we will be inclined to say that they do have "intrinsic value."[11]

The second approach to environmental ethics is not to argue by analogy but simply to try to persuade us as valuers that there are certain things or states of affairs in nature that we as rational, morally sensitive people ought to regard as having a value independent of our needs and interests and that there are other states of affairs (like defoliated jungles or exotic pine plantations) that we ought to regard as having a disvalue. We simply have to come to recognize that these values or disvalues are there, and the job of the proponent of environmental ethics is to encourage us to do this by persuading us to appreciate certain aspects of nature and by trying to show us that an ethic which does not acknowledge these values cannot satisfy our intuitive understanding of what is bad or good, right or wrong. The Routleys take this approach, and so do Rodman and sometimes Rolston.

The Routleys argue in "Human Chauvinism and Environmental Ethics" that environmental systems are to be valued according to their possession of a mix of factors: diversity, naturalness, integrity, stability, and harmony,[12] and that people who appreciate wilderness, who are reluctant to destroy natural systems even if the destruction does not harm sentient creatures, should accept this criterion of value. Rolston maintains that not only organisms as self-maintaining systems deserve to be valued, but also species as entities with a history and an essence and ecosystems as "integrated cybernetic systems." He argues that only if we are prepared to value these things for themselves do we have an ethical basis for preserving and protecting what many sensitive people want to preserve and protect.

Because both approaches claim to be laying the foundations of an environmental ethic, it is presupposed that they can satisfy the formal requirements of an ethic. Indeed, it seems that they do satisfy these requirements. Each claims to have the virtue of consistency—unlike ethics which are described as being "human chauvinist." Each tells us that some things or states of affairs are valuable and some are not; and each presents criteria that we are supposed to be able to use to decide what is valuable and to what extent.

But what exactly is valuable? On this matter environmental ethicists do not speak with one voice. Taylor insists that it is individual organisms that have intrinsic value and not environmental systems or species. The Routleys regard environmental systems as holders of value. Rolston thinks that individual organisms, species, and ecosystems all have value, though perhaps to different degrees. Is this disagreement about what in nature has value a little problem that environmental ethicists should be able to solve among themselves, or is it a symptom of a larger difficulty? To answer this question let us look more closely at each of the two approaches.

Once again I take Taylor's argument as illustrating what goes wrong with the analogical approach. Taylor argues that if a thing has a good of its own, then it is a candidate for having intrinsic value. He assumes that it is individual living organisms and only individual living organisms that can have this value. But there is nothing in the criterion, or the mode of argument used to support it, that requires this limitation. It is not difficult to use Taylor's way of determining what is of value to insist that other kinds of things must also have the same intrinsic value if we are to be true to the consistency requirement.

Why can't we say, for example, that hearts, lungs, livers, and kidneys have intrinsic value and thus deserve in themselves to be objects of our moral concern? Once we come to appreciate how a kidney or some other internal organ develops within the embryo, how it functions and maintains itself, what makes it flourish and what harms it, then surely as in the case of the butterfly or the bacteria we have to recognize that it has a good of its own.

But isn't the good of a kidney defined in terms of the good of the organism that has the kidney? It is true that my own good and the good of my kidneys are intimately related. We depend upon each other (though modern technology has made it possible for me to get on without my kidneys and my kidneys to continue to exist without me). But my purposes and goals do not define what is good for a kidney. This can be determined independently to the same extent that the good of a woodboring insect can be determined independently of the good of the tree it feeds on or that the good of intestinal bacteria can be defined independently of the good of the intestine or the good of the creature who has the intestine. Kidneys, like insects and bacteria, need certain kinds of nourishment: they are healthy under some conditions and are caused harm by others. These conditions can be specified without mentioning the organism in which the organs reside.

So using the same kind of argument which Taylor uses to persuade us that organisms have a good of their own, we have to conclude that internal organs

have such a good too. For the same reason, it seems that we also ought to say that individual leaves, buds, and bits of bark have a good of their own and are equally candidates for having intrinsic value. And what will stop us from saying that a piece of skin, a bodily cell, or a DNA molecule has a good of its own?

Why discriminate against rocks? Once we appreciate how crystals form according to a pattern determined by molecular structure, what conditions make it possible for this pattern to form in a characteristic way, what maintains its structural integrity, and what conditions cause it to be deformed or to break up, then surely we will want to say that in an extended sense of the phrase a crystal has a "good of its own." It is true that it sounds odd to say this. But why should we be any more impressed by the fact that crystals, strictly speaking, do not have a good of their own than Taylor is impressed by the fact that nonsentient creatures, strictly speaking, do not have interests? Surely it is the relevant similarities between bacteria, cells, and crystals that should be crucial for our ethical reasoning, just as it is the relevant similarities between sentient creatures and nonsentient creatures that are crucial for Taylor. The same thing that is said about crystals can be said about any natural entity, whether a rock, a molecule, an atom, or a solar system. Each has an integrity of its own which it can maintain under certain conditions, but which will be destroyed under others.

It is time to reassess the status of machines. Although it is true that we think that the purpose of a machine is to serve a human need, the matter is really not so simple, for machines, because of their structure, have a potential, a way of doing things, of their own, and in order to accomplish their purposes people often have to conform to the ways of the machine. In fact, it is frequently the case that people have to redefine their goals or are caused to discover new ones as a consequence of realizing the potential of a machine or in the course of adapting themselves to it. It seems as if the good of a machine is best defined in terms of the structures and capacities it has and what operations will realize its potential and which ones will tend to destroy it or not allow it to fulfill its potential. Moreover, if a machine has a good of its own, then so do the parts of a machine for the same reason that a liver or a heart have a good of its own.

What can be said about a machine might also be said about other constructed entities like social institutions and societies, for these also have a structure, a potential, a way of operating which the individuals in them don't necessarily appreciate. The same can be said of ecological systems. Taylor objects to regarding systems as being objects of respect, probably because he assumes that the good of a system is reducible to the goods of the individual animal and plant populations that make it up; however, ecological systems, like social systems, have a potential for change and development and a dynamic which may be compatible with the destruction of particular populations—as when a forest develops toward a climax state. So why not admit that ecological systems have a good of their own and are thus in themselves candidates for our moral concern? If ecological systems are entities with a good of their own, then why not parts of ecological systems— e.g., the relation between a predator population and a prey population? Why not a whole wilderness? Why not the relations between plants and animals on a continent? Why not nature as a whole?

One of the problems which this vigorous use of analogy brings out in the open is the problem of determining what should count as an individual for the purposes of environmental ethics. It is perhaps natural to think that particular plants and animals are the individuals that we need to be concerned with. But why shouldn't we count the parts of an animal or plant as individuals, their cells, organs, or molecules? Why not the complex consisting of an animal or a plant and its various parasites and bacteria? Why not the plant and the soil that nourishes it? Why not an interrelated system of animals and plants? There doesn't seem to be any good reason why one thing should be counted as an individual and others not. How we divide up the world depends upon context and convenience. But surely an environmental ethic which claims to discover intrinsic value in nature shouldn't depend upon the way we happen to look at things.

Once we do (somehow) pick out the individuals we are concerned with it is still a problem to decide what is good for them. So far, like Taylor, I have assumed that this is generally obvious. However, there is another way of viewing the matter. An individual plant or animal has a genetic potential to manifest a range of properties, but what properties it realizes depends on its environment. Why should we regard it to be for the good of a plant if it realizes one aspect of its potential rather than another? Once again it is natural to think that it is for the good of a plant to be raised in conditions which encourage it to be vigorous and healthy and that disease and poor nutrition are bad for a plant. Nevertheless, a diseased plant displays properties, realizes a potential, which it would not have manifested if it had been healthy. Why should we

regard it as a worse thing for it if it has these properties? The answer might be that if the ability of a plant to survive and reproduce is threatened, then this is not to its good. However, if this is our criterion of what is bad for natural things, why should we say that it is bad for the plant's sake that it dies of disease rather than that this is bad for its genes or bad for the species? Moreover, why should it be bad for the plant's sake to live a short time rather than a longer time? One reason why we find it so natural to suppose that it is better for an organism's sake that it be healthy and have a long, productive life is because this is what we want for ourselves and what we want for the plants we grow. Nevertheless, plants don't want anything. Thus, as this discussion shows, determining what a nonsentient organism's own good is is not as straightforward as it sometimes appears and this difficulty throws into question the analogy between sentient creatures and nonsentient organisms upon which Taylor's approach to environmental ethics depends.

Other attempts to argue by analogy have not been any more successful. Rolston suggests that what living creatures from the most complex to the simplest have in common is that they are self-contained systems and that it is this which makes them deserving of respect. Nevertheless, virtually anything can be regarded as a self-contained system in the same sense, be it a liver, a molecule, or a solar system. Moreover, Rolston, like Taylor, faces the problem of determining in a nonarbitrary way what states of a system count as good.

Because of these problems, I conclude that neither Taylor nor Rolston succeed in providing the foundations for an environmental ethic. The criteria they use to determine what is of value not only fail to rule out many things that they would probably wish to exclude (e.g., lungs and livers), but also fail to satisfy the formal requirements of an ethic. First, their proposals probably fail to satisfy the requirement of non-vacuity, for if we push the analogies that they depend upon to their logical conclusion, then we end up regarding virtually everything as valuable. Second, even if we can somehow resist this result, it is clear that the proposals won't satisfy the decidability requirement, for the criteria leave us radically uncertain about what counts as an object of moral concern and what states of affairs should be regarded as good.

Of course, the fact that a few proponents of environmental ethics have failed to establish that there can be such an ethic is not conclusive. Is there a way of improving the argument from analogy and/or sharpening up the criteria of value so that they satisfy the requirements? It might be suggested that environmental ethicists should simply declare that what is of intrinsic value are living creatures, or wilderness, or ecological systems. The obvious problem with this idea, however, is that in making this declaration they would be committing the same sin of arbitrariness which they accuse human chauvinists of committing. If they claim to be uncovering intrinsic values in nature, then we are entitled to get an answer to the question, "What is it about living creatures or wilderness that is valuable?" and when the answer is given, in attempting to satisfy the consistency requirement for the ethic, they are likely once again to encounter the problems I have already discussed above.

Maybe the environmental ethicist can give a better answer than the ones so far considered. What distinguishes living things from nonliving things is their complexity. They are not only self-contained systems, but also systems with parts that are related in a complex way, systems which carry out complex processes. Perhaps we should say that something is intrinsically valuable if it has a certain degree of complexity, or that things are valuable according to their degree of complexity. The latter is sometimes suggested by Rolston.

If we adopt the complexity criterion, we might be able to satisfy the requirement of non-vacuity. However, accusations of arbitrariness can still be made. Why should the cutoff point that determines what is of value or what degree of value something has be in one place rather than another? Why should a slightly lesser degree of complexity be regarded as a relevant difference? In addition, it is doubtful whether the criterion can satisfy the decidability requirement. How is complexity to be defined in general and how are we to compare the complexity of different kinds of things? Is an individual less complex than the ecological system or social institution to which he/she/it belongs? Is a heart or liver or brain less complex than the creature it belongs to? Moreover, it is not clear what systems we are talking about. Virtually anything, as I have pointed out, can be regarded as a system: an individual animal or plant, the relationship between several animals and plants, an ecological system, the planet Earth, a heart or kidney, a molecule, an interacting system of molecules, etc. Until we know what we are comparing and how, it is not going to be possible to answer the question, "What should be the object of our moral concern?" Finally, even if we can determine what systems we ought to be concerned with, there remains the difficulty of how we should determine, in a nonarbitrary way, what states of these systems count as good.

Given that there are so many problems with the analogical approach to environmental ethics, one might suppose that the second approach is bound to be preferable. I argue, however, that it encounters the same difficulties. Let us begin with the Routleys' multifactored criterion for evaluating natural systems: diversity, naturalness, integrity, stability, and harmony. The Routleys allow that there can be difficulties in determining how these different factors should be weighed, for example, whether and in what cases a greater diversity can make up for a lack of naturalness. They would also undoubtedly admit that there may be difficulties in determining what "stability" or "harmony" amount to in a dynamic system. But they do claim that this criterion gives us clear reasons for preferring a wilderness over a monoculture pine plantation and for condemning the defoliation of a jungle or the clear-cutting of a forest, and they argue that the judgments that we make using it correspond to our intuitions about what is of value in nature.

That the Routleys don't escape the problems we have already encountered becomes evident as soon as we ask the question: "What is it exactly that we are supposed to be evaluating?" Although they assume that their criterion applies primarily to large environmental systems, such as wilderness, why should we assume this? What prevents us from applying the criterion more widely?[13] For example, compost and dung heaps are little environmental systems that can be evaluated according to the diversity of creatures or processes which they contain, their naturalness, integrity, stability, and harmony. Likewise, individual animals and plants can be regarded as environmental systems containing a greater or lesser diversity of parts and functions, parts that tend to maintain harmony and stability. And, of course, parts of these systems, e.g., livers and lungs, are also systems with a complexity of parts, with an integrity, harmony, etc., of their own. Finally, why should we suppose that the criterion must apply only to systems of living things? How about a solar system, a molecule, or an atom? Why can't a society be regarded as a diverse, stable, harmonious cybernetic system?

Once again we have a problem of determining and limiting the scope of the application of the value criterion. It won't do any good to insist that it is only to be applied to ecological systems. This is a mere piece of legislation. If other systems are like ecological systems in relevant respects, then they too should be judged as valuable. If we don't want to say that they are valuable, then we have to find a relevant respect in which they are different.

The difficulty involved in determining what should be the objects of our moral concern translates into a difficulty about what states of affairs we should be promoting. Is the diversity, integrity, naturalness, etc., contained in a compost heap or a tree less worthy of our concern than the diversity, integrity, naturalness, etc., of a forest? Is a monoculture pine plantation full of creatures, which in themselves have diversity, integrity, etc., necessarily of less worth than the wilderness that it replaced?

Even if we focus on ecological systems, it is difficult to determine what ought to be preserved and protected and why. If we degrade an environmental system, make it less diverse, natural, stable, etc., then we have rendered it less valuable according to our criterion. But in the future this system may recover, becoming as diverse and integrated as before (though perhaps with different species), or another system just as diverse, etc., may eventually replace it (perhaps in a thousand or a million years). If we have good reason to think that this will happen, then why should we be terribly concerned about what we now do to our environment? What counts as harm?

One answer might be that a state of affairs is worse if it is brought about by our tampering. What environmental ethics above all wants to condemn is unnecessary human interventions in nature. Its message is "Leave it alone." The Routleys, for example, place a lot of weight on "naturalness." Even if our interventions increase the diversity of a system and do not damage its stability and harmony, they can still be condemned because they make it less natural.

It is puzzling that an ethic which purports to find objective value in nature should be so concerned about what states of affairs human beings bring about. Although it is true that human actions do have a detrimental effect on environmental systems, so do storms, floods, volcanoes, and glaciers. Exotic species can be introduced into a system by winds or the migration of birds. Given these natural disturbances, how can environmental ethicists justify condemning a human action when it does not (in the long term, at least) make a system any less stable, diverse, harmonious, etc.? Moreover, why aren't they concerned to prevent (if possible) natural occurrences that threaten the stability, integrity, and diversity of an environmental system? The emphasis environmental ethicists place on limiting human interventions, on preserving and protecting the natural communities which we are in contact with, suggests that their real concern is to encourage a better relationship between humans and their environment. Their ideas about what we should value and why—that, for example, we should value the creatures and systems that now happen to exist—depend on a covert reference to the human point of view, to our interests and concerns.

Other recent attempts to develop a criterion for making value judgments have been no more successful than the Routleys' criterion. Rolston, for example, argues that species deserve to be respected because they are discrete entities with a history of their own. A species, he says, is a kind of an essence.[14] But what history a species has, what turns out to be its essence, depends upon the environmental forces which act upon it. Why should one outcome be regarded as better than another? Why should existing species be regarded as better than others that could take their place (whether now or in several thousand or million years)? If a species is an essence, then why not say that any population with a distinct genetic character is an essence? Why not an individual, etc.?

Although I cannot rule out the possibility that someone might someday state a criterion of value which would include in its scope all and only those things and states that environmental ethicists want included and which would satisfy the formal requirements of ethics, it seems to me to be unlikely. The problem, as I have suggested, is that how we view the world, how we divide it up into individuals and systems, what we regard as good or bad for an individual or a system is too arbitrary—i.e., too dependent on point of view, interest, and convenience—to support an ethic that purports to be based on value in nature independent of our interests and concerns. Every criterion of environmental value seems to depend for its application on our taking a particular point of view, or on using a particular set of concepts, and there does not seem to be any nonarbitrary reason (as far as ethics is concerned) for taking up one point of view or using one set of concepts rather than another. As a result, the attempt to be objective and to avoid assuming an interest or a point of view risks vacuity or at the very least producing something too indeterminate in scope to be useful as an ethic.

If there is something so fundamentally wrong with environmental ethics, then two questions are critical. First, is any ethic possible at all? If environmental ethics is flawed, then what reason do we have for supposing that a nonenvironmental ethic is any less arbitrary or any more likely to satisfy formal requirements? Second, if environmental ethics is impossible, what we are going to say about those practices—our destruction of wilderness, species, environmental systems, creatures—which environmental ethicists believe that they need an environmental ethics to condemn?

To establish the possibility of ethics it is enough to give an example of a system of ethics which satisfies the formal criteria for an ethic and includes reference to intrinsic values. I believe that an ethic which takes individuals who have a point of view (i.e., that are centers of consciousness) as having intrinsic value—an ethic which supports the satisfaction of the interests, needs, and preferences of those individuals—is such an ethic. The fact that individuals have a point of view, and can therefore be caused anguish, frustration, pleasure, or joy as the result of what we do, is one good reason for valuing such individuals and requiring that their interests and preferences be a matter of moral concern to all rational, morally sensitive agents. Equally important, in satisfying the formal requirements of an ethic, is the fact that individuals with a point of view—with consciousness, desires, feelings, goals, etc.,—are self-defining. What in the framework of the ethic counts as an individual is not an arbitrary matter, not a question of the valuer's point of view. That they have a point of view decides the matter. It is also not an arbitrary matter, not a question of the valuer's point of view, that counts as the good of such individuals. They themselves define their good by how they feel, what they say, by how they behave. Because we are able to use the value criteria of this ethic consistently, nonvacuously, and without any overwhelming problems of undecidability, it is clear that a nonarbitrary ethic is possible, though, of course, much more discussion is needed to determine what an ethic which values sentient beings requires of us.[15]

If environmental ethics is nonviable, if we are stuck with a sentient-being-centered ethic, then what about the needs of the environment? What do we say about the intuitions and attitudes of those people who think that we ought to preserve wilderness, species, and nonsentient organisms even when these things have no instrumental value for human beings or other sentient creatures? Do we really need an environmental ethic in order to do justice to the standpoint of the environmentalist who abhors a defoliated jungle or a strip-mined hillside?

Perhaps the reason why so many people think we do is because they are operating within an unnecessarily narrow conception of what is instrumentally valuable. They think that within the framework of a human-centered or sentient-being-centered ethic we can only value natural things if they satisfy a well-defined need which we (or some other sentient creatures) have. Dissatisfied with this ethic, they mistakenly want to argue for the preservation of something that is not valuable in this sense and thus feel obliged to embark on the project of constructing an environmental ethic. Fortunately, there is another possibility. We might be able to argue that something is valuable and therefore ought to be preserved because our lives and our conception of ourselves will be enhanced—in a spiritual sense—if we learn to appreciate it for what it is and we learn how to live with it in harmony.[16] Although such an approach does not pretend to go beyond the human point of view, beyond our concerns and interests, it is not confined to a concern with obvious and traditional material and psychological needs, for it permits us to define a new conception of what we are as individuals and what a good life is. My view is that those who want to develop a deep approach to environmental concerns have everything to gain and nothing to lose by following this approach. Environmental ethics is not only a dead end, but also an unnecessary diversion.

Endnotes

1. Arne Naess, "The Shallow and the Deep, Long Range Ecology Movement: A Summary," *Inquiry* 16 (1973): 96.

2. John Rodman, "Liberation of Nature," *Inquiry* 20 (1977): 89.

3. Val and Richard Routley, "Human Chauvinism and Environmental Ethics," in *Environmental Philosophy,* edited by Don Mannison, Michael McRobbie, and Richard Routley, Monograph Series 2, Department of Philosophy, Research School of Social Sciences (Canberra: Australian National University, 1980). See also Val and Richard Routley, "Against the Inevitability of Human Chauvinism," in Kenneth Goodpaster and Kenneth Sayre, eds., *Ethics and the Problems of the 21st Century* (Notre Dame: University of Notre Dame Press, 1987).

4. Holmes Rolston III, *Environmental Ethics* (Philadelphia: Temple University Press, 1988). See also *Philosophy Gone Wild: Essays in Environmental Ethics* (Buffalo: Prometheus Books, 1986).

5. Paul W. Taylor, *Respect for Nature: A Theory of Environmental Ethics* (Princeton: Princeton University Press, 1986).

6. The Routleys ("Human Chauvinism and Environmental Ethics") hold that there are no values without valuers, but that valuers can and should value things which are not instrumental to their needs and purposes (p. 152). Rolston (*Environmental Ethics*) argues that values are as much in the world as objects like trees (see chap. 3); see also Holmes Rolston, III, "Are Values in Nature Subjective or Objective?"

in Robert Elliot and Arran Gare, eds., *Environmental Philosophy* (University Park: Pennsylvania University Press, 1983). Although these accounts of values are metaphysically diverse, they nevertheless satisfy what I call the minimum conditions for being intrinsic values.

7. See for example the Routleys' arguments against human chauvinism in "Against the Inevitability of Human Chauvinism."

8. One might distinguish between being decidable in principle and being decidable in practice. For example, hedonistic utilitarianism might satisfy "in principle" decidability because it gives us a formula for determining what we should do (in terms of the net balance of pleasure and pain). However, in practice it may be impossible to apply this formula, and if this is so, then hedonistic utilitarianism gives us no way in practice of determining what we ought to do. It is undecidability in practice with which I am concerned here.

9. Taylor, *Respect for Nature*, p. 129.

10. Ibid., p. 66.

11. Taylor's strategy is, first, to persuade us that nonsentient organisms have a good of their own, and thus are plausible candidates for having what he calls an *inherent worth*, and, second, to argue that if we adopt a biocentric outlook (which includes accepting the argument against the

superiority of human beings and sentient creatures criticized above), we will then believe that they do indeed have inherent worth.

12. Routley and Routley, "Human Chauvinism and Environmental Ethics," p. 170.

13. In Richard Sylvan, "Critique of Deep Ecology," *Radical Philosophy* no. 40 (1984): 2–12, and no. 41 (1985): 1–22, Richard Sylvan (Routley) does suggest that natural systems are not the only things which satisfy his criterion of value. However, he does not attempt to say exactly what satisfies.

14. Rolston's *Environmental Ethics*, chap. 7.

15. Peter Singer in *Expanding Circle* (Oxford: Clarendon Press, 1981) also insists that distinction between sentient and nonsentient creatures is not an arbitrary one from a moral point of view. He stresses the importance of creatures being capable of feeling pleasure or pain, whereas I emphasize the importance of their having a point of view. Whether this difference makes a difference to the content of an ethic is not something I can explore here.

16. I argue in more detail for this position in "Preservation of Wilderness and the Good Life," in Elliot and Gare, *Environmental Philosophy*.

---

52. *Lifeboat Ethics: The Case against Helping the Poor*

Garrett Hardin

> In his essay, Garrett Hardin critically assesses the environmentalists' metaphor that the earth is a "spaceship" and that all persons and institutions should share equally in its resources. Instead of conceiving of the earth as a spaceship, Hardin argues that it is more accurately described as a lifeboat, in which are found the rich of the world and on which the poor of the world seek to come aboard. Unfortunately, the survival of those on the lifeboat will be threatened if too many of the poor are accommodated. As a result, Hardin concludes that it is in the best interests of the world community to allocate resources to the poor only sparingly, lest we severely deplete the earth's resources to the detriment of all.

Environmentalists use the metaphor of the earth as a "spaceship" in trying to persuade countries, industries, and people to stop wasting and polluting our natural

Reprinted with permission from "Living on a Lifeboat," *Bioscience* 24(10) (1974): 561–568.

resources. Since we all share life on this planet, they argue, no single person or institution has the right to destroy, waste, or use more than a fair share of its resources.

But does everyone on earth have an equal right to an equal share of its resources? The spaceship metaphor can be dangerous when used by misguided idealists to justify suicidal policies for sharing our resources through uncontrolled immigration and foreign aid. In their enthusiastic but unrealistic generosity, they confuse the ethics of a spaceship with those of a lifeboat.

A true spaceship would have to be under the control of a captain, since no ship could possibly survive if its course were determined by committee. Spaceship Earth certainly has no captain; the United Nations is merely a toothless tiger, with little power to enforce any policy upon its bickering members.

If we divide the world crudely into rich nations and poor nations, two thirds of them are desperately poor, and only one third comparatively rich, with the United States the wealthiest of all. Metaphorically each rich nation can be seen as a lifeboat full of comparatively rich people. In the ocean outside each lifeboat swim the poor of the world, who would like to get in, or at least to share some of the wealth. What should the lifeboat passengers do?

First, we must recognize the limited capacity of any lifeboat. For example, a nation's land has a limited capacity to support a population and as the current energy crisis has shown us, in some ways we have already exceeded the carrying capacity of our land.

Adrift in a Moral Sea

So here we sit, say fifty people in our lifeboat. To be generous, let us assume it has room for ten more, making a total capacity of sixty. Suppose the fifty of us in the lifeboat see 100 others swimming in the water outside, begging for admission to our boat or for handouts. We have several options: we may be tempted to try to live by the Christian ideal of being "our brother's keeper," or by the Marxist ideal of "to each according to his needs." Since the needs of all in the water are the same, and since they can all be seen as "our brothers," we could take them all into our boat, making a total of 150 in a boat designed for sixty. The boat swamps, everyone drowns. Complete justice, complete catastrophe.

Since the boat has an unused excess capacity of ten more passengers, we could admit just ten more to it. But which ten do we let in? How do we choose? Do we pick the best ten, the neediest ten, "first come, first served"? And what do we say to the ninety we exclude? If we do let an extra ten into our lifeboat, we will have lost our "safety factor," an engineering principle of critical importance. For example, if we don't leave room for excess capacity as a safety factor in our country's agriculture, a new plant disease or a bad change in the weather could have disastrous consequences.

Suppose we decide to preserve our small safety factor and admit no more to the lifeboat. Our survival is then possible, although we shall have to be constantly on guard against boarding parties.

While this last solution clearly offers the only means of our survival, it is morally abhorrent to many people. Some say they feel guilty about their good luck. My reply is simple: "Get out and yield your place to others." This may solve the problem of the guilt-ridden person's conscience, but it does not change the ethics of the lifeboat. The needy person to whom the guilt-ridden person yields his place will not himself feel guilty about his good luck. If he did, he would not climb aboard. The net result of conscience-stricken people giving up their unjustly held seats is the elimination of that sort of conscience from the lifeboat.

This is the basic metaphor within which we must work out our solutions. Let us now enrich the image, step by step, with substantive additions from the real world, a world that must solve real and pressing problems of overpopulation and hunger.

The harsh ethics of the lifeboat become even harsher when we consider the reproductive differences between the rich nations and the poor nations. The people inside the lifeboats are doubling in numbers every eighty-seven years; those swimming around outside are doubling, on the average, every thirty-five years, more than twice as fast as the rich. And since the world's resources are dwindling, the difference in prosperity between the rich and the poor can only increase.

As of 1973, the U.S. had a population of 210 million people, who were increasing by 0.8 percent per year. Outside our lifeboat, let us imagine another 210 million people, (say the combined populations of Colombia, Ecuador, Venezuela, Morocco, Pakistan, Thailand, and the Philippines) who are increasing at a rate of 3.3 percent per year. Put differently, the doubling time for this aggregate population is twenty-one years, compared with eighty-seven years for the U.S.

Multiplying the Rich and the Poor

Now suppose the U.S. agreed to pool its resources with those seven countries, with everyone receiving an equal share. Initially the ratio of Americans to non-Americans in this model would be one-to-one. But consider what the ratio would be after eighty-seven years, by which time the Americans would have doubled to a population of 420 million. By then, doubling every twenty-one years, the other group would have swollen to 354 billion. Each American would have to share the available resources with more than eight people.

But, one could argue, this discussion assumes that current population trends will continue, and they may not. Quite so. Most likely the rate of population increase will decline much faster in the U.S. than it will in the other countries, and there does not seem to be much we can do about it. In sharing with "each according to his needs," we must recognize that needs are determined by population size, which is determined by the rate of reproduction, which at present is regarded as a sovereign right of every nation, poor or not. This being so, the philanthropic load created by the sharing ethic of the spaceship can only increase.

The Tragedy of the Commons

The fundamental error of spaceship ethics, and the sharing it requires, is that it leads to what I call "the tragedy of the commons." Under a system of private property, the men who own property recognize their responsibility to care for it, for if they don't they will eventually suffer. A farmer, for instance, will allow no more cattle in a pasture than its carrying capacity justifies. If he overloads it, erosion sets in, weeds take over, and he loses the use of the pasture.

If a pasture becomes a commons open to all, the right of each to use it may not be matched by a corresponding responsibility to protect it. Asking everyone to use it with discretion will hardly do, for the considerate herdsman who refrains from overloading the commons suffers more than a selfish one who says his needs are greater. If everyone would restrain himself, all would be well; but it takes only one less than everyone to ruin a system of voluntary restraint. In a crowded world of less than perfect human beings, mutual ruin is inevitable if there are no controls. This is the tragedy of the commons.

One of the major tasks of education today should be the creation of such an acute awareness of the dangers of the commons that people will recognize its many varieties. For example, the air and water have become polluted because they are treated as commons. Further growth in the population or per capita conversion of natural resources into pollutants will only make the problem worse. The same holds true for the fish of the oceans. Fishing fleets have nearly disappeared in many parts of the world; technological improvements in the art of fishing are hastening the day of complete ruin. Only the replacement of the system of the commons with a responsible system of control will save the land, air, water and oceanic fisheries.

The World Food Bank

In recent years there has been a push to create a new commons called a World Food Bank, an international depository of food reserves to which nations would contribute according to their abilities and from which they would draw according to their needs. This humanitarian proposal has received support from many liberal international groups, and from such prominent citizens as Margaret Mead, U.N. Secretary General Kurt Waldheim, and Senators Edward Kennedy and George McGovern.

A world food bank appeals powerfully to our humanitarian impulses. But before we rush ahead with such a plan, let us recognize where the greatest political push comes from, lest we be disillusioned later. Our experience with the "Food for Peace program," or Public Law 480, gives us the answer. This program moved billions of dollars worth of U.S. surplus grain to food-short, population-long countries during the past two decades. But when P.L. 480 first became law, a headline in the business magazine *Forbes* revealed the real power behind it: "Feeding the World's Hungry Millions: How It Will Mean Billions for U.S. Business."

And indeed it did. In the years 1960 to 1970, U.S. taxpayers spent a total of $7.9 billion on the Food for Peace program. Between 1948 and 1970, they also paid an additional $50 billion for other economic-aid programs, some of which went for food and food-producing machinery and technology. Though all U.S. taxpayers were forced to contribute to the cost of P.L. 480, certain special interest groups gained handsomely under the program. Farmers did not have to contribute the grain; the Government, or rather the taxpayers, bought it from them at full market prices. The increased demand raised prices of farm products generally. The manufacturers of farm machinery, fertilizers and pesticides benefited by the farmers' extra efforts to grow more food. Grain elevators profited from storing the surplus until it could be shipped. Railroads made money hauling it to ports, and shipping lines profited from carrying it overseas. The implementation of P.L. 480 required the creation of a vast Government bureaucracy, which then acquired its own vested interest in continuing the program regardless of its merits.

Extracting Dollars

Those who proposed and defended the Food for Peace program in public rarely mentioned its importance to any of these special interests. The public emphasis was always on its humanitarian effects. The combination of silent selfish interests and highly vocal humanitarian apologists made a powerful and successful lobby for extracting money from taxpayers. We can expect the same lobby to push now for the creation of a World Food Bank.

However great the potential benefit to selfish interests, it should not be a decisive argument against a truly humanitarian program. We must ask if such a program would actually do more good than harm, not only momentarily but also in the long run. Those who propose the food bank usually refer to a current "emergency" or "crisis" in terms of world food supply. But what is an emergency? Although they may be infrequent and sudden, everyone knows that emergencies will occur from time to time. A well-run family, company, organization or country prepares for the likelihood of accidents and emergencies. It expects them, it budgets for them, it saves for them.

Learning the Hard Way

What happens if some organizations or countries budget for accidents and others do not? If each country is solely responsible for its own well-being, poorly managed ones will suffer. But they can learn from experience. They may mend their ways, and learn to

budget for infrequent but certain emergencies. For example, the weather varies from year to year, and periodic crop failures are certain. A wise and competent government saves out of the production of the good years in anticipation of bad years to come. Joseph taught this policy to Pharaoh in Egypt more than 2,000 years ago. Yet the great majority of the governments in the world today do not follow such a policy. They lack either the wisdom or the competence, or both. Should those nations that do manage to put something aside be forced to come to the rescue each time an emergency occurs among the poor nations?

"But it isn't their fault!" some kindhearted liberals argue. "How can we blame the poor people who are caught in an emergency? Why must they suffer for the sins of their governments?" The concept of blame is simply not relevant here. The real question is, What are the operational consequences of establishing a world food bank? If it is open to every country every time a need develops, slovenly rulers will not be motivated to take Joseph's advice. Someone will always come to their aid. Some countries will deposit food in the world food bank, and others will withdraw it. There will be almost no overlap. As a result of such solutions to food shortage emergencies, the poor countries will not learn to mend their ways, and will suffer progressively greater emergencies as their populations grow.

The Ratchet Effect

An "international food bank" is really, then, not a true bank but a disguised one-way transfer device for moving wealth from rich countries to poor. In the absence of such a bank, in a world inhabited by individually responsible sovereign nations, the population of each nation would repeatedly go through a cycle of the sort shown in Figure 1. P_2 is greater than P_1, either in absolute numbers or because a deterioration of the

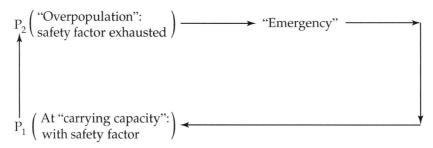

Figure 1

food supply has removed the safety factor and produced a dangerously low ratio of resources to population. P_2 may be said to represent a state of overpopulation which becomes obvious upon the appearance of an "accident," e.g., a crop failure. If the "emergency" is not met by outside help, the population drops back to the "normal" level—the "carrying capacity" of the environment—or even below. In the absence of population control by a sovereign, sooner or later the population grows to P_2 again and the cycle repeats. The long-term population curve is an irregularly fluctuating one, equilibrating more or less about the carrying capacity.

A demographic cycle of this sort obviously involves great suffering in the restrictive phase, but such a cycle is normal to any independent country with inadequate population control. The third century theologian Tertullian expressed what must have been the recognition of many wise men when he wrote: "The scourges of pestilence, famine, wars, and earthquakes have come to be regarded as a blessing to overcrowded nations, since they serve to prune away the luxuriant growth of the human race."

Only under a strong and farsighted sovereign—which theoretically could be the people themselves, democratically organized—can a population equilibrate at some set point below the carrying capacity, thus avoiding the pains normally caused by periodic and unavoidable disasters. For this happy state to be achieved it is necessary that those in power be able to contemplate with equanimity the "waste" of surplus food in times of bountiful harvests. It is essential that those in power resist the temptation to convert extra food into extra babies. On the public relations level it is necessary that the phrase "surplus food" be replaced by "safety factor."

But wise sovereigns seem not to exist in the poor world today. The most anguishing problems are created by poor countries that are governed by rulers insufficiently wise and powerful. If such countries can draw on a world food bank in times of "emergency," the population *cycle* of Figure 1 will be replaced by the population *escalator* of Figure 2. The input of food from a food bank acts as the pawl of a rachet, preventing the population from retracing its steps to a lower level. Reproduction pushes the population upward; inputs from the world bank prevent its moving downward. Population size escalates, as does the absolute magnitude of "accidents" and "emergencies." The process is brought to an end only by the total collapse of the whole system, producing a catastrophe of scarcely imaginable proportions.

Such are the implications of the well-meant sharing of food in a world of irresponsible reproduction. . . .

Population Control the Crude Way

On the average, poor countries undergo a 2.5 percent increase in population each year; rich countries, about 0.8 percent. Only rich countries have anything in the way of food reserves set aside, and even they do not have as much as they should. Poor countries have none. If poor countries received no food from the outside, the rate of their population growth would be

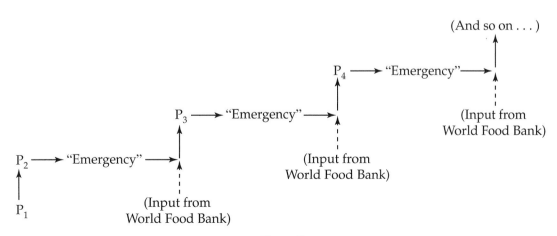

Figure 2

periodically checked by crop failures and famines. But if they can always draw on a world food bank in time of need, their population can continue to grow unchecked, and so will their "need" for aid. In the short run, a world food bank may diminish that need, but in the long run it actually increases the need without limit.

Without some system of worldwide food sharing, the proportion of people in the rich and poor nations might eventually stabilize. The overpopulated poor countries would decrease in numbers, while the rich countries that had room for more people would increase. But with a well-meaning system of sharing, such as a world food bank, the growth differential between the rich and the poor countries will not only persist, it will increase. Because of the higher rate of population growth in the poor countries of the world, 88 percent of today's children are born poor, and only 12 percent rich. Year by year the ratio becomes worse, as the fast-reproducing poor outnumber the slow-reproducing rich.

A world food bank is thus a commons in disguise. People will have more motivation to draw from it than to add to any common store. The less provident and less able will multiply at the expense of the abler and more provident, bringing eventual ruin upon all who share in the commons. Besides, any system of "sharing" that amounts to foreign aid from the rich nations to the poor nations will carry the taint of charity, which will contribute little to the world peace so devoutly desired by those who support the idea of a world food bank.

As past U.S. foreign-aid programs have amply and depressingly demonstrated, international charity frequently inspires mistrust and antagonism rather than gratitude on the part of the recipient nation.

Chinese Fish and Miracle Rice

The modern approach to foreign aid stresses the export of technology and advice, rather than money and food. As an ancient Chinese proverb goes: "'Give a man a fish and he will eat for a day; teach him how to fish and he will eat for the rest of his days." Acting on this advice, the Rockefeller and Ford Foundations have financed a number of programs for improving agriculture in the hungry nations. Known as the "Green Revolution," these programs have led to the development of "miracle rice" and "miracle wheat," new strains that offer bigger harvests and greater resistance to crop damage. Norman Borlaug, the

Nobel Prize winning agronomist who, supported by the Rockefeller Foundation, developed "miracle wheat," is one of the most prominent advocates of a world food bank.

Whether or not the Green Revolution can increase food production as much as its champions claim is a debatable but possibly irrelevant point. Those who support this well-intended humanitarian effort should first consider some of the fundamentals of human ecology. Ironically, one man who did was the late Alan Gregg, a vice president of the Rockefeller Foundation. Two decades ago he expressed strong doubts about the wisdom of such attempts to increase food production. He likened the growth and spread of humanity over the surface of the earth to the spread of cancer in the human body, remarking that "cancerous growths demand food; but, as far as I know, they have never been cured by getting it."

Overloading the Environment

Every human born constitutes a draft on all aspects of the environment: food, air, water, forests, beaches, wildlife, scenery and solitude. Food can, perhaps, be significantly increased to meet a growing demand. But what about clean beaches, unspoiled forests, and solitude? If we satisfy a growing population's need for food, we necessarily decrease its per capita supply of the other resources needed by men.

India, for example, now has a population of 600 million, which increases by 15 million each year. This population already puts a huge load on a relatively impoverished environment. The country's forests are now only a small fraction of what they were three centuries ago, and floods and erosion continually destroy the insufficient farmland that remains. Every one of the 15 million new lives added to India's population puts an additional burden on the environment, and increases the economic and social costs of crowding. However humanitarian our intent, every Indian life saved through medical or nutritional assistance from abroad diminishes the quality of life for those who remain, and for subsequent generations. If rich countries make it possible, through foreign aid, for 600 million Indians to swell to 1.2 billion in a mere twenty-eight years, as their current growth rate threatens, will future generations of Indians thank us for hastening the destruction of their environment? Will our good intentions be sufficient excuse for the consequences of our actions?

My final example of a commons in action is one for which the public has the least desire for rational discussion—immigration. Anyone who publicly questions the wisdom of current U.S. immigration policy is promptly charged with bigotry, prejudice, ethnocentrism, chauvinism, isolationism or selfishness. Rather than encounter such accusations, one would rather talk about other matters, leaving immigration policy to wallow in the crosscurrents of special interests that take no account of the good of the whole, or the interests of posterity.

Perhaps we still feel guilty about things we said in the past. Two generations ago the popular press frequently referred to Dagos, Wops, Polacks, Chinks and Krauts, in articles about how America was being "overrun" by foreigners of supposedly inferior genetic stock. But because the implied inferiority of foreigners was used then as justification for keeping them out, people now assume that restrictive policies could only be based on such misguided notions. There are other grounds.

A Nation of Immigrants

Just consider the numbers involved. Our Government acknowledges a net inflow of 400,000 immigrants a year. While we have no hard data on the extent of illegal entries, educated guesses put the figure at about 600,000 a year. Since the natural increase (excess of births over deaths) of the resident population now runs about 1.7 million per year, the yearly gain from immigration amounts to at least 19 percent of the total annual increase, and may be as much as 37 percent if we include the estimate for illegal immigrants. Considering the growing use of birth-control devices, the potential effect of educational campaigns by such organizations as Planned Parenthood Federation of America and Zero Population Growth, and the influence of inflation and the housing shortage, the fertility rate of American women may decline so much that immigration could account for all the yearly increase in population. Should we not at least ask if that is what we want?

For the sake of those who worry about whether the "quality" of the average immigrant compares favorably with the quality of the average resident, let us assume that immigrants and nativeborn citizens are of exactly equal quality, however one defines that term. We will focus here only on quantity; and since our conclusions will depend on nothing else, all charges of bigotry and chauvinism become irrelevant.

Immigration vs. Food Supply

World food banks *move food to the people*, hastening the exhaustion of the environment of the poor countries. Unrestricted immigration, on the other hand, *moves people to the food*, thus speeding up the destruction of the environment of the rich countries. We can easily understand why poor people should want to make this latter transfer, but why should rich hosts encourage it?

As in the case of foreign-aid programs, immigration receives support from selfish interests and humanitarian impulses. The primary selfish interest in unimpeded immigration is the desire of employers for cheap labor, particularly in industries and trades that offer degrading work. In the past, one wave of foreigners after another was brought into the U.S. to work at wretched jobs for wretched wages. In recent years the Cubans, Puerto Ricans and Mexicans have had this dubious honor. The interests of the employers of cheap labor mesh well with the guilty silence of the country's liberal intelligentsia. White Anglo-Saxon Protestants are particularly reluctant to call for a closing of the doors to immigration for fear of being called bigots.

But not all countries have such reluctant leadership. Most educated Hawaiians, for example, are keenly aware of the limits of their environment, particularly in terms of population growth. There is only so much room on the islands, and the islanders know it. To Hawaiians, immigrants from the other forty-nine states present as great a threat as those from other nations. At a recent meeting of Hawaiian government officials in Honolulu, I had the ironic delight of hearing a speaker, who like most of his audience was of Japanese ancestry, ask how the country might practically and constitutionally close its doors to further immigration. One member of the audience countered: "How can we shut the doors now? We have many friends and relatives in Japan that we'd like to bring here some day so that they can enjoy Hawaii too." The Japanese-American speaker smiled sympathetically and answered: "Yes, but we have children now, and someday we'll have grandchildren too. We can bring more people here from Japan only by giving away some of the land that we hope to pass on to our grandchildren some day. What right do we have to do that?"

At this point, I can hear U.S. liberals asking: "How can you justify slamming the door once you're inside? You say that immigrants should be kept out. But aren't we all immigrants, or the descendents of immigrants? If we insist on staying, must we not admit all others?"

Our craving for intellectual order leads us to seek and prefer symmetrical rules and morals: a single rule for me and everybody else; the same rule yesterday, today, and tomorrow. Justice, we feel, should not change with time and place.

We Americans of non-Indian ancestry can look upon ourselves as the descendants of thieves who are guilty morally, if not legally, of stealing this land from its Indian owners. Should we then give back the land to the now living American descendants of those Indians? However morally or logically sound this proposal may be, I, for one, am unwilling to live by it and I know no one else who is. Besides, the logical consequence would be absurd. Suppose that, intoxicated with a sense of pure justice, we should decide to turn our land over to the Indians. Since all our wealth has also been derived from the land, wouldn't we be morally obliged to give that back to the Indians too?

Pure Justice vs. Reality

Clearly, the concept of pure justice produces an infinite regression to absurdity. Centuries ago, wise men invented statutes of limitations to justify the rejection of such pure justice, in the interest of preventing continual disorder. The law zealously defends property rights, but only relatively recent property rights. Drawing a line after an arbitrary time has elapsed may be unjust, but the alternatives are worse.

We are all the descendants of thieves, and the world's resources are inequitably distributed. But we must begin the journey to tomorrow from the point where we are today. We cannot remake the past. We cannot safely divide the wealth equitably among all peoples so long as people reproduce at different rates. To do so would guarantee that our grandchildren, and everyone else's grandchildren, would have only a ruined world to inhabit.

To be generous with one's own possessions is quite different from being generous with those of posterity. We should call this point to the attention of those who, from a commendable love of justice and equality, would institute a system of the commons, either in the form of a world food bank, or of unrestricted immigration. We must convince them if we wish to save at least some parts of the world from environmental ruin.

Without a true world government to control reproduction and the use of available resources, the sharing ethic of the spaceship is impossible. For the foreseeable future, our survival demands that we govern our actions by the ethics of a lifeboat, harsh though they may be. Posterity will be satisfied with nothing less.

Part 8

Human Cloning

53. Cloning Human Beings: An Assessment of the Ethical Issues Pro and Con

DAN W. BROCK

Assessing the possibility of human cloning from a utilitarian perspective, Dan Brock offers an evaluation of the short- and long-term benefits and liabilities that could be expected. Brock focuses carefully on six discernible benefits: (1) the relief of infertility for various individuals, (2) the removal of some of the risk of hereditary disease in reproduction, (3) the creation of organs or tissue for research and transplantation, (4) the possible cloning of persons who held special meaning for others, such as loved ones, (5) the possibility of cloning geniuses or the extraordinarily talented, and (6) the new areas of research and knowledge that cloning could generate. On the negative side, Brock principally explores concerns about the violation of one's right to a unique identity and the right to ignorance about one's own future. Brock sees no decisive moral case either way but urges no legal prohibition at this time of further research or possible future cloning.

The world of science and the public at large were both shocked and fascinated by the announcement in the journal *Nature* by Ian Wilmut and his colleagues that they had successfully cloned a sheep from a single cell of an adult sheep (Wilmut, 1997). But many were troubled or apparently even horrified at the prospect that cloning of adult humans by the same process might be possible as well. The response of most scientific and political leaders to the prospect of human cloning, indeed of Dr. Wilmut as well, was of immediate and strong condemnation.

A few more cautious voices were heard both suggesting some possible benefits from the use of human

This essay is a shorter version of a paper prepared for the National Bioethics Advisory Commission.

I want to acknowledge with gratitude the invaluable help of my research assistant, Insoo Hyun, on this paper. He not only made it possible to complete the paper on the National Bioethics Advisory Commission's tight schedule, but also improved it with a number of insightful substantive suggestions.

cloning in limited circumstances and questioning its too quick prohibition, but they were a clear minority. A striking feature of these early responses was that their strength and intensity seemed far to outrun the arguments and reasons offered in support of them— they seemed often to be "gut level" emotional reactions rather than considered reflections on the issues. Such reactions should not be simply dismissed, both because they may point us to important considerations otherwise missed and not easily articulated, and because they often have a major impact on public policy. But the formation of public policy should not ignore the moral reasons and arguments that bear on the practice of human cloning—these must be articulated in order to understand and inform people's more immediate emotional responses. This essay is an effort to articulate, and to evaluate critically, the main moral considerations and arguments for and against human cloning. Though many people's religious beliefs inform their views on human cloning, and it is often difficult to separate religious from secular positions, I shall restrict myself to arguments and reasons that can be given a clear secular formulation.

On each side of the issue there are two distinct kinds of moral arguments brought forward. On the one hand, some opponents claim that human cloning would violate fundamental moral or human rights, while some proponents argue that its prohibition would violate such rights. While moral and even human rights need not be understood as absolute, they do place moral restrictions on permissible actions that an appeal to a mere balance of benefits over harms cannot justify overriding; for example, the rights of human subjects in research must be respected even if the result is that some potentially beneficial research is more difficult or cannot be done. On the other hand, both opponents and proponents also cite the likely harms and benefits, both to individuals and to society, of the practice. I shall begin with the arguments in support of permitting human cloning, although with no implication that it is the stronger or weaker position.

Moral Arguments in Support of Human Cloning

Is There a Moral Right To Use Human Cloning?

What moral right might protect at least some access to the use of human cloning? A commitment to individual liberty, such as defended by J. S. Mill, requires that individuals be left free to use human cloning if they so choose and if their doing so does not cause significant harms to others, but liberty is too broad in scope to be an uncontroversial moral right (Mill, 1859; Rhodes, 1995). Human cloning is a means of reproduction (in the most literal sense) and so the most plausible moral right at stake in its use is a right to reproductive freedom or procreative liberty (Robertson, 1994a; Brock, 1994), understood to include both the choice not to reproduce, for example, by means of contraception or abortion, and also the right to reproduce.

The right to reproductive freedom is properly understood to include the right to use various assisted reproductive technologies (ARTs), such as in vitro fertilization (IVF), oocyte donation, and so forth. The reproductive right relevant to human cloning is a negative right, that is, a right to use ARTs without interference by the government or others when made available by a willing provider. The choice of an assisted means of reproduction should be protected by reproductive freedom even when it is not the only means for individuals to reproduce, just as the choice among different means of preventing conception is protected by reproductive freedom. However, the case for permitting the use of a particular means of reproduction is strongest when it is necessary for particular individuals to be able to procreate at all, or to do so without great burdens or harms to themselves or others. In some cases human cloning could be the only means for individuals to procreate while retaining a biological tie to their child, but in other cases different means of procreating might also be possible.

It could be argued that human cloning is not covered by the right to reproductive freedom because whereas current ARTs and practices covered by that right are remedies for inabilities to reproduce sexually, human cloning is an entirely new means of reproduction; indeed, its critics see it as more a means of manufacturing humans than of reproduction. Human cloning is a different means of reproduction than sexual reproduction, but it is a means that can serve individuals' interest in reproducing. If it is not protected by the moral right to reproductive freedom, I believe that must be not because it is a new means of reproducing, but instead because it has other objectionable or harmful features; I shall evaluate these other ethical objections to it later.

When individuals have alternative means of procreating, human cloning typically would be chosen because it replicates a particular individual's genome. The reproductive interest in question then is not simply reproduction itself, but a more specific interest in choosing what kind of children to have. The right to reproductive freedom is usually understood to cover at least some choice about the kind of children one will have. Some individuals choose reproductive partners in the hope of producing offspring with desirable traits. Genetic testing of fetuses or preimplantation embryos for genetic disease or abnormality is done to avoid having a child with those diseases or abnormalities. Respect for individual self-determination, which is one of the grounds of a moral right to reproductive freedom, includes respecting individuals' choices about whether to have a child with a condition that will place severe burdens on them, and cause severe burdens to the child itself.

The less a reproductive choice is primarily the determination of one's own life, but primarily the determination of the nature of another, as in the case of human cloning, the more moral weight the interests of that other person, that is the cloned child, should have in decisions that determine its nature (Annas, 1994). But even then parents are typically accorded substantial, but not unlimited, discretion in shaping the persons their children will become, for example, through education and other childrearing decisions. Even if not part of reproductive freedom, the right to raise one's children as one sees fit, within limits mostly determined by the interests of the children, is also a right to determine within limits what kinds of persons one's children will become. This right includes not just preventing certain diseases or harms to children, but selecting and shaping desirable features and traits in one's children. The use of human cloning is one way to exercise that right.

Public policy and the law now permit prospective parents to conceive, or to carry a conception to term, when there is a significant risk or even certainty that the child will suffer from a serious genetic disease. Even when others think the risk or certainty of genetic disease makes it morally wrong to conceive, or to carry a fetus to term, the parents' right to reproductive freedom permits them to do so. Most possible harms to a cloned child are less serious than the genetic harms with which parents can now permit their offspring to be conceived or born.

I conclude that there is good reason to accept that a right to reproductive freedom presumptively includes both a right to select the means of reproduction, as well as a right to determine what kind of children to have, by use of human cloning. However, the specific reproductive interest of determining what kind of children to have is less weighty than are other reproductive interests and choices whose impact falls more directly and exclusively on the parents rather than the child. Even if a moral right to reproductive freedom protects the use of human cloning, that does not settle the moral issue about human cloning, since there may be other moral rights in conflict with this right, or serious enough harms from human cloning to override the right to use it; this right can be thought of as establishing a serious moral presumption supporting access to human cloning.

What Individual or Social Benefits Might Human Cloning Produce?

Largely Individual Benefits

The literature on human cloning by nuclear transfer or by embryo splitting contains a few examples of circumstances in which individuals might have good reasons to want to use human cloning. However, human cloning seems not to be the unique answer to any great or pressing human need and its benefits appear to be limited at most. What are the principal possible benefits of human cloning that might give individuals good reasons to want to use it?

1. Human cloning would be a new means to relieve the infertility some persons now experience. Human cloning would allow women who have no ova or men who have no sperm to produce an offspring that is biologically related to them (Eisenberg, 1976; Robertson, 1994b, 1997; LaBar, 1984). Embryos might also be cloned, by either nuclear transfer or embryo splitting, in order to increase the number of embryos for implantation and improve the chances of successful conception (NABER, 1994). The benefits from human cloning to relieve infertility are greater the more persons there are who cannot overcome their infertility by any other means acceptable to them. I do not know of data on this point, but the numbers who would use cloning for this reason are probably not large.

The large number of children throughout the world possibly available for adoption represents an alternative solution to infertility only if we are prepared to discount as illegitimate the strong desire of many persons, fertile and infertile, for the experience of pregnancy and for having and raising a child biologically related to them. While not important to all infertile (or fertile) individuals, it is important to many and is respected and met through other forms of assisted reproduction that maintain a biological connection when that is possible; that desire does not become illegitimate simply because human cloning would be the best or only means of overcoming an individual's infertility.

2. Human cloning would enable couples in which one party risks transmitting a serious hereditary disease to an offspring to reproduce without doing so (Robertson, 1994b). By using donor sperm or egg donation, such hereditary risks can generally be avoided now without the use of human cloning. These procedures may be unacceptable to some couples, however, or at least considered less desirable than human cloning because they introduce a third party's genes into their reproduction instead of giving their offspring only the genes of one of them. Thus, in some cases human cloning could be a reasonable means of preventing genetically transmitted harms to offspring. Here too, we do not know how many persons would want to use human cloning instead of other means of avoiding the risk of genetic transmission of a disease or of accepting the risk of transmitting the disease, but the numbers again are probably not large.

3. Human cloning to make a later twin would enable a person to obtain needed organs or tissues for transplantation (Robertson, 1994b, 1997; Kahn, 1989; Harris, 1992). Human cloning would solve the problem of finding a transplant donor whose organ or tissue is an acceptable match and would eliminate, or drastically reduce, the risk of transplant rejection by the host. The availability of human cloning for this purpose would amount to a form of insurance to enable treatment of certain kinds of medical conditions. Of course, sometimes the medical need would be too urgent to permit waiting for the cloning, gestation, and development that is necessary before tissues or organs can be obtained for transplantation. In other cases, taking an organ also needed by the later twin, such as a heart or a liver, would be impermissible because it would violate the later twin's rights.

Such a practice can be criticized on the ground that it treats the later twin not as a person valued and loved for his or her own sake, as an end in itself in Kantian terms, but simply as a means for benefiting another. This criticism assumes, however, that only this one motive defines the reproduction and the relation of the person to his or her later twin. The well-known case some years ago in California of the Ayalas, who conceived in the hopes of obtaining a source for a bone marrow transplant for their teenage daughter suffering from leukemia, illustrates the mistake in this

assumption. They argued that whether or not the child they conceived turned out to be a possible donor for their daughter, they would value and love the child for itself, and treat it as they would treat any other member of their family. That one reason they wanted it, as a possible means to saving their daughter's life, did not preclude their also loving and valuing it for its own sake; in Kantian terms, it was treated as a possible means to saving their daughter, but not *solely as a means,* which is what the Kantian view proscribes.

Indeed, when people have children, whether by sexual means or with the aid of ARTs, their motives and reasons for doing so are typically many and complex, and include reasons less laudable than obtaining lifesaving medical treatment, such as having someone who needs them, enabling them to live on their own, qualifying for government benefit programs, and so forth. While these are not admirable motives for having children and may not bode well for the child's upbringing and future, public policy does not assess prospective parents' motives and reasons for procreating as a condition of their doing so.

4. Human cloning would enable individuals to clone someone who had special meaning to them, such as a child who had died (Robertson, 1994b). There is no denying that if human cloning were available, some individuals would want to use it for this purpose, but their desire usually would be based on a deep confusion. Cloning such a child would not replace the child the parents had loved and lost, but would only create a different child with the same genes. The child they loved and lost was a unique individual who had been shaped by his or her environment and choices, not just his or her genes, and more importantly who had experienced a particular relationship with them. Even if the later cloned child could not only have the same genes but also be subjected to the same environment, which of course is impossible, it would remain a different child than the one they had loved and lost because it would share a different history with them (Thomas, 1974). Cloning the lost child might help the parents accept and move on from their loss, but another already existing sibling or a new child who was not a clone might do this equally well; indeed, it might do so better since the appearance of the cloned later twin would be a constant reminder of the child they had lost. Nevertheless, if human cloning enabled some individuals to clone a person who had special meaning to them and doing so gave them deep satisfaction, that would be a benefit to them even if their reasons for wanting to do so, and the satisfaction they in turn received, were based on a confusion.

Largely Social Benefits

5. Human cloning would enable the duplication of individuals of great talent, genius, character, or other exemplary qualities. Unlike the first four reasons for human cloning which appeal to benefits to specific individuals, this reason looks to benefits to the broader society from being able to replicate extraordinary individuals— a Mozart, Einstein, Gandhi, or Schweitzer (Lederberg, 1966; McKinnell, 1979). Much of the appeal of this reason, like much support and opposition to human cloning, rests largely on a confused and false assumption of genetic determinism, that is, that one's genes fully determine what one will become, do, and accomplish. What made Mozart, Einstein, Gandhi, and Schweitzer the extraordinary individuals they were was the confluence of their particular genetic endowments with the environments in which they were raised and lived and the particular historical moments they in different ways seized. Cloning them would produce individuals with the same genetic inheritances (nuclear transfer does not even produce 100 percent genetic identity, although for the sake of exploring the moral issues I have followed the common assumption that it does), but it is not possible to replicate their environments or the historical contexts in which they lived and their greatness flourished. We do not know the degree or specific respects in which any individual's greatness depended on "nature" or "nurture," but we do know that it always depends on an interaction of them both. Cloning could not even replicate individuals' extraordinary capabilities, much less their accomplishments, because these too are the product of their inherited genes and their environments, not of their genes alone.

None of this is to deny that Mozart's and Einstein's extraordinary musical and intellectual capabilities, nor even Gandhi's and Schweitzer's extraordinary moral greatness, were produced in part by their unique genetic inheritances. Cloning them might well produce individuals with exceptional capacities, but we simply do not know how close their clones would be in capacities or accomplishments to the great individuals from whom they were cloned. Even so, the hope for exceptional, even if less and different, accomplishment from cloning such extraordinary individuals might be a reasonable ground for doing so.

Worries here about abuse, however, surface quickly. Whose standards of greatness would be used to select individuals to be cloned? Who would control use of human cloning technology for the benefit of society or mankind at large? Particular groups, segments of society, or governments might use the technology for their own benefit, under the cover of benefiting society or even mankind at large.

6. Human cloning and research on human cloning might make possible important advances in scientific knowledge, for example, about human development (Walters, 1982; Smith, 1983). While important potential advances in scientific or medical knowledge from human cloning or human cloning research have frequently been cited, there are at least three reasons for caution about such claims. First, there is always considerable uncertainty about the nature and importance of the new scientific or medical knowledge to which a dramatic new technology like human cloning will lead; the road to new knowledge is never mapped in advance and takes many unexpected turns. Second, we do not know what new knowledge from human cloning or human cloning research could also be gained by other means that do not have the problematic moral features to which its opponents object. Third, what human cloning research would be compatible with ethical and legal requirements for the use of human subjects in research is complex, controversial, and largely unexplored. Creating human clones solely for the purpose of research would be to use them solely for the benefit of others without their consent, and so unethical. But if and when human cloning was established to be safe and effective, then new scientific knowledge might be obtained from its use for legitimate, nonresearch reasons.

Although there is considerable uncertainty concerning most of human cloning's possible individual and social benefits that I have discussed, and although no doubt it could have other benefits or uses that we cannot yet envisage, I believe it is reasonable to conclude at this time that human cloning does not seem to promise great benefits or uniquely to meet great human needs. Nevertheless, despite these limited benefits, a moral case can be made that freedom to use human cloning is protected by the important moral right to reproductive freedom. I shall turn now to what moral rights might be violated, or harms produced, by research on or use of human cloning.

Moral Arguments Against Human Cloning

Would the Use of Human Cloning Violate Important Moral Rights?

Many of the immediate condemnations of any possible human cloning following Wilmut's cloning of Dolly claimed that it would violate moral or human rights, but it was usually not specified precisely, or often even at all, what rights would be violated (WHO, 1997). I shall consider two possible candidates for such a right: a right to have a unique identity and a right to ignorance about one's future or to an open future. Claims that cloning denies individuals a unique identity are common, but I shall argue that even if there is a right to a unique identity, it could not be violated by human cloning. The right to ignorance or to an open future has only been explicitly defended, to my knowledge, by two commentators, and in the context of human cloning, only by Hans Jonas; it supports a more promising, but in my view ultimately unsuccessful, argument that human cloning would violate an important moral or human right.

Is there a moral or human right to a unique identity, and if so would it be violated by human cloning? For human cloning to violate a right to a unique identity, the relevant sense of identity would have to be genetic identity, that is, a right to a unique unrepeated genome. This would be violated by human cloning, but is there any such right? It might be thought that cases of identical twins show there is no such right because no one claims that the moral or human rights of the twins have been violated. However, this consideration is not conclusive (Kass, 1985; NABER, 1994). Only human actions can violate others' rights; outcomes that would constitute a rights violation if deliberately caused by human action are not a rights violation if a result of natural causes. If Arthur deliberately strikes Barry on the head so hard as to cause his death, he violates Barry's right not to be killed; if lightning strikes Cheryl, causing her death, her right not to be killed has not been violated. Thus, the case of twins does not show that there could not be a right to a unique genetic identity.

What is the sense of identity that might plausibly be what each person has a right to have uniquely, that constitutes the special uniqueness of each individual (Macklin 1994; Chadwick 1982)? Even with the same genes, homozygous twins are numerically distinct and

not identical, so what is intended must be the various properties and characteristics that make each individual qualitatively unique and different from others. Does having the same genome as another person undermine that unique qualitative identity? Only on the crudest genetic determinism, according to which an individual's genes completely and decisively determine everything else about the individual, all his or her other nongenetic features and properties, together with the entire history or biography that constitutes his or her life. But there is no reason whatever to believe that kind of genetic determinism. Even with the same genes, differences in genetically identical twins' psychological and personal characteristics develop over time together with differences in their life histories, personal relationships, and life choices; sharing an identical genome does not prevent twins from developing distinct and unique personal identities of their own.

We need not pursue whether there is a moral or human right to a unique identity—no such right is found among typical accounts and enumerations of moral or human rights—because even if there is such a right, sharing a genome with another individual as a result of human cloning would not violate it. The idea of the uniqueness, or unique identity, of each person historically predates the development of modern genetics. A unique genome thus could not be the ground of this long-standing belief in the unique human identity of each person.

I turn now to whether human cloning would violate what Hans Jonas called a right to ignorance, or what Joel Feinberg called a right to an open future (Jonas, 1974; Feinberg, 1980). Jonas argued that human cloning in which there is a substantial time gap between the beginning of the lives of the earlier and later twin is fundamentally different from the simultaneous beginning of the lives of homozygous twins that occur in nature. Although contemporaneous twins begin their lives with the same genetic inheritance, they do so at the same time, and so in ignorance of what the other who shares the same genome will by his or her choices make of his or her life.

A later twin created by human cloning, Jonas argues, knows, or at least believes she knows, too much about herself. For there is already in the world another person, her earlier twin, who from the same genetic starting point has made the life choices that are still in the later twin's future. It will seem that her life has already been lived and played out by another, that her fate is already determined; she will lose the sense of human possibility in freely and spontaneously creating her own future and authentic self. It is tyrannical, Jonas claims, for the earlier twin to try to determine another's fate in this way.

Jonas's objection can be interpreted so as not to assume either a false genetic determinism, or a belief in it. A later twin might grant that he is not determined to follow in his earlier twin's footsteps, but nevertheless the earlier twin's life might always haunt him, standing as an undue influence on his life, and shaping it in ways to which others' lives are not vulnerable. But the force of the objection still seems to rest on the false assumption that having the same genome as his earlier twin unduly restricts his freedom to create a different life and self than the earlier twin's. Moreover, a family environment also importantly shapes children's development, but there is no force to the claim of a younger sibling that the existence of an older sibling raised in that same family is an undue influence on the younger sibling's freedom to make his own life for himself in that environment. Indeed, the younger twin or sibling might gain the benefit of being able to learn from the older twin's or sibling's mistakes.

A closely related argument can be derived from what Joel Feinberg has called a child's right to an open future. This requires that others raising a child not so close off the future possibilities that the child would otherwise have as to eliminate a reasonable range of opportunities for the child autonomously to construct his or her own life. One way this right might be violated is to create a later twin who will believe her future has already been set for her by the choices made and the life lived by her earlier twin.

The central difficulty in these appeals to a right either to ignorance or to an open future is that the right is not violated merely because the later twin is likely to *believe* that his future is already determined, when that belief is clearly false and supported only by the crudest genetic determinism. If we know the later twin will falsely believe that his open future has been taken from him as a result of being cloned, even though in reality it has not, then we know that cloning will cause the twin psychological distress, but not that it will violate his right. Jonas's right to ignorance, and Feinberg's right of a child to an open future, are not violated by human cloning, though they do point to psychological harms that a later twin may be likely to experience and that I will take up later.

Neither a moral or human right to a unique identity, nor one to ignorance and an open future, would be violated by human cloning. There may be other moral or human rights that human cloning would violate, but I do not know what they might be. I turn now to consideration of the harms that human cloning might produce.

What Individual or Social Harms Might Human Cloning Produce?

There are many possible individual or social harms that have been posited by one or another commentator and I shall only try to cover the more plausible and significant of them.

Largely Individual Harms

1. *Human cloning would produce psychological distress and harm in the later twin.* No doubt knowing the path in life taken by one's earlier twin might often have several bad psychological effects (Callahan, 1993; LaBar, 1984; Macklin, 1994; McCormick, 1993; Studdard, 1978; Rainer, 1978; Verhey, 1994). The later twin might feel, even if mistakenly, that her fate has already been substantially laid out, and so have difficulty freely and spontaneously taking responsibility for and making her own fate and life. The later twin's experience or sense of autonomy and freedom might be substantially diminished, even if in actual fact they are diminished much less that it seems to her. She might have a diminished sense of her own uniqueness and individuality, even if once again these are in fact diminished little or not at all by having an earlier twin with the same genome. If the later twin is the clone of a particularly exemplary individual, perhaps with some special capabilities and accomplishments, she might experience excessive pressure to reach the very high standards of ability and accomplishment of the earlier twin (Rainer, 1978). These various psychological effects might take a heavy toll on the later twin and be serious burdens to her.

While psychological harms of these kinds from human cloning are certainly possible, and perhaps even likely in some cases, they remain at this point only speculative since we have no experience with human cloning and the creation of earlier and later twins. Nevertheless, if experience with human cloning confirmed that serious and unavoidable psychological harms typically occurred to the later twin, that would be a serious moral reason to avoid the practice. Intuitively at least, psychological burdens and harms seem more likely and more serious for a person who is only one of many identical later twins cloned from one original source, so that the clone might run into another identical twin around every street corner. This prospect could be a good reason to place sharp limits on the number of twins that could be cloned from any one source.

One argument has been used by several commentators to undermine the apparent significance of potential psychological harms to a later twin (Chadwick, 1982; Robertson, 1994b, 1997; Macklin, 1994). The point derives from a general problem, called the nonidentity problem, posed by the philosopher Derek Parfit, although not originally directed to human cloning (Parfit, 1984). Here is the argument. Even if all these psychological burdens from human cloning could not be avoided for any later twin, they are not harms to the twin, and so not reasons not to clone the twin. That is because the only way for the twin to avoid the harms is never to be cloned, and so never to exist at all. But these psychological burdens, hard though they might be, are not so bad as to make the twin's life, all things considered, not worth living. So the later twin is not harmed by being given a life even with these psychological burdens, since the alternative of never existing at all is arguably worse—he or she never has a worthwhile life—but certainly not better for the twin. And if the later twin is not harmed by having been created with these unavoidable burdens, then how could he or she be wronged by having been created with them? And if the later twin is not wronged, then why is any wrong being done by human cloning? This argument has considerable potential import, for if it is sound it will undermine the apparent moral importance of any bad consequence of human cloning to the later twin that is not so serious as to make the twin's life, all things considered, not worth living.

I defended elsewhere the position regarding the general case of genetically transmitted handicaps, that if one could have a *different* child without comparable burdens (for the case of cloning, by using a different method of reproduction which did not result in a later twin), there is as strong a moral reason to do so as there would be not to cause similar burdens to an already existing child (Brock, 1995). Choosing to create the later twin with serious psychological burdens instead of a different person who would be free of them, without weighty overriding reasons for choosing the former, would be morally irresponsible or wrong, even if doing so does not harm or wrong the later twin who could only exist with the burdens. These issues are too detailed and complex to pursue here and the nonidentity problem remains controversial and not fully resolved, but at the least, the argument for disregarding the psychological burdens to the later twin because he or she could not exist without them is controversial, and in my view mistaken. Such psychological harms, as I shall continue to call them, are speculative, but they should not be disregarded because of the nonidentity problem.

2. Human cloning procedures would carry unacceptable risks to the clone. There is no doubt that attempts to clone a human being at the present time would carry unacceptable risks to the clone. Further research on the procedure with animals, as well as research to establish its safety and effectiveness for humans, is clearly necessary before it would be ethical to use the procedure on humans. One risk to the clone is the failure to implant, grow, and develop successfully, but this would involve the embryo's death or destruction long before most people or the law consider it to be a person with moral or legal protections of its life.

Other risks to the clone are that the procedure in some way goes wrong, or unanticipated harms come to the clone; for example, Harold Varmus, director of the National Institutes of Health, raised the concern that a cell many years old from which a person is cloned could have accumulated genetic mutations during its years in another adult that could give the resulting clone a predisposition to cancer or other diseases of aging (Weiss, 1997). Risks to an ovum donor (if any), a nucleus donor, and a woman who receives the embryo for implantation would likely be ethically acceptable with the informed consent of the involved parties.

I believe it is too soon to say whether unavoidable risks to the clone would make human cloning forever unethical. At a minimum, further research is needed to better define the potential risks to humans. But we should not insist on a standard that requires risks to be lower than those we accept in sexual reproduction, or in other forms of ART.

Largely Social Harms

3. Human cloning would lessen the worth of individuals and diminish respect for human life. Unelaborated claims to this effect were common in the media after the announcement of the cloning of Dolly. Ruth Macklin explored and criticized the claim that human cloning would diminish the value we place on, and our respect for, human life because it would lead to persons being viewed as replaceable (Macklin, 1994). As I have argued concerning a right to a unique identity, only on a confused and indefensible notion of human identity is a person's identity determined solely by his or her genes, and so no individual could be fully replaced by a later clone possessing the same genes. Ordinary people recognize this clearly. For example, parents of a child dying of a fatal disease would find it insensitive and ludicrous to be told they should not grieve for their coming loss because it is possible to replace him by cloning him; it is *their child who is dying* whom they love and value, and that child and his importance to them is not replaceable by a cloned later twin. Even if they would also come to love and value a later twin as much as they now love and value their child who is dying, that would be to love and value that *different child* for its own sake, not as a replacement for the child they lost. Our relations of love and friendship are with distinct, historically situated individuals with whom over time we have shared experiences and our lives, and whose loss to us can never be replaced.

A different version of this worry is that human cloning would result in persons' worth or value seeming diminished because we would come to see persons as able to be manufactured or "handmade." This demystification of the creation of human life would reduce our appreciation and awe of human life and of its natural creation. It would be a mistake, however, to conclude that a person created by human cloning is of less value or is less worthy of respect than one created by sexual reproduction. At least outside of some religious contexts, it is the nature of a being, not how it is created, that is the source of its value and makes it worthy of respect. For many people, gaining a scientific understanding of the truly extraordinary complexity of human reproduction and development increases, instead of decreases, their awe of the process and its product.

A more subtle route by which the value we place on each individual human life might be diminished could come from the use of human cloning with the aim of creating a child with a particular genome, either the genome of another individual especially meaningful to those doing the cloning or an individual with exceptional talents, abilities, and accomplishments. The child then comes to be objectified, valued only as an object and for its genome, or at least for its genome's expected phenotypic expression, and no longer recognized as having the intrinsic equal moral value of all persons, simply as persons. For the moral value and respect due all persons to come to be seen as resting only on the instrumental value of individuals and of their particular qualities to others would be to fundamentally change the moral status properly accorded to persons. Individuals would lose their moral standing as full and equal members of the moral community, replaced by the different instrumental value each has to others.

Such a change in the equal moral value and worth accorded to persons should be avoided at all costs, but it is far from clear that such a change would result from permitting human cloning. Parents, for example, are quite capable of distinguishing their children's intrinsic value, just as individual persons, from their instrumental value based on their particular qualities or properties. The equal moral value and respect due all persons simply as persons is not incompatible with the different instrumental value of different individuals; Einstein and an untalented physics graduate student have vastly different value as scientists, but share and are entitled to equal moral value and respect as persons. It is a confused mistake to conflate these two kinds of value and respect. If making a large number of clones from one original person would be more likely to foster it, that would be a further reason to limit the number of clones that could be made from one individual.

4. Human cloning might be used by commercial interests for financial gain. Both opponents and proponents of human cloning agree that cloned embryos should not be able to be bought and sold. In a science fiction frame of mind, one can imagine commercial interests offering genetically certified and guaranteed embryos for sale, perhaps offering a catalogue of different embryos cloned from individuals with a variety of talents, capacities, and other desirable properties. This would be a fundamental violation of the equal moral respect and dignity owed to all persons, treating them instead as objects to be differentially valued, bought, and sold in the marketplace. Even if embryos are not yet persons at the time they would be purchased or sold, they would be being valued, bought, and sold for the persons they will become. The moral consensus against any commercial market in embryos, cloned or otherwise, should be enforced by law whatever the public policy ultimately is on human cloning.

5. Human cloning might be used by governments or other groups for immoral and exploitative purposes. In *Brave New World*, Aldous Huxley imagined cloning individuals who have been engineered with limited abilities and conditioned to do, and to be happy doing, the menial work that society needed done (Huxley, 1932). Selection and control in the creation of people was exercised not in the interests of the persons created, but in the interests of the society and at the expense of the persons created; nor did it serve individuals' interests in reproduction and parenting. Any use of human cloning for such purposes would exploit the clones solely as means for the benefit of others, and would violate the equal moral respect and dignity they are owed as full moral persons. If human cloning is permitted to go forward, it should be with regulations that would clearly prohibit such immoral exploitation.

Fiction contains even more disturbing or bizarre uses of human cloning, such as Mengele's creation of many clones of Hitler in Ira Levin's *The Boys from Brazil* (Levin, 1976), Woody Allen's science fiction cinematic spoof *Sleeper* in which a dictator's only remaining part, his nose, must be destroyed to keep it from being cloned, and the contemporary science fiction film *Blade Runner*. These nightmare scenarios may be quite improbable, but their impact should not be underestimated on public concern with technologies like human cloning. Regulation of human cloning must assure the public that even such far-fetched abuses will not take place.

Conclusion

Human cloning has until now received little serious and careful ethical attention because it was typically dismissed as science fiction, and it stirs deep, but difficult to articulate, uneasiness and even revulsion in many people. Any ethical assessment of human cloning at this point must be tentative and provisional. Fortunately, the science and technology of human cloning are not yet in hand, and so a public and professional debate is possible without the need for a hasty, precipitate policy response.

The ethical pros and cons of human cloning, as I see them at this time, are sufficiently balanced and uncertain that there is not an ethically decisive case either for or against permitting it or doing it. Access to human cloning can plausibly be brought within a moral right to reproductive freedom, but its potential legitimate uses appear few and do not promise substantial benefits. It is not a central component of the moral right to reproductive freedom and it does not uniquely serve any major or pressing individual or social needs. On the other hand, contrary to the pronouncements of many of its opponents, human cloning seems not to be a violation of moral or human rights. But it does risk some significant individual or social harms, although most are based on common public confusions about genetic determinism, human identity, and the effects of human cloning. Because most potential harms feared from human cloning remain speculative, they seem insufficient to warrant at this time a complete legal prohibition of either research on or later use of human cloning,

if and when its safety and efficacy are established. Legitimate moral concerns about the use and effects of human cloning, however, underline the need for careful public oversight of research on its development, together with a wider public and professional debate and review before cloning is used on human beings.

References

Annas, G. J. (1994). "Regulatory Models for Human Embryo Cloning: The Free Market, Professional Guidelines, and Government Restrictions." *Kennedy Institute of Ethics Journal* 4,3:235–249.

Brock, D. W. (1994). "Reproductive Freedom: Its Nature, Bases and Limits," in *Health Care Ethics: Critical Issues for Health Professionals*, eds. D. Thomasma and J. Monagle. Gaithersbrug, MD: Aspen Publishers.

Brock, D. W. (1995). "The Non-Identity Problem and Genetic Harm." *Bioethics* 9:269–275.

Callahan, D. (1993). "Perspective on Cloning: A Threat to Individual Uniqueness." *Los Angeles Times,* November 12, 1993:B7.

Chadwick, R. F. (1982). "Cloning." *Philosophy* 57:201–209.

Eisenberg, L. (1976). "The Outcome as Cause: Predestination and Human Cloning." *The Journal of Medicine and Philosophy* 1:318–331.

Feinberg, J. (1980). "The Child's Right to an Open Future," in *Whose Child? Children's Rights, Parental Authority, and State Power,* eds. W. Aiken and H. LaFollette. Totowa, NJ: Rowman and Littlefield.

Harris, J. (1992). *Wonderwoman and Superman: The Ethics of Biotechnology.* Oxford: Oxford University Press.

Huxley, A. (1932). *Brave New World.* London: Chalto and Winders.

Jonas, H. (1974). *Philosophical Essays: From Ancient Creed to Technological Man.* Englewood Cliffs, NJ: Prentice-Hall.

Kahn, C. (1989). "Can We Achieve Immortality?" *Free Inquiry* 9:14–18.

Kass, L. (1985). *Toward a More Natural Science.* New York: The Free Press.

LaBar, M. (1984). "The Pros and Cons of Human Cloning." *Thought* 57:318–333.

Lederberg, J. (1966). "Experimental Genetics and Human Evolution." *The American Naturalist* 100:519–531.

Levin, I. (1976). *The Boys from Brazil.* New York: Random House.

Macklin, R. (1994). "Splitting Embryos on the Slippery Slope: Ethics and Public Policy." *Kennedy Institute of Ethics Journal* 4:209–226.

McCormick, R. (1993). "Should We Clone Humans?" *Christian Century* 110:1148–1149.

McKinnell, R. (1979). *Cloning: A Biologist Reports.* Minneapolis, MN: University of Minnesota Press.

Mill, J. S. (1859). *On Liberty.* Indianapolis, IN: Bobbs-Merrill Publishing.

NABER (National Advisory Board on Ethics in Reproduction) (1994). "Report on Human Cloning Through Embryo Splitting: An Amber Light." *Kennedy Institute of Ethics Journal* 4:251–282.

Parfit, D. (1984). *Reasons and Persons.* Oxford: Oxford University Press.

Rainer, J. D. (1978). "Commentary." *Man and Medicine: The Journal of Values and Ethics in Health Care* 3:115–117.

Rhodes, R. (1995). "Clones, Harms, and Rights." *Cambridge Quarterly of Healthcare Ethics* 4:285–290.

Robertson, J. A. (1994a). *Children of Choice: Freedom and the New Reproductive Technologies.* Princeton, NJ: Princeton University Press.

Robertson, J. A. (1994b). "The Question of Human Cloning." *Hastings Center Report* 24:6–14.

Robertson, J. A. (1997). "A Ban on Cloning and Cloning Research is Unjustified." Testimony Presented to the National Bioethics Advisory Commission, March 1997.

Smith, G. P. (1983). "Intimations of Immortality: Clones, Cyrons and the Law." *University of New South Wales Law Journal* 6:119–132.

Studdard, A. (1978). "The Lone Clone." *Man and Medicine: The Journal of Values and Ethics in Health Care* 3:109–114.

Thomas, L. (1974). "Notes of a Biology Watcher: On Cloning a Human Being." *New England Journal of Medicine* 291: 1296–1297.

Verhey, A. D. (1994). "Cloning: Revisiting an Old Debate." *Kennedy Institute of Ethics Journal* 4:227–234.

Walters, W. A. W. (1982)."Cloning, Ectogenesis, and Hybrids: Things to Come?" in *Test-Tube Babies,* eds. W. A. W. Walters and P. Singer. Melbourne: Oxford University Press.

Weiss, R. (1997). "Cloning Suddenly Has Government's Attention." *International Herald Tribune,* March 7, 1997.

WHO (World Health Organization Press Office). (March 11, 1997). "WHO Director General Condemns Human Cloning." World Health Organization, Geneva, Switzerland.

Wilmut, I., et al. (1997). "Viable Offspring Derived from Fetal and Adult Mammalian Cells." *Nature* 385:810–813.

54. *The Wisdom of Repugnance: Why We Should Ban the Cloning of Humans*

Leon Kass

Leon Kass traces the scientific and cultural developments that gave rise to cloning and suggests that the practice in many ways embodies the current opinions of the age. In particular, he cites the growing acceptance of divorce, out-of-wedlock births, and the erosion of the consensus that stable marriages provide the ideal setting for the producing and raising of children as central factors in the movement toward social acceptance of cloning. For Kass, our initial reactions to such a practice are, and should continue to be, repugnance, disgust, and revulsion. Cloning is to be rejected because it violates, fundamentally, the ontological meaning of reproduction and compromises the identity and the individuality of the cloned.

Our habit of delighting in news of scientific and technological breakthroughs has been sorely challenged by the birth announcement of a sheep named Dolly. Though

This article originally appeared in the *New Republic, 1997.* Reprinted with permission from the author.

Dolly shares with previous sheep the "softest clothing, woolly bright," William Blake's question, "Little Lamb, who made thee?" has for her a radically different answer: Dolly was, quite literally, made. She is the work not of nature or nature's God but of man, an Englishman, Ian Wilmut, and his fellow scientists. What's more, Dolly came into being not only asexually—ironically, just like "He [who] calls Himself a Lamb"—but also as, the genetically identical copy (and the perfect incarnation of the form or blueprint) of a mature ewe, of whom she is a clone. This long-awaited yet not quite expected success in cloning a mammal raised immediately the prospect— and the specter—of cloning human beings: "I a child and Thou a lamb," despite our differences, have always been equal candidates for creative making, only now, by means of cloning, we may both spring from the hand of man playing at being God.

After an initial flurry of expert comment and public consternation, with opinion polls showing overwhelming opposition to cloning human beings, President Clinton ordered a ban on all federal support for human cloning research (even though none was being supported) and charged the National Bioethics Advisory Commission to report in ninety days on the ethics of human cloning research. A fateful decision is at hand. To clone or not to clone a human being is no longer an academic question.

Taking Cloning Seriously, Then and Now

Cloning first came to public attention roughly thirty years ago, following the successful asexual production, in England, of a clutch of tadpole clones by the technique of nuclear transplantation. Much has happened in the intervening years. It has become harder, not easier, to discern the true meaning of human cloning. We have in some sense been softened up to the idea—through movies, cartoons, jokes and intermittent commentary in the mass media, some serious, most lighthearted. We have become accustomed to new practices in human reproduction: not just *in vitro* fertilization, but also embryo manipulation, embryo donation and surrogate pregnancy. Animal biotechnology has yielded transgenic animals and a burgeoning science of genetic engineering, easily and soon to be transferable to humans.

Perhaps the most depressing feature of the discussions that immediately followed the news about Dolly was their ironical tone, their genial cynicism, their moral fatigue: "an udder way of making lambs" (*Nature*), "who will cash in on breakthrough in cloning?" (*The Wall Street Journal*), "is cloning baaaaaaaad?" (*The Chicago Tribune*). Gone from the scene are the wise and courageous voices of Theodosius Dobzhansky (genetics), Hans Jonas (philosophy) and Paul Ramsey (theology) who, only twenty-five years ago, all made powerful moral arguments

against ever cloning a human being. We are now too sophisticated for such argumentation; we wouldn't be caught in public with a strong moral stance, never mind an absolutist one. We are all, or almost all, postmodernists now.

Cloning turns out to be the perfect embodiment of the ruling opinions of our new age. Thanks to the sexual revolution, we are able to deny in practice, and increasingly in thought, the inherent procreative teleology of sexuality itself. But if sex has no intrinsic connection to generating babies, babies need have no necessary connection to sex. Thanks to feminism and the gay rights movement, we are increasingly encouraged to treat the natural heterosexual difference and its preeminence as a matter of "cultural construction." But if male and female are not normatively complementary and generatively significant, babies need not come from male and female complementarity. Thanks to the prominence and the acceptability of divorce and out-of-wedlock births, stable, monogamous marriage as the ideal home for procreation is no longer the agreed-upon cultural norm. For this new dispensation, the clone is the ideal emblem: the ultimate "single-parent child."

Thanks to our belief that all children should be wanted children (the more high-minded principle we use to justify contraception and abortion), sooner or later only those children who fulfill our wants will be fully acceptable. Through cloning, we can work our wants and wills on the very identity of our children exercising control as never before. Thanks to modern notions of individualism and the rate of cultural change, we see ourselves not as linked to ancestors and defined by traditions, but as projects for our own self-creation, not only as self-made men but also man-made selves; and self-cloning is simply an extension of such rootless and narcissistic self-recreation.

Unwilling to acknowledge our debt to the past and unwilling to embrace the uncertainties and the limitations of the future, we have a false relation to both: cloning personifies our desire fully to control the future, while being subject to no controls ourselves. Enchanted and enslaved by the glamour of technology, we have lost our awe and wonder before the deep mysteries of nature and of life. We cheerfully take our own beginnings in our hands and, like the last man, we blink.

Part of the blame for our complacency lies, sadly, with the field of bioethics itself, and its claim to expertise in these moral matters. Bioethics was founded by people who understood that the new biology touched and threatened the deepest matters of our humanity: bodily integrity, identity and individuality, lineage and kinship, freedom and self-command, eros and aspiration, and the relations and strivings of body and soul. With its capture by analytic philosophy, however, and its inevitable routinization and professionalization, the field has by and large come to content itself with analyzing moral arguments, reacting to new technological developments and taking on emerging issues of public policy, all performed with a naive faith that the evils we fear can all be avoided by compassion, regulation, and a respect for autonomy. Bioethics has made some major contributions in the protection of human subjects and in other areas where personal freedom is threatened; but its practitioners, with few exceptions, have turned the big human questions into pretty thin gruel.

One reason for this is that the piecemeal formation of public policy tends to grind down large questions of morals into small questions of procedure. Many of the country's leading bioethicists have served on national commissions or state task forces and advisory boards, where, understandably, they have found utilitarianism to be the only ethical vocabulary acceptable to all participants in discussing issues of law, regulation and public policy. As many of these commissions have been either officially under the aegis of NIH or the Health and Human Services Department, or otherwise dominated by powerful voices for scientific progress, the ethicists have for the most part been content, after some "values clarification" and wringing of hands, to pronounce their blessings upon the inevitable. Indeed, it is the bioethicists, not the scientists, who are now the most articulate defenders of human cloning: the two witnesses testifying before the National Bioethics Advisory Commission in favor of cloning human beings were bioethicists, eager to rebut what they regard as the irrational concerns of those of us in opposition. For human cloning, though it is in some respects continuous with previous reproductive technologies, also represents something radically new—in itself and in its easily foreseeable consequences. The stakes are very high indeed. I exaggerate, but in the direction of the truth, when I insist that we are faced with having to decide nothing less than whether human procreation is going to remain human, whether children are going to be made rather than begotten, whether it is a good thing, humanly speaking, to say yes in principle to the road which leads (at best) to the dehumanized rationality of *Brave New World.* This is not business as usual, to be fretted about for a while but finally to be given our seal of approval.

We must rise to the occasion and make our judgments as if the future of our humanity hangs in the balance. For so it does.

The State of the Art

Some cautions are in order and some possible misconceptions need correcting. For a start, cloning is not Xeroxing. As has been reassuringly reiterated, the clone of Mel Gibson, though his genetic double, would enter the world hairless, toothless and peeing in his diapers, just like any other human infant. Moreover, the success rate, at least at first, will probably not be very high: the British transferred 277 adult nuclei into enucleated sheep eggs, and implanted twenty-nine clonal embryos, but they achieved the birth of only one live lamb clone. For this reason, among others, it is unlikely that, at least for now, the practice would be very popular, and there is no immediate worry of mass-scale production of multicopies. The need of repeated surgery to obtain eggs and, more crucially, of numerous borrowed wombs for implantation will surely limit use, as will the expense; besides, almost everyone who is able will doubtless prefer nature's sexier way of conceiving.

Still, for the tens of thousands of people already sustaining over 200 assisted-reproduction clinics in the United States and already availing themselves of *in vitro* fertilization, intracytoplasmic sperm injection and other techniques of assisted reproduction, cloning would be an option with virtually no added fuss (especially when the success rate improves). Should commercial interests develop in "nucleus-banking," as they have in sperm-banking; should famous athletes or other celebrities decide to market their DNA the way they now market their autographs and just about everything else; should techniques of embryo and germline genetic testing and manipulation arrive as anticipated, increasing the use of laboratory assistance in order to obtain "better" babies—should all this come to pass, then cloning, if it is permitted, could become more than a marginal practice simply on the basis of free reproductive choice, even without any social encouragement to upgrade the gene pool or to replicate superior types. Moreover, if laboratory research on human cloning proceeds, even without any intention to produce cloned humans, the existence of cloned human embryos in the laboratory, created to begin with only for research purposes, would surely pave the way for later baby-making implantations.

In anticipation of human cloning, apologists and proponents have already made clear possible uses of the perfected technology, ranging from the sentimental and compassionate to the grandiose. They include: providing a child for an infertile couple; "replacing" a beloved spouse or child who is dying or has died; avoiding the risk of genetic disease; permitting reproduction for homosexual men and lesbians who want nothing sexual to do with the opposite sex; securing a genetically identical source of organs or tissues perfectly suitable for transplantation; getting a child with a genotype of one's own choosing, not excluding oneself; replicating individuals of great genius, talent or beauty—having a child who really could "be like Mike"; and creating large sets of genetically identical humans suitable for research on, for instance, the question of nature versus nurture, or for special missions in peace and war (not excluding espionage), in which using identical humans would be an advantage. Most people who envision the cloning of human beings, of course, want none of these scenarios. That they cannot say why is not surprising. What is surprising, and welcome, is that, in our cynical age, they are saying anything at all.

The Wisdom of Repugnance

"Offensive." "Grotesque." "Revolting." "Repugnant." "Repulsive." These are the words most commonly heard regarding the prospect of human cloning. Such reactions come both from the man or woman in the street and from the intellectuals, from believers and atheists, from humanists and scientists.

People are repelled by many aspects of human cloning. They recoil from the prospect of mass production of human beings, with large clones of look-alikes, compromised in their individuality; the idea of father-son or mother-daughter twins; the bizarre prospects of a woman giving birth to and rearing a genetic copy of herself, her spouse, or even her deceased father or mother; the grotesqueness of conceiving a child as an exact replacement for another who has died; the utilitarian creation of embryonic genetic duplicates of oneself, to be frozen away or created when necessary, in case of need for homologous tissues or organs for transplantation; the narcissism of those who would clone themselves and the arrogance of others who think they know who deserves to be cloned or which genotype any child-to-be should be thrilled to receive; the Frankensteinian hubris to create human

life and increasingly to control its destiny; man playing God. Almost no one finds any of the suggested reasons for human cloning compelling; almost everyone anticipates its possible misuses and abuses. Moreover, many people feel oppressed by the sense that there is probably nothing we can do to prevent it from happening. This makes the prospect all the more revolting.

Revulsion is not an argument; and some of yesterday's repugnances are today calmly accepted—though, one must add, not always for the better. In crucial cases, however, repugnance is the emotional expression of deep wisdom, beyond reason's power fully to articulate it. Can anyone really give an argument fully adequate to the horror which is father-daughter incest (even with consent), or having sex with animals, or mutilating a corpse, or eating human flesh, or even just (just!) raping or murdering another human being? Would anybody's failure to give full rational justification for his or her revulsion at these practices make that revulsion ethically suspect? Not at all. On the contrary, we are suspicious of those who think that they can rationalize away our horror, say, by trying to explain the enormity of incest with arguments only about the genetic risks of inbreeding.

The repugnance at human cloning belongs in this category. We are repelled by the prospect of cloning human beings not because of the strangeness or novelty of the undertaking, but because we intuit and feel, immediately and without argument, the violation of things that we rightfully hold dear. Repugnance, here as elsewhere, revolts against the excesses of human willfulness, warning us not to transgress what is unspeakably profound. Indeed, in this age in which everything is held to be permissible so long as it is freely done, in which our given human nature no longer commands respect, in which our bodies are regarded as mere instruments of our autonomous rational wills, repugnance may be the only voice left that speaks up to defend the central core of our humanity. Shallow are the souls that have forgotten how to shudder.

The goods protected by repugnance are generally overlooked by our customary ways of approaching all new biomedical technologies. The way we evaluate cloning ethically will in fact be shaped by how we characterize it descriptively, by the context into which we place it, and by the perspective from which we view it. The first task for ethics is proper description. And here is where our failure begins.

Typically, cloning is discussed in one or more of three familiar contexts, which one might call the technological, the liberal, and the meliorist. Under the first, cloning will be seen as an extension of existing techniques for assisting reproduction and determining the genetic makeup of children. Like them, cloning is to be regarded as a neutral technique, with no inherent meaning or goodness, but subject to multiple uses, some good, some bad. The morality of cloning thus depends absolutely on the goodness or badness of the motives and intentions of the cloners: as one bioethicist defender of cloning puts it, "the ethics must be judged [only] by the way the parents nurture and rear their resulting child and whether they bestow the same love and affection on a child brought into existence by a technique of assisted reproduction as they would on a child born in the usual way."

The liberal (or libertarian or liberationist) perspective sets cloning in the context of rights, freedoms, and personal empowerment. Cloning is just a new option for exercising an individual's right to reproduce or to have the kind of child that he or she wants. Alternatively, cloning enhances our liberation (especially women's liberation) from the confines of nature, the vagaries of chance, or the necessity for sexual mating. Indeed, it liberates women from the need for men altogether, for the process requires only eggs, nuclei and (for the time being) uteri—plus, of course, a healthy dose of our (allegedly "masculine") manipulative science that likes to do all these things to mother nature and nature's mothers. For those who hold this outlook, the only moral restraints on cloning are adequately informed consent and the avoidance of bodily harm. If no one is cloned without her consent, and if the clonant is not physically damaged, then the liberal conditions for licit, hence moral, conduct are met. Worries that go beyond violating the will or maiming the body are dismissed as "symbolic"—which is to say, unreal.

The meliorist perspective embraces valetudinarians and also eugenicists. The latter were formerly more vocal in these discussions, but they are now generally happy to see their goals advanced under the less threatening banners of freedom and technological growth. These people see in cloning a new prospect for improving human beings—minimally, by ensuring the perpetuation of healthy individuals by avoiding the risks of genetic disease inherent in the lottery of sex, and maximally, by producing "optimum babies," preserving outstanding genetic material, and (with the help of soon-to-come techniques for precise genetic engineering) enhancing inborn human capacities on many fronts. Here the morality of cloning as a means is justified solely by the excellence of the end, that is,

by the outstanding traits or individuals cloned—beauty, or brawn, or brains.

These three approaches, all quintessentially American and all perfectly fine in their places, are sorely wanting as approaches to human procreation. It is, to say the least, grossly distorting to view the wondrous mysteries of birth, renewal and individuality, and the deep meaning of parent-child relations, largely through the lens of our reductive science and its potent technologies. Similarly, considering reproduction (and the intimate relations of family life!) primarily under the political-legal, adversarial and individualistic notion of rights can only undermine the private yet fundamentally social, cooperative, and duty-laden character of child-bearing, child-rearing, and their bond to the covenant of marriage. Seeking to escape entirely from nature (in order to satisfy a natural desire or a natural right to reproduce!) is self-contradictory in theory and self-alienating in practice. For we are erotic beings only because we are embodied beings, and not merely intellects and wills unfortunately imprisoned in our bodies. And, though health and fitness are clearly great goods, there is something deeply disquieting in looking on our prospective children as artful products perfectible by genetic engineering, increasingly held to our willfully imposed designs, specifications and margins of tolerable error.

The technical, liberal, and meliorist approaches all ignore the deeper anthropological, social and, indeed, ontological meanings of bringing forth new life. To this more fitting and profound point of view, cloning shows itself to be a major alteration, indeed, a major violation, of our given nature as embodied, gendered and engendering beings—and of the social relations built on this natural ground. Once this perspective is recognized, the ethical judgment on cloning can no longer be reduced to a matter of motives and intentions, rights and freedoms, benefits and harms, or even means and ends. It must be regarded primarily as a matter of meaning: Is cloning a fulfillment of human begetting and belonging? Or is cloning rather, as I contend, their pollution and perversion? To pollution and perversion, the fitting response can only be horror and revulsion; and conversely, generalized horror and revulsion are prima facie evidence of foulness and violation. The burden of moral argument must fall entirely on those who want to declare the widespread repugnances of humankind to be mere timidity or superstition.

Yet repugnance need not stand naked before the bar of reason. The wisdom of our horror at human cloning can be partially articulated, even if this is finally one of those instances about which the heart has its reasons that reason cannot entirely know.

The Profundity of Sex

To see cloning in its proper context, we must begin not as I did before, with laboratory technique, but with the anthropology—natural and social—of sexual reproduction.

Sexual reproduction—by which I mean the generation of new life from (exactly) two complementary elements, one female, one male, (usually) through coitus—is established (if that is the right term) not by human decision, culture or tradition, but by nature; it is the natural way of all mammalian reproduction. By nature, each child has two complementary biological progenitors. Each child thus stems from and unites exactly two lineages. In natural generation, moreover, the precise genetic constitution of the resulting offspring is determined by a combination of nature and chance, not by human design; each human child shares the common natural human species genotype, each child is genetically (equally) kin to each (both) parent(s), yet each child is also genetically unique.

These biological truths about our origins foretell deep truths about our identity and about our human condition altogether. Every one of us is at once equally human, equally enmeshed in a particular familial nexus of origin, and equally individuated in our trajectory from birth to death—and, if all goes well, equally capable (despite our mortality) of participating, with a complementary other, in the very same renewal of such human possibility through procreation. Though less momentous than our common humanity, our genetic individuality is not humanly trivial. It shows itself forth in our distinctive appearance through which we are everywhere recognized, it is revealed in our signature marks of fingerprints and our self-recognizing immune system, it symbolizes and foreshadows exactly the unique, never-to-be-repeated character of each human life.

Human societies virtually everywhere have structured child-rearing responsibilities and systems of identity and relationship on the bases of these deep natural facts of begetting. The mysterious yet ubiquitous "love of one's own" is everywhere culturally exploited, to make sure that children are not just produced but well cared for, and to create for everyone clear ties of meaning, belonging, and obligation. But it is wrong to treat such naturally rooted social practices as mere cultural constructs (like left- or right-driving, or like burying or cremating the dead) that we can alter with little human cost. What would kinship be without its clear natural grounding? And what would identity be without kinship? We must resist those who have begun to refer to sexual reproduction as the "traditional method of reproduction," who would have us regard as merely traditional, and by implication arbitrary, what is in truth not only natural but most certainly profound.

Asexual reproduction, which produces "single-parent" offspring, is a radical departure from the natural human way, confounding all normal understandings of father, mother, sibling, grandparent, etc., and all moral relations tied thereto. It becomes even more of a radical departure when the resulting offspring is a clone derived not from an embryo, but from a mature adult to whom the clone would be an identical twin; and when the process occurs not by natural accident (as in natural twinning), but by deliberate human design and manipulation; and when the child's (or children's) genetic constitution is pre-selected by the parent(s) (or scientists). Accordingly, as we will see, cloning is vulnerable to three kinds of concerns and objections, related to these three points: cloning threatens confusion of identity and individuality, even in small-scale cloning; cloning represents a giant step (though not the first one) toward transforming procreation into manufacture, that is, toward the increasing depersonalization of the process of generation and, increasingly, toward the "production" of human children as artifacts, products of human will and design (what others have called the problem of "commodification" of new life); and cloning—like other forms of eugenic engineering of the next generation—represents a form of despotism of the cloners over the cloned, and thus (even in benevolent cases) represents a blatant violation of the inner meaning of parent-child relations, of what it means to have a child, of what it means to say "yes" to our own demise and "replacement." Before turning to these specific ethical objections, let me test my claim of the profundity of the natural way by taking up a challenge recently posed by a friend. What if the given natural human way of reproduction were asexual, and we now had to deal with a new technological innovation—artificially induced sexual dimorphism and the fusing of complementary gametes—whose inventors argued that sexual reproduction promised all sorts of advantages, including hybrid vigor and the creation of greatly increased individuality? Would one then be forced to defend natural asexuality because it was natural? Could one claim that it carried deep human meaning?

The response to this challenge broaches the ontological meaning of sexual reproduction. For it is impossible, I submit, for there to have been human life—or even higher forms of animal life—in the absence of sexuality and sexual reproduction. We find asexual reproduction only in the lowest forms of life: bacteria, algae, fungi, some lower invertebrates. Sexuality brings with it a new and enriched relationship to the world. Only sexual animals can seek and find complementary others with whom to pursue a goal that transcends their own existence. For a sexual being, the world is no longer an indifferent and largely homogeneous otherness, in part edible, in part dangerous. It also contains some very special and related and complementary beings, of the same kind but of opposite sex, toward whom one reaches out with special interest and intensity. In higher birds and mammals, the outward gaze keeps a lookout not only for food and predators, but also for prospective mates; the beholding of the many-splendored world is suffused with desire for union, the animal antecedent of human eros and the germ of sociality. Not by accident is the human animal both the sexiest animal—whose females do not go into heat but are receptive throughout the estrous cycle and whose males must therefore have greater sexual appetite and energy in order to reproduce successfully—and also the most aspiring, the most social, the most open and the most intelligent animal.

The soul-elevating power of sexuality is, at bottom, rooted in its strange connection to mortality, which it simultaneously accepts and tries to overcome. Asexual reproduction may be seen as a continuation of the activity of self-preservation. When one organism buds or divides to become two, the original being is (doubly) preserved, and nothing dies. Sexuality, by contrast, means perishability and serves replacement; the two that come together to generate one soon will die. Sexual desire, in human beings as in animals, thus serves an end that is partly hidden from, and finally at odds with, the self-serving individual. Whether we know it or not, when we are sexually active we are voting with our genitalia for our own demise. The salmon swimming upstream to spawn and die tell the universal story: Sex is bound up with death, to which it holds a partial answer in procreation.

Through children, a good common to both husband and wife, male and female achieve some genuine unification (beyond the mere sexual "union," which fails to do so). The two become one through sharing generous (not needy) love for this third being as good. Flesh of their flesh, the child is the parents' own commingled being externalized, and given a separate and persisting existence. Unification is enhanced also by their commingled work of rearing. Providing an opening to the future beyond the grave, carrying not only our seed but also our names, our ways and our hopes that they will surpass us in goodness and happiness, children are a testament to the possibility of transcendence. Gender duality and sexual desire, which first draws our love upward and outside of ourselves, finally provide for the partial overcoming of the confinement and limitation of perishable embodiment altogether.

Human procreation, in sum, is not simply an activity of our rational wills. It is a more complete activity precisely because it engages us bodily, erotically, and spiritually, as well as rationally. There is wisdom in the mystery of nature that has joined the pleasure of sex, the inarticulate longing for union, the communication of the loving embrace, and the deep-seated and only partly articulate desire for children in the very activity by which we continue the chain of human existence and participate in the renewal of human possibility. Whether or not we know it, the severing of procreation from sex, love and intimacy is inherently dehumanizing, no matter how good the product.

We are now ready for the more specific objections.

The Perversities of Cloning

First, an important if formal objection: Any attempt to clone a human being would constitute an unethical experiment upon the resulting child-to-be. As the animal experiments (frog and sheep) indicate, there are grave risks of mishaps and deformities. Moreover, because of what cloning means, one cannot presume a future cloned child's consent to be a clone, even a healthy one. Thus, ethically speaking, we cannot even get to know whether or not human cloning is feasible.

I understand, of course, the philosophical difficulty of trying to compare a life with defects against nonexistence. Several bioethicists, proud of their philosophical cleverness, use this conundrum to embarrass claims that one can injure a child in its conception, precisely because it is only thanks to that complained-of conception that the child is alive to complain. But common sense tells us that we have no reason to fear such philosophisms. For we surely know that people can harm and even maim children in the very act of conceiving them, say, by paternal transmission of the AIDS virus, maternal transmission of heroin dependence or, arguably, even by bringing them into being as bastards, or with no capacity or willingness to look after them properly. And we believe that to do this intentionally, or even negligently, is inexcusable and clearly unethical.

Cloning creates serious issues of identity and individuality. The cloned person may experience concerns about his distinctive identity not only because he will be in genotype and appearance identical to another human being, but, in this case, because he may also be twin to the person who is his "father" or "mother"—if one can still call them that. What would be the psychic burdens of being the "child" or "parent" of your twin? The cloned individual, moreover, will be saddled with a genotype that has already lived. He will not be fully a surprise to the world.

People are likely always to compare his performances in life with that of his alter ego. True, his nurture and his circumstance in life will be different; genotype is not exactly destiny. Still, one must also expect parental and other efforts to shape this new life after the original—or at least to view the child with the original version always firmly in mind. Why else did they clone from the star basketball player, mathematician and beauty queen—or even dear old dad—in the first place?

Since the birth of Dolly, there has been a fair amount of doublespeak on this matter of genetic identity. Experts have rushed in to reassure the public that the clone would in no way be the same person, or have any confusions about his or her identity; as previously noted, they are pleased to point out that the clone of Mel Gibson would not be Mel Gibson. Fair enough. But one is shortchanging the truth by emphasizing the additional importance of the intrauterine environment, rearing, and social setting: genotype obviously matters plenty. That, after all, is the only reason to clone, whether human beings or sheep. The odds that clones of Wilt Chamberlain will play in the NBA are, I submit, infinitely greater than they are for clones of Willie Shoemaker.

Curiously, this conclusion is supported, inadvertently, by the one ethical sticking point insisted on by friends of cloning: no cloning without the donor's consent. Though an orthodox liberal objection, it is in fact quite puzzling when it comes from people (such as Ruth Macklin) who also insist that genotype is not identity or individuality, and who deny that a child could reasonably complain about being made a genetic copy. If the clone of Mel Gibson would not be Mel Gibson, why should Mel Gibson have grounds to object that someone had been made his clone? We already allow researchers to use blood and tissue samples for research purposes of no benefit to their sources: my falling hair, my expectorations, my urine and even my biopsied tissues are "not me" and not mine. Courts have held that the profit gained from uses to which scientists put my discarded tissues do not legally belong to me. Why, then, no cloning without consent—including, I assume, no cloning from the body of someone who just died? What harm is done the donor, if genotype is "not me"? Truth to tell, the only powerful justification for objecting is that genotype really does have something to do with identity, and everybody knows it. If not, on what basis could Michael Jordan object that someone cloned "him," from cells, say, taken from a "lost" scraped-off piece of his skin? The insistence on donor consent unwittingly reveals the problem of identity in all cloning.

Troubled psychic identity (distinctiveness), based on all-too-evident genetic identity (sameness), will be made much worse by the utter confusion of social identity and kinship ties. For, as already noted, cloning radically confounds lineage and social relations, for "offspring" as for "parents." As bioethicist James Nelson has pointed out, a female child cloned from her "mother" might develop a desire for a relationship to her "father," and might understandably seek out the father of her "mother," who is after all also her biological twin sister. Would "grandpa," who thought his paternal duties concluded, be pleased to discover that the clonant looked to him for paternal attention and support?

Social identity and social ties of relationship and responsibility are widely connected to, and supported by, biological kinship. Social taboos on incest and adultery everywhere serve to keep clear who is related to whom (and especially which child belongs to which parents), as well as to avoid confounding the social identity of parent-and-child (or brother-and-sister) with the social identity of lovers, spouses, and co-parents. True, social identity is altered by adoption (but as a matter of the best interest of already living children: we do not deliberately produce children for adoption). True, artificial insemination and *in vitro* fertilization with donor sperm, or whole embryo donation, are in some way forms of "prenatal adoption"—a not altogether unproblematic practice. Even here, though, there is in each case (as in all sexual reproduction) a known male source of sperm and a known single female source of egg—a genetic father and a genetic mother—should anyone care to know (as adopted children often do) who is genetically related to whom.

In the case of cloning, however, there is but one "parent." The usually sad situation of the "single-parent child" is here deliberately planned, and with a vengeance. In the case of self-cloning, the "offspring" is, in addition, one's twin; and so the dreaded result of incest—to be parent to one's sibling—is here brought about deliberately, albeit without any act of coitus. Moreover, all other relationships will be confounded. What will father, grandfather, aunt, cousin, sister mean? Who will bear what ties and what burdens? What sort of social identity will someone have with one whole side—"father's" or "mother's"—necessarily excluded? It is no answer to say that our society, with its high incidence of divorce, remarriage, adoption, extramarital childbearing and the rest, already confounds lineage and confuses kinship and responsibility for children (and everyone else), unless one also wants to argue that this is, for children, a preferable state of affairs.

Human cloning would also represent a giant step toward turning begetting into making, procreation into manufacture (literally, something "handmade"), a process already begun with *in vitro* fertilization and genetic testing of embryos. With cloning, not only is the process in hand, but the total genetic blueprint of the cloned individual is selected and determined by the human artisans. To be sure, subsequent development will take place according to natural processes; and the resulting children will still be recognizably human. But we here would be taking a major step into making man himself simply another one of the man-made things. Human nature becomes merely the last part of nature to succumb to the technological project, which turns all of nature into raw material at human disposal, to be homogenized by our rationalized technique according to the subjective prejudices of the day. How does begetting differ from making? In natural procreation, human beings come together, complementarily male and female, to give existence to another being who is formed, exactly as we were, by what we are: living, hence perishable, hence aspiringly erotic, human beings. In clonal reproduction, by contrast, and in the more advanced forms of manufacture to which it leads, we give existence to a being not by what we are but by what we intend and design. As with any product of our making, no matter how excellent, the artificer stands above it, not as an equal but as a superior, transcending it by his will and creative prowess. Scientists who clone animals make it perfectly clear

that they are engaged in instrumental making; the animals are, from the start, designed as means to serve rational human purposes. In human cloning, scientists and prospective "parents" would be adopting the same technocratic mentality to human children: human children would be their artifacts.

Such an arrangement is profoundly dehumanizing, no matter how good the product. Mass-scale cloning of the same individual makes the point vividly; but the violation of human equality, freedom, and dignity are present even in a single planned clone. And procreation dehumanized into manufacture is further degraded by commodification, a virtually inescapable result of allowing babymaking to proceed under the banner of commerce. Genetic and reproductive biotechnology companies are already growth industries, but they will go into commercial orbit once the Human Genome Project nears completion. Supply will create enormous demand. Even before the capacity for human cloning arrives, established companies will have invested in the harvesting of eggs from ovaries obtained at autopsy or through ovarian surgery, practiced embryonic genetic alteration, and initiated the stockpiling of prospective donor tissues. Through the rental of surrogate-womb services, and through the buying and selling of tissues and embryos, priced according to the merit of the donor, the commodification of nascent human life will be unstoppable.

Finally, and perhaps most important, the practice of human cloning by nuclear transfer—like other anticipated forms of genetic engineering of the next generation—would enshrine and aggravate a profound and mischievous misunderstanding of the meaning of having children and of the parent-child relationship. When a couple now chooses to procreate, the partners are saying yes to the emergence of new life in its novelty, saying yes not only to having a child but also, tacitly, to having whatever child this child turns out to be. In accepting our finitude and opening ourselves to our replacement, we are tacitly confessing the limits of our control. In this ubiquitous way of nature, embracing the future by procreating means precisely that we are relinquishing our grip, in the very activity of taking up our own share in what we hope will be the immortality of human life and the human species. This means that our children are not our children: they are not our property, not our possessions. Neither are they supposed to live our lives for us, or anyone else's life but their own. To be sure, we seek to guide them on their way, imparting to them not just life but nurturing, love, and a way of life; to be sure, they bear our hopes that they will live fine and flourishing lives, enabling us in small measure to transcend our own limitations. Still, their genetic distinctiveness and independence are the natural foreshadowing of the deep truth that they have their own and never-before-enacted life to live. They are sprung from a past, but they take an uncharted course into the future.

Meeting Some Objections

The defenders of cloning, of course, are not wittingly friends of despotism. Indeed, they regard themselves mainly as friends of freedom: the freedom of individuals to reproduce, the freedom of scientists and inventors to discover and devise and to foster "progress" in genetic knowledge and technique. They want large-scale cloning only for animals, but they wish to preserve cloning as a human option for exercising our "right to reproduce"—our right to have children, and children with "desirable genes." As law professor John Robertson points out, under our "right to reproduce" we already practice early forms of unnatural, artificial and extramarital reproduction, and we already practice early forms of eugenic choice. For this reason, he argues, cloning is no big deal.

We have here a perfect example of the logic of the slippery slope, and the slippery way in which it already works in this area. Only a few years ago, slippery slope arguments were used to oppose artificial insemination and *in vitro* fertilization using unrelated sperm donors. Principles used to justify these practices, it was said, will be used to justify more artificial and more eugenic practices, including cloning. Not so, the defenders retorted, since we can make the necessary distinctions. And now, without even a gesture at making the necessary distinctions, the continuity of practice is held by itself to be justificatory.

The principle of reproductive freedom as currently enunciated by the proponents of cloning logically embraces the ethical acceptability of sliding down the entire rest of the slope—to producing children ectogenetically from sperm to term (should it become feasible) and to producing children whose entire genetic makeup will be the product of parental eugenic planning and choice. If reproductive freedom means the right to have a child of one's own choosing, by whatever means, it knows and accepts no limits.

But, far from being legitimated by a "right to reproduce," the emergence of techniques of assisted reproduction and genetic engineering should compel us to reconsider the meaning and limits of such a putative right. In truth, a "right to reproduce" has always been a peculiar and problematic notion. Rights generally belong to individuals, but this is a right which (before cloning) no one can exercise alone. Does the right then inhere only in couples? Only in married couples? Is it a (woman's) right to carry or deliver or a right (of one or more parents) to nurture and rear? Is it a right to have your own biological child? Is it a right only to attempt reproduction, or a right also to succeed? Is it a right to acquire the baby of one's choice?

The assertion of a negative "right to reproduce" certainly makes sense when it claims protection against state interference with procreative liberty, say, through a program of compulsory sterilization. But surely it cannot be the basis of a tort claim against nature, to be made good by technology, should free efforts at natural procreation fail. Some insist that the right to reproduce embraces also the right against state interference with the free use of all technological means to obtain a child. Yet such a position cannot be sustained: for reasons having to do with the means employed, any community may rightfully prohibit surrogate pregnancy, or polygamy, or the sale of babies to infertile couples, without violating anyone's basic human "right to reproduce." When the exercise of a previously innocuous freedom now involves or impinges on troublesome practices that the original freedom never was intended to reach, the general presumption of liberty needs to be reconsidered.

We do indeed already practice negative eugenic selection, through genetic screening and prenatal diagnosis. Yet our practices are governed by a norm of health. We seek to prevent the birth of children who suffer from known (serious) genetic diseases. When and if gene therapy becomes possible, such diseases could then be treated, *in utero* or even before implantation—I have no ethical objection in principle to such a practice (though I have some practical worries), precisely because it serves the medical goal of healing existing individuals. But therapy, to be therapy, implies not only an existing "patient." It also implies a norm of health. In this respect, even germline gene "therapy," though practiced not on a human being but on egg and sperm, is less radical than cloning, which is in no way therapeutic. But once one blurs the distinction between health promotion and genetic enhancement, between so-called negative and positive eugenics, one opens the door to all future eugenic designs. "To make sure that a child will be healthy and have good chances in life": this is Robertson's principle, and owing to its latter clause it is an utterly elastic principle, with no boundaries. Being over eight feet tall will likely produce some very good chances in life, and so will having the looks of Marilyn Monroe, and so will a genius-level intelligence.

Proponents want us to believe that there are legitimate uses of cloning that can be distinguished from illegitimate uses, but by their own principles no such limits can be found. (Nor could any such limits be enforced in practice.) Reproductive freedom, as they understand it, is governed solely by the subjective wishes of the parents-to-be (plus the avoidance of bodily harm to the child). The sentimentally appealing case of the childless married couple is, on these grounds, indistinguishable from the case of an individual (married or not) who would like to clone someone famous or talented, living or dead. Further, the principle here endorsed justifies not only cloning but, indeed, all future artificial attempts to create (manufacture) "perfect" babies.

A concrete example will show how, in practice no less than in principle, the so-called innocent case will merge with, or even turn into, the more troubling ones. In practice, the eager parents-to-be will necessarily be subject to the tyranny of expertise. Consider an infertile married couple, she lacking eggs or he lacking sperm, who wants a child of their (genetic) own, and propose to clone either husband or wife. The scientist-physician (who is also co-owner of the cloning company) points out the likely difficulties—a cloned child is not really their (genetic) child, but the child of only one of them; this imbalance may produce strains on the marriage; the child might suffer identity confusion; there is a risk of perpetuating the cause of sterility, and so on—and he also points out the advantages of choosing a donor nucleus. Far better than a child of their own would be a child of their own choosing. Touting his own expertise in selecting healthy and talented donors, the doctor presents the couple with his latest catalog containing the pictures, the health records and the accomplishments of his stable of cloning donors, samples of whose tissues are in his deep freeze. Why not, dearly beloved, a more perfect baby?

The "perfect baby," of course, is the project not of the infertility doctors, but of the eugenic scientists and their supporters. For them, the paramount right is not the so-called right to reproduce but what biologist Bentley Glass called, a quarter of a century ago, "the right of every child to be born with a sound physical and mental constitution, based on a sound genotype, . . . the inalienable right to a sound heritage." But to secure this right, and to achieve the requisite quality control over new human life, human conception and gestation will need to be brought fully into the bright light of the laboratory, beneath which it can be fertilized, nourished, pruned, weeded, watched, inspected, prodded, pinched, cajoled, injected, tested, rated, graded, approved, stamped, wrapped, sealed, and delivered. There is no other way to produce the perfect baby.

Yet we are urged by proponents of cloning to forget about the science fiction scenarios of laboratory manufacture and multiple-copied clones, and to focus only on the homely cases of infertile couples exercising their reproductive rights. But why, if the single cases are so innocent, should multiplying their performance be so off-putting? (Similarly, why do others object to people making money off this practice, if the practice itself is perfectly acceptable?) When we follow the sound ethical principle of universalizing our choice—"Would it be right if everyone cloned a Wilt Chamberlain (with his consent, of course)? Would it be right if everyone decided to practice asexual reproduction?"—we discover what is wrong with these seemingly innocent cases. The so-called science fiction cases make vivid the meaning of what looks to us, mistakenly, to be benign.

Though I recognize certain continuities between cloning and, say, *in vitro* fertilization, I believe that cloning differs in essential and important ways. Yet those who disagree should be reminded that the "continuity" argument cuts both ways. Sometimes we establish bad precedents, and discover that they were bad only when we follow their inexorable logic to places we never meant to go. Can the defenders of cloning show us today how, on their principles, we will be able to see producing babies ("perfect babies") entirely in the laboratory or exercising full control over their genotypes (including so-called enhancement) as ethically different, in any essential way, from present forms of assisted reproduction? Or are they willing to admit, despite their attachment to the principle of continuity, that the complete obliteration of "mother" or "father," the complete depersonalization of procreation, the complete manufacture of human beings, and the complete genetic control of one generation over the next would be ethically problematic and essentially different from current forms of assisted reproduction? If so, where and how will they draw the line, and why? I draw it at cloning, for all the reasons given.

Ban the Cloning of Humans

What, then, should we do? We should declare that human cloning is unethical in itself and dangerous in its likely consequences. In so doing, we shall have the backing of the overwhelming majority of our fellow Americans, and of the human race, and (I believe) of most practicing scientists. Next, we should do all that we can to prevent the cloning of human beings. We should do this by means of an international legal ban, if possible, and by a unilateral national ban, at a minimum. Scientists may secretly undertake to violate such a law, but they will be deterred by not being able to stand up proudly to claim the credit for their technological bravado and success. Such a ban on clonal baby-making, moreover, will not harm the progress of basic genetic science and technology. On the contrary, it will reassure the public that scientists are happy to proceed without violating the deep ethical norms and intuitions of the human community.

This still leaves the vexed question about laboratory research using early embryonic human clones, specially created only for such research purposes, with no intention to implant them into a uterus. There is no question that such research holds great promise for gaining fundamental knowledge about normal (and abnormal) differentiation, and for developing tissue lines for transplantation that might be used, say, in treating leukemia or in repairing brain or spinal cord injuries—to mention just a few of the conceivable benefits. Still, unrestricted clonal embryo research will surely make the production of living human clones much more likely. Once the genies put the cloned embryos into the bottles, who can strictly control where they go (especially in the absence of legal prohibitions against implanting them to produce a child)?

I appreciate the potentially great gains in scientific knowledge and medical treatment available from embryo research, especially with cloned embryos. At the same time, I have serious reservations about creating human embryos for the sole purpose of experimentation. There is something deeply repugnant and fundamentally transgressive about such a utilitarian treatment of prospective human life. This total, shameless exploitation is worse, in my opinion, than the "mere" destruction of nascent life. But I see no added objections, as a matter of principle, to creating and using cloned early embryos for research purposes, beyond the objections that I might raise to doing so with embryos produced sexually.

And yet, as a matter of policy and prudence, any opponent of the manufacture of cloned humans must, I think, in the end oppose also the creating of cloned human embryos. Frozen embryonic clones (belonging to whom?) can be shuttled around without detection. Commercial ventures in human cloning will be developed without adequate oversight. In order to build a fence around the law, prudence dictates that one oppose—for this reason alone—all production of cloned human embryos, even for research purposes. We should allow all cloning research on animals to go forward, but the only safe trench that we can dig across the slippery slope, I suspect, is to insist on the inviolable distinction between animal and human cloning.

Some readers, and certainly most scientists, will not accept such prudent restraints, since they desire the benefits of research. They will prefer, even in fear and trembling, to allow human embryo cloning research to go forward.

Very well. Let us test them. If the scientists want to be taken seriously on ethical grounds, they must at the very least agree that embryonic research may proceed if and only if it is preceded by an absolute and effective ban on all attempts to implant into a uterus a cloned human embryo (cloned from an adult) to produce a living child. Absolutely no permission for the former without the latter.

The proposal for such a legislative ban is without American precedent, at least in technological matters, though the British and others have banned cloning of human beings, and we ourselves ban incest, polygamy, and other forms of "reproductive freedom." Needless to say, working out the details of such a ban, especially a global one, would be tricky, what with the need to develop appropriate sanctions for violators. Perhaps such a ban will prove ineffective; perhaps it will eventually be shown to have been a mistake. But it would at least place the burden of practical proof where it belongs: on the proponents of this horror, requiring them to show very clearly what great social or medical good can be had only by the cloning of human beings.

The president's call for a moratorium on human cloning has given us an important opportunity. In a truly unprecedented way, we can strike a blow for the human control of the technological project, for wisdom, prudence, and human dignity. The prospect of human cloning, so repulsive to contemplate, is the occasion for deciding whether we shall be slaves of unregulated progress, and ultimately its artifacts, or whether we shall remain free human beings who guide our technique toward the enhancement of human dignity. If we are to seize the occasion, we must, as the late Paul Ramsey wrote, raise the ethical questions with a serious and not a frivolous conscience. A man of frivolous conscience announces that there are ethical quandaries ahead that we must urgently consider before the future catches up with us. By this he often means that we need to devise a new ethics that will provide the rationalization for doing in the future what men are bound to do because of new actions and interventions science will have made possible. In contrast a man of serious conscience means to say in raising urgent ethical questions that there may be some things that men should never do. The good things that men do can be made complete only by the things they refuse to do.

55. *The Judeo-Christian Case against Cloning*

STEPHEN G. POST

Proceeding on the scientific assumption that human cloning is possible, Stephen G. Post examines the possible moral implications of the practice. In this essay, Post outlines seven basic objections to cloning, the seventh of which he believes is the most significant: (1) it diminishes the distinctive newness of each human life; (2) it makes males reproductively obsolete; (3) it puts the power of eugenics to seek human perfection into the hands of one generation at the expense of the generations to follow; (4) it makes possible the harvesting of organs from humans cloned for that purpose; (5) it heightens the risks of serious genetic mishaps; (6) it lends itself to a focus on physiological rather than characterological traits as the source of human good, and (7) it trespasses on the very structure of nature and can be described as "encroaching on the Creator's domain." Above all, then, cloning violates God's purposes for marriage and the fidelity, unity, and intentional procreative decisions made within that union.

For purposes of discussion, I will assume that the cloning of humans is technologically possible. This supposition raises Einstein's concern: "Perfection of means and confusion of ends seems to characterize our age." Public reaction to human cloning has been strongly negative, although without much clear articulation as to why. My task is the Socratic one of helping to make explicit what is implicit in this uneasiness.

Some extremely hypothetical scenarios might be raised as if to justify human cloning. One might speculate, for example: If environmental toxins or pathogens

From *America*, Vol. 176 (June 21–28, 1997), pp. 19–22.
© 1997. All rights reserved. Reprinted with permission from America Press. For subscription information, visit www.americamagazine.org.

should result in massive human infertility, human cloning might be imperative for species survival. But in fact recent claims about increasing male infertility worldwide have been found to be false. Some apologists for human cloning will insist on other strained "What ifs." 'What if' parents want to replace a dead child with an image of that child? "What if" we can enhance the human condition by cloning the best among us?

I shall offer seven unhypothetical criticisms of human cloning, but in no particular priority. The final criticism, however, is the chief one to which all else serves as preamble.

1. The Newness of Life. Although human cloning, if possible, is surely a novelty, it does not corner the market on newness. For millennia, mothers and fathers have marveled at the newness of form in their newborns.

I have watched newness unfold in our own two children, wonderful blends of the Amerasian variety. True, there probably is, as Freud argued, a certain narcissism in parental love, for we do see our own form partly reflected in the child, but, importantly, never entirely so. Sameness is dull, and as the French say, *vive la différence.* It is possible that underlying the mystery of this newness of form is a creative wisdom that we humans will never quite equal.

This concern with the newness of each human form (identical twins are new genetic combinations as well) is not itself new. The scholar of constitutional law Laurence Tribe pointed out in 1978, for example, that human cloning could "alter the very meaning of humanity." Specifically, the cloned person would be "denied a sense of uniqueness." Let us remember that there is no strong analogy between human cloning and natural identical twinning, for in the latter case there is still the blessing of newness in the newborns, though they be two or more. While identical twins do occur naturally, and are unique persons, this does not justify the temptation to impose external sameness more widely.

Sidney Callahan, a thoughtful psychologist, argues that the random fusion of a couple's genetic heritage "gives enough distance to allow the child also to be seen as a separate other," and she adds that the egoistic intent to deny uniqueness is wrong because ultimately depriving. By having a different form from that of either parent, I am visually a separate creature, and this contributes to the moral purpose of not reducing me to a mere copy utterly controlled by the purposes of a mother or father. Human clones will not look exactly alike, given the complex factors influencing genetic imprinting, as well as environmental factors affecting gene expression. But they will look more or less the same, rather than more or less different.

Surely no scientist would doubt that genetic diversity produced by procreation between a man and a woman will always be preferable to cloning, because procreation reduces the possibility for species annihilation through particular diseases or pathogens. Even in the absence of such pathogens, cloning means the loss of what geneticists describe as the additional hybrid vigor of new genetic combinations.

2. Making Males Reproductively Obsolete. Cloning requires human eggs, nuclei and uteri, all of which can be supplied by women. This makes males reproductively obsolete. This does not quite measure up to Shulamith Firestone's notion that women will only be able to free themselves from patriarchy through the eventual development of the artificial womb, but of course, with no men available, patriarchy ends—period.

Cloning, in the words of Richard McCormick, S.J., "would involve removing insemination and fertilization from the marriage relationship, and it would also remove one of the partners from the entire process." Well, removal of social fatherhood is already a *fait accompli* in a culture of illegitimacy chic, and one to which some fertility clinics already marvelously contribute through artificial insemination by donor for single women. Removing male impregnators from the procreative dyad would simply drive the nail into the coffin of fatherhood, unless one thinks that biological and social fatherhood are utterly disconnected. Social fatherhood would still be possible in a world of clones, but this will lack the feature of participation in a continued biological lineage that seems to strengthen social fatherhood in general.

3. Under My Thumb: Cookie Cutters and Power. It is impossible to separate human cloning from concerns about power. There is the power of one generation over the external form of another, imposing the vicissitudes of one generation's fleeting image of the good upon the nature and destiny of the next. One need only peruse the innumerable texts on eugenics written by American geneticists in the 1920s to understand the arrogance of such visions.

One generation always influences the next in various ways, of course. But when one generation can, by the power of genetics, in the words of C. S. Lewis, "make its descendants what it pleases, all men who live after it are the patients of that power." What might our medicalized culture's images of human perfection become? In Lewis's words again, "For the power of Man to make himself what he pleases means, as we have seen, the power of some men to make other men what they please."

A certain amount of negative eugenics by prenatal testing and selective abortion is already established in American obstetrics. Cloning extends this power from the negative to the positive, and it is therefore even more foreboding.

This concern with overcontrol and overpower may be overstated because the relationship between genotype and realized social role remains highly obscure. Social role seems to be arrived at as much through luck and perseverance as anything else, although some innate capacities exist as genetically informed baselines.

4. Born to Be Harvested. One hears regularly that human clones would make good organ donors. But we ought not to presume that anyone wishes to give away body parts. The assumption that the clone would choose to give body parts is completely unfounded. Forcing such a harvest would reduce the clone to a mere object for the use of others. A human person is an individual substance of a rational nature not to be treated as object, even if for one's own narcissistic gratification, let alone to procure organs. I have never been convinced that there are any ethical duties to donate organs.

5. The Problem of Mishaps. Dolly the celebrated ewe represents one success out of 277 embryos, nine of which were implanted. Only Dolly survived. While I do not wish to address here the issue of the moral status of the entity within the womb, suffice it to note that in this country there are many who would consider proposed research to clone humans as far too risky with regard to induced genetic defects. Embryo research in general is a matter of serious moral debate in the United States, and cloning will simply bring this to a head.

As one recent British expert on fertility studies writes, "Many of the animal clones that have been produced show serious developmental abnormalities, and, apart from ethical considerations, doctors would not run the medicolegal risks involved."

6. Sources of the Self. Presumably no one needs to be reminded that the self is formed by experience, environment and nurture. From a moral perspective, images of human goodness are largely virtue-based and therefore characterological. Aristotle and Thomas Aquinas believed that a good life is one in which, at one's last breath, one has a sense of integrity and meaning. Classically the shaping of human fulfillment has generally been a matter of negotiating with frailty and suffering through perseverance in order to build character. It is not the earthen vessels, but the treasure within them that counts. A self is not so much a genotype as a life journey. Martin Luther King Jr. was getting at this when he said that the content of character is more important than the color of skin.

The very idea of cloning tends to focus images of the good self on the physiological substrate, not on the journey of life and our responses to it, some of them compensations to purported "imperfections" in the vessel. The idea of the designer baby will emerge as though external form is as important as the inner self.

7. Respect for Nature and Nature's God. In the words of Jewish bioethicist Fred Rosner, cloning goes so far in violating the structure of nature that it can be considered as "encroaching on the Creator's domain." Is the union of sex, marriage, love and procreation something to dismiss lightly?

Marriage is the union of female and male that alone allows for procreation in which children can benefit developmentally from both a mother and father. In the Gospel of Mark, Jesus draws on ancient Jewish teachings when he asserts, "Therefore what God has joined together, let no man separate." Regardless of the degree of extendedness in any family, there remains the core nucleus: wife, husband, and children. Yet the nucleus can be split by various cultural forces (e.g., infidelity as interesting, illegitimacy as chic), poverty, patriarchal violence, and now cloning.

A cursory study of the Hebrew Bible shows the exuberant and immensely powerful statements of Genesis 1, in which a purposeful, ordering God pronounces that all stages of creation are "good." The text proclaims, "So God created humankind in his image, in the image of God he created them, male and female he created them" (Gen. 1:27). This God commands the couple, each equally in God's likeness, to "be fruitful and multiply." The divine prototype was thus established at the very outset of the Hebrew Bible: "Therefore a man leaves his father and his mother and clings to his wife, and they become one flesh" (Gen. 2:24).

The dominant theme of Genesis I is creative intention. God creates, and what is created procreates, thereby ensuring the continued presence of God's creation. The creation of man and woman is good in part because it will endure.

Catholic natural law ethicists and Protestant proponents of "orders of creation" alike find divine will and principle in the passages of Genesis 1.

A major study on the family by the Christian ethicist Max Stackhouse suggests that just as the Presocratic philosophers discovered still valid truths about geometry, so the biblical authors of Chapters One and Two of Genesis "saw something of the basic design, purpose, and context of life that transcends every sociohistorical epoch." Specifically, this design includes "fidelity in communion" between male and female oriented toward "generativity" and an enduring family, the precise social details of which are worked out in the context of political economies.

Christianity appropriated the Hebrew Bible and had its origin in a Jew from Nazareth and his Jewish followers. These Hebraic roots that shape the words of Jesus stand within Malachi's prophetic tradition of emphasis on inviolable monogamy. In Mk. 10:2–12 we read:

> The Pharisees approached and asked, "Is it lawful for a husband to divorce his wife?" They were testing him. He said to them in reply, "What did Moses command you?" They replied, "Moses permitted him to write a bill of divorce and dismiss her." But Jesus told them, "Because of the hardness of your hearts he wrote you this commandment. But from the beginning of creation, 'God made them male and female. For this reason a man shall leave his father and mother (and be joined to his wife), and the two shall become one flesh.' So they are no longer two but one flesh. Therefore what God has joined together, no human being must separate." In the house the disciples again questioned him about this. He said to them, "Whoever divorces his wife and marries another commits adultery against her; and if she divorces her husband and marries another, she commits adultery."

Here Jesus quotes Gen. 1:27 ("God made them male and female") and Gen. 2:24 ("the two shall become one flesh").

Christians side with the deep wisdom of the teachings of Jesus, manifest in a thoughtful respect for the laws of nature that reflect the word of God. Christians simply cannot and must not underestimate the threat of human cloning to unravel what is both naturally and eternally good.

---

56. *Contingency, Tragedy, and the Virtues of Parenting*

Sondra Wheeler

> Sondra Wheeler assesses the prospective implications of human cloning through an assessment of its possible impact on the role of parenting. To date, the discussion of cloning has focused on the costs and benefits associated with deliberately duplicating existing individuals, but Wheeler argues that a serious and overlooked consideration is the effect that cloning may have on the very meaning of the terms *mother* and *father*. After explaining with some care how cloning would undermine the virtues associated with parenthood under God, she concludes that the choice to put cloning into practice would demonstrate, not a richer appreciation of family, but a fundamental misunderstanding of it.

The immediate furor sparked by the birth of Dolly the cloned sheep has now died down. We have turned our attention to other things, perhaps revealing that as a nation we have the cultural equal of attention deficit disorder. More deeply, I suspect, we have run out of things to say about human cloning, and this is the reflection of our lack of a shared and generally available language in which to talk about our hopes, fears, and intuitions concerning the control of human genetic inheritance.

Discussion continues, mostly in specialized settings, academic and professional contexts, or scientific and philosophical journals. There, experts debate the possible benefits and foreseeable risks of cloning applications that would result in the birth of a child who was the deliberate genetic copy of some existing template, whether of one of the rearing parents or of some other person. These discussions are important. It is quite reasonable to look to scientists and ethicists to help us

From: Ronald Cole-Turner (Ed.), *Beyond Cloning* (Harrisburg PA: Trinity Press International, 2001), pp. 111–123. Reprinted with permission from T&T Clark/Continuum International.

understand the technical possibilities, and to frame the questions that the fast-maturing discipline of bioethics teaches us to ask about their moral acceptability. But such debates among specialists are not sufficient.

All proposed forays into human genetic engineering are significant because they have the capacity, by changing what we *do,* to change what we *mean* by terms as basic as mother and father. Accepting such new practices requires us to make a subtle shift in what we understand and intend in entering into the most fundamental of all human relationships, that between parent and child. There is no academic specialty in what it means to be the fruit of the previous generation or the progenitors of the next. No degrees are available that confer the wisdom necessary to judge the terms on which, or the ends *for* which, we ought to undertake to determine the genetic complement of those other human beings whom we will call our children. Moreover, whether they realize it or not, there are no human beings on the planet to whom the moral character of these basic social ties is irrelevant. Therefore it is important to continue the discussion in the broadest possible terms and among the widest possible segment of the society that stands to be affected by these developments.

My intention here is to explore the implications of human reproductive cloning for our understanding of the relationship between parents and children. I propose to do this in a language as close as I can manage to the ordinary terms in which people think about their own relationships with their parents and their children. I want to talk about certainty and uncertainty, about control and randomness, and about the interplay of power and helplessness that are part of the ordinary experience of conceiving, bearing, and raising children. I want to talk about how we make moral judgments about the use of power in this realm. And whether I want to or not, I will be forced to talk about suffering, about how we as human beings can and should respond to it.

However, before entering on that extended reflection, I will begin by reviewing some of the things that have been said about the possibility of cloning, by those in favor of it and by those deeply opposed to it. I do this to capture something of the flavor of the public conversation, the concerns that have animated it, and the reasons that have been offered for and against cloning human beings. Against this background, I will be in a position to consider whether the character of parenting as a moral practice has received enough attention within this discussion.

Revisiting the Arguments for Cloning

Positive arguments for human reproductive cloning are actually hard to come by. Those who support the pursuit of that goal[1] generally do so for what might be called negative reasons (that is, they find no convincing reasons to ban the practice) rather than for the sake of some particular good cloning is expected to bring about. There are, in fact, a number of rationales for supporting cloning of preimplantation embryos as a tool in basic and clinical research, and a wide range of possible therapeutic benefits projected to come from such research. But these do not depend upon implanting cloned embryos or the result of nuclear transfers and bringing them to term, and thus do not fall into the category of reproductive cloning. Just to be clear, there are also serious arguments against these research protocols, rooted in respect for the embryo as a form of nascent human life that should not be manipulated and discarded. These objections, however, are not particular to procedures that involve cloning, applying as well to any creation of human embryos not destined for implantation.

Some of the arguments that have been made in favor of reproductive cloning proceed on libertarian grounds, that only direct and demonstrated harm to a recognized other should limit individual autonomy. These depend on the supposition that the procedure can be made safe for the cloned child-to-be and for the gestating mother, and on the prior supposition that failures on the way to such a technical development do not harm any being who is morally eligible for protection. On these premises, libertarians argue that no one has the right to limit what researchers or prospective cloners wish to do. Cloning is to be supported because it might provide a way for prospective parents to obtain the offspring they want, whether that means overcoming disease or just exercising "quality control." The substantive good in view in this position is thus individual liberty.

Most people do not find such arguments for unconstrained cloning convincing on the face of it, for the same reason that they do not find libertarian arguments in favor of ending tax support for public education convincing. It is entirely too evident how much common stake we all have in the bearing and upbringing of children, who are after all destined to be our

---

[1]Estimates of the likelihood of overcoming the practical barriers to human cloning, and of the time frame needed to do so, vary widely. All informed sources agree; however, that we are still some distance scientifically from the possibility.

neighbors and inheritors, to suppose that such practices should be matters of purely private judgment.
Even those who have supported some uses of human
cloning have generally recognized that proposals must
pass greater public scrutiny than this.

More appealing to some have been arguments
based on benefits that might be obtained using this
technique for individuals in particular circumstances.
Rabbi Moshe Tendler, for example, envisions a case in
which someone, all of whose relatives were killed in
the Holocaust, is unable to produce gametes, but has a
great stake in continuing his or her family line.[2] The
use of nuclear transfer cloning technology might allow
this person to have posterity by first producing
a genetic twin. Ronald Cole-Turner asks whether a couple who loses a late-term pregnancy at a point when
they can no longer conceive might be justified in
cloning the dead fetus to obtain a child who was genetically related to both of them.[3] A number of commentators have proposed that cloning might enable couples
who carry certain serious genetic defects to be certain
of not passing these to their offspring. And a few have
noted that cloning could allow lesbian couples to have
children genetically related to them and to no one else,
extending the contemporary notion of a right to procreate to those now excluded by biology. These are not,
of course, routine circumstances, and such unusual scenarios raise the question of whether "hard cases" make
better ethics than they do law. But the exploration of
quandaries can help to clarify what is at the heart of
our intuitions and our considered judgments and help
us articulate what might be at stake in our decisions.
I will return to such particular justifications for reproductive cloning near the end of the discussion.

Arguments Against Cloning

Arguments against the moral permissibility of cloning
can also be divided into types. The first and simplest
type argues on grounds of scientific safety and relia-
bility that such experimental procedures are too risky
to apply to human beings. Those who would make
this the grounds for an ongoing or permanent ban contend that any research that would reduce the uncertainty is morally prohibited because it would involve

helpless and unconsenting subjects in high-risk,
nontherapeutic research. They deny that animal studies can ever give us sufficient confidence to justify proceeding to human trials.

Many have objected to cloning because they see
a threat to human dignity and individuality in a technique that creates a genetic replica of an existing genotype. Popular commentators have raised questions
about the personal identity, value, and social status to
be accorded a clone. While others counter that cloning
poses no greater threat to genetic uniqueness than natural twinning, opponents point to a distinction between
what one accepts as a random event and what one sets
out to do. They also point out that it makes a difference
if one of the twins is a deliberately chosen template,
already fully developed, who may function socially as
the "parent" of the other.

Related but distinct are the concerns of those who
worry about compromising genetic diversity in favor of
the replication of a few highly valued genotypes. Along
with the biological risks if it were to be done on a large
scale, cloning raises philosophical questions about
human nature and the value of human differences.
Further along this same trajectory of concern for human
freedom and dignity, some have speculated about the
uses of cloning to create whole categories of people specially adapted for some social purpose, ranging from
soldiers to worker drones to sources of "replacement
parts" for their cloners. Some have proposed these possibilities with full seriousness as moral barriers to
the application of this technique to human beings.
Whatever the criteria or motives for selection, the replication of a desirable genotype has seemed to many to
be a fatal step toward treating infants as commodities.

Changing the Focus

Common to all these objections is the fear of making
a human being a merely instrumental good, a being created at someone else's direction and to his or her specifications to fulfill a human purpose outside the child's
own flourishing. This is seen as a basic violation of the
duty of respect for persons, which forbids treating them
solely as means to other ends, rather than as ends in
themselves. This concern is evident even among those
thinkers, both religious and secular, who do not find the
asexual character of replication and the lack of genetic
uniqueness compelling arguments against cloning. Ted
Peters, for example, untroubled by these issues, nevertheless worries that "reproduction will come to look

---

[2]In the unpublished proceedings of a public forum on
cloning at the American Association for the Advancement of
Science in June 1997.

[3]In private correspondence, June 2000.

more and more like production . . . with quality control and babies will come to look more and more like products."[4] Karen Lebacqz, in considering sympathetically whether cloning might serve social justice by extending the putative right to a genetically related child to disadvantaged groups, asks a more basic question: "Is there something fundamentally flawed with the notion that children must be genetically ours? Is the very language of 'rights' out of place when it comes to procreation and families?" She concludes: "Our individualistic, 'rights'-based assumptions about families and procreation need to be challenged, and fundamentally new understandings of family need to be developed."[5]

Although there are aspects of both Peters's and Lebacqz's analyses with which I would take issue, they share a central insight that seems to me exactly right: it is the moral character of human relationships within the family, rather than simply the mechanics of embryo generation or the raw biochemistry of genetic identity, that is the heart of the matter. Even the most sensitive analysis of the dignity of procreation as a natural process, or the respect to be accorded the human embryo as an individual entity, will leave something crucial out of the picture, namely, the social practice of parenting as a central human activity. This returns me to the matters with which I began, with the implications of reproductive cloning for how we think about family life, and how we understand and protect the bearing and rearing of children as a moral practice.

Welcoming the Stranger: Contingency, Uncertainty, and the Virtues of Parenting

In trying to think morally about a possibility for which there is no precedent, it sometimes helps to think carefully about the familiar pattern it proposes to replace. This can be surprisingly difficult to do, for the same familiarity that makes us comfortable also makes us blind to important features of our ordinary experience. This makes it necessary to say some very obvious things about the experience of becoming a parent.

Ian Wilmut, Dolly's scientific progenitor, speaks of people having children in what he calls "the ordinary, fun way." The truth is, it **is** fun; not just the lovemaking, but pregnancy itself. Despite its many discomforts, pregnancy is a perennial wonder, as the child within makes its presence more and more known and felt, as the curiosity and anticipation grow, and parents ponder a thousand variations on the question, "I wonder who it will be?" For the fact is, we don't know. However often we go for ultrasounds, however much we submit to prenatal testing to learn about the gender and size and health of our soon-to-be offspring, even those who embark upon parenting in the most considered and controlled and rational way possible *do not know who is coming*. Having a child is, arguably, the deepest and most enduring connection of which we are capable, and we don't know who it is we are proposing to devote our work and worry to for the next eighteen or twenty years. This has to be the ultimate blind date! Only it is more like an arranged marriage, for when this stranger arrives you are not just courting: you are already committed. If it were not so commonplace, we would think it was madness.

Here is a social arrangement in which rational, self-sufficient actors, perfectly capable of judging their own best interests and maximizing them, commit themselves sight unseen to a being who will reliably cost them enormous time, money, labor, anxiety, and grief for a mixed and unreliable long-range return. Sometimes we do it by conscious choice, carefully timing a pregnancy to fit in with other life activities. Often enough we do it by accident or by default, or for reasons that may be good or bad or foolish. But however it comes about, with an amazing degree of regularity, we accept our children as they come to us, receive them for no other reason than that they somehow belong to us and we to them, and we do our best through the years that follow to figure out what is good for them and provide it as well as we can.

Of course, we do not merely passively receive our children, but also actively shape who they will become, socializing and educating them, forming and directing their development according to our own judgments and convictions. Along with devotion to our children in the present go plans and dreams about their future, and all the goods we hope to see realized in their lives. But no one with any real involvement in the upbringing of a child could subscribe to Locke's theory that a child is a blank tablet upon which anything at all can be written. Children from birth both absorb and resist our influence, bringing to the equation their own inclinations

---

[4]Ted Peters, "Cloning Shock: A Theological Reaction," in Ronald Cole-Turner, editor, *Human Cloning: Religious Responses,* (Louisville, Ky.:Westminster John Knox Press), 23.

[5]Karen Lebacqz, "Genes, Justice, and Clones," in Cole-Turner, *Human Cloning,* 55–56.

and abilities, their own preferences and limitations, their own nature, and, very soon, their own choices about who they wish to become. The actual experience of parenting is always an interplay between planning and happenstance, between the weighty sense of responsibility and the frustration of helplessness. Experienced parents know they cannot, and wise parents know they should not, undertake to impose their own version of the ideal child upon their offspring. And they also know something of the grief that goes with accepting all the things they care passionately about but cannot control.

What all this underscores is the complexity and delicacy of the moral task that parents undertake, to be thoroughly interested and invested participants in the nurture of another human being who will in the end meet them as an equal, and will certainly not always please them. Parenting is the risky enterprise in which one merely human being sets out to form another, and it requires a whole panoply of virtues: flexibility and courage and humility, humor and restraint and above all a deep generosity of spirit. For here human beings are asked to use an enormous disparity of power unselfishly and with a deliberate intent to see it overturned in the end in favor of the liberty and responsibility of one who stands in primary relation to God. We discover our children's good rather than determine it, and in the end we will complete our duties to our children by stepping back from their lives as they become in actuality what they have always been in origin and in destiny: our peers and not our subjects, fellow creatures with us and "coheirs of the grace of life."

Cloning as a Technique of Selection

On this specifically theological note I want to pause, to propose that we think about what difference it will make to us and to our children if we move from this basic stance of receiving and welcoming and cherishing the children who are born to us to one of selecting them, or more properly selecting in advance a template that is to be reproduced in them. What will it mean to our understanding of our offspring and our relation to them if they are not gifts who surprise us but projects we have engineered, whose most basic biological attributes are the product of our will? What will it do to parenting if we go to such lengths as asexual replication in order to exercise control over every element of the individual genome?

One of the things such a practice will do is to place parental desires, not simply the general desire to have a baby but the desire for a *particular* baby, squarely in the center of what constitutes the parent-child relationship. We will have moved from the experience at once routine and extraordinary of being presented with a child who is one's to nurture and to celebrate, to the quite different experience of the delivery of a specific and intended result, inevitably measured against the prototype chosen for replication. It is not hard to see why so many fear that our attitude about this relationship among both technicians and prospective parents will shift toward child-as-commodity afforded to parent-as-consumer. The traditional language of Christians and Jews, that children are gifts of God, can only seem quaint and out of place in a context in which people can speak without blushing of "quality control."

On the other hand, what cloning will not do is successfully eliminate uncertainty. Some of the rationales proposed for human cloning reflect not only an unseemly desire to control who our offspring will be but also a great lack of sophistication in understanding human development. Any behavioral scientist can tell you that a person is far too complex an interaction of genotype, physical environment, social context, and individual life experience to be engineered reliably. The odds are overwhelming that you cannot make yourself another Michael Jordan or another Yo-Yo Ma, or even another you, even if it were morally legitimate to set out to do so. But the fact that it will not work is little comfort, for what would it be like to live as a failed copy or to be the parent of one? Successful or not, our readiness to engineer the genome of our offspring to obtain a desirable result expresses a lack of fundamental respect for the otherness of our children, who not only are not us but are finally not ours.

In my judgment, human reproductive cloning as a technique of genetic engineering represents a basic distortion of parenting. It displays a failure of the reticence rooted in religious awe with which people of faith should approach intervention in the being of another human creature. This reticence is most important precisely where it is most in danger of subversion, in the intense and emotion-laden relationship between parent and child, where such enormous influence is exerted and such disparate power is exercised. By making our offspring the product not of our bodies and our relationships but of our will, we give a new and peculiarly intimate form to a most fundamental human corruption: the readiness to make ourselves each the center of our own universe and to regard all others in relation to ourselves.

Cloning as a Remedy for Deprivation

Now finally I come around to the arguments for reproductive cloning as a means of providing a child under special circumstances that rule out other methods. Rationales have included the desire to produce a child who is genetically related to a sterile donor, as in Tendler's example; the wish to replace a dead fetus or child in cases like that proposed by Cole-Turner; and the possibility of providing a genetically related child to a lesbian couple, in Lebacqz's discussion. I will not pretend that such circumstances do not represent real losses, even in some cases real tragedies. But I question whether it is always possible to offer a technical solution to a human reality such as sterility or premature death, and whether it is always desirable to do so simply because it is possible. Such questions are always subject to the charge of heartlessness, especially when they are raised by people who do not confront in their own lives the realities with which these proposals try to grapple. Nevertheless, I think we are in danger of serious distortions of life and thought if we do not think long and hard about what we are trying to do with biomedical technology and why, and if we don't stop to consider who we turn ourselves and each other into along the way. Taking these examples as instances of a larger class of exceptional cases, I will treat them in the order given. My aim is to achieve some clarity about what possibilities cloning would or would not offer in such cases.

Rabbi Tendler's scenario proposes to use cloning to continue a family line for a sterile man whose relatives have all died in the Holocaust. He speaks of a religious and cultural value placed on familial continuity, and of the peculiar horror of the Nazi genocide as destroying whole families, root and branch. These are matters of enormous weight and seriousness, not to be passed off lightly. What the world has lost in the destruction of so much of European Jewry is incalculable, as indeed are the losses of every such slaughter, both those known and those buried in the silence of history. But it is important to be clear about what cloning can and cannot offer here. It cannot restore either the children who were or the children who would have been, not as individuals and not as collective carriers of all the particular genetic mix that might be thought to underlie a "family line." It cannot even give the hypothetical man a child in the normal sense of the word, a descendant half of whose genetic complement comes from the father without replicating any of his genome. It can only give the sterile man a delayed genetic twin, a child who, far from rescuing familial continuity, is not exactly anyone's son or daughter. The idea that this is the only or the best way to resist the destruction of a family strikes me as wrongheaded, as if the transmission of DNA decisively constituted human identity and belonging, and gave meaning to what we express when we call our families "ours." It seems to me that Rabbi Tendler's hypothetical survivor would be better served by adopting a child and raising her or him in the history and the traditions, the memories and the love that are the real stuff of family life and continuity.

The case envisioned by Cole-Turner is at once more poignant and more troubling. It presents us with a grief more imaginable and distinct: the loss of a child late in pregnancy by a couple who can conceive no more. There is no issue here of genetic replication of parent or living donor, and no actual developed human being who would have been selected in the person of the clone. What there is instead is a chance to cheat death by cloning the fetus from salvaged tissue, and thus to replace for the couple what, one might argue, nature and even God intended: a living child born of their union. It seems we have here the opportunity to provide a technical fix for tragedy. But do we? Even if we do, is it one we ought to use?

The reality is that such a couple has experienced a real loss, an actual death, and that fact must not be denied or minimized lest it come back to haunt both the parents and any child to be born. Neither by cloning nor by any other technique is it possible to give back the dead child; the question is whether we ought to try to give the grieving parents a twin to replace it. In more ordinary circumstances, parents experiencing such a late-term loss would be counseled to take time to live with and come to terms with their grief before making an effort to conceive a "new" baby, precisely because of the moral and psychological problems inherent in trying to replace one human being with another. Such concerns could only be dramatically heightened if the new fetus were a clone of the child now dead. As harsh as it may seem, I am convinced that this utterly understandable impulse is a temptation we should resist. Rather than finding a technical circumvention of mortality, we must find the courage to face it squarely, to endure the suffering it imposes, and to move toward the recovery of faith and hope through grief rather than around it. As human beings, our task is not to outwit death, but to become people who can live mortal lives, loving other mortals wisely and well. Since the natural conception of another child is (hypothetically) impossible, the alternatives for such a couple would be other means of assisted reproduction (the specific means would depend on the nature of the infertility, now unspecified), or the adoption of a child who would be their second child, not a re-creation of the first; a child made theirs by love and the thousand shared tasks of parenting, rather than by genetic relationship.

Finally, I turn to the question of whether cloning should be used to extend the right to a child related to them and no one else to couples who in the nature of the case cannot conceive one in the ordinary fashion: lesbian couples. Here I want to affirm Lebacqz's insight that to pose the question in this way reveals how far, and how far astray, we have come in our pursuit of technological reproduction. In our urgency to provide would-be parents with whatever they want, and can pay for, we have allowed ourselves to forget a lesson that should have been burned into our brains with the abolition of slavery and the repeal of laws that made women and children property: no one can have a right to another human being.

In our lives as members of families, however constituted, we are gifted with one another rather than entitled to one another. In living and loving, in giving birth and nurture and care to the next generation, we are charged with the stewardship of the gift of life that we rightly call holy, which at root means simply "belonging to God." We do have responsibilities to one another, and claims not to have our liberty in fulfilling those responsibilities arbitrarily restricted. But none of this amounts to the right to a child, however conceived. A child comes always from beyond us and is oriented beyond us ultimately to the friendship with God for which human beings are made. If we belong to one another, we do so by our devotion to one another's well-being in all its dimensions, by our wisdom about it as well as our commitment to it. Our children are ours, or perhaps more deeply we are theirs, because we receive and welcome them, because we put ourselves in service to them, and finally because we understand both the depth and the limits of human belonging. Our insistence on "children of our own" and our readiness to go to any expense, any risk, any length to obtain offspring who carry our genes and no one else's, reveal not so much our prizing of family as our misunderstanding of it.

---

57. *Clone Wars*

Mark D. Eibert

In this essay, Mark Eibert strongly opposes all legislative bans on human cloning. Citing the fact that approximately 15 percent of Americans are infertile, and that many of these cannot be helped by existing technology, Eibert argues that cloning could provide these patients the reproductive opportunity they seek. Eibert insists that procreation is a basic right and that the government should exercise no legal control over reproductive freedom. Fears about the negative impact of cloning, he argues, are exaggerated.

"There are some avenues that should be off limits to science. If scientists will not draw the line for themselves,

Published originally as "Clone Wars" in *Reason*, vol. 30 (June 1998). Reprinted with permission from Reason Foundation.

it is up to the elected representatives of the people to draw it for them."

Thus declared Senator Christopher "Kit" Bond (Republican–Missouri) one of the sponsors of S. 1601, the official Republican bill to outlaw human cloning.

The bill would impose a 10-year prison sentence on anyone who uses "human somatic cell nuclear transfer technology" to produce an embryo, even if only to study cloning in the laboratory. If enacted into law, the bill would effectively ban all research into the potential benefits of human cloning. Scientists who use the technology for any reason—and infertile women who use it to have children—would go to jail.

Not to be outdone, Democrats have come up with a competing bill. Senators Ted Kennedy (Massachusetts) and Dianne Feinstein (California) have proposed S. 1602, which would ban human cloning for at least 10 years. It would allow scientists to conduct limited experiments with cloning in the laboratory, provided any human embryos are destroyed at an early stage rather than implanted into a woman's uterus and allowed to be born.

If the experiment goes too far, the Kennedy–Feinstein bill would impose a $1 million fine and government confiscation of all property, real or personal, used in or derived from the experiment. The same penalties that apply to scientists appear to apply to new parents who might use the technology to have babies.

The near unanimity on Capitol Hill about the need to ban human cloning makes it likely that some sort of bill will be voted on this session and that it will seriously restrict scientists' ability to study human cloning. In the meantime, federal bureaucrats have leapt into the breach. In January, the U.S. Food and Drug Administration announced that it planned to "regulate" (that is, prohibit) human cloning. In the past, the FDA has largely ignored the fertility industry, making no effort to regulate *in vitro* fertilization, methods for injecting sperm into eggs, and other advanced reproductive technologies that have much in common with cloning techniques.

An FDA spokesperson told me that although Congress never expressly granted the agency jurisdiction over cloning, the FDA can regulate it under its statutory authority over biological products (like vaccines or blood used in transfusions) and drugs. But even Representative Vernon Ehlers (Republican-Michigan), one of the most outspoken congressional opponents of cloning, admits that "it's hard to argue that a cloning procedure is a drug." Of course, even if Congress had granted the FDA explicit authority to regulate cloning, such authority would only be valid if Congress had the constitutional power to regulate reproduction—which is itself a highly questionable assumption (more on that later).

Nor have state legislatures been standing still. Effective January 1, California became the first state to outlaw human cloning. California's law defines "cloning" so broadly and inaccurately—as creating children by the transfer of nuclei from any type of cell to enucleated eggs—that it also bans a promising new infertility treatment that has nothing to do with cloning. In that new procedure, doctors transfer nuclei from older, dysfunctional eggs (not differentiated adult cells as in cloning) to young, healthy donor eggs, and then inseminate the eggs with the husband's sperm—thus conceiving an ordinary child bearing the genes of both parents. Taking California as their bellwether, many other states are poised to follow in passing very restrictive measures.

Constitutional Principles Conflict with Any Cloning Ban

What started this unprecedented governmental grab for power over both human reproduction and scientific inquiry? Within days after Dolly, the cloned sheep, made her debut, President Clinton publicly condemned human cloning. He opined that "any discovery that touches upon human creation is not simply a matter of scientific inquiry. It is a matter of morality and spirituality as well. Each human life is unique, born of a miracle that reaches beyond laboratory science."

Clinton then ordered his National Bioethics Advisory Commission to spend all of 90 days studying the issue—after which the board announced that it agreed with Clinton. Thus, Clinton succeeded in framing the debate this way: Human cloning was inherently bad, and the federal government had the power to outlaw it.

But in fact, it's far from clear that the government has such far-reaching authority. Several fundamental constitutional principles conflict with any cloning ban. Chief among them are the right of adults to have children and the right of scientists to investigate nature.

The Supreme Court has ruled that every American has a constitutional right to "bear or beget" children. This includes the right of infertile people to use sophisticated medical technologies like *in vitro* fertilization. As the U.S. District Court for the Northern District of Illinois explained, "Within the cluster of constitutionally protected choices that includes the right to have access to contraceptives, there must be included . . . the right to submit to a medical procedure that may bring about, rather than prevent, pregnancy."

About 15 percent of Americans are infertile, and doctors often cannot help them. Federal statistics show that *in vitro* fertilization and related technologies have an average national success rate of less than 20 percent. Similarly, a Consumer Reports study concludes that fertility clinics produce babies for only 25 percent of patients. That leaves millions of people who still cannot have children, often because they can't produce viable eggs or sperm, even with fertility drugs. Until recently, their only options have been to adopt or to use eggs or sperm donated by strangers.

Once cloning technology is perfected, however, infertile individuals will no longer need viable eggs or sperm to conceive their own genetic children—any body cell will do. Thus, cloning may soon offer many Americans the only way possible to exercise their constitutional right to reproduce. For them, cloning bans are the practical equivalent of forced sterilization.

In 1942, the Supreme Court struck down a law requiring the sterilization of convicted criminals, holding that procreation is "one of the basic civil rights of man," and that denying convicts the right to have children constitutes "irreparable injury" and "forever deprived them of a basic liberty." To uphold a cloning ban, then, a court would have to rule that naturally infertile citizens have less right to try to have children than convicted rapists and child molesters do.

Many politicians and bureaucrats who want to ban human cloning say they need their new powers to "protect" children. Reciting a long list of speculative harms, ranging from possible physical deformities to the psychic pain of being an identical twin, they argue in essence that cloned children would be better off never being born at all.

But politicians and the media have grossly overstated the physical dangers of cloning. The Dolly experiment started with 277 fused eggs, of which only 29 became embryos. All the embryos were transferred to 13 sheep. One became pregnant, with Dolly. The success rate per uterine transfer (one perfect offspring from 13 sheep, with no miscarriages) was better than the early success rates for *in vitro* fertilization. Subsequent animal experiments in Wisconsin have already made the process much more efficient, and improvements will presumably continue as long as further research is allowed.

Government Control over Reproduction Goes against American Tradition

More fundamentally, the government does not have the constitutional authority to decide who gets born—although it once thought it did, a period that constitutes a dark chapter of our national heritage. In the early twentieth century, 30 states adopted eugenics laws, which required citizens with conditions thought to be inheritable (insanity, criminal tendencies, retardation, epilepsy, etc.) to be sterilized—partly as a means of "protecting" the unfortunate children from being born.

In 1927, the U.S. Supreme Court upheld such a law, with Oliver Wendell Holmes writing for the majority, "It would be better for all the world, if instead of waiting to execute degenerate offspring for crime, or to let them starve for their imbecility, society can prevent those who are manifestly unfit from continuing their kind . . . Three generations of imbeciles are enough."

California's eugenics law in particular was admired and emulated in other countries—including Germany in 1933. But during and after World War II, when Americans learned how the Nazis had used their power to decide who was "perfect" enough to be born, public and judicial opinion about eugenics began to shift. By the 1960s, most of the eugenics laws in this country had been either repealed, fallen into disuse, or were struck down as violating constitutional guarantees of due process and equal protection.

Indeed, those old eugenics laws were a brief deviation from an American tradition that has otherwise been unbroken for over 200 years. In America, it has always been the prospective parents, never the government, who decided how much risk was acceptable for a mother and her baby—even where the potential harm was much more certain and serious than anything threatened by cloning.

Hence, *in vitro* fertilization and fertility drugs are legal, even though they create much higher risks of miscarriages, multiple births, and associated birth defects. Individuals who themselves have or are known carriers of serious inheritable mental or physical defects such as sickle cell anemia, hemophilia, cystic fibrosis, muscular dystrophy, and Tay-Sachs disease are allowed to reproduce, naturally and through *in vitro* fertilization, even though they risk having babies with serious, or even fatal, defects or diseases. Older mothers at risk of having babies with Down syndrome, and even women with AIDS, are also allowed to reproduce, both naturally and artificially. Even if prenatal testing shows a fetus to have a serious defect like Down Syndrome, no law requires the parents to abort it to save it from a life of suffering.

In short, until science revealed that human cloning was possible, society assumed that prospective parents could decide for themselves and their unborn children how much risk and suffering were an acceptable part of life. But in the brave new world of the federal bureaucrat, that assumption no longer holds true.

Ironically, some cloning opponents have turned the eugenics argument on its head, contending that cloning could lead to "designer children" and superior beings who might one day rule mankind. But allowing infertile individuals to conceive children whose genome is nearly identical to their already existing genomes no more creates "designer children" that it creates "designer parents." More important, these opponents miss the point that only government has the broad coercive power over society as a whole necessary to make eugenics laws aimed at "improving the race." It is those who support laws to ban cloning who are in effect urging the passage of a new eugenics law, not those who want to keep government out of the business of deciding who is perfect enough or socially desirable enough to be born.

Another significant driving force behind attempts to restrict or reverse an expansion in human knowledge stems from religious convictions. Interestingly, there is no necessary theological opposition to cloning: For example, two leading rabbis and a Muslim scholar who testified before the National Bioethics Advisory Commission had no objection to the practice and even advanced religious arguments for cloning.

Still, politicians from both major parties have already advanced religious arguments against cloning. President Clinton wants to outlaw cloning as a challenge to "our cherished concepts of faith and humanity." House Majority Leader Dick Armey also opposes cloning, saying that "to be human is to be made in the image and likeness of a loving God," and that "creating multiple copies of God's unique handiwork" is bad for a variety of reasons. Senator Bond warns that "humans are not God and they should not be allowed to play God"—a formulation similar to that of Albert Moraczewski, a theologian with the National Conference of Catholic Bishops, who told the president's commission, "Cloning exceeds the limits of the delegated dominions given to the human race."

Earlier Advances Were Attacked on Similar Grounds

Of course, virtually every major medical, scientific, and technological advance in modern history was initially criticized as "playing God." To give just two recent examples, heart transplants and "test tube babies" both faced religious opposition when first introduced. Today, heart transplants save 2,000 lives every year, and *in vitro* fertilization helped infertile Americans have 11,000 babies in 1995 alone.

Religious belief doesn't require opposition to these sorts of expansions in human knowledge and technology. And basing a cloning ban primarily on religious grounds would seem to violate the Establishment Clause. But that's not the only potential constitutional problem with a ban.

Many courts and commentators say that a constitutional right of scientific inquiry is inherent in the rights of free speech and personal liberty. To be sure, certain governmental attempts to restrict the methods scientists can use have been upheld—for example, regulations requiring free and informed consent by experimental subjects. But those have to do with protecting the rights of others. Cloning bans try to stop research that everyone directly concerned wants to continue. As one member of the National Bioethics Advisory Commission observed, if the group's recommendation to ban cloning is enacted, it would apparently be the first time in American history that an entire field of medical research has been outlawed.

Prohibiting scientific and medical activities would also raise troubling enforcement issues. How exactly would the FBI—in its new role as "reproductive police" and scientific overseer—learn, then prove, that scientists, physicians, or parents were violating the ban? Would they raid research laboratories and universities? Seize and read the private medical records of infertility patients? Burst into operating rooms with their guns drawn? Grill new mothers about how their babies were conceived? Offer doctors reduced sentences for testifying against the patients whose babies they delivered? And would the government really confiscate, say, Stanford University Medical Center, if one of its many researchers or clinicians "goes too far"?

The year since the announcement of Dolly's birth has seen unprecedented efforts by government to expand its power over both human reproduction and science. Decisions traditionally made by individuals—such as whether and how to have children, or to study the secrets of nature—have suddenly been recast as political decisions to be made in Washington.

The Nightmares are Based on Misunderstandings

Human cloning, when it actually arrives, is not apt to have dire consequences. Children conceived through cloning technology will be not "Xerox copies" but unique individuals with their own personalities and full human rights. Once this basic fact is understood, the only people likely to be interested in creating children through cloning technology are incurably infertile individuals. There are already tens of millions of identical twins walking the earth, and they have posed no threat so far to God, the family, or country. A few more twins, born to parents who desperately want to have, raise, and love them as their own children, will hardly be noticed.

As for the nightmare fantasies spun by cloning opponents, even the president's special commission has admitted that fears of cloning being used to create hordes of Hitlers or armies of identical slaves are "based . . . on gross misunderstandings of human biology and psychology." And laws already prohibit criminal masterminds from holding slaves, abusing children, or cutting up people for spare body parts.

As harmless as the fact of cloning may be, the fear of cloning is already bearing bitter fruit: unprecedented extensions of government power, based either on unlikely nightmare scenarios or on an unreasoning fear that humans were "not meant" to know or do certain things. Far from protecting the "sanctity" of human life, such an attitude, if consistently applied, would doom the human race to a "natural" state of misery.

---

58. In God's Garden: Creation and Cloning in Jewish Thought

Jonathan R. Cohen

> In this essay, Jonathan R. Cohen responds to the challenge that cloning addresses to core Western beliefs about the nature of creation and of our relationship to God. Tracing the references to these two themes in the Hebrew Bible, Cohen argues that cloning requires a reconsideration of traditional notions of our creation in God's image, and our notions of God as "Father," but it does not render them inoperative. In conclusion, Cohen suggests that children brought into the world through genetic engineering or through traditional means may be equally pleasing to God.

The possibility of cloning human beings challenges Western beliefs about creation and our relationship to God. If we understand God as the Creator and creation as a completed act, cloning will be a transgression. If, however, we understand God as the Power of Creation and creation as a transformative process, we may find a role for human participation, sharing that power as beings created in the image of God.

From The Hastings Center Report 4, 1999, pp. 7–12. Reprinted with permission from The Hastings Center and the author.

Some scientific revolutions change what people believe about the world. The Copernican and Darwinian revolutions, while not significantly changing what people could then use science to achieve, forced people to re-examine their understanding of the universe, of humanity and its place in the universe, and of God's agency within the universe. Other scientific revolutions, like Faraday and Maxwell's work on the physics of electric fields, pose little challenge to fundamental beliefs but dramatically change society through their technological application. We are now in the midst of a genetic revolution that may both profoundly influence our beliefs and dramatically change how society functions. Will designing our offspring someday be as easy and common as "cut and paste" on a word processor? Are we on the cusp of an evolutionary advance toward being an "autocreative" species, or in attempting to "play God" has our hubris reached its zenith? Such are the questions we face.

My purpose here is to explore how the genetic revolution could affect our beliefs. My strategy is to examine several challenges that human cloning and, to a lesser extent, genetic engineering raise for certain basic Jewish beliefs—though by no means exclusively Jewish beliefs—about humans and God, using as a lens for my thoughts the Biblical account of creation presented in the first few chapters of Genesis.[1] Not only are many basic Jewish beliefs about humans and God embedded in that account, but even if one believes that Genesis is inaccurate as a literal account of the world's creation, or even if one does not believe in God, Genesis provides an excellent framework for addressing some of the existential challenges posed by the genetic revolution. Although I address challenges human cloning presents for certain basic Jewish beliefs, such Biblically rooted beliefs influence much Christian and Western thought. Moreover, such beliefs play an important part in developing public policy toward human cloning. For example, the National Bioethics Advisory Commission devoted roughly one quarter of its report on human cloning to religious views, focusing in particular on the Biblical account of creation.

The Biblical account is open to two different interpretations, of creation as a completed act and creation as a transformative process, which carry quite different implications for human cloning. Understanding creation in these different ways suggests different answers to how human cloning might impinge on our beliefs about the worth of a human life, about God's role as Creator and Sovereign, and about how meaning can be found in a human life. I want to suggest that if its implications are properly understood, human cloning can be integrated with many of our basic beliefs and can encourage us to view God's act of creation as a transformative process.

This is not to advocate that human cloning be permitted—that is a very different question. However, the possibility of human cloning challenges our beliefs irrespective of whether we ultimately permit or ban such practice, or of whether human cloning actually occurs.

A note before I begin. Although for simplicity I use terms such as "Jewish beliefs" and "Jewish thought," I do not mean to suggest that all Jews do hold or should hold similar beliefs about these topics or that Judaism requires one to hold a particular view about these topics. Indeed, I pretend no special expertise in Jewish thought, but speak as a lay Jew who seeks to make some existential "sense" out of the possibility of human cloning.

Completed Act or Transformative Process?

The Bible begins, "*Bereshit bara Elohim et hashamayim v'et haaretz . . .*" It is a mysterious phrase. Under one common interpretation, it is translated as a declarative sentence—"In the beginning, God created the heavens and the earth." The import is that God created the universe out of nothing, and essentially all at once. In this reading, God engages in two primary activities in Genesis: bringing into existence various elements, and dividing them from one another, each to have a distinct role. Light is separated from darkness; land is separated from sea; birds are to fly in the sky while fish are to swim in the sea. The patterns of reproduction also appear Divinely set. Each form of vegetation is to produce offspring of its own type, and there are two genders of humans, with reproduction to occur through the union of a male and a female.[2] We are also told that by the seventh day, "The heavens and the earth and all their hosts were complete" (Gen. 2:1). The structure of the universe had been set. Creation is essentially completed.

From such an interpretation, an argument arises: if God created the structure of our world, who are we to tamper with it? Further, the Bible describes humans as created "in God's image" (Gen. 1: 27). If "in God's image" means "after God's likeness," how could that likeness be improved upon? If "in God's image" means "in accordance with God's plan," who are we to create a better plan?

If God's stamp in creating the world and the life within it alone does not lead one to think that the structure of the world should be left as is, other sources might. The Bible depicts transgressing the boundaries God gave as the paradigm of sin. Eating the forbidden fruit leads to the expulsion from Eden, and the commingling of divine and human beings precedes the flood. Sex between humans and animals is prohibited, as is sex between two men (Lev. 18: 22–24; 20: 12, 15–16). So too crossbreeding animals and planting a field with different types of seed (Lev. 19: 19; Deut. 22: 9). The concern for nature's structure is even applied to clothing: it is forbidden to construct a garment of both linen and wool (Lev. 19: 19, Deut. 22: 12). Conversely, many Biblical passages, especially in Leviticus, indicate that holiness can be found by respecting boundaries. As Mary Douglas has argued, "Holiness requires that individuals shall conform to the class to which they belong. And holiness requires that different classes of things shall not be confused."[3]

Against such a reading of the Bible, human cloning would be wrong. Although human cloning would not bring into existence a new species—a potential criticism of transgenic activities such as making hybrid plants or animals—it would transgress the structure of sexual reproduction that God created. Human cloning supplants the structure by which God designed humans to reproduce. Our current genetic quandary might be cast as a second fall from Eden. Driven by our lust for Godlike power, we have picked of the tempting fruit of the tree of genetic knowledge. We ought not to use that knowledge to pervert the structure of the world.[4]

Like most great literature, however, the Biblical account of creation can be interpreted in different ways. A second, contrasting interpretation of Genesis may be offered that has quite different implications for how we view human cloning. Often the opening phrase of Genesis is translated not as a declarative sentence, but as a constructive clause—"When God began creating the heavens and the earth . . ." or "At the beginning of God's creation of the heavens and the earth . . ."[5] So construed, creation may be seen not as a completed act cast in a particular structure, but as a transformative process.[6] In this interpretation, the miracle of creation is not the specific world God produced, but rather God's moving the world from a chaotic nothingness to an ordered, light-filled, life-bearing place. Further, one might point to the Bible's repeated emphasis that God created things called "good" and "very good." Put differently, the miracle was that God improved what existed. Good purpose, rather than a particular form, lies at the heart of creation.[7]

If God is seen as Creator, and if we are created in the image of God, then might we not have a role to play as creators ourselves?[8] Abraham is viewed as praiseworthy when, exercising an independent conception of what is moral, he argues with God over the fate of Sodom and Gomorrah.[9] Might we be praiseworthy if we put our technology to work to pursue our independently formed conception of the good?[10] People get sick naturally, and yet most feel that medical intervention to aid the sick is morally permissible, perhaps even obligatory, as in Jewish law. God, rather than nature, is to be worshipped.

If creation is a transformative process of bettering our world in which humans are to play a part, then in assessing human cloning the normative focus would turn to whether we use human cloning to do good or evil. As Rabbi Elliot Dorff has written, "Cloning, like all other technologies, is morally neutral. Its moral valence depends on how we use it."[11] It is in this respect like our use of drugs: when used to improve health, they are a blessing; when taken by addicts, a curse. And some think that the use of human cloning would sometimes be merited, even obliged. Rabbi Moshe Tendler has declared, "Show me a young man who is sterile, whose family was wiped out in the Holocaust, and [who] is the last of a genetic line [and] I would certainly clone him."[12] Other candidates include more common cases of infertility, such as parents who could not otherwise reproduce and want to clone their recently deceased newborn, or of saving someone's life, such as cloning an infant who has suffered severe kidney damage in the hope that the clone might someday willingly donate a kidney to the clonee.[13]

In sum, different interpretations of Genesis have quite different implications for how we judge human cloning. If we believe structuring our world a particular way lies at the heart of God's creation, then we will likely view human cloning as transgressing that structure. In contrast, if we believe that transforming what exists for the better lies at the heart of creation, then our view of human cloning will likely depend on whether we use human cloning to accomplish good or evil.

Cloning and Humanity

Central to the Western conception of human nature is the Biblical view that we were created by God and "in God's image." The idea has been historically as well as philosophically important, for it has done much to protect and elevate the status of humans. Yet the genetic revolution, and especially the possibility of human cloning, deeply challenges that view. While humans have long produced other humans through traditional reproduction, they have never been able to control the exact genetic structure of their offspring. Traditional conception has always involved much randomness and uncertainty. Seeing God's hand in the uncertain and mysterious is relatively easy; seeing God's hand in what we can control may be difficult.

Cloning and genetic engineering offer the prospect of removing that randomness and uncertainty, and so threaten to undermine the belief that humans are created by God, in God's image.

Commenting on the Biblical account of creation, the Mishnaic Rabbis (c. 200 CE) explained;

> For this reason was man created alone, to teach you that whoever destroys a single soul of Israel, Scripture imputes (guilt) to him as though he had destroyed a complete world; and whosoever preserves a single soul of Israel, Scripture ascribes (merit) to him as though he had preserved a complete world. Furthermore, (he was created alone) for the sake of peace among men, that one might not say to his fellow, "My father was greater than thine", ...[and] to proclaim the greatness of The Holy One, Blessed be He: for if a man strikes many coins from one mould, they all resemble one another, but The Supreme King of Kings, The Holy One, Blessed be He, fashioned every man in the stamp of the first man, and yet not one of them resembles his fellow.[14]

The commentary exemplifies the traditional Jewish view that three central values are imputed by the Biblical account of creation to every human life: pricelessness, uniqueness, and equality. Arguably, cloning could undermine each of these values.

Consider pricelessness tint. Belief in the pricelessness of human life seems to fall naturally out of the belief that humans are created in God's image, for if each of us is created in God's image, then each of us is of infinite worth, indeed is sacred. The worry is that if we clone our offspring, then rather than seeing them as created in the Divine image, we might come to see them as mere objects of production, genetically replaceable like other products. The art market provides analogies: An original oil painting is typically much more valuable than copies of it, and objects that can be readily duplicated, such as photographs, usually sell for far less than those that cannot. In economic language, cloning increases the potential "supply" of each of us and so might cause our value to decline.

Yet this fear should not be overstated. If someone were cloned a thousand times over, perhaps it would be hard to see each as a priceless being. But such use seems unlikely. In contrast, if cloning were used to make only one or two "copies" of a person, maintaining the belief that each has infinite worth would be much easier. Few would argue that natural genetic twins have diminished worth.[15]

As interpreted by the Mishnaic Rabbis, the fact that God began by creating not a group of people but the individual Adam also shows that every human being is unique.[16] To this day, a belief in individual uniqueness has played an important part in Jewish thought. As was expressed by Rabbi Zusya of Anipol shortly before his death, "In the world to come I shall not be asked: 'Why were you not Moses?' Rather I shall be asked: 'Why were you not Zusya?'"[17] Martin Buber also put great weight on the concept of human uniqueness:

> Every person born into this world represents something new, something that never existed before, something original and unique . . . Every man's foremost task is the actualization of his unique, unprecedented and never-recurring potentialities, and not the repetition of something that another, and be it even the greatest, has already achieved. (p. 17)

To many (myself included), the thought of being cloned is frightening. Indeed, the very thought that one could be cloned may be disturbing. If I can be copied, what is so special about me?

Of course, as many have pointed out, two clones would not really be identical. Raised in different environments, perhaps at different times, they will become different people. Even if physically identical, each will have a different character—a different soul. Yet for many, this observation only ducks the question; even if a clone will not be in all ways identical to the one cloned, he or she will be similar in many ways and identical in one fundamental way—namely, in having the same genetic composition.

Ultimately, cloning challenges us to consider how important our genetic structure is to our sense of self. Specifically, it challenges us to consider to what extent a person is more than a physical being—or, to the degree that behavior is genetically influenced, more than just a set of particular behaviors. The less one's sense of identity is based on physical being, the less threatening cloning becomes. If when one looks in the mirror one sees only one's physical being, then a genetic duplicate might destroy one's sense of uniqueness.

Cloning also forces one to ask how important uniqueness is to one's sense of self. Why should one be a lesser person simply because there are copies of one? Contra Buber's view, perhaps a person's foremost task is not the actualization of his or her "unique, unprecedented and never-recurring potentialities," but simply the actualization of his or her potentialities, whether or not others possess those potentialities as well.

When first exposed to photography, some people refused to be photographed for fear that a photograph—an inanimate, two-dimensional copy—would "capture their souls." Over time, most of us have learned to tolerate the camera. For those who do not mind being photographed but are repulsed at the thought of being cloned, a useful thought experiment is to ask at what point our repulsion toward cloning begins. Would we be repulsed by an inanimate, three-dimensional copy—a statue? A three-dimensional copy that is mechanically animated? That is biologically animated? That can think?

The third lesson often tied in the Jewish tradition to the Biblical account of human creation is that of equality. If God initially created one person (Adam), and we are all descended from Adam, then we must all be equal.[18] Our common descent implies our equality.

What are the implications of cloning—and of genetic engineering—for equality? Would lesser people be squeezed out? Would we produce a basketball team of Michael Jordans or a university of Albert Einsteins? Would neo-Nazis produce their "master" race? Would we breed docile workers? Would the rich become genetically advantaged? Would we see people produced by genetic engineering as better or worse than those produced by traditional means?

Yet the challenge to equality, like the challenges to pricelessness and uniqueness, is also conceptually no greater than challenges we already face. Already there are significant genetic differences between people, and yet we view all people as equal. Already identical twins exist, and yet we view each as priceless and unique. Human choice, rather than genetic structure, has long determined the values we attach to human life.

Theological Implications

Just as the possibility of human cloning challenges our belief that humans are created in God's image, it also challenges our image of God as our Creator—our "Parent" or "Father." Of course, advances in genetic knowledge will not solve the great mystery of where the universe in toto came from, but because it suggests that we can "autocreate," it does seem likely to affect our own relationship to the creative power of God.

Again, it seems, we could turn to the transformative view of creation, augmented by the view that we participate in the creation. And perhaps it can be admitted that we participate in the transformation. Perhaps, instead of seeing God as an agent who acted in the distant past, we will see God as the Power of Creation, and hold that we too share in that Power.[19] If asked whether we are "playing God" by engaging in human cloning, we might respond, "Yes, for God is in us too." We might even stress that creation lies not merely in changing the world, but in changing it for the better.

A similar point holds for our image of God as Sovereign—as "Ruler" or "King." Under the view that creation is a completed act, our autocreativity seems to usurp God's sovereignty. But if our understanding of God's sovereignty can parallel the changed understanding of our relationship to God's creative power, it need not. If creation involves changing the world for the better, not merely tampering with it, then we might see God's sovereignty as requiring the responsible exercise of the Godliness within ourselves.

Perhaps all this seems arrogant, but I do not find it so. Recognizing that responsibilities attach to the powers we have, and accepting those responsibilities, may form the basis of a more mature understanding of ourselves and of God and God's sovereignty. Children must eventually become adults, and works of art must stand on their own.

Death and the Search for Meaning

The Biblical account of creation concludes with expulsion. As punishment for eating the forbidden fruit of the tree of knowledge, Adam and Eve are expelled from Eden and blocked from eating the fruit of the tree of (eternal) life, lest they, like God, become immortal (Gen. 3: 22). Despite a presumed desire for immortality, death awaits, and Adam and Eve must live in its shadow.

Some might think that cloning (and perhaps other new genetic technologies, such as those derived by replicating embryonic stem cells) offers a way to escape death—a way to make themselves "immortal." Through cloning a person might try to ensure that he or she does not really die; indeed, one might suppose it possible to achieve immortality by spawning a series of clones over time. Others might seek immortality of a different sort by producing multiple replicates all at once, so as to spread their genes as widely as possible and ensure their perpetuation in the human stock. Or one might try to preserve oneself by creating clones to supply genetically identical, but more youthful, body parts.

Of course, there are a variety of specific reasons that such attempts either must fail or are morally abhorrent. A general response is also available, however. As the author of Ecclesiastes asked, what point is there in living, if death awaits us all (Eccles. 3: 18–19)? Yet even if, *arguendo,* immortality or near immortality could be achieved through human cloning, rather than asking, "What point is there in living if death awaits?" a simpler question would remain, namely, "What point is there in living?"

The Biblical author was well acquainted with the human search for meaning and well aware that personal immortality can be a seductive, yet fruitless, goal in that search. In contradistinction to other Near Eastern religions concerned with death and immortality (as seen, for example, in Egyptian embalmment and mummification), the Bible strictly limited contact with the dead (Numbers 19: 11–16). The approach advocated in the Hebrew Bible is to live in connection with the Eternal in the life one leads, rather than to seek eternal life. Indeed, death was later taken as an impetus for spiritual growth. As the Psalmist expressed, "Teach us to number our days so that we may maintain a heart of wisdom" (Psalms 90: 12).

For many, the greatest human existential dilemma is not death but isolation and loneliness, and the greatest source of meaning comes from finding a mate and having children. In the Biblical narrative, shortly after Adam's creation but before Eve's creation—and before Adam's mortality or immortality is clearly established— God offers a rare comment on the human condition: "It is not good for man to be alone" (Gen. 2: 18). God then creates Eve to be Adam's counterpart.

Cloning would be a poor substitute for what is achieved through mating, understood in the richest sense, as involving bonding with another and sharing of life's joys and sorrows, and joining with that other to create an original and genetically intertwined life. By contrast, in cloning oneself one would be focused primarily on one's own life, trapped within one's own ego.

Perhaps the Biblical verb used to indicate sexual relations—*yodeah* (to know)—hints at the deep role that bonding with another person, including joining physically and genetically, may play in finding meaning in life. At its best, joining with another to create a child is an act not merely of reproduction, but of love. While there are many sources of meaning in life, it is hard to imagine one greater than love.

Wild Strains and Cultivars

A Jerusalem rabbi once shared with me a story that I have found helpful, indeed comforting, in thinking about the genetic revolution. I had asked this rabbi about raising my children, may I someday be so blessed, in the United States, versus raising them in Israel. Would one option provide a better life for them as Jews than the other? He responded with a story that he attributed to the Ba'al Shem Tov, the mythical, eighteenth-century founder of Hassidic Judaism. The Ba'al Shem Tov taught that there are two types of fruit in the world: fruit that grows in vineyards, and fruit that grows in the wild. Usually, fruit that grows in vineyards is large, shapely, tasty, and consistent. Fruit that grows in the wild often has blemishes or defects, and much of it is lost to insects and disease. However, it may be quite strong in flavor. How do these two types of fruit compare? Both are pleasing in God's eyes.

In time, we may well see a world in which many people will be cloned or genetically engineered, while others will be created through traditional means. Perhaps both will be pleasing in God's eyes.

References

1. For an overview of religious issues raised by the possibility of human cloning, see National Bioethics Advisory Commission, *Cloning Human Beings: Report and Recommendations of the National Bioethics Advisory Commission* (Rockville MD, 1997); Ethics and Theology: A Continuation of the National Discussion on Human Cloning: Hearing Before the Subcommittee on Public Health and Safety of the Senate Committee on Labor and Human Resources, 105th Cong. (1997). For analyses of genetic engineering from a Jewish perspective before the "Dolly" breakthrough, see Azriel Rosenfeld, "Judaism and Gene Design," and Fred Rosner, "Genetic Engineering and Judaism," both in *Jewish Bioethics,* ed. Fred Rosner and J. David Bleich (New York 1979), pp. 401–408 and 409–420, respectively. For Christian perspectives on human cloning, see Ronald Cole-Turner, ed., *Human Cloning: Religious Responses* (Louisville 1997).

2. Arguably, different accounts of how the genders arise can be found in the first and the second chapters of Genesis, which many have observed appear to provide not one but two accounts of creation. Traditional commentators have sought to reconcile these accounts (and thereby defend the view that the entire Bible is the word of God as transcribed by Moses). For one such recent work, see Joseph B. Soloveitchik, *The Lonely Man of Faith* (New York 1992). For the view that the Bible is composed of many documents,

see E. A. Spieser, *Anchor Bible: Genesis* (New York 1962), pp. xx–xxii, 3–28.

3. Mary Douglas, "The Abominations of Leviticus," in *Purity and Danger: An Analysis of the Concepts of Pollution and Taboo* (London 1984), pp. 41–57, at 53.

4. A parallel argument can be made in evolutionary terms. The genetic structure of our world evolved over billions of years into an interwoven and equilibrated system. While we often use science to modify nature, such modifications function within an existing evolutionary structure. In contrast, human cloning (and genetic engineering more generally) changes the very rules of the game of genetic evolution. Such a profound shift may shatter the entire system.

5. See, for example, *Torah* (New York: Jewish Publication Society, 1962); Everett Fox, *Five Books of Moses* (New York 1995); and Robert Alter, *Genesis* (New York 1996). Under this second translation, a formless and void earth might, though need not necessarily, be supposed to have existed before God first acted by creating light.

6. For a similar argument from a Christian perspective, see Ted Peters, *Playing God? Genetic Determinism and Human Freedom* (New York 1997), p. 14, distinguishing between *creatio ex nihilo* and *creatio continua;* and Philip Hefner, "The Evolution of the Created Co-Creator," in *Cosmos as Creation: Science and Theology in Consonance,* ed. Ted Peters (Nashville 1989), pp. 212–33.

7. To explain the textual claim that by the seventh day God had completed the structure of the universe, various points might be made. For example, the text stresses that God rested from the work he had completed (Gen. 2: 2–3), but does not explicitly say that God did not engage in further work later. Indeed, the second chapter of Genesis proceeds to offer a second account of creation.

8. When describing Divine creation, the Bible uses two verbs: bara (to bring into existence) and yatzar (to form or shape). However, when describing creation by humans, the Bible uses only one verb: yatzar. Some might feel that even if we humans should view ourselves as creators, we should limit ourselves to yatzar, a category that might exclude human cloning. The questions would then become: (1) What does one mean by bara and yatzar? and (2) Where on that spectrum do the various uses of genetic technology fall? I do not seek to resolve these questions here, but I do believe that how one resolves them depends in part on the extent to which one views creation as a completed act versus a transformative process.

9. Arguing with God is a recurrent theme in Jewish thought. See Anson Laytner, *Arguing with God: A Jewish Tradition* (Northvale NJ, 1990).

10. Some may ask whether creation by humans should be judged differently from creation by God. If God created something, then we can presume that something to be good; but if humans create, we can make no such presumption, the argument would run. Yet the Biblical text supports a different view. The Bible suggests that the merits of God's creations must also be judged and cannot simply be deduced from their source or fully foreseen in advance. See Gen. 1: 3, 10, 12, 18, 21, 25, and 30, where God assesses God's own creations as "good" and "very good." See also Gen. 5: 5–13, especially 12, where God's destroys most of the world by flood after assessing the earth as corrupt. Similarly, one might think that the merits of human creation cannot be fully foreseen but must await later assessment.

11. Elliot Dorff, "Human Cloning: A Jewish Perspective," Testimony before the National Bioethics Advisory Commission (14 March 1997), p. 5. Contrast J. M. Haas, Letter from the Pope John Center, submitted to the Nation Bioethics Advisory Commission (31 March 1997), p. 4.

12. Rabbi Moshe Tendler, Testimony before the National Bioethics Advisory Commission (14 March 1997), 10–11, at 10.

13. See James F. Childress, "The Challenges of Public Ethics: Reflections on NBAC's Report," *Hastings Center Report* 27, no. 5 (1997): 9–11, at 10.

14. Babylonian Talmud: Seder Nezikin, vol. 1, tr. Isidore Epstein (London, 1935), pp. 233–234 (Sanhedrin 37a). Epstein points out that the term "of Israel" is omitted in some versions (p. 234, note 2). No doubt the editors of those versions were aware of the tension the phrase "of Israel" created with the ensuing verse proclaiming human equality.

15. However, natural genetic twins, unlike clones, are not produced with the intention of achieving genetic identicalness.

16. In one interpretation, God did not begin human creation with a single individual. See particularly Gen. 1: 26–28.

17. Quoted in Martin Buber, *The Way of Man* (Chicago 1951), p. 18.

18. Scholars debate whether the Biblical accounts of creation reflect men and women as equal. See Gen. 2: 16.

19. For such an approach, see Mordecai M. Kaplan, *The Meaning of God in Modern Jewish Religion* (New York 1937), pp. 25–29, 51–57, and 62.

59. What Exactly Is Wrong with Cloning People?

Ronald Bailey

Examining the negative reaction to the cloning of a sheep by Scottish biotechnologists, Ronald Bailey finds the arguments against human cloning unconvincing. Most of the objections, Bailey believes, can be reduced to the claim that cloning violates the will of God, but he can see little ethical force in such assertions except in the religious communities to which they are directed. As for the concerns that clones will lack a unique genetic identity, he points out that they will be comparable to twins or triplets and that such beings have created no particular moral dilemmas for us. Over time, Bailey sees cloning as inevitable since it will be impossible to ban, and he foresees that as with other medical advances, we will and should experiment to discover its best uses.

By now everyone knows that Scottish biotechnologists have cloned a sheep. They took a cell from a 6-year-old sheep, added its genes to a hollowed out egg from another sheep, and placed it in the womb of yet another sheep, resulting in the birth of an identical twin sheep that is six years younger than its sister. This event was followed up by the announcement that some Hawaiian scientists had cloned mice. The researchers say that in principle it should be possible to clone humans. That prospect has apparently frightened a lot of people, and quite a few of them are calling for regulators to ban cloning since we cannot predict what the consequences of it will be.

President Clinton rushed to ban federal funding of human cloning research and asked privately funded researchers to stop such research at least until the National Bioethics Advisory Commission issues a report on the ethical implications of human cloning. The commission, composed of scientists, lawyers, and ethicists, was appointed last year to advise the federal government on the ethical questions posed by biotechnology research and new medical therapies. But Sen. Christopher Bond (R-MO) wasn't waiting around for the commission's recommendations; he'd already made up his mind. Bond introduced a bill to ban the federal funding of human cloning or human cloning research. "I want to send a clear signal," said the senator, "that this is some-

From Ronald Bailey, "The Twin Paradox: What Exactly Is Wrong with Cloning People?" *Reason,* vol. 29 (May 1997). Reprinted with permission from Reason Foundation.

thing we cannot and should not tolerate. This type of research on humans is morally reprehensible."

Carl Feldbaum, president of the Biotechnology Industry Organization, hurriedly said that human cloning should be immediately banned. Perennial Luddite Jeremy Rifkin grandly pronounced that cloning "throws every convention, every historical tradition, up for grabs." At the putative opposite end of the political spectrum, conservative columnist George Will chimed in: "What if the great given—a human being is a product of the union of a man and woman—is no longer a given?" In addition to these pundits and politicians, a whole raft of bioethicists declared that they, too, oppose human cloning. Daniel Callahan of the Hastings Center said flat out: "The message must be simple and decisive: The human species doesn't need cloning." George Annas of Boston University agreed: "Most people who have thought about this believe it is not a reasonable use and should not be allowed . . . This is not a case of scientific freedom vs. the regulators."

Given all of the brouhaha, you'd think it was crystal clear why cloning humans is unethical. But what exactly is wrong with it? Which ethical principle does cloning violate? Stealing? Lying? Coveting? Murdering? What? Most of the arguments against cloning amount to little more than a reformulation of the old familiar refrain of Luddites everywhere: "If God had meant for man to fly, he would have given us wings. And if God had meant for man to clone, he would have given us spores." Ethical reasoning requires more than that.

What would a clone be? Well, he or she would be a complete human being who happens to share the

487

same genes with another person. Today, we call such people identical twins. To my knowledge no one has argued that twins are immoral. Of course, cloned twins would not be the same age. But it is hard to see why this age difference might present an ethical problem—or give clones a different moral status. "You should treat all clones like you would treat all monozygous [identical] twins or triplets," concludes Dr. H. Tristam Engelhardt, a professor of medicine at Baylor and a philosopher at Rice University. "That's it." It would be unethical to treat a human clone as anything other than a human being. If this principle is observed, he argues, all the other "ethical" problems for a secular society essentially disappear. John Fletcher, a professor of biomedical ethics in the medical school at the University of Virginia, agrees: "I don't believe that there is any intrinsic reason why cloning should not be done."

Let's take a look at a few of the scenarios that opponents of human cloning have sketched out. Some argue that clones would undermine the uniqueness of each human being. "Can individuality, identity and dignity be severed from genetic distinctiveness, and from belief in a person's open future?" asks George Will. Will and others have apparently fallen under the sway of what Fletcher calls "genetic essentialism." Fletcher says polls indicate that some 30 percent to 40 percent of Americans are genetic essentialists, who believe that genes almost completely determine who a person is. But a person who is a clone would live in a very different world from that of his genetic predecessor. With greatly divergent experiences, their brains would be wired differently. After all, even twins who grow up together are separate people—distinct individuals with different personalities and certainly no lack of Will's "individuality, identity and dignity."

In addition, a clone that grew from one person's DNA inserted in another person's host egg would pick up "maternal factors" from the proteins in that egg, altering its development. Physiological differences between the womb of the original and host mothers could also affect the clone's development. In no sense, therefore, would or could a clone be a "carbon copy" of his or her predecessor. What about a rich jerk who is so narcissistic that he wants to clone himself so that he can give all his wealth to himself? First, he will fail. His clone is simply not the same person that he is. The clone may be a jerk too, but he will be his own individual jerk. Nor is Jerk Sr.'s action unprecedented. Today, rich people, and regular people too, make an effort to pass along some wealth to their children when they die. People will their estates to their children not only because they

are connected by bonds of love but also because they have genetic ties. The principle is no different for clones.

Senator Bond and others worry about a gory scenario in which clones would be created to provide spare parts, such as organs that would not be rejected by the predecessor's immune system. "The creation of a human being should not be for spare parts or as a replacement," says Bond. I agree. The simple response to this scenario is: Clones are people. You must treat them like people. We don't forcibly take organs from one twin in and give them to the other. Why would we do that in the case of clones?

The technology of cloning may well allow biotechnologists to develop animals that will grow human-compatible organs for transplant. Cloning is likely to be first used to create animals that produce valuable therapeutic hormones, enzymes, and proteins. But what about cloning exceptional human beings? George Will put it this way: "Suppose a cloned Michael Jordan, age 8, preferred violin to basketball? Is it imaginable? If so, would it be tolerable to the cloner?" Yes, it is imaginable, and the cloner would just have to put up with violin recitals. Kids are not commercial property—slavery was abolished some time ago. We all know about Little League fathers and stage mothers who push their kids, but given the stubborn nature of individuals, those parents rarely manage to make kids stick forever to something they hate. A ban on cloning wouldn't abolish pushy parents.

One putatively scientific argument against cloning has been raised. As a National Public Radio commentator who opposes cloning quipped, "Diversity isn't just politically correct, it's good science." Sexual reproduction seems to have evolved for the purpose of staying ahead of evermutating pathogens in a continuing arms race. Novel combinations of genes created through sexual reproduction help immune systems devise defenses against rapidly evolving germs, viruses, and parasites. The argument against cloning says that if enough human beings were cloned, pathogens would likely adapt and begin to get the upper hand, causing widespread disease. The analogy often cited is what happens when a lot of farmers all adopt the same corn hybrid. If the hybrid is highly susceptible to a particular bug, then the crop fails. That warning may have some validity for cloned livestock, which may well have to live in environments protected from infectious disease. But it is unlikely that there will be millions of clones of one person. Genomic diversity would still be the rule for humanity. There might be more identical twins, triplets, etc., but unless there are millions of clones of one person, raging epidemics sweeping through hordes of human beings with identical genomes seem very unlikely. But even if someday millions of clones of one person existed, who is to say that novel technologies wouldn't by then be able to control human pathogens? After all, it wasn't genetic diversity that caused typhoid, typhus, polio, or measles to all but disappear in the United States. It was modern sanitation and modern medicine.

There's no reason to think that a law against cloning would make much difference anyway. "It's such a simple technology, it won't be banable," says Engelhardt. "That's why God made offshore islands, so that anybody who wants to do it can have it done." Cloning would simply go underground and be practiced without legal oversight. This means that people who turned to cloning would not have recourse to the law to enforce contracts, ensure proper standards, and hold practitioners liable for malpractice.

Who is likely to be making the decisions about whether human cloning should be banned? When President Clinton appointed the National Bioethics Advisory Commission last year, his stated hope was that such a commission could come up with some sort of societal consensus about what we should do with cloning. The problem with achieving and imposing such a consensus is that Americans live in a large number of disparate moral communities. "If you call up the Pope in Rome, do you think he'll hesitate?" asks Engelhardt. "He'll say, 'No, that's not the way that Christians reproduce.' And if you live Christianity of a Roman Catholic sort, that'll be a good enough answer. And if you're fully secular, it won't be a relevant answer at all. And if you're in-between, you'll feel kind of generally guilty."

Engelhardt questions the efficacy of such commissions: "Understand why all such commissions are frauds. Imagine a commission that really represented our political and moral diversity. It would have as its members Jesse Jackson, Jesse Helms, Mother Teresa, Bella Abzug, Phyllis Schafly. And they would all talk together, and they would never agree on anything . . . Presidents and Congresses rig—manufacture

fraudulently—a consensus by choosing people to serve on such commissions who already more or less agree. . . Commissions are created to manufacture the fraudulent view that we have a consensus."

Unlike Engelhardt, Fletcher believes that the National Bioethics Advisory Commission can be useful, but he acknowledges that "all of the commissions in the past have made recommendations that have had their effects in federal regulations. So they are a source eventually of regulations." The bioethics field is littered with ill-advised bans, starting in the mid-1970s with the two-year moratorium on recombining DNA and including the law against selling organs and blood and Clinton's recent prohibition on using human embryos in federally funded medical research. As history shows, many bioethicists succumb to the thrill of exercising power by saying no. Simply leaving people free to make their own mistakes will get a bioethicist no perks, no conferences, and no power. Bioethicists aren't the ones suffering, the ones dying, and the ones who are infertile, so they do not bear the consequences of their bans. There certainly is a role for bioethicists as advisers, explaining to individuals what the ramifications of their decisions might be. But bioethicists should have no ability to stop individuals from making their own decisions, once they feel that they have enough information.

Ultimately, biotechnology is no different from any other technology—humans must be allowed to experiment with it in order to find its best uses and, yes, to make and learn from mistakes in using it. Trying to decide in advance how a technology should be used is futile. The smartest commission ever assembled simply doesn't have the creativity of millions of human beings trying to live the best lives that they can by trying out and developing new technologies. So why is the impulse to ban cloning so strong? "We haven't gotten over the nostalgia for the Inquisition," concludes Engelhardt. "We are people who are postmodernist with a nostalgia for the Middle Ages. We still want the state to have the power of the Inquisition to enforce good public morals on everyone, whether they want it or not."